The University of Chicago Spanish Dictionary

Universidad de Chicago Diccionario Español–Inglés,
Inglés–Español

Universidad de Chicago Diccionario Español–Inglés, Inglés–Español

Compilación original de Carlos Castillo y Otto F. Bond

QUINTA EDICIÓN

David Pharies
Director

María Irene Moyna
Redactora Adjunta

Gary K. Baker
Asistente de Dirección

Erica Fischer Dorantes
Ayudante de Dirección

POCKET BOOKS
NEW YORK   LONDON   TORONTO   SYDNEY   SINGAPORE

The University of Chicago Spanish Dictionary
Spanish–English • English–Spanish

Originally Compiled by Carlos Castillo and Otto F. Bond

FIFTH EDITION

David Pharies
Editor in Chief

María Irene Moyna
Associate Editor

Gary K. Baker
Assistant Editor

Erica Fischer Dorantes
Editorial Assistant

POCKET BOOKS
NEW YORK   LONDON   TORONTO   SYDNEY   SINGAPORE

POCKET BOOKS, a division of Simon & Schuster, Inc.
1230 Avenue of the Americas, New York, NY 10020

Copyright © 2002 by The University of Chicago

Published by arrangement with The University of Chicago Press

All rights reserved, including the right to reproduce
this book or portions thereof in any form whatsoever.
For information address The University of Chicago Press,
1427 East 60th Street, Chicago, IL 60637

ISBN: 0-7434-7013-3

First Pocket Books printing of this revised edition July 2003

10 9 8 7 6 5 4 3 2 1

POCKET and colophon are registered trademarks of
Simon & Schuster, Inc.

Manufactured in the United States of America

For information regarding special discounts for bulk purchases,
please contact Simon & Schuster Special Sales at 1-800-456-6798
or business@simonandschuster.com

Contents

Preface to the Fifth Edition

The University of Chicago Spanish Dictionary has been compiled for the general use of the American English-speaking learner of Spanish and the Spanish-speaking learner of American English.

With this purpose in mind, the editors of the fifth edition have introduced a number of significant improvements. One of the most important changes is the addition of many new words and meanings in order to bring the dictionary up to date with the latest technical advancements and cultural changes. Especially significant are additions in the fields of medicine (*anorexia, antioxidant, clone, defibrillate, gene splicing, HIV, hypoglycemia, liposuction, mammography, melanoma, metastasis, progesterone, scoliosis*), electronics (*CD, fax, magnetic resonance imaging, microwave, satellite dish*), computers (*browser, cache, chat room, megabyte, on-line, scanner, search engine, URL, website*), and science and technology (*entropy, genome, nanosecond, polyurethane, pulsar, smart bomb*). Recent cultural phenomena are captured in items such as *bungee jumping, e-commerce, mountain bike, politically correct, pro-life, sexual harassment,* and *surrogate mother*, as well as in slang terms such as *bigtime, bimbo, ditsy, douchebag, hype,* and *no-brainer*. In order to provide the most up-to-date picture of the language, many obsolescent or obsolete terms have been eliminated, such as *aught, ere, forenoon, fortnight, kerchief, knave, morrow,* and *o'er*.

Another significant improvement in the fifth edition is the consistent use of parenthetical words meant to guide the choice of equivalents from a series. For example, among the various equivalents of *soft*, the user is advised to choose *blando* to apply to butter, *suave* to apply to skin, and *tenue* to apply to light. Similarly, users are enabled by these parenthetical words to choose appropriate equivalents for *sheet* according to whether reference is being made to a sheet of paper (*hoja*), of ice (*capa*), of glass (*lámina*), or to a bed covering (*sábana*).

A change that will enhance the usability of the dictionary is the integration into the entries themselves of material that was formerly presented in charts and lists, such as idioms, proverbs, names of nations, and cardinal and ordinal numbers.

The amount and quality of grammatical information has been expanded. For the first time, gender markings for Spanish noun equivalents are provided on the English–Spanish side, thus freeing users from having to seek this information on the Spanish–English side. Additionally, transitive and intransitive verbal meanings are distinguished.

The frequent references to regional usage characteristic of the fourth edition have been de-emphasized here, partly for reasons of space, partly because of the notorious unreliability of the available information on regional dialects. In the present edition, such information is provided only where a word of more general currency might not be understood (see the various equivalents of Eng. *bean*), where the use of a particular word might cause embarrassment (see Sp. *coger*), or where the word is universally recognized as being characteristic of a given dialect (see Sp. *che, cuate*).

Acknowledgments

The Editor in Chief and the University of Chicago Press wish to acknowledge with thanks the contributions to early project planning made by the following Advisory Board, all from the University of Chicago: Paolo Cherchi, Gene B. Gragg, Eric P. Hamp, Salikoko Mufwene, and Michael Silverstein.

Preámbulo a la quinta edición

Este libro se ha compilado para el uso general del anglohablante estadounidense que estudia español y para el hispanohablante que estudia el inglés americano.

Con este propósito, los editores de la presente edición han incorporado una cantidad sustancial de mejoras. Uno de los cambios más importantes es la adición de muchos términos y significados nuevos que han puesto el diccionario al día con los avances tecnológicos y las transformaciones culturales. De especial importancia son las incorporaciones en los campos de la medicina (*anorexia, antioxidante, clon, desfibrilar, empalme genético, escoliosis, hipoglucemia, VIH, liposucción, mamografía, melanoma, metástasis, progesterona*), la electrónica (*CD, fax, imagen por resonancia magnética, microondas, parabólica, píxel*), la informática (*bit, caché, en línea, escáner, megabyte, motor de búsqueda, navegador, protector de tensión, sitio web, URL*) y la ciencia y la tecnología (*bomba inteligente, entropía, genoma, nanosegundo, púlsar, poliuretano*). Los recientes fenómenos culturales se ven reflejados en términos tales como *antiaborto, bicicleta de montaña, lifting, limpieza étnica, madre de alquiler, políticamente correcto,* y *puénting* además de palabras familiares, tales como *chute, coca, curro, gachí, mala leche, mamado, truja.* Al mismo tiempo, para captar la lengua en su forma más actualizada se han eliminado muchas palabras arcaicas o caídas en desuso como *acullá, albéitar, asaz, luengo* y *postrer.*

Otra mejora considerable de la quinta edición es el uso sistemático de indicadores semánticos, que van entre paréntesis y cuyo objetivo es guiar en la elección del equivalente apropiado a partir de una serie de posibilidades. Por ejemplo, entre los diferentes equivalentes de *destino*, se advierte al usuario que opte por *fate* cuando significa 'hado', por *destination* cuando significa 'lugar adonde se viaja' y por *use* cuando significa 'uso'. Del mismo modo, la presencia de estos indicadores semánticos posibilita al usuario elegir con certeza entre los equivalentes de *calmar* según se hable de los nervios (*to calm*), dolor (*to soothe*), miedo (*to allay, to quell*) o sed (*to quench*).

Otro cambio que sin duda facilitará el empleo del diccionario es la integración, en el cuerpo del mismo, de material que en ediciones anteriores se presentaba en forma de cuadros y listas, tal como expresiones idiomáticas, refranes, nombres de países y números cardinales y ordinales.

También se ha incrementado la cantidad y calidad de la información gramatical. Por primera vez se proporcionan las marcas de género gramatical para los sustantivos en la sección inglés–español, lo cual elimina la necesidad de consultar la sección español–inglés para obtener esta información. Además, se distinguen los significados verbales transitivos e intransitivos.

En comparación con la edición anterior, la nueva insiste mucho menos en las diferencias dialectales en el vocabulario del español, en parte por razones de espacio y en parte porque la información disponible sobre ese aspecto del vocabulario es incompleta y poco fidedigna. En la presente edición las referencias al léxico regional se limitan a unos cuantos tipos de términos, concretamente, aquellos que pueden resultar desconocidos en una determinada comunidad lingüística (como los muchos

equivalentes españoles del ingl. *bean*), aquellos que pueden resultar ofensivos (ver *coger*)
y aquellos que son universalmente reconocidos como típicos de un dialecto dado (ver
che, cuate).

Agradecimiento

El Director y la Editorial de la Universidad de Chicago desean expresar su gratitud por
las contribuciones a la planificación de la obra hechas por los miembros del Consejo
Editorial, concretamente por Paolo Cherchi, Gene B. Gragg, Eric P. Hamp, Salikoko
Mufwene y Michael Silverstein.

How to Use *The University of Chicago Spanish Dictionary*

Order of Entries

Alphabetical order is observed irrespective of hyphens or spaces, such that *air conditioner* precedes *aircraft* and *middle school* precedes *middle-sized*. Homographs are placed under a single entry (*lie* 'to prevaricate', *lie* 'to recline', both pronounced [laɪ]), with different pronunciations if applicable (e.g., *bow* [baʊ] 'forward end of a vessel', *bow* [bo] 'bend, curve'). Regarding Spanish, according to the current policy of the Spanish Royal Academy,[1] *ch* and *ll* are no longer recognized as separate letters, such that *ch* now follows *ce* and precedes *ci*, and *ll* follows *li* and precedes *lo* in alphabetization.

Compounds listed within entries are also alphabetized. However, the need to list compounds under their first element sometimes interferes with alphabetization, as when *slumlord*, a compound listed under *slum*, comes before the next headword, *slumber*, even though strict alphabetization would require the reverse.

Spelling

Spelling of English words reflects common American usage, variants being noted where applicable (*ax*, *axe*; *sulphur*, *sulfur*; *stymie*, *stymy*). The spelling of Spanish words, where possible, follows the conventions of the Spanish Royal Academy. For the orthography of problematic Spanish words such as recent borrowings (*escáner*, *scooter*), country names (*Malí*, *Irak*) and adjectives of nationality (*zimbabuo*), a variety of authorities were consulted, including the *Diccionario del español actual*, the *Diccionario de dudas*, the *Libro de estilo* published by the Madrid newspaper *El País*, and various Internet sources.[2] It should be noted that there is vacillation in some cases, cf. *Bahrain*, which is listed as *Bahrein* in the *Libro de estilo* and as *Bahráin* or *Bahréin* in the *Diccionario de dudas*. In these cases, we either opt for the form that appears to be most generally accepted or provide multiple equivalents.

1. Real Academia Española, *Ortografía de la lengua española* (Madrid: Espasa-Calpe, 1999), p. 2.

2. Manuel Seco, Olimpia Andrés, and Gabino Ramos, *Diccionario del español actual* (Madrid: Aguilar, 1999); Manuel Seco, *Diccionario de dudas y dificultades de la lengua española*, 10th ed. (Madrid: Espasa-Calpe, 1998), *El País: Libro de estilo*, 9th ed. (Madrid: Ediciones El País, 1990).

Omissions

Some categories of words are systematically omitted from the vocabulary entries. First, irregular English past tense and participial forms (e.g., *drunk*, *smitten*), formerly included among the entries, have been removed and are presented instead in a verb table (p. 282). Second, adverbial forms in *-ly* (English) and *-mente* (Spanish) are included only when their usage and meaning are not transparently derivable from their adjectival bases. Thus, *clearly* is omitted, as its usage is predictable from its adjectival base ('in a clear way'), while *surely* is included, since it means, in addition to 'in a sure way', also 'undoubtedly' or 'without fail'. Similarly, *claramente* 'clearly' is omitted, while *atentamente* is retained, since the latter, in addition to meaning 'in an attentive manner', is also used as a farewell, equivalent to 'yours truly'. Third, English nouns in *-ing* and adjectives in *-ed*, which may appear as glosses of Spanish words, are not always accorded separate entries on the English–Spanish side, due to their derivational regularity and to considerations of space.

Structure of Entries

1. HEADWORD. Spelling variants, if any, follow the most frequent form, which appears first. In Spanish, occupational designations, titles, and kinship terms are shown in both masculine and feminine forms, as in *abogado -da*.
2. PRONUNCIATION. Pronunciation of English words is indicated through a modified version of the International Phonetic Alphabet, whose conventions are explained on p. 276. No individual transcription of Spanish words is required, given the simplicity and consistency of the Spanish orthographic system. See "The Spanish Spelling System and the Sounds Represented" (p. 2) for an explanation.
3. GRAMMATICAL CATEGORY. Meanings are marked according to whether they reflect usage as a noun (*n*), adjective (*adj*), adverb (*adv*), conjunction (*conj*), preposition (*prep*), pronoun (*pron*), interjection (*interj*), transitive verb (*vt*), or intransitive verb (*vi*). The exception to this rule is that nouns on the Spanish–English side are marked only by gender, i.e., *m* (masculine noun) or *f* (feminine noun).

    Order of meanings within an entry reflects frequency of usage. Where more than one grammatical category can be rendered by the same gloss, the two are listed together, cf. Eng. *red*, which can be glossed as Sp. *rojo* in both its adjective and noun meanings.

    Traditionally, Spanish adjectives are listed in their masculine form only. However, where the adjective normally functions as a noun as well, it is shown with both masculine and feminine forms if both are possible, cf. the case of *africano -na*, which can mean *African* in the adjectival sense as well as *African* (*man*) and *African* (*woman*).

    Special mention must be made of the combination "vi/vt." Occasionally, a single verb form may function both transitively and intransitively, e.g., both *to eat* and its Spanish equivalent *comer*. Not infrequently, however, Spanish glosses of English intransitives require the addition of the pronominal particle *-se*. Thus, in cases such as *to bathe*, marked "vi/vt" and glossed *bañar(se)*, it should be understood that the bare form is transitive, and the *-se* form intransitive. Finally, where transitivity differs between a headword and its equivalent in the second language, particles must be added to reflect this, as in the case of the transitive English verb *to regret*, which is glossed in Spanish as *arrepentirse de*, since *arrepentirse* alone is intransitive. Where an English verb can be used both transitively and intransitively and its Spanish equivalent is only intransitive, the latter may sometimes be made transitive through the addition of a preposition, which appears in parentheses. Thus, English *fight* is glossed as *pelear (con)* to show that its intransitive equivalent is *pelear*, whereas its transitive equivalent is *pelear con*.

Again for reasons of economy, pronominal forms of Spanish verbs are omitted in two cases: First, when the particle *-se* functions as a direct object, either reflexive or reciprocal, cf. *mirarse*, which can mean both *to look at oneself*, and *to look at each other*, and second, when the addition of *-se* does not affect the English translation, cf. *bañar(se)*, glossed in both meanings as *to bathe*. In contrast, pronominal forms of verbs are included when they differ substantially in meaning from the bare forms, cf. *ir*, glossed as *to go*, vs. *irse*, which means *to leave*.

4.   DELIMITERS.   Whenever a word, within a grammatical category, is considered to have two or more meanings, these are differentiated by means of delimiters, that is, explanatory markers. Most commonly, synonyms are used, cf. *retort*, which in the meaning 'reply' is glossed as *réplica* and in the meaning 'vessel' as *retorta*, though on occasion other strategies may be adopted. Thus, transitive verbs are sometimes best differentiated according to the objects they take, cf. *to negotiate* (a contract), which is glossed *negociar*, while *to negotiate* (an obstacle) is glossed *salvar*. Similarly, adjectives may be most easily distinguished by showing the referents to which they regularly apply, cf. *refreshing*, which applied to drink is *refrescante*, to sleep is *reparador*, and to honesty is *amable*. Not infrequently, a single equivalent covers almost all meanings of a headword in a single grammatical category. In such cases, only the "exceptional" meaning, placed second, is delimited. For example, the equivalent of Eng. *net* in almost all its meanings is Sp. *red*, though when it refers specifically to a hairnet it is *redecilla*. Although delimiters typically precede the gloss they are meant to distinguish, occasionally they are placed afterward. In these cases they are meant to erase doubts about the applicability of a given gloss in a specific secondary context, cf. *site*, whose gloss *sitio* is followed by the delimiter "also Internet."

5.   GLOSSES.   Insofar as is possible, glosses are intended to match the headword in terms of meaning, register, and frequency. Thus, *cop* is glossed as *poli* rather than the more formal *policía*. Similarly, *orinar* is glossed as *to urinate* rather than the informal and vulgar *to piss*. Glosses separated by a comma are to be considered interchangeable, if not perfectly synonymous. Semicolons, on the other hand, indicate separate meanings.

6.   REGIONAL USAGE.   No systematic attempt has been made to reflect regional usage in either English or Spanish, since in the great majority of cases a word of more general currency is available as a gloss. Thus, among the many Spanish equivalents of Eng. *peasant*, Sp. *campesino* is understood everywhere, even where a local term also exists, such as Puerto Rican *jíbaro*, Cuban *guajiro*, and Chilean *guaso*. However, Spanish regional usage is marked where any of the following conditions are met: (1) there is no term of international currency, or it might not be understood in a given location (cf. the various regional Spanish equivalents of Eng. *bean*), (2) the use of a given term in a given region could cause embar-

rassment or misunderstanding, as in the case of *coger*, which means 'to catch' or 'to get' in Spain and Cuba, but is a vulgar term meaning 'to have sexual relations with' in large parts of Spanish America, or (3) a specific regionalism is known throughout the Spanish-speaking world to be typical of a given dialect, cf. River Plate *che*, Mexican *ándale*, *cuate*.

7. STYLISTIC MARKERS. Because, as mentioned earlier, equivalents are chosen in order to match headwords in all aspects of their meaning, including register and frequency, stylistic markers are only infrequently employed. They are included, redundantly, in the case of taboo or offensive words, in order to provide a second level of warning to potential users. Thus, whereas there is no need to mark the Spanish gloss *tonto* as familiar, since it is meant to be equivalent to the equally familiar Eng. *fool*, the gloss of Eng. *whore*, viz., *puta*, is marked "offensive," on the chance that a given user might not realize that this is also true of *whore*. Only five register markers are employed: literary (*lit*), which also includes poetic and formal language, familiar (*fam*), which designates words used among family and friends, vulgar (*vulg*), for words whose use is socially censured, pejorative (*pej*), which implies a negative evaluation, and *offensive* (not abbreviated), for words meant to insult people.

Taboo and offensive words are included in this dictionary because of its purely descriptive rather than prescriptive nature; that is, this dictionary is intended to reflect how the vocabularies of English and Spanish are actually used by their speakers, rather than how we or other people may feel that they should be used. The inclusion of vulgar and offensive words here should not be construed as an indication that we condone or encourage their use.

8. COMPOUNDS. Ease of usage would dictate that each lexical item receive its own entry, but for reasons of economy this is not possible in a concise dictionary. This explains why compound words, which are composed of two or more preexisting words, are listed in almost all cases under the entry of their initial constituent, at the end of the corresponding grammatical category. Thus, *doghouse* is listed as —*house*, under *dog*. There are certain exceptions to this convention, however. First, compounds are listed under the headword of their second constituent when the first is extremely frequent, as are the so-called empty verbs such as Eng. *keep*, *take*, *turn*, Sp. *hacer*, *tener*, *tomar*. Thus, *to have a good time*, glossed *divertirse*, is listed under *time* rather than *have*, and *tener paciencia*, glossed *to be patient*, is under *paciencia* rather than *tener*. Second, English compounds whose first element is a preposition (*offsides*, *outcast*, *overcome*) are listed as separate headwords, chiefly because of their frequent grammatical complexity, cf. *overhead*, which can be an adverb (*it flew overhead*), an adjective (*overhead projector*), or a noun (*overhead from grant money*). Conversely, derived words, that is, words that contain one or more affixes (e.g., *antiabortion*, composed of the prefix *anti-* plus *abortion*, and *kingdom*, composed of *king* plus the suffix *-dom*), are listed as separate headwords.

9. ILLUSTRATIVE PHRASES. Appearing together with the compound words pertinent to any given grammatical category are illustrative phrases, a category defined so as to include idioms, collocations, proverbs, and, especially, sentences required to clarify usage in some way, as when the usage of *gustarle a uno* as a gloss of *to like* is illustrated by the phrase *he likes dogs*, with the translation *le gustan los perros*.

Cómo usar el *Universidad de Chicago Diccionario Español–Inglés, Inglés–Español*

Orden de las entradas

Se respeta el orden alfabético, independientemente de la presencia de guiones o espacios, de tal manera que *air conditioning* precede a *aircraft* y *middle school* precede a *middle-sized*. Los homógrafos se ubican en una sola entrada (*lie* 'mentir' y *lie* 'yacer', ambos con la pronunciación [laɪ]), y se indican sus distintas pronunciaciones si corresponde (e.g., *bow* [baʊ] 'proa' y *bow* [bo] 'curva'). En cuanto al español y siguiendo la política oficial de la Real Academia Española,[1] *ch* y *ll* ya no se reconocen como letras independientes, de tal manera que *ch* ahora sigue a *ce* y precede a *ci*, y *ll* sigue a *li* y precede a *lo* en el orden alfabético.

Asimismo, los compuestos incluidos dentro de una entrada determinada aparecen en orden alfabético a continuación de su primer elemento, lo cual a veces interfiere con el orden alfabético general. Así, por ejemplo, *rompeolas* aparece a continuación de *romper*, porque se trata de un compuesto de dicho verbo, si bien el orden alfabético requeriría lo contrario.

Ortografía

La ortografía de los vocablos ingleses refleja el uso general en inglés americano, y las variantes se incluyen en los casos pertinentes (*ax, axe; sulphur, sulfur; stymie, stymy*). La ortografía española sigue las convenciones de la Real Academia Española. Para la grafía española de palabras problemáticas, tales como préstamos recientes (*escáner, scooter*), nombres de países (*Malí, Irak*) y gentilicios (*zimbabuo*), se consultaron fuentes tales como el *Diccionario del español actual*, el *Diccionario de dudas*, el *Libro de estilo* de *El País* de Madrid y varios sitios en el Internet.[2] Corresponde hacer notar que la grafía de algunos términos vacila entre varias posibles, cf. la versión española de *Bahrain*, que aparece como *Bahrein* en el *Libro de estilo* y como *Bahráin* o *Bahréin* en el *Diccionario de dudas*, en cuyo caso damos la forma que parece más generalmente aceptada u ofrecemos varias.

---

1. Real Academia Española, *Ortografía de la lengua española* (Madrid: Espasa-Calpe, 1999), p. 2.

2. Manuel Seco, Olimpia Andrés y Gabino Ramos, *Diccionario del español actual* (Madrid: Aguilar, 1999); Manuel Seco, *Diccionario de dudas y dificultades de la lengua española*, 10ª ed. (Madrid: Espasa-Calpe, 1998), *El País: Libro de estilo*, 9ª ed. (Madrid: Ediciones El País, 1990).

Omisiones

Algunas categorías de palabras se omiten sistemáticamente de las entradas del diccionario. En primer lugar, las formas irregulares de los pretéritos y participios pasados del inglés (e.g., *drunk, smitten*), que en ediciones anteriores aparecían incluidas en el cuerpo del diccionario, se han eliminado y se presentan ahora tabuladas (p. 282). En segundo lugar, las formas adverbiales en *-mente* (español) y en *-ly* (inglés), se incluyen solamente cuando su uso y significado no pueden deducirse claramente de sus bases adjetivas. De esta forma, *claramente* se omite, ya que su significado es predecible a partir de su base adjetiva ('de manera clara'), mientras que *atentamente* se incluye, ya que además de significar 'de manera atenta', también se usa como fórmula de despedida epistolar. Del mismo modo, se omite *clearly*, porque su equivalente, *de manera clara*, se deduce de su base adjetiva, mientras que se incluye *surely* porque además de significar *de forma segura* también quiere decir *sin duda*. Finalmente, debe notarse que los sustantivos ingleses terminados en *-ing* y los adjetivos en *-ed*, que pueden aparecer como traducción de palabras españolas en la parte español–inglés, no figuran siempre como cabezas de artículo en la parte inglés–español debido a la total regularidad de su formación y a consideraciones de espacio.

Estructura de las entradas

1. PALABRAS CABEZA DE ARTÍCULO. Las variantes ortográficas, si las hay, siguen a la forma más frecuente, que aparece en primer término. En español, las designaciones de profesiones y oficios, los títulos y las relaciones de parentesco aparecen tanto en la forma masculina como en la femenina, como por ejemplo, *abogado -da*.

2. PRONUNCIACIÓN. La pronunciación de las palabras inglesas se indica mediante una versión modificada del Alfabético Fonético Internacional, cuyas convenciones se explican en la p. 276. No se requiere transcripción individual de las palabras españolas, gracias a la simplicidad y sistematicidad de la ortografía española. Para detalles, ver la sección titulada "El sistema ortográfico español" en la p. 2.

3. CATEGORÍA GRAMATICAL. Los significados se marcan según reflejen el uso de la palabra como sustantivo masculino (*m*), sustantivo femenino (*f*), adjetivo (*adj*), adverbio (*adv*), conjunción (*conj*), preposición (*prep*), pronombre (*pron*), interjección (*interj*), verbo transitivo (*vt*) o verbo intransitivo (*vi*). En inglés, en cambio, los sustantivos se marcan con *n*, abreviación de *noun*.

     Los significados dentro de una entrada aparecen ordenados de manera que el más frecuente figure primero. Cuando la misma traducción cubre el significado de dos categorías gramaticales, ambas aparecen juntas, cf. el inglés *red*, que puede traducirse como *rojo* tanto en su significado sustantivo como en el adjetivo.

     Siguiendo la tradición, los adjetivos españoles aparecen exclusivamente en su forma masculina. Sin embargo, cuando el adjetivo frecuentemente funciona además como sustantivo, se muestra tanto en la forma masculina como en la femenina si ambas son posibles, cf. el caso de *africano -na*, traducido al inglés como *African*, forma adecuada para todos sus usos.

     La combinación "vi/vt" merece mención especial. En ocasiones, una única forma verbal funciona tanto transitiva como intransitivamente, v.g., tanto *comer* como su equivalente inglés *to eat*. Sin embargo, es también frecuente que las traducciones españolas de verbos intransitivos ingleses requieran el agregado de una partícula pronominal *-se*. Así, en casos tales como *to bathe* que se marca "vi/ vt," y se traduce como *bañar(se)*, debe entenderse que la forma no pronominalizada es transitiva y la forma con *-se* es intransitiva. En aquellos casos en los que la palabra cabeza de artículo y su equivalente en la otra lengua difieren en transitividad, se deben agregar partículas para reflejar esta diferencia. Tal es el caso del verbo *aprobar*, que se traduce al inglés como *to approve of* en algunos de sus significados, ya que *to approve* es intransitivo si no va acompañado de preposición. Finalmente, en los casos en los que un verbo español puede usarse tanto intransitiva como transitivamente y su equivalente inglés es exclusivamente intransitivo, este último puede a veces volverse transitivo mediante el agregado de una preposición entre paréntesis. Así, el esp. *chivar* se traduce como *to snitch (on)* para mostrar que su forma intransitiva en inglés es *to snitch* mientras que el equivalente transitivo es *to snitch on*.

Por razones de espacio se omiten las formas pronominales de los verbos españoles en dos casos. En primer lugar, se omiten si la partícula pronominal hace las veces de complemento directo reflexivo o recíproco, cf. *mirarse* (a sí mismo o el uno al otro). En segundo lugar no se incluyen tampoco si la partícula pronominal no afecta la traducción al inglés, como en el caso de *bañar* y *bañarse*, ambos *to bathe*. Sí se incluyen aquellas formas pronominales que difieren semánticamente de sus verbos de base, cf. *ir* vs. *irse*.

4. INDICADORES SEMÁNTICOS. En aquellos casos en los que una palabra, dentro de una misma categoría gramatical, tiene dos o más acepciones, estas se distinguen por medio de indicadores semánticos, o sea, explicaciones parentéticas. Lo más frecuente es que se empleen sinónimos, cf. *arco*, que se traduce *arc* cuando se trata de una curva, como *arch* cuando se refiere a una estructura arquitectónica, y como *bow* cuando se trata de un arma, aunque en otras ocasiones se adoptan otras estrategias. Así, los verbos transitivos a veces se distinguen con mayor facilidad mediante los tipos de complementos directos que los acompañan, cf. *acordonar* (un zapato) *to lace*, (un lugar) *to rope off*, (una moneda) *to mill*, mientras que la forma más sencilla de distinguir adjetivos es mostrar los tipos de referentes a los cuales se aplican con mayor frecuencia, cf. *inseguro*, que aplicado a una personalidad se traduce por *insecure*, a un vehículo por *unsafe*, y al andar por *unsteady*. Es frecuente que un único equivalente abarque casi todas las acepciones de una palabra cabeza de artículo dentro de una categoría gramatical determinada. En esos casos, solamente el significado "excepcional," que aparece en segundo lugar, se acompaña de un indicador semántico. Por ejemplo, el equivalente de *acceso* en casi todas sus acepciones es *access*, excepto cuando se refiere a un ataque de tos o rabia, en cuyo caso se traduce como *fit*. Aunque los indicadores semánticos normalmente preceden a la traducción que les corresponde, en ocasiones se ubican después. En estos casos tienen como objetivo eliminar dudas acerca del empleo de una traducción determinada en un contexto secundario específico, cf. *acompañar*, cuya traducción *to accompany* va seguida de un indicador semántico "también en música" para confirmar al lector su aplicación a ese contexto.

5. TRADUCCIONES. En la medida de lo posible, se ha tratado de que las traducciones sean equivalentes a la palabra cabeza de artículo en cuanto a su significado,

registro y frecuencia. Así, *poli* se traduce como *cop* y no como *policeman*, palabra más formal. De la misma forma, *to urinate* se traduce como *orinar* y no como *mear*, palabra más familiar. Las traducciones separadas por una coma deben considerarse equivalentes, aunque no sean exactamente sinónimas. El uso del punto y coma indica acepciones distintas.

6.   USO REGIONAL. No se ha hecho ningún esfuerzo sistemático por reflejar usos regionales, ni en inglés ni en español, ya que en la gran mayoría de los casos existe una palabra de uso general. Así, entre los muchos equivalentes españoles de la palabra inglesa *peasant*, su equivalente español *campesino* se entiende en todo el mundo de habla hispana, aun cuando existan términos locales, tales como *jíbaro* en Puerto Rico, *guajiro* en Cuba y *guaso* en Chile. Sin embargo, el uso regional se indica para el español en tres casos específicos. En primer lugar se encuentran los casos en los que una palabra determinada podría resultar desconocida en una región dada, como los varios equivalentes españoles del ingl. *bean*. En segundo lugar, hay casos en que el empleo de una palabra podría dar lugar a situaciones bochornosas o equívocas. Tal es el caso de *coger*, que significa 'tomar' u 'obtener' en España y Cuba, pero es un vulgarismo para 'tener relaciones sexuales con' en gran parte de Hispanoamérica. En tercer término, se han incluido regionalismos que se reconocen en todo el mundo de habla hispana como típicos de un dialecto determinado, cf. español rioplatense *che*, mexicano *ándale*, *cuate*.

7.   INDICADORES DE ESTILO. Ya que, como se mencionó anteriormente, los equivalentes se eligen para que correspondan a las palabras cabeza de artículo en todos los aspectos de su significado, incluyendo nivel de lengua y frecuencia, los indicadores de estilo se usan poco. Aunque son redundantes, se incluyen en los casos de palabras tabú o términos ofensivos para reforzar la advertencia a los usuarios potenciales del término. Así, aunque no hay necesidad de indicar que la palabra inglesa *fool* es familiar, ya que figura como equivalente del español *tonto*, la traducción de *puta* como *whore* va acompañada del indicador *ofensivo* por si el usuario ignora las connotaciones de la palabra española. Se han empleado cinco indicadores de estilo: literario (*lit*), que incluye lenguaje poético y formal, familiar (*fam*), que designa palabras que se usan en situaciones de intimidad, vulgar (*vulg*), que designa términos cuyo uso está censurado socialmente, peyorativo (*pey*), que designa palabras que tienen una carga connotativa negativa hacia el referente y *ofensivo* (sin abreviar), que designa insultos. Las palabras tabú y los términos ofensivos se incluyen en el diccionario debido a la naturaleza descriptiva y no prescriptiva del mismo. Es decir, el diccionario tiene como objetivo reflejar el uso que los hablantes nativos dan a los términos y no las opiniones nuestras o ajenas de cómo deberían usarse, de manera que la inclusión de estas palabras no debe interpretarse como una indicación de que preconizamos su empleo.

8.   COMPUESTOS. El criterio de facilidad de uso requeriría que cada palabra recibiera su propia entrada, pero por razones de economía de espacio esto no es posible en un diccionario conciso. Por lo tanto, las palabras compuestas, que están formadas por dos o más vocablos preexistentes, aparecen en casi todos los casos en la entrada de su primer constituyente, al final de la categoría gramatical correspondiente. De tal forma, *hombre rana* aparece como — *rana*, en la entrada de *hombre*. Hay ciertas excepciones a esta regla, sin embargo. En primer lugar, los compuestos aparecen bajo la cabeza de artículo de su segundo constituyente cuando el primero es extremadamente frecuente, tal como lo son los verbos se-

mánticamente "vacíos" como el español *hacer, tener, tomar* y el inglés *keep, take, turn*. De este modo, *tener paciencia* aparece en la entrada de *paciencia* y no en la de *tener*, y *to have a good time* figura bajo *time* y no bajo *to have*. En segundo lugar, los compuestos ingleses cuyo primer elemento es una preposición (*offsides, overcome, outcast*), aparecen como cabezas de artículo independientes, sobre todo debido a su complejidad gramatical, cf. *overhead*, que puede ser adverbio (*it flew overhead*, que equivale a *voló en lo alto*), adjetivo (*overhead projector*, es decir, *retroproyector*) y sustantivo (*overhead from grant money*, o sea, *gastos generales de una subvención*). No obstante, las palabras derivadas, i.e., aquellas que contienen uno o más afijos (e.g., *anticuerpo*, compuesta del prefijo *anti-* y *cuerpo*, y *cabezón*, compuesta por *cabeza* y el sufijo *-ón*), figuran como cabezas de artículo independientes.

9. FRASES ILUSTRATIVAS. Junto con las palabras compuestas de una determinada categoría gramatical figuran las frases ilustrativas, una categoría que incluye expresiones idiomáticas, colocaciones típicas, refranes y especialmente, oraciones necesarias para aclarar el uso de alguna palabra, como cuando el uso de *like* como traducción de *gustar* se ilustra con la frase *he likes dogs*, que se traduce *le gustan los perros*.

Spanish–English · Español–Inglés

List of Abbreviations / Lista de abreviaturas

adj	adjetivo	adjective
adv	adverbio, adverbial	adverb, adverbial
Am	América	America
art	artículo	article
conj	conjunción	conjunction
def	definido	definite
dem	demostrativo	demonstrative
Esp	España	Spain, Spanish
f	femenino	feminine
fam	familiar	familiar
indef	indefinido	indefinite
interj	interjección	interjection
interr	interrogativo	interrogative
inv	invariable	invariable
lit	literario	literary
loc	locución	locution
m	masculino	masculine
Méx	México	Mexico
num	numeral	numeral
pej	peyorativo	pejorative
pers	personal	personal
pl	plural	plural
pos	posesivo	possessive
prep	preposición, preposicional	preposition, prepositional
pron	pronombre	pronoun
rel	relativo	relative
RP	Río de la Plata	River Plate
sg	singular	singular
v aux	verbo auxiliar	auxiliary verb
vi	verbo intransitivo	intransitive verb
vt	verbo transitivo	transitive verb
vulg	vulgar	vulgar

Spanish Pronunciation

Spanish orthography very closely mirrors Spanish pronunciation, much more so than is the case in English. This explains why, in bilingual dictionaries such as this, each English entry must be accompanied by a phonetic representation, while Spanish pronunciation may be presented in synoptic form.

This synopsis is only meant as an introduction, however. In spite of the clarity of the orthographical system of Spanish, the individual sounds of the language are difficult for adult native speakers of English to pronounce, and this difficulty is compounded by the syllabic structure of the language. For these reasons, readers who wish to perfect their pronunciation of Spanish are strongly advised to seek the help of a competent teacher.

To say that orthography mirrors pronunciation means that there is a close correlation between letters and sounds. Thus, most Spanish letters correspond to a single sound, or to a single family of closely related sounds, as is the case for all vowels, and the consonants *f*, *l*, *m*, *n*, *p*, *t*, and *s*. In a few cases a single letter represents two very different sounds, as *c*, which is pronounced as *k* before *a*, *o*, and *u*, but *th* (as in *thin*, or as *s* in America) before *e* or *i*. Rarely, two letters represent a single sound, as in the case of *ch*.

The overarching differences between Spanish and English pronunciation are tenseness of articulation and syllabification within the breath group. Due to the tenseness of their articulation, for example, all Spanish vowels have a clear nondiphthongal character, unlike English long vowels, which tend to be bipartite (e.g., *late*, pronounced [leⁱt]). Syllabification is a problem for English speakers because in Spanish, syllables are formed without respect to word boundaries, such that *el hado* 'fate' and *helado* 'ice cream' are both pronounced as e-la-do, and the phrase *tus otras hermanas* 'your other sisters' is syllabified as tu-so-tra-ser-ma-nas. In fast speech, vowels may combine, as in *lo ofendiste* 'you offended him', pronounced lo-fen-dis-te. Finally, when Spanish consonants occur in clusters, very often the articulation of the second influences that of the first, as when *un peso* 'one peso' is pronounced um-pe-so, and *en que* 'in which' is pronounced eŋ ke, where ŋ represents the sound of the letters *ng* in English.

The Spanish Spelling System and the Sounds Represented

I.   VOWELS

   i as a single vowel always represents a sound similar to the second vowel of *police*. Examples: **hilo, camino, piso.** As a part of a diphthong, it sounds like the *y* of English *yes, year.* Examples: **bien, baile, reina.**

   e is similar to the vowel of *late* ([leⁱt]), but without the diphthong. Examples: **mesa, hablé, tres.**

   a is similar to the vowel of *pod*. Examples: **casa, mala, América.** Notably, **a** is always pronounced this way, even when not stressed. This contrasts with the English tendency to reduce unstressed vowels to schwa ([ə]), as in *America*, pronounced in English as [ə-mé-rɪ-kə].

o has a value similar to that of the vowel in Eng. *coat* [ko^{w}t], but without the diphthong. Examples: **no, modo, amó.**

u has a value similar to that of English *oo*, as in *boot* [bu^{w}t], but without the diphthong. Examples: **cura, agudo, uno.** Note that the letter **u** is not pronounced in the syllables **qui, que, gui,** and **gue** (unless spelled with dieresis, as in *bilingüe*). When **u** occurs in diphthongs such as those of **cuida, cuento, deuda,** it has the sound of *w* (as in *way*).

II. CONSONANTS

b and **v** represent the same sounds in Spanish. At the beginning of a breath group or when preceded by the *m* sound (which may be spelled *n*), they are both pronounced like English *b*. Examples: **bomba, en vez de, vine, invierno.** In other environments, especially between vowels, both letters are pronounced as a very relaxed *b*, in which the lips do not completely touch and the air is not completely stopped. This sound has no equivalent in English. Examples: **haba, uva, la vaca, la banda.**

c represents a *k* sound before **a, o, u, l,** and **r.** However, this sound is not accompanied by a puff of air as it is in Eng. *can* and *coat* (compare the *c* in *scan*, which is more similar to the Spanish sound). Examples: **casa, cosa, cuna, quinto, queso, crudo, aclamar.** (Note that, as mentioned above, the vowel **u** is not pronounced in **quinto** and **queso.**) In contrast, when appearing before the vowels **e** and **i, c** is pronounced as *s* in Spanish America and the southwest of Spain, and as *th* (as in *thin*) in other parts of Spain (see **s** for more information).

ch is no longer considered to be a separate letter in the Spanish alphabet. However, it represents a single sound, which is similar to the English *ch* in *church* and *cheek.* Examples: **chato, chaleco, mucho.**

d is phonetically complex in Spanish. In terms of articulation, it is pronounced by the tongue striking the teeth rather than the alveolar ridge as in English. Second, it is represented by two variants. The first of these, which is similar to that of English *dame* and *did*, occurs at the beginning of breath groups or after **n** and **l.** Examples: **donde, falda, conde.** In all other situations the letter represents a sound similar to the *th* of English *then.* Examples: **hado, cuerda, cuadro, usted.** This sound tends to be very relaxed, to the point of disappearing in certain environments, such as word-final and intervocalic.

f is very similar to the English *f* sound. Examples: **faro, elefante, alfalfa.**

g is phonetically complex. Before the vowels **e** and **i,** it is pronounced as *h* in most American dialects, while in northern Spain it is realized like the *ch* in the German word *Bach.* Examples: **gente, giro.** At the beginning of breath groups before the vowels **a, o, u,** and before the consonants **l** and **r,** it is pronounced like the **g** of English *go.* Examples: **ganga, globo, grada.** In all other environments it is pronounced as a very relaxed *g.* Examples: **lago, la goma, agrado.**

3

h is silent. Examples: **hoja, humo, harto.**

j is realized in most American dialects as *h*, while in northern Spain it is pronounced like the *ch* in the German word *Bach*. Examples: **jamás, jugo, jota.**

k sounds like Eng. *k*, but without the accompanying puff of air. Examples: **kilo, keroseno.**

l is pronounced forward in the mouth, as the *l* in *leaf, leak*, never in the back, as in *bell, full*. Examples: **lado, ala, sol.**

ll is no longer considered to be a separate letter in the Spanish alphabet. However, it does represent a single sound, which differs widely in pronunciation throughout the Spanish-speaking world. In most areas, it is pronounced like the *y* of Eng. *yes*, though with greater tension. In extreme northern Spain and in parts of the Andes, it sounds like the *lli* in Eng. *million*. In the River Plate area it is pronounced like the *g* in *beige* or the *sh* in *ship*. Examples: **calle, llano, olla.**

m is essentially the same as in English. Examples: **madre, mano, cama.** However, in final position, as in **álbum** 'album', it is pronounced *n*.

n is normally pronounced like Eng. *n*. Examples: **no, mano, hablan.** There are exceptions, however. For example, before **b, v, p,** and **m**, it is pronounced *m*, as in **en Barcelona, en vez de, un peso**, while before **k, g, j, ge-,** and **gi-**, it is realized as [ŋ], the final sound of Eng. *sing*, as in **anca, tengo, naranja, engendrar.**

ñ is similar to but more tense than the *ny* of Eng. *canyon*. Examples: **cañón, año, ñato.**

p is like English *p* except that it is not accompanied by a puff of air, as it is in Eng. *pill* and *papa* (compare the *p* in *spot*, which is more similar to the Spanish sound). Examples: **padre, capa, apuro.**

q combined with **u** has the sound of *k*. Examples: **queso, aquí, quien.**

r usually represents a sound similar to that of the *tt* in Eng. *kitty*, and the *dd* in *ladder*. Examples: **caro, tren, comer.** In contrast, at the beginning of words, and after **n, l, s,** the letter **r** is realized as a trill, as in **rosa, Enrique, alrededor, Israel.** The double letter **rr** always represents a trill, as in **carro, correr, guerrero.**

s is pronounced the same as in standard American English in most parts of Spanish America and in parts of southern Spain. In most of Spain, in contrast, it is realized with the tip of the tongue against the alveolar ridge, producing a whistling sound that is also common in southern dialects of American English. Examples: **solo, casa, es.** In the Caribbean and in coastal Spanish generally, there is a strong tendency to pronounce **s** in certain environments (usually preconsonantal) as *h*, or to eliminate it entirely. In these dialects, *esta* may be pronounced as *ehta* or *eta*.

t differs from English *t* in two respects: first, it is articulated by the tongue touching the teeth rather than the alveolar ridge, and second, it is not accompanied by a puff of air, as it is in English *too* and *titillate* (compare the *t* in *stop*, which is more similar to the Spanish sound). Examples: **tela, tino, tinta.**

x has a wide range of phonetic realizations. Between vowels, it is usually pronounced *ks* or *gs* (but never *gz*), as in **examen, próximo,** though in a few words it is pronounced as *s*, e.g., *exacto, auxilio*. Before a consonant, **x** is almost always pronounced *s*, as in **extranjero, experiencia.** In many Mexican and Central American words of indigenous origin, **x** represents *h*, as in **México.**

y varies regionally in its pronunciation. In most areas it is pronounced like the *y* of Eng. *yes*, though with greater tension. In the River Plate area it is pronounced like the *g* in *beige* or the *sh* in *ship*. Examples: **yo, ayer.**

z is subject to dialectal variation as well. In most parts of Spain, except the southwest, it is pronounced as the *th* in Eng. *thin, cloth.* In southwestern Spain and all of Spanish America, in contrast, it is pronounced *s*. Examples: **zagal, hallazgo, luz.**

Stress Assignment in Spanish and the Use of the Written Accent

Spanish words are normally stressed on the next-to-last syllable when they end in a vowel or the consonants **n** or **s**. Examples: **mesa, zapato, acontecimiento, hablan, mujeres.** Words whose pronunciation does not conform to this rule are considered exceptions, and their stressed syllable is indicated with an accent mark. Examples: **lámpara, estómago, género, acá, varón, además.**

Conversely, Spanish words are normally stressed on the final syllable when they end in a consonant other than **n** or **s**. Examples: **mujer, actualidad, pedal, voraz.** Words whose pronunciation does not conform to this rule are considered exceptions, and their stressed syllable is indicated with an accent mark. Examples: **nácar, volátil, lápiz.**

For the purposes of stress assignment, diphthongs are considered the same as simple vowels. Thus, **arduo** and **industria** are considered to have two and three syllables respectively, with regular stress on the penultimate syllable. However, some sequences of vowels are not considered diphthongs. For example, **alegría** and **continúo** are both considered to have four syllables, with the stress mark indicating the absence of a diphthong.

Until recently certain words received written accents in order to differentiate functions, even though they are pronounced identically (this is still true in certain cases, such as **de** 'of', **dé** 'give'). Thus, the orthography **esta** was assigned to the demonstrative adjective ('this', fem.), while the demonstrative pronoun ('this one', fem.) was written **ésta.** This convention is no longer observed by most writers.

Notes on Spanish Grammar

The Noun

Gender. All Spanish nouns, not just those that denote male or female beings, are assigned either masculine or feminine gender. As a general rule, male beings (**muchacho** 'boy', **toro** 'bull') and all nouns ending in **-o** (**lodo** 'mud') are assigned masculine gender (exceptions: **mano** 'hand', **radio** 'radio', **foto** 'photo', all feminine). Similarly, female beings (**mujer** 'woman', **vaca** 'cow') and nouns ending in **-a** (**envidia** 'envy') tend to be assigned feminine gender (exceptions: **mapa** 'map', **drama** 'drama', **día** 'day', all masculine). In addition, nouns ending in **-ción, -tad, -dad, -tud,** and **-umbre** are always feminine: **canción** 'song', **facultad** 'college', **ciudad** 'city', **virtud** 'virtue', and **muchedumbre** 'crowd'. Otherwise, nouns ending in consonants and vowels other than **-o** and **-a** are of unpredictable gender. Some are feminine (**barbarie** 'savagery', **clase** 'class', **nariz** 'nose', **tribu** 'tribe'), while others are masculine (**antílope** 'antelope', **corte** 'cut', **mesón** 'lodge', **nácar** 'mother of pearl').

Nouns in **-o** that denote human beings (and to some extent, animals) form the feminine by replacing **-o** with **-a**, as in **tío** 'uncle' / **tía** 'aunt', **niño** 'boy' / **niña** 'girl', **oso** 'bear' / **osa** 'she-bear'. Where the masculine noun does not end in **-o**, the rules of formation are more complex. For example, nouns ending in **-ón, -or,** and **-án** require the addition of **-a**, as in the pairs **patrón** / **patrona** 'patron', **pastor** / **pastora** 'shepherd', **holgazán** / **holgazana** 'lazy person'. In other cases the difference is more unpredictable: **poeta** / **poetisa** 'poet', **emperador** 'emperor' / **emperatriz** 'empress', **abad** 'abbot' / **abadesa** 'abbess'.

Some nouns have different genders according to their meanings: **corte** (m) 'cut', (f) 'court', **capital** (m) 'money capital', (f) 'capital city', while others have invariable endings which are used for both the masculine and the feminine: **artista** 'artist' (and all nouns ending in **-ista**), **amante** 'lover', **aristócrata** 'aristocrat', **homicida** 'murderer', **cliente** 'customer'. Finally, some words vacillate as to gender, e.g., **mar** 'sea', which is normally masculine but is feminine in certain expressions (**en alta mar** 'on the high seas') and in poetic contexts, and **arte**, which is masculine in the singular but feminine in the plural. Some words, such as **armazón** and **esperma,** can be both masculine and feminine.

Pluralization. Nouns ending in an unaccented vowel and **-é** add **-s** to form the plural: **libro** / **libros, casa** / **casas, café** / **cafés,** while nouns ending in a consonant, in **-y,** or in an accented vowel other than **-é** add **-es:** **papel** / **papeles, canción** / **canciones, ley** / **leyes, rubí** / **rubíes.** Exceptions to this rule include the words **papá** / **papás, mamá** / **mamás,** and the small group of nouns ending in unaccented **-es** and **-is,** which do not change in the plural: **lunes** 'Monday', 'Mondays', **tesis** 'thesis', 'theses'.

Articles

Definite Article. The equivalent of English **the** is as follows: masculine singular, **el;** feminine singular, **la;** masculine plural, **los;** feminine plural, **las.** Feminine words beginning with stressed **a** or **ha** take **el** in the singular and **las** in the plural: **el alma** 'the soul' / **las almas** 'the souls', **el hacha** 'the hatchet' / **las hachas** 'the hatchets'. In spite of this, these nouns remain feminine in the singular, as shown by adjective agreement: **el alma bendita** 'the blessed soul'. When preceded by the prepositions **a** and **de,** the masculine singular article **el** forms the contractions **al** and **del.**

Indefinite Article. The equivalent of English **a, an** is as follows: masculine singular, **un;** feminine singular, **una.** In the plural, masculine **unos** and feminine **unas** are equivalent to English **some.** Feminine words beginning with stressed **a** or **ha** take **un** in the singular and **unas** in the plural: **un alma** 'a soul' / **unas almas** 'some souls', **un hacha** 'a hatchet' / **unas hachas** 'some hatchets'.

Adjectives

Agreement. The adjective in Spanish agrees in gender and number with the noun it modifies: **el lápiz rojo** 'the red pencil', **la casa blanca** 'the white house', **los libros interesantes** 'the interesting books', **las flores hermosas** 'the beautiful flowers'.

Formation of the Plural. Adjectives follow the same rules as nouns for the formation of the plural: **pálido, pálidos** 'pale', **fácil, fáciles** 'easy', **cortés, corteses** 'courteous', **capaz, capaces** 'capable'.

Formation of the Feminine. Adjectives ending in **-o** change to **-a**: **blanco, blanca** 'white'. Adjectives ending in other vowels are invariable: **verde** 'green', **fuerte** 'strong', **indígena** 'indigenous, native', **pesimista** 'pessimistic', **baladí** 'trivial', as are adjectives ending in a consonant: **fácil** 'easy', **cortés** 'courteous', **mayor** 'older', 'larger'. Some cases are more complex: (a) adjectives ending in **-ón, -án, -or** (except comparatives like **mayor**) add **-a** to form the feminine: **holgazán, holgazana** 'lazy', **preguntón, preguntona** 'inquisitive', **hablador, habladora** 'talkative', (b) adjectives of nationality ending in a consonant add **-a** to form the feminine: **francés, francesa** 'French', **español, española** 'Spanish', **alemán, alemana** 'German'.

Adverbs

Most adverbs are formed by adding **-mente** to the feminine form of the adjective: **clara** 'clear' / **claramente** 'clearly', **fácil** 'easy' / **fácilmente** 'easily'.

Comparison of Inequality in Adjectives and Adverbs

The comparative of inequality is formed by placing **más** or **menos** before the positive form of the adjective or adverb: **más rico que** 'richer than', **menos rico que** 'less rich than', **más tarde** 'later', **menos tarde** 'less late'. The superlative is formed by placing the definite article **el** before the comparative: **el más rico** 'the richest', **el menos rico** 'the least rich'.

The following adjectives and adverbs have irregular forms of comparison:

Positive	Comparative	Superlative
bueno	mejor	el (la) mejor
malo	peor	el (la) peor
grande	mayor	el (la) mayor
pequeño	menor	el (la) menor

Common Spanish Suffixes

-aco   is a pejorative suffix: **pajarraco** 'ugly bird' (from **pájaro** 'bird'), **libraco** 'large, bulky book' (**libro** 'book')

-ada   *a.*   attaches to verbal stems to indicate an action: **mirada** 'look' (**mirar** 'to look'), **empujada** 'push' (**empujar** 'to push')

     b.   attaches to noun stems to indicate a blow: **cachetada** 'blow on the cheek' (**cachete** 'cheek'), **puñalada** 'stab with a dagger' (**puñal** 'dagger')

     c.   attaches to nominal stems to indicate an action characteristic of a person or group: **bobada** 'foolish act' (**bobo** 'fool'), **niñada** 'childish act' (**niño** 'child')

-al, -ar   attach to nouns indicating trees to form nouns that denote a grove: **naranjal** 'orange grove' (from **naranjo** 'orange tree'), **pinar** 'pine grove' (**pino** 'pine tree')

-azo   attaches to noun stems, forming nouns that indicate

     a.   augmentation: **hombrazo** 'big man' (**hombre** 'man'), **marranazo** 'large hog' (**marrano** 'hog')

     b.   a blow or explosion: **porrazo** 'blow with a club' (**porra** 'club'), **cañonazo** 'cannon shot' (**cañón** 'cannon')

-cito   is a diminutive suffix: **cochecito** 'a little car' (**coche** 'car'), **mujercita** 'little woman' (**mujer** 'woman')

-dor   forms agent nouns from verbs: **hablador** 'talker' (**hablar** 'to talk'), **regulador** 'regulator' (**regular** 'to regulate'), which are sometimes used as adjectives: **hablador** 'talkative', **regulador** 'regulating'

-ejo   is a pejorative suffix: **librejo** 'worthless book' (**libro** 'book'), **lugarejo** 'Podunk' (**lugar** 'place')

-ería   attaches to noun stems to denote

     a.   a place where something is made or sold: **zapatería** 'shoestore' (**zapato** 'shoe'), **pastelería** 'pastry shop' (**pastel** 'pastry')

     b.   a profession, business, or occupation: **carpintería** 'carpentry' (**carpintero** 'carpenter'), **ingeniería** 'engineering' (**ingeniero** 'engineer')

     c.   a group: **chiquillería** 'bunch of children' (**chiquillo** 'little kid')

-ero   *a.*   attaches to nouns to indicate a person who makes, sells, or is in charge of something: **librero** 'bookseller' (**libro** 'book'), **zapatero** 'shoemaker' (**zapato** 'shoe'), **carcelero** 'jailer' (**cárcel** 'jail')

     b.   attaches to nominal stems to form adjectives: **guerrero** 'warlike' (**guerra** 'war'), **conejero** 'for hunting rabbits' (**conejo** 'rabbit')

-ez, -eza	are used to make abstract nouns from adjectival bases: **vejez** 'old age' (**viejo** 'old'), **niñez** 'childhood' (**niño** 'child'), **grandeza** 'greatness' (**grande** 'large, great'), **rareza** 'rarity' (**raro** 'rare')
-ía	forms adjective abstracts: **valentía** 'courage' (**valiente** 'brave'), **cobardía** 'cowardice' (**cobarde** 'coward')
-ico	is a diminutive suffix: **ratico** 'little while' (**rato** 'while'), **momentico** 'brief moment' (**momento** 'moment')
-(i)ento	attaches to adjectives to indicate attenuation, as in **amarillento** 'yellowish' (**amarillo** 'yellow'), or an undesirable quality, as in **hambriento** 'hungry' (**hambre** 'hunger')
-illo	is sometimes a diminutive suffix: **politiquillo** 'insignificant politician' (**político** 'politician'), **chiquillo** 'little kid' (**chico** 'child')
-ísimo	attaches to adjectives to indicate an extreme degree of a quality: **hermosísimo** 'very beautiful' (**hermoso** 'beautiful')
-ito	is a diminutive suffix: **librito** 'small book' (**libro** 'book'), **casita** 'little house' (**casa** 'house')
-izo	forms adjectives from nominal stems, indicating a tendency or attenuation: **rojizo** 'reddish' (**rojo** 'red'), **olvidadizo** 'forgetful' (**olvidar** 'to forget')
-mente	is the adverbial ending attached to the feminine form of the adjective: **generosamente** 'generously' (**generoso** 'generous'), **claramente** 'clearly' (**claro** 'clear')
-ón *a.*	is an augmentative adjectival suffix: **barrigón** 'pot-bellied' (**barriga** 'belly'), **cabezón** 'large-headed' (**cabeza** 'head')
b.	attaches to verb stems to denote sudden actions: **tirón** 'pull, jerk' (**tirar** 'to pull'), **apretón** 'push' (**apretar** 'to push')
-oso	forms adjectives from nouns, indicating abundance or character: **rocoso** 'rocky' (**roca** 'rock'), **tormentoso** 'stormy' (**tormenta** 'storm')
-ote, -ota	is an augmentative and pejorative suffix attached to nouns: **discursote** 'long, boring speech' (**discurso** 'speech'), **narizota** 'big ugly nose' (**nariz** 'nose')
-udo	forms adjectives from nouns, indicating an excess: **peludo** 'hairy' (**pelo** 'hair'), **panzudo** 'big-bellied' (**panza** 'belly')

-ura	forms abstract nouns from adjectives: **negrura** 'blackness' (**negro** 'black'), **altura** 'height' (**alto** 'high')
-uzco	forms adjectives from other adjectives, indicating attenuation: **blancuzco** 'whitish' (**blanco** 'white'), **negruzco** 'blackish' (**negro** 'black')

Spanish Regular Verbs

First Conjugation

Infinitive	**hablar**
Pres. Indic.	hablo, hablas, habla, hablamos, habláis, hablan
Pres. Subj.	hable, hables, hable, hablemos, habléis, hablen
Pret. Indic.	hablé, hablaste, habló, hablamos, hablasteis, hablaron
Imp. Indic.	hablaba, hablabas, hablaba, hablábamos, hablabais, hablaban
Imp. Subj.	hablara, hablaras, hablara, habláramos, hablarais, hablaran, *or* hablase, hablases, hablase, hablásemos, hablaseis, hablasen
Fut. Indic.	hablaré, hablarás, hablará, hablaremos, hablaréis, hablarán
Cond.	hablaría, hablarías, hablaría, hablaríamos, hablaríais, hablarían
Imperatives	habla (tú), hable (usted), hablad (vosotros), hablen (ustedes)
Pres. Part.	hablando
Past Part.	hablado

Second Conjugation

Infinitive	**comer**
Pres. Indic.	como, comes, come, comemos, coméis, comen
Pres. Subj.	coma, comas, coma, comamos, comáis, coman
Pret. Indic.	comí, comiste, comió, comimos, comisteis, comieron
Imp. Indic.	comía, comías, comía, comíamos, comíais, comían
Imp. Subj.	comiera, comieras, comiera, comiéramos, comierais, comieran, *or* comiese, comieses, comiese, comiésemos, comieseis, comiesen
Fut. Indic.	comeré, comerás, comerá, comeremos, comeréis, comerán
Cond.	comería, comerías, comería, comeríamos, comeríais, comerían
Imperatives	come (tú), coma (usted), comed (vosotros), coman (ustedes)
Pres. Part.	comiendo
Past Part.	comido

Third Conjugation

Infinitive	**vivir**
Pres. Indic.	vivo, vives, vive, vivimos, vivís, viven
Pres. Subj.	viva, vivas, viva, vivamos, viváis, vivan
Pret. Indic.	viví, viviste, vivió, vivimos, vivisteis, vivieron
Imp. Indic.	vivía, vivías, vivía, vivíamos, vivíais, vivían

Imp. Subj.	viviera, vivieras, viviera, viviéramos, vivierais, vivieran, *or*
	viviese, vivieses, viviese, viviésemos, vivieseis, viviesen
Fut. Indic.	viviré, vivirás, vivirá, viviremos, viviréis, vivirán
Cond.	viviría, vivirías, viviría, viviríamos, viviríais, vivirían
Imperative	vive (tú), viva (usted), vivid (vosotros), vivan (ustedes)
Pres. Part.	viviendo
Past Part.	vivido

Spanish Irregular and Orthographic Changing Verbs

The superscript number or numbers listed as part of a verb entry indicate that the verb is to be conjugated like the model verb in this section that has the corresponding number. Only the tenses that have irregular forms or spelling changes are given, wherein irregular forms and spelling changes are shown in boldface type.

1. **pensar**

Pres. Indic.	**pienso, piensas, piensa,** pensamos, pensáis, **piensan**
Pres. Subj.	**piense, pienses, piense,** pensemos, penséis, **piensen**
Imper.	**piensa** (tú), **piense** (usted), pensad (vosotros), **piensen** (ustedes)

2. **contar**

Pres. Indic.	**cuento, cuentas, cuenta,** contamos, contáis, **cuentan**
Pres. Subj.	**cuente, cuentes, cuente,** contemos, contéis, **cuenten**
Imper.	**cuenta** (tú), **cuente** (usted), contad (vosotros), **cuenten** (ustedes)

3. *a.* **sentir**

Pres. Indic.	**siento, sientes, siente,** sentimos, sentís, **sienten**
Pres. Subj.	**sienta, sientas, sienta, sintamos, sintáis, sientan**
Pret. Indic.	sentí, sentiste, **sintió,** sentimos, sentisteis, **sintieron**
Imp. Subj.	**sintiera, sintieras, sintiera, sintiéramos, sintierais, sintieran,** or **sintiese, sintieses, sintiese, sintiésemos, sintieseis, sintiesen**
Imperative	**siente** (tú), **sienta** (usted), sentid (vosotros), **sientan** (ustedes)
Pres. Part.	**sintiendo**

   b. **erguir**

Pres. Indic.	**yergo, yergues, yergue,** erguimos, erguís, **yerguen**
Pres. Subj.	**yerga, yergas, yerga, irgamos, irgáis, yergan**
Pret. Indic.	erguí, erguiste, **irguió,** erguimos, erguisteis, **irguieron**
Imp. Subj.	**irguiera, irguieras, irguiera, irguiéramos, irguierais, irguieran,** or **irguiese, irguieses, irguiese, irguiésemos, irguieseis, irguiesen**
Imperative	**yergue** (tú), **yerga** (usted), erguid (vosotros), **yergan** (ustedes)
Pres. Part.	**irguiendo**

4. **dormir**

Pres. Indic.	**duermo, duermes, duerme,** dormimos, dormís, **duermen**
Pres. Subj.	**duerma, duermas, duerma, durmamos, durmáis, duerman**
Pret. Indic.	dormí, dormiste, **durmió,** dormimos, dormisteis, **durmieron**
Imp. Subj.	**durmiera, durmieras, durmiera, durmiéramos, durmierais, durmieran,** or **durmiese, durmieses, durmiese, durmiésemos, durmieseis, durmiesen**
Imperative	**duerme** (tú), **duerma** (usted), dormid (vosotros), **duerman** (ustedes)
Pres. Part.	**durmiendo**

5. **pedir**

Pres. Indic.	**pido, pides, pide,** pedimos, pedís, **piden**
Pres. Subj.	**pida, pidas, pida, pidamos, pidáis, pidan**
Pret. Indic.	**pedí,** pediste, **pidió,** pedimos, pedisteis, **pidieron**
Imp. Subj.	**pidiera, pidieras, pidiera, pidiéramos, pidierais, pidieran,** or **pidiese, pidieses, pidiese, pidiésemos, pidieseis, pidiesen**
Imperative	**pide** (tú), **pida** (usted), pedid (vosotros), **pidan** (ustedes)
Pres. Part.	**pidiendo**

6. **buscar**

Pres. Subj.	**busque, busques, busque, busquemos, busquéis, busquen**
Pret. Indic.	**busqué,** buscaste, buscó, buscamos, buscasteis, buscaron
Imperative	busca (tú), **busque** (usted), buscad (vosotros), **busquen** (ustedes)

7. **llegar**

Pres. Subj.	**llegue, llegues, llegue, lleguemos, lleguéis, lleguen**
Pret. Indic.	**llegué,** llegaste, llegó, llegamos, llegasteis, llegaron
Imperative	llega (tú), **llegue** (usted), llegad (vosotros), **lleguen** (ustedes)

8. **averiguar**

Pres. Subj.	**averigüe, averigües, averigüe, averigüemos, averigüéis, averigüen**
Pret. Indic.	**averigüé,** averiguaste, averiguó, averiguamos, averiguasteis, averiguaron
Imperative	averigua (tú), **averigüe** (usted), averiguad (vosotros), **averigüen** (ustedes)

9. **abrazar**

Pres. Subj.	**abrace, abraces, abrace, abracemos, abracéis, abracen**

Pret. Indic.	**abracé,** abrazaste, abrazó, abrazamos, abrazasteis, abrazaron
Imperative	abraza (tú), **abrace** (usted), abrazad (vosotros), **abracen** (ustedes)

10. *a.* **convencer**

Pres. Indic.	**convenzo,** convences, convence, convencemos, convencéis, convencen
Pres. Subj.	**convenza, convenzas, convenza, convenzamos, convenzáis, convenzan**
Imperative	convence (tú), **convenza** (usted), convenced (vosotros), **convenzan** (ustedes)

b. **esparcir**

Pres. Indic.	**esparzo,** esparces, esparce, esparcimos, esparcís, esparcen
Pres. Subj.	**esparza, esparzas, esparza, esparzamos, esparzáis, esparzan**
Imperative	esparce (tú), **esparza** (usted), esparcid (vosotros), **esparzan** (ustedes)

c. **cocer**

Pres. Indic.	**cuezo,** cueces, cuece, cocemos, cocéis, cuecen
Pres. Subj.	**cueza, cuezas, cueza, cozamos, cozáis, cuezan**
Imperative	cuece (tú), **cueza** (usted), coced (vosotros), **cuezan** (ustedes)

11. *a.* **dirigir**

Pres. Indic.	**dirijo,** diriges, dirige, dirigimos, dirigís, dirigen
Pres. Subj.	**dirija, dirijas, dirija, dirijamos, dirijáis, dirijan**
Imper.	dirige (tú), **dirija** (usted), dirigid (vosotros), **dirijan** (ustedes)

b. **coger**

Pres. Indic.	**cojo,** coges, coge, cogemos, cogéis, cogen
Pres. Subj.	**coja, cojas, coja, cojamos, cojáis, cojan**
Imperative	coge (tú), **coja** (usted), coged (vosotros), **cojan** (ustedes)

12. **distinguir**

Pres. Indic.	**distingo,** distingues, distingue, distinguimos, distinguís, distinguen
Pres. Subj.	**distinga, distingas, distinga, distingamos, distingáis, distingan**
Imperative	distingue (tú), **distinga** (usted), distinguid (vosotros), **distingan** (ustedes)

13. *a.* **conocer**

Pres. Indic.	**conozco,** conoces, conoce, conocemos, conocéis, conocen
Pres. Subj.	**conozca, conozcas, conozca, conozcamos, conozcáis, conozcan**
Imperative	conoce (tú), **conozca** (usted), conoced (vosotros), **conozcan** (ustedes)

13

b. **lucir**

Pres. Indic.	**luzco,** luces, luce, lucimos, lucís, lucen
Pres. Subj.	**luzca, luzcas, luzca, luzcamos, luzcáis, luzcan**
Imperative	luce (tú), **luzca** (usted), lucid (vosotros), **luzcan** (ustedes)

14. **creer**

Pret. Indic.	creí, creíste, **creyó,** creímos, creísteis, **creyeron**
Imp. Subj.	**creyera, creyeras, creyera, creyéramos, creyerais, creyeran,** or **creyese, creyeses, creyese, creyésemos, creyeseis, creyesen**
Pret. Part.	**creyendo**

15. **reír**

Pres. Indic.	**río, ríes, ríe,** reímos, reís, **ríen**
Pres. Subj.	**ría, rías, ría, riamos, riáis, rían**
Pret. Indic.	reí, reíste, **rió,** reímos, reísteis, **rieron**
Imp. Subj.	**riera, rieras, riera, riéramos, rierais, rieran,** or **riese, rieses, riese, riésemos, rieseis, riesen**
Imperative	**ríe** (tú), **ría** (usted), reíd (vosotros), **rían** (ustedes)
Pres. Part.	**riendo**

16. **enviar**

Pres. Indic.	envío, envías, envía, enviamos, enviáis, envían
Pres. Subj.	envíe, envíes, enviemos, enviéis, envíen
Imperative	envía (tú), envíe (usted), enviad (vosotros), envíen (ustedes)

17. **continuar**

Pres. Indic.	continúo, continúas, continúa, continuamos, continuáis, continúan
Pres. Subj.	continúe, continúes, continúe, continuemos, continuéis, continúen
Imperative	continúa (tú), continúe (usted), continuad (vosotros), continúen (ustedes)

18. **gruñir**

Pret. Indic.	gruñí, gruñiste, **gruñó,** gruñisteis, **gruñeron**
Imp. Subj.	**gruñera, gruñeras, gruñera, gruñéramos, gruñerais, gruñeran,** or **gruñese, gruñeses, gruñese, gruñésemos, gruñeseis, gruñesen**
Pres. Part.	**gruñendo**

19. **bullir**

Pret. Indic.	bullí, bulliste, **bulló,** bullimos, bullisteis, **bulleron**
Imp. Subj.	**bullera, bulleras, bullera, bulléramos, bullerais, bulleran,** or **bullese, bulleses, bullese, bullésemos, bulleseis, bullesen**
Pres. Part.	**bullendo**

20. **andar**
   Pret. Indic. **anduve, anduviste, anduvo, anduvimos, anduvisteis, anduvieron**
   Imp. Subj. **anduviera, anduvieras, anduviera, anduviéramos, anduvierais, anduvieran,** or
   anduviese, anduvieses, anduviese, anduviésemos, anduvieseis, anduviesen

21. **asir**
   Pres. Indic. **asgo,** ases, ase, asimos, asís, asen
   Pres. Subj. **asga, asgas, asga, asgamos, asgáis, asgan**
   Imperative ase (tú), **asga** (usted), asid (vosotros), **asgan** (ustedes)

22. **caber**
   Pres. Indic. **quepo,** cabes, cabe, cabemos, cabéis, caben
   Pres. Subj. **quepa, quepas, quepa, quepamos, quepáis, quepan**
   Pret. Indic. **cupe, cupiste, cupo, cupimos, cupisteis, cupieron**
   Imp. Subj. **cupiera, cupieras, cupiera, cupiéramos, cupierais, cupieran,** or **cupiese, cupieses, cupiese, cupiésemos, cupieseis, cupiesen**
   Fut. Indic. **cabré, cabrás, cabrá, cabremos, cabréis, cabrán**
   Cond. **cabría, cabrías, cabría, cabríamos, cabríais, cabrían**
   Imperative cabe (tú), **quepa** (usted), cabed (vosotros), **quepan** (ustedes)

23. **caer**
   Pres. Indic. **caigo,** caes, cae, caemos, caéis, caen
   Pres. Subj. **caiga, caigas, caiga, caigamos, caigáis, caigan**
   Pret. Indic. caí, caiste, **cayó,** caímos, caísteis, **cayeron**
   Imp. Subj. **cayera, cayeras, cayera, cayéramos, cayerais, cayeran,** or **cayese, cayeses, cayese, cayésemos, cayeseis, cayesen**
   Imperative cae (tú), **caiga** (usted), caed (vosotros), **caigan** (ustedes)
   Pres. Part. **cayendo**

24. **conducir**
   Pres. Indic. **conduzco,** conduces, conduce, conducimos, conducís, conducen
   Pres. Subj. **conduzca, conduzcas, conduzca, conduzcamos, conduzcáis, conduzcan**
   Pret. Indic. **conduje, condujiste, condujo, condujimos, condujisteis, condujeron**
   Imp. Subj. **condujera, condujeras, condujera, condujéramos, condujerais, condujeran,** or **condujese, condujeses, condujese, condujésemos, condujeseis, condujesen**
   Imperative conduce (tú), **conduzca** (usted), conducid (vosotros), **conduzcan** (ustedes)

25. **dar**
    Pres. Indic.   **doy,** das, da, damos, dais, dan
    Pres. Subj.   **dé,** des, **dé,** demos, deis, den
    Pret. Indic.   **di, diste, dio, dimos, disteis, dieron**
    Imp. Subj.   **diera, dieras, diera, diéramos, dierais, dieran,** or
                       diese, dieses, diese, diésemos, dieseis, diesen

26. **decir**[1]
    Pres. Indic.   **digo, dices, dice,** decimos, decís, **dicen**
    Pres. Subj.   **diga, digas, diga, digamos, digáis, digan**
    Pret. Indic.   **dije, dijiste, dijo, dijimos, dijisteis, dijeron**
    Imp. Subj.   **dijera, dijeras, dijera, dijéramos, dijerais, dijeran,** or
                       dijese, dijeses, dijese, dijésemos, dijeseis, dijesen
    Fut. Indic.   **diré, dirás, dirá, diremos, diréis, dirán**
    Cond.   **diría, dirías, diría, diríamos, diríais, dirían**
    Imperative   **di** (tú), **diga** (usted), decid (vosotros), **digan** (ustedes)
    Pres. Part.   **diciendo**
    Past Part.   **dicho**

27. **errar**
    Pres. Indic.   **yerro, yerras, yerra,** erramos, erráis, **yerran**
    Pres. Subj.   **yerre, yerres, yerre,** erremos, erréis, **yerren**
    Imperative   **yerra** (tú), **yerre** (usted), errad (vosotros), **yerren** (ustedes)

28. **estar**
    Pres. Indic.   **estoy, estás, está,** estamos, estáis, **están**
    Pres. Subj.   **esté, estés, esté,** estemos, estéis, **estén**
    Pret. Indic.   **estuve, estuviste, estuvo, estuvimos, estuvisteis,
                       estuvieron**
    Imp. Subj.   **estuviera, estuvieras, estuviera, estuviéramos,
                       estuvierais, estuvieran,** or **estuviese, estuvieses,
                       estuviese, estuviésemos, estuvieseis, estuviesen**
    Imperative   **está** (tú), **esté** (usted), estad (vosotros), **estén** (ustedes)

29. **haber**
    Pres. Indic.   **he, has, ha, hemos,** habéis, **han**
    Pres. Subj.   **haya, hayas, haya, hayamos, hayáis, hayan**
    Pret. Indic.   **hube, hubiste, hubo, hubimos, hubisteis, hubieron**
    Imp. Subj.   **hubiera, hubieras, hubiera, hubiéramos, hubierais,
                       hubieran,** or **hubiese, hubieses, hubiese, hubiésemos,
                       hubieseis, hubiesen**
    Fut. Indic.   **habré, habrás, habrá, habremos, habréis, habrán**

1. The compound verbs of *decir* have the same irregularities with the exception of the following: The future and conditional of the compound verbs *bendecir* and *maldecir* are regular: *bendeciré, maldeciré,* etc.; *bendeciría, maldeciría,* etc. The familiar imperative is regular: *bendice tu, maldice tu, contradice tu,* etc. The past participles of *bendecir* and *maldecir* are regular when used with haber or in the passive with ser: *bendecido, maldecido.*

	Cond.	**habría, habrías, habría, habríamos, habríais, habrían**

30. **hacer**
	Pres. Indic.	**hago,** haces, hace, hacemos, hacéis, hacen
	Pres. Subj.	**haga, hagas, haga, hagamos, hagáis, hagan**
	Pret. Indic.	**hice, hiciste, hizo, hicimos, hicisteis, hicieron**
	Imp. Subj.	**hiciera, hicieras, hiciera, hiciéramos, hicierais, hicieran,** or **hiciese, hicieses, hiciese, hiciésemos, hicieseis, hiciesen**
	Fut. Indic.	**haré, harás, hará, haremos, haréis, harán**
	Cond.	**haría, harías, haría, haríamos, haríais, harían**
	Imperative	**haz** (tú), **haga** (usted), haced (vosotros), **hagan** (ustedes)
	Past Part.	**hecho**

31. *a.* **huir**
	Pres. Indic.	**huyo, huyes, huye,** huimos, huís, **huyen**
	Pres. Subj.	**huya, huyas, huya, huyamos, huyáis, huyan**
	Pret. Indic.	huí, huiste, **huyó,** huimos, huisteis, **huyeron**
	Imp. Subj.	**huyera, huyeras, huyera, huyéramos, huyerais, huyeran,** or **huyese, huyeses, huyese, huyésemos, huyeseis, huyesen**
	Imperative	**huye** (tú), **huya** (usted), huid (vosotros), **huyan** (ustedes)
	Pres. Part.	**huyendo**

    b. **argüir**
	Pres. Indic.	**arguyo, arguyes, arguye,** argüimos, argüís, **arguyen**
	Pres. Subj.	**arguya, arguyas, arguya, arguyamos, arguyáis, arguyan**
	Pret. Indic.	argüí, argüiste, **arguyó,** argüimos, argüisteis, **arguyeron**
	Imp. Subj.	**arguyera, arguyeras, arguyera, arguyéramos, arguyerais, arguyeran,** or **arguyese, arguyeses, arguyese, arguyésemos, arguyeseis, arguyesen**
	Imperative	**arguye** (tú), **arguya** (usted), argüid (vosotros), **arguyan** (ustedes)
	Pres. Part.	**arguyendo**

32. **ir**
	Pres. Indic.	**voy, vas, va, vamos, vais, van**
	Pres. Subj.	**vaya, vayas, vaya, vayamos, vayáis, vayan**
	Imp. Indic.	**iba, ibas, iba, íbamos, ibais, iban**
	Pret. Indic.	**fui, fuiste, fue, fuimos, fuisteis, fueron**
	Imp. Subj.	**fuera, fueras, fuera, fuéramos, fuerais, fueran,** or **fuese, fueses, fuese, fuésemos, fueseis, fuesen**
	Imperative	**ve** (tú), **vaya** (usted), id (vosotros), **vayan** (ustedes)
	Pres. Part.	**yendo**

33. **jugar**
    Pres. Indic.   **juego, juegas, juega,** jugamos, jugáis, **juegan**
    Pres. Subj.   **juegue, juegues, juegue,** juguemos, juguéis, **jueguen**
    Pret. Indic.   **jugué,** jugaste, jugó, jugamos, jugasteis, jugaron
    Imperative   **juega** (tú), **juegue** (usted), jugad (vosotros), **jueguen**
                     (ustedes)

34. **adquirir**
    Pres. Indic.   **adquiero, adquieres, adquiere,** adquirimos, adquirís,
                     adquieren
    Pres. Subj.   **adquiera, adquieras, adquiera,** adquiramos, adquiráis,
                     adquieran
    Imperative   **adquiere** (tú), **adquiera** (usted), adquirid (vosotros),
                     adquieran (ustedes)

35. **oír**
    Pres. Indic.   **oigo, oyes, oye,** oímos, oís, **oyen**
    Pres. Subj.   **oiga, oigas, oiga, oigamos, oigáis, oigan**
    Pret. Indic.   oí, oíste, **oyó,** oímos, oísteis, **oyeron**
    Imp. Subj.   **oyera, oyeras, oyera, oyéramos, oyerais, oyeran,** or
                     oyese, oyeses, oyese, oyésemos, oyeseis, oyesen
    Imperative   **oye** (tú), **oiga** (usted), oíd (vosotros), **oigan** (ustedes)
    Pres. Part.   **oyendo**

36. **oler**
    Pres. Indic.   **huelo, hueles, huele,** olemos, oléis, **huelen**
    Pres. Subj.   **huela, huelas, huela,** olamos, oláis, **huelan**
    Imperative   **huele** (tú), **huela** (usted), oled (vosotros), **huelan**
                     (ustedes)

37. **placer**
    Pres. Indic.   **plazco,** places, place, placemos, placéis, placen
    Pres. Subj.   **plazca, plazcas, plazca, plazcamos, plazcáis, plazcan**

38. **poder**
    Pres. Indic.   **puedo, puedes, puede,** podemos, podéis, **pueden**
    Pres. Subj.   **pueda, puedas, pueda,** podamos, podáis, **puedan**
    Pret. Indic.   pude, pudiste, pudo, pudimos, pudisteis, pudieron
    Imp. Subj.   pudiera, pudieras, pudiera, pudiéramos, pudierais,
                     pudieran, or pudiese, pudieses, pudiese, pudiésemos,
                     pudieseis, pudiesen
    Fut. Indic.   podré, podrás, podrá, podremos, podréis, podrán
    Cond.   podría, podrías, podría, podríamos, podríais,
                     podrían
    Pres. Part.   pudiendo

39. **poner**
    Pres. Indic.   **pongo,** pones, pone, ponemos, ponéis, ponen

Pres. Subj.	**ponga, pongas, ponga, pongamos, pongáis, pongan**
Pret. Indic.	**puse, pusiste, puso, pusimos, pusisteis, pusieron**
Imp. Subj.	**pusiera, pusieras, pusiera, pusiéramos, pusierais, pusieran,** or **pusiese, pusieses, pusiese, pusiésemos, pusieseis, pusiesen**
Fut. Indic.	**pondré, pondrás, pondrá, pondremos, pondréis, pondrán**
Cond.	**pondría, pondrías, pondría, pondríamos, pondríais, pondrían**
Imperative	**pon** (tú), **ponga** (usted), poned (vosotros), **pongan** (ustedes)
Past Part.	**puesto**

40. **querer**

Pres. Indic.	**quiero, quieres, quiere,** queremos, queréis, **quieren**
Pres. Subj.	**quiera, quieras, quiera,** queramos, queráis, **quieran**
Pret. Indic.	**quise, quisiste, quiso, quisimos, quisisteis, quisieron**
Imp. Subj.	**quisiera, quisieras, quisiera, quisiéramos, quisierais, quisieran,** or **quisiese, quisieses, quisiese, quisiémos, quisieseis, quisiesen**
Fut. Indic.	**querré, querrás, querrá, querremos, querréis, querrán**
Cond.	**querría, querrías, querría, querríamos, querríais, querrían**
Imperative	**quiere** (tú), **quiera** (usted), quered (vosotros), **quieran** (ustedes)

41. **saber**

Pres. Indic.	**sé,** sabes, sabe, sabemos, sabéis, saben
Pres. Subj.	**sepa, sepas, sepa, sepamos, sepáis, sepan**
Pret. Indic.	**supe, supiste, supo, supimos, supisteis, supieron**
Imp. Subj.	**supiera, supieras, supiera, supiéramos, supierais, supieran,** or **supiese, supieses, supiese, supiésemos, supieseis, supiesen**
Fut. Indic.	**sabré, sabrás, sabrá, sabremos, sabréis, sabrán**
Cond.	**sabría, sabrías, sabría, sabríamos, sabríais, sabrían**
Imperative	sabe (tú), **sepa** (usted), sabed (vosotros), **sepan** (ustedes)

42. **salir**

Pres. Indic.	**salgo,** sales, sale, salimos, salís, salen
Pres. Subj.	**salga, salgas, salga, salgamos, salgáis, salgan**
Fut. Indic.	**saldré, saldrás, saldrá, saldremos, saldréis, saldrán**
Cond.	**saldría, saldrías, saldría, saldríamos, saldríais, saldrían**
Imperative	**sal** (tú),[2] **salga** (usted), salid (vosotros), **salgan** (ustedes)

2. The compound *sobresalir* is regular in the familiar imperative: **sobresale tú.**

43. **ser**

Pres. Indic.	**soy, eres, es, somos, sois, son**
Pres. Subj.	**sea, seas, sea, seamos, seáis, sean**
Imp. Indic.	**era, eras, era, éramos, erais, eran**
Pret. Indic.	**fui, fuiste, fue, fuimos, fuisteis, fueron**
Imp. Subj.	**fuera, fueras, fuera, fuéramos, fuerais, fueran,** or **fuese, fueses, fuese, fuésemos, fueseis, fuesen**
Imperative	**sé** (tú), **sea** (usted), sed (vosotros), **sean** (ustedes)

44. **tener**

Pres. Indic.	**tengo, tienes, tiene,** tenemos, tenéis, **tienen**
Pres. Subj.	**tenga, tengas, tenga, tengamos, tengáis, tengan**
Pret. Indic.	**tuve, tuviste, tuvo, tuvimos, tuvisteis, tuvieron**
Imp. Subj.	**tuviera, tuvieras, tuviera, tuviéramos, tuvierais, tuvieran,** or **tuviese, tuvieses, tuviese, tuviésemos, tuvieseis, tuviesen**
Fut. Indic.	**tendré, tendrás, tendrá, tendremos, tendréis, tendrán**
Cond.	**tendría, tendrías, tendría, tendríamos, tendríais, tendrían**
Imperative	**ten** (tú), **tenga** (usted), tened (vosotros), **tengan** (ustedes)

45. **traer**

Pres. Indic.	**traigo,** traes, trae, traemos, traéis, traen
Pres. Subj.	**traiga, traigas, traiga, traigamos, traigáis, traigan**
Pret. Indic.	**traje, trajiste, trajo, trajimos, trajisteis, trajeron**
Imp. Subj.	**trajera, trajeras, trajera, trajéramos, trajerais, trajeran,** or **trajese, trajeses, trajese, trajésemos, trajeseis, trajesen**
Imperative	trae (tú), **traiga** (usted), traed (vosotros), **traigan** (ustedes)
Pres. Part.	**trayendo**

46. **valer**

Pres. Indic.	**valgo,** vales, vale, valemos, valéis, valen
Pres. Subj.	**valga, valgas, valga, valgamos, valgáis, valgan**
Fut. Indic.	**valdré, valdrás, valdrá, valdremos, valdréis, valdrán**
Cond.	**valdría, valdrías, valdría, valdríamos, valdríais, valdrían**
Imperative	**val** or vale (tú), **valga** (usted), valed (vosotros), **valgan** (ustedes)

47. **venir**

Pres. Indic.	**vengo, vienes, viene,** venimos, venís, **vienen**
Pres. Subj.	**venga, vengas, venga, vengamos, vengáis, vengan**
Pret. Indic.	**vine, viniste, vino, vinimos, vinisteis, vinieron**
Imp. Subj.	**viniera, vinieras, viniera, viniéramos, vinierais, vinieran,** or **viniese, vinieses, viniese, viniésemos, vinieseis, viniesen**

Fut. Indic.	**vendré, vendrás, vendrá, vendremos, vendréis, vendrán**
Cond.	**vendría, vendrías, vendría, vendríamos, vendríais, vendrían**
Imperative	**ven** (tú), **venga** (usted), venid (vosotros), **vengan** (ustedes)
Pres. Part.	**viniendo**

48. **ver**

Pres. Indic.	**veo**, ves, ve, vemos, veis, ven
Pres. Subj.	**vea, veas, vea, veamos, veáis, vean**
Imp. Indic.	**veía, veías, veía, veíamos, veíais, veían**
Imperative	ve (tú), **vea** (usted), ved (vosotros), **vean** (ustedes)
Past Part.	**visto**

49. **yacer**

Pres. Indic.	**yazco** or **yazgo**, yaces, yace, yacemos, yacéis, yacen
Pres. Subj.	**yazca, yazcas, yazca, yazcamos, yazcáis, yazcan**, or **yazga, yazgas, yazga, yazgamos, yazgáis, yazgan**
Imperative	yace (tú), **yazca** or **yazga** (usted), yaced (vosotros), **yazcan** or **yazgan** (ustedes)

50. Defective Verbs

The following verbs are used only in the forms that have an **i** in the ending: **abolir, agredir, aterirse, empedernirse, transgredir.**

The verb **atañer** is used only in the third person, most frequently in the present indicative: atañe, atañen.

The verb **concernir** is used only in the third person of the following tenses:

Pres. Indic.	**concierne, conciernen**
Pres. Subj.	**concierna, conciernan**
Imp. Indic.	concernía, concernían
Imp. Subj.	concerniera *or* concerniese, concernieran *or* concerniesen
Pres. Part.	concerniendo

The verb **roer** (also **corroer**) has three forms in the first person of the present indicative: **roo, royo, roigo,** all of which are infrequently used. In the present subjunctive the preferable form is **roa, roas, roa,** etc., although the forms **roya** and **roiga** are found.

The verb **soler** is used most frequently in the present and imperfect indicative. It is less frequently used in the present subjunctive.

Pres. Indic.	**suelo, sueles, suele,** solemos, soléis, **suelen**
Pres. Subj.	**suela, suelas, suela,** solamos, soláis, **suelan**
Imp. Indic.	solía, solías, solía, solíamos, solíais, solían

51. Additional Irregular Past Participles

absolver—**absuelto**
abrir—**abierto**
circunscribir—**circunscrito**
componer—**compuesto**
cubrir—**cubierto**
decir—**dicho**
deponer—**depuesto**
descomponer—**descompuesto**
describir—**descrito**
descubrir—**descubierto**
desenvolver—**desenvuelto**
deshacer—**deshecho**
devolver—**devuelto**
disolver—**disuelto**
encubrir—**encubierto**
entreabrir—**entreabierto**
entrever—**entrevisto**
envolver—**envuelto**
escribir—**escrito**
hacer—**hecho**
imprimir—**impreso** (often regular, **imprimido**)
inscribir—**inscrito**
morir—**muerto**
poner—**puesto**
prescribir—**prescrito**
proscribir—**proscrito**
proveer—**provisto** (often regular, **proveído**)
pudrir—**podrido**
reabrir—**reabierto**
reescribir—**reescrito**
resolver—**resuelto**
revolver—**revuelto**
romper—**roto**
satisfacer—**satisfecho**
subscribir—**subscrito**
transcribir—**transcrito**
ver—**visto**
volver—**vuelto**

Aa

a PREP **voy — Londres** I'm going to London; **te lo doy — ti** I'm giving it to you; **se sentó — la sombra** she sat down in the shade; **tumbarse —l sol** to lie down in the sun; **una soga —l cuello** a rope around his neck; **lo miraba — la luz de una vela** she looked at him by the light of a candle; **— dos pesetas cada uno** at two pesetas each; **— las tres y media** at three-thirty; **sentarse — la mesa** to sit down at the table; **prestar dinero —l 15%** to lend money at 15%; **en grupos de — cinco** in groups of five; **cocina — gas** gas cooker; **fotos — todo color** full-color photos; **nadie le gana — testaruda** no one touches her for stubbornness; **terminaron — puñetazos** they ended up fighting; **¡— jugar!** let's play! **¿— qué vienen?** what are they coming for? **veo — mi mamá** I see my mother

abacá M manila

abad -esa M abbot; F abbess

abadejo M cod

abadía F abbey

abajo ADV (dirección) down; (posición relativa) below; **mirar para —** to look down; **el piso de —** the apartment below; **véase —** see below; **— de** under, underneath; **Stefan está — del coche** Stefan is under / underneath the car; **¡— el rey!** down with the king! **—firmante** undersigned; **echar —** to knock down; **río —** downstream; **venirse —** to go to ruin

abalanzarse⁹ VI to lunge at, to swoop down upon

abanderado -da MF standard-bearer

abandonado ADJ abandoned; **es una persona muy abandonada** she's very unkempt

abandonar VT (a una persona, a una familia) to leave, to desert; (el hogar, un partido) to abandon; (una carrera, el poder) to give up; (una carrera, a un enamorado, el hábito de fumar) to quit; (en los naipes) to fold; (un curso) to drop out of

abandono M (acción de descuidar) neglect; (acción de abandonar, condición de abandonado) abandonment; **por —** by default

abanicar⁶ VT to fan

abanico M (utensilio) fan; (de posibilidades) array; **abrirse en —** to fan out

abaratar VT (bajar el precio) to lower the price of; (desprestigiar) to cheapen

abarcar⁶ VT (categorías) to embrace, to encompass; (un período de tiempo) to span

abarrotería F *Méx* grocery store

abarrotero -ra MF *Méx* grocer

abarrotes M PL *Méx* groceries; **tienda de —** *Méx* grocery store

abastecer¹³ VT (un ejército, una ciudad) to supply; (una tienda) to stock

abastecimiento M supply

abasto M supply; **mercado de —s** farmers' market; **yo sola no doy —** I can't cope alone

abatido ADJ dejected, despondent, downcast

abatimiento M dejection, despondency

abatir VT (bajar) to lower; (derribar) to knock down; (desanimar) to depress; (matar a tiros) to shoot; **—se** to swoop down

abdicar⁶ VI/VT to abdicate

abdomen M abdomen

abdominal ADJ abdominal; M sit-up

abecedario M alphabet

abedul M birch

abeja F bee; **— asesina** killer bee

abejón M bumblebee

abejorro M bumblebee

aberración F aberration

abertura F (acción) opening; (de una cueva) mouth

abeto M fir

abierto ADJ (no cerrado, no determinado, sin cubierta) open; (franco) frank; **— de par en par** wide open

abigarrado ADJ motley

abigeato M cattle rustling

abismal ADJ abysmal

abismo M abyss, chasm; **— generacional** generation gap

ablandar VT to soften

abnegación F self-denial

abobado ADJ silly

abocar⁶ VI to turn onto; **—se a** to devote oneself to

abochornar VT (calentar) to make too hot; (avergonzar) to embarrass; **—se** to get embarrassed

abocinar VT to flare

abofetear VT to slap

abogacía F legal profession; **ejercer la —** to practice law

abogado -da MF lawyer, attorney

abogar⁷ VI **— por** to advocate, to plead for

abolengo M ancestry
abolición F abolition
abolir[50] VT to abolish
abollado ADJ dented
abolladura F dent
abollar VT to dent; **—se** to get dented
abolsarse VI to sag
abombar VT to make bulge
abominable ADJ abominable, loathsome
abominación F abomination
abominar VI to detest
abonado -da MF subscriber
abonar VT (suscribir) to subscribe; (pagar) to make a payment; (poner abono) to fertilize; **—se** to subscribe
abono M (a una revista) subscription; (para una temporada deportiva) season ticket; (para el autobús) pass; (para la tierra) fertilizer
abordar VT (un avión, un buque) to board; (un problema) to tackle, to approach; (a una persona en la calle) to accost
aborigen ADJ aboriginal; M primitive inhabitant; **— australiano** Australian aborigine
aborrascarse[6] VI to become stormy
aborrecer[13] VT to abhor, to loathe
aborrecible ADJ hateful, abhorrent
aborrecimiento M abhorrence
abortador -ora MF abortionist
abortar VI to miscarry, to have a miscarriage; VI/VT to abort
abortero -ra MF abortionist
aborto M (espontáneo) miscarriage; (provocado) abortion
abotargarse[7] VI to bloat
abotonar VT to button; **—se** to button up
abovedar VT (una iglesia) to vault, to cover with a vault; (una calle) to arch, to cover as a vault
abozalar VT to muzzle
abracadabra M abracadabra
abrasador ADJ burning
abrasar VT to burn; **—se** to be consumed
abrasión F abrasion
abrasivo ADJ abrasive
abrazadera F clamp
abrazar[9] VT (rodear con los brazos) to hug, to embrace; (rodear una cosa sujetando) to clasp; (una opinión) to espouse
abrazo M hug, embrace
abrevadero M trough
abrevar VT (dar de beber) to water; (beber) to drink
abreviación F abbreviation
abreviar VT to abbreviate, to abridge
abreviatura F abbreviation

abridor M opener
abrigado ADJ (ropa) warm; (lugar) sheltered
abrigar[7] VT to shelter; (emociones) to harbor; **—se** to bundle up
abrigo M (refugio) shelter; (prenda de vestir) coat, wrap
abril M April
abrillantar VT to make shiny
abrir[51] VI/VT to open; VT (con llave) to unlock; (un grifo) to turn on; **— el apetito** to whet one's appetite; **— paso** to make way; M SG **abrebotellas** bottle opener; **abrelatas** can opener; VI (el cielo) to clear up; **—se** to open up; **—se paso** to press through; **en un — y cerrar de ojos** in the twinkle of an eye
abrochar VT to fasten; **—se** to buckle (up)
abrogación F repeal
abrogar[7] VT to repeal
abrojo M bur, sticker
abrumador ADJ overwhelming
abrumar VT to overwhelm, to weigh down; **—se** to become foggy
abrupto ADJ abrupt
absceso M abscess
absolución F acquittal
absoluto ADJ absolute; **en —** absolutely not
absolver[2,51] VT to absolve, to acquit
absorbente ADJ absorbent
absorber VT to absorb
absorción F absorption
absorto ADJ absorbed, engrossed
abstemio -mia ADJ abstemious; MF teetotaler
abstenerse[44] VI to abstain; **— de** to abstain from, to refrain from
abstinencia F abstinence
abstracción F abstraction
abstracto ADJ abstract
abstraer[45] VT to abstract; **—se de** to shut out
abstraído ADJ lost in thought
absurdo ADJ absurd, preposterous; M absurdity
abuchear VI/VT to boo, to jeer
abucheo M boo, jeer
abuelo -la M grandfather; F grandmother; **—s** grandparents
abulia F apathy
abultado ADJ bulgy
abultar VI to bulge
abundancia F abundance, plenty
abundante ADJ abundant, plentiful
abundar VI to abound; **— en** to abound in
aburrido ADJ (sin entretenimiento) bored; (pesado) boring, tiresome
aburrimiento M boredom
aburrir VT to bore; **—se** to become bored

abusar VT — **de** to abuse; (sexualmente) to molest

abuso M abuse; — **de confianza** breach of trust; — **de sustancias** substance abuse

abyecto ADJ abject

acá ADV (en este lugar) here; (a este lugar) over here, *lit* hither; — **y allá** here and there

acabado ADJ finished; M finish

acabar VT to finish; VI to end; (llegar al orgasmo) *vulg* to come; — **de** to have just; — **por** to end up by; — **con** (la corrupción) to put an end to; (las cucarachas) to get rid of; **él y yo hemos acabado** he and I are through; **se nos acabaron los dulces** the candy is all gone; **se nos acabaron las ideas** we ran out of ideas; **y se acabó** and that's that

academia F (corporación, escuela militar) academy; (centro privado de enseñanza) private school

académico ADJ academic

acallar VT to silence, to quiet

acalorado ADJ heated

acaloramiento M **sufrió un** — he got too hot

acalorarse VI/VT (sofocarse) to overheat; (emocionarse) to get excited

acampada F camping

acampante MF camper

acampar VT to camp

acanalar VT to groove

acantilado ADJ sheer, steep; M bluff, cliff

acantonar VT to quarter

acaparar VT (productos) to hoard; (atención) to capture; (monopolizar) *fam* to hog

acaramelar VT to candy

acariciar VT to caress; — **una esperanza** to harbor a hope

ácaro M mite

acarrear VT (transportar) to cart, to transport; (ocasionar) to bring about

acarreo M cartage, carriage, transport

acaso ADV perhaps; **por si** — just in case

acatamiento M compliance

acatar VT to abide by, to comply with

acatarrarse VI to chill; —**se** to catch cold

acaudalado ADJ wealthy

acceder VI — **a** to accede to

accesible ADJ accessible, convenient

acceso M access; (de ira) fit

accesorio ADJ & M accessory

accidentado -da ADJ (viaje) eventful; (terreno) uneven; MF accident victim

accidental ADJ accidental

accidentarse VI to have an accident

accidente M (suceso imprevisto) accident; (del terreno) feature; (automovilístico) wreck; **por** — by accident

acción F (acto) action; (valor de bolsa) share of stock; — **de gracias** thanksgiving; **las buenas acciones** good deeds; **acciones preferenciales** preferred stock; **acciones ordinarias** common stock

accionar VT to operate

accionista MF shareholder, stockholder

acebo M holly

acechar VT (emboscar) to lie in ambush; (amenazar) to stalk

acecho M **rondar en** — to prowl; **estar al** — to lie in wait

aceitar VT to oil

aceite M oil; — **de linaza** linseed oil; — **de oliva** olive oil; — **de ricino** castor oil; — **vegetal** vegetable oil

aceitera F oilcan

aceitoso ADJ oily

aceituna F olive

aceleración F acceleration

acelerador M accelerator

acelerar VT to accelerate, to speed up; VI to accelerate, to step on the gas; — **en vacío** to rev, to race; —**se** to get nervous

acémila F pack animal

acento M (rasgos fonéticos, signo) accent; (especial intensidad) stress

acentuar[17] VT (la hermosura) to accentuate; (ortográficamente) to accent; (oralmente) to stress; —**se** to accentuate

acepción F gloss, meaning

aceptable ADJ acceptable

aceptación F acceptance

aceptar VT to accept

acequia F irrigation ditch

acera F sidewalk

acerado ADJ made of steel

acerar VT to steel

acerca PREP — **de** about, concerning

acercamiento M approach

acercar[6] VT to bring near; **os acerco a la estación** I'll give you a ride to the station; —**se** to come near, to approach

acería F steel mill

acero M steel; — **inoxidable** stainless steel

acérrimo ADJ bitter

acertado ADJ right

acertar[1] VT to hit; VI to be right; — **con** to hit upon; — **a** to happen to; **no** — to miss the mark

acertijo M riddle, conundrum

acervo M heritage

acetona F acetone

achacar[6] VI to blame

achacoso ADJ infirm

achaparrado ADJ (planta) stunted; (persona) squat

achaque M affliction, ailment; **—s** aches and pains

achicado ADJ weak-kneed

achicar[6] VT (empequeñecer) to make small; (un vestido) to take in; (agua) to bail; **—se** (acobardarse) to feel intimidated; (empequeñecerse) to get smaller

achicoria F chicory

aciago ADJ unlucky

acicalado ADJ clean-cut

acicalarse VI to dress up

acicate M incentive

acidez F (de un ácido) acidity; (del vinagre) sourness; **— de estómago** heartburn

ácido M acid; ADJ (como el ácido) acidic; (fruta) sour, tart

acierto M (contestación correcta) right answer; (buena elección) felicitous choice

aclamación F acclamation, acclaim; **por —** by acclamation

aclamar VT to acclaim, to hail

aclaración F clarification

aclarar VT (con explicaciones) to clarify; (con agua) to rinse; (la voz) to clear; VI to dawn; **aclaró después de la tormenta** it cleared up after the storm; **—se** to lighten

aclimatar VT to acclimate

acné M acne

acobardar VT to intimidate

acogedor ADJ (persona) hospitable; (cuarto) cozy

acoger[11b] VT (una sugerencia) to receive; (a un refugiado) to shelter; **—se** to take refuge; **—se a la ley** to have recourse to the law

acogida F reception

acogimiento M reception

acolchar VT (pespuntear) to quilt; (rellenar) to pad

acollarar VT to collar

acometer VT (atacar) to attack; (emprender) to undertake

acometida F attack

acomodado ADJ well-off

acomodador -ora MF usher

acomodar VT (arreglar) to arrange; (ajustar) to adjust; (adaptar) to adapt; **—se** (ponerse cómodo) to make oneself comfortable; (adaptarse) to adapt oneself

acomodo M position

acompañamiento M (acción, música) accompaniment; (grupo de personas que acompaña) retinue; (comida) side dish

acompañante ADJ accompanying; MF (compañero) companion; (en música) accompanist

acompañar VI/VT to accompany (también en música); (escoltar) to escort; (en una carta) to enclose; **—se de** to be accompanied by; **esperemos que el tiempo acompañe** we hope the weather cooperates; **te acompaño en el sentimiento** my thoughts are with you

acompasado ADJ rhythmical, measured

acomplejado ADJ self-conscious

acondicionar VT to prepare

acongojar VT to distress; **—se** to become distressed

aconsejable ADJ advisable

aconsejar VT to advise, to counsel

acontecer[13] VI to take place

acontecimiento M event; **todo un —** quite a happening; **a esta altura de los —s** at this point in the proceedings

acopiar VT to stockpile

acopio M (acción de guardar) storing; (cosas guardadas) stockpile

acoplamiento M coupling; **— universal de cardán** universal joint

acoplar VT to couple; **—se** (juntarse) to couple, to join; (parlantes) to have feedback

acople M coupling, connection

acorazado ADJ armored; M battleship, warship

acorazar[9] VT to armor

acordar[2] VI **— en** to arrange to; **—se (de)** to remember

acorde ADJ in agreement; **— con** in agreement with; M chord

acordeón M accordion

acordonar VT (un zapato) to tie with a lace; (un lugar) to rope off, to seal off; (una moneda) to mill

acorralar VT (meter en un corral) to corral; (impedir la salida) to corner

acortamiento M shortening

acortar VT to shorten

acosar VT (perseguir) to harry; (atacar) to beset; (atormentar) to badger; (solicitar sexualmente) to harass

acostar[2] VT to put to bed; **—se** to go to bed; **—se con** to sleep with

acostumbrado ADJ accustomed; (habitual) customary; **estar — a** to be used / accustomed to

acostumbrar VT to accustom; (soler) to be accustomed to; **—se (a)** to get accustomed (to)

acotación F (anotación) marginal note; (en una obra de teatro) stage directions

acotar VT (un terreno) to mark off; (un texto) to make marginal notes on

acre ADJ acrid, pungent, sharp; M acre

acrecentamiento M growth, increase

acrecentar[1] VI to grow

acreditar VT (una cuenta) to credit; (a un profesional) to accredit; **a quien pueda — ser el dueño de** to whoever can prove he is the owner of

acreedor -ora ADJ deserving; **saldo —** positive balance; MF creditor

acribillar VI (a balazos) to riddle; (a pedradas) to pelt

acrílico ADJ & M acrylic

acritud F acrimony

acrobacia F (arte) acrobatics; (ejercicio de acróbata) stunt

acróbata MF INV acrobat

acrobático ADJ acrobatic

acrofobia F acrophobia

acrónimo M acronym

acta F (de nacimiento) certificate; (de una reunión) minutes; (de un congreso) proceedings

actitud F attitude

activar VT to activate

actividad F activity

activismo M activism

activista MF activist

activo ADJ active; **en —** working; M assets; **— líquido** liquid assets

acto M (solemne, sexual, de una obra de teatro) act; (acción) action; **— seguido** immediately after; **— fallido** Freudian slip; **en el —** on the spot; **hacer — de presencia** to show up

actor -triz M actor; F actress; **— de carácter** character actor

actuación F (acción de actuar) acting; (modo de actuar) performance

actual ADJ current, present

actualidad F present time; **—es** latest news; **de —** up-to-date

actualización F (de información) update; (de ordenador) upgrade

actualizado ADJ up-to-date

actualizar[9] VT to update; (ordenador) to upgrade

actualmente ADV presently

actuar[17] VI to act; (ante el público) to perform

actuario -ria MF (judicial) clerk; (de seguros) actuary

acuarela F watercolor

acuario M aquarium

acuartelar VT to quarter

acuático ADJ aquatic

acuchillar VT to stab, to slash

acuclillado ADJ squatting

acuclillarse VI to squat

acudir VI (ir) to go; (asistir) to attend; **— a** to turn to; **— al llamado** to respond to the call; **— al socorro de** to go to the rescue of; **— en masa** to flock

acueducto M aqueduct

acuerdo M agreement; **estar de —** to be in agreement; **ponerse de —** to come to an agreement; **de — con** in accordance with

acumulación F accumulation, build-up

acumulador M storage battery

acumular VT to accumulate; (una fortuna) to amass; **—se** to collect

acumulativo ADJ cumulative

acuñación F coinage, minting

acuñar VT (hacer monedas, una expresión) to coin; (meter cuñas) to wedge

acuoso ADJ watery

acupuntor -ora MF acupuncturist

acupuntura F acupuncture

acurrucarse[6] VI to nestle, to huddle

acusación F accusation, charge

acusado -da MF accused; (en un juicio) defendant

acusador -ora MF accuser

acusar VT (señalar como culpable) to accuse; (detectar) to detect; (revelar) to betray; (entre niños) to tattle, to tell; **— el golpe** to feel the blow; **— recibo** to acknowledge receipt

acuse M acknowledgment

acusetas MF SG tattletale

acusica MF INV tattletale

acústica F acoustics

acústico ADJ acoustic

adagio M adage

adaptabilidad F resilience

adaptación F adaptation

adaptar VT to adapt

adecuado ADJ appropriate

adecuar VT to adapt; **—se a** to be suitable for

adefesio M sight, hideous thing

adelantado ADJ (economía, alumno) advanced; (reloj) fast; (tren) ahead of time, ahead of schedule; **por —** in advance

adelantamiento M (de una fecha) bringing forward; (de un coche) overtaking

adelantar VT (una fecha, dinero) to advance; (la mano) to move forward; (un coche) to pass; (una noticia) to tell before; VI (un reloj) to gain; **— en** to make progress in; **—se** (sacar ventaja) to get ahead; (actuar antes) to go ahead; (innovar) to be ahead; (hablar antes) to get ahead of oneself

adelante ADV forward; — **con los faroles** let's get started; — **de mí** in front of me; **de aquí en** — from now on; **hacia** — forward; **ir** — to go ahead; **más** — later; **sacar** — to make prosper; **seguir** — to go on

adelanto M (de la ciencia) advance, breakthrough; (de un coche) passing; (pago) advance; **el** — **de los relojes** setting the clocks forward

adelfa F oleander

adelgazar[9] VI to lose weight; VT to lose; (hacer perder peso) to make one lose weight; (hacer menos espeso) to thin; (hacer parecer delgado) to make one look thinner; —**se** to get thinner

ademán M gesture; **hacer un** — **a alguien** to motion to someone

además ADV moreover, besides, in addition; — **de deberme dinero** besides / in addition to owing me money

adentro ADV inside; **ir para / hacia** — to go inside; **hablar para sus** —**s** to talk to oneself; **con lo de** — **para afuera** inside out

aderezar[9] VT (embellecer) to adorn; (condimentar) to season, to garnish

aderezo M (adornar) adornment; (de un alimento) seasoning; (de una ensalada) salad dressing

adeudar VT (deber) to owe; (cargar en cuenta) to debit

adeudo M (endeudamiento) indebtedness; (a una cuenta) debit

adherencia F adhesion

adherir[3] VI to adhere; —**se a** (una cosa) to stick to; (una huelga) to join; (una idea) to subscribe to

adhesión F (a una cosa) adhesion; (a una doctrina) adherence

adhesivo ADJ adhesive; M (pegamento) cement, adhesive; (calcomanía) sticker

adicción F addiction

adición F addition

adicional ADJ additional

adictivo ADJ addictive

adicto -ta ADJ addicted; MF addict

adiestramiento M training

adiestrar VT to train

adinerado ADJ wealthy, well-to-do

adiós INTERJ goodbye; **hacer — con la mano** to wave goodbye

adiposo ADJ fatty

aditivo M additive

adivinanza F riddle

adivinar VT to guess

adivino -na MF fortune teller

adjetivo ADJ & M adjective

adjudicación F award

adjudicar[6] VT to award; —**se** to be awarded

adjuntar VT (incluir en una carta) to enclose; (añadir) to add

adjunto ADJ (unido) attached; (en un mismo envío) enclosed; (asistente) adjunct; ADV herewith

adminículo M gadget

administración F administration; — **pública** civil service

administrador -ora MF administrator

administrar VT (una empresa, un medicamento) to administer; (justicia) to dispense; —**se** to budget

administrativo ADJ administrative

admirable ADJ admirable

admiración F admiration

admirador -ora MF admirer; (de una estrella de cine) fan

admirar VT to admire; —**se** to be amazed; —**se de** to wonder at

admisible ADJ admissible, allowable

admisión F (aceptación) admission; (reconocimiento) acknowledgment

admitir VT (dejar entrar, reconocer) to admit; (aceptar) to accept; (permitir) to allow

ADN (**ácido desoxirribonucleico**) M DNA

adobar VT (aderezar una comida) to fix; (curtir una piel) to tan; (encurtir) to pickle

adobe M adobe

adobo M sauce for seasoning

adoctrinar VT to indoctrinate

adolecer[13] VI — **de** to suffer from

adolescencia F adolescence

adolescente ADJ adolescent; MF adolescent, teenager

adonde ADV REL **esa es la casa** — **vamos** that's the house (where) we're going to

adónde ADV INTERR & PRON where

adopción F adoption

adoptar VT to adopt

adoptivo ADJ adoptive

adoquín M cobblestone

adorable ADJ adorable

adoración F (a un ser amado) adoration; (a un dios) worship

adorador -ora MF worshiper

adorar VT (a una persona) to adore; (a un dios) to worship

adormecer[13] VT (dar sueño) to make drowsy; (entumecer) to numb; —**se** (de sueño) to become drowsy; (de frío) to go numb

adormilado ADJ sleepy

adornar VT to adorn, to embellish

adorno M adornment, ornament, decoration

adquirir[34] VT to acquire; (una característica)

to take on
adquisición F acquisition; (a una colección, al personal) addition; (de una compañía) takeover
adrede ADV on purpose
adrenalina F adrenaline
aduana F customs; (edificio) customshouse
aduanero -ra MF customs officer
aducir[24] VT to offer as proof
adueñarse VI to take possession
adulación F flattery
adulador -ora ADJ flattering; MF flatterer
adular VI/VT to flatter
adulón -ona ADJ flattering; MF *fam* brown-noser
adulterar VT to adulterate
adulterio M adultery
adúltero -ra MF adulterer
adulto -ta ADJ & MF adult
adusto ADJ stern
advenedizo ADJ upstart
advenimiento M advent
adverbio MF adverb
adversario -ria MF adversary, opponent
adversidad F adversity
adverso ADJ adverse
advertencia F (aviso) notice; (amonestación) warning, admonition
advertir[3] VT (avisar) to warn; (notar) to notice; (notificar) to advise, to tip off
Adviento M Advent
adyacente ADJ adjacent
aéreo ADJ aerial; **correo —** air mail
aeróbic M aerobics
aeróbico ADJ aerobic
aerobio ADJ aerobic
aerodeslizador M hovercraft
aerodinámica F aerodynamics
aerodinámico ADJ aerodynamic, streamlined
aeródromo M airport
aeroespacial ADJ aerospace
aeronáutica F aeronautics
aeronave F aircraft
aeropuerto M airport
aerosol M (suspensión) aerosol; (aparato) spray can
aerotransportado ADJ airborne
aerotransportar VT to airlift
afabilidad F affability, friendliness
afable ADJ affable, friendly
afamado ADJ famed
afán M eagerness
afanar VT *fam* to swipe; **—se** to work hard
afanoso ADJ hardworking
afasia F aphasia
afear VT to make ugly; **—se** to become ugly
afección F condition

afectación F affectation
afectado ADJ (por un desastre) affected, stricken; (modales) affected, unnatural
afectar VT to affect
afecto M affection, fondness; **— a** fond of
afectuoso ADJ affectionate, loving
afeitado ADJ clean-shaven; M shave
afeitadora F shaver
afeitar VT to shave
afelpado ADJ & M plush
afeminado ADJ effeminate, sissy
aferrado ADJ stubborn, obstinate
aferrar VT (agarrar) to grasp; (atar) to grapple; **—se** to cling
affaire M affair
Afganistán M Afghanistan
afgano -na ADJ & MF Afghan, Afghani
afianzar[9] VT to secure; (un préstamo) to guarantee
afiche M poster
afición F (inclinación) inclination; (afecto) fondness; (conjunto de aficionados) fans
aficionado -da ADJ **— a** fond of; MF (no profesional) amateur; (hincha) fan
aficionarse VI **— a** to become fond of
afilado ADJ sharp; M sharpening
afilador -ora MF grinder, sharpener
afilar VT to sharpen, to grind
afiliarse VI **— con** to affiliate oneself with
afín ADJ kindred, related
afinación F tune-up
afinado ADJ in tune
afinador -ora MF tuner
afinar VT (una destreza) to perfect; (un plan) to fine-tune; (un piano) to tune; **—se** to become thinner
afinidad F (afecto) affinity; (parentesco) kinship
afirmación F (aseveración) assertion; (aseveración positiva) affirmation
afirmar VT (decir) to assert, to declare; (decir que algo es cierto) to affirm; (sujetar) to secure; **—se** to steady oneself
afirmativa F affirmative answer
afirmativo ADJ affirmative
aflicción F affliction, woe
afligir[11] VT (dar dolor) to afflict; (entristecer) to distress
aflojar VT (una soga) to slacken, to loosen; (la vigilancia) to relax; **— el dinero** to hand over the money; VI to ease up, to slack off; **—se** to work loose
afluencia F influx
afluente M tributary
afluir[31] VI (ríos) to flow (into); (turistas) to flock
afortunado ADJ fortunate, lucky

afrecho M bran
afrenta F affront
afrentar VT to offend
África F Africa
africano -na ADJ & MF African
afroamericano -na ADJ & MF African-American
afrodisíaco M aphrodisiac
afrontar VT to face
afuera ADV outdoors, outside; F PL **—s** outskirts
agachar VT to lower; **—se** to crouch, to stoop
agalla F (de pez) gill; (de roble) gallnut; **tener —s** to have guts/spunk
agarrado ADJ tight-fisted
agarrar VT (sujetar) to seize, to grasp, to grab; (capturar) to catch; (adherirse) to grip; **— por sorpresa** to catch by surprise; **—le la onda a algo** to get the swing of something; **—se una sífilis** to catch a case of syphilis; **—se** to hold on; **—se de** to latch onto; **agarré por la calle ocho** I took eighth street; **agarró y se fue** he up and went
agarre M grip
agarrón M grab
agarrotarse VI (el cuerpo) to stiffen up; (un motor) to seize (up)
agasajar VT to entertain
agasajo M entertainment
agazaparse VI to crouch
agencia F agency, bureau; **— de viajes** travel agency
agenciar VT to wrangle
agente MF agent; (espía) operative; **— de policía** police officer
ágil ADJ agile, nimble
agilidad F agility
agitación F (acción de agitar, nerviosismo) agitation; (protesta) turmoil, unrest
agitado ADJ (estado) agitated; (vida) eventful, hectic; (mar) choppy; (sueño) uneasy
agitador -ora M (aparato) agitator; MF agitator, troublemaker
agitar VT (sacudir) to agitate, to shake up; (incitar a la protesta) to agitate; **—se** (ponerse nervioso) to get worked up; (moverse) to thrash around
aglomeración F crowd
aglomerado M particle board
aglomerarse VI to crowd together
agnóstico -ca ADJ & MF agnostic
agobiado ADJ (por los enemigos) embattled; (por el trabajo) overwhelmed
agobiante ADJ overwhelming
agobiar VT (con una carga excesiva) to weigh down; (con el trabajo) to overwhelm; (con impuestos) to burden
agolparse VI to crowd together
agonía F throes of death; **ser un —s** to be a whiner
agonizante ADJ dying
agonizar[9] VI to be in the throes of death
agorafobia F agoraphobia
agorero -ra ADJ ominous; MF soothsayer
agosto M August; **hacer su —** to make hay while the sun shines
agotado ADJ (una persona) worn-out; (un libro) out-of-print; (una mercancía) out-of-stock
agotamiento M (de una persona) exhaustion; (de un recurso) depletion
agotar VT (un recurso) to exhaust, to use up, to deplete; (la energía) to sap; (un libro) to go out of print; (a una persona) to wear down; **—se** (acabarse) to be all gone; (venderse) to sell out; (secarse) to dry up
agraciado ADJ attractive
agraciar VT to grace
agradable ADJ (persona) agreeable, pleasant, congenial; (situación) pleasant, enjoyable
agradar VT to please
agradecer[13] VT (dar las gracias) to thank; (sentir gratitud) to be grateful for; **se agradece** thank you
agradecido ADJ thankful, grateful
agradecimiento M thankfulness, appreciation; (en un libro) acknowledgment
agrado M pleasure; **de su —** to his liking
agrandamiento M enlargement
agrandar VT to enlarge
agrario ADJ agrarian
agravar VT to aggravate, to make worse; **—se** to get worse
agraviar VT to outrage
agravio M outrage
agredir[50] VT to assault
agregado -da MF (funcionario de embajada) attaché; (profesor asociado) adjunct; M (mezcla) aggregate
agregar[7] VT to add
agresión F (violencia) aggression; (ataque) assault; **— con lesiones** assault and battery
agresivo ADJ aggressive
agresor -ora MF aggressor, assailant
agreste ADJ rough
agriar[16] VT to make sour; **—se** to go sour
agrícola ADJ INV agricultural
agricultor -ora MF agriculturist, farmer
agricultura F agriculture, farming
agridulce ADJ (sabor) sweet-and-sour;

(memoria) bittersweet

agrietarse VI to crack; (los labios) to chap

agrimensor -ora MF surveyor

agrimensura F surveying

agrio ADJ sour

agrisarse VI to gray

agropecuario ADJ agricultural

agrumarse VI to lump

agrupación F group

agrupar VT to group

agua F water; — **con gas** sparkling water; — **corriente** running water; — **de colonia** cologne; — **de grifo** tap water; — **de manantial** spring water; — **dulce** fresh water; —**marina** aquamarine; — **mineral** mineral water; — **oxigenada** hydrogen peroxide; — **salada** salt water; —**s abajo** downstream; —**s arriba** upstream; —**s negras** sewer water; **hacer** — *fam* to take a leak; **se me hace — la boca** my mouth is watering

aguacate M avocado

aguacero M shower, cloudburst, downpour

aguada F watering hole

aguadero M watering hole

aguado ADJ (fruta) watery; (vino, sopa) watered-down

aguantar VT (miserias) to endure; (a una persona molesta) to bear, to stand; (un peso) to bear; (la respiración) to hold; VI (mantenerse) to stand; (durar) to last; (esperar) to wait; (no pudrirse) to keep; **aguántate** grin and bear it

aguante M (para el trabajo) endurance, stamina; (para el vino) tolerance

aguar[8] VT (añadir agua, despojar de fuerza) to water down; (estropear) to spoil; —**se** to become diluted; MF SG **aguafiestas** killjoy, wet blanket

aguardar VI to wait; VT to wait for, to await

aguardentoso ADJ hoarse

aguardiente M brandy

aguarrás M turpentine

agudeza F (visual) sharpness, keenness; (del ingenio) quickness; (para los negocios) acumen; (dicho agudo) witticism

agudo ADJ (dolor, enfermedad, ángulo) acute; (vista, mente) sharp, keen; (mentón) pointed; (voz) high-pitched; (chiste) witty

agüero M portent, omen; **de mal —** portentous

aguijada F goad

aguijar VT to goad

aguijón M (de planta) spur; (de insecto) sting, stinger

aguijonear VT (a un animal) to goad, to prod; (insecto) to sting

águila F eagle; **es un —** he is sharp

aguilucho M eaglet

aguinaldo M Christmas bonus

aguja F (para coser, tejer, de tocadiscos, de pino, de velocímetro) needle; (de reloj) hand; (riel móvil) railroad switch; (chapitel) steeple, spire; — **de croché** crochet hook; — **de punto** knitting needle; — **de zurcir** darning needle; **como una — en un pajar** like a needle in a haystack

agujerear VT to pierce

agujero M hole; (de una ley) loophole; (déficit) shortfall; — **negro** black hole; **tapar** —**s** to pay debts

aguzar[9] VT to sharpen; — **el oído** to prick up one's ears

ahechaduras F PL chaff

ahí ADV there; **por —** over there, thereabouts; **de —** hence; — **te quiero ver** I want to see you in that situation

ahijado -a M godson; F goddaughter

ahínco M **trabajar con —** to work hard

ahogar[7] VT (asfixiar en agua) to drown; (inundar un motor con combustible) to flood; (asfixiar por falta de aire) to smother; (reprimir un grito) to stifle; (asfixiar por presión al cuello) to throttle, to strangle, to choke; — **las penas bebiendo** to drown one's sorrows in drink; —**se** (en agua) to drown

ahogo M (por calor, falta de aire) suffocation; (por un esfuerzo) breathlessness; **vivir sin** —**s** to live a comfortable life

ahondar VT (un hoyo) to deepen; (un asunto) to dig deeper into; —**se** to become deeper

ahora ADV now; — **bien** now then; — **mismo** right now; **por —** for the present, for now; **hasta —** to date, up to now, so far

ahorcar[6] VT to hang, *fam* to string up

ahorrar VT to save; (librar de una molestia) to spare

ahorrativo ADJ frugal, thrifty

ahorro M thriftiness; —**s** savings

ahuecar[6] VT to hollow out; — **la voz** to speak in a hollow voice

ahumado ADJ smoked; M smoking

ahumar VT to smoke

ahuyentar VT to drive away, to scare away; —**se** to get scared

airado ADJ irate

airarse VI to get angry

airbag M airbag

aire M air; (melodía) tune; (manera de ser) manner; — **acondicionado** air

conditioning; — **libre** outdoors; **al —
libre** outdoors; **andar con el culo al —**
to walk around buck naked; **cambiar de
—s** to change surroundings; **darse —s** to
posture; **en el —** up in the air; **estar en
el —** to be on the air; **tener — de** to look
like; **tomar —** to breathe in; **tomar el —**
to get some air

airear VT to air out

airoso ADJ graceful

aislacionismo M isolationism

aislado ADJ (persona) isolated; (lugar)
secluded

aislador M insulator; ADJ insulating

aislamiento M (acción de aislarse) isolation;
(cosa que aísla) insulation; (soledad)
seclusion

aislante M insulator

aislar VT (dejar separado, separar) to isolate;
(poner fuera de contacto) to insulate;
(rechazar socialmente) to ostracize

ajar VT (una planta) to wither; (las manos) to
make rough; (la piel) to age

ajedrez M chess

ajeno ADJ (de otro) belonging to someone
else; (extraño) alien; **— a un peligro**
oblivious to a danger; **— a mi voluntad**
beyond my control; **— a mi experiencia**
foreign to my experience

ajetrearse VI to bustle about

ajetreo M bustle, hustle and bustle

ají M chili

ajo M garlic

ajuar M (de novia) trousseau; (mobiliario)
furnishings

ajustado ADJ tight, snug; **— a la ley** in
accordance with the law

ajustar VT (hacer corresponder, retocar una
prenda) to adjust; (retocar un contrato) to
tweak; (apretar) to tighten; VI to fit tight;
— cuentas to settle accounts; **—se a
derecho** to be in accordance with the law

ajuste M (acción de ajustar) adjustment; (del
cinturón) tightening; (de una máquina)
fine-tuning; (de cuentas) settlement; (de
una prenda) alteration; **hacer —s** to
tinker with

ala F (de ave) wing; (de sombrero) brim;
cortarle las —s a alguien to clip
someone's wings

alabanza F praise

alabar VT to praise

alabeo M warp

alacena F pantry

alacrán M scorpion

alamar M (adorno con flecos) frog; (presilla)
clasp

alambique M still

alambrada F wire fence

alambrado M (barrera) wire fence; (acción
de alambrar) wiring

alambrar VT to wire

alambre M wire; **— de púas** barbed wire

alameda F poplar grove

álamo M poplar (tree)

alancear VT to wound with a lance, to spear

alano M mastiff

alarde M show; **hacer — de** to boast of, to
show off

alardear VI **— de** to boast about

alargar[7] VT (hacer más largo) to lengthen;
(un brazo, un guiso) to stretch (out); **— la
vista** to peer into the distance; **—se** to go
on (longer than expected)

alarido M scream, howl

alarma F alarm; **— antirrobo** burglar alarm;
— contra incendios fire alarm

alarmar VT to alarm

alba F dawn

albacea MF INV executor

albanés -esa ADJ & MF Albanian

Albania F Albania

albañal M sewer

albañil M mason, bricklayer

albañilería F masonry

albaricoque M apricot

albatros M albatross

alberca F (depósito) reservoir; (piscina) *Méx*
swimming pool

albergar[7] VT (dar refugio) to shelter;
(hospedar) to lodge; (ser sede de) to
house; (guardar rencor, un secreto) to
harbor; **—se** to take shelter

albino -na MF albino

albóndiga F meatball

albor M dawn

alborada F dawn; reveille

albornoz M bathrobe

alborotador -ora ADJ rowdy; MF
troublemaker

alborotar VT (el pelo) to muss; (la casa) to
mess up; (la calle) to cause trouble in; (a
los niños) to excite; **—se** to get excited

alboroto M hubbub, fuss

alborozado ADJ joyful

alborozar[9] VT to gladden; **—se** to rejoice

alborozo M joy

albricias F PL & INTERJ congratulations

álbum M album

alcachofa F artichoke

alcahuete -ta MF (soplón) tattletale;
(mediador, encubridor) procurer

alcaide M warden

alcalde -esa MF mayor

álcali M alkali

alcalino ADJ alkaline

alcance M (de una persona) reach; (de los deseos) attainment; (de un misil) range; (de una ley) scope; **de corto(s) —(s)** meager intellect; **al —** at hand, within reach; **a su —** within his reach; **al — del oído** within hearing; **dar — a** to catch up with; **de gran —** far-reaching; **de largo —** long-range

alcancía F piggybank

alcanfor M camphor

alcantarilla F (para agua sucia) sewer; (para lluvias) gully, gutter

alcantarillado M sewage system

alcanzar[9] VT (llegar a un punto, cumplir un deseo) to reach; (igualar) to catch up with; (pasar, poner en la mano) to pass; (herir a balazos) to get; **no alcanzo a verlo** I can't quite see it; **no me alcanza el dinero** I don't have enough money; **alcancé a conocer a mi abuela** I was born soon enough to meet my grandmother

alcaparra F caper

alcaucil M artichoke

alcázar M fortress

alce M elk; (norteamericano) moose

alcoba F bedroom

alcohol M alcohol; **— etílico** ethyl alcohol

alcohólico -ca ADJ & MF alcoholic

alcoholismo M alcoholism

alcornoque M (árbol) cork tree; (persona) blockhead

alcuza F oilcan

aldaba F (para llamar) knocker; (para cerrar) bolt

aldabón M large knocker

aldea F village, hamlet

aldeano -na MF villager; **joven aldeana** village girl

aleación F alloy

alear VT (metales) to alloy; (alas) to flap

aleatorio ADJ random

aleccionar VT to teach a lesson

aledaños M PL vicinity

alegar[7] VT (aducir) to adduce; (pretender) to claim

alegato M (a favor de) plea; (en contra de) allegation

alegoría F allegory

alegrar VT (a una persona) to gladden; (una fiesta) to brighten up; **—se** to be glad; (por efecto del alcohol) to get tipsy

alegre ADJ joyful, cheerful, lighthearted; (ebrio) tipsy, lit

alegría F joy, merriment, cheer

alejamiento M withdrawal

alejar VT (distanciar) to move away; (ahuyentar) to scare off; **—se** (físicamente) to move away; (emocionalmente) to withdraw

alelar VT to stupefy

alemán -ana ADJ & MF German; M (lengua) German

Alemania F Germany

alentar[1] VT (animar) to encourage, to cheer up; VI to breathe

alergia F allergy

alérgico ADJ allergic

alergólogo -ga MF allergist

alero M eaves

alerón M (de avión) aileron, flap; (de coche) spoiler

alerta ADJ INV, ADV & F alert

alertar VT to alert

aleta F (de pez) fin; (de ballena) fluke; (de buceador) flipper

aletargado ADJ sluggish

aletargarse[7] VI to fall into a lethargy

aletazo M flap of a wing

aletear VI to flap, to flutter

aleteo M flapping, flutter

alevín M small fry

alevosía F treachery

alevoso ADJ treacherous

alfabetismo M literacy

alfabetización F literacy

alfabetizar[9] VI (enseñar a leer y a escribir) to teach to read and write; VT (disponer en orden alfabético) to alphabetize

alfabeto M alphabet

alfalfa F alfalfa

alfanumérico ADJ alphanumeric

alfarería F pottery

alfarero -ra MF potter

alféizar M windowsill

alfeñique M (golosina) sugar paste; (persona) weakling

alférez MF second lieutenant; **— de fragata** ensign

alfil M bishop

alfiler M pin; **— de corbata** tiepin; **no cabe un —** it's totally full

alfiletero M pincushion

alfombra F carpet; (suelta) rug

alfombrar VT to carpet

alfombrilla F mat

alforja F saddlebag

alga F seaweed; **—s** algae

algarabía F uproar

algarrobo M locust tree

algazara F merriment

álgebra F algebra

algo PRON something, anything; ADV somewhat; **— es —** something is better than nothing; **por — será** there must be reason

algodón M cotton; **— de azúcar** cotton candy; **se crió entre algodones** he had a protected childhood

algoritmo M algorithm

alguacil M sheriff, marshal; (en un tribunal) bailiff

alguien PRON INDEF somebody, someone; **vino — a hablarte** someone came to talk to you; (en preguntas) anybody, anyone; **¿— lo vio?** did anyone see him?

alguno ADJ some; **—s** some, a few; **sin ruido** — without a sound; **en alguna parte** somewhere; **de alguna manera** somehow; **en algún momento** sometime; **¿lo has visto alguna vez?** have you ever seen him? **¿hay alguna forma de hacer esto?** is there any way to do this?

alhaja F jewel (también persona); **—s** jewelry

alhajero M jewelry box

alharaca F fuss

alhelí M wallflower

aliado -da ADJ allied; MF ally

alianza F alliance; (de Dios) covenant

aliar[16] VT to ally

alias M alias

alicaído ADJ crestfallen

alicates M PL pliers

aliciente M inducement

aliento M (aire respirado) breath; (ánimo) encouragement; **cobrar —** to catch one's breath; **contener el —** to hold one's breath; **sin —** out of breath, breathless

aligerar VT to lighten; **— el paso** to quicken one's pace

alijo M cache, stash

alimentación F (de una persona) nourishment, food; (de una máquina) feeding

alimentar VT (a una persona) to feed, to nourish; (un fuego) to stoke

alimenticio ADJ nutritious, nourishing; **industria alimenticia** food industry; **pensión alimenticia** alimony

alimento M food, nourishment

alineación F (de un equipo deportivo) lineup; (de un coche) alignment

alinear VT (un grupo de cosas) to line up; (a un deportista) to put in the lineup; **—se con** to align oneself with

aliño M condiment, seasoning

alisar VT to smooth; (pelo) to straighten

alistamiento M enlistment

alistar VT to enlist

aliviar VT (hacer menos pesado) to lighten; (mitigar) to alleviate, to relieve; (tranquilizar) to relieve; **—se** (mejorarse) to get better; (hacer sus necesidades) to relieve oneself

alivio M relief

aljaba F quiver

aljibe M cistern

allá ADV there, over there; **más —** farther, beyond; **el más —** the hereafter; **— tú** that's your problem

allanamiento M raid; **— de morada** forcible entry

allanar VT (la tierra) to level, to smooth; (una dificultad) to iron out; (una casa) to raid; **— el camino** to smooth the way

allegado -da ADJ close to; MF relative

allegar[7] VT to gather; **—se** to arrive

allí ADV (punto en el espacio) there; (punto en el tiempo) then; **por —** through there

alma F soul; **con toda el —** from the bottom of one's heart; **hasta el —** to the bone; **ni un —** not a soul; **no me cabía el — en el cuerpo** I was overjoyed; **se me fue el — al piso** my heart sank

almacén M (depósito) warehouse, storehouse, depot; (tienda) department store; **almacenes** department store

almacenaje M storage

almacenamiento M storage

almacenar VT to store, to stock up on

almacenista MF wholesaler

almáciga F nursery

almádena F sledgehammer

almanaque M (publicación anual) almanac; (calendario) calendar

almeja F clam

almendra F almond

almendro M almond tree

almiar M haystack

almíbar M syrup

almidón M starch

almidonado ADJ stiff

almidonar VT to starch

almirante M admiral

almohada F pillow; **consultarlo con la —** to sleep on it

almohadilla F (para sentarse) cushion; (en las patas de los perros) pad

almohadón M cushion

almohaza F currycomb

almohazar[9] VT to groom

almorranas F PL piles, hemorrhoids

almorzar[2,9] VT to lunch, to eat lunch

almuerzo M lunch

alocado ADJ wild

áloe M aloe vera

alojamiento M lodging, accommodations; (militar) quarters

alojar VT (a un invitado) to lodge, to accommodate; (a unos huérfanos) to house; (a las tropas) to quarter; **—se** (una bala) to lodge; (una persona) to board, to room

alondra F lark

alpaca F alpaca

alpinismo M mountain climbing

alpinista MF mountain climber, mountaineer

alpino ADJ alpine

alpiste M birdseed

alquería F farmhouse

alquilar VT to rent; **se alquila** for rent

alquiler M (pago mensual) rent; (acción de alquilar) renting; **coche de —** rental car; **dar en —** to hire out

alquitrán M tar

alquitranar VT to tar

alrededor ADV around; **— de la casa** around the house; M **—es** (de un área) surroundings; (de una ciudad) outskirts

alta F discharge; **dar de —** to discharge

altanería F haughtiness

altanero ADJ haughty

altar M altar

alteración F alteration; **alteraciones al orden público** public disturbances

alterar VT to alter; **— el ánimo** to upset; **—se** to get upset

altercado M altercation

altercar[6] VT **— con** to quarrel with

alternador M alternator

alternar VT to alternate; **— con** to rub elbows with

alternativa F alternative

alternativo ADJ (cambiante) alternating; (optativo) alternative

alterno ADJ alternate; **alterna y continua** AC/DC

alteza F highness

altibajos M PL ups and downs

altillo M attic

altímetro M altimeter

altiplano M high plateau

altisonante ADJ high-sounding

altitud F altitude

altivez F haughtiness

altivo ADJ haughty

alto ADJ (que está arriba) high; (que tiene mayor altura vertical) tall; **de alta fidelidad** high fidelity; **de alta potencia** high-powered; **de alta velocidad** high-speed; **en — grado** to a great extent; **en alta mar** on the high seas; M **altavoz** loudspeaker; **altoparlante** loudspeaker; M (altura) height; (piso) upper story; **— el fuego** cease-fire; ADV loud; **hablar —** to talk loud; **cotizarse —** to be set high; INTERJ halt!

altruismo M altruism

altura F (de persona, edificio, ola, epidemia) height; (de avión) altitude; (del suelo sobre el mar, lugar alto) elevation; **a estas —s** at this stage; **a la — de la calle ocho** at eighth street; **a la — de las circunstancias** equal to the circumstances

alubia F bean

alucinar VT (causar alucinaciones) to hallucinate; (fascinar) to fascinate; (deslumbrar) to bowl over; VI (sufrir alucinaciones) to hallucinate

alud M avalanche

aludir VI **— a** to allude to, to refer to

alumbrado M lighting; ADJ lit

alumbramiento M childbirth

alumbrar VT to light up; (dar a luz) to give birth

aluminio M aluminum

alumnado M student body

alumno -na MF (de enseñanza primaria) pupil; (de enseñanza secundaria) student

alusión F allusion

aluvión M (de preguntas, pedidos) barrage; (de personas) flood

alza F appreciation; **— de precios** boost in prices

alzamiento M (acción de alzar) raising; (insurrección) uprising

alzaprima F crowbar

alzar[9] VT (la mano, la voz, una casa) to raise; (a un niño) to lift up; **— la vista** to look up; **—se** to rise up in rebellion; **—se con** to make off with

amabilidad F kindness; **¿tendría la — de...?** would you mind...?

amable ADJ kind, nice

amado -da MF beloved

amaestrador -ora MF trainer

amaestramiento M training

amaestrar VT to train

amagar[7] VI/VT **amagó que iba a llover** it looked like it was going to rain; **amagó con llover** it threatened to rain

amago M **— hacer** to make as if

amalgamar VT to amalgamate

amamantar VT to nurse, to breast-feed

amanecer[13] VI to dawn; **— enfermo** to wake up ill; **amanecí en Londres** I woke up in London; M dawn, sunrise, daybreak

amanerado ADJ effete

amansar VT to tame

amante MF lover; ADJ — **de** fond of

amañar VT (una elección) to rig; (un documento) to tamper with

amapola F poppy

amar VT to love

amargar[7] VT to embitter

amargo ADJ bitter

amargor M bitterness

amargura F bitterness

amarillear VI/VT to yellow, to turn yellow

amarillento ADJ yellowish

amarillo -lla ADJ yellow; MF (esquirol) scab

amarra F cable, rope; —**s** moorings; **soltar —s** to cast off

amarrar VT (un barco) to moor; (una cosa) to secure, to tie down

amartillar VT (pegar con martillo) to hammer; (un arma) to cock

amasar VT (masa) to knead; (una fortuna) to amass

amateur ADJ & MF amateur

amatista F amethyst

Amazonas M Amazon River

ambages M hablar sin — to not mince words, to speak plainly

ámbar M amber

ambición F ambition

ambicionar VT to have the ambition of

ambicioso ADJ ambitious; (codicioso) overambitious

ambidiestro ADJ ambidextrous

ambiental ADJ environmental; (temperatura) ambient

ambiente ADJ ambient; M (condiciones biológicas) environment; (atmósfera) atmosphere, ambiance; (sector social) milieu

ambigüedad F ambiguity

ambiguo ADJ ambiguous

ámbito M (ambiente) scene; (alcance) scope; (esfera) sphere

ambivalente ADJ ambivalent

ambos ADJ & PRON both

ambulancia F ambulance

ambulante ADJ itinerant

ameba F ameba

amedrentar VT to scare

amén INTERJ amen; **decir —** to approve without discussion; **— de** besides

amenaza F threat, menace

amenazador ADJ threatening

amenazar[9] VT to threaten; **— con** to threaten to

amenidad F (cualidad de ameno) pleasantness; (placer) pleasure

amenizar[9] VT to make entertaining

ameno ADJ enjoyable, entertainment

América F America

americano -na ADJ & MF American; F sport coat

ametrallador -ora MF gunner; F (arma) machine gun

ametrallar VT to strafe

amianto M asbestos

amigable ADJ friendly

amígdala F tonsil

amigdalitis F tonsillitis

amigo -ga ADJ friendly; — **de** fond of; — **de lo ajeno** thieving; MF friend

aminoácido M amino acid

aminorar VT to lessen

amistad F (relación) friendship; (amigo) friend; **trabar —** to strike up a friendship

amistoso ADJ friendly, amicable

amnesia F amnesia

amniocentesis F amniocentesis

amnistía F amnesty

amo -ma M (de esclavo, sirviente) master; (de animal) owner; F (de esclavo, de sirviente) mistress; (de animal) owner; **ama de leche** wet nurse; **ama de llaves** housekeeper; **ama de casa** homemaker

amodorrado ADJ drowsy

amodorrar VT to make drowsy; —**se** to become drowsy

amolar[2] VT to annoy

amoldar VT to mold

amonestación F admonition, warning

amonestar VT to admonish, to warn

amoníaco M ammonia

amontonamiento M pile

amontonar VT to pile up

amor M love; — **propio** self-esteem; **de mil —es** gladly; **hacerle el — a** to make love to; **por el — de Dios** for God's sake; **por — al arte** unremunerated

amoral ADJ amoral

amoratado ADJ (de golpes) black-and-blue; (de frío, por falta de oxígeno) blue

amordazar[9] VT (a una persona) to gag; (a un perro, a los críticos) to muzzle

amorfo ADJ amorphous

amorío M love affair

amoroso ADJ loving, amorous

amortajar VT to shroud

amortiguador M shock absorber

amortiguar[8] VT (un sonido) to muffle, to absorb; (un golpe) to cushion, to absorb; (un dolor) to deaden, to dull

amortizar[9] VT (recuperar a plazos) to amortize; (depreciar) to depreciate

amoscarse[6] VI to get peeved

amostazarse[9] VI to get peeved
amotinarse VI (en un barco) to mutiny; (en una ciudad) to riot
amparar VT (proteger) to protect; (refugiar) to shelter; **—se** to protect oneself
amparo M (protección) protection; (refugio) shelter; **al — de** under the protection of
amperio M ampere
ampicilina F ampicillin
ampliación F (de una foto) enlargement; (de una casa) extension
ampliar[16] VT (una foto) to enlarge; (una calle) to extend; (una explicación) to expand; (un volumen) to amplify
amplificador M amplifier
amplificar[6] VT (un sonido) to amplify; (una imagen) to magnify
amplio ADJ (información, tiempo) ample; (piso) spacious, roomy; (región, resonancia, sonrisa) broad; (vestido) full; **de amplias miras** open-minded
amplitud F (de comprensión) breadth; (de onda) amplitude
ampolla F (de la epidermis) blister; (vasija) vial
ampollar VT to blister
ampuloso ADJ bombastic
amputar VT to amputate
amueblar VT to furnish
amuleto M amulet, charm
anacronismo M anachronism
ánade M duck
anadear VI to waddle
anadeo M waddle
anaerobio ADJ anaerobic
anal ADJ anal
anales M PL annals
analfabetismo M illiteracy
analfabeto -ta ADJ & MF illiterate
analgésico ADJ & M analgesic
análisis M analysis
analítico ADJ analytical, analytic
analizar[9] VT to analyze
analogía F analogy
analógico ADJ (relativo a la analogía) analogical; (no digital) analog
análogo ADJ analogous
ananás M pineapple
anaquel M shelf
anaranjado ADJ & M (color) orange
anarquía F anarchy
anarquista MF anarchist
anatema M anathema
anatomía F anatomy
anatómico ADJ anatomical
anca F haunch, rump
ancho ADJ wide, broad; **a sus anchas** at his

ease; **me viene —** it's too wide for me; M width, breadth; **a lo —** widthwise; **tiene un metro de —** it's one meter wide
anchoa F anchovy
anchura F width, breadth
ancianidad F old age
anciano -na ADJ elderly, aged; MF old person
ancla F anchor
anclar VI/VT to anchor
andada F **volver a las —s** to backslide
andador -ora MF walker
Andalucía F Andalusia
andaluz -za ADJ & MF Andalusian
andamiaje M (para construcción) scaffolding; (fundamento) framework
andamio M scaffold
andanada F broadside
andante ADJ walking
andanzas F PL adventures
andar[20] VI to walk; (coche, motor, reloj) to run; (el tiempo) to pass; (un aparato) to work; **— con cuidado** to be careful; **— en coche** to travel by car, to ride in a car; **— mal** to be in bad shape, to be a mess; **— mal del corazón** to have heart trouble; **—se por las ramas / con vueltas** to beat around the bush; **no —se con rodeos** to make no bones about it; **en eso ando** that's what I'm up to; **¡andando!** move on! **¿dónde anda a estas horas?** where is he at this hour? **¡ándale!** *Méx* (apresúrate) come on! (de acuerdo) OK; M gait
andariego ADJ fond of walking
andas F **llevar en —** *RP* to carry on one's shoulders
andén M platform
Andes M PL Andes
andino ADJ Andean
Andorra F Andorra
andorrano -na ADJ & MF Andorran
andrajo M rag, tatter
andrajoso ADJ ragged, tattered
andrógino ADJ androgynous
anécdota F anecdote
anegar[7] VT to flood
anejo ADJ attached; M accompanying volume
anemia F anemia; **— falciforme** sickle cell anemia
anémico ADJ anemic
anestesia F (acción de anestesiar) anesthesia; (sustancia) anesthetic
anestésico ADJ & M anesthetic
anestesiología F anesthesiology
aneurisma M aneurysm
anexar VT to annex; (con una carta) to enclose

anexión F annexation

anexo ADJ attached; M (de un edificio) annex, extension; (a una ley) rider

anfeta F *fam* speed

anfetamina F amphetamine

anfibio ADJ & M amphibian

anfiteatro M amphitheater

anfitrión -ona M host; F hostess

ángel M angel; — **de la guarda** guardian angel

angelical ADJ angelic

angélico ADJ angelic

angina F —s tonsillitis; — **del pecho** angina pectoris

angioplastia F angioplasty

anglosajón -ona ADJ & MF Anglo-Saxon

Angola F Angola

angolano -na, angoleño -ña, angolés -esa ADJ & MF Angolan

angostar VT to narrow, to contract

angosto ADJ narrow

angostura F (cualidad de angosto) narrowness; (desfiladero) narrows

anguila F eel; — **eléctrica** electric eel

angular ADJ angular

ángulo M (figura geométrica, enfoque) angle; (rincón, esquina) corner; — **muerto** blind spot; — **recto** right angle

anguloso ADJ angular

angustia F (desasosiego) anguish, anxiety, distress; (congoja) heartache; (desazón existencial) angst

angustiado ADJ distraught

angustiante ADJ nerve-wracking

angustiar VT to distress; —**se** to feel distressed

angustioso ADJ distressing

anhelante ADJ longing

anhelar VT to long for, to yearn for

anhelo M longing, yearning

anidar VI to nest

anillas F PL gymnastics rings

anillo M ring; — **de boda** wedding ring; **me queda como** — **al dedo** it fits me like a glove

ánima F soul of the departed

animación F (viveza) animation, liveliness; (en películas) animation

animado ADJ (vivo) animate; (bullicioso) lively

animador -ora MF (de un espectáculo) host; (de un equipo) cheerleader

animal ADJ & M animal

animar VT (dar vida) to animate, to enliven; (incitar) to encourage, to urge on; (dar aliento) to cheer up; —**se** (alegrarse) to cheer up; (atreverse) to gather courage

ánimo M (espíritu) spirit; (aliento) encouragement; (humor) mood; (intención) intention; **no estoy de** — **para eso** I'm not in the mood for that; INTERJ hang in there!

animosidad F animosity

animoso ADJ spirited

aniñado ADJ childlike

aniquilar VT to annihilate, to wipe out

anís M anise

aniversario M anniversary

ano M anus

anoche ADV last night

anochecer[13] VI to get dark; **anochecimos en París** night found us in Paris; M nightfall, dusk

anomalía F anomaly

anómalo ADJ anomalous

anonadado ADJ dumbfounded

anonadar VT (aniquilar) to annihilate; (desconcertar) to dumbfound; —**se** to become dumbfounded

anónimo ADJ anonymous; M anonymous letter

anorak M anorak

anorexia F anorexia

anoréxico ADJ anorexic

anormal ADJ abnormal; MF freak

anotación F (nota) annotation, notation; (en fútbol) goal

anotar VT (apuntar) to note; (marcar un tanto) to score; —**se** to sign up

anquilosarse VT (las articulaciones) to become stiff; (una institución) to become stagnant

ansia F (deseo) eagerness; (congoja) anguish

ansiar[16] VT to covet

ansiedad F anxiety

ansioso ADJ anxious, eager

antagonismo M antagonism

antagonista MF antagonist

antagonizar[9] VT to antagonize

antaño ADV in the old days

antártico ADJ antarctic

Antártida F Antarctica

ante PREP before; — **este problema** in the face of this problem; — **todo** above all; M suede

anteanoche ADV night before last

anteayer ADV day before yesterday

antebrazo M forearm

antecedente ADJ & M antecedent; —**s** (profesionales) background; (criminales) record

antecesor -ora MF (antepasado) ancestor; (predecesor) predecessor

antedicho ADJ aforesaid

antelación LOC ADV **con** — beforehand
antemano LOC ADV **de** — beforehand
antena F (de radio) antenna, aerial; (de insecto) antenna, feeler
anteojera F blinder
anteojos M PL glasses, spectacles; — **de sol** sunglasses; — **bifocales** bifocals
antepasado -da MF ancestor, forebear
antepecho M sill
anteponer[39] VT (poner delante, poner antes) to place before; (dar preferencia) to give priority to
anterior ADJ (en el tiempo) previous; (en el espacio) anterior, front; — **a** prior to
antes ADV before; — **de** before; — **la muerte** I'd rather die; — **bien** rather
antiaborto ADJ antiabortion, right-to-life
antiácido ADJ & M antacid
antiaéreo ADJ antiaircraft
antibacteriano ADJ antibacterial
antibalas ADJ INV bulletproof
antibalístico ADJ antiballistic
antibiótico ADJ & M antibiotic
antibloqueo ADJ INV antilock
anticipación LOC ADV **con** — in advance
anticipado LOC ADV **por** — in advance
anticipar VT (una fecha) to move up; (dinero) to advance; (el porvenir) to anticipate; —**se a los acontecimientos** to jump the gun
anticipo M advance, deposit
anticoncepción F contraception
anticonceptivo ADJ & M contraceptive
anticongelante M antifreeze
anticuado ADJ antiquated, out-of-date, outdated
anticuerpo M antibody
antidepresivo ADJ & M antidepressant
antídoto M antidote
antieconómico ADJ wasteful
antiestético ADJ unsightly
antígeno M antigen
antigualla F old piece of junk
antiguano -na ADJ & MF Antiguan
Antigua y Barbuda F Antigua and Barbuda
antigüedad F (cualidad de antiguo) antiquity; (objeto) antique; (tiempo en un cargo) seniority
antiguo ADJ (era, historia) ancient; (ropa) old; (mueble) antique; **a la antigua** in the old style; **la antigua capital** the former capital; **más** — with more seniority
antihistamínico M antihistamine
antiinflamatorio ADJ & M anti-inflammatory
Antillas F PL West Indies

antílope M antelope
antimonio M antimony
antimonopolio ADJ antitrust
antioxidante ADJ & M antioxidant
antiparras F PL goggles
antipatía F antipathy
antipático ADJ unfriendly, unkind
antipoliomielítico ADJ antipolio
antisemitismo M anti-Semitism
antiséptico ADJ & M antiseptic
antisocial ADJ antisocial
antítesis F antithesis
antitranspirante M antiperspirant
antitrust ADJ antitrust
antojadizo ADJ whimsical
antojarse VI **se le antojó comer salchicha** he took a notion to eat sausage; **esa tarea se me antoja difícil** that task seems hard to me
antojo M (deseo) whim, craving; (mancha de nacimiento) birthmark
antología F anthology, reader
antónimo M antonym
antorcha F torch
antracita F anthracite
ántrax M anthrax
antro M (bar) dive, joint; — **de perdición** den of iniquity
antropología F anthropology
antropólogo -ga MF anthropologist
anual ADJ annual, yearly
anualidad F annuity
anuario M annual, yearbook
anudar VT to knot; **se le anudó la garganta** he got all choked up
anulación F (de un contrato) cancellation; (de un matrimonio) annulment
anular VT (un matrimonio) to annul; (un contrato, un evento) to cancel; (una sentencia) to overrule, to overturn; (un talón) to void; M ring finger
anunciador -ora MF announcer
anunciante MF advertiser
anunciar VT (información) to announce; (un producto) to advertise
anuncio M (de información) announcement; (de un producto) advertisement; — **clasificado** classified advertisement; — **publicitario** advertisement; **poner un** — to place an ad
anzuelo M fishhook; **morder / picar el** — to take the bait
añadidura F addition; **por** — in addition
añadir VT to add
añejo ADJ aged, vintage
añicos M **hacerse** — to break into a thousand pieces

añil M indigo, bluing

año M year; (de la escuela) grade; (de vino) vintage; **— bisiesto** leap year; **— luz** light-year; **de cuarenta —s** aged forty; **el — pasado** last year; **en los —s veinte** in the 1920s; **entrado en —s** getting on in years; **¿cuántos —s tienes?** how old are you?

añojo -ja MF yearling

añoranza F longing; (del hogar) homesickness

añorar VT to long for, to be homesick for

añoso ADJ old

añublo M blight

aorta F aorta

apabullar VT (impresionar) to bowl over; (derrotar) to crush

apacentar[1] VI to graze, to pasture

apacible ADJ good-natured

apaciguar[8] VT (pacificar) to pacify; (aplacar) to mollify, to appease; **—se** to calm down

apadrinar VT to sponsor; (en un bautismo) to act as godfather to; (en una boda) to act as best man for; (en un duelo) to second

apagado ADJ (no llamativo) flat; (no intenso) dull

apagar[7] VT (un fuego) to put out, to extinguish; (una luz) to turn off, to turn out; (motor) to turn off, to kill; (una vida) to kill, to snuff out; (la sed) to quench; **—se** (luz) to go out; (un color) to fade; (una voz) to trail off; (un volcán) to become extinct

apagón M blackout, outage

apalabrarse VI **— con** to make a verbal agreement with

apalear VT to thrash

aparador M sideboard, buffet, cupboard

aparato M (de gimnasia) apparatus; (de cocina) appliance; (teléfono) telephone; (máquina, dirigencia política) machine; (boato) pomp; **— circulatorio** circulatory system; **— de televisión** television set; **— ortodóntico** braces; **— ortopédico** leg brace

aparatoso ADJ pompous

aparcamiento M (lugar para aparcar) parking lot; (acción de aparcar) parking

aparcar[6] VI/VT to park; MF SG **aparcacoches** valet

aparcero -ra MF sharecropper

aparear VT (animales) to mate; (calcetines) to match, to pair; **—se** (animales) to mate; (en un baile) to pair off

aparecer[13] VI (ponerse a la vista, publicarse) to appear; (hacer acto de presencia) to show up; **se me apareció un ángel** an angel appeared to me

aparejar VT (un cuarto, un ejército) to prepare; (problemas) to entail; (una embarcación) to rig

aparejo M (de caballo) harness; (de buque) rigging; (para pescar) tackle; **—s** equipment

aparentar VT to feign; VI to show off; **aparenta la edad que tiene** she looks her age

aparente ADJ apparent; **un precio —** an acceptable price

aparición F (fantasma) apparition; (acción de aparecer) appearance

apariencia F (aspecto) appearance; (fingimiento) pretense, semblance; **las —s engañan** appearances are deceiving; **guardar las —s** to keep up appearances

apartado M section; **— postal** post office box; ADJ (recóndito) secluded; (distante) distant; **muy —** far apart

apartamento M apartment

apartamiento M separation

apartar VT **aparta las monedas de veinticinco centavos** set aside/sort out the quarters; **apartó la silla de la pared** he moved the chair away from the wall; **lo aparté para hablarle** I took him aside to talk to him; **apartó la cacerola del fuego** she took the pan off the fire; **lo apartó de un empujón** she pushed him away; **apartaron al ministro de su cargo** they removed the minister from his post; **apartó la vista** he looked away; VI **se apartaron del buen camino** they strayed from the straight and narrow; **los resultados se apartan de lo esperado** the results depart/deviate from the norm; **se apartó para que no lo atropellara el coche** he got out of the way so the car wouldn't hit him

aparte ADJ separate; ADV **bromas —** kidding aside; **dejar —** to exclude; **punto y —** new paragraph; PREP **— de** (además de) besides; (salvo) except for

apasionado ADJ (amor, hombre) passionate; (defensa, comentario) impassioned

apasionar VT **eso me apasiona** I love that; **—se por** to be passionate about

apatía F apathy

apático ADJ apathetic

apear VT to get down; **—se** to dismount

apechugar[7] VI **— con** to put up with

apedrear VT to stone

apegado ADJ attached

apegarse[7] VI to become attached

apego M attachment

apelación F appeal

apelar VI/VT to appeal

apellidarse VI to have the surname of

apellido M surname, last name

apelotonarse VI (una almohada) to ball up; (gente) to bunch together

apenado ADJ grieved

apenar VT to grieve, to pain; **—se** to be grieved

apenas ADV hardly, scarcely, barely; **— llegó, se desmayó** no sooner had he arrived than he fainted

apéndice M (órgano, parte de un libro) appendix; (añadido) appendage

apendicectomía F appendectomy

apendicitis F appendicitis

apercibir VT to warn; **—se de** to notice

aperitivo M appetizer

apero M farm implement

apertura F opening

apesadumbrado ADJ doleful

apestar VT (hacer heder) to stink up; (causar la peste) to plague; VI to stink, to reek

apestoso ADJ smelly

apetecer[13] VI **no me apetece ir contigo** I don't feel like going with you

apetecible ADJ appetizing

apetito M appetite

apetitoso ADJ appetizing

apiadarse VI **— de** to pity, to take pity on

ápice M apex; (de la lengua) tip; **no apartarse ni un —** not to diverge a jot

apio M celery

apisonadora F steamroller

apisonar VT to pack down

aplacamiento M appeasement

aplacar[6] VT (a una persona) to appease, to mollify; (miedo) to allay; (sed, pasión) to quench; **—se** to relent

aplanadora F steamroller

aplanamiento M flattening, leveling

aplanar VT (un terreno) to level, to flatten; (con una aplanadora) to roll

aplastado ADJ flattened

aplastamiento M crushing

aplastante ADJ (derrota) crushing; (victoria) sweeping

aplastar VT (achatar) to squash, to crush; (derrotar) to plaster, to stomp; (una revolución) to squelch, to smash, to crush; **—se** to crumple

aplaudir VI/VT to applaud

aplauso, aplausos M (PL) applause

aplazamiento M postponement; (de un proceso legal) continuance

aplazar[9] VT to postpone, to put off

aplicable ADJ applicable

aplicación F (acción de aplicarse) application; (de un castigo) administration

aplicado ADJ industrious

aplicar[6] VT to apply; **—se** to work hard, to apply oneself

aplomado ADJ (equilibrado) poised; (vertical) plumb

aplomar VT to plumb

aplomo M poise

apnea M apnea

apocado ADJ timid

apocalipsis MF apocalypse

apocamiento M timidity

apocarse[6] VT to become intimidated

apodar VT to nickname

apoderado -da MF proxy, agent

apoderarse VI **— de** to take possession of, to seize

apodo M nickname

apogeo M apogee; **en su —** (una fiesta) in full swing; (un estilo) in its heyday, at its peak

apolillado ADJ (comido por las polillas) moth-eaten; (anticuado) antiquated

apología F apology

aporrear VT to club, to cudgel

aportación F contribution

aportar VT (posibilidades, evidencia) to provide; (dinero) to contribute

aporte M contribution

aposento M chamber

apostador -ora MF bettor

apostar[2] VI/VT to bet, to wager; (a un centinela) to station, to post; **— por** to bet on

apóstol M apostle

apóstrofe MF apostrophe, invocation

apóstrofo M apostrophe

apostura F bearing

apoyar VT (sostener) to rest; (respaldar) to support, to back; (votar por) to second; (respaldar un argumento) to buttress; **—se en** (recostarse contra) to lean on, to prop against; (basarse en) to be based on; M SG **apoyabrazos** armrest

apoyo M support

apreciable ADJ (digno de aprecio) esteemed; (perceptible) noticeable; (registrable) appreciable

apreciación F appreciation

apreciado ADJ dear

apreciar VT (reconocer la valía) to appreciate; (percibir) to notice; (registrar) to measure; (considerar) to take into consideration; (sentir afecto) to cherish;

—**se** (un fenómeno) to be noticeable;
(moneda) to appreciate

aprecio M appreciation

aprehender VT (a un delincuente) to
apprehend; (contrabando) to seize; (una
idea) to grasp

aprehensión F (arresto) apprehension;
(incautación) seizure

apremiante ADJ pressing

apremiar VT to pressure

apremio M pressure

aprender VI/VT to learn; — **de memoria** to
memorize, to learn by heart

aprendiz -za MF (de un oficio) apprentice,
trainee; (de una lengua, canto) learner

aprendizaje M (de un oficio) apprenticeship;
(acto de aprender) learning

aprensión F apprehension, misgivings

aprensivo ADJ apprehensive

apresar VT (aprisionar) to imprison;
(incautar) to seize

aprestar VT to prepare; —**se a** to get ready
to

apresurado ADJ hasty, hurried

apresurar VT to hurry, to hasten

apretado ADJ (zapato) tight; (beso) hard;
(racimo) compact; (síntesis) succinct;
(jornada) busy; (situación) difficult,
dangerous

apretar¹ VT (un botón) to press; (un gatillo)
to squeeze; (un tornillo) to tighten; (los
dientes, puños) to clench; (a un bebé) to
clasp; **me apretó para que le diera
dinero** he pressured me to give him
money; **ese profesor nos aprieta
mucho** that teacher demands a lot of us;
VI (zapatos) to be tight, to pinch; (sol) to
be intense; (esforzarse) to try hard, to bear
down; —**se** to crowd together

apretón M squeeze; — **de manos** handshake

aprieto M jam, fix, predicament; **en —s** in
need, hard-pressed, in dire straits; **estar
en un —** to be in a tight spot, to be in
trouble, to be in a pickle; **poner en —s** to
embarrass

aprisa ADV quickly

aprisco M (para el ganado) fold

aprisionar VT to trap

aprobación F (aceptación) approval; (de una
ley) passage, adoption; (nota) passing
grade

aprobar² VT (una medida, una opinión) to
approve of; (una ley) to pass, to approve;
(un examen) to pass; VI to pass

aprontar VT to ready

apropiación F appropriation; — **indebida**
embezzlement

apropiado ADJ appropriate, suitable

apropiarse VT to appropriate

aprovechable ADJ usable

aprovechado ADJ opportunistic

aprovechamiento M use

aprovechar VT (una ocasión) to take
advantage of; (el espacio) to utilize; (la
enseñanza) to profit from; VI to be useful;
—**se de** to take advantage of; **¡que
aproveche!** enjoy your meal!

aproximación F approach

aproximado ADJ approximate

aproximar VT to bring near; —**se** to
approach; — **a** to approximate

aptitud F aptitude; —**es musicales** musical
aptitude

apto ADJ apt, suitable; — **para menores** for
general audiences

apuesta F bet, wager

apuesto ADJ good-looking

apuntalar VT to prop up, to shore up

apuntar VT (señalar) to point out; (dirigir a
un blanco) to aim; (matricular) to enroll;
(escribir) to write down, to note; (ayudar a
un actor) to prompt; VI (una flecha) to
point; (canas) to sprout; —**se** to score; —
a un blanco to aim at a target; **me
apunto para ir con vosotros** I'm game
to go with you

apunte M notation; —**s** notes; **tomar —s** to
take notes; **llevar el — a alguien** to pay
attention to someone

apuñalar VT to stab

apurado ADJ (situación) difficult; (persona)
in dire straits; *Am* (apresurado) in a hurry

apurar VT (consumir) to drink up; (apremiar)
to put under pressure

apuro M predicament, fix; *Am* (prisa) hurry;
estar en —s to be in distress

aquejado ADJ stricken

aquejar VT to afflict, to trouble

aquel ADJ that; **aquella chica se llama
María** that girl is named María; **aquellas
ciudades son antiguas** those cities are
old; PRON that one; — **es el mayor** that
one is the oldest; **aquellos son mis
hijos** those are my children; **de mis dos
hijos, Juan y Pedro, este es gordo y
— es flaco** of my two sons, Juan and
Pedro, the latter is fat and the former is
thin; **en / por — entonces** back then

aquí ADV here; **está por —** it is around here;
ven por — come this way; **hasta —** this
far; **de — a cuatro horas** four hours
from now; **de — en adelante** from now
on; **de — para allá** to and fro, back and
forth; — **y ahora** here and now

aquietar VT to quiet; **—se** (los nervios) to calm down; (una tormenta) to subside

ara LOC ADV **en —s de** for the sake of

árabe MF (persona) Arab; (caballo) Arabian; (lengua) Arabic; ADJ Arabian; (costumbre, arte) Arab

Arabia Saudí, Arabia Saudita F Saudi Arabia

arácnido M arachnid

arado M plow

Aragón M Aragon

aragonés -esa ADJ Aragonese; MF (persona) Aragonese; M (dialecto) Aragonese

arancel M (impuesto) tariff; (lista de honorarios) list of fees

arancelario ADJ **acuerdo —** tariff agreement

arándano M cranberry

arandela F washer

araña F (arácnido) spider; (candelabro) chandelier

arañar VT (rayar) to scratch; (herir con garras) to claw, to scratch; (raspar) to scrape, to score

arañazo M scratch

arañero M warbler

arar VI/VT to plow, to till

arbitraje M arbitration

arbitrar VT (un desacuerdo) to arbitrate; (un partido) to referee, to officiate; (un partido de béisbol) to umpire

arbitrario ADJ arbitrary

arbitrio M (libre albedrío) free will; (capricho) whim; (decisión) discretion; (deseos) wishes

árbitro -tra MF (del buen gusto) arbiter; (de conflictos) arbitrator; (de encuentros deportivos) referee

árbol M tree; (mástil) mast; **— de Navidad** Christmas tree; **— de levas** camshaft; **— genealógico** family tree

arbolado ADJ woody, wooded

arboleda F grove, clump

arbóreo ADJ arboreal

arbusto M shrub, bush

arca F ark; **— de Noé** Noah's ark; **las —s municipales** municipal coffers

arcada F arcade, archway; **tener / dar —s to** gag

arcaico ADJ archaic

arcaísmo M archaism

arcano ADJ arcane

arce M maple (tree)

arcén M shoulder of a road

archienemigo -ga MF archenemy

archipiélago M archipelago

archisabido ADJ very well-known

archivador M filing cabinet

archivar VT (guardar en un archivo) to file; (arrinconar) to shelve

archivo M (lugar) archive; (fichero de ordenador) file; (acción de archivar) filing

arcilla F clay

arco M (curva, eléctrico) arc; (estructura arquitectónica) arch; (arma, varilla de violín) bow; **— iris** rainbow

arder VT to burn; **la cosa está que arde** things are really getting hot; **el trigo se ardió** the wheat spoiled

ardid M scheme, artifice

ardiente ADJ (de deseo) ardent; (de calor, fuego, deseo) burning

ardilla F squirrel; **— de tierra** gopher; **— listada** chipmunk

ardite M **no valer un —** not to be worth a penny

ardor M (de pasión) ardor; (de fuego) heat; **— de estómago** heartburn

arduo ADJ arduous, grueling

área F area

arena F (tierra) sand; (plaza) arena; **— movediza** quicksand

arenero M sandbox

arenga F harangue

arengar[7] VT to harangue

arenisca F sandstone

arenisco ADJ sandy

arenoso ADJ sandy

arenque M herring

arete M earring

argamasa F mortar

Argelia F Algeria

argelino -na ADJ & MF Algerian

Argentina F Argentina

argentino -na ADJ Argentine, Argentinian; (propio de la plata) silvery; MF Argentine, Argentinian

argolla F iron ring

argón M argon

argot M slang

argucias F PL trickery

argüir[31] VT to argue

argumentar VT to argue

argumento M (razonamiento) argument; (conjunto de sucesos) plot

aridez F dryness

árido ADJ (seco) arid, dry, barren; (aburrido) dry; **—s** dry goods

ariete M battering ram

arisco ADJ surly

arista F (borde) edge; (de trigo) beard; **limar —s** to overcome difficulties

aristocracia F aristocracy

aristócrata MF INV aristocrat

aristocrático ADJ aristocratic

aritmética F arithmetic

aritmético ADJ arithmetical

arma F (instrumento bélico) arm, weapon; (división del ejército) branch; — **blanca** sharp weapon; — **de fuego** firearm; **a las** — to arms; **de** —**s tomar** resolute; **tomar las** —**s** to take up arms

armada F armada, fleet

armado ADJ armed; **a mano armada** at gunpoint; M assembly, putting together

armador -ora MF shipowner

armadura F (piezas de hierro) armor; (de un edificio) framework; (de gafas) frame; (de música) key signature

armamento M armament

armar VT (proveer de armas) to arm; (abastecer una embarcación) to equip; (reforzar) to reinforce; (ensamblar) to assemble, to put together; (levantar una tienda de campaña) to pitch; — **jaleo** to whoop it up; — **relajo** to make a mess; —**se de** to arm oneself with; — **una pendencia** to pick a fight, to start a quarrel

armario M (de ropa) wardrobe, closet; (de cocina) cabinet, armoire

armatoste M unwieldy object

armazón MF framework, skeleton

Armenia F Armenia

armenio -nia ADJ & MF Armenian

armería F (depósito de armas) armory; (tienda de armas) gun shop

armiño M ermine

armisticio M armistice

armonía F harmony

armónico ADJ & M harmonic

armonioso ADJ harmonious

armonizar[9] VI/VT to harmonize, to blend

ARN (ácido ribonucleico) M RNA

arnés M harness

aro M (de baloncesto) hoop; (de rueda) rim

aroma M (olor agradable) aroma; (del vino) bouquet

aromático ADJ aromatic

arpa F harp

arpía F shrew

arpillera F burlap

arpón M harpoon

arponear VT to harpoon

arqueado ADJ arched

arquear VT to arch

arqueología F archaeology

arquetipo M archetype

arquitecto -ta MF architect

arquitectónico ADJ architectural

arquitectura F architecture

arrabal M outlying slum

arraigar[7] VT to take root

arrancar[6] VT (una planta) to uproot; (el pelo) to tear out; (un diente) to pull; (un vicio) to eradicate; (una flor) to pick; (una confesión) to extract; — **de** to wrest from; VI/VT (un vehículo) to start; **arrancó para el valle** he took off for the valley; **arrancó a sudar** he began to sweat; **sus problemas arrancan de su niñez** his problems are rooted in his childhood; —**se los cabellos** to tear one's hair (out)

arranque M (proceso de arrancar un coche) starting; (dispositivo para arrancar un coche) starter; (decisión, empuje) gumption; — **de ira** fit of rage

arrasar VT (destruir) to level, to raze; (derrotar) to crush; — **con** to obliterate; VI to win

arrastrado ADJ wretched

arrastrar VT (mover por el suelo) to drag; (llevarse consigo) to sweep away; (atraer) to draw; (soportar) to bear; (pronunciar lentamente) to draw out; — **los pies** (moverse con dificultades) to shuffle; (ser renuente) to stall; VI to hang down to the floor; —**se** (una serpiente) to slither; (una lagartija, un insecto) to crawl; (una persona) to grovel; M SG **arrastrapiés** shuffle

arrayán M myrtle

arrear VT to drive, to herd

arrebatar VT (quitar) to snatch away, to wrest away; (quemar) to burn on the outside; —**se** to have a fit

arrebatiña F mad scramble

arrebato M fit, outburst

arreciar VI to increase in intensity

arrecife M reef

arreglar VT (poner en orden, concertar, adaptar música) to arrange; (ordenar) to tidy up; (reparar) to fix, to repair; (resolver) to settle; — **cuentas** to settle accounts; **ya te arreglo** I'll fix you; —**se** (embellecerse) to fix oneself up; (llevarse bien con) to get along with; (entablar relaciones amorosas) to start dating; (reconciliarse) to make up; (conformarse) to make do; (despejarse) to clear up; —**se en** to agree on; **arreglárselas** to cope, to manage

arreglo M arrangement; **con** — **a** in accordance with; **no tiene** — it can't be helped; **llegar a un** — to settle; —**s** alterations

arrellanarse VI to lounge, to loll

arremangado ADJ turned up

arremangar[7] VT to roll up; —**se** to roll up

one's sleeves, to knuckle down

arremeter VI to attack; **— contra** to lunge at

arremetida F thrust, lunge

arremolinarse VT (viento) to whirl around; (agua) to eddy

arrendajo M bluejay

arrendamiento M rental

arrendar VI/VT to rent, to lease

arrendatario -ria MF tenant

arreo M adornment; **—s** tack, harness

arrepentido ADJ repentant, rueful

arrepentimiento M (contrición) repentance; (disgusto) regret

arrepentirse[3] VI (de los pecados) to repent; (de los errores) to regret

arrestar VT to arrest

arresto M arrest

arriar[16] VT (la bandera) to lower; (un cabo) to slacken

arriate M flower bed

arriba ADV above; **¡—!** get up! **¡— las manos!** stick 'em up! **¡— Juan!** long live Juan! **de — abajo** from top to bottom; **lleno hasta —** full to the brim; **te vas para —** you are doing well; **viven —** they live upstairs

arribar VI LIT to arrive; (buque) to put into port

arribista MF social climber

arribo M LIT arrival

arriendo M leasing, rental

arriero -ra MF animal driver

arriesgado ADJ (peligroso) risky; (valiente) daring

arriesgar[7] VT to risk; **—se** to take a chance

arrimar VT (acercar) to bring near; (golpear) to strike; **—se a** (apoyarse) to lean on; (acercarse) to get near

arrinconar VT (acorralar) to corner; (poner en un rincón) to put in a corner; (abandonar) to abandon

arritmia F arrhythmia

arrobamiento M rapture

arrobarse VI to be enraptured

arrodillarse VI to kneel

arrogancia F arrogance

arrogante ADJ arrogant

arrogarse[7] VT to assume

arrojadizo ADJ projectile

arrojar VT (lanzar) to throw, to hurl; (expulsar) to throw out; (botar) to throw away; (vomitar) to throw up, to vomit; (proyectar una luz) to shed, to throw; **— un saldo de** to show a balance of; **—se** to hurl oneself

arrojo M boldness, daring

arrollador ADJ overwhelming

arrollar VT (poner en forma de rollo) to roll up; (arrastrar) to run over; (derrotar) to defeat

arropar VT to wrap up; (en la cama) to tuck in; **—se** to pull up the covers

arroyo M stream, creek

arroz M rice; **— integral** brown rice

arrozal M rice field

arruga F wrinkle

arrugar[7] VT to wrinkle; **— el ceño** to knit one's brow; **—se** (pasar a tener arrugas) to get wrinkles; (asustarse) to be afraid

arruinar VT (estropear) to ruin; (destruir) to destroy, to ravage; (aguar) to spoil; (dejar en la quiebra) to bankrupt, to ruin; **—se** to go to ruin

arrullar VI (una paloma) to coo; VT (a un enamorado) to whisper sweet nothings to; (a un niño) to rock to sleep, to lull to sleep

arrullo M (de la tórtola) cooing; (del agua) babbling

arrumbar VT (arrinconar) to put aside; (marginalizar) to marginalize

arsenal M (depósito) arsenal; (astillero) navy yard

arsénico M arsenic

arte M SG art; F PL arts; M (destreza) skill, ability; (actividad técnica) craft; **bellas —s** fine arts; **el — por el —** art for art's sake; **malas —s** wiles; **no tener ni — ni parte en algo** to have nothing to do with something; **por — de** by means of

artefacto M (aparato útil) contrivance, device; (bomba) bomb

arteria F artery

arteriosclerosis F arteriosclerosis

artero ADJ artful, wily

artesanía F (trabajo, obra) craft; (habilidad) craftsmanship

artesano -na MF artisan, craftsman

ártico ADJ arctic

articulación F (acción de articular) articulation; (juntura) joint

articular VT (pronunciar) to articulate, to enunciate; (unir) to join

artículo M article; (entrada en un diccionario) article, entry; **— de fondo** editorial; **— definido** definite article; **hacer el —** to give a sales pitch

artífice MF (autor) architect; M (artesano) craftsman; F craftswoman

artificial ADJ artificial

artificio M artifice

artificioso ADJ affected, contrived

artillería F artillery

artillero -ra MF gunner
artimaña F trick, wile
artista MF artist
artístico ADJ artistic
artritis F arthritis
artroscópico ADJ arthroscopic
Aruba F Aruba
arveja F pea
arzobispo M archbishop
arzón M saddletree
as M ace (también atleta)
asa F handle
asado ADJ roasted; M (carne asada) roast; (acción de asar) roasting
asador -ora M spit; MF barbecue cook
asalariado -da MF wage-earner
asaltante MF mugger
asaltar VT (a una persona) to assault, to assail; (un banco) to hold up; (con preguntas) to assail; **—le a uno una idea** to be struck by an idea
asalto M (ataque) assault; (de un banco) holdup, stickup; **tomar por —** to storm
asamblea F assembly, gathering
asar VT to roast; **— a la parrilla** to grill; **— con adobo** to barbecue
asbesto M asbestos
ascendencia F ancestry
ascendente ADJ (que incrementa) ascending, rising; (hacia arriba) upward
ascender[1] VI (a un empleado) to promote; (una montaña) to climb; VI to ascend; **— a** to amount to
ascendiente MF ancestor
ascenso M (acción de ascender) ascent; (en el trabajo) promotion
ascensor M elevator
asceta MF INV ascetic
ascético ADJ ascetic
asco M disgust, revulsion; **hacer —s a** to reject; **me da —** it makes me sick, it disgusts me; **ese hombre está hecho un —** that man is a mess
ascórbico ADJ ascorbic
ascua F ember; **estar en —s** to be on pins and needles; **tener en —s** to string along
aseado ADJ well-groomed
asear VT to clean up
asediar VT to besiege
asedio M siege
asegurar VT (una victoria) to assure; (una frontera, una cerradura) to secure; (con un contrato de seguro) to insure; **—se (de)** to make sure (of); **te lo aseguro** I assure you
asemejarse VI **— a** to resemble
asentaderas F PL buttocks

asentar VT (datos) to enter; (una población) to establish; **—se** (posarse) to settle; (madurar) to settle down
asentimiento M assent, acquiescence
asentir[3] VI to assent, to acquiesce; **— con la cabeza** to nod
aseo M (acción de asearse) cleaning; (cualidad de aseado) cleanliness; (cuarto de baño) bathroom; (servicio) toilet, restroom
asequible ADJ (que se puede obtener) available; (que se puede pagar) affordable
aserción F assertion
aserradero M sawmill, lumber mill
aserrado ADJ serrated; M sawing
aserrar[1] VT to saw
aserrín M sawdust
aserto M assertion
asesinar VT to murder; (a una figura pública) to assassinate
asesinato M murder, killing; (de una figura pública) assassination
asesino -na ADJ murderous; MF killer, murderer; (de una figura pública) assassin
asesor -ora MF consulting, advisor
asesoramiento M consulting, advising
asesorar VT to advise
asestar VT **— un golpe** to inflict/deal a blow
aseveración F assertion
aseverar VT to assert
asexual ADJ asexual
asfalto M asphalt
asfixia F suffocation, asphyxiation
asfixiar VT to suffocate, to smother
así ADV so, thus, like this; **— —** so-so; **— como** in the same way that; **— de grande** that big; **— que** so that; **¿— que no vienes?** so you're not coming?
Asia F Asia
asiático -ca ADJ & MF Asian
asidero M hold; **eso no tiene — en la realidad** that has no basis in reality
asiduo ADJ (lector) assiduous; (cliente) steady
asiento M (lugar donde sentarse, parte de una silla, de válvula) seat; (de nóminas) entry, record; **tomar —** to take a seat
asignación F (acción de asignar) assignment; (acción de dar fondos) appropriation; (pago) allowance
asignar VT (una tarea) to assign; (fondos) to allot, to allocate
asignatura F subject
asilado -da MF inmate
asilar VT (a un político) to give asylum to; (un animal) to shelter
asilo M (para los perseguidos) asylum; (para huérfanos, ancianos) home

asimétrico ADJ asymmetric

asimilar VT (vitaminas, un grupo étnico) to assimilate; (información) to absorb

asimismo ADV likewise

asir[21] VT to grasp, to grip; **—se a** to hold onto

asistencia F (presencia, personas presentes) attendance; (ayuda) assistance, aid; (servicio para averías) roadside assistance; **— médica** health care; **— social** (ayuda) welfare; (profesión) social work

asistente -ta ADJ assistant; MF assistant, helper; **— social** social worker

asistir VT **— a** (estar presente) to attend; (ayudar) to help, to assist

asma F asthma

asmático ADJ asthmatic

asno M ass, donkey

asociación F association

asociado -da MF associate

asociar VT to associate; **—se** to join

asolamiento M desolation

asolar VT to desolate, to devastate

asomar VI to show; VT to poke out, to stick out; **—se a** to look out

asombrar VT to astonish, to amaze, to astound; **—se** to be astonished

asombro M astonishment, amazement

asombroso ADJ astonishing, amazing

asomo LOC ADV **ni por —** by no means

asonancia F assonance

aspa F (de hélice) blade; (de ventilador) vane

aspecto M (faceta) aspect, feature; (apariencia) looks

aspereza F roughness, harshness; **limar —s** to smooth over disagreements

áspero ADJ (terreno, mano) rough; (lucha) bitter; (tiempo, voz) harsh

aspiración F (ambición) aspiration, ambition; (respiración) breathing in; (succión) suction

aspiradora F vacuum cleaner

aspirante MF applicant, candidate

aspirar VT to breathe in, to inhale; **— a** to aspire to

aspirina F aspirin

asqueado ADJ disgusted

asquear VT to disgust

asquerosidad F nastiness; **¡estás hecho una —!** you're gross!

asqueroso ADJ nasty, disgusting, gross

asta F (de toro) horn; (de ciervo) antler; (de bandera) flagpole; (de lanza) shaft; **a media —** at half mast

asterisco M asterisk, star

asteroide M asteroid

astigmatismo M astigmatism

astilla F (de madera) chip, splinter; (de vidrio) sliver; **—s** kindling

astillar VT to chip, to splinter

astillero M shipyard

astringente ADJ & M astringent

astro M (del cielo) celestial body; (de cine) movie star

astrofísica F astrophysics

astrología F astrology

astronauta MF astronaut

astronáutica F astronautics

astronomía F astronomy

astrónomo -ma MF astronomer

astucia F (listeza) cunning, guile; (treta) trick

asturiano -na ADJ & MF Asturian

Asturias F SG Asturias

astuto ADJ shrewd, wily, cunning

asueto M time off

asumir VT (una responsabilidad) to assume, to shoulder; (una mala noticia) to accept; **— un cargo** to take office

asunto M (cuestión) matter; (de una obra artística) theme

asustadizo ADJ easily frightened, jumpy

asustado ADJ frightened

asustar VT to frighten, to scare; **—se** to become frightened

atacante ADJ attacking; MF assailant

atacar[6] VT to attack, to assault; **—se de risa** to have a laughing fit

atado M bundle

atadura F **sin —s** with no strings attached

atajador M tackle

atajar VT (interrumpir) to cut off; VI (tomar un atajo) to take a shortcut

atajo M shortcut

atalaya F watchtower

atañer[18, 50] VI to concern, to pertain to

ataque M (violento, de asma) attack; (de rabia, de tos) fit; (de epilepsia) seizure; **— cardíaco** heart attack; **— de nervios** nervous breakdown; **— relámpago** blitz

atar VT (sujetar) to tie, to bind; **— cabos** to make sense of something; **—se los zapatos** to tie one's shoes

atardecer[13] VI to get dark; M late afternoon, dusk, evening; **al —** at dusk

atareado ADJ busy

atarearse VI to busy oneself

atascadero M (lodazal) quagmire; (de tránsito) bottleneck

atascado ADJ stuck

atascar[6] VT (un tubo) to stop up; (una máquina) to jam; (el tráfico) to obstruct; **—se** (un vehículo) to get stuck; (una máquina) to get jammed

ataúd M coffin, casket

ataviar[16] VT to attire, to array; **—se** to dress up

atavío M attire, garb

ateísmo M atheism

atemorizar[9] VT to frighten

atención F attention; (médica) care; (acto de cortesía) courtesy; **a la — de** to the attention of; **llamar la —** (hacer notar) to call attention; (ser llamativo) to attract attention; (interesar) to interest; INTERJ watch out!

atender[1] VI **— a** to pay attention to; (el trabajo) to attend to, to take care of; (a un enfermo) to take care of, to look after; (una súplica) to heed; (a un cliente) to serve

atenerse[44] VI **— a los hechos** to bear the facts in mind; **— a la ley** to abide by the law

atentado M assassination; assassination attempt; **un — contra** an affront to

atentamente ADV (con atención) attentively; (despedida en cartas) yours truly / sincerely

atentar[1] VI **— contra la vida de alguien** to make an attempt on someone's life

atento ADJ (que presta atención) attentive; (amable) thoughtful

atenuar[17] VT (la violencia) to attenuate; (una luz) to dim; **—se** to abate

ateo -a MF atheist

aterciopelado ADJ velvety

aterido ADJ stiff with cold

aterirse[50] VI to become stiff with cold

aterrador ADJ terrifying

aterrar VT to terrify

aterrizaje M landing; **— forzoso** crash landing

aterrizar[9] VI/VT to land

aterrorizar[9] VT to terrify

atesorar VT (memorias) to treasure; (dinero) to hoard

atestado ADJ crowded, crammed

atestar VT (certificar) to attest to; (llenar) to jam, to pack

atestiguar[8] VT to bear witness, to testify

atiborrar VT to stuff; **—se** to stuff one's face

atiesar VT to stiffen

atildado ADJ spruced up

atinar VT (dar en el blanco) to hit the mark; (adivinar) to guess right; **no — a decir palabra** not to manage to get a word out

atisbar VT (mirar con disimulo) to peek at, to peep at; (vislumbrar) to catch a glimpse of; VI to peek

atisbo M glimpse, hint

atizar[9] VT (un fuego) to poke, to stake; (las pasiones) to stir up, to stoke

atlántico ADJ Atlantic; M **Océano Atlántico** Atlantic Ocean

atlas M atlas

atleta MF athlete

atlético ADJ athletic

atletismo M track and field

atmósfera F atmosphere

atmosférico ADJ atmospheric

atolladero M quagmire

atolondrado ADJ scatterbrained; (muchacha) ditsy

atómico ADJ atomic

atomizar[9] VT to atomize

átomo M atom

atónito ADJ dumbfounded

atontado ADJ stupefied

atontar VT to stupefy

atorar VT to jam; **—se** to choke

atormentar VT to torment; **—se por** to agonize over

atornillar VT to bolt

atracadero M dock

atracar[6] VT (amarrar) to dock; (robar) to hold up, to mug; **—se** to gorge oneself

atracción F attraction

atraco M holdup, stickup

atracón M **darse un —** to gorge

atractivo ADJ (capacidad de atraer) attractiveness, appeal; M (cosa que atrae) attraction; **— sexual** sex appeal

atraer[45] VT to attract

atragantarse VI to choke

atrancar[6] VT to bolt, to bar

atrapada F catch

atrapar VT (en una trampa) to trap, to ensnare, to catch; (una pelota, el interés) to catch

atrás ADV **— de la casa** behind the house; **cuatro años —** four years back; **hacia —** backward; **para —** back / backwards; **quedarse —** to fall behind

atrasado ADJ (pasado) late; (en el pago) in arrears, behind; (país) backward; (un libro de biblioteca) overdue; **tengo sueño —** I'm behind in my sleep; **el reloj anda —** the clock is slow; **feliz cumpleaños —** happy belated birthday

atrasar VT (un plazo) to delay; (una mesa) to push back; (un reloj) to turn back; VI (un reloj) to run slow; **—se** to fall behind, to lag

atraso M (condición de atrasado) backwardness; (pago) back payment; (de trabajo) backlog; **con dos meses de —** two months in arrears

atravesar[1] VT (cruzar) to cross; (ir de lado a lado) to span; (penetrar) to impale, to run through; — **un momento difícil** to go through a difficult moment; **se me atravesó un caballo** a horse crossed in front of me; **—se en la cama** to lie crossways in bed

atreverse VI to dare

atrevido ADJ (audaz) bold, daring; (insolente) insolent

atrevimiento M (cualidad de atrevido) boldness, daring, audacity; (acción atrevida) daring act

atribución F attribution; **atribuciones** powers

atribuir[31] VT to attribute, to ascribe

atribular VT to distress; **—se** to be distressed

atributo M attribute

atril M stand

atrincherar VT to entrench

atrio M atrium

atrocidad F atrocity

atrofia F atrophy

atrofiar VT to atrophy, to stunt

atronador ADJ thunderous, deafening

atronar[2] VI to make a racket

atropellar VT (a un peatón) to run over, to run down; (los derechos de alguien) to trample upon

atropello M (de un peatón) running over; (ultraje) outrage; (de derechos) trampling

atroz ADJ (modales, crimen) atrocious; (dolor) excruciating; (ofensa) grievous

atuendo M getup

atún M tuna

aturdido ADJ bewildered; **estar —** to be in a daze

aturdimiento M bewilderment

aturdir VT to bewilder, to daze

atusar VT to smooth, to fix

audacia F audacity, boldness

audaz ADJ audacious, bold

audible ADJ audible

audición F audition

audiencia F (tribunal) court; (reunión, conjunto de oyentes) audience; (hecho de oír un pleito) hearing

audífono M (para los sordos) earphone; (para música) headphones

audio M audio; **—libro** book on tape; **—visual** audiovisual

audiología F audiology

auditar VI/VT to audit

auditivo ADJ auditory

auditor -ora MF auditor

auditoría F audit

auditorio M (público) audience; (local) auditorium

auge M (del mercado) boom; (de una moda) heyday; (de una carrera) peak

augurar VT to foretell; **no — nada bueno** not to bode well

aula F (de clase) classroom; (de conferencia) lecture hall

aullar VI to howl

aullido M howl

aumentar VT to augment, to increase; VI (los precios) to rise, to escalate; (población) to swell; (violencia) to escalate

aumento M increase; (de expectativas) buildup; (de población) growth; (de precios) rise, upturn; (de peso) gain

aun ADV even; **— así** even so; **— cuando** even though/if

aún ADV still

aunque CONJ though, although

aura F aura

áureo ADJ golden

aureola F halo

auricular M (de teléfono) receiver; **—es** headphones, earphones

aurora F dawn, aurora; **— boreal** aurora borealis, northern lights

auscultar VT to listen to with a stethoscope

ausencia F absence

ausentarse VT to absent oneself

ausente ADJ absent, missing

ausentismo M absenteeism

auspicios M PL auspices

austeridad F austerity

austero ADJ austere, stern

Australia F Australia

australiano -na ADJ & MF Australian

Austria F Austria

austríaco -ca ADJ & MF Austrian

autenticar[6] VT to authenticate

auténtico ADJ authentic

autismo M autism

auto M (coche) auto; (orden judicial) writ; **— de choques** bumper car

autoadhesivo M decal; (para el parachoques) bumper sticker

autoayuda F self-help

autobiografía F autobiography

autobomba M fire engine

autobús M bus

autocine M drive-in movie theater

autocompasión F self-pity

autocontrol M self-control

autócrata MF INV autocrat

autóctono ADJ indigenous

autodestructivo ADJ self-destructive

autodisciplina F self-discipline

autoestima F self-esteem

autogobierno M self-government

autógrafo M autograph

autoimagen F self-image
automático ADJ automatic
automatización F automation
automatizar[9] ADJ (mecanizar) to automate; (hacer automáticamente) to do automatically
automóvil M automobile
automovilista MF motorist
automovilístico ADJ automotive
autonomía F autonomy; (de un vehículo) range
autopista F freeway, turnpike
autopropulsado ADJ self-propelled
autopsia F autopsy
autor -ora MF author
autoridad F authority
autoritario ADJ (tiránico) authoritarian; (respetado) authoritative
autorización F authorization
autorizar[9] VT to authorize; (dar propiedad intelectual) to license
autosatisfacción F self-satisfaction
autoservicio M (sistema de venta) self-service; (tienda) convenience store
autosuficiente ADJ self-sufficient; (presumido) smug
autovía F freeway
auxiliar VT to help; ADJ auxiliary; MF assistant; — **de vuelo** (hombre) steward; (mujer) stewardess
auxilio M help
avalancha F avalanche
avalar VT to guarantee, to co-sign
avaluar[17] VT to appraise
avalúo M appraisal
avance M (acción de avanzar, adelanto) advance, headway; (sinopsis de película) trailer
avanzada F scouting party
avanzado ADJ advanced
avanzar[9] VI (ir hacia adelante) to advance; (progresar) to make headway; **a medida que avanzaba la mañana** as the morning progressed; VT to move forward; (una cinta) to fast-forward
avaricia F avarice
avariento ADJ avaricious, miserly
avaro ADJ miserly, avaricious
avasallar VT to subjugate
ave F bird; — **de corral** poultry; — **de rapiña** bird of prey; — **canora** songbird; — **zancuda** wading bird
avecindarse VI to take up residence
avellana F hazelnut
avellano M hazel
avena F oats
avenencia F agreement

avenida F avenue
avenir[47] VI to reconcile; —**se a** to come around; —**se bien** to get along
aventadora F fan, blower
aventajar VT (ser mejor) to be superior to; (sobrepasar) to get ahead of
aventón M **dar un** — *Méx* to give a lift
aventura F (suceso que implica riesgo) adventure; (relación amorosa) fling, affair
aventurado ADJ (arriesgado) risky; (atrevido) daring
aventurar VT (arriesgar) to risk; (sugerir) to venture; —**se a** to dare to
aventurero -ra ADJ adventurous; MF adventurer
avergonzado ADJ (tímido) abashed; (arrepentido) ashamed
avergonzar[2,9] VT to shame, to embarrass; —**se** to be ashamed/embarrassed
avería F (de frutas) damage; (de coche) breakdown, mechanical trouble
averiado ADJ (un coche) broken-down; (un televisor) on the blink
averiarse[16] VI (fruta) to become damaged; (un coche) to break down
averiguar[8] VT to find out, to ascertain
aversión F aversion, dislike
avestruz MF ostrich
avezado ADJ seasoned
aviación F aviation
aviador -ora MF aviator
aviar[16] VT to fix
avidez F eagerness
ávido ADJ eager, avid
avinagrado ADJ sour
avinagrar VT to sour; —**se** to become sour
avío M tidying up; —**s de pescar** fishing tackle
avión M (máquina) airplane; (ave) martin; — **comercial** airliner; — **a reacción** jet airplane; — **caza** fighter airplane
avisar VT (notificar) to advise; (a la policía) to alert
aviso M notice; — **publicitario** advertisement; **estar sobre** — to be forewarned; **poner sobre** — to forewarn; **sin previo** — without warning
avispa F wasp
avispado ADJ lively
avisparse VI to wise up
avispero M wasp's nest; **alborotar el** — to stir up a wasp's nest
avispón M hornet
avistar VT to catch sight of
avivar VT (una fiesta) to enliven; (un fuego, un debate) to fuel; (una llama) to fan
avizorar VT to spy on

axila F underarm

ay INTERJ (de dolor) ouch; (de decepción) oh, no; (de sorpresa desagradable) oh; — **de mí** poor me

ayer ADV yesterday

ayuda F help; (después de un desastre) relief

ayudante -ta MF assistant, helper; — **de médico** physician's assistant

ayudantía F assistantship

ayudar VT to help, to aid

ayunar VI to fast

ayunas F PL **en** — (antes de comer) without having eaten; (despistado) clueless; **estoy en** — I am fasting

ayuno M fast

ayuntamiento M (gobierno) municipal government; (edificio) city hall

azabache M jet; ADJ jet-black, raven

azada F hoe

azadón M hoe

azafato -ta MF (en aviones) flight attendant; (en ferias) host

azafrán M saffron

azahar M orange blossom

azar M chance; **al** — by chance, at random

azaroso ADJ (arriesgado) risky; (aleatorio) random

azerbaijano -na, azerbaiyano -na ADJ & MF Azerbaijani, Azerbaijanian

Azerbaiyán F Azerbaijan

azogar[7] VT to silver

azogue M (sustancia) quicksilver, mercury; (niño inquieto) restless child; **tener** — **en el cuerpo** to be restless

azorar VT to embarrass

azotaina F flogging

azotar VT (con azote) to whip, to lash, to flog; VI/VT (el viento) to whip, to buffet; (el sol) to beat down; (la lluvia) to sting

azote M (instrumento) whip; (golpe) lash; (aflicción) scourge; (golpe de viento) buffet

azotea F flat roof

azúcar MF sugar; — **moreno -na** brown sugar

azucarar VT to sugar

azucarera F (fábrica) sugar mill; (recipiente) sugar bowl

azucarero M sugar bowl

azucena F white lily

azufre M sulfur/sulphur

azul ADJ blue; — **acero** steel blue; — **celeste** sky-blue; — **claro** light blue; — **marino** navy blue

azulado ADJ bluish

azular VT to color blue

azulear VI (tener color azul) to be blue;

(ponerse azul) to become blue; VT (dar color azul) to color blue

azulejar VT to tile

azulejo M tile

azuzar[9] VT (a un perro) to sic; (a una persona) to egg on

Bb

baba F drivel, drool, slobber; (de un caracol, de agua estancada) slime; **se le cae la baba por el coche nuevo** he's drooling over the new car

babear VI to drivel, to drool

babero M bib

babor M portside

babosa F slug

babosear VI/VT to slobber (on)

baboso ADJ (caracol) slimy; (persona que babea) driveling; (persona tonta) idiotic; (adulador) fawning

babuino M baboon

baca F luggage rack

bacalao M cod

bache M pothole; (momento) bad time; (de aire) air pocket

bacheado ADJ bumpy

bachiller -ra M (graduado) high school graduate; (alumno) high school student

bachillerato M baccalaureate

bacilo M bacillus

backgammon M backgammon

bacteria F bacteria

bacteriología F bacteriology

badajo M bell clapper

badana F sheepskin

bagaje M baggage

bagatela F trifle

bagazo M pulp

Bahamas F PL Bahamas

bahameño -ña ADJ & MF Bahamian

bahía F bay

Bahrein M Bahrain

bahreiní ADJ & MF Bahraini

bailador -ora MF folk dancer; ADJ dancing

bailar VI/VT to dance; **me bailan los pantalones** my pants are falling off; **me tocó** — **con la más fea** I was left holding the bag; **que me quiten lo bailado** I enjoyed it anyway

bailarín -ina MF dancer

baile M (movimiento rítmico) dance; (fiesta) dance, ball; — **aeróbico** aerobic dance; —

de máscaras masked ball; — **folklórico** folk dance; — **zapateado** clog dance

bailongo M hop

bailotear VI to jig

baivel M bevel

baja F (caída barométrica) drop; (de precios) decline; (víctima de guerra) casualty; (del ejército) discharge, dismissal; (licencia) leave; **dar de** — to discharge; **darse de** — to call in sick

bajada F (acción de bajar, pendiente) descent; (de un caballo) dismount; — **contra-reloj** downhill ski race

bajar VI to go down; (corriendo) to run down; (de un árbol) to climb down; (de un caballo) to get down; (de un ómnibus) to step off, to get off; (empeorar) to worsen; (alcanzar) to reach down; (la marea) to ebb; (una creciente) to subside; VT (las escaleras) to go down; (un avión de un tiro) to shoot down; (comida con agua) to wash down; (la cabeza) to lower; (un cargamento) to let down; (el volumen) to turn down; (focos) to dim; (la voz) to lower, to soften; — **de categoría** to demote; — **el cursor** to scroll down; — **en picada** to dive; — **los pantalones** to pull down one's pants

bajeza F (cualidad) baseness; (acción) vile act

bajío M shoal

bajista ADJ (bolsa) bearish

bajo ADJ (nubes, estante, precio, voz grave) low; (persona) short; (voz débil) soft; (río) lower; (vista, persianas) lowered; (acto) base; **baja espalda** small of the back; **de baja ley** base; PREP under; — **control** under control; — **cuerda** under-the-table; — **fianza** on bail; — **fuego** under fire; — **sospecha** under a cloud; — **tierra** underground; **poner** — **llave** to lock up; **por lo** — under one's breath; M (voz grave) bass; (de pantalón) cuff; **hacer los** —**s** to cuff; ADV low

bala F (de pistola) bullet; (de prueba olímpica) shot; (de cañón) ball

balada F ballad

baladí ADJ trivial

balance M (cálculo) balance; (documento) balance sheet; (de víctimas) toll; (movimiento) sway; **hacer un** — to take stock

balancear VT to swing; VI to sway; —**se** to sway

balanceo M (de un cuerpo) swinging, swing; (de un barco) rolling, roll

balancín M seesaw

balanza F scale; — **comercial** balance of trade; — **de pagos** balance of payments

balar VI to bleat

balasto M ballast

balaustrada F banister

balazo M (disparo) shot; (herida) bullet wound

balbucear VI to stammer; (un bebé) to babble

balbuceo M stammer; stammering; (de bebé) babble, babbling

balcón M balcony

balde M pail, bucket; **de** — gratis; **en** — in vain

baldear VT to flush

baldío ADJ (terreno) fallow; (acción) useless

baldosa F (en una casa) floor tile; (en una calle) flagstone

balido M bleat, bleating

balística F ballistics

balístico ADJ ballistic

ballena F whale; (hueso) whalebone

ballenato M whale calf

ballet M ballet

balneario M summer resort; (con aguas medicinales) spa

balón M ball; **baloncesto** basketball; **balonmano** European handball; F **balonvolea** volleyball

balsa F raft, balsa; (lago) pond

bálsamo M balsam, balm

baluarte M bulwark, stronghold

bambolear VT to sway, to swing; —**se** to sway, to swing

bamboleo M swinging, swaying

bambú M bamboo

banal ADJ banal; **una respuesta** — a pat answer

banana F banana

banano M banana tree

banca F (industria) banking; (en el juego) bank

bancario -ria ADJ bank, banking; MF banker

bancarrota F bankruptcy

banco M (establecimiento) bank; (asiento) bench; (de peces) school; (de arena) shoal, spit; — **de datos** data bank; — **de niebla** fog bank

banda F (musical) band; (cinta ancha) band, sash; (grupo) gang, band, ring; (dibujo) stripe; (de un neumático) tread; (lindero) side, edge, border; (de un barco) side; — **de frecuencia** frequency band; — **horaria** time slot; — **magnética** magnetic strip; — **sonora** sound track

bandada F (de aves) flock, flight; (de peces) school

bandeja F tray; **me lo sirvieron en** — (de

plata) they served it to me on a silver platter

bandera F flag; **jurar la —** to pledge allegiance to the flag

banderín M pennant

banderola F pennant

bandido -da MF bandit, outlaw; (como epíteto) rascal

bando M (decreto) edict; (partido) camp

bandolero -ra MF bandit

Bangladesh M Bangladesh

banjo M banjo

banquero -ra MF banker

banqueta F (taburete) stool; (acera) *Méx* sidewalk

banquete M banquet

banquetearse VI to feast

banquillo M bench

bañar VT to bathe; (una torta) to ice, to frost; **—se** to take a bath, to bathe

bañera F bathtub

bañista MF bather

baño M (acción) bath; (cuarto) bathroom, lavatory; (de torta) icing, frosting; **darse un —** (bañarse) to take a bath; (nadar) to take a swim; **— (de) María** double boiler; **— de sangre** bloodbath

bar M bar

barahúnda F ruckus, racket

baraja F pack / deck of cards

barajada F shuffle

barajar VI/VT (naipes) to shuffle; (alternativas) to weigh

baranda F railing, guard rail

barandal M banister

barandilla F rail, railing

barata F *Méx* sale

baratear VT to sell cheap

baratija F trinket, knickknack

barato ADJ cheap

baratura F cheapness

barba F beard; **—s** whiskers; **hacer algo en las —s de alguien** to do something right under someone's nose

barbacoa F barbecue

barbadense ADJ & MF Barbadian

barbado ADJ bearded

Barbados M Barbados

barbaridad F atrocity; **una — de** a lot of; **¡qué —!** what nonsense!

barbarie F savagery

bárbaro -ra ADJ (salvaje) barbarous, barbaric; (estupendo) cool, super; MF barbarian

barbecho M fallow land

barbería F barbershop

barbero -ra MF barber

barbilla F chin

barbitúrico M barbiturate

barbudo ADJ bearded

barca F rowboat

barcaza F barge

barco M boat

bardo M bard

bario M barium

barítono ADJ & M baritone

barlovento M windward

barniz M (para madera) varnish; (para cerámica) glaze; (de cultura) veneer

barnizar[9] VT (madera) to varnish; (cerámica) to glaze

barómetro M barometer

barón M baron

barquero -era M boatman; F boatwoman

barquillo M rolled wafer

barquinazo M **dar —s** to lurch

barra F (de hierro, arena, chocolate, en un bar) bar; (en gimnasia) crossbar; (signo ortográfico) slash; **— de jabón** bar of soap; **— espaciadora** space bar

barrabasada F mischief

barraca F (en las fiestas) stall, stand; (casucha) hovel

barracuda F barracuda

barranca M ravine

barranco M gully, ravine

barrena F (de un taladro) bit; (de un avión) tailspin; **entrar en —** to go into a tailspin

barrenar VT to drill

barrendero -ra MF street sweeper

barrer VI/VT to sweep; (derrotar) to defeat decisively; M SG **barreminas** mine-sweeper

barrera F barrier; (valla) barrier, bar; **— arancelaria** tariff barrier; **— de coral** barrier reef; **— del sonido** sound barrier

barrica F vat

barricada F barricade

barrida F sweep

barrido M (acción de barrer) sweeping; (movimiento) sweep

barriga F belly; (gorda) paunch; **rascarse la —** to do nothing

barrigón ADJ pot-bellied

barril M barrel, keg, drum

barrio M neighborhood, quarter; **— residencial** residential neighborhood; **—s bajos** slums

barritar VI to trumpet

barro M (lodo) mud; (arcilla) clay; (acné) pimple; **de —** earthen

barroco ADJ & M baroque

barroso ADJ muddy

barrote M bar

barruntar VT to suspect
barrunto M suspicion
bártulos M PL stuff
barullo M hubbub
basal ADJ basal
basalto M basalt
basar VT to base; **—se en** (depender de) to rely on; (fundamentar en) to be based on
basca F nausea
báscula F scale
base F (apoyo, área militar, química) base; (punto de partida) basis; (de maquillaje) foundation; (de una campaña) plank; **— de concurso** contest rules; **— de datos** database; **— de lanzamiento** launching pad; **con — en** on the basis of; **en — a** on the basis of; **las —s** (de un partido) grass roots; (de un sindicato) rank and file; **salario —** base salary; **tener una — sólida** to be on a strong footing
basic M (lenguaje de programación) basic
básico ADJ basic; (comida) staple
bastante ADJ & PRON enough, sufficient; ADV (suficientemente) enough; (mucho) quite a lot; (algo) quite, pretty
bastar VI to be enough, to suffice; **¡basta!** enough!
bastardilla F italics
bastardo -da ADJ & MF *ofensivo* bastard
bastedad F coarseness
bastidor M (de un teatro) wing; (para bordado) frame; (de un coche) chassis; (de una ventana) sash; **entre —es** (en teatro) offstage; (en privado) behind the scenes
bastimentos M PL provisions
basto ADJ coarse, crude; M suit in the Spanish deck of cards
bastón M (para andar) cane, walking stick; **— de esquí** ski pole
basura F rubbish, garbage, trash
basural M *Am* dump
basurero -ra MF (persona) garbage collector; M (lugar) dump
bata F (para llevar en casa) robe, housecoat; (de laboratorio) lab coat; (de pacientes) hospital gown; **— de baño** bathrobe
batahola F racket
batalla F battle; (de coches) wheelbase; **— naval** sea battle; **ropa de —** everyday clothing; **trabar —** to engage in battle
batallar VI to battle
batallón M battalion
batata F sweet potato
bate M baseball bat
batea F tray
bateador -ora MF batter
batear VI to bat

batería F (de coche, artillería) battery; (de cocina) pots and pans; **en —** lined up
baterista MF drummer
batiburrillo M hodgepodge
batido M shake, milk shake
batidor M whisk, beater
batidora F mixer
batintín M gong
batir VT (una alfombra) to beat; (un terreno) to comb; (mantequilla) to cream, to churn; (un récord) to break; (huevos) to beat; (crema) to whip; (alas) to flap, to beat; **—se en duelo** to duel; **—se en retirada** to retreat; **— palmas** to clap, to applaud
batuta F baton; **llevar la —** to call the shots
baudio M baud
baúl M trunk
bautismo M baptism, christening; **— de fuego** baptism of fire
bautizar[9] VT to baptize, to christen
bautizo M christening, baptism
baya F berry
bayeta F cleaning cloth
bayo ADJ bay
bayoneta F bayonet
baza F card trick; **meter — en una conversación** to participate in a conversation
bazar M bazaar
bazo M spleen
bazofia F slop
bazuca F bazooka
beagle M beagle
beato ADJ (bendito) blessed; (piadoso) beatified; (santurrón) overly pious
bebé M baby, infant
bebedero M (recipiente) drinking trough; (lugar) watering hole
bebedor -ora MF drinker
beber VI/VT to drink
bebercio M *fam* booze
bebida F drink, beverage
beca F scholarship, fellowship
becario -ria MF scholar, fellow
becerro M calf; (piel) calfskin
becuadro M natural sign
befa F jeer
befar VT to jeer at
beicon M *Esp* bacon
beige ADJ INV & M beige
beldad F beauty
belga ADJ & MF Belgian
Bélgica F Belgium
Belice M Belize
beliceño -ña ADJ & MF Belizean
bélico ADJ warlike

belicoso ADJ (guerrero) bellicose; (agresivo) feisty

beligerante ADJ & MF belligerent

bellaco M rascal, scoundrel

bellaquería F mischief

belleza F beauty

bello ADJ beautiful

bellota F acorn

bemol ADJ & M flat; **tener —es** to be tricky

bencina F benzine

bendecir[26b] VT to bless

bendición F (parte de la misa) benediction; (acción y efecto de bendecir) blessing; (cosa excelente) boon, blessing

bendito ADJ (agua) holy; (alma) blessed; **— sea** may he be blessed; **dormir como un —** to sleep like a log; **es un —** he is a saint

benefactor -ora M benefactor, patron; F benefactress, patroness

beneficencia F charity; **— pública** welfare

beneficiar VT to benefit; **—se de** to benefit from

beneficiario -ria MF (de una herencia, perdón, acto de bondad) beneficiary; (de un cheque) payee

beneficio M benefit (también espectáculo)

beneficioso ADJ beneficial

benéfico ADJ beneficent

benemérito ADJ worthy of esteem

benevolencia F benevolence

benévolo ADJ benevolent

bengala F flare

benigno ADJ benign

Benín M Benin

beninés -esa ADJ & MF Beninese

benjamín -ina MF youngest child

beodo ADJ drunk

berbiquí M carpenter's brace

berenjena F eggplant

bermejo ADJ reddish

bermellón ADJ vermilion

berrear VI (animal) to bellow, to bawl; (bebé) to squall

berrido M (de animal) bellowing, bawling; (de bebé) squall, squalling

berrinche M tantrum

berro M watercress

berza F cabbage

besar VT to kiss

beso M kiss

bestia F beast

bestial ADJ bestial

best-seller ADV best seller

besuquear VT to kiss repeatedly; **—se** to make out

betabel M *Méx* beet

betún M shoe polish

Biblia F Bible

bíblico ADJ biblical

bibliografía F bibliography

biblioteca F library; (estante) bookcase

bibliotecario -ria MF librarian

bicarbonato M bicarbonate; **— de sosa** bicarbonate of soda

bíceps M SG bicep(s)

bicho M (insecto) bug (también en informática); (animal) *fam* critter; **— raro** odd bird; **mal —** creep; **¿qué — te ha picado?** what's gotten into you? **—s** vermin

bici F bike

bicicleta F bicycle; **— de montaña** mountain bike; **— estática** stationary bike

biela F connecting rod

Bielorrusia F Belarus

bien ADV well; **—aventurado** blessed; **— arreglado** well groomed; **— hecho** well-made, well-done; **— poco** very little; **agarrarse —** to hold on tight; **ahora —** now then; **apretar —** to press hard; **está —** she is fine; **más —** rather; **me doy — cuenta** I'm perfectly aware; **pues —** now; **qué —** how wonderful; **si —** although; **ya está —** that's enough; M good; **—es** property, assets; **—es inmuebles** real estate; **—es muebles** personal property; **—es raíces** real estate; **—estar** well-being, welfare; **—hechor** benefactor; **persona de —** a good person

bienio M biennium

bienvenida F welcome

bienvenido ADJ welcome

bifurcación F fork, forking; (en un programa de computadora) branch

bifurcarse[6] VI to fork, to branch off

bigamia F bigamy

bigote M mustache; (de animal) whisker

bikini M bikini

bilateral ADJ bilateral

bilingüe ADJ & MF bilingual

bilingüismo M bilingualism

bilis F bile

billar M billiards, pool; (mesa) pool table

billete M (de viaje, para espectáculos) ticket; (de banco) bill, banknote

billetera F billfold

billón M trillion

bimestral ADJ bimonthly

bimestre M two-month period

binario ADJ binary

bingo M bingo

binomial ADJ binomial

binomio M binomial
biodegradable ADJ biodegradable
biofeedback M biofeedback
biografía F biography
bioingeniería F bioengineering
biología F biology
biombo M folding screen
biopsia F biopsy
bioquímica F biochemistry
biorritmo M biorhythm
biotecnología F biotechnology
bipartidista ADJ bipartisan
bipolar ADJ bipolar
birlar VT *fam* to pinch, to swipe
Birmania F Burma
birmano -na ADJ & MF Burmese, from Myanmar
birrete M mortarboard
bis M encore
bisabuelo -la M great-grandfather; F great-grandmother
bisagra F hinge
bisecar[6] VT to bisect
bisel M bevel
biselar VT to bevel
bisexual ADJ bisexual
bisiesto ADJ **año —** leap year
bisnieto -ta M great-grandson; F great-granddaughter
bisonte M bison, buffalo
bistec M beefsteak
bisturí M scalpel
bisutería F costume jewelry
bit M bit
bizarría F gallantry
bizarro ADJ gallant
bizco ADJ cross-eyed
bizcocho M sponge cake
bizcochuelo M sponge cake
bizquear VI to be cross-eyed
black-jack M black-jack
blanca F half note
blanco ADJ (color) white; (tez) fair; M (color) white (también de huevos, ojos); (de tiro) target; (de una burla) butt; **— fácil** sitting duck; **dar en el —** to hit the target; **en —** (hoja de papel, mente) blank; (sin dormir) sleepless; **en — y negro** in black and white
blancura F whiteness; (de tez) fairness
blancuzco ADJ whitish
blandir VT to brandish, to wield
blando ADJ soft; (sensiblero) mushy
blandura F softness
blanqueador M bleach
blanquear VT (una pared) to whitewash; (dinero) to launder; (verduras) to blanch; **—se** to whiten
blanquecino ADJ whitish
blanqueo M whitening
blasfemar VI/VT to blaspheme
blasfemia F blasphemy
blasón M coat of arms
blasonar VI to boast
blazer M blazer
blindado ADJ armored
blindaje M armor
blindar VT to armor
bloc M writing tablet, pad of paper
bloque M block (también de motor, político); (edificio) building; **en —** together
bloquear VT (una carretera, un asalto, un pase) to block; (un puerto) to blockade; (cuentas bancarias) to freeze; **—se** to choke
bloqueo M block; (militar) blockade
blues M PL blues
bluff M bluff
blusa F blouse, top
boa F boa constrictor
boato M pomp
bobada F foolish act; (fruslería) trifle
bobalicón -ona ADJ goofy; MF nincompoop
bobear VI to fool around, to monkey around
bobería F (cualidad) foolishness; (dicho) foolish remark; (hecho) foolish act
bobina F (de hilo) bobbin; (de alambre, de coche) coil; (de película) reel
bobinar VT to reel
bobo -ba ADJ (tonto) dumb, dimwit, silly; (estupefacto) flabbergasted; MF booby, fool
boca F mouth (también de río); (de un arma de fuego) muzzle; (del estómago) pit; (de una cueva) opening; **— a —** mouth-to-mouth; **— abajo** face down; **— arriba** face up; **—calle** intersection; **a — de jarro** at close range; **callarse la —** to shut up
bocadillo M snack; *Esp* sandwich
bocado M bite, morsel, mouthful; (de una brida) bit
bocanada F (de líquido) mouthful; (de humo) puff; (de aire) sniff
bocazas MF SG loudmouth
boceto M sketch
bochorno M (calor) oppressive heat; (vergüenza) embarrassment
bochornoso ADJ (caluroso) sultry, oppressive, muggy; (vergonzoso) embarrassing
bocina F (de coche) horn; (megáfono) megaphone
bocinazo M honk, toot
boda F wedding; **— de oro** golden anniversary; **— de plata** silver

anniversary

bodega F (despensa subterránea) cellar; (para vinos) wine cellar; (vinería) winery; (espacio en un barco, avión) hold; (tienda de comestibles) *Caribbean, Central America* grocery store

bodeguero -ra MF wine producer; *Caribbean, Central America* grocer

bofe M (de animal) lung; **echar los — s** to tire oneself out

bofetada F slap

boga LOC ADV **en —** in vogue, fashion

bogar[7] VI/VT to row

bohemio -mia ADJ & MF Bohemian

boicot M boycott

boicotear VT to boycott

boicoteo M boycott

boina F beret

bol M bowl

bola F (pelota) ball; (canica) marble; (de helado) dip; **— blanca** cue ball; **en —s** in the buff; **no dar pie con —** to be lost; **no dar ni —** not to pay attention

bolera F bowling alley

boleta F (de lotería) ticket; (de votación) *Méx* ballot

boletín M bulletin

boleto M ticket

boliche M (juego) bowling; (bolera) bowling alley

bolígrafo M ballpoint pen

bolita F pellet

Bolivia F Bolivia

boliviano -na ADJ & MF Bolivian

bollo M bun, roll

bolo M bowling pin; **jugar a los —s** to bowl

bolsa F bag, purse; (de canguro) pouch; (de valores) stock market; **— de aire** airbag; **— de estudio** scholarship; **— de miseria** pocket of poverty; **hace —s** it pooches out

bolsillo M pocket; **de —** pocket-sized

bolsista MF stockbroker

bolso M (grande) bag; (pequeño) purse

bomba F (para agua, gasolina) pump; (noticia, mujer) *fam* bombshell; (artefacto explosivo) bomb; **— atómica** atomic bomb; **— de hidrógeno** hydrogen bomb; **— de neutrones** neutron bomb; **— de tiempo** time bomb; **— fétida** stink bomb; **— incendiaria** incendiary bomb; **— inteligente** smart bomb; **lo pasamos —** we had a blast

bombacha F *RP* panties, underpants

bombardear VT to bombard

bombardeo M bombardment, bombing

bombardero -era MF (tripulante) bombardier; M (avión) bomber

bombear VT to pump

bombero -era MF firefighter

bombilla F lightbulb

bombo M bass drum; **dar —** to extol; **con — y platillo** with great fanfare

bombón M (dulce de chocolate) bonbon, candy; (mujer atractiva) *fam* dish

bombonería F candy store

bonachón ADJ (amable) good-natured; (inocente) naïve

bonanza F (buen tiempo) fair weather; (prosperidad) prosperity

bondad F goodness, kindness; **—es** virtues; **tenga la —** de would you please

bondadoso ADJ kind, kindly

boniato M sweet potato

bonito ADJ pretty; M tuna

bono M (financiero) bond; (vale) voucher

boñiga F dung

boqueada F gasp

boquear VI to gasp

boquete M opening

boquiabierto ADJ openmouthed, astonished

boquilla F (para cigarros) cigarette holder; (para una trompeta) mouthpiece; **defender de —** to pay lip-service to

bórax M borax

borbollar VI to bubble

borbollón M bubbling; (alboroto) *Am* commotion; **a borbollones** bubbling over

borbotar VI to bubble, to gurgle

borboteo M bubbling, gurgling

bordado M embroidery, needlework

bordar VI/VT to embroider

borde M edge, border; (de un vaso) rim, brim; (de un desastre) brink; (de una calle) *Méx* curb

bordear VT (rodear) to skirt, go along the edge of; (adornar) to trim

bordillo M curb

bordo LOC ADV **a —** on board

bordó, bordeaux ADJ & M maroon

borla F (de birrete) tassel; (algodón) powder puff

boro M boron

borra F dregs

borrachera F (estado) drunkenness; (juerga) drunken spree

borrachín -ina M drunkard

borracho -cha ADJ drunk, wasted; **no lo hago ni —** I would never do such a thing; MF drunkard, wino

borrador M (bosquejo) rough draft; (goma) eraser

borrar VT to erase; **—se de un club** to

withdraw from a club
borrasca F squall
borrego M lamb
borrico M donkey; (persona) *pey* ass
borrón M blot, blotch, smudge; **hacer — y cuenta nueva** to start over at square one
borronear VT to smudge
borroso ADJ blurry, fuzzy
boscaje M thicket
Bosnia-Herzegovina F Bosnia and Herzegovina
bosnio -nia ADJ & MF Bosnian
bosque M forest, woods
bosquecillo M grove
bosquejar VT to sketch, to outline
bosquejo M sketch, outline
bosta F dung
bostezar[9] VI to yawn
bostezo M yawn
bota F (calzado) boot; (bolsa) leather wine bag
botadura F launch
botánica F botany
botánico ADJ botanical
botar VT (una pelota) to bounce; (un buque) to launch; (a un borracho) to throw out
botarate M fool
bote M (jarro) can; (embarcación) boat; (rebote) bounce; **— de basura** garbage can; **— de remos** rowboat; **— de salvamento** lifeboat; **de — en —** filled to overflowing
botella F bottle
botero M boatman
botija F earthen jug
botijo M earthen jar
botín M (de guerra) booty, plunder; (de ladrón) loot, haul
botiquín M (en el baño) medicine cabinet; (de primeros auxilios) first-aid kit
botón M (de planta) bud; (de aparato, de camisa) button; (remache) stud; **botones** bellboy, page
Botsuana F Botswana
bouquet M bouquet
boutique F boutique
bóveda F (techo) arched roof, vault; **— celeste** the vault of heaven
bowling M bowling
box M pit
boxeador -ora MF boxer, prizefighter
boxear VI/VT to box
boxeo M boxing
bóxer M boxer
boya F (en el mar) buoy; (corcho) float
boyante ADJ buoyant
boyar VI to buoy

bozal M muzzle
bozo M fuzz on the lip
bracear VI to move one's arms
bracero -ra MF migrant worker
bragas F PL. underpants, panties
bragueta F fly
brainstorming M brainstorming
bramar VI (ciervo, cochino) to bellow; (león, viento) to roar
bramido M (de ciervo, cochino) bellow; (de león, viento) roar
brandy M brandy
brasa F ember
brasero M brazier
Brasil M Brazil
brasileño -ña ADJ & MF Brazilian
brasilero -ra ADJ & MF Brazilian
bravata F act of bravado
bravío ADJ wild
bravo ADJ (animal, río) wild; (terreno) rugged; (persona) brave; (barrio) tough; INTERJ bravo!
bravucón -ona ADJ bullying; MF bully
bravuconería F bullying
bravura F (de bestia) fierceness; (de persona) courage
braza F fathom
brazada F (cantidad) armful; (en natación) stroke
brazalete M bracelet
brazo M arm (también de silla); (de cornamenta) branch; (de balanza) beam; **— de mar** sound; **— derecho** right-hand man; **—s** day laborers; **con los —s abiertos** with open arms; **con los —s cruzados** with crossed arms; **ir del — to** go arm in arm; **luchar a — partido** to fight to the end
brea F pitch, tar
brecha F breach, gap
brécol M broccoli
bregar[7] VI to struggle, to toil
breña F scrubland
breve ADJ brief, short; (bikini) scanty; **en —** shortly
brevedad F brevity, shortness; **a la — as** soon as possible
bribón -ona ADJ roguish; MF rascal, rogue, scoundrel
brida F bridle
brigada F brigade
brillante ADJ brilliant, bright; M brilliant, gem
brillantez F brilliance
brillantina F glitter
brillar VI to shine; (los ojos) to sparkle, to twinkle; (nieve) to glisten; **— por su**

ausencia to be conspicuous by its absence

brillo M shine, luster, sparkle; (de los ojos) twinkle; (de nieve) glistening; (del pelo, plumas) sheen; (de diamantes) sparkle; **dar —** to give luster; **sacar —** to polish

brilloso ADJ shiny

brincar[6] VI to hop, to skip

brinco M hop, skip

brindar VI to toast; **— por alguien** to toast someone; **—se a hacer algo** to volunteer to do something

brindis M toast

brío M spirit

brioso ADJ spirited

brisa F breeze

británico ADJ British

brizna F blade of grass

broca F drill bit

brocado M brocade

brocal M curb

brocha F paint brush; **de — gorda** coarse

broche M (alhaja) brooch; (sujetador) clasp, clip; (para el pelo) barrette; **— de oro** grand finale

brocheta F skewer

brócoli, bróculi M broccoli

broma F (chiste) joke; (réplica) jest, wisecrack; **— pesada** practical joke; **—s aparte** kidding aside; **en —** in jest; **gastar una —** to play a joke; **ni en —** no way; **no estoy para —s** I'm not in the mood for kidding

bromear VI to joke, to kid

bromista MF wag, joker

bromo M bromine

bromuro M bromide

bronca F row; **armar una —** to cause a disturbance, to raise a rumpus; **echarle — a alguien** to bawl someone out

bronce M bronze

bronceado ADJ (cubierto de bronce) bronzed; (piel) tanned; (de color bronce) bronze; M suntan

broncear VT (un objeto) to bronze; (a una persona) to tan; **—se** to get a tan

bronco ADJ (voz) gruff; (terreno) rough; (caballo) wild

bronquio M bronchial tube

bronquitis F bronchitis

brotar VI (planta) to sprout; (enfermedad eruptiva) to break out; (agua) to gush, to flow, to issue

brote M (de una enfermedad) outbreak; (retoño) sprout, spear

broza F brushwood

bruces LOC ADV **de —** face down

brujería F deviltry, witchcraft

brujo -ja M wizard, sorcerer; F witch

brújula F compass

bruma F mist

brumoso ADJ misty

brunch M brunch

bruneano -na ADJ & MF Bruneian

Brunéi M Brunei

bruñir[18] VT to burnish

brusco ADJ (descortés) brusque, curt; (repentino) sudden

brusquedad F (descortesía) brusqueness; (lo repentino) suddenness

brutal ADJ brutal

brutalidad F brutality

bruto -ta ADJ (ignorante) ignorant; (maleducado, burdo) uncouth; (violento) brutish; (no neto) gross; **a lo —** roughly; **en —** in the rough; **recaudar en —** to gross; MF (ignorante) blockhead; (persona violenta) brute; (mal educado) lout, brute

bu INTERJ boo

bucal ADJ oral

bucear VI to scuba-dive; (indagar) to explore

buche M (en las aves) crop; (bocado) mouthful

bucle M curl, ringlet; (en informática) loop

budín M pudding

bueno ADJ good; **buena voluntad** willingness; **a la buena de Dios** haphazardly; **de buenas a primeras** out of the blue; **estar —** to be sexy; **hace buen tiempo** it is fine weather; **lo —** the good thing; **por las buenas o por las malas** by hook or by crook; **ser — con los números** to be good at figures; INTERJ OK! **—s días** good day/morning; **buenas noches** good night/evening; **buenas tardes** good afternoon

buey M ox, steer

búfalo M buffalo, bison

bufanda F scarf, muffler

bufar VI to snort; **está que bufa** he is incensed

bufete M (despacho) lawyer's office; (negocio) practice

buffet M buffet

bufido M snort

bufón -ona MF buffoon, jester

bufonear VI to clown

buhardilla F (desván) attic, garret; (ventana) dormer

búho M owl

buhonero -ra MF peddler

buitre M vulture, buzzard

buje M bushing

bujía F spark plug

bulbo M bulb
buldog M bulldog
bulevar M boulevard
Bulgaria F Bulgaria
búlgaro -ra ADJ & MF Bulgarian
bulla F uproar, fuss, bustle
bulldozer M bulldozer
bullicio M uproar, racket, bustle
bullicioso ADJ boisterous, rowdy
bullir[19] VI (hervir) to boil; (hacer burbujas) to bubble; (ajetrearse) to bustle; (moverse) to stir
bullón M puff
bulto M (paquete) bundle; (tumor) lump, growth; (silueta) shape; (saliente) bulge; **a —** approximately; **escurrir el —** to slack off
bungaló M bungalow
bungee M bungee jumping
búnker M bunker
buñuelo M fritter
buque M ship
burbuja F bubble
burdel M brothel, *fam* whorehouse
burdo ADJ coarse
burgués ADJ bourgeois
burla F ridicule, mockery; **hacer — a alguien** to mock someone
burlar VT to mock; **—se de** to scoff at, to make fun of
burlesco ADJ burlesque
burlón ADJ mocking
burocracia F bureaucracy
burócrata MF INV bureaucrat
burrez F stupidity
burro M (animal) donkey, ass; (persona) dunce; ADJ dense
burundés -esa ADJ & MF Burundian
Burundi M Burundi
bus M bus
busca LOC ADV **en — de** in search of
buscar[6] VT to seek, to look for, to search for; (datos, palabras) to look up; (provocar) to provoke; (la verdad) to seek after; (minerales) to prospect for; (talento) to scout for; **—se problemas** to invite trouble; **tú te lo buscaste** you asked for it; **ir a —** to fetch; M SG **buscapersonas** beeper
búsqueda F search; **— del tesoro** treasure hunt
busto M bust
butaca F armchair; (en el teatro) orchestra seat
Bután M Bhutan
butanés -esa ADJ & MF Bhutanese
butano M butane

buzo M diver
buzón M mailbox; **— de sugerencias** suggestion box
bypass M bypass operation
byte M byte

Cc

cabal ADJ (completo) complete; (exacto) exact; (honrado) upright; **estar uno en sus —es** to be in one's right mind
cabalgar[7] VI to ride horseback
caballa F mackerel
caballada F herd of horses
caballejo M nag
caballeresco ADJ chivalrous
caballería F (tropas a caballo) cavalry; (equino) equine; (condición de caballero) knighthood
caballeriza F stable
caballerizo M groom
caballero M (señor) gentleman; (hidalgo) knight, cavalier; **— andante** knight errant; ADJ gentlemanly
caballerosidad F chivalry
caballeroso ADJ chivalrous, gentlemanly
caballete M (soporte de madera) sawhorse; (de la nariz) bridge; (de pintor) easel; (de tejado) ridge
caballo M (animal) horse; (en ajedrez) knight; (heroína) *fam* smack; **a —** on horseback; **— de carreras** racehorse; **— de batalla** hobbyhorse; **— de fuerza** horsepower; **— de Troya** Trojan horse
cabaña F (casa tosca) hovel; (casa de campo) cabin, cottage; (conjunto de ganado) livestock
cabaret M cabaret
cabecear VI (con la cabeza) to nod; (dormirse) to nod off; (un barco) to bob, to pitch
cabeceo M (de la cabeza) nodding; (de un barco) pitching
cabecera F (de cama) headboard; (de mesa) head
cabecilla MF INV ringleader
cabellera F head of hair
cabello M hair; **traido por los —s** far-fetched
caber[22] VI to fit; **no cabe duda** there is no doubt; **no cabe nadie más** there is no room for anybody else; **no — uno en sí** to be puffed up with pride; **no cabe en**

lo posible it is absolutely impossible; **¿en qué cabeza cabe?** who would believe that?

cabestrillo M sling

cabestro M halter

cabeza F head; **— de chorlito** scatterbrain, airhead; **— de playa** beachhead; **— de puente** bridgehead; **— de turco** scapegoat, fall guy; **— rapada** skinhead; **a la —** at the forefront; **caerse de —** to fall headfirst; **echarse de —** to plunge headlong; **ir a la —** to lead the way; **por —** each; **romperse la —** to rack one's brains; **se le fue la —** it went to his head; **sentar —** to settle down; **tiene la — cuadrada** she's a square

cabezada F nod; **dar —s** to nod off

cabezal M magnetic head

cabezazo M butt (with the head)

cabezón ADJ (de cabeza grande) big-headed; (testarudo) pig-headed; (fuerte) strong

cabezudo ADJ (de cabeza grande) big-headed; (testarudo) pig-headed

cabida F capacity; **dar —** to include; **tener — en** to fit in

cabina F (de pasajeros) cabin; (de piloto) cockpit; (de camión) cab; (de teléfono, control) booth

cabizbajo ADJ crestfallen, downcast

cable M cable

cableado M wiring

cablevisión F cable television

cabo M (parte extrema) end; (hilo) thread; (cuerda) rope; (saliente de la costa) cape; (rango militar) corporal; **— suelto** loose end; **al — de** at the end of; **atar —s** to make sense of; **de — a rabo** from beginning to end; **llevar a —** to carry out

cabotaje M coastal trade

Cabo Verde M Cape Verde

caboverdiano -na ADJ & MF Cape Verdean

cabra F goat; **— montés** mountain goat; **como una —** completely crazy

cabrearse VI to get mad

cabrestante M winch

cabrillas F PL whitecaps

cabrio M rafter

cabrío ADJ **macho —** he-goat

cabriola F caper

cabriolar VI to cavort

cabritilla F kid (leather)

cabrito M kid (goat)

cabrón -ona M (macho de cabra) he-goat; (hombre cuya mujer le engaña) cuckold; (hijo de puta) *ofensivo* bastard; F (hija de puta) *ofensivo* bitch; MF (cobarde) wimp

caca F poop; **hacer —** to poop

cacahuate M *Méx* peanut

cacahuete M *Esp* peanut

cacao M cocoa

cacarear VI to cackle, to squawk

cacareo M cackling, squawking

cacatúa F cockatoo

cacería F hunt; **— de brujas** witch hunt

cacerola F saucepan

cacha F (de navaja) handle; (nalga) hip; **hasta la —** completely

cachalote M sperm whale

cacharro M (vasija) earthen pot; (coche viejo) clunker, jalopy

cachaza F slowness

cachazudo ADJ slow

caché M (en informática) cache; (distinción) cachet

cachear VT to body-search, to frisk

cachet M artist's fee

cachetada F slap

cachete M cheek

cachiporra F blackjack

cachivaches M PL stuff, odds and ends

cacho M hunk

cachondo ADJ *fam* horny

cachorro M (de oso, lobo, tigre, león) cub; (de perro) puppy

cacique -ca M (de indios) chief, chieftain; MF (caudillo) political boss

cacofonía F cacophony

cacto M cactus

cactus M cactus

cada ADJ each; **— uno** each one; **— vez más** more and more; **— vez menos gente** fewer and fewer people; **— vez menos harina** less and less flour; **— vez peor** worse and worse; **doscientas pesetas — una** two hundred pesetas each / apiece

cadalso M gallows

cadáver M corpse; (para disecar) cadaver

cadavérico ADJ ghastly

caddie, caddy MF caddie

cadena F (serie de piezas) chain; (de televisión) network; (cordillera) mountain range; **— alimenticia** food chain; **— de montaje** assembly line; **— perpetua** life sentence; **—s** shackles; **tirar la —** to flush

cadencia F cadence

cadera F hip

cadete MF cadet

cadmio M cadmium

caducar[6] VI to lapse, to expire

caducidad F expiration

caduco ADJ (destinado a caer) deciduous; (decrépito) decrepit

caer[23] VI to fall; (perder el equilibrio) to fall down; (colgar) to hang; (ir a parar) to end

up; **al — la noche** at nightfall; **— en
desgracia** to fall into disfavor; **— en
desuso** to fall into disuse; **— en cama** to
fall ill; **— en cuenta** to catch on; **— en
ruina** to fall into disrepair; **—le bien /
mal a uno** (una persona) to make a
good / bad impression; (una comida) to
agree with; **—le en suerte a uno** to fall
to one's lot; **— muy bajo** to fall so low;
caiga quien caiga let fall who may;
dejar — to drop; **está al —** he's about to
show up; **—se** to fall down; **—se de culo**
to fall on one's bottom

café M (bebida) coffee; (color) brown;
(establecimiento público) coffee shop

cafeína F caffeine

cafetal M coffee plantation

cafetera F coffeepot

cafetería F snack bar, cafeteria, diner

cafetero -ra MF coffee dealer; ADJ **industria
cafetera** coffee industry

cafeto M coffee bush

cagada F (acción de cagar) *vulg* dump;
(desacierto) *vulg* screw-up; **este libro es
una —** *fam* this book sucks

cagalera F *vulg* the trots, the shits

cagar[7] VI/VT *vulg* to shit, to take a crap; **—la**
vulg to screw up, to fuck up; **me cago en
diez / la mar** *fam* I'll be damned; **me
cago en tu madre** *ofensivo* fuck you! **me
cagué la chaqueta** *vulg* I fucked up my
jacket; **—se de miedo** *vulg* to shit a brick

caída F (acción de caer) fall, tumble, spill; (de
presión arterial) drop; (de un ordenador)
crash; (de una cortina) hang; **— libre** free
fall; **— del sol** sunset

caído ADJ (orejas) floppy; (arco del pie) fallen;
los —s the fallen

caimán M alligator

caja F box; **— chica** petty cash; **— de
ahorros** savings bank; **— de cambios**
transmission; **— de escalera** stairwell; **—
de fusibles** fuse box; **— de
herramientas** tool kit; **— de
jubilaciones** pension fund; **— de
música** music box; **— de reloj**
watchcase; **— fuerte** safe; **—
registradora** (aparato) cash register, till;
(lugar) checkout counter; **— tonta** idiot
box; **— torácica** rib cage; **entrar en —**
to get going

cajero -ra MF cashier; (en un banco) teller; **—
automático** ATM

cajetilla F pack (of cigarettes)

cajilla F pack (of cigarettes)

cajón M (para transportes) crate; (parte de un
mueble) drawer; **eso es de —** that's a

foregone conclusion

cajuela F *Méx* car trunk

cal F lime; **cerrar a — y canto** to close
hermetically

calabacín M zucchini

calabaza F (grande y redonda) pumpkin;
(pequeña y / o alargada) squash; (vaciado)
gourd; **dar —s** to turn down

calabozo M dungeon

calado M draft

calamar M squid

calambre M cramp

calamidad F calamity

calamina F calamine

calandria F lark

calar VT (agujerear) to perforate; (empapar)
to soak, to drench; **— a alguien** to see
through someone; **— hondo** to resonate;
—se to get drenched

calavera F skull; M libertine

calcar[6] VT (sobre papel) to trace; (imitar) to
copy

calcetería F hosiery

calcetín M sock

calcinar VT to bake

calcio M calcium

calco M (acción de calcar) tracing; **es el — de
su padre** he's the spitting image of his
father

calcomanía F decal

calculador ADJ calculating

calculadora F calculator

calcular VT (averiguar una cantidad) to
calculate, to figure; (sopesar) to weigh;
(prever) to reckon

cálculo M (acción de calcular) calculation;
(aritmética) arithmetic; (integral,
diferencial) calculus; **— biliar** gallstone;
— renal kidney stone

caldear VT to warm up; **— los ánimos** to
get everyone upset

caldera F (en una máquina de vapor) boiler;
(recipiente con asas) kettle; (de la
calefacción) furnace

calderón M hold

caldo M broth, stock; **— de cultivo** culture
medium

calefacción F heat, heating; **— central**
central heating

calendario M calendar

caléndula F marigold

calentador M heater; **— de agua** water
heater

calentamiento M warming; (en deportes)
warm-up; **— global** global warming

calentar[1] VI/VT (poner caliente) to warm, to
heat; **—se** (ponerse caliente, prepararse

para un partido) to warm up, to heat up; (excitarse sexualmente) *fam* to get horny

calentura F (fiebre) fever; (excitación sexual) *fam* horniness

calesa F buggy

caletre M **no tener —** to have no brains

calibrador M caliper

calibrar VT to gauge, to calibrate

calibre M (de pistola, tubo) caliber; (de alambre) gauge; (instrumento para medir) caliper

calicó M calico

calidad F quality; **de —** of good quality; **estoy aquí en — de representante** I'm here in my capacity as representative

cálido ADJ warm

caliente ADJ (agradable) warm; (excesivo) hot; (excitado sexualmente) *fam* horny

calificación[6] F (nota) grade, mark; (acción de asignar notas) grading; (juicio) rating; **le dieron la — de genio** they called him a genius

calificar[6] VT (expresar la calidad) to rate, to adjudge; (asignar nota) to grade; **—se como** to be characterized as

caligrafía F (calidad de letra) penmanship; (arte) calligraphy

calina F haze

callado ADJ silent, quiet; **estarse —** to keep quiet

callar VT (no manifestar, hacer que calle) to quiet; (no hablar) to remain silent; (dejar de hablar) to shut up; **—se la boca** to shut up, to pipe down

calle F street; (en un campo de golf) fairway; **— abajo** down the street; **— arriba** up the street; **— de sentido único** one-way street; **hacer la —** *fam* to cruise for Johns; **no pisar la —** to stay home

calleja F narrow street

callejear VI to walk the streets

callejero ADJ **perro —** stray dog; **caos —** chaos in the streets

callejón M alley; **— sin salida** blind alley, dead end

callo M callus, corn

calloso ADJ callous

calma F calm; **— chicha** absolute calm; **mantener la —** to keep one's temper; **tomar las cosas con —** to take things easy

calmante ADJ & M sedative

calmar VT (los nervios) to calm; (dolor) to sooth; (miedo) to allay, to quell; (sed) to quench; **—se** (una persona) to calm down; (una tormenta, la ira) to subside, to abate

calmo ADJ calm

calmoso ADJ easygoing

calor M heat, warmth; (actitud acogedora) warmth; **hace — hoy** it's hot today; **los —es** hot flashes; **tengo —** I'm hot

caloría F calorie

calumnia F calumny, slander

calumniar VT to slander, to malign

calumnioso ADJ slanderous

caluroso ADJ (día) hot; (recepción) warm

calva F bald spot

calvario M **mi vida es un —** *fam* my life is hell

calvo ADJ bald, baldheaded; **ni tanto ni tan — ** *fam* it ain't necessarily so; **quedarse —** to go bald

calza F long sock

calzada F pavement

calzado M footwear

calzador M shoehorn

calzar[9] VT (poner zapatos) to shoe; (hacer zapatos para) to make shoes for; **— a la familia** to buy shoes for the family; **calzo 42** I take size 10; **—se** to put on shoes

calzones M PL (de mujer) panties; (de hombre) shorts

calzonazos M SG *vulg* pussy-whipped man

calzoncillos M PL underpants, briefs; **— largos** long johns

cama F bed; **— de agua** waterbed; **— doble** double bed; **— elástica** trampoline; **— individual** twin bed; **guardar —** to be confined to bed; **meterse en la —** con to sleep with

camada F litter

camafeo M cameo

camaleón M chameleon

cámara F (espacio) chamber; (de neumático) inner tube; (fotográfica) camera; **— de comercio** chamber of commerce; **— de diputados** lower house; **— de gas** gas chamber; **— de oxígeno** oxygen tent; **— frigorífica** locker; **— legislativa** legislature; **en — lenta** in slow motion; MF INV (persona que maneja una cámara) camera operator

camarada MF INV comrade

camarero -ra M (en un restaurante) waiter, server; (en un coche cama) steward; F (en un restaurante) waitress, server; (en un coche cama) stewardess; (en un hotel) maid

camarilla F clique

camarógrafo -fa M cameraman; F camerawoman

camarón M shrimp

camarote M cabin, stateroom

cambalache M fraudulent swap

cambalachear VI/VT to swap fraudulently

cambiante ADJ (que cambia) changing; (propenso a cambiar) changeable; (temperamento) volatile

cambiar VI/VT to change; VT (una cosa por otra) to exchange, to swap, to trade; **— de marcha** to shift gears; **— de opinión / parecer** to change one's mind; **— de sitio** to move

cambio M (acción de cambiar) change; (marcha) gear; (cotización) exchange rate; (de ferrocarril) railway switch; **— de divisas** foreign exchange; **— para peor** a turn for the worse; **— y fuera** over and out; **a — (de)** in return (for); **en —** on the other hand

cambista MF money changer

Camboya F Cambodia

camboyano -na ADJ & MF Cambodian

camellear VT to push (drugs)

camello -lla M (animal) camel; (vendedor de droga) pusher; F (animal) female camel; (vendedora de droga) pusher

camerino M dressing room

Camerún M Cameroon

camerunés -esa ADJ & MF Cameroonian

camilla F stretcher, litter

camillero -ra MF hospital orderly

caminante MF walker, wayfarer

caminar VI/VT to walk

caminata F long walk; (por un lugar agreste) hike

camino M (carretera) road; (itinerario, dirección que hay que seguir) way; **— de** on the way to; **— de mesa** table runner; **— de rosas** bed of roses; **abrirse —** to make way; **a medio —** halfway; **en — (a)** on the way (to); **llevar por mal —** to lead astray; **mostrar el —** to lead the way; **ponerse en —** to set out; **señalar el —** to show the way

camión M truck; *Méx* bus; **— de la basura** garbage truck; **— de mudanzas** moving van; **— de remolque** tow truck, wrecker; **— de reparto** delivery truck; **— volteador** dump truck

camionero -ra MF truck driver; *Méx* bus driver

camioneta F (furgoneta) van, minivan; (camioncito) pickup truck; (coche sin maletero) station wagon

camisa F shirt; **— de fuerza** straitjacket; **meterse en — de once varas** to get into a jam

camiseta F (exterior) T-shirt; (interior) undershirt

camisón M nightgown

camorrista MF hell-raiser, rowdy

campamento M (de refugiados, exploradores) camp; (recreativo) campground

campana F bell; **tocar una —** to ring a bell

campanario M belfry, bell tower

campanilla F (campana pequeña) small bell; (flor) bluebell; (órgano en la boca) uvula

campanilleo M ringing

campánula F bellflower

campaña F campaign; **de —** on the front; **hacer —** to campaign

campechano ADJ straightforward

campeón -ona MF champion

campeonato M championship

campero ADJ **hombre —** a man from the country

campesino -na MF peasant; ADJ **casa —** peasant house

campestre ADJ rural

camping M (lugar) campground; (actividad) camping

campiña F open country

campista MF camper

campo M (fuera de la ciudad) country, countryside; (para cultivos, deportes, ámbito) field; (grupo en un conflicto) camp; **— abierto** range; **— de acción** field of action; **— de batalla** battlefield; **— de concentración** concentration camp; **— de golf** golf course; **— de tiro** shooting range; **— libre** free rein; **— magnético** magnetic field; **— minado** minefield; **—santo** churchyard; **— visual** visual field; **a — traviesa** cross-country

campus M campus

camuflaje M camouflage

camuflar VT to camouflage

can M dog

cana F white hair; **echar una — al aire** to go out for a good time

Canadá M Canada

canadiense ADJ & MF Canadian

canal M (cauce artificial de agua) canal; (estrecho marítimo, banda de frecuencia) channel; (emisora) station

canalé M ribbed fabric

canalizar[9] VT to channel

canalla MF *ofensivo* scum, lowlife

canalón M spout

canana F cartridge belt

canapé M divan

canario -ria M canary; ADJ of / from the Canary Islands; MF Canary Islander

canasta F basket

canasto M hamper

cancelación F cancellation

cancelar VT (un contrato, un sello) to cancel; (una deuda) to pay off; (una actividad) to call off

cáncer M cancer; **— de mama** breast cancer

cancerígeno ADJ carcinogen

canceroso -sa MF cancer patient

cancha F (de baloncesto, tenis) court; (de fútbol) field; **¡abran —!** gangway! **falta —** there's no room

canciller MF (de Alemania, de universidades) chancellor; (de EEUU) Secretary of State

canción F song; **— de cuna** lullaby

candado M padlock

candela F candle

candelabro M candelabrum

candelero M candlestick; **en —** in the limelight

candente ADJ red-hot

candidato -ta MF candidate

candidatura F (hecho de ser candidato) candidacy; (conjunto de candidatos en equipo) ticket

candidez F innocence

cándido ADJ naïve

candil M oil lamp

candilejas F PL footlights

candor M innocence

canela F (especia) cinnamon; (árbol) cinnamon tree

canesú M yoke of a shirt

cangrejo M crab

canguro M kangaroo; MF INV *Esp* baby-sitter

caníbal ADJ & MF cannibal

canica F toy marble

caniche M poodle; **— enano** toy poodle

canilla F (espinilla) shin; (pantorrilla) calf; (grifo) faucet

canino ADJ canine; **tener un hambre canina** to be ravenous; M canine (tooth)

canje M exchange

canjear VT (prisioneros, libros) to exchange; (un cupón) to redeem

cano ADJ gray-haired

canoa F canoe

canon M (regla, modelo) canon; (canción) round

canónigo M canon

canoso ADJ gray-haired

cansado ADJ (fatigado) tired, weary; (fatigoso) wearing, tiring

cansancio M weariness

cansar VT (fatigar) to tire, to tire out; (aburrir) to bore; **—se** to get tired

cantante MF singer

cantar VI/VT to sing; VT (anunciar) to call out; (confesar) to confess; **— a tono** to sing on key; **—le a alguien las cuarenta** to give someone a piece of one's mind; **— victoria** to declare victory; **en menos que cante un gallo** before you can say Jack Robinson; M epic poem; **eso es otro —** that's another story

cántaro M pitcher; **llover a —s** to rain cats and dogs

cantera F quarry

cantero M *RP* flowerbed

cántico M chant

cantidad F quantity, amount; (de dinero) amount, sum; **— de gente** a lot of people

cantimplora F canteen

cantina F (lugar donde comer) mess hall, mess, canteen; (bar) tavern

cantinela F chant

cantinero -ra MF bartender

canto M (cosa cantada) song; (piedra) pebble; **— de cisne** swan song; **— llano** chant; **— rodado** rounded pebble; **de —** on edge

cantor -ora MF singer

canturrear VI to hum

canturreo M hum, humming

caña F (planta gramínea) reed; (de azúcar) cane; (cerveza) *Esp* beer; (vaso para cerveza) *Esp* beer glass; **— de pescar** fishing pole; **dale —** floor it

cañada F (barranco) ravine; (arroyo) brook

cáñamo M hemp

cañaveral M reed patch

cañería F (en la calle) piping; (en la casa) plumbing

caño M (tubo) pipe; (grifo) spout; (de arma) barrel; **de doble —** double-barreled

cañón M (arma) cannon; (pieza hueca) barrel; (cañada profunda) canyon; (de pluma, bolígrafo) shaft

cañonero M gunboat

caoba F mahogany

caos M chaos

caótico ADJ chaotic

capa F (prenda) cape, cloak; (de pintura, animal) coat; (de tierra) layer; (de hielo) sheet; **— de ozono** ozone layer; **— freática** water table; **de — y espada** cloak and dagger

capacidad F capacity; **—es** aptitude, ability, capability

capacitar VT (entrenar) to train; (habilitar) to qualify

capar VT to castrate

caparazón M shell

capataz -za MF boss, overseer

capaz ADJ (que puede hacer algo) capable, able; (apto) apt; (espacioso) spacious,

roomy; (competente) competent
capear VT to ride out; **— un temporal** to weather a storm
capellán M chaplain
caperuza F pointed hood
capilar ADJ & M capillary
capilla F chapel; **estar en —** (castigado) to be in the doghouse; (esperando una noticia) to be on pins and needles
capital M (dinero) capital; (de préstamo) principal; **— de riesgo** venture capital; **el gran —** big business; F capital (city); ADJ main
capitalino ADJ **atmósfera capitalina** capital city atmosphere
capitalismo M capitalism
capitalista MF capitalist; ADJ capitalistic
capitalización F capitalization
capitalizar[9] VT (aportar capital) to capitalize; (aprovechar) to capitalize on
capitán -ana MF captain
capitanear VT to captain
capitel M capital
capitolio M capitol
capitular VI to capitulate
capítulo M chapter
capó M hood (of a car)
capo M mafia boss
capota F top
capote M cloak; (de coche) *Méx* hood; **decir para su —** to say under one's breath
capricho M caprice, whim, notion
caprichoso ADJ (impredecible) capricious; (impulsivo) whimsical, fanciful; (malcriado) willful
cápsula F capsule
captar VT (un concepto) to grasp; (atención, interés) to capture; (una emisión) to receive; (una indirecta) to get; **— la onda** to get the drift
captor -ora MF captor
captura F (acción de capturar) capture; (pesca capturada) catch
capturar VT to capture; (pescado) to catch
capucha F (de cabeza) hood, cowl; (de lapicero) cap
capuchina F nasturtium
capuchino M cappuccino
capullo M (de insecto) cocoon; (de flor) bud; (tonto) *vulg* dickhead
caqui M khaki
cara F (rostro) face; (de cubo) surface; (de papel, moneda) side; (morro) nerve; **— a —** face to face; **— o cruz** heads or tails; **dar la —** to face up to things; **de — al sur** facing south; **decir en la —** to tell to one's face; **de dos —s** two-sided; **la otra**

— de la moneda the other side of the coin; **poner buena —** to put on a good face; **se le ve en la —** it's written all over his face; **tener — (dura)** to have a lot of nerve; **un ojo de la —** an arm and a leg; **volverle la — a** to snub
caracol M (molusco) snail; (concha) snail shell; **¡—es!** *fam* darn!
carácter M (temperamento, signo) character; (rasgo) characteristic; (índole) kind
característica F characteristic, feature
característico ADJ characteristic
caracterizar[9] VT to characterize
carajo INTERJ *vulg* shit! **irse al —** *vulg* to go to hell; **no sabe un —** *vulg* he doesn't know shit; **¿qué — quieres?** *vulg* what the fuck do you want? **un artista del —** *vulg* a shitty artist; M *Esp vulg* dick
caramba INTERJ *fam* darn! good grief! heck!
carámbano M icicle
carambola F carom; **por —** indirectly
caramelo M (azúcar fundido) caramel; (dulce pequeño) bonbon
caramillo M reed pipe
carátula F (máscara) mask; (portada) title page
caravana F (en el desierto, convoy) caravan; (remolque) trailer
caray INTERJ *fam* shoot!
carbohidrato M carbohydrate
carbón M (sustancia sólida) coal; (pedazo) piece of coal; **— de leña** charcoal
carboncillo M charcoal drawing
carbonera F coal bin
carbono M carbon
carburador M carburetor
carca MF INV *fam* fossil, old fogey
carcaj M quiver
carcajada F burst of laughter, guffaw
carcamal MF INV *fam* fossil, old fogey
cárcel F jail, prison
carcelero -ra MF jailer
carcinógeno M carcinogen
carcinoma M carcinoma; **— de célula basal** basal cell carcinoma
carcomido ADJ worm-eaten
carda F card, comb
cardán M universal joint
cardar VT (lana) to card, to comb; (pelo) to rat, to tease
cardenal M (pájaro, prelado) cardinal; (moretón) bruise
cardíaco -ca ADJ cardiac; MF heart patient
cardinal ADJ cardinal
cardiología F cardiology
cardiovascular ADJ cardiovascular
cardo M thistle

cardumen M school of fish
carear VT to bring face to face; **—se** to meet face to face
carecer[13] VI to lack
carencia F lack; (en la dieta) deficiency
carenciado ADJ disadvantaged
carente ADJ lacking; **— de** lacking in
carero ADJ expensive
carestía F (escasez) scarcity; (costo alto) high cost
careta F mask
carga F (cosa cargada) load, freight; (de la prueba, impuesto) burden; (hipoteca) lien; (de encendedor) refill; (de explosivo, electricidad) charge; **— de municiones** round of ammunition; **— útil** payload; **volver a la —** to insist
cargado ADJ (bebida) stiff; (pausa) pregnant; (cartucho) live; **— de deudas** deep in debt; **— de espaldas** stooping
cargador M (de batería) charger; (de arma de fuego) clip, magazine
cargamento M cargo, load, shipment
cargar[7] VT (cargamentos, dados, un arma, un programa de ordenador) to load; (una batería, a una cuenta) to charge; (de obligaciones) to burden with; (a un niño) to carry; (a un estudiante) *Esp* to flunk; (molestar) to bother; **— a alguien de responsabilidades** to saddle someone with responsibilities; **— al hombro** to shoulder; **— con la culpa** to saddle with blame; **— de combustible** to fuel; VI to charge; **— sobre** to charge, to attack
cargo M (función en una empresa) position; (en una factura, a una cuenta) charge; (acusación) count, charge; **— de conciencia** guilt feelings; **a mi —** under my charge; **hacerse — de** (responsabilizarse de) to take charge of; (ser consciente de) to understand; **investir de un —** to induct into office; **los niños están a — de la maestra** the children are under the care of the teacher; **la maestra está a(l) — de los niños** the teacher is in charge of the children
cargoso ADJ fussy
carguero ADJ freight-carrying
caribeño ADJ Caribbean
caricatura F (retrato) caricature; (con texto) cartoon
caricaturista MF cartoonist
caricaturizar[9] VT to caricature
caricia F caress
caridad F charity
caries F cavity, tooth decay
carillón M chimes

cariño M (amor) affection, fondness; (apodo) honey; **darle —s a alguien** to send love to someone; **ella y el perro se hacen —s** she and the dog nuzzle each other; **hacer con —** to do with great care; **tenerle — a alguien** to be fond of someone
cariñoso ADJ affectionate, loving
carisma M charisma
caritativo ADJ charitable
cariz M complexion
carmesí ADJ & M crimson
carmín M (carmesí) crimson; (lápiz de labios) lip gloss
carnal ADJ carnal
carnaval M carnival
carne F (para comer) meat; (de animal vivo, de persona, de tomate) flesh; **— de cañón** cannon fodder; **— de cerdo** pork; **— de cordero** mutton; **— de gallina** goose bumps; **— de res** beef; **— de venado** venison; **— y hueso** flesh and blood; **como — y uña** *fam* thick as thieves; **en — viva** raw; **metido en —s** overweight
carnear VT to butcher
carnero M ram
carnet M **— de conducir** driver's license; **— de identidad** identification card
carnicería F (tienda) butcher's shop; (matanza) carnage, bloodbath
carnicero -ra MF butcher; ADJ (carnívoro) carnivorous; (cruel) cruel
carnívoro ADJ carnivorous
carnoso ADJ fleshy
caro ADJ expensive, costly, high-priced; ADV at a high price
carona F saddle pad
carótida F carotid artery
carozo M *RP* pit
carpa F (pez) carp; (tienda de circo) circus tent
carpeta F (para documentos, también en ordenador) folder; (cartera) portfolio
carpintería F (oficio) carpentry; (taller) carpenter's shop
carpintero -ra MF carpenter
carraspear VI to clear one's throat
carraspera F scratchy throat
carrera F (conjunto de estudios, trayectoria profesional) career; (competición) race; (en las medias) run; (recorrido corto) run, dash; (de pistón) stroke; **— a pie** footrace; **— de caballos** horse race; **— de relevos** relay race; **a la —** running; **hacer —** to succeed in a profession; **tomar —** to get a running start

carreta F wagon

carrete M (de película) reel; (de hilo) bobbin; (de alambre) spool

carretera F highway; — **de circunvalación** bypass; — **de peaje** toll road

carretero ADJ **sistema** — highway system

carretilla F (de una rueda) wheelbarrow; (de más de una rueda) dolly; **de** — by memory

carretón M large wagon

carril M (de ferrocarril) rail; (de calle) lane

carrillo M cheek; **a dos/cuatro** —s voraciously

carrillón M chimes

carrizo M reed

carro M (vehículo de dos ruedas) cart; (automóvil) car; (de máquina de escribir) roll; — **alegórico** parade float; — **blindado** armored car; — **de guerra** chariot; **poner el** — **delante de los bueyes** to put the cart before the horse; **subirse al** — to get on the bandwagon

carrocería F auto body

carroña F carrion

carroza F (coche de caballos) coach; (de desfile) parade float; (fúnebre) hearse

carruaje M carriage, coach

carta F (misiva) letter; (naipe) card; (de restaurante) menu; (constitución) charter; (mapa) chart; — **blanca** free hand; **a la** — à la carte; **echarle las** —s **a alguien** to do a card-reading for someone; **tomar** —s **en la situación** to take charge of a situation

cartearse VI to correspond

cartel M poster, placard; **en** — showing

cartelera F (de periódico) entertainment section; (publicitaria) billboard; (tablón para anuncios) bulletin board

cárter M oil pan

cartera F (para dinero) wallet, billfold; (para papeles) briefcase; (de alumnos) satchel; (bolsa) handbag; (de valores) portfolio

carterista MF pickpocket

cartero -ra MF letter carrier; M mailman, postman

cartílago M cartilage

cartilla F (libro para aprender a leer) reader; (librito de información) booklet; — **de racionamiento** ration book

cartografiar[16] VT to chart

cartón M cardboard, pasteboard; — **de cigarrillos** carton of cigarettes

cartuchera F cartridge belt

cartucho M (de arma de fuego) cartridge, shell; (de monedas) roll; (de dinamita) stick; — **de fogueo** blank cartridge;

quemar el último — to exhaust one's resources

cartulina F thin cardboard

casa F (edificio) house; (hogar) home; (negocio) business firm; — **de ancianos** old folks' home; — **de citas** cheap motel for rendezvous; — **de empeños** pawnshop; — **de la moneda** mint; — **de muñecas** dollhouse; — **de pompas fúnebres** funeral home; — **de putas** vulg whorehouse; — **de reposo** rest home; — **embrujada** haunted house; — **rodante** house trailer; — **solariega** manor house; **de** — **en** — from house to house; **en** — at home; **entró como Perico por su** — he made himself right at home; **estás en tu** — make yourself at home; **ir a** — to go home; **la** — **paga** on the house; **poner una** — to set up a household; **quedarse en** — to stay home; **tirar la** — **por la ventana** to live it up

casaca F riding jacket

casadero ADJ marriageable

casado ADJ married

casamentero -ra MF matchmaker

casamiento M wedding, marriage ceremony

casar VT to marry off; —**se** to get married, to wed; —**se con** to get married to; **no** —**se con nadie** to remain independent

cascabel M (cosa que tintinea) jingle bell; (de víbora) rattle; **ser un** — to be lively; **poner el** — **al gato** to stick one's neck out

cascada F cascade, waterfall

cascajo M old wreck

cascar[6] VT (quebrar) to crack; (dar bofetadas) to slap around; —**se** to crack open; M SG **cascanueces** nutcracker

cáscara F (de huevo, fruto seco) shell; (de granos, arvejas) husk; (de fruto seco) hull; (de fruta) rind; (de naranja, manzana) peel

cascarrabias MF SG crab, grouch; ADJ INV grouchy

casco M (de ciclista, militar) helmet; (de obrero) hard hat; (de barco) hull; (de naranja) shell; (uña del pie de caballería) hoof; — **urbano** limits of the city

cascote M rubble

caserío M (aldea) hamlet; (casa) Esp farmhouse

casero -ra ADJ (doméstico) domestic; (hecho en casa) homemade; MF caretaker; M landlord; F landlady

caseta F (en un mercado) booth, stall; (de guardia) guardhouse; (de perro) doghouse

casete MF cassette

casi ADV almost, nearly; — **diez mil** almost/

nearly ten thousand; **— lo hago** I almost
did it; **— siempre** almost always; **—
nadie** hardly anyone; **— nunca** hardly
ever

casilla F (en el tablero de ajedrez) square; (en
una tabla) box; (en un casillero)
pigeonhole, cubbyhole; **— de perro**
doghouse; **sacarle a alguien de sus —s**
to drive someone up the wall

casino M (club) men's club; (lugar de recreo)
casino

caso M case; **en — de** in the event of; **en —
de que** in case that; **el — es que** the deal
is that; **en todo —** in any case, at any
rate; **en último —** as a last resort; **eso no
viene al —** that is beside the point;
hacer — (de) to pay attention (to);
hacer — omiso de to disregard; **no hay
—** there's no point; **pongamos por —**
let's suppose that; **venir al —** to come to
the point

caspa F dandruff

casquillo M (de bala) case; (de lámpara)
socket

cassette MF cassette

casta F caste

castaña F chestnut; **— de cajú** cashew

castañetear VI to chatter; **— con los dedos**
to snap one's fingers

castañeteo M (de dientes) chattering; (de
dedos) snapping

castaño M (árbol) chestnut tree; (color,
madera) chestnut; ADJ chestnut-colored,
brown

castañuela F castanet

castellano ADJ & MF Castilian; M (lengua)
Castilian

castidad F chastity

castigar[7] VT to chastise, to punish

castigo M chastisement, punishment; **¡qué
—!** what a nuisance!

Castilla F Castile

castillo M castle; **— de arena** sand castle;
—s en el aire *fam* pie in the sky

casting M casting

castizo ADJ traditional

casto ADJ chaste

castor M beaver

castrar VT (a un hombre, animal) to castrate;
(a una mascota) to neuter, to fix; (a
mascotas hembras) to spay

casual ADJ chance, accidental

casualidad F (chance, coincidence; **da la —
que** it so happens that; **oír por —** to
overhear; **por —** by chance

casucha F shack

cata F **— de vinos** wine-tasting

catalán -ana ADJ (del catalán) Catalan; (de
Cataluña) Catalonian; MF Catalan; M
(lengua) Catalan

catalejo M spyglass

catalizador M catalyst

catalogar[7] VT to catalog, catalogue

catálogo M catalog, catalogue

Cataluña F Catalonia

catar VT to taste

catarata F (cascada) cataract, waterfall; (de
los ojos) cataract

catarí ADJ & MF Qatari

catarro M cold

catástrofe F catastrophe

catecismo M catechism

cátedra F (puesto de profesor) chair,
professorship; (enseñanza) teaching;
(división académica) department; **sentar
—** to hold forth

catedral F cathedral

catedrático -ca MF (full) professor

categoría F category; **de —** important; **de —
mundial** world-class; **de poca —** third-
rate

caterpillar M caterpillar

catéter M catheter

cátodo M cathode

catolicismo M Catholicism

católico -ca ADJ Catholic; MF Catholic

catorce NUM fourteen

catre M cot

cátsup M catsup, ketchup

cauce M channel; **— de río** riverbed

cauchero -ra MF rubber gatherer; ADJ
industria cauchera rubber industry

caucho M rubber; **— sintético** synthetic
rubber

caución F security payment

caudal M (conjunto de bienes) wealth;
(cantidad de agua) volume of water

caudaloso ADJ mighty

caudillo M leader

causa F cause; (proceso) case; **— noble**
worthy cause; **— perdida** lost cause; **a —
de** on account of, because of; **con
conocimiento de —** wittingly; **hacer —
común** to work together

causar VT to cause; **— problemas** to make
trouble

cáustico ADJ caustic

cautela F caution

cauteloso ADJ cautious, wary

cauterizar[9] VT to cauterize

cautivar VT (tomar cautivo) to capture;
(atraer la simpatía) to captivate

cautiverio M captivity

cautivo -va MF captive

cauto ADJ cautious, wary
cavar VT to dig
caverna F cavern, cave
cavidad F cavity
cavilar VI to muse
cayado M shepherd's crook, staff
cayo M key
caza F (acción de cazar) hunt, hunting; (conjunto de animales) wild game; — **mayor** big game; — **menor** small game; **andar a la — de** to hunt; **dar — a** to hunt down; M (avión) fighter
cazador -ora ADJ hunting; MF hunter; F windbreaker[tm]
cazar[9] VI/VT (buscar presas) to hunt; (matar presas) to shoot, to bag; (atrapar presas) to trap; MF SG **cazatalentos** talent scout; **cazatorpedero** destroyer, torpedo-boat
cazo M (para agua) dipper; (para sopa) ladle
cazoleta F pipe bowl
cazuela F (recipiente) casserole; (cazo) pan
CD M CD; — **ROM** CD-ROM
cebada F barley
cebador M pump primer
cebar VT (un animal) to fatten; (bombas) to prime; (anzuelos) to bait; —**se** to vent one's anger
cebo M (para peces) bait, lure; (para animales) feed
cebolla F onion
cebollar M onion patch
cebollino M scallion
cebra F (animal) zebra; (paso) crosswalk
cecear VI to lisp
ceceo M lisp
cecina F jerky
cedazo M sieve
ceder VT (propiedad) to cede, to assign; (un sitio) to yield, to give up; VI (disminuir) to diminish; (perder resistencia) to give way
cedro M cedar
cédula F — **de identidad** identification card
céfiro M zephyr
cegar[1,7] VT to blind
ceguera F blindness
ceja F (sobre el ojo) eyebrow; (en una encuadernación) tab; **quemarse las —** to cram for an exam
cejar VI to back down
cejijunto ADJ with thick eyebrows
celada F ambush
celador -ora MF school monitor
celar VT to watch over jealously
celda F cell
celebración F (fiesta) celebration; (acto solemne) performance
celebrar VT (festejar) to celebrate; (una

reunión) to hold; (un rito) to perform
célebre ADJ famous, noted
celebridad F celebrity
celeste ADJ (relativo al firmamento) celestial; (del color del cielo) azure, light blue
celestial ADJ celestial, heavenly
célibe ADJ celibate; MF unmarried person
cellisca F sleet; **caer —** to sleet
celo M (diligencia) zeal; (excitación sexual) heat; **estar en —** to be in heat; —**s** jealousy; **tener —s** to be jealous
celofán M cellophane
celosía F window lattice
celoso ADJ (que tiene celos) jealous; (diligente) zealous
célula F cell; — **adiposa** fat cell; — **estaminal embrional** stem cell
celular ADJ cellular; M mobile phone
celulitis F cellulite
celuloide M celluloid
celulosa F cellulose
cementar VT to cement
cementerio M cemetery, graveyard
cemento M cement; — **armado** reinforced concrete
cena F supper, dinner
cenagal M quagmire, swamp
cenagoso ADJ marshy, swampy
cenar VI to eat supper, to eat dinner; **vamos a — pescado** we're having fish for dinner
cencerro M cowbell
cenicero M ashtray
ceniciento ADJ ashen
cenit M zenith
cenizas F PL ashes, cinders
censar VI/VT to take a census (of)
censo M census
censor -ora MF censor; — **de cuentas** auditor
censura F (reprobación) censure; (control) censorship
censurador ADJ censuring
censurar VT (criticar) to censure; (examinar) to censor
centavo M cent
centella F sparkle; **pasar como una —** to go by in a flash
centelleante ADJ sparkling
centellear VI to sparkle, to scintillate
centelleo M sparkle
centenar M group of a hundred; —**es** hundreds
centenario M centennial; ADJ centenarian
centeno M rye
centésimo ADJ & M hundredth
centígrado ADJ centigrade
centímetro M centimeter

céntimo M cent

centinela MF INV sentry, sentinel

centrado ADJ true; M truing

central ADJ central; F plant; **— de teléfonos** telephone exchange; **— eléctrica** power plant; **— lechera** milk processing plant; **— nuclear** nuclear power plant

centralita F switchboard

centrar VT to center; **—se** to focus, to be focused

céntrico ADJ central

centrífugo ADJ centrifugal

centrípeto ADJ centripetal

centro M center; (de ciudad) downtown; **— comercial** shopping center; **— de gravedad** center of gravity; **— de mesa** centerpiece

Centroamérica F Central America

ceñido ADJ tight

ceñir[5,18] VT (rodear) to gird; (abrazar) to encircle; **— la corona** to be crowned; VI (estar apretado) to be tight; **—se a** (limitarse) to limit oneself to; (arrimarse) to get close to

ceño M **fruncir el —** to frown, to scowl

cepa F (de árbol) stump; (de viña) stock; (de bacteria) strain; **de pura —** of good stock

cepillar VT (dientes, pelo) to brush; (madera) to plane, to shave

cepillo M (para el pelo, los dientes) brush; (para madera) carpenter's plane; **— de dientes** toothbrush

cepo M (para cazar) trap; (para inmovilizar coches) boot

cera F wax; **— de oídos** earwax; **— para muebles** polish

cerámica F (arte) ceramics; (conjunto de artículos) pottery, earthenware

cerámico ADJ ceramic

cerbatana F blowpipe

cerca ADV near, nearby, close; **— de** near, close to; **de —** at close range; F fence

cercado M (terreno cercado) enclosure; (cerca) fence

cercanía F proximity, nearness, closeness

cercano ADJ (lugar) near, nearby; (pariente) close; **— Oriente** Near East

cercar[6] VT (rodear con una cerca) to fence, to enclose; (sitiar) to besiege

cercenar VT (cortar) to chop off; (reducir) to curtail, to encroach upon

cerciorarse VI **— (de)** to make sure (of)

cerco M (sitio) siege; (cerca) *Am* fence

cerda F bristle

cerdo -da M (animal, persona sucia) hog, pig; (carne) pork; F sow

cerdoso ADJ bristly

cereal M cereal; **—es** breakfast cereal; **cultivo —** cereal crop

cerebral ADJ cerebral

cerebro M brain (también genio); **lavarle el — a** to brainwash

ceremonia F ceremony

ceremonial ADJ & M ceremonial

ceremonioso ADJ ceremonious

cereza F cherry

cerezo M cherry tree

cerilla F match

cerner[1] VT to sift; **—se** (un ave) to hover; (un desastre) to loom

cernícalo M kestrel

cero M zero; (en deportes) nothing, goose egg, zip; (en tenis) love; **— absoluto** absolute zero; **partir de —** to start from scratch; **ser un — a la izquierda** to be a nobody

cerrado ADJ (no abierto) closed; (denso, tonto) dense; (poco comunicativo) reserved; (intransigente) closed-minded; (curva) sharp; M enclosure

cerradura F lock; **— de combinación** combination lock

cerrajería F locksmith's shop

cerrajero -ra MF locksmith

cerrar[1] VT (la puerta, un cajón) to close, to shut; (un trato) to close, to clinch; (un terreno) to enclose; (el gas, un grifo) to turn off; (una fábrica) to shut down, to close; **— filas** to close ranks; **— el paso** to block passage; VI to close; **—se** (una flor, una tienda) to close; (un plazo) to end; **—se el cielo** to become overcast

cerrazón F closed-mindedness

cerro M hill

cerrojo M bolt

certamen M contest; **— de belleza** beauty contest

certero ADJ sure

certeza F certainty

certidumbre F certainty

certificación F certification

certificado ADJ certified; M certificate; **— de nacimiento** birth certificate

certificar[6] VT (la autenticidad de algo) to certify; (una carta) to register

cervatillo M fawn

cervecera F brewery

cervecería F bar

cerveza F beer; **— de barril** draft beer

cérvix M (uterino) cervix

cerviz F (del cuello) cervix

cesar VI to cease; **— de trabajar** to stop working; **— en un cargo** to resign from a position; **— a** to dismiss

cesárea F Caesarean section
cese M cessation; — **el fuego** ceasefire; — **de actividades** shutdown
cesión F (de propiedad) assignment; (de derechos) waiver
césped M lawn, grass; (para deportes) turf
cesta F basket
cestería F basketry
cesto M (cesta) basket; (para ropa) hamper
cetrino ADJ olive-colored
chabacano ADJ (modales) crude; (gustos) tacky; M *Méx* apricot
chacal M jackal
chacha F servant girl
cháchara F small talk
chacota F joke; **tomarse algo a la** — to take lightly
chacra F small farm
Chad M Chad
chadiano -na ADJ & MF Chadian
chal M shawl, wrap
chala F *Am* husk; **quitar la** — to husk
chalán M horse trader
chalé M cottage
chaleco M galoshes, vest; — **antibalas** bulletproof vest; — **de fuerza** straitjacket; — **salvavidas** life jacket
chalupa F small canoe; *Méx* tortilla with sauce
chamaco -ca M *Méx* boy; F *Méx* girl
chamarra F sheepskin jacket
chambergo M wide-brimmed hat
chambón ADJ clumsy
champán M champagne
champaña F champagne
champiñón M mushroom
champú M shampoo
chamuscadura F scorch
chamuscar[6] VT to scorch, to singe; **—se** to get scorched, to get singed
chamusquina F scorching, singeing
chance MF chance
chancearse VI — **de** to make fun of
chancho M hog
chanchullo M *fam* monkey business
chancleta F thong, flip-flop; **tirar la** — to kick up one's heels
chanclo M galosh, overshoe; **—s** rubbers
chándal M sweatsuit
chantaje M blackmail
chantajear VT to blackmail
chanza F jest
chao INTERJ bye-bye
chapa F (de metal) sheet metal; (identificación de policía) badge; (tapa de botella) bottle top; (cópula de prostituta) trick; (de madera) veneer; — **en la**

puerta shingle on the door; **hacer —s** to turn tricks; **hacerle — y pintura** to fix the bodywork and paint
chapado ADJ — **a la antigua** old-fashioned
chapalear VI to splash
chapar VT to plate
chaparro M scrub oak; ADJ *Méx* short
chaparrón M cloudburst
chaperón -ona MF chaperon(e); **ir de** — to chaperon(e)
chapitel M spire, steeple
chapotear VI to splash
chapoteo M splash, splashing
chapucear VT to botch, to bungle
chapucería F (cosa chapuceada) botched job; (cualidad de chapucero) sloppiness
chapucero ADJ shoddy, slipshod
chapurrear VT to speak a language poorly
chapuz M dive
chapuza F botched job
chapuzar[9] VI to dive
chaqueta F jacket; — **de sport** sport jacket
charada F charades
charca F pond
charco M puddle, pool; **cruzar el** — to cross the ocean
charcutería F (tienda) delicatessen; (industria) sausage-making
charla F chat, talk
charlar VI to chat, to gab
charlatán -ana ADJ talkative; MF (parlanchín) chatterbox, windbag; (curandero) charlatan, quack
charlotear VI to chatter, to jabber
charloteo M chatter, jabber
charol M (barniz) varnish; (cuero barnizado) patent leather
charolar VT to varnish
charqui M beef jerky
charro ADJ flashy, tawdry
chárter M charter flight
chascar VT (los nudillos, un hueso) to crack; (los labios) to smack; (la lengua) to click
chascarrillo M funny anecdote
chasco M (broma) prank; (decepción) dud; **llevarse un** — to be disappointed
chasis M frame, chassis
chasquear VT (decepcionar) to disappoint; (una cerradura, la lengua) to click; (un látigo) to crack; (los labios) to smack; (los dedos) to snap; **—se** to be disappointed
chasquido M (de látigo, madera, las articulaciones) crack; (de los labios) smack; (de la lengua, una cerradura) click; (de los dedos) snap
chata F bedpan
chatarra F scrap iron

chatarrería F junkyard

chato ADJ (nariz) snub-nosed; (zapatos, pecho) flat; — **como una tabla** as flat as a pancake

chaucha F green bean

chaval -la M *Esp* boy; F *Esp* girl

chaveta F cotter pin; **perder la** — *fam* to go bonkers

che INTERJ *RP* say! hey!

checo -ca ADJ & MF Czech

chef MF chef

cheque M check; — **de viajero** traveler's check

chequear VT to check

chequera F checkbook

chic ADJ & M chic

chicha F (bebida alcohólica) *Am* corn liquor; (carne) *Esp fam* meat; **de** — **y nabo** two-bit; **ni** — **ni limonada** neither fish nor fowl

chicharra F (insecto) cicada; (timbre eléctrico) buzzer

chiche M *Am vulg* tit, boob

chichi M *Am vulg* tit, boob; *Esp vulg* beaver, cunt

chichón M bump, lump, knot

chicle M chewing gum; — **de globo** bubblegum

chico -ca ADJ small, little; M boy; F girl; **mis** —**s** my kids

chicote M *Am* whip

chicotear VT *Am* to whip

chicoteo M *Am* whipping

chiflado ADJ *fam* nuts, cuckoo, loony

chifladura F craziness

chiflar VI (silbar) to whistle; VT (volver loco) to drive crazy; —**se** to go crazy

chiflido M whistle

chifón M chiffon

chile M chili

Chile M Chile

chileno -na ADJ & MF Chilean

chillar VI (persona) to shriek; (puerta, ratón) to squeak; (cerdo) to squeal

chillido M (de persona) shriek; (de puerta, ratón) squeak; (de cerdo) squeal

chillón ADJ (sonido) shrill; (color) loud, gaudy

chimenea F (de casa) chimney; (hogar) fireplace; (de volcán, baño, mina) vent; (de fábrica) smokestack

chimpancé M chimpanzee

china F (porcelana) china; (piedra) pebble

China F China

chinche MF (insecto) bedbug; (chincheta) thumbtack; (persona molesta) pain

chinchilla F chinchilla

chinchorro M rowboat

chingar[7] VT (fastidiar) *vulg* to screw with; (estropear) *vulg* to screw up; VI/VT *Méx vulg* to fuck

chino -na ADJ Chinese; M (lengua) Chinese; MF Chinese; **eso es** — that's Greek to me

chip M (de ordenador, en golf) chip; (de patata) potato chip

Chipre M Cyprus

chipriota ADJ & MF Cypriot(e)

chiquilín -ina M little boy; F little girl

chiquito ADJ tiny, wee

chiripa F stroke of good luck; **por / de** — by a fluke

chirivía F parsnip

chirona F jail

chirriante ADJ squeaky

chirriar[16] VI (puerta, freno) to squeak; (ave, freno) to screech

chirrido M (de puerta, freno) squeak; (de ave, freno) screech

chisgarabís M pipsqueak

chisguete M squirt

chisme M (noticia) gossip, piece of gossip; (objeto) *fam* gizmo, thingamajig

chismear VI to gossip

chismoso -sa ADJ gossipy; MF gossip

chispa F (partícula incandescente) spark; (ingenio) wit; **echar** —**s** to be furious; **pasar echando** —**s** to whiz by

chispeante ADJ (que echa chispas) sparkling; (ingenioso) witty

chispear VI (echar chispas) to spark; (lloviznar) to sprinkle

chisporrotear VI (leña) to sputter; (cigarrillo) to fizzle; (carne) to sizzle

chisporroteo M (de leña) sputter; (de carne) sizzle

chiste M (verbal) joke; (visual) cartoon; (ocurrencia) wisecrack; — **verde** dirty joke; **no le veo el** — I don't see the humor in it

chistera F top hat

chistoso ADJ funny, amusing, humorous

chivar VI/VT to snitch (on), to rat (on)

chivatar VI/VT to squeal (on), to snitch (on)

chivato -ta MF (delator) informer, snitch, stool pigeon; (chivito) kid

chivo M kid; — **expiatorio** scapegoat; **estar como un** — to be crazy as a loon

chocante ADJ shocking, jarring

chocar[6] VI (dar con) to bump, to collide; (estar en conflicto) to clash; VT (sorprender) to shock; (causar un accidente) to wreck; — **los cinco** to shake hands

chocarrería F coarseness

chochear VI to be in one's dotage
chochera F senility, dotage
chochez F senility, dotage
chocho ADJ senile; **estar —** to be in one's dotage; **estar — con** to dote on; M *vulg* cunt
choclo M ear of corn
chocolate M chocolate; (bebida) cocoa, hot chocolate; (hachís) *Esp* pot
chocolatera F chocolate pot
chocolatina F chocolate bar
chófer, chofer MF chauffeur, driver
cholo -la M (mestizo) person of mixed race; (indio) Europeanized Indian
chopo M poplar
choque M (de objetos móviles) collision, bump, crash; (eléctrico, emocional, cultural) shock
chorizo M sausage
chorlito M plover
chorrear VI/VT (poco) to drip; (mucho) to gush
chorro M spurt, jet; **a —s** in buckets
chotearse VI **— de** to make fun of
choteo M mocking
chovinismo M chauvinism
choza F hut, shack, hovel
chubasco M squall, shower
chuchería F trinket, knick-knack
chueco ADJ *Am* crooked
chuleta F (papel para copiar) cheat sheet; **— de cerdo** pork chop; **— de ternera** veal cutlet
chulo -la M (proxeneta) pimp; (dandi) dandy, dude; (bravucón) tough guy; MF working-class resident of Madrid; ADJ (fanfarrón) boastful; (bonito) cute
chupada F (de cigarro) puff; (de bebida) sip
chupar VI/VT (succionar) to suck; (fumar) to puff (on); VT (absorber) to absorb; (vivir a costa de) to sponge off of; **chupársela** *vulg* to suck (a dick); **chúpate esa** put that in your pipe and smoke it; M SG **chupasangre** leech
chupete M pacifier
chupetín M *RP* lollipop, sucker
churrasco M *Am* barbecued steak
churro M fritter
chusma F rabble, riffraff
chutar VI (drogas) to shoot up; (un balón) to shoot
chute M narcotic fix
chuzo M watchman's pike
CIA F CIA
cianotipo M blueprint
cianuro M cyanide
ciberespacio M cyberspace

cibernética F cybernetics
ciberpunk M cyberpunk
cicatero ADJ stingy
cicatriz F scar
cicatrizar VI to form a scar, to heal up
cíclico ADJ cyclical
ciclista MF bicycle rider, cyclist
ciclo M cycle; **—motor** moped; **— vital** life cycle
ciclón M cyclone
ciclotrón M cyclotron
cicuta F hemlock
ciego ADJ (que no ve) blind; (por borrachera) plastered; (por los efectos de drogas) high; **quedarse —** to go blind; **a ciegas** blindly
cielo M (firmamento) sky; (paraíso) heaven; **— abierto** open mining; **— raso** ceiling; **¡—s!** good heavens! **estar en el séptimo —** to be in seventh heaven; **me cayó del —** it's a godsend; **poner el grito en el — ** *fam* to hit the ceiling
ciempiés M centipede
cien, ciento NUM hundred; **por ciento** percent
ciénaga F swamp, mire, marsh
ciencia F (campo de estudio) science; (conocimiento) knowledge; (arte) art; **—ficción** science fiction; **—s políticas** political science; **a — cierta** with certainty; **las — ocultas** the occult; **no tiene —** nothing to it
cieno M mud, mire, ooze
científico -ca ADJ scientific; MF scientist
cierre M (cosa para cerrar) clasp, fastener; (de cremallera) zipper; (acción de cerrar) closing, closure; **— patronal** lock-out; **al — ** at press time
cierto ADJ certain; (verdadero) true; (seguro) sure; **en — sentido** in a sense; **hasta — punto** to a certain extent; **por —** by the way; INTERJ you're right!
ciervo -va M deer; (macho) stag; **— volante** stag beetle; F (hembra) doe, hind
cierzo M north wind
cifra F (0-9) digit; (número) figure; (clave) cipher, key; **poner en —** to encode
cifrar VT to write in code; **— la esperanza en** to place one's hopes on; **—se en** to amount to
cigarra F cicada
cigarrera F cigar case, cigarette case
cigarrillo M cigarette
cigarro M cigarette; (puro) cigar
cigoto M zygote
cigüeña F stork
cigüeñal M crankshaft

cilíndrico ADJ cylindrical
cilindro M cylinder
cima F summit
cimarrón -ona ADJ wild; MF runaway slave
címbalo M cymbal
cimbel M decoy
cimbrar VT to sway, to vibrate
cimentar VT (una casa) to lay the foundation of; (una victoria) to secure
cimiento M foundation
cinc M zinc
cincel M chisel
cincelar VT to chisel
cincha F cinch, girth
cinchar VT to cinch, to girth
cinco NUM five
cincuenta NUM fifty
cine M cinema, movies
cinematografiar VI/VT to film
cinematográfico ADJ **industria cinematográfica** motion-picture industry
cingalés -esa ADJ & MF Sri Lankan
cínico -ca ADJ cynical; MF cynic
cinismo M cynicism
cinta F (para adornar) ribbon; (adhesiva) tape; (cinematográfica) film; — **aislante** electrical tape; — **de vídeo** video tape; — **magnetofónica** recording tape; — **métrica** tape measure; — **rodante** treadmill; — **transportadora** conveyor belt
cinto M belt
cintura F (de persona) waist; (de cosa) middle
cinturón M belt; — **de seguridad** safety belt
ciprés M cypress
circo M circus
circonio M zirconium
circuitería F circuitry
circuito M circuit; — **cerrado** closed circuit; — **impreso** circuit board; — **integrado** integrated circuit
circulación F circulation; **poner en** — to circulate
circular VI to circulate; **hay que** — **por la derecha** you have to drive on the right; F circular letter
círculo M circle; — **vicioso** vicious circle
circuncidar VT to circumcise
circundante ADJ surrounding
circundar VT to surround
circunferencia F circumference
circunlocución F circumlocution
circunscribir[51] VT to circumscribe
circunspecto ADJ circumspect

circunstancia F circumstance
circunstancial ADJ circumstantial
cirio M candle
cirro M cirrus
cirrosis F cirrhosis
ciruela F plum; — **pasa** prune
ciruelo M plum tree
cirujano -na MF surgeon
cirujía F surgery; — **de corazón abierto** open-heart surgery; — **plástica / estética** plastic surgery
cisne M swan
cisterna F cistern
cita F (romántica) date; (con el médico) appointment; (textual) quotation, quote; — **a ciegas** blind date; **darse** — to meet
citación F citation, summons
citar VT (a un testigo) to summon; (a un autor) to cite, to quote; —**se con** (el médico) to make an appointment with; (un amigo) to make a date with
cítrico ADJ citric; M citrus
ciudad F city
ciudadanía F citizenship
ciudadano -na MF citizen
Ciudad del Vaticano F Vatican City
ciudadela F citadel
cívico ADJ civic
civil ADJ (no criminal, no religioso) civil; (no militar) civilian
civilidad F civility
civilización F civilization
civilizador ADJ civilizing
civilizar[9] VT to civilize; —**se** to become civilized
cizalla F metal shears
cizaña F **sembrar** — to sow discord
clamar VT to clamor for; — **por** to clamor for
clamor M clamor, outcry
clamorear VI/VT to shout
clamoreo M shouting
clamoroso ADJ clamorous
clan M clan
clandestino ADJ clandestine
claqué M tap dance
clara F egg white
claraboya F skylight
clarear VI (ponerse claro) to become clear; (amanecer) to grow light; (volverse menos espeso) to grow less dense; VT to illuminate; —**se** to grow light
claridad F clarity; (luz) brightness, lightness
clarificar[6] VT to clarify, to clear
clarín M bugle
clarinete M clarinet
clarividente ADJ & MF clairvoyant

claro ADJ clear; (franco) straightforward; (que tiene mucha luz) light, bright; **azul** — light blue; **a las claras** clearly; ADV clearly; INTERJ of course! M (espacio) gap; (en un bosque) clearing; — **de luna** moonlight

clase F (grupo social, sesión docente, conjunto de alumnos) class; (aula) classroom; (tipo) kind, sort; — **alta** upper class; — **obrera** working class; — **turista** economy class; **dar** — to teach a class; **toda** — **de** all sorts of

clasicismo M classicism

clásico ADJ (destacado, consabido) classic; (de un período histórico) classical; M classic

clasificación F classification; (deportiva) qualification

clasificado M want ad

clasificar[6] VT to classify; (en deportes) to qualify; **—se para** to qualify for; **—se segundo** to come in second

claustro M cloister; — **de profesores** university faculty

claustrofobia F claustrophobia

claustrofóbico ADJ claustrophobic

cláusula F clause

clausura F closing

clavadista MF diver

clavado ADV exactly; M nailing

clavar VT to nail, to drive a nail into; (pinchar) to stick, to poke; **—le la mirada / los ojos a alguien** to stare at someone; — **los frenos** to stomp on the brakes; **me clavaron** I got a raw deal

clave F (sistema de signos) code; (tabla de correspondencias, base) key; (signo musical) clef; (clavicémbalo) harpsichord; (de mapa) legend; — **de fa** bass clef; — **de seguridad** password; — **de sol** treble clef; ADJ key

clavel M carnation

clavetear VT to put pegs on

clavicémbalo M harpsichord

clavícula F collarbone, clavicle

clavija F (de guitarra) peg; (de enchufe) pin

clavo M (pieza de metal) nail; (capullo) clove; (de zapato) spike; **dar en el** — to hit the nail on the head

claxon M car horn

clearing M clearing

clemencia F clemency, mercy

clemente ADJ forgiving

clerecía F (funciones de clérigo) ministry; (conjunto de clérigos) clergy

clerical ADJ clerical

clérigo M clergyman, minister

clero M clergy

clic M click; **hacer** — to click; **hacer doble** — to double-click

cliché M (placa fotográfica) photographic plate; (expresión muy usada) cliché

cliente MF (de un profesional) client; (de un negocio) customer; (de un restaurante) patron; (de un hotel) guest

clientela F clientele

clientelismo M patronage

clima M climate

climatización F air conditioning

clímax M climax

clinch M clinch

clínica F clinic

clip M paper clip

clítoris M clitoris

cloaca F sewer

clon M clone

clonación F cloning

clonaje M cloning

clonar VT to clone

cloquear VI to cluck

cloqueo M cluck, clucking

cloro M chlorine

clorofila F chlorophyll

cloroformo M chloroform

cloruro M chloride

club M club (también palo de golf); — **nocturno** nightclub

coacción F compulsion, coercion; **bajo** — under duress

coagular VI to coagulate; (sangre) to clot

coágulo M clot

coalición F coalition

coartada F alibi

coartar VT (una libertad) to restrict; (a una persona) to inhibit; (la creatividad) to strangle

cobalto M cobalt

cobarde ADJ cowardly; MF coward

cobardía F cowardice

cobertizo M shed

cobertor M cover

cobertura F (de nieve, aérea) cover; (de noticias, telecomunicativa) coverage

cobija F cover; (manta) blanket

cobijar VT to shelter; **—se** to seek shelter

cobra F cobra

cobrador -ora MF (persona que cobra) collector; M (perro) retriever

cobranza F collection

cobrar VT (impuestos) to collect; (una cuenta) to charge; (un cheque) to cash; (el sueldo) to earn; (víctimas) to claim; (adquirir) to gain; — **ánimo** to take heart; — **caro** to charge a lot; — **de más** to overcharge; **vas a** — you're in for it

cobre M (elemento) copper; (objetos de cobre) copper utensils
cobrizo ADJ copper-colored
cobro M collection
coca F (planta, hoja) coca; (cocaína) *fam* coke
cocaína F cocaine
cocear VI/VT to kick
cocer[2, 10c] VI/VT (huevos) to boil; (verduras) to cook; (cerámica) to fire; — **al vapor** to steam; **a medio** — half-cooked; **romper a** — to break into a boil; **¿qué se cuece aquí?** what's up?
coche M (automóvil, vagón) car; (autobús) coach; (vehículo tirado por caballerías) carriage; — **bomba** car bomb; — **cama** sleeper; —**-comedor** dining car; — **de bebé** stroller, baby carriage; — **de bomberos** fire engine; — **de choque** bumper car; — **de línea** city bus; — **deportivo** sports car; — **fúnebre** hearse; **ir en** — to go by car, to drive; **pasear en** — to go on a drive
cochera F carport
cochinada F (acto asqueroso) filthy action; (acto perverso) dirty trick
cochinilla F woodlouse
cochino ADJ filthy; M pig
cocido M stew
cociente M quotient
cocina F (habitación) kitchen; (aparato para cocinar) range, stove; (arte de guisar) cuisine, cookery
cocinar VI/VT to cook; (tramar) to cook up
cocinero -ra MF cook
cócker MF cocker spaniel
coco M (fruto del cocotero) coconut; (cabeza) *fam* dome; (fantasma) bogeyman; **comerse el** — to get all worked up
cocodrilo M crocodile
cóctel M (fiesta) cocktail party; (bebida) cocktail, mixed drink
codazo M jab with the elbow; **dar —s** to elbow
codear VI/VT to elbow, to jab; —**se** to nudge one another; —**se con** to rub elbows with
codeína F codeine
codicia F (deseo de poseer) greed; (deseo sexual) lust
codiciar VT (una cosa) to covet; (sexualmente) to lust after
codicioso ADJ covetous, greedy
codificar[6] VT to codify, to encrypt
código M code; — **de barras** bar code; — **genético** genetic code; — **postal** zip code
codo M elbow; — **a** — side by side; — **de tenista** tennis elbow; **empinar el** — to

drink too much; **hablar por los —s** to talk one's head off; **hasta los —s** up to one's elbows
codorniz F quail
coeficiente M coefficient; — **de inteligencia** intelligence quotient
coerción F compulsion
coetáneo ADJ contemporary
coexistencia F coexistence; — **pacífica** peaceful coexistence
cofre M coffer
coger[11b] VT (a un criminal) to catch; (con las manos) to grasp; (flores) to gather; to pick; (a un empleado) to hire; (una emisora) to receive; (cosas del suelo) to pick up; (espacio) to take up; (un pez) to land, to catch; (un camino, tren, curso) to take; (poseer sexualmente) *Am vulg* to screw, to fuck; — **de sorpresa** to catch by surprise; — **el sueño** to fall asleep; — **hacia el castillo** to turn toward the castle; —**le miedo a algo** to get scared of something; —**le el tranquillo a algo** to get into the swing of things; —**se un resfriado** to come down with a cold; **coge y le dice** he ups and says
cognado ADJ & M cognate
cognitivo ADJ cognitive
cogollo M heart
cogote M neck
cohabitar VI to live (with); (sin casarse) to cohabitate
cohecho M bribe
coheredero -ra MF joint heir
coherencia F (consecuencia) consistency; (lógica) coherence
coherente ADJ (consecuente) consistent; (lógico) coherent
cohesión F cohesion
cohesivo ADJ coherent
cohete M rocket
cohetería F rocketry
cohibición F inhibition
cohibido ADJ inhibited, self-conscious
cohibir VT to inhibit
coincidencia F coincidence
coincidir VI to coincide
coito M coitus
cojear VI to limp; **saber de qué pie cojea alguien** to know someone's weaknesses
cojera F limp
cojín M cushion
cojinete M bushing; — **de bolas** ball bearing
cojo ADJ lame, crippled
cojón M (testículo) *vulg* ball, nut; (valor) guts, grit; **estoy hasta los cojones** I've had it; **¿qué cojones quieres?** *vulg* what the

hell do you want? **tener cojones** to be brave, to be impassive; **tu doctorado me lo paso por los cojones** *vulg* I don't give a shit about your doctorate

cojonudo ADJ (estupendo) cool; (valeroso) gutsy

cok M coke

col F cabbage; **— de Bruselas** Brussels sprouts

cola F (de perro, ave, avión) tail; (de vestido) train; (hilera de gente) line; (pegamento) glue; **— de caballo** ponytail; **hacer —** to stand in line; **no pegar ni con —** not to go together; **traer —** to have consequences

colaboración F collaboration

colaborador -ora MF (de periódico) contributor; (con el gobierno) collaborator

colaborar VI to collaborate; (con un periódico) to contribute

colación F **sacar a —** to bring up

colacionar VT to collate

colador M (para té) strainer; (para verduras) colander

colágeno M collagen

colapso M collapse

colar[2] VT (té) to strain; (metal líquido) to pour; VI to go through, to slip through; **esa excusa no va a —** that excuse won't wash; **—se en una fiesta** to crash a party

colateral ADJ collateral

colcha F bedspread

colchón M mattress; (recurso de emergencia) cushion

colchoneta F mat

colear VI (un perro) to wag the tail; (un tema) to be pending; (un auto) to fishtail

colección F collection

coleccionar VT to collect

coleccionista MF collector

colecta F charity collection

colectivo M (grupo) collective; (autobús) *Am* bus

colector M (de aguas negras) sewer; (eléctrico) collector; (de coche) manifold

colega MF INV colleague

colegio M (escuela privada) private school; (centro de enseñanza primaria) elementary school; (asociación de profesionales) association, college

colegir[5, 11] VI to gather

cólera F rage, wrath; **montar en —** to fly into a rage; M cholera

colérico ADJ irritable

colesterol M cholesterol

coleta F pigtail

coletilla F tag

coleto M **decir para su —** to say to oneself

colgadero M hanger; ADJ hanging

colgado ADJ high and dry

colgadura F drapery; **—s** hangings

colgante ADJ hanging; M pendant

colgar[2, 7] VT (suspender, ahorcar) to hang; (un teléfono, un abrigo) to hang up; VI (un espejo) to hang; (un andrajo) to dangle; (un asunto) to be pending; **esa falda te cuelga por atrás** that dress hangs down in the back; **— (un ordenador)** to crash; **—se de** to get hooked on; **—se del teléfono** to tarry on the phone

colibrí M hummingbird

cólico M colic

coliflor F cauliflower

colilla F cigarette butt

colina F hill, knoll

colindante ADJ neighboring

colindar VI **— con** to border (on), to adjoin

coliseo M coliseum

colisión F collision

collage M collage

collar M (de perlas) necklace; (de perro) collar; **— antipulgas** flea collar

collera F horse collar

collie M collie

colmar VT (un vaso) to fill; (una demanda) to satisfy; **— de alabanzas** to lavish praise upon

colmena F beehive

colmillo M (de persona) eyetooth; (de elefante) tusk; (de víbora) fang

colmo M **— de la locura** height of folly; **¡eso es el —!** that takes the cake; **para —** to top it all

colocación F (ubicación) placement; (puesto) position

colocar[6] VT (poner, encontrar un puesto para) to place; (casar) to marry off; (invertir) to invest; **—se** (drogarse) to get stoned; (encontrarse empleo) to get a job

coloide M colloid

Colombia F Colombia

colombiano -na ADJ & MF Colombian

colon M colòn

colón M (moneda de El Salvador y Costa Rica) colon

colonia F (territorio, grupo de insectos) colony; (comunidad de inmigrantes) community, settlement; (vivienda) development; (perfume) cologne

colonial ADJ colonial

colonización F colonization

colonizador -ora MF colonist

colonizar[9] VT to colonize, to settle

colono -na MF (habitante de una colonia) colonist, settler; (arrendatario) tenant farmer

coloquial ADJ colloquial

coloquio M colloquium

color M color; (pintura) paint; (maquillaje) rouge; (de naipes) flush; **—es primarios** primary colors; **a todo —** full color; **de —** of color

coloración F coloring

colorado ADJ & M red; **ponerse —** to blush

colorante ADJ & M coloring

coloreado ADJ colored; M coloring

colorear VT to color

colorete M rouge

colorido M (de un caballo) coloring; (de un comentario, paisaje) color; ADJ colorful

colosal ADJ (grande) colossal; (estupendo) wonderful

columbrar VT to glimpse

columna F column; **— de dirección** steering column; **— vertebral** spinal column, backbone

columnista MF columnist

columpiar VI/VT to swing

columpio M swing

colza F (planta) rape; (aceite) rapeseed oil

coma F (signo) comma; M (falta de conciencia) coma

comadre F (chismosa) gossip; (partera) midwife

comadreja F weasel

comadrona F midwife

comandancia F command

comandante M (rango militar) major; (militar que ejerce el mando) commander; **— en jefe** commander in chief

comandar VT to command; **— un avión** to pilot an airplane

comando M (militar) commando; (orden dada al ordenador) command

comarca F district

comatoso ADJ comatose

comba F (de una pared) bulge; (de madera) warp; **saltar a la —** to jump rope

combar VI (una pared) to sag; (madera) to warp

combate M combat; **fuera de —** out of the competition

combatiente MF combatant

combatir VI/VT to combat

combativo ADJ combative

combinación F combination; (billete) transfer ticket

combinar VT to combine; **—se para hacer algo** to agree to do something

combo M combo

combustible ADJ combustible; M fuel

combustión F combustion

comedero M trough

comedia F comedy; (farsa) farce; **— de situación** situation comedy, sitcom; **hacer la — de** to play the part of

comediante MF comedian

comedido ADJ moderate; *Am* obliging

comedirse[5] VI to show restraint; **— a hacer algo** *RP* to volunteer to do something

comedor M dining room; (de empresa) cantina

comensal MF fellow diner

comentador -ora MF commentator

comentar VI/VT to comment (on), to remark (on)

comentario M (análisis) commentary; (observación) comment, remark

comentarista MF commentator

comenzar[1,9] VI/VT to begin, to start; **— a comer** to begin to eat; **— comprando** to begin by buying

comer VI/VT to eat; (al mediodía) to eat lunch; (en ajedrez) to take; (en el juego de las damas) to jump; **dar de —** to feed; **sin —lo ni beberlo** through no fault of one's own; **—se** (ácido) to eat away; (completamente) to eat up; **—se las eses** to drop s; **—se las palabras** to eat one's words; **—se un semáforo rojo** to run a red light

comercial ADJ commercial

comercialización F marketing, merchandising

comercializar[9] VT (dar carácter comercial) to commercialize; (llevar al mercado) to market

comerciante MF merchant, trader, dealer

comerciar VI to trade

comercio M commerce, trade; **— exterior** foreign trade; **— minorista** retail trade

comestible ADJ edible; M **—s** groceries

cometa M (cuerpo celeste) comet; F (juguete) kite

cometer VT to commit

cometido M function

comezón F itch; **tener —** to itch

comic M comic book

comicios M PL polls

cómico -ca ADJ comic, comical; MF comedian

comida F (alimento que se toma de una vez) meal; (conjunto de cosas para alimentarse) food; (de mediodía) lunch; **— basura** junk food; **— macrobiótica** health food; **— rápida** fast food

comienzo M beginning; **a —s de** toward the beginning of; **al —** at first; **desde un / el**

— from the start
comilla F quotation mark; **entre —s** in quotes
comilón -ona MF big eater; F binge
comino M cumin seed; **me importa un —** *fam* I don't give a hoot; **no vale un —** *fam* it's not worth a hoot
comisaría F **— de policía** police station, precinct
comisario -ria MF (comisionado) commissioner; (jefe de policía) police chief
comisión F (acción de cometer, porcentaje ganado) commission; (conjunto de personas) committee
comisionar VT to commission
comistrajo M bad food
comisura F **— de los labios** corner of the mouth
comité M committee
comitiva F retinue
como ADV (del mismo modo que) as, like; **ella pinta — yo** she paints like I do; (aproximadamente) about; **pesa — diez kilos** it weighs about ten kilos; CONJ (puesto que) since; **— no tenemos dinero** since we have no money; **— no me pagues** if you don't pay me; **era — que muy viejo** he was, like, real old; **— que te voy a permitir** like I would let you; **— quieras** as you please; **— si** as if; **— si me lo fuera a creer** a likely story
cómo ADV INTERR & PRON (de qué manera) how; (¿perdón?) what? **¡— brillan las estrellas!** how the stars are shining! **¿— no?** of course; **¿a — me lo vende?** what does that cost?
cómoda F bureau, chest of drawers, dresser
comodidad F (cualidad de cómodo) comfort; (cosa cómoda) convenience; **—es** amenities
comodín M joker, wild card
cómodo ADJ (mueble) comfortable; (horario) convenient; (persona) lazy
Comoras F PL Comoros
compactar VT to compact
compacto ADJ compact
compadecer [13] VT to pity; **—se de** to take pity on
compadre M pal, crony
compañero -ra MF companion; (de un zapato) mate; **— de clase** classmate; **— de cuarto** roommate
compañía F company; **en — de** in the company of
comparable ADJ comparable
comparación F comparison
comparar VI/VT to compare; **—se con** to compare with
comparativo ADJ comparative
comparecer [13] VI to appear
compartimiento M compartment
compartir VT (bienes) to share; (el tiempo) to divide
compás M (instrumento de dibujo) compass; (ritmo) beat; (espacio entre barras) measure, bar; (división de música en partes iguales) time signature; **marcar el —** to beat time
compasión F compassion
compasivo ADJ compassionate, sympathetic
compatible ADJ compatible
compatriota MF compatriot
compeler VT to compel
compendiar VT to summarize
compendio M digest, condensation
compenetración F bonding
compensación F compensation
compensar VT to compensate
competencia F (pugna, competición deportiva, conjunto de competidores) competition; (cualidad de competente) competence
competente ADJ competent
competición F athletic competition, meet
competidor -ora ADJ competing; MF competitor
competir [5] VI to compete, to vie
competitivo ADJ competitive
compilador M compiler
compilar VT to compile
compinche M chum, crony
complacencia F satisfaction
complacer [37] VT to please, to gratify; **—se (en)** to take pleasure (in)
complaciente ADJ (que complace) obliging; (que consiente) indulgent
complejidad F complexity
complejo ADJ complex; M complex; **— de inferioridad** inferiority complex
complementar VT to complement, to supplement
complemento M complement; **— alimenticio** dietary supplement; **— directo** direct object; **— indirecto** indirect object; **—s** fringe benefits
completar VT to complete; **—se** to be completed
completo ADJ complete; (baño, pensión, hotel) full; **hoy tenemos el —** today we have a full house; **por —** completely
complexión F build
complicación F complication
complicado ADJ complicated
complicar [6] VT to complicate; **—le a**

alguien la vida to give someone trouble
cómplice MF accomplice
complicidad F complicity
complot M plot
componenda F (arreglo provisional) quick fix; (arreglo ilegal) shady deal
componente ADJ & M component
componer[39] VT (un grupo) to compose, to make up; (imprenta) to set; (un coche descompuesto) to fix; (música) to compose; **—se de** to be composed of; **componérselas** to deal with one's problems alone
comportamiento M conduct, behavior
comportarse VI/VT to conduct oneself, to behave
composición F composition
compositor -ora MF composer
compostura F (arreglo) repair; (dignidad) composure
compra F purchase; **ir de —s** to go shopping
comprador -ora MF (persona que compra) buyer, purchaser; (persona que está de compras) shopper
comprar VT to buy, to purchase
comprender VT (entender) to understand, to comprehend; (abarcar) to cover, to include
comprensible ADJ comprehensible, understandable
comprensión F (intelectual) understanding, comprehension; (emocional) sympathy, understanding
comprensivo ADJ understanding
compresa F compress
compresión F compression
comprimido ADJ compressed; M tablet
comprimir VT to compress
comprobación F verification, check
comprobante M proof; **— de compra** proof of purchase
comprobar[2] VT (verificar) to verify, to check; (probar) to prove; (darse cuenta) to realize
comprometer VT (obligar) to commit; (poner en peligro) to jeopardize, to compromise; **—se** (prometer) to promise; (tomar partido) to commit oneself; (para casarse) to get engaged
compromiso M (ideología, obligación, promesa) commitment; (acuerdo) agreement; (cita) appointment, engagement; (de matrimonio) engagement; (solución) compromise; **no me pongas en —** don't compromise me; **sin — de compra** without obligation to buy
compuerta F sluice gate, floodgate
compuesto ADJ (ojos, tiempo, interés)

compound; **estar — de** to be composed of; M compound
compulsión F compulsion
compulsivo ADJ compulsive
compungirse[11] VI to feel sorry
computación F computing
computadora F *Am* computer; **— personal** *Am* personal computer
computar VT to compute
computarizar[9] VT to computerize
cómputo M computation
comulgar[7] VI (recibir el sacramento) to take communion; (estar de acuerdo) to agree
común ADJ common; **en —** in common; **por lo —** generally; **el — de las gentes** the majority of the people
comuna F commune
comunicable ADJ communicable
comunicación F communication; (ponencia) presentation; **se nos cortó la —** we got disconnected
comunicar[6] VI/VT to communicate; **—se con** (entenderse) to communicate with; (tener acceso a) to open into; (ponerse en contacto con) to reach
comunicativo ADJ communicative
comunidad F community
comunión F communion
comunismo M communism
comunista ADJ & MF communist
con PREP with; **— lo que come, tendría que estar obesa** given what she eats, she should be obese; **— mucho** by far; **— que le digas alcanza** just telling him is enough; **— tal que** provided that; **— todo** all things considered
conato M minor problem
concavidad F hollow
cóncavo ADJ concave
concebible ADJ conceivable
concebir[5] VT (engendrar) to conceive; (explicarse) to conceive of
conceder VT (dar) to grant; (admitir) to concede, to allow
concejal MF councilor
concejo M council
concentración F concentration; (manifestación) rally, demonstration
concentrar VT to concentrate; **—se** (prestar atención) to concentrate; (manifestar) to rally
concepción F conception
concepto M concept; (literario) conceit
concernir[50] VT to concern
concertar[1] VT (arreglar) to arrange; (concretar) to finalize; (planear) to concert; **—se** to agree

concesión F (admisión) concession; (otorgamiento) grant; (permiso comercial) franchise

concha F shell; (genitales femeninos) *Am vulg* pussy

conchabarse VI to conspire

conciencia F (vida moral) conscience; (vida mental) consciousness; **tomar — de** to come to grips with

concienzudo ADJ conscientious, thorough

concierto M (música) concert; (armonía) harmony; (acuerdo) agreement

conciliar VT (personas) to conciliate; (ideas) to reconcile; **— el sueño** to get to sleep

concilio M council

concisión F conciseness

conciso ADJ concise, brief

conciudadano -na MF fellow citizen

concluir[31] VI/VT to conclude

conclusión F conclusion

concluyente ADJ conclusive

concomitante ADJ attendant

concordancia F agreement

concordar[2] VI to agree

concordia F concord

concretar VT (cerrar) to finalize; (especificar) to be specific about; (realizar) to realize; **—se a** to focus on

concreto ADJ concrete; **en—** specifically

concubina F concubine

concurrencia F gathering

concurrido ADJ well-attended

concurrir VI (confluir) to come together; (asistir) to attend

concursante MF contestant

concurso M (para un premio) contest; (como parte de una licitación) call for bids; (para un puesto de trabajo) competitive examination; **— de belleza** beauty pageant

concusión F graft

concusionario -ria MF grafter

condado M county

conde M count

condecoración F decoration

condecorar VT to decorate

condena F (castigo) sentence; (crítica) condemnation; **¡qué —!** what a pain!

condenación F condemnation

condenar VT (criticar) to condemn; (sentenciar) to sentence; **eso le condenó al fracaso** that doomed him to failure; **—se** to go to hell

condensación F condensation

condensar VI to condense

condesa F countess

condescendencia F (tolerancia)

acquiescence; (superioridad) condescension

condescender[1] VI (acomodarse) to acquiesce; (dignarse) to condescend

condición F condition; **— social** social station; **a — de que** on the condition that; **condiciones** (físicas) condition; (de un contrato) terms, provisos

condicional ADJ & M conditional

condicionamiento M conditioning

condicionar VT to condition

condimentar VT to season

condimento M condiment, seasoning

condiscípulo -la MF classmate

condolencias F PL condolences; **dar las —** to offer one's condolences

condolerse[2] VI to offer one's condolences

condominio M condominium

condón M condom, rubber

cóndor M condor

conducente ADJ conducive

conducir[24] VT (a un grupo) to lead; (una orquesta, electricidad) to conduct; (un coche) to drive, to steer; **—se** to behave

conducta F (moral) conduct, behavior; (biológica) behavior

conducto M (de agua) conduit; (anatómico) duct; **por — de** through

conductor -ora M (de electricidad, calor) conductor; MF (de coches) driver

conectar VI/VT to connect

conejillo M **— de Indias** Guinea pig

conejo M rabbit; (genitales femeninos) *Esp vulg* pussy

conexión F connection

confabulación F collusion

confección F (fabricación) confection; (calidad) workmanship; **de —** ready-made

confeccionar VT to manufacture

confederación F confederation

confederado -da ADJ & MF confederate

confederar VI to form a confederacy

conferencia F (discurso) lecture; (reunión) conference; **— de prensa** press conference; **dar una —** to give a lecture

conferenciante MF lecturer

conferenciar VI to confer

conferencista MF lecturer, speaker

conferir[3] VT to confer, to bestow; (un título) to confer

confesar[1] VI/VT to confess

confesión F confession

confesionario M confessional

confesor -ora MF confessor

confiabilidad F reliability

confiable ADJ reliable

confiado ADJ (seguro de sí) confident;

(crédulo) trusting
confianza F confidence, trust; **en —** in confidence; **tener —** to be confident; **tener — en** to have confidence in; **tomar —s** to be overly familiar with
confianzudo ADJ over-familiar
confiar[16] VT (un secreto) to confide; (una cosa) to entrust; **— en** to rely on; **confío que Dios me proteja** I trust that God will protect me
confidencia F confidence
confidencial ADJ confidential
confidente MF confidant; M (mueble) love seat
configuración F configuration
confinamiento M confinement
confinar VT to confine
confines M PL bounds, confines
confirmación F confirmation
confirmar VT to confirm
confiscación F confiscation, seizure
confiscar[6] VT to confiscate
confitar VT to candy
confite M candy
confitería F confectionery
confitura F confection
conflicto M conflict
confluencia F (de calles) junction; (de ríos) confluence
conformar VT to adapt; **—se con** to settle for
conforme ADJ in agreement, content; **— a** in accordance with; **— amanece** as dawn breaks
conformidad F conformity, agreement; **estar de / en — con** to be in accordance with
conformismo M conformity
confort M comfort
confortable ADJ comfortable
confortar VT to comfort
confraternidad F fraternity, fellowship
confraternizar[9] VI to fraternize
confrontar VT (a un enemigo) to confront; (dos listas) to compare
confundido ADJ confused, mixed-up
confundir VT to confuse, to perplex, to baffle; **—se** (personas) to become confused; (cosas) to mingle
confusión F (mental) confusion; (de cosas) clutter, disarray
confuso ADJ (que no comprende, falto de orden) confused; (difícil de comprender) confusing
congelación F freezing
congelado ADJ frozen
congelador M freezer

congelar VT to freeze
congeniar VI **— con** to get along with
congénito ADJ congenital
congestión F congestion
conglomeración F conglomeration
conglomerado M conglomeration
Congo M Congo
congoja F anguish, grief
congoleño -ña ADJ & MF Congolese
congregación F congregation
congregar[7] VI to congregate
congresista MF (representante) member of Congress; (asistente a un congreso) conventioneer
congreso M (cuerpo legislativo, edificio) congress; (reunión periódica) convention
congresual ADJ congressional
congruencia F congruence
conífera F conifer
conjetura F conjecture, surmise
conjeturar VT to conjecture, to surmise
conjugación F conjugation
conjugar[7] VT to conjugate
conjunción F conjunction
conjuntivitis F conjunctivitis
conjunto M (grupo de cosas) set; (totalidad) total, aggregate; (de ropa) outfit; **— musical** ensemble; **en —** as a whole, all told; ADJ joint
conjuración F conspiracy
conjurado -da MF conspirator
conjurar VT (conspirar) to conspire, to plot; (alejar un daño) to ward off
conjuro M incantation, spell
conmemorar VT to commemorate
conmemorativo ADJ memorial
conmigo PRON with me
conmiseración F commiseration
conmoción F commotion; **— cerebral** brain concussion
conmovedor ADJ moving, touching
conmover[2] VT to move, to touch
conmovido ADJ moved, touched
conmutador M switch
conmutar VT to commute
connatural ADJ inborn
connotación F connotation
cono M cone
conocedor -ora ADJ who know(s); MF connoisseur, expert
conocer[13] VT to know (también en sentido carnal); (reconocer) to recognize; (tratar por primera vez) to meet; **— el paño** to know the ropes; **se conoce que** it is clear that
conocido -da ADJ well-known; MF acquaintance

conocimiento M knowledge, acquaintance; **— de embarque** bill of lading; **perder el —** to lose consciousness; **poner en —** to inform; **—s** knowledge

conque CONJ so

conquista F conquest

conquistador -ora MF conqueror; ADJ conquering

conquistar VT (un terreno) to conquer; (el amor de alguien) to win

consabido ADJ habitual

consagración F consecration

consagrar VT (declarar consagrado) to consecrate; (dedicar) to devote

consciente ADJ conscious; **— del problema** aware of the problem

consecución F attainment, achievement

consecuencia F (hecho que resulta de otro) consequence; (cualidad de consecuente) consistency; **a — de** as a result of

consecuente ADJ (que se sigue de) consequent, logical; (fiel en sus actos) consistent

consecutivo ADJ consecutive

conseguible ADJ obtainable

conseguir[5,12] VT (to get; (un objetivo) to achieve; (un puesto de trabajo) to land, to get; **— hacer algo** to manage to do something

consejero -ra MF (persona que da consejos) adviser; (miembro del consejo) board member

consejo M (opinión) counsel, advice; (comité) council; **— de guerra** court-martial

consenso M consensus

consentimiento M consent, acquiescence

consentir[3] VT (permitir) to consent to, to acquiesce to; (mimar) to pamper, to indulge; **— en** to permit

conserje MF (limpiador) janitor; (portero) superintendent; (recepcionista) hotel clerk

conserva F canned food; **en —** canned

conservación F conservation, preservation

conservador -ora MF (en política) conservative; (de museo) curator; ADJ (de las tradiciones) conservative; (de comida) preservative

conservadurismo M conservatism

conservante M preservative

conservar VT (guardar) to keep; (seguir teniendo) to retain; (no destruir) to preserve; (no malgastar) to conserve

conservatorio M conservatory

considerable ADJ considerable

consideración F consideration; **de —** considerable; **tomar / tener en —** to take into consideration

considerado ADJ considerate, thoughtful

considerar VT to consider

consigna F watchword

consignación F consignment

consignar VT to consign

consignatario -ria MF consignee

consigo PRON with oneself / himself / herself / themselves

consiguiente ADJ consequent; **por —** consequently

consistencia F consistency

consistente ADJ (que consiste) which consists; (firme) consistent

consistir VI **— en** to consist of

consocio -cia MF fellow member

consola F console

consolación F consolation

consolar[2] VT to console

consolidar VT to consolidate

consonante ADJ & F consonant

consorcio M consortium

consorte MF consort

conspicuo ADJ conspicuous

conspiración F conspiracy, plot

conspirador -ora MF conspirator, plotter

conspirar VI to conspire, to plot

constancia F (en el amor) constancy; (en el esfuerzo) perseverance; (en el trabajo) steadiness; (prueba) documentary proof

constante ADJ & F constant; **—s vitales** vital signs

constar VI to be stated; **— de** to consist of, to be composed of; **hacer —** to mention; **me consta que** I am aware that; **que conste** let it be known

constatar VT to verify

constelación F constellation

consternación F consternation, dismay

consternar VT to dismay

constipación F constipation

constipado ADJ *Esp* suffering from a cold; *Am* constipated; M *Esp* head cold

constitución F constitution

constitucional ADJ constitutional

constituir[31] VT to constitute

constitutivo ADJ (constituyente) constituent; (inherente) inherent; **— de un delito** which constitutes a crime

constituyente ADJ constituent

constreñimiento M constraint

constreñir[5,18] VT (limitar) to constrain; (apretar) to constrict, to constrain

constricción F constriction

construcción F (acción y actividad de construir, cosa construida) construction, building; (gramatical) construction; **construcciones** building blocks

constructivo ADJ constructive

construir[31] VI/VT to construct, to build

consuelo M consolation, comfort, solace

consuetudinario ADJ (acción) habitual; (derecho) common

cónsul MF consul

consulado M consulate

consulta F (acción de consultar) consultation; (pregunta) question; (consultorio del médico) doctor's office

consultar VT to consult; **—lo con la almohada** to sleep on it

consultoría F consulting

consultorio M doctor's office

consumado ADJ consummate, accomplished

consumar VT to consummate

consumidor -ora MF consumer; ADJ consuming

consumir VT to consume; **—se (agua)** to boil off; **(neumático)** to wear out; **—se de** to be consumed by

consumismo M consumerism

consumo M consumption

consunción F consumption

contabilidad F accounting, bookkeeping

contable MF accountant, bookkeeper

contactar VI/VT to contact; **—(se) con** to get in contact with

contacto M contact; **en — con** in touch with

contado M **al —** in cash; ADJ **—s** few

contador -ora ADJ counting; M (de dinero) counter; (de electricidad) meter; **— Geiger** Geiger counter; MF accountant; **— público** certified public accountant

contaduría F accountant's office

contagiar VT to infect

contagio M contagion; (de ordenador) infection

contagioso ADJ contagious, catching, infectious

contaminación F (del agua, de la comida) contamination; (del medio ambiente) pollution

contaminante M contaminate

contaminar VT (agua, alimentos, cultura) to contaminate; (el medio ambiente) to pollute; **—se (agua)** to become contaminated; (medio ambiente) to become polluted

contar[2] VI/VT (medir una cantidad) to count; (decir historias) to tell; **el hotel cuenta con una piscina** the hotel has a swimming pool; **cuento con mi hermano** I count on my brother; **esto no cuenta** this doesn't count; **¿me lo vas a contar a mí?** you can say that

again; **mi padre cuenta 55 años** my father is 55 years old; **tienes que — con el tiempo** you have to watch the time; M SG **cuentakilómetros** (marcador de kilómetros) odometer; (velocímetro) speedometer

contemplación F contemplation

contemplar VT (mirar, tener en cuenta) to contemplate; (consentir) to spoil; VI to contemplate

contemporáneo ADJ contemporary

contender[1] VI to contend

contenedor M container

contener[44] VT (un líquido) to contain; (risa, lágrimas) to hold back; (entusiasmo) to restrain; (el aliento) to hold

contenido ADJ restrained; M content(s)

contentar VT to satisfy; **—se** to be satisfied

contento ADJ (conforme) content, contented; (feliz) happy; M contentment

contera F (de paraguas) tip; (de bolígrafo) cap

contestación F answer, reply

contestador M answering machine

contestar VT to answer; VI to talk back, to mouth off

contexto M context

contextura F makeup; (de persona) build

contienda F (guerra) conflict; (encuentro deportivo) competition

contigo PRON with you

contiguo ADJ contiguous; **estar — a** to adjoin

continental ADJ continental

continente M continent, mainland; ADJ continent

contingencia F contingency

contingente ADJ & M contingent

continuación F continuation; (de película) sequel; **a —** after that; **a — hubo una guerra** there ensued a war

continuar[17] VI/VT to continue

continuidad F continuity

continuo ADJ (ininterrumpido) continuous; (repetido) continual

contonearse VI (mujer) to swing one's hips; (hombre) to swagger

contoneo M (de mujer) swinging of the hips; (de hombre) swagger

contorno M (forma) outline, contour; (tamaño de árbol, persona) girth

contorsión F contortion

contra PREP against; M **el pro y el —** the pros and cons; **en —** against; F drawback; **llevar a alguien la —** to contradict someone

contraatacar[6] VI/VT to counterattack

contraataque M counterattack
contrabajo M double bass; MF INV double bass player
contrabandear VI/VT to smuggle
contrabandista MF smuggler
contrabando M (introducción de mercancías) smuggling; (mercancías introducidas) contraband; **hacer —** to smuggle
contracción F contraction
contrachapado M plywood
contractual ADJ contractual
contracultura F counterculture
contradecir²⁶ᵇ VT to contradict
contradicción F contradiction
contradictorio ADJ contradictory
contraejemplo M counterexample
contraer⁴⁵ VT to contract; (limitar) to limit; **— matrimonio** to get married
contraespionaje M counterespionage
contrafuerte M (de muro) buttress; (de zapato) counter
contrahecho ADJ deformed
contralor -ora MF comptroller, controller
contralto M (voz) alto; MF (persona) alto
contramandar VT to countermand
contraoferta F counteroffer
contraorden F countermand
contrapartida F compensation
contrapelo LOC ADV **a —** against the grain
contrapesar VT to counterbalance
contrapeso M counterbalance
contraproducente ADJ counterproductive
contrariar¹⁶ VT to annoy; **—se** to get annoyed
contrariedad F (fastidio) annoyance; (dificultad) snag
contrario ADJ (opuesto) opposite; (discrepante) conflicting; **al —** on the contrary; **de lo —** otherwise; **llevar la contraria** to be contrary; **por el —** on the contrary; **soy — al doblaje de películas** I'm against the dubbing of films; **todo lo —** just the opposite
contrarrestar VT to counteract
contrarrevolución F counterrevolution
contraseña F password, watchword
contrastar VI/VT to contrast
contraste M contrast
contrata F contract
contratación F hiring
contratar VT (a un empleado) to hire; (un servicio) to contract for; **—se** to be hired
contratiempo M mishap
contratista MF contractor, builder
contrato M contract
contravenir⁴⁷ VT to contravene

contraventana F shutter
contribución F (cosa contribuida) contribution; (impuesto) tax
contribuir³¹ VT to contribute
contribuyente MF taxpayer
contrincante MF opponent
contrito ADJ contrite
control M (dominio, dirección) control; (médico) checkup; (vigilancia) check; (puesto) checkpoint; **— de calidad** quality control; **— de la natalidad** birth control; **— remoto** remote control; **bajo —** under control
controlador -ora MF comptroller
controlar VT (ejercer control) to control; (llevar a cabo un control) to check on
controversia F controversy
contumacia F obstinacy
contumaz ADJ stubborn
contusión F bruise
convalecer¹³ VI to convalesce
convección F convection
convencer¹⁰ᵃ VT (por medio de la lógica) to convince; (por insistencia) to persuade
convencimiento M (creencia) conviction; (acción de convencer) convincing
convención F convention
convencional ADJ conventional
conveniencia F (lo cómodo) convenience; (lo aconsejable) desirability; **a su —** at your convenience
conveniente ADJ (cómodo) convenient; (aconsejable) advisable
convenio M agreement; **— colectivo** collective bargaining
convenir⁴⁷ VI (ser apropiado) to be suitable; (llegar a un acuerdo) to agree
convento M convent
converger¹¹ᵇ VI to converge
conversación F conversation; **trabar — con** to engage in a conversation with
conversar VI to converse
conversión F conversion
converso -sa MF convert
convertible ADJ convertible
convertidor M converter
convertir³ VT to convert; **—se en** to become
convexo ADJ convex
convicción F conviction
convicto -ta ADJ convicted; MF convict
convidar VT to invite; *Am* to offer
convincente ADJ convincing, compelling
convite M (invitación) invitation; (banquete) banquet
convocación F convocation
convocar⁶ VT to convoke, to call together; (una reunión, un concurso) to convene

convoy M convoy
convoyar VT to convoy
convulsión F convulsion
conyugal ADJ conjugal, marital
cónyuge MF spouse
coñac M cognac, brandy
coñazo M (persona molesta, molestia) *vulg* pain in the butt; (cosa de mala calidad) *vulg* piece of crap
coño M *vulg* pussy, cunt; **en el quinto —** in the boondocks; INTERJ *fam* damn!
cooperación F cooperation
cooperar VI to cooperate
cooperativa F cooperative, co-op
cooperativo ADJ cooperative
coordenada F coordinate
coordinación F coordination
coordinado ADJ coordinate
coordinar VT to coordinate
copa F (vaso) goblet, wineglass; (de árbol) top; (de sombrero) crown; (palo de la baraja) card in the suit of copas; (trofeo, parte de un sujetador) cup; **ir de —s** to go for a drink
copete M (de pelo) tuft; (de plumas) crest; **estar hasta el —** to be fed up
copia F copy; (de foto) print; **— de seguridad** backup copy
copiadora F copy machine
copiar VT (reproducir) to copy; (en un examen) to cheat
copión -ona MF copycat
copioso ADJ copious, plentiful
copla F (canción) popular song; (estrofa) stanza
copo M (de nieve) snowflake; (masa de lana) wad; **—s de maíz** cornflakes
copropietario -ria MF joint owner
coprotagonista MF co-star
copular VI to copulate
copyright M copyright
coque M coke
coqueta F (mujer) coquette; (mueble) dressing table
coquetear VI to flirt
coquetería F flirtation
coqueto ADJ flirtatious
coraje M (valentía) courage; (enojo) anger
coral M (marino) coral; (musical) chorale
coralino ADJ coral
coraza F armor
corazón M heart; (de manzana) core; (vocativo) honey; **con el — en la boca** really tired; **de buen —** kindhearted; **de todo —** wholeheartedly; **romper el — a alguien** to break someone's heart
corazonada F hunch

corbata F necktie, tie, cravat
corcel M charger, steed
corchea F eighth note; **— con puntillo** dotted eighth note
corchete M (en costura) hook and eye; (paréntesis recto) square bracket; (llave) brace
corcho M (para botella) cork; (para pescar) float
corcova F hump, hunchback
corcovear VI to buck
cordel M string
cordero M lamb; (piel) lambskin
cordial ADJ cordial
cordillera F mountain range
cordón M cord; (al borde de la calle) *Am* curb; **— de apertura** rip cord; **— de zapatos** shoelace, shoestring; **— policial** police cordon; **— umbilical** umbilical cord
cordoncillo M ridge, rib
cordura F sanity
Corea F Korea; **— del Norte** North Korea; **— del Sur** South Korea
coreano -na ADJ & MF Korean
corear VI/VT to chant
coreografía F choreography
cornada F goring
cornear VT to gore
corneja F crow
corneta F cornet; M bugler
cornisa F cornice, ledge
corno M horn; **— francés** French horn
cornudo ADJ horned; M cuckold
coro M (grupo de cantantes) choir, chorus; (pieza de música) chorus; (parte de la iglesia) loft; **cantar a —** to sing in unison
corolario M corollary
corona F crown
coronación F coronation
coronar VT to crown
coronel M colonel
coronilla F crown of the head; **estar hasta la —** to be fed up
corpiño M bodice; (sujetador) *Am* bra
corporación F guild
corporal ADJ corporal, bodily
corpulento ADJ stout, corpulent
corpus M corpus
corpúsculo M corpuscle
corral M (de granja) barnyard, farmyard; (para ganado) corral, pen
correa F leather strap; (de ventilador) belt; (de perro) leash
corrección F (acción de corregir) correction; (cualidad de correcto) correctness
correcto ADJ (apropiado) correct, proper;

(acertado) right

corrector -ora MF editor; **— de pruebas** proofreader

corredizo ADJ sliding

corredor -ora ADJ running; MF (persona que corre) runner; (deportista automovilístico, ciclista) racer; (intermediario) broker, agent; M (pasillo) hallway, corridor

corregir[5,11] VT to correct; (exámenes) to grade; **—se** to mend one's ways

correlacionar VT to correlate

correlato M correlate

correo M mail; (edificio) post office; **— aéreo** air mail; **— certificado** certified mail; **— electrónico** e-mail; **echar al —** to mail

correoso ADJ tough

correr VI (persona, agua, calle) to run; (coche) to go fast; (una puerta) to slide; (dinero, tiempo) to pass; **— con los gastos** to take on the costs; VT (una cortina) to draw; (una carrera, un riesgo) to run; **—se** (moverse) to scoot over; (colores) to run, to bleed; (tinta) to smear; (tener orgasmo) *Esp fam* to come

correría F foray

correspondencia F correspondence

corresponder VI (ser adecuado, estar en consonancia) to correspond; (pertenecer) to belong; VT (amor, favores) to reciprocate; **a mí me corresponde llamarla** it's up to me to call her

correspondiente ADJ corresponding; MF correspondent

corresponsal MF correspondent

corretaje M broker's / agent's commission

corretear VI to run around

corrida F (acción de correr) running; (competición) race; (orgasmo) *Esp* orgasm; (de banco) run; **— de toros** bullfight; **de —** without stopping

corrido ADJ (que tiene mucha experiencia) worldly; (continuo) uninterrupted; **de —** without stopping; M ballad

corriente ADJ (que corre) running; (común) usual; (franco) frank; **el — mes** the current month; **estar al —** to be up-to-date; F (de agua, electricidad) current; (de dinero) flow; (de pesimismo) wave; (de aire) draft; **— alterna** alternating current; **— continua** direct current; **— del Golfo** Gulf Stream; **dejarse llevar por la —** to conform; **llevarle la — a alguien** to humor someone

corrillo M group of gossips

corro M circle of people

corroborar VT to corroborate

corroer[50] VT to corrode

corromper VT (a una persona) to corrupt; (un alimento) to rot; **—se** (una persona) to become corrupt; (un alimento) to rot

corrompido ADJ corrupt

corrosión F corrosion

corrupción F corruption

corrupto ADJ corrupt

corsé M corset

cortada F shortcut

cortador -ora MF (persona) cutter; F (aparato) cutter; **cortadora de césped** lawn mower

cortadura M cut

cortante ADJ (comentario, instrumento) cutting; (frío, viento) biting; (tono, instrumento) sharp

cortar VT to cut; (un vestido, el uso de algo) to cut out; (a un locutor, una rama, el gas) to cut off; (un árbol) to cut down; (las uñas) to clip; (el césped) to mow; **— el paso** to block; **— por lo sano** to take drastic action; M SG **cortacésped** lawn mower; **cortacircuitos** circuit breaker; **cortafuego** fire line; **cortapapeles** paper cutter; **cortaplumas** penknife; **cortauñas** nail cutter; VI (el frío) to bite; (la piel) to crack; **—se** (una persona) to be intimidated; (la leche) to curdle, to sour; **—se el pelo** to get a haircut

corte M (de un traje, herida) cut; (acción de cortar) cutting; (de televisión) commercial break; (estilo) style; **— de pelo** haircut; **— transversal** cross section; **— y confección** dressmaking; **eso me da —** that embarrasses me; F court; (séquito) retinue; **—s** Spanish parliament; **hacer la —** to court

cortedad F shortness

cortejar VT to court, to woo

cortejo M (séquito) entourage; (acción de cortejar) courtship

cortés ADJ courteous, polite

cortesano -na MF courtier

cortesía F courtesy

córtex M cortex

corteza F (de árbol) bark; (de pan, de la Tierra) crust; (de queso, fruta) rind; **— cerebral** cerebral cortex

cortijo M country house

cortina M (de ventana) curtain; (de lluvia) sheet; **— de humo** smokescreen

cortisona F cortisone

corto ADJ (bajo, no largo) short; (no inteligente) short on brains; (encogido) bashful; **—circuito** short circuit; **— de vista** short-sighted; **a — plazo** in the short run; **quedarse —** to come up short;

vestirse de — to wear a short dress; M short (film)

cosa F thing; **como quien no quiere la —** without realizing it; **como si tal —** as cool as a cucumber; **como son las —s** what a surprise; **decir una — por otra** to tell a lie; **esperamos — de cinco minutos** we waited about five minutes; **las —s como son** let's be honest; **las —s de la vida** that's life; **no es gran —** it's no big deal; **otra —** something else

cosecha F crop, harvest; **de su —** of his invention; **vino — 1975** wine of 1975 vintage

cosechadora F combine

cosechar VT (cultivos) to harvest; (resultados) to reap

coser VI/VT to sew

cosignatario -ria MF cosigner

cosmético ADJ & M cosmetic

cósmico ADJ cosmic

cosmología F cosmology

cosmonauta MF cosmonaut

cosmopolita ADJ cosmopolitan

cosmos M cosmos

cosmovisión F worldview

coso M doodad

cosquillas F **hacer —** to tickle; **tener —** to be ticklish

cosquillear VT to tickle

cosquilleo M tickle

cosquilloso ADJ ticklish

costa F (del mar) coast, shore; **a toda —** at all costs; **—s** costs

Costa de Marfil F Ivory Coast

costado M side; **al —** alongside; **de —** edgewise; **por los cuatro —s** from all sides

costal M sack

costanero ADJ coastal

costar² VI/VT to cost; **— trabajo** to be difficult; **— un dineral** to cost a fortune; **— un ojo de la cara** to cost an arm and a leg

Costa Rica F Costa Rica

costarricense, costarriqueño -ña ADJ & MF Costa Rican

coste M cost; **— de (la) vida** cost of living

costear VT (pagar) to defray costs; VI to sail along the coast

costero ADJ coastal

costilla F rib; **lo hizo a —s de su padre** he did it at his father's expense

costo M cost; **— de (la) vida** cost of living

costoso ADJ costly

costra F (de pan) crust; (de herida) scab

costroso ADJ (de pan) crusty; (de heridas) scabby

costumbre F (manera habitual) habit; (uso tradicional) custom; **de —** habitual; **tener la — de** to be accustomed to

costura F (acción de coser) sewing; (línea de puntadas) stitching; (unión de dos piezas) seam; **alta —** high fashion

costurero -ra F (caja) sewing box; (sastre) tailor; F seamstress

costurón M large scar

cota F (nivel del agua) height above sea level; (estándar) benchmark

cotejar VT to check against

cotejo M comparison

cotidiano ADJ everyday

cotización F price quote/quotation

cotizar⁹ VT to quote

coto M **— de caza** game preserve; **poner — a** to put an end to

cotorra F (loro) parrot; (persona) chatterbox

cotorrear VI to chatter

covacha F small cave

coyote M coyote

coyuntura F joint; **aprovechar la —** to take advantage of the situation

coz F kick; **dar coces** to kick

crack M (cocaína) crack; (deportista) ace

cráneo M cranium, skull

craso ADJ crass

cráter M crater

crayola® F crayon

creación F creation

creacionismo M creationism

creador -ora MF creator; ADJ creative

crear VI/VT to create

creativo ADJ creative

crecer¹³ VI to grow; (masa, río) to rise; (madera, mar) to swell; (la luna) to wax

crecida F rise of a river

crecido ADJ (adulto) grown; (grande) large; (demasiado alto) overgrown

creciente ADJ (que crece) growing; (luna) crescent; M (luna) crescent; (marea) high tide

crecimiento M growth

credencial F credential

crédito M (solvencia, unidad de estudios) credit; (hecho de creer) credence; (fama) reputation; (préstamo) loan; **dar — a** to believe; **—s** film credits; **vender a —** to sell on credit

credo M creed

crédulo ADJ credulous, gullible

creencia F belief

creer¹⁴ VI/VT (tomar como cierto) to believe; (opinar) to think, to feel; **—se** to fall for; **¿quién se cree que es?** who does he think he is? **se cree artista** he fancies himself an artist; **¡ya lo creo!** I should say so!

creíble ADJ credible, believable

crema F cream (también cosmético); **— de espárragos** cream of asparagus

cremallera F (de coche) rack; (de prenda) zipper; **— y piñón** rack and pinion

cremar VT to cremate

cremoso ADJ creamy

creosota F creosote

crepitación F crackle

crepitar VI to crackle

crepúsculo M twilight

crespo ADJ wiry, kinky

crespón M crepe

cresta F (de ola, montaña) crest; (de ave) tuft; (de gallo) comb

creyente MF believer; ADJ believing

cría F (acción de criar) breeding; (camada) litter; (animal joven) young

criadero M **— de peces** hatchery; **— de pollos** chicken farm

criado -da MF servant; F maid

criador -ora MF breeder

crianza F (de animales) breeding; (de hijos) upbringing; (modales) manners

criar[16] VT (animales) to breed; (hijos) to bring up, to rear, to raise; **estar criando malvas** *fam* to be pushing up daisies; **—se** to grow up

criatura F (ser extraño) creature; (bebé) baby

criba F sieve

cribar VT to sift

crimen M (delito grave) serious crime; (asesinato) murder; **— de guerra** war crime

criminal ADJ & MF criminal

criminalidad F crime

crin F mane

criollo ADJ (nacido en América) born in Spanish America; (tradicionalmente americano) traditionally Spanish American; M (lengua) Creole

críquet M cricket

crisálida F chrysalis

crisantemo M chrysanthemum

crisis F crisis

crisma F crown of the head

crisol M crucible, melting pot

crisparse VI (un músculo) to contract; (los puños) to clench; (los nervios) to be on edge

cristal M (mineral, vidrio de gran calidad) crystal; (vidrio de ventana) *Esp* glass, pane; (lente) lens; **— labrado** cut glass

cristalería F (objetos de cristal) glassware; (establecimiento) glassware store; (fábrica) glassworks

cristalino ADJ (de cristal) crystalline; (transparente) crystal clear; M lens of the eye

cristalizar[9] VI/VT to crystallize

cristiandad F Christendom

cristianismo M Christianity

cristiano -na ADJ & MF Christian; **hablar en —** (claramente) to speak clearly; (español) to speak Spanish

criterio M criterion

crítica F criticism; (de un libro) review

criticar[6] VT to criticize

crítico -ca ADJ critical; MF critic; (de un libro) reviewer

criticón -ona ADJ critical; MF faultfinder

Croacia F Croatia

croar VI to croak

croata ADJ & MF INV Croatian

crocante ADJ crisp, crunchy

croché, crochet M crochet; **hacer —** to crochet

croissant M croissant

crol M crawl

cromado ADJ chroming

cromo M chromium, chrome

cromosoma M chromosome

crónica F (narración de eventos) chronicle; (reportaje) feature; **— policial** police report

crónico ADJ chronic

cronología F chronology

cronológico ADJ chronological

cronometrador -ora MF timer, timekeeper

cronometraje M timing

cronometrar VT to time

cronómetro M chronometer, stopwatch

croquet M croquet

croquis M rough sketch

cross M cross-country race

cruasán M croissant

cruce M (acción de cruzar, lugar donde cruzar) crossing; (de dos calles) crossroads, intersection; (de razas) crossbreeding; (animal procedente de una mezcla) cross; **— peatonal** crosswalk

crucero M (buque) cruiser; (viaje de placer) cruise

cruceta F crosspiece

crucial ADJ crucial

crucificar[6] VT to crucify

crucifijo M crucifix

crucigrama M crossword puzzle

crudo ADJ (comida, seda) raw; (tiempo, invierno, imágenes) harsh; (petróleo, lenguaje) crude; **agua cruda** hard water;

color — yellowish white
cruel ADJ cruel, mean
crueldad F cruelty, meanness
cruento ADJ grisly, gruesome
crujido M (de puerta, piso) creak; (de un
  tallo al quebrarse) crack; (de hojas) rustle;
  (de un fuego) crackle
crujiente ADJ (manzana, tocino) crisp, crispy;
  (nueces) crunchy
crujir VI (puerta, piso) to creak; (dientes) to
  grate; (hojas) to rustle; (nueces) to crunch;
  (fuego) to crackle
cruz F cross; (de moneda) tails; **hacerse
  cruces de** to dread
cruzada F crusade
cruzado -da MF crusader; ADJ (cheque)
  crossed; (fuego) cross; (traje) double-
  breasted
cruzamiento M (de piernas, razas) crossing;
  (de calles) crossroads; (de razas) cross
cruzar[9] VT to cross; (un cheque) to write
  across; **—le la cara a alguien** to
  backhand someone's face; **cruzo los
  dedos** I'll keep my fingers crossed; **—se
  con alguien** to bump into someone; **—se
  de brazos** to fold one's arms; **se me
  cruzó un ciervo** a deer crossed in front
  of me
cuaderno M notebook; **— de bitácora**
  logbook; **— de espiral** spiral notebook
cuadra F (establo) stable; (distancia entre
  calles) Am block
cuadrado ADJ square; **estar —** to be fat; M
  square; **es (un) —** he's a square; **dos al —**
  two squared; **elevar al —** to square
cuadrar VT (trabajar en ángulo recto) to
  square; VI (corresponder) to fit; (ser
  conveniente) to be convenient; (ser
  iguales) to balance, to add up; **— con** to
  be in agreement with
cuadricular VT to divide into squares
cuadrilátero ADJ quadrilateral; M (en boxeo)
  ring; (polígono) quadrilateral
cuadrilla F (de ladrones) gang; (de obreros)
  crew; (baile) square dance
cuadro M (cuadrado) square; (pintura)
  picture; (de bicicleta) frame; (de jardín)
  bed; (de tela) checker; (de fútbol) team; **—
  clínico** symptoms; **— sinóptico** table; **a /
  de —s** checked
cuadrúpedo ADJ & M quadruped
cuajada F curd
cuajar VI (leche) to curdle; (queso, cemento)
  to set; (gelatina) to jell; (un movimiento
  literario) to come about; **—se** to curdle; **la
  cosa no cuajó** that didn't pan out
cuajarón M clot

cual PRON REL which; **el / la —** (cosa) which;
  (persona) who; **lo —** which; **sea — sea**
  whichever it may be; ADV like; **— hoja al
  viento** like a leaf in the wind
cuál PRON INTERR which; **¿cuáles son los
  tuyos?** which ones are yours?
cualidad F quality
cualquiera ADJ INDEF any; **de cualquier
  manera / forma** anyhow; **en cualquier
  lado** anywhere; PRON INDEF (cosa) any;
  (persona) anyone; **— que sea su
  nacionalidad** whatever his nationality
  may be; **— que elijas** whichever one you
  choose; **— podría hacer eso** anyone
  could do that
cuando ADV REL when; **— la guerra** during
  the war; **— menos** at least; **— mucho** at
  most; **se rompió — lo usaba** it broke
  while she was using it
cuándo ADV INTERR & PRON when
cuantía F (cantidad) quantity; (importancia)
  importance
cuantificar[6] VT to quantify
cuantioso ADJ considerable
cuanto ADJ REL any; **lee — libro** ve she
  reads any book she sees; PRON REL **unos
  —s** a few; CONJ **hice — pude** I did as
  much as I could; ADV **— antes** as soon as
  possible; **— más trabajo, menos
  consigo** the more I work, the less I
  accomplish; **en —** as soon as possible; **en
  — a** regarding; **en — que** as
cuánto ADJ, ADV & PRON INTERR (dinero, agua)
  how much; (personas, libros) how many;
  ¿cada —? how often? **¿— piensas
  quedarte?** how long do you plan to
  stay?
cuarenta NUM forty; **cantarle las — a
  alguien** to bawl someone out
cuarentena F quarantine; **una — de libros**
  forty-odd books
cuarentón -ona MF person in his or her
  forties
cuaresma F Lent
cuarta F (marcha) fourth gear; (palmo) span
  of a hand
cuartear VT (una res) to quarter; (los labios)
  to chap; **—se** to chap
cuartel M barracks; **— general** headquarters;
  no dar — to give no quarter
cuartelada F military coup
cuartelazo M military coup
cuarteto M quartet
cuartilla F sheet of paper
cuarto ADJ one-fourth, quarter; M (cuarta
  parte) fourth, quarter; (habitación) room;
  (cantidad) quarter, one fourth; **— de**

baño bathroom; **— de estar** living room; **— de final** quarter finals; **— oscuro** darkroom; **¡ni que ocho —s!** no way!

tres —s three fourths

cuarzo M quartz

cuásar M quasar

cuate M *Méx* pal, buddy

cuatrero -ra MF cattle rustler

cuatrillizo -za MF quadruplet

cuatro NUM four; **— ojos** four-eyes; **más de — a good number**

cuba F (barril) cask, barrel; (tina) tub, vat

Cuba F Cuba

cubano -na ADJ & MF Cuban

cubeta F (recipiente triangular) tray; (balde) pail; **— de hielo** ice tray

cúbico ADJ cubic

cubículo M cubicle

cubierta F (de libro) cover; (cosa para cubrir) covering; (neumático) tire; (de buque) deck

cubierto M place setting; **— de plata** silverware; **a —** sheltered

cubismo M cubism

cubo M (cuerpo geométrico, tercera potencia) cube; (balde) bucket; (de rueda) hub; (juguete) building block; **— de basura** trash can

cubrir[51] VT to cover; (con carteles) to plaster; (una vacante) to fill; (con pintura) to coat; (con crema batida) to smother; (de niebla) to shroud; **—se** (nublarse) to fog up; (ponerse el sombrero) to put on one's hat

cucaracha F cockroach

cuchara F spoon; (de excavadora) bucket; (para helado) scoop; **— sopera** soup spoon; **meter la —** to butt in

cucharada F (lo que cabe en una cuchara) spoonful; (medida) tablespoonful; (de helado) dip

cucharadita F teaspoonful

cucharear VT to spoon

cucharita F teaspoon

cucharón M (para helado) scoop, dipper; (para sopa) ladle

cuchichear VI/VT to whisper

cuchicheo M whisper

cuchilla F (cuchillo grande) large knife, cleaver; (de afeitar, de licuadora) blade; (de patín) runner

cuchillada F (golpe) stab, slash; (herida) stab wound, gash

cuchillería F (conjunto de cuchillos) cutlery; (tienda) cutlery store

cuchillo M knife; **pasar a —** to kill with a knife

cuclillas LOC ADV **en —** squatting; **sentarse en —** to squat

cuclillo M cuckoo

cuco ADJ cute

cucú INTERJ cuckoo

cucurucho M (de papel) paper cone; (para helado) ice-cream cone; (capirote) hood

cuello M (parte del cuerpo) neck; (parte de una prenda) collar; **— de botella** bottleneck; **— uterino** cervix; **— vuelto** turtleneck; **estoy hasta el — en deudas** I'm up to my neck in debts

cuenca F (conjunto de tierras) basin; (cavidad del ojo) eye socket

cuenco M earthen bowl

cuenta F (cálculo) count, calculation; (factura) bill, check; (relación de ingresos y gastos) account; (bolita) bead; (depósito bancario) bank account; **— conjunta** joint account; **— corriente** checking account; **— de ahorros** savings account; **— de crédito** charge account; **— de gastos** expense account; **— regresiva / atrás** countdown; **abrir / cerrar una —** to open / close an account; **a fin de —s** when all is said and done; **ajustar —s** to settle old scores; **caí en (la) — de que** it just dawned on me that; **dar — de** to finish off; **dar —s** to give an accounting; **darse —** to realize; **en resumidas —s** in short; **eso corre por mi —** that is my responsibility; **habida — de** bearing in mind; **más de la —** more than necessary; **pasar la —** to call in a favor; **tomar / tener en —** to take into account; **trabajar por — propia** to freelance; M SG **cuentagotas** eyedropper

cuento M story, tale; **— chino** tall tale; **— de hadas** fairy tale; **— de nunca acabar** never-ending tale; **déjese de —s** come to the point; **traer a —** to bring up; **venir a —** to be to the point

cuerda F (soga) cord, rope; (parte de un arco) bowstring; (de guitarra) string; (de reloj) spring; **— floja** tight rope; **—s vocales** vocal cords; **bajo —** under-the-table; **contra las —s** on the ropes; **dar — a** to wind

cuerdo ADJ sane

cuerno M horn (también instrumento de viento); (de caracol) feeler; (de ciervo) antler; **— de la abundancia** horn of plenty; **coger el toro por los —s** to take the bull by the horns; **irse al —** *vulg* to go to hell; **poner —s a** to be unfaithful to

cuero M (piel de animal) hide; (piel curtida) leather; **— cabelludo** scalp; **en —s** naked

cuerpo M body; (torso) torso; ¡— **a tierra!** hit the deck! — **de bomberos** fire department; — **de policía** police force; — **de prensa** press corps; — **docente** teaching staff; **a — de rey** in great luxury; **dar — a** to flesh out; **de — entero** through and through; **ganó por tres —s de ventaja** he won by three lengths; **ir de —** to have a bowel movement

cuervo M crow, raven

cuesta F slope; — **abajo** downhill; — **arriba** uphill; **a —s** piggyback

cuestión F question; **en — de** in a matter of; **poner en —** to question; **ser — de** to be a matter of

cuestionable ADJ questionable

cuestionador ADJ questioning

cuestionar VT to question

cuestionario M questionnaire

cueva F cave

cuidado M (atención) care; (preocupación) worry; — **con el perro** beware of the dog; — **de la casa** housekeeping; **al — de** in care of; **eso me trae sin —** I don't care about that; **tener —** to be careful; **un enfermo de —** a severely ill patient; INTERJ look out!

cuidador -ora MF caregiver, caretaker

cuidadoso ADJ careful

cuidar VT to take care of, to look after; — **de** to take care of; — **la casa** to keep house; — **niños** to babysit; —**se de** to beware of

culata F (anca) haunch; (de rifle) butt; (de motor) cylinder head

culatazo M (golpe) blow with the butt of a rifle; (rebote al disparar) recoil

culear VI/VT Am vulg to fuck, to screw

culebra F snake

culebrear VI to slither

culebrilla F shingles

culinario ADJ culinary

culminar VI to culminate

culo M (trasero) vulg ass, butt; (ano) anus; — **de botella** bottle bottom; — **del mundo** boondocks; — **veo, — quiero** I want everything I see; **caerse de —** to be astounded; **dar por el —** (fastidiar) to bother; (sodomizar) to sodomize; **hacer de —** to be lucky; **lamer —s** fam to suck up to someone, to brown-nose; **rascarse el —** vulg to fart around; **romperse el —** vulg to bust one's ass

culpa F (responsabilidad) fault, blame; (sentimiento) guilt; **echar la — a** to blame; **por — de** because of; **tener la —** to be to blame

culpabilidad F guilt

culpable ADJ guilty; MF culprit

culpar VT to blame

cultivado ADJ (tierra) cultivated; (perlas) cultured

cultivador -ora MF (persona) cultivator; F (aparato) cultivator

cultivar VT (cosechas) to grow, to raise; (la tierra) to farm; (relaciones, inteligencia) to cultivate; (microbios) to culture

cultivo M (de plantas) growing; (de la tierra) farming; (de microbios) culture; (de relaciones) cultivation; **de —** cultured

culto ADJ educated, cultured; M worship; **libertad de —** freedom of religion

cultura F culture; — **general** general knowledge

cultural ADJ cultural

culturismo M body-building

cumbre F summit

cumplido ADJ (cortés) polite; (perfecto) perfect; M compliment; **hacer algo de —** to do something out of duty; **hacer un —** to pay a compliment

cumplimiento M (de un contrato) performance; (de una promesa, obligación) fulfillment; (de un plazo) expiration

cumplir VT (una obligación) to fulfill, to discharge; (una promesa) to keep; (una condena) to complete, to serve; — **diez años** to turn ten; **hacer —** to enforce; VI (acceder a las relaciones sexuales) to have sexual relations; (vencer) to expire; — **con** to meet a goal; **me cumple informarle que** it is my duty to inform you that

cúmulo M (grupo) host; (tipo de nube) cumulus

cuna F (que se puede mecer) cradle; (con barandas) crib

cundir VI (extenderse) to spread; (rendir) to go a long way

cuneta F roadside ditch; **en la —** out to pasture

cuña F (pieza para hender) wedge; (recipiente de excrementos) bedpan

cuñado -da M brother-in-law; F sister-in-law

cuño M die; **de — hispano** with a Hispanic stamp

cuota F (cantidad que le corresponde a uno) quota; (cantidad que hay que pagar) dues; (mensualidad) installment

cupé M coupé

cupo M (cantidad) quota; (capacidad) Am room

cupón M coupon

cúpula F dome

cura F cure, remedy; M priest
curable ADJ curable
curación F cure
curandero -ra MF healer
curar VT (una enfermedad, carne) to cure; (una herida) to heal; VI to heal; **—se** to heal; **—se en salud** to take precautionary measures
curiosear VI to look around; (en asuntos ajenos) to pry
curiosidad F curiosity
curioso ADJ curious
curita F *Am* adhesive bandage, Band-Aid™
currículum M résumé
curro M *Esp* job
curruca F warbler
curry M curry
cursar VT (un curso) to take; (un telegrama) to send
cursi ADJ (afectado) affected; (de mal gusto) tacky
cursivo ADJ cursive; **escribir en —** to write in cursive
curso M (de río, enfermedad, acontecimientos, moneda) course; (período docente) academic year; (grupo de estudiantes que siguen el mismo curso) class; (libro de texto) textbook; **— legal** legal currency; **el mes en —** the current month
cursor M cursor
curtiduría F tannery
curtiembre F tannery
curtir VT (cuero) to tan; (cutis) to weather; (hacer adquirir experiencia) to harden; **—se** (envejecerse) to get weathered; (acostumbrarse a las dificultades) to become accustomed to hardships
curva F curve
curvatura F curvature
curvo ADJ curved
cúspide F summit
custodia F custody, keeping; **en —** in escrow
custodiar VT to guard
custodio -dia MF guardian
cutícula F cuticle
cutis M facial skin
cuyo ADJ REL whose
cyborg M cyborg

Dd

dádiva F gift
dadivoso ADJ generous

dado ADJ given; M die; **jugar a los —s** to throw dice
dador -ora MF giver; **— de sangre** blood donor
daga F dagger
dalia F dahlia
daltónico ADJ color-blind
dama F lady; (en el juego de la dama) king; **jugar a las —s** to play checkers; **— de honor** bridesmaid
damajuana F demijohn
damasco M (fruta) apricot; (árbol) apricot tree
damisela F damsel
dandi M dandy
danés -esa ADJ Danish; MF Dane; M (lengua) Danish
danza F dance; **— del vientre** belly dance; **en —** in action
danzante MF dancer
danzar[9] VI/VT to dance
dañar VT to harm, to damage; **—se** to suffer harm
dañino ADJ harmful
daño M damage, harm; **— emergente** actual damage; **— físico** bodily harm; **—s y perjuicios** damages; **hacer —** to harm
dañoso ADJ harmful
dar[25] VT (un regalo) to give; (un golpe, naipes) to deal; (sal) to add; (una fiesta) to throw; (la hora) to strike; (un olor) to give off; (la alarma) to raise; (un paseo) to take; **— a** (un edificio) to face; (una calle) to lead to; **— a conocer** to announce; **— a entender** to intimate; **— con** to hit upon, to find; **— de alta** to discharge, to release from the hospital; **— de baja** to discharge; **— de comer** to feed; **— de sí** to perform at capacity; **esta tela da de sí** this fabric gives; **— en la pared** to hit the wall; **—le con** to scrub with; **lo misma da** it makes no difference; **¿qué más da?** what difference does it make? **dale que dale** on and on; **hoy no doy una** today I can't get anything right; **le doy cincuenta años** he must be about fifty; **me da rabia / miedo** that makes me angry / afraid; **no me da el tiempo para ir al cine** I don't have time to go to the movie; **que no le dé el sol** don't let the sun shine on it; **y dale** enough already; **—se** to be found; **—se a** to indulge in; **—se por conforme** to be satisfied; **dárselas de** to boast of being
dardo M dart
dársena F dock
datar VT to date; **— de** to date from

dátil M date
dato M piece of information; **—s** data
de PREP — **la familia** of the family; —
  Madrid from Madrid; **habló — la
  guerra** he talked about the war; **el
  hombre — gafas** the man with glasses;
  el mejor estudiante — la clase the
  best student in the class; **fácil — hacer**
  easy to do; **más — tres** more than three;
  llevar — la mano to lead by the hand;
  — regreso a España upon returning to
  Spain; **— venta en farmacias** on sale in
  pharmacies; **ancianos — respeto** older
  people to be respected; **— lo más lindo**
  really pretty; **tonto — mí** silly me
deambular VI to amble, to saunter
deán M dean
debacle M debacle
debajo ADV under, underneath; PREP — **de**
  under, below; **por — de** under
debate M debate
debatir VT to debate; **—se** to struggle
debe M debit
deber V AUX **deben apoyarme** they should
  support me; **debe de ser** it must be;
  deberías sentarte you should sit down;
  VT to owe; **me debes una** you owe me
  one; **me debo a mis alumnos** I'm
  devoted to my students; M duty; **—es**
  homework
debidamente ADV duly
debido ADJ due; **— a** due to, owing to; **a su
  — tiempo** in due time
débil ADJ (que tiene poca fuerza) weak;
  (endeble) frail, feeble; (sonido) faint
debilidad F weakness; (cualidad de endeble)
  frailty; (de un sonido) faintness
debilitamiento M weakening
debilitar VT to weaken, to debilitate
débito M debit
debutar VI to make a debut
década F decade
decadencia F (moral) decadence, decay;
  (cultural, económica) decline
decadente ADJ decadent
decaer[23] VI (fuerza) to weaken; (energía) to
  ebb; (salud) to fail; (ánimo) to flag
decaimiento M (decadencia) decline;
  (debilidad) weakness
decano -na ADJ senior; MF dean
decapitar VT to behead, to decapitate
decatlón M decathlon
decencia F decency
decenio M decade
decente ADJ decent; **muy —** rather good
decepción F disappointment
decepcionante ADJ disappointing

decepcionar VT to disappoint
decibelio M decibel
decidido ADJ resolute, determined; **una
  decidida preferencia** a decided
  preference
decidir VI/VT to decide; **—se** to make up
  one's mind; **—se a** to resolve to
deciduo ADJ deciduous
décima F tenth
decimal ADJ decimal
décimo ADJ & M tenth
decir[26] VT (palabras, oraciones) to say; (una
  mentira, un chiste, la verdad) to tell; —
  tonterías to talk nonsense; **con —te
  que** suffice it to say that; **este tipo no
  me dice nada** this guy leaves me cold;
  ¿que me lo digan a mí? you're telling
  me that? VI to say; **diga** hello (al
  contestar el teléfono); **es —** that is to say;
  he dicho I have spoken; **no es
  prometedor que digamos** it's hardly
  promising; **no me digas** you don't say;
  querer — to mean; M saying
decisión F decision; **tomar una —** to make
  a decision
decisivo ADJ decisive
declaración F (de amor, independencia,
  guerra) declaration; (de un hecho)
  statement; (de un testigo) deposition; **—
  de derechos** bill of rights; **— de
  impuestos / de la renta** tax return; **—
  jurada** affidavit
declarar VT (amor, independencia, ingresos)
  to declare; (un hecho) to state; **—
  culpable** to find guilty; **os declaro
  marido y mujer** I pronounce you man
  and wife; VI (como testigo) to testify; **—se**
  (un amante) to declare one's love; **—se
  culpable** to plead guilty; **—se en huelga**
  to go on strike; **—se en quiebra** to
  declare bankruptcy
declinar VI/VT to decline
declive M (pendiente) slope, drop;
  (decadencia) decline
decoración F decoration; **— de interiores**
  interior decorating
decorado M (de una casa) decoration; (de un
  escenario) scenery
decorar VT to decorate
decorativo ADJ decorative
decoro M decorum, propriety
decoroso ADJ decorous, proper
decrépito ADJ decrepit
decretar VT to decree
decreto M (disposición ejecutiva) decree; (ley)
  act
dedal M thimble

dedicación F dedication

dedicar[6] VT (la vida) to dedicate, to devote; (un libro) to dedicate; **—se** to dedicate oneself; (a los estudios) to apply oneself

dedicatoria F dedication

dedo M (de la mano) finger; (del pie) toe; **— anular** ring finger; **— índice** index finger; **— mayor / del corazón** middle finger; **— meñique** little finger; **— pulgar** thumb; **chuparse el —** to be a fool; **chuparse los —s** to lick one's fingers; **cruzar los —s** to keep one's fingers crossed; **elegir a —** to appoint directly; **hacer —** to hitch a ride; **no mover un —** not to lift a finger

deducción F deduction

deducible ADJ deductible

deducir[24] VT (concluir) to deduce, to conclude; (descontar) to deduct

defecar[6] VI/VT to defecate

defección F defection

defecto M defect, flaw

defectuoso ADJ defective, faulty

defender[1] VT to defend; (una causa) to champion; (los derechos) to stand up for, to stick up for; **se defiende en francés** he can hold his own in French

defendible ADJ defensible

defensa F defense; **aprende — personal** he's learning self-defense; **lo dijo en — propia** he said it in self-defense

defensivo ADJ defensive; **a la defensiva** on the defensive

defensor -ora MF defender; (de una causa) champion

deferencia F deference

deficiencia F deficiency

deficiente ADJ deficient

déficit M deficit

definición F definition

definido ADJ definite

definir VT to define

definitivo ADJ (superior) definitive; (final) final; **en definitiva** all things considered

deflación F deflation

deflector M baffle

deforestación F deforestation

deformación F deformation

deformar VT to deform; **—se** to become deformed

deforme ADJ deformed

deformidad F deformity

defraudar VT (cometer fraude) to defraud; (decepcionar) to disappoint

defunción F death

degenerado -da ADJ & MF degenerate

degenerar VI to degenerate

degollar[2] VT to slash someone's throat

degradación F degradation

degradar VT (envilecer) to degrade, to debase; (rebajar el rango) to demote; **—se** to degrade

degüello M throat-slashing; **lucha a —** fight to the death

dehesa F pasture

deidad F deity

dejadez F slovenliness

dejado ADJ slovenly

dejar VT (abandonar, no comer, legar) to leave; (a un enamorado) to leave, to dump; (permitir) to let; (soltar) to let go; **— de** to stop; **— caer** to drop; **déjame en paz** leave me alone; **me dejó atónito** it left / rendered me speechless; **no dejes de venir** don't fail to come; **te lo dejo en mil dólares** I'll sell it to you for one thousand dollars; **—se** to let oneself go; **—se crecer la barba** to grow a beard; **déjate de joder** give me a break

deje M slight accent

dejo M (sabor) aftertaste; (acento) slight accent; (toque) hint; **tener un — de** smack of

delantal M apron

delante ADV in front; **— de** in front of, ahead of

delantera F (de carrera) lead; (de vestido) front; **llevar la —** to be in the lead; **tomar la —** to take the lead

delantero ADJ (pata) front; (línea) forward; M front

delatar VT to inform against, to squeal on; **— la edad** to betray one's age

delator -ora MF accuser, informer

delegación F delegation

delegado -da MF delegate

delegar[7] VT to delegate

deleitar VT to delight; **—se en algo** to revel in something; **—se la vista con** to feast one's eyes on

deleite M delight

deletrear VT to spell; **— mal** to misspell

deleznable ADJ despicable

delfín M dolphin

delgadez F thinness

delgado ADJ thin, slender, slim

deliberación F deliberation

deliberado ADJ deliberate

deliberar VI/VT to deliberate

delicadeza F (tacto) gentleness; (fineza) delicacy; **con — gently; tuvo la — de llamar** he was kind enough to call

delicado ADJ (suave, fácil de romper, controvertido) delicate; (enfermizo) frail;

(exquisito) dainty; (quisquilloso) squeamish

delicatessen F PL delicacies

delicia F delight

delicioso ADJ delicious, delectable

delimitar VT to delimit

delincuencia F crime

delincuente ADJ & MF delinquent, criminal; **— juvenil** juvenile delinquent

delineador M eyeliner

delinear VT to delineate, to outline

delirante ADJ delirious, raving

delirar VI to be delirious, to rave

delirio M delirium; **— paranoico** paranoid delusion; **—s de grandeza** delusions of grandeur

delito M crime, offense

demacrado ADJ drawn, gaunt, haggard

demagogo -ga MF demagog

demanda F (de mercancías) demand; (de seguros) insurance claim; (pleito) lawsuit; **por —** on demand; **entablar una —** to file a lawsuit

demandado -da MF defendant

demandante MF plaintiff

demandar VT (pedir) to ask for; (poner pleito) to sue, to file a suit against

demarcar[6] VT to demarcate

demás ADJ (restante) remaining; PRON the others, the rest; **lo —** the rest; **y —** and whatnot; ADV **por lo —** moreover; **por —** useless

demasía LOC ADV **en —** excessively

demasiado ADV too; too much; **eso es — para mí** that's too much for me; **él es — alto** he's too tall; ADJ too much; too many; **— dinero** too much money; **demasiadas cosas** too many things

demencia F (locura) insanity; (senilidad) senility

demente ADJ demented, insane, deranged

democracia F democracy

demócrata MF INV democrat

democrático ADJ democratic

demografía F demographics

demográfico ADJ demographic

demoler[2] VT to demolish, to tear down

demonio M demon; **al — con los libros** *vulg* to hell with books; **mandar al —** *vulg* to tell someone to go to hell; **¿qué —s haces?** what the heck are you doing? **un frío de —s** bitter cold

demora F delay

demorar VT to delay; **—se** to linger

demostración F demonstration; **— de fuerza** show of force

demostrar[2] VT (mostrar) to demonstrate, to

show; (hacer ver la verdad) to prove, to demonstrate

demostrativo ADJ demonstrative

demudar VT to change, to alter

denigrar VT to denigrate, to disparage

denodado ADJ untiring

denominación F (valor) denomination; (nombre) designation

denominar VT to designate, to term

denostar[2] VT to revile

denotación F denotation

denotar VT to denote

densidad F density

denso ADJ dense; (líquido) heavy

dentado ADJ (rueda) toothed; (montaña) ragged

dentadura F set of teeth; **— postiza** false teeth

dental ADJ dental

dentellada F (mordedura) bite; (señal de diente) tooth mark; **a —s** biting

dentífrico M dentifrice

dentista MF dentist

dentro ADV inside; PREP **— de la casa** inside the house; **— de la ley** within the law; **— de quince días** (en el plazo de) within two weeks; (al cabo de) in two weeks; **por —** within

denuncia F (acusación) denunciation; (de mina, de seguro) claim

denunciar VT (un hecho negativo) to denounce; (una mina) to claim; (un delito) to report

deparar VT to have in store for

departamento M (división) department; (piso) small apartment

departir VI *lit* to commune

dependencia F (hecho de depender) dependence; (habituación) dependency; (filial) branch office

depender VI to depend; **— de** to depend on

dependiente -ta ADJ dependent; MF clerk

depilar VT to remove hair

depilatorio ADJ & M depilatory

deplorable ADJ deplorable

deplorar VT to deplore

deponer[39] VT (las armas) to lay down; (a un ministro) to depose, to remove; VI to defecate

deportar VT to deport

deporte M sport; **me gusta el —** I like sports/athletics

deportista ADJ athletic; MF athlete

deportivo ADJ athletic; **revista deportiva** sports magazine

deposición F (de un testigo) deposition; (de un ministro) removal; (movimiento de

vientre) bowel movement
depositante MF depositor
depositar VT to deposit; **—se** to settle
depositario -ria MF repository
depósito M (en el banco) deposit; (de
    gasolina) tank; (de agua) reservoir; (de
    cadáveres) morgue; (de armas) depot,
    dump; (de mercancías) stock room,
    storehouse; **hacer un —** to make a
    deposit; **en —** on consignment
depravado ADJ depraved
depreciar VI to depreciate
depredador -ora MF predator
depresión F depression
deprimente ADJ depressing
deprimido ADJ depressed
deprimir VT to depress
deprisa ADV quickly
depuración F purification; (de un programa)
    debugging
depurar VT to purify; (un programa) to
    debug
derby M derby
derecha F (política) right wing; **a la —** to
    the right; **de —s** right-wing
derechista ADJ right-wing; MF rightist
derecho ADJ (no izquierdo) right; (recto)
    straight; **ponerse —** to hold oneself erect;
    ADV straight; **volver — a casa** to go
    straight home; **todo —** straight ahead; M
    (preceptos, disciplina) law; (posibilidad
    legal) right; **— consuetudinario**
    common law; **— de admisión** fee; **—
    internacional** international law; **—**
    fees; **—s aduaneros** tax on imports; **—s
    civiles** civil rights; **—s de autor**
    copyright; **—s de la mujer** women's
    rights; **—s de los animales** animal
    rights; **estar en su —** to be entitled;
    poner al — to put on right side out;
    registrar los —s to copyright
derechura F straightness
deriva F drift; **ir a la —** to be adrift
derivación F derivation
derivado M (subproducto) by-product;
    (palabra) derivative
derivar VT to derive
dermatología F dermatology
dermatólogo -ga MF dermatologist
derogación F repeal
derogar[7] VT to repeal
derramamiento M spill, spilling; **— de
    sangre** bloodshed
derramar VT (un líquido) to spill; (sangre,
    lágrimas) to shed; **—se** to spill over, to
    run over
derrame M spill; **— cerebral** stroke, cerebral

hemorrhage
derredor LOC ADV **en —** all around
derrengar[7] VT (dañar la espalda) to sprain
    one's back; (cansar) to exhaust
derretir[5] VT to melt; **—se por alguien** to
    be crazy about someone
derribar VT (un edificio) to demolish, to tear
    down; (a una persona) to knock down;
    (un gobierno) to topple, to overthrow; (un
    avión) to shoot down, to down
derrocamiento M overthrow
derrocar[6] VT (un gobierno) to overthrow, to
    topple; (a un dictador) to depose
derrochador -ora ADJ extravagant; MF (de
    dinero) spendthrift; (de recursos)
    squanderer
derrochar VT (dinero) to squander; (salud) to
    radiate
derroche M (de recursos) waste,
    extravagance; (de color) profusion
derrota F defeat
derrotar VT to defeat
derrotero M course
derrubio M washout
derruido ADJ dilapidated
derrumbadero M precipice
derrumbamiento M collapse
derrumbar VT to demolish; **—se** (edificio) to
    collapse; (túnel, caverna) to cave in
derrumbe M (de tierra) landslide; (de un
    edificio) collapse
desabotonar VT to unbutton, to undo
desabrido ADJ (comida) tasteless; (persona)
    Am dull; Esp surly
desabrigado ADJ exposed
desabrochado ADJ undone, unfastened
desabrochar VT to undo; (ganchos) to
    unhook; (hebillas, cinturones) to
    unbuckle; (botones) to unbutton; **—se** to
    come undone
desacato M disrespect; **— al tribunal**
    contempt of court
desacelerar VI to decelerate
desacierto M mistake
desaconsejable ADJ inadvisable
desaconsejar VT to caution against
desacoplar VT to uncouple, to disconnect
desacostumbrado ADJ unusual
desacostumbrar VT to break of a habit; **—se**
    to lose a habit
desacreditar VT to discredit
desactivar VT (explosivo, situación) to
    defuse; (mecanismo) to disable; (virus) to
    deactivate
desacuerdo M disagreement; **estar en —** to
    be at odds
desafiar[16] VT (retar) to challenge, to dare;

(enfrentar) to defy

desafilado ADJ dull

desafilar VT to dull; **—se** to become dull

desafinado ADJ out of tune, off-key

desafinar VT to be out of tune

desafío M (reto) challenge; (desobediencia) defiance

desafortunado ADJ unfortunate, unlucky

desafuero M (de un diputado) withdrawal of immunity; (ultraje) outrage

desagradable ADJ disagreeable, unpleasant

desagradar VT to displease

desagradecido ADJ ungrateful

desagrado M displeasure

desagraviar VI to make amends, to redress

desagravio M redress

desaguadero M drainpipe

desaguar[8] VI to drain

desagüe M (acción de desaguar) drainage; (de lavabo) drain, drainpipe; (en la azotea) gutter

desaguisado M mess

desahogado ADJ (cómodo) comfortable; (espacioso) spacious

desahogar[7] VT (aliviar) to relieve; (expresar) to pour out one's feelings

desahogo M relief; **vivir con —** to live an easy life

desairar VT to slight, to snub, to rebuff

desaire M slight, snub, rebuff

desajustar VT to loosen; **—se** to come loose

desalentado ADJ despondent

desalentador ADJ disheartening

desalentar[1] VT to discourage, to dishearten; **—se** to get discouraged

desaliento M discouragement, dismay

desaliñado ADJ disheveled, slovenly, unkempt

desaliño M slovenliness

desalmado ADJ heartless

desalojar VT (una piedra) to dislodge; (un tribunal) to clear; (por peligro) to evacuate; (por no pagar) to evict; (dejar vacío) to vacate

desamparado ADJ helpless, forlorn

desamparar VT to forsake

desamparo M abandonment, helplessness

desamueblado ADJ unfurnished

desangrar VT to bleed

desanimado ADJ (persona) discouraged; (jornada) dull

desanimar VT to discourage

desánimo M discouragement

desaparecer[13] VI to disappear, to vanish; (morir) to pass away

desaparición F disappearance; (muerte) demise

desapasionado ADJ dispassionate

desapego M detachment

desapercibido ADJ unnoticed

desaprobación F disapproval

desaprobar[2] VT to disapprove of

desarmado ADJ unarmed

desarmar VT (quitar las armas) to disarm; (desmontar) to take apart

desarme M disarmament

desarraigar[7] VT to uproot

desarreglar VT to disturb, to mess up

desarreglo M (nervioso) disorder; (falta de arreglo) mess

desarrollar VT (aumentar) to develop; (extender algo arrollado) to unroll; (llevar a cabo) to carry out; (aclarar) to elaborate, to flesh out; **—se** to unfold

desarrollo M development; (de una ecuación) expansion; **en —** developing

desarticulado ADJ disjointed

desaseado ADJ slovenly

desaseo M slovenliness

desasir[21] VT to let go of

desasosiego M uneasiness

desastrado ADJ (desaseado) untidy; (funesto) ill-fated

desastre M disaster

desastroso ADJ disastrous

desatado ADJ (ambición) unfettered; (zapatos) untied

desatar VT (un nudo) to untie, to loosen; (una ola de violencia) to unleash; **—se** to come untied; **—se en insultos** to let out a string of insults

desatascador M plunger

desatascar[6] VT (un inodoro) to unclog; (una cosa) to dislodge

desatención F lack of attention

desatender[1] VT (no ocuparse de algo) to neglect; (ignorar) to ignore

desatendido ADJ (descuidado) neglected; (ignorado) ignored

desatento ADJ inattentive

desatinado ADJ imprudent

desatornillar VT to unscrew

desatracar[6] VI/VT to shove off

desavenencia F discord

desayunar VT **desayuné huevos** I had eggs for breakfast; **—se** to have breakfast; **—se (con que)** to find out (that)

desayuno M breakfast

desazón F uneasiness

desbandarse VI to disband

desbaratar VT (un plan) to disrupt; (un hechizo) to break

desbocado ADJ (caballo) runaway; (collar) loose

desbordamiento M overflow
desbordante ADJ overflowing
desbordar VI (derramar) to overflow; VT (abrumar) to overwhelm; —**se** to overflow, to spill over
desbravar VT to break
descabalgar[7] VI to dismount
descabellado ADJ harebrained
descabezar[9] VT to behead; — **un sueño** to take a nap
descafeinado ADJ decaffeinated
descalabrar VT to split someone's head open
descalabro M disaster
descalificar VT to disqualify
descalzar[9] VT to take off someone's shoes; —**se** to take off one's shoes
descalzo ADJ barefoot
descaminado ADJ **andar** / **ir** — to be on the wrong track
descamisado ADJ (sin camisa) shirtless; (pobre) poor
descansar VI/VT to rest; — **en paz** to rest in peace; —**se en** to rely on
descanso M (acción de descansar) rest; (de escalera) staircase landing; (tiempo en que se descansa) break; **en** — at ease
descapotable ADJ & M convertible
descarado ADJ shameless, impudent, brazen; **a la descarada** shamelessly
descarga F (de batería, agua, armas) discharge; (de buques) unloading; (emocional) outpouring; (de electricidad) shock
descargar[7] VT (una batería, agua) to discharge; (un buque, un arma de fuego) to unload; (bombas) to drop; (un programa de computadora) to download; —**se** (una batería) to drain; (ira) to vent
descargo M **en su** — in his defense
descarnado ADJ (realidad) stark; (cara) emaciated
descaro M effrontery, impudence, nerve
descarriar[16] VT to lead astray; —**se** to go astray
descarrilarse VI to derail, to jump the track
descartar VT (un naipe) to discard; (una posibilidad) to dismiss, to discard
descarte M discard; **por** — by elimination
descascararse VI (en jirones) to peel; (en fragmentos) to chip, to flake
descendencia F (linaje) descent; (descendientes) descendants
descendente ADJ descending, downward
descender[1] VI to descend; — **de** to descend from
descendiente MF descendant
descenso M descent

descifrar VT to decipher
descodificar[6] VT to decode
descolgar[2,7] VT (una cortina) to take down; (un teléfono) to pick up; —**se con** to come up with; —**se de** to come down from
descollar[2] VI to excel
descolorido ADJ (persona) pale; (cosa) colorless
descomponer[39] VT (disgustar) to upset; (dar diarrea) to give diarrhea; (dar náuseas) to make nauseous; (productos químicos) to break down; (cadáveres) to decompose; (un reloj) to break; — **en factores** to factor; —**se** (productos químicos) to break down; (cadáveres) to decompose; (un reloj) to break; (sentir náuseas) to be nauseous; (tener diarrea) to have diarrhea; (disgustarse) to go to pieces
descomposición F (de cadáveres) decomposition; (de productos químicos) breaking down; (diarrea) diarrhea
descompuesto ADJ (roto) broken; (caótico) chaotic; (con diarrea) having diarrhea
descomunal ADJ enormous
desconcertado ADJ disconcerted
desconcertante ADJ disconcerting
desconcertar[1] VT to disconcert, to puzzle, to baffle; —**se** to become disconcerted
desconchar VT to chip
desconcierto M confusion
desconectado ADJ disconnected
desconectar VT to disconnect
desconexión F (acción de desconectar) disconnecting; (incomunicación) disconnect
desconfiado ADJ mistrustful, suspicious
desconfianza F mistrust
desconfiar[16] VT to distrust, to mistrust, to be wary of
descongelación F thawing
descongestionante M decongestant
desconocer[13] VT (no reconocer) to fail to recognize; (no saber) not to know
desconocido -da ADJ unknown; **un actividad desconocida** an unheard-of activity; MF stranger
desconocimiento M ignorance
desconsideración F thoughtlessness
desconsiderado ADJ thoughtless, inconsiderate
desconsolado ADJ disconsolate, dejected
desconsolador ADJ disheartening
desconsolar[2] VT to dishearten; —**se** to become disheartened
desconsuelo M dejection
descontar[2] VT (bajar el precio) to discount;

(excluir) to exclude; (quitar del sueldo) to dock

descontentadizo ADJ hard to please

descontentar VT to displease

descontento ADJ & M discontent

descorazonado ADJ disheartened

descortés ADJ discourteous, impolite

descortesía F discourtesy, impoliteness

descortezar [7] VT to strip the bark from

descoser VT to rip; —**se** to come unsewn

descosido ADJ unsewn; M unsewn place; **hablar como un —** to talk one's head off

descostrar VT to remove the crust from

descoyuntado ADJ dislocated, out of joint

descoyuntar VT to dislocate; —**se** to become dislocated

descrédito M discredit

descreído -da ADJ unbelieving; MF unbeliever

descreimiento M unbelief

describir [51] VT to describe

descripción F description

descriptivo ADJ descriptive

descuartizar [9] VT to quarter

descubierto ADJ (destapado) uncovered; (sin sombrero) hatless; **al —** in the open; **estar al —** to be exposed; **poner al —** to expose, to lay bare; **en —** overdrawn; M overdraft

descubridor -ora MF discoverer

descubrimiento M discovery

descubrir [51] VT (hallar) to discover; (destapar) to uncover; —**se** to take off one's hat; — **el pastel** to spill the beans

descuento M discount

descuidado ADJ (en lo que se hace) careless, negligent; (en el arreglo de su persona) slovenly

descuidar VT to neglect; **descuida, yo me ocupo de eso** don't worry, I'll take care of that; —**se** to be negligent

descuido M (falta de cuidado) neglect; (acción descuidada) oversight; **al —** off-hand; **por —** by chance

desde PREP (origen) from; (tiempo) since; — **Madrid** from Madrid; — **el martes** since Tuesday; — **luego** of course; — **el principio** from the start; — **el vamos** from the word go; — **entonces** ever since

desdecirse [26] VI (decir lo contrario) to contradict oneself; (negar lo dicho) to retract

desdén M disdain, scorn

desdentado ADJ toothless

desdeñar VT to disdain, to scorn

desdeñoso ADJ disdainful, scornful

desdicha F misfortune; **por —** unfortunately

desdichado ADJ wretched

desdoblamiento M division

desdoblar VT (desplegar) to unfold; (dividir) to divide

deseabilidad F desirability

deseable ADJ desirable

desear VT to desire

desecación F drying

desecar [6] VT to dry; —**se** to dry up

desechar VT (ropa vieja) to discard; (una oferta) to refuse; (una posibilidad) to dismiss

desecho M waste material; —**s** refuse, waste

desembalar VT to unpack

desembarazar [9] VT to rid of; —**se** to get rid of

desembarcadero M dock

desembarcar [6] VI (de un buque) to disembark, to go ashore; (de un avión) to deplane

desembarco M landing

desembarque M landing

desembocadura F mouth

desembocar [6] VI to flow; — **en** to flow into; **la calle Ocho desemboca en la Rambla** eighth street feeds into la Rambla

desembolsar VT to disburse, to pay out

desembolso M disbursement, outlay

desembragar [7] VI/VT to disengage (the clutch)

desempacar [6] VT to unpack

desempañar VT to wipe clean

desempeñar VT to redeem; — **un cargo** to perform the duties of a position; — **un papel** to play a part; —**se** to get out of debt

desempeño M (de un cargo o papel) performance; (de una cosa en prenda) redemption

desempleado ADJ unemployed

desempleo M unemployment

desempolvar VT to dust off

desencadenar VT (quitar las cadenas) to unchain; (producir algo) to trigger, to spark

desencajado ADJ (mandíbula) dislocated; (mirada) wild; **estaba — en el funeral** he was deeply disturbed at the funeral

desencajar VT (un cajón) to unstick; (la mandíbula) to dislocate

desencantar VT (desilusionar) to disillusion; (quitar un hechizo) to remove a spell from

desencanto M disillusion

desenchufar VI/VT to unplug

desenfadado ADJ uninhibited

desenfado M lack of inhibition

desenfrenadamente ADV with wild abandon

desenfrenado ADJ (sin moderación) unbridled, wanton, rampant; (muy rápido) reckless

desenganchar VT to unhook

desengañar VT to disabuse; **—se** (de un error) to become disabused; (de una ilusión) to become disillusioned

desengaño M disillusion

desengranar VT to take out of gear

desenmarañar VT to disentangle

desenmascarar VT to unmask, to expose

desenredar VT to disentangle

desenrollar VT to unroll

desenroscar VT to untwist

desentenderse[1] VI to pay no attention

desentendido ADJ **hacerse el —** to pretend not to notice / know

desenterrar[1] VT (una cosa) to unearth, to dig up; (un cadáver) to disinter

desentonado ADJ out of tune

desentonar VI (cantar mal) to sing off key; (estar fuera de lugar) to be out of place

desentrañar VT to unravel

desenvoltura F self-assurance

desenvolver[2,51] VT (desenrollar) to unroll; (quitar la envoltura) to unwrap; **—se** to behave

desenvuelto ADJ self-assured

deseo M desire, wish; (sexual) desire; **pedir un —** to make a wish

deseoso ADJ desirous

desequilibrado -da ADJ unbalanced; MF unbalanced person

desequilibrar VT to unbalance

desequilibrio M imbalance

deserción F desertion

desertar VI/VT to desert; **— de** to defect from

desértico ADJ desert

desertor -ora MF deserter

desesperación F desperation

desesperado ADJ desperate

desesperanza F despair, hopelessness

desesperanzado ADJ hopeless

desesperanzar[9] VT to discourage, to deprive of hope; **—se** to despair

desesperar VI to despair; VT to drive crazy

desestabilizar[9] VT to destabilize

desestimación F rejection

desestimar VT to reject

desfachatez F audacity

desfalcar[6] VT to embezzle

desfalco M embezzlement

desfallecer[13] VI (debilitarse) to grow weak; (desmayarse) to faint

desfallecimiento M (debilidad) weakness;

(desmayo) faint

desfavorable ADJ unfavorable

desfibrilar VT to defibrillate

desfigurar VT (el rostro) to disfigure; (una estatua) to deface

desfiladero M narrow passage

desfilar VI to file by; (soldados, modelos) to parade

desfile M parade

desgana F (falta de apetito) lack of appetite; (falta de entusiasmo) lack of enthusiasm

desganado ADJ without enthusiasm

desgarbado ADJ ungainly, gawky

desgarrado ADJ (prenda) torn; (grito) heart-rending

desgarradura F tear

desgarrar VT (rasgar) to tear; (causar dolor) to break one's heart; **—se** to tear, to pull

desgarro M muscle pull

desgarrón M tear

desgastar VT to wear away; **—se** to get worn away

desgaste M wear and tear

desglosar VT (una suma) to itemize; (un documento) to separate out

desgracia F (infortunio) misfortune; (infelicidad) unhappiness; **—s personales** casualties; **caer en —** to fall into disgrace / disfavor

desgraciado -da ADJ (desafortunado) unfortunate; (infeliz) unhappy; MF (persona desafortunada) unfortunate person; (hombre despreciable) *vulg* bastard; F (mujer desgraciada) *vulg* bitch

desgranar VT (granos) to thrash, to thresh; (guisantes) to shell

desgravable ADJ tax-deductible

desgreñado ADJ disheveled, unkempt

desgreñar VT to dishevel; **—se** to muss up one's hair

desguazar[9] VT to scrap

deshabitado ADJ (territorio) uninhabited; (casa) vacant

deshacer[30] VT (una acción) to undo; (una cama) to strip; (una cosa) to destroy; (un sólido en un líquido) to dissolve; (un nudo) to untie; **— la maleta** to unpack the suitcase; **—se de** to get rid of; **—se en elogios** to rave about

desharrapado ADJ ragged

deshelar[1] VT to thaw

desheredar VT to disinherit

deshielo M thaw

deshierbar VT to weed

deshilachar VT to unravel

deshojado ADJ leafless

deshojar VT to strip of leaves; **—se** (un árbol)

to shed leaves; (un libro) to lose pages

deshonestidad F (falta de honradez) dishonesty; (falta de recato) immodesty

deshonesto ADJ (no honrado) dishonest; (no modesto) immodest

deshonra F dishonor, disgrace

deshonrar VT to dishonor, to disgrace

deshonroso ADJ dishonorable

deshora LOC ADV **a** — at an inopportune time; **comer a** — to eat between meals

deshuesar VT (un fruto) to stone; (un animal) to bone

deshumanizar[9] VT to dehumanize

desidia F indolence

desierto ADJ (lugar) deserted; (premio) unawarded; M (región árida) desert; (región poco fértil y no habitada) wilderness

designación F (acción de designar, nombre) designation; (nombramiento) appointment

designar VT to designate; (a un funcionario) to appoint

designio M design

desigual ADJ (pelea) one-sided; (actuación) uneven; (números) not equal; (rango) unequal; (terreno) uneven

desigualdad F inequality; (del terreno) roughness

desilusión F disillusion, disappointment

desilusionar VT to disillusion, to disappoint; —**se** to become disillusioned/ disappointed

desinencia F ending

desinfectante ADJ & M disinfectant

desinfectar VT to disinfect

desinflado ADJ (globo, persona) deflated; (neumático) flat; M flat tire

desinflar VT to deflate

desinformación F disinformation

desinformar VT to misinform

desinhibido ADJ uninhibited

desintegración F disintegration; — **atómica** atomic decay

desintegrarse VI to disintegrate; (materia radiactiva) to decay

desinterés M (falta de interés) lack of interest; (generosidad) unselfishness

desinteresado ADJ (que no muestra interés) disinterested; (generoso) unselfish, selfless

desistir VI to desist

deslavado ADJ faded

deslavar VT (quitar color) to fade; (lavar ligeramente) to wash superficially

desleal ADJ (persona) disloyal, faithless; (competencia) unfair

desleír[15] VT to mix with a liquid

deslindar VT to mark off

desliz M slipup

deslizamiento M slide, glide

deslizar[9] VT (un patín) to slip, to slide, to glide; (una tarjeta) to swipe; —**se** (un patín) to slide, to glide; (un error) to slip by

deslucido ADJ (actuación) dull; (color) dingy

deslucir[13b] VT (un espectáculo) to tarnish; (color) to make dingy

deslumbramiento M dazzle

deslumbrante ADJ dazzling

deslumbrar VT to dazzle; —**se** to be dazzled

deslustrar VT to tarnish

deslustre M tarnish

desmadejado ADJ (fatigado) exhausted; (desgarbado) ungainly

desmadejar VT to exhaust

desmán M abuse

desmantelar VT to dismantle

desmañado ADJ awkward, clumsy

desmayar VI to lose courage; —**se** to faint, to pass out

desmayo M faint, swoon; **peleó sin** — he fought unflaggingly

desmedido ADJ excessive

desmejorar VI (empeorar el aspecto) to look worse; (debilitarse) to get worse

desmembrar VT to dismember

desmentido M denial

desmentir[3] VT to deny

desmenuzar[9] VT (pan) to crumble; (zanahorias) to mince

desmerecer[13] VI **no** — **de** to compare favorably with

desmesurado ADJ (esfuerzo) inordinate; (orejas) too large

desmigajar VT to crumb, to crumble

desmitificar[6] VT to debunk

desmochar VT to top, to cut the top off of

desmontar VT (limpiar un monte) to clear; (desarmar) to dismantle, to take apart; (derribar de una caballería) to throw; —**se** to dismount

desmoralizar[9] VT to demoralize; —**se** to become demoralized

desmoronar VT to crumble

desmovilizar[9] VT to demobilize

desnatar VT to skim

desnaturalizado ADJ (madre) unnatural; (aceite) denatured

desnudar VT to undress; —**se** to get undressed

desnudez F nakedness

desnudo ADJ nude, naked

desnutrición F malnutrition

desnutrido ADJ underfed, malnourished

desobedecer[13] VT to disobey
desobediencia F disobedience; **— civil** civil disobedience
desobediente ADJ disobedient
desocupación F (paro) unemployment; (abandono de vivienda) vacating
desocupado ADJ (asiento, casa) unoccupied, empty; (tiempo) idle; (que no trabaja) unemployed
desocupar VT to vacate; **—se** to get free
desodorante M deodorant
desoír[35] VT to turn a deaf ear to
desolación F desolation
desolado ADJ desolate, bleak
desolar VT to lay waste to, to desolate; **—se** to be desolated
desollar[2] VT to skin; **— vivo** to skin alive
desorbitado ADJ out of proportion; (ojos) bulging
desorden M disorder, disarray; **— público** public disturbance; **en —** in disarray
desordenado ADJ (persona, situación) messy; (niño, vida) wild; (cuarto) untidy, disorderly; (archivo) disorganized
desordenar VT to mess up
desorganización F disorganization
desorganizado ADJ disorganized
desorientar VT to disorient; (confundir) to confuse; **—se** to lose one's bearings, to become disoriented
desovar VT to spawn
desoxidar VT to deoxidize
despabilado ADJ (despierto) wide-awake; (listo) on the ball
despabilar VT (cortar el pabilo) to trim the wick of; (despertar) to awaken; **—se** to wake up
despachar VT (problemas) to dispatch; (una carta) to mail; (a un cliente) to take care of; (mercancías) to ship; (a una víctima) to bump off; (un pedido) to fill; **— al público** to sell to the public; **—se a su gusto** to speak one's mind
despacho M (oficina) office; (comunicación) dispatch; (envío de cartas) mailing; (envío de mercancías) shipping
despachurrar VT to squash
despacio ADV slow, slowly
desparasitar VT to worm
desparejo ADJ uneven
desparpajo M (desenvoltura) ease; (descaro) impudence
desparramar VT to scatter; **—se** to be scattered
desparramo M (lío) commotion; (de libros) clutter
despatarrarse VT (caerse) to sprawl; (abrirse

de piernas) to spread one's legs
despecho M spite; **por —** out of spite
despectivo ADJ derogatory, pejorative
despedazar[9] VT to tear to pieces
despedida F farewell; **— de soltero** bachelor party
despedir[5] VT (acompañar a una persona que se va) to see off; (echar de un empleo) to fire, to dismiss; (emitir un dolor) to emit, to give off; **despídeme de tus padres** say good-bye to your parents for me; **—se (de)** to take leave (of), to say good-bye (to)
despegar[7] VT (dos cosas pegadas) to detach; VI (un avión) to take off; (un cohete) to blast off; **—se** to become detached
despegue M (de avión) takeoff; (de cohete) blastoff, liftoff
despeinado ADJ unkempt
despejado ADJ (el cielo) clear, cloudless; (un camino) clear; (la frente) with one's hair pulled back; (una persona) bright
despejar VT (el campo) to clear; VI (una duda, el cielo) to clear up; **—se** to sober up
despellejar VT to skin
despensa F pantry
despeñadero M cliff
despeñar VT to push off a precipice; **—se** to fall down a precipice
despepitar VT (una granada) to seed; (una manzana) to core; **—se por una cosa** to be crazy about something
desperdiciar VT to waste; **—se** to go to waste
desperdicio M waste; **—s** scraps
desperdigar[7] VT to scatter; **—se** to be scattered
desperezarse[9] VI to stretch
desperezo M stretch
desperfecto M damage; **— mecánico** mechanical breakdown
despertador M alarm clock
despertar[1] VT (a una persona) to awaken, to wake up; (sospecha) to arouse; (interés, deseo) to kindle; **—se** to wake up
despiadado ADJ merciless, heartless, ruthless
despido M dismissal, termination
despierto ADJ (no dormido) awake; (vivaracho) alert
despilfarrador ADJ wasteful
despilfarrar VT to squander
despilfarro M waste
despistado ADJ absent-minded
despistar VT to throw off the track; (a un perseguidor) to lose; **—se** to get confused
desplantador M trowel

desplante M rude remark

desplazar[9] VT to displace; **—se** to move

desplegar[1,7] VT (algo plegado) to unfold; (una bandera) to unfurl; (tropas) to deploy; (interés) to display

despliegue M display

desplomarse VI (edificio, precios) to collapse; (una persona) to slump

desplome M collapse

desplumar VT (un ave) to pluck; (a una víctima) to fleece

despoblado ADJ uninhabited; **— de árboles** treeless; M open country

despojar VT to despoil; **—se** to shed leaves

despojos M PL (de batalla) spoils; (mortales) remains

desportilladura F chip

desportillar VT to chip

desposeer VT to dispossess

déspota MF INV despot

despótico ADJ despotic

despotismo M despotism

despotricar[6] VI to rant

despreciable ADJ (vil) contemptible, despicable, worthless; (insignificante) negligible

despreciar VT (menospreciar) to despise, to look down on; (rechazar) to snub

desprecio M (menosprecio) contempt, disdain; (rechazo) snub

desprender VT (un cierre) to unfasten; (algo prendido) to detach; (gases) to give off; **—se de algo** to part with something; **—se la ropa** to undo one's clothes; **de lo dicho se desprende que** from what has been said it follows that

desprendimiento M (de retina) detachment; (de energía) release; (de tierra) landslide; (generosidad) generosity

despreocupado ADJ carefree

desprestigiar VT to discredit; **—se** to lose one's prestige

desprestigio M loss of prestige

desprevenido ADJ unprepared; **tomar —** to take by surprise

desproporcionado ADJ disproportionate, out of proportion

despropósito M nonsense

desprovisto ADJ **— de** lacking in

después ADV after, afterward; **— de** after; **— de todo** after all

despuntar VI/VT to blunt; **—se** to become blunt

desquiciar VT to unhinge; **—se** to come unhinged

desquitarse VI to get even

desquite M getting even

desregular VT to deregulate

destacado ADJ outstanding

destacamento M military detachment, military detail

destacar[6] VT (tropas) to detach; (una cualidad) to accentuate; VI to stand out; **—se** to stand out

destajo LOC ADV **a —** by the job

destapar VT (una cacerola) to take the top off of; (un plan, a un niño) to uncover; **—se** (en la cama) to uncover; (desnudarse) to bare all

destartalado ADJ dilapidated

destellar VI to flash

destello M flash

destemplado ADJ (persona) feverish; (sonido) out of tune

desteñido ADJ washed-out

desteñir[5,18] VI/VT to fade; VI to run; **—se** to fade

desternillarse VI **— de risa** to die laughing

desterrado -da ADJ exiled, banished; MF exile

desterrar[1] VT to exile, to banish

destetar VT to wean

destierro M exile, banishment

destilación F distillation

destilar VT to distill

destilería F distillery

destinar VT (determinar el destino) to destine; (dirigir) to address; (asignar) to commit

destinatario -ria MF addressee, recipient

destino M (hado) destiny, fate, lot; (uso) use; (lugar adonde se viaja) destination

destitución F dismissal

destituir[31] VT to dismiss

destornillador M screwdriver

destoxificación F detoxification

destrabar VT to untie

destreza F dexterity, skill

destripar VT to gut

destronar VT to dethrone

destrozar[9] VT (estropear) to ruin; (causar grandes daños) to destroy; (derrotar) to rout

destrozo M damage

destrucción F destruction

destructible ADJ destructible

destructivo ADJ destructive

destructor -ra ADJ destructive; M (buque) destroyer; MF (persona) destroyer

destruir[31] VT (reducir a pedazos) to destroy, to obliterate; (estropear) to ruin

desunir VT to divide; **—se** to come apart

desusado ADJ (no frecuente) unusual; (no usado) obsolete

desuso M disuse, obsolescence; **caer en —** to fall into disuse

desvaído ADJ faded

desvainar VT to hull, to husk

desvalido ADJ helpless

desvalijar VT (un cuarto) to ransack; (a una persona) to clean out

desvalimiento M helplessness

desván M attic

desvanecer[13] VT (un color) to fade; (un contorno) to blur; **—se** (una persona) to faint; (un color, arrugas) to fade; (un sonido) to trail off

desvanecido ADJ (una persona) fainted; (un color) faded; (un contorno) blurred

desvanecimiento M (de una persona) fainting; (de colores) fading; (de un contorno) blurring

desvariar[16] VI to rave

desvarío M raving

desvelado ADJ sleepless

desvelar VT to keep awake; **—se** to be sleepless

desvelo M (falta de sueño) sleeplessness; **—s** (esfuerzos) efforts

desvencijado ADJ dilapidated, rickety; **estoy —** I'm all beat up

desventaja F disadvantage; **estar en —** to be at a disadvantage

desventura F misfortune

desventurado ADJ unfortunate

desvergonzado ADJ shameless

desvergüenza F shamelessness

desvestir[5] VT to undress; **—se** to get undressed, to undress

desviación F (de una norma) deviation, divergence; (para coches) detour; (de fondos) diversion; (de la columna vertebral) curvature; **— estándar** standard deviation

desviar[16] VT (la vista) to avert; (fondos, tráfico) to divert; (un golpe) to ward off; (una conversación) to steer; (un tren) to sidetrack; **—se de** (un camino) to stray from; (una norma) to deviate from

desvío M (camino secundario) side road; (desviación) detour

desvirtuar[17] VT to distort; **—se** to become distorted

desvivirse VI **— por hacer algo** to bend over backward to do something; **— por alguien** to go out of one's way for someone

detallado ADJ detailed

detallar VT to detail, to go into detail about

detalle M (pormenor) detail; (venta al por menor) retail; (lista) list; **¡qué —!** how thoughtful! **con / al / en —** in detail

detallista ADJ (cuidadoso) meticulous; (considerado) thoughtful; M (comercio) retail; MF retailer

detectar VT to detect

detective M detective; **— privado** private eye

detención F (arresto) detention, arrest; (de un vehículo) stop; **— domiciliaria** house arrest; **— ilegal** false arrest

detener[44] VT (arrestar) to detain, to arrest; (parar) to stop; **—se** to stop; **—se en** to linger on; **—se a pensar** to stop to think

detenido ADJ thorough

detenimiento LOC ADV **con —** with care

detergente ADJ & M detergent

deteriorar VT to deteriorate

deterioro M deterioration

determinación F determination

determinar VT to determine

detestable ADJ detestable

detestar VT to detest

detonación F detonation; **hacer detonaciones** to backfire

detonar VI/VT to detonate

detrás ADV behind; **— de** (en el espacio) behind; (en el tiempo) after; **por —** behind

detritus M debris

deuda F debt

deudor -ora ADJ & MF debtor; **— hipotecario** mortgagor

devaluación F devaluation

devanar VT to spool; **—se los sesos** to rack one's brain

devaneo M (acción de pasatiempo) idle pursuit; (amorío) fling

devastar VT to devastate

devengar[7] VT to earn

devoción F devotion

devolución F return

devolver[2,51] VT (volver al dueño) to return; VI (vomitar) to throw up

devorar VT to devour

devoto ADJ (pío) devout; (que muestra devoción) devoted

dextrosa F dextrose

día M day; **— a —** day-to-day; **— tras —** day after day; **al —** up-to-date; **al otro —** on the next day; **de — by** by day; **de todos los —s** everyday; **el — de mañana** in the future; **hoy —** nowadays; **no veo el —** I can't wait; **ponerse al —** to catch up; **por —** by the day; **todo el —** all day; **todos los —s** every day; **un — sí y otro no** every other day; **vivir al —** to live from hand to mouth

diabetes F SG diabetes

diablo M devil; **irse al —** *vulg* to go to hell; **pobre —** poor devil; **¿por qué —s dices eso?** *fam* why the heck are you saying that?

diablura F deviltry, mischief

diabólico ADJ diabolic, devilish

diácono M deacon

diacrítico ADJ & M diacritic

diafragma M diaphragm

diagnosticar[6] VT to diagnose

diagonal ADJ & F diagonal

diagrama M diagram; **— de flujo** flow chart

dial M dial

dialéctica F dialectic

dialéctico ADJ dialectic

dialecto M dialect

dialectología F dialectology

diálisis F dialysis

dialogar[7] VI to dialog, to hold talks

diálogo M dialog, conversation; **— de sordos** conversation in which no one listens

diamante M diamond; **— en bruto** diamond in the rough

diámetro M diameter

diana F bull's eye

diapasón M tuning fork

diapositiva F slide

diario ADJ daily; M (periódico) newspaper; (de sucesos personales) journal, diary; (de navegación) log; **a —** every day; **de —** everyday; **llevar un —** to keep a diary

diarrea F diarrhea

diatriba F diatribe

dibujante MF illustrator

dibujar VT to draw; **—se** to appear, to loom

dibujo M (arte de dibujar, cosa dibujada) drawing; (diseño) design; **— al carbón** charcoal drawing; **—s animados** animated cartoon

dicción F diction

diccionario M dictionary

dicha F happiness

dicharachero ADJ witty

dicho ADJ aforementioned; M saying

dichoso ADJ happy; **todo el — día** the whole blessed day

diciembre M December

dicotomía F dichotomy

dictado M (ejercicio) dictation; (orden) dictate; **escribir al —** to take dictation

dictador -ora MF dictator

dictadura F dictatorship

dictamen M (opinión) report; (judicial) ruling

dictaminar VI (dar una opinión) to report;

(fallar) to rule

dictar VT to dictate; **— clase** to teach class; **— sentencia** to rule

diecinueve NUM nineteen

dieciocho NUM eighteen

dieciséis NUM sixteen

diecisiete NUM seventeen

diente M (de persona, sierra) tooth; (de víbora) fang; (de rueda dentada) cog; (de tenedor) prong; **— de león** dandelion; **— de leche** baby tooth; **—s postizos** false teeth; **entre —s** under one's breath; **tener buen —** to have a good appetite

diesel M diesel

diestra F right hand

diestro -tra ADJ (habilidoso) skillful, deft; (no zurdo) right-handed; MF right-handed person; **a diestra y siniestra** on all sides

dieta F diet; **estar a —** to be on a diet

diez NUM ten

diezmar VT to decimate

diezmo M tithe; **pagar el —** to tithe

difamación F (oral) slander; (escrito) libel

difamar VT to defame, to malign; (oralmente) to slander; (por escrito) to libel

difamatorio ADJ slanderous

diferencia F difference; **a — de** unlike; **hacer —s entre** to treat differently; **partir la —** to split the difference

diferencial ADJ & M (distancia, pieza de coche) differential; F (matemática) differential

diferenciar VT to differentiate; **—se de** to differ from

diferente ADJ different

diferir[3] VT (aplazar) to defer; VI (ser diferente) to differ

difícil ADJ difficult, hard

dificultad F difficulty

dificultar VT to make difficult

dificultoso ADJ difficult

difteria F diphtheria

difundir VT (luz) to diffuse; (noticias) to broadcast

difunto -ta ADJ & MF deceased

difusión F (de luz) diffusion; (de noticias) broadcasting

difuso ADJ diffuse

digerible ADJ digestible

digerir[3] VT to digest

digestible ADJ digestible

digestión F digestion

digestivo ADJ digestive

digesto M digest

digital ADJ digital

dígito M digit

dignarse VI to deign
dignatario -ria MF dignitary
dignidad F dignity
digno ADJ (respetable) worthy; (orgulloso) dignified; — **de confianza** trustworthy; — **de elogio** praiseworthy
digresión F digression
dije M charm
dilación LOC ADV **sin** — without delay
dilatación F (de un metal, parte dilatada) expansion; (del ojo) dilation
dilatar VT (pupila, capilares, útero) to dilate; (metal, músculo) to expand; (posponer) to defer; —**se en un asunto** to dwell on a subject
dilema M dilemma
diletante MF dilettante
diligencia F (laboriosidad) diligence, industry; (vehículo) stagecoach
diligente ADJ diligent, industrious
dilucidar VT to elucidate
diluido ADJ dilute
diluir[31] VT (una solución) to dilute; (pintura, sopa) to thin
diluvio M deluge
dimensión F dimension
dimes M PL — **y diretes** gossip; **andar en** — **y diretes** to quibble
diminutivo ADJ & M diminutive
diminuto ADJ (tamaño) diminutive; (cantidad) minute
dimisión F resignation
dimitir VI to resign
Dinamarca F Denmark
dinámica F dynamics
dinámico ADJ dynamic
dinamismo M vigor
dinamita F dynamite
dinamitar VT to dynamite
dínamo M dynamo
dinastía F dynasty
dineral M fortune
dinero M money; — **contante y sonante** ready cash, hard cash; — **de plástico** plastic, credit card; — **sucio** dirty money
dinosaurio M dinosaur
diodo M diode; — **electroluminiscente** light-emitting diode
Dios M God; **dios** god; — **dirá** we'll see; — **los cría y ellos se juntan** birds of a feather flock together; — **mediante** God willing; **¡— mío!** my God! — **te lo pague** may God reward you; — **y su madre** everybody and their dog; **a la buena de** — any old way; **como** — **manda** as it should be; **¡por —!** oh, my! **que** — **te oiga** I hope you're right

diosa F goddess
diploma M diploma
diplomacia F diplomacy
diplomático -ca ADJ diplomatic; MF diplomat
diptongo M diphthong
diputación F council
diputado -da MF representative
dique M (presa) dike; (al lado de un río) levee; — **seco** dry dock
dirección F (sentido, rumbo) direction; (domicilio) address; (administración) management; (oficina de administración de una escuela) principal's office; (mecanismo para conducir, acción de conducir) steering; — **asistida** power steering
directiva F (orden) directive; (norma) guideline; (junta de directores) board of directors
directivo -va ADJ leadership; MF officer
directo ADJ (sin desviaciones, intermediarios) direct; (derecho) straight; **en** — live
director -ora MF (de una empresa) director, manager; (de una escuela) principal; (de orquesta) conductor; — **de correos** postmaster
directorio M (índice) directory; (junta directiva) board of directors
dirigente MF leader; — **sindical** union leader
dirigible M dirigible
dirigir[11] VT (una obra teatral) to direct; (una empresa) to manage; (una orquesta) to conduct; (a un turista) to guide; (un saludo, una carta, una pregunta, una crítica) to address; —**se a** (hablar con) to address; (ir a) to go to; (tratar de) to be aimed at
discar[6] VI/VT Am to dial
discernimiento M discernment, insight
discernir[1] VT to discern
disciplina F discipline
disciplinar VT to discipline
discípulo -la MF disciple
disco M (cartílago, objeto plano y circular) disk; (fonográfico) record; — **compacto** compact disk; — **duro** hard disk; **es un** — **rayado** he's a broken record
díscolo ADJ unruly
disconforme ADJ dissatisfied
discontinuo ADJ discontinuous
discordancia F discord
discordia F discord
discoteca F (lugar donde bailar) discotheque; (colección de discos) record collection
discreción F discretion; **a** — at one's own

discretion

discrepancia F discrepancy

discrepar VI to disagree; **— de** to take issue with

discreto ADJ (prudente) discreet; (de unidades indivisibles) discrete; **un partido —** a sorry game

discriminación F discrimination; **— positiva** affirmative action

discriminar VI to discriminate; **— a** to discriminate against

disculpa F (excusa) excuse; (perdón) apology

disculpable ADJ excusable

disculpar VT (excusar) to excuse; (perdonar) to forgive, to pardon; **—se** to apologize

discurrir VI (transcurrir) to pass; (exponer) to discourse

discursear VI to make speeches

discurso M (enunciado) discourse; (alocución pública) speech, address; **— de apertura** keynote address

discusión F (charla) discussion; (riña) argument

discutible ADJ debatable, questionable

discutir VT (hablar sobre) to discuss; (oponerse a) to dispute; VI (reñir) to argue

disecar[6] VT (cortar) to dissect; (preparar para conservar) to stuff

diseminación F dissemination

diseminar VT to disseminate

disensión F dissension, dissent

disenso M dissent

disentería F dysentery

disentir[3] VI to dissent, to disagree

diseñador -ora MF designer

diseñar VT to design

diseño M design; **— de interiores** interior design; **— gráfico** graphic design

disertación F lecture

disertar VI to lecture

disfraz M (para ocultarse) disguise; (de carnaval) costume

disfrazar[9] VT to disguise

disfrutar VI/VT to enjoy; **— de** to enjoy

disfrute M enjoyment

disfunción F dysfunction

disgustado ADJ (molesto) upset; (enojado) angry

disgustar VT to upset; **—se** (molestarse) to get upset; (enfadarse) to get angry

disgusto M (desagrado) unpleasantness; (discusión) quarrel; **a —** (con desgana) against one's will; (con incomodidad) uncomfortably; (en disconformidad) in conflict; **esa niña no da más que —s** that girl keeps us upset all the time

disidente ADJ & MF dissident

disimulado ADJ **hacerse el —** to pretend not to notice

disimular VI (fingir) to dissemble; (ocultar) to conceal

disimulo M (fingimiento) dissimulation; (ocultamiento) concealment

disipación F dissipation

disipar VT (niebla, calor) to dissipate; (dudas) to dispel; (miedo) to allay; (dinero) to squander; **—se** to dissipate; (miedo, dudas) to allay, to lift

dislocar[6] VT to dislocate; **—se** to get dislocated

disminuir[31] VT to diminish, to decrease, to lessen; (despreciar) to belittle

disolución F dissolution

disoluto ADJ dissolute, loose

disolvente M solvent; **— de pintura** paint thinner

disolver[2,51] VT to dissolve; (una reunión) to break up

disonancia F discord

dispar ADJ disparate

disparar VT (un arma de fuego) to shoot, to fire; (una cámara) to click; (la inflación) to trigger; VI (en fútbol) to shoot; **—le a alguien** to shoot at someone; **—se** (aumentar) to take off; (salir) to shoot out

disparatado ADJ absurd

disparatar VI to talk nonsense

disparate M absurdity, nonsense; **decir —s** to talk nonsense; **un — de plata** a ton of money; **puros —s** *vulg* pure bullshit

disparo M (acción de disparar) shooting; (tiro, herida) shot

dispensa F dispensation

dispensación F dispensation

dispensar VT to dispense; **— de** to exempt from

dispensario M dispensary

dispersar VT to disperse

dispersión F dispersal

display M display

displicencia F flippancy

displicente ADJ (comportamiento) flippant; (actitud) cavalier

disponer[39] VT (colocar) to arrange; (preparar) to prepare, to dispose; (mandar) to order; **— de** to have; **—se** to get ready; **—se a** to set about

disponible ADJ available

disposición F (voluntad) disposition; (colocación) arrangement; (de ánimo) mood; **a — de** at the disposal of

dispositivo M device; **— intrauterino** intrauterine device

dispuesto ADJ ready; **bien —** willing; **no**

estar — a to be unwilling to

disputa F (controversia) dispute; (riña) argument

disputar VI/VT to dispute; **—se el poder** to vie/challenge/contend for power; **—se la posición** to jockey for position

disquete M floppy disk

disquetera F disk drive

distancia F distance; **a —** at arm's length; **guardar —s** to keep at a distance; **¿a qué — está?** how far away is it?

distanciar VT to distance

distante ADJ distant

distar VI **dista mucho de** it's a far cry from; **dista diez kilómetros de** it's ten kilometers from

distender[1] VT (aflojar) to relax; (dilatar) to expand

distinción F distinction

distinguido ADJ distinguished

distinguir[12] VT to distinguish

distintivo ADJ distinctive, distinguishing; M distinguishing characteristic

distinto ADJ (diferente, no el mismo) different; (que se percibe con claridad) distinct

distorsión F distortion

distorsionar VT to distort

distracción F distraction

distraer[45] VT (la atención) to distract; (fondos, mano de obra) to divert; **—se** to entertain oneself

distraído ADJ distracted, absent-minded; **hacerse el —** to play dumb

distribución F distribution

distribuidor -ora MF (persona) distributor; M (pieza de un motor) distributor

distribuir[31] VT to distribute

distrito M district

Distrito de Columbia M District of Columbia

disturbio M disturbance, trouble

disuadir VT (mediante palabras) to dissuade; (mediante acciones) to deter

diurético ADJ & M diuretic

diurno ADJ (actividad) daytime; (animal) diurnal

divagación F rambling

divagar[7] VI to ramble on, to digress

diván M divan; (de psiquiatra) couch

divergencia F divergence

divergir[11] VI to diverge

diversidad F diversity

diversión F (pasatiempo) amusement, entertainment, fun; (hecho de distraer la atención) diversion

diverso ADJ diverse; **—s** various

divertido ADJ amusing, entertaining

divertir[3] VT to amuse, to entertain; **—se** to have a good time, to have fun

dividendo M dividend

dividir VT to divide; (un territorio conquistado) to partition

divieso M boil

divinidad F divinity

divino ADJ divine; **estuvo —** it was heavenly; **lo pasé —** I had a wonderful time

divisa F (señal) emblem; (moneda) currency; (moneda extranjera) foreign currency

divisar VT to make out, to catch sight of

división F division; (de un territorio conquistado) partition

divisorio ADJ dividing

divorciar VT to divorce; **—se** to get divorced

divorcio M divorce

divulgar[7] VT (un secreto) to divulge; (información) to disseminate

dobladillo M hem; **hacer —s** to hem

doblaje M dubbing

doblar VT (una sábana) to fold; (el capital) to double; (una esquina) to turn; (la voz de un actor) to dub; VI (un coche) to turn; (una campana) to knell; **—se** to bend over

doble ADJ double; **— agente** double agent; **— personalidad** split personality; **— visión** double vision; **de — caño** double-barreled; **de — filo** double-edged; **de — sentido** two-way; MF (persona muy parecida, actor sustituto) double; M (repique) knell; **—s** doubles; **el —** double

doblegar[7] VT to break

doblez M fold; F deceitfulness

doce NUM twelve

docena F dozen; **— del fraile** baker's dozen

docente ADJ teaching

dócil ADJ (persona, animal) docile, pliant; (pelo) manageable

docto ADJ learned

doctor -ora MF doctor

doctorado M doctorate

doctrina F doctrine

documental ADJ & M documentary

documentar VT to document

documento M document

dogma M dogma

dogmático ADJ dogmatic

dogo M pug

dólar M dollar

dolencia F ailment

doler[2] VI to ache, to hurt; **me duele el brazo** my arm aches, my arm is sore; **—se de** (compadecerse) to feel sorry for; (arrepentirse) to regret

doliente MF mourner

dolor M (físico) pain, ache; (espiritual) sorrow, pain; **— de barriga** bellyache; **— de cabeza** headache; **— de espalda** backache; **— de muela** toothache; **— de oídos** earache; **— de garganta** sore throat

dolorido ADJ aching, sore

doloroso ADJ painful

doma F (de caballos) breaking; (de leones) taming

domado ADJ (caballo) broken; (león) tamed

domador -ora MF (de perros) trainer; (de leones) lion tamer

domar VT (caballos, personas) to break; (leones) to tame

domesticar[6] VT to domesticate, to tame

doméstico -ca ADJ domestic; MF servant

domiciliarse VI to take up residence; **¿dónde se domicilia usted?** where do you reside?

domicilio M (casa) dwelling; (dirección) address

dominación F domination

dominador ADJ (predominante) dominant; (tiránico) domineering

dominante ADJ (predominante) dominant; (tiránico) domineering, overbearing

dominar VT (tener bajo su autoridad, ser más alto) to dominate; (reprimir los impulsos) to control, to rein in; (tener sometido a su voluntad) to domineer

domingo M Sunday; **— de Ramos** Palm Sunday; **— de Pascua** Easter Sunday

Dominica F Dominica

dominicano -na ADJ & MF Dominican

dominio M (sobre una tierra, derecho de usar una cosa) dominion; (de sí mismo) control; (de una lengua) mastery, command; (hecho de dominar) domination; (ámbito, campo) domain; **— público** public domain

dominiqués -esa ADJ & MF Dominican

dominó M (pieza) domino; (juego) dominoes

domo M dome

don M (gracia) gift; (título, jefe mafioso) don; **un — nadie** a nobody

dona F *Méx* doughnut

donación F donation

donador -ora MF donor

donaire M grace

donante MF donor

donar MF to donate

doncella F *lit* maiden

donde ADV REL where; **de —** whence, from which; **ir — el herrero** to go to the blacksmith's shop; **— no** otherwise;

—quiera wherever

dónde ADV INTERR where

donoso ADJ graceful

doña F doña

dopar VT to dope

dorado ADJ (cubierto de oro) gilt; (del color de oro) golden; M dolphinfish

dorar VT to gild; **— la píldora** to sweeten the pill

dormido ADJ asleep

dormir[4] VI/VT to sleep; **— a** to put to bed; **— a un paciente** to anesthetize a patient; **— la mona** to sleep it off; **— la siesta** to take a nap; **se me ha dormido el brazo** my arm has fallen asleep; **—se** to fall asleep

dormitar VI to doze, to snooze

dormitorio M bedroom

dorso M back, reverse

dos NUM two; **— puntos** colon; **— veces** twice; **cada — por tres** constantly; **en un — por tres** in a jiffy; **los —** both of them

DOS M DOS

dosel M canopy

dosificar[6] VT to dose

dosis F (de medicamento) dose; (de droga) hit

dotación F (de fondos) endowment; (de personal) complement

dotar VT to endow

dote F dowry; **—s** talents

draga F dredge

dragado M dredging

dragar[7] VT (para limpiar) to dredge; (para buscar objetos) to drag; M SG **dragaminas** minesweeper

dragón M (animal fantástico) dragon; (planta) snapdragon

drama M drama

dramático ADJ dramatic

dramatizar[9] VT to dramatize

dramaturgo -ga MF playwright, dramatist

drapear VI to drape

drástico ADJ drastic

drenaje M drainage

drenar VI/VT to drain

dribbling M dribble, dribbling

driblar VI/VT to dribble

dril M drill

drive M drive

drive-in M drive-in

driver M (de golf) driver

droga F drug; **— de recreo** recreational drug; **—s de diseño** designer drugs; **tomar —s** to do drugs; MF **drogadicto -ta** drug addict

drogar[7] VT to drug

drogata MF INV junkie

drogota MF INV junkie

droguería F (tienda) drugstore; (industria) drug industry

droguero -ra MF druggist

ducado M dukedom

ducha F shower; — **vaginal** vaginal douche

ducharse VI to shower

ducho ADJ skillful

dúctil ADJ (metal) ductile; (persona) flexible, supple

duda F doubt; **en** — in doubt; **fuera de** — beyond doubt; **no cabe** — there's no doubt; **poner en** — to cast doubt on; **sin** — without a doubt, undoubtedly; **sin lugar a** —**s** without doubt; **tengo una** — I have a question

dudar VT to doubt; (vacilar) to hesitate; — **de** to have doubts about

dudoso ADJ doubtful; **de dudosa honestidad** of dubious honesty

duela F stave

duelo M (combate) duel; (luto) mourning; (pena) grief; (dolientes) mourners; **estar de** — to be in mourning

duende M (gnomo) goblin, gremlin; (gracia) charm

dueño -ña MF owner; **me sentí** — **de la situación** I felt like I was in control of the situation; M landlord; F landlady

dueto M duet

dulce ADJ (sabor, personalidad) sweet; (clima) pleasant; (agua) fresh; —**amargo** bittersweet; M (cosa dulce) sweet; (mermelada) preserves, conserve

dulcería F confectionery

dulcificar[6] VT to sweeten

dulzón ADJ unpleasantly sweet

dulzor M sweetness

dulzura F sweetness

duna F dune

dúo M duet; **decir a** — to say in unison

dúplex M duplex

duplicado ADJ & M duplicate; **por** — in duplicate

duplicar[6] VT to duplicate

duplicidad F duplicity

duque M duke

duquesa F duchess

durabilidad F durability

duración F duration; (de una película, vocal) length

duradero ADJ (ropa) durable, serviceable; (pilas) long-lasting

durante PREP during; — **el mandato de los demócratas** under the Democrats; — **muchos años** for/over many years

durar VI/VT to last

duraznero M peach tree

durazno M (fruto) peach; (árbol) peach tree

dureza F (de metal) hardness; (del clima, de la expresión, de una tempestad) severity; (del invierno) harshness; (de un boxeador) toughness; (del cuero) stiffness

durmiente ADJ sleeping; M railroad tie, sleeper

duro ADJ (metal, golpe, droga, agua) hard; (clima, tormenta) severe; (invierno, expresión, sonido) harsh; (soldado) tough; (grifo) stuck; (viento) strong; (autoridad) inflexible; (pan) stale; (cuero) stiff; — **de corazón** hard-hearted; — **de entendederas** slow on the uptake; **a duras penas** barely; M five peseta coin; **no tengo un** — I'm flat broke

DVD M DVD

Ee

e CONJ and

ebanista MF cabinetmaker

ébano M ebony

ebrio ADJ drunk, inebriated

ebullición F boiling

eccema M eczema

echar VT (una pelota, redes) to throw, to cast; (yemas, hojas) to sprout; (a un empleado) to fire; (humo, olor) to give off; (un líquido) to pour; (a un borracho) to throw out; — **abajo** to knock down; — **a la basura** to throw away; — **al mar** to put to sea; — **al correo** to mail; — **anclas** to drop anchor; — **a pique** to sink; — **carnes** to get fat; — **de menos** to miss; — **de ver** to notice; — **mano de** to seize upon; — **la culpa** to blame; — **por la borda** to jettison; — **raíces** to take root; — **sangre** to bleed; — **suertes** to draw lots; — **una carta** to mail a letter; — **una siesta** to take a nap; — **un vistazo a** to glance at, to take a look at; **te echo una carrera** I'll race you; —**le el muerto a alguien** to pass the buck to someone; —**se** to lie down; —**se a correr** to bolt; —**se a** to start to; —**se a perder** to spoil; —**se a reír** to burst out laughing; —**se para atrás** to lean back; —**se atrás** to back down

ecléctico ADJ eclectic

eclesiástico ADJ & M ecclesiastic

eclipsar VT to eclipse; (superar) to eclipse, to outshine, to overshadow; **—se** to fade

eclipse M eclipse; **— de sol** solar eclipse; **— de luna** lunar eclipse

eco M echo; **hacer —** to echo; **hacerse — de** to repeat

ecología F (medio ambiente) environment; (ciencia) ecology

ecológico ADJ environmental

ecologista ADJ environmental; MF environmentalist

economato M commissary

economía F (conjunto de actividades de producción) economy; (ciencia) economics; (familiar) finances; **— doméstica** home economics; **—s** savings; **hacer —s** to be thrifty

económico ADJ (relativo a la economía) economic; (que gasta poco) frugal, thrifty; (que cuesta poco) economical

economista MF economist

economizar[9] VT to economize, to save

ecosistema M ecosystem

ecuación F equation

ecuador M equator

Ecuador M Ecuador

ecualizar[9] VT to equalize

ecuatoriano -na ADJ & MF Ecuadorian

ecuménico ADJ ecumenical

edad F age; **— avanzada** ripe old age; **— mental** mental age; **— de Piedra** Stone Age; **— Media** Middle Ages; **— de merecer** marriageable age

edición F (tienda, ejemplar) edition; (acción de editar) publication; **— de sobremesa** desktop publishing

edicto M edict

edificación F building

edificar[6] VT (construir) to build; (infundir sentimientos morales) to edify, to uplift

edificio M building

editar VT to edit, to publish

editor -ora ADJ publishing; MF editor

editorial ADJ publishing; F publishing house; M editorial

editorializar[9] VI to editorialize

edredón M comforter

educación F (en la escuela) education; (de normas sociales) breeding; **— a distancia** distance learning; **— cívica** civics; **— especial** special education; **— física** physical education

educado ADJ (cortés) well-bred; (instruido) educated

educador -ora MF educator

educar[6] VT (a una persona en la escuela) to educate; (a una persona en la casa, la voz) to train

educativo ADJ educational

edulcorante M sweetener

EEUU (Estados Unidos) M SG USA

efectivo ADJ (eficaz) effective; (real) actual; **hacer —** (un cheque) to cash; (una deuda) to pay off; (una amenaza) to make good on; M cash; **en —** in cash; **—s** troops

efecto M (resultado) effect, result; (letra comercial) bill of exchange; (rotación) English, spin; **en —** in fact; **llevar a —** to carry out; **surtir —** to work; **— invernadero** green house effect; **—s especiales** special effects; **—s personales** personal effects; **perder —** to wear off; **rebotar con —** to glance off; **a estos —s** to this effect; **para los —s** to all intents and purposes; **por — de** as a consequence of

efectuar[17] VT to effect; **—se** to be carried out

eficacia F efficacy; **— de una ley** force of law

eficaz ADJ effective

eficiencia F efficiency

eficiente ADJ efficient

efigie F effigy; **quemar en —** to burn in effigy

efímero ADJ ephemeral, fleeting

efusivo ADJ effusive

egipcio -cia ADJ & MF Egyptian

Egipto M Egypt

égloga F pastoral

ego M ego

egocéntrico ADJ egocentric, self-centered

egoísmo M selfishness

egoísta ADJ selfish; MF selfish person

egotismo M egotism

egresado -da MF graduate

eje M (de la Tierra) axis; (de un vehículo) axle; **— del pistón** piston rod; **eso me parte por el —** that messes me up

ejecución F (de un condenado) execution; (de un plan, una orden) carrying out, execution; (de una tarea) performance; (de una propiedad) foreclosure

ejecutar VT (a un condenado) to execute; (un plan, una orden) to carry out; (una tarea, música) to perform; (una propiedad) to foreclose on

ejecutivo -va ADJ & MF executive

ejemplar ADJ exemplary, model; M (libro) copy; (individuo) specimen

ejemplificar[6] VT to exemplify

ejemplo M (cosa típica) example; (modelo) model; **a — de** on the example of; **dar —** to set an example; **por —** for example

ejercer [10a] VT (una profesión) to practice; (influencia, fuerza) to exert; (poder) to wield

ejercicio M exercise; (de una profesión) practice; **hacer —** to take exercise; **— contable** accounting period; **— físico** physical exercise; **en —** active

ejercitar VT (la vista, los músculos) to exercise; (a soldados) to drill; (a alumnos) to train; **—se** to train

ejército M army; **el —** the military

ejido M common

ejote M *Méx* green bean

el ART DEF M the; **— de la derecha** the one on the right; **— que** the one that; **— que sepa** whoever knows

él PRON PERS M SG (como sujeto) he; **— dijo** he said; (como objeto) him; **para —** for him; **le di el libro a —** I gave the book to him; **estamos hablando de —** we're talking about him; **el libro de —** his book

elaboración F (de miel, comida) making; (de un método) development; (de un informe) drafting

elaborado ADJ elaborate

elaborar VT (un método) to elaborate, to develop; (comida) to make; (un informe) to draft

elasticidad F elasticity

elástico ADJ (sustancia) elastic; (cuerpo) supple; (horario) flexible; M elastic

elección F (votación) election; (selección) choice, selection; **no tuve —** I had no choice

electo ADJ elect

elector -ora ADJ electoral; MF elector

electoral ADJ electoral

electricidad F electricity; **— estática** static electricity

electricista MF electrician

eléctrico ADJ (aparato) electric; (instalación, corriente) electrical

electrificar [6] VT to electrify

electrizado ADJ electrified

electrizante ADJ electrifying

electrizar [9] VT (suministrar electricidad) to electrify; (emocionar) to galvanize, to electrify

electrocardiograma M electrocardiogram

electrocutar VT to electrocute

electrodo M electrode

electrodoméstico M electrical appliance

electroencefalograma M electroencephalogram

electroimán M electromagnet

electrólisis F electrolysis

electromagnético ADJ electromagnetic

electrón M electron

electrónica F electronics

electrónico ADJ electronic

elefante M elephant

elegancia F elegance

elegante ADJ (que tiene gracia) elegant; (en el vestir) stylish, smart

elegible ADJ eligible

elegir [5, 11] VT to choose, to select; (votar) to elect

elemental ADJ (sencillo) elementary; (básico) elemental

elemento M element

elenco M cast

elevación F elevation; **tirar por —** to throw high in the air

elevado ADJ (pensamiento, estilo) elevated; (fiebre, montaña) high; (precios) high

elevador M elevator

elevar VT (en una jerarquía) to elevate; (precios, voz, objeto) to raise; (el espíritu) to uplift; **— la vista** to look up; **— al cuadrado** to square; **— al cubo** to cube; **—se a** to go up to, to rise to; **el rascacielos se eleva sobre la ciudad** the skyscraper towers over the city

elfo M elf

eliminación F elimination

eliminar VT to eliminate

eliminatoria F heat

elíptico ADJ elliptical

elite / élite F elite

elitista ADJ & MF elitist

ella PRON PERS F SG (como sujeto) she; **— dijo** she said; (como objeto) her; **para —** for her; **le di el libro a —** I gave the book to her; **el libro de —** her book

ellas PRON PERS F PL (como sujeto) they; **— dijeron** they said; (como objeto) them; **para —** for them; **les di el libro a —** I gave them the book; **el libro de —** their book

ello PRON it; **— es que** the fact is that

ellos PRON M PL (como sujeto) they; **— dijeron** they said; (como objeto) them; **para —** for them; **les di el libro a —** I gave them the book; **el libro de —** their book

elocuencia F eloquence

elocuente ADJ eloquent; **las estadísticas son —s** the statistics speak for themselves

elogiar VT to praise

elogio M praise

elote M *Méx* corn on the cob

elucidación F elucidation

elucidar VT to elucidate

eludir VT to elude, to avoid, to dodge
emanación F emanation, flow
emanar VI/VT to emanate
emancipación F emancipation
emancipar VT to emancipate; **—se** to become free
emascular VT to emasculate
embadurnar VT to daub
embajada F embassy
embajador -ora MF ambassador
embalador -ora MF packer
embalaje M packing
embalar VT to pack; VI to accelerate
embaldosar VT to tile
embalsamar VT (a un muerto) to embalm; (un animal) to stuff
embalse M reservoir
embanderar VT to adorn with flags
embarazada ADJ pregnant
embarazar[9] VT (impedir) to hamper; (fecundar) to make pregnant; **—se** to get pregnant
embarazo M (obstáculo) impediment; (estado de embarazada) pregnancy
embarazoso ADJ embarrassing, awkward
embarcación F boat, embarkation, craft
embarcadero M wharf, pier
embarcar[6] VT (pasajeros) to embark; (mercancías) to load; **—se** to embark, to go aboard; **—se en** to embark upon
embargar[7] VT to seize; **estar embargado de emoción** to be overcome with emotion
embargo M embargo; **— judicial** seizure; **imponer un —** to embargo; **sin —** nevertheless, however
embarque M (de mercancías) loading; (de pasajeros) embarkation
embarrado ADJ smeared with mud
embarrar VT to smear with mud, to muddy
embate M lashing
embaucador M confidence man
embaucar[6] VT to dupe
embeber VT to soak up; **—se** to be enraptured
embelesar VT to enrapture
embeleso M rapture
embellecer[13] VI/VT to beautify
embestida F charge
embestir[5] VI/VT to charge
embetunar VT to polish
emblanquecer[13] VI/VT to whiten
emblema M emblem
embobar VT to amaze; **—se** to be amazed
embolia F embolism
émbolo M piston, plunger
embolsar VT (dinero) to pocket; (una compra) to bag
emborrachar VT (a una persona) to intoxicate; (el carburador) to flood; **—se** to get drunk
emborronar VT (manchar) to blot; (hacer impreciso) to blur
emboscada F ambush
emboscar[6] VT to ambush; **—se** to lie in ambush
embotamiento M (efecto de embotar) dullness, bluntness; (acción de embotar) dulling
embotar VT to dull
embotelladora F bottling plant
embotellamiento M (acción de embotellar) bottling; (de tráfico) traffic jam, bottleneck
embotellar VT (cerveza) to bottle; (tráfico) to bottle up
embozar[9] VT to conceal
embragar[7] VI to engage the clutch
embrague M clutch
embriagado ADJ drunken
embriagar[7] VT to intoxicate; **—se** to become intoxicated
embriaguez F intoxication, drunkenness
embridar VT to bridle
embrión M embryo
embrollar VT to embroil
embrollo M muddle
embromar VT to kid
embrujar VT to bewitch
embrujo M spell
embrutecer[13] VT to stupefy
embudo M funnel
embuste M lie
embustero -ra MF liar, trickster
embutido M sausage
embutir VT to cram, to jam
emergencia F emergency
emerger[11b] VI to emerge; (del agua) to surface
emigración F (de personas) emigration; (de animales) migration
emigrante ADJ & MF emigrant
emigrar VI (personas) to emigrate; (animales) to migrate
eminencia F eminence; **— gris** gray eminence
eminente ADJ eminent
emisario -ria MF emissary; M outlet
emisión F (de acciones, billetes) issue; (de un olor) discharge; (de programas) broadcast; (de vapor) emission
emisor ADJ emitting; M transmitter
emisora F radio/television station
emitir VT (un olor, vapor) to emit; (juicios) to pronounce; (dinero, acciones) to issue;

vɪ/vᴛ (programas) to broadcast; —**se** to be on the air

emoción ꜰ emotion; **¡qué —!** what a thrill!

emocional ᴀᴅᴊ emotional

emocionante ᴀᴅᴊ (conmovedor) touching; (apasionante) exciting

emocionar vᴛ (apasionar) to excite; (conmover) to move, to touch; —**se** (estar apasionado) to be excited; (estar conmovido) to be touched

emotivo ᴀᴅᴊ emotional

empacador -ora ᴍꜰ packer

empacar[6] vᴛ (regalos, mercancías) to pack; (algodón) to bale

empachar vᴛ to cause indigestion; —**se** to suffer indigestion; —**se de** to get sick on, to stuff oneself with

empacho ᴍ (indigestión) indigestion; (cohibición) inhibition; **no tener — en** to have no qualms about

empalagar[7] vɪ/vᴛ to cloy

empalagoso ᴀᴅᴊ cloying, saccharine

empalar vᴛ to impale

empalizada ꜰ stockade, palisade

empalmar vᴛ to splice; **— con** to join

empalme ᴍ (de caminos) junction; (de cuerdas) splice; **— genético** gene splicing

empanada ꜰ turnover, pie

empanar vᴛ to bread

empañado ᴀᴅᴊ (vidrio) misty, foggy; (metal, reputación) tarnished

empañar vᴛ (vidrio) to fog up, to blur; (metal, reputación) to tarnish

empapado ᴀᴅᴊ soggy, sopping wet

empapamiento ᴍ soaking

empapar vᴛ (mojar) to soak, to drench; (recoger con algo) to soak up; —**se** (mojarse) to get soaked; (enterarse) to find out all about

empapelado ᴍ wallpapering

empapelar vᴛ to paper, to wallpaper; **— las calles** to plaster the streets

empaque ᴍ (acción de empacar) packing; (envoltorio) packaging

empaquetadura ꜰ gasket

empaquetar vᴛ to pack, to package; —**se** to get dolled up

emparedado ᴍ sandwich

emparejar vᴛ (una carga, un partido) to even up; vɪ/vᴛ (los enamorados) to pair up

emparentado ᴀᴅᴊ akin, related

emparentarse vɪ to become related by marriage

empastar vᴛ to fill

empaste ᴍ filling

empatar vɪ to tie

empate ᴍ tie

empatía ꜰ empathy

empecinado ᴀᴅᴊ stubborn

empedernido ᴀᴅᴊ (criminal) hardened; (mujeriego) incorrigible; (solterón) confirmed

empedernirse[50] vɪ to become hardened

empedrado ᴍ (acción) paving with stones; (cosa) cobblestone pavement; ᴀᴅᴊ paved with stones

empedrar[1] vᴛ to pave with stones

empeine ᴍ (del pie) instep; (del vientre) groin

empellón ᴍ shove; **a empellones** with shoves, shoving

empeñar vᴛ to pawn; **— la palabra** to pledge; —**se** (endeudarse) to go into debt; (obstinarse) to insist; (esforzarse) to apply oneself; —**se en** to engage in

empeño ᴍ (prenda) pawn; (insistencia) insistence; (deseo) desire; (esfuerzo) exertion; **poner — en** to strive for

empeorar vᴛ to make worse, to aggravate; vɪ to worsen; —**se** to get worse

empequeñecer[13] vᴛ to make smaller; vɪ to get smaller

emperador -triz ᴍ emperor; ꜰ empress

emperifollarse vɪ to deck oneself out, to doll oneself up

empezar[1,9] vɪ/vᴛ to begin, to start; **— a** to start to; **— de cero** to start from scratch; **para —** for starters; **no tengo ni para — con él** I can't touch him; **— por** to begin with; **empezamos mal** we got off to a bad start; **un tubo sin —** an unopened tube; **por algo se empieza** you have to start somewhere

empinado ᴀᴅᴊ steep

empinar vᴛ to raise; **— el codo** to drink; —**se** (una persona) to stand on tiptoes; (un caballo) to rear; (una torre) to tower

empírico ᴀᴅᴊ empirical

empizarrar vᴛ to cover with slate

emplastar vᴛ to plaster

emplasto ᴍ plaster

empleado -da ᴍꜰ employee

emplear vᴛ (usar) to employ, to use; (dar trabajo) to employ; —**se en** to be employed in

empleo ᴍ (ocupación) employment, work; (puesto de trabajo) job; (utilización) use

emplumado ᴀᴅᴊ feathery

emplumar vᴛ (poner plumas a algo) to adorn with feathers; (pegar plumas en el cuerpo) to tar and feather; vɪ (echar plumas) to grow feathers

empobrecer[13] vɪ/vᴛ to impoverish

empollar vᴛ (huevos) to hatch, to brood; vɪ/

VT (para un examen) to cram

empollón -ona MF grind, egghead

empolvar VT to cover with dust; **—se** (con cosméticos) to powder oneself; (con polvo) to get dirty

emponzoñar VT to poison

empotrado ADJ built-in

emprendedor ADJ enterprising

emprender VT (una tarea) to undertake; (un viaje) to embark on; **—la con alguien** to attack someone

empresa F (cosa que se emprende) undertaking; (compañía) company, enterprise; **— libre** free enterprise; **— privada** private enterprise; **— pública** public company

empresario -ria MF entrepreneur

empréstito M loan

empujar VT to push; (con violencia) to shove; (apresurar) to hurry

empuje M (ánimo) drive; (fuerza de propulsión) thrust; (fuerza hacia arriba) lift

empujón M shove, push; **dar empujones** to jostle

empuñadura F hilt

empuñar VT to grasp

emular VT to emulate

en PREP in; **— Asturias** in Asturias; (sobre una superficie) on, upon; **— la mesa** on the table; **sentarse — el suelo** to sit down on the floor; **me lo vendió — mil pesetas** she sold it to me for a thousand pesetas; **— la parada del autobús** at the bus stop; **— la noche** at night; **ir — tren** to go by train

enaguas F PL petticoat

enajenación M (mental) insanity; (cambio de dueño) transfer

enajenar VT (trasladar) to transfer; (alienar) to alienate; **—se** (a los amigos) to alienate

enaltecer[13] VT to extol

enamorado -da ADJ in love; MF lover

enamoramiento M crush

enamorar VT to make fall in love; **—se (de)** to fall in love (with)

enano -na MF (de los cuentos de hada, persona deforme) dwarf; (de proporciones normales) midget

enarbolar VT (una bandera) to raise on high; (un garrote) to brandish

enardecer[13] VT to inflame; **—se** to become inflamed

enardecimiento M inflaming

encabezamiento M heading

encabezar[9] VT (una carta, una obra, un gobierno) to head; (un desfile) to lead

encabritarse VI (un caballo) to rear (up);

(enfurecerse) to get furious

encadenar VT (poner en cadenas) to chain; (unir) to link

encajar VI/VT to fit; **el policía me encajó una multa** the policeman stuck me with a fine; **tu historia no encaja** your story doesn't hold water

encaje M (tejido) lace; (reserva bancaria) reserve; (acción de encajar) fitting together

encajonar VT (meter en una caja) to box; (apretar) to squeeze in

encallar VI to run aground, to strand; (una ballena) to beach; VT to ground

encamarse VI **— con** to go to bed with

encaminar VT to direct; **—se hacia** to head for

encanecer[13] VI to go gray; VT to cause to go gray

encanijado ADJ sickly

encanijarse VI to get sickly

encantado ADJ (a gusto) delighted; (hechizado) enchanted; **— de conocerla** pleased to meet you

encantador -ora ADJ charming, delightful; MF charmer

encantamiento M enchantment

encantar VT to enchant; **eso me encanta** I love that

encanto M (encantamiento) enchantment; (atractivo) charm; **un — de persona** a delightful person; **como por —** as if by magic

encapotado ADJ overcast

encapotarse VI to become overcast

encapricharse VI **— con / de / por** to become infatuated with

encapuchar VT (a una persona) to hood; (un bolígrafo) to put the top on

encaramar VT to raise; **—se** to climb up on; **—se al primer puesto** to rise to first place

encarar VT to face; **me encaró el fusil** he pointed the rifle at me; **—se con** to face

encarcelamiento M imprisonment

encarcelar VT to imprison, to jail, to incarcerate

encarecer[13] VI (subir de precio) to increase in price; VT (rogar) to beg

encarecidamente ADV earnestly

encargado -da MF person in charge; **— de curso** lecturer

encargar[7] VT (dar cargo) to put in charge; (pedir) to order; (mandar) to commission, to order; **— a alguien una tarea** to charge someone with a task; **—se de** to take care of

encargo M (pedido) order; (tarea)

assignment, charge, errand; **construido por / de** — custom-built; **hecho por** — made-to-order

encariñarse VI — **de** to become fond of

encarnado ADJ (rojo) red; (uña) ingrown

encarnar VT (un ideal) to embody; (a un personaje) to play; **se me encarnó una uña** one of my nails got ingrown

encarnizado ADJ fierce

encarnizarse[9] VI — **con alguien** to attack someone viciously

encarte M insert

encasillar VT to pigeonhole

encauzamiento M channeling

encauzar[9] VT to channel

encendedor M cigarette lighter

encender[1] VT (un cigarro, fuego) to light; (un fósforo) to strike; (una luz, radio) to switch on, to turn on; (pasión) to arouse; VI —**se** (una persona, sexualmente) to get aroused; (una lámpara) to turn on

encendido ADJ (rojo) bright; (sexualmente) aroused; M ignition

encerado M (pizarrón) blackboard; (acción de encerar) waxing; (capa de cera) wax coating; ADJ waxed

encerar VT to wax, to polish

encerrar[1] VT (palabras entre paréntesis) to enclose; (una oveja) to pen; (a una persona) to lock up; (un contenido) to contain; (un peligro) to involve; —**se** (aislarse) to isolate oneself; (obstinarse) to become fixated

enchapar VT (metal) to plate; (madera) to veneer

enchilada F enchilada

enchufar VT (un aparato eléctrico) to plug in; (a un protegido) to fix up; — **un tubo con otro** to fit one pipe into another

enchufe M (de aparatos eléctricos) socket, plug-in, electrical outlet; (situación ventajosa) connection

encías F PL gums

enciclopedia F encyclopedia

encierro M (confinamiento) confinement; (lugar) enclosure

encima ADV (arriba) on top; (además) in addition; — **de** on top of; **por** — **de** above; **sacar de** — to get rid of; **orinarse** — to urinate on oneself; **ya tenía el coche** — the car was already on top of me; **no lleves tanto dinero** — don't carry so much money on you; **los exámenes están** — the exams are upon us; **mi madre siempre me está** — my mother is always on me; **lo leí por** — I scanned it

encimera F counter

encina F oak

encinta ADJ pregnant

enclaustrar VT to cloister

enclavarse VI to be located

enclave M enclave

enclenque ADJ (endeble) sickly; (desvencijado) rickety

encoger[11b] VI/VT to shrink; —**se** (una prenda) to shrink; (una persona) to be intimidated; —**se de hombros** to shrug one's shoulders

encogido ADJ (tímido) shy; M (acción de encoger) shrinkage

encogimiento M (acción de encoger) shrinking; — **de hombros** shrug

encolar VT to glue

encolerizar[9] VT to incense; —**se** to become incensed, to lose one's temper

encomendar[1] VT to entrust; —**se** to commend oneself

enconar VT to inflame; VI —**se** (discusión) to become inflamed; (herida) to fester

encono M animosity

encontrado ADJ contrary, opposing

encontrar[2] VT (hallar) to find; (converger) to meet; — **a** to run into; —**se** (estar ubicado) to be located; (hallarse) to feel; —**se con** (verse, según plan) to meet with; (verse, por coincidencia) to run into; (enterarse) to find out; **vas a encontrarte la casa en obras** you'll find the house under construction

encontronazo M collision

encordar[2] VT to string

encorvado ADJ stoop-shouldered

encorvamiento M slouch, stoop

encorvar VT to stoop; —**se** to bend over

encostrarse VI to scab

encrespar VT (el pelo) to curl; (el mar) to make choppy; —**se** (el pelo) to get curly; (el mar) to get choppy

encrucijada F crossroads

encuadernación F (oficio) bookbinding; (lo encuadernado) binding

encuadernar VT to bind

encuadrar VT to frame; **la poesía de esta época se encuadra en tres tendencias** the poetry of this period can be classified into three tendencies

encubierto ADJ covert

encubrimiento ADJ (de un delincuente) concealment; (de un escándalo) cover-up

encubrir[51] VT (un secreto) to conceal; (un escándalo) to cover up, to hush up

encuentro M (casual) encounter; (planeado) meeting; (partido) game; (de atletismo) meet; **salir al — de** (ir a encontrar) to go out to meet; (prevenir) to counter

encuerar VT to strip

encuesta F survey, poll

encuestar VI/VT to survey, to poll

encumbrado ADJ elevated, lofty

encumbramiento M elevation

encumbrar VT to elevate

encurtido M pickle

encurtir VT to pickle

ende LOC ADV **por —** hence

endeble ADJ (persona) feeble; (material, argumento) flimsy; (mesa) rickety

endémico ADJ endemic

endemoniado ADJ (poseído por el diablo) possessed by the devil; (niño) devilish; (pregunta) tough

enderezar[9] VT to straighten; **enderézate** stand up straight; **la niña se enderezó con los años** the girl straightened out after a few years

endeudarse VI to get into debt

endiablado ADJ devilish

endócrino ADJ endocrine

endomingado ADJ dressed in one's Sunday best

endorfina F endorphin

endosante MF endorser

endosar VT to endorse

endoso M endorsement

endulzante M sweetener

endulzar[9] VT to sweeten; **se endulzó el tiempo** the weather became milder

endurecer[13] VT to harden; VI **—se** (músculos) to get hard; (cola) to set

endurecimiento M hardening

enebro M juniper

eneldo M dill

enema MF enema

enemigo -ga ADJ & MF enemy; **buques —s** enemy ships; **ser — de una cosa** to dislike a thing

enemistad F enmity

enemistar VT to cause enmity between; **—se con** to become an enemy of

energético ADJ (politica energética) energy policy

energía F energy; **— nuclear** nuclear energy; **— hidráulica** water power; **— solar** solar energy; **— térmica** thermal energy

enérgico ADJ (persona) energetic; (protesta, medida, tono) forceful

enero M January

enervar VT (debilitar) to enervate; (irritar) to irritate

enfadado ADJ angry

enfadar VT to anger; VI **—se** to get angry

enfado M anger

enfadoso ADJ annoying

enfardar VT to bale

énfasis M emphasis

enfático ADJ emphatic

enfatizar[9] VT to emphasize

enfermar VT to sicken; VI to become sick; **—se** to become ill

enfermedad F (estado de enfermo) sickness, illness; (cardiovascular, de Parkinson) disease; (social) ill; **— contagiosa** contagion; **— coronaria** heart disease; **— mental** mental illness; **— venérea** venereal disease

enfermería F infirmary

enfermero -ra M male nurse; F nurse

enfermizo ADJ (persona) sickly, infirm; (obsesión, aspecto) unhealthy; (imaginación) sick

enfermo -ma ADJ sick, ill; **me tiene — que vengan tarde** I'm sick of them coming late; MF patient; **— del corazón** person with a heart condition

enfisema M emphysema

enflaquecer[13] VI to get thin

enfocar[6] VT (los ojos) to focus; (un faro) to point; (una cámara) to train; (un tema) to approach

enfoque M approach

enfrentamiento M clash

enfrentar VT to confront; (una dificultad) to face, to tackle; **— a** to pit against; **—se con** to clash with

enfrente ADV opposite; **— de** in front of, opposite

enfriamiento M (del aire) cooling; (de una persona) chill; (de la economía, las relaciones) cooling off

enfriar[16] VT to cool, to chill; VI **—se** to cool off

enfundar VT to sheathe

enfurecer[13] VT to infuriate, to enrage; VI **—se** to become enraged, to rage

enfurruñado ADJ sulky

enfurruñarse VI to sulk

engalanar VT (una mesa) to decorate; (a una muchacha) to dress up; **—se** to dress up

enganchar VT (bueyes) to hitch; (una red) to snag; (un teléfono) to hook up; (a los televidentes, a un adicto) to hook; VI **—se** to get hooked

enganche M (del gas, teléfono) connection, hookup; (de drogas) addictiveness; (de vagones) coupling; (de caballos) team; (entrada) *Méx* down payment

enganchón M snag

engañador ADJ deceitful

engañar VT (mentir) to deceive; (ser infiel) to cheat on; — **el hambre** to ward off hunger; **—se** to deceive oneself

engaño M deceit, deception

engañoso ADJ deceitful

engastar VT to set

engaste M setting

engatusar VT to coax, to cajole

engendrar VT (emociones) to engender; (hijos) to procreate

englobar VT to encompass

engomar VT to glue

engordar VI to get fat, to put on weight; VT to make fat, to fatten; **esta semana he engordado dos kilos** I gained two kilos this week

engorroso ADJ irksome

engoznar VT to hinge

engranado ADJ meshed, interlocking; **estar —** to be in gear

engranaje M gears, gearing; **el — del partido** the party apparatus

engranar VT (meter una marcha) to put in gear, to throw into gear; (encajar) to mesh; — **la marcha atrás** to put (the car) in reverse

engrandecer[13] VT (la fama) to aggrandize; (un palacio) to make more grandiose

engrapar VT to staple, to cramp

engrasar VT (untar) to grease; (manchar) to make greasy; (sobornar) to grease someone's palm; **—se** to get greasy

engrase M grease job

engreído ADJ conceited

engreírse[15] VI to get conceited

engrillar VT to shackle

engrosar VT (una manifestación) to swell; (un volumen) to grow; (una persona) to get fat

engrudo M paste

engullir[19] VT to gobble

enhebrar VT (un hilo) to thread; (cuentas) to string; — **idioteces** to string together a bunch of idiocies

enhorabuena F congratulation; INTERJ congratulations

enigma M (misterio) enigma, conundrum; (adivinanza) riddle; (problema) puzzle

enjabonar VT (poner jabón) to soap, to lather; (adular) to flatter

enjaezar[9] VT to harness

enjalbegar[7] VT to whitewash

enjambre M swarm

enjaular VT (un animal) to cage; (a una persona) to jail

enjuagar[7] VT to rinse; (ropa) to rinse out; (platos) to rinse off

enjuague M (limpieza) rinse, rinsing; (trama) scheme; — **bucal** mouthwash

enjugar[7] VT (la frente) to wipe; (lágrimas) to wipe away

enjuiciar VT to prosecute, to try

enjuto ADJ dry; (delgado) thin

enlace M (de trenes) link; (químico) bond; (boda) marriage; (persona) liaison

enladrillado M brick pavement

enladrillar VT to brick, to pave with bricks

enlatar VT to can

enlazar[9] VT (unir) to link; (sujetar con lazo) to rope, to lasso; VI to connect; **—se** to connect

enlodar VT to muddy; **—se** to get muddy

enloquecedor ADJ maddening

enloquecer[13] VT to drive crazy; VI to go crazy; **—se** to go crazy

enlosado M flagstone pavement

enlosar VT to pave with flagstones

enmantecar[6] VT to butter

enmarañar VT (pelo) to entangle; (problema) to complicate

enmarcar[6] VT (un cuadro) to frame; **se enmarca dentro de** it takes place in the context of

enmascarar VT to mask

enmendar[1] VT (una ley) to amend; (un texto) to revise; — **la situación** to mend matters; **no me enmiendes la plana** don't correct me; VI **—se** to mend one's ways

enmienda F (de una ley) amendment; (de un texto) revision

enmohecer[13] VT to mold; **—se** to get moldy, to mold

enmudecer[13] VT to silence; VI to go silent

ennegrecer[13] VI/VT to blacken

ennoblecer[13] VT to ennoble

enojadizo ADJ hotheaded

enojado ADJ angry, mad

enojar VT to anger; **—se** to get angry

enojo M anger

enojoso ADJ bothersome

enorgullecer[13] VT to fill with pride; **—se de** to take pride in

enorme ADJ enormous

enramada F bower

enrarecido ADJ thin, rare

enrarecimiento M rarity, thinness

enredadera F creeper

enredar VT (enmarañar) to entangle; (complicar) to complicate; (involucrar) to mix up; VI to cause trouble; **—se** to get tangled up; **—se con** to become involved with

enredijo M tangle, snarl

enredo M (enredijo) snarl; (lío) mess; (amancebamiento) affair

enredoso ADJ complicated

enrejado M (conjunto de rejas) grating, grate; (entrecruzamiento de varillas) lattice

enrejar VT to install a grate on

enrevesado ADJ involved

enriquecer[13] VT to enrich; —se to become rich

enrojecer[13] VI/VT to redden

enrollar VT (manga, alfombra) to roll up; (hilo, cuerda, cinta magnética) to wind up; —se con to become involved with

enronquecer[13] VT to make hoarse; VI to become hoarse

enroscar[6] VT (soga) to coil, to roll up; (tuerca) to screw in; (tapa) to screw on; —se (vid) to twine; (serpiente) to coil up

ensacar[6] VT to sack

ensalada F salad

ensalzar[9] VT to extol

ensanchar VT to widen; —se (una calle) to widen; (una falda) to flare

ensanche M (de una calle) widening; (de una ciudad) expansion

ensangrentado ADJ gory, bloody

ensangrentar VT to smear blood on; —se to get covered with blood

ensartar VT (cuentas) to string; (aguja) to thread; (con un pincho) to pierce; (historias) to rattle off

ensayar VT (probar) to try out; (intentar) to try; (analizar un metal) to assay; (practicar una obra teatral) to rehearse

ensayo M (intento) trial, attempt; (de teatro) rehearsal; (obra literaria) essay; (nuclear) testing; (de un metal) assay; — **general** dress rehearsal; **por — y error** by trial and error

ensenada F cove

enseña F ensign

enseñanza F teaching, education; —s teachings

enseñar VT (mostrar) to show; (instruir) to teach; — **a** to teach how to

enseres M PL household utensils

ensillar VT to saddle, to saddle up

ensimismarse VI to lose oneself in thought

ensoberbecer[13] VT to make haughty; —se to become haughty

ensombrecer[13] VT (oscurecer) to make shadowy; (entristecer) to sadden

ensoñación F dream

ensordecedor ADJ deafening

ensordecer[13] VT to deafen

ensortijar VT to curl

ensuciar VT to dirty, to sully; —se (ponerse sucio) to get dirty; (defecar) to soil oneself; —se en to defecate on

ensueño M reverie, dream

entablar VT (relaciones) to establish; (un conflicto) to start; (una conversación) to strike up; (una demanda) to file; (una pelea) to pick

entablillar VT to splint

entallar VT to take in

entarimar VT to floor with planks

ente M (ser) entity; (excéntrico) weirdo; (agencia) agency

enteco ADJ sickly

entender[1] VT to understand; (oír) to hear; (ser homosexual) *Esp* to be homosexual; — **de** to know about; —se con (comunicar) to communicate with; (llevarse bien) to get along with; **dar a —** to intimate; **yo me entiendo** I know what I'm doing; **se entiende** of course

entendido -da ADJ (comprendido) understood; (experto) expert; **tengo — que** I understand that; **caridad mal entendida** misguided charity; MF expert

entendimiento M understanding

enterado ADJ informed; **darse por —** to acknowledge; **estar — de** to be privy to

enterar VT to inform; —se (de) to find out (about); **recién me entero** I just found out; **para que te enteres** just so you know

entereza F fortitude

enternecedor ADJ touching

enternecer[13] VT to touch; —se to be touched

entero ADJ (completo) entire, whole; (número) whole; **se mantuvo — durante el funeral** he held himself together during the funeral; M integer, whole number

enterrar[1] VT to bury

entibiar VT to make lukewarm; —se to become lukewarm

entidad F entity; **de —** significant; — **bancaria** banking institution

entierro M burial, funeral

entintar VT to stain with ink

entoldar VT to cover with an awning

entomología F entomology

entonación F intonation

entonar VT to sing; VI to sing in tune; — **con** to go well with; —se to get tipsy

entonces ADV then; **desde —** ever since; **hasta —** until then; **el — presidente** the then president; CONJ (así que) so

entornado ADJ half-open

entornar VT (una puerta) to leave ajar; (los ojos) to partially close

entorpecer[13] VT (los sentidos) to dull; (el paso) to hinder; **—se** to become sluggish

entorpecimiento M (de los sentidos) dullness; (del paso) hindrance

entrada F (sitio por donde se entra, de un actor) entrance; (acción de entrar, artículo de diccionario) entry; (conjunto de personas que asisten) gate; (oportunidad para actuar) opening; (billete, derecho, precio de entrar) admission; (llegada) arrival; (primer plato) entrée; (pago inicial) down payment; (tiempo en béisbol) inning; **—s** cash receipts; **— de coches** driveway; **— por partida doble** double entry; **de —** from the start

entramado M lattice

entrante ADJ (alcalde, etc.) incoming; (año) next; M recess

entrañas F PL (intestinos) entrails, *fam* guts; (sentimientos) heart, core; **— de la tierra** bowels of the earth; **de mis —** of my own flesh and blood

entrar VI to enter; (a trabajar) to come in; (en un lugar) to fit; VT (datos) to enter, to input; **le entré dos pastillas** I brought in two pills for him; **me entró miedo** I became afraid; **me entró sueño** I got sleepy; **no sé cómo —le a esa chica** I don't know how to approach that girl; **la física no me entra** I can't learn physics; **no entra entre mis favoritos** it is not included among my favorites; **la semana que entra** next week; **este vestido no me entra** this dress doesn't fit me; **seis entra dos veces en doce** six goes into twelve two times; **dejar —** to let in; **hacer — en razón** to bring to reason; **hazle —** show him in; **— a medicina** to go into medicine; **— en calor** to warm up; **— en coma** to go into a coma; **— en / a un cuarto** to enter a room; **— en una discusión** to take part in a discussion; **— en materia** to get to the meat of a matter; **— en vigencia / vigor** to go into effect

entre PREP (dos) between; (muchos) among; **— vaso y vaso** between glasses; **— dientes** under one's breath

entreabierto ADJ ajar, half-open

entreabrir[51] VT (puerta) to crack open; (los ojos) to half-open

entreacto M intermission

entrecano ADJ graying

entrecejo M space between the eyebrows

entrecortado ADJ (voz) faltering; (respiración) irregular

entrecortarse VI to falter

entrecruzar[9] VT to interlace; **—se** to cross

entredicho LOC ADV **en —** in doubt

entrega F (de un paquete) delivery; (de un manuscrito) submission; (al vicio) surrender; (de una novela) installment; (de revista) issue; **por —s** serial; **— a domicilio** home delivery; **— de premios** presentation of awards; **— inicial** down payment

entregar[7] VT (un paquete) to deliver; (a un rehén, prisionero) to hand over; (a un delincuente) to turn in; (a una hija en matrimonio) to give; (premios) to hand out, to present; (los deberes) to hand in; (el coche) to trade in; **—se (a)** to surrender (to), to dedicate oneself to

entrelazar[9] VT to intertwine

entremés M (obra de teatro) interlude; (comida) hors d'oeuvre

entremeter VT to insert; **—se en** (meterse) to get mixed up in; (inmiscuirse) to meddle in

entremetido -da ADJ meddlesome, nosy; MF meddler

entremezclar VT to intermingle

entrenador -ora MF trainer, coach

entrenamiento M training

entrenar VI/VT to train

entrepierna F (de personas) crotch; (de pantalón) inseam

entrepiso M mezzanine

entresacar[6] VT (seleccionar) to cull; (hacer menos espeso) to thin

entresuelo M (de hotel) mezzanine; (de cine) balcony

entretanto ADV meanwhile

entretejer VT (el pelo, una tela) to weave; (una historia) to weave together

entretener[44] VT (hacer atrasar) to delay; (distraer) to distract; (divertir) to entertain; **—se** (divertirse) to amuse oneself; (detenerse) to delay

entretenido ADJ entertaining

entretenimiento M entertainment, amusement

entrever[48] VT (apenas) to catch a glimpse of; (a lo lejos) to make out

entreverar VT to intersperse; **—se** to meddle

entrevía F gauge

entrevista F interview

entrevistar VT to interview; **—se con** to have an interview with

entristecer[13] VT to sadden; **—se** to become sad

entrometerse VI to meddle, to interfere

entrometido -da ADJ meddlesome, nosy; MF meddler, busybody

entronque M (ferroviario) junction; (parentesco) relationship

entropía F entropy

entumecido ADJ (dedo, diente) numb; (músculo) stiff

entumecimiento M (de los dedos, dientes) numbness; (de los músculos) stiffness

enturbiar VT (el agua) to muddy; (una decisión) to muddle; (el juicio, la alegría) to cloud; **—se** (agua) to get muddy; (alegría) to be marred

entusiasmado ADJ enthusiastic

entusiasmar VT to excite; **—se** to be excited

entusiasmo M enthusiasm, excitement

entusiasta MF enthusiast; ADJ enthusiastic

enumerar VT to enumerate

enunciado M utterance

enunciar VT (palabras) to enunciate; (una teoría) to articulate, to enunciate

envainar VT to sheathe

envalentonar VT to make bold; **—se** to get bold

envanecer[13] VT to make vain; **—se** to become vain

envarado ADJ stiff

envaramiento M stiffness

envasar VT to package; **— al vacío** to vacuum-pack

envase M packaging

envejecer[13] VT to make old; **ese maquillaje te envejece** that makeup makes you look old; VI to grow old, to age

envenenamiento M poisoning

envenenar VT to poison

envergadura F (de un avión) wingspan; (de un ave) wingspread; (de un evento, proyecto) importance

envés M back

enviado -da MF (político) envoy; (periodístico) correspondent

enviar[16] VT to send

enviciar VT to corrupt; **—se con** to get hooked on

envidia F envy

envidiable ADJ enviable

envidiar VT to envy

envidioso ADJ envious, jealous

envilecer[13] VT to debase

envío M (de mercancías) shipment; (de un manuscrito) submission

envite M bet

envoltorio M (cosa envuelta) bundle; (envoltura) wrapper

envoltura F wrapping, wrapper

envolver[2,51] VT (involucrar) to involve;

(cubrir) to wrap; (atrapar) to entangle; (rodear) to surround; **—se** to become involved

enyesar VT (enlucir con yeso) to plaster; (escayolar) to put in a cast

enzima MF enzyme

épica F epic

epicentro M epicenter

épico ADJ epic

epidemia F epidemic

epidémico ADJ epidemic

epidermis F epidermis

epifanía F epiphany

epilepsia F epilepsy

epílogo M epilog

episódico ADJ episodic

episodio M episode

epitafio M epitaph

epítome M epitome

época F (momento) time, period; (período histórico) age; (temporada) season; (período geológico) epoch

epopeya F epic poem

equidad F equity

equidistante ADJ equidistant

equilibrar VT to balance

equilibrio M equilibrium, balance; **perder el —** to lose one's balance; **hacer —s** to do a balancing act

equino ADJ & M equine

equinoccio M equinox

equipaje M baggage, luggage

equipamiento M equipment

equipar VT to equip, to outfit

equiparar VT to equate

equipo M (materiales) equipment; (grupo de personas) team; **— de vida** life-support system; **— deportivo** sweatsuit; **— de esquí** ski gear

equitación F horsemanship

equitativo ADJ equitable

equivalente ADJ equivalent

equivaler[46] VI to be equivalent; **lo que equivale a decir** which amounts to saying

equivocación F mistake

equivocado ADJ mistaken, wrong; **estar —** to be wrong/mistaken

equivocar[6] VT to mistake; **—se** to be mistaken, to make a mistake; **—se de sala** to choose the wrong room; **si no me equivoco** unless I'm mistaken

equívoco ADJ (ambiguo) equivocal; (moralmente dudoso) questionable; M misunderstanding

era F (período) era, age; (lugar donde se trilla) threshing floor; (parcela) plot

erario M treasury
erección F erection
erecto ADJ (órgano) erect; (postura) upright
erguido ADJ erect, upright
erguir[3b] VT to lift, to raise; **—se** to rise
erial M uncultivated land
erigir[11] VT (construir) to erect; (fundar) to found; **—se en** to set oneself up as
Eritrea F Eritrea
eritreo -a ADJ & MF Eritrean
erizado ADJ bristly; **— de** bristling with
erizar[9] VT to set on end; **—se** to bristle
erizo M hedgehog; **— de mar** sea urchin; **ser un —** to be a grouch
ermitaño -ña MF (persona) hermit; M (cangrejo) hermit crab
erógeno ADJ erogenous
erosión F erosion
erótico ADJ erotic
erradicar[6] VT to eradicate, to root out
errado ADJ erroneous, in error
errante ADJ wandering
errar[27] VT to miss; **— el cálculo** to miscalculate; VI (estar equivocado) to be mistaken; (vagar) to roam, to rove, to wander
errata F misprint, typographical error
errático ADJ erratic
erróneo ADJ erroneous
error M error, mistake; **— de imprenta** misprint
eructar VI to belch, to burp
eructo M belch, burp
erudición F learning, scholarship
erudito -ta ADJ (persona) erudite; (obra) scholarly, learned; MF scholar
erupción F eruption; **hacer —** to erupt
esbelto ADJ slender
esbozar[9] VT to outline; **— una sonrisa** to give a hint of a smile
esbozo M sketch, outline; **— de una sonrisa** hint of a smile
escabechar VT to pickle
escabroso ADJ (agreste) rugged; (espinoso) thorny; (sórdido) lurid, sordid
escabullirse[19] VI (ladrones) to slip away, to steal away; (lagartijas) to scurry away / off; **— de** to wriggle out of
escafandra F (en el agua) scuba gear; (en el espacio) spacesuit
escala F (escalera, escalafón) ladder; (serie de grados, notas, relación de importancia) scale; (parada) stopover; **hacer —** to stop over at; **— salarial** wage scale; **a — nacional** nationwide; **de gran —** large-scale; **sin —s** nonstop
escalada F (de una montaña) climb; (de violencia) escalation
escalador -ora MF climber
escalar VT to scale, to climb
escaldadura F scald
escaldar VT (la piel) to scald; (las verduras) to blanch; **—se** to get scalded
escalera F (en un edificio) stairs, staircase; (de mano) ladder; (de naipes) flush; **— mecánica** escalator; **— de caracol** spiral / winding staircase; **— de color** straight flush; **— de incendios** fire escape; **— real** royal flush
escalfar VT to poach
escalinata F grand staircase
escalofriante ADJ chilling, hair-raising
escalofrío M chill; **—s** the shivers
escalón M (peldaño) step, stair; (terraza) terrace; (de escalera de mano, de escalafón) rung; (formación militar) echelon
escalonar VT (distribuir) to stagger; (aterrazar) to terrace
escalope M scallop
escama F (de animal) scale; (de piel, de corteza) flake
escamar VT to scale
escamoso ADJ (animal) scaly; (piel) flaky
escamotear VT (esconder) to palm; (robar) to snatch; (eludir) to shirk
escampar VI to clear up
escandalizar[9] VT (chocar) to scandalize; (causar escándalo) to cause a scandal; **—se** to be shocked
escándalo M (suceso vergonzoso) scandal; (riña) uproar
escandaloso ADJ (chocante) scandalous, shocking; (ruidoso) raucous
escandir VT *lit* to scan
escanear VT to scan
escáner M scanner
escaño M seat in parliament
escapada F (escape) escape
escapar VI (de un lugar, una situación) to escape; (de una persona, responsabilidad) to run away; **—se** (persona) to escape; (gas) to leak; **se me escapó una sonrisa** I inadvertently smiled; **Matilde se me está escapando de las manos** Matilde is getting out of hand
escaparate M shop window
escapatoria F escape, way out
escape M (de fantasía, escapatoria) escape; (de motor) exhaust; (de gas, agua) leak
escarabajo M beetle
escaramuza F skirmish
escaramuzar[9] VI to skirmish
escarbar VI/VT to dig, to scratch; **— en los**

archivos to dig around in the files; —
  los dientes to pick one's teeth
escarcha F frost
escarchar VI to frost
escardar VT to weed
escarlata ADJ & M (color) scarlet; F
  (enfermedad) scarlet fever
escarlatina F scarlet fever
escarmentar[1] VI to learn one's lesson; VT to
  teach a lesson
escarmiento M lesson; **que te sirva de —**
  let that be a lesson to you
escarnecer[13] VT to deride
escarnio M derision
escarpa F steep slope
escarpado ADJ steep, precipitous; M steep
  slope
escasear VI (estar escaso) to be scarce;
  (acabarse) to grow scarce
escasez F (falta) shortage; (carestía) scarcity,
  want
escaso ADJ sparse, scarce; **una docena
  escasa** a scant dozen; **— de** short on; **—
  de personal** short-handed
escatimar VT to skimp on; **no — gastos** to
  spare no expense
escena F (fragmento de una obra de teatro,
  episodio) scene; (escenario) stage; **montar
  una —** to make a scene; **en —** on stage;
  poner en — to stage; **entrar en —** to go
  on stage
escenario M stage
escenificación F staging
escepticismo M skepticism
escéptico -ca ADJ skeptical; MF skeptic
escisión F split
esclarecer[13] VT to elucidate
esclavitud F slavery
esclavizar[9] VT to enslave
esclavo -va MF slave
esclerosis F sclerosis; **— múltiple** multiple
  sclerosis
esclusa F (de un canal) lock; (de una presa)
  floodgate, sluice gate
escoba F broom
escobilla F whisk broom
escocer[2,10c] VI to sting
escocés -esa ADJ Scottish; **(cuadros)
  escoceses** plaid; MF Scot; M (whisky)
  Scotch; (lengua) Scottish
Escocia F Scotland
escoger[11b] VT to choose
escolar MF pupil; ADJ **año —** school year
escoliosis F scoliosis
escollo M (en el mar) reef; (obstáculo)
  obstacle
escolta F (policial) escort; MF INV (persona)

escort
escoltar VT to escort
escombros M PL rubble, debris
esconder VT to hide; **—se** to hide
escondidas LOC ADV **a —** on the sly; **entrar
  a —** to sneak in; **meter algo a —** to
  sneak something in; **jugar a las —** to
  play hide and seek
escondite M hiding place; (de ladrón)
  hideout; (de cazador) blind; **jugar al —**
  to play hide and seek
escondrijo M hiding place
escopeta F shotgun
escoplo M chisel
escora F listing
escorar VI to list
escoria F (de metales) slag; (de la sociedad)
  scum, dregs
escorpión M scorpion
escotado ADJ low-cut
escote M (parte del vestido) neckline; (parte
  del cuerpo) cleavage; **pagar a —** to go
  Dutch
escotilla F hatch
escozor M smarting sensation
escribiente MF clerk
escribir[51] VI/VT to write; **¿cómo se escribe?**
  how do you spell it? **— a máquina** to
  type
escrito ADJ written; **— a máquina**
  typewritten; **no —** unwritten; **por —** in
  writing; M document
escritor -ora MF writer, author
escritorio M (mueble) desk; (oficina) office
escritura F (acción de escribir) writing;
  (certificado de propiedad) deed; **— de
  traspaso** conveyance; **— de venta** bill of
  sale
escroto M scrotum
escrúpulo M scruple, qualm; **sin —s**
  unscrupulous
escrupuloso ADJ scrupulous
escrutar VT (a una persona) to scrutinize; (el
  horizonte) to scan; (votos) to count
escrutinio M (examen) scrutiny; (recuento)
  vote count
escuadra F (de buques, soldados) squadron;
  (instrumento) square
escuadrilla F (de aviones) flight of aircraft;
  (de buques) squadron
escuadrón M squadron; **— de la muerte**
  death squad
escualidez F (delgadez) skinniness; (suciedad)
  squalor
escuálido ADJ (sucio) squalid; (delgado) thin
escuchar VT to listen to; (oír) to hear; VI to
  listen; **— a hurtadillas** to eavesdrop

escudar VT to shield

escudo M (arma defensiva) shield; (moneda de Portugal) escudo; **— de armas** coat of arms

escudriñar VT (a una persona) to scrutinize, to peer at; (el horizonte) to scan

escuela F school; **— industrial** trade school; **— normal** school of education; **— pública** public school; **— primaria** elementary school; **— secundaria** secondary school; **tener —** to have good technique

escueto ADJ (explicación) succinct; (verdad) simple

esculpir VI/VT to sculpture, to sculpt

escultor -ora MF sculptor

escultura F sculpture

escupir VI/VT to spit

escupitajo M spit

escurridizo ADJ (acera) slippery; (ladrón) elusive, slippery

escurrir VI/VT (platos, verduras) to drain; (ropa) to wring out; **—se** to slink away

ese ADJ that, those; **esa chica se llama Matilde** that girl is named Matilde; **esas ciudades son antiguas** those cities are old; PRON that one, those; **ese es el mayor** that one is the oldest; **esos son mis hijos** those are my children

esencia F essence

esencial ADJ essential; **lo —** gist, bottom line, name of the game

esfera F (sólido) sphere; (espacio, ámbito) realm, sphere; (de reloj) face, dial

esférico ADJ spherical; M soccer ball

esforzado ADJ valiant

esforzarse⁹ VI to try hard, to exert oneself; **— por** to strive to, to make an effort to

esfuerzo M effort

esfumar VT to tone down; **—se** to vanish

esgrima F fencing; **practicar —** to fence

esgrimir VT (armas) to brandish, to wield; (argumentos) to employ

eslabón M chain link; **— perdido** missing link

eslabonar VT to link

eslavo -va ADJ Slavic; MF Slav

eslogan M slogan

eslovaco ADJ & MF Slovakian; M (lengua) Slovakian

Eslovaquia F Slovakia

Eslovenia F Slovenia

esloveno -na ADJ & MF Slovene; M (lengua) Slovene

esmaltar VT to enamel

esmalte M enamel; **— de uñas** nail polish

esmerado ADJ painstaking, careful

esmeralda F emerald

esmerarse VI to take pains

esmerilado ADJ frosted; M frosting

esmerilar VT to frost

esmero M care

esmirriado ADJ scrawny

esmoquin M tuxedo

esnifar VT to snort

esnob M snob

esnórquel M snorkel

eso PRON DEM that; **— es** that's true; **— sí** granted; **a — de las tres** at about three o'clock; **de —, nada** no way! **en — llega y me dice** at that moment he arrives and says to me; **y — que le dije que viniese temprano** even when I told him to come early

esófago M esophagus

esotérico ADJ esoteric

espaciado M pitch, spacing

espacial ADJ spatial; **nave —** space ship

espaciar VT to space; **—se** to space out

espacio M (capacidad) space, room; (superficie) expanse; (separación entre líneas) space, spacing; (en un formulario) blank space; (porción de tiempo) span; **— aéreo** aerospace; **— exterior** outer space; **— noticioso** newscast; **a doble —** double-spaced; **a un —** single-spaced; **por — de una semana** for a week

espacioso ADJ spacious, roomy

espada F sword; **—s** (palo de naipes) swords; **— de doble filo** double-edged sword; **estar entre la — y la pared** to be between a rock and a hard place

espalda F back; **— mojada** pey wetback; **a —s de alguien** behind one's back; **caerse de —s** to fall on one's back; **nadar de —s** to do the backstroke; **tener las —s anchas** to take a lot of abuse; **volver las —s** to turn one's back

espaldar M chair back

espantadizo ADJ easily scared

espantado ADJ frightened

espantajo M scarecrow

espantar VT to frighten, to scare; (ahuyentar) to frighten away, to scare away; **—se** to get scared; M SG **espantapájaros** scarecrow

espanto M fright, dread; **estás hecho un —** you look a sight; **estoy curado de —** nothing surprises me anymore

espantoso ADJ frightful, dreadful

España F Spain

español -ola ADJ Spanish; MF Spaniard; M (lengua) Spanish

esparadrapo M surgical tape

esparcimiento M (recreo) relaxation; (reparto) spreading

esparcir[10b] VT to scatter, to spread; **—se** to amuse oneself

espárrago M asparagus

espasmo M spasm, jerk

espasmódico ADJ jerky

espástico ADJ spastic

espátula F spatula

especia F spice

especial ADJ & M special; **en —** in particular

especialidad F specialty, specialization

especialista MF specialist

especialización F specialization

especializar[9] VT to specialize; **—se en** to specialize in

especie F (en ciencias naturales) species; (clase) kind; **—s en peligro de extinción** endangered species; **pagar en — to** pay in kind; **una — de** a kind of

especiero M spice rack

especificar[6] VT to specify

específico ADJ & M specific

espécimen M specimen

espectacular ADJ spectacular

espectáculo M (escándalo) spectacle; (actuación pública) show; (vista) sight; **dar el —** to make a spectacle of oneself

espectador -ora MF (de un espectáculo) spectator; (de un suceso) onlooker

espectro M (fantasma) specter; (de luz, medicina) spectrum

especulación F speculation

especulador -ora MF speculator

especular VT to speculate; ADJ mirror; **imagen —** mirror image

espejismo M (en el desierto) mirage; (ilusión) illusion

espejo M mirror; **— de cuerpo entero** full-length mirror; **— retrovisor** rearview mirror

espeluznante ADJ hair-raising

espeluznar VT to terrify; **—se** to be terrified

espera F (acción de esperar) wait; (aplazamiento) extension; **estar en — de** to be waiting for

esperanza F hope; **— de vida** life expectancy; **con una — de voto de 12,5%** expected to get 12.5% of the vote

esperanzado ADJ hopeful

esperanzador ADJ hopeful

esperanzar[9] VT to give hope to

esperar VT (tener esperanza) to hope; (llevar a un hijo, creer que sucederá algo) to expect; (aguardar) to wait for; VI to wait; **era de —** it was to be expected; **espera sentado** don't hold your breath; **estoy**

esperando un milagro I'm hoping for a miracle; **todavía espera confirmación** it still awaits confirmation

esperma MF sperm

esperpento M grotesque person or thing

espesar VT to thicken

espeso ADJ (pelo, sopa, niebla) thick; (cejas) bushy

espesor M thickness

espesura F (espesor) thickness; (lugar poblado de matorrales) thicket

espetar VT (decir bruscamente) to blurt out; (atravesar con un espeto) to run a spit through

espía MF INV spy

espiar[16] VI to spy; VT to spy on

espichar VI *fam* to croak, to bite the dust

espiga F spike

espigar[7] VT to glean; VI to grow spikes; **—se** to grow tall

espina F (de planta) thorn; (de pez) fish bone; **— dorsal** spinal column; **me quedé con la —** I was left wondering

espinaca F spinach

espinal ADJ spinal

espinazo M spine, backbone

espinilla F (de persona) shin; (de animal) shank; (grano) blackhead

espino M thorny shrub

espinoso ADJ thorny

espionaje M espionage

espiración F expiration

espiral ADJ & F spiral

espirar VI/VT to exhale, to breathe out, to expire

espíritu M (ser no físico, fantasma, de una ley) spirit; (alma) soul; **— fuerte** free spirit; **— deportivo** sportsmanship; **— emprendedor** can-do attitude; **— Santo** Holy Spirit

espiritual ADJ & M spiritual

espita F spigot

espléndido ADJ (estupendo) splendid; (generoso) lavish

esplendor M splendor

esplendoroso ADJ magnificent

espliego M lavender

espolear VT to spur

espoleta F bomb fuse

espolón M (de gallo, planta, estímulo) spur; (de buque) ram

espolvorear VT to dust, to sprinkle

esponja F (animal, utensilio) sponge; (borracho) souse

esponjado ADJ spongy

esponjar VT to make spongy; **—se** to become spongy

esponjoso ADJ spongy
esponsales M PL betrothal
espontaneidad F spontaneity
espontáneo ADJ spontaneous
espora F spore
esposar VT to handcuff
esposo -sa M husband; F wife; **esposas** handcuffs
espuela F spur
espulgar[7] VT to delouse
espuma F (de cerveza) froth; (de jabón) suds, lather; (de la boca) foam; (de colchón) foam rubber; (de mar) foam, spray; **echar — por la boca** to foam at the mouth; **hacer —** to make suds
espumar VT (quitar la espuma) to skim; (formar espuma) to foam
espumarajo M foam; **echar —s por la boca** to foam at the mouth
espumillón M tinsel
espumoso ADJ foamy
esputo M sputum
esquela F note; **— mortuoria** death notice
esqueleto M (huesos) skeleton; (armazón) framework; **mover el —** (bailar) to dance; (moverse) to move
esquema M outline; **romperle los —s a alguien** (planes) to ruin one's plans; (conceptos) to shatter one's preconceptions
esquí M (tabla) ski; (deporte) skiing; **— acuático** (tabla) water ski; (deporte) water skiing; **hacer — acuático** to water-ski
esquiar[16] VI to ski
esquila F (cencerro) cowbell; (acción de esquilar) shearing
esquilador -ora MF sheep shearer
esquilar VT to shear, to clip
esquileo M shearing
esquimal ADJ & MF Eskimo; M (lengua) Eskimo
esquina F corner; **en cada —** everywhere
esquirol M strikebreaker; *pey* scab
esquivar VT (a una vecina) to avoid; (un golpe) to dodge
esquivo ADV (tímido) shy, coy; (huraño) aloof; (reservado) elusive
esquizofrenia F schizophrenia
estabilidad F stability
estabilizar[9] VT to stabilize
estable ADJ (mesa) stable; (precio) firm; (huésped) long-term
establecer[13] VT to establish; (averiguar) to ascertain; **— una cita** to set up an appointment; **—se** to settle
establecimiento M establishment
establishment M establishment

establo M stable
estaca F (con punta) stake; (gruesa) club
estacada F stockade; **dejar en la —** to leave in the lurch
estacar[6] VT (atar) to stake; (delimitar) to stake off
estación F (de tren, autobús, radio) station; (parte del año) season; **— bípeda** bipedal stance; **— de bomberos** fire station; **— de esquí** ski resort; **— de servicio** filling station; **— de trabajo** work station; **— espacial** space station
estacionamiento M (acción) parking; (lugar) parking lot
estacionar VT (tropas) to station; (un vehículo) to park; **—se** (un coche) to park; (precios) to level off
estacionario ADJ stationary
estadía F stay
estadio M (recinto con graderías) stadium; (fase) stage
estadista M statesman; F stateswoman
estadística F (ciencia) statistics; **—s** (datos numéricos) statistics
estado M (manera de estar, unidad política) state; **— civil** marital status; **— de cuenta** bank statement; **— de alarma** state of emergency; **— de ánimo** state of mind; **— de excepción** martial law; **— de guerra** state of war; **— de sitio** state of siege; **— mayor** chiefs of staff; **— policíaco** police state; **de — sólido** solid state; **en — interesante** expecting; **en — vegetativo** brain-dead
Estados Unidos M PL / SG United States
estadounidense ADJ & MF American
estafa F swindle, scam, racket
estafador -ora MF swindler
estafar VT to swindle
estalactita F stalactite
estalagmita F stalagmite
estallar VI (una bomba) to explode; (un globo) to burst; (una guerra) to break out; (una persona) to snap; **— de risa** to burst with laughter; **— en una carcajada** to burst out laughing; **hacer —** to set off
estallido M (de bomba, color) explosion; (ruido) bang, report
estampa F (de revista) illustration; (imagen) image; (apariencia) appearance; **de buena —** good-looking; **la viva — de la madre** the spitting image of her mother; **la viva — de la desolación** the very picture of desolation
estampado ADJ printed; M (tela) print; (acción) printing
estampar VT (en tela, papel) to print; (con

un molde, en metal) to stamp; **—le un beso a alguien** to plant a kiss on someone
estampida F stampede
estampido M bang
estampilla F stamp
estampillar VT to stamp
estancado ADJ stagnant
estancar[6] VT to stem; to dam; to block; **—se** to stagnate
estancia F (estadía) stay; (habitación) hall; (hacienda) *RP* cattle ranch
estanco ADJ waterproof; M government store
estándar ADJ INV & M standard
estandarización F standardization
estandarizar[9] VT to standardize
estandarte M standard, banner
estanque M pond
estante M (tabla) shelf; (mueble) bookcase
estantería F (mueble) bookcase; (en una biblioteca) stack
estañar VT to tin-plate
estaño M tin
estar[28] VI to be; **— a tres kilómetros de aquí** to be three kilometers from here; **— bien** to be all right; **— del corazón** to have heart trouble; **— de más** to be unnecessary; **— para** to be about to; **— por** (a favor de) to be in favor of; (a punto de) to be about to; **— trabajando duro** to be working hard; **¿a cuántos estamos?** what day of the month is it? **ahí está** that's it; **¿está Alice?** is Alice there? **están muy buenos tus zapatos nuevos** your new shoes are nice; **estáte tranquilo** don't worry; **no —** to be out; **cuarto de —** living room
estático ADJ static
estatua F statue
estatura F (importancia) stature; (altura de una persona) height
estatuto M (ley) statute; (de una sociedad) bylaw
este ADJ DEM this, these; **esta chica se llama Hilary** this girl is named Hilary; **estas ciudades son antiguas** these cities are old; PRON DEM this one, these; **— es el mayor** this one is the oldest; **estos son mis hijos** these are my children; M & ADJ east; **hacia el —** eastward
estela F (de una embarcación) wake; (de humo, polvo) trail; **dejar una —** to leave a trail
estelar ADJ stellar
estenotipista MF court reporter
estentóreo ADJ booming
estepa F steppe

estera F mat
estercolar VT to fertilize with manure
estercolero M dunghill
estérco ADJ & M stereo; **en —** in stereo
estereotipo M stereotype
estéril ADJ sterile; (mujer) barren
esterilidad F sterility
esterilizar[9] VT to sterilize
esternón M sternum
esteroide M steroid
estertor M death rattle
estética F aesthetics
estético ADJ aesthetic
estetoscopio M stethoscope
estibador M longshoreman
estibar VT to stow
estiércol M manure
estigma M stigma
estigmatizar[9] VT to stigmatize
estilarse VI to be in style
estilo M (literario, estético) style; (de natación) stroke; **— de vida** lifestyle; **— espalda** backstroke; **— indirecto** reported speech; **— libre** freestyle; **— mariposa** butterfly stroke; **— pecho** breaststroke; **— perrito** dog paddle; **cosas por el —** things like that
estima F esteem, regard
estimación F (cálculo) estimate; (estima) estimation
estimado ADJ esteemed; **— Sr.** Dear Sir
estimar VT (apreciar) to esteem; (determinar el valor) to estimate; (opinar) to think
estimulación F stimulation
estimulante ADJ stimulating; M stimulant
estimular VT to stimulate; (alentar) to encourage
estímulo M stimulus
estío M *lit* summer
estipendio M stipend
estipulación F stipulation
estipular VT to stipulate
estirado ADJ stuck-up
estirar VT (alargar) to stretch; **— el cuello** to crane one's neck; **— la pata** *fam* to kick the bucket; (crecer) to grow; **—se** to stretch
estirón M growth spurt; **pegar un —** to have a growth spurt
estirpe F lineage
estival ADJ **vacaciones —es** summer vacation
esto ADJ & PRON this; **— es** that is to say; **a todo —** meanwhile; **en —** at this point
estocada F thrust; **lanzar una —** to thrust
estofa F type; **de baja —** low-class
estofado M stew

estofar VT to stew

estoico -ca ADJ & MF stoic

estolón M runner

estómago M stomach

Estonia F Estonia

estonio -nia ADJ & MF Estonian; M (lengua) Estonian

estopa F tow

estorbar VT (obstaculizar) to hinder, to impede; (ser una molestia) to be a nuisance

estorbo M (obstáculo) hindrance, impediment; (molestia) nuisance

estornino M starling

estornudar VI to sneeze

estornudo M sneeze

estrado M bench

estrafalario ADJ bizarre, outlandish

estragar[7] VT (físicamente) to devastate; (moralmente) to corrupt

estrago M havoc; **hacer —s** to wreak havoc

estrangular VT to strangle

estratagema F stratagem

estrategia F strategy

estratégico ADJ strategic

estrato M stratum, layer; **— social** social class

estratosfera F stratosphere

estrechamiento M constriction

estrechar VT (hacer más estrecho) to narrow; (abrazar) to embrace; **la estrechó en sus brazos** he held her in his arms; **—se** to get narrower; **—se la mano** to shake hands

estrechez F (cualidad de estrecho) narrowness; (estrechamiento) narrowing; (aprietos) dire straits

estrecho ADJ narrow; **la falda le quedaba estrecha** the skirt was too tight for her; M strait

estrella F star; **— binaria** binary star; **— de cine** movie star; **— de mar** starfish; **— fugaz** shooting star, falling star; **ver las —s** to see stars

estrellado ADJ (como una estrella) starlike; (cubierto de estrellas) starry

estrellar VT (aplastar) to smash; (romper) to crack; **—se** (avión) to crash; (intento) to fail; **—se contra** to smash into

estremecer[13] VT to make shudder; **el terremoto estremeció París** the earthquake rocked París; VI to shudder

estremecimiento M shudder

estrenar VT (un vestido) to wear for the first time; (una obra de cine, teatro) to debut; (una bicicleta) to try out for the first time; (un título) to use for the first time; **—se** to debut

estreno M (de una película) premiere; (de un objeto) first use; (de una actividad) debut

estreñido ADJ (constipado) constipated; (antipático) uptight

estreñimiento M constipation

estreñir[5,18] VT to constipate; **—se** to become constipated

estrépito M racket, clatter; **causar —** to clatter

estrepitoso ADJ noisy

estrés M stress

estresar VT to stress (out)

estría F (en la piel) stretch mark; (en una columna) flute

estriado ADJ (piel) covered with stretch marks; (columna) fluted; (piedra) streaked

estriar[16] VT to flute; **—se** to get stretch marks

estribación F spur

estribar VI **— en** (apoyarse en) to lean on; (radicar en) to lie in

estribillo M refrain

estribo M (de silla, oído) stirrup; (de coche) running board; **perder los —s** to fly off the handle

estribor M starboard

estricnina F strychnine

estricto ADJ strict

estridente ADJ strident

estrofa F verse, stanza

estrógeno M estrogen

estropajo M scrubber; **tengo la boca que es un —** my mouth is as dry as a bone

estropajoso ADJ sinewy

estropear VT to ruin

estructura F structure

estructural ADJ structural

estruendo M din, racket

estruendoso ADJ thunderous

estrujamiento M (para romper) crushing; (para sacar jugo) squeezing

estrujar VT (aplastar) to crush; (apretar) to squeeze

estrujón M squeeze

estuario M estuary

estucar[6] VT to stucco

estuche M (para joyas) jewelry box; (para pastillas) pill box; (para lentes) glasses case

estuco M stucco

estudiantado M student body

estudiante MF student

estudiantil ADJ **— vida** student life

estudiar VI/VT to study

estudio M (acción de estudiar, investigación, habitación de casa) study; (habitación de artista) studio; (apartamento pequeño)

studio apartment; **en** — understudy
estudioso -sa ADJ studious; MF scholar
estufa F (para calentar) heater, stove; (para cocinar) *Méx* stove
estupefaciente ADJ & M narcotic
estupefacto ADJ stunned, speechless
estupendo ADJ stupendous, terrific; **me la pasé — en la casa de Hilary** I had a great time at Hilary's house
estupidez F stupidity; **estupideces** nonsense
estúpido ADJ stupid
estupor M stupor
estupro M statutory rape
etapa F stage; **por —s** by stages
etcétera CONJ etcetera, and so forth
éter M ether
eternidad F eternity
eternizarse[9] VI to drag on
eterno ADJ eternal, everlasting
ética F ethics
ético ADJ ethical
etimología F etymology
etíope ADJ & MF Ethiopian
etiqueta F (normas de comportamiento) etiquette; (en una lata, botella) label; (en una prenda) tag; **— adhesiva** sticker; **— de identificación** name tag; **— de precio** price tag; **nos trataron con —** they treated us very formally; **vestirse de —** to dress formally
etiquetar VT (latas, botellas, personas) to label; (prendas) to tag
etnicidad F ethnicity
étnico ADJ ethnic
etnografía F ethnography
etnología F ethnology
ETS (enfermedad de transmisión sexual) F STD
eucalipto M eucalyptus
eufemismo M euphemism
euforia F euphoria
eunuco M eunuch
euro M euro
Europa F Europe
europeo -a ADJ & MF European
eutanasia F euthanasia
evacuación F (de un lugar) evacuation; (del vientre) bowel movement; (de agua) drainage
evacuar VT (un lugar, a una persona) to evacuate; (el vientre, los excrementos) to void; (agua) to drain
evadir VT to evade; **—se** to escape
evaluación F evaluation
evaluar[17] VT (analizar) to evaluate, to assess; (tasar) to estimate; (calificar) to test
evangélico ADJ evangelical

evangelio M gospel
evaporación F evaporation
evaporar VT to evaporate; **—se** to vanish
evasión F (fiscal) evasion; (de prisioneros, de la realidad) escape; **— de capitales** capital flight
evasiva F **salirse con —s** to beat around the bush
evasivo ADJ evasive
evasor -ora MF evader
evento M event
evidencia F evidence; **dejar / poner en —** to show up; **quedar / ponerse en —** to become apparent
evidenciar VT to make evident; **—se** to become evident
evidente ADJ evident, obvious
evitar VT (eludir) to avoid; (ahorrar) to spare
evocar[6] VT (una memoria) to evoke; (a los espíritus) to conjure up
evolución F evolution
evolucionar VI to evolve
ex MF *fam* ex
exacerbar VT (intensificar) to exacerbate; (irritar) to aggravate
exactitud F accuracy, precision
exacto ADJ exact, precise, accurate; INTERJ exactly
exageración F exaggeration
exagerado ADJ exaggerated; **Jorge es un —** Jorge always exaggerates
exagerar VI/VT to exaggerate
exaltar VT to exalt; **—se** to get excited
examen M (inspección) examination; (prueba) examination, test, exam; **— de ingreso** entrance examination; **— final** final examination; **— médico** checkup; **dar un —** to take a test; **poner un —** to give a test
examinar VT (inspeccionar) to examine; (someter a un examen) to test
exasperar VT to exasperate, to aggravate
excavación F excavation; (arqueológica) dig
excavador -ora MF (persona) excavator; F (aparato) excavator, earthmover
excavar VT to excavate, to dig
excedente ADJ & M surplus
exceder VT (sobrepasar) to exceed; (superar) to surpass; **— de** to go beyond
excelencia F excellence; **por —** par excellence
excelente ADJ excellent, great
excentricidad F eccentricity
excéntrico ADJ eccentric
excepción F exception; **a — de** with the exception of
excepcional ADJ exceptional

excepto ADV & PREP except

exceptuar[17] VT to except

excesivo ADJ excessive

exceso M excess; **— de equipaje** excess baggage; **beber en —** to drink to excess; **comer en —** to overeat

excitación F (de músculos) excitement; (sexual) arousal

excitante ADJ stimulating

excitar VT (un órgano) to excite; (sexualmente) to arouse; **—se** (sexualmente) to get aroused; (átomos) to be excited

exclamación F exclamation

exclamar VT to exclaim

excluir[31] VT to exclude

exclusión F exclusion

exclusivo ADJ exclusive

excomulgar[7] VT to excommunicate

excremento M excrement

excretar VT to excrete

excursión F excursion, outing

excusa F excuse

excusable ADJ excusable

excusado M Méx toilet

excusar VT to excuse

exención F exemption

exento ADJ exempt; **— de impuestos** tax-exempt

exequias F PL funeral rites

exhalar VI/VT (aire) to exhale, to breathe out; (un olor) to give off; **— un suspiro** to sigh

exhaustivo ADJ exhaustive, thorough

exhausto ADJ exhausted

exhibición F (manifestación) exhibition; (despliegue) display

exhibir VT (fotos) to exhibit; (mercancías) to display; (el carnet de identidad) to show; **—se** to be shown

exhortar VT to exhort, to urge

exigencia F demand

exigente ADJ demanding, exacting

exigir[11] VT to demand; **exigen a alguien que sepa inglés** they require someone who knows English

exiguo ADJ meager; **exigua mayoría** scant majority

exiliado -da MF exile

exiliar VT to exile

exilio M exile

eximio ADJ illustrious

eximir VT (de impuestos) to exempt; (de sospecha) to clear; (de una responsabilidad) to excuse

existencia F existence; **complicarle la — a alguien** to cause someone trouble; **la**

lucha por la — the fight for survival; **—s** stock on hand; **en —** in stock, on hand

existente ADJ extant, existing

existir VI to exist

éxito M success; (musical) hit; **— de taquilla** blockbuster; **tener —** to be successful; **tiene — con las mujeres** he's popular with women

exitoso ADJ successful

éxodo M exodus

exonerar VT to exonerate

exorbitante ADJ exorbitant

exorcisar VT to exorcise

exorcismo M exorcism

exótico ADJ exotic

expansión F (crecimiento) expansion; (diversión) relaxation

expansivo ADJ (que expande) expansive; (efusivo) effusive

expatriado -da MF expatriate

expatriar VT to expatriate, exile

expectación F anticipation

expectativa F (esperanza) expectation; (posibilidad) prospect; **estar en — de algo** to be on pins and needles; **— de vida** life expectancy

expectorar VI/VT to expectorate, to cough up

expedición F (viaje) expedition; (de documentos) issuing; (de mercancías) delivery

expedicionario -ria ADJ expeditionary; MF member of an expedition

expedidor -ora ADJ shipping; MF shipper

expediente M (administrativo) file, dossier; (policial, académico) record

expedir[5] VT (enviar) to dispatch; (emitir) to issue

expeler VT to expel

experiencia F experience

experimentado ADJ experienced

experimental ADJ experimental

experimentar VI (hacer experimentos) to experiment; VT (tener experiencia de) to experience

experimento M experiment

experto -ta ADJ & MF expert

expiación F atonement

expiar[16] VT to atone for

expirar VI to expire

explayarse VI to become extended; **— sobre** to enlarge upon

explicable ADJ explainable, explicable

explicación F explanation

explicar[6] VT to explain; **—se** to make oneself clear; **no me explico por qué** I can't figure out why

explicativo ADJ explanatory

explícito ADJ explicit
exploración F exploration
explorador -ora ADJ exploring; MF (expedicionario) explorer; (militar) scout
explorar VI/VT to explore; (con fines diagnósticos) to scan; (con fines militares) to scout
explosión F explosion; **hacer —** to explode
explosivo ADJ & M explosive
explotación F exploitation
explotar VT (sacar provecho) to exploit; (hacer explosión) to explode
exponente M exponent
exponer[39] VT (al sol, al peligro) to expose; (al público) to exhibit, to display; (explicar) to state, to set forth; **—se al peligro** to expose oneself to danger
exportación F (acción) exportation, export; (cosa) export
exportar VI/VT to export
exposición F (feria) exposition; (de arte) exhibition; (explicación) explanation; (al sol, a una influencia, al peligro) exposure
expresar VT to express
expresión F expression; **valga la —** so to speak
expresivo ADJ expressive
expreso ADJ (explícito) express; (rápido) fast; M express train
exprimidor M juicer
exprimir VT (naranjas) to squeeze; (zumo) to squeeze out
expropiar VT to expropriate
expuesto ADJ exposed; **lo —** what has been said
expulsar VT to expel; (de un bar) to throw out; (de un partido) to eject
expulsión F expulsion
exquisito -ta ADJ exquisite; (comida) delicious; MF effete snob
extasiado ADJ rapt
extasiarse[16] VI to be enraptured
éxtasis M ecstasy (también droga)
extender[1] VT (el brazo, radio de acción, gratitud) to extend; (un tapete, una masa, un idioma) to spread; (un cheque) to draw up; **—se** to extend; **—se sobre** to enlarge upon; **la fiesta se extendió hasta las 3** the party lasted until 3 o'clock
extendido ADJ (brazos) outstretched; (costumbre) widespread
extensión F (del antebrazo, semántica, telefónica) extension; (de terreno) expanse; (de un texto) length; (eléctrica) extension cord; **por —** by extension; **tener mucha —** to be widespread
extensivo ADJ extensive; **hacer —** to extend

extenso ADJ (calendario, plan, grupo) extensive; (narración, programa de radio) extended
extenuado ADJ exhausted
exterior ADJ (de fuera) exterior, outer; (mundo) outside; (política) foreign; M (parte de afuera) exterior, outside; (aspecto) outward appearance; **en —es** on location
exteriorizar[9] VT to externalize
exterminación F extermination
exterminar VT to exterminate
exterminio M extermination
externo ADJ external
extinción F extinction
extinguidor M fire extinguisher
extinguir[12] VT (un fuego) to extinguish, to put out; (una especie) to make extinct, to wipe out; **—se** (animal, volcán) to go extinct
extinto ADJ extinct
extintor M fire extinguisher
extirpación F removal
extirpar VT to remove
extorsión F extortion
extorsionar VT to extort money from
extorsionista MF racketeer
extra ADJ extra; **horas —s** overtime; MF INV (de película) extra; M (cosa accesoria) extra; F (pago extraordinario) bonus
extracto M (resumen) abstract; (de café) extract
extraditar VT to extradite
extraer[45] VT (esencia) to extract; (minerales) to mine; (un diente) to pull
extramarital ADJ extramarital
extranjero -ra ADJ foreign; MF foreigner; **en el —** abroad
extrañar VT (sorprender) to surprise; (echar de menos) to miss; **no es de — que** it's no wonder that; **no me extraña** it doesn't surprise me; **—se** to be surprised
extrañeza F surprise
extraño -ña ADJ (persona, costumbre) strange; (partícula) foreign; MF stranger
extraoficial ADJ unofficial
extraordinario ADJ extraordinary
extrapolar VI/VT to extrapolate
extrasensorial ADJ extrasensory
extraterrestre ADJ & M alien, extraterrestrial
extravagancia F (cualidad de extravagante) extravagance; (comportamiento extravagante) outrageous behavior
extravagante ADJ flamboyant, outrageous
extraviar[16] VT (perder) to misplace; (confundir) to lead astray; **—se** to lose one's way, to get lost

extravío M loss
extremado ADJ extreme
extremar VT to maximize
extremidad F extremity
extremo ADJ (máximo, mínimo, extraordinario) extreme; (más lejos) farthest; **con — cuidado** with utmost care; M (punto más alejado) extreme; (de una región) end; **llegar al — de** to go so far as to; **— Oriente** Far East; **extrema izquierda** far left; **extrema unción** last rites
extrovertido -da ADJ extroverted; MF extrovert
exuberante ADJ (vegetación, jóvenes) exuberant; (mujer) voluptuous
exudar VI/VT to exude
exultante ADJ exhilarated, exultant
exultar VI to exult
eyacular VI/VT to ejaculate
eyectar VT to eject

Ff

fábrica F factory, plant; (de acero, de textiles) mill
fabricación F manufacture, manufacturing
fabricante MF manufacturer; (de coches) maker
fabricar[6] VT (producir) to manufacture, to make; (construir) to build; (inventar) to concoct, to fabricate
fabril ADJ manufacturing
fábula F (relato) fable; (mentira) falsehood
fabuloso ADJ (imaginario) imaginary; (magnífico) awesome, fabulous
facción F faction; **facciones** facial features
faceta F facet
facha F **estaba hecho una —** he was a sight
fachada F façade
facial ADJ facial
fácil ADJ easy; (promiscuo) easy, loose; **— de entender** self-explanatory; **— de usar** user-friendly
facilidad F ease; (habilidad) facility, knack
facilitar VT (hacer más fácil) to facilitate; (proporcionar) to furnish
facsímil M fax
factible ADJ feasible
fáctico ADJ factual
factor M factor
factoría F trading post

factura F bill, invoice
facturable ADJ billable
facturación F billing
facturar VT to invoice; (equipaje) to check
facultad F (habilidad) faculty; (autoridad) authority; (división de una universidad) college
facundia F gift of gab
faena F (trabajo corporal) chore; (labor) task; (molestia) nuisance
fagot M bassoon
fairway M fairway
faisán M pheasant
faja F (en la cintura) sash; (prenda interior) girdle; (de tierra) ribbon, strip
fajar VT (ceñir) to gird; (envolver) to wrap up; (golpear) to thrash
fajo M (de dinero) wad; (de papel, paja) sheaf
falacia F fallacy
falaz ADJ fallacious
falda F (prenda de vestir) skirt (también mujer o mujeres); (de una montaña) slope
faldón M (de una camisa) tail, shirttail; (de un saco) coattail
falible ADJ fallible
falla F (en un argumento) flaw; (en un motor) miss; (de una máquina) failure; (geológica) fault; **las Fallas** Valencian holiday
fallar VI (no funcionar) to fail; (un motor) to miss; VI/VT (un juez) to find, to rule
fallecer[13] VI to pass away, to decease
fallecimiento M demise, decease
fallo M (de una computadora) bug, failure; (de la memoria) lapse; (de un juez) ruling, finding
falo M phallus
falsear VT to falsify
falsedad F (dicho falso) falsehood; (condición de falso) falseness
falsificación F (de dinero) counterfeit; (de un documento) forgery
falsificar[6] VT to falsify, to fake; (dinero) to counterfeit; (una firma) to forge
falso ADJ (incorrecto) false, untrue; (no auténtico) fake, phony; (dinero) counterfeit; (promesa) hollow; (amigo) faithless, two-faced; (excusa) made-up; **falsa alarma** false alarm; **jurar en —** to perjure oneself; **paso en —** a false step; **salida en —** false start
falta F (defecto) fault; (carencia) lack, want; (ausencia) absence, miss; (jugada ilícita) foul; (de ortografía) mistake; **— de aire** shortness of breath; **— de respeto** disrespect; **a — de** for want of, in the absence of; **hacer —** to be necessary; **me**

hace — I need; **sin** — without fail

faltar VI (ausentarse) to be absent; (no haber) to be lacking; **— a la palabra** to break a promise; **— a la verdad** to misstate oneself; **—le el respeto a** to disrespect; **— poco para las cinco** to be almost five o'clock; **me falta tiempo** I don't have enough time; **¡no faltaba más!** (con indignación) that's the last straw; (no hay de qué) don't mention it! (no te molestes) I wouldn't hear of it

falto ADJ lacking; **— de esperanza** devoid of hope

fama F (condición de conocido) fame; (reputación) reputation

famélico ADJ ravenous

familia F family; **— nuclear** nuclear family; **en —** in the family; **jefe de —** head of household; **la señora de Juan tuvo —** John's wife had a baby

familiar ADJ (de familia) (of the) family; (amistoso, coloquial, conocido) familiar; (de tamaño grande) family-size; **coche —** family car; **vida —** family life; MF relative; **—es** next of kin

familiaridad F familiarity

familiarizar[9] VT to familiarize, to acquaint; **—se** to acquaint oneself, to become familiar with

famoso ADJ famous

fanático -ca ADJ fanatic; MF fanatic, zealot; (de deportes) freak

fanatismo M fanaticism

fanega F bushel

fanfarria F fanfare

fanfarrón -ona MF braggart, show-off; ADJ blustering

fanfarronear VI to bluster

fanfarronería F bluster, swagger

fango M mire

fangoso ADJ miry

fantasear VI to fantasize

fantasía F (imaginación) imagination; (imagen) fantasy; **de —** fake, artificial

fantasioso ADJ (niño) imaginative; (idea) fanciful

fantasma M ghost, phantom

fantasmagórico ADJ ghostly

fantástico ADJ fantastic

farándula F show business

fardo M (paquete) bundle; (de heno, algodón) bale

farfolla F husk

farfulla F jabber

farfullar VI to jabber

faringe F pharynx

faríngeo ADJ pharyngeal

farmacéutico -ca MF pharmacist, druggist; ADJ pharmaceutical

farmacia F pharmacy, drugstore

farmacología F pharmacology

faro M (torre) lighthouse; (luz) beacon; **— delantero** headlight

farol M (portátil) lantern; (del alumbrado público) street lamp, streetlight; (pie de hierro) lamppost; (jactancia, envite) bluff; **darse —** to show off, to put on airs

farra F spree; **ir de —** to go on a spree

farsa F (engaño) sham, hoax; (obra teatral, imitación ridícula) farce, mockery

farsante MF fraud, fake

fascículo M installment

fascinación F fascination

fascinante ADJ fascinating

fascinar VI/VT to fascinate

fascismo M fascism

fascista ADJ & MF fascist

fase F phase

fastidiado ADJ irked

fastidiar VT to irk

fastidio M annoyance

fastidioso ADJ annoying, wearisome

fatal ADJ (mortal) fatal; (terrible) terrible; **mujer —** femme fatale; ADV very badly

fatalidad F (desgracia) misfortune; (destino) destiny

fatídico ADJ ill-fated

fatiga F fatigue, exhaustion; **—s** hardships

fatigado ADJ tired, weary

fatigar[7] VT to tire out

fatigoso ADJ (cansado) tiring; (aburrido) tiresome

fauces F PL jaw

favor M favor; **a — de** in favor of; **por —** please

favorable ADJ favorable

favorecer[13] VT to favor

favoritismo M favoritism

favorito -ta ADJ favorite; MF favorite; (en una elección) front-runner; (de la maestra) pet

fax M fax

faxear VT to fax

faz F face

FBI M FBI

fe F faith; **— de bautismo** baptismal certificate; **— de erratas** list of errors; **— de nacimiento** birth certificate; **de buena —** in good faith; **dar — de** to vouch for

fealdad F ugliness

febrero M February

febril ADJ (con fiebre) feverish; (actividad) feverish, hectic

fecha F date

fechado ADJ dated
fechar VT to date
fechoría F misdeed
fecundar VT to fertilize; (una hembra) to impregnate
fecundo ADJ fertile
federación F federation
federal ADJ federal
felicidad F happiness; **¡—es!** congratulations
felicitación F congratulation; **¡felicitaciones!** congratulations!
felicitar VT to congratulate
feligrés -esa MF parishioner; **feligreses** congregation
felino ADJ feline; M cat
feliz ADJ happy
felpa F plush
felpudo M door mat
femenino ADJ (como una mujer, de género gramatical) feminine; (de la mujer) female
feminidad F femininity
feminismo F feminism
fémur M femur
fenómeno M phenomenon
feo ADJ ugly, homely; (dentadura) bad; (accidente) nasty
féretro M coffin
feria F (mercado) market; (exposición) fair; (espectáculo) carnival; (celebración) holiday
feriante MF trader at fairs
fermentación F fermentation
fermentar VT to ferment; (cerveza) to brew
fermento M ferment
ferocidad F ferocity
feroz ADJ ferocious, fierce
férreo ADJ iron; (disciplina) harsh
ferretería F (tienda) hardware store; (artículos) hardware
ferrocarril M railroad, railway
ferroviario -ria ADJ railroad; MF railroad employee
ferry M ferryboat
fértil ADJ fertile
fertilidad F fertility
fertilizante M fertilizer
fertilizar[9] VT to fertilize
ferviente ADJ fervent
fervor M fervor, zeal
fervoroso ADJ zealous
festejar VT to celebrate
festejo M celebration
festín M feast; **darse un —** to treat oneself
festival M festival
festividad F festivity
festivo ADJ festive, gay; **día —** holiday
festón M scallop

festonear VT to scallop
fetal ADJ fetal
fetiche M fetish
fétido ADJ foul-smelling
feto M fetus
feudal ADJ feudal
feudo M manor
fiabilidad F reliability
fiable ADJ reliable
fiador -ora MF guarantor, voucher; (prestamista) backer; (de un preso) bondsman
fiambre M (carne) cold cut; (cadáver) *fam* stiff
fianza F security, guaranty; (de un preso) bail
fiar[16] VT (garantizar) to vouch for; **—se de** to trust
fiasco M fiasco
fibra F fiber; **— de vidrio** fiberglass; **— óptica** optical fiber
fibroso ADJ fibrous
ficción F fiction
ficha F (pieza) token; (de dominó) domino; (de damas) checker; (en poker, ruleta) chip; (tarjeta) index card; MF INV (persona con antecedentes penales) delinquent
fichar VT to open a file on; VI to punch in
fichero M (de computadora) file; (archivador) filing cabinet
ficticio ADJ (no real) fictitious; (novelesco) fictional
fidedigno ADJ trustworthy
fideicomisario -ria MF trustee
fideicomiso M trusteeship
fidelidad F fidelity, faithfulness; (de una traducción) closeness; (a la bandera) allegiance
fideo M noodle
fiduciario -ria ADJ & MF fiduciary
fiebre F fever; **— aftosa** foot-and-mouth disease; **— amarilla** yellow fever; **— de candilejas** stage fight; **— del oro** gold rush; **— tifoidea** typhoid fever; **tener —** to run a fever
fiel ADJ faithful; (exacto) true, accurate; M pointer on a scale; **los —es** the congregation
fieltro M felt; (sombrero de fieltro) felt hat
fiera F beast; **ponerse hecho una —** to go berserk
fiereza F ferocity
fiero ADJ fierce; (muy grande) huge
fierro M piece of iron
fiesta F (festejo) party; (día feriado) holiday; **aguar una —** to ruin a party
fiestero -ra ADJ fond of parties; MF merrymaker, party animal

figura F figure
figurado ADJ figurative
figurar VI (aparecer) to feature; (lucirse) to be seen; (incluirse) to figure, to enter into; **—se** (imaginarse) to imagine; **¡figúrate!** imagine!
figurativo ADJ figurative
figurín M fashion plate
figurón M dummy
fijación F fixing
fijador M hairspray
fijar VT (un cartel) to fix, to fasten; (una fecha) to set; **—se en** (notar) to notice; (prestar atención) to pay attention to, to focus on
fijo ADJ (sujeto, que no cambia) fixed; (inmóvil) fixed, stationary; (firme) firm; (definitivo) definite; (permanente) permanent
fila F (uno detrás del otro) row, file; (hombro a hombro) rank; (de espera) line; **— india** single file; **cerrar —s** to close ranks; **romper —s** to break ranks
filamento M filament
filantropía F philanthropy
filarmónica F philharmonic
filarmónico ADJ philharmonic
filete M (de carne) fillet; (de un plato) rim
filetear VT to fillet
filial ADJ filial; F affiliate
filibusterismo M filibustering
filigrana F filigree
Filipinas F Philippines
filipino -na ADJ & MF Philippine
filmar VT to film, to shoot
filo M (de una navaja) cutting edge; (biológico) phylum; **de doble —** two-edged; **al — de las dos** at around two o'clock
filón M seam, vein, pocket
filoso ADJ sharp
filosofía F philosophy
filosófico ADJ philosophical
filósofo -fa MF philosopher
filtración F (acción de filtrar) filtration; (de información) leak
filtrar VT to filter; **—se** to leak through
filtro M filter; **— de aire** air filter; **— de amor** love potion
fin M (conclusión, objetivo) end; **— de año** New Year's Eve; **— del mundo** (lugar apartado) boondocks; **— de semana** weekend; **— de siglo** turn of the century; **al —** at last; **al — y al cabo** at any rate; **a — de que** so that; **a — de mes** toward the end of the month; **en —** in conclusion; **poner — a** to put an end to;

por — at last; **sin —** (ilimitado) myriad; (continuo) endless
finado ADJ late
final ADJ final, last; F (deportiva) final; M (de una historia) ending; (de un terreno) end; (de una carrera) finish; (de una filmación) wrap
finalista MF finalist
finalización F completion
finalizar[9] VT to finish
finalmente ADV at last
financiación F (para una compra) financing; (para un proyecto científico) funding
financiamiento M (para una compra) financing; (para un proyecto científico) funding
financiar VT (una compra) to finance; (un proyecto) to fund, to underwrite
financiero -ra ADJ financial; MF financier
finanza F finance; **—s** finances
finca F property
finés -esa MF Finn; M (lengua) Finnish; ADJ Finnish
fineza F (atención) courtesy; (suavidad) smoothness
fingir[11] VI/VT (sorpresa) to feign; (un ataque al corazón) to fake; **fingió que la quería** he pretended to love her
finiquito M settlement
finito ADJ finite
finlandés -esa MF Finn; M (lengua) Finnish; ADJ Finnish
Finlandia F Finland
fino ADJ (vino, arena, pelo, metal) fine; (sentidos) keen, sharp; (medias) sheer; (hielo, alambre, voz) thin; (modales) smooth, refined
firma F (compañía) firm; (rúbrica) signature
firmamento M sky
firmante MF signer
firmar VI/VT to sign
firme ADJ firm; (control) tight; (colores) fast; (amarras) secure; (mano) steady, sure; (resistencia) stiff; (apoyo, resistencia) strong, staunch, steadfast; **mantenerse —** to stand one's ground; **¡—s!** attention!
firmeza F firmness; (de la mano) steadiness; (de la resistencia) stiffness; (del apoyo) strength
fiscal ADJ fiscal; MF public prosecutor, district attorney
fiscalía F prosecution
fisgar[7] VI to snoop
fisgón -ona ADJ snooping; MF snoop
fisgonear VI to snoop
física F physics
físico -ca ADJ physical; MF (persona)

physicist; M (cuerpo) physique
fisiología F physiology
fisiológico ADJ physiological
fisonomía F features
fisura F fissure
fiyano ADJ Fijian
Fiyi M Fiji
fláccido, fláccido ADJ (sin firmeza) limp; (gordo) flabby
flaco ADJ thin, skinny; **su lado —** his weakness
flacura F thinness
flagrante ADJ (injusticia) gross; **en — delito** in the act
flamante ADJ brand-new
flamear VI (llamear) to flame; (ondear) to flap
flamenco -ca ADJ Flemish; MF Flemish person; M (lengua) Flemish; (ave) flamingo; (baile) flamenco
flamígero ADJ flaming
flan M caramel custard
flanco M (de un animal, ejército) flank; (de un neumático) sidewall
flanquear VT to flank
flaquear VI (intención) to waver; (salud) to wane
flaqueza F weakness
flash M (noticias, visión) flash; (lámpara) flashbulb, flash
flashback M flashback
flatulencia F flatulence
flauta F flute; **— dulce** recorder
flautín M piccolo
flecha F arrow
flechar VT to wound with an arrow
flechazo M (herida) wound from an arrow; (enamoramiento) love at first sight
fleco M (de una alfombra) fringe; (de pelo) bangs
flema F phlegm
flequillo M bangs
fletamento M charter
fletar VT to charter
flete M (contratación) charter; (envío) transport; (precio de transporte) freight
flexibilidad F flexibility; (libertad) latitude
flexible ADJ flexible; (cuerpo humano) limber, supple; (opinión) pliant, pliable
flojear VT to slacken
flojedad F laxity, looseness; (debilidad) weakness
flojera F (debilidad) weakness; (pereza) laziness
flojo ADJ (no ajustado) loose, slack; (holgazán) lazy; (inferior) crummy; (débil) weak; (sin fundamento) flimsy

floppy M floppy disk
flor F flower, blossom, bloom; (cumplido) compliment; **— de la edad** prime of life; **— de Pascua** poinsettia; **— y nata** the cream of the crop; **a — de** flush with; **en — in bloom
floración F blooming, blossoming
floral ADJ flowery
floreado ADJ flowery
florear VT (adornar con flores) to decorate with flowers; (adornar) to adorn
florecer[13] VI (echar flores) to flower, to bloom; (prosperar) to flourish, to thrive
floreciente ADJ (que prospera) flourishing, prosperous; (que echa flores) blooming
florecimiento M flourishing
floreo M flourish
florería F florist's shop
florero M flower vase
florete M fencing foil
florido ADJ flowery
florista MF florist
floritura F flourish
flota F fleet
flotador M (cosa que flota) float; (de un avión) pontoon; ADJ floating
flotante ADJ floating, buoyant
flotar VI (estar suspendido, variar en valor) to float; (moverse en la superficie) to drift; (en el aire) to waft
flote M flotation; **a — afloat; poner a — to set afloat
fluctuación F fluctuation; (amplitud de variación) range
fluctuar[17] VI to fluctuate
fluidez F (lo fluido) fluency; (lo aguado) thinness
fluido ADJ (que fluye) fluid, flowing; (no vacilante) fluent; M fluid
fluir[31] VI to flow
flujo M flow; (uterino) discharge; **— de caja** cash flow
flúor M (elemento gaseoso) fluorine; (sal) fluoride
fluorescente ADJ fluorescent
fluoruro M fluoride
flux M flush
fluyente ADJ flowing
fobia F phobia
foca F seal
foco M (punto central) focus; (bombilla) bulb; (lámpara potente) spotlight
fofo ADJ mushy
fogata F bonfire; (en un campamento) campfire
fogonazo M flash
fogonero M fireman

fogoso ADJ fiery, spirited
folclore M folklore
folio M folio
folíolo M leaflet
follaje M foliage
follar VT *vulg* to fuck, to screw
folleto M pamphlet, brochure
follón M (confusión) mess; (alboroto) ruckus
fomentar VT (estudio) to promote; (amistad) to foster; (discordia) to foment; (apoyo) to drum up
fomento M encouragement
fonda F inn
fondear VI to anchor
fondillos M PL seat of pants
fondista MF (posadero) innkeeper; (corredor) long-distance runner
fondo M (parte más profunda de algo) bottom; (de un salón) rear; (del mar) bed; (de un cuadro, foto) background; (de dinero) fund; (de una biblioteca) holdings; **— común** pool; **— físico** endurance; **— musical** background music; **— mutuo** mutual fund; **—s** funds; **a —** in depth; **carrera de —** long-distance race; **de cuatro en —** four abreast; **de —** in depth; **sin —** bottomless; **tocar —** to hit rock bottom
fonética F phonetics
fonógrafo M phonograph
fonología F phonology
fontanería F plumbing
fontanero -ra MF plumber
forajido -da MF outlaw
foráneo ADJ foreign; **influencia foranéa** outside influence
forastero -ra MF stranger, outsider
forcejear VI to struggle
forcejeo M struggle
fórceps M forceps
forense ADJ forensic; MF forensic scientist
forja F (fogón) forge; (acción de forjar) forging; (taller) blacksmith's shop
forjado ADJ wrought
forjar VT (metales, un acuerdo) to forge; (un acuerdo) to hammer out; (un documento) to frame
forma F (figura) form, shape; (manera) manner; **ponerse en —** to get in shape; **no hay —** no way; **dar — a** to shape
formación F formation
formal ADJ (que atañe a la forma) formal, serious; (fiable) reliable
formalidad F (convencionalidad) formality; (fiabilidad) reliability
formalismo M formality
formalizar[9] VT to make official; **—se** to

settle down
formar VT to form; (reunir tropas) to muster; (entrenar) to train; **—se** (montañas) to form; (estudiantes) to be educated
formatear VT to format
formateo M formatting
formativo ADJ formative
formato M format
formidable ADJ formidable
formón M wood chisel
fórmula F formula
formular VT to formulate; (un plan, una pregunta) to frame; (un documento) to word
formulario M form
fornicar[6] VI to fornicate
fornido ADJ stout, sturdy
foro M forum; (de un escenario) back
forrado ADJ (con un forro) lined; (bien provisto) flush
forraje M forage, fodder
forrajear VI to forage
forrar VT (un saco) to line; **—se** to line one's pockets
forro M lining; (de un libro) jacket
fortalecer[13] VT to fortify, to strengthen
fortaleza F (construcción) fortress, fort; (fuerza) fortitude
fortificación F fortification
fortificar[6] VT to fortify
fortuito ADJ fortuitous, accidental
fortuna F fortune; **por —** fortunately; **probar —** to try one's luck; **hacer —** to become rich
forúnculo M boil
forzar[9] VT to force, to coerce; **— la entrada** to break into
forzoso ADJ (por la fuerza) forcible; (inevitable) necessary; (aterrizaje) forced
fosa F (sepultura) grave; (de la nariz) cavity; (en el fondo del mar) trench
fosfato M phosphate
fósforo M (sustancia) phosphorus; (cerilla) match
fósil ADJ & M fossil
foso M (de un castillo) moat; (de un taller, teatro) pit
foto F snapshot, photo
fotocopia F photocopy
fotocopiadora F photocopier
fotocopiar VI/VT to photocopy
fotoeléctrico ADJ photoelectric
fotogénico ADJ photogenic
fotografía F (foto) photograph; (arte) photography
fotografiar[16] VT to photograph
fotógrafo -fa MF photographer

fotón M photon
fotosíntesis F photosynthesis
foul M foul
frac M tails
fracasar VI to fail; (una película) to bomb; (una embarcación) to break up
fracaso M failure; (una película) flop, bomb
fracción F fraction
fractura F fracture, break
fracturar VT to fracture, to break; **se fracturó la cadera** she broke her hip
fragancia F fragrance
fragante ADJ fragrant; **en —** in the act
fragata F frigate
frágil ADJ (delicado) delicate; (que se quiebra) fragile, brittle; (una paz) tenuous
fragilidad F (condición de quebradizo) brittleness, delicacy; (debilidad) frailty
fragmento M fragment; (de metal, piedra) scrap; (de una conversación) snatch; (de un texto) extract, excerpt
fragoso ADJ rugged
fragua F (fogón) forge; (taller) blacksmith's shop
fraguar[8] VT to forge; (una trama) to hatch; VI (cemento, yeso) to set
fraile M friar
frambuesa F raspberry
frambueso M raspberry bush
francés -esa ADJ French; M (lengua) French; (hombre) Frenchman; F (mujer) Frenchwoman
franchute -uta MF pey frog
Francia F France
franco ADJ (sincero) frank, candid; (exento) free; **una franca mayoría** a clear majority; **un tratado —-americano** a Franco-American treaty
francotirador -ora MF sniper
franela F flannel
franja F ribbon
franquear VT (una frontera) to cross; (una carta) to frank; **—se** to be frank
franqueo M postage
franqueza F frankness
franquicia F (concesión) franchise; (exención) exemption
frasco M (recipiente de vidrio) flask; (de medicina, perfume) bottle; (de mermelada) jar
frase F phrase
frasear VI/VT to phrase
fraternal ADJ fraternal, brotherly
fraternidad F fraternity
fraternizar[9] VI fraternize
fraterno ADJ fraternal
fraude M fraud

fraudulento ADJ fraudulent
frazada F blanket
frecuencia F frequency; **con —** frequently
frecuentar VT to frequent; (una tienda) to patronize
frecuente ADJ frequent
fregadero M sink
fregado M scrubbing
fregar[7] VT to scour, to scrub
fregona F (persona) scrubwoman, drudge; (utensilio) mop
freír[15] VI/VT to fry
frenar VT (un coche) to brake; (la inmigración) to restrain; (los impulsos) to bridle; VI to brake, to apply the brakes
frenesí M frenzy; (de actividad) flurry
frenético ADJ frantic
freno M (de coche) brake; (de caballo) bit; (contra el contrabando) curb
frente F forehead; **el sudor de la —** the sweat of one's brow; M (parte delantera, zona de combate, zona meteorológica) front; (de un edificio) face; **— a** (ante) in the face of; (al otro lado) facing; **— a** face to face; **de —** head-on; **en — de** in front of; **hacer —** to face; **pasar al —** to come to the fore
fresa F (fruta) strawberry; (herramienta) mill
fresadora F milling machine
fresar VT to mill
frescachona F buxom woman
fresco ADJ (que acaba de producirse, descansado) fresh; (frío) cool, brisk; (de poco abrigo) light; (no cocinado) raw; (pintura) wet; M (frío) coolness; (pintura) fresco
frescor M (de verduras) freshness; (del aire) coolness
frescura F (de verduras, del carácter) freshness; (del tiempo) coolness; (comentario) impudent remark
fresno M ash tree
friabilidad F looseness
frialdad F coldness, coolness
fricción F friction, rubbing
friccionar VT to rub
friega F rubbing, massage
frigorífico M (electrodoméstico) refrigerator; (cámara) refrigeration chamber
frijol M bean
frío ADJ cold; (muy frío) frigid; M cold; **tener —** to be cold
friolento ADJ sensitive to cold
friolera la — de $50,000 a trifling $50,000
fritada F dish of fried food
frito ADJ fried; M dish of fried food

fritura F (acción de freír) frying; (comida frita) dish of fried food

frivolidad F frivolity

frívolo ADJ frivolous

fronda F foliage

frondoso ADJ leafy

frontera F frontier, border

fronterizo ADJ frontier

frontón M (juego) jai alai; (pista) jai alai court

frotación F rubbing

frotar VI/VT to rub

frote M rub

frotis M smear

fructífero ADJ fruitful

fructificar[6] VI to bear fruit

fructosa F fructose

frugal ADJ frugal

frunce M (volante) ruffle; (defecto) pucker

fruncir[10b] VT to gather; **— el ceño** to frown, to knit one's brow; **— los labios** to purse one's lips

fruslería F trifle

frustración F frustration

frustrar VT (los planes) to frustrate, to thwart, to foil; (las esperanzas) to shatter, to dash; **—se** to fail, to miscarry

fruta F fruit

frutero -era MF fruit vendor; M fruit dish

fruto M fruit; **—s del mar** seafood

fuego M fire; (para un cigarro) light; **— antiaéreo** anti-artillery fire; **—s artificiales** fireworks; **abrir el —** to begin to fire; **alto el —** cease-fire; **bajo —** under fire; **arma de —** firearm; **entre dos —s** between a rock and a hard place; **hacer —** to fire; **poner / pegar / prender — a** to set fire to

fuelle M bellows

fuel-oil M fuel oil

fuente F (surtidor) fountain; (manantial, referencia) spring; (caracteres de imprenta) font; **de buena —** from the horse's mouth

fuera ADV outside, out; **— de** outside of; **— de borda** outboard; **— de combate** out of commission; **— de serie** one of a kind; INTERJ out!

fuero M (jurisdicción) jurisdiction; (privilegio) privilege, charter

fuerte ADJ strong; (ruido) loud; (cuero) tough; (personalidad) forceful; (estantería) sturdy; (comida) hearty; M (castillo) fort; (talento especial) strong point; ADV (tirar) strongly; (respirar) heavily; (gritar) loud; **soplar —** to bluster; **pisar —** to stomp; **atar —** to tie tight

fuerza F (capacidad de mover algo) force; (de una persona, animal) strength; **— aérea** air force; **— bruta** brute force; **— de la naturaleza** force of nature; **— de tarea** task force; **— de voluntad** willpower; **—s armadas** armed forces; **a — de** by dint of; **hacer —** to press on; **por la —** by force; **sacar — de flaqueza** to pull oneself together

fuga F (escape) escape, flight; (de la cárcel) jailbreak; (de gas) leak; (de capitales) drain

fugarse[7] VI to flee, to escape; **— con** to abscond with

fugaz ADJ fleeting

fugitivo -va ADJ fugitive; MF fugitive

fulano -na MF so-and-so; **—, zutano y mengano** Tom, Dick and Harry; F tart, tramp

fulgor M radiance

fulgurar VI to flash

full M full house

fullero -ra MF (tramposo) cheat; (en naipes) card sharp

fulminante M cap; ADJ devastating

fulminar VT to strike with lightning; to thunder; **lo fulminó con la mirada** she gave him a withering look

fumadero M crackhouse

fumador -ora MF smoker

fumar VI/VT to smoke; **—se mucho dinero** to blow a lot of money

fumigar[7] VT to fumigate, to fog

función F (uso) function; (de una obra de teatro) performance; (cargo) office

funcionamiento M operation, working

funcionar VI to function, to work; (motor) to run

funcionario -ria MF government employee, official

funda F cover; (de una almohada) pillowcase, slip; (de navaja) sheath

fundación F foundation

fundador -ora MF founder

fundamental ADJ (básico) fundamental; (importante) crucial

fundamentarse VI to be based

fundamento M foundation, basis; **—s** fundamentals

fundar VT (un instituto) to found, to establish; (un argumento) to base

fundición F (fábrica) foundry; (acción de fundirse) fusing

fundido ADJ molten; M (en cinematografía) fade-in / out

fundidor -ora MF foundry worker

fundir VT (combinar) to fuse; (derretir) to melt; (moldear) to mold; **—se**

(combinarse) to fuse; (romperse una bombilla) to burn out

fúnebre ADJ funeral

funeral ADJ & M funeral

funerario -ria ADJ funeral; F funeral parlor; MF funeral director

funesto ADJ ill-fated, unlucky

funicular M cable car

funky ADJ funky

furgón M (vagón) boxcar; (camioneta de policía) police van; **— de cola** caboose

furia F fury

furibundo ADJ furious, livid

furioso ADJ furious; (tempestad) fierce

furor M fury; **hacer —** to be all the rage

furtivo ADJ furtive, stealthy

fuselaje M fuselage

fusible M electric fuse

fusil M rifle

fusilar VT to execute with firearms

fusión F (derretimiento) melting; (nuclear) fusion; (empresarial) merger

fusionar VT (metales) to fuse; (compañías) to merge

fusta F crop

fustigar[7] VT to lash, to whip; (criticar) to lash out at

fútbol M soccer; **— americano** football

fútil ADJ futile, trivial

futilidad F triviality

futuro ADJ future; M future; **—s** futures

Gg

gabacho -cha ADJ & MF (francés) *pey* frog; (americano) *pey* American

gabán M overcoat

gabardina F trench coat

gabinete M (ministerial) cabinet; (oficina) office

Gabón M Gabon / Gabun

gabonés -esa ADJ & MF Gabonese

gacela F gazelle

gaceta F gazette

gacetilla F short news item

gachas F PL **— de avena** oatmeal

gachí F bimbo

gacho ADJ (orejas) drooping; (cabeza) bowed; (ojos) lowered

gachupín -ina MF *Méx pey* Spaniard

gafar VT to jinx

gafas F PL glasses

gafe M jinx

gaffe M gaffe, faux pas

gag M gag

gaita F bagpipe

gaje M **—s del oficio** occupational hazards

gajo M (rama) branch; (de naranja) section

gala F (cena) banquet; **—s** finery; **hacer — de** to boast of, to flaunt; **vestirse de —** to dress up

galán M gallant, suitor; (en un drama) leading man

galante ADJ gallant

galantear VT to court

galanteo M courting

galantería F (caballerosidad) gallantry; (cumplido) compliment

galardón M award

galaxia F galaxy

galera F galley (también prueba de imprenta); *RP* top hat

galerada F galley proof

galería F gallery; (pasillo) corridor; (tiendas) mall, gallery; (de coro) loft; (subterráneo) tunnel; **—s** *Esp* department store

Gales M Wales

galés -esa ADJ & MF Welsh

galgo M greyhound

Galicia F Galicia

gallardete M pennant

gallardía F (elegancia) elegance; (valentía) bravery

gallardo ADJ (elegante) elegant; (valiente) brave

gallego -ga ADJ Galician; M (lengua) Galician; MF Galician

gallera F cockpit

galleta F (salada) cracker; (dulce) cookie

gallina F (pollo) chicken; (hembra) hen; MF coward; **— ciega** blind man's bluff; **la — de los huevos de oro** the goose that laid the golden egg

gallinero M (de gallinas) chicken coop; (de teatro) gallery; **alborotarse el —** to raise a ruckus

gallito ADJ cocksure, cocky

gallo M cock, rooster; (de la voz) break; **tener —s en la garganta** to have a frog in one's throat; **en menos que canta un —** before you can say Jack Robinson

galón M (de líquido) gallon; (de tela) stripe

galopar VI/VT to gallop

galope M gallop; **al —** at a gallop

galvanizar[9] VT to galvanize

gama F gamut, range

gamba F large shrimp

gamberro -rra MF punk, hoodlum

Gambia F Gambia

gambiano -na ADJ & MF Gambian

gamo M buck

gamuza F chamois (también piel); (piel de venado) buckskin, deerskin; (de vaca) suede

gana F urge; **con —s** with a vengeance; **de buena —** willingly; **tener —s de** to feel like; **tengo —s** I have to go (to the bathroom); **no me da la —** I absolutely don't want to

ganadero -ra M cattleman; F cattlewoman; ADJ **industria ganadera** cattle industry

ganado M livestock; **— ovino** sheep; **— porcino** swine; **— vacuno** cattle

ganador -ora MF winner; ADJ winning

ganancia F profit, gain, return; **—s** (recaudación de un evento) proceeds; (de un juego) winnings; (de un negocio) earnings

ganapán M (obrero) menial worker; (trabajo) bread-and-butter

ganar VI/VT (una guerra, la lotería) to win; (kilos, en eficacia) to gain; VT (un sueldo) to earn; (tiempo, espacio) to save; (tierra) to reclaim; **dejarse — por algo** to give in to something; **nos ganaron el partido** they beat us; **—se la vida** to make a living

ganchillo M crochet

gancho M hook (también en boxeo, baloncesto); (rama) snag; (para sujetar) clip; (atractivo) lure; **echar a uno el —** to hook someone; **tener —** to be attractive

gandul -la MF loafer

ganga F bargain, steal

gangoso ADJ twangy

gangrena F gangrene

gangrenarse VI to gangrene

gángster M gangster

ganguear VI to twang

ganso M (animal) goose; (macho) gander; (tonto) *fam* ding-a-ling

ganzúa F picklock

gañido M yelp

gañir[18] VI to yelp

garabatear VI to scribble

garabato M scribble; **hacer —s** to scribble

garaje M garage

garante MF voucher

garantía F (de producto) guarantee, warranty; (de promesa) security, guaranty; (de un derecho) guarantee

garantizar[9] VT (un producto) to guarantee, to warranty; (prometer) to warrant

garañón M stud, horse

garbanzo M chickpea

garbo M grace

garboso ADJ graceful

garfio M hook

garganta F (interno) throat; (todo) neck; (valle estrecho) gorge

gárgara F gargle; **hacer —s** to gargle

gargarismo M gargle

garita F sentry box

garito M gambling house

garra F (de ave) claw; (de león) paw with claws; **caer en las —s de alguien** to fall into someone's clutches

garrafa F decanter

garrapata F tick

garrapatear VI to scribble

garrapiñar VT to candy

garrocha F pole

garrote M club

garrucha F pulley

gárrulo ADJ garrulous

garza F heron

gas M gas; **—es** (de motor) fumes; (de intestino) gas; **— lacrimógeno** tear gas; **— mostaza** mustard gas; **— natural** natural gas; **— nervioso** nerve gas; **a todo —** at full speed

gasa F gauze; (para heridas) dressing

gaseosa F soda, soft drink

gaseoso ADJ gaseous

gasoducto M pipeline

gasolina F gasoline, gas

gasolinera F gas station

gastado ADJ (neumático) smooth; (ropa) worn-out, shabby

gastador -ora ADJ extravagant, wasteful; MF spendthrift

gastar VT (dinero, tiempo) to spend; (energía) to expend; (neumáticos, ropa) to wear out, to use up; **— una broma** to play a trick; **—se** to wear out

gasto M (dinero) expense, expenditure, outlay; (desgaste) wear

gástrico ADJ gastric

gastritis F gastritis

gastroenteritis F gastroenteritis

gastrointestinal ADJ gastrointestinal

gastronomía F gastronomy

gatas LOC ADV **a —** on all fours

gatear VI to creep, to crawl

gatillo M (en un arma de fuego) trigger; (de dentista) forceps

gatito M kitten

gato M (felino) cat; (aparato para levantar) jack; **— montés** wildcat, mountain lion; **aquí hay — encerrado** I smell a rat; **a gatas** on all fours; **dar — por liebre** to sell someone a pig in a poke

gaucho M gaucho

gaveta F small drawer
gavilán M hawk
gavilla F (de maíz) sheaf; (de maleantes) gang
gaviota F seagull
gayola F big house
gazmoñería F prudery
gazmoño -ña MF prude; ADJ prudish
gaznate M gullet
gazpacho M *Esp* cold vegetable soup
geco M gecko
géiser M geyser
gel M gel
gelatina F gelatin
gélido ADJ frigid
gema F gem, jewel
gemelo -la ADJ & MF twin; **—s** (mellizos) twins; (binoculares) binoculars, opera glasses; (de camisa) studs
gemido M (de dolor) moan, groan; (de queja) whine
gemir[5] VI (gruñir) to moan, to groan; (lloriquear) to whine
gen, gene M gene
genealogía F genealogy
generación F generation
generador M generator
general ADJ & M general; **por lo —** generally
generalidad F generality
generalizar[9] VI/VT to generalize; **—se** to become widespread
generar VT generate
genérico ADJ generic
género M (clase) kind; (gramatical) gender; (tela) material; (literario) genre; (biológico) genus; **— humano** human race; **—s** dry goods
generosidad F generosity
generoso ADJ generous
genética F genetics
genético ADJ genetic
genial ADJ brilliant
genio MF (persona inteligente) genius; M (inteligencia) genius, brilliance; (temperamento) temperament, nature; (mal humor) temper; **de mal —** mean; **de buen —** genial
genital ADJ genital; M PL **—es** genitals
geniudo ADJ quick-tempered
genocidio M genocide
genoma M genome
gente F (personas) people; **— de campo** country folk; **— de color** persons of color; **— joven** young people; **— menuda** small fry; **buena —** good person
gentil ADJ (cortés) gracious; (no judío) gentile; MF gentile

gentileza F graciousness
gentío M crowd
gentuza F rabble, riffraff
genuino ADJ genuine
geocéntrico ADJ geocentric
geoestacionario ADJ geostationary
geofísica F geophysics
geografía F geography
geográfico ADJ geographical
geología F geology
geológico ADJ geological
geometría F geometry
geométrico ADJ geometric
Georgia F Georgia
georgiano -na ADJ & MF Georgian
geotérmico ADJ geothermal
geranio M geranium
gerencia F management
gerente -ta MF manager
geriátrico ADJ geriatric
germen M germ
germinar VI to germinate, to sprout
gerundio M gerund, present participle
gestación F gestation
gesticular VI to gesture; (exageradamente) to gesticulate
gestión F (acción) step, maneuver; (empresarial) management; (política) administration; **—es** negotiations; **hacer —es para** to take steps to
gestionar VT (negociar) to negotiate; (administrar) to administer
gesto M (con la cara) face; (con las manos) gesture; **hacer —s a** to make faces at
Ghana F Ghana
ghanés -esa ADJ & MF Ghanaian
giba F hump, hunch
gibón M gibbon
Gibraltar M Gibraltar
gibraltareño -ña ADJ & MF Gibraltarian
giga F jig
gigabyte M gigabyte
gigante ADJ giant, gigantic; MF giant
gigantesco ADJ gigantic
gilipollas MF *ofensivo* idiot, schmuck
gimnasia F gymnastics
gimnasio M gymnasium, gym
gimotear VI to whimper
gimoteo M whimper
ginebra F gin
ginecología F gynecology
ginecólogo -a MF gynecologist
gingivitis F gingivitis
gira F tour
girar VI/VT (una llave, un volante, un coche, a la derecha) to turn; VI (repetidas veces)

to revolve, to spin, to whirl; VT (dinero) to wire

girasol M sunflower

giratorio ADJ rotary, revolving

giro M (movimiento circular) rotation, spin; (cambio de dirección) turn; (expresión) turn of phrase; (monetario) draft, remittance; — **postal** money order

giroscopio M gyroscope

gitano -na ADJ & MF gypsy

glacial ADJ glacial, bitter

glaciar M glacier

gladiador M gladiator

glamoroso ADJ glamorous

glamour M glamour

glándula F gland

glandular ADJ glandular

glaseado M (de una torta) glaze; ADJ (papel) glossy

glasear VT to glaze

glaucoma M glaucoma

glicerina F glycerin

global ADJ (mundial) global; (de conjunto) blanket, overall

globo M (esfera) globe; (de árbol de Navidad) ball; (lleno de gas) balloon; (en tenis) lob; — **ocular** eyeball; — **terráqueo** globe

glóbulo M globule; (de sangre) corpuscle

gloria F glory

glorieta F (pérgola) arbor; (rotonda) traffic circle

glorificar[6] VT to glorify

glorioso M glorious

glosa F gloss

glosar VT to gloss

glosario M glossary

glotón -ona ADJ gluttonous; MF glutton

glotonería F gluttony

glucosa F glucose

gluglutear VI to gobble

gobernador -ora ADJ governing; MF governor

gobernante ADJ governing; MF ruler

gobernar[1] VI/VT to govern, to rule; (un buque) to steer

gobierno M government

goce M enjoyment

gofre M waffle

gol M goal

goleador -ora MF shooter

goleta F schooner

golf M golf

golfo -fa M (mar) gulf; (sinvergüenza) rascal; F tramp

gollería F delicacy

golondrina F swallow

golosina F sweet, goody, tidbit

goloso ADJ sweet-toothed

golpazo M bang, whack

golpe M (físico) blow, knock, whack; (emocional) blow; (estafa) sting; (robo) holdup; (de viento) buffet; (con el codo) to jab; (con los nudillos) rap; — **bajo** low blow; — **de calor** heat stroke; — **de estado** coup; — **de gracia** coup de grâce; — **de sol** sunstroke; **de** — suddenly; **de un** — all at once

golpear VI/VT to strike, to hit; (a la puerta) to knock, to rap; (dar una paliza a una persona) to beat, to batter; (con el codo) to jab

golpecito M tap

golpetear VI to tap; (lluvia) to patter; (motor) to knock; (algo suelto) to rattle

golpeteo M tap; (de lluvia) patter; (de un motor) knock; (de algo suelto) rattle

goma F (de mascar) gum; (caucho) rubber; (neumático) tire; — **de borrar** eraser; — **de mascar** chewing gum; — **elástica** rubber band; — **espuma** foam

gomero M rubber tree

gomoso ADJ slimy

góndola F gondola

gong M gong

gonorrea F gonorrhea, *fam* the clap

gordinflón ADJ *pey* fatso

gordito ADJ chubby

gordo ADJ fat; **se armo la gorda** all hell broke loose; **hacer la vista gorda** to turn a blind eye

gordura F (cualidad de gordo) fatness; (sebo) fat

gorgojo M weevil

gorila M gorilla; (en un bar) bouncer; (guardaespaldas) bodyguard

gorjear VI (ave) to warble, to chirp, to twitter; (niño) to gurgle

gorjeo M (de ave) warble, twitter, chirp; (de niño) gurgle

gorra F cap; **de** — at someone else's expense; **vivir de** — to sponge

gorrino M piglet

gorrión M sparrow

gorro M cap, bonnet

gorrón M sponge, sponger

gorronear VI/VT to mooch, to freeload

gospel M gospel

gota F (de líquido) drop; (de sudor) bead; (enfermedad) gout; — **a** — drop by drop; **ser dos** —**s de agua** to be like two peas in a pod; **sudar la** — **gorda** (sudar) to sweat profusely; (trabajar) to work hard

gotear VI (caer gota a gota) to drip; (rápidamente) to dribble, to trickle;

(salirse) to leak; (llover) to sprinkle

goteo M drip (también intravenoso); (rápido) dribble, trickle

gotera F leak

gotero M dropper

gótico ADJ Gothic; M (lengua) Gothic

gourmet ADJ & MF gourmet

gozar[9] VT to enjoy; — **de** to enjoy

gozne M hinge

gozo M pleasure, enjoyment

gozoso ADJ enjoyable

grabación F recording

grabado M engraving; (con ácido) etching

grabador -ora MF (persona) engraver; F (instrumento) tape recorder; (empresa) recording company

grabar VI/VT (marcar) to engrave; (con ácido) to etch; (en cinta magnetográfica) to record, to tape; — **en la memoria** to etch / imprint on one's memory

gracejo M wit

gracia F (garbo, desenvoltura) grace, gracefulness; (humor) humor; (monería) antic; (favor) favor; (indulto) pardon; ¡—**s!** thanks! thank you! **—s a Dios** thank God; **caer en —** to please; **dar —s** to say the blessing; **dar las —s** to thank; **hacer —** to amuse; **tener —** to be funny

grácil ADJ supple, graceful

gracioso ADJ (chistoso) amusing, funny; (gentil) gracious

grada F step, bleachers

gradación F gradation

graderías F PL bleachers

grado M (de temperatura, de parentesco, de un ángulo, de universidad) degree; (militar) rank; (de alcohol) proof; **de buen —** willingly; **en alto —** to a great extent; **en mayor o menor —** to some extent; **quemadura de primer —** first-degree burn

graduación F (de una escuela) graduation, commencement; (rango militar) military rank; (de alcohol) proof; (de un lente óptico) correction

graduado -da MF graduate

gradual ADJ gradual

graduar[17] VT (ajustar) to adjust; (regular) to calibrate; **—se** to graduate, to get a degree

graffiti M graffiti

grafiar[16] VT to graph

gráfica F (arte) graphics; (representación) graph, chart

graficar[6] VT to chart

gráfico -ca ADJ graphic; **acento —** written accent; M (representación) graph, chart; MF (empleado) printer

grafito M graphite

grama F lawn

gramática F grammar

gramatical ADJ grammatical

gramo M gram

grana ADJ INV & F scarlet

granada F (fruta) pomegranate; (proyectil) grenade; — **de mano** hand grenade

Granada F Grenada

granadino -na ADJ & MF Grenadian

granado M pomegranate tree; ADJ notable

granate M garnet

Gran Bretaña F Great Britain

grande ADJ large, big; (importante) great; **un gran poeta** a great poet; **divertirse en — ** to have a whale of a time; **a —s alturas** at high altitudes; **de gran alcance** far-reaching; **de gran escala** large-scale; **en gran parte** in large measure; **gran almacén** department store

grandeza F greatness; **delirios de —** delusions of grandeur

grandiosidad F grandeur

grandioso ADJ grandiose, grand

granero M (edificio) granary, grain barn; (recipiente) bin, crib

granito M granite

granizada F hailstorm

granizar[9] VI to hail

granizo M hail

granja F farm

granjearse VI to win for oneself

granjero -ra MF farmer

grano M (de una foto, arena, semilla) grain; (cereal) cereal, grain; (barrito) pimple; — **de café** coffee bean; **ir al —** to come to the point

granuja MF ragamuffin

granular VT to granulate; **—se** to become granulated

grapa F (para sujetar madera) clamp; (para sujetar papel) staple

grapadora F stapler

grasa F (aceite) grease; (animal) fat

grasiento ADJ greasy

grasoso ADJ greasy

gratificación F bonus

gratificar[6] VT to gratify

gratis ADV free

gratitud F gratitude, thankfulness

grato ADJ pleasant

gratuito ADJ (gratis) free; (arbitrario) wanton, gratuitous

grava F gravel

gravamen M (impuesto) tax, assessment; (carga sobre una propiedad) lien

gravar VT to tax, to assess

grave ADJ (enfermedad, decisión) grave, serious; (sonido) low, deep; (injuria) grievous; (de carácter) earnest

gravedad F (fuerza de atracción) gravity; (de una situación) seriousness; (de una tormenta) severity; (de un tono) depth; (de una personalidad) earnestness

gravitación F gravitation

gravoso ADJ burdensome

graznar VI (cuervo) to caw, to croak; (pato) to quack; (ganso) to honk

graznido M (de cuervo) caw, croak; (de pato) quack; (de ganso) honk

Grecia F Greece

greda F clay

green M (de golf) green

gregario ADJ gregarious

gremial ADJ **acuerdo —** union agreement

gremio M (conjunto de personas) trade; (asociación histórica) guild; (sindicato) trade union

greña F mop of hair

grey F flock, fold

griego -ga ADJ & MF Greek

grieta F crevice, crack

grifo M faucet, spigot, tap

grillete M fetter, shackle

grillo M (insecto) cricket; **—s** shackles

grima F uneasiness; **dar —** (disgustar) to be upsetting; (dar asco) to be disgusting

gringo -ga ADJ & MF *pey* American

gripe F flu, influenza

gris ADJ & M gray

grisáceo ADJ grayish

gritar VI/VT to shout, to yell; (chillar) to scream

gritería F shouting

grito M shout, cry; (chillido) scream; **el último —** the last word; **estar en un —** to be in agony; **pedir a —s** to clamor for; **poner el — en el cielo** to hit the ceiling

grosella F currant

grosellero M currant

grosería F (cualidad) rudeness; (hecho, dicho) profanity, something rude

grosero ADJ (descortés) rude, ill-mannered, boorish; (vulgar) vulgar, profane; (sin arte) coarse, unrefined

grosor M thickness

grotesco ADJ grotesque

grúa F (máquina) crane; (automóvil para remolcar coches) wrecker, tow truck

gruesa F gross

grueso ADJ (persona) thick-set, heavy; (tabla) thick; (palabra, arena) coarse; M (grosor) thickness; (parte más numerosa) majority

grulla F crane

grumo M lump

grumoso ADJ lumpy

gruñido M (de perro) growl, snarl; (de cerdo) grunt; (humano) grumble

gruñir[18] VI (el cerdo) to grunt; (el perro) to growl, to snarl; (el ser humano) to grumble

gruñón -ona ADJ grumpy; MF grumpy person

grupa F rump; **volver —s** to turn around

grupo M group; **— de apoyo** support group; **— de presión** lobby; **— étnico** ethnicity; **— paritario** peer group; **— sanguíneo** blood type

gruta F grotto, cavern

guacal M crate

guacamole M *Méx* guacamole

guacho M (cría de ave) chick; *Am* (animal huérfano) orphan

guadaña F scythe

guagua F (fruslería) trifle; *Caribbean* bus; MF *Chile* baby; LOC ADV **de —** for nothing, free

guaje -ja MF urchin

guano M guano, bird dung

guantada F slap

guante M glove; **— de boxeo** boxing glove; **arrojar el —** to challenge; **echarle el — a alguien** to capture someone; **te queda como un —** it fits you like a glove

guantelete M gauntlet

guantera F glove compartment

guapetón -ona MF *fam* fox

guapo ADJ (de hombre) good-looking, handsome; (de mujer) good-looking, pretty; (valiente) brave; **¡hola —!** hello, big boy!

guarapo M cane syrup

guarda MF INV (guardián) guard; F (almacenamiento) storage

guardar VT (almacenar) to keep, to store; (observar) to observe; (datos) to save; (proteger) to guard; **— rencor** to hold a grudge; **— un secreto** to keep a secret; **—se de** to guard against; M SG **guardabarros** fender; **guardacostas** Coast Guard cutter; **guardaespaldas** bodyguard; **guardafangos** fender; **guardapelo** locket; **guardarropa** (armario, ropa) wardrobe; (en un local) cloakroom; MF SG **guardabosques** forest ranger, forester; **guardafrenos** brake operator; **guardagujas** switch operator; **guardameta** goalie

guardería F nursery, day-care center

guardia MF (persona) guard; **— civil** civil guard; F (vigilancia) guard; **bajar la —** to let down one's guard; **de** — on duty, on watch; **en** — en garde; **hacer / montar** — to stand guard

guardián -ana MF guardian, keeper

guarecerse[13] VT to take shelter

guarida F den, lair

guarismo M cipher

guarnecer[13] VT (un plato) to garnish; (un vestido) to trim; (una fortaleza) to man, to garrison

guarnición F (de tropas) garrison; (de comida) trimmings; **guarniciones** harness

guarro ADJ filthy; M pig

guasa LOC ADV **de / a** — in jest, as a joke

guasón -ona MF joker

guata F padding

Guatemala F Guatemala

guatemalteco -ca ADJ & MF Guatemalan

guau INTERJ woof

guay ADJ cool, great

guayaba F guava

guayabera F tropical pleated shirt

gubernamental ADJ governmental

gubernativo ADJ governmental

gubia F gouge

guedeja F shock of hair

guepardo M cheetah

guerra F war, warfare; **dar** — to aggravate; **en pie de** — at war; — **fría** cold war

guerrear VI to war

guerrero -rra MF warrior; **operación** — war operation; **espíritu** — warrior spirit

guerrilla F group of guerrillas

guerrillero -ra MF guerrilla

gueto M ghetto

guía MF (persona) guide, leader; F (cosa o animal) guide; — **telefónica** telephone directory

guiar[16] VT to guide, to lead; —**se por** to follow

guijarro M pebble

güinche M hoist

guinda F cherry

guindilla F *Esp* small hot pepper

Guinea F Guinea

guineano -na ADJ & MF Guinean

guingán M gingham

guiñada F wink

guiñapo M rag

guiñar VI/VT to wink

guiño M wink

guión M (ortografía) hyphen; (libreto) script, screenplay

guionista MF screenwriter

guirnalda F garland; (de Navidad) tinsel

guisa F **a** — **de** by way of

guisado M stew, hash

guisante M pea

guisar VI/VT to cook; (en guisado) to stew

guiso M stew, casserole

guitarra F guitar

gula F gluttony

gusano M worm; — **de seda** silkworm

gustar VT (agradar) to be pleasing to; **ella me gusta** I like her; **le gustan los perros** he likes dogs; **no me gustan las fiestas** I dislike parties; **te guste o no te guste** whether you like it or not; **cuando gustes** whenever you want; — **de** to be fond of; (saborear) to taste

gusto M (sentido, sabor, aprecio estético) taste; (agrado) pleasure; (preferencia personal) like; **a** — at ease; **a mi** — to my liking; **dar** — to be a pleasure; **darle** — **a alguien** to humor someone; **darse el** — to indulge oneself; **de mal** — in bad taste; **el** — **es mío** the pleasure is mine; **estar a** — to be comfortable; **mucho** — nice to meet you; **por** — for fun; **tener el** — **de** to have the pleasure of; **tomar el** — **a una cosa** to become fond of something

gustoso ADJ (que gusta de) fond of; (agradable) pleasant; ADV willingly

Guyana F Guyana

guyanés -esa ADJ & MF Guyanese

Hh

haba F bean; (verde) Lima bean

habano M cigar

haber[29] V AUX to have; — **comido cuatro veces en un día** to have eaten four times in a day; **habérselas con** (un problema) to grapple with; (una persona) to have it out with; **ha de llegar mañana** he is to arrive tomorrow; **hay** there is, there are; **hay viento** it is windy; **hubo** there was / were; **había** there was / were; **hay que** it is necessary to; **no hay de qué** don't mention it; **no hay forma** no way; **no hay problema** no problem; **¿qué hay?** what's up; **todo lo habido y por haber** everything possible; M (hacienda) assets; (columna en una cuenta) credit; —**es** earnings

habichuela F bean; — **verde** string bean

hábil ADJ adept, able; **día** — workday

habilidad F ability, skill

habilidoso ADJ deft, skillful

habilitar VT (equipar) to outfit; (autorizar) to authorize

habitación F (vivienda) dwelling; (cuarto) room

habitante MF inhabitant; (de un barrio) resident

habitar VT to inhabit

hábitat M habitat

hábito M habit (también vestimenta religiosa)

habitual ADJ habitual, usual

habituar[17] VT to accustom; —**se** to get used to

habla F (lenguaje) speech; (modalidad local) dialect; — **infantil** baby talk; **al** — in communication with; **quedarse sin** — to be left speechless

hablador ADJ talkative

habladurías F idle talk, gossip

hablar VI/VT to talk, to speak; — **de** to talk about; — **hasta por los codos** to talk one's head off; — **no cuesta nada** talk is cheap; — **por señas** to use sign language; — **por teléfono** to talk on the phone; — **sin rodeos** to speak one's mind; — **solo / para sí** to talk to oneself; **hablando mal y pronto** pardon my French; **no** —**se** not to be on speaking terms; **no me hagas** — don't get me started on it

hablilla F malicious tale

hacedor -ora MF maker

hacendado -da MF landowner

hacendoso ADJ industrious, diligent

hacer[30] VT (crear) to do, to make; (causar) to make; (decir) to go; (resolver) to do; — **frío / calor / viento** to be cold / hot / windy; — **una torta** to make a cake; — **un crucigrama** to do a crossword puzzle; **me hizo llorar** he made me cry; **la vaca hace 'mu'** the cow goes moo; **hace mucho tiempo** a long time ago; **hace poco** a short while ago; **hizo como si estuvieras presente** he acted as if you were here; **a lo hecho, pecho** you've got to face the music; **la hiciste buena** you've really screwed up; **¿qué le vamos a hacer?** that's life; **¿qué se hizo de Juan?** whatever became of Juan? **haz el trabajo** do the work; —**se rico** to become rich; —**se el tonto** to play the fool; —**se el listo** to pull a stunt; —**se pasar por el jefe** to pose as the boss; —**se a un lado** to step aside; —**se amigo de** to befriend; —**se a la oscuridad** to get used to the dark; —**se rogar** to play hard to get

hacha F (grande) ax(e); (pequeña) hatchet

hachís M hashish

hacia PREP (en dirección) toward; (aproximadamente) about; — **abajo** downward; — **adelante** forward; — **adentro** inward; — **afuera** outward; — **arriba** upward; — **atrás** backward; — **el este** eastward; — **la izquierda** to the left; **dar** — to face

hacienda F estate; (de ganado) ranch; (impositiva) Internal Revenue Service

hacina F shock

hacinar VT (liar) to shock; (atestar) to crowd in

hada F fairy

hado M fate

Haití M Haiti

haitiano -na ADJ & MF Haitian

halagar[7] VT to flatter

halago M flattery

halagüeño ADJ (palabras) flattering; (perspectiva) promising

halcón M falcon

hálito M breath

hallar VT to find; —**se** to be; —**se en un aprieto** to be in a pickle; —**se mal de salud** to be in a bad way

hallazgo M (resultado científico) finding; **ese documento fue un — sensacional** that document was a real find

halo M halo

halógeno ADJ & M halogen

halterofilia F weight training, weightlifting

hamaca F hammock

hambre F (deseo de comer) hunger; (hambruna) famine; **tener** — to be hungry; **pasar** — to hunger; **morirse de** — to starve

hambrear VI/VT to starve

hambriento ADJ (que tiene hambre) hungry; (que se muere de hambre) famished, starving

hambruna F famine

hamburguesa F hamburger

hampa F underworld

hámster M hamster

handicapar VT to handicap

hangar M hangar

haragán -ana ADJ indolent; MF loafer

haraganear VI to loaf

haraganería F laziness

harapiento ADJ ragged, tattered

harapo M rag, tatter

hardware M hardware

harén M harem

harina F (fino) flour; (grueso) meal; — **de avena** oatmeal; — **de maíz** cornmeal; **es**

— **de otro costal** that's another kettle of fish

hartar VT to satiate; **—se** (de comida) to have one's fill; (de aburrimiento) to get sick

hartazgo M surfeit, excess

harto ADJ (satisfecho) full; **estar —** to be fed up; **ese asunto me tiene —** I'm sick and tired of the whole business

hasta PREP (temporal) till, until; (espacial) (up) to; **— ahora** to date / so far; **— cierto punto** to a certain extent; **— luego** good-bye, see you later; **— pronto** see you later; **caminó — la esquina** he walked to the corner; **lo llenó — el borde** he filled it up to brim; **estar — la coronilla** to be fed up; ADV even; **— mi madre lo notó** even my mother noticed it; **— que** until

hastiado ADJ jaded

hastial M gable

hastiar[16] VT to cloy, to tire; **—se** to grow weary of

hastío M tedium

hato M (envoltorio) bundle; (rebaño) herd

hay ver haber

haya F beech

hayuco M beechnut

haz M (de leña) bundle; (de luz) beam; (de flechas) sheaf

hazaña F deed, exploit, feat

hazmerreír M laughingstock

he VT IMPERSONAL **he aquí la lista** here's the list

hebilla F buckle

hebra F (de hilo) thread; (vegetal) fiber

hebreo -a ADJ & MF Hebrew

heces F PL (de vino, cafe) dregs; (excremento) feces

hechicería F enchantment

hechicero -ra ADJ bewitching; M sorcerer; F sorceress

hechizar[9] VT to bewitch, to enchant; (al público) to enthrall

hechizo M charm, spell

hecho M fact; **los —s de la noche del 17** the events of the night of the 17th; **de —** in fact

hechura F cut

hectárea F hectare

heder[1] VI to stink, to reek

hediondez F stench

hediondo ADJ stinking, smelly

hedonismo M hedonism

hedor M stink, stench

hegemonía F hegemony

helada F (frente frío) freeze; (escarcha) frost

heladera F refrigerator

heladería F ice-cream parlor

helado ADJ (muy frío) frozen, freezing; (con hielo) icy; M ice cream

helar[1] VI/VT to freeze

helecho M fern

hélice F (espiral) helix; (de avión) propeller; (de barco) screw, propeller

helicóptero M helicopter

helio M helium

hematoma M hematoma

hembra F (de animal) female; (del venado) doe; (de la ballena, foca) cow; (ave) hen

hemisferio M hemisphere

hemofilia F hemophilia

hemoglobina F hemoglobin

hemorragia F hemorrhage

hemorroides F PL hemorrhoids

henchir[5] VT to swell

hender[1] VI/VT to cleave, to split

hendido ADJ cleft, split

hendidura F rift, rent

henil M hayloft

heno M hay; **fiebre de —** hay fever

hepatitis F hepatitis

heraldo M herald

herbicida M weedkiller, herbicide

herbívoro ADJ herbivorous; M herbivore

herboso ADJ grassy

heredad F homestead

heredar VI/VT (recibir en herencia) to inherit; (dar en herencia) to bequeath

heredero -ra M heir; F heiress

hereditario ADJ hereditary

hereje MF heretic

herejía F heresy

herencia F (económica) inheritance; (cultural) heritage; (genética) heredity

herida F injury; (abierta) wound; **respirar por la —** to reopen an old wound

herido ADJ injured; (con herida abierta) wounded

herir[3] VI/VT to injure; (con herida abierta) to wound; (sentimientos) to hurt

hermanastro -tra M stepbrother; F stepsister

hermandad F (de hombres) brotherhood; (de mujeres) sisterhood

hermanito -ta M little brother; F little sister

hermano -na M brother (también religioso); **— mayor** big brother; **— menor** little brother; F sister (también religiosa); **— mayor** big sister; **— menor** little sister

herméticamente ADV tight

hermético ADJ hermetic, airtight; (a prueba de agua) watertight; (que no revela secretos) secretive

hermosear VT to beautify

hermoso ADJ beautiful, lovely
hermosura F beauty
hernia F hernia
héroe M hero
heroico ADJ heroic
heroína F (droga) heroin; (personaje) heroine
heroísmo M heroism
herpes M herpes; (en la boca) cold sore
herradura F horseshoe
herraje M ironwork
herramienta F tool
herrar[1] VT (un caballo) to shoe; (una vaca) to brand
herrería F blacksmith's shop
herrero -ra MF blacksmith
herrumbre F rust
hervidero M swarm
hervidor M kettle
hervir[3] VI/VT to boil; — **a fuego lento** to simmer; — **de** to be swarming with; **me hervía la sangre** I was seething
hervor M (acción de hervir) boiling; **levantar el —** to come to a boil
heterodoxo ADJ unorthodox
heterogéneo ADJ heterogeneous
heterosexual ADJ heterosexual; *fam* straight
hexágono M hexagon
hiato M hiatus
hibernar VI to hibernate
híbrido ADJ & M hybrid
hidalgo M hidalgo
hidalguía F (nobleza) nobility; (generosidad) generosity
hidrato M hydrate
hidráulico ADJ hydraulic
hidroavión M hydroplane, seaplane
hidrocarburo M hydrocarbon
hidroeléctrico ADJ hydroelectric
hidrofobia F hydrophobia
hidrógeno M hydrogen
hiedra F ivy
hiel F gall
hielo M ice; — **seco** dry ice; **romper el —** to break the ice
hiena F hyena
hierba F (pasto) grass; (especia) herb; (marihuana) *fam* weed; — **buena** mint; **mala —** weed; **y otras —s** and so on
hierro M iron (también de golf); — **corrugado** corrugated iron; — **forjado** wrought iron; — **fundido** cast iron; —**s** handcuffs
hígado M liver; **malos —s** ill will
higiene F hygiene
higo M fig; **me importa un —** I couldn't care less
higuera F fig tree

hijastro -tra M stepson; F stepdaughter
hijo -ja M son; — **de perra** *ofensivo* son of a bitch; — **de puta** *ofensivo* son of a bitch; — **de su madre** *vulg* son of a gun; **John Smith, —** John Smith, Jr.; **sin —s** childless; F daughter; **hija de puta** *ofensivo* bitch
hilachas F loose threads
hilado M spinning
hilandería F (fábrica) spinning mill; (técnica) spinning
hilandero -ra MF spinner
hilar VI/VT to spin; — **fino** to split hairs
hilaridad F mirth
hilera F row, line
hilo M (para coser) thread; (para tejer, hilar) yarn; (alambre) filament; — **de agua** trickle; — **de pensamiento** train of thought; — **de perlas** string of pearls; — **de voz** thin voice; — **dental** floss; **al —** in a row; **mover —s** to pull strings; **seguir el — de** to keep track of; **pender de un —** to be hanging by a thread; **perder el —** to lose track
hilván M basting
hilvanar VT to baste, to tack
himno M (religioso) hymn; (patriótico) anthem
hincapié M emphasis; **hacer — to** emphasize
hincar[6] VT — **los dientes en** to sink one's teeth into; —**se** to kneel
hincha MF INV (aficionado) supporter; F (antipatía) *Esp* grudge
hinchado ADJ (inflamado) swollen; (exagerado) inflated
hinchar VI to swell; (un globo) to blow up; — **por el equipo de Uruguay** to pull for the Uruguayan team; —**se** (cuerpo) to swell; (pulmones) to inflate; (las mejillas) to bulge; (de orgullo) to puff up; (el pan) to rise
hinchazón F swelling
hindi M Hindi
hindú ADJ & MF Hindu
hinojos LOC ADV **de —** on one's knees
hipar VI hiccup
hiperactivo ADJ hyperactive, overactive
hipermétrope ADJ farsighted
hipersensible ADJ hypersensitive; (a la crítica) touchy
hipertensión F high blood pressure
hiperventilar VI to hyperventilate
hipnosis F hypnosis
hipnotizar VI/VT to hypnotize, to mesmerize
hipo M (espasmo) hiccup; (sollozo) sob; **tengo —** I have the hiccups

hipoalérgico ADJ hypoallergenic

hipocondríaco -ca, hipocondriaco -ca ADJ & MF hypochondriac

hipocresía F hypocrisy

hipócrita ADJ INV hypocritical, two-faced; MF INV hypocrite

hipódromo M racetrack

hipogloso M halibut

hipoglucemia F hypoglycemia

hipopótamo M hippopotamus

hipoteca F mortgage

hipotecar[6] VT to mortgage

hipotecario banco — mortgage bank

hipótesis F hypothesis

hiriente ADJ hurtful; (comentario) nasty, catty

hirviente ADJ boiling

hisopo M swab

hispano -na ADJ Hispanic, Spanish-speaking; MF Spanish-speaking person

Hispanoamérica F Spanish America

hispanoamericano ADJ Spanish-American

histamina F histamine

histerectomía F hysterectomy

histérico ADJ hysterical

historia F (el pasado, estudio del pasado) history; (relato) story; — **clínica** case history; **dejarse de —s** to stop fooling around; **esa es otra** — that's another story; **la — se repite** history repeats itself; **pasar a la** — to be a thing of the past

historiador -ora MF historian

historial M record

histórico ADJ (de importancia histórica) historic; (pertinente a la historia) historical

historietas F PL funnies

histrionismo M histrionics

hito M landmark, milestone; **de — en** — fixedly; **marcar un** — to be a milestone

hobby M hobby

hocicar[6] VI/VT (un cerdo) to root; (un caballo) to nose

hocico M snout, muzzle

hockey M hockey

hogaño ADV LIT nowadays

hogar M (lumbre) hearth, fireplace; (casa, asilo) home

hogareño ADJ domestic; **persona hogareña** homebody

hoguera F bonfire, campfire

hoja F (de planta) leaf; (de mesa plegadiza) flap; (de papel) sheet; (de un libro) page; (de navaja) blade; — **de afeitar** razor blade; — **de metal** foil; **echar —s** to leaf; — **de servicio** record; —**lata** tin plate

hojaldre M puff pastry

hojarasca F fallen leaves

hojear VT to page through, to flip through, to browse

hojuela F flake; —**s de maíz** cornflakes

hola INTERJ hello

Holanda F Holland

holandés -esa ADJ Dutch; M (hombre) Dutchman; (lengua) Dutch; F Dutchwoman

holding M holding company

holgado ADJ (vida) comfortable; (pantalón) loose-fitting, baggy; (cuarto) roomy

holganza F (haraganería) idleness; (diversión) leisure

holgar[2,7] VI to loaf; **huelga decir** it is needless to say

holgazán -ana ADJ lazy, idle; MF idler, loafer, slouch

holgazanear VI to idle, to loaf

holgazanería F laziness

holgura F (de movimiento) ease; (financiera) comfort; (de la ropa) looseness

holístico ADJ holistic

hollejo M skin

hollín M soot, smut

holocausto M holocaust

hombre M man; — **anuncio** sandwich man; — **de bien** a man of good will; — **de familia** family man; — **de las cavernas** caveman; — **de la calle** man in the street; — **de negocios** businessman; — **del saco** bogeyman; — **de paja** straw man; — **lobo** werewolf; — **orquesta** one-man band; — **rana** frogman; **es bien** — he's a real he-man; INTERJ come on!

hombro M shoulder; **encogerse de —s** to shrug; **cargar al** — to shoulder; **en / a** —**s** piggyback; **poner el** — to lend a hand

hombruno ADJ mannish

homenaje M homage, tribute

homeopatía F homeopathy

homeopático ADJ homeopathic

homicida MF INV murderer

homicidio M homicide, murder

homogeneizar VT to homogenize

homogéneo ADJ homogeneous

homólogo -ga MF counterpart

homóplato M shoulder blade

homosexual ADJ homosexual; *fam* gay

honda F sling, slingshot

hondo ADJ deep; M hollow

hondonada F hollow, dell

hondura F depth; **meterse en —s** to get in over one's head

Honduras F Honduras

hondureño -ña ADJ & MF Honduran

honestidad F (castidad) chastity, modesty; (honradez) honesty

honesto ADJ chaste, modest; (honrado) honest, straightforward

hongo M (seta) mushroom; (moho) fungus; **aburrirse como un —** to be bored stiff

honor M honor; **con —es** with honors; **tener el — de** to have the honor of; **hacer los —es a** to be appreciative of

honorable ADJ honorable

honorario ADJ honorary; M **—s** fee

honra F honor

honradez F honesty

honrado ADJ honest

honrar VT to honor; (hacer más digno) to do credit to

honroso ADJ honorable

hora F hour; **— de dormir** bedtime; **— oficial** standard time; **—s extras** overtime; **a esta —** at this time; **¿a qué —?** at what time? **a todas —s** at all hours; **a última —** at the last minute; **decir la —** to tell time; **en —** on time; **es — de** it is time to; **es — de que me vaya** it's time for me to go; **kilómetros por —** kilometers per hour; **no ver la — de** to be dying to; **por —** by the hour; **¿qué — es?** what time is it? **ya era —** it was about time

horadar VT to bore

horario M schedule, timetable; (manecilla del reloj) hour hand

horca F (cadalso) gallows; (herramienta con púas) pitchfork; **— de ajos** string of garlic

horcajadas LOC ADV **a —** astraddle, astride

horda F horde

horizontal ADJ horizontal

horizonte M horizon; (de una ciudad) skyline

horma F (de zapato) shoe last; (de queso) wheel

hormiga F ant; **— blanca** termite

hormigón M concrete

hormigonera F cement mixer

hormiguear VI (moverse animales) to swarm; (sentir hormigueo) to tingle

hormigueo M tingle

hormiguero M anthill

hormona F hormone

hornada F batch

horneado M baking

hornear VI/VT to bake

hornilla F burner

horno M (industrial) furnace; (doméstico) oven; (para cerámica) kiln; **— de microondas** microwave oven; **alto —** blast furnace; **el — no está para bollos**

it's not a good time; **recién salido del —** brand-new

horóscopo M horoscope

horquilla F (para el pelo) hairpin; (horca) pitchfork

horrendo ADJ horrendous, horrid; (feo) hideous, ghastly

horrible ADJ horrible

horripilante ADJ gruesome, hair-raising

horror M (miedo, repulsión) horror; (cosa monstruosa) abomination; (espectáculo) sight; **tenerle — a** to be scared of

horrorizar[9] VT to horrify, to shock, to appall

horroroso ADJ appalling, awful

hortaliza F vegetable; **—s** produce, truck

hortera ADJ INV tacky, uncool, cheesy

horticultura F horticulture

hosco ADJ sullen, surly

hospedaje M lodging

hospedar VT to lodge, to accommodate; **—se** to lodge, to room

hospicio M (para peregrinos) hospice; (para huérfanos) orphanage

hospital M hospital

hospitalario ADJ hospitable

hospitalidad F hospitality

hostal M hostel

hostería F hostelry

hostia F (oblea) host, wafer; (golpe) whack; **¡—s!** *vulg* shit! **me cago en la —** *vulg* God damn it!

hostigar[7] VT to harass, to harry

hostil ADJ hostile

hostilidad F hostility

hotel M hotel

hotelero -ra MF hotel keeper

hoy ADV today; **— (en) día** nowadays; **de — en adelante** from now on; **— por —** at present

hoya F river basin

hoyo M hole (también de golf); (muy profundo) pit

hoyuelo M dimple

hoz F sickle

hozar[9] VI to root

HTML M HTML

hucha F piggy bank

hueco ADJ (vacío) hollow; (vanidoso) vain, affected; **palabras huecas** empty words; M (entre los dientes) gap; (cavidad) hollow; (del ascensor) shaft

huelga F strike, work stoppage; **— de hambre** hunger strike; **declararse en —** to strike; **en —** on strike

huelguista MF striker

huella F (señal dejada al pasar) trace, trail;

(de pie) footprint, track; (de rueda) track;
— **dactilar / digital** fingerprint; **seguir
las —s de alguien** to follow in
someone's footsteps

huérfano -na ADJ & MF orphan

huerta F (de verduras) large vegetable
garden; (de árboles frutales) large orchard;
la — valenciana the farming region of
Valencia

huerto M (de verduras) vegetable garden; (de
árboles frutales) orchard

hueso M (de animal) bone; (de una fruta)
stone, pit; **calado hasta los —s** soaked
to the bone; **la sin —** the tongue; **no
dejarle un — sano** to break someone's
bones; **un — duro de roer** a hard pill to
swallow

huésped MF (invitado) guest; (anfitrión) host
(también de parásitos)

hueste F host

huesudo ADJ bony

hueva F spawn

huevo M egg; **— de Pascua** Easter egg; **—
duro** hard-boiled egg; **— estrellado /
frito** fried egg; **— pasado por agua**
soft-boiled egg; **—s** (testículos, valentía)
vulg balls; **—s revueltos** scrambled eggs;
ir pisando —s to walk on eggshells; **me
importa un —** *vulg* I don't give a shit; **¡y
un —!** *vulg* my ass!

huída F flight

huir[31] VI to flee, to fly

hule M oilcloth

hulla F soft coal; **— blanca** hydroelectric
power

humanidad F (cualidad y condición)
humanity; (conjunto de los seres
humanos) mankind; **—es** humanities

humanismo M humanism

humanitario ADJ (organización, ayuda)
humanitarian; (generoso) humane

humano ADJ (del hombre) human;
(generoso) humane; M human

humareda F cloud of smoke

humeante ADJ smoking

humear VI (echar humo) to give off smoke;
(echar vapor) to give off steam

humedad F (del aire) humidity; (de un paño)
dampness; (en la tierra) moisture;
(mancha) moisture stain

humedal M wetland

humedecer[13] VT (sello, ojo) to moisten;
(paño) to dampen; **se le humedecieron
los ojos** his eyes grew teary

húmedo ADJ damp; (aire) humid; (tierra)
moist; (tiempo) wet, soggy

humero M flue, funnel

humidificar[6] VT to humidify

humildad F (actitud de humilde) humility;
(condición) lowliness

humilde ADJ (actitud) humble; (condición)
low, lowly, mean

humillación F humiliation

humillar VT (dañar el amor propio) to
humiliate; (hacer sentirse disminuido) to
humble; **—se** to grovel

humo M smoke; (vapor) vapor; **—s**
conceitedness; **bajarle los —s a alguien**
to cut someone down to size; **echar —** to
put out smoke; **estar que echa —** to be
fuming; **hacerse —** to vanish into thin
air

humor M (actitud risueña) humor; (estado de
ánimo) mood

humorada F witty remark

humorismo M (humor) humor; (profesión)
comedy

humorístico ADJ humorous

humoso ADJ smoky

hundimiento M (acción de hundirse)
sinking; (hoyo) sinkhole

hundir VT (un barco) to sink, to scuttle;
(arruinar) to destroy; (enterrar) to bury;
—se (barco) to sink; (empresa, edificio,
precios) to collapse; (tierra) to subside;
(sol) to go down

húngaro -ra MF Hungarian

Hungría F Hungary

huracán M hurricane

huraño ADJ sullen, unsociable

hurgar[7] VI (en una bolsa) to rummage; (en
la basura) to scavenge; **—se las narices**
to pick one's nose

hurón M ferret

huronear VI to ferret out

hurra INTERJ hurrah

hurtadillas LOC ADV **a —** stealthily

hurtar VT to steal, to swipe; **— el cuerpo** to
dodge; **—se** to hide

hurto M theft, larceny; **— con escalo** break-
in

husky M (perro) husky

husmear VT (un pedazo de carne) to sniff at;
(a un delincuente) to smell out; (peligro)
to smell; (en los asuntos ajenos) to nose
around in, to poke around in

husmeo M sniff

huso M spindle; **— horario** time zone

huy INTERJ (sorpresa) wow; (pena) oh

Ii

ibérico ADJ Iberian
iceberg M iceberg
ictericia F jaundice
ida F —s y venidas comings and goings
idea F (reflexión) idea, thought; (intuición) inkling
ideal ADJ & M ideal
idealismo M idealism
idealista ADJ idealistic; MF idealist
idear VT to devise, to think out, to plan; (un método) devise; (un plan) to conceive; (una solución) to engineer; (un complot) to hatch
ídem PRON & ADV ditto
idéntico ADJ identical
identidad F identity
identificación F identification
identificar[6] VT to identify
ideología F ideology
idilio M idyll
idioma M language
idiosincrasia F idiosyncrasy
idiota ADJ INV idiotic, lamebrained; MF INV fam idiot, dork, twerp
idiotez F idiocy
idolatrar VT to idolize
idolatría F idolatry
ídolo M idol
idóneo ADJ (calificado) expert; (ideal) ideal
iglesia F church
iglú M igloo
ignición F ignition
ignifugar[7] VT to fireproof
ignorancia F ignorance
ignorante ADJ ignorant, uneducated
ignorar VT (no saber) to be unaware of; (hacer caso omiso de) to ignore, to disregard; (despreciar) to shrug off, to discount
igual ADJ (idéntico) equal; (semejante) same, alike; (liso) even; me da — it's all the same to me; al — que just like; M equal sign
igualar VT (alisar) to level; (ser igual a) to equal; (hacer iguales) to equalize; (compararse con) to match
igualdad F equality
ijada F loin
ijar M loin
ilegal ADJ illegal, unlawful, lawless
ilegítimo ADJ illegitimate

ileso ADJ unharmed, unhurt
ilícito ADJ illicit
ilimitado ADJ unlimited; (energía) boundless; (horizonte) limitless
iluminación F illumination, lighting; (moral) enlightenment
iluminado ADJ lit
iluminar VT (un cuarto) to illuminate, to brighten; (moralmente) to enlighten
ilusión F (idea o imagen falsa) illusion; (deseo) dream, fond hope; (entusiasmo) thrill; — óptica optical illusion; me da — I'm looking forward to
iluso ADJ naive
ilusorio ADJ illusory
ilustración F illustration; la — the Enlightenment
ilustrador -ora MF illustrator
ilustrar VT to illustrate; (intelectualmente) to enlighten
ilustre ADJ illustrious
imagen F (representación, reputación) image; (foto, televisión) picture; (unidad de película fotográfica) frame; — especular mirror image; la — del tacto the soul of tact; — por resonancia magnética magnetic resonance imaging
imaginable ADJ conceivable
imaginación F imagination
imaginar VT to imagine, to picture; (idear) to dream up
imaginario ADJ imaginary
imaginativo ADJ imaginative
imán M magnet
imantar VT to magnetize
imbatible ADJ unbeatable
imbécil ADJ idiotic; MF ofensivo imbecile, moron
imbuir[31] VT to imbue
imitación F imitation
imitador -ora MF (que imita) imitator; (que imita gestos y voces) mimic; un — de Elvis an Elvis wannabe
imitar VT to imitate; (en gestos y voces) to mimic, to impersonate
impaciencia F impatience
impaciente ADJ impatient; fam antsy
impactar VI/VT to impact
impacto M impact
impagado ADJ unpaid
impala M impala
impar ADJ odd, uneven
imparcial ADJ impartial, unbiased; (justo) evenhanded; (que no toma partido) nonpartisan
imparcialidad F impartiality
impartir VT to impart

impasible ADJ impassive

impasse M impasse

impávido ADJ undaunted

impeachment M impeachment

impecable ADJ (perfecto) flawless; (limpio) spick and span

impedimento M impediment, hindrance; (incapacidad) handicap

impedir[5] VT to impede, to prevent, to hinder; (acceso) to bar

impeler VT (empujar) to impel; (inducir) to drive

impenetrable ADJ impenetrable

impensable ADJ unthinkable

imperar VI to prevail

imperativo ADJ & M imperative

imperceptible ADJ imperceptible

imperdible M safety pin

imperecedero ADJ undying

imperfecto ADJ & M imperfect

imperial ADJ imperial

imperialismo M imperialism

impericia F lack of skill

imperio M (forma de gobierno) empire; (hecho de imperar) rule

imperioso ADJ (mandón) imperious; (necesario) imperative

impermeabilizar[9] VT to waterproof

impermeable ADJ (al agua) waterproof; (a la crítica) impervious; M raincoat, slicker

impersonal ADJ impersonal

impertinencia F (actitud) impertinence, impudence; (réplica) backtalk

impertinente ADJ impertinent, impudent

ímpetu M impetus

impetuoso ADJ impetuous, brash

impío ADJ godless

implacable ADJ implacable, relentless

implantar VT to implant

implante M implant

implementar VT to implement

implemento M implement

implicar[6] VT (involucrar) to implicate, to involve; (conllevar) to entail

implícito ADJ implicit

implorar VI/VT to implore

imponente ADJ (impresionante) imposing; (espantoso) forbidding

imponer[39] VT to impose, to force upon; (gravar) to assess; **—se** to get one's way

impopular ADJ unpopular

importación F import

importancia F importance

importante ADJ important; (cantidad) substantial; (tema, asunto) weighty; (suceso, ocasión) momentous

importar VI (ser de importancia) to matter;

me importa un comino I don't give a hoot; **no importa** it makes no difference; VT (introducir bienes) to import

importe M amount

importunar VT to besiege

importuno ADJ inopportune

imposibilidad F impossibility

imposibilitar VT to make impossible

imposible ADJ impossible

imposición F imposition; (de impuestos) assessment

impostor -ora MF impostor, fraud

impotencia F impotence

impotente ADJ powerless; (sexualmente) impotent

impreciso ADJ inaccurate

impredecible ADJ unpredictable

impregnar VT to impregnate

impremeditado ADJ unpremeditated

imprenta F (arte, oficio) printing; (máquina) press, printing press

imprescindible ADJ indispensable

impresión F (efecto en el ánimo) impression; (acción de imprimir) printing; (huella) imprint

impresionante ADJ (logro) impressive, imposing; (edificio) grand, imposing; (panorama) breathtaking

impresionar VT to impress; **—se** to be overwhelmed

impreso M printed matter

impresor -ora MF (persona) printer; F (aparato) printer; **impresora de inyección de tinta** ink-jet printer; **impresora gráfica** plotter; **impresora láser** laser printer

imprevisible ADJ unpredictable

imprevisto ADJ unforeseen; M unforeseen event

imprimir[51] VI/VT to print; (marcar con presión) to imprint

improbable ADJ improbable, unlikely

improductivo ADJ unproductive

impromptu M impromptu

impropio ADJ (inadecuado) unbecoming; (atípico) atypical

improvisación F improvisation, role-playing

improvisado ADJ impromptu

improvisando ADV ad lib

improvisar VI/VT to improvise

improviso LOC ADV **de —** all of a sudden

imprudencia F (actitud) recklessness; (acción) reckless act

imprudente ADJ imprudent, unwise

impublicable ADJ unprintable

impúdico ADJ immodest

impuesto M tax, duty; **— de sucesión**

inheritance tax; **—s** taxation; **— sobre ingresos** income tax; **— sobre las ventas** sales tax; **— sobre rentas** income tax

impugnar VT to contest, to dispute

impulsar VT (empujar) to propel, to drive; (estimular) to boost

impulsivo ADJ impulsive

impulso M (estímulo) boost; (deseo espontáneo) impulse, urge

impunidad F impunity

impureza F impurity

impuro ADJ (sustancia) impure; (pensamiento) impure, unclean

inacabado ADJ unfinished

inaccesible ADJ inaccessible

inaceptable ADJ unacceptable, inadequate

inacostumbrado ADJ unwonted

inactividad F inactivity

inactivo ADJ inactive

inadaptado -da ADJ maladjusted; MF misfit

inadecuado ADJ unsuitable

inadvertido ADJ unnoticed, unobserved

inagotable ADJ (recursos) inexhaustible; (optimismo) unfailing

inaguantable ADJ unbearable

inalámbrico ADJ cordless, wireless

inalterable ADJ unalterable, unchangeable

inalterado ADJ unchanged

inamovible ADJ immovable

inanición F starvation

inanimado ADJ inanimate

inapetencia F lack of appetite

inapreciable ADJ (invalorable) invaluable; (muy pequeño) too small to be seen

inapropiado ADJ unsuitable

inasequible ADJ inaccessible

inaudible ADJ inaudible

inaudito ADJ unheard-of, unprecedented; (sufrimiento) untold

inauguración F (de un gobierno) inauguration; (de una carretera, etc.) dedication

inaugurar VT (un gobierno) to inaugurate; (una carretera) to dedicate

incalculable ADJ untold

incandescencia F glow

incandescente ADJ incandescent, glowing

incansable ADJ untiring, tireless

incapacidad F inability

incapacitar VT to disable, to incapacitate

incapaz ADJ incapable

incautación F seizure

incauto ADJ unwary

incendiar VT to set fire to; VI/VT to burn; **—se** to catch fire, to burn down

incendiario -ria ADJ incendiary; MF arsonist

incendio M conflagration, fire, blaze; **— doloso** arson; **— forestal** forest fire

incentivo M incentive, inducement

incertidumbre F uncertainty, suspense

incesante ADJ incessant, ceaseless

incesto M incest

incidencia F incidence

incidental ADJ incidental

incidente M incident

incienso M incense

incierto ADJ uncertain

incinerar VT to incinerate

incipiente ADJ incipient

incisión F incision

incisivo ADJ incisive; M incisor

incitar VT to incite, to whip up

incivilizado ADJ uncivilized

inclemencia F **las —s del tiempo** foul weather

inclemente ADJ inclement, foul

inclinación F (de personalidad) inclination, bent, disposition; (acto de inclinar) tilting; (estado de inclinado) tilt; (de un techo) slant; (del terreno) slope; (sesgo) bias

inclinar VT (ladear) to tilt; (bajar la cabeza) to hang; **—se** (doblarse en la cintura) to bend over; (tener tendencia a) to tend; (hacer una reverencia) to bow

incluir[31] VT (incorporar) to include; (abarcar) to include, to comprise

inclusive ADV even

inclusivo ADJ inclusive

incluso ADJ even

incógnita F unknown (quantity)

incógnito LOC ADV **de —** incognito

incoherente ADJ incoherent

incoloro ADJ colorless

incomestible ADJ inedible

incomformista ADJ & MF nonconformist

incomible ADJ inedible

incomodar VT to inconvenience

incomodidad F uneasiness

incómodo ADJ (silla) uncomfortable; (situación) awkward, inconvenient; (baúl) cumbersome; (silencio) uneasy; (que siente molestia) ill at ease

incomparable ADJ incomparable, peerless

incompatible ADJ incompatible

incompetente ADJ incompetent

incompleto ADJ incomplete

incomprensible ADJ incomprehensible

incomunicación F disconnect

inconcebible ADJ inconceivable

inconcluso ADJ unfinished

incondicional ADJ unconditional, unqualified

inconexo ADJ disconnected

inconformista MF nonconformist
inconfundible ADJ unmistakable
inconsciente ADJ (sin sentido) unconscious, senseless; (ignorante) unaware, oblivious
inconsecuencia F inconsistency
inconsecuente ADJ inconsistent
inconsolable ADJ heartbroken
inconstancia F inconstancy
inconstante ADJ inconstant, changeable
inconstitucional ADJ unconstitutional
incontable ADJ countless
incontenible ADJ uncontrollable
incontinente ADJ incontinent
incontrolable ADJ uncontrollable
incontrovertible ADJ incontrovertible
inconveniencia F inconvenience
inconveniente ADJ improper; M inconvenience, downside
incorporado ADJ built-in
incorporar VT to incorporate, to build into; (incluir) to incorporate; **—se** (erguirse) to sit up
incorrecto ADJ incorrect, wrong
incorregible ADJ incorrigible
incredulidad F disbelief
incrédulo ADJ incredulous
increíble ADJ (que no puede creerse) incredible, unbelievable; (extraordinario) amazing
incrementar VT to augment
incremento M increment, increase
incriminar VT to incriminate
incrustación F inlay
incrustado ADJ (en piedra) embedded; (joyas) inlaid
incrustar VT to embed; (oro) to inlay; **—se en** to become embedded in
incubadora F incubator
incuestionable ADJ unquestionable
inculcar[6] VT to inculcate, to instill
inculto ADJ (sin modales) uncultured, unrefined; (sin instrucción) uneducated
incumbencia F **no es de tu —** it's none of your business
incurable ADJ incurable
incurrir VI **— en** (una deuda) to incur; (un error) to fall into
incursión F raid, foray
incursionar VI to foray
indagación F investigation, probe
indagar[7] VI/VT to investigate, to inquire into
indebido ADJ undue
indecencia F indecency
indecente ADJ indecent
indecible ADJ unspeakable
indecisión F indecision
indeciso ADJ (que no ha decidido) undecided; (que suele vacilar) wishy-washy
indecoroso ADJ improper
indefendible ADJ indefensible
indefenso ADJ defenseless
indefinible ADJ indefinable
indefinido ADJ indefinite
indeleble ADJ indelible
indelicado ADJ indelicate
indemnización F indemnity; (de guerra) reparation; (de un pleito) recovery
indemnizar[9] VT to indemnify
independencia F independence; (de un individuo) self-reliance
independiente ADJ independent
indescriptible ADJ indescribable
indeseable ADJ undesirable, unwelcome
indestructible ADJ indestructible
indeterminado ADJ indeterminate
indexar VT to index
India F India
indicación F indication; (instrucción) instruction; **indicaciones** directions
indicador M pointer
indicar[6] VT to indicate, to point out; (aparato de medida) to read, to register; (mostrar) to show
indicativo ADJ & M indicative
índice M (lista alfabética) index; (tabla de materias) table of contents; (dedo) index finger
indicio M clue, sign
Índico M Océano **—** Indian Ocean
indiferencia F indifference; (frialdad) coolness
indiferente ADJ (apático) indifferent, unconcerned; (frío) cool; (sin entusiasmo) lukewarm; (no conmovido) unmoved; **esa chica me es —** I don't care about that girl
indígena ADJ INV indigenous; MF INV native
indigente ADJ destitute, indigent
indigestión F indigestion
indignación F indignation
indignado ADJ indignant
indignar VT to make indignant; **—se** to become indignant
indigno ADJ unworthy
índigo M indigo
indio -dia ADJ & MF Indian
indirecta F hint
indirecto ADJ indirect; (ruta) roundabout
indisciplinado ADJ unruly
indiscreción F indiscretion
indiscreto ADJ indiscreet
indiscutible ADJ unquestionable
indispensable ADJ indispensable

indisponer[39] VT to indispose; **—se** to become indisposed

indispuesto ADJ (disgustado) upset; (enfermo) indisposed

indistinto ADJ indistinct, vague

individual ADJ individual; (habitación) single

individualidad F individuality

individualismo M individualism

individualista MF individualist

individuo ADJ & M individual

indivisible ADJ indivisible

índole F type

indolencia F indolence

indolente ADJ indolent

indoloro ADJ painless

indomable ADJ indomitable

indomado ADJ unbroken

Indonesia F Indonesia

indonesio -sia ADJ & MF Indonesian

inducción F induction

inducir[24] VT to induce, to prompt

indudablemente ADV undoubtedly

indulgencia F indulgence

indulgente ADJ indulgent, lenient

indultar VT to pardon

indulto M pardon

indumentaria F apparel

industria F industry, trade

industrial ADJ industrial; MF industrialist

industrioso ADJ industrious

inédito ADJ unpublished

inefable ADJ ineffable

ineficaz ADJ ineffective, ineffectual

ineficiente ADJ inefficient

inelegible ADJ ineligible

inepto ADJ inept

inequívoco ADJ unequivocal

inercia F inertia

inerte ADJ inert

inescrutable ADJ inscrutable

inesperado ADJ unexpected

inestabilidad F instability

inestable ADJ unstable; (andar) unsteady

inestimable ADJ inestimable, invaluable

inevitable ADJ inevitable; (accidente) unavoidable

inexacto ADJ inaccurate

inexcusable ADJ inexcusable

inexorable ADJ inexorable

inexperto ADJ inexperienced, unskilled; (ojo) untrained

inexplicable ADJ inexplicable

inexpresivo ADJ inexpressive, wooden

infalible ADJ infallible, foolproof; (confiable) unfailing

infame ADJ infamous

infamia F infamy

infancia F childhood

infante -ta MF (hijo -ja del rey) infante -ta; M (soldado) infantrymen

infantería F infantry; **— de marina** marine corps

infantil ADJ (como niño) childlike; (aniñado) childish, infantile

infección F infection

infeccioso ADJ infectious

infectar VT to infect; **—se** to become infected

infecto ADJ foul, repugnant

infelicidad F misery

infeliz ADJ unhappy, wretched, miserable; MF poor wretch

inferencia F inference

inferior ADJ (en calidad) inferior; (en posición) lower

inferioridad F inferiority

inferir[3] VT to infer

infernal ADJ infernal; (ruido) unholy

infestar VT to infest

infiel ADJ unfaithful, faithless, untrue

infierno M hell; (lugar donde hace mucho calor) inferno; **en el quinto —** in the middle of nowhere

infinidad F infinity; **una — de** a large number of

infinitivo ADJ & M infinitive

infinito ADJ infinite; M infinity

inflación F inflation

inflado M inflation

inflamable ADJ flammable

inflamación F inflammation

inflamar VT to inflame; **—se** to become inflamed

inflar VT (neumáticos) to inflate, to pump up; (globos) to blow up; (precios) to balloon

inflexible ADJ (rígido) inflexible; (testarudo) unbending, adamant

infligir[11] VT to inflict

influencia F influence, pull, clout; (sobre las masas) sway

influir[31] VI **— en / sobre** to influence; (las masas) to sway

influjo M influence

influyente ADJ influential

infomercial M infomercial

información F information; (periodística) story

informal ADJ (no formal) informal, casual; (poco fiable) unreliable

informante MF (para un estudio) informant; (de la policía) informer

informar VT to inform, to appraise; (un

militar) to debrief; (un periodista) to
report; (un abogado) to advise; **—se** to
become informed

informática F computer science

informatizar[9] VT to computerize

informe M report; (militar) debriefing; **—s**
information; ADJ shapeless

infortunio M misfortune

infracción F (de reglamentos) infraction; (de
contrato) breach; (de tránsito) violation

infractor -ora MF lawbreaker

infraestructura F infrastructure

infrarrojo ADJ & M infrared

infrascrito -ta MF undersigned

infringir[11] VT to infringe, to breach, to
violate

infructuoso ADJ fruitless, unsuccessful

ínfulas F PL airs; **darse —** to put on airs

infundado ADJ groundless, unfounded

infundir VT to infuse, to imbue

infusionar VT to steep

ingeniar VT to contrive; **ingeniárselas
para** to contrive to

ingeniería F engineering; **— genética**
genetic engineering; **— química**
chemical engineering

ingeniero -ra MF engineer; **— civil** civil
engineer; **— electricista** electrical
engineer

ingenio M (mental) ingenuity, cleverness;
(verbal) wit; (artefacto) artifact; **— de
azúcar** (refinería) sugar refinery, sugar
mill; (plantación) sugar plantation

ingeniosidad F ingenuity

ingenioso ADJ ingenious, resourceful

ingenuo -nua ADJ (inocente) naive; (crédulo)
gullible; MF dupe

ingerir VI/VT to ingest

ingestión F ingestion

ingle F groin

inglés -esa ADJ English; M Englishman;
(lengua) English; F Englishwoman

ingobernable ADJ unruly

ingratitud F ingratitude

ingrato -ta ADJ thankless, ungrateful; MF
ingrate

ingrávido ADJ weightless

ingrediente M ingredient; **—s** makings

ingresar VT (datos) to input; (dinero en una
cuenta) to deposit; VI (a un hospital) to be
admitted

ingreso M (permiso para entrar) entrance,
entry; (depósito bancario) deposit; (renta)
income; **—s** (de una firma) earnings; (del
Estado) revenue

inhábil ADJ unskilled

inhabilidad F inability

inhabilitar VT to disqualify

inhalar VI/VT to breathe in, to inhale

inherente ADJ inherent

inhibición F inhibition

inhibir VT to inhibit

inhospitalario ADJ inhospitable

inhóspito ADJ inhospitable

inhumano ADJ inhuman

iniciación M initiation, induction

inicial ADJ initial; (pago) up-front; F initial

inicializar[9] VT to initialize

iniciar VT (comenzar) to initiate; (admitir) to
induct

iniciativa F initiative

inimitable ADJ inimitable

ininflamable ADJ fireproof

ininteligible ADJ unintelligible

ininterrumpido ADJ continuous, unbroken

injertar VT to graft

injuria F (insulto) insult, verbal abuse;
(daño) damage

injuriar VT to insult, to abuse verbally

injurioso ADJ insulting, injurious, verbally
abusive

injusticia F injustice; (acto injusto) wrong;
(error judicial) miscarriage of justice

injustificable ADJ unjustifiable

injustificado ADJ uncalled-for, unwarranted

injusto ADJ unjust, unfair

inmaculado ADJ immaculate, spotless

inmaduro ADJ immature

inmanejable ADJ unmanageable

inmaterial ADJ immaterial

inmediación F vicinity

inmediato ADJ immediate, instant; **de —** at
once

inmensidad F immensity, vastness

inmenso ADJ immense, vast

inmigración F immigration

inmigrante ADJ & MF immigrant

inmigrar VI to immigrate

inminente ADJ imminent, impending

inmiscuir[31] VI to mix; **—se** to meddle

inmoral ADJ immoral

inmoralidad F immorality

inmortal ADJ & MF immortal

inmortalidad F immortality

inmóvil ADJ motionless, immobile

inmovilizar[9] VT to immobilize; (en una
pelea) to pin

inmune ADJ immune

inmunidad F immunity

inmutable ADJ unchangeable, immutable

innato ADJ innate, inborn

innecesario ADJ unnecessary, needless

innegable ADJ undeniable

innoble ADJ ignoble

innocuo ADJ innocuous
innovación F innovation
innumerable ADJ innumerable, countless
inocencia F innocence
inocente ADJ innocent, guiltless; MF dupe
inocuo ADJ harmless
inodoro ADJ odorless; M toilet, commode
inofensivo ADJ inoffensive, harmless
inolvidable ADJ unforgettable
inoperable ADJ inoperable
inoportuno ADJ inopportune, untimely
inorgánico ADJ inorganic
inoxidable ADJ rustproof
inquietar VT to worry
inquieto ADJ (movedizo) restless;
 (preocupado) uneasy
inquietud F (intranquilidad) restlessness;
 (preocupación) alarm
inquilino -ina MF (de un apartamento)
 tenant, renter; (de una pensión) lodger
inquina F spite
inquirir[34] VI/VT to inquire
inquisición F inquisition
inquisitivo ADJ inquisitive
insaciable ADJ insatiable
insalubre ADJ unhealthy
insatisfactorio ADJ unsatisfactory
insatisfecho ADJ dissatisfied, unhappy
inscribir[51] VT (grabar) to inscribe;
 (matricular) to register, to enroll; **—se**
 register, to enroll
inscripción F (grabado) inscription;
 (matriculación) registration, enrollment
insecticida M insecticide
insectívoro ADJ insectivorous
insecto M insect
inseguro ADJ (personalidad) insecure;
 (vehículo) unsafe; (el andar) unsteady
insensato -ta ADJ foolish; MF fool
insensibilizar[9] VT to desensitize
insensible ADJ (cruel) insensitive, callous;
 (imperturbable) unfeeling, thick-skinned;
 (entumecido) numb
inseparable ADJ inseparable
inserción F insertion
insertar VT to insert
inservible ADJ useless
insidioso ADJ insidious
insigne ADJ famous
insignia F insignia, badge
insignificante ADJ insignificant,
 unimportant
insincero ADJ insincere
insinuación F insinuation; (sexual)
 innuendo
insinuante ADJ suggestive
insinuar[17] VT to insinuate, to suggest; **—se**

to insinuate oneself
insípido ADJ insipid, flavorless
insistencia F insistence; (perseverancia)
 persistence
insistente ADJ insistent; (perseverante)
 persistent
insistir VI/VT to insist; (perseverar) to persist;
 — en to insist on; **— sobre** to harp on
insolación F (por sol) sunstroke; (por calor)
 heatstroke
insolencia F insolence; (comentario) smart
 remark
insolente ADJ insolent, sassy
insólito ADJ unusual; (accidente) freak,
 freakish
insoluble ADJ insoluble
insolvente ADJ insolvent
insomne ADJ wakeful, unable to sleep
insoportable ADJ unbearable, impossible;
 (dolor) excruciating
insospechado ADJ unsuspected
insostenible ADJ untenable
inspección F inspection; (encuesta) canvass
inspeccionar VT to inspect, to survey
inspector -ora MF inspector
inspiración F (idea) inspiration; (inhalación)
 inhalation
inspirar VI/VT to inspire; VI to inhale, to
 breathe in
instalación F installation
instalar VT to install; **—se** to take up
 residence
instancia LOC ADV **a —s de** at the request of
instantánea F snapshot
instantáneo ADJ instantaneous
instante M instant; **al —** right away
instar VT to enjoin
instigar[7] VT to instigate, to abet
instintivo ADJ instinctive
instinto M instinct; **— suicida** death wish
institución F institution; **— benéfica**
 charity
instituir[31] VT to institute
instituto M institute; (escuela secundaria)
 high school
institutriz F governess
instrucción F instruction, schooling
instructivo ADJ instructive
instructor -ora MF instructor
instruir[31] VT to instruct, to school
instrumental ADJ instrumental
instrumentar VT (un plan) to implement;
 (música) to do the instrumentation for
instrumento M instrument; **— de metal**
 brass instrument; **— de viento** wind
 instrument
insubordinado ADJ insubordinate

insuficiencia F insufficiency; (de los órganos) failure

insuficiente ADJ insufficient, inadequate

insufrible ADJ insufferable

insulina F insulin

insulso ADJ bland

insultar VT to insult

insulto M insult, put-down

insuperable ADJ (resultado) insuperable; (obstáculo) insurmountable

insurgente ADJ & MF insurgent

insurrección F insurrection

insurrecto -ta ADJ rebellious; MF rebel

intachable ADJ blameless

intacto ADJ intact, unbroken

intangible ADJ intangible

integral ADJ integral; (harina) whole-grain

integrante ADJ integral

integrar VT to form; (ser miembro de) to be a member of

integridad F integrity

íntegro ADJ whole; (moralmente) upright

intelecto M intellect

intelectual ADJ & MF intellectual

inteligencia F intelligence (también militar); (persona) mind; — **artificial** artificial intelligence

inteligente ADJ intelligent, bright, smart

inteligible ADJ intelligible

intemperie LOC ADV **a la** — exposed to the weather

intención F intention, intent

intencional ADJ intentional

intensidad F intensity

intensificar[6] VT to intensify; —**se** to intensify; (violencia) to escalate

intensivo ADJ intensive

intenso ADJ intense; (debate) fierce; (calor) severe

intentar VI/VT to try; VT to attempt

intento M (tentativa) try, attempt; (propósito) intention

interactivo ADJ interactive

interactuar[17] VI to interact

intercalación F insertion

intercalar VT to insert

intercambiador M interchange

intercambiar VI/VT to exchange

intercambio M exchange

interceder VI to intercede

interceptación F interception

interceptar VT to intercept

intercesión F intercession

intercesor -ora MF advocate

interés M (intelectual, financiero) interest; (preocupación) concern; (participación comercial) stake; — **compuesto** compound interest

interesado ADJ interested; (preocupado) concerned; (egoísta) self-serving

interesante ADJ interesting

interesar VT to interest; —**se por** to become interested in

interestatal ADJ interstate

interestelar ADJ interstellar

interface MF interface

interfaz MF (electrónica/informática) interface

interferencia F interference; (en una transmisión) interference, static

interferir VT to jam; VI to interfere

ínterin M interim; **en el** — meanwhile

interino ADJ acting, interim

interior ADJ (de un edificio) interior; (no costeño) inland; (dentro de una organización) internal; (hacia dentro) inward; M interior

interiorizar[9] VT to internalize

interjección F interjection

interlineal ADJ interlinear

interlock M interlock

interlocutor -ora MF interlocutor

interludio M interlude

intermediario -ria M middleman; MF (mensajero) go-between

intermedio ADJ intermediate; M intermission; **por** — **de** through

interminable ADJ interminable, unending, endless

intermitente ADJ intermittent; M turn signal

internacional ADJ international

internado -da M (escuela) boarding school; (período de práctica) internship; MF (alumno) boarding student; (en un hospital) inmate

internalizar[9] VT to internalize

internar VT (en una cárcel) to intern; (en un hospital) to admit; (en un manicomio) to commit

internet M Internet

internista MF internist

interno -na ADJ internal; MF (alumno) boarding-school student; (prisionero, médico) intern

interpersonal ADJ interpersonal

interponer[39] VT to interpose; —**se** to intervene

interpretación F interpretation; (artístico) performance, rendition

interpretar VT to interpret; (música) to perform; (intenciones) to construe

intérprete MF interpreter; (músico) artist

interracial ADJ interracial

interrelacionado ADJ interrelated

interrogación F interrogation
interrogador -ora MF questioner; ADJ questioning
interrogar[7] VI/VT (por la policía) to interrogate; (con intensidad) to grill; (a un testigo) to question, to cross-examine
interrogativo ADJ interrogative
interrogatorio M interrogation, questioning
interrumpir VI/VT to interrupt; VT (servicios) to disrupt, to cut off; (producción de un modelo) to discontinue; (en una conversación) to intrude, to cut in
interrupción F interruption; (en una conversación) intrusion; (de producción) stoppage
interruptor M switch
intersección F intersection
intersticio M interstice
intervalo M interval; (en el teatro) intermission, interlude
intervención F intervention; — **de teléfono** wiretap
intervenir[47] VI to intervene; — **un teléfono** to wiretap
interviú F interview
intestino ADJ & M intestine; — **delgado** small intestine; —**s** bowels
intimar VI to become friendly
intimidad F intimacy
intimidar VT (una persona) to intimidate; (una tarea) to daunt
íntimo ADJ intimate, close
intitular VT to entitle; —**se** to be entitled
intolerable ADJ intolerable
intolerancia F intolerance, bigotry
intolerante ADJ intolerant, narrow-minded
intoxicación F intoxication, poisoning; — **con plomo** lead poisoning; — **por alimentos** food poisoning
intoxicar[6] VT to poison, to intoxicate
intransigente ADJ intransigent, uncompromising
intransitivo ADJ intransitive
intravenoso ADJ intravenous
intrepidez F fearlessness
intrépido ADJ (sin miedo) intrepid, fearless; (aventurero) adventurous
intriga F intrigue
intrigante MF schemer; ADJ scheming
intrigar[7] VI/VT to intrigue, to scheme
intrincado ADJ intricate
intrínseco ADJ intrinsic
introducción F introduction
introducir[24] VT (incorporar) to introduce; (colocar) to put in, to insert
introspección F introspection
introvertido -da ADJ introverted; MF introvert

intrusión F intrusion
intrusivo ADJ intrusive
intruso -sa ADJ intruding; MF intruder
intuición F intuition
intuir[31] VT to sense
intuitivo ADJ intuitive
inundación F flood
inundar VI/VT to inundate, to flood; (de regalos) to shower
inusitado ADJ unusual
inútil ADJ useless, pointless; (esfuerzo) futile; (persona) worthless, good-for-nothing
inutilidad F uselessness; (de un esfuerzo) futility
inutilizar[9] VT to render useless, to put out of commission
invadir VI/VT to invade
invalidar VT to render invalid
inválido -da ADJ (discapacitado) invalid; (nulo) void; MF invalid
invalorable ADJ priceless, invaluable
invariable ADJ invariable
invasión F invasion
invasor -ora MF invader; ADJ invading
invencible ADJ invincible
invención F invention (también mentira); (mental) construct
inventar VT to invent; (una historia) to fabricate, to make up
inventariar[16] VT to inventory
inventario M inventory
inventiva F ingenuity
inventivo ADJ inventive
invento M invention
inventor -ora MF inventor
invernadero M greenhouse, hothouse
invernal ADJ wintry
invernar[1] VI to winter
inverosímil ADJ unlikely, farfetched
inversión F (trueque) inversion; (financiero) investment
inversionista MF investor
inverso ADJ inverse, reverse; **a la inversa** the other way around
inversor -ora MF investor
invertir[3] VT to invert, to reverse; VI/VT (dinero) to invest
investidura F inauguration, investment
investigación F (policial) investigation, inquiry; (científico) research
investigador -ora MF investigator; (científico) researcher
investigar[7] VI/VT to investigate, to look into; (científico) to research
investir VI/VT to invest; — **de un cargo** to induct into office

invicto ADJ unbeaten
invierno M winter
invisible ADJ invisible; (oculto) unseen
invitación F invitation
invitado -da MF guest
invitar VI/VT to invite
invocación F invocation
invocar[6] VT to invoke; (espíritus) to conjure
involucrar VT (implicar) to implicate; (consistir de) to involve
involuntario ADJ involuntary; (accidental) inadvertent
inyección F injection, shot; (en coches) fuel injection
inyectado ADJ — **de sangre** bloodshot
inyectar VT to inject
ión M ion
ionizar[9] VT to ionize
ir[32] VI to go; (deber estar situado) to belong; — **a caballo** to ride horseback; — **a pie** to walk; —**a por** to fetch; — **aprendiendo** to learn gradually; — **corriendo** to run; — **de mal en peor** to go from bad to worse; — **en coche** to drive/ride in a car; — **tirando** to scrape along/ **no me va ni me viene** it's all the same to me; **¿cómo te va?** how are you? **¡vaya!** well now! **¡vaya a saber uno!** go figure! **¡vamos!** let's go! come on! **¡vaya hombre!** what a man! **¡ve a freír espárragos!** take a hike! **va por dos años que me casé** it's going on two years since I got married; **voy a comer** I'm going to eat; **va y se come un hongo venenoso** she goes and eats a poisonous mushroom; **en lo que va del año** since the beginning of the year; **ya van siete veces que me lo dice** that makes seven times that she's told me; **voy a ir de rojo** I'm going dressed in red; **para que no vayas a creer** lest you should think; **no vayas a caerte** don't fall; **¡qué va!** no way! —**se** to go away, to leave; —**se a la quiebra** to go broke; —**se a las manos** to come to blows; —**se a pique** to founder; —**se de vacaciones** to take a vacation
ira F ire, wrath
Irak M Iraq
Irán M Iran
iraní ADJ & MF Iranian
iraquí ADJ & MF Iraqi
irascible ADJ irascible, quick-tempered
iridiscente ADJ iridescent
iris M iris
Irlanda F Ireland
irlandés -esa MF Irish; ADJ Irish

ironía F irony
irónico ADJ ironic, wry
irracional ADJ irrational, unreasonable
irradiar VT to radiate, to irradiate
irreal ADJ unreal
irreconocible ADJ unrecognizable
irrecuperable ADJ irretrievable
irreflexivo ADJ thoughtless
irrefutable ADJ irrefutable
irregular ADJ irregular; (borde, filo) ragged; (pulso) unsteady; (superficie) rough, uneven; (comportamiento) erratic, haphazard
irremediable ADJ hopeless
irremplazable ADJ irreplaceable
irreparable ADJ irreparable
irreprochable ADJ irreproachable, flawless
irresistible ADJ irresistible
irrespetuoso ADJ disrespectful
irresponsable ADJ irresponsible
irreverente ADJ irreverent
irrevocable ADJ irrevocable
irrigación F irrigation
irrigar[7] VI/VT to irrigate
irritable ADJ irritable
irritación F irritation
irritante ADJ (molesto) irritating, grating; (agresivo) abrasive
irritar VI/VT to irritate, to aggravate
irrumpir VI to burst into
isla F island, isle; —**s Fiyi** Fiji Islands; —**s Malvinas** Falkland Islands; —**s Marshall** Marshall Islands; —**s Salomón** Solomon Islands; —**s Vírgenes** Virgin Islands
islamismo M Islam
islandés -esa MF Icelander; ADJ Icelandic
Islandia F Iceland
isleño -ña MF islander
isobara F isobar
isométrico ADJ isometric
isótopo M isotope
Israel M Israel
israelí ADJ & MF Israeli
istmo M isthmus
Italia F Italy
italiano -na ADJ & MF Italian
itálico ADJ italic
ítem M item
itinerante ADJ itinerant
itinerario M itinerary
IVA (impuesto al valor añadido / agregado) M sales tax
izar[9] VT to hoist, to raise
izquierda F left (también política); (mano) left hand; **a la** — to the left
izquierdista ADJ & MF leftist
izquierdo ADJ left

Jj

jab M jab
jabalí M (wild) boar
jabalina F javelin
jabón M soap
jabonera F soap dish
jabonoso ADJ soapy
jaca F nag
jacinto M hyacinth
jactancia F boastfulness
jactancioso ADJ boastful, blustering
jactarse VI to boast, to brag
jacuzzi M Jacuzzi™, hot tub
jade M jade
jadear VI to pant, to gasp
jadeo M panting, gasping
jaez M harness
jaguar M jaguar
jalar VI/VT to pull, to tug
jalea F jelly
jaleo M (lío) mess; (barahúnda) ruckus
jam M jam session
Jamaica F Jamaica
jamaicano -na ADJ & MF Jamaican
jamaiquino -na ADJ & MF Jamaican
jamás ADV never
jamelgo M hack
jamón M ham
jamona F buxom woman
Japón M Japan
japonés -esa ADJ & MF Japanese
jaque M check; **— mate** checkmate; **tener a uno en —** *fam* to have someone by the short hairs
jaqueca F migraine
jarabe M syrup
jarana F revelry; **ir de —** to paint the town red
jarcia F rigging
jardín M (de flores) garden; (de césped) yard; **— de niños** kindergarten; **— infantil** nursery
jardinero -ra MF gardener
jarra F (cántaro) jug, pitcher; (taza) mug; **en —s** akimbo
jarro M pitcher, jug
jarrón M vase
jaspe M jasper; (mármol) veined marble
jaula F cage, coop
jauría F pack
jazmín M jasmine
jazz M jazz

jeans M PL jeans
jefatura F headquarters
jefe -fa MF (en un lugar de trabajo) boss; (militar) commander; (departamental) chair, head; (policial) chief; **— del estado mayor** chief of staff
jején M gnat
jengibre M ginger
jerarquía F hierarchy
jerez M sherry
jerga F jargon, slang
jerigonza F gibberish, gobbledygook; (juego lingüístico) pig Latin
jeringa F syringe
jeringar[7] VT to annoy
jeroglífico ADJ & M hieroglyphic
jersey M sweater
jesuita ADJ INV & M Jesuit
Jesús INTERJ God bless you! gesundheit!
jeta F (hocico) snout; (cara) mug
jet-set M jet set
jilguero M goldfinch
jinete -ta MF rider
jinetear VI to ride horseback
jingle M jingle
jirafa F giraffe
jobar INTERJ holy cow! holy Moses! holy mackerel!
jockey M jockey
jocoso ADJ jocular
joder INTERJ *vulg* fuck! shit! VI/VT (tener relaciones sexuales) *vulg* to fuck; VT (dañar) *vulg* to fuck up; (fastidiar) *vulg* to jerk around
jodido ADJ (de mierda) *vulg* fucking; (estropeado) *vulg* fucked up
jofaina F basin
jolgorio M rumpus
Jordania F Jordan
jordano -na ADJ & MF Jordanian
jornada F (día laboral) workday; (coloquio) colloquium
jornal M daily wage
jornalero -ra MF day laborer
joroba F hump
jorobado -da ADJ & MF hunchback
jorobar VT (molestar) to hassle; (estropear) to gum up
jota F jay; **no saber ni —** to know zilch
joven ADJ young; M (muchacho) youth
jovial ADJ jolly
joya F jewel; (persona apreciada) gem; **—s** jewelry
joyería F jewelry store
joyero -ra MF jeweler
joystick M joystick
juanete M bunion

jubilación F retirement; (pagos) pension

jubilar VT to pension, to retire; **—se** to retire

jubileo M jubilee

júbilo M glee

jubiloso ADJ jubilant, joyous

judía F bean; **— blanca** navy bean; **— pinta** pinto bean; **— verde** green bean

judicial ADJ judicial

judío -ía ADJ Jewish; MF Jew

judo M judo

juego M (actividad recreativa) play; (partido de pelota) game; (conjunto de tazas) set; (conjunto de muebles) suite; **— de damas** checkers; **— de palabras** pun, play on words; **—s Olímpicos** Olympic Games; **estar en —** to be at stake; **hacer — to match**

juerga F binge; **irse de —** to go on a binge

juerguista MF merrymaker

jueves M Thursday

juez -za MF judge; (en deportes) referee; **— de paz** justice of the peace

jugada F play, move

jugador -ora MF player; (apostador) gambler

jugar[33] VI to play; (apostar) to gamble; **— a la baraja / a los naipes** to play cards; **— con fuego** to play with fire; **— limpio** to play fair; **—se** to risk

jugarreta F bad turn

jugo M juice

jugoso ADJ juicy

juguete M plaything, toy

juguetear VI to toy with, to fiddle with

juguetón -ona ADJ playful

juicio M (criterio) judgment; (proceso) trial; **perder el —** to lose one's mind; **a mi —** in my estimation

juicioso ADJ judicious

juke-box M jukebox

julio M July

jumbo ADJ jumbo; M jumbo jet

jumper M jumper

junco M rush, reed; (barco chino) junk

jungla F jungle

junio M June

junta F (reunión) meeting; (concejo) council; (juntura) joint; (pieza de coche) gasket

juntar VT (tubos) to attach; (valentía) to muster; (flores) to gather, to pick; (ganado) to round up, to wrangle; **— polvo** to gather dust; **— valor** to muster courage; **—se** (acumularse) to gather; (asociarse) to band together; (reunirse) to come together

junto ADJ together; LOC ADV **— a** next to; **— con** together with

juntura F (lugar) juncture; (articulación) joint

jurado -da MF juror; M (conjunto de jurados) jury

juramentar VI/VT to swear in; **—se** to be sworn in

juramento M oath

jurar VI/VT to swear, to vow; **— en falso** to perjure oneself; **— la bandera** to pledge allegiance to the flag

jurisdicción F jurisdiction

jurisprudencia F (doctrina) jurisprudence; (derecho) law

justa F joust, tilt

justamente ADV precisely, fairly

justicia F justice

justificación F justification

justificar[6] VT to justify

justo ADJ just; (equitativo) equitable; (pío) righteous, upright; **— después de** right after; **— en ese momento** exactly at that moment

juvenil ADJ (inmaduro) juvenile; (de apariencia joven) youthful

juventud F youth

juzgado M court

juzgar[7] VI/VT to judge, to pass judgment (on); **— mal** to misjudge

Kk

kaki M khaki

kart M go-cart

kayak M kayak

Kazajstán M Kazakhstan

kazako -ka ADJ & MF Kazak(h)

Kenia F Kenya

keniata ADJ INV & MF INV Kenyan

kermés F bazaar

keroseno M kerosene

ketchup M catsup, ketchup

kilo M kilo

kilobyte M kilobyte

kilociclo M kilocycle

kilogramo M kilogram

kilometraje M mileage

kilómetro M kilometer

kilovatio M kilowatt; F **—-hora** kilowatt-hour

Kirguistán M Kyrgyzstan

Kiribati M Kiribati

kosher ADJ kosher

Kuwait M Kuwait

kuwaití ADJ & MF Kuwaiti

Ll

la ART DEF F the; **— de** the one with, that one with; PRON PERS it, her; PRON REL **— que** she who, the one that
laberinto M labyrinth, maze
labia F gift of gab
labio M lip; **— leporino** harelip
labor F (trabajo) labor; (tarea) task; (manualidad) handiwork
laboral ADJ **legislación —** labor legislation
laboratorio M laboratory
laborioso ADJ (trabajoso) laborious; (amante del trabajo) hard-working
labrado ADJ carved
labranza F plowing
labrar VT to till; **—se una carrera** to carve out a career
laca F lacquer
lacar[6] VT to lacquer
lacayo M lackey, flunky
laciar VT RP to straighten
lacio ADJ straight
lacónico ADJ (persona) laconic; (comentario) terse
lacra F (física) scar; (moral) blight
lacre M sealing wax
lacrimógeno ADJ tear-producing
lactar VT to nurse
lácteo ADJ (parecido a la leche) milky; (hecho de leche) dairy
ladeado ADJ (torcido) awry, askew; (asimétrico) lopsided
ladear VT to tilt; (la cabeza) to cock; (un avión) to bank; (ignorar) to snub, to ignore; **—se** to tilt, to lean
ladeo M tilt
ladera F hillside
ladillas F PL crabs
ladino ADJ artful
lado M side; **— a —** side by side; **al —** nearby; **¡a un —!** gangway! **de —** sideways; **hacerse a un —** to move over
ladrar VI to bark; VI/VT (hablar de modo áspero) to snap (at)
ladrido M bark, barking
ladrillo M brick
ladrón -ona MF (de casas) burglar; (con violencia) robber; (con astucia) thief
lagartija F lizard; (ejercicio) push-up
lagarto M alligator
lago M lake
lágrima F tear, teardrop

lagrimear VI to weep
laguna F lagoon; (de la memoria, conocimiento) gap; (legal) loophole
laico -ca MF layperson; ADJ lay
laja F slab
lamentable ADJ (desafortunado) lamentable, regrettable; (ruinoso) woeful
lamentación F lamentation
lamentar VT to lament, to regret; **—se** to lament, to wail
lamento M lament, lamentation
lamer VT to lick; **— culos** fam to brown-nose; VI/VT (el mar) to lap
lamida F lick
lámina F (de vidrio, metal) sheet; (de metal) plate; (grabado) print
laminar VT to laminate
lámpara F lamp
lamparilla F night-light
lampiño ADJ (sin pelo) hairless; (sin barba) beardless
lana F wool; **— de acero** steel wool
lanar ADJ wool-bearing
lance M incident
lancear VT to lance, to spear
lanceta F lancet, lance
lancha F launch, boat; **— a motor** motorboat
langosta F (crustáceo) lobster; (insecto) locust
langostino M prawn
languidecer[13] VI to languish, to wilt
languidez F languor
lánguido ADJ languid, listless
lanilla F flannel
lanolina F lanolin
lanudo ADJ wooly, shaggy
lanza F lance, spear; **romper una — por alguien** to stick one's neck out for someone; M SG **—llamas** flame thrower
lanzadera F shuttle
lanzador -ora MF pitcher
lanzamiento M (de un cohete, producto) launch; (de suministros) drop; (de una roca grande) heave; (de una pelota) pitch
lanzar[9] VT (un cohete, un producto) to launch; (una pelota) to throw; (una bala) to fire; (algo pesado) to heave; (lodo) to sling; VI/VT (vomitar) to puke; **—se** to launch forth / out
lanzazo M thrust with a lance
Laos M Laos
laosiano -na ADJ & MF Laotian
lápida F stone tablet; (de sepultura) gravestone, tombstone
lapidar VT to stone
lapidario ADJ & M lapidary

lápiz M pencil; **— de color** crayon; **— de labios** lipstick

lapso M lapse, span

lapsus M lapse, slip of the tongue

laptop M laptop

laquear VT to lacquer

largar[7] VI (soltar) to cough up; **—se** *fam* to scram, to buzz off, to shove off

largo ADJ long; (discurso) lengthy; **¡— de aquí!** scram! **—metraje** feature film; **a la larga** in the long run; **a lo —** lengthwise; M length

largueza F generosity

larguirucho ADJ lanky

largura F length

laringe F larynx

laringitis F laryngitis

larva F larva

lascivia F (deseo) lust; (perversión) lewdness

lascivo ADJ (pervertido) lascivious, lewd; (cachondo) *fam* horny

láser M laser

lástima F (compasión) pity; **¡qué —!** what a shame!

lastimadura F hurt

lastimar VT to hurt; (insultar) to hurt one's feelings; **—se** to get hurt

lastimoso ADJ pitiful

lastrar VT to ballast

lastre M ballast

lata F tin can, can; (con tapa) canister; (pesadez) bore; **dar la —** to be a nuisance

latente ADJ latent, dormant

lateral ADJ lateral, side

látex M latex

latido M (individual) beat, throb; (colectivo) beating; (del corazón) heartbeat

latifundio M large estate

latigazo M (golpe) lash; (chasquido) crack of a whip

látigo M whip

latín M Latin

latino -na ADJ (relativo a los hispanos) Latino; (relativo a la lengua latina) Latin; M Latino; F Latina

Latinoamérica F Latin America

latinoamericano ADJ Latin American

latir VI to beat, to throb

latitud F latitude (también flexibilidad)

latón M brass

latrocinio M larceny

laudable ADJ laudable

laurel M laurel; **dormirse sobre los —es** to rest on one's laurels

lava F lava

lavable ADJ washable

lavabo M (retrete) lavatory, toilet; (recipiente) sink

lavadero M laundry

lavado M wash, washing; **— de cerebro** brain washing; **— de dinero** money laundering; **— en seco** dry cleaning

lavadora F washing machine

lavanda F lavender

lavandera F washerwoman

lavandería F laundry

lavar VI/VT to wash; (ropa) to launder; **—se** to wash up; **—se las manos** to wash one's hands; M SG **lavaplatos / lavavajillas** dishwasher

lavativa F enema

lavatorio M washroom

laxante M laxative

laxitud F laxity

laxo ADJ lax

lazada F bowknot

lazar[9] VT to lasso

lazarillo M (persona) guide for the blind; (perro) guide dog

lazo M (soga) lasso, rope; (vuelta) loop; (nudo corredizo) noose; (relación) tie, bond

le PRON PERS **— dije** I told you / him / her; **— vi** *Esp* I saw him; **se — murió el perro** his / her dog died on him / her

leal ADJ loyal, trusty

lealtad F loyalty, allegiance

lección F lesson, assignment; **darle una — a alguien** to teach someone a lesson

lechada F whitewash

leche F (de vaca) milk; (semen) *vulg* come; **— desnatada** skim milk; **— en polvo** powdered milk; **— entera** whole milk; **— homogeneizada** homogenized milk; **— malteada** malted milk; **¿qué —s quieres?** *Esp fam* what the hell do you want? **mala —** nasty disposition; **ir a toda —** to barrel along; **ese tío es la —** that guy's a case; **es un mala —** *Esp fam* he's a nasty creep

lechería F dairy

lechero -ra ADJ dairy; M milkman; F milkmaid

lecho M bed (también de río)

lechón M suckling pig

lechoso ADJ milky

lechuga F lettuce

lechuza F screech owl, barn owl

lector -ora MF reader

lectura F (acción) reading; (material) reading matter

leer[14] VI/VT to read

legación F legation

legado M legacy, bequest

legajo M file

legal ADJ legal, lawful
legalizar[9] VT to legalize
legar[7] VT to will, to bequeath
legendario ADJ legendary
leggings M PL leggings
legible ADJ legible
legión F legion
legislación F legislation
legislador -ora MF legislator, lawmaker
legislar VI/VT to legislate
legislativo ADJ legislative
legislatura F legislature
legítimo ADJ legitimate, lawful, rightful
lego -ga MF layperson; ADJ lay
legua F league
leguleyo -ya MF *pey* shyster
legumbre F legume
leído ADJ well-read
lejanía F distance
lejano ADJ distant, faraway; (parentesco) remote
lejía F (producto de limpieza) bleach; (de sosa) lye
lejos ADV far away, far; **a lo —** in the distance; **— de** far from; **desde —** from afar
lelo ADJ silly
lema M motto; (político) slogan
lencería F lingerie
lengua F (órgano) tongue; (idioma) language; **— materna** mother tongue
lenguado M sole
lenguaje M language (también en informática); **— corporal** body language; **— de máquina** machine language; **— de signos** sign language; **— ensamblador** assembly language
lenguaraz ADJ gossipy
lengüeta F (de un instrumento de viento) reed; (de un zapato) tongue
lengüetazo M lick
lente MF lens; **— filtrador** filter lens; **—s** eyeglasses; **—s de contacto** contact lenses; **—s negros / oscuros** sunglasses, shades
lenteja F lentil
lentitud F slowness
lento ADJ (no rápido) slow; (no inteligente) dull; (letárgico) sluggish
leña F firewood
leñador -ora MF woodcutter, lumberjack
leñera F woodshed
leño M log
leñoso ADJ woody
león M lion; **— marino** sea lion
León M Leon
leona F lioness

leonés ADJ Leonese
leopardo M leopard
lepra F leprosy
lerdo ADJ slow
lesbiano -na ADJ lesbian; F lesbian
lesión F injury, lesion
lesionar VT to injure; **—se** to get injured
Lesotho M Lesotho
letal ADJ lethal
letargo M lethargy
letón -ona ADJ & MF Latvian
Letonia F Latvia
letra F (del alfabeto) letter; (caligrafía) handwriting; (de una canción) lyrics, words; **— bastardilla / cursiva** italics; **— chica** fine print; **— de cambio** bill of exchange; **— de imprenta** block letter; **— manuscrita** longhand; **sin —s** uneducated
letrado ADJ learned, literate
letrero M sign
letrina F latrine
leucemia F leukemia
leudar VI to rise; VT to leaven
leva F (de tropas) levy; (de motor) cam
levadura F leaven, yeast
levantamiento M (revuelta) uprising; (suspensión) suspension; **— de pesas** weight-lifting
levantar VT (la mano) to raise; (una caja) to lift; (un interruptor) to switch; (algo caído) to pick up; (perdices) to flush; (a un dormido) to wake up, to rouse; (un edificio) to put up; **— el campamento** to break camp; **— falso testimonio** to bear false witness; **— la mesa** to clear the table; **— la sesión** to adjourn the meeting; **— vuelo** to take flight; **—se** (de la cama) to get up, to rise, to arise; (de una silla) to stand up, to get up; (un edificio) to go up
levar VT **— anclas** to weigh anchor
leve ADJ (brisa) light; (resfrío) mild; (problema) slight
levedad F (de una brisa) lightness; (de un resfrío) mildness
léxico M lexicon, dictionary; ADJ lexical
lexicografía F lexicography
ley F law, statute; **— de prescripción** statute of limitations; **— marcial** martial law; **de buena —** of good quality
leyenda F (mitología) legend; (texto que acompaña una figura) caption
liar[16] VT (paquetes) to bundle; (cigarros) to roll; **—se** to get involved
libanés -esa ADJ & MF Lebanese
Líbano M Lebanon

libelo M libel
libélula F dragonfly
liberación F liberation; (de pecados) deliverance; (de presos) release
liberal ADJ & MF liberal
liberalidad F liberality
liberalismo M liberalism
liberar VT (de un deber) to relieve; (a un pueblo) to liberate; (del sufrimiento) to deliver; (a un preso) to free, to release
Liberia F Liberia
liberiano -na ADJ & MF Liberian
libertad F liberty, freedom; — **condicional** parole; — **de expresión** free speech; **poner en** — to set free; **poner en** — **bajo fianza** to let out on bail; **poner en** — **condicional** to parole
libertador -ora MF liberator
libertar VT to liberate
libertinaje M licentiousness
libertino -na MF libertine
Libia F Libya
libido F libido
libio -bia ADJ & MF Libyan
libra F pound (también moneda británica)
librar VT to free, to set free; (de una obligación) to release; (un cheque) to write; (una letra de cambio) to draft; (una guerra) to wage; **—se de** to get rid of
libre ADJ free; (asiento) vacant; (camino) clear; (traducción) loose; (de una obligación) exempt; — **albedrío** free will; — **cambio / comercio** free trade; — **de impuestos** duty-free; — **pensador** free thinker
librería F bookstore
librero -ra MF bookseller
libresco ADJ bookish
libreta F small notebook
libreto M libretto
libro M book; — **de bolsa** pocket book; — **de cocina** cookbook; — **de texto** textbook; — **en rústica** paperback; — **mayor** ledger
licencia F (carnet de conducir, libertad poética) license; (permiso) leave
licenciado -da MF college graduate
licenciar VT to discharge; **—se** to graduate from college
licenciatura F bachelor's degree
licencioso ADJ licentious
liceo M high school
licitación F bid
lícito ADJ lawful, permissible
licor M liqueur, cordial
licuadora F blender
líder MF leader

lidiar VI/VT to contend, to grapple
liebre F hare; **levantar la** — to let the cat out of the bag
Liechtenstein M Liechtenstein
liechtensteiniano -na MF Liechtensteiner
lienzo M canvas
lifting M face-lift
liga F (alianza, grupo deportivo) league; (cinta elástica) garter; — **mayor** major league
ligado M slur
ligadura F ligature
ligamento M ligament
ligar[7] VT to bind; (conectar notas) to slur; (perseguir sexualmente) to hit on; (conquistar sexualmente) to score; VI **—se** to bind; **—se las trompas** to have one's tubes tied
ligereza F (de peso) lightness; (de temperamento) levity
ligero ADJ (poco pesado) light; (rápido) swift; (pequeño) slight; **a la ligera** lightly
ligue M (amistad casual) pickup; (conquista sexual) score
liguero M garter belt
lija F sandpaper
lijar VI/VT to sandpaper, to sand
lila ADJ & MF INV lilac
lima F (fruta) lime; (árbol) lime tree; — **de uñas** nail file
limar VI/VT to file
limero M lime tree
limitación F (restricción) limitation; (defecto) shortcoming
limitar VT to limit; (gastos) to curb; **—se a** to limit oneself to
límite M limit; (de una región) boundary; (de la paciencia) bounds; — **de velocidad** speed limit
limítrofe ADJ bordering
limo M slime
limón M lemon
limonada F lemonade
limonero M lemon tree
limosna F alms, handout
limpiador M cleanser
limpiar VI/VT to clean; VT (una superficie) to wipe; (la piel) to cleanse; (un camino, una pantalla de computadora, la reputación) to clear; (animales) to dress; (zapatos) to shine; (un derrame) to mop up, to wipe up; (dejar sin dinero) to clean out; M SG **limpiaparabrisas** windshield wiper; **limpiavidrios** squeegee
límpido ADJ limpid
limpieza F cleanliness, neatness; (operación militar) mop-up; — **étnica** ethnic

cleansing

limpio ADJ clean, neat; (piel, conciencia) clear; (juego) fair; (sin dinero) broke; **pasar en —** to make a clean copy

limusina F limousine

linaje M lineage, ancestry

linaza F linseed

lince M (animal) lynx; (persona astuta) sly fox; **con ojos de —** sharp-eyed

linchar VT to lynch

lindante ADJ neighboring

lindar VI to border, to adjoin

linde MF boundary

lindero ADJ adjoining; M boundary

lindo ADJ pretty; **un día —** a nice day; **de lo — —** a lot

línea F line; **— de conducta** course of action; **— de crédito** credit line; **— de montaje** assembly line

lineal ADJ linear

linfa F lymph

lingüista MF linguist

lingüística F linguistics

lingüístico ADJ linguistic

linimento M liniment

lino M (tela) linen; (fibra) flax

linóleo M linoleum

linterna F flashlight; (de un faro) lantern

lío M (bulto) bundle; (enredo, molestia) mess, hassle; (amorío) affair, fling; **armar un —** to raise a rumpus; **meterse en un —** to get oneself into a mess

liposucción F liposuction

liquidación F (ajuste de cuentas, de bienes) settlement, liquidation; (rebaja) sale, clearance sale; (pago completo) payment in full

liquidar VT (bienes, mercancías) to liquidate; (una cuenta, herencia) to settle; (a una persona) *fam* to waste, to off

liquidez F liquidity

líquido ADJ & M liquid

lira F lira

lírico ADJ lyric, lyrical

lirio M iris; **— de los valles** lily of the valley

lirismo M lyricism

lisiado ADJ (descapacitado) handicapped; (lesionado) injured

lisiar VT to handicap

liso ADJ (neumático) bald; (camino) even, smooth; (terreno) flat; (pelo) straight; **azul —** solid blue

lisonja F flattery

lisonjear VI/VT to flatter

lisonjero -ra MF flatterer; ADJ flattering

lista F list; (de miembros) roster; (de alumnos) roll; (banda) stripe; (de precios) schedule, list; **— de control** checklist; **— de espera** waiting list; **pasar —** to call the roll

listado ADJ striped; M listing, printout

listo ADJ (preparado) ready, set; (inteligente) clever, smart; **hacerse el —** to pull a stunt

listón M (tabla) board; (en salto de altura) crossbar

lisura F smoothness

litera F (cama en el tren, barco) berth; (cama superpuesta) bunk bed

literal ADJ literal

literario ADJ literary

literato -ta MF writer

literatura F literature

litigio M (pleito) lawsuit; (acción de litigar) litigation

litio M lithium

litoral ADJ seaside; M seaboard, seacoast

litro M liter

Lituania F Lithuania

lituano -na ADJ & MF Lithuanian

liviano ADJ (leve) light; (promiscuo) promiscuous

lívido ADJ livid

living M living room

llaga F sore

llama F (fuego) flame; (animal) llama

llamada F call; (grito) hail; (nota al pie) footnote; **— de cobro revertido / por cobrar** collect call

llamador M knocker

llamamiento M (conversación) call; (exhortación) appeal; **hacer un —** to appeal

llamar VT (un nombre, una huelga, por teléfono) to call; (a la puerta) to knock; (grito) to hail; **— la atención** to call attention; **me llamo Juan** my name is Juan

llamarada F blaze, flare

llamativo ADJ (impactante) striking, bold; (chabacano) gaudy, flashy

llameante ADJ flaming

llamear VI to flare, to flame

llana F trowel

llano ADJ (sencillo) plain; (liso) flat, smooth, level; (de poca profundidad) shallow; M plain

llanta F (reborde metálico) rim; (neumático) tire

llanto M crying, weeping

llanura F plain, prairie

llave F (para puertas) key; (de armas de fuego) lock; (en lucha libre) lock, hold; (grifo) faucet, tap; (interruptor) light

switch; (de gas) cock; — **de tuercas**
wrench; — **inglesa** pipe wrench; —
maestra master key

llavero M key ring

llegada F arrival

llegar[7] VI (arribar) to arrive, to get there/
here; (alcanzar) to reach; — **a las manos**
to come to blows; — **a ser** to become; —
a un arreglo to cut a deal; — **tarde**
to be late

llenar VT to fill; (un formulario) to fill out; —
el tanque to tank up, to gas up; — **el
vacío** to take up the slack; —**se** to fill up;
—**se de** to get filled with; —**se de oro** to
make a killing

lleno ADJ full; — **de** full of; **de** — totally; **un
— completo** a full house

llevadero ADJ bearable

llevar VT (transportar) to carry, to take;
(transportar en coche) to drive; (tener
puesto) to wear; (contener) to hold;
(inducir) to lead, to drive; — **a cabo** to
carry out; — **la cuenta** to keep score; —
la ventaja to have an advantage; — **los
libros** to keep the books; — **un mes
aquí** to have been here one month; **le
llevo dos años a mi hermano** I'm two
years older than my brother; **llevo las de
perder** the odds are against me; —**se** to
carry away, to take away; —**se bien con**
to get along with

llorar VI (con ruido) to cry, to bawl; (con
lágrimas) to weep; VT (una pérdida) to
lament; (una muerte) to mourn

lloriquear VI to whimper

lloriqueo M whimper

llorón -ona ADJ weeping; MF crybaby, whiner

lloroso ADJ tearful, weeping

llovedizo ADJ **agua llovediza** rainwater

llover[2] VI/VT to rain; — **a cántaros** to rain
cats and dogs; **llueva o truene** rain or
shine

llovizna F drizzle

lloviznar VI to drizzle, to mist

lluvia F rain; (de preguntas, críticas) barrage;
(de protestas, flechas, piedras) volley; (de
golpes, de chispas) shower; — **ácida** acid
rain

lluvioso ADJ rainy

lo PRON PERS — **bueno** the good thing; — **de
la protesta** the matter of the protest; —
que quiero what I want; **sé** — **bueno
que eres** I know how good you are; **yo
— vi** I saw it/him/you

loable ADJ laudable, praiseworthy

loar VT to laud

lobato M wolf cub

lobbista, lobista MF lobbyist

lobby M lobby

lobezno M wolf cub

lobo M wolf

lobotomía F lobotomy

lóbrego ADJ gloomy

lóbulo M lobe

local ADJ local; M premises

localidad F (pueblo) town, locality; (en un
teatro) seat

localización F location

localizar[9] VT (encontrar) to locate; (limitar)
to localize

loción F lotion

loco -ca ADJ insane, mad, crazy; — **de
remate** stark raving mad; MF lunatic,
insane person; M madman

locomotora F locomotive, train engine

locuaz ADJ garrulous, loquacious

locura F madness, insanity

locutor -ora MF radio announcer

lodazal M quagmire

lodo M mud

lodoso ADJ muddy

logaritmo M logarithm

logia F lodge

lógica F logic

lógico ADJ logical; (bien fundado) sound

logística F logistics

lograr VT to achieve, to accomplish; **logré
convencerle** I managed to/succeeded in
convincing him

logro M accomplishment, achievement;
(hazaña) feat

lola F (teta) *fam* boob

loma F knoll

lombriz F (de tierra) earthworm; (de
estómago) tapeworm

lomo M (de animal) back ridge; (corte de
carne) loin

lona F canvas

longaniza F cured sausage

longevidad F longevity

longevo ADJ long-lived

longitud F (distancia angular) longitude;
(largo) length; — **de onda** wavelength

lonja F (mercado) commodity exchange;
(loncha) slice of meat

loquería F *fam* booby hatch, funny farm

loquero -ra MF (psiquiatra) *fam* shrink; M
(manicomio) *fam* funny farm

lord M lord

loro M parrot

losa F slab; (baldosa) flagstone

lote M lot

lotería F lottery

loza F (basto) crockery; (fino) china

lozanía F freshness, bloom
lozano ADJ fresh, blooming
LSD M LSD
lubina F bass
lubricante ADJ & M lubricant
lubricar[6] VI/VT to lubricate
lucero M morning star; — **del alba** morning star
lucha F (de clases) struggle; (pelea) fight; — **libre** wrestling
luchador -ora MF fighter; (en lucha libre) wrestler
luchar VI/VT (contra un enemigo) to fight; (con un problema) to struggle; (en lucha libre) to wrestle; — **por** to strive for
lúcido ADJ lucid, clear-headed
luciérnaga F firefly, glowworm
lucio M pike
lucir[13b] VI (mostrarse) to look; VT (llevar) to model, to sport; (alardear de) to flaunt; —**se** (sobresalir) to excel; (ostentar) to show off
lucrativo ADJ lucrative, profitable
lucro M **sin fines de** — not for profit
luctuoso ADJ sad, mournful, dismal
luego ADV afterwards, then, next; — **de** after; **desde** — of course; **hasta** — so long
lugar M place; — **común** platitude; — **de nacimiento** birthplace; — **de trabajo** workplace; **dar** — **a** to give rise to; **no hay** — there's no room; **en** — **de** instead of
lúgubre ADJ mournful, gloomy
lujo M luxury; **darse un** — to indulge oneself; **con** — **de detalles** in great detail
lujoso ADJ luxurious; (hotel) plush
lujuria F lust
lujurioso ADJ lustful
lumbre F fire
luminosidad F brilliance
luminoso ADJ luminous
luna F moon; (espejo) large mirror; — **de miel** honeymoon; **estar en la** — to be distracted; — **llena** full moon
lunar ADJ lunar; M (en la piel) mole; (en una tela) polka dot
lunático -ca ADJ & MF lunatic
lunes M Monday
lupa F magnifying glass
lúpulo M hops
lustrar VT to shine, to polish
lustre M luster, shine
lustroso ADJ (revista) glossy; (pelo) shining, sleek
luto M mourning
Luxemburgo M Luxembourg

luxemburgués -esa MF Luxembourger; ADJ Luxembourgian
luz F light (también aparato); (del sol) sunshine; (abertura) aperture; — **trasera** tail light; — **verde** green light; **dar a** — to give birth; **sacar a** — to disclose

Mm

macabro ADJ grim
macanudo ADJ cool
Macao M Macao
macarrones M PL macaroni
Macedonia F Macedonia
macedonio -nia ADJ & MF Macedonian
maceta F flowerpot
machacar[6] VT (aplastar) to pound, to crush; (insistir) to harp on
machacón ADJ persistent
machetazo M hack with a machete
machete M machete
machismo M (male) chauvinism
macho M (animal masculino) male; (mulo) he-mule; (varón) man; (hombre muy varonil) he-man; — **cabrío** he-goat; — **y hembra** hook and eye; ADJ (masculino) male; (fuerte) strong; INTERJ man!
machote ADJ butch
machucar[6] VT to bruise
macilento ADJ pale
macizo ADJ massive; M plateau
Madagascar M Madagascar
madama F madam
madeja F skein
madera F wood; (árboles maderables) timber; (madera para construcción) lumber; — **contrachapada** plywood; — **flotante** driftwood; — **noble** hardwood; —**s** woodwinds; **tocar** — to knock on wood
maderaje M woodwork
madero M trunk
madrastra F stepmother
madre F mother; — **de alquiler** surrogate mother; — **patria** mother country; —**perla** mother-of-pearl; — **política** mother-in-law; —**selva** honeysuckle; **ciento y la** — everybody and their dog
madriguera F burrow, hole
madrileño -ña ADJ & MF (person) from Madrid
madrina F godmother
madrugada F early morning hours; **a las dos de la** — at two in the morning

madrugador -ra ADJ & MF early bird
madurar VI to mature, to grow up
madurez F (de personas) maturity; (de frutas) ripeness
maduro ADJ (de personas) mature; (de frutas) ripe
maestría F master's degree
maestro -tra MF (docente) (school)teacher; (artesano) master
mafia F mafia
mafioso -sa MF mafioso
magia F magic
mágico ADJ magic, magical
magistrado -da MF magistrate
magistral ADJ masterful, masterly
magma M magma
magnánimo ADJ magnanimous
magnate MF magnate, tycoon
magnesia F magnesia
magnesio M magnesium
magnético ADJ magnetic
magnetismo M magnetism
magnetizar[9] VT to magnetize
magnificar[6] VT to magnify
magnificencia F magnificence
magnífico ADJ magnificent; (día) glorious
magnitud F magnitude
magno ADJ great
magnolia F magnolia
magnolio M magnolia tree
mago M magician, wizard
magro ADJ lean
magulladura F bruise
magullar VI/VT (machucar) to bruise; (mutilar) to mangle
mahonesa F mayonnaise
maicena® F cornstarch
maíz M corn, maize
maizal M cornfield
majadería F stupidity
majadero ADJ stupid
majar VT to pound
majestad F majesty
majestuoso ADJ majestic, stately
majo ADJ (atractivo) good-looking; (agradable) charming
mal M (maldad) evil; (enfermedad) malady, affliction; (daño) harm; **— de altura** altitude sickness; **— de ojo** evil eye; ADV wrong, badly; **— aconsejado** misguided; **— adquirido** ill-gotten; **— hablado** foulmouthed; **hablar — de alguien** to speak ill of someone; **hacer —** to do wrong
malabarista MF juggler
malandanza F misfortune
malaria F malaria

Malasia F Malaysia
malasio -sia ADJ & MF Malaysian
Malawi M Malawi
malawiano -na ADJ & MF Malawian
malbaratar VT to undersell
malcontento ADJ discontented
malcriado ADJ spoiled
malcriar VT to spoil
maldad F evil, wickedness
maldecir[26b] VI/VT to curse
maldición F curse
maldito ADJ accursed; **¡— sea!** *fam* damn it!
Maldivas F PL Maldives
maldivo -va ADJ & MF Maldivian
maleable ADJ malleable
maleante MF gangster, hoodlum
malear VT to corrupt
maleducado ADJ ill-mannered, ill-bred
maleficio M evil spell
maléfico ADJ evil
malentendido M misunderstanding
malestar M (de estómago) upset; (físico) discomfort; (espiritual) malaise; (social) unrest
maleta F suitcase, bag; **hacer la —** to pack one's suitcase
maletín M briefcase
malévolo ADJ malevolent; (comentario) snide
maleza F underbrush, scrub
malgache ADJ & MF Madagascan
malgastar VI/VT to waste, to throw away
malgasto M waste
malhechor -ora MF evildoer, criminal
malhumorado ADJ grumpy, ill-humored
Malí M Mali
malí ADJ & MF Malian
malicia F malice
malicioso ADJ malicious, spiteful
maligno ADJ vicious, evil; (tumor) malignant
malinterpretar VI/VT to misunderstand
malla F (de armadura) mail; (de metal) mesh
malo ADJ bad; (calidad, letra) poor; (enfermo) ill; **mal estado** disrepair; **mal humor** bad mood; **mal tiempo** rough weather; **mala fama** ill repute; **mala hierba** weed; **mala pasada** bad turn; **mala racha** slump; **mala suerte** bad luck; **mala voluntad** ill will
malograr VT to spoil, to ruin; **—se** to miscarry
malpagar[7] VI/VT to underpay
malparto M miscarriage
malsano ADJ unhealthy, unwholesome
malta F malt
Malta F Malta
maltés -esa ADJ & MF Maltese
maltratar VT to mistreat, to abuse

maltrato M mistreatment, abuse

maltrecho ADJ battered

malvado ADJ wicked, evil

malversación F misuse, misappropriation

malversar VT to misuse, to embezzle

mamá F mama, mamma, mom

mamada F suck; (felación) *vulg* blow job

mamado ADJ drunk

mamar VI (un bebé) to suckle, to nurse; VI/VT to suck; **—la** *vulg* to blow

mamarracho M sight

mami F mommy

mamífero ADJ mammalian, mammal; M mammal

mamografía F mammography

mampara F partition

mamut M mammoth

manada F (de ballenas) pod; (de vacas) herd; (de lobos) pack

manantial M (naciente) spring; (cantidad inagotable de algo) wellspring

manar VI to stream out

mancha F (marca) stain, spot; (de tinta) blot; (cosa borrosa) blur; (aceitosa) smear, smudge; (menoscabo) tinge; (en la piel) blemish

manchado ADJ spotted

manchar VI/VT (ensuciar) to spot; (menoscabar) to stain, to blemish

manchón M large spot

mancilla F blemish

mancillar VT to defile, to sully

manco ADJ one-armed

mancuerna F dumbbell

mandado M errand

mandamiento M commandment

mandante MF principal

mandar VI/VT (dar órdenes) to command, to order; (enviar) to send; **— buscar a** to send for; **— decir** to send word; **¿quién manda?** who's in charge? **—se hacer un traje** to have a suit made

mandarina F tangerine

mandatario -ria MF (mediante contrato) agent; (de estado) head of state

mandato M (orden) command, order; (cargo político) term, mandate

mandíbula F jaw; (hueso) jawbone

mandil M apron

mandioca F manioc

mando M (de un estado) rule; (de un aparato) control; **— a distancia** remote control

mandolina F mandolin

mandón -ona ADJ bossy, domineering; MF bossy person, control freak

mandonear VI/VT to domineer, to boss

around

manea F hobble

manear VT to hobble

manecilla F clock hand

manejable ADJ manageable

manejar VT (un vehículo) to drive, to steer; (un negocio) to run, to manage; (una máquina) to operate

manejo M (de un negocio) running, management; (de asuntos) handling; (de una máquina) operation

manera F manner, way; **a — de** like; **de alguna —** somehow; **de cualquier —** anyway; **de ninguna —** on no account; **de — que** so that

manga F (de una camisa) sleeve; (de una nave) beam; (de agua) hose; **— de viento** windsock; **en —s de camisa** not wearing a jacket; **ser de — ancha** to be broadminded; **sacar algo de la —** to pull something out of a hat

manganeso M manganese

mangle M mangrove

mango M (agarradera) handle, grip; (fruta, árbol) mango

mangosta F mongoose

manguera F hose

manguito M muff

maní M peanut

manía F (moda, estado patológico) mania; (hábito) bad habit; (tic) tic

maníaco -ca ADJ maniacal; MF maniac

maníacodepresivo ADJ manic-depressive

maniatar VT to tie the hands; (manear) to hobble

maniático ADJ (que tiene manías) crotchety; (melindroso) fastidious

manicomio M insane asylum

manicura F manicure

manicurar VT to manicure

manido ADJ hackneyed

manifestación F (muestra) manifestation; (protesta) demonstration

manifestar[1] VT to manifest, to show; (expresar) to air; (protestar en público) to demonstrate; (declarar) to state

manifiesto ADJ & M manifest; **poner de —** to underscore; M (dogma) manifesto

manija F handle

maniobra F (militar) maneuver; (para llamar la atención) stunt

maniobrar VI/VT to maneuver

manipulación F (de la opinión pública) manipulation; (de alimentos) handling

manipular VT (influir) to manipulate; (tocar con las manos) to handle

maniquí M (muñeco) mannequin; MF

(modelo) model

manivela F crank

manjar M delicacy

mano F hand (también de naipes); (de pintura) coat; **— a —** one on one; **— de obra** workforce; **—s a la obra** let's get to work; **—s de mantequilla** butterfingers; **a —** (presente) at hand; (con la mano) by hand; **a — armada** at gunpoint; **dar una —** to lend a hand; **dar una — de pintura** to put on a coat of paint; **darle una — a alguien** to lend someone a hand; **darse la —** (saludo) to shake hands; (señal de afecto) to hold hands; **de primera —** firsthand; **de segunda —** secondhand; **estar a — con alguien** to be even with someone; **hecho a —** handmade; **poner las —s en el fuego por alguien** to go out on a limb for someone; **quedar a —** to break even; **se le fue la —** he got carried away; **ser — to** lead (in a card game); **tener buena — con / para algo** to have a knack for something; **tomarse de la —** to hold hands

manojo M handful; (de llaves) bunch

manómetro M pressure gauge

manopla F mitten

manosear VT (a una persona) to fondle, to grope; (tocar una cosa) to feel, to finger

manoseo M feel, grope

manotazo M swat; **tirarle un — a alguien** to take a swipe at someone

manotear VI to swat at

mansalva LOC ADV **a —** at will

mansedumbre F gentleness

mansión F mansion

manso ADJ (humilde) meek; (domesticado) tame; (apacible) gentle

manta F blanket, cover; (liviana) throw

manteca F lard, shortening; *RP* butter; **— de cacao** cocoa butter

mantecoso ADJ rich, buttery

mantel M tablecloth

mantener[44] VT (conservar, sostener) to maintain; (dejar prolongadamente) to keep; (alimentar, costear a alguien) to provide for; (apoyar a lo largo del tiempo) to sustain; **— a flote** to buoy up; **— el orden público** to keep the peace; **— en suspenso** to keep in suspense; **— la calma** to remain calm; **—se** (quedarse) to remain; (ganarse la vida) to support oneself; **—se al corriente** to keep abreast; **—se al tanto** to stay informed; **—se firme** to stand pat, to stick to one's guns

mantenimiento M maintenance, upkeep

mantequera F (platillo) butter dish; (aparato para hacer mantequilla) churn

mantequilla F butter; **— de maní** peanut butter

mantilla F mantilla

manto M mantle (también geológico); (de juez) robe

mantón M shawl

mantra M mantra

manual ADJ & M manual

manubrio M handlebar

manufactura F manufacture

manufacturar VT to manufacture

manufacturero -ra ADJ manufacturing; MF manufacturer

manuscrito ADJ written by hand; M manuscript

manutención F maintenance

manzana F (fruta) apple; (de calles) block; **— de discordia** bone of contention

manzanar M apple orchard

manzano M apple tree

maña F (destreza) skill, knack; (artimaña) cunning

mañana F (división del día) morning; (futuro) tomorrow; ADV tomorrow; **— por la —** tomorrow morning

mañanero -ra MF early bird

mañoso ADJ tricky

mapa M map; **— en relieve** relief map

mapache M raccoon

maple M maple

maqueta F mock-up

maquillaje M makeup

maquillarse VI to put on makeup

máquina F (aparato) machine; (motor) engine; **— de búsqueda** search engine; **— de coser** sewing machine; **— de escribir** typewriter; **— de lavar** washing machine; **— de vapor** steam engine; **— expendedora** vending machine; **— fotográfica** camera

maquinación F scheming, plotting

maquinador -ora MF schemer

maquinal ADJ automatic

maquinar VI/VT to plot, to scheme

maquinaria F machinery, apparatus; (de un gobierno) machine

maquinilla F clipper; **— de afeitar** razor

maquinista M (de locomotora) locomotive engineer; (obrero) machinist

mar MF sea; **— de fondo** undercurrent; **llover a mares** to rain cats and dogs; **en alta —** on the high seas; **un — de cosas** a lot of things; **hacerse a la —** to put to sea

maraca F maraca

maraña F tangle, snarl; (de pelo) mat

marañón M cashew

maratón M marathon

maravilla F wonder, marvel; (flor) marigold; **a las mil —s** wonderfully

maravillar VT to amaze; **—se** to be amazed, to marvel

maravilloso ADJ marvelous, wonderful

marca F (récord) record; (de ganado) brand; (de producto) brand, brand-name, label; (de coche) make; **— de fábrica** trademark; **— registrada** registered trademark; **de —** name-brand

marcado ADJ (acento) thick; (contraste) sharp, stark; (descenso) steep; (parecido) strong

marcador M marker; **— de libros** bookmark; **— genético** genetic marker

marcar[6] VT to mark; (ganado) to brand; (el ritmo) to beat; (la hora) to say; (un tanto) to score; (medida) to read, to show; (un número telefónico) to dial

marcha F (caminata, pieza musical) march; (partida) leaving; (progreso) course; (modo de andar) gait; (cambio en un coche) gear; (animación) nightlife; **— atrás** reverse; **ponerse en —** to get going; **puesta en —** beginning; **sobre la —** as you go

marchante M (vendedor) art dealer; (cliente) customer

marchar VI (soldado) to march; (máquina, vehículo) to run; **—se** to go away

marchista MF walker

marchitar VT to wither; **—se** to wither, to shrivel up

marchito ADJ withered, shriveled up

marcial ADJ martial

marco M (de un cuadro, de una puerta, de referencia) frame; (moneda alemana) mark

marea F tide; **— baja** low tide

mareado ADJ (en una embarcación) seasick; (en un coche) carsick; (de alegría) giddy; (con vértigo) dizzy, lightheaded

marear VT to make dizzy; (en un barco) to make seasick; **—se** to get dizzy; (en un barco) to get seasick

marejada F tidal wave

maremoto M tidal wave

mareo M (en una embarcación) seasickness; (en un vehículo) motion sickness; (vértigo) dizziness

marfil M ivory

marfileño -ña ADJ & MF Ivorian

margarina F margarine

margarita F daisy; **echar —s a los cerdos** to cast pearls before swine

margen M margin; (de la sociedad) fringe; MF (de un río) bank; **al —** on the outside

marginado -da ADJ & MF outcast

marginal ADJ marginal

marginar VT to marginalize

mariachi M mariachi

marica ADJ (homosexual) *ofensivo* queer; (cobarde) sissy; M (cobarde) sissy, pansy; (homosexual) *ofensivo* queer, fruit

maricón ADJ (cobarde) sissy; (homosexual) *ofensivo* queer; M (cobarde) sissy; (homosexual) *ofensivo* queer, fruit

marido M husband

marihuana F marijuana; *fam* grass, pot

marimacho ADJ (niña) tomboyish; (mujer) butch; MF (niña) tomboy; (mujer) butch woman

marimba F marimba

marina F navy; **— mercante** merchant marine

marinar VT to marinate

marinero -ra ADJ (buque) seaworthy; (nación) seafaring; MF sailor

marino -na ADJ marine; MF sailor; (oficial) naval officer

marioneta F marionette

mariposa F (insecto) butterfly (también natación); (tuerca) wing nut; **— nocturna** moth

mariquita F ladybug

mariscal M marshal; **— de campo** field marshal

mariscos M PL shellfish

marítimo ADJ maritime

marketing M marketing

marmita F pot

mármol M marble

marmóreo ADJ marble

marmota F groundhog

maroma F rope

marrano M hog

marrón ADJ brown

marroquí ADJ & MF Moroccan

Marruecos M Morocco

marshalés -esa ADJ & MF Marshallese

marsopa F porpoise

martes M Tuesday

martillar VI/VT to hammer

martillo M hammer (también hueso del oído, pieza de revólver); (de juez) gavel; **— neumático** jackhammer

martinete M (martillo grande) pile driver; (pieza de piano) piano hammer

martini M martini

mártir MF martyr

martirio M martyrdom

martirizar[9] VT to martyr, to torment

marxismo M Marxism

marzo M March

mas CONJ but

más ADJ more; PREP plus; ADV more; (más tiempo) longer; — **allá de** beyond; — **bien** rather; — **de tres** more than three; — **o menos** more or less; — **que nunca** more than ever; — **que tú** more than you; **a lo** — at best; **a** — **tardar** at the latest; **de** — extra; **el** — **allá** the hereafter; **es de lo** — **simpático** he's really nice; **es** — furthermore; **está de** — it is superfluous; **otro** — yet another; **por** — **que** no matter how much; **y** — **todavía** and then some

masa F mass; (de agua) body; (harina líquida) batter; (harina para amasar) dough; **en** — en masse, in large numbers; **las** —**s** the masses; — **de hojaldre** puff pastry

masacrar VT to massacre, to slaughter

masacre M massacre

masaje M massage

masajear VT to massage

masajista M masseur; F masseuse

mascar[6] VI/VT to chew; (con ruido) to crunch

máscara F mask; — **de gas** gas mask

mascarada F masquerade

mascota F (animal doméstico) pet; (emblema de un equipo) mascot

masculino ADJ (como un hombre) masculine; (del hombre) male

mascullar VI/VT to mumble

masilla F putty

masivo ADJ massive

masón M mason

masonería F masonry

masoquismo M masochism

mastectomía F mastectomy

masticar[6] VT to chew

mástil M (en un barco) mast; (para una bandera) flagpole, flagstaff

mastín M mastiff

masturbar VI to masturbate

mata F bush; — **de pelo** head of hair

matadero M slaughterhouse

matador ADJ horrendous; M bullfighter

matanza F slaughter, killing

matar VT to kill; (animales) to butcher, to slaughter; — **a tiros** to gun down; — **con hambre** to starve; **matasellar** to cancel a stamp; M SG **matamoscas** flyswatter; **matasellos** postmark; **matasanos** quack (doctor)

mate M (en ajedrez) checkmate; (planta, bebida) mate; ADJ (pintura) flat

matemática, matemáticas F mathematics

matemático -ca ADJ mathematical; MF mathematician

materia F matter; (tema de estudio) school subject; (tema) topic; — **extraña** extraneous matter; — **fecal** fecal matter; — **gris** gray matter; — **prima** raw material

material ADJ (necesidades) material; (autor) real; M material

maternal ADJ (instinto) maternal; (amor) motherly

maternidad F (pertinente al nacimiento) maternity; (estado de ser madre) motherhood

materno ADJ maternal

matiné M matinee

matiz M (de un color) tint, shade, hue; (de ironía) tinge; (de sentido) nuance

matizar[9] VT (mezclar colores) to blend, to tinge; (moderar) to qualify

matón M (que intimida a los pequeños) bully; (pendenciero) thug

matorral M (mata) thicket; (región) bush

matraz M flask

matriarca F matriarch

matrícula F (de alumnos) enrollment, matriculation; (de un coche) registration; (placa) license plate; (en la universidad) tuition fees

matriculación F matriculation

matricular VT to matriculate, to enroll

matrimonio M matrimony, marriage; (pareja) married couple

matriz F (en matemáticas) matrix; (útero) womb; (plantilla) stencil; **casa** — main office

matrona ADJ frumpy; F matron

matutino ADJ of the morning

maullar VI to mew

maullido M mew

mauriciano -na ADJ & MF Mauritian

Mauricio M Mauritius

Mauritania F Mauritania

mauritano -na MF Mauritanian

maxilar M jawbone

máxima F maxim

máximo ADJ & M maximum; (autoridad) ultimate; (cuidado) utmost

mayo M May; (palo) maypole

mayonesa F mayonnaise

mayor ADJ (de tamaño) greater, larger; (de edad) older, elder; (rango, clave) major; **al por** — wholesale; **dedo** — middle finger; **el** — **número de votos** the most votes; M (adulto) adult

mayoral M boss

mayordomo M butler

mayoreo M wholesale
mayoría F majority; — **de edad** legal age, majority
mayorista M wholesale dealer
mayúsculo -la ADJ (letra) capital; (problema) major; F capital letter
mazmorra F dungeon
mazo M mallet
mazorca F ear of corn; (sin maíz) corncob
me PRON PERS **él — vio me** he saw me; **él — habló** he talked to me; **se — murió el perro** my dog died on me
meadero M *fam* john
mear VI/VT *fam* to pee, to piss
mecánico -ca ADJ mechanical; MF mechanic; F mechanics
mecanismo M mechanism; — **de seguridad** safety device
mecanografía F typewriting
mecanografiar[16] VI/VT to type
mecanógrafo -fa MF typist
mecedora F rocking chair, rocker
mecenas MF SG/PL patron, sponsor
mecenazgo M patronage
mecer[10a] VI/VT (cuna) to rock; (columpio) to swing
mecha F (de una vela) wick; (de explosivos) fuse; —s (en el pelo) highlights
mechar VT (rellenar con tocino) to lard; (robar) to shoplift
mechero -ra MF shoplifter; M burner; — **Bunsen** Bunsen burner
mechón M lock, strand
medalla F medal
médano M dune
media F (hasta el muslo) stocking; (hasta la cintura) pantyhose; (calcetín) sock; (promedio) mean
mediación F mediation
mediador -ra MF mediator
mediados LOC ADV **a — de mayo** in mid-May
mediana F median
mediano ADJ (intermedio en tamaño) medium; (intermedio en calidad) average; **de tamaño** — middle-sized; **de mediana edad** middle-aged
medianoche F midnight
mediante PREP by means of
mediar VI (intervenir en un asunto) to mediate, to intervene; (transcurrir tiempo) to intervene; **mediaba febrero** it was mid-February
medible ADJ measurable
medicación F medication
medicamento M medicine, drug
medicina F medicine

medición F measurement; (de un terreno) survey
médico -ca MF doctor, physician; — **forense** coroner; — **general** general practitioner; ADJ medical
medida F (dimensión) measure; (acto de medir) measurement; — **para áridos** dry measure; **a — que** as; **en la — en que** to the extent that; **hacer a la** — to make to measure; **hecho a la** — made-to-measure; **tomar** —s to take measures; **tomarle las** —s a alguien to measure someone
medidor M gauge, meter
medieval ADJ medieval
medio ADJ —**día** noon, midday; — **hermano** half brother; **a media asta** at half mast; **clase media** middle class; **el americano** — the average American; **hacer una cosa a medias** to do something halfway; **ir a medias** to go halves; **media hora** half an hour; **mi media naranja** my better half; **temperatura media** mean temperature; ADV half; **a — camino** halfway; **a — derretir** half-melted; **de — tiempo** part-time; M (centro) middle; (ambiente) medium; — **ambiente** environment; — **tiempo** halftime; —s means, resources; **en (el)** — **de** in the middle of; **en — de la calle** in the middle of the street; **meterse de por** — to intervene; **por** — **de** by means of; —**s de comunicación** the media; **por todos los** —s by all possible means
medioambiental ADJ environmental
mediocre ADJ mediocre; (actuación) lackluster
mediocridad F mediocrity
medir[5] VI/VT to measure; VT (consecuencias) to gauge; (terreno) to survey; — **a pasos** to step off; —**se** to be moderate
meditación F meditation
meditar VI to meditate, to ponder
médium MF medium, psychic
medroso ADJ fearful
médula F marrow, pith; — **espinal** spinal cord; — **ósea** bone marrow
medusa F jellyfish, man-of-war
megabyte M megabyte
megáfono M megaphone
megahercio, megahertz M megahertz
mejilla F cheek
mejor ADJ better; **el** — the best; **en el** — **de los casos** at best; **te deseo lo** — I wish you the best; ADV better; **a lo** — maybe; **tanto** — so much the better
mejora F improvement

mejoramiento M improvement

mejorar VT to improve, to improve upon; (las posibilidades de uno) to better; VI (ventas) to pick up; **—se** to get better / well

mejoría F improvement

melancolía F melancholy, gloom

melancólico ADJ melancholy, gloomy

melanoma M melanoma

melaza F molasses

melena F mane

melindre M affectation

melindroso ADJ affected, finicky

mella F notch; **hacer —** to make a dent

mellar VT to notch

mellizo -za ADJ & MF twin

melocotón M peach

melocotonero M peach tree

melodía F melody

melodioso ADJ melodious

melodrama M melodrama

melómano -na ADJ music-loving; MF music-lover

melón M melon, cantaloupe

membrana F membrane; (en los patos) web

membrete M letterhead

membrillo M (fruta) quince; (árbol) quince tree

membrudo ADJ stout

memorable ADJ memorable

memorándum M memorandum

memoria F (facultad de recordar, recuerdo) memory; (obra autobiográfica) memoir; (actas) proceedings; **— de acceso directo** random access memory (RAM); **— de sólo lectura** read only memory (ROM); **— intermedia** buffer; **— residente** internal memory; **de —** by heart; **hacer —** to try to remember / recollect

memorial M memorial

memorizar[9] VI/VT to memorize

mención F mention

mencionar VT to mention

mendigar[7] VI to beg

mendigo -ga MF beggar

mendrugo M large crumb

menear VT (las caderas) to wiggle, to wriggle, to shake; (la cola) to wag

meneo M (de las caderas) wiggle; (de la cola) wag

menesteroso ADJ needy, destitute

mengua F diminution, waning

menguante ADJ waning

menguar[8] VI (luna) to wane; (energía) to flag; (provisiones) to dwindle

meningitis F meningitis

menjurje M concoction

menopausia F menopause

menor ADJ (de tamaño) smaller; (de cantidad) lesser, smaller; (de edad) younger; (de importancia, en música) minor; **el —** (de tamaño) the smallest; (de cantidad) the least, the smallest; (de edad) the youngest; MF **— de edad** minor; **al por —** retail

menos ADV less; **— de** less than; **— mal** just as well; **a — que** unless; **al —** at least; **dar de —** to shortchange; **echar de —** to miss; **lo —** the least; **no es para menos** there is good reason; **por lo —** at least; **signo de menos** minus sign; **venir a —** to decline; **el que trabaja —** the one who works the least; **las cinco — cuarto** quarter to five; **no puede — de hacerlo** he cannot help doing it; **tienes — que yo** you have less than I; **trabaja — que yo** she works less than I; PREP (salvo) except, but; ADJ & PRON less, least; **— agua** less water; **— problemas** fewer problems; M minus

menoscabar VT to impair, to undermine

menoscabo M impairment

menospreciar VI/VT (despreciar) to despise; VT (burlarse de) to belittle, to demean

menosprecio M contempt

mensaje M message

mensajería F carrier

mensajero -ra MF messenger, courier

menstruación F menstruation

mensual ADJ monthly

mensualidad F (recibida) monthly allowance; (pagada) monthly installment

mensuario ADJ monthly

mensurable ADJ measurable

menta F mint, peppermint; **—verde** spearmint

mental ADJ mental

mentalidad F mentality

mente F mind

mentecato -ta ADJ foolish, simple; MF simpleton

mentir[3] VI to lie

mentira F lie, falsehood

mentirilla F fib, white lie

mentiroso -sa ADJ lying; MF liar

mentón M chin

mentor -ora MF mentor

menú M menu (también de computadoras); **— del día** daily special

menudeo LOC ADV **al —** retail

menudo ADJ (pequeño) small; (insignificante) insignificant; **a —** often; **dinero —** small change; **— perro** that's some dog; M (entrañas) entrails

meñique ADJ little (finger); M little finger, *fam* pinkie

meollo M (médula) marrow; (parte sustancial de un asunto) marrow, pith, core; (seso) brain

mequetrefe M runt, pipsqueak

mercachifle M peddler, huckster

mercadear VT to market

mercadeo M merchandising

mercader M merchant

mercadería F merchandise

mercado M market; — **alcista** bull market; — **bajista** bear market; — **de pulgas** flea market; — **de valores** stock market; — **libre** free market; — **negro** black market

mercadotecnia F marketing

mercancía F merchandise, goods

mercante ADJ merchant

mercantil ADJ mercantile

merced LOC ADV — **a** thanks to; **a (la) — de** at the mercy of

mercenario -ria ADJ & MF mercenary

mercería F notions

mercurio M mercury, quicksilver

merecedor ADJ deserving

merecer[13] VT to deserve, to merit

merecido M deserved punishment, due

merendar[1] VI to have a snack

merendero M picnic area

meridiano ADJ & M meridian

meridional ADJ southern; MF southerner

merienda F afternoon snack

mérito M merit

meritorio ADJ meritorious, worthy

merluza F hake

merma F decrease

mermar VI/VT to decrease, to dwindle

mermelada F jam; (de cítricos) marmalade

mero ADJ mere; **la mera idea** the very idea; M grouper

merodear VI to loiter

mes M month

mesa F table; (consejo) board; (formación geológica) mesa; — **de noche** nightstand; **levantar la —** to clear the table; **poner la —** to set the table

mesada F monthly allowance

mesero -ra M waiter; F waitress

meseta F plateau

mesón M inn, lodge

mesonero -ra MF innkeeper

mestizo -za ADJ (persona) *pey* half-breed; (perros) mongrel; MF *pey* half-breed; (mezcla de europeo e india) mestizo; (perro de raza mezclada) mongrel

mesura F moderation

mesurado ADJ moderate; (respuesta) measured

meta F (objetivo) goal; (en una carrera) finish line

metabolismo M metabolism

metafísica F metaphysics

metáfora F metaphor

metafórico ADJ metaphorical

metal M metal; — **precioso** precious metal

metálico ADJ metallic; M cash

metalurgia F metallurgy

metamorfosis F metamorphosis

metano M methane

metástasis F metastasis

meteorito M meteorite

meteoro M meteor

meteorología F meteorology

meteorólogo -ga M weatherman; F weatherwoman

meter VT to put (into), to stick (into); (un lío) to get (into); (invertir) to invest; — **el estómago** to suck in one's stomach; — **la pata** to make a mistake; — **miedo** to scare; — **ruido** to make noise; — **un gol** to score a goal; —**se** to meddle; —**se a bailar** to begin to dance; —**se con** to mess with; —**se en camisa de once varas** to get oneself into a fix

metódico ADJ methodical

método M method

metralleta F portable machine gun

métrico ADJ metric

metro M (medida) meter; (cinta de medir) measuring tape; (tren subterráneo) subway

metrónomo M metronome

metrópoli F metropolis

metropolitano ADJ metropolitan; M subway

mexicano -na ADJ & MF Mexican

México M Mexico

mezcla F mixture, mix; (en albañilería) mortar; (de café, especias) blend

mezclador -ora MF (persona) mixer; F (aparato) mixer

mezclar VT to mix, to blend; (naipes) to shuffle; (números) to scramble; —**se** (combinarse) to mix; (tener trato con) to mingle; (entrometerse) to meddle

mezcolanza F hodgepodge

mezquindad F (crueldad) meanness; (tacañería) stinginess

mezquino ADJ (cruel) mean, mean-spirited, petty; (insignificante) small, petty; (tacaño) tight, stingy

mezquita F mosque

mi ADJ POS my

mí PRON PERS me; **es para —** it's for me; **me vio a —** he saw me; **me la dio a —** he gave it to me

miau M meow

mico M long-tailed monkey

micra F micron

micro M (autobús) bus; (micrófono) microphone

microbio M microbe, germ

microcirujía F microsurgery

microcomputadora F microcomputer

microeconomía F microeconomics

microficha F microfiche

microfilm M microfilm

micrófono M microphone

Micronesia F Micronesia

micronesio -sia ADJ & MF Micronesian

microonda F microwave; M SG —**s** microwave oven

microordenador M microcomputer

microorganismo M microorganism

microprocesador M microprocessor

microscópico ADJ microscopic

microscopio M microscope; — **electrónico** electron microscope

miedo M fear; — **al escenario** stage fright; **tener** — to be afraid

miedoso ADJ fearful

miel F honey

miembro M member; (extremidad) limb; — **viril** penis

mientras CONJ (durante) while, as; (siempre y cuando) as long as; — **que** while; — **tanto** meanwhile; ADV in the meantime

miércoles M Wednesday

mierda F (excremento) *vulg* shit, crap; (droga) *vulg* shit; (persona o cosa despreciable) *vulg* piece of shit, piece of crap; **una** — **de coche** *vulg* a crappy / shitty car; **mandar a alguien a la** — *vulg* to tell somebody to go to hell; ¡—! *vulg* shit!

mies F grain; —**es** fields of grain

miga F crumb; **hacer buenas** —**s** to get along well

migaja F crumb

migración F migration

migrante ADJ migrant

migraña F migraine

mil NUM thousand; — **millones** billion; **llegamos a las** — **y quinientas** we got there very late

milagro M miracle, wonder

milagroso ADJ miraculous

milano M kite

milenio M millennium

milicia F militia

miligramo M milligram

mililitro M milliliter

milímetro M millimeter

militante ADJ & MF militant

militar ADJ military; MF soldier; VI to militate

milla F mile

millaje M mileage

millar M thousand

millón M million

millonario -ria MF millionaire

millonésimo ADJ & M millionth

mimar VT to pamper, to spoil, to coddle

mimbre M wicker

mímico ADJ mimic; F mimicry

mimo M (trato cariñoso) caressing, cuddling; MF (actor) mime

mimoso ADJ cuddly

mina F (yacimiento) mine; (explosivo) (land) mine; (de un lápiz) lead; (fuente) storehouse

minado M mining

minar VT (sembrar minas) to mine; (socavar) to undermine; VI (cavar) to burrow

mineral M mineral; (de oro) ore; ADJ mineral

minería F mining

minero -ra MF miner; ADJ mining

mingitorio M urinal

miniatura F miniature

minicomputadora F minicomputer

minifalda F miniskirt

minifundio M subsistence farm

minimizar[9] VT (gastos) to minimize; (a una persona) to belittle; VI (un incidente) to play down

mínimo ADJ (cantidad) least; (tamaño) smallest; M minimum; **como** — at least; **en lo más** — at all

minino M kitty

miniordenador M minicomputer

ministerio M (religioso) ministry; (gubernamental) ministry, department

ministro -tra MF minister, secretary; — **de Justicia** Attorney General

minoría F minority

minoridad F minority

minorista MF retailer

minoritario ADJ minority

minucioso ADJ (detalle) minute; (trabajo) thorough; (persona) fastidious

minúsculo ADJ small, minuscule; **letra** — lowercase letter

minusválido ADJ disabled

minuta F (honorarios) lawyers' fees; (actas) minutes

minutero M minute hand

minuto M minute

mío PRON mine; **este libro es** —— this book is mine; **un amigo** — a friend of mine

miope ADJ shortsighted, nearsighted

miopía F near-sightedness, myopia

mira F (dispositivo de arma) gun sight; (intención) intention; **con —s a** with a view to

mirada F gaze, look; **— asesina** dirty look; **— de soslayo** side glance; **— fija** stare

mirador M vantage point, overlook

miramiento M consideration

mirar VI/VT to look (at); (un partido, televisión) to watch; **— de soslayo** to look askance (at); **— fijamente** to stare (at); **¡mira (tú)!** you don't say!

miríada F myriad

mirilla F peephole

mirlo M blackbird

mirón M onlooker; (erótico) voyeur

mirto M myrtle

misa F mass

misántropo -pa MF misanthrope

misceláneo ADJ miscellaneous

miserable ADJ (vil, pobre) wretched, unhappy; (insignificante) paltry; (tacaño) miserly

miseria F (desgracia) misery; (pobreza) poverty, squalor; (cantidad despreciable) trifle

misericordia F mercy

misericordioso ADJ merciful, gracious

mísero ADJ miserable

misil M missile; **— balístico** ballistic missile; **— crucero** cruise missile

misión F mission

misionero -ra MF missionary

mismo ADJ same; **ese — día** that very day; **se nombró a sí —** he named himself; **lo — the same thing; me da lo —** it's all the same to me; **yo —** I myself

misoginia F misogyny

misterio M mystery

misterioso ADJ mysterious

místico -ca ADJ mystical; MF mystic

mitad F half; **por la —** in half; **en la — de** in the middle of; **a — del camino** midway

mitigar[7] VT to mitigate

mitin M political meeting

mito M myth

mitología F mythology

mixto ADJ mixed; **escuela mixta** coed school

mobiliario M furniture

mocasín M (zapatilla de indio, culebra) moccasin; (zapato sin cordones) loafer

mochar VT to chop off

mochila F knapsack, backpack

moción F motion

moco M mucus; (líquido) *fam* snot

mocoso -sa ADJ snotty; MF *fam* brat, punk

moda F fashion; **de —** fashionable, in style; **ponerse de —** to catch on

modales M PL manners

modelar VI/VT to model

modelo ADJ & MF model

módem M modem

moderación F moderation, restraint

moderado -da ADJ moderate; (invierno) mild; (precio) reasonable; (respuesta) measured; (clima) temperate; MF moderate

moderar VT (restringir) to moderate, to restrain; (presidir) to moderate

moderno ADJ modern

modestia F modesty

modesto ADJ modest

módico ADJ moderate, reasonable

modificación F modification

modificar[6] VT to modify

modismo M idiom

modista MF dressmaker

modo M (manera) mode, manner, way; (categoría gramatical) mood; (de computadora / ordenador) mode; **a — de** by way of; **del mismo —** in like manner; **de ningún —** by no means; **de — que** so that; **de otro —** otherwise; **de ningún — not at all; de todos —s** anyway; **en cierto —** in a way; **ni —** no dice; **no hay —** no way

modorra F drowsiness

modular VT to modulate

mofa F jeer, ridicule

mofarse VT **— de** to make fun of, to scoff at

mofeta F skunk

moflete M fat cheek

mohair M mohair

mohín M grimace

moho M mold, mildew

mohoso ADJ moldy

mojado -da ADJ wet; MF (inmigrante ilegal) *pey* wetback

mojadura F wetting

mojar VT to wet; (impregnar) to dip; **—se** to get wet; *vulg* to get laid

mojigatería F prudery

mojigato -ta ADJ prudish; MF prude

mojo M dip

mojón M (hito) landmark; (zurullo) turd

molar ADJ molar

Moldavia F Moldova

moldavo -va ADJ & MF Moldovan

molde M (norma) mold, cast; (tortera) cakepan; (patrón) pattern; (de imprenta) die; **letras de —** block letters

moldeado M molding

moldear VT to mold, to cast

moldura F molding

mole F mass

molécula F molecule

moler[2] VI/VT to mill, to grind; **— a palos** to beat thoroughly

molestar VT to bother, to pester; **no te molestes** don't bother

molestia F bother, nuisance; **no te tomes la —** don't go to the trouble

molesto ADJ bothersome, irksome; (situación) uneasy

molibdeno M molybdenum

molienda F grinding

molinero -ra MF miller

molinete M (puerta) turnstile; (juguete) pinwheel

molinillo M mill, grinder

molino M mill; **— de viento** windmill

mollete M muffin

molusco M mollusk

momentáneo ADJ momentary

momento M (tiempo) moment; (movimiento) momentum; **al —** immediately; **a cada —** continually; **en todo —** all the time; **no veo el —** I can't wait; **se oscurecía por —s** it was getting darker by the minute

momia F mummy

Mónaco M Monaco

monada F (acción graciosa) antic; (persona atractiva) *fam* peach

monarca MF INV monarch

monarquía F monarchy

monasterio M monastery

mondar VT to pare; **—se los dientes** to pick one's teeth; M SG **mondadientes** toothpick

moneda F (dinero metálico) coin; (divisa) currency; **— corriente** common currency; **— de curso legal** legal tender; **— falsa** counterfeit money

monegasco -ca ADJ & MF Monegasque

monería F antic

monetario ADJ monetary

mongol -la ADJ & MF Mongolian

Mongolia F Mongolia

monigote M puppet

monitor -ora M (aparato) monitor; MF (persona) monitor

monja F nun

monje M monk

mono -na MF (simio) monkey; **— araña** spider monkey; M (mimo) mimic; (prenda de trabajo) overalls, coverall; (síndrome de abstinencia) withdrawal symptoms; **dormir la mona** to sleep it off; ADJ cute

monogamia F monogamy

monokini M topless swimsuit

monólogo M monolog, monologue

mononucleosis F mononucleosis

monopatín M skateboard; (con manillar) scooter; (de nieve) snowboard

monopolio M monopoly

monopolizar[9] VT to monopolize; (un mercado) to corner

monotonía F monotony

monótono ADJ monotonous

monserga F nonsense

monstruo M monster; (persona grotesca) freak

monstruosidad F monstrosity

monstruoso ADJ monstrous

monta F mount; **de poca —** of little value

montaje M (de un aparato) assembly, set up; (de una película) editing

montante M (total) total; (ventana de puerta) transom; (columna) upright

montaña F mountain; **— rusa** roller coaster

montañés -esa ADJ mountain; MF mountain dweller

montañismo M mountaineering

montañoso ADJ mountainous

montar VT (ir a caballo, en bicicleta) to ride; (un aparato) to assemble; (una película) to edit; (subirse al caballo) to mount, to get on; **— en cólera** to fly into a rage; **— una escena** to make a scene; **—se a caballo** to mount a horse

montaraz ADJ coarse

monte M (montaña) mount; (zona agreste) wilderness; **— de piedad** pawnshop

montés ADJ (salvaje) wild; (de la montaña) of the mountains

montículo M mound

montón M pile, heap; (de papel) stack; (de nieve) drift; (de flores) basketful; (de gente) bunch; **a montones** in abundance; **del —** run-of-the-mill

montura F (animal) mount; (silla) saddle; (armazón de gafas) frame, rim

monumental ADJ monumental

monumento M monument

moño M (de pelo) bun; (adorno) bow

mopa F mop

moquearse VI to be snotty

moquillo M distemper

mora F blackberry, mulberry; **en —** in default

morada F dwelling, abode

morado ADJ purple; **ojo —** black eye

morador -ora MF dweller

moral ADJ moral; F (principios éticos) morals; (estado de ánimo) morale; M mulberry tree

moraleja F moral

moralidad F morality

moralista MF moralist

moralizar[9] VI/VT to moralize
morar VI to dwell, to abide
mórbido ADJ morbid
morboso ADJ morbid, sick
morcilla F black pudding
mordacidad F sharpness
mordaz ADJ (comentario) cutting, sharp; (persona) sharp-tongued
mordaza F (de la boca) gag; (de un torno) vise jaw
mordedor ADJ biting, snappy
mordedura F bite
morder[2] VI/VT to bite; **—se la lengua** to bite one's tongue
mordida F (mordisco) bite; (comisión ilegal) bribe, kickback
mordiscar[6] VI/VT to nibble; to nip
mordisco M nibble, nip
mordisquear VI/VT to nip; to nibble
mordisqueo M nibble
moreno ADJ (piel) dark, dark-skinned, swarthy; (pelo) dark, brunette; **un señor — a** man of color
moretón M bruise
morfina F morphine
morgue F morgue
moribundo ADJ dying, moribund
morir[4,51] VI to die; (una calle) to end; **—se de envidia** to eat one's heart out; **—se de hambre** to starve; **—se de miedo** to die of fear; **—se de risa** to die laughing; **—se por algo** to crave something; **—se por alguien** to be crazy about someone
morisco ADJ Moorish
moro -ra ADJ Moorish; MF Moor; **—s y cristianos** beans and rice; **no hay —s en la costa** the coast is clear
morocho ADJ dark-haired, brunet, brunette
moroso ADJ delinquent, deadbeat
morrear VI to make out
morriña F homesickness
morro M (monte) knoll; (caradura) gall, nerve; (de un avión) nose; (de animal) snout
morrón M bell pepper
morsa F walrus
mortaja F shroud
mortal ADJ mortal, deadly; MF mortal
mortalidad F mortality
mortandad F death toll
mortecino ADJ fading
mortero M mortar
mortífero ADJ deadly
mortificación F chagrin
mortificar[6] VT to mortify, to chagrin
mortuorio ADJ **casa mortuaria** funeral home

mosaico M mosaic
mosca F fly; (dinero) dough; **— muerta** hypocrite; **no se oía volar una —** you could have heard a pin drop
mosquear VT (crear desconfianza) to cause distrust; (hacer enfadarse) to enrage; **—se** (desconfiar) to distrust; (enfadarse) to become enraged
mosquitero M (de ventana) window screen; (de tienda de campo) mosquito net
mosquito M mosquito
mostacho M mustache, moustache
mostaza F mustard
mostrador M counter
mostrar[2] VT to show; **—se reticente** to appear reticent
mostrenco ADJ stray
mota F speck, speckle
mote M nickname
moteado ADJ speckled, spotted
motear VT to speck, to speckle
motejar VI **— de** to brand as
motel M motel
motín M (en un barco) mutiny; (de prisioneros) riot
motivación F motivation
motivar VT (impulsar) to motivate; (causar) to cause
motivo M (causa) motive, reason; (figura repetida) motif, theme; **con — de** on the occasion of
moto F bike, motorcycle
motocicleta F motorcycle
motociclista MF biker, motorcyclist
motor ADJ of motion; M motor, engine; **— de reacción** jet engine; **— de búsqueda** search engine; **— de combustión interna** internal combustion engine; **— fuera de borda** outboard engine
motriz ADJ **fuerza —** motive power
movedizo ADJ restless
mover[2] VT to move; **— palancas** to pull strings; **—se** to move, to budge
movible ADJ movable
movido ADJ eventful; (foto) blurred
móvil M (motivo) motive; (teléfono) mobile telephone; (adorno, juguete) mobile; ADJ (que se mueve) mobile; (que puede ser movido) movable; **un blanco — a** moving target
movilizar[9] VI/VT to mobilize
movimiento M movement, motion; (organización, pieza de reloj) movement; (comercial) traffic; **los rojos tienen poco — the** red ones don't sell well; **un cuerpo en — a** moving body
Mozambique M Mozambique

mozambiqueño -ña ADJ & MF Mozambican

mozárabe ADJ Mozarabic

mozo -za ADJ young; **en mis años —s** in my youth; M (joven) young man; **buen —** handsome man; (siervo) servant; **— de cordel** porter; F (joven) young woman; (sierva) servant

mucama F chambermaid

muchacho -cha M boy, youngster; F girl; (de servicio) maid

muchedumbre F crowd, throng

mucho ADJ a lot of; (cosas contables) many; (cosas incontables, en oraciones interrogativas y/o negativas) much; **¿tienes — tiempo?** do you have much time? **no tenemos — tiempo** we don't have much time; **tenemos —s problemas** we have many problems; ADV much; (demasiado) too much; **hace — que no lo veo** I haven't seen him for a long time; **ni con —** not by a long shot; **ni — menos** not by any means; **por — que** no matter how much; PRON a lot, many; (en preguntas y oraciones negativas) much

mucoso ADJ mucous

muda F (de ropa, voz) change; (de plumas, piel de serpiente) molt

mudable ADJ fickle

mudanza F move

mudar VT to change; (el pelo) to shed; **— la piel** to molt; **— las plumas** to molt; **—se (de casa)** to move (house); **—se de ropa** to change clothes

mudez F dumbness, muteness

mudo -da ADJ mute, dumb; (por emoción) speechless; (película) silent; MF mute

mueble M piece of furniture; **—s** furniture

mueblería F (tienda) furniture store; (fábrica) furniture factory

mueca F grimace; **hacer —s** to grimace

muela F (diente) molar tooth; (piedra) grindstone; **— del juicio** wisdom tooth

muelle M (para embarcaciones) wharf, pier; (resorte) spring; **— en espiral** coil; **— real** mainspring

muérdago M mistletoe

muerte F death; **dar —** to kill; **sus clases son la —** his classes are unbearable; **de mala —** disreputable

muerto ADJ dead, lifeless; **— de cansancio** dead tired; **— de hambre** famished; **estoy — de sed** I'm parched; **echarle el — a uno** to pass the buck; **ni —** not in a million years

muesca F notch, indentation

muestra F (ejemplo) sample; (señal) sign, token; **— de orina** urine specimen; **dar —s de impaciencia** to show impatience

muestrear VT to sample

muestreo M sampling

mugido M moo, lowing

mugir[11] VI to moo, to low

mugre F dirt, grime, crud

mugriento ADJ grimy, dirty

mujer F woman; (esposa) wife

mujeriego ADJ womanizing; M womanizer

mujerzuela F *pey* slut

mulato -ta ADJ & MF mulatto

muleta F crutch

muletilla F cliché

mullido ADJ fluffy

mullir[19] VT to fluff

mulo -la MF mule (también en el tráfico de drogas)

multa F fine, penalty; (de tránsito) ticket

multar VT to fine; (en tránsito) to ticket

multicultural ADJ multicultural

múltiple ADJ multiple

multiplicación F multiplication

multiplicar[6] VI/VT to multiply; **—se** to breed

multiplicidad F multiplicity

múltiplo M multiple

multitarea F multitasking

multitud F multitude, throng

mundano ADJ mundane, worldly

mundial ADJ global, worldwide; **la guerra —** the world war

mundo M world; **todo el —** everybody; **tener —** to be worldly; **el tercer —** the third world; **el — al revés** the world upside-down

munición F ammunition, munition

municipal ADJ municipal; **servicios —es** city services

municipalidad F municipality

municipio M municipality; (ayuntamiento) city hall

muñeca F (juguete) doll; (articulación del brazo) wrist; **— de trapo** ragdoll

muñeco M (juguete) boy doll; (de ventrílocuo) dummy; **— de nieve** snowman

muñón M stump

mural ADJ & M mural

muralla F wall

murciélago M bat

murmullo M murmur; (de agua) babble

murmuración F gossip

murmurar VI/VT to murmur; VI (agua) to babble

muro M wall

murria F the blues; **tener —** to have the

blues
musa F muse
musaraña F shrew
muscular ADJ muscular
músculo M muscle
musculoso ADJ muscular
muselina F muslin
museo M museum
musgo M moss
musgoso ADJ mossy
música F music; — **de cámara** chamber music; — **folclórica** folk music; — **incidental** incidental music
musical ADJ & M musical
músico -ca ADJ musical; MF musician
musitar VI to mutter
muslo M thigh
mustio ADJ sad, humble; (marchito) limp; (deslucido) faded
musulmán -ana ADJ & MF Moslem, Muslim
mutación F mutation
mutante ADJ & MF mutant
mutilar VT to mutilate, to mangle; (a un ser vivo) to maim, to mutilate; (una estatua) to deface
mutuo ADJ mutual
muy ADV very; **estás — grande para eso** you're too big for that
Myanmar M Myanmar

Nn

nabo M turnip
nácar M mother-of-pearl
nacarado ADJ pearly
nacer[13] VI to be born; (una calle) to begin; — **de** (río) to spring from; — **de nuevo** to have a new lease on life
naciente ADJ (tendencia) incipient; (sol) rising; M (de río) origin
nacimiento M birth; (pesebre) nativity scene; (naciente) origin (of a river)
nación F nation
nacional ADJ national; MF national
nacionalidad F nationality
nacionalismo M nationalism
nacionalizar[9] VT to nationalize
nada PRON nothing; — **del otro mundo** nothing special; — **en absoluto** nothing at all; **como si** — as if nothing were going on; **de** — you are welcome, don't mention it; **no es por** —, **pero** I hope you don't mind my saying this, but; **no**

sirve para — it's useless; **no tener** — **que ver con** to have nothing to do with; **no tengo** — **de dinero** I don't have any money; **para** — in the least; **quedar en la** — to fall through; **salir de la** — to come out of nowhere; ADV not at all; **no me gusta** — I don't like it at all; F nothingness
nadador -ora MF swimmer
nadar VI/VT to swim; — **en la abundancia** to be in the lap of luxury
nadería F trifle, nothing
nadie PRON nobody; — **más** no one else; **no vi a** — **en el parque** I didn't see anyone in the park; **un don** — a nobody
nafta F gasoline
nailón M nylon
naipe M playing card
nalgada F smack on the bottom
nalgas F PL buttocks
Namibia F Namibia
namibio -bia ADJ & MF Namibian
nana F (canción de cuna) lullaby; (lastimadura) boo-boo; (niñera) baby-sitter
nanosegundo M nanosecond
napalm M napalm
napias F PL *fam* snout
naranja F (fruta) orange; ADJ & M (color) orange; — **de ombligo** navel orange; **mi media** — my better half
naranjal M orange grove
naranjo M orange tree
narcisismo M narcissism
narciso M narcissus, daffodil
narcolepsia F narcolepsy
narcótico ADJ & M narcotic
narcotizar[9] VT to drug
narcotráfico M narco-trafficking
nariz F nose; — **chata** pug nose; **sonarse la** — to blow one's nose; F PL **narices** nostrils; **se dio de narices contra la ventana** he bumped his nose on the window; **estoy hasta las narices** I've had it up to here
narración F narration
narrador -ora MF narrator
narrar VT to narrate, to recount
narrativa F narrative
narrativo ADJ narrative
NASA F NASA
nasal ADJ nasal
nata F skin of boiled milk; *Esp* cream
natación F swimming
natal ADJ natal; (suelo) native
natillas F PL custard
nativo -va ADJ & MF native
nato ADJ **es un músico** — he's a born

musician

natural ADJ natural; (nacido en un lugar) native; (nacido fuera del matrimonio) illegitimate; M nature; **al —** unprocessed; (sin afectación) unaffected

naturaleza F nature; **— muerta** still life

naturalidad F naturalness

naturalista MF naturalist

naturalización F naturalization

naturalizar[9] VT to naturalize; **—se** to become naturalized

naturalmente ADV (de forma natural) naturally; (desde luego) of course

naufragar[7] VI to shipwreck; (una empresa) to fail

naufragio M shipwreck

náufrago -ga MF shipwrecked person

Nauru M Nauru

nauruano -na ADJ & MF Nauruan

náusea F nausea; **—s** morning sickness; **dar —s** to nauseate; **hasta la —** ad nauseam; **tener —s** to be nauseated, to be sick to one's stomach

nauseabundo ADJ nauseating

nauseoso ADJ queasy

náutica F navigation

náutico ADJ nautical

navaja F jackknife, pocketknife; (de barbero) razor

navajazo M (golpe) stab with a jackknife; (herida) stab wound

naval ADJ naval

nave F (embarcación) vessel; (parte de una catedral) nave; **— espacial** spaceship

navegable ADJ navigable

navegación F navigation; (deportiva) boating

navegador M computer browser

navegante MF navigator; ADJ navigating

navegar[7] VI/VT to navigate; (barco o vela) to sail; (en el Internet) to browse, to surf

Navidad F Christmas

navideño ADJ **fiesta navideña** Christmas party

navío M ship

neblina F mist

neblinoso ADJ misty

nebuloso ADJ (poco claro) nebulous; (que tiene niebla) foggy

necesario ADJ necessary

neceser M toiletry bag

necesidad F need; (cosa necesaria) necessity; **hacer sus —es** to relieve oneself; **de primera —** indispensable

necesitado ADJ needy

necesitar VT to need

necio -cia ADJ asinine, foolish; MF pey clod

necrología F necrology

néctar M nectar

nectarina F nectarine

nefasto ADJ unholy

nefritis F nephritis

negación F (que sirve para negar) negation; (que no acepta) denial

negar[1,7] VT (decir que no es verdad) to deny; (no dar a alguien algo que ha pedido) to refuse; (no reconocer públicamente) to disavow; **—se** to refuse; **—se a** to refuse to

negativa F (rechazo verbal) denial; (ausencia de cooperación) refusal

negativo ADJ negative; **signo —** minus sign; M (photographic) negative

negligencia F negligence, neglect; (médica) malpractice

negligente ADJ negligent, neglectful

negociación F negotiation

negociante MF business person

negociar VI/VT (tratar condiciones) to negotiate; (realizar un negocio) to trade

negocio M (tienda, actividad comercial) business; (transacción) business deal, business transaction; **hombre de —s** businessman; **mujer de —s** businesswoman; **hacer —** to make a profit

negrear VI to appear black; VT to blacken

negritas F boldface type

negro -ra ADJ black (también aplicado al café sin leche); (futuro) bleak; **pasarlas negras** to undergo hardships; F (nota) quarter note; MF (persona) person of color, black

negrura F blackness

negruzco ADJ blackish

némesis F nemesis

nene -na M baby boy; F baby girl

nenúfar M water lily

neologismo M neologism

neón M neon

neozelandés -esa MF New Zealander

Nepal M Nepal

nepalés -esa ADJ & MF Nepalese

nepalí ADJ & MF Nepalese

nepotismo M nepotism

nervado ADJ veined

nervio M nerve; **perder los —s** to lose one's cool; **tener los —s de punta** to be on edge

nerviosismo M nervousness

nervioso ADJ (relativo a los nervios) nervous; (inquieto) nervous, jumpy; (carne) sinewy

nervudo ADJ sinewy, wiry

neto ADJ (mejoría) distinct; (ganancia) net

neumático M tire; ADJ pneumatic

neural ADJ neural

neurona F nerve cell
neurosis F neurosis
neurótico -ca ADJ & MF neurotic
neutral ADJ neutral
neutralidad F neutrality
neutralizar[9] VT to neutralize
neutro ADJ neutral; (género) neuter
neutrón M neutron
nevada F snowfall
nevado ADJ snowy
nevar[1] VI to snow
nevera F icebox, refrigerator
nevisca F snow flurry
ni CONJ & ADV — **con mucho** not by a long
      shot; — **hablar** forget it; — **habló**
      conmigo he didn't even talk to me; —
      idea (it) beats me; — **modo** no way; —
      que esto fuera un hotel it's not like
      this is a hotel; — **siquiera** not even; —
      soñar fat chance; — **trabaja** — **estudia**
      he neither works nor studies; — **una**
      palabra not a word; **no tiene amigos**
      — **enemigos** he has no friends nor
      enemies; **no es rico** — **mucho menos**
      he's not even close to being rich
Nicaragua F Nicaragua
nicaragüense ADJ & MF Nicaraguan
nicho M niche, recess
nicotina F nicotine
nidada F (huevos) nest of eggs; (crías) hatch,
      brood
nido M nest
niebla F fog
nieto -ta M grandson; F granddaughter; —**s**
      grandchildren
nieve F snow (también cocaína, heroína)
Níger M Niger
Nigeria F Nigeria
nigeriano -na ADJ & MF Nigerian
nigerino -na ADJ & MF Nigerien
nigua F chigger
nihilismo M nihilism
nilón M nylon
nimio ADJ insignificant
ninguno PRON **no tengo** — I have none/I
      don't have any; **ningún amigo mío** no
      friend of mine; **no tengo ningún libro**
      I don't have any books; — **de los dos**
      neither one; **de ningún modo** in no way
niñera F (ocasional) baby-sitter;
      (permanente) nanny
niñería F childish act
niñez F childhood; (de niño) boyhood; (de
      niña) girlhood
niño -ña M child, kid, boy; F child, kid, girl;
      — **del ojo** pupil (of the eye); ADJ childish
níquel M nickel

niquelado ADJ nickel-plated
níspero M loquat
nitidez F sharpness
nítido ADJ sharp
nitrato M nitrate
nitrógeno M nitrogen
nitroglicerina F nitroglycerine
nivel M level (también herramienta); (grado
      jerárquico) echelon; — **de mar** sea level;
      — **de vida** standard of living; **a** —
      straight; **a** — **de** level with
nivelar VT to level; (un camino de tierra) to
      grade
níveo ADJ snowy
no ADV no; — **quiero** I don't want to; —
      bien llegaron no sooner had they
      arrived; — **sólo** not only; — **sea que** lest;
      a — **ser que** unless
noble ADJ noble; M nobleman; F noblewoman
nobleza F nobility
nócaut M knockout
noche F night; (horas de la noche) nighttime;
      —**buena** Christmas Eve; —**vieja** New
      Year's Eve; — **y día** day and night; **de** —
      at night; **de la** — **a la mañana**
      overnight; **esta** — tonight; **por la** — at
      night
noción F notion; **no tener ni** — to have no
      clue
nocivo ADJ harmful, noxious
nocturno ADJ (que actúa de noche)
      nocturnal; (que sucede todas las noches)
      nightly
nodo M node
nodriza F wet nurse
nódulo M node
nogal M walnut tree
nómada MF INV nomad
nombramiento M appointment; (militar)
      commission
nombrar VT to name, to appoint; (a un
      oficial militar) to commission
nombre M name; — **de pila** first name; —
      de soltera maiden name; **en** — **de** on
      behalf of; **eso no tiene** — that's unheard
      of; **hacerse un** — to make a name for
      oneself
nomenclatura F nomenclature
nomeolvides M SG forget-me-not
nómina F payroll
nominación F nomination
nominal ADJ nominal
nominar VT to nominate
non ADJ odd; M odd number
nopal M prickly pear
noquear VT to knock out
norcoreano -na ADJ & MF North Korean

nordeste ADJ & M northeast

nórdico ADJ Nordic

noreste ADJ & M northeast

norma F norm, standard

normal ADJ normal, standard; F (escuela) teacher's college; (línea) perpendicular line

normalizar[9] VT to normalize

noroeste ADJ & M northwest

norte ADJ & M north

norteamericano -na ADJ & MF (de América del Norte) North American; (de EEUU) American

norteño -ña ADJ northern; MF northerner

Noruega F Norway

noruego -ga ADJ & MF Norwegian

nos PRON us; **él — vio** he saw us; **— dio el libro** he gave us the book, he gave the book to us

nosotros -as PRON we; **para —** for us

nostalgia F nostalgia

nostálgico ADJ nostalgic

nota F (musical) note; (anotación) annotation; (calificación) grade, mark; **— al pie de página** footnote; **de —** of note; **exagerar la —** to overdo something

notable ADJ notable, noteworthy, remarkable

notación F notation

notar VT (percibir) to note, to notice; (señalar) to note

notariar VT to notarize

notario -ria MF notary

noticia F piece of news; **—s** news; **tener —s de alguien** to hear from someone

noticiario M newscast, news bulletin

noticiero M newscast

notificación F notification; (policial) summons

notificar[6] VT to notify

notorio ADJ (conocido públicamente) well-known; (evidente) obvious

novato -ta MF novice; (policía, atleta) rookie

novedad F novelty; **—es** news; **sin —** all's well

novedoso ADJ novel

novela F novel

novelesco ADJ fictional

novelista MF novelist

noveno ADJ ninth

noventa NUM ninety

noviazgo M engagement

novicio -cia MF novice

noviembre M November

novillo -lla M steer; **hacer —s** to play hooky; F heifer

novio -via M (comprometido) fiancé; (no formal) boyfriend; (de boda) bridegroom; F (comprometida) fiancée; (no formal) girlfriend; (de boda) bride

nubarrón M thunderhead

nube F cloud; (de humo) billow; **poner por las —s** to praise to the skies; **está en las —s** his head is in the clouds; **los precios están por las —s** prices have gone through the roof

nublado ADJ (cielo) cloudy, overcast; (los ojos, de emoción) misty; (los ojos, por falta de sueño) bleary

nublar VT to blur; **—se** (cielo) to become overcast; (ojos) to cloud over

nuboso ADJ cloudy

nuca F nape

nuclear ADJ nuclear

núcleo M nucleus; (de imán, reactor) core

nudillo M knuckle

nudismo M nudism

nudista ADJ & MF nudist

nudo M knot (también en la madera, medida de velocidad); (de una obra teatral) turning point; (en el pelo) tangle; (en plantas) node; (en la garganta) lump; **— corredizo** slipknot; **— de rizo** square knot

nudoso ADJ knotty, gnarled

nuera F daughter-in-law

nuestro ADJ POS our; **— hijo** our son; PRON ours; **esto es —** this is ours

nueve NUM nine

nuevo ADJ new; **de —** again; **¿qué hay de — ?** what's new?

nuez F walnut; **— de Adán** Adam's apple; **— moscada** nutmeg

nulidad F nonentity

nulo ADJ null and void, invalid

numeral ADJ & M numeral

numerar VT to number

numérico ADJ numerical

número M (dígito) number; (en un espectáculo) act; (de una revista) issue; (cifra) figure

numeroso ADJ numerous

nunca ADV never, not ever; **no viene —** he never comes, he doesn't ever come; **más que —** more than ever; **casi —** hardly ever; **peor que —** worse than ever

nupcial ADJ nuptial, bridal

nupcias F PL nuptials

nutria F otter

nutrición F nutrition

nutrido ADJ **el congreso tuvo una nutrida concurrencia** the conference was well attended

nutriente M nutrient

nutrir VT to nourish

nutritivo ADJ nutritious, nourishing

Ññ

ñandú M rhea
ñato ADJ *Am* pug-nosed
ñoño ADJ bland
ñu M gnu

Oo

o CONJ or; **— se casa — lo mato** either he
    gets married or I'll kill him; **— sea** that is
oasis M oasis
obedecer[13] VI/VT to obey; **esto obedece a**
    que this is due to the fact that
obediencia F obedience
obediente ADJ obedient
obertura F musical overture
obesidad F obesity
obeso ADJ obese
obispo M bishop
obituario M obituary
objeción F objection
objetar VI/VT to object, to take exception (to)
objetivo ADJ objective; M (lente) objective;
    (meta) aim, objective
objeto M object
oblea F wafer
oblicuo ADJ (inclinado) oblique; (sesgado)
    biased
obligación F (deber) obligation, duty; (título
    financiero) bond
obligar[7] VT to force, to compel, to oblige;
    —se (a) to obligate oneself (to)
obligatorio ADJ obligatory, compulsory
oboe M oboe
obra F (artística, literaria, de construcción)
    work; (lugar de construcción) construction
    site; **— maestra** masterpiece; **en —s**
    under construction
obrar VI to act; **obra en nuestro poder** we
    acknowledge receipt of
obrero -ra MF worker; ADJ working
obscenidad F obscenity; **—es** filth
obsceno ADJ obscene
obsequiar VT to present, to give; **me**
    obsequió perfume he gave me perfume
obsequio M gift

obsequioso ADJ obsequious
observación F observation; (comentario)
    remark
observador -ora MF observer; ADJ observant
observancia F observance
observar VI/VT to observe; (hacer un
    comentario) to remark, to observe
observatorio M observatory
obsesión F obsession
obsesionar VT to obsess; **—se con** to obsess
    over, to be obsessed with
obsesivo-compulsivo ADJ obsessive-
    compulsive
obstaculizar VT to impede
obstáculo M obstacle, hindrance,
    impediment; (en carreras) hurdle
obstante LOC PREP **no — tu oposición**
    notwithstanding your opposition; LOC ADV
    no —, voy a ir nevertheless, I am going
    to go
obstar VT to preclude
obstetricia F obstetrics
obstinación F obstinacy
obstinado ADJ obstinate, bullheaded
obstinarse VI to be obstinate
obstrucción F obstruction, blockage
obstruir[31] VT to obstruct, to block; (un
    aparato) to jam; VI **—se** to get jammed
obtención F acquisition
obtener[44] VT to obtain, to get; (permiso) to
    secure; (con dificultad) to procure
obturador M (de una cámara fotográfica)
    shutter; (de un coche) choke
obviar VT to circumvent
obvio ADJ obvious
ocasión F occasion; (oportunidad)
    opportunity; (ganga) bargain; **de —**
    reduced
ocasional ADJ occasional
ocasionar VT to occasion, to cause
ocaso M sunset, twilight
occidental ADJ occidental, western; MF
    westerner
occidente M west
océano M ocean
oceanografía F oceanography
ocelote M ocelot
ochenta NUM eighty
ocho NUM eight
ocio M (diversión) leisure; (inacción) idleness
ociosidad F idleness
ocioso ADJ (inactivo) idle; (no usado) unused
octágono M octagon
octano M octane
octava F octave
octavilla F tract
octavo ADJ & M eighth

octeto M byte
octógono M octagon
octubre M October
ocular M eyepiece; ADJ **infección** — eye
infection
oculista MF oculist
ocultar VT to conceal; (información) to
withhold
ocultismo M the occult
oculto ADJ unseen, occult
ocupación F occupation
ocupado ADJ busy; (asiento, aseo) occupied
ocupante MF occupant
ocupar VT to occupy; (contratar) to employ;
—**se de** to take care of
ocurrencia F witticism, quip
ocurrente ADJ witty
ocurrir VI to occur
oda F ode
odiar VI/VT to hate
odio M hatred, hate
odioso ADJ (tarea) odious; (persona) hateful
odontología F dentistry
odre M wineskin
**OEA (Organización de Estados
Americanos)** F OAS
oeste ADJ & M west
ofender VI/VT to offend; —**se** to get
offended, to take offense
ofensa F offense
ofensiva F (militar) offensive; (deportiva)
offense
ofensivo ADJ offensive, obnoxious
oferta F offer; (rebaja) special offer; **en** — on
sale
offset M offset
oficial -la ADJ official; MF (militar) officer;
(obrero calificado) skilled worker; —
general high-ranking officer
oficiar VI to officiate; — **de** to serve as
oficina F office; (dependencia
gubernamental) bureau
oficinista MF office worker
oficio M (actividad laboral) trade, craft;
(comunicación oficial) official
communication; **tiene mucho** — he
knows his stuff; **buenos** —**s** good offices
oficioso ADJ (entrometedor) officious; (no
oficial) unofficial
ofrecer[13] VT to offer; (en una subasta) to bid;
(una cena) to give; — **resistencia** to put
up resistance; **¿qué se le ofrece a Vd.?**
how can I help you?
ofrecimiento M (acción de ofrecer) offering;
(oferta) offer
ofrenda F offering
ofuscar[6] VT to bewilder

ogro M ogre
ohmio M ohm
oído M (facultad) hearing; (órgano) inner ear;
(musical) ear; — **medio** middle ear; **al** —
confidentially; **de** — by ear
oír[35] VI/VT (percibir) to hear; (atender) to
listen; — **decir que** to hear that; —
hablar de to hear about; — **misa** to
attend mass; **¡oye!** listen! hey!
ojal M buttonhole
ojalá INTERJ — **estuviera aquí** I wish he
were here; — **que venga** I hope that he
comes
ojeada F glimpse
ojear VT to glimpse
ojera F dark circle under the eye
ojeriza F animosity
ojeroso ADJ with dark circles under the eyes
ojiva F (arco) pointed arch; (explosivo)
warhead
ojo M (órgano, centro de huracán, instinto,
yema de patata) eye; **¡—!** careful! look out!
a — de buen cubero as a rule of thumb;
a —**s vistas** clearly; **me costó un** — **de
la cara** it cost me an arm and a leg; **¿no
tienes** —**s en la cara?** are you blind?
dichosos los —**s que te ven** you're a
sight for sore eyes; — **de buey** porthole;
— **de la cerradura** key hole; — **de
lince** eagle-eye; — **morado** black eye; —
por — an eye for an eye
ola F wave; (de un olor) waft; (de protesta)
storm
oleada F wave, surge
oleaje M swell, surge
óleo M oil painting
oleoducto M pipeline
oleoso ADJ oily
oler[36] VI/VT to smell (también sospechar); —
a to smell of
olfatear VI/VT to scent, to sniff
olfateo M sniff, sniffing
olfato M (facultad) sense of smell; (instinto)
nose
olfatorio ADJ olfactory
olimpiada F Olympiad; —**s** Olympic games
olímpico ADJ Olympian
oliva F olive
olivar M olive grove
olivo M olive tree
olla F pot; — **de grillos** snake pit; —
podrida stew of mixed vegetables and
meat
olmo M elm
olor M smell, odor
oloroso ADJ odorous
olvidadizo ADJ forgetful

olvidar VI/VT to forget; **—se (de)** to forget; **se me olvidó algo** I forgot something

olvido M oblivion; **caer en el —** to be forgotten; **echar al —** to cast into oblivion; **tus —s** your forgetfulness

Omán M Oman

omaní ADJ & MF Omani

ombligo M navel

omisión F omission

omiso ADJ **hacer caso — (de)** to ignore

omitir VT to omit, to leave out; **(no notar)** to overlook

ómnibus M bus

omnipotencia F omnipotence

omnipotente ADJ omnipotent

omnisciencia F omniscience

omnisciente ADJ omniscient

omnívoro ADJ omnivorous

once NUM eleven

oncología F oncology

onda F wave; **— corta** short wave; **— expansiva** shock wave; **— sonora** sound wave; **agarrarle la — a algo** to get in the swing of things; **captar la —** to get the drift

ondeado ADJ wavy

ondeante ADJ flying

ondear VI to wave

ondulación F ripple, ruffle, roll

ondulado ADJ wavy

ondulante ADJ undulating

ondular VI to undulate; VI/VT to wave

ónix M onyx

onomatopeya F onomatopoeia

ONU (Organización de las Naciones Unidas) F UN

onza F ounce

opacar[6] VT **(oscurecer)** to dull; **(eclipsar)** to overshadow

opaco ADJ **(no transparente)** opaque; **(no brillante)** dull

ópalo M opal

opción F option; **opciones** stock options

opcional ADJ optional

OPEP (Organización de Países Exportadores de Petróleo) F OPEC

ópera F **(composición)** opera; **(teatro)** opera house

operable ADJ operable

operación F operation

operador -ora M **(en matemáticas)** operator; MF **(de teléfono)** operator

operar VI/VT to operate; VT **(intervenir quirúrgicamente)** to operate on; **(llevar a cabo)** to carry out; VI **(hacer cuentas)** to do mathematical operations

operario -ria MF operator, operative

opinar VI/VT to hold an opinion, to think

opinión F opinion, view, feeling; **cambiar de —** to change one's mind

opio M opium

oponer[39] VT to oppose; **—se** to conflict; **—se a** to oppose, to be against

oporto M port wine

oportunidad F opportunity, chance; **(pretexto)** opening

oportunista ADJ & MF opportunistic

oportuno ADJ **(en el momento conveniente)** opportune, timely; **(adecuado)** appropriate

oposición F opposition; **oposiciones** competitive examinations

opositor -ora MF opponent

opresión F oppression

opresivo ADJ oppressive

opresor -ora MF oppressor

oprimir VT **(al pueblo)** to oppress; **(un botón)** to press

optar VI to choose; **— por** to choose

optativo ADJ optional

óptico -ca ADJ optical; MF optician; F optics

optimismo M optimism

optimista ADJ optimistic; MF optimist

optometría F optometry

opuesto ADJ opposite, contrary; **se mostró — al casamiento** he was against the marriage; **dos fuerzas opuestas** two opposing forces; **lo —** the opposite; **dirección opuesta** the opposite / reverse direction

opulencia F opulence

opulento ADJ opulent; **(sociedad)** affluent

oración F **(frase)** sentence; **(súplica)** prayer

oráculo M oracle

orador -ora MF orator, speaker

oral ADJ oral

orangután M orangutan

orar VI/VT to pray

oratoria F oratory

oratorio M oratory

órbita F **(de los cuerpos celestes)** orbit; **(de los ojos)** eye socket

orbitador M orbiter

orbital ADJ orbital

orbitar VI/VT to orbit

orca F killer whale

orden M **(limpieza, secuencia)** order; **— del día** order of the day; **perturbar el — público** to disturb the peace; **sin — ni concierto** haphazard; F **(mando)** command, order; **(de religiones)** order; **(de cateo)** warrant; **a sus órdenes** at your service

ordenado ADJ orderly, neat

ordenador M computer

ordenanza F ordinance; M orderly

ordenar VT (arreglar) to put in order; (mandar) to order, to command; (conferir órdenes) to ordain; **—se** to become ordained

ordeñar VT to milk

ordeño M milking

ordinal ADJ ordinal

ordinariez F vulgarity

ordinario ADJ (corriente) ordinary; (vulgar) vulgar

orear VT to air out

orégano M oregano

oreja F (outer) ear; (de un martillo) claw; (en un utensilio) flap; **aguzar la —** to prick up one's ears; **sonreír de — a —** to smile from ear to ear; **estar hasta las —s en algo** to be up to one's neck in something

orejera F ear muff

orfanato M orphanage

orfebre MF (con oro) goldsmith; (con plata) silversmith

orgánico ADJ organic

organismo M organism

organista MF organist

organización F organization

organizador -ora MF organizer

organizar[9] VT to organize; (un ataque) to stage; (una fiesta) to give, to throw

órgano M organ

orgía F orgy

orgullo M pride; **es mi —** she's my pride and joy

orgulloso ADJ proud

orientación F orientation, guidance; (de velas) trim; (de estudios) track; (de un objeto) lie; (del terreno) lay

oriental ADJ oriental, eastern; MF oriental

orientar VT to orient; **—se** to get one's bearings

oriente M orient, east

orificio M orifice

origen M origin; (de un problema, conflicto) source; (antecedentes familiares) birth

original ADJ original; M original; (de una cinta magnética) master

originalidad F originality

originar VT to originate, to give rise to; **—se** to originate, to arise

orilla F (de un lago, mar) shore, bank; (de una cama) edge; (de una prenda) hem

orillar VT (una calle) to border; (una prenda) to hem

orín M rust; M PL **orines** urine

orina F urine

orinal M chamber pot

orinar VI/VT to urinate

oriundo ADJ **ser — de** (persona) to hail from; (cosa) to originate in

orla F (de un uniforme) trimming; (de una alfombra) fringe

orlar VT to fringe

orlón[tm] M Orlon[tm]

ornamental ADJ ornamental

ornamentar VT to ornament, to embellish

ornamento M ornament

ornar VT to adorn

ornitología F ornithology

oro M gold; **— blanco** white gold; **— en lingotes** gold bullion; **— negro** black gold; **— puro** solid gold; **prometer el — y el moro** to promise the moon

orondo ADJ self-satisfied

oropel M tinsel

oropéndola F oriole

orquesta F orchestra

orquestar VT to orchestrate

orquídea F orchid

ortiga F nettle

ortodoncia F orthodontics

ortodoxo ADJ orthodox

ortografía F orthography, spelling

oruga F caterpillar

orujo M rape

orzuelo M sty

osadía F boldness, daring

osado ADJ bold, daring

osamenta F skeleton

osar VI/VT to dare

oscilación F oscillation

oscilar VI to oscillate, to seesaw; **— entre** to range between

oscuridad F (lugar sin luz) dark, darkness; (condición de oscuro) darkness; (falta de claridad conceptual, anonimato) obscurity

oscuro ADJ (sin luz) dark; (nublado) murky; (poco claro, poco conocido) obscure; **lentes —s** dark glasses; **gris —** dark gray; **a oscuras** in the dark

óseo ADJ bony

osezno M bear cub

ósmosis F osmosis

oso -sa M bear; F she-bear; **— blanco / polar** polar bear; **— hormiguero** anteater

ostentación F ostentation, show, display; **hacer de —** to flaunt

ostentar VI/VT to display, to show off, to flaunt

ostentoso ADJ ostentatious, showy

osteoporosis F osteoporosis

ostión M large oyster

ostra F oyster

OTAN (Organización del Tratado del Atlántico Norte) F NATO

otero M hillock
otoñal ADJ autumnal
otoño M autumn, fall
otorgamiento M grant
otorgar[7] VT (permiso) to grant, to concede; (un premio) to award
otro ADJ (uno adicional) another; (uno diferente) other; **otra vez** again; **otra cosa** something else; — **más** another one; **al — día** the next day; **de — modo** otherwise; **en otra parte** somewhere else; **la otra cara de la moneda** the flip side; **por otra parte** on the other hand; PRON (uno más) another one; (una persona diferente) someone else; (una cosa diferente) something else
ovación F ovation, acclaim
oval ADJ oval
ovalado ADJ oval
óvalo M oval
ovario M ovary
oveja F sheep; (hembra) ewe
ovejero M sheepdog
overoles M PL overalls
ovillar VT to ball; **—se** to curl up into a ball
ovillo M ball of yarn; **hacerse un —** to curl up
OVNI (objeto volador no identificado) M UFO
ovular VI to ovulate
óvulo M egg
oxidado ADJ oxidized, rusty
oxidar VI/VT to oxidize, to rust
óxido M (cuerpo químico) oxide; (herrumbre) rust
oxígeno M oxygen
oyente MF (que oye) listener, hearer; (alumno no oficial) auditor
ozono M ozone

Pp

pabellón M (de feria) pavilion; (parte de un edificio) wing; (bandera) flag; (departamento de hospital) ward; — **de la oreja** outer ear
pabilo M wick
paca F bale
pacana F (fruto) pecan; (árbol) pecan tree
pacer[13] VI to pasture, to graze; VT to crop, to graze
paciencia F patience; **tener —** to be patient
paciente ADJ & MF patient

pacificar[6] VT to pacify
pacífico ADJ peaceful; M **Océano Pacífico** Pacific Ocean
pacifismo M pacifism
pacto M pact, covenant
paddock M (de caballos) paddock; (de coches) pit
padecer[13] VI/VT to suffer; — **de cáncer** to suffer from cancer
padecimiento M suffering
padrastro M (marido de la madre) stepfather; (uñero) hangnail
padre M father; **—s** parents, folks; — **de familia** male head of the household; **—nuestro** the Lord's Prayer; **John Smith, —** John Smith, senior; **ser —** to become a father; **un lío —** a real mess
padrino M (de bautizo) godfather; (de boda) best man; (en un duelo) second
paella F paella
paga F pay; (para un niño) allowance
pagadero ADJ payable, due
pagado ADJ — **de sí mismo** self-satisfied
pagador -ora MF payer
paganismo M paganism
pagano -na ADJ & MF pagan
pagar[7] VT (cuentas, deudas) to pay; (mercancías) to pay for; **—se de** to be proud of; — **el pato** to be left holding the bag; **pagan justos por pecadores** the just pay for the sins of others; — **a plazos** to pay in installments; — **al contado** to pay cash; — **con la misma moneda** to pay in kind; — **en especie** to pay in kind
pagaré M promissory note
página F page
paginar VT to paginate
pago M payment; — **en efectivo** cash payment
paila F large pan
país M country
paisaje M landscape, scenery
paisajismo M landscape architecture
paisano -na M countryman; F countrywoman
paja F straw (también para beber de un vaso); **a humo de —s** thoughtlessly; **hacerse una —** *vulg* to jack off; **no caberle a alguien una — por el culo** to be self-satisfied; **por un quítame allá esas —s** for a trifle
pajar M hayloft
pájaro M bird; — **carpintero** woodpecker; — **pinto** cautious person; **un — francés** a French guy
paje M page

pajizo ADJ straw-colored
pajonal M *Am* grassland
pala F (para cavar) shovel; (para recoger basura) dustpan; (de hélice, remo) blade; (de zapato) upper; (para remar, de ping-pong) paddle; **— mecánica** power shovel; **lo tuvimos que recoger con —** he was exhausted
palabra F (unidad léxica) word; (facultad) speech; **— clave** key word; **—s mayores** a big deal; **cuatro —s** a few words; **cumplir con la —** to keep one's word; **dejar con la — en la boca** to cut someone off in mid-sentence; **en pocas —s** in a nutshell; **faltar a la —** to break a promise; **la última —** the final say; **ni una —** not a word; **no dijo —** he didn't breathe a word; **un hombre de —** a man of his word; **tener la —** to have the floor; **tomar la —** to take the floor; **traducción — por —** word for word translation; **tragarse / comerse las propias —s** to eat one's words
palabrerío M verbiage
palabrero ADJ long-winded
palabrota F curse word, four-letter word; **—s** profanity
palacio M palace
paladar M palate; **— hendido** cleft palate
paladear VT to relish
paladín M champion, crusader
palanca F (mecanismo para levantar algo) lever; (para abrir algo) crowbar; (fuerza) leverage; **— del cambio** gearshift lever; **— de juegos** joystick; **— del regulador** throttle lever; **hacer —** to use leverage
palangana F basin
Paláu M Palau
palco M box
palenque M fence
paleontología F paleontology
paleta F (de pintor) palette; (de albañil) trowel; (de ping-pong, para mezclar, batir) paddle; (hélice) blade; (pirulí) lollipop, sucker
paletilla F shoulder
paleto -ta MF hayseed, hick
paliar VT to alleviate
palidecer[13] VI to turn pale
palidez F pallor, paleness
pálido ADJ pallid, pale
palillo M (de dientes) toothpick; (de tambor) drumstick; (para comida china) chopstick; **tocar todos los —s** to try everything
palique M chit-chat
paliza F beating, whipping; **dar una —** to beat, to whip

palma F (árbol) palm (tree); (hoja) palm leaf; (de mano) palm (of the hand); **batir —s** to clap; **llevarse la —** to take the prize; **conocer como la — de la mano** to know like the back of one's hand
palmada F (en la espalda) slap; (aplauso) clap; (en el trasero) spank; **dar una —** (en la espalda) to slap; (en el trasero) to spank
palmear VT to slap on the back
palmera F palm tree
palmípedo M web-footed bird
palmo M span; **— a —** inch by inch
palmotear VT to slap on the back
palo M (de madera) stick; (de barco) mast; (de naipes) suit; **— de golf** golf club; **— de escoba** broomstick; **dar —s** to hit with a stick; **de tal — tal astilla** a chip off the old block
paloma F dove, pigeon
palomar M pigeon loft
palomilla F wing nut
palomitas F PL popcorn; **hacer —** to pop corn
palote M rolling pin
palpable ADJ palpable
palpar VT to feel
palpitación F palpitation
palpitante ADJ palpitating; **una cuestión —** a burning question
palpitar VI to palpitate
palta F *Am* avocado
paludismo M malaria
pampa F *Am* prairie
pamplinas F PL baloney, hogwash
pan M bread; (pieza) loaf of bread; **— comido** piece of cake, cinch; **— de cada día** everyday occurrence; **— rallado / molido** bread crumbs; **al —, — y al vino, vino** to call a spade a spade; **contigo, — y cebolla** love is all we need; **ganarse el —** to make a living
pana F corduroy
panacea F panacea, magic bullet
panadería F bakery
panadero -ra MF baker
panal M honeycomb
Panamá M Panama
panameño -ña ADJ & MF Panamanian
panamericano ADJ Pan-American
panceta F bacon
páncreas M pancreas
panda M panda bear
pandearse VT to buckle, to sag
pandeo M sag
pandereta F tambourine
pandilla F gang, band

panecillo M roll

panegírico M eulogy

panel M panel

panera F breadbasket

panfleto M pamphlet

pánico ADJ & M panic

panoja F ear of corn

panorama M panorama; (horizonte) outlook

panorámico ADJ panoramic

panqueque M pancake

pantaletas F PL panties

pantalla F (de lámpara) lampshade; (de monitor, para películas) screen; (para actividades ilícitas) cover, front; **la grande** the silver screen; — **dividida** split screen; — **táctil** touchscreen

pantalón M trousers, pants; — **corto** shorts; **pantalones** trousers, pants; **llevar bien puestos los pantalones** to be master in one's own house

pantano M swamp, marsh

pantanoso ADJ swampy, marshy

panteón M vault

pantera F panther

pantomima F mime, pantomime

pantorrilla F calf

pantufla F slipper

panty M pantyhose

panza F paunch, belly

panzudo ADJ pot-bellied

pañal M diaper; **estar en —es** to be in infancy

paño M (trozo de tela) cloth; (de lana) woolen cloth; (para limpiar) rag; — **higiénico** sanitary napkin; — **mortuorio** pall; — **de manos** towel; — **de cocina** dishcloth; — **de mesa** tablecloth; **ella es mi — de lágrimas** I always cry on her shoulder; —**s menores** underwear

pañuelo M (para la nariz) handkerchief; (de cuello) scarf

papa M pope; F *Am* potato; **no saber ni —** not to know a thing; —**s fritas** French fries

papá M papa, dad

papacito M daddy

papada F double chin

papado M papacy

papagayo M parrot

papaíto M daddy

papar VT to eat; MF SG **papamoscas** (pájaro) flycatcher; (tonto) half-wit; **papanatas** twerp

paparruchas F PL baloney, bull

papaya F papaya

papel M paper; (dramático) role, part; —

aluminio aluminum foil; — **carbón** carbon paper; — **cuadriculado** graph paper; — **de cartas** stationery; — **de estaño** tin foil; — **de estraza** brown paper; — **de lija** sandpaper; — **de seda** tissue paper; — **encerado** wax paper; — **higiénico** toilet paper; — **moneda** paper money; — **tisú** tissue paper; **desempeñar un —** to play a role; **en el — on paper; hacer buen — to cut a good figure

papelera F (fábrica) paper factory; (cubo) wastepaper basket

papelería F stationery store

papeleta F slip of paper; (para votar) ballot

paperas F PL mumps

papito M daddy

páprika F paprika

papú ADJ & MF Papua New Guinean

paquete M (envuelto) package; (atado) bundle; (conjunto de programas) package

Paquistán M Pakistan

paquistano -na ADJ & MF Pakistani

par ADJ even; M (de cosas idénticas) pair; (de cosas diferentes) couple; (título) peer; (en golf) par; **a la —** at par; **sin —** peerless; **de — en —** wide-open

para PREP in order to, for; **lo hice — ganar dinero** I did it in order to earn money; **demasiado — mí** too much for me; **trabajo — mi padre** I work for my father; — **ser perro es inteligente** for a dog he's smart; — **mi sorpresa** to my surprise; **voy — Madrid** I'm going to Madrid; — **las dos** by two o'clock; — **atrás** backwards; — **empezar** for starters; — **llevar** to go; **¿— qué?** what for? — **que** so that, so as to; — **siempre** forever; **habla — sí** he talks to himself; — **mis adentros** to myself; — **morirse de risa** hilarious; **no es — tanto** it's no big deal; **sin qué ni — qué** without rhyme or reason

parabién M congratulations; **dar el —** to congratulate

parada F (acción de parar) stop; (de perro de caza) point; (de taxis) stand; (militar) parade; (relevo de guardia) changing the guard; (de balón) parry

paradero M whereabouts

paradigma M paradigm

parado ADJ (que no se mueve) stationary; (que no tiene trabajo) unemployed, idle; **salir bien —** to come out on top

paradoja F paradox

paradójico ADJ paradoxical

parafernalia F paraphernalia

parafina F paraffin
parafrasear VI/VT to paraphrase
paráfrasis F paraphrase
paraguas M SG umbrella
Paraguay M Paraguay
paraguayo -ya ADJ & MF Paraguayan
paraíso M paradise
paraje M spot
paralela F parallel line; **—s** parallel bars
paralelo ADJ & M parallel; **hacer —s** to draw
  parallels
parálisis F paralysis
paralítico -ca ADJ & MF paralytic
paralización F (de tránsito) gridlock; (del
  cuerpo) paralysis
paralizar[9] VT to paralyze; (negociaciones) to
  stall; **—se** to gridlock
paramédico -ca ADJ & MF paramedic
parámetro M parameter
paramilitar ADJ & MF paramilitary
páramo M cold highland, moor
parangón M comparison; **sin —**
  incomparable
parangonar VT to compare
paraninfo M auditorium
paranoia F paranoia
paranoico -ca ADJ & MF paranoid
paranormal ADJ paranormal
parapsicología F parapsychology
parar VI/VT (detener) to stop; (motor) to stall;
  VT (un pase de pelota) to block; (un golpe)
  to parry; **— de hacer algo** to stop doing
  something; **y para de contar** and that's
  it; **— en seco** to stop short; **ir a —** to end
  up; **habló sin —** he talked non-stop; **—se**
  to stop; *Am* to stand up; **—se a pensar** to
  stop to think; M SG **parabrisas**
  windshield; **paracaídas** parachute;
  paracaidismo skydiving; **parachoques**
  bumper; **pararrayos** lightning rod;
  parasol parasol; MF **paracaidista**
  parachutist
parásito M parasite
parcela F parcel, plot
parcelación F subdivision
parcelar VT to parcel (out)
parche M (para remendar) patch; (de tambor)
  drum head; **— de ojo** eye patch
parcial ADJ partial
pardillo M linnet
pardo ADJ (color) gray-brown; (mulato)
  mulatto
pareado M couplet
parear VT to match
parecer[13] VI to seem; **— que** to seem like, to
  look like; **¿qué te parece?** what do you
  think? **—se a** to resemble, to look like; M

(opinión) opinion; (aspecto) appearance;
  al — apparently; **a mi —** to my mind /
  way of thinking; **del mismo —** like-
  minded
parecido ADJ alike, similar; **bien —** good-
  looking; M similarity, resemblance
pared F wall; **poner a alguien contra la
  —** to corner; **subirse por las —es** to be
  furious; **de — a —** wall-to-wall; **reloj de
  —** wall clock
paredón M execution wall
pareja F (de personas) couple; (de cosas) pair,
  match; (compañero) partner
parejo ADJ (hermanos) alike; (carrera) even;
  (dientes) straight; **correr al —** to go hand
  in hand
parental ADJ parental
parentela F kin
parentesco M kinship, relation
paréntesis M parenthesis
pargo M red snapper
paria MF INV pariah, outcast
paridad F parity
pariente -ta MF relative, relation; **—
  consanguíneo** blood relative
parir VI/VT to give birth (to)
parlamentar VI to parley
parlamentario -ria ADJ parliamentary; MF
  member of parliament
parlamento M (en una obra de teatro)
  speech; (negociación) parley; (cuerpo
  legislativo) parliament
parlanchín ADJ talkative
parlotear VI to chatter, to rattle on
parloteo M chatter
paro M (pequeña huelga) stoppage; (situación
  de no tener trabajo) unemployment; (ave)
  tit; **— cardiaco** cardiac arrest
parodia F parody
parodiar VT to parody
parpadear VI (un ojo) to blink; (una vela) to
  flicker; (una estrella) to twinkle
parpadeo M (del ojo) blink; (de una vela)
  flicker; (de una estrella) twinkle
párpado M eyelid
parque M park; **— automotor** fleet of cars;
  — de atracciones amusement park; **—
  zoológico** zoo
parra F grapevine
párrafo M paragraph; **echar un — con** to
  have a chat with
parral M grape arbor
parranda F binge, spree; **andar de —** to go
  on a spree
parrandear VI to revel
parrandero -ra MF party animal
parrilla F (sobre el fuego) grill; (en el horno)

broiler; (de calles) grid; (de coche) grille

parrillada F barbecue dish

párroco M parish priest

parroquia F (distrito) parish; (iglesia) parish church

parroquial ADJ parochial

parroquiano -na MF (de iglesia) parishioner; (de tienda) regular

parte F (sección) part; (lugar) place; (papel en un drama) lines; (persona) party; **—s pudendas** private parts; **a otra —** somewhere else; **a —s iguales** fifty-fifty; **de un tiempo a esta —** for some time; **de — de** on behalf of; **de — a —** completely; **echar a mala —** to take amiss; **en —** partly; **en gran —** in large measure; **en otra —** elsewhere; **en / por todas —s** everywhere; **formar — de** to be part of; **ir por —s** to proceed by steps; **la mayor — de** most of; **la — del león** the lion's share; **no está en ninguna —** it's nowhere to be found; **no va a ninguna —** it's going nowhere; **por otra —** on the other hand; **tomar — en** to take part in; M report; **dar — to** report; **dar — de enfermo** to report sick; **dar — de un crimen** to report a crime

partera F midwife

participación F participation; (en un negocio) interest; **— de nacimiento** birth announcement

participante MF participant; (en una carrera) entrant; (en un concurso) contestant

participar VI to participate; VT to announce; **— de / en** to participate in, to share in

partícipe MF participant

participio M participle

partícula F particle

particular ADJ (específico) particular; (poco usual) peculiar; (privado) private; **en —** in particular; **clases —es** private lessons; M (detalle) particular; (asunto) matter; MF private citizen

partida F (fondos) appropriation; (de caza) party; (cantidad de mercancía) parcel, lot; (de ajedrez) game; (acción de partir) departure; **— de nacimiento** birth record; **jugar una mala —** to play a mean trick; **por — doble** double-entry

partidario -ria MF (de una medida) supporter, advocate; (de partido político) partisan

partido M (grupo político) party; (de golf) round; (de tenis, fútbol) game, match; **es un buen —** he's a good match; **sacar — de** to take advantage of; **tomar —** to take sides; ADJ split, cleft

partir VT (dividir) to divide; (repartir) to share; (quebrar) to break; **eso me parte por el eje** that screws me up; **que te parta un rayo** go jump in the lake; VI (salir) to depart, to leave; **a — de entonces** since then; **a — del lunes** starting Monday; **—se de risa** to die of laughter

partisano -na MF partisan

partitura F musical score

parto M childbirth, delivery; **estar en trabajo de —** to be in labor

parvulario M kindergarten, nursery

párvulo -la MF nursery school child

pasa F raisin

pasable ADJ passable

pasada F (acción de pasar) passing; (con una máquina) pass; **una mala —** a mean trick; **de —** by the way

pasadizo M secret passage

pasado M past; ADJ (anterior) past; (demasiado maduro) overripe; **— mañana** day after tomorrow; **el año —** last year; **el — mes de septiembre** last September

pasador M pin

pasaje M (sitio por donde se pasa, fragmento de texto) passage; (billete) ticket; (pasajeros) passengers

pasajero -ra ADJ fleeting, transitory; MF passenger

pasaporte M passport

pasar VI (no querer jugar, ir de un lado a otro, seguir su proceso, transcurrir) to pass; (ocurrir) to happen; (mantenerse) to get by on; **— a ser** to become; **— de moda** to go out of style; **— por** to pass by; **—le por la cabeza a alguien** to occur to someone; **pasan de los 80 años** they're over 80 years old; **te pasaste la casa** you missed the house; **—se de la raya** to cross the line; **—se de sol** to get too much sun; **—se de listo** to outsmart oneself; **—se** to spoil; **se me pasó ir a buscarte** I totally forgot to pick you up; **me la paso bien** I have a good time; VT (la sal, una prueba, la plancha) to pass; (un sofocón) to endure; (una tarde) to spend; **—las de Caín** to go through hell; **— en limpio** to make a new copy; **— por alto** to overlook; **— los 50 kmh** to exceed 50 kmh; **— revista** to pass in review; **nos pasó un Volvo** a Volvo passed us; **no lo paso** I can't stand him; M **tienen un buen —** they have a comfortable life; **pasamano** (de barco) guard rail, gangway; (de escalera) banister, railing; **pasatiempo** pastime

pasarela F (en un barco) gangplank; (para modelos) runway

Pascua F Easter; (fiesta judía) Passover; — **Florida / de Resurrección** Easter Sunday; — **de Navidad** Christmas

pase M pass

pasear VI (a pie) to take a walk; (en bici, a caballo) to go on a ride; (en coche) to go for a drive, to go on a ride; —**se** to parade, to take a walk; —**se a caballo** to go horseback riding; VT (un perro) to walk a dog

paseo M (a pie) walk, stroll; (a caballo, en bicicleta) ride; (en coche) drive, ride; (lugar donde pasear) mall; **irse a** — to go jump in a lake; **dar un** — (a pie) to take a walk; (a caballo, en bicicleta) to go on a ride; (en coche) to go on a drive

pasillo M (de un teatro) aisle; (de un edificio) hallway, corridor; (para vuelo aéreo) corridor

pasión F passion

pasivo ADJ passive; **voz pasiva** passive voice; M SG (en un negocio) liabilities; (de una cuenta) debit side

pasmado ADJ astounded

pasmar VT to astound, to stun; —**se** to be astounded, to be stunned

pasmo M astonishment

pasmoso ADJ astonishing, stunning

paso M (acción de pasar, lugar donde pasar) pass; (de pie, de danza, distancia, de un proceso) step; (velocidad) pace; (de caballerías) walk; (de tornillo) pitch; (de coche) wheelbase; — **elevado** overpass; — **a nivel** grade crossing; — **de tortuga** snail's pace; — **a paso** step by step; **dar** — (dejar pasar) to let pass; (dejar actuar) to make possible; **dar** —**s** to take steps; **de** — by the way, in passing; **estar de** — to be passing through; **marcar el** — to set the pace; **al** — **que** while; **salir del** — to get out of a difficulty; **dicho sea de** — incidentally; **a cada** — at every turn; — **del tiempo** passage of time; **abrir** — **para** to make way for; **abrirse** — to plow through, to press through; ADJ dried

pasta F (de almidón) paste; (de harina) dough; (de fideos) pasta; (de libro) hard cover, binding; (dinero) *fam* dough; **de buena** — of good disposition; — **dentífrica / dental** toothpaste

pastar VI/VT to pasture, to graze

pastel M (torta) cake; (tarta) pie; (pintura, cuadro) pastel; — **de cumpleaños** birthday cake; — **de limón** lemon pie; —

de carne meat pie; **descubrir el** — to spill the beans; ADJ pastel

pastelería F (establecimiento) pastry shop; (conjunto de pasteles) pastry

pastelero -ra M pastry cook

pasterizar, pasteurizar[9] VT to pasteurize

pastilla F (de medicina) tablet, pill; (para la tos) drop; (de jabón) bar

pastizal M grassland

pasto M (terreno) pasture, grassland; (hierba) grass; **ser** — **de** to be a victim of

pastor -ora MF (de ovejas) shepherd; (sacerdote protestante) pastor, minister; M — **alemán** German shepherd

pastoral ADJ pastoral; F pastoral letter

pastoril ADJ pastoral

pastoso ADJ pasty

pastura F feed

pata F (de animal, mueble) foot, leg; (de pollo) drumstick; (de un enchufe) pin; — **palmada** webfoot; — **de gallo** crow's-foot; **en cuatro** —**s** on all fours; **a (la) coja** skipping on one leg; **estirar la** — *fam* to kick the bucket; **mala** — bad luck; **metedura de** — faux pas; **meter la** — to slip up; —**s arriba** upside down; **patihendido** cloven-hoofed; **patitieso** dumbfounded; **patizambo** (hacia adentro) knock-kneed; (hacia afuera) bow-legged

patada F kick; **libros a** —**s** tons of books; **en dos** —**s** in a jiffy; **dar** —**s** to kick; **echar a** —**s** to kick out

patalear VI (en el aire) to kick; (en el suelo) to stamp

pataleo M (en el aire) kick; (en el suelo) stamp

pataleta F fit; **dar una** — to throw a fit

patán M boor

patata F *Esp* potato; —**s fritas** French fries; — **caliente** hot potato

patear VT (algo, a alguien) to kick; (el suelo) to stamp; VI to tramp around

patentar VT to patent

patente ADJ & F patent; **se hizo** — **su ignorancia** he betrayed his ignorance; — **en trámite** patent pending

paternal ADJ (del padre) paternal; (como padre) fatherly

paternidad F paternity, fatherhood; **prueba de** — paternity test

paterno ADJ paternal

patético ADJ moving

patetismo M pathos

patíbulo M gallows scaffold, gallows

patilla F (de gafas) arm; —**s** sideburns

patín M skate; (de trineo) runner; — **de**

ruedas roller skate; **— de cuchilla / de hielo** ice skate
patinaje M skating
patinar VI (una persona) to skate; (un coche sobre hielo) to skid; (un embrague) to slip; (en un examen) to blank out
patinazo M (de embrague) slip; (de coche) skid
patio M (de casa) patio, courtyard; (de escuela) playground
pato M duck; (macho) drake; **pagar el —** to take the rap
patochada F blunder
patógeno M pathogen
patología F pathology
patológico ADJ pathological
patoso ADJ clumsy
patraña F tall tale
patria F fatherland, homeland
patriarca M patriarch
patriarcal ADJ patriarchal
patrimonio M patrimony; **— cultural** cultural heritage; **— personal** personal assets
patriota MF patriot
patriótico ADJ patriotic
patriotismo M patriotism
patrocinador -ora MF sponsor
patrocinar VT to sponsor
patrocinio M sponsorship
patrón -ona MF (protector) patron; (jefe) employer; (de navío) skipper; M (dueño de pensión) landlord; (de costura) pattern; (punto de referencia) yardstick, standard; (planta) stock; (de un parásito) host; **— de oro** gold standard; F (dueña de pensión) landlady
patronato M board of trustees
patrono -na MF patron
patrulla F (grupo de policías o soldados) patrol, squad; (coche) squad car
patrullar VI/VT to patrol
patrullero M patrol car, squad car
pausa F (musical) pause, rest; **trabajar con —** to work slowly; **hacer —** to pause
pauta F guideline
pavimentar VT to pave
pavimento M pavement
pavo M turkey; **— real** peacock; **— frío** cold turkey; ADJ silly
pavón M peacock
pavonearse VI to strut, to swagger
pavoneo M strut, swagger
pavor M dread
pavoroso ADJ frightful
payasada F clownish act or remark; **—s** antics, horseplay

payasear VI to clown around, to horse around
payaso M (de circo) clown; (persona poco seria) buffoon; **hacer el —** to clown around
paz F peace; **estamos en —** we are even; **en — descanse** may she rest in peace; **hacer las paces** to make up; **dejar en —** to leave alone
PC M PC
peaje M toll; (lugar donde se paga) tollbooth
peatón -ona MF pedestrian
peca F freckle
pecado M sin; **— mortal** mortal sin
pecador -ora MF sinner; ADJ sinful
pecaminoso ADJ sinful
pecar[6] VI to sin; **— contra** to transgress against; **— de bueno** to be too good; **— de generoso** to be too generous; **— de oscuro** to be exceedingly unclear
pecera F aquarium
pechera F (de camisa) front; (de delantal) bib
pecho M (parte del cuerpo) chest; (mama) breast; **dar el —** to nurse; **nadar —** to do the breaststroke; **tomar a —(s)** to take to heart; **sacar —** to puff out one's chest
pechuga F breast
pechugona ADJ buxom
pecio M flotsam and jetsam
pecoso ADJ freckled
pectoral ADJ & M pectoral
peculado M embezzlement
peculiar ADJ peculiar
peculiaridad F peculiarity
pedagogía F pedagogy, education
pedagogo -ga MF pedagogue
pedal M pedal
pedalear VI/VT to pedal
pedante ADJ pedantic; MF pedant
pedazo M piece; **— de idiota** absolute idiot; **él es un — de pan** he's a saint; **hacer —s** to tear to pieces; **caerse a —s** to fall to pieces; **— por —** piece by piece
pedernal M flint
pedestal M pedestal
pedestre ADJ pedestrian
pediatra MF INV pediatrician
pediatría F pediatrics
pedido M order, requisition; **hacer un —** to place an order; **— fijo** standing order; **— urgente** rush order
pedigrí M pedigree
pedigüeño ADJ **no seas —** stop asking me for things
pedir[5] VT (requerir) to ask for, to request; (exigir) to demand; (encargar) to order, to requisition; **— limosna** to beg; **—**

prestado to borrow; **— socorro** to cry for help; **— un deseo** to make a wish; **— que** to ask/pray that; **— la mano** to ask in marriage; **— por alguien** to ask to speak to someone

pedo M fart; **tener/cogerse un —** to be drunk; **tirarse —s** to fart

pedrada F **dar una —** to hit with a stone; **matar a —s** to stone to death

pedregal M rocky ground

pedregoso ADJ stony

pedrería F precious stones

pedrusco M boulder

pedúnculo M stem

pega F snag

pegadizo ADJ catchy

pegajoso ADJ sticky, tacky

pegamento M glue

pegar[7] VT (con el puño) to hit, to strike; (algo con pegamento) to stick, to glue; (botones) to sew on; (una devisa) to peg; **— con** to match; **— contra** to touch; **— un grito** to yell; **— un susto** to give a scare; **— un salto** to jump; **—le un tiro a alguien** to shoot someone; **—se** (adherir) to stick together, to cling; (contagiarse) to be contagious; **—se a** to latch onto; **no — un ojo** not to sleep a wink

pegote M glob

pegotear VT to gum up

peinado M (estilo) coiffure, hairdo; (acción) combing

peinador -ora MF hairdresser

peinar VT to comb (también registrar); (en una peluquería) to style; **— a contrapelo** to rub the wrong way

peine M comb

pelada F bald spot

pelado ADJ (pobre) poor; (sin cáscara) peeled; (sin pelo) hairless; (sin árboles) treeless; (sin plumas) plucked; (sin dinero) broke

pelador M peeler

pelaje M coat, fur

pelar VT (el pelo) to cut the hair of; (las plumas) to pluck the feathers from; (frutas, verduras) to peel; (a un jugador) to fleece; **duro de —** hard to deal with; **el agua está que pela** the water is really hot; **—se** to peel; M SG **pelagatos** nobody

peldaño M step, stair

pelea F (de palabra) fight, quarrel; (de obra) fight, scrape; (de boxeo) fight; **— a puñetazos** fistfight; **— de perros** dogfight

pelear VI (con palabras) to fight, to quarrel; (con obras) to fight, to scuffle; **—se con**

alguien to have a fight with someone

pelechar VI (perder la piel) to shed; (mejorar) to get better

pelele M (persona sin carácter) wimp; (muñeca) straw doll

peletería F (tienda) fur store; (comercio) fur trade

pelícano M pelican

película F film (también membrana); (obra cinematográfica) motion-picture film, movie; **de —** extraordinary; **dar una —** to show a film; **— muda** silent film

peligrar VI to be in danger

peligro M danger, peril; **ese muchacho es un —** that boy is dangerous; **en — ** in danger; **poner en —** to imperil/ endanger/jeopardize

peligroso ADJ dangerous, perilous

pellejo M (piel de animal) hide, pelt; (odre) wineskin; **salvar el —** to save one's skin; **ser todo —** to be skin and bones; **jugarse el —** to risk one's life

pellizcar[6] VT to pinch

pellizco M pinching

pelma MF jerk

pelo M (de persona) hair; (de animal) fur; (de alfombra) pile; **con —s y señales** with every possible detail; **de medio —** low-class; **eso me viene al —** that suits me perfectly; **montar en —** to ride bareback; **ni un —** not at all; **no tener —s en la lengua** not to mince words; **se le ponen los —s de punta** his hair stands on end; **se salvó por un —** he was saved by the skin of his teeth; **tomar el — a** to make fun of; **traído de los —s** far-fetched; ADJ **pelirrojo** redheaded

pelón ADJ bald

pelota F (objeto) ball (también testículo); (juego) ball game; **— vasca** jai-alai; **en —s** naked; **pasar la —** to pass the buck

pelotera F brawl

pelotón M (pelota grande) large ball; (de tierra seca) clod; (de ciclistas) pack; (de soldados) platoon; (de fusilamiento) firing squad

peltre M pewter

peluca F wig

peludo ADJ (persona) hairy; (animal) furry; (perro) shaggy

peluquería F (para hombres) barbershop; (para mujeres) salon

peluquero -ra MF (de hombres) barber; (de mujeres) hairdresser

peluquín M toupee

pelusa F (de tela) lint; (de melocotón, cara) fuzz; (de plantas) hair; (de ropa) fluff, lint;

(de polvo) dust bunny

pelvis F pelvis

pena F (castigo) penalty; (tristeza) sorrow; — **de muerte** death penalty, capital punishment; —**s** hardships; **a duras** —**s** with great difficulty; **me da** — it grieves me; **hecho una** — in a mess; **sería una** — **perder** it would be a shame to lose; **so** — **de** on pain of; **valer la** — to be worthwhile

penacho M (de plumas) tuft, crest; (de humo) plume

penal ADJ penal; M penitentiary

penalidad F (penuria) hardship; (castigo) penalty

penalizar[9] VT to penalize

penalty M penalty kick

penar VI to suffer; VT to punish

penco M plug, nag

pendejo -ja MF (persona licenciosa) *pey* swine; (persona tonta) *fam* dummy; M (hombre despreciable) *pey* schmuck; (pelo púbico) pubic hair

pendencia F wrangle, fight

pendenciero ADJ quarrelsome

pender VI to hang, to dangle

pendiente F slope, incline; M *Esp* earring; ADJ (aretes) dangling; (negocio) pending, unfinished; (pago) outstanding; **vive** — **de su hija** she lives for her daughter

pendón M banner

péndulo M pendulum

pene M penis

penetración F penetration

penetrante ADJ (mirada, sonido) penetrating, piercing; (frío) biting; (comentario) cutting; (inteligencia) keen

penetrar VT (pasar al interior) to penetrate, to pierce; (comprender) to comprehend

penicilina F penicillin

península F peninsula

peninsular ADJ peninsular

penitencia F penance

penitenciaría F penitentiary

penitente ADJ & MF penitent

penoso ADJ (que produce tristeza) painful, grievous; (que lleva consigo penalidades) trying

pensador -ora MF thinker; ADJ reflective

pensamiento M (facultad, acción, efecto) thought; (flor) pansy

pensar[1] VI/VT to think; — **en** to think about/over; — **hacer algo** to intend to do something; **eso da que** — that seems questionable; **no lo pienses dos veces** don't think twice

pensativo ADJ pensive, thoughtful

pensión F (asignación periódica) pension, allowance; (comidas) board; (hostal) boardinghouse; — **completa** room and board; **tener en** — to have as a boarder

pensionado M boarding school

pensionar VT to pension

pensionista MF (que vive en una pensión) boarder; (que cobra una pensión) pensioner

pentágono M pentagon

pentagrama M musical staff

penthouse M penthouse

penúltimo ADJ next to the last, penultimate

penumbra F semi-darkness, dimness

penuria F (escasez) shortage; (pobreza) poverty

peña F boulder; — **folklórica** folklore club

peñasco M crag

peñascoso ADJ craggy

peñón M crag

peón -ona MF (obrero) unskilled laborer, farm hand; — **caminero** road worker; M (en ajedrez) pawn; (en damas) piece

peonada F gang of laborers

peonaje M gang of laborers

peonza F toy top

peor ADJ worse, worst; **este libro es** — this book is worse; **el** — **libro** the worst book; ADV worse; **trabaja** — he works worse; — **que** worse than; — **que nunca** worse than ever; **en el** — **de los casos** if worst comes to worst; **lo** — the worst (thing); **tanto** — so much the worse

pepa F **es un viva la** — it's bedlam

pepino M cucumber

pepita F (simiente) seed; (tumor de gallina) pip; (masa de oro) nugget

pequeñez F (cualidad de pequeño) smallness; (cosa insignificante) trifle

pequeño -ña ADJ (de poco tamaño) small, little; (de corta edad) young; (de poca importancia) trivial

pera F pear; **pedirle** —**s al olmo** to ask the impossible

peral M pear tree

perca F perch; — **americana** black bass

percal M percale

percance M accident, mishap

percebe M barnacle

percepción F perception

perceptible ADJ perceptible, noticeable

perceptivo ADJ perceptive

percha F (para el armario) clothes hanger; (palo para colgar cosas) peg; (palo para aves) perch; (perchero) coat rack

perchero M coat rack

percibir VT (experimentar) to perceive, to

sense; (recibir) to collect

percudir VT to make grimy; **—se** to get grimy

percusión F percussion

percutor M firing pin

perdedor -ora MF loser

perder[1] VT (dejar de tener algo, extraviar) to lose, to mislay; (echar a perder) to spoil, to ruin; (ser derrotado) to lose; (no sacar el provecho debido) to waste; (no llegar a tiempo, no disfrutar) to miss; **— el conocimiento** to lose consciousness; **— el tiempo** to waste time; **— los estribos** to fly off the handle; **— hojas** to shed leaves; **— pie** to lose one's footing; **— terreno** to lose ground; **echarse a —** to spoil; **el vaso pierde agua** the glass leaks water; **llevo las de —** the odds are against me; **—se** (extraviarse) to lose one's way, to get lost; (pervertirse) to go astray, to go astray; **se han perdido las llaves** the keys have gotten lost; **—se de vista** to disappear; **—(se) una oportunidad** to pass up an opportunity

perdición F perdition, damnation

pérdida F (acción de perder, cosa perdida) loss; **entrar en —** to nosedive; **— de tiempo** waste of time

perdido -da ADJ (extraviado) lost, missing; (aislado) isolated; (promiscuo) promiscuous; **un borracho —** an utter drunkard; **estar — por alguien** to be crazy about someone; M degenerate; F slut

perdigón M (pollo de perdiz) young partridge; (grano de plomo) birdshot, buckshot

perdiz F partridge

perdón M forgiveness; (oficial) pardon; **con — de los presentes** present company excepted; **no tener —** to be unforgivable; INTERJ excuse me

perdonar VT to forgive; (oficial) to pardon

perdurable ADJ lasting

perdurar VI to last

perecedero ADJ perishable

perecer[13] VI to perish

peregrinación F pilgrimage

peregrinar VI to go on a pilgrimage

peregrino -na MF pilgrim; ADJ far-fetched

perejil M parsley

perenne ADJ perennial

pereza F laziness, idleness, sloth

perezoso ADJ lazy, idle; M (animal) sloth

perfección F perfection; **a la —** to perfection

perfeccionamiento M perfecting

perfeccionar VT to perfect

perfecto ADJ perfect, flawless; **es un —**

tarado he's an utter idiot

perfil M profile; **de —** from the side

perfilar VT to outline; **—se** (marcarse) to be outlined; (definirse) to become clear

perforación F perforation; (de un pozo) drilling

perforar VT (agujerear) to perforate; (para petróleo) to drill

perfumar VT to perfume, to scent

perfume M perfume, scent

perfumería F perfumery

pergamino M parchment

pérgola F arbor

pericia F expertness

perico M (loro) parakeet; (cocaína) *fam* snow

periferia F periphery, fringe

periférico ADJ & M peripheral

perilla F (adorno, remate) knob; (pelo de barbilla) goatee; **de —** apt

perímetro M perimeter

periódico M newspaper; **— mensual** monthly periodical; ADJ periodic

periodismo M journalism

periodista MF journalist

periodístico ADJ journalistic

período M period (también menstruación); (de materia radiactiva) half-life; **— glaciar** ice age

peripecia F vicissitude

peripuesto ADJ dressed up, dolled up, decked out

periquito M parakeet

periscopio M periscope

perito -ta ADJ expert, practiced; MF technician

peritonitis F peritonitis

perjudicar[6] VT to harm

perjudicial ADJ harmful, detrimental

perjuicio M harm

perjurar VT to swear; VI to commit perjury; **—se** to commit perjury

perjurio M perjury

perla F (de nácar) pearl; (persona) gem; (gota de sudor) bead; (de sabiduría) nugget; (frase desafortunada) blooper; **de —s** perfectly

perlado ADJ pearly

permanecer[13] VI to remain, to stay

permanencia F (carácter de permanente) permanence; (acción de permanecer) stay

permanente ADJ permanent

permeable ADJ permeable

permear VT to permeate

permisible ADJ permissible

permisivo ADJ permissive

permiso M permission; (para faltar al servicio militar) furlough; (para faltar al trabajo) leave; (licencia) license, permit; **con —** excuse me

permitir VT (dar posibilidad moral) to permit, to allow; (dar posibilidad física) to enable; **—se** (una libertad) to take the liberty of; (un lujo) to allow oneself; **¿me permite?** may I cut in?

permuta F exchange

permutación F permutation

permutar VT to exchange

pernetas LOC ADV **en —** barelegged

pernicioso ADJ pernicious

pernicorto ADJ short-legged

perno M bolt, pin

pero CONJ but; ADV **muy — muy lindo** very, very pretty; M objection; **no hay — que valga** no buts about it

perogrullada F platitude

perorar VI to hold forth

perorata F lecture

peróxido M peroxide

perpendicular ADJ perpendicular

perpetrar VT to perpetrate

perpetuar[17] VT to perpetuate

perpetuo ADJ perpetual

perplejidad F perplexity, bewilderment

perplejo ADJ perplexed, bewildered; VT **dejar — to** perplex

perrera F (lugar donde guardar perros) pound; (rabieta) tantrum

perrero -ra MF dogcatcher; ADJ dog-loving

perro M dog; **— caliente** hot dog; **— cobrador** retriever; **— de caza** hunting dog; **— faldero** lapdog; **— callejero** stray dog; **— de lanas** poodle; **— esquimal** husky; **— guía** guide dog; **— guardián** watchdog, guard dog; **— pastor** sheepdog; **— policía** police dog; **hijo de —** vulg son of a bitch; ADJ miserable; **en la perra vida** never

perruno ADJ canine

persa ADJ & MF Persian; M (lengua) Persian

persecución F (religiosa) persecution; (acción de seguir) pursuit, chase

perseguidor -ora MF (que sigue) pursuer; (que acosa) persecutor

perseguir[5,12] VT (seguir para alcanzar) to pursue, to chase; (seguir para encontrar) to track down; (acosar) to hound; (tratar de destruir) to persecute

perseverancia F perseverance

perseverar VI to persevere

persiana F blind, shade

persistencia F persistence

persistente ADJ persistent

persistir VI to persist

persona F person; **— legal** legal entity; **en**

— in person; **— mayor** adult

personaje M (persona importante) personage; (de obra literaria) character; **es todo un — he's** quite a character

personal ADJ personal; M personnel, staff

personalidad F personality

personificar[6] VT to personify, to embody

perspectiva F (punto de vista, distancia, técnica de representación) perspective; (panorama) view, vista; (posibilidad) prospect; **tener en — to** have planned

perspicacia F insight, sharpness

perspicaz ADJ perspicacious, perceptive

persuadir VT to persuade

persuasión F persuasion

persuasivo ADJ persuasive

pertenecer[13] VI to belong

perteneciente ADJ belonging

pertenencias F PL belongings

pértiga F pole

pertinente ADJ pertinent, relevant

pertrechos M PL military supplies

perturbación F disturbance

perturbar VT to perturb, to disturb

Perú M Peru

peruano -na ADJ & MF Peruvian

perversidad F (distorsión) perversity; (maldad) wickedness

perversión F perversion

perverso ADJ (distorsionante) perverse; (malvado) wicked

pervertido -da MF pervert

pervertir[3] VT (hacer vicioso) to pervert; (alterar negativamente) to distort; **—se** to become perverted

pesa F weight; **—s y medidas** weights and measures

pesadez F (cualidad de pesado) heaviness; (tedio) tiresomeness; (persona pesada) tiresome person

pesadilla F nightmare

pesado -da ADJ (que pesa mucho, difícil de digerir) heavy; (aburrido) tiresome; (robusto) heavy-set; (tardo) slow; MF bore, pest

pesadumbre F grief, sorrow

pésame M condolence, expression of sympathy

pesar VT (apenar) to sadden; (medir el peso de) to weigh; (recaer sobre) to weight down; VI (tener peso, importancia) to weigh; M grief, sorrow; LOC ADV **a — de** in spite of

pesaroso ADJ (triste) sad; (arrepentido) repentant

pesca F (acción de pescar) fishing; (lo pescado) catch; **ir de — to** go fishing

pescadería F fish market

pescado M fish

pescador -ora MF fisherman

pescar[6] VI/VT (capturar peces) to fish; (sacar del agua, coger, comprender, sorprender, pillar) to catch; (obtener) to land, to nail

pescozón M blow to the back of the head

pescuezo M neck

pesebre M (para pienso) manger, crib; (belén) nativity scene

peseta F peseta

pesimismo M pessimism

pesimista MF pessimist

pésimo ADJ dismal, wretched

peso M (fuerza, importancia) weight; (que oprime moralmente) burden; (cosa pesada) load; **vender al —** to sell by weight; **levantar en —** to lift off the ground

pesquería F fishery

pesquero ADJ fishing; M fishing boat

pesquisa F inquiry

pestaña F (del ojo) eyelash; (en costura) fringe; (de papel) tab; **quemarse las —s** to burn the midnight oil

pestañear VI to blink; **sin —** unflinchingly

pestañeo M blink

peste F (enfermedad) plague; (persona molesta) pest; (hedor) stench; **— bubónica** bubonic plague; **— negra** black death; **hablar —s de alguien** to speak badly of someone

pestilencia F pestilence

pestillo M deadbolt, latch

petaca F (para tabaco) tobacco pouch; (para whisky) flask

pétalo M petal

petardear VI to backfire

petardeo M backfire

petate M bundle; **liar el —** to pack up and go

petición F petition, request

peticionar VT to petition

petirrojo M robin

pétreo ADJ stony

petróleo M petroleum; **— crudo** crude oil

petrolera F oil company

petrolero M oil tanker

petulancia F smugness

petulante ADJ smug

petunia F petunia

peyorativo ADJ pejorative

peyote M peyote

pez M fish; **— dorado** goldfish; **— espada** sword fish; **— gordo** *fam* fat cat, big shot; **— vela** sail fish; **— volador** flying fish; **como — en el agua** perfectly at ease; F pitch

pezón M nipple

pezuña F hoof

piadoso ADJ pious, saintly

piafar VI to stamp

piano M piano; **— de cola** grand piano; **— vertical** upright piano

pianola F player piano

piar[16] VI to peep, to chirp

pica F (lanza) pike; (palo de baraja) spade

picada F (de insecto) bite; (de avión) nosedive; **bajar en —** to dive

picadillo M meat and vegetable hash

picado ADJ (mar) rough, choppy; (carne) chopped; (de viruela) pocked; M (de avión) nosedive

picador M picador; ADJ stinging

picadora F grinder

picadura F (de serpiente) bite; (de insecto) sting, bite

picante ADJ (obsceno) risqué; (especia) spicy, hot; (queso) sharp; M (especia fuerte) strong seasoning; (cualidad) spiciness

picar[6] VI/VT (un pez) to bite; (un ave) to peck; (comer en pequeñas cantidades) to nibble; VT (tomates) to chop up; (carne) to mince; (una vaca) to goad, to poke; (la curiosidad) to pique; (con espuelas) to spur; VI (una comida picante) to sting; (el sol) to burn; (la piel) to itch, to smart; (un avión) to dive; **— alto** to aim high; **— en** to border on; **—se** to spoil; **—se heroína** to shoot up heroin; **se pica el mar** the sea is getting rough; **se me picó un diente** I got a cavity; M SG **picapleitos** *pey* shyster; **picaporte** latch

picardía F mischief

picaresco ADJ picaresque

pícaro -ra MF rogue, rascal; ADJ roguish, mischievous

picazón F (en la piel) itch; (en la garganta) tickle

picea F spruce

pichi M jumper

pichón M (paloma) pigeon; (cría de ave) chick

picnic M picnic

pico M (de ave) beak, bill; (de montaña) peak; (herramienta) pick; (de tetera) spout; **cuarenta y —** forty-odd; **cerrar el —** to shut one's mouth; **tener el — de oro** to be very eloquent

pícolo M piccolo

picotazo M peck

picotear VI/VT (aves) to peck; (personas) to nibble

pídola F leapfrog

pie M (del cuerpo, de calcetín, de cama,

medida) foot; (de foto) caption; (de copa) stem; (de lámpara) stand; (de página) bottom; (para un actor) cue; (de árbol) trunk; (de mueble) leg; — **de atleta** athlete's foot; — **de autor** byline; — **de imprenta** printer's mark; **a** — on foot; **un soldado de** — a foot soldier; — **de banco** silly remark; **a** — **juntillas** firmly; **al** — **de la letra** to the letter; **caer de** — to have good luck; **con un** — **en el estribo** with one foot out of the door; **dar** — (a una crítica) to give rise to; (a un actor) to cue; **de / en**— standing; **en** — **de guerra** on the warpath; **estar de** — to be standing; **estar en** — **de igualdad con** to be on a par with; **esto no tiene ni** —**s ni cabeza** I can't make heads or tails of this; **ir a** — to walk; **perder** — to lose one's footing; **poner** —**s en polvorosa** to take a powder; **ponerse de** — to stand up

piedad F (cualidad de pío) piety; (misericordia) mercy; **tener** — to show mercy

piedra F stone; — **angular** cornerstone, keystone; — **caliza** limestone; — **de afilar** whetstone; — **de toque** touchstone; — **pómez** pumice; — **preciosa** gemstone; **ser** — **de escándalo** to be an object of scandal

piel F (humana) skin; (animal) hide, pelt; (prenda de piel) fur; — **de gallina** goose bumps; — **de naranja** cellulite

pienso M feed; **ni por** — no way

pierna F leg; — **de ternera** leg of lamb; **dormir a** — **suelta** to sleep like a log

pieza F (de artillería, de tela, de música, de teatro, mueble) piece; (habitación) room; **de una** — astonished; **menuda** — a piece of work

pífano M fife

pifia F goof, miscue

pifiar VT to goof up, to miscue

pigmento M pigment

pigmeo -a MF pygmy

pija F *vulg* cock, dick

pijama M pajamas

pila F (recipiente) basin; (bautismal) baptismal font; (cúmulo) pile, heap, stack; (generador) battery; — **atómica** atomic reactor

pilar M pillar

píldora F pill; —**s para dormir** sleeping pills

pillaje M pillage, plunder

pillar VT (saquear) to pillage, to plunder; (atrapar, coger) to catch; (en el juego infantil) to tag

pillo -lla ADJ (travieso) naughty; (taimado) sly; MF (adulto) scoundrel; (niño) scamp

pilluelo -la MF urchin

pilón M (de fuente) large basin; (de puente) pylon

pilotar, pilotear VT to pilot, to fly

pilote M pile, stilt

piloto MF pilot; (llama pequeña de gas) pilot light; — **automático** autopilot; — **de pruebas** test pilot

pimentar VT to pepper

pimentero M pepper shaker

pimentón M paprika

pimienta F pepper; — **de cayena** red pepper; — **negra** black pepper

pimiento M pepper, bell pepper; — **verde** green pepper

pimpollo M (de rosa) rosebud; (de vid) shoot

PIN M PIN

pináculo M pinnacle

pinar M pine grove

pincel M artist's brush

pincelada F stroke; **dar las últimas** —**s** to put on the final touches

pinchadura F flat tire

pinchar VT to prick, to puncture; (apuñalar) to poke; (inyectar) to inject; (intervenir un teléfono) to wiretap; (provocar) to needle; VI to have a flat; **ni corta ni pincha** he doesn't count; M SG **pinchadiscos** disk jockey, DJ

pinchazo M (acción de pinchar) puncture, prick; (neumático) flat tire; (puñalada) stab; (de teléfono) wiretap

pincho M (palo afilado) spike; (de rotisería) spit

pingajo M (harapo) tatter; (persona harapienta) person dressed in rags

ping-pong M ping-pong

pingüe ADJ abundant

pingüino M penguin

pino M (árbol) pine; (ejercicio) handstand; **en el quinto** — in the boondocks

pinta F (mancha) dot; (aspecto) looks; (medida de líquidos) pint

pintar VT (colorear) to paint; (describir) to depict; **este marcador no pinta** this marker won't write; **no** — **nada** to count for nothing; **las cosas no pintaban bien** things did not look well; —**se** to put on makeup

pintarrajear VT to daub, to smear with paint

pinto ADJ paint, dapple(d)

pintor -ora MF painter; — **de brocha gorda** house painter

pintoresco ADJ picturesque, colorful

pintorrear VT to smear with paint

pintura F (acción de pintar, obra) painting; (sustancia) paint; — **al óleo** oil painting; — **en aerosol** spray paint; — **fresca** wet paint

pinza F (de cangrejo) claw; (de vestido) dart; (instrumento) clothespin; —**s** tweezers

piña F (fruto del pino) pine cone; (ananás) pineapple; (bomba) hand grenade

piñata F piñata

piñón M (semilla del pino) pine nut; (rueda del engranaje) pinion; (de bicicleta) sprocket

pío ADJ pious; INTERJ peep; **ni** — not a word

piojo M louse; **como** —**s en costura** like sardines

piojoso ADJ lousy

pionero -ra MF pioneer

pipa F pipe; (semilla) sunflower seed; **pasarlo** — to have a great time

pipí M pee; **hacer** — *fam* to pee

pipiolo -la MF novice

pique M (rivalidad) rivalry; (desavenencia) falling-out; **echar a** — to sink; **irse a** — to capsize

piquete M picket

piragua F dugout canoe

pirámide F pyramid

pirata MF INV pirate

piratear VT to pirate

pirómano -na MF pyromaniac

piropo M compliment

pirotecnia F pyrotechnics

pirulí M sucker, lollipop

pisada F (paso) footstep; (huella) footprint; **seguir las** —**s de** to follow in the footsteps of

pisar VT (oprimir con el pie) to step on, to tread on; (apisonar) to mash; **jamás pisó una plaza de toros** he never set foot in a bullfight; **ir pisando huevos** to walk on eggshells; M SG **pisapapeles** paperweight; VI to step on; — **fuerte** to throw one's weight around

piscifactoría F fishery

piscina F swimming pool

piso M (suelo) floor; (planta) story; (vivienda) apartment; **de** — **a techo** from the ground up

pisotear VT to tramp on, to trample, to stomp on

pisotón M stamp; **dar un** — to stamp

pista F (rastro) track, scent; (noticia) clue; (de aterrizaje) runway; (de circo) arena, ring; (de patinaje) skating ring; (de tenis) court; (de baile) floor; (de carreras) track, racetrack; **seguir la** — to track; — **para bicicletas** bike lane

pistola F pistol; (para pintura) gun

pistolera F holster

pistolero M gunman

pistón M piston; (explosivo) cap

pitada F drag, puff

pitar VI to toot, to whistle; VI/VT (rechiflar) to boo

pitazo M honk

pitido M whistle, toot

pitillo M cigarette

pito M (silbato) whistle; (pene) *fam* dick; **no vale un** — *fam* it is not worth a damn; **entre** —**s y flautas** when all is said and done; **¿qué** —**s toca?** what's his role here?

pitón M (serpiente) python; (punta de cuerno) tip of a bull's horn

pituitario ADJ pituitary

pivotar VI to pivot

pivote M pivot; — **central** kingpin

píxel M pixel

pizarra F (roca) slate; (tablero de escuela) blackboard, chalkboard

pizarrón M blackboard, chalkboard

pizca F (de sal) pinch, dash; (de evidencia) shred; (de verdad) grain; (de suciedad) speck; **no entiendo ni** — I don't understand a bit/jot

pizza F pizza

placa F (fotográfica) plate; (de policía) badge; (condecoración, dental) plaque; (de coche) license plate; (de computadora) board, card

placaje M tackle

placar[6] VI/VT to tackle

placebo M placebo

placenta F placenta, afterbirth

placentero ADJ pleasant

placer[37] M pleasure, enjoyment; VT *lit* to please

plácido ADJ placid

plaf INTERJ plop

plaga F plague; (persona, insecto) pest

plagar[7] VT to infest; —**se de** to become infested with

plagio M plagiarism

plan M (proyecto) plan; (ligue) pickup; — **de estudios** curriculum; **se vistió en** — **de vampiresa** she was dressed to kill

plana F newspaper page; — **mayor** top brass; **enmendar la** — **a uno** to correct a person's mistakes

plancha F (electrodoméstico) iron; (lámina) metal plate; (parrilla) griddle; **hacer la** — to float; **tirarse una** — to fall flat on

one's face
planchado M ironing
planchar VT to iron, to press; **me dejó planchado** it left me speechless
plancton M plankton
planeador M glider
planear VI/VT to plan; VI (volar) to glide, to plane; VT (madera) to plane
planeo M gliding
planeta M planet
planetario M planetarium
planificar[6] VI/VT to plan
planilla F payroll; *Am* **— de cálculo** spreadsheet
plano ADJ flat, even; M (superficie) plane; (de un edificio) plan; (de calles) map; **— inclinado** inclined plane; **caer de —** to fall flat; **de —** flatly; **primer —** foreground
planta F (vegetal) plant; (del pie) sole; **— baja** ground floor
plantación F plantation
plantar VT (una planta, cruz) to plant; (a un novio) to dump; (a un colega) to make wait; **—se** to stand firm, to refuse to move; **— a alguien una bofetada** to give someone a slap; **dejar plantado** to stand up
plantear VT (presentar) to present; **me planteó sus planes** she explained her plans to me; (provocar) to give rise to; **eso plantea un problema** that gave rise to a problem; **—se** to occur to; **¿te has planteado lo que pasa si te quedas sin trabajo?** have you thought about what will happen if you become unemployed?
plantel M (personal) staff; (almáciga) nursery
plantilla F (pieza suelta) insole; (patrón) pattern, stencil
plantío M grove
plasma M plasma
plasta ADJ INV tiresome; F (cosa informe) lump; (persona) bore
plástico ADJ & M plastic
plata F (metal, color, objeto de plata) silver; *Am* money; **hablar en —** to speak in plain language
plataforma F platform (también política); **— de lanzamiento** launching pad; **— petrolífera** oil rig; **— continental** continental shelf
platanar M banana grove
plátano M (fruta) banana; (bananero) banana tree; (árbol ornamental) plane tree
platea F main floor of a theatre
plateado ADJ & M (color) silver; M (acción de platear) silver-plating
platear VT to silver-plate
platero -ra MF silversmith
plática F chat
platicar[6] VI to chat
platija F flounder
platillo M (plato pequeño) saucer; (instrumento musical) cymbal; **— volador** flying saucer
platino M platinum
plato M (recipiente) plate; (comida) dish; **— fuerte** main dish / course; **— hondo** bowl; **— sopero** soup dish
plausible ADJ plausible
playa F beach
playboy M playboy
plaza F (espacio amplio) plaza, public square; (puesto de trabajo) job; **de cuatro —s** four-seater; **— de toros** bullring; **— mayor** main square
plazo M term; **a corto —** short-term; **a largo —** long-term; **a — fijo** fixed-term; **a —s** on credit; **cumplir un —** to meet a deadline
plazoleta F court
plazuela F court
pleamar M high tide
plebe F rabble
plebeyo -ya ADJ & MF plebeian
plegable ADJ folding
plegadera F paper folder
plegadizo ADJ folding
plegar[1,7] VT to fold; **—se (a)** to yield (to)
pleitesía F compliance
pleito M dispute; (judicial) litigation, lawsuit; **poner —** to sue
plenario ADJ & M plenary
plenitud F **— de la vida** prime of life
pleno ADJ complete; **en — día** in broad daylight; **en — invierno** in the dead of winter; **en — rostro** right on the face; **en — verano** in midsummer; **en plena vista** in plain sight; M full session
pliego M leaflet
pliegue M (en papel) fold; (en tela) pleat
plomada F plumb
plomería F plumbing
plomero -ra MF plumber
plomizo ADJ leaden
plomo M (metal, color) lead; (pesos) lead weight; (perdigón) shot; **a —** plumb; **caer a —** to fall vertically; **sin —** unleaded; ADJ tiresome
pluma F (de ave) feather, quill; (para escribir) pen; **— fuente** fountain pen
plumaje M plumage
plumero M dust mop, duster

plumífero ADJ feathery
plumón M down
plural ADJ & M plural
pluralidad F plurality
pluscuamperfecto ADJ & N pluperfect
plutonio M plutonium
pluvial ADJ **aguas —es** rain water
pluviómetro M rain gauge
PNB (producto nacional bruto) M GNP
población F (conjunto de personas)
    population; (acción de poblar) settlement;
    (pueblo) town
poblado M hamlet
poblador -ora MF settler
poblar[2] VT (habitar) to populate; (colonizar)
    to settle; **—se** to become covered with
pobre ADJ poor; MF **los —s** the poor
pobrecito -ta MF poor thing
pobreza F poverty; (escasez) scarcity
pocilga F pigsty, pigpen
pocillo M cup
poción F potion
poco ADJ (no mucho) little; **poca paciencia**
    little patience; **al — rato** after a little
    while; (no muchos) few; **—s pasajeros**
    few passengers; **al — tiempo** shortly; **a
    los —s meses** after a few months; **como
    — at least; de pocas luces** stupid; **en
    pocas palabras** in a nutshell; ADV
    trabaja — he works little; **— caritativo**
    not very charitable; **— a —** little by little;
    — más o menos about; **hace — a** short
    while ago; **por — me caigo** I almost fell;
    tener en — to hold in low esteem; M a
    little, a bit; **un —** a little bit, a little while;
    unos —s a few
poda F trim
podadera F pruning hook
podar VT to prune, to trim
poder[38] VI to be able to; **no puedo llegar
    antes de las cinco** I can't get there
    before five; **¿puedo sentarme?** may I be
    seated? **puede que venga** she may come;
    a más no — to the utmost; **no puedo
    más** I can't go on; **nadie puede con
    ella** nobody can deal with her; **no puede
    menos que venir** he can't help but
    come; **no puede menos de hacerlo** he
    cannot help doing it; M (fuerza) power;
    (escrito que da autoridad) proxy, power of
    attorney; **— judicial** the judiciary
    branch; **por —** by proxy
poderío M power, might
poderoso ADJ powerful, mighty
podio M podium
podredumbre F rot
podrido ADJ rotten

podrir ver pudrir
poema M poem
poesía F poetry; (poema) poem
poeta -tisa MF poet
poética F poetics
poético ADJ poetic
polaco -ca ADJ Polish; M (lengua) Polish; MF
    Pole
polaina F legging
polar ADJ polar
polaridad F polarity
polarización F polarization
polca F polka
polea F pulley
polémica F polemic, controversy
polémico ADJ polemic
polen M pollen
poli MF cop; F cops
policía F (en conjunto) police; (mujer)
    policewoman; M policeman
policíaco ADJ police
poliéster M polyester
poliestireno M Styrofoam[tm]
poligamia F polygamy
políglota ADJ & MF INV polyglot
polígrafo M polygraph
poliinsaturado ADJ polyunsaturated
polilla F moth
polímero M polymer
polinizar[9] VT to pollinate
polio F polio
pólipo M polyp
política F (actividad relativa al gobierno)
    politics; (conjunto de orientaciones)
    policy; **— exterior** foreign policy
político -ca ADJ (relativo a la política)
    political; (diplomático) politic; MF
    politician
poliuretano M polyurethane
póliza F policy; **— de seguros** insurance
    policy
polizón M stowaway
polizonte M *pey* cop
polla F (cría de ave) pullet; (pene) *vulg* cock,
    dick; **y una —** *vulg* bullshit!
pollada F brood
pollera F woman who raises and sells
    chickens; *Am* skirt
pollo M (cría de ave) young chicken; (carne)
    chicken
polo M (extremo) pole; (juego) polo; **—
    acuático** water polo; **— de atención**
    focus of attention; **— Norte** North Pole
Polonia F Poland
poltrona F easy chair
polvareda F cloud of dust; **levantar una —**
    (causar escándalo) to raise a ruckus;

(causar una nube de polvo) to kick up the
dust
polvera F compact
polvo M (suciedad) dust; (partículas) powder;
(acto sexual) *vulg* screwing; **— de
hornear** baking powder; **echarse un —**
fam to get laid; **juntar —** to gather dust;
limpio de — y paja net
pólvora F gunpowder
polvoriento ADJ dusty
polvorín M (almacén de pólvora) magazine;
(situación explosiva) powder keg
pomada F salve
pomelo M grapefruit
pómez M pumice
pomo M doorknob
pompa F (boato) pomp; (burbuja) soap
bubble; **—s fúnebres** funeral
pomposo ADJ pompous
pómulo M cheekbone
ponche M punch
ponchera F punch bowl
poncho M poncho
ponderación F (acción de ponderar)
pondering; (valor relativo) weighting
ponderar VT (considerar) to ponder, to
consider; (exagerar) to exaggerate; (ajustar
estadísticas) to weight
ponencia F presentation
poner[39] VT to put, to place; (la mesa, un
reloj) to set; (huevos) to lay; (azúcar) to
add; (un examen) to give; (el televisor) to
turn on; (un pleito) to file; **— a alguien
a hacer algo** to have someone do
something; **— en claro** to clarify; **— en
limpio** to recopy, to make a clean copy;
—- nombre a un niño to name a child;
cada uno pone mil pesetas each
person contributes a thousand pesetas;
pongamos que let us suppose that; **—se**
(volverse) to become; (el sol) to set; (ropa)
to put on; (sexualmente) to get turned on;
—se a to begin to; **—se al corriente** to
become informed; **—se de acuerdo** to
come to an agreement; **—se de pie** to
stand up
póney M pony
poniente M (oeste) west; (viento del oeste)
west wind
pontón M pontoon
ponzoña F poison
ponzoñoso ADJ poisonous
pool M pool
popa F poop, stern
populacho M mob
popular ADJ (conocido y citado) popular;
(del pueblo) folk

popularidad F popularity
populoso ADJ populous
popurrí M potpourri; (musical) medley
por PREP **— barco** by boat; **— casualidad**
by chance; **— Dios** by God; **— etapas** by
stages; **— las buenas o — las malas** by
hook or by crook; **— litro** by the liter;
multiplicar — to multiply by; **lo
agarró por la mano** he grabbed him by
the throat; **mi amor — ella** my love for
her; **— poco tiempo** for a short time; **—
primera vez** for the first time; **— vía de
argumento** for the sake of argument; **—
ejemplo** for instance; **— el momento**
for the time being; **hazlo — mí** do it for
my sake; **trabaja — mí** work on my
behalf; **no me gustan — su olor** I don't
like them because of their smell; **lo supe
— él** I found out through him; **pasé —
Londres** I passed through London; **un
viaje — la costa** a trip along the coast;
— lo que cuentas from what you're
telling me; **— adelantado** in advance; **—
escrito** in writing; **— la mañana** in the
morning; **— lo general** in general; **—
rachas** in spurts; **está — Badajoz** it's
near Badajoz; **— fin** at last; **— el mes de
marzo** around the month of March; **—
ciento** percent; **— consiguiente**
consequently; **— escrito** in writing; **—
poco se muere** he almost died; **está —
hacer** it is yet to be done; **él está —
hacerlo** he is in favor of doing it;
recibir — esposa to take as a wife;
tener — to consider, to think of as; **¿—
qué?** why? for what reason?
porcelana F porcelain, china
porcentaje M percentage
porche M porch, stoop
porcino ADJ **ganado —** swine; M pig
porción F (parte) portion, share; (de
alimento) helping
pordiosear VT to panhandle
pordiosero -ra MF panhandler
porfía F obstinacy
porfiado ADJ willful
porfiar[16] VT to insist
pormenor M detail
pormenorizar[9] VT to detail, to go into
detail about
pornografía F pornography
pornográfico ADJ pornographic
poro M pore
poroso ADJ porous
poroto M *Am* bean
porque CONJ because
porqué M why

porquería F (suciedad) filth; (acción despreciable) dirty trick; (cosa de mala calidad) crud; (comida de mala calidad) junk food; (persona despreciable) *pey* douchebag, dirtbag

porra F club, cudgel

porrista MF cheerleader

porro M joint

portada F title page

portador -ora MF (de enfermedad) carrier; (de cheque) bearer; **— del féretro** pallbearer

portal M portal, doorway

portar VT to carry; **—se** to behave; **—se mal** to misbehave; M SG **portaaviones** aircraft carrier; **portaequipajes** luggage bin; **portaestandarte** standard-bearer; **portafolio** briefcase; **portalámparas** socket; **portaligas** garter belt; **portamonedas** coin purse; **portaobjeto** slide

portátil ADJ portable

portavoz MF spokesperson

portazo M slam; **dar un —** to slam the door

porte M (envío) freight; (por correo) postage; (aspecto) bearing, carriage; (capacidad de carga) capacity; (tamaño) size; **— de armas** the carrying of arms; **enviar — pagado** to send prepaid

portear VT to carry

portentoso ADJ portentous

portería F (de un edificio) entrance area; (en fútbol) goal

portero -ra MF (de un edificio) doorkeeper, superintendent; (en fútbol) goalkeeper; M **— automático** intercom

portón M gate

Portugal M Portugal

portugués -esa ADJ & MF Portuguese; M (lengua) Portuguese

porvenir M future

pos LOC PREP **en — de** after

posada F inn, lodge

posaderas F PL *fam* rear end

posadero -ra MF innkeeper

posar VT (la mano, los ojos) to rest; VI (en el suelo) to sit down; (como modelo) to pose; **—se** (partículas) to settle; (mariposa) to alight; (pájaro) to perch

posdata F postscript

pose F pose

poseedor -ora MF possessor

poseer[14] VT to possess

posesión F possession

posesivo ADJ & M possessive

posibilidad F possibility

posible ADJ possible; **hacer lo —** to do one's best; **es —** it's possible

posición F position; (opinión) stance; (rango) standing; **— del misionero** missionary position; **— fetal** fetal position

positivo ADJ & M positive

poso M dregs; (de café) grounds

posponer[39] VT (aplazar) to postpone, to defer, to put off; (relegar) to put after

posta F (relevo) relay; (perdigón) buckshot

postal ADJ postal; F (tarjeta) postcard

poste M post; (de portería) upright

póster M poster

postergar[7] VT to neglect

posteridad F posterity

posterior ADJ (en el espacio) back, rear; (anatómico) posterior; (temporal) later; **nuestro divorcio fue posterior a nuestra boda** our divorce came after our wedding

postigo M shutter

postizo ADJ false; **familia postiza** adoptive family; M hairpiece

postrado ADJ prostrate, prone

postrar VT to prostrate

postre M dessert; **a la —** at last

postulado M postulate

postulante MF candidate

postular VT to postulate

póstumo ADJ posthumous

postura F posture (también opinión)

potable ADJ drinkable, potable

potasio M potassium

pote M (cilíndrico) jar; (panzudo) jug

potencia F (sexual) potency; (de una fuerza, nación) power; **es un asesino en —** he's a potential murderer; **— naval** sea power; **de alta —** high-powered; **segunda —** the second power

potencial ADJ & M potential

potentado -da MF potentate

potente ADJ potent, powerful

potranco -ca M colt; F filly

potrero M pasture; *Am* cattle ranch, stock farm

potro M (caballo) colt; (en gimnasia) vaulting horse; **— de tormento** rack

pozo M (de agua, petróleo) well; (hoyo profundo) pit; (minero) mine shaft; **sacar del —** to rescue; **— negro** sink; **— sin fondo** bottomless pit; **— séptico** septic tank

práctica F (repetición, costumbre) practice; (destreza) skill; **en la —** in practice; **poner en —** to put into practice

practicante ADJ practicing; MF (que practica) practitioner; (asistente de médico) physician's assistant

practicar[6] VI/VT to practice; (un agujero) to make
práctico ADJ practical; (adiestrado) skillful; M **— de puerto** harbor pilot
pradera F prairie, grassland
prado M meadow, pasture
pragmático ADJ pragmatic
preadolescente ADJ & MF preteen, preadolescent
preámbulo M preamble
precalentamiento M warmup
precario ADJ precarious
precaución F precaution
precaverse VT to take precautions
precavido ADJ cautious
precedencia F precedence
precedente ADJ preceding; M precedent; **sin — ** unprecedented; **sentar — ** to set a precedent
preceder VI/VT to precede
precepto M precept
preciado ADJ (estimado) prized; (valioso) valuable
preciarse VI **— de** to be proud of
precintar VT to seal
precinto M seal
precio M price; **poner — a** to put a price on; **no tener — ** to be priceless; **— de lista** list price; **— de mercado** market price
preciosista ADJ precious
precioso ADJ (de gran valor, metal, piedra) precious; (muy bonito) beautiful, adorable
precipicio M precipice, cliff
precipitación F precipitation (también atolondramiento)
precipitado ADJ precipitate, hasty, rash; M precipitate
precipitar VI to precipitate; VT to hurl; **—se** (apresurarse) to be hasty; (arrojarse) to plunge, to plummet; (depositarse) to precipitate; (adelantarse) to come to a head
precisar VT (determinar) to determine precisely; (necesitar) to need
precisión F precision, accuracy; **precisiones** clarifications
preciso ADJ precise, accurate; **es — que vengas** you must come; **en este — instante** at this very moment
precoz ADJ (niño) precocious; (diagnóstico) early
precursor -ora MF precursor, forerunner
predecesor -ora MF predecessor
predecir[26b] VT to predict, to foretell
predestinar VT to predestine
predicación F preaching
predicado ADJ & M predicate

predicador -ora MF preacher
predicar[6] VI/VT to preach
predicción F prediction
predilección F predilection
predilecto ADJ favorite, pet
predisponer[39] VT to predispose
predominante ADJ predominant, prevailing
predominar VI to predominate
predominio M predominance
preeminente ADJ foremost
preescolar ADJ nursery; MF nursery school child
preestreno M preview
prefacio M preface
preferencia F preference; (en el tráfico) right of way; **de — ** predominately
preferente ADJ preferential; (acciones) preferred
preferible ADJ preferable
preferido ADJ preferred, favorite
preferir[3] VT to prefer
prefijar VT to prefix
prefijo M prefix
pregonar VT (noticias) to make public; (mercancías) to hawk
pregunta F question; **hacer una — ** to ask a question
preguntar VI/VT to ask, to inquire; **— por** (pedir información) to inquire about; (pedir para hablar) to ask for; **—se** to wonder
preguntón ADJ inquisitive
prehistórico ADJ prehistoric
prejuicio M prejudice, bias
prejuzgar[7] VT to prejudge
preliminar ADJ & M preliminary
preludiar VT to prelude
preludio M prelude
prematrimonial ADJ premarital
prematuro ADJ premature; (muerte) untimely
premeditado ADJ premeditated
premiar VT to reward; **las obras premiadas** the award-winning works
première M premiere
premio M (galardón) prize, award; (de la moneda) appreciation; **Juan Pérez, — nacional de poesía** Juan Pérez, winner of the national poetry award; **— gordo** jackpot
premisa F premise
premonición F premonition
prenatal ADJ prenatal
prenda F (fianza) pawn, pledge; (de vestir) article of clothing, garment; **dejar en — ** to pawn; **en — de** as a token of
prendar VT to charm; **—se de** to fall in love

with
prendedor M brooch, pin
prender VT (agarrar) to grab; (sujetar) to clasp; (enganchar) to fasten; (detener) to arrest; (arraigar) to take root; (encender) to turn on, to switch on; — **fuego** to set on fire; **la vacuna no prendió** the vaccination didn't take
prensa F press; **tener mala** — to have bad press
prensar VT to press
prensil ADJ prehensile
prenupcial ADJ prenuptial
preñada ADJ pregnant
preñar VT *vulg* to knock up
preñez F pregnancy
preocupación F worry, concern
preocupado ADJ worried, concerned, anxious
preocupante ADJ worrisome
preocupar VT to worry, to concern; **—se de** to worry about; **—se por** to be concerned about
preocupón -ona MF worrywart
preparación F preparation
preparado ADJ ready; M preparation
preparar VT to prepare; **—se** to get ready, to brace oneself
preparativo ADJ preparatory; M preparation
preparatorio ADJ preparatory
preponderancia F preponderance
preponderante ADJ preponderant
preponderar VI to predominate
preposición F preposition
prepucio M foreskin
prerequisito M prerequisite
prerrogativa F prerogative
presa F (animal de caza) prey, quarry; (dique) dam
presagiar VT to forebode
presagio M omen, sign
présbita ADV & MF INV farsighted
prescindible ADJ dispensable
prescindir VI — **de** to dispense with
prescribir[51] VT to prescribe
prescripción F prescription
presencia F presence; — **de ánimo** presence of mind
presenciar VT to witness
presentable ADJ presentable
presentación F presentation; (a una persona) introduction
presentador -ora MF (de televisión) host; (de noticiero) anchor
presentar VT to present; (a una persona) to introduce; (la declaración de impuestos, una demanda) to file; (un informe) to submit; (documentos) to produce; (una

queja) to lodge; (una renuncia) to tender; **—se** (aparecer) to appear; (hacerse conocer) to introduce oneself
presente ADJ present; M (tiempo) present; (regalo) present, gift; **al** — at the present time; **tener** — to bear in mind; **en el** — (**contrato**) herein; **por la** — (**carta**) hereby
presentimiento M presentiment, foreboding, hunch
presentir[3] VT to have a presentiment of
preservación F (protección) preservation; (ahorro) conservation
preservar VT (proteger) to preserve; (ahorrar) to conserve
preservativo M condom
presidencia F presidency
presidencial ADJ presidential
presidente -ta MF (de un país) president; (de una reunión, junta) chair
presidiario -ria MF prisoner
presidio M prison
presidir VI to preside; VT to preside over
presilla F loop
presión F pressure; — **atmosférica** atmospheric pressure; — **arterial** blood pressure; — **de aire** air pressure
presionar VT (un botón) to press; (al gobierno) to lobby
preso -sa MF prisoner, inmate
prestación F provision; **prestaciones** benefits
prestador -ora MF lender
prestamista MF lender; (en un montepío) pawnbroker
préstamo M loan
prestar VT to loan, to lend; — **ayuda** to give help; — **atención** to pay attention; — **juramento** to take an oath; — **servicio** to render service
prestatario -ria MF borrower
prestidigitación F sleight of hand
prestigio M prestige
prestigioso ADJ prestigious
presumido ADJ conceited, presumptuous
presumir VT (suponer) to presume; VI (ostentar) to show off; — **de valiente** to boast of one's valor
presunción F presumption
presunto ADJ (autor) presumed; (asesino) alleged; — **heredero** heir apparent
presuntuoso ADJ presumptuous
presuponer[39] VT to presuppose
presupuesto M (de gastos e ingresos) budget; (de costo) estimate
presuroso ADJ hasty
pretencioso ADJ pretentious

pretender VI (sostener) to claim, to purport;
— **ser** to claim to be; — **al trono** to
pretend to the throne; VT (intentar) to
attempt

pretendiente -ta MF (al trono) pretender; (a
un puesto) aspirant; M (de una mujer)
suitor, admirer

pretensión F pretension

pretérito ADJ past; M past tense; — **perfecto**
present perfect

pretexto M pretext, pretense; **so — de** under
pretense of

pretil M railing

pretina F waistband

prevalecer[13] VI to prevail

prevaleciente ADJ prevalent

prevención F (protección) prevention;
(recelo) caution

prevenido ADJ forewarned

prevenir[47] VT (precaver) to prevent; (prever)
to foresee; (advertir) to warn; — **contra**
to protect oneself against

preventivo ADJ preventive

prever[48] VT to foresee, to anticipate

previo ADJ previous, prior; — **examen de
salud** after undergoing a health
examination

previsión F foresight, anticipation

prieto ADJ swarthy

prima F (cuota de seguro) premium; (recargo)
surcharge; (pago extraordinario) bonus

primario ADJ primary

primate M primate

primavera F spring

primaveral ADJ springlike

primero ADJ & ADV first; **primer ministro**
prime minister; — **piso** second floor;
primer plano foreground; **primera
enseñanza** primary education; **primera
persona** first person; —**s auxilios** first
aid; **a primera vista** at first sight; **de —
grado** first degree; **de primera** top-
notch; **de primera mano** firsthand; **por
primera vez** for the first time; — **del
mes** first of the month; F (marcha) first
gear; (clase) first-class

primicia F (fruto primero) first fruit; (noticia)
scoop

primitivo ADJ primitive

primo -ma MF (hijo de tío) cousin; (persona
incauta) sucker, dupe; — **hermano** first
cousin; — **segundo** second cousin; ADJ
prime

primogénito -ta ADJ & MF firstborn

primogenitura F birthright

primor M (esmero) care; (cosa fina) lovely
thing

primordial ADJ primordial

primoroso ADJ exquisite

princesa F princess

principal ADJ principal, main; **la causa —
de muerte** the leading cause of death; **el
dormitorio —** the master bedroom

príncipe M prince

principesco ADJ princely

principiante MF beginner; ADJ beginning

principiar VT to commence

principio M (fundamento, regla de
conducta) principle, tenet; (hecho de
empezar, tiempo, lugar) beginning, start; **a
—s de** towards the beginning of; —
activo active ingredient; **al —** at the
beginning, at first; **de — a fin** from
beginning to end; **desde el —** from the
beginning; **en —** in principle

pringar[7] VT (ensuciar) to get greasy; (mojar)
to dip

pringoso ADJ greasy

pringue MF grease

prioridad F (autoridad, preferencia) priority,
precedence; (en el tráfico) right of way

prisa F haste, hurry; **a toda —** at full speed;
correr — to be urgent; **darse —** to
hurry; **las —s comienzan a la una** the
rush starts at one; **tener —** to be in a
hurry; **sin —** leisurely

prisión F prison; — **perpetua** life in prison

prisionero -ra MF prisoner; — **de guerra**
prisoner of war

prisma M prism

prismáticos M PL binoculars

privacidad F privacy

privación F privation; **pasar privaciones**
to suffer want

privado ADJ private; **en —** in private

privar VT to deprive; —**se de** to deprive
oneself of

privativo ADJ exclusive

privilegiado ADJ privileged

privilegiar VT to favor, to give a privilege to

privilegio M privilege

pro M advantage; **en — de** in favor of; **en —
y en contra** for and against

proa F prow, bow

proaborto ADJ pro-choice

probabilidad F probability; **tienes pocas
—es de ganar** you have little chance of
winning; **¿qué —es tiene?** what are her
odds?

probable ADJ probable, likely

probador M dressing room

probar[2] VT (alimento, bebida) to taste, to
try, to sample; (una hipótesis) to prove;
(una guitarra) to try out; (un coche) to

test-drive; **—se un vestido** to try on a dress; **prueba a venir más temprano** try to come earlier; **no — bocado** not to eat a bite; **— fortuna** to try one's luck

probeta F test tube

problema M problem; **él sólo da —s** he's nothing but trouble

problemático ADJ problematic

procedente ADJ **— de** from

proceder VI to proceed; **— de** to come from; **— a** to proceed to; **— contra** to take action against

procedimiento M procedure; **—s** proceedings

procesado -da MF accused; M processing

procesamiento M prosecution; **— de datos** data processing; **— de textos** word processing

procesar VT to prosecute, to try

procesión F procession; **la — va por dentro** he doesn't let it show

proceso M (conjunto de fases) process; (juicio) trial, legal proceedings

proclama F proclamation

proclamación F proclamation

proclamar VT to proclaim; **—se campeón** to be proclaimed winner

proclive ADJ prone

procrear VI/VT to procreate

procurador -ora MF attorney

procurar VT (intentar) to endeavor; (obtener) to procure, to obtain

prodigar[7] VT to lavish; **—se** to be lavish

prodigio M prodigy

prodigioso ADJ prodigious

pródigo -ga ADJ (derrochador) prodigal; (muy generoso) lavish; MF spendthrift

producción F (acción de producir) production; (cantidad producida) production, yield; **— masiva** mass production

producir[24] VT (efectos, mercancías, películas) to produce; (fruta, resultados) to yield, to bear; **—se** to happen

productivo ADJ productive

producto M product; **— interno bruto** gross national product

productor -ora MF producer; ADJ **un país — de petróleo** an oil-producing country

proeza F exploit

profanación F desecration

profanar VT to profane, to desecrate

profano ADJ profane

profecía F prophecy

proferir[3] VT to utter

profesar VT to profess

profesión F profession

profesional ADJ & MF professional

profesionista MF *Méx* professional

profesor -ora MF (universitario) professor; (de enseñanza secundaria) teacher; (de tenis, perros) instructor

profesorado M faculty

profeta MF INV prophet

profético ADJ prophetic

profetizar[9] VI/VT to prophesy

profilaxis F prevention

prófugo -ga ADJ & MF fugitive

profundidad F (del mar, de comprensión, de un armario) depth; (sabiduría) profundity

profundizar[9] VT to deepen; VI to do into deeply

profundo ADJ (trascendente) profound; (mar, pozo, armario, voz) deep

profuso ADJ profuse

progesterona F progesterone

programa M (de boxeo) card; (de televisión) show, program; (de un curso) syllabus

programación F programming

programador -ora MF programmer

programar VT (una computadora) to program; (un evento) to schedule

progresar VT to progress, to advance

progresista ADJ & MF progressive

progresivo -va ADJ & MF progressive

progreso M progress

prohibición F prohibition, ban

prohibido ADJ forbidden; **prohibida la entrada** no admittance

prohibir VT to prohibit, to ban; **se prohibe fumar** no smoking

prohijar VT to adopt

prójimo -ma MF fellow human

prole F offspring

proletariado M proletariat

proletario -ria ADJ & MF proletarian

proliferación F spread

prolífico ADJ prolific

prolijo ADJ (verboso) wordy; (esmerado) overly careful

prologar[7] VT to preface

prólogo M prologue, foreword, preface

prolongación F prolongation

prolongado ADJ extended

prolongar[7] VT to prolong; **—se** to wear on

promediar VT to average

promedio M average, mean; **de / en —** on average

promesa F promise; **romper una —** to break a promise; **un joven —** a promising young player

prometedor ADJ promising

prometer VT to promise; VI to show promise; **—se** to trust that

prometido -da ADJ engaged; M fiancé; F
fiancée
prominente ADJ prominent
promiscuo ADJ promiscuous
promisorio ADJ promissory
promoción F promotion; (conjunto de
personas) class
promocionar VT to promote
promontorio M promontory
promotor -ora MF promoter
promover[2] VT (ideas, producto, a un
alumno) to promote; (mutua
comprensión, una causa) to foster, to
further
promulgación F enactment
promulgar[7] VT to promulgate, to enact
pronombre M pronoun
pronominal ADJ pronominal
pronosticar[6] VT to forecast
pronóstico M (del tiempo, de la economía)
forecast; (de una enfermedad) prognosis
pronto ADJ (rápido) quick; (listo) ready; ADV
soon, promptly; **de —** suddenly; **¡hasta
—!** see you soon! **tan — como** as soon as
pronunciación F pronunciation
pronunciado ADJ pronounced
pronunciar VT (un sonido, una sentencia) to
pronounce; (un discurso) to make, to
deliver; **—se** (acusarse) to be pronounced;
(expresarse) to declare one's opinion
propagación F propagation, spread
propaganda F (de ideas) propaganda; (de
mercancías) advertising, publicity; **hacer
—** to advertise
propagar[7] VT to propagate
propalar VT to spread
propano M propane
propasarse VI to go too far
propensión F propensity
propenso ADJ prone
propiciar VT to favor
propicio ADJ propitious, auspicious
propiedad F (cualidad, pertenencia, finca)
property; (derecho de dueño) ownership;
(corrección) precision; **—es** estate
propietario -ria M (de una tienda)
proprietor, owner; (de un apartamento)
landlord; F (de una tienda) owner; (de un
apartamento) landlady
propina F tip, gratuity; **dar (una) —** to tip
propinar VT **— una paliza** to give a
beating
propio ADJ (correcto) proper; **el significado
—** the proper meaning; (típico) like; **no es
— de él quejarse así** it's not like him to
complain like that; (conveniente)
appropriate; **una expresión propia** an

appropriate expression; (que le pertenece)
own; **su — hijo** his own son; **un hijo —**
a son of his own; **por tu — bien** for your
own good; (mismo) same; **al — tiempo**
at the same time
proponente MF proponent
proponer[39] VT to propose; **—se** to set out to
proporción F proportion, ratio;
proporciones dimensions
proporcionar VT (ajustar a proporción) to
proportion; (brindar) to furnish, to
provide
proposición F proposition; (de matrimonio)
proposal; **proposiciones deshonestas**
indecent proposals
propósito M purpose, intent; **a —** (adecuado)
apropos; (voluntariamente) on purpose,
intentionally; (además) by the way,
incidentally; **a — de** apropos of
propuesta F proposal
propugnar VT to urge
propulsar VT to propel
propulsión F propulsion; **— a chorro** jet
propulsion
propulsor -ora ADJ propelling; MF promoter
prorratear VT to prorate
prórroga F (plazo) extension of time; (de un
préstamo) renewal; (de un encuentro
deportivo) overtime
prorrogar[7] VT (un pago) to put off, to defer;
(un tiempo) to extend; (un préstamo) to
renew
prorrumpir VI to burst; **— en llanto** to
burst into tears; **— en carcajadas** to
burst out laughing
prosa F prose
prosaico ADJ prosaic
proscribir[51] VT to banish, to disenfranchise
proscripción F banishment
proseguir[5,12] VI to proceed
prosódico ADJ prosodic
prospectar VT to prospect
prospector -ora MF prospector
prosperar VI to prosper, to flourish, to thrive
prosperidad F prosperity
próspero ADJ prosperous
próstata F prostate (gland)
prostituir[31] VT to prostitute
prostituta F prostitute
protagonista MF protagonist
protagonizar[9] VT to star in
protección F protection
proteccionista ADJ & MF protectionist
protector -ora ADJ protective; MF protector;
— de tensión surge protector; **— solar**
sunblock
protectorado M protectorate

proteger[11b] VT to protect; (a un artista) to sponsor

protegido -da MF protégé(e)

proteína F protein

prótesis F prosthesis

protesta F protest

protestante MF Protestant

protestar VI/VT to protest

protocolo M protocol

protón M proton

protoplasma M protoplasm

prototipo M prototype

protozoario M protozoan

protuberancia F protuberance, bulge, bump

protuberante ADJ bulging

provecho M (beneficio) benefit; (eructo) burp; **¡buen —!** bon appétit! **sacar — (de)** to benefit (from), to profit (from)

provechoso ADJ beneficial, advantageous

proveedor -ora MF provider

proveer[14,51] VT to provide; **— de** to provide with; **—se de** to provide oneself with

provenir[47] VI to arise; **— de** to stem from

proverbio M proverb

providencia F providence

providencial ADJ providential

provincia F province

provincial ADJ provincial

provinciano -na ADJ & MF provincial

provisión F provision, supply, store

provisional ADJ temporary, provisional

provisorio ADJ temporary

provocación F provocation

provocar[6] VT (ira) to provoke; (sexualmente) to excite; (un incendio) to start; (una respuesta) to elicit

provocativo ADJ provocative

proxeneta MF pander, pimp

proximidad F proximity, nearness; **en las —es** in the vicinity

próximo ADJ (después) next; (cercano) near, nearby; **el lunes — pasado** last Monday; **de próxima aparición** forthcoming

proyección F projection

proyectar VT to project; (una película) to screen; (una sombra) to cast; **—se** to overhang, to jut

proyectil M projectile

proyecto M project; (arquitectónico) plan; **— de ley** bill

proyector M (para películas) projector; (en el teatro) spotlight

prudencia F prudence

prudente ADJ prudent

prueba F (de imprenta, argumento irrefutable) proof; (argumento parcial) evidence; (intento, dificultad) trial, test;

(examen) examination; (de ropa) fitting; **a — de incendio** fireproof; **— de fuego** trial by fire; **poner — a** to put to the test

psicodélico ADJ & M psychedelic

psicología F psychology

psicológico ADJ psychological

psicólogo -ga MF psychologist

psicópata MF INV psychopath

psicosis F psychosis

psicosomático ADJ psychosomatic

psicoterapia F psychotherapy

psicótico ADJ psychotic

psiquiatra MF INV psychiatrist

psiquiatría F psychiatry

psíquico ADJ psychic

psoriasis F psoriasis

púa F (con punta aguda) spike; (de alambre) barb; (de guitarra) pick; (de erizo) quill; (de horca) prong

puaf, puaj INTERJ yuck, ugh

pubertad F puberty

publicación F publication

publicar[6] VT to publish; (revelar) to divulge

publicidad F publicity, advertising; **hacer —** to advertise

público ADJ public; M (la gente) public; (en un espectáculo) audience; **en —** in public

puchero M (vasija) pot; (gesto) pout; **hacer —s** to pout

puck M puck

pudiente ADJ wealthy

pudor M (sexual) modesty; (reserva) reserve

pudrir[5] VI to rot

pueblerino ADJ provincial

pueblo M (población) town; (nación) people, folk

puente M bridge (también dental, de gafas, de nariz); (fin de semana) long weekend; **— aéreo** (regular) shuttle; (de emergencia) airlift; **— colgante** suspension bridge; **— levadizo** drawbridge

puénting M bungee jumping

pueril ADJ childish

puerta F door; (de aeropuerto, de ciudad) gate; (medio de acceso) entrance; **vender de — en —** to sell door-to-door; **dar a alguien con la — en las narices** to slam the door in someone's face; **llamar a la —** to knock on the door; **— trasera** back door; **a — cerrada** behind closed doors

puerto M port (también en informática); **llegar a buen —** to bring to a satisfactory conclusion

puertorriqueño -ña ADJ & MF Puerto Rican

pues CONJ (puesto que) since, for; ADV (entonces) then; **— bien** well then, now

puesta F **— al día** update; **— del sol** sunset, setting of the sun; **— en marcha** (de un proyecto) setting in motion; (de un coche) starting; **— en libertad** freeing

puestero -ra MF vendor, seller

puesto ADJ **bien —** (casa) well-appointed; (persona) well made-up; **llevar —** to have on; M (posición) place; (de venta) booth, stand; (de trabajo) post, position; **— de socorros** first-aid station; **quedarse con lo —** to be left with only the clothes on one's back; CONJ **— que** since

pugilato M boxing

pugilista M boxer, prizefighter

pugna F struggle; **estar en — con** to be in conflict with

pugnaz ADJ feisty

puja F (del viento) push; (en una subasta) bid

pujanza F vigor

pujar VI (para dar a luz) to push; (en una subasta) to bid; **— por** to strive to

pujo M contraction

pulcritud F neatness

pulcro ADJ neat

pulga F flea; **tener malas —s** to be ill-tempered

pulgada F inch

pulgar M thumb

pulido ADJ polished; M polishing

pulimento M (de modales) refinement; (de metales) buffing; (sustancia) scouring powder

pulir VT (metal, oración) to polish; (madera) to sand

pulla F taunt, dig

pulmón M lung; **— de acero** iron lung

pulmonar ADJ **capacidad —** lung capacity

pulmonía F pneumonia

pulpa F pulp

púlpito M pulpit

pulpo M octopus

pulque M *Méx* pulque

pulquería F *Méx* pulque bar

pulsación F pulse

pulsar VT (una tecla) to hit; (cuerdas de guitarra) to pluck; (la opinión pública) to gauge

púlsar M pulsar

pulsera F bracelet; (de reloj) watchband; **reloj de —** wristwatch

pulso M pulse; (firmeza de mano) steadiness; **echar un —** to arm-wrestle; **tomar el —** to take the pulse; **a —** with great effort

pulular VI to swarm, to teem with

pulverizar[9] VT to pulverize

puma F mountain lion, cougar

puna F cold, arid tableland of the Andes

punitivo ADJ punitive

punk ADJ & M punk

punkero -ra MF punk

punta F (de cuchillo, lengua) point; (de espárrago, lápiz) tip; (de calcetín) toe; **— de lanza** spearhead; **una — de** a bunch of; **a — de cuchillo** at knifepoint; **— de flecha** arrowhead; **de —** on end; **iba caminando de —s** he was tiptoeing; **sacar — a un lápiz** to sharpen a pencil; **en la — de la lengua** on the tip of the tongue; **me pone los nervios de —** it makes me nervous; M **—pié** kick; ADJ **puntiagudo** sharp, pointed

puntada F stitch, prick

puntal M (de un edificio) prop; (de la economía) mainstay

puntear VT (una guitarra) to pluck; (un mapa) to make dots on; (una lista) to check off

puntería F aim; **tener buena —** to be a good shot

puntero M pointer

puntilla F point lace; **de —s** on tiptoe

punto M (puntuación) period; (de cinturón) notch; (signo) point, dot; (tanteo, tema, lugar) point; (puntada) stitch; **— álgido** fever pitch; **— de apoyo** foothold; **— de condensación** dewpoint; **— de congelación** freezing point; **— de ebullición** boiling point; **— de partida** point of departure; **— de referencia** point of reference, benchmark; **— de vista** viewpoint, point of view; **— muerto** (en un negocio) stalemate, deadlock; (en un coche) neutral; **— y coma** semicolon; **al —** at once; **a — ready; a — de** on the point / verge of; **cogerle el —** to figure out; **dos —s** colon; **el — medio** the halfway mark; **en — on the dot; hacer —** to knit; **hasta cierto —** to a certain extent; **poner los —s sobre las íes** to dot the i's and cross the t's

puntuación F punctuation

puntual ADJ punctual, prompt; (específico) specific

puntualidad F punctuality

puntualizar[9] VT to point out

puntuar[17] VT to punctuate

punzada F (de dolor) stab; (de remordimiento, hambre) pang, twinge

punzante ADJ sharp, piercing

punzar[9] VT to prick

punzón M (en papel) hole punch; (en cuero) awl

puñado M handful; **a —s** by the handful

puñal M dagger

puñalada F stab; **coser a —s** to stab to death

puñetazo M punch, slug; **dar un —** to punch; **dar un — en la mesa** to bang on the table

puño M (mano cerrada) fist; (en un mango) cuff; (de espada) handle; **arreglarlo con los —s** to duke it out; **de mi — y letra** by my own hand

pupa F *Esp* boo-boo

pupila F pupil

pupilo -la MF ward

pupitre M school desk

puré M purée; **— de patatas** mashed potatoes; **hacer —** to smash

pureza F purity

purga F (política) purge; (medicinal) purgative

purgación F atonement

purgante ADJ & M purgative, laxative

purgar[7] VT (el vientre, a un rival) to purge; (frenos) to bleed; (pecados) to atone for

purgatorio M purgatory

purificar[6] VT to purify

purista S & MF purist

puritano ADJ puritanical

puro ADJ pure; **lo hizo de — bueno** he did it out of sheer kindness; **a pura fuerza** by sheer force; **la pura verdad** the plain truth; **son puras mentiras** that's a lot of bull; **de purasangre** thoroughbred; M cigar

púrpura ADJ & M purple

pus M pus

puta F (prostituta) *ofensivo* whore; (mujer fácil) *ofensivo* slut; **de — madre** *vulg* very good; **de la gran —** *vulg* huge

putañero M john

putón M *ofensivo* slut

putrefacto ADJ putrid

putter M putter

Qq

Qatar M Qatar

quásar M quasar

que PRON REL that; (antecedentes no humanos) which; (antecedentes humanos) who, whom; **el / la —** the one that; **lo — tú dices** what you say; **vino la suegra, lo — complicó la visita** the mother-in-law came, which complicated the visit;

CONJ that; **no creo — haya tiempo** I don't think (that) there's time; **estoy — me muero** I feel like I'm about to die; **Carlos es más alto — Luis** Carlos is taller than Luis; **más (menos) —** more (less) than; **déjalo aquí — lo voy a necesitar después** leave it here because I will need it later; **por mucho —** no matter how much; **a — gana** I bet he'll win; **— yo sepa** as far as I know

qué ADJ INTERR & PRON what, which; **¿— libro vas a usar?** what / which book are you going to use? **¿— dices?** what are you saying? **no sé — dijo** I don't know what he said; **¡— bonito!** how beautiful! **¡— de gente!** what a lot of people! **y eso —** so what! **no hay de —** don't mention it; **¿— sé yo?** what do I know? **¿— tal?** how are you? **¡— más da!** what's the difference! **¡a mí —!** so what!

quebrada F ravine

quebradizo ADJ breakable, brittle

quebrado ADJ (roto) broken; (rajado) cracked; (sin dinero) broke; M fraction

quebrantar VT (una casa, la salud) to weaken; (la ley) to violate

quebranto M weakening

quebrar[1] VT (romper) to break; (rajar) to crack; VI (irse a bancarrota) to go bankrupt, to go under, to fail; **—se** to break (up); **se quebró la muñeca** he broke his wrist; **—se uno la cabeza** to rack one's brain

queda F curfew

quedar VI (permanecer) to remain; (no haberse terminado) to be left; (estar ubicado) to be located; (sentar bien la ropa) to suit; **queda leche en el vaso** there's milk in the glass; **la iglesia queda en la esquina** the church is located on the corner; **— bien** to come out well; **— en** to agree to; **—se** to remain, to stay; **—se con una cosa** to take (buy) something

quehacer M chore

queja F complaint; (oficial) grievance

quejarse VI to complain; (ruidosamente) to gripe, to squawk; (incesantemente) to whine

quejica ADJ INV whiny; MF INV nag, whiner

quejido M (de sonido grave) moan, groan; (agudo) squawk

quejoso ADJ whiny

quema F burning

quemado -da MF burn victim

quemador M burner

quemadura F (lugar quemado) burn;

(enfermedad de plantas) blight

quemar VT to burn; (del sol) to sunburn; **—se** to burn up/down

quemazón F burning sensation

querella F lawsuit

querellante MF plaintiff

querellarse VI to file suit

querer[40] VI/VT (desear) to want; (amar) to love; **como quieras** as you please; **cuando quieras** whenever you want; **no quiso hacerlo** he refused to do it; **quiere llover** it is about to rain; **sin —** unwillingly; **— decir** to mean

querido -da ADJ beloved, dear; MF sweetheart; (como tratamiento) dear, darling

queroseno M kerosene

quesería F dairy, cheese factory

queso M cheese; **— crema/de untar** cream cheese; **— suizo** Swiss cheese

quiche M quiche

quicio M hinge; **sacar a uno de —** to drive someone up the wall

quiebra F bankruptcy (también moral); (de un mercado) crash; (de un comercio) failure

quiebre M break

quien PRON REL who, whom; **Juan, — recién cumplió cuarenta años** Juan, who just turned forty; **— hizo eso** whoever did that; **a — corresponda** to whom it may concern; **—quiera** whoever; **de —** whose; **con —** with whom

quién PRON INTERR & PRON who; **¿— es?** who is it? **no sé — entró** I don't know who came in; **¿a — se lo diste?** who did you give it to? to whom did you give it?

quieto ADJ still

quietud F stillness

quijada F jaw

quilate M carat

quilla F keel

química F chemistry

químico -ca ADJ chemical; MF chemist

quimioterapia F chemotheraphy

quince NUM fifteen

quincena F (de cosas) group of 15; (de días) two-week period

quincha F thatch

quinchar VT to thatch

quingombó M okra

quinqué M oil lamp

quinta F (casa) villa; (reclutamiento) draft

quinto ADJ, ADV, & M fifth

quiosco M kiosk, newsstand

quiquiriquí INTERJ cock-a-doodle-doo

quirófano M surgery, operating room

quiropráctico -ca ADJ chiropractic; MF chiropractor; F chiropractic

quirúrgico ADJ surgical

quisquilloso ADJ particular, fussy

quiste M cyst

quitar VT (una mancha) to remove; (una prenda de vestir) to take off; (despojar de) to take away; M SG **quitaesmalte** nail polish remover; **quitanieves** snowplow; **quitamanchas** spot remover; VI **—se** to take off; **—se a alguien de encima** to get rid of someone; **quítate de ahí** move over

quite M **salir al — de** to go to the rescue of

quizá, quizás ADV perhaps, maybe

Rr

rabadilla F (coxis) tailbone; (de un ave) rump

rábano M radish; **me importa un —** I couldn't care less

rabia F (hidrofobia) rabies; (enojo) rage; **me tiene —** he hates me; **dar —** to anger

rabiar VI to rage, to fume; **guapa a —** drop-dead beautiful

rabieta F tantrum

rabino -na MF rabbi

rabioso ADJ (hidrofóbico, apasionado) rabid, mad; (enojado) mad, furious

rabo M (cola) tail; (pene) *fam* dick; (cabo) stem; **mirar con el — del ojo** to look out of the corner of one's eye; **con el — entre las piernas** with his tail between his legs

rabón ADJ bobtail

racha F (de suerte) streak; (de viento) gust

racial ADJ racial

racimo M (de plátanos, personas) bunch; (de uvas) cluster

raciocinio M reasoning

ración F ration, allowance; (de comida) portion

racional ADJ rational (también número)

racionalizar[9] VT to rationalize

racionamiento M rationing

racionar VT to ration

racismo M racism

racista ADJ & MF racist

radar M radar

radiación F radiation

radiactivo ADJ radioactive

radiador M radiator

radial ADJ radial

radiante ADJ radiant

radiar VT to radiate; (por radio) to broadcast

radical ADJ (extremo) radical; (hojas, células) root; M (en ciencias) radical; (en gramática) root

radicalismo M radicalism

radicar[6] VI to be located; **— en** to lie in; **—se** to take up residence

radio M (hueso, segmento de un círculo) radius; (elemento radiactivo) radium; F (aparato, difusión) radio; (emisora) radio station; **— de acción** sphere of influence

radiodifusión F broadcasting

radiodifusora F radio station

radioescucha MF INV radio listener

radiofónico ADJ radio

radiografía F x-ray

radiografiar[16] VT to x-ray; (examinar con cuidado) to examine carefully

radiología F radiology

radiotelescopio M radio telescope

radiotransmisor M radio transmitter

radón M radon

raer[23] VI/VT to scrape (off); (un artículo de ropa) to wear out

ráfaga F (de viento) gust, blast; (de luz) flash; (de ametralladora) burst

raído ADJ threadbare

raigón M stump

raíz F root; **— cuadrada** square root; **a — de** due to; **arrancar de —** to uproot; **cortar de —** to nip in the bud; **echar raíces** to take root

raja F (de melón) slice; (de falda) slit; (del culo) *vulg* crack; (de leña) stick

rajadura F (en piedra, metal) crack; (en tela) rent, rip

rajar VT (una piedra) to crack; (un tronco) to split; **—se** (partir) to split open; (acobardarse) to chicken out, to blink; ADV **a rajatabla** strictly

ralea F ilk

ralear VI to thin out

ralentización F (de la economía) slump; (de un motor) idle

rallador M grater

rallar VT to grate, to shred

ralo ADJ sparse, thin

rama F branch, limb; (delgada) twig; **andarse por las —s** to beat around the bush; **algodón en —** raw cotton

ramaje M foliage

ramal M (de soga) strand; (de vía férrea) branch, spur

ramera F whore

ramificarse[6] VI to divide into branches, to branch off

ramillete M bouquet, bunch, spray

ramo M (de flores) bouquet; (de una ciencia) branch; (de una actividad) line; **— de olivo** olive branch

rampa F ramp

ramplón ADJ vulgar

rana F frog

ranchero -ra MF rancher

rancho M (comida para soldados) mess; (comida mala) swill; (finca) ranch; **hacer — aparte** to keep to oneself

rancio ADJ (alimento) rancid; **de — abolengo** of ancient lineage

rango M (militar) rank; (categoría) standing

ranilla F frog (of a hoof)

ranura F (corte) groove; (para insertar monedas, cartas) slot

rapar VT (pelo) to shave off; (cabeza) to shave

rapaz ADJ (animal) predatory; (destructivo) rapacious

rape M **cortar al —** to crop

rapé M snuff

rapear VI to rap

rapidez F (de un coche) speed; (de un movimiento) rapidity, quickness

rápido ADJ (con mucha velocidad) fast; (en poco tiempo) quick; M rapids; ADV (con mucha velocidad) fast; (en poco tiempo) quickly

rapiña F pillage

raptar VT to kidnap, to abduct

rapto M (secuestro) abduction, kidnapping; (arrebato) fit

raqueta F racket

raquítico ADJ feeble, sickly

raramente ADV seldom

rareza F (escasez) rarity; (cosa rara) oddity; (cualidad de extraño) strangeness

raro ADJ (infrecuente, de gases, tierras) rare; (extraño) strange, funny; **rara vez** seldom; **sentirse —** to feel funny

ras LOC ADV **a — de la tierra** low to the ground

rascar[6] VT to scratch; **—se el culo** *vulg* to fart around; M SG **rascacielos** skyscraper

rasgado ADJ **ojos —s** slit eyes

rasgadura F tear, rip

rasgar[7] VT to tear, to rip

rasgo M (propiedad) trait, feature; **a grandes —s** in broad strokes

rasgón M tear

rasguñar VT to scratch

rasguño M scratch

raso ADJ (superficie) smooth; (cucharada)

level; **al** — in the open air; M satin

raspado M scrape

raspador M scraper

raspadura F scrape

raspar VT to scrape

raspón M scrape

rastra F harrow; **a —s** dragging, pulling

rastrear VT (a un animal) to trail, to track, to trace; (un terreno) to search

rastreo M sweep, search

rastrero ADJ (planta) creeping; (persona) contemptible

rastrillar VT to rake

rastrillo M rake

rastro M (huella) track, trail; (olor) scent; (mercado) flea market; **ni —s** no trace

rastrojo M stubble

rasurado M shave

rasurador -ora MF razor

rasurar VT to shave

rata F rat

ratear VT to pilfer

ratería F petty larceny

ratero -ra MF pickpocket

ratificar[6] VT to ratify

rato M while; **—s perdidos** leisure hours; **a cada** — frequently; **a —s** from time to time; **pasar el** — to kill time; **pasar un buen** — (divertirse) to have a pleasant time; (permanecer) to spend a long time; **un largo** — a great while

ratón M mouse; — **almizclero** muskrat

ratonera F mousetrap

raudal LOC ADV **a —es** in great quantities

raudo ADJ swift

raya F line; (linde) boundary; (lista) stripe; (en el pelo) part; (en un pantalón) crease; (ortografía) dash; (en un zapato) scuff; (pez marino) stingray; **tener a** — to hold in check; **pasarse de la** — to be out of line

rayado ADJ (papel) lined; (vestido) striped; **hablaba como disco** — he talked like a broken record

rayar VT (papel) to rule, to make lines on; (discos, espejo) to scratch; (zapatos) to scuff; — **el alba** to dawn; — **en** to border on

rayo M (de luz) ray, beam, streak; (de relámpago) flash of lightning; (de rueda) spoke; (de esperanza) ray, flicker; **—s infrarrojos** infrared rays; **—s X** X-rays

rayón M rayon

raza F (de personas) race; (de animal) breed

razón F (facultad) reason; (proporción) ratio; — **social** company name; **a** — **de** at the rate of; **¡con —!** no wonder! **entrar en**

— to listen to reason; **te doy la** — I admit you're right; **perder la** — to lose one's mind; **tener** — to be right

razonable ADJ reasonable

razonamiento M reasoning

razonar VI (pensar) to reason; (arguir) to argue

reabastecer[13] VT to replenish

reabrir[51] VT to reopen

reacción F reaction; — **en cadena** chain reaction; — **nuclear** nuclear reaction

reaccionar VI to react

reaccionario ADJ & MF reactionary

reacio ADJ averse, reluctant

reacondicionar VT to rebuild

reactivo M reagent

reactor M reactor; — **nuclear** nuclear reactor

readaptación F readjustment

readaptar VT to readjust

reagrupar VT to regroup

reajustar VT to readjust

reajuste M readjustment

real ADJ (verdadero) real, actual; (del rey) royal; M fairground

realce M **dar** — to enhance

realeza F royalty

realidad F reality, actuality; **en** — really, actually; — **virtual** virtual reality

realismo M realism

realista ADJ (auténtico) realistic; (partidario del rey) royalist; MF (no idealista) realist; (partidario del rey) royalist

realización F (de un sueño) realization, fulfillment; (de una tarea) realization; (de una película) production

realizar[9] VT (un sueño) to realize, to fulfill; (película) to produce

realzar[9] VT (mejorar) to enhance; (destacar) to accentuate; (intensificar) to heighten

reanimar VT (devolver fuerzas) to revive; (dar ánimos) to rally

reanudación F renewal

reanudar VT (una amistad) to renew; (una reunión) to resume

reaparecer[13] VI to reappear

reasumir VT to resume

reata F lariat, lasso

reavivar VT to revive

rebaja F markdown, price cut; **de —s** cut-rate

rebajar VT (precios) to cut, to lower, to slash; (una bebida) to water down; (una crítica) to tone down; VI/VT (los cambios) to downshift; **—se** to lower oneself; **—se a** to stoop to

rebanada F slice

rebanar VT to slice

rebaño M flock, fold

rebasar VT (un coche) to overtake; (un límite) to exceed

rebatir VT to refute

rebato M alarm

rebelarse VI to rebel, to revolt

rebelde ADJ rebellious; (pelo) unruly; MF rebel

rebeldía F rebelliousness, defiance; (no comparecencia) default

rebelión F rebellion

rebenque M whip

rebobinar VT to rewind

reborde M edge

rebosante ADJ (de líquido) brimming, overflowing; (de salud) flush, glowing

rebosar VI (líquido) to overflow, to brim over; (de alegría) to bubble over; (de salud) to glow

rebotar VI (botar para atrás) to rebound, to bounce; (chocar) to bounce; (cambiar de dirección una bala) to ricochet; (cambiar de dirección una pelota) to carom

rebote M rebound, bounce; (de bala) ricochet

rebozar[9] VT to cover with batter; **—se** to muffle up

rebozo M shawl; **sin —** frankly

rebullir[19] VI to stir

rebuscado ADJ (estilo) overly elaborate; (persona) affected

rebuscar[6] VT (espigar) to glean; VI **— en** (la memoria) to search through; (un cajón) to rummage in

rebuznar VI to bray

rebuzno M bray, braying

recabar VT to raise (money)

recado M (mensaje) message; (quehacer) errand; **— de escribir** writing materials

recaer[23] VI to relapse; **— sobre** to fall to

recaída F relapse

recalar VI to make a stop at

recalcar[6] VT to accentuate

recalcitrante ADJ obstinate

recalentar[1] VT (volver a calentar) to warm over; (calentar en exceso) to overheat

recamar VT to embroider

recámara F (de un arma de fuego) chamber; *Méx* bedroom

recapitular VI/VT to recapitulate, to sum up

recargado ADJ busy, fussy

recargar[7] VT to overload, to burden

recargo M (emocional) burden; (de precio) surcharge, premium

recatado ADJ (cauteloso) cautious; (modesto) modest

recato M (cautela) caution; (modestia) modesty

recaudación F collection, levy; **— de fondos** fund-raising

recaudador -ora MF tax collector

recaudar VT (impuestos) to collect, to levy; (fondos) to raise; **— en bruto** to gross; **lo recaudado** proceeds

recaudo M **estar a buen —** to be in a safe place

rección F government

recelar VT to suspect; **— de** to be suspicious of

recelo M misgivings

receloso ADJ mistrustful

recepción F reception

receptáculo M receptacle, holder

receptor M receiver

recesión F recession

receta F (de cocina) recipe; (de médico) prescription

recetar VT to prescribe

rechazar[9] VT to reject; (un ataque) to repel, to repulse; (una oferta) to decline, to turn down, to refuse; (una acusación) to deny; (a un amante) to spurn, to reject

rechazo M (de un amante) rejection; (de un ataque) repulse; (de una oferta) refusal; (de una acusación) denial

rechifla F whistling, booing

rechiflar VT to whistle, to boo

rechinamiento M (de una puerta) creaking, squeaking; (de los dientes) grinding

rechinante ADJ squeaky

rechinar VI (una puerta) to squeak, to creak; VI/VT (los dientes) to grind; **eso me rechina** that grates on my nerves

rechoncho ADJ plump, chubby, roly-poly

recibidor -ora MF receiver; M reception room

recibimiento M reception

recibir VT to receive, to get; (visitas) to receive, to welcome; (una noticia trágica) to take; **— noticias de** to hear from; **—se** to graduate; **—se de médico** to graduate from medical school

recibo M receipt; **de —** acceptable; **al — de** upon receipt of; **acusar —** to acknowledge receipt; **acuse de —** acknowledgment of receipt

reciclar VI/VT to recycle

recién ADV recently; **— casado** newlywed; **— comprado** brand-new; **— llegado** newly arrived; **— me entero** it's news to me; **— nacido** newborn

reciente ADJ recent

recinto M enclosure

recio ADJ strong, rugged

recipiente M container

recíproco ADJ reciprocal

recitación F recitation

recital M recital

recitar VT to recite, to speak

reclamación F (protesta) protest; (demanda) claim

reclamante MF claimant

reclamar VT (protestar) to protest; (demandar) to claim; VI (aves) to call

reclamo M (reclamación) claim; (voz de animal) call, cry; (dispositivo) bird call; (señuelo) decoy

reclinar VT to lean; **—se** to recline

recluir[31] VT to confine; **—se** to be a recluse

recluso -sa MF inmate

recluta F recruitment; M (voluntario) recruit; (forzoso) conscript

reclutamiento M (voluntario) recruitment; (forzoso) conscription

reclutar VT (voluntariamente) to recruit; (por la fuerza) to draft, to conscript

recobrar VI to recover, to recuperate; VT to recover, to regain

recodo M bend, turn

recoger[11b] VT (el cabello) to gather; (un cuarto) to tidy up; (citas en un texto) to collect; (la mesa) to clear; (polvo) to sweep up; (a un desamparado) to shelter; (los frutos del campo) to glean; **—se** (retirarse) to retire, to withdraw; (acumularse) to gather

recogida F (del cabello) gathering; (de un cuarto) tidying up; (de la mesa) clearing; (de un desamparado) sheltering

recogimiento M (aislamiento) seclusion; (meditación) meditation

recolección F (de frutos, datos) collecting, gathering; (de carga) pickup; (cosecha) harvest

recolectar VT to gather, to forage

recomendable ADJ advisable

recomendación F recommendation

recomendar[1] VT to recommend

recompensa F recompense, reward

recompensar VT to recompense, to reward

reconcentrar VI to concentrate intensely; **—se** to concentrate, to become absorbed in thought

reconciliación F reconciliation

reconciliar VT to reconcile

recóndito ADJ remote

reconfortante ADJ heart-warming, comforting

reconfortar VT to comfort

reconocer[13] VT (identificar) to recognize; (admitir) to admit, to acknowledge; (explorar) to reconnoiter

reconocimiento M (identificación) recognition; (admisión, agradecimiento) acknowledgment; (exploración) scouting; **hacer un —** to reconnoiter

reconsiderar VT to reconsider

reconstrucción F reconstruction

reconstruir[31] VT to reconstruct, to rebuild

recopilar VT to compile

récord M record

recordar[2] VT (acordarse) to remember, to recollect, to recall; (hacer acordar) to remind

recordatorio M reminder

recorrer VT (andar una distancia) to cover; (examinar) to go over, to look over

recorrido M (ruta) run; (distancia) distance

recortado ADJ jagged

recortar VT (pelo, hilos, presupuesto) to trim; (uñas, periódicos) to clip; (una película) to shorten; **—se** to be outlined

recorte M (de pelos, hilos) trimming; (de uñas, periódicos) clipping; (de sueldo) cut; (sobrante) trimming

recostar[2] VT (sobre) to lay; (contra) to lean; **—se** to recline

recoveco M (en un camino) turn; (rincón) cranny

recreación F recreation

recrear VT to entertain; **—se** to amuse oneself

recreo M recreation, relaxation; (tiempo de descanso) recess; (lugar de juego) playground

recriminar VT to recriminate

recrudecer[13] VI to flare up

recrudecimiento M flareup

rectángulo M rectangle

rectificar[6] VT to rectify

rectitud F uprightness, righteousness

recto ADJ (no curvo) straight; (honrado) upright, righteous; (estricto) strict; **todo —** straight ahead; M rectum

rector -ora MF university president, chancellor

recua F herd

recuento M account; **— sanguíneo** blood count

recuerdo M (acción de recordar, cosa recordada) memory, recollection; (objeto que hace recordar) souvenir, token; **—s** regards

recular VI (ir hacia atrás) to move backward; (en un coche) to back up; (ante un desafío) to back down

recuperación F recovery

recuperar VT (una cosa perdida) to recover; (tiempo perdido) to make up; **—se** to recuperate

recurrir VT to appeal; — **a** to resort to, to have recourse to

recurso M (acción de recurrir) recourse; (reclamación) appeal; —**s** resources; —**s naturales** natural resources

recusar VT (a una persona) to reject; (a un juez) to challenge

red F (para pescar) net; (tejido de mallas) mesh; (conjunto de mallas) network; (para engañar) snare; (internet) World Wide Web, Internet

redacción F (ensayo) composition; (acción de redactar) drafting; (en un periódico) editorial department

redactar VT to draft; (en la escuela) to compose

redactor -ora MF editor

redada F (de peces) catch, haul; (por la policía) raid

redar VT to net

redecilla F hairnet

redención F redemption

redil M sheepfold, sheep pen; **volver al —** to come back into the fold

redimir VT (a un pecador) to redeem; (a un esclavo) to set free

rédito M (de ahorros) interest; (de acciones) yield

redituar[17] VT to yield

redoblar VT to double; VI/VT (un tambor) to roll

redoble M drumroll

redoma F flask

redonda F whole note; **a la —** all around

redondear VT to make round

redondel M ring

redondez F roundness

redondo ADJ round; **en —** all around; **caer — ** to collapse; **salir —** to turn our perfect

reducción F reduction, cutback; **hacer — de personal** to cut back on personnel

reducir[24] VT to reduce; (un hueso) to set; (actividades) to curtail, to cut down on; —**se** to limit oneself; —**se a** to boil down to

redundante ADJ redundant

reedificar[6] VT to rebuild

reelección F reelection

reelegir[11] VT reelect

reembolsar VT to reimburse, to refund

reembolso M reimbursement, refund

reemplazable ADJ replaceable

reemplazar[9] VT to replace

reemplazo M replacement, substitute

reencarnación F reincarnation

reescribir[51] VT to rewrite

reexpedir[5] VT to forward

referencia F reference

referéndum M referendum

referente LOC ADV — **a** relative to

referir[3] VT (narrar) to narrate; —**se a** to refer to

refinación F refinement

refinado ADJ refined, genteel

refinamiento M refinement

refinar VT to refine

refinería F refinery

reflector M (en una bicicleta) reflector; (en deportes) floodlight; (militar, policial) searchlight

reflejar VT (luz) to reflect; (imagen) to mirror; —**se** to be reflected

reflejo M (luz) reflection; (movimiento) reflex; —**s** frosting; ADJ reflex

reflexión F reflection

reflexionar VI to reflect; — **sobre** to think over

reflexivo ADJ (gramatical) reflexive; (pensativo) thoughtful

reflujo M ebb

reforma F (política) reform; (religiosa) reformation

reformador -ora MF reformer

reformar VT (un gobierno, a un delincuente) to reform; (ropa) to make alterations in; —**se** to mend one's ways

reformatorio M reformatory

reformista MF reformer

reforzar[2,9] VT to reinforce; (las defensas) to beef up; (un argumento) to bolster, to buttress

refracción F refraction

refractario ADJ refractory

refrán M proverb, saying

refrenar VT (un caballo) to rein in; (emociones) to restrain, to check

refrendar VT (una sentencia) to uphold; (un documento) to countersign, to endorse

refrendario -ria MF endorser

refrendo M endorsement

refrescante ADJ refreshing

refrescar[6] VT to refresh; (el tiempo) to get cool; —**se** to cool off

refresco M refreshment

refriega F fray, scuffle

refrigeración F refrigeration

refrigerador ADJ refrigerating; M refrigerator

refrigerante ADJ cooling; M coolant

refrigerar VT to cool, to refrigerate

refrigerio M refreshment

refrito ADJ (comida) refried; M (obra) rerun

refuerzo M (acción de reforzar) reinforcement; (de tela) backing; (de una vacuna) booster

refugiado -da MF refugee

refugiar VT to shelter; **—se** to take shelter

refugio M refuge, shelter; **— antiaéreo** bomb shelter; **— fiscal** tax shelter

refulgente ADJ resplendent

refundir VT to recast

refunfuñar VI to grumble, to mutter

refunfuño M grumbling, muttering

refunfuñón -ona ADJ grouchy, grumpy; MF grouch

refutar VT to refute

regadera F watering can

regadío M (tierra irrigada) irrigated land; (riego) irrigation

regalar VT (dar como presente) to give as a gift; (vender barato, donar) to give away; (agasajar) to regale

regaliz M licorice

regalo M (presente, cosa barata) present, gift; (para los sentidos) treat, delight

regañar VI (un perro) to snarl; VT (a un niño) to scold, to reprimand; (constantemente) to nag; **a regañadientes** reluctantly

regaño M scolding, reprimand

regañón -ona MF scold

regar[1,7] VT (campos) to irrigate; (flores) to water

regatear VI to haggle, to bargain

regateo M bargaining

regazo M lap

regente MF regent; ADJ ruling

reggae M reggae

régimen M (gobierno) regime; (dieta) diet; **— de vida** lifestyle

regimiento M regiment

regio ADJ regal

región F region

regir[5,11] VT to govern; VI to be in force; **—se por** to be guided by

registrar VT (buscar en) to search; (indicar) to record, to register

registro M (de la voz, lingüístico) register; (de nacimientos) record, register; (del equipaje) search; (de un órgano) stop

regla F (norma) rule; (utensilio para medir) ruler; (menstruación) period; **en —** in order; **por — general** as a general rule

reglamento M regulations

regocijar VT to gladden; **—se** to rejoice

regocijo M joy, rejoicing

regodearse VI (en la desgracia propia) to wallow; (en la desgracia ajena) to gloat

regodeo M (en la desgracia propia) wallowing; (en la desgracia ajena) gloating

regordete ADJ plump

regresar VI to return

regreso M return; **estar de —** to be back

reguero M trail; **correr como un — de pólvora** to spread like wildfire

regulación F (acción de regular) regulation; (de una máquina) adjustment

regulador M regulator, governor, throttle; **— de voltaje** dimmer

regular VT to regulate; (ajustar una máquina) to adjust; ADJ regular; **una paliza —** quite a beating; ADV so-so

regularidad F regularity

regularizar[9] VT to regulate; (formalizar) to formalize; **—se** to become regular

regurgitar VI/VT to regurgitate

rehabilitador ADJ remedial

rehacer[30] VT to remake; **—se** to recover

rehén MF hostage

rehuir[31] VT to shun; (responsabilidades) to shirk

rehusar VT to refuse; **—se a** to refuse to

reimpresión F reprint

reina F queen

reinado M reign

reinante ADJ prevailing

reinar VI to reign

reincidencia F relapse

reincidir VI to relapse

reino M (territorio de un rey) kingdom, realm; (período de reinado) reign; (división biológica) kingdom; (ámbito) realm

reintegrar VT to rebate; **—se a** to return to

reintegro M rebate

reír[15] VI to laugh; **—se de** to laugh at

reiterar VT to reiterate

reivindicar[6] VT to vindicate

reja F grate, grating; (pieza de arado) plowshare; **entre —s** behind bars

rejilla F (para equipaje) luggage rack; (de coche) grille

rejuvenecer[13] VT to rejuvenate; VI to become rejuvenated

relación F relation, connection; (interpersonal) relationship; (relato) account, report; (lista) list; **relaciones** (conocidos) connections; (trato) dealings; **relaciones públicas** public relations; **con — a** in relation to

relacionado ADJ related, germane

relacionar VT to relate, to connect; **—se con** to relate to

relajación F relaxation

relajamiento M relaxation

relajar VT to relax; **—se** to become lax

relajo M (aflojamiento) relaxation; (desorden) mess

relamerse VI to lick one's lips

relámpago M lightning

relampaguear VI to lightning; (los ojos, cosa reluciente) to flash

relampagueo M flash of lightning

relatar VT to relate, to recount

relativo ADJ relative; **— a** relative to

relato M (informe) account; (cuento) story, tale

relé M relay

relegar[7] VT to relegate

relevar VT to relieve

relevo M (soldado) relief; (carrera) relay

relicario M reliquary, locket

relieve M relief; **de —** (mapa) relief; (persona) prominent; **poner de —** to emphasize; **letras en —** raised letters

religión F religion

religioso -sa ADJ religious; M monk; F nun

relinchar VI to neigh

relincho M neigh

reliquia F relic

rellenado M filling

rellenar VT (un vaso) to refill, to replenish; (un tanque de gasolina) to fill, to fill up; (un formulario) to fill out; (un hueco) to fill in; (una almohada) to stuff

relleno ADJ (un pimiento) stuffed; (el cuerpo) full; M (de comida) stuffing, dressing; (de un colchón) padding

reloj M (de pared) clock; (de muñeca, bolsillo) watch; (de horno) timer; **— pulsera** wristwatch; **— de sol** sundial; **— despertador** alarm clock; **contra —** against the clock; **como un —** regularly, like clockwork

relojería F (tienda) watch shop; (actividad) clock-making

relojero -ra MF watchmaker

reluciente ADJ shining

relucir[13b] VI to shine; **sacar a —** to bring up

relumbrar VI to glare

relumbre M glare

REM M REM

remachar VT (una victoria, un clavo) to clinch; (un remache) to rivet

remache M (acción de remachar) clinching; (clavo) clinching; (clavija) rivet

remanente M remainder

remar VI/VT to row, to paddle

rematador -ora MF auctioneer

rematar VT (acabar) to finish; (matar) to finish off; (perfeccionar) to give the finishing touches to; (patear un balón) to take a shot; (subastar) to auction

remate M (de una obra) finishing touch; (tiro) shot; (subasta) auction; **— de un**

chiste punch line; **loco de —** stark raving mad

remedador -ora MF mimic

remedar VT to mimic, to ape, to mock

remediar VT to remedy

remedio M remedy, cure; **sin —** unavoidable; **no tiene —** it can't be helped; **no tengo más —** I can't help it; **el — es peor que la enfermedad** the remedy is worse than the disease

remedo M mockery

remendar[1] VT to mend, to patch; (calcetines) to darn; (zapatos) to repair

remendón -ona MF cobbler

remero -ra MF rower

remesa F (de mercancías) shipment; (de dinero) remittance

remiendo M (de ropa) patch; (de zapatos) repair

remilgado ADJ fussy, prim

remilgo M fussiness, primness

reminiscencia F reminiscence

remisión F remission

remitente MF sender

remitir VT (enviar) to remit; (mandar a otra parte) to refer; **—se** to yield; **a las pruebas me remito** the evidence speaks for itself

remo M (pala) oar, paddle; (deporte) rowing

remodelar VI/VT to remodel

remojar VT to soak

remojo M soaking; **poner en —** to soak

remojón M soaking

remolacha F beet

remolcador M tugboat

remolcar[6] VT to tow

remolino M swirl, whirl; (de viento) whirlwind; (de agua) whirlpool, eddy; (de pelo) cowlick; (juguete) pinwheel; **— de gente** throng, crowd

remolón -ona ADJ dallying; MF dallier

remolonear VI to dally

remolque M (acción de remolcar) tow; (vehículo remolcado) towed vehicle; (vehículo que remolca) tow truck; (de camión) trailer; **llevar a —** to tow

remontar VT (una cometa) to fly; (una pendiente, un río) to go up; **—se** to rise; **el coche se remonta a los años 20** the car dates from the '20s; **para comprenderlo, debemos remontarnos a su juventud** in order to understand him, we must go back to his youth

remorder[2] VT to gnaw at

remordimiento M remorse

remoto ADJ remote, distant; **no tiene la**

más remota idea he doesn't have the slightest idea

remover[2] VT (un cargo, un obstáculo) to remove; (un asunto problemático) to stir up

remuneración F compensation

remunerado ADJ gainful

renacer[13] VI to be reborn

renacimiento M revival; (período histórico) Renaissance

renacuajo M tadpole; (hombre esmirriado) shrimp

rencilla F quarrel

rencor M rancor; **guardar —** to bear a grudge

rencoroso ADJ resentful

rendición F surrender

rendido ADJ exhausted

rendija F crack

rendimiento M (lo rendido) yield, output; (productividad) performance

rendir[5] VT (someter) to subdue; (producir) to yield; (fatigar) to fatigue; **— homenaje** to pay homage; **— cuentas a** to answer to; VI (obtener buenos resultados) to perform well; **—se** (darse por vencido) to surrender, to give in; (fatigarse) to become fatigued

renegado -da MF renegade

renegar[1,7] VT (negar) to deny insistently; (repudiar) to renounce; **— de** to gripe about

renglón M line; **a —** seguido immediately following

rengo ADJ lame

renguear VI to limp

renguera F limp

reno M reindeer

renombrado ADJ renowned

renombre M renown; **de —** of note

renovación F renewal; **— urbana** urban renewal

renovar[2] VT (un edificio) to renovate; (ataques, temores) to renew

renquear VT to limp

renta F (de una persona) income; (de un gobierno) revenue; (alquiler) rent; **— anual** annuity; **—s internas** internal revenue; **vivir de la —** to live on the interest

rentable ADJ profitable; (idea) viable

renuencia F reluctance

renuente ADJ reluctant, loath; **ser — a** to be loath to

renuevo M sprout

renuncia F (dimisión) resignation; (de un derecho) waiver; (de una herencia) renunciation

renunciar VI **— a** (un cargo) to resign; (la ciudadanía) to renounce; (un derecho) to relinquish, to waive

reñido ADJ contested

reñir[5,18] VI (discutir) to quarrel, to bicker, to argue; (pelear) to fight, to scuffle; (rezongar) to scold

reo -a MF defendant, accused

reojo M **mirar de —** to look out of the corner of one's eye

reorganizar[9] VT to reorganize, to regroup

repantigarse[7] VI to lounge

reparación F (compensación) reparation, redress; (arreglo) repair

reparador ADJ refreshing; M serviceman

reparar VT (arreglar) to repair; (compensar) to redress; **— en** to notice

reparo M **no tener —s en** to have no qualms about; **sin —s** freely; **hacer —s to** object

repartición F distribution

repartir VT (tierras, un botín) to distribute; (volantes) to hand out; (periódicos) to deliver; (naipes) to deal; (días libres) to space out

reparto M (de tierras) distribution; (entrega de periódicos) delivery; (de naipes) dealing; (ruta de entrega) route; (lista de actores) cast; **— proporcional** apportionment

repasar VT (una lección) to review, to go over again; (en la memoria) to retrace; (leer por encima) to skim

repaso M review

repelente ADJ repellent

repeler VT to repel, to repulse

repente M **de —** suddenly

repentino ADJ sudden

repercusión F repercussion

repercutir VI to have repercussions

repertorio M repertoire

repetición F repetition

repetido ADJ repeated; **repetidas veces** repeatedly

repetir[5] VI/VT to repeat; VI to belch; (tomar una segunda ración) to have seconds; **— como loro** to parrot; **—se** to recur

repicar[6] VI/VT to ring

repique M ringing, ring

repiquetear VI/VT to ring

repiqueteo M ringing

repisa F shelf

replegar[1,7] VT to fold; **—se** to retreat

repleto ADJ replete

réplica F (contestación) reply, comeback; (copia) replica; (temblor secundario) aftershock

replicar[6] VI/VT to reply, to rejoin; (una célula) to replicate

repliegue M (pliegue marcado) crease; (retirada) retreat

repollo M cabbage

reponer[39] VT (reemplazar) to replace; (restituir) to restore; (replicar) to reply; (una obra de teatro) to revive; (una película) to show again; **—se** to recover one's health

reportaje M feature story

reportar VT (beneficios) to yield; VI (en una jerarquía) to answer to; **—se enfermo** to call in sick

reportero -ra MF reporter

reposado ADJ quiet, calm

reposar VI to repose, to rest; **dejar —** to let steep; M SG **reposacabezas** headrest

reposición F (reemplazo) replacement; (de una obra de teatro) revival

reposo M (descanso) repose, rest; (sosiego) calm

repostería F (establecimiento) pastry shop; (actividad) baking

repostero -ra MF pastry cook

reprender VT to reprimand, to scold, to rebuke

reprensión F rebuke

represa F (dique) dam; (reservorio de agua) reservoir

represalia F reprisal

represar VT to dam

representación F representation; (delegación) delegation; (de un papel) portrayal; (de una obra de teatro) performance

representante MF representative; (comercial) agent

representar VT to represent, to depict; (una obra de teatro) to perform; (un personaje) to portray; **tiene treinta años, pero no los representa** he's thirty years old, but he doesn't look it; **tu presencia representa mucho para mí** your presence means a lot to me

representativo ADJ representative

represión F (psicológica) repression; (política) suppression, crackdown

reprimenda F reprimand, rebuke

reprimido ADJ repressed, pent-up

reprimir VT (impulsos) to repress; (una tendencia) to check; (enemigos políticos) to suppress, to crack down on; (una rebelión) to quell

reprobación F reproof

reprobar[2] VT to reprove; VI/VT (no aprobar

un examen) to flunk, to fail

reprochar VT to reproach, to rebuke

reproche M reproach, rebuke

reproducción F reproduction

reproducir[24] VI/VT to reproduce; **—se** to reproduce, to breed

reproductor -ora ADJ breeding; MF breeding animal; F (aparato) VCR

reptar VI to crawl

reptil M reptile

república F republic

republicano -na ADJ & MF republican

repudiar VT (a la sociedad) to repudiate; (a un hijo) to disown; (una herencia) to renounce

repuesto M (pieza de reemplazo) spare part; **de —** spare

repugnancia F repugnance, disgust, revulsion

repugnante ADJ repugnant, disgusting, loathsome

repugnar VI to be repugnant; VT to disgust, to cloy

repulir VT to polish up

repulsa F rebuff, repulse

repulsar VT to repulse

repulsivo ADJ repulsive, creepy

repuntar VI to rally

reputación F reputation

reputado ADJ reputable

requemar VT to burn

requerimiento M request

requerir[3] VT to require

requesón M cottage cheese

requiebros M PL advances

requisa F requisition

requisar VT to commandeer, to requisition; (registrar) to search

requisito M requirement, requisite

res F animal; **— lanar** sheep; **— vacuna** cow

resabio M (dejillo) aftertaste; (vicio) bad habit

resaca F (de mar) undertow; (malestar físico) hangover

resaltar VI (sobresalir) to stand out; (poner de relieve) to highlight

resarcir[10b] VT to compensate for

resbaladizo ADJ slippery, slick

resbalar VI (deslizar) to slip; (ser/estar resbaladizo) to be slippery

resbalón M slip; **darse un —** to slip

resbaloso ADJ slippery; *Méx fam* sleazy

rescatar VT (a un secuestrado) to ransom; (a una persona en peligro) to rescue

rescate M (para un secuestrado) ransom; (de una persona en peligro) rescue

rescindir VT to rescind
rescoldo M embers
resecar[6] VT to dry; **—se** to dry out
reseco ADJ dried-up, parched
resentido ADJ resentful
resentimiento M resentment, grudge; **guardar —** to hold a grudge
resentirse[3] VI to hurt, to suffer; **— de** to resent
reseña F book review
reseñar VT to review
reserva F (de provisiones, de oro, de jugadores, del ejército) reserve; (de localidades, de hotel, de indios) reservation; (de animales) preserve; **sin —s** without reservations; **tener —s** to have reservations
reservación F Am reservation
reservado ADJ (distante) aloof; (discreto) reserved
reservar VT to reserve; **me reservo mi opinión** I'll spare you my opinion
resfriado M common cold; **estoy —** I've got a cold
resfriarse VI to catch cold
resfrío M cold, head cold
resguardar VT to shelter; **—se de** to seek shelter from
resguardo M (abrigo) shelter; (comprobante) deposit slip
residencia F residence
residencial ADJ residential; (en las afueras) suburban
residente ADJ & MF resident
residir VI to reside
residuo M residue
resignación F resignation
resignarse VI to resign oneself
resina F resin
resistencia F resistance; (de la calefacción) element; (aguante) endurance, stamina
resistente ADJ resistant, tough
resistir VT (una tentación) to resist; (un ataque) to withstand; **—se a un arresto** to resist arrest; VI to resist, to hold (up)
resollar[2] VI (por enfermedad) to wheeze; (después de un esfuerzo) to pant; (por alivio) to sigh
resolución F (acción de resolver) resolution; (ánimo) determination, resolve
resolver[2,51] VT (decidir) to decide; (solucionar) to solve; **—se a** to resolve to
resonancia F resonance
resonar[2] VI (sonidos) to resound, to boom; (una polémica) to resonate
resoplar VI (con enfado) to huff and puff; (un caballo) to snort

resoplido M (con enojo) puff; (de caballo) snort
resorte M spring
respaldar VT to back, to stand behind
respaldo M (parte de una silla) back; (apoyo) support, backing
respectivo ADJ respective
respecto LOC ADV **— a / de** with respect to, concerning; **a ese —** on that score; **con — a** with regard to, regarding, vis-à-vis
respetable ADJ respectable
respetar VT to respect
respeto M respect, regard; **con todo —** with all due respect; **faltar el / al —** to slight, to disregard
respetuoso ADJ respectful
respingar[7] VI (dar respingos) to buck; (asustarse) to shy away
respingo M (salto) buck; (susto) start
respiración F respiration, breathing; **— boca a boca** mouth-to-mouth resuscitation
respirar VI/VT to breathe; (sentir alivio) to breathe easy; **dejar —** to give a breather
respiro M (acto de respirar) breathing; (descanso) respite
resplandecer[13] VI (brillar) to glare; (de felicidad) to glow
resplandeciente ADJ resplendent, radiant
resplandor M brilliance, radiance
responder VI (reaccionar) to respond; VT (contestar) to answer; (corresponder) to correspond
respondón ADJ saucy
responsabilidad F (obligación de aceptar consecuencias) responsibility; (obligación de informar) accountability
responsable ADJ (que debe aceptar las consecuencias) responsible; (obligado legalmente) liable for; (que tiene que informar) accountable
respuesta F response, answer
resquebrajadura F crack
resquebrajar VI to crack
resquicio M (rendija) crack; (laguna legal) loophole
resta F subtraction
restablecer[13] VT to reestablish; (una costumbre) to revive; **—se** to recover
restante ADJ remaining
restañar VT to stanch / staunch
restar VT (sustraer) to subtract; (quitar) to take away from; (quedar) to remain; **— importancia a** to make light of
restauración F restoration
restaurante M restaurant
restaurar VT to restore; (muebles) to refurbish

restitución F restitution

restituir[31] VT to pay back, to give back

resto M (lo demás) rest; (sobrante) remainder; **—s** (de un edificio) remains; (de una comida) leftovers; **echar el —** to go all out

restorán M restaurant

restregar[1,7] VT to scrub, to scour

restricción F restriction

restringir[11] VT to restrict, to curtail

resucitación F resuscitation, revival

resucitar VT to resuscitate, to revive

resuello M (por enfermedad) wheeze; (por fatiga) panting

resuelto ADJ (de carácter decidido) resolute, strong-willed; (de actitud decidida) determined

resulta LOC ADV **de —s** as a result

resultado M result; (de un suceso) outcome; (de un partido) score; **—s científicos** findings; **—s electorales** returns; **como — as** a result; **dar buen —** to pan out; **dar por —** to result in

resultante ADJ resulting, consequent

resultar VI to result; (acabar siendo) to turn out, to prove; **— de** to result from; **resulta que** it turns out that

resumen M summary, abstract; **en —** in sum, in brief

resumir VT to summarize, to sum up; **—se a** to be condensed to, to boil down to

resurgimiento M revival

resurgir[11] VI to arise again

resurrección F resurrection

retablo M altarpiece

retaguardia F rear guard

retal M remnant

retama F broom

retar VT to challenge

retardar VI/VT to retard

retardo M lag

retazo M remnant

retén M (aparato) retainer; (de vigilancia) squad

retención F retention

retener[44] VT (una pelota, la atención) to hold; (salarios, fondos) to garnish, to withhold

retina F retina

retintín M (en los oídos) ringing; (de cascabeles) jingle

retirada F (de tropas) retreat, withdrawal; (de un diplomático, producto) recall

retirar VT (apartar) to move away; (dinero) to withdraw; (algo dicho) to take back, withdraw; (un producto) to recall; **—se** (para descansar, de un trabajo) to retire;

(un ejército) to retreat, to pull back

retiro M (refugio) retreat; (jubilación) retirement; (de fondos) withdrawal

reto M challenge

retocar[6] VT to retouch, to touch up

retoñar VI to sprout

retoño M sprout, shoot, bud

retoque M retouching

retorcer[2,10c] VT (una toalla mojada) to wring out; (la muñeca) to wrench, to twist; **—se** (de dolor) to writhe; (de inquietud) to squirm

retorcido ADJ (persona) devious; (rama) gnarled

retorcimiento M (de dolor) writhing; (de inquietud) squirming

retórica F rhetoric

retornar VT to return

retorno M return; (de una costumbre, moda) revival

retozar[9] VI to frolic, to romp; (en juegos eróticos) to cavort

retozo M frolic, romp

retractarse VI to take back one's words

retraer[45] VT (las garras) to retract; **—se** to withdraw

retraído ADJ shy

retraimiento M shyness

retrasado ADJ (falto de desarrollo) backward; (deficiente mental) retarded

retrasar VT to delay; (un reloj) to set back; **—se** to fall behind

retraso M delay, lag

retratar VT to portray; (pintar un retrato) to paint a portrait

retrato M (pintura) portrait; (descripción) portrayal

retreta F retreat

retrete M lavatory

retroactivo ADJ retroactive

retroalimentación F feedback

retroceder VI to step back; (de horror) to recoil, to shrink back; (en un coche) to back up; (al mecanografiar) to backspace; (dar marcha atrás) to backtrack; (tropas) to retreat, to fall back; (una inundación) to recede

retroceso M (de un arma de fuego) recoil; (económico) recession; (en un teclado) backspace

retrogradismo M backwardness

retrógrado ADJ backward

retroproyector M overhead projector

retrovirus M retrovirus

retrucar[6] VT to counter

retruécano M play on words

retumbar VI to rumble, to roll

retumbo M rumble
reubicar[6] VT to relocate
reuma M rheumatism
reumatismo M rheumatism
reunión F meeting; (informal) get-together; (de ex-alumnos) reunion
reunir VT (juntar) to gather; (hacer que acudan al mismo lugar) to reunite, to bring together; (coleccionar) to collect; (juntar coraje) to muster; (juntar dinero) to raise; **—se** (formal) to meet; (mucha gente) to gather; (informal) to get together
revancha F (venganza) revenge; (en deportes) return game
revelación F revelation
revelado M film development
revelador ADJ revealing
revelar VT to reveal; (película) to develop; (un escándalo) to expose; (información) to disclose; **—se** to show oneself
revendedor -ora MF (de mercadería) middleman; (de entradas) scalper
revender VT (vender de nuevo) to resell; (billetes) to scalp
reventar[1] VI/VT (estallar) to burst, to bust; (morir) to die; (fastidiar) to annoy
reventón M (acción de reventar) bursting; (de un neumático) blowout
reverberar VI to reverberate
reverdecer[13] VI (ponerse verde de nuevo) to become green again; (renovarse) to gain new strength
reverencia F reverence; (gesto) bow
reverenciar VT to revere
reverendo -da ADJ & MF reverend
reverente ADJ reverent
reverso M reverse
revertir[3] VI to revert; **— en beneficio de** to be of benefit to
revés M (cosa opuesta) reverse; (en tenis) backhand; (contratiempo) setback, downturn; **al —** (con lo de adelante hacia atrás) backwards; (con lo de arriba hacia abajo) upside down; **dar vuelta al —** to turn inside out
revestimiento M overlay
revestir[5] VT (un camino) to surface; (una pared) to cover; (conllevar) to be marked by
revisar VT (examinar) to review, to go over; (un coche) to service
revisión F review; (de una película vieja) revival
revisor -ora MF (en un tren, autobús) conductor
revista F (inspección) inspection; (de tropas) muster; (publicación) magazine, journal;

periodical; (espectáculo) revival; **— de historietas** comic book; **— electrónica** e-zine; **pasar —** to pass in review
revistar VT to inspect
revivir VI/VT to revive
revocación F revocation; (de una ley) repeal
revocar[6] VT (un fallo) to reverse; (una ley) to repeal; (una pared) to plaster
revolcar[6] VT (derribar) to knock over; **—se** (cerdos) to wallow; (niños) to roll around
revolear VT to roll
revolotear VI to flutter, to flit
revoltijo M (de cosas) jumble; (de pelo) muss
revoltoso -sa ADJ unruly, disorderly; MF troublemaker
revolución F (cambio radical) revolution; (giro) revolution, turn; **revoluciones por minuto** revolutions per minute
revolucionario -ria ADJ revolutionary, earthshaking; MF revolutionary
revolver[2,51] VT (remover) to stir up; (registrar) to rummage in; (desordenar) to mess up; (huevos) to scramble; (ensalada) to toss; **eso me revuelve el estómago** that makes my stomach turn; **—se** to toss and turn
revólver M revolver, pistol
revuelo M stir, commotion
revuelta F revolt
revuelto ADJ (el mar) rough; (los ánimos) restless; (el pelo) disheveled; **huevos —s** scrambled eggs
rey M king; **los —es Magos** the Wise Men
reyerta F melee, squabble
rezagarse[7] VI to straggle behind, to lag behind
rezar[9] VI/VT (a Dios) to pray; (un letrero) to say
rezo M prayer
rezongar[7] VI/VT (murmurar) to grumble; (quejarse) to gripe
rezongón -ona ADJ grumpy; MF grouch
rezumar VT to ooze
riachuelo M brook
riada F flash flood
ribazo M steep bank
ribera F shore, bank; (de río) riverbank
ribereño ADJ on the bank
ribete M (de uniforme) trimming; (de alfombra) binding; (de ropa) piping; (de mosaico) border; **tener —s de** to have hints of
ribetear VT (un uniforme) to trim; (una alfombra) to bind; (un diseño) to border
ricacho ADJ very rich
rico ADJ (persona) rich, wealthy, affluent; (suelo) rich; (piso) exquisite; (manjar)

delicious; (niño) cute

ridiculizar[9] VT to ridicule, to deride

ridículo ADJ ridiculous; (medio absurdo) ludicrous; **hacer el —** to act the fool; **poner en —** to ridicule; **ponerse en —** to make a spectacle of oneself

riego M irrigation

riel M rail

rienda F rein; **dar — suelta** to give a free hand

riesgo M risk; **correr un —** to run a risk

rifa F raffle

rifar VT to raffle

rifirrafe M free-for-all

rifle M rifle

rigidez F rigidity

rígido ADJ rigid

rigor M (exactitud) rigor; (del invierno) harshness; **en —** in reality; **de —** indispensable

riguroso ADJ rigorous; (invierno) harsh

rima F rhyme

rimar VI/VT to rhyme

rimbombante ADJ grandiose

rímel M mascara

rin M rim

rincón M corner; (lugar retirado) nook, alcove

rinconera F (mueble) corner cupboard; (mesa) corner table

ring M boxing ring

ringlera F row

rinoceronte M rhinoceros

rinoplastia F *fam* nose job

rinovirus M rhinovirus

riña F (discusión) quarrel; (pelea) scrap, fight, spat

riñón M kidney; (región lumbar) lower back

río M river; **— abajo** downstream

ripio M rubble

riqueza F wealth; **—s** riches

risa F (carcajada) laugh; (acción, sonido de reír) laughter; **reventar / desternillarse de —** to burst with laughter; **morirse de —** to die laughing; **¡qué —!** what a joke!

risco M crag, bluff

risible ADJ laughable

risita F (burlona) snicker; (ahogada) chuckle

risotada F guffaw, gale of laughter

ristra F string

risueño ADJ (sonriente) smiling; (alegre) cheerful

rítmico ADJ rhythmical

ritmo M rhythm; **— cardíaco** heart rate; **— de vida** pace of life

rito M rite

ritual ADJ & M ritual

rival ADJ & MF rival

rivalidad F rivalry

rivalizar[9] VI to rival; **— con** to compete with

rizado ADJ curly; M curling

rizar[9] VT (pelo) to curl, to crimp; (agua) to ripple

rizo M (en el pelo) curl, ringlet; (en el agua) ripple, ruffle; (hecho por un avión) loop

robar VT (algo a una persona) to rob; (dinero) to steal

roble M oak tree

robledal M oak grove

robo M (violento) robbery; (furtivo) theft; **— con allanamiento** burglary

robot M robot

robótica F robotics

robusto ADJ robust; (grueso) stout, stocky; (sólido) sturdy

roca F rock

roce M (acción de rozar) graze; (en una prenda) rub; (conflicto) brush

rociada F (acción de rociar) sprinkling, spraying; (de insultos) volley

rociar[16] VI/VT to spray, to sprinkle; (carne) to baste

rocín M nag

rocío M (del alba) dew; (en aerosol) spray, mist

rock M rock

rocoso ADJ rocky

rodada F track; (profunda) rut

rodadura F rolling

rodaja F flat round slice

rodaje M (de un coche) running; (de una película) shoot

rodar[2] VI (girar) to roll; (caer) to tumble down; (vagar) to roam; (filmar) to shoot

rodear VT (cercar) to surround; (cubrir) to wrap around; (evitar) to go around

rodeo M (desvío) detour; (modo de expresarse) circumlocution; (fiesta) rodeo

rodilla F knee; **de —s** on one's knees; **hincarse de —s** to kneel down

rodillo M (para pintar) roller; (para cocinar) rolling pin; (para caminos) road roller

rododendro M rhododendron

roedor M rodent

roer[50] VI/VT to gnaw

rogar[2,7] VT to pray, to beg, to beseech; **hacerse —** to play hard to get; **se ruega no molestar** please do not disturb

rojez F redness

rojizo ADJ reddish

rojo ADJ & M red; **al — vivo** red-hot

rollizo ADJ plump; M log

rollo M (de papel, de película, de grasa) roll;

(de árbol) log; (de cuerda) reel; (de tela) bolt; (discurso aburrido) story; (mentira) lie; (lío) mess, hassle; (relación amorosa) affair; (manuscrito) scroll; (de alambre) coil; **dar el —** to hassle

ROM M ROM

romance ADJ Romance; M (lengua románica) Romance language; (español) Spanish language; (relación amorosa) romance; (composición métrica) ballad; **en buen —** in plain language

románico ADJ (arte) Romanesque; (lengua) Romance

romano -na ADJ & MF Roman

romanticismo M (corriente literaria) romanticism; (sentimentalismo) romance

romántico -ca ADJ & MF romantic

rombo M diamond

romería F pilgrimage

romero -ra MF (persona) pilgrim; M rosemary

romo ADJ (sin punta) blunt; (sin filo) dull

romper[51] VI/VT to break; VT (relaciones) to sever; **— a** to start to; **— con** to break up with; **— el alba** to dawn; **— filas** to break ranks; **rompió las aguas / la fuente** her water broke; **de rompe y rasga** coarse; M SG **rompecabezas** jigsaw puzzle; **rompehuelgas** strikebreaker; **rompeolas** breakwater

rompible ADJ breakable

rompientes M PL surf

rompimiento M (con el pasado) break; (de una promesa) breach

rompope M *Méx* eggnog

ron M rum

roncar[6] VI to snore

roncha F (de sarampión) spot; (de mosquito) bite

ronco ADJ hoarse, raspy

ronda F (de policía) patrol, beat; (de niños) circle; (de bebidas, de negociaciones) round

rondar VT (patrullar) to patrol; (acercarse por interés) to hang around; (cantar serenatas) to serenade; **rondaba los cuarenta** she was around forty years old

ronquera F hoarseness

ronquido M snore

ronronear VI to purr

ronroneo M purr

ronzal M halter

roña F (enfermedad de plantas) scab; (sorna) mange; MF INV (tacaño) skinflint

roñoso ADJ (planta) scabby; (animal) mangy; (persona) stingy

ropa F clothing, clothes; **— blanca** linen; **— vieja** stew made from leftover meat

ropaje M apparel

ropería F checkroom

ropero M (armario) wardrobe; (cuarto) closet

roque M castle

rorro M baby

rosa F (flor) rose; (marca) blemish; **— de los vientos** mariner's compass; ADJ (rosado) rose colored, pink; (homosexual) *fam* gay

rosado ADJ (saludable) rosy; (de color de rosa) rose-colored, pink; M rosé wine

rosal M rosebush

rosario M rosary

rosbif M roast beef

rosca F (de tornillo) screw; (pan) ring-shaped roll; **pasarse de —** to go off the deep end

rostro M (cara) face; (morro) nerve

rotación F rotation

rotar VI/VT to rotate

rotativo ADJ (movimiento) rotary; (cultivos) rotating; M *Esp* newspaper

rotatorio ADJ rotary

roto ADJ (broken); (cansado) exhausted; (ropa, voz) ragged

rotor M rotor

rótula F kneecap

rotular VT to label

rótulo M (título) title; (etiqueta) label

rotundo ADJ resounding; **una negativa rotunda** a categorical denial

rotura F break; (de un órgano, tubo) rupture

roturar VT to plow

round M (asalto) round

rozadura F chafing

rozamiento M friction

rozar[9] VT (herir levemente) to graze; (arañar) to scrape; (irritar) to rub, to chafe; (limpiar un terreno) to clear; **—se con alguien** to have dealings with someone; **rozaba en los cuarenta** she was almost forty years old

Ruanda F Rwanda

ruandés -esa ADJ & MF Rwandan

rubí M ruby; (en un reloj) jewel

rubicundo ADJ (permanente) ruddy; (temporal) flush

rubio -a ADJ & MF blond

rubor M blush, flush; (de las mejillas) bloom, glow

ruborizarse[9] VI to blush

rúbrica F (trazo) flourish; (título) title

rucio ADJ gray

rudeza F rudeness, coarseness

rudo ADJ rude, coarse; **— golpe** hard blow

rueca F spinning wheel

rueda F (de coche) wheel; (de personas) circle; (rodaja) slice; **— de prensa** news conference; **ir sobre —s** to be smooth sailing

ruedo M ring; (de vestido) hem

ruego M prayer, plea, entreaty

rufián M (matón) ruffian; (proxeneta) pimp

rugby M rugby

rugido M roar

rugir[11] VI to roar; (estómago) to growl

rugoso ADJ rough

ruibarbo M rhubarb

ruido M noise; **mucho — y pocas nueces** much ado about nothing

ruidoso ADJ noisy, loud

ruin ADJ (persona, cosa) vile; (animal) puny

ruina F (acción de arruinar) destruction; (edificio, estado de pobreza) ruin; (persona) wreck; (perjuicio) downfall; **en —s** in ruins

ruindad F (actitud) vileness; (acto) vile act

ruinoso ADJ ruinous

ruiseñor M nightingale

rulero M *RP* roller, curler

ruleta F roulette

rulo M roller, curler

Rumania F Romania, Rumania

rumano -na ADJ & MF Romanian, Rumanian

rumba F rumba

rumbear VI to head in a certain direction

rumbo M course, route; **— a** toward

rumiar VI (meditar) to ruminate; (reflexionar) to ruminate, to mull over, to brood over

rumor M rumor

runrún M (rumor) rumor; (sonido sordo) humming

ruptura F (de relaciones) break; (de órganos internos) rupture

rural ADJ rural

Rusia F Russia

ruso -sa ADJ & MF (persona) Russian; M (lengua) Russian

rústico ADJ (rural) rustic, rural; (tosco) coarse; **en rústica** paperback

ruta F route; (carretera) highway

rutina F routine

Ss

sábado M Saturday

sábalo M shad

sábana F bed sheet

sabañón M chilblain

saber[41] VI/VT to know; **— nadar** to know how to swim; **supo la verdad** he found

out the truth; **— a** to taste like; **— a ciencia cierta** to know for sure; **— de biología** to know all about biology; **a —** namely; **hacer —** to let know; **las vacaciones me han sabido a poco** my vacation was too short; **para que sepas** for your information; **sabe bien** it tastes good; **sabérselas todas** to know the ropes; **vaya a —** who knows? M knowledge, learning; **a mi leal — y entender** as far as I know; **sabelotodo** know-it-all

sabiduría F wisdom

sabiendas LOC ADV **a —** knowingly

sabihondo -da ADJ & MF wise guy; know-it-all

sabio -bia ADJ wise, sage; MF (estudioso) scholar; (sabedor) sage, wise person

sable M saber

sabor M taste, flavor

saborear VT to savor, to relish

sabotaje M sabotage

sabotear VT to sabotage

sabroso ADJ (comida) savory, tasty; (cuento) juicy

sabueso M (perro) bloodhound; (detective) sleuth

sacar[6] VT (cosas de la maleta, a pasear) to take out; (manchas, dinero del banco) to get out; (los zapatos) to take off; (malas notas, carnet de conducir) to get; (una copia) to make; (una foto) to take; (una conclusión) to draw; (la lengua, la cabeza por la ventana) to stick out; (una pelota de tenis) to serve; (una asignatura escolar) *Esp* to pass; **— ampollas** to blister; **— brillo** to polish up; **— provecho (de)** to benefit (from); **— a bailar** to ask to dance; **— a colación** to broach; **— a luz** to divulge; **— de un apuro** to bail out; **me saca de quicio** he gets my goat, he gets on my nerves; **— el cuerpo** to dodge; **— el mejor partido de** to make the best of; **—le el jugo a algo** to make the most of; **— en limpio** to deduce; **— el sombrero** *Am* to take off one's hat; **¡sáquese de allí!** *Am* get out of there! **— punta** to sharpen; M SG **sacabocados** punch; **sacacorchos** corkscrew; **sacamuelas** quack dentist; **sacapuntas** pencil sharpener

sacarina F saccharine

sacerdocio M priesthood

sacerdote M priest

saciar VT to satiate; **—se** to be satiated

saco M (bolsa) sack; (prenda) blazer, sport coat; (de boxeo) punching bag; **— de**

dormir sleeping bag; **— de noche** overnight bag; **echar en — roto** to waste one's effort

sacramento M sacrament

sacrificar[6] VT to sacrifice; (una mascota) to put to sleep

sacrificio M sacrifice

sacrilegio M sacrilege

sacrílego ADJ sacrilegious

sacristán M sexton

sacudida F shake, jolt; (de terremoto) tremor; (de la cabeza) toss; (eléctrica) shock

sacudir VT to shake; (las alfombras) to beat; (el polvo) to dust; **ir sacudiéndose** to rattle along, to jolt along; **—se de alguien** to get rid of someone

sádico ADJ sadistic

sadismo M sadism

sadomasoquismo M sadomasochism

saeta F arrow

safari M safari

sagaz ADJ shrewd, astute

sagrado ADJ sacred, holy; **Sagrada Escritura** Holy Scripture

sahumar VT to perfume with incense

sahumerio M burning of incense

sainete M one-act farce; **esa familia es un — that family is a complete mess

sal F (mineral) salt; (gracia) wit; **— gorda** cooking salt; **— yodada** iodized salt; **— de mesa** table salt; **dar — ** to spice up; **— y pimienta** life, spark

sala F (de estar) parlor, living room; (grande) large room; **— de justicia** courtroom; **— de clase** classroom; **— de espera** waiting room; **— de directorio** boardroom; **— de lectura** reading room; **— de operaciones** operating room

salado ADJ salty; (gracioso) witty; M (acción) salting

salamandra F salamander

salar VT to salt; **—se** to become salty

salario M pay, wages; **— base** base pay; **— mínimo** minimum wage

salchicha F sausage

saldar VT to settle

saldo M (resultado final) balance; (venta especial) sale

salegar[7] VT to give salt to; M salt lick

salero M (dispensador) saltcellar, saltshaker; (gracia) charm

saleroso ADJ charming

salida F (partida) departure; (puerta) exit, way out; (de una carrera) start; (militar) sally; (eléctrica, computadora) output; (de una crisis) way out; **este artículo tiene mucha — ** this article sells well; **dar la —**

to start a race; **— del sol** sunrise; **— de emergencia** emergency exit; **— en falso** false start

saliente ADJ (roca) salient, projecting; (gobierno) outgoing; M salient, projection, overhang

salina F salt mine

salino ADJ saline

salir[42] VI (del interior al exterior, para divertirse) to go out; (de un país) to depart, to leave; (del trabajo) to quit; (manchas de tinta) to come out; (un anillo del dedo) to come off; (el sol) to rise; (una publicación) to appear; (flores) to sprout; **trabajando no se puede — de pobre** you can't work your way out of poverty; **salió a su madre** she takes after her mother; **— a la luz** to surface; **— adelante** to overcome difficulties; **— bien** to turn out well; **— con** to date; **— ganando** to come out ahead; **— mal** to go wrong; **¿a cuánto sale?** how much is it? **no me sale ser amable con él** I can't bring myself to be nice to him; **—se** (gotear) to leak; (rebosar) to overflow; (proyectarse) to stick out

saliva F saliva

salmón M salmon

salmonela F salmonella

salmuera F brine

salobre ADJ salty

salomonense ADJ & MF Solomon Islander

salón M (de estar) living room, parlor; (de conferencias) hall; **— de belleza** beauty parlor; **— de clase** classroom; **— de exposición y ventas** showroom; **— de exhibición** exhibition hall; **— de té** tearoom

salpicadero M dashboard

salpicadura F spatter, splash, splatter

salpicar[6] VI/VT to sprinkle, to spatter, to splash; (adornar) to punctuate; (dispersar) to intersperse

salpicón M meat salad

salpimentar[1] VT to salt and pepper

salsa F sauce; **en su — ** in her element; **— tártara** tartar sauce; **— de soya** soy sauce; **— de tomate** ketchup

saltar VI (brincar) to jump, to leap; (cinco metros) to jump; (una cerca) to jump over, to vault; (un renglón) to skip; VT (los fusibles) to trip; (una ley) to ignore; **— a la vista** to be obvious; **— sobre** to pounce on; **se le saltaron los ojos** his eyes bugged out; **se le saltó un botón** one of his buttons popped off; **se me saltaban las lágrimas** it brought tears to my eyes; M SG **saltamontes** grasshopper

salteador -ora MF bandit

saltear VT to stir-fry

salto M jump, leap; — **de agua** waterfall; **a — de mata** from hand to mouth; — **de cama** dressing gown; **dar un —** (saltar) to jump; (el corazón) to skip a beat; — **alto** high jump; — **con esquí** ski jump; — **con pértiga** pole vault; — **de longitud** broad jump; — **del ángel** swan dive; — **mortal** somersault; — **triple** triple jump

saltón ADJ jumping; (ojo) bulging; M grasshopper

salubridad F sanitation

salud F health; — **mental** mental health; **curarse en —** to take precautions; INTERJ cheers!

saludable ADJ healthy, healthful

saludar VT (decir hola) to greet; (recibir bien) to salute, to hail; (en el militar) to salute; (hacer un gesto amistoso con la mano) to wave

saludo M (hola) greeting, salutation; (gesto) wave; (militar) salute; **retirar el — a alguien** to stop speaking to someone; **—s** best wishes, regards

salva F salvo

salvación F salvation

salvado M bran

salvador -ora MF savior; ADJ saving

salvadoreño -ña ADJ & MF Salvador(i)an

salvaguarda F safeguard

salvaguardar VT to safeguard

salvajada F (acción) savage act; (comentario) savage remark

salvaje ADJ (feroz) savage; (no domesticado) wild; MF savage

salvajismo M savagery

salvamento M (de gente) rescue; (de propiedad) salvage

salvar VT (la vida, el alma) to save; (de un peligro) to rescue; (propiedad) to salvage; (un obstáculo) to clear; (un camino difícil) to negotiate; — **el pellejo** to save one's skin; **el puente salva el río** the bridge spans the river; **—se** to pull through; **—se por poco** to have a narrow escape; **sálvese quien pueda** every man for himself; M SG **salvavidas** (aparato) life preserver, life jacket; MF (persona) lifeguard

salvia F sage

salvo ADJ safe; **a —** safe; **—conducto** safe-conduct; PREP save, except; — **en caso de desastre** barring a disaster

Samoa F Samoa

samoano -na ADJ & MF Samoan

sanar VI/VT to heal; M **sanalotodo** cure-all

sanatorio M (para convalecientes) sanitarium; (hospital) hospital

sanción F sanction

sancionar VT to sanction

sandalia F sandal

sandez F (acción) stupidity, foolishness; (dicho) foolish remark

sandía F watermelon

saneamiento M sanitation

sanear VT to drain

sangrar VI/VT to bleed; VT (un árbol) to tap; (un párrafo) to indent

sangre F blood; — **fría** coolness under pressure; **a — fría** in cold blood; **hacerse mala —** to get upset; **eso lo llevo en la — that's in my blood; de — caliente** warm-blooded; — **azul** blue blood; **sudar — to sweat bullets; de pura —** thoroughbred; **chupar la — a alguien** to be a parasite on someone

sangría F (bebida) wine punch; (acción de sangrar) bleeding; (espacio tipográfico) indentation; (pérdida de recursos) drain

sangriento ADJ (manchado de sangre, que provoca la pérdida de sangre) bloody; (sanguinario) bloodthirsty

sanguijuela F leech

sanguinario ADJ bloody, vicious

sanidad F public health

sanitario ADJ sanitary; M **—s** bathroom fittings

sanmarinense ADJ & MF San Marinese

sanmarinés -esa ADJ & MF San Marinese

sano ADJ (persona) healthy; (juicio) sound; (dieta) healthful; (vaso) unbroken; — **y salvo** safe and sound; **en su — juicio** of sound mind

sánscrito M Sanskrit

sanseacabó INTERJ **te quedas y —** you're staying and that's that

santalucense ADJ & MF St. Lucian

santiamén LOC ADV **en un —** in a jiffy, lickety-split

santidad F sanctity, holiness

santificar[6] VT to sanctify

santiguarse[8] VI to cross oneself

santo -ta ADJ saintly, holy; **esperar todo el — día** to wait the whole blessed day; MF saint; **día del —** saint's day; **quedarse para vestir —s** to be a spinster; **¿a — de qué?** for what reason? **¡por todos los —s!** my goodness!

santotomense ADJ & MF São Tomean

santuario M sanctuary

santurrón -ona ADJ & MF goody-goody

saña F fury

sañudo ADJ furious

sapo M toad (también hombre); **echar —s y culebras** to swear, to curse; **sentirse como un — de otro pozo** to feel like a fish out of water

saque M tennis serve, tennis service

saquear VT to sack, to plunder, to pillage

saqueo M sacking, plundering, pillaging

sarampión M measles

sarape M *Méx* serape

sarcasmo M sarcasm

sarcástico ADJ sarcastic

sarcófago M sarcophagus

sarcoma M sarcoma

sardina F sardine

sardo -da ADJ & MF Sardinian

sardónico ADJ sardonic

sargento -ta MF sergeant; F battle-ax(e)

sarmentoso ADJ gnarled

sarmiento M vine

sarna F mange

sarnoso ADJ mangy

sarpullido M rash

sarro M tartar, plaque

sarta F string

sartén F frying pan, skillet

sastre -tra MF tailor

sastrería F tailor shop

satánico ADJ satanic

satélite M satellite; **— artificial** man-made satellite

satén M satin

sátira F satire

satírico ADJ satirical

satirizar[9] VT to satirize

satisfacción F satisfaction

satisfacer[30,51] VT to satisfy; (una deuda) to pay; **—se** to be satisfied

satisfactorio ADJ satisfactory

satisfecho ADJ contented, satisfied

saturar VT to saturate; (un mercado) to glut; (líneas de teléfono) to overload

sauce M willow; **— llorón** weeping willow

saudí, saudita ADJ & MF Saudi Arabian

savia F sap

saxofón M saxophone

sazón F season; **a la —** at that time; **en —** ripe

sazonar VT (condimentar) to season, to flavor; (llegar a su sazón) to ripen

scooter M scooter

scout MF scout

se PRON PERS **— coronó a sí mismo** he crowned himself; **— lavó la cara** he washed his face; **— besaron** they kissed each other; **— habla español** Spanish is spoken; **— lo puede combatir** it can be fought

sebo M tallow, fat

secador M hair dryer

secadora F clothes dryer

secante ADJ drying

secar[6] VT to dry; (las manos) to dry off; **—se** (planta) to dry up; (río) to run dry; (madera) to season

sección F (militar) platoon; (de un almacén) department

seccionar VT to section

seco ADJ dry; (río) dried-up; (planta) withered; (respuesta) curt, brief; **en —** on dry land; **parar en —** to stop short; **quedar —** to fall dead; **estar —** to be broke; **lavar en —** to dry-clean; **a secas** plain

secreción F secretion

secretar VT to secrete

secretaría F secretariat

secretariado M (profesión) secretarial profession; (secretaría) secretariat; (conjunto de secretarias) secretarial pool

secretario -ria MF secretary; **— general** secretary general

secretear VI to whisper

secreto ADJ secret; (de policía sin uniforme) undercover; M (cosa oculta) secret; (condición de oculto) secrecy; **— a voces** open secret; **en —** in secret; **— bancario** client confidentiality

secta F sect

sector M sector

secuaz M henchman

secuela F consequence; **—s** aftermath

secuencia F sequence

secuenciar VT to sequence

secuestrador -ora MF kidnapper

secuestrar VT (a una persona) to kidnap, to abduct; (propiedad) to seize; (un avión) to hijack

secuestro M (de una persona) kidnapping; (de propiedad) seizure; (de un avión) hijacking

secular ADJ secular

secundar VT to second; (imitar) to imitate; (seguir) to follow suit

secundaria F secondary school

secundario ADJ secondary

sed F thirst; **tener —** to be thirsty

seda F silk; **como una —** (suave) soft as silk; (afable) sweet-tempered

sedación F sedation

sedán M sedan

sedante ADJ & M sedative

sedar VT to sedate

sedativo ADJ & M sedative
sede F (gubernamental) seat; (religiosa) see
sedentario ADJ sedentary
sedería F (conjunto de artículos de seda) silk goods; (tienda de sedas) silk shop
sedero -ra MF (que vende) silk dealer; (que fabrica) silk weaver; ADJ **industria sedera** silk industry
sedición F sedition
sediento ADJ thirsty; **estar — de** to thirst for
sedimento M sediment
sedoso ADJ silken, silky
seducción F seduction
seducir[24] VT (corromper) to seduce; (atraer) to entice; (persuadir con argucias) to lure
seductivo ADJ alluring
seductor -ora ADJ alluring; M seducer; F seductress
sefardí ADJ Sephardic; MF Sephardi; M (variedad del español) Sephardi
sefardita ADJ & M Sephardi
segador -ora MF (persona) mower, reaper; F (máquina) mower, reaper
segar[1,7] VT (hierba) to mow; (mies) to reap
seglar ADJ secular; M layman; F laywoman
segmento M segment
segregar[7] VT (separar) to segregate; (producir una sustancia) to secrete
seguida LOC ADV **en —** at once, immediately
seguido ADJ in a row; **dos horas seguidas** two hours in a row; ADV straight through; **trabajaron —** they worked continuously
seguidor -ora MF follower
seguimiento M (persecución) pursuit; (atención continuada) follow-up
seguir[5,12] VT to follow; (estudios) to pursue; (progreso de un avión) to track; **sigue trabajando** he keeps on working; **sigue allí** he is still there; **de lo anterior se sigue que** from the preceding it follows that; **— los pasos de** to follow in the footsteps of; **—le la corriente a alguien** to play along with someone; **— el tren** to keep up; **— el hilo de** to keep track of; **— la pista de** to trail
según PREP according to; **— se mire** depending on how you see it; **— pasa el tiempo** as time goes by; **— tus instrucciones** per your instructions; CONJ as; **lo haré — me digas** I will do it as you tell me to
segundero M (de reloj) second hand
segundo -da ADV, ADJ & M second; **segunda intención** ulterior motive; **de —** secondrate; **de segunda mano** secondhand; MF second in command
segundón -ona MF (hijo) second-born child;

(persona mediocre) also-ran
seguridad F (contra el delito) security; (contra accidentes) safety; **— en sí mismo** self-confidence; **— social** social security
seguro ADJ (a prueba de delincuencia) secure; (que no ofrece, siente duda) sure, certain; (libre de peligro) safe; (firme) stable; **es — que** it is certain that; **su — servidor** yours truly; **— de sí mismo** self-assured; M (contrato contra riesgos) insurance; (dispositivo) safety device, restraint; **— contra daños a terceros** liability insurance; **— contra incendios** fire insurance; **— contra todo riesgo** comprehensive insurance; **— médico** health insurance; **— de vida** life insurance; **en —** in safety; **sobre —** without risk
seis NUM six
selección F selection, choice; **— natural** natural selection; **— nacional** national team
seleccionar VT to select, to choose
selectivo ADJ selective
selecto ADJ select, choice
sellar VT (poner sello) to stamp; (precintar) to seal
sello M (de correo) stamp; (de documento oficial) seal; (instrumento) seal, stamp; (de discos) label; **— de goma** rubber stamp; **— fiscal** revenue stamp
selva F forest; (tropical) jungle; **— virgen** virgin forest
semáforo M traffic light
semana F week; **entre —** during the week
semanal ADJ weekly
semanario M weekly publication
semántica F semantics
semblante M countenance
semblanza F biographical sketch
sembrado M sown ground
sembradora F planting machine
sembrar[1] VT (plantar) to sow, to plant; (esparcir) to scatter; (minas) to lay; (pánico, alegría) to spread
semejante ADJ similar, like; **— afirmación** such a statement; **un tipo —** such a guy; MF fellow human being
semejanza F resemblance, similarity; **a — de** in the manner of
semejar VT to resemble
semen M semen, sperm
semental ADJ stud; M stud, stallion
semestre M semester
semicírculo M semicircle
semiconductor M semiconductor

semifinal ADJ & F semifinal

semilla F seed

semillero M seedbed; **— de vicios** hotbed of vice

seminario M (religioso) seminary; (universitario) seminar

semítico ADJ Semitic

senado M senate

senador -ora MF senator

sencillez F simplicity

sencillo ADJ (no complicado, de clase humilde) simple; (fácil) easy, simple; (sin adornos) plain; (no afectado) straightforward

senda F (construida) path, pathway; (natural) track, trail

sendero M (construido) path, pathway; (natural) track, trail

sendos ADJ one for each

Senegal M Senegal

senegalés -esa ADJ & MF Senegalese

senil ADJ senile

senilidad F senility

seno M (pecho) breast; (hueco) sinus; (útero) womb; **— de la familia** bosom of the family

sensación F (física) sensation; (mental) feeling, impression; **tengo la — de que** I have the feeling that; **fue la — de la fiesta** she was the life of the party

sensacional ADJ sensational

sensatez F common sense

sensato ADJ sensible, level-headed

sensibilidad F (modo de pensar) sensibility; (percepción) sensitiveness

sensibilizar[9] VT to sensitize

sensible ADJ sensitive; (notable) perceptible; **tengo el brazo muy — por el accidente** my arm is very tender because of the accident; **Juana es muy — en estas ocasiones** Juana is very emotional on these occasions

sensiblería F sentimentality

sensiblero ADJ sentimental, mushy

sensitivo ADJ sensitive

sensor M sensor

sensorial ADJ sensory

sensual ADJ (carnal) sensual; (de los sentidos) sensuous

sensualidad F sensuality

sentada F sitting; (protesta) sit-in; **de una —** at one sitting

sentado ADJ **dar por —** to take for granted

sentar[1] VT to seat; **— bien** to agree with; **me sentó muy mal lo que dijo** what he said did not sit well with me; **este peinado no te sienta** this hairdo does

not become you; **no te sienta ese traje** that suit does not fit you; **— precedente** to set a precedent; **—se** to sit down

sentencia F maxim; (fallo) ruling; (condena) sentence; (indemnización) award

sentenciar VT (condenar) to sentence; (fallar) to rule

sentido ADJ heartfelt; M (facultad) sense; (significado) meaning; (dirección) way; **— común** common sense; **aguzar el —** to prick up one's ears; **de un sólo —** one-way; **de dos —s** two-way; **dejar sin —** to render unconscious; **en cierto —** in a sense; **perder el —** to faint; **quedar —** to have one's feelings hurt; **sin —** meaningless; **tener —** to make sense

sentimental ADJ sentimental

sentimentalismo M sentimentality

sentimiento M feeling, sentiment

sentir[3] VT to feel; (oír) to hear; (lamentar) to regret; **—se** to feel; **—se capaz de** to feel up to; **—se de los pies** to have pains in the feet

seña F (gesto) sign; (rasgo) trait; (marca) mark; **—s** name and address; **por mas —s** as an additional proof; **—s de vida** life signs; **hablar por —s** to use sign language; **hacer —s** to signal

señal F (de tráfico, violencia, vida, de la cruz) sign; (de violencia) mark; (de radio) signal; (pago anticipado) deposit; **en — de** in token of

señalar VT (marcar, señalar) to mark; (mostrar, mencionar) to point out; (fijar) to fix; **—se** to distinguish oneself

señor M (título) mister; (forma de tratamiento) sir; (dueño) lit master, lord; **el Señor** the Lord; **un gran —** a great man

señora F (dama) lady; (forma de tratamiento) madam, ma'am; (título) Mrs., Ms.; (esposa) wife

señorear VI to dominate

señoría F lordship; **su —** your honor

señorial ADJ lordly

señorío M (dominio) dominion; (dignidad) lordship

señorita F miss

señorito M (joven) master; (dandi) dandy

señuelo M decoy, lure

separación F separation

separado ADJ (apartado) separate; (estado civil) separated; **por —** separately

separar VT to separate; (clasificar) to sort out; (despedir de un cargo) to remove; **—se** to separate, to part company

separata F offprint, reprint

septentrional ADJ northern

septicemia F blood poisoning

septiembre, setiembre M September

séptimo ADJ & M seventh

sepulcro M tomb

sepultar VT to bury, to inter

sepultura F (acción) burial; (lugar) grave, tomb; **dar —** to bury

sepulturero -ra MF gravedigger

sequedad F dryness

sequía F drought

séquito M retinue, entourage

ser[43] VI to be; **— de Valencia** to be from Valencia; **— de madera** to be made of wood; **a no — que** unless; **así es** that's right; **érase una vez** once upon a time; **es decir** that is to say; **es de esperar** it is to be expected; **es más** what's more; **la boda es hoy** the wedding takes place today; **son las nueve** it is nine o'clock; **somos cuatro** there are four of us; V AUX to be; **fue elegido presidente** he was elected president; M (entidad viviente) being; (esencia) essence; (existencia) existence; **un — humano** a human being

serenar VI to quiet; **—se** (el alma) to become serene, to calm down; (el tiempo) to clear up

serenata F serenade; **dar —** to serenade

serenidad F serenity

sereno ADJ (mar, alma) serene; (cielo) clear; **al —** in the night air; M night watchman

serie F series; **en —** serial

seriedad F seriousness, earnestness

serio ADJ serious; (persona) earnest, serious; **en —** seriously

sermón M (prédica) sermon; (reprimenda) lecture

sermonear VI/VT (predicar) to preach; (reprender) to lecture

serpentear VI to wind, to meander

serpiente F snake

serrado ADJ serrated

serranía F mountainous region

serrano -na M mountain man; F mountain woman; ADJ **zona —** mountain region

serrín M sawdust

serrucho M handsaw

servicial ADJ helpful

servicio M service; (sirvientes) servants; (para un comensal) place setting; (aseo) rest room, facilities; **— militar** military service; **— de entrega** delivery service; **— a la habitación** room service; **poner en —** to commission, to put into service; **estar en —** to be in commission; **a su —** at your service

servidor -ora MF (persona) servant; **un —** yours truly; **su seguro —** yours truly; M (ordenador) server

servidumbre F servitude

servil ADJ (personalidad) servile; (trabajo) menial

servilleta F napkin

servir[5] VI to serve; **— de** to serve as; **— para** to be used for; **para —le** at your service; **no — para nada** to be of no use; **¿en qué le puedo —?** how can I help you? **—se de** to make use of; **sírvase usted hacerlo** please do it

sésamo M sesame; **¡abre —!** open sesame!

sesenta NUM sixty

sesgado ADJ biased

sesgar[7] VT (una tela) to cut on the bias; (una opinión) to slant; (las estadísticas) to skew

sesgo M (en la tela) bias; (de los ojos, de orientación) slant; **al —** obliquely

sesión F (reunión, periodo) session; (para fotografías) sitting; (de una película) showing

seso M brain; **de poco —** foolish; **devanarse los —s** to rack one's brain

sestear VI to take a nap

sesudo ADJ (persona) brainy; (explicación) intelligent; (testarudo) *Méx* stubborn

set M set

seta F mushroom

setenta NUM seventy

seto M hedge

sétter M setter

seudónimo M pseudonym, pen name

severidad F severity, harshness

severo ADJ severe, stern, harsh

sexar VT to sex

sexismo M sexism

sexo M sex; (órganos) genitals; **el — bello** the fair sex; **— seguro** safe sex

sexto ADV, ADJ & M sixth

sexual ADJ sexual

sexualidad F sexuality

sexy ADJ sexy

Seychelles F PL Seychelles

shock M shock

short, shorts M shorts

si CONJ if; **yo voy — tú vas** I'm going if you're going; **no sé — viene o no** I don't know whether she's coming or not; **¡— ya te lo dije!** but I already told you! **— bien** although; **por — acaso** just in case; **— Dios quiere** God willing; **— no me equivoco** unless I'm mistaken

sí ADV yes; **¿—? really? — que fui** I did go; **creo que —** I think so; M consent; **me dio el —** she said yes; PRON himself, herself, itself, oneself, themselves; **de por** — in itself; **estar sobre** — to be on the alert; **volver en** — to come to; **pagado de** — self-satisfied; **estar fuera de** — to be beside oneself; **hablar para** — to talk to oneself; **dio todo de** — she gave her all; **cada cual para** — every man for himself

sicario M hitman

sicomoro M sycamore

SIDA (síndrome de inmunodeficiencia adquirida) M AIDS

siderurgia F steel industry

sidra F cider

siega F (de la hierba) mowing; (de las mieses) reaping

siembra F (acción de sembrar) sowing; (época) sowing time

siempre ADV always; **desde** — since forever; **para / por** — forever; **por — jamás** forevermore; **— que** (en cualquier momento) whenever; (con tal que) provided that; **— y cuando** provided that; **como** — as usual; **hoy no eres el mismo de** — you're not yourself today

sien F temple

sierpe F *lit* serpent

sierra F saw; (cordillera) small mountain range; **— de cadena** chain saw

siesta F siesta, afternoon nap; **dormir la —** to take an afternoon nap

siete NUM seven

sífilis F syphilis

sifón M (para líquidos) siphon; (tubo) trap

sigilo M stealth

sigla F acronym

siglo M century

signatario -ria MF signer

significación F (sentido) meaning; (importancia) significance

significado M meaning, sense

significar[6] VT to mean, to signify

significativo ADJ significant

signo M sign; **— de admiración** exclamation point; **— de igual** equal sign; **— de interrogación** question mark; **— de más** plus sign; **— de menos** minus sign; **— de multiplicación** multiplication sign; **—s vitales** vital signs

siguiente ADJ following; **al día —** the next day

sílaba F syllable

silbar VI to whistle; (rechiflar) to hiss

silbato M whistle

silbido M whistle

silenciador M (de arma) silencer; (de coche) muffler

silenciar VT to silence

silencio M silence, quiet; **guardar —** to keep quiet

silencioso ADJ silent, quiet

silicio M silicon

silla F chair; (de montar) saddle; **— de ruedas** wheelchair; **— eléctrica** electric chair; **— plegadiza** folding chair

sillín M saddle, seat

sillón M armchair

silo M silo

silogismo M syllogism

silueta F silhouette

siluro M catfish

silvestre ADJ wild

silvicultura F forestry

sima F chasm

simbiosis F symbiosis

simbólico ADJ symbolic

simbolismo M symbolism

símbolo M symbol; **— de status** status symbol; **— sexual** sex symbol

simetría F symmetry

simétrico ADJ symmetrical

simiente F seed

símil M simile

similar ADJ similar

simio M ape

simpatía F friendliness; **no le tengo mucha —** I don't like him much

simpático ADJ (amistoso) nice, friendly, congenial; (sistema nervioso) sympathetic

simpatizar[9] VI (con alguien) to like; (con una idea) to be sympathetic toward

simple ADJ (no complicado) simple; (mero) mere; (tonto) simpleminded

simpleza F (sencillez) simplicity; (estupidez) stupidity

simplicidad F simplicity

simplificar[6] VT to simplify

simplista ADJ simplistic; (explicación) glib, simplistic

simplón -ona ADJ simpleminded; MF simpleton

simposio M symposium

simulacro M **— de batalla** mock battle; **— de incendio** fire drill

simular VT to simulate, to feign

simultáneo ADJ simultaneous

sin PREP without; **— aliento** out of breath; **— amueblar** unfurnished; **— azúcar** sugar-free; **— comentarios** no comment; **— compromiso** without obligation; **— duda** without doubt, undoubtedly; **— embargo** nevertheless; **— escrúpulos** unscrupulous; **— falta** without fail; **— sentido** meaningless

sinagoga F synagogue

sincerarse VI to clear the air

sinceridad F sincerity

sincero ADJ sincere; (opinión) candid; (agradecimiento) heartfelt, wholehearted

sincronización F timing

sincronizar VT to synchronize

sindicar[6] VT to unionize, to syndicate

sindicato M syndicate, trade union, labor union

síndico -ca MF receiver, trustee

síndrome M syndrome; **— de Down** Down's syndrome; **— de abstinencia** withdrawal symptoms

sinfín M un **— de cosas** a lot of things

sinfonía F symphony

Singapur M Singapore

singapurense ADJ & MF Singaporean

singular ADJ (número) singular; (excepcional) unique

siniestro ADJ sinister; M disaster

sinnúmero M myriad

sino CONJ but; **no vino — que llamó** she didn't come, but instead called; **no tengo dos — tres** I don't have two but three; **no es — madera** it's only wood

sinónimo ADJ synonymous; M synonym

sinopsis F synopsis

sinrazón F injustice

sinsabor M trouble

sinsonte M mockingbird

sintaxis F syntax

síntesis F synthesis

sintético ADJ synthetic; (fibras) man-made

sintetizar[9] VT to synthesize

síntoma M symptom

sintonía F tuning

sintonizador M tuner

sintonizar[9] VT (una emisora) to tune in; (un sintonizador) to fine-tune; **los dos sintonizan bien** the two are on the same wavelength

sinuoso ADJ (camino) sinuous, winding; (comportamiento) devious

sinvergüenza MF creep

siquiera ADV at least; **dame — unos días** give me a few days at least; **ni —** not even

sirena F (ninfa, bocina) siren; (mitad mujer, mitad pez) mermaid

Siria F Syria

sirio -ria ADJ & MF Syrian

sirviente -ta MF servant

sisar VT to pilfer, to swipe

sisear VI to hiss

siseo M hiss, hissing

sísmico ADJ seismic

sistema M system; **— operativo** operating system; **— binario** binary system; **— mundial de posicionamiento** global positioning system; **— experto** expert system; **— inmune** immune system; **— nervioso central** central nervous system; **— solar** solar system

sistemático ADJ systematic

sistematizar[9] VI/VT to systematize

sistémico ADJ systemic

sitial M seat of honor

sitiar VT to besiege

sitio M (espacio vacío) room; (ubicación) place, site; (asedio) siege; **no hay —** there's no room; **esto no está en su —** this is out of place; **— web** website; **poner — a** to lay siege to; **poner a alguien en su —** to put someone in his place

sito ADJ situated

situación F situation; (legal, financiero, social) status

situado ADJ situated; **estar —** to be located

situar[17] VT to locate, to place; **—se** to be located

sketch M sketch, skit

slalom M slalom

smog M smog

smoking M dinner jacket

so PREP **— pena de** under penalty of; **— pretexto de** under the pretext of; INTERJ whoa; ADV **— tonto** you stupid idiot!

sobaco M armpit

sobar VT (la masa) to knead; (a una persona) to fondle; (un traje) to wear out

soberanía F sovereignty

soberano -na ADJ & MF sovereign

soberbia F pride, haughtiness

soberbio ADJ proud, haughty

sobornar VT to bribe

soborno M (acción) bribery; (mordida) bribe

sobra F surplus; **—s** leftovers, leavings; **de — sabes** you know full well; **está de —** it is superfluous; **las piezas de —** spare parts

sobrado ADJ more than enough

sobrante ADJ leftover; M surplus

sobrar VI (dinero, libros) to be left over, to remain; (personas) to be in the way

sobre PREP (encima de) above, over; (en contacto con) on, upon; (acerca de) about; **un préstamo — su coche** a loan on his car; **— todo** above all; **— las 9:30** at about 9:30; **marchar — Madrid** to march toward Madrid; M (para cartas) envelope; (de sopa) packet; **— manila** manila envelope; **irse al —** to hit the sack

sobreactuar[17] VI to ham it up
sobrealimentador M supercharger
sobrecalificado ADJ overqualified
sobrecarga F overload
sobrecargar[7] VT to overload
sobrecogedor ADJ awesome
sobrecoger[11b] VI/VT to awe; **—se** to be in awe; **—se de pánico** to be panic-stricken
sobrecogimiento M awe
sobredosis F overdose
sobreentenderse[1] VI to be understood
sobreentendido ADJ understood; M assumption
sobreexcitado ADJ overexcited, wired
sobreexcitar VT to overexcite
sobregirar VT to overdraw
sobregiro M overdraft
sobrehumano ADJ superhuman
sobrellevar VT to bear, to endure
sobremanera ADV beyond measure
sobremesa F after-dinner conversation
sobrenadar VI to float
sobrenatural ADJ supernatural
sobrenombre M nickname
sobrepasar VT to exceed
sobrepeso M overweight
sobreponerse[39] VT to superimpose; VI **— a** (valer más que) to outweigh; (recuperarse) to get over
sobreproteger[11b] VT to smother
sobrepujar VT to surpass
sobresaliente ADJ outstanding; MF understudy
sobresalir[42] VI (ser notable) to stand out; (estar en un plano más saliente) to project, to jut out; (ser excelente) to excel
sobresaltar VT to startle, frighten; **—se** to be startled, to start
sobresalto M start, scare
sobrestante M foreman
sobresueldo M extra pay
sobretodo M overcoat
sobrevenir[47] VI to happen unexpectedly
sobrevivencia F survival
sobreviviente MF survivor; ADJ surviving
sobrevivir VI/VT to survive
sobriedad F sobriety
sobrino -na M nephew; **— nieto** great-nephew; F niece
sobrio ADJ sober
socarrar VT to singe
socarrón ADJ sarcastic
socarronería F sarcasm
socavar VT (excavar por debajo) to dig under; (debilitar) to undermine, to undercut
socavón M sinkhole; shaft, tunnel
sociable ADJ sociable, gregarious

social ADJ social
socialismo M socialism
socialista ADJ & MF socialist
socializar[9] VT to socialize
sociedad F society; (firma) company, partnership; **— anónima** corporation; **— de consumo** consumer society; **alta —** high society
socio -ia MF (de una firma) partner; (de un club) member
socioeconómico ADJ socioeconomic
sociología F sociology
sociópata MF INV sociopath
socorrer VT to help
socorro INTERJ & M help; **acudir al — de** to go to the rescue of; **pedir —** to cry out for help
soda F soda
sodio M sodium
sodomía F sodomy
soez ADJ vulgar
sofá M sofa, couch; **—-cama** sleeper, sofa bed
sofisma M fallacy
sofisticado ADJ sophisticated
sofocante ADJ suffocating, oppressive
sofocar[6] VI/VT to suffocate; (una rebelión) to quash, to quell, to suppress; (un incendio) to put out
sofoco M suffocation
softball M softball
software M software
soga F rope; **estar con la — al cuello** to have a rope around one's neck
soja F (planta) soy; (semilla) soybean
sojuzgar[7] VT to subjugate, to subdue
sol M sun; **de — a —** from sunrise to sunset; **hace —** it is sunny; **tomar el —** to sunbathe; **ella es un —** she's a gem; **arrimarse al — que más calienta** to know which side one's bread is buttered on
solamente ADV only
solana F sunny place
solapa F lapel
solapado ADJ underhanded
solar M (terreno) lot; (casa ancestral) manor; ADJ solar
solaz M *lit* recreation
soldado M soldier; **— raso** private; **— de línea** regular soldier
soldador M soldering iron
soldadura F (acción, con estaño) soldering; (resultado) solder; (acción, sin estaño) welding; (resultado) weld; **— autógena** arc welding
soldar[2] VI/VT (con estaño) to solder; (sin

estaño) to weld; **—se** to mend
soleado ADJ sunny
solear VT to put in the sun; **—se** to sun
   oneself
soledad F solitude, loneliness
solemne ADJ solemn; **— disparate**
   downright foolishness
solemnidad F solemnity
solenoide M solenoid
soler[2,50] VI **suelo levantarme a las siete** I
   usually get up at seven; **solía acostarme**
   tarde I used to go to bed late
solferino ADJ reddish-purple
solicitante MF applicant
solicitar VT (permiso) to request; (un puesto,
   una beca) to apply for
solícito ADJ solicitous
solicitud F (para beca, puesto) application;
   (de información, permiso) request; **a — de**
   at the request of
solidaridad F solidarity
solidez F solidity
solidificar[6] VT to solidify
sólido ADJ solid; (mueble) sturdy;
   (argumento) strong; M solid
solista MF soloist
solitario -ria ADJ solitary; MF (persona)
   recluse; M (juego de cartas, brillante)
   solitaire; F tapeworm
sollozar[9] VI to sob
sollozo M sob
solo ADJ (desamparado) lonely, lonesome; (no
   acompañado) alone; **tengo un — coche** I
   only have one car; **a solas** alone; **habla**
   solo he talks to himself; **ni una sola**
   palabra not a single word; M solo
sólo ADV just, only; **— quiero saber** I just/
   only want to know
solomillo M sirloin
solsticio M solstice
soltar[2] VT (a un prisionero) to let go, to
   release; (el vientre) to loosen; (una
   carcajada) to let out; (bombas) to drop;
   (un disparate) to say; **— amarras** to cast
   off; **— el hervor** to come to a boil; **—**
   tacos to swear; **—se** to loosen up; **—se el**
   pelo to kick up one's heels
soltero -ra ADJ single, unmarried; M
   bachelor; F unmarried woman
solterón -ona M old bachelor; F *pey* spinster
soltura F ease; **hablar con —** to speak
   fluently
soluble ADJ soluble
solución F solution
solucionar VT to solve
solventar VT to settle
solvente ADJ & M solvent

somalí ADJ & MF Somalian
Somalia F Somalia
sombra F (de una figura) shadow; (protección
   del sol) shade; (para ojos) eye shadow;
   hacer — to overshadow; **dar —** to shade;
   no fiarse ni de su propia — to be
   scared of one's own shadow; **a la —** in
   the shade; **sin — de duda** without a
   shadow of a doubt
sombreado ADJ (con protección del sol)
   shady; (oscuro) shadowy
sombrear VT to shade
sombrerería F millinery
sombrerero -ra MF milliner
sombrero M hat; **— de copa** top hat; **—**
   hongo derby
sombrilla F parasol
sombrío ADJ (oscuro) dark; (triste) somber,
   gloomy
somero ADJ shallow
someter VT (proponer algo) to submit; (poner
   bajo dominio) to subject; **—se a** to
   undergo
sometimiento M (proposición) submission;
   (dominio) subjection
somnífero M sleeping pill
somnolencia F drowsiness, sleepiness
somnoliento ADJ drowsy
son LOC ADV **al — de** to the sound of;
   venimos en — de paz we come in peace
sonaja F rattle
sonajero M rattle
sonámbulo -la MF sleepwalker
sonar[2] VI (hacer un sonido) to sound;
   (mencionarse) to be mentioned; (ser
   familiar) to sound familiar; **— a** to sound
   like; VT (bocina) to sound; (tambor) to
   beat; (campana, timbre) to ring; **—se la**
   nariz / los mocos to blow one's nose;
   suena que it is rumored that; M sonar
sonda F (de médico) catheter; (cohete) probe;
   tirar una — to sound
sondear VT (medir la oportunidad) to sound,
   to fathom; (investigar la opinión) to
   sound out
sondeo M survey
soneto M sonnet
sonido M sound
sonoro ADJ sonorous
sonreír[15] VI to smile
sonriente ADJ smiling
sonrisa F smile
sonrojarse VI to blush
sonrojo M blush, flush
sonrosado ADJ rosy
sonsacar[6] VT to extract
soñador -ora MF dreamer

soñar[2] VI/VT to dream; **— con / en** to dream of; **— despierto** to daydream; **— que** to dream that; **ni —** *fam* fat chance

soñoliento ADJ sleepy

sopa F (líquido) soup; (pan mojado) sop; **estar hecho una —** to be sopping wet; **— crema** cream soup

sopapo M smack

sopera F soup tureen

sopesar VT to weigh

sopetón LOC ADV **de —** all of a sudden

soplador -ora MF blower

soplar VI/VT to blow; (la sopa) to blow on; (en un examen) to whisper; (a un amante) to steal

soplete M blowtorch

soplo M breath, puff; **en un —** in a jiffy; **— cardíaco** heart murmur

soplón -ona MF informer, snitch, stool pigeon

sopor M lethargy

soportar VT (apoyar) to support, to bear; (aguantar) to stand, to endure

soporte M support; (de una bicicleta) kickstand

soprano M (voz) soprano; F (cantante) soprano

sorber VI/VT to sip; **—se los mocos** to sniffle

sorbete M sherbet

sorbo M sip; **de un —** in one gulp

sordera F deafness

sórdido ADJ sordid, tawdry, sleazy

sordina F mute

sordo -da ADJ (que no oye) deaf; (dolor) dull; (sonido) dull, muffled; **hacerse oídos —s** to turn a deaf ear; MF deaf person; **hacerse el —** to pretend not to hear

sordomudo -da ADJ deaf and dumb; MF deaf-mute

sorna F irony

sorprendente ADJ surprising, startling

sorprender VT to surprise; **—se** to be surprised

sorpresa F surprise; **— de cumpleaños** party favor; **para mí —** to my surprise; **pillar por —** to catch by surprise

sortear VT (elegir al azar) to draw lots, to raffle; (esquivar) to dodge

sorteo M drawing, raffle

sortija F (anillo) ring; (de pelo) ringlet

sortilegio M spell, charm

SOS M SOS

sosa F soda

sosegado ADJ composed, sedate

sosegar[1,7] VT to calm, to quiet; **—se** to quiet down, to compose oneself

sosiego M quiet, calm

soslayo LOC ADV **de —** oblique, slanting; **mirar de —** to look at out of the corner of one's eye

soso ADJ tasteless, insipid; (persona) dull

sospecha F suspicion

sospechar VT to suspect

sospechoso -sa ADJ suspicious; MF suspect

sostén M (apoyo, sustento) support, prop; (persona que sostiene) supporter, provider; (prenda) brassiere; **— de la familia** breadwinner

sostener[44] VT (una nota musical) to hold, to sustain; (una familia) to support; (un peso) to support, to hold; (una opinión) to claim, to uphold

sostenido ADJ sustained; M sharp

sota F jack, knave

sótano M cellar, basement

soto M thicket

soya F (semilla) soybean; (planta) soy

squash M squash

Sr. M Mr.

Sra. F (casada) Mrs.; (sin indicación de estado civil) Ms.

S.R.C. (Se Ruega Contestar) LOC RSVP

status M status

stop M stop sign

strip-tease M striptease

striptisero -ra MF stripper

su ADJ POS (de él) his; (de ella) her; (de usted, ustedes) your; (de ellos, ellas) their

suave ADJ (pelo, piel) soft; (tiempo, droga) mild; (brisa, persona, animal) gentle; (coñac) smooth; **hablan —** they speak gently

suavidad F (pelo, piel) softness; (coñac) smoothness; (tiempo, droga) mildness; (brisa, persona, animal) gentleness

suavizante M fabric softener

suavizar[9] VT to soften

suazi ADJ & MF Swazi

Suazilandia F Swaziland

subalterno -na ADJ & MF subordinate

subarrendar VI/VT to sublet

subasta F auction

subastador -ora MF auctioneer

subastar VT to sell at auction, to auction

subconsciente ADJ subconscious

subcontratar VT to subcontract

subdesarrollado ADJ underdeveloped

súbdito -ta MF subject

subdivisión F subdivision

subempleado ADJ underemployed

subestimar VT to underestimate

subida F (de precios, de río) rise; (de montaña) climb; (de drogas) high; (cuesta) slope; **—s y bajadas** ups and downs

subido ADJ (color) bright; — **de tono** risqué
subir VI to rise, to go up; (la marea) to surge; (a un tren) to board; (a un autobús, coche) to get into; VT (algo del sótano) to bring up; (una montaña) to climb; (precios) to raise; —**se** to ride up; **el vino se me sube a la cabeza** the wine goes to my head; M **subibaja** seesaw
súbito ADJ sudden
subjetivo ADJ subjective
subjuntivo ADJ & M subjunctive
sublevación F revolt
sublevar VT to incite to rebellion; (indignar) to infuriate; —**se** to revolt
sublime ADJ sublime
submarino ADJ underwater; M submarine
subordinado -da ADJ & MF subordinate
subordinar VT to subordinate
subproducto M by-product
subproletariado M underclass
subrayar VT (con una línea) to underline; (enfatizar) to emphasize
subrepticio ADJ surreptitious
subrutina F subroutine
subsanar VT (una deficiencia) to remedy; (un error) to correct
subsecretario -ia MF undersecretary; — **de Justicia** Solicitor General
subsidiario ADJ subsidiary
subsiguiente ADJ subsequent
subsistencia F survival
subsistir VI to subsist, to survive
subteniente MF second lieutenant
subterfugio M subterfuge
subterráneo ADJ subterranean, underground; M subway
subtítulo M (de un capítulo, película) subtitle; (pie de foto) caption
suburbano -na ADJ of shantytowns; MF shantytown resident
suburbio M shantytown
subvaluar[17] VT to underestimate
subvención F subsidy
subvencionar VT to subsidize
subversivo ADJ subversive
subyacer[49] VI to underlie
subyugar[7] VT (dominar) to subjugate; (hechizar) to charm
succión F suction
sucedáneo -a MF substitute
suceder VI to happen, to occur; — **al trono** to succeed to the throne; VT to succeed
sucesión F succession; (heredero) descendant
sucesivo ADJ successive; **en lo** — in the future
suceso M (evento) event, occurrence; (incidente) incident

sucesor -ora MF successor
suciedad F (porquería) dirt, filth; (cualidad de sucio) filthiness
sucinto ADJ concise
sucio ADJ dirty, filthy; (trabajo, chiste) dirty; (conciencia) guilty; **blanco** — off-white; **este traje es** — this suit gets dirty easily
sucumbir VI to succumb
sucursal F branch, subsidiary
sudadera F sweatshirt
sudado ADJ sweaty
Sudáfrica F South Africa
sudafricano -na ADJ & MF South African
Sudamérica F South America
sudamericano -na ADJ & MF South American
Sudán M Sudan
sudanés -esa ADJ & MF Sudanese
sudar VT to sweat; — **la gota gorda** to sweat blood
sudeste ADJ southeast, southeastern; M southeast
sudoeste ADJ southwest, southwestern; M southwest
sudor M sweat
sudoroso ADJ sweaty
Suecia F Sweden
sueco -ca ADJ Swedish; M (lengua) Swedish; MF Swede; **hacerse el** — to pretend not to understand
suegro -a M father-in-law; F mother-in-law
suela F (de zapato) sole; (pez) flounder
sueldo M salary
suelo M (tierra) soil, ground; (piso) floor; **arrastrar por el** — to drag; **por los** —**s** at rock-bottom
suelto ADJ (no atado) loose, unattached; (flojo) loose; (libre) free; M loose change
sueño M (hecho de dormir) sleep; (hecho de soñar) dream; (ganas de dormir) sleepiness; **en** —**s** dreaming; **conciliar el** — to get to sleep; **tener** — to be sleepy; **ni en** —(**s**) never; **perder el** — to lose sleep; — **húmedo** wet dream; — **profundo** sound sleep; **estar en el séptimo** — to be deeply asleep
suero M serum; — **de leche** buttermilk; — **fisiológico** saline solution
suerte F (destino) fate; (fortuna) luck; (clase) kind; **de** — in luck; **dejar a su** — to leave to his own devices; **echar** —**s** to cast lots; **mala** — (desgracia) bad luck; (lo siento) too bad; **tener** — to be lucky; **tentar a la** — to court danger; **tocarle en** — to be one's lot
suertudo -da ADJ lucky; MF lucky devil
suéter M sweater

suficiencia F adequacy; **tiene una —** she's so arrogant

suficiente ADJ (adecuado) sufficient, adequate; (arrogante) smug; M (calificación mínima) lowest passing grade; PRON enough; **ser —** to be enough; **más que —** ample

sufijo M suffix

sufragar[7] VT to defray; **— los gastos** to meet the expenses

sufragio M suffrage

sufrido ADJ (madre) long-suffering; (pantalón) durable

sufrimiento M suffering

sufrir VI/VT to suffer; VT to stand; (una lesión) to sustain; (un cambio) to undergo; (una pena) to grieve; **— de** to suffer from; **— de los pies** to have foot pains

sugerencia F suggestion

sugerir[3] VT to suggest

sugestión F suggestion

suicida MF suicide

suicidarse VI to commit suicide

suicidio M suicide

suite F suite

Suiza F Switzerland

suizo -za ADJ & MF Swiss; M sweet roll

sujeción LOC ADV **con — a** subject to

sujetar VT (fijar) to attach; (unir) to hold; (someter) to subdue, to hold down; **—se** to hold on; M SG **sujetalibros** bookend; **sujetapapeles** paper clip

sujeto ADJ held by; **— a** subject to; M (de oración, de experimento) subject; (individuo) individual

sulfato M sulphate

sulfurarse VI to hit the roof

sulfúrico ADJ sulfuric

sulfuro M sulfide

suma F (resultado aritmético) sum; (operación aritmética) addition; (cantidad) amount, sum; **en —** in sum

sumadora F adding machine

sumar VT to add, to add up; **—se a** to join

sumario M brief; ADJ summary

sumergible ADJ waterproof

sumergir[11] VT to submerge, to dip; **—se** to dive; **—se en** to immerse oneself in

sumidero M (socavón) sinkhole; (desagüe) drain

suministrar VT to furnish, to supply with

suministros M PL supplies

sumir VT to immerse

sumisión F submission

sumiso ADJ submissive

súmmum M ultimate; **el — de la moda** the cat's meow

sumo ADJ utmost, paramount; **a lo —** at the most

suntuoso ADJ sumptuous, luxurious

superar VT (las expectativas) to surpass; (un límite) to exceed; (una dificultad) to overcome, to surmount; (una prueba) to pass; **—se** to improve oneself

superávit M surplus

supercomputadora F supercomputer

superdirecta F overdrive

superdotado ADJ gifted

superego M superego

superestrella F superstar

superficial ADJ (conocimiento, herida, persona) superficial; (persona) shallow

superficialidad F shallowness

superficie F (parte exterior) surface; (de una figura geométrica) area

superfluo ADJ superfluous

superintendente MF superintendent

superior ADJ (mejor) superior; (más alto) higher; (más grande, intenso) greater; MF superior

superioridad F superiority

superlativo ADJ & M superlative

supermercado M supermarket

superordenador M supercomputer

superponer[39] VT to superimpose

superpotencia F superpower

supersónico ADJ supersonic

superstición F superstition

supersticioso ADJ superstitious

supervisar VT to supervise

supervisión F supervision

supervisor -ora MF supervisor

supervivencia F survival; **la — del más apto** the survival of the fittest

superyó M superego

suplantar VT to supplant

suplementar VT to supplement

suplemento M supplement

suplente ADJ & MF substitute

súplica F entreaty, plea

suplicar[6] VT to plead, to beseech

suplicio M ordeal

suplir VT (sustituir) to substitute for; (compensar) to make up for

suponer[39] VT (dar por sentado) to suppose, to presume, to surmise; (implicar) to involve

suposición F supposition, surmise

supositorio M suppository

supremacía F supremacy

supremo ADJ supreme

supresión F (de una idea) suppression; (de una palabra) deletion

suprimir VT (una idea) to suppress; (la

esclavitud) to abolish; (una palabra) to
delete

supuesto ADJ supposed; **— que** supposing
that; **dar por —** to consider certain; **por
— of course;** M supposition

supuración F discharge

supurante ADJ festering, running

supurar VI to fester, to discharge

sur ADJ & M south; **hacia el —** southward;
rumbo al — southward

surcar[6] VT to plow

surco M (en la tierra) furrow; (en un camino)
rut; (en un disco) groove; (en el rostro)
wrinkle

surcoreano -na ADJ & MF South Korean

sureño -ña ADJ southern; MF southerner

sureste ADJ southeast, southeastern; M
southeast

surfear VI/VT to surf (también en el internet)

surfing M surfing; **hacer —** to surf

surgimiento M rise

surgir[11] VI (situación) to arise; (manantial) to
rise; (problema) to emerge, to crop up

Surinam M Surinam, Suriname

surinamés -esa ADJ & MF Surinamer

surmenage M burnout

suroeste ADJ southwest, southwestern; M
southwest

surrealismo M surrealism

surtido M stock, assortment; ADJ assorted

surtidor M (bomba) pump; (chorro, pieza de
carburador) jet

surtir VT to provide; **— efecto** to produce
the desired effect; **— un pedido** to fill an
order

susceptible ADJ susceptible

suscitar VT to stir up

suscribir[51] VT (una opinión) to subscribe to,
to endorse; (un seguro) to underwrite;
—se a to subscribe to

suscripción F subscription

suscriptor -ora MF subscriber

susodicho ADJ above-mentioned

suspender VT (colgar) to suspend, to hang;
(interrumpir) to suspend, to stop;
(cancelar) to cancel; (no dejar trabajar) to
suspend; VI/VT (no aprobar) to fail, to
flunk

suspense M suspense

suspensión F suspension

suspenso ADJ hanging; **quedarse —** to
freeze; M (en un examen) failure; (en una
película) suspense; **en —** in suspense

suspensorio M jock (strap)

suspicaz ADJ suspicious

suspirar VT to sigh; **— por** to yearn for

suspiro M sigh; **dame un —** give me a

breather

sustancia F substance

sustancial ADJ substantial

sustancioso ADJ substantial

sustantivo M noun; ADJ substantive

sustentar VT to sustain

sustento M (alimento) sustenance; (apoyo)
support; **ganarse el —** to earn a living

sustitución F substitution

sustituible ADJ replaceable

sustituir[31] VI/VT to substitute for, to replace;
Juan sustituyó a María John
substituted for Mary; **sustituí la leche
por agua** I substituted water for milk

sustituto -ta MF substitute

susto M scare, fright

sustracción F subtraction

sustraer[45] VT to take away; **—se a** to avoid

susurrar VI/VT (una persona, el viento) to
whisper; (agua) to murmur, to ripple;
(hojas) to rustle

susurro M (de una persona, del viento)
whisper; (del agua) murmur; (de las hojas)
rustle

sutil ADJ subtle

sutileza F subtlety; (exagerada) nicety,
quibble

sutilizar[9] VT to quibble over

sutura F suture

suyo ADJ (de él) his; (de ella) her; (de usted,
de ustedes) your; (de ellos, de ellas) their;
PRON (de él) his; (de ella) hers; (de usted,
de ustedes) yours; (de ellos, de ellas)
theirs; **salirse con la suya** to get one's
own way; **hacer de las suyas** to be up to
one's tricks; **los —s** his/her/your/their
family

swing M swing

Tt

tabaco M tobacco

tábano M horsefly

tabaquismo M smoking

taberna F tavern, saloon

tabernero -ra MF bartender

tabicar[6] VT to partition

tabique M partition

tabla F (tablero) board, plank; (teatro) stage;
(pliegue) pleat; (gráfica) table, chart; **— de
surf** surfboard; **— de planchar** ironing
board; **—s** (escenario) stage; **—s de la ley**
the tables of the law; **—s de multiplicar**

multiplication tables; — **periódica** periodic table; — **de contenidos** table of contents; — **de cortar** cutting board; **hacer** —**s** to tie

tablado M stage

tablero M (para juegos de mesa) board; (de instrumentos) panel, instrument panel; (de coche) dashboard; (pizarra) blackboard; (para noticias) bulletin board; — **de mando** control panel

tableta F (de aspirina) tablet; (de chocolate) bar

tablilla F (de arcilla) tablet; (de cama) slat; (para fracturas) splint

tabloide M tabloid

tablón M plank

tabú M taboo

tabulador M tab

tabular VT to tabulate, to chart

taburete M stool, footstool

TAC (tomografía axial computarizada) F CAT scan

tacañería F stinginess, tightness

tacaño -ña ADJ stingy, miserly; MF miser

tacha F blemish; (al honor) blot

tachar VT (borrar) to cross out, to delete; (atribuir una tacha) to accuse of

tachón M crossing out

tachonar VT to stud

tachuela F tack, thumbtack

tácito ADJ tacit

taciturno ADJ taciturn

taco M (de artillería) wad; (palo de billar) billiard cue; (comida ligera) snack; (palabrota) swear word; (comida mexicana) *Méx* taco; **soltar** —**s** *Esp* to swear

tacómetro M tachometer

tacón M heel

taconear VI to click the heels

taconeo M clicking

táctica F tactics

táctil ADJ tactile

tacto M (acción de tocar) touch; (sentido) sense of touch; (habilidad diplomática) tact

tahúr -ura MF gambler

tailandés -esa ADJ & MF Thai, Thailander

Tailandia F Thailand

taimado ADJ sly, devious

Taiwán M Taiwan

taiwanés -esa ADJ & MF Taiwanese

tajada F (de pan, carne) slice; (de carne) slab; **sacar** — to take one's cut

tajante ADJ (inequívoco) unequivocal; (cortante) sharp

tajar VT to slice

tajear VI/VT to slash

tajo M (corte) slash, hack; (cañón) gorge; (separación) gap

tal ADJ such; — **cual** just so; — **vez** perhaps; **un** — **García** a certain García; **a** — **grado** to such an extent; **de** — **palo** — **astilla** a chip off the old block; **en** — **caso** in such a case; CONJ — **como** like, just as; **con** — **(de) que** provided that; ADV **¿qué** —**?** how is it going? PRON **y** — and so on; **como si** — as if nothing had happened

taladrar VT to bore, to drill

taladro M drill

talante M temperament

talar VT (un árbol) to chop down; (un bosque) to lumber

talco M talcum

talento M talent

talentoso ADJ talented, gifted

talismán M charm

talla F (altura) height; (moral, intelectual) stature; (de ropa) size; (de madera) carving

tallado M carving

tallar VT to carve; (madera) to whittle, to carve; (naipes) to deal

tallarín M noodle

talle M (cintura) waist, waistline; **tiene buen** — she has a good figure; **corto de** — short-waisted

taller M (para trabajo manual, para enseñanza artística) workshop; (de artista plástico) studio; (de mecánico) garage, shop

tallo M stalk, stem

talón M (de pie, calcetín) heel; (de cheque) stub; — **de Aquiles** Achilles' heel; **girar sobre los talones** to turn on one's heels; **pisarle los talones a alguien** to be hot on someone's heels

talonario M checkbook

talonear VI to walk briskly

tamal M *Méx* tamale

tamaño M size; — **mediano** medium-sized; **de** — **natural** life-sized; ADJ such a big, so big a

tambalearse VI (un borracho) to stagger; (un boxeador) to reel; (un viejo) to dodder

tambaleo M stagger

también ADV also, too, as well

tambor M (instrumento musical, pieza de máquina) drum; (músico) drummer; (cilindro) cylinder; **a** — **batiente** with fanfare

tamborilear VI to drum, to tap

tamborilero -ra MF drummer

tamiz M sieve

tamizar[9] VT to sift

tampoco CONJ either; **no lo hizo** — he did not do it either; **ni yo** — me either

tampón M tampon

tan ADV **es** — **rica** she is so rich; — **alto como Juan** as tall as Juan; — **pronto como** as soon as; **es** — **idiota** he's such an idiot; **vecinos** — **simpáticos** such nice neighbors

tanda F (de personas) group; (de galletas) batch; (de ejercicios) set

tándem M tandem

tanga F thong

tangente ADJ & F tangent; **salirse por la** — (irse de tema) to go off on a tangent; (evadir) to beat about the bush

tangerina F tangerine

tangible ADJ tangible

tango M tango

tanque M tank

tantán M African drum

tantear VT (calcular) to estimate roughly; (averiguar) to sound out, to feel out; (apuntar) to score; (palpar) to grope

tanteo M (cálculo) estimate; (número de tantos) score; **al** — approximately

tanto ADJ, PRON & ADV **lloró** — **que se le enrojecieron los ojos** he cried so much his eyes got red; **yo tengo** — **como tú** I have as much as you do; **me quiere** — he loves me so; **no te quiero** — I don't love you that much; **a cada** —**s pasos** every so many steps; **cuarenta y** —**s** forty-odd; **a** — **el kilo** at so much per kilo; **el** — **por ciento** at such and such a percentage; **estar al** — to be in the know; **no es para** — it's not such a big deal; — **da** it's all the same; — **como** as much as; — **en la ciudad como en el campo** both in the city and in the country; **entre / mientras** — meanwhile; **mantenerse al** — to stay informed; **otros** —**s** just so many more; **por lo** — therefore; **a las tantas** until late at night; M (en los juegos) points

Tanzania F Tanzania

tanzano -na ADJ & MF Tanzanian

tañer[18] VT *lit* (una guitarra) to play; VI (una campana) to ring, to toll

tañido M (de guitarra) twang; (de campanas) toll

tapa F (de botella) cap; (de libro) cover; (de coche) hood; (de olla, bote) lid, top; *Esp* bar snack

tapadera F (de recipiente) lid; (de un fraude) cover

tapar VT (una olla) to cover; (una salida) to

block; (un caño) to plug up, to stop up; (encubrir) to cover up for; M SG

tapacubos hubcap; **tapajuntas** flashing; **taparrabos** loincloth

tapete M runner

tapia F garden wall

tapiar VT to board up

tapicería F (para paredes) tapestry; (para muebles) upholstery; (tienda de textiles de decoración) tapestry shop; (arte de hacer tapices) tapestry making; (tienda de tapicero) upholstery shop

tapioca F tapioca

tapir M tapir

tapiz M tapestry, wall hanging

tapizar[9] VT to upholster

tapón M stopper; (de lavabo) plug; (de corcho) cork; — **de oídos** earplug

taponazo M pop of a cork

taquigrafía F shorthand

taquígrafo -fa MF stenographer

taquilla F ticket office, box office

tarambana MF INV dork, knucklehead

tarántula F tarantula

tararear VI/VT to hum

tarareo M hum, humming

tarascada F (mordedura) snap, bite; (réplica) rude answer

tardanza F lateness

tardar VI to take time; **¿cuánto tarda el trámite de divorcio?** how long does it take to get divorced? —**se** to take a long time; **tu padre se tarda** your father is taking a long time; **a más** — at the latest

tarde F afternoon; (hacia el anochecer) evening; **buenas** —**s** good afternoon; ADV late; **ya es** — it is late; — **o temprano** sooner o later; **más** — later on; **llegar** — to be late

tardío ADJ late

tardo ADJ *lit* slow

tarea F task, chore; (escolar) homework

tarifa F (impuesto) tariff; (lista de precios) list of prices; (de transporte) fare; (precio estipulado) rate

tarima F platform

tarjeta F card (también dispositivo de computadora); — **comercial** business card; — **postal** postcard; — **de cobro automático / de débito** debit card; — **de crédito** credit card; — **de Navidad** Christmas card; **marcar** — to punch in

tarro M jar

tarta F tart, pie

tartajear VI to stutter

tartamudear VI to stutter, to stammer

tartamudeo M stammer, stutter

tartamudez F stuttering
tartamudo -da MF stutterer, stammerer; ADJ stuttering, stammering
tártaro M tartar
tartera F round baking pan
tarugo M (trozo de madera) piece of wood; (tonto) blockhead
tasa F (índice) rate; (impuesto) tax; — **de desempleo** rate of unemployment; — **de interés** interest rate; — **de mortalidad** death rate; — **de natalidad** birth rate; — **prima** prime rate
tasación F valuation, appraisal
tasajo M jerky
tasar VT to appraise, to assess
tatarabuelo -la M great-great-grandfather; F great-great-grandmother
tataranieto -ta M great-great-grandson; F great-great-granddaughter
tatuaje M tattoo
tatuar[17] VT to tattoo
tauromaquia F bullfighting
taxi M taxi, taxicab
taxidermia F taxidermy
taxista MF taxi driver, cab driver
taxonomía F taxonomy
Tayikistán M Tajikistan
tayiko -ka ADJ & MF Tajik
taza F (de té, café) cup; (del inodoro) bowl
tazón M (para beber) mug; (de comida) bowl
té M (bebida) tea; (fiesta) tea party
te PRON you; **yo — amo** I love you; — **digo mañana** I'll tell you tomorrow; **no — mires en el espejo** don't look at yourself in the mirror
teatral ADJ theatrical
teatro M theater; — **de títeres** puppet show; **no hagas** — don't make such a production
techado M (techo) roof; (acción de techar) roofing
techar VT to roof
techo M (exterior) roof; (interior) ceiling
techumbre F roof
tecla F key; — **para mayúsculas** capital letter key; — **de cambio** shift key; — **control** control key; — **de función** function key; — **de retroceso** backspace key; — **de tabulación** tab key; **dar uno en la** — to hit the nail on the head
teclado M keyboard; — **numérico** keypad
teclear VT (pulsar las teclas) to key in; (hacer ruido) to click
tecleo M keying in, clicking
técnica F (método) technique; (tecnología) technology
técnico -ca ADJ technical; MF technician

tecnología F technology
tectónica F tectonics
tedio M boredom
tedioso ADJ tedious
tee M tee
teja F (de cerámica) tile; (de madera u otros materiales) shingle
tejado M roof
tejar M tile factory; VT to cover with tiles
tejedor -ora MF weaver
tejer VI/VT (cesta, tela) to weave; (suéter) to knit; M **tejemaneje** (fraude) hanky-panky; (actividad) goings-on
tejido M (tela) textile, fabric; (de células) tissue; (acción de tejer tela) weaving; (acción de tejer un suéter) knitting
tejo M disk
tejón M badger
tela F (paño) cloth, fabric; (lienzo para pintar) canvas; (de araña) web; (dinero) money; (película) film; — **adhesiva** adhesive tape; — **de cebolla** onion skin; **en** — hardbound; **poner en** — **de juicio** to call into question
telar M loom
telaraña F cobweb, spider's web
tele F TV
telebobo -ba MF couch potato
telecomunicaciones F PL telecommunications
teleconferencia F teleconference
teledifusión F telecast
teledirección F remote guidance
teleférico M cable car
telefonazo M buzz, ring
telefonear VI/VT to telephone, to phone
telefónico ADJ **llamada telefónica** telephone call
telefonista MF telephone operator
teléfono M telephone, phone; (número) telephone number
telegrafiar[16] VI/VT to telegraph, to wire
telegráfico ADJ telegraphic
telégrafo M telegraph
telegrama M Telegram
telemarketing M telemarketing
telemercadeo M telemarketing
telémetro M range finder
telenovela F soap opera
teleobjetivo M zoom lens
telepatía F telepathy
telescopio M telescope
telesquí M ski lift
teletipo M Teletype[tm]
televidente MF television viewer
televisión F television
televisor M television set; — **a / en color**

color television

telón M theater curtain; **— de acero** iron curtain

tema M (de una obra literaria, musical) theme; (de conversación) topic, subject; (de un CD) song

temario M agenda

temático ADJ thematic

temblar[1] VI (la mano, la tierra) to tremble; (la voz) to shake, to quaver; (de frío) to shiver; (de miedo) to shudder; (la luz) to flicker

temblequear VI to dodder

temblón ADJ trembling

temblor M (acción de temblar) trembling; (de tierra) tremor; (de una llama) flicker; (de la voz) quaver; (de frío) shiver; (de miedo) shudder; **— de tierra** earthquake

tembloroso ADJ (mano) shaky; (llama) flickering; (voz) quavering; (de miedo) shuddering; (de frío) shivering

temer VI/VT to fear, to be afraid (of); **— por** to fear for; **mucho me temo que** I fear that

temerario ADJ rash, reckless

temeridad F temerity, recklessness

temeroso ADJ fearful

temible ADJ dreadful, dread

temor M fear

témpano M (bloque de hielo) block of ice; (persona fría) cold fish

temperamento M temperament, disposition

temperancia F temperance

temperatura F temperature

tempestad F tempest, storm; **una — en un vaso de agua** a tempest in a teapot

tempestuoso ADJ tempestuous, stormy

templado ADJ (clima) moderate, temperate; (ánimo) serene; (actitud) moderate

templanza F temperance

templar VT (moderar, dar fuerza) to temper; (calentar) to warm up; (una guitarra) to tune

temple M (dureza) temper; (coraje) mettle; **de mal —** in a bad mood

templo M temple

temporada F season; **— baja** off-season; **— de caza** hunting season

temporal ADJ (del tiempo) temporal; (secular) worldly; (no permanente) temporary; M storm; **capear el —** to weather the storm

tempranero -ra ADJ early rising; MF early riser

temprano ADJ & ADV early

tenacidad F tenacity

tenaz ADJ tenacious

tenazas F PL (de cangrejo) pincers; (de mecánico) pliers; (de dentista) forceps; (para hielo) tongs

tendedero M clothesline

tendencia F tendency; (orientación) orientation; (de la moda) trend; **de — mayoritaria** mainstream; **— a la baja** downturn; **— al alza** upturn

tender[1] VT (un mantel) to spread out; (la ropa) to hang out; (la mano) to extend; (un cable) to lay; (una trampa) to set; VI **— a** to tend to; **—se** to stretch out

tendero -ra MF storekeeper; (de comestibles) grocer

tendido M (de cables) laying; (de ropa mojada) hanging out; (conjunto de cables) cables

tendinitis F tendonitis

tendón M tendon, sinew; **— de Aquiles** Achilles' tendon

tenebroso ADJ (oscuro) dark; (sombrío) gloomy

tenedor -ora M (utensilio) table fork; MF holder, payee; **— de libros** bookkeeper

teneduría F **— de libros** bookkeeping

tener[44] VT to have; **tiene el pelo castaño** she has brown hair, her hair is brown; **— en mucho** to esteem highly; **— por** to consider; **— que** to have to; **— ganas** to feel like; **tengo escrita la carta** I have the letter written; **— éxito** to be successful; **— miedo** to be afraid; **— sueño** to be sleepy; **— frío** to be cold; **— hambre** to be hungry; **tiene cinco años** she is five years old; **—se** to stand straight; **no — más remedio** to have no other choice; **— que ver con** to have to do with

tenería F tannery

tenia F tapeworm

teniente MF lieutenant

tenis M (juego) tennis; (zapatos) sneakers, tennis shoes

tenista MF tennis player

tenor M (voz, estilo) tenor; (tono) tone, tenor; ADJ **saxofón —** tenor saxophone

tensión F tension

tenso ADJ tense; (extendido) taut

tentación F temptation

tentáculo M tentacle

tentador ADJ tempting

tentar[1] VT to tempt; **— a la suerte** to court danger; **— por todos los medios** to try everything

tentativa F attempt, try

tentativo ADJ tentative

tentempié M snack

tenue ADJ (tela) delicate; (luz) tenuous, dim, faint; (sonido) feeble

tenuidad F faintness, softness

teñir[5,18] VT (de color) to dye; (de tristeza) to tinge

teología F theology

teoría F theory

teórico ADJ theoretical

tepe M sod

tequila M tequila

terabyte M terabyte

terapeuta MF INV therapist

terapéutico ADJ therapeutic

terapia F therapy

tercero ADJ third; **tercera persona** third person; **tercera edad** old age; **tercer mundo** third world; M third party

terciar VI/VT to arbitrate

tercio M third

terciopelo M velvet

terco ADJ obstinate, stubborn

tergiversación F distortion, misrepresentation

tergiversar VT (palabras) to distort; (datos) to skew

termal ADJ thermal

terminación F termination, completion; (de una palabra, cuento) ending; (de un piso) finish

terminal ADJ terminal; MF (de aeropuerto, de omnibus) terminal; M (de computadora, eléctrico) terminal

terminante ADJ (negativa) flat; (prohibición) absolute

terminar VI/VT (completar) to finish, to conclude; VI (tener como final) to end; — **por** to end up; **no termino de entender** I still can't understand; **terminó con las ratas** he got rid of the rats; **sin —** unfinished

término M (final) end; (período de tiempo) period; (límite) boundary; (palabra) term; **a —** with a deadline; **estar en buenos —s** to be on good terms; **por — medio** on average; **— medio** medium; **en primer —** first of all; **poner — to** to end; **en —s generales** in general terms; **en último —** as a last resort

terminología F terminology

termita F termite

termo M thermos

termodinámico ADJ thermodynamic

termómetro M thermometer

termonuclear ADJ thermonuclear

termostato M thermostat

ternero -ra MF (animal) calf; F (carne) veal

terneza F tenderness

terno M three-piece suit

ternura F tenderness

terquedad F obstinacy, stubbornness

terraplén M embankment

terrateniente MF landholder

terraza F (terreno) terrace; (de casa) veranda; (delante de un bar) deck; (azotea) flat roof

terremoto M earthquake

terrenal ADJ earthly

terreno M (campo) piece of land, tract of land; (lote) lot; (formación geológica) terrain; (campo científico) field; **todo —** with four-wheel drive; **ganarle — a alguien** to gain on someone; **tantear el —** to put out feelers; **perder —** to lose ground

terrestre ADJ terrestrial, earthly

terrible ADJ terrible, awful

terrier M terrier

territorio M territory

terrón M (de tierra) clod; (de azúcar) lump

terror M terror, dread

terrorismo M terrorism

terrorista MF INV terrorist

terso ADJ (liso) smooth; (pulido) polished

tersura F smoothness

tertulia F social gathering

tesis F thesis; **— doctoral** dissertation

tesón M determination

tesonero ADJ determined

tesorería F treasury

tesorero -ra MF treasurer

tesoro M treasure; (público) treasury

test M test

testaferro M straw man

testamentaría F (gestiones) execution; (bienes) estate

testamento M testament, will

testarudez F stubbornness

testarudo ADJ stubborn, headstrong

testículo M testicle

testificar[6] VI to testify

testigo -ga MF witness; **— de cargo** witness for the prosecution; **— ocular** eyewitness; M proof

testimoniar VI to give testimony

testimonio M testimony, proof, evidence; **levantar falso —** to bear false witness; **en — de su amor** as a testament to his love

testosterona F testosterone

teta F (de animal) teat; (de mujer) vulg tit, jug

tétanos M tetanus

tetera F teapot, teakettle

tetilla F nipple

tetina F nipple

tetraplégico -ca ADJ & MF quadriplegic

tétrico ADJ gloomy

teutónico ADJ Teutonic

textil ADJ & M textile

texto M text; (libro de texto) textbook

textual ADJ verbatim

textura F texture

tez F complexion

ti PRON PERS you; **para** — for you; **te lo doy a** — I give it to you

tibieza F (poco fervor, afecto) lukewarmness; (calor) warmth

tibio ADJ (ni caliente ni frío) tepid, lukewarm; (templado) warm

tiburón M shark

tic M twitch, tic

tictac M **hacer** — to tick

tiempo M (cronológico) time; (climático) weather; (gramatical) tense; (de un partido de cuatro tiempos) quarter; (de un partido de dos tiempos) half; **— completo** full time; **— extra** overtime; **— y medio** time and a half; **— libre** leisure hours, free time; **— pretérito** past tense; **a —** on time; **al mismo —** at the same time; **antes de —** ahead of time; **a su —** in due course; **a un —** at the same time; **con —** in advance; **de medio —** part-time; **en aquel —** back then; **en mis —s** in my day; **hace buen —** the weather is nice; **hace mucho —** a long time ago; **mal —** rough weather; **motor de dos —s** two-stroke motor; **perder el —** to goof off, to waste time; **tener — de sobra** to have time to spare; **todo el —** all the time; **tomar el —** to clock

tienda F (de venta) store; (de campaña) tent

tientas LOC ADV **a —** blindly; **andar a —** to feel one's way

tiento M care; **coger el —** to get the hang of something

tierno ADJ (fácil de cortar) tender; (joven) young; (cariñoso) affectionate

tierra F (planeta) earth; (superficie seca) land; (país) country; (suelo) soil; **— adentro** inland; **—s altas** highlands; **—s bajas** lowlands; **— de nadie** no-man's land; **—firme** mainland; **—s raras** rare earths; **bajo —** underground; **caer a —** to fall to the ground; **dar en — con alguien** to overthrow someone; **echar por —** to knock down; **por —** overland; **tomar —** to land

tieso ADJ stiff; (persona) erect; **quedarse —** fam to kick the bucket

tiesto M flowerpot

tiesura F stiffness

tifoideo -a ADJ & F typhoid

tifón M typhoon

tifus M typhoid fever

tigre M tiger

tijeretada F snip

tijeretazo M snip

tijeretear VT to snip

tildar VT to brand

tilde F (en la ñ) tilde; (en las vocales) accent (mark)

tilín M *fam* ding-a-ling

timador M confidence man

timbrar VT to stamp

timbrazo M ring

timbre M (aparato) buzzer, doorbell; (cualidad de la voz) timbre; (sello) stamp; (insignia heráldica) crest

timidez F timidity, shyness

tímido ADJ timid, shy, bashful

timo M confidence game, scam

timón M helm, rudder

timonear VT to steer

timonel M pilot

timorato ADJ timorous, faint-hearted

tímpano M eardrum

tina F (bañera) tub; (de tintorero) vat

tinaja F large earthen jar

tinglado M (armazón) shed; (plataforma) platform

tinieblas F PL darkness; **en —** in the dark

tino M (buen juicio) good judgment; (puntería) marksmanship

tinta F ink; **medias —s** wishy-washiness

tinte M (sustancia) dye, stain; (matiz) tint

tintero M inkwell; **eso se me quedó en el — I** never got to that

tintín M clink

tintinear VI to tinkle, to clink

tintineo M tinkle, tinkling

tinto ADJ red

tintorería F dry cleaner

tintorero -ra MF dry cleaner

tintura F (medicina) tincture; (tinte) dye, tint

tiñoso ADJ scabby

tío -a M (hermano de madre o padre) uncle; **— abuelo** great uncle; (tipo) guy; F (hermana de madre o padre) aunt; (tipa) woman, gal; *pey* whore

tiovivo M merry-go-round

típico ADJ typical

tiple M treble

tipo -pa M (especie, imprenta) type; (tío) *fam* guy, dude; *Am* rate of interest; *Am* **— de cambio** rate of exchange; **— de interés** interest rate; **un buen —** a good-looking fellow, a regular guy; **tiene buen —** he's good looking; F (tía) woman, gal

tipografía F printing
tipología F typology
tira F (de papel, tocino, tela) strip; (de cuero, zapato) strap; **— cómica** comic strip
tirada F (de una pelota) throw; (de una publicación) issue, print run; (distancia) stretch; **de una —** all at once
tirador -ora MF (persona que dispara) shooter; M (tirachinas) slingshot; (pomo) knob
tiranía F tyranny
tiránico ADJ tyrannical
tirano -na ADJ tyrannical; MF tyrant
tirante ADJ (cable) taut; (relaciones) strained; M (de caballería) trace; (de vestido) strap; (apoyo) brace, strut; **—s** suspenders
tirantez F tension, strain
tirar VT (pelota) to throw, to toss, to pitch; (derechos, dinero) to throw away; (una bala) to shoot; (una moneda) to flip, to toss; (dados) to cast; (una cuerda) to pull, to tug; **— la cadena** to flush; **— la casa por la ventana** to live it up; **— la chancleta** to kick up one's heels; **no me tira la política** I'm not attracted to politics; **el coche tira a un lado** the car pulls to one side; **— al suelo** to throw down; **— a** to tend toward; **— abajo** to knock over; **— de** to tug at; **ir tirando** to get along; **—se** to lie down; **—se pedos** to fart; **—se solo** to go it alone; **tirárselas de** to pretend to be; **trabajar con él es un constante tira y afloja** working with him is a roller-coaster; M **tirabuzón** (sacacorchos) corkscrew; (espiral) coil; M SG **tirachinas** slingshot
tiritar VI (de frío) to shiver; (de miedo) to shudder
tiro M (lanzamiento) throw; (disparo) shot; (deporte) shooting; (de cocaína) hit; (de dados) roll; (de caballos) team; (de chimenea) draft; **— al arco** archery; **— al blanco** target practice; **— de penalidad** penalty kick; **errar el —** to miss the mark; **matar a —s** to gun down; **ni a —s** absolutely not; **pegarle un — a alguien** to shoot someone; **me salió el — por la culata** the plan backfired on me
tiroides ADJ & M thyroid
tirón M jerk, tug, pull; (atracción fuerte, lesión de un músculo) pull; **de un —** all at once; **un — de orejas** a slap on the wrist
tironear VI/VT to jerk, to tug at
tirotear VI to shoot; **—se** to exchange shots
tiroteo M shooting, gunfire
tirria F dislike; **tenerle — a una persona**

to have a strong dislike for someone
tisana F herbal tea
tísico ADJ consumptive
tisis F consumption
titánico ADJ titanic
titanio M titanium
títere M (marioneta) puppet; (persona) puppet, dupe; **—s** puppet show; **no dejar — sin cabeza** to leave no one standing
titilación F flicker
titilar VI to flicker, to twinkle
titileo M twinkle
titubear VI (vacilar) to hesitate, to waver; (oscilar) to totter, to dodder
titubeo M hesitation
titular VT to entitle; **—se** to graduate; ADJ permanent; M (de periódico) headline; MF (de cargo) incumbent
titularidad F tenure
título M (de una obra, persona, liga) title; (derecho) claim, legal right; (universitario) degree, diploma; **— de crédito** credits; **— de propiedad** title deed; **a — de** by way of
tiza F chalk
tiznado ADJ sooty
tiznar VT to smear with soot
tizne M soot
tizón M (leña) burning log; (parásito) smut
TNT M TNT
toalla F towel; **tirar la —** to throw in the towel
toallero M towel rack
tobillo M ankle
tobogán M slide
tocado M headdress; ADJ touched
tocador M (mueble) dressing table, vanity table; (habitación) *lit* boudoir
tocante a PREP concerning
tocar[6] VT (con los dedos) to touch; (un instrumento musical) to play; (una campana) to ring; (un timbre) to buzz; (a la puerta) to knock; (la bocina) to honk, to blast; (una alarma) to sound; (mencionar) to touch upon; **— en** to stop over in; **—le a uno** to be one's turn; **— fondo** to hit bottom; M SG **tocadiscos** record player
tocayo -ya MF namesake
tocino M bacon
tocón M stump
todavía ADV still, as yet, yet; **— está aquí** she's still here; **¿— no has comido?** have you not eaten yet? **— no ha llegado** she still has not arrived, as yet she has not arrived; **me dio — más** she gave me even more

todo ADJ all; (cada uno) every, each; — **hombre** every man; —**s los días** every day; **a — correr** at top speed; **a toda costa** at all costs; **a toda marcha** in high gear; **a toda vela** under full sail; **a toda velocidad** at full speed; **a — volumen** at full blast; **de — corazón** whole-heartedly; **con —s modos** still, anyway, all the same; **del — entirely; en — caso** in any case, at any rate, in any event; **es — un personaje** he's quite a character; **por — lados** everywhere; **— el día** all day; **— el tiempo** all the time; **— el mundo** everyone; **todas las noches** nightly; **toda la noche** all through the night; **toda clase de** all sorts of; **en / por todas partes** everywhere, for and wide; **con toda el alma** from the bottom of one's heart; **con toda sinceridad** in all earnestness; PRON **de una vez por todas** once and for all; **— se vale** anything goes; **—s** everybody; **—s juntos** all together; ADV **— derecho** straight ahead; **— lo contrario** quite the opposite; **— recto** straight ahead; **— sucio** all dirty; **ante —** first of all; **así y — in spite of that; con — in spite of that; del — completely; sobre — especially; M whole; —poderoso** almighty

toga F (de catedrático) gown; (de juez) robe

Togo M Togo

togolés -esa ADJ & MF Togolese

toldería F Indian village

toldo M awning, canopy

tolerancia F tolerance

tolerante ADJ tolerant, broad-minded

tolerar VT to tolerate; **no lo puedo —** I can't stand it

tolete M oarlock

toma F (de una ciudad) taking; (cinematográfica) take; (de juramento) administration; (de teléfono) jack; **— de agua** faucet; **— de corriente** electric outlet; **— de poder** takeover; **toma y daca** give and take

tomar VT to take; (un juramento) to administer; (un vestido) to take in; (a un criado) to hire; (una bebida) to drink; **— a pecho** to take to heart; **— asiento** to take a seat; **— desprevenido** to take by surprise; **— el sol** to sunbathe; **—lo a mal** to take the wrong way; **— el pelo a** to make fun of, to kid, to pull someone's leg; **— medidas** to take action; **— una decisión** to make a decision; **—le las medidas a alguien** to measure someone for clothes; **—se de la mano** to hold hands; **—se la molestia** to bother to

tomate M tomato

tomillo M thyme

tomo M volume

tomografía F scan; **— axial computarizada** CAT scan

ton LOC ADV **sin — ni son** for no reason

tonada F tune

tonel M (barril) barrel; (persona) *pey* fatso

tonelada F ton

tóner M toner

Tonga F Tonga

tongano -na ADJ & MF Tongan

tongo M setup

tónica F (tono) tone; (agua) tonic (water)

tónico ADJ & M tonic

tono M tone; (tono musical) pitch; (intervalo musical) step; **— de ocupado** busy signal; **— menor** low key; **a — on key; bajar el — to lower the volume; darse — to put on airs; de buen — in good taste; fuera de — out of place; subido de — risqué

tontear VI to fool around

tontería F (cualidad de tonto) stupidity; (hecho o dicho) foolishness, nonsense

tonto -ta ADJ (ingenuo) foolish; (de poca inteligencia) stupid, dumb; **a tontas y a locas** haphazardly; MF (persona ingenua) fool; (persona de poca inteligencia) *fam* dummy, blockhead, dimwit; **— de capirote** dunce; **hacer(se) el —** to play the fool

topacio M topaz

topar VT to butt; **—se con** to bump into

tope M (de precios) ceiling, cap; (de tren) bumper; (de puerta) doorstop; **a — a lot; hasta el — to the maximum; estar hasta el — to be completely full

topetazo M butt

tópico M (lugar común) cliché; (tema) topic; ADJ topical

topless ADJ topless

topo M mole (también espía)

toque M (con la mano) touch; (de campana) ringing; (de tambor) beat; (de trompeta) blare; (de pintura) dab; **— de queda** curfew; **dar los últimos —s** to put the finishing touches on; **dar —s** to dab; **un — femenino** a woman's touch

toquetear VI/VT (mercancías) to finger; (por placer sexual) *vulg* to grope, to feel up / off

toqueteo M feel

tórax M thorax

torbellino M whirlwind

torcedura F twist, sprain, strain

torcer[2,10] VT to twist; (una articulación) to sprain, to strain; (tergiversar) to distort;

—le el pescuezo a alguien to wring someone's neck; VI (un río) to bend

torcido ADJ crooked

tordo M thrush

torear VT (lidiar) to fight a bull; (provocar) to provoke

torero -ra MF bullfighter

tormenta F storm; **— de arena** sandstorm; **— eléctrica** electrical storm

tormento M torment

tormentoso ADJ stormy

tornadizo ADJ changeable

tornado M tornado, twister

tornar VI (regresar) to return; VT (cambiar) to turn; **— a hacer algo** to do something again

tornasolado ADJ iridescent

tornear VT to turn on a lathe

torneo M tournament

tornillo M screw; **— de banco** vise; **faltarle a uno un —** to have a screw loose

torniquete M (eje giratorio) turnstile; (contra hemorragia) tourniquet

torno M (para levantar pesos) hoist, winch; (para cerámicas) lathe, pottery wheel; **en —** around

toro M bull; **coger / agarrar el — por los cuernos** to take the bull by the horns

toronja F grapefruit

torpe ADJ (poco habilidoso) clumsy, awkward; (lento) slow, sluggish

torpedear VT to torpedo

torpedero M (barco) torpedo boat; (avión) torpedo plane

torpedo M torpedo

torpeza F (falta de habilidad) clumsiness; (lentitud) slowness, sluggishness

torpor M torpor

torrar VT to roast

torre F (de castillo) tower; (de buque de guerra) turret; (en ajedrez) castle; **— de control** control tower; **— de marfil** ivory tower; **— de perforación** oil derrick; **— de vigilancia** watch tower

torrencial ADJ torrential

torrente M torrent; **— de lágrimas** flood of tears; **— sanguíneo** bloodstream

torreón M large tower

torreta F turret

tórrido ADJ torrid

torsión F torsion

torso M torso

torta F (postre) cake; (bofetada) slap

tortícolis F kink

tortilla F (de huevo) omelet; (de harina) *Méx* tortilla; **se dio vuelta la —** the tables

have turned

tortillera F *ofensivo* dyke

tórtola F turtledove

tortuga F tortoise, turtle; **— marina** sea turtle; **a paso de —** at a snail's pace

tortuoso ADJ (camino) tortuous; (carácter) devious

tortura F torture

torturante ADJ torturous

torturar VT to torture

torvo ADJ fierce

tos F cough; **— ferina** whooping cough

tosco ADJ coarse, crude

toser VI to cough

tosquedad F coarseness, crudeness

tostada F toast

tostado ADJ (pan) toasted; (café) roasted; M (acción de tostar pan) toasting; (color, bronceado) tan; (acción de tostar café) roasting

tostador -ora MF toaster

tostar² VT (el pan) to toast; (la piel) to tan; (el café) to roast

total ADJ & M total; **en —** altogether; **—, a mí no me importa** anyway, I don't care

totalidad F **la — del dinero** all the money; **en su —** as a whole

totalitario ADJ totalitarian

tour M tour

tóxico ADJ toxic

toxina F toxin

traba F (estorbo) hindrance; (de caballo) hobble

trabajador -ora ADJ (esforzado) hard-working; (proletario) working; MF worker

trabajar VI/VT to work; **— un taxi** to drive a taxi; VI (una tienda) to be open; **— duro** to work hard

trabajo M work; (acción de trabajo) working; (puesto) job; (informe académico) paper; **da mucho —** it's a lot of work; **sin —** unemployed

trabajoso ADJ laborious

trabar VT (una puerta) to jam; (un caballo) to hobble; (a un boxeador) to clinch; (una salsa) to thicken; (negociaciones) to impede; **— amistad con alguien** to strike up a friendship with someone; **— batalla** to join battle; **— conversación** to strike up a conversation; M SG **trabalenguas** tongue twister

tracción F traction

tractocamión M tractor-trailer

tractor M tractor

tradición F tradition

tradicional ADJ traditional

traducción F translation

traducir[24] VI/VT to translate
traductor -ora MF translator
traer[45] VT to bring; (llevar puesto) to have on; (contener) to feature; — **a colación** to bring up; — **a mal a alguien** to mistreat someone; **este niño se las trae** this child is something else; **¿qué te traes entre manos?** what are you up to? —**se secretos** to have secrets
tráfago M bustle
traficante MF dealer
traficar[6] VI to traffic, to trade
tráfico M traffic
tragar[7] VI/VT to swallow; (comer) *fam* to feed one's face; (consumir gasolina) to guzzle; (aguantar) to stand; (hacer desaparecer) to engulf; —**se algo** to swallow (accidentally); **no me lo trago** I don't buy that; M **tragaluz** skylight; MF SG **tragamonedas / tragaperras** slot machine
tragedia F tragedy
trágico ADJ tragic
trago M swallow; (bebida alcohólica) shot, slug; **a —s** (bebiendo) in sips; (poco a poco) little by little; **echar / tomar un —** to take a drink; **pasar un mal —** to suffer a difficulty
traición F (política) treason; (personal) betrayal; (acto desleal) treachery; **a —** by treachery
traicionar VT to double-cross
traicionero ADJ treacherous
traidor -ora ADJ treacherous; MF (político) traitor; (personal) betrayer
trailer M trailer
traílla F leash
traje M (conjunto) suit; (de fiesta) gown; — **de baño** swimsuit
trajeado ADJ **bien —** well-dressed
trajín M hustle and bustle
trajinar VI to rush around
trama F (argumento) plot; (intriga) scheme; (conjunto de hilos) woof
tramador -ora MF plotter
tramar VT (con hilos) to weave; (intrigar) to plot, to scheme
tramitar VT to take steps to obtain
trámite M procedure, paperwork
tramo M (de carretera) stretch; (de puente) span; (de hielo) patch; (de escalera) flight
tramoyista MF stagehand
trampa F (de caza) trap, snare; (engaño) trick; **hacer —** to cheat, to trick; **tender una —** to set a trap
trampear VI to cheat
trampilla F trap door

trampolín M (de piscina) springboard; (de circo) trampoline
tramposo -sa ADJ deceitful; MF cheat
tranca F crossbar
trance M (momento difícil) pass, difficult moment; (estado de suspensión) trance; **el último —** the last moment of life; **a todo —** at any cost
tranco M stride; **a —s** hurriedly; **en dos —s** in a jiffy
tranquera F wooden fence
tranquilidad F tranquility, calm, quiet
tranquilizante M tranquilizer
tranquilizar[9] VT to quiet, to calm down; —**se** to calm down, to wind down
tranquilo ADJ (no ruidoso) quiet, peaceful; (no excitado) calm, cool; (no preocupado) calm, at ease; (no excitable) sedate; (mar) smooth, tranquil
transacción F transaction; — **comercial** business transaction
transar VI to compromise
transatlántico ADJ transatlantic; M transatlantic liner
transbordar VI to transfer
transbordo M transfer
transcribir[51] VT to transcribe
transcripción F transcript
transcultural ADJ cross-cultural
transcurrir VI to elapse
transcurso M passing, passage; **en el — de un año** in the course of a year
transeúnte MF passer-by, transient
transexual ADJ & MF transsexual
transferencia F transfer
transferible ADJ transferable
transferir[3] VT to transfer
transformación F transformation
transformador M transformer
transformar VT to transform
transfusión F transfusion
transgredir[50] VT to transgress
transgresión F transgression
transgresor -ora MF lawbreaker
transición F transition
transigir[11] VI to compromise
transistor M transistor
transitable ADJ passable
transitar VI/VT to travel
transitivo ADJ transitive
tránsito M (acción de viajar) transit, passage; (tráfico) traffic; **de / en —** in transit
transitorio ADJ transitory
transmisible ADJ communicable
transmisión F transmission; — **automática** automatic transmission
transmisor M transmitter; ADJ transmitting

transmitir VI/VT to transmit; (una
enfermedad) to communicate; (por radio o
televisión) to broadcast
transparencia F transparency
transparente ADJ transparent
transpiración F perspiration
transpirar VI/VT to transpire, to perspire
transportación F transportation, transport
transportar VT (mercancías, gente) to
transport; (mercancías) to ship, to haul
transporte M (acción) transport,
transportation; (vehículo de transporte)
transport (vessel); **— de locura** fit of
madness; **— público** mass transit
transportista MF teamster, trucker
transversal ADJ transverse; F transversal
transverso ADJ transverse
tranvía M (transporte urbano) streetcar,
trolley; (tren de cercanías) local train
trapacería F racket
trapacero -ra MF racketeer
trapeador M mop
trapear VT *Am* to mop
trapecio M trapeze
trapezoide ADJ & M trapezoid
trapiche M sugar mill
trapisonda F trick
trapo M rag; **—s** *fam* duds; **a todo** — at full
speed; **tratar a alguien como un** — to
treat someone like dirt; **—s sucios** dirty
laundry
tráquea F trachea, windpipe
traquetear VI (hacer sonido) to rattle, to
clatter; (llevar a todos lados) to drag from
place to place
traqueteo M rattle, clatter
tras PREP (temporal) after; (espacial) after,
behind, in back of; **correr** — to run after;
día — **día** day after day; **una vez** —
otra time after time
trascendencia F transcendence
trascendental ADJ transcendental;
(importante) momentous
trascendente ADJ transcendental
trascender VT to transcend; VI (surgir) to
emerge; (extender) to extend
trasegar[1,7] VT (vino) to pour from one
container to another; (objetos) to move
around; (papeles) to shuffle
trasero ADJ (punto, asiento) rear, back; (pata)
hind; M (de persona) *fam* rear, rear end,
bottom
traslación F transfer
trasladar VT (a un empleado) to transfer;
(una reunión) to postpone; **—se** to travel
traslado M transfer
traslapo M overlap

trasnochar VI to stay up late
traspapelar VT to mislay, to misplace; **—se**
to become mislaid
traspasar VT (pasar por) to transfix; (ir más
allá de) to go beyond; (pasar un límite) to
transgress, to cross over; (una propiedad)
to transfer
traspaso M transfer
traspié M stumble, slip; **dar un** — to
stumble
trasplantar VT to transplant
trasplante M transplant
trasponer[39] VT to transpose
trasquilar VT (una oveja) to shear; (a una
persona) to fleece
trastabillar VI to stumble
trastazo M bump
traste M (de guitarra) fret, stop; (trasero)
buttocks; **dar al** — **con** to destroy; **irse
al** — to go down the drain
trasto M piece of junk; **—s** stuff
trastocar[6] VT to disrupt
trastornar VT (alterar psíquicamente) to
disturb; (alterar el funcionamiento) to
disrupt; **—se** to go crazy
trastorno M (molestia) trouble; (patología)
disorder; **— bipolar** bipolar disorder; **—
de personalidad múltiple** multiple
personality disorder
trasudar VI/VT to perspire
trata F trade
tratable ADJ (curable) treatable; (amistoso)
approachable
tratado M (acuerdo) treaty; (libro) treatise
tratamiento M (acción de tratar) treatment;
(fórmula de cortesía) form of address; **—
de textos** *Esp* word processing
tratante MF dealer, trader
tratar VT (una enfermedad, a un paciente,
un asunto) to treat; VI (intentar) to try; **—
como** to treat like; **— con** to have
dealings with; **— de** to try to, to attempt;
— sobre to be about; **lo trató de
imbécil** she called him an idiot; **—le a
uno de** to address someone as; **— en** to
deal in; **—se con** to have to do with; **—se
de** to be a question of, to be
trato M (acuerdo) treatment; (acción de
tratar) dealings; (convenio) deal;
(comercio) trade; (modales) manners; **¡—
hecho!** it's a deal! **tener buen** — to have
good manners; **cerrar un** — to strike a
bargain
trauma M trauma
traumático ADJ traumatic
traumatismo M trauma
través LOC ADV **a / al** — **de** through, across;

a — de las declaraciones throughout the declarations; **de —** across; **mirar de —** to look askance (at)

travesaño M crossbar

travesía F crossing, sea voyage, passage

travestí, travesti MF cross-dresser, transvestite

travestido -da MF transvestite

travesura F mischief, prank; **hacer —s** to play pranks

traviesa F railway tie

travieso ADV mischievous, naughty

trayecto M course, route

trayectoria F (de proyectil) trajectory, path; (profesional) career

traza F (huella) trace; (aspecto) appearance; **tiene —s de no acabar nunca** it looks as if it will never end

trazado M (de ciudad) layout; (de edificio) blueprint; (de un plan) outline

trazador M **— gráfico** plotter

trazar[9] VT to trace, to sketch; (un plan) to outline; (un edificio) to blueprint; **— el curso** to plot a course

trébol M clover

trece NUM thirteen

trecho M (distancia) stretch; **a —s** at intervals; **de — en —** at intervals

tregua F (de guerra) truce; (descanso) lull, respite

treinta NUM thirty

tremendo ADJ (extraordinario) tremendous; (terrible) terrible

trementina F turpentine

tremolar VI (bandera) to flutter; (voz) to trill

trémolo M quaver

trémulo ADJ tremulous, trembling

tren M train; **— de aterrizaje** landing gear; **— de carga / de mercancías** freight train; **— de cercanías** local train; **— de vida** lifestyle; **— expreso** express train; **a todo —** at top speed; **perder el —** to miss the boat; **seguir el —** to keep up

trenza F braid

trenzar[9] VT to braid

trepador ADJ (planta) climbing; (ciclista) climber

trepadora F climbing plant

trepar VI to climb

trepidar VI to tremble

tres NUM three

treta F trick, wile

triaje M triage

triangular ADJ triangular

triángulo M triangle; **— recto** right triangle

tribu F tribe

tribulación F tribulation

tribuna F (de orador) rostrum; (de un público) grandstand

tribunal M (judicial) tribunal, court; (cuerpo de jueces) body of judges

tributar VT to pay tribute with; VI to pay taxes

tributario ADJ & M tributary

tributo M (pago obligatorio) tribute; (impuesto) tax

triceps M triceps

triciclo M tricycle

tridimensional ADJ three-dimensional

trifulca F fight

trigo M wheat

trigueño ADJ (tez) swarthy; (pelo) dark-blond

trillado ADJ trite

trilladora F threshing machine

trillar VT to thresh

trillizo -za ADJ & MF triplet

trilogía F trilogy

trimestral ADJ quarterly

trimestre M quarter

trinar VI to trill; **está que trina** she is furious

trinchante M carving knife

trinchar VT to carve

trinche M pitchfork

trinchera F trench; (gabardina) trench coat

trinchero M carving table

trineo M sleigh, sled

trinitense ADJ & MF Trinidadian

trino M trill

trinquete M ratchet

trio M trio

tripas F PL guts; **hacer de — corazón** to pluck up one's courage

triple ADJ triple

triplicar[6] VT to triple, to treble

trípode M tripod

triptongo M triphthong

tripulación F crew

tripular VT to man

triquiñuela F caper

triquitraque M firecracker

triscar[6] VI to frisk

triste ADJ sad, sorrowful

tristeza F sadness, sorrow

tristón ADJ glum

tritón M newt

trituradora F (para desechos) garbage disposal unit; (para papel) paper shredder

triturar VI/VT (documentos) to shred; (granos) to grind

triunfal ADJ triumphal

triunfante ADJ triumphant

triunfar VT to triumph

triunfo M triumph

trivial ADJ trivial, commonplace, trite

trizas F PL **hacer —** to tear into shreds

trocar[2,6] VT (transformar) to change into; (cambiar una cosa por otra) to exchange

trocear VT to divide into pieces

trocha F trail

trofeo M trophy

troje M granary

trola F whopper

trole M trolley

trolebús M trolley bus

tromba F waterspout; **salir en —** to storm out

trombón M trombone

trompa F (de elefante) trunk; (instrumento musical) horn; **— de Falopio** Fallopian tube

trompada F blow with the fist

trompeta F trumpet

trompetazo M trumpet blast

trompetear VI to trumpet

trompo M spinning top

tronada F thunderstorm

tronar[2] VI to thunder

tronchar VT to chop off

tronco M (de árbol) trunk, log; (del cuerpo) trunk, torso; **dormir como un —** to sleep like a log

tronera F (de buque) gun port; (de mesa de billar) pocket

trono M throne (también wáter)

tropa F (grupo) troop; (oficiales) rank and file; **—s de asalto** storm troops; **—s de choque** shock troops

tropel LOC ADV **en —** in droves

tropezar[1,9] VI to stumble, to trip; **—(se) con alguien** to meet up with someone; **— con algo** to come across something

tropezón M stumble, trip; **salir a tropezones** to stumble out; **darse un —** to stumble

tropical ADJ tropical

trópico M tropic

tropiezo M stumble

troquel M die

trotar VI to trot

trote M trot; **al —** at a trot; **no estoy para estos —s** I'm too old for this

troza F log

trozar[9] VT to cut up

trozo M (de roca, madera, torta) piece; (de un texto) section; (de carbón) lump; (de carne) slab

trucha F trout

truco M clever trick

truculento ADJ gruesome

trueno M thunder

trueque M barter

truhán -ana MF scoundrel

truja F cigarette

trust M trust

tu ADJ POS your

tú PRON PERS you

tuba F tuba

tuberculosis F tuberculosis

tubería F (tubo) pipe; (conjunto de tubos) piping

tubo M (cilindro hueco) tube; (de agua, órgano) pipe; (digestivo) tract; **— de ensayo** test tube; **— de escape** tailpipe

tubular ADJ tubular

tuerca F nut

tuerto ADJ one-eyed

tuétano M marrow; **hasta los —s** through and through

tufillo M whiff

tufo M (humo) fumes; (hedor) stench

tugurio M hovel; **—s** slums

tulipán M tulip

tullido -da ADJ crippled; MF *pey* cripple

tullir VT to cripple; **—se** to become crippled

tumba F (panteón) tomb; (sepultura) grave; **soy una —** my lips are sealed

tumbar VT to knock down, to flatten; **—se** to lie down, to stretch out

tumbo M tumble, somersault; **dar —s** (persona) to stagger; (coche) to bump along

tumor M tumor

tumulto M (alboroto) tumult, uproar; (muchedumbre) mob

tumultuoso ADJ tumultuous

tuna F prickly pear; *Esp* minstrel group

tunante -ta MF scamp

tunda F thrashing

túnel M tunnel

tunesino -na ADJ & MF Tunisian

Túnez M Tunisia

tungsteno M tungsten

túnica F tunic; **— de laboratorio** lab gown

tupido ADJ dense, compact

tupir VT (hacer tupido) to compact; (cubrir) to cover; **—se** to stuff oneself

turba F (muchedumbre) mob; (carbón fósil) peat

turbación F confusion

turbamulta F throng

turbante M turban

turbar VT to disturb; **—se** to become disturbed

turbina F turbine

turbio ADJ (pasado, secreto) dark; (agua, materia) murky

turbocompresor M turbocharger

turborreactor M turbojet
turbulento ADJ turbulent
turco -ca ADJ Turkish; MF Turk; M (lengua) Turkish
turcomano -na ADJ & MF Turkmen
turismo M (actividad) tourism; (conjunto de turistas) tourists; **hacer —** to go sightseeing
turista MF tourist
Turkmenistán M Turkmenistan
turnarse VI to take turns
turno M turn; (de trabajo) shift
turquesa F turquoise
Turquía F Turkey
turrón M nougat
tutear VT to address as "tú"
tutela F guardianship
tutelar VT to have charge of
tutor -ora MF (de un menor) guardian; M (de planta) prop
Tuvalu M Tuvalu
tuvaluano -na ADJ & MF Tuvaluan
tuyo PRON your, yours; **el amigo —** your friend; **esto es —** this is yours
tweed M tweed

Uu

u CONJ or
ubicación F location
ubicar[6] VT (situar) to locate; (identificar) to place; **-se** to be located
ubicuo ADJ ubiquitous
ubre F udder
UCP (unidad central de proceso) F CPU
Ucrania F Ukraine
ucraniano -na ADJ & MF Ukrainian
ufanarse VI to glory (in), to be proud (of)
ufano ADJ proud
Uganda F Uganda
ugandés -esa ADJ & MF Ugandan
ujier M bailiff
úlcera F (lesión superficial) sore; (en el estómago) sore; (en la boca) canker, sore
ulterior ADJ ulterior
últimamente ADV of late
ultimar VT to finalize
ultimátum M ultimatum
último ADJ last, final; (destino) ultimate; (más reciente) latest; **estar en las últimas** to be on one's last legs; **la última palabra** the last word; **en los —s tiempos** lately; **a última hora** at

the last moment
ultrajante ADJ outrageous
ultrajar VT to outrage
ultraje M outrage, indignity
ultraligero M ultralight
ultramar LOC ADV **de —** overseas
ultramoderno ADJ ultramodern
ultratumba LOC ADV **de —** from beyond the grave
ultravioleta ADJ INV & M ultraviolet
ulular VI to howl, to hoot
ululato M hoot
umbral M threshold, doorstep
umbrío ADJ shady
un, uno, una ART INDEF a, an; **un hombre** a man; **un actor** an actor; **una mujer** a woman; **una manzana** an apple; NUM one; **de a —** one at a time; **es la una** it is one o'clock; **yo tengo —** I have one; PRON one; **— por —** one by one; **—s** some; **—s cuantos** some; **— tiene que cuidarse** you've got to take care of yourself; **— tras otro** one after the other; **— al lado del otro** side by side; **los —s a los otros/el — al otro** one another/each other
unánime ADJ unanimous
unanimidad F unanimity
uncir[10b] VT to yoke; (a un carro) to hitch
ungüento M ointment, salve
único ADJ only; (extraordinario) unique
unidad F (indivisibilidad) unity; (ejemplar) unit; (fracción militar) unit, outfit; **— central de proceso** central processing unit
unificar[6] VT to unify
uniformar VT (estandarizar) to standardize; (dar uniformes) to furnish with uniforms
uniforme ADJ & M uniform
uniformidad F uniformity
unilateral ADJ unilateral
unión F (acción de unir, cosas unidas) union; (lugar en que se unen dos cosas) junction; (indivisibilidad) unity
unir VT to unite; (dos construcciones) to join; (cinta magnética, genes) to splice; (caños) to couple; VI/VT (con lazos) to bind
unisex ADJ unisex
unísono ADJ unison; **al —** in unison
universal ADJ universal
universidad F (de enseñanza e investigación) university; (de enseñanza) college
universitario ADJ university; (relativo a los deportes) collegiate
universo M universe
untar VT (la piel con crema) to oil; (pan con

mantequilla) to spread on; (la cara con
pintura) to smear; — **la mano a alguien**
to grease someone's palm

untuoso ADJ (graso) oily; (zalamero) slick,
unctuous

uña F fingernail; (de gato) claw; **como — y
carne** thick as thieves; **con —s y
dientes** tooth and nail

uranio M uranium

urbanidad F refinement, polish

urbanización F development

urbanizar[9] VT to build up

urbano ADJ (relativo a la ciudad) urban;
(refinado) suave; **autobus —** city bus

urbe F metropolis

urdimbre F warp

urdir VT (una tela) to weave; (una historia)
to concoct; (un plan) to devise, to work
out

uretra F urethra

urgencia F (prisa) urgency; (crisis médica)
emergency; **con —** urgently; **—s**
emergency room

urgente ADJ urgent, pressing

urgir[11] VT to urge; VI to be urgent

úrico ADJ uric

urinario ADJ urinary; M urinal

URL M URL

urna F (para cenizas) urn; (electoral) ballot
box; **acudir a las —** s to go to the polls

urólogo -ga MF urologist

urraca F (ave) magpie; (persona acaparadora)
packrat

urticaria F hives

Uruguay M Uruguay

uruguayo -ya ADJ & MF Uruguayan

usado ADJ used; (desgastado) worn

usar VT to use; (ropa) to wear; **—se** to be in
use; **sin —** unused

uso M (empleo) use; (costumbre) usage,
custom; **al — de la época** according to
the custom of the time

usted PRON PERS you; **—es** you, you all, y'all

usual ADJ usual

usuario -ria MF user; (en una biblioteca)
borrower

usufructo M enjoyment

usufructuar[17] VT to enjoy the use of

usura F usury

usurero -ra MF usurer, loan shark

usurpar VT to encroach upon, to usurp

utensilio M utensil

útero M uterus, womb

útil ADJ useful, helpful; M PL **—es** utensils

utilidad F usefulness, utility

utilitario ADJ utilitarian

utilización F use, utilization

utilizar[9] VT to utilize; (explotar) to use

utopía F utopia

uva F grape

úvula F uvula

uvular ADJ uvular

Uzbekistán M Uzbekistan

uzbeko -ka ADJ & MF Uzbek

Vv

vaca F cow; — **marina** sea cow

vacaciones F PL vacation

vacante ADJ vacant; F vacancy, opening

vaciar[16] VT to empty; (una naranja) to
hollow out; (una estatua) to cast

vacilación F hesitation

vacilante ADJ vacillating, hesitating;
(tembloroso) shaky

vacilar VI to vacillate, to hesitate, to waver;
— **(con)** *Esp fam* to make fun (of)

vacío ADJ empty; (casa) vacant; (comentarios)
idle; (expresión) blank; M (condición)
emptiness; (lugar) void; (espacio sin aire)
vacuum; **envasado al —** vacuum-packed;
hacer el — to give the cold shoulder

vacuna F vaccine

vacunación F vaccination

vacunar VI/VT to vaccinate

vadear VT to ford

vado M ford, crossing

vagabundear VI to wander idly

vagabundo -da ADJ vagabond, vagrant; MF
(pordiosero) tramp, bum; (trabajador
errante) drifter, transient; (en la playa)
beachcomber

vagancia F vagrancy

vagar[7] VI to wander, to roam

vagina F vagina

vago -ga ADJ (idea) vague; (silueta) shadowy;
(impresión) faint, vague; (persona) lazy;
MF vagrant, tramp

vagón M railway car; — **restaurante** dining
car

vaguedad F faintness

vahído M dizzy spell

vaho M steam

vaina F (de una espada) sheath; (de
legumbres) pod, shell; (molestia) nuisance

vainilla F vanilla

vaivén M swaying, swinging; **vaivenes** ups
and downs

vajilla F tableware, dishes; — **de barro**
earthenware; — **de porcelana** chinaware

vale M voucher
valedero ADJ valid
valentía F courage, valor, bravery
valentón -ona ADJ cocky; MF cocky person
valer[46] VT (tener un determinado valor) to be worth; VI (ser válido) to be valid; (estar permitido) to be allowed; (ser de utilidad) to be useful; **— la pena** to be worthwhile; **— más que** to outweigh; **—se de** to avail oneself of; **—se por sí mismo** to be self-sufficient; **¿cuánto vale?** how much is it? **hacer — los derechos** to assert one's rights; **hacerse —** to stand up for oneself; **le valió una paliza** that earned him a beating; **más vale sólo que mal acompañado** better alone than in poor company; **no hay pero que valga** no buts about it; **no vale ni un comino** it's not worth a hoot; **no vale** that's not fair; **¡vale!** OK; **¡válgame Dios!** gracious! **todo —** anything goes
valeroso ADJ valorous, brave
valía F worth
validez F validity
válido ADJ valid; (cheque) good; (argumento) solid
valiente ADJ valiant, brave, courageous
valija F valise, suitcase; (para el correo) pouch
valioso ADJ valuable
valla F fence; (en carreras) hurdle
vallar VT to fence
valle M valley, vale
valor M (precio) value, worth; (valentía) valor, mettle; **— contable** book value; **—es securities; —es en cartera** holdings; **— nominal** face value; **armarse de —** to muster up one's courage
valoración F valuation
valorar VT (apreciar el valor) to value; (determinar el valor) to appraise
valorizar[9] VT to make more valuable; **—se** to become more valuable
vals M waltz
valsar VI to waltz
valuación F valuation, appraisal
valuar[17] VT to appraise
valva F valve
válvula F valve; **— reguladora de aceleración** throttle
vampiresa F vamp
vampiro M vampire
vanagloria F boastfulness
vanagloriarse VI to boast
vanaglorioso ADJ boastful
vándalo -la MF vandal

vanguardia F vanguard; **a la —** at the forefront
vanidad F vanity, conceit
vanidoso ADJ vain
vano ADJ vain; **en —** in vain
Vanuatu M Vanuatu
vanuatuense ADJ & MF Vanuatuan
vapor M (de agua) vapor, steam; (buque) steamship; **—es** fumes; **cocer al —** to steam; **echar —** to give off steam
vapulear VT to thrash
vapuleo M thrashing
vaquería F cowshed
vaqueriza F cowshed
vaquero -ra M cowboy; **—s** blue jeans; F cowgirl; ADJ **botas —s** cowboy boots
vaqueta F cowhide
vaquilla F heifer
vara F (rama) stick; (palo) rod
varadero M dry dock
varano M monitor lizard
varar VT to beach, to strand; VI to run aground
varear VT to whip with a stick
variable ADJ variable, changeable; F variable
variación F variation
variado ADJ varied
variante F variant
variar[16] VI/VT to vary
varicela F chicken pox
várices, varices F PL varicose veins
varicoso ADJ varicose
variedad F variety, assortment
varilla F small rod; (para azotar) switch; (de paraguas) rib
vario ADJ varied; **—s** various, several
variopinto ADJ variegated
varita F wand
varón M male (person)
varonil ADJ manly; (hombruno) mannish
vasco -ca ADJ & MF Basque; M (lengua) Basque
vascuence ADJ Basque; M (lengua) Basque
vascular ADJ vascular
vasectomía F vasectomy
vaselina F Vaseline[tm]
vasija F vessel
vaso M (de vidrio) glass; (de papel, plástico) cup; (corto y grueso) tumbler; (sanguíneo) vessel; **— de precipitado** beaker
vástago M (de planta) shoot, sprout; (de persona) offspring; (de motor) rod
vasto ADJ vast
vataje M wattage
vaticinar VT to foretell
vaticinio M prediction
vatio M watt

vecindad F (cercanía) vicinity; (barrio) neighborhood

vecindario M neighborhood

vecino -na MF (de al lado) neighbor; (residente) resident; ADJ neighboring

vedar VT to prohibit

vega F fertile plain

vegan ADJ & MF INV vegan

vegetación F vegetation

vegetal ADJ vegetable; M plant; MF (persona paralizada) vegetable

vegetar VI to vegetate

vegetariano -na ADJ & MF vegetarian

vehemencia F vehemence

vehemente ADJ vehement

vehículo M vehicle

veinte NUM twenty

veintena F (aproximadamente) group of (about) twenty; (exactamente) score

veintiuno NUM twenty-one; M (juego de naipes) blackjack

vejancón -ona M codger; F old woman

vejar VT to humiliate

vejestorio -ria M codger; F old woman

vejete M codger

vejez F old age

vejiga F bladder; (ampolla) blister

vela F (período de vigilancia) vigil, watch; (de cera) candle; (de un navío) sail; **a toda —** under full sail; **en —** without sleep; **hacerse a la —** to set sail

velada F (noche) evening; (fiesta) evening party

velador M nightstand

velar VI (no dormir) to keep vigil, to stay awake; (cubrir con velo) to veil; (exponer a la luz una película fotográfica) to expose; **— por** to look after

velatorio M wake

veleidoso ADJ fickle

velero M sailboat; ADJ swift-sailing

veleta F weathervane; MF INV fickle person

vello M (del cuerpo) body hair; (de frutas) fuzz

vellón M fleece

velloso ADJ fuzzy

velludo ADJ hairy

velo M veil; **— del paladar** soft palate

velocidad F velocity, speed; **a toda —** at full speed

velocímetro M speedometer

velorio M wake

veloz ADJ swift, fast

vena F (vaso sanguíneo, veta) vein; (estado de ánimo) mood; (de locura) streak; **estar en —** to be in the mood, to be inspired

venado M deer; (macho) stag; (carne de venado) venison

vencedor -ora ADJ winning; MF winner, victor

vencer[10a] VT (a un enemigo) to conquer, to vanquish; (a un equipo) to defeat, to beat; (obstáculos) to overcome; (en valor, inteligencia) to surpass; VI **—se** (un plazo) to expire; (el asiento de una silla) to cave in

vencido ADJ (derrotado) defeated; (a pagar) due, overdue; **darse por —** to give up, to surrender

vencimiento M (de una deuda) maturity; (de un contrato) expiration

venda F bandage; (sobre los ojos) blindfold

vendaje M bandage

vendar VT (una herida) to bandage; (los ojos) to blindfold

vendaval M gale

vendedor -ora MF vendor, seller, salesperson; **— mayorista** wholesaler

vender VI/VT to sell; (traicionar) to betray; **—se a** to go over to; **se vende** for sale

vendetta F vendetta

vendible ADJ marketable

vendimia F vintage

veneciana F venetian blind

veneno M poison; (de víboras) venom

venenoso ADJ poisonous; (de víboras) venomous

venerable ADJ venerable

veneración F veneration, reverence

venerar VT (a una persona) to venerate, to revere; (a Dios) to worship

venéreo ADJ venereal

venezolano -na ADJ & MF Venezuelan

Venezuela F Venezuela

vengador -ora ADJ avenging; MF avenger

venganza F vengeance, revenge

vengar[7] VT to avenge; **—se de** to retaliate for, to avenge, to take revenge

vengativo ADJ vindictive, vengeful

venida F coming

venidero ADJ forthcoming

venir[47] VI to come; **— a colación** to come up (in conversation); **— al caso / a cuento** to be relevant; **— bien** to be convenient; **—le a uno bien** to be suitable to someone; **—se** fam to come (sexually); **—se abajo** to collapse; **¿a qué viene eso?** what is the point of that? **el año que viene** next year; **lo mejor esta por —** the best is yet to come; **no me vengas con excusas** no excuses; **venga lo que venga** come what may

venta F sale; **— al por mayor** wholesale; **— al por menor** retail; **en —** for sale;

poner a la — to put up for sale
ventaja F advantage; (en una carrera) head start
ventajoso ADJ advantageous
ventana F window; **tirar por la —** to throw out the window
ventanilla F (de coche, avión) window; (de la nariz) nostril
ventarrón M gale, high wind
ventear VI to sniff the wind
ventilación F ventilation; (hueco para el aire) vent
ventilado ADJ airy
ventilador M (abertura) ventilator; (aparato) electrical fan
ventilar VT to ventilate, to air out; (una cuestión) to air
ventisca F blizzard
ventisquero M (lugar ventoso) place prone to blizzards; (lugar nevado) snowfield
ventolera F gust of wind; **darle a uno la — de** to take a notion to
ventosear VI to break wind
ventoso ADJ windy, breezy
ventrículo M ventricle
venturoso ADJ **futuro —** bright future
ver[48] VI/VT to see; (televisión, espectáculos) to watch; **a —** let's see; **eso aún está por —se** that is still to be seen; **no lo puedo —** I can't stand him; **no — la hora de** to be dying for something to happen; **no tener nada que — con** not to have anything to do with; **te veo preocupado** you look worried; **a mi modo de —** in my opinion; **—se obligado a** to be obliged to; **vérselas con algo** to confront something; **vérselas negras** to have a hard time
vera LOC ADV **a la —** beside
veracidad F truthfulness
veranear VI to spend the summer
veraneo M summer vacation
veraniego ADJ summer
verano M summer
veras LOC ADV **de —** really
veraz ADJ truthful
verbal ADJ verbal
verbena F carnival
verbo M verb
verborrágico ADJ long-winded
verboso ADJ verbose, wordy
verdad F truth; **¿—?** really? **de —** indeed; **una pistola de —** a real pistol; **faltar a la —** to fib
verdadero ADJ true, real
verde ADJ green (también inmaduro, sin experiencia, ecologista); (chiste) off-color;

— oliva olive-green; **ponerse —** to stuff oneself; M green; **poner — a alguien** to run someone down
verdear VI/VT to turn green
verdín M scum
verdor M greenness
verdoso ADJ greenish
verdugo M executioner, hangman
verdugón M welt
verdulero -ra MF vegetable vendor
verduras F PL produce
vereda F Am sidewalk; **entrar en —** to toe the line
veredicto M verdict
verga F (percha para vela) yard; (pene) vulg dick
vergonzoso ADJ (que da vergüenza) shameful, disgraceful; (que siente vergüenza) sheepish, bashful
vergüenza F (humillación) shame; (incomodidad) embarrassment; (escándalo) disgrace; **tener —** to be ashamed; **es una —** it's a shame
vericueto M twists and turns
verídico ADJ truthful, true
verificación F verification, cross-check
verificar[6] VT to verify, to check; **—se** to take place
verja F grate
vermú M vermouth
vernáculo ADJ & M vernacular
verruga F wart; **— genital** genital wart
versado ADJ versed
versar VI **— sobre** to deal (with), to treat
versátil ADJ versatile
versículo M Bible verse
versión F version; (traducción) translation; (de una canción) rendition; **— original** original (of a film)
verso M line (of poetry); **— libre** free verse; **— suelto / blanco** blank verse
versus PREP versus
vértebra F vertebra
vertebrado ADJ & M vertebrate
vertebral ADJ spinal
vertedero M dump, landfill
verter[1] VT (echar líquido) to pour; (vaciar) to pour out; (derramar) to spill; **— en** to empty into; **—se** to spill
vertical ADJ vertical; (erguido) upright; (empinado) sheer
vertiente F (pendiente) slope; (cuenca) watershed; ADJ flowing
vertiginoso ADJ dizzy, giddy
vértigo M (falta de equilibrio) vertigo; (frenesí) hectic pace
vertigoso ADJ dizzy, giddy

vesícula F gall bladder

vestíbulo M (de un edificio) vestibule, lobby; (de una casa) hallway

vestido M dress; **— de noche** evening gown; **— de novia** bridal dress

vestidura F attire

vestigio M vestige, trace, remnant

vestimenta F attire, dress; (estrafalaria) get-up

vestir S VT to dress, to clothe; **—se** to get dressed; **—se de gala** to dress up

vestuario M wardrobe; (en el teatro) costumes; (lugar para vestirse) changing room

veta F (de minerales) vein, seam; (de madera) grain; (de humor) strain

vetar VT to veto

veteado ADJ veined

veterano -na ADJ & MF veteran

veterinario -ria MF veterinarian; ADJ veterinary; F veterinary medicine

veto M veto

vetusto ADJ ancient

vez F time; **a la —** at the same time; **a su —** in turn; **a veces** sometimes; **cada — más** more and more; **cada — que** whenever; **de — en cuando** from time to time; **de una —** (por entero) all at once; (por fin) one and for all; **de una — por todas** once and for all; **en — de** instead of; **por primera —** for the first time; **otra —** again; **una — (que)** once; **una — tras otra** over and over; **una y otra —** over and over again; **raras veces** seldom; **hacer las veces de** to take the place of

vía F (camino) road; (de ferrocarril) track; (medio de acceso) avenue; **— Láctea** Milky Way; **— navegable** waterway; **por — de** by means of; **en —s de** in the process of; PREP via

viable ADJ viable

viaducto M tunnel

viajante MF traveler; **— de comercio** traveling salesman/saleswoman

viajar VI to travel, to journey; (por mar) to voyage; (con drogas) to trip

viaje M trip, journey; (por mar) voyage; (en coche, caballo) ride; (por efecto de las drogas) trip; **— de ida y vuelta** round trip; **buen —** have a nice trip; **de —** out of town

viajero -ra MF traveler

viandante MF passer-by

viático M (de viaje) per diem; (religioso) last rites

víbora F viper; **— de cascabel** rattlesnake

vibración F vibration; (de la lengua) trill

vibrador M vibrator

vibrante ADJ vibrating

vibrar VI/VT to vibrate

vicegobernador -ora MF lieutenant governor

vicepresidente -ta MF vice-president

vicerrector -ora MF provost

viceversa ADV vice versa

viciado ADJ (aire) stale; (costumbre) stuffy; (corrupto) foul

viciar VT to foul; (corromper) to corrupt

vicio M (mala costumbre) vice, bad habit; **de —** unjustifiably; **quitarse el — de** to wean oneself of

vicioso ADJ (persona) having bad habits; (gasto) unjustifiable; (gramática) faulty

vicisitud F vicissitude

víctima F victim; (en un accidente) casualty, victim

victimizar [9] VT to victimize

victoria F victory

victorioso ADJ victorious

vid F vine, grapevine

vida F life; **— mía** sweetheart; **— nocturna** night life; **así es la —** that's life; **de toda la —** lifelong; **de — o muerte** life and death; **en la — voy a hacer eso** I would never do that; **esto es —** this is the life; **ganarse la —** to earn a living; **mujer de mala —** fam hooker; **sin —** lifeless

vidente MF seer; ADJ seeing

vídeo, video M (aparato) VCR; (técnica) video; (cinta) videocassette

videocasete F videocassette

videoconferencia F videoconference

videojuego M video game

vidriado M glaze; ADJ glazed

vidriar VT to glaze

vidriera F show window

vidriero -ra MF glazier, glassmaker

vidrio M (sustancia) glass; (en una ventana) pane; **pagar los —s rotos** to be left holding the bag

vidrioso ADJ glassy

vieira F scallop

viejo -ja ADJ old; (chiste) stale; M old man; (padre) father; **— verde** dirty old man; **los —s** the old folks; F old woman; (madre) mother

viento M wind; **hace —** it is windy; **a los cuatro —s** in all directions

vientre M abdomen; (barriga) belly; (de mujer) womb

viernes M Friday

Vietnam M Vietnam

vietnamita ADJ & MF INV Vietnamese

viga F (de madera) beam, rafter; (de metal) girder

vigencia F **entrar en —** to go into effect; **estar en —** to be in force

vigente ADJ effective, in force

vigía F lookout, reef; MF INV lookout

vigilancia F vigilance; (en una tienda) surveillance

vigilante ADJ vigilant; M watchman; F watchwoman

vigilar VI/VT to keep watch (over); VT to keep an eye on; (policía) to stake out

vigilia F vigil, watch

vigor M vigor; **en —** in force; **entrar en —** to become effective

vigorizar[9] VT to invigorate

vigoroso ADJ vigorous

VIH (virus de inmunodeficiencia humana) M HIV

vil ADJ vile, base, low

vileza F villainy, baseness

vilipendiar VT to revile

villa F village

villancico M Christmas carol

villanía F villainy

villano -na ADJ villainous; MF villain

vilo LOC ADV **en —** (en el aire) suspended; (en ascuas) in suspense

vinagre M vinegar

vincular VT to link; **—se** to link up

vínculo M link, tie

vindicar[6] VT to vindicate

vinilo M vinyl

vino M wine; **— blanco** white wine; **— espumoso** sparkling wine; **— rosado** rosé wine; **— tinto** red wine

viña F vineyard

viñatero -ra MF winegrower

viñedo M vineyard

viola F viola

violación F violation; (sexual) rape

violado ADJ violet; M violet

violar VT (una ley) to violate, to break; (una mujer) to rape, to ravish; (una promesa) to breach; (una cerradura) to pick; (derechos) to infringe upon; (mandamientos) to trespass against

violencia F violence; **— doméstica** domestic violence

violentar VT (a una persona) to manhandle; (una casa) to break into; **—se** to get mortified

violento ADJ violent, rough; (marido) abusive; (entrada) forcible; (ataque) vicious

violeta ADJ INV & M violet

violín M violin; (para música folklórica) fiddle

violinista MF violinist

violonchelo M cello

virada F veer

viraje M swerve

virar VI/VT (vehículo) to swerve, to veer; VI (barco) to tack

virgen ADJ & MF virgin; ADJ (cassette) blank; (selva) undisturbed

virginal ADJ virginal

viril ADJ virile, manly

virilidad F virility, manhood

virreinato M viceroyalty

virrey M viceroy

virtual ADJ virtual

virtud F (moral) virtue; (práctica) asset

virtuoso -sa ADJ (moral) virtuous; ADJ & MF (artístico) virtuoso

viruela F smallpox

virulento ADJ virulent

virus M virus (también de computadoras)

viruta F wood shaving

visa F visa

visado M visa

visar VT to endorse

visceral ADJ visceral

viscoso ADJ viscous

visera F visor

visible ADJ visible

visigodo -da ADJ Visigothic; MF Visigoth

visillo M window shade

visión F vision; (persona fea) sight

visionario -ria ADJ & MF visionary

visita F (acción de visitar) visit; (persona) visitor, caller; (a un edificio) tour; **— de médico** house call

visitación F visitation

visitador -ora MF visitor, caller; (inspector) inspector; (vendedor de medicamentos) pharmaceutical sales representative

visitante MF caller, visitor; ADJ visiting

visitar VT to visit; (un médico) to make a house call

vislumbrar VT to make out

viso M slip

visón M mink

víspera LOC ADV **en —s de** on the eve of

vista F (panorama) view, vista; (visión) eyesight; **a la —** in sight; **a primera —** at first sight; **a simple —** with the naked eye; **bajar la —** to lower one's eyes; **conocer de —** to know by sight; **con — a** with a view to; **en — de** considering; **hacer la — gorda** to look the other way; **¡hasta la —!** good-bye; **perder de —** to lose sight of; **tener a la —** to have before one's eyes; **tener — a** to look out on

vistazo M glance, glimpse, look; **dar / echar**

un — a to glance over
visto ADJ **bien —** well thought of; **mal —** looked down upon; **— que** whereas; M **— bueno** approval; **dar el — bueno** to approve
vistoso ADJ showy
visual ADJ visual
visualizador M display
visualizar[9] VT to visualize; (en pantalla) to display
vital ADJ vital; **fuerzas —es** life force
vitalicio ADJ life; M lifetime pension
vitalidad F vitality
vitamina F vitamin
viticultor -ora MF winegrower
vítor M cheer
vitorear VI/VT to cheer
vitral M stained-glass window
vitrina F (ventana) shop window; (armario) showcase
vituperación F vituperation
vituperar VT to revile
vituperio M vituperation
viudo -da M widower; F widow; **viuda negra** black widow spider
vivacidad F vivacity
vivaracho ADJ vivacious
vivaz ADJ vivacious, lively
víveres M PL provisions
vivero M nursery
viveza F (vivacidad) liveliness; (inteligencia) cleverness
vívido ADJ vivid
vivienda F (casa) dwelling; (alojamiento) housing
viviente ADJ living
vivir VI/VT to live; **vive una vida normal** he leads a normal life; **¡viva!** hurrah! long live!
vivisección F vivisection
vivo ADJ (no muerto) alive, living; (ágil) lively; (vistoso, intenso) vivid; (listo) clever; **en —** before a live audience; **en — y en directo** live; **de viva voz** by word of mouth
vocablo M word
vocabulario M vocabulary
vocación F vocation, calling; (religioso) call
vocal ADJ vocal; (no consonántico) vowel; F vowel; MF member
vocálico ADJ vocalic
vocear VI/VT to cry out; (anunciar) to page
vocerío M clamor
vocero -ra MF spokesperson
vociferante ADJ vociferous
vociferar VI to clamor
vodevil M vaudeville

vodka M vodka
volado ADJ (drogado) high; (escrito arriba) superscript
volador ADJ flying
volante ADJ flying; M (en un vestido) ruffle, frill; (en un coche) steering wheel; (en un motor) flywheel; (folleto) leaflet, handbill
volar[2] VI/VT to fly; **— por su cuenta** to fly solo; **ir volando** to hurry; VT (un puente) to blow up; VI (hojas) to blow; **—se** (hacer explosión) to blow up; (enojarse) to lose one's temper; (irse volando) to fly away; (drogarse) *fam* to get stoned
volátil ADJ volatile
volcán M volcano
volcánico ADJ volcanic
volcar[2,6] VT (voltear) to tip over, to knock over; (derramar) to spill; (vaciar) to empty; VI to roll over; **—se** to tip over, to overturn
volea F volley
volear VI/VT to volley
voleibol M volleyball
volición F volition
volquete M dump truck
voltaje M voltage
voltear VT (la lámpara) to knock over, to turn over; (la cara) to turn away
voltereta F somersault, tumble; **dar una —** to somersault; **dar —s** to tumble
voltio M volt
voluble ADJ (malhumorado) moody; (mercado de valores) volatile
volumen M volume
voluminoso ADJ voluminous, bulky
voluntad F will; **a —** at will; **buena —** good will, willingness; **mala —** ill will; **por su propia —** of his own volition
voluntario -ria ADJ (por la propia voluntad) voluntary; MF volunteer
voluntarioso ADJ (bien dispuesto) willing; (testarudo) willful
voluptuoso ADJ voluptuous
voluta F scroll; **—s de humo** spirals of smoke
volver[2,51] VI (ir al punto de partida) to return, to come back; (ir de nuevo) to return, to go back, to go again; **— a comer** to eat again; **— del revés** to turn inside out; **— en sí** to regain consciousness; **—se** (regresar) to go back; (ponerse) to become; **—se contra** to turn against; **—se atrás** to turn back; **—se hacia** to go toward; **—se loco** to go crazy; VT (la cara) to turn away; **— las espaldas** to turn one's back
vomitar VI/VT to vomit, to throw up

vómito M vomit
voraz ADJ voracious, ravenous
vórtice M vortex
vosotros -as PRON PERS you, you guys; (sur de EEUU) you all, y'all
votación F vote
votante MF voter
votar VI to vote; VT (elegir) to vote for; (aprobar) to vote into law; — **a / por** to vote for
voto M (opinión) vote; (promesa) vow; — **de confianza** vote of confidence
voz F (sonido, aptitud, voto) voice; (cabeza de entrada) headword; **a — en cuello** at the top of one's lungs; **alzar la —** to raise one's voice; **correr la —** to be rumored; **en — alta** aloud; **a voces** shouting; **dar voces** to shout
vozarrón M loud voice
vudú M voodoo
vuelco M **todo daría un —** everything would change radically; **me dio un — el corazón** my heart skipped a beat; **dar un —** to overturn, to turn over
vuelo M flight; (de una falda) flare; **al —** on the fly; **de alto —** prestigious; **levantar / alzar el —** to fly away
vuelta F (movimiento circular) turn; (regreso, devolución) return; (carrera ciclista) tour; (en una pista) lap; (curva) twist; (de un collar) loop; (en deportes) round; (dinero) change; — **de tuerca** unforeseen event; **a la — de la esquina** around the corner; **a — de correo** by return mail; **dar —** to turn upside down; **dar — al revés** to turn inside out; **dar — a una página / una llave** to turn a page / a key; **dar —s** to spin; **dar —s en la cama** to toss and turn; **dar — a algo** to turn something upside down; **dar la —** to turn around; **dar una —** to take a walk, to take a spin; **darse —** to roll over; **estar de —** (de regreso) to be back; (desencantado) to be jaded; **me da —s la cabeza** my head is spinning; **no tiene — de hoja** there are no two ways about it
vuelto M *Am* change
vuestro ADJ POS — **hermano** your bother; **un amigo —** a friend of yours; PRON **el —** yours
vulgar ADJ (común) ordinary; (tosco) vulgar
vulgo M common people
vulnerable ADJ vulnerable
vulva F vulva

Ww

wafle M waffle
waflera F waffle iron
wáter M toilet
web F World Wide Web
whisky M whisk(e)y; — **escocés** scotch
windsurf M windsurfing
wok M wok

Xx

xenofobia F xenophobia
xilofón, xilófono M xylophone

Yy

y CONJ and
ya ADV (desde antes) already; (ahora) now; (pronto) soon; ¡—! enough! — **era hora** it was about time; ¡— **lo creo!** I should say so! — **no** no longer; — **que** since; — **sea que** whether; — **te arreglo** I'll fix you; — **verás** mark my words; — **voy** I am coming
yacer[49] VI to lie
yacimiento M (de minerales) deposit; (de petróleo) field
yanqui ADJ & MF *pey* American
yarda F yard
yate M yacht
yegua F mare
yelmo M helmet
yema F (de huevo) egg yolk; (de una planta) bud, shoot; — **del dedo** fingertip
Yemen M Yemen
yemení ADJ & MF Yemeni
yen M yen
yermo ADJ (estéril) barren; (desolado) bleak, stark
yerno M son-in-law
yesca F tinder
yeso M (mineral) gypsum; (en construcción, medicina) plaster (of Paris); (escayola) cast
Yibuti M Djibouti

yibutiano -na ADJ & MF Djiboutian
yo PRON PERS I; M (ego) ego
yodo M iodine
yoduro M iodide
yoga M yoga
yogur M yogurt
yo-yo M yo-yo
yuca F (ornamental) yucca; (comestible) manioc
yugo M yoke
Yugoslavia F Yugoslavia
yugoslavo -va ADJ & MF Yugoslavian
yugular ADJ & F jugular
yunque M anvil
yunta F yoke
yuppie MF yuppie
yuxtaponer[39] VT juxtapose

Zz

zafar VT to release; **—se** (soltarse) to slip off; (no cumplir) to cop out; **—se de un aprieto** to squirm out of a difficulty
zafio ADJ boorish
zafiro M sapphire
zafra F (sugar) harvest
zaga LOC ADV **a la** — behind; F **ir a la** — to be behind; **quedar a la** — to fall behind
zaguán M vestibule, hall
zaino ADJ chestnut-colored
zalamería F (tacto) smoothness; (lisonja) flattery
zalamero -ra MF flatterer; ADJ (empalagoso) smooth, unctuous; (lisonjero) flattering
Zambia F Zambia
zambiano -na ADJ & MF Zambian
zambo ADJ knock-kneed
zambullida F dive, plunge
zambullir[19] VT to plunge, to dip; **—se** to dive, to plunge
zanahoria F carrot
zanca F leg of a wading bird
zancada F stride; **dar —s** to stride
zancadilla F intentional tripping; **hacer una —** to trip
zanco M stilt
zancudo ADJ long-legged, lanky; M *Am* mosquito
zángano M drone (también holgazán)
zangolotear VI/VT to jiggle
zangoloteo M jiggle
zanja F ditch, trench
zanjar VT to settle

zapapico M pickax(e)
zapata F brake shoe
zapatear VI to tap the feet in dancing
zapateo M tapping with the feet in dance
zapatería F shoe store
zapatero -ra MF (que fabrica) shoemaker; (que vende) shoe dealer; (que remienda) cobbler
zapatilla F (pantufla) slipper; (de vestir) pump; **—s** sneakers
zapato M shoe
zar M czar
zarandear VT to jiggle; **—se** to flop around
zarandeo M jiggle
zarcillo M (arete) earring; (de planta) tendril
zarigüeya F opossum
zarpa F claw
zarpar VI to sail, to set sail
zarpazo M blow with a claw; **dar —s** to claw
zarza F bramble, briar
zarzamora F blackberry
zepelín M blimp, zeppelin
zigoto M zygote
zigzag M zigzag
zigzaguear VI to zigzag, to weave one's way
Zimbabue M Zimbabwe
zimbabuo -ua ADJ & MF Zimbabwean
zirconio M zirconium
zócalo M baseboard
zodíaco M zodiac
zombi M zombie
zona F (área) zone; (culebrilla) shingles; **— gris** gray area; **— tampón** buffer zone
zonzo ADJ silly, foolish
zoo M zoo
zoología F zoology
zoológico ADJ zoological; M zoo
zoom M zoom lens
zopenco -ca MF dolt, numbskull
zorrillo M skunk
zorro -a MF fox; F (hembra) vixen; (prostituta) *pey* prostitute; ADJ (astuto) foxy, cunning; (promiscuo) loose
zorzal M thrush
zozobra F anxiety, worry
zozobrar VI to founder
zueco M clog
zumbar VI (hacer sonidos los insectos) to buzz, to drone, to hum; (hacer ruidos las máquinas) to whir, to whiz; (tintinear los oídos) to ring; (dar golpe) to sock
zumbido M (sonido de insectos) buzz, drone, hum; (sonido de máquinas) whir, whiz; (sonido en los oídos) ring
zumo M fruit juice
zurcido M (remiendo) darn; (acción de remendar) darning

zurcir [10b] VT to darn
zurdo ADJ left-handed, southpaw
zuro M corncob
zurra F whipping
zurrar VT to whip, to thrash
zurullo M turd
zutano -na M so-and-so, what's-his-name; F
    what's-her-name

Inglés–Español · English–Spanish

Lista de abreviaturas / List of Abbreviations

adj	adjective	adjetivo
adv	adverb, adverbial	adverbio, adverbial
Am	America	América
art	article	artículo
conj	conjunction	conjunción
def	definite	definido
dem	demonstrative	demostrativo
f	feminine	femenino
fam	familiar	familiar
indef	indefinite	indefinido
interj	interjection	interjección
interr	interrogative	interrogativo
inv	invariable	invariable
lit	literary	literario
loc	locution	locución
m	masculine	masculino
Mex	Mexico	México
n	noun	sustantivo
num	numeral	numeral
pej	pejorative	peyorativo
pl	plural	plural
poss	possessive	posesivo
prep	preposition, prepositional	preposición, preposicional
pron	pronoun	pronombre
rel	relative	relativo
RP	River Plate	Río de la Plata
sg	singular	singular
Sp	Spain, Spanish	España
v aux	auxiliary verb	verbo auxiliar
vi	intransitive verb	verbo intransitivo
vt	transitive verb	verbo transitivo
vulg	vulgar	vulgar

Pronunciación inglesa

I. VOCALES

Símbolo fonético	Ortografía inglesa	Explicación
[i]	see, pea	como la *i* en hilo
[ɪ]	bit	el sonido más aproximado es la *i* en *virtud,* pero la [ɪ] inglesa es más abierta, tirando a *e*
[e]	late, they	equivale aproximadamente a *ei*
[ɛ]	set	semejante a la *e* de *perro,* pero más abierta
[ɝ]	work, bird	como la *u* de *cud* (ver abajo) pero articulada simultáneamente con una *r*
[æ]	sat	sonido intermedio entre *e* y *a*
[ɑ]	hot	como la vocal de *pan*
[ɔ]	saw, laud	sonido intermedio entre *a* y *o*
[o]	low, mode	equivale aproximadamente a *ou*
[ʊ]	book, pull	como la *u* de *turrón,* pero más abierta
[u]	June, moon	como la *u* de *uno*
[ʌ]	cud	una *e* muy relajada
[ə]	adept	una *e* muy relajada y átona
[ɚ]	teacher	una *e* átona relajada articulada simultáneamente con una *r*

II. DIPTONGOS

Símbolo fonético	Ortografía inglesa	Explicación
[aɪ]	pie, aisle	como *ai* en *aire*
[aʊ]	now, foul	como *au* en *causa*
[ɔɪ]	boy	como *oy* en *hoy*
[ju]	use	como *iu* en *ciudad*

III. CONSONANTES

Símbolo fonético	Ortografía inglesa	Explicación
[b]	bat	semejante a la *b* española, pero seguida de aspiración
[d]	day	semejante a la *d* española, pero articulada en los alvéolos y con más tensión
[f]	fun, photo	como la *f* española
[g]	go	como la *g* de *goma,* pero con más tensión

276

[h]	hat	muy suave como la *j* de los dialectos caribeños del español
[j]	year	como la *i* del diptongo de *hielo*
[k]	cat, kill	como la *c* de *carro*, pero seguida de aspiración
[l]	let	como la *l* de *lado*
[ɫ]	ball	como la *l* final catalana
[m]	much	como la *m* española
[n]	no	como la *n* española
[p]	pea	como la *p* española, pero seguida de aspiración
[r]	red	no tiene equivalente en español; se pronuncia con la punta de la lengua enrollada hacia arriba, sin tocar el paladar
[s]	sea	como la *s* hispanoamericana (no la castellana)
[t]	tea	como la *t* española pero articulada en los alvéolos y seguida de aspiración
[v]	very	se articula con los dientes incisivos superiores colocados en el labio inferior
[w]	weed	equivale a la *u* del diptongo de *fui*
[z]	zero, rose	como la *s* de *mismo* cuando se sonoriza, pero aun más sonora
[ɒ]	latter, ladder	como la *r* de *para*
[θ]	thin	como la *z* del español castellano en *zagal*
[ð]	this	como la *d* de *cada*
[ʃ]	sheet, machine, notation	una *s* muy palatal como en francés *chapeau* o italiano *lasciare*
[ʒ]	measure, beige	como la *ll* argentina en *valle*, cuando es sonora
[tʃ]	church	como la *ch* de *charla*
[dʒ]	judge	como la *y* de *inyectar*
[ṇ]	eaten, button	representa la *n* silábica, articulada sin la vocal anterior
[ŋ]	ring	como la *n* española en *mango* y *banco*
[ḷ]	able	representa la *l* silábica, articulada sin la vocal anterior
[hw]	where	combinación de los sonidos [h] y [w] arriba descritos

Notas sobre gramática inglesa

El sustantivo

Género. En la gramática inglesa el género solo desempeña un papel importante en el sistema pronominal, p. ej. **he runs** 'él corre', **she runs** 'ella corre', **I see him** 'lo veo', **I see her** 'la veo'. En los sustantivos que designan a personas, se emplean varios métodos para distinguir entre los sexos, v. gr. por el agregado de un sufijo, como en **actor** 'actor', **actress** 'actriz', por el agregado de una palabra, como en **baby boy** 'niño', **baby girl** 'niña', **she-bear** 'osa', **male nurse** 'enfermero', o utilizando palabras completamente distintas, como en **uncle** 'tío', **aunt** 'tía'.

Número. Generalmente se forma el plural añadiendo -s al singular: **paper, papers** 'papel, papeles', **books, books** 'libro, libros', **chief, chiefs** 'jefe, jefes'.

Los sustantivos que terminan en **-ss, -x, -sh, -z,** y **-o** añaden **-es** para formar el plural: **kiss, kisses** 'beso, besos', **box, boxes** 'caja, cajas', **dish, dishes** 'plato, platos', **buzz, buzzes** 'zumbido, zumbidos', **hero, heroes** 'héroe, héroes'. Esto vale también por **-ch** cuando se pronuncia [č], como en **arch, arches** 'arco, arcos', pero no cuando se pronuncia [k], como en **monarch, monarchs** 'monarca, monarcas'.

Los sustantivos que terminan en **-fe**, y ciertos sustantivos que terminan en **-f,** cambian estas letras en **v** y añaden **-es** en el plural: **leaf, leaves** 'hoja, hojas', **life, lives** 'vida, vidas', **wife, wives** 'esposa, esposas', **knife, knives** 'cuchillo, cuchillos' (pero **reef, reefs** 'arrecife, arrecifes').

Para el plural de los sustantivos terminados en **-y** precedida de consonante se cambia la **-y** en **-ies: fly, flies** 'mosca, moscas', **family, families** 'familia, familias'. En cambio, los sustantivos terminados en **-y** precedida de vocal forman el plural añadiendo **-s** al singular: **day, days** 'día, días'.

Ciertos sustantivos forman el plural de una manera irregular: **man, men** 'hombre, hombres', **woman, women** 'mujer, mujeres', **mouse, mice** 'ratón, ratones', **louse, lice** 'piojo, piojos', **goose, geese** 'ganso, gansos', **tooth, teeth** 'diente, dientes', **foot, feet** 'pie, pies', **ox, oxen** 'buey, bueyes'.

Ciertos sustantivos que terminan en **-is** forman el plural cambiando la **i** de la terminación en **e: axis, axes** 'eje, ejes', **crisis, crises** 'crisis' (sg., pl.).

El adjetivo

El adjetivo inglés es invariable en cuanto a género y número. Normalmente se coloca delante del sustantivo: **an interesting woman** 'una mujer interesante', **a large man** 'un hombre grande', **beautiful birds** 'aves hermosas'.

Los comparativos y superlativos. Aunque no hay una regla general, por lo común los adjetivos monosílabos, los adjetivos acentuados en la última sílaba y algunos bisílabos comunes forman el comparativo de aumento y el superlativo añadiendo **-er** y **-est** (como en **tall**). Los demás adjetivos van precedidos de **more** (para el comparativo) y **most** (para el superlativo) (como en **careful**). Nótese que (1) si la palabra termina en **-e** muda, se añaden **-r** y **-st** en vez de **-er** y **-est** (ver **wise**), (2) los adjetivos terminados en **-y** cambian esta letra en **i** (ver **happy**), (3) los adjetivos terminados en consonante precedida de vocal doblan la consonante (ver **fat**):

Positivo	*Comparativo*	*Superlativo*
tall alto	**taller** más alto	**the tallest** el más alto
careful cuidadoso	**more careful** más cuidadoso	**the most careful** el más cuidadoso
wise sabio	**wiser** más sabio	**the wisest** el más sabio
happy feliz	**happier** más feliz	**the happiest** el más feliz
fat gordo	**fatter** más gordo	**the fattest** el más gordo

Los adjetivos siguientes forman el comparativo y el superlativo de una manera irregular:

good	**better**	**best**
bad, ill	**worse**	**worst**
much	**more**	**most**

El adverbio

Muchos adverbios se forman añadiendo **-ly** al adjetivo: **courteous** 'cortés', **courteously** 'cortésmente', **bold** 'atrevido', **boldly** 'atrevidamente'. Existen las irregularidades ortográficas siguientes en la formación de los adverbios que terminan en **-ly**: (1) los adjetivos terminados en **-ble** cambian la **-e** en **-y: possible, possibly,** (2) los terminados en **-ic** añaden **-ally: poetic, poetically,** (3) los terminados en **-ll** añaden sólo **-y: full, fully,** (4) los terminados en **-ue** pierden la **-e** final: **true, truly,** (5) los terminados en **-y** cambian la **-y** en **i: happy, happily.**

La mayor parte de los adverbios forman el comparativo y el superlativo con los adverbios **more** 'más' y **most** 'el/la más'. Asimismo los adverbios monosílabos añaden **-er** y **-est:**

Positivo	*Comparativo*	*Superlativo*
boldly	**more boldly**	**most boldly**
generously	**more generously**	**most generously**
soon	**sooner**	**soonest**
early	**earlier**	**earliest**
late	**later**	**latest**
fast	**faster**	**fastest**

Los adverbios siguientes forman el comparativo y el superlativo de una manera irregular:

well	**better**	**best**
badly	**worse**	**worst**
little	**less**	**least**
far	**farther, further**	**farthest, furthest**

Sufijos comunes del inglés

-dom   a partir de bases nominales, forma sustantivos con los sentidos de dominio, jurisdicción, estado, condición: **kingdom** 'reino' (**king** 'rey'), **martyrdom** 'martirio' (**martyr** 'mártir'), **freedom** 'libertad' (**free** 'libre')

-ee   a partir de verbos, forma sustantivos indicando a la persona que recibe una acción: **addressee** 'destinatario' (**to address** 'dirigir'), **employee** 'empleado' (**to employ** 'emplear').

-eer   a partir de bases diversas, forma sustantivos que denotan oficio u ocupación: **auctioneer** 'subastador' (**to auction** 'subastar'), **puppeteer** 'titiritero' (**puppet** 'títere')

-en *a.* forma adjetivos que denotan la sustancia de que está hecha una cosa: **golden** 'dorado' (**gold** 'oro'), **wooden** 'de madera' (**wood** 'madera')

   b. forma verbos a partir de adjetivos: **to whiten** 'blanquear' (**white** 'blanco), **to darken** 'oscurecer' (**dark** 'oscuro')

-er *a.* forma sustantivos a partir de verbos para indicar agente: **player** 'jugador' (**to play** 'jugar'), **speaker** 'hablante' (**to speak** 'hablar'), **baker** 'panadero' (**to bake** 'hornear')

   b. forma sustantivos a partir de sustantivos para denominar al residente de un lugar: **New Yorker** 'neoyorkino' (**New York** 'Nueva York'), **islander** 'isleño' (**island** 'isla')

-ess   se usa para formar el género femenino de ciertos sustantivos: **princess** 'princesa' (**prince** 'príncipe'), **countess** 'condesa' (**count** 'conde')

-fold   indica el número de veces que se repite algo: **twofold** 'dos veces' (**two** 'dos'), **hundredfold** 'cien veces' (**hundred** 'cien')

-ful *a.* forma adjetivos a partir de sustantivos para indicar la presencia de una cualidad: **hopeful** 'esperanzado' (**hope** 'esperanza'), **careful** 'cuidadoso' (**care** 'cuidado'), **willful** 'voluntarioso' (**will** 'voluntad')

   b. forma adjetivos a partir de verbos para indicar tendencia: **forgetful** 'olvidadizo' (**to forget** 'olvidar')

   c. forma sustantivos a partir de sustantivos indicando la capacidad: **handful** 'puñado' (**hand** 'mano'), **spoonful** 'cucharada' (**spoon** 'cuchara')

-hood   forma abstractos a partir de sustantivos concretos: **motherhood** 'maternidad' (**mother** 'madre'), **childhood** 'niñez' (**child** 'niño'), **likelihood** 'probabilidad' (**likely** 'probable')

-ing *a.* forma adjetivos a partir de verbos: **running water** 'agua corriente' (**to run** 'correr'), **drinking water** 'agua potable' (**to drink** 'beber'), **waiting room** 'sala de espera' (**to wait** 'esperar'), **washing machine** 'máquina lavadora' (**to wash** 'lavar')

   b. se usa para formar sustantivos que denominan la acción de un verbo: **understanding** 'entendimiento' (**to understand** 'entender'), **supplying** 'abastecimiento' (**to supply** 'abastar')

   c. se usa para formar sustantivos que denominan una cosa que desempeña una acción: **clothing** 'ropa' (**to clothe** 'vestir'), **covering** 'cobertura' (**to cover** 'cubrir')

-ish   forma adjetivos a partir de sustantivos indicando semejanza o atenuación: **boyish** 'como un niño' (**boy** 'niño'), **womanish** 'como mujer, mujeril' (**woman** 'mujer'), **whitish** 'blancuzco' (**white** 'blanco')

-less   se agrega a sustantivos para indicar falta de algo: **childless** 'sin hijos' (**child** 'hijo'), **penniless** 'sin dinero' (**penny** 'centavo'), **endless** 'interminable, sin fin' (**end** 'fin')

-like   se añade a sustantivos para indicar semejanza: **lifelike** 'que parece vivo' (**life** 'vida'), **childlike** 'infantil' (**child** 'niño'), **tigerlike** 'como un tigre' (**tiger** 'tigre')

-ly   *a.*   se añade a adjetivos para formar adverbios: **slowly** 'lentamente' (**slow** 'lento'), **happily** 'felizmente' (**feliz** 'happy')

      b.   deriva adjetivos a partir de sustantivos indicando manera: **motherly** 'maternal' (**mother** 'madre'), **gentlemanly** 'caballeroso' (**gentleman** 'caballero'), **friendly** 'amistoso' (**friend** 'amigo')

      c.   deriva adjetivos o adverbios de tiempo a partir de sustantivos: **daily** 'diario', 'diariamente' (**day** 'día'), **weekly** 'semanal', 'semanalmente' (**week** 'semana')

-ness   forma sustantivos abstractos a partir de adjetivos: **goodness** 'bondad' (**good** 'bueno'), **darkness** 'oscuridad' (**dark** 'oscuro'), **foolishness** 'tontería' (**fool** 'tonto')

-ship   se emplea para derivar sustantivos a partir de sustantivos y verbos para denotar

      a.   cualidades abstractas: **friendship** 'amistad' (**friend** 'amigo')

      b.   arte o destreza: **horsemanship** 'equitación' (**horseman** 'jinete')

      c.   dignidad, oficio, cargo, o título: **professorship** 'cátedra' (**professor** 'catedrático'), **lordship** 'señoría' (**lord** 'señor')

      d.   la duración de una acción: **courtship** 'cortejo' (**to court** 'cortejar')

-some   se añade a verbos para formar adjetivos que expresan tendencia excesiva: **tiresome** 'aburrido' (**to tire** 'aburrir'), **quarrelsome** 'pendenciero' (**to quarrel** 'discutir')

-th   es el sufijo que forma números ordinales a partir de los cardinales: **fifth** 'quinto' (**five** 'cinco'), **tenth** 'décimo' (**ten** 'diez')

-ward   se añade a sustantivos y adverbios para indicar movimiento hacia un lugar: **homeward** 'hacia casa' (**home** 'casa'), **downward** 'hacia abajo' (**down** 'abajo')

| -wise, | se añaden a sustantivos para indicar dirección o posición: **edgewise** |
| -ways | 'de lado' (**edge** 'borde'), **lengthwise** 'a lo largo' (**length** 'largo'), **sideways** 'de lado' (**side** 'lado') |

-y	*a.*	es un sufijo diminutivo: **doggy** 'perrito' (**dog** 'perro'), **Johnny** 'Juanito' (**John** 'Juan')
	b.	se añade a sustantivos para formar adjetivos que indican abundancia: **rocky** 'rocoso' (**rock** 'roca'), **rainy** 'lluvioso' (**rain** 'lluvia'), **hairy** 'peludo' (**hair** 'pelo'), **angry** 'enojado' (**anger** 'enojo')
	c.	se añade a sustantivos para formar adjetivos que expresan semejanza: **rosy** 'rosado' (**rose** 'rosa')

Verbos irregulares de la lengua inglesa

Se denominan verbos irregulares los que no forman el pretérito o el participio pasivo con la adición de **-d** o **-ed** al presente. Obsérvese que en ciertos verbos (aquí señalados con asterisco) coexiste la forma regular al lado de la irregular. Las formas poco usadas aparecen entre paréntesis.

Presente	*Pretérito*	*Participio pasivo*
*abide	(abode)	abode
am, is, are	was, were	been
arise	arose	arisen
*awake	awoke	awoke, awoken
bear	bore	borne
beat	beat	beat, beaten
become	became	become
befall	befell	befallen
beget	begat	begotten
begin	began	begun
behold	beheld	beheld
bend	bent	bent
beseech	(besought)	(besought)
beset	beset	beset
bet	bet	bet
bid 'offer'	bid	bid
bid 'command'	bade	bidden
bind	bound	bound
bite	bit	bitten, bit
bleed	bled	bled
blow	blew	blown
break	broke	broken
breed	bred	bred
bring	brought	brought
build	built	built
*burn	burnt	burnt

Presente	Pretérito	Participio pasivo
burst	burst	burst
buy	bought	bought
cast	cast	cast
catch	caught	caught
choose	chose	chosen
cling	clung	clung
*clothe	(clad)	(clad)
come	came	come
cost	cost	cost
creep	crept	crept
*crow	crew	crowed
cut	cut	cut
deal	dealt	dealt
dig	dug	dug
*dive	dove	dived
do	did	done
draw	drew	drawn
*dream	dreamt	dreamt
drink	drank	drunk
drive	drove	driven
*dwell	dwelt	dwelt
eat	ate	eaten
fall	fell	fallen
feed	fed	fed
feel	felt	felt
fight	fought	fought
find	found	found
*fit	fit	fit
flee	fled	fled
fling	flung	flung
fly	flew	flown
forbear	forbore	forborne
forbid	forbade	forbidden
foresee	foresaw	foreseen
foretell	foretold	foretold
forget	forgot	forgotten, forgot
forgive	forgave	forgiven
forsake	forsook	forsaken
freeze	froze	frozen
get	got	got, gotten
*gild	gilt	gilt
*gird	girded	girt
give	gave	given
go	went	gone
grind	ground	ground

Verbos irregulares

Presente	Pretérito	Participio pasivo
grow	grew	grown
hang[1]	hung	hung
have, has	had	had
hear	heard	heard
*hew	hewed	hewn
hide	hid	hidden, hid
hit	hit	hit
hold	held	held
hurt	hurt	hurt
keep	kept	kept
*kneel	knelt	knelt
*knit	knit	knit
know	knew	known
lay	laid	laid
lead	led	led
*lean	(leant)	(leant)
*leap	leapt	leapt
*learn	(learnt)	(learnt)
leave	left	left
lend	lent	lent
let	let	let
lie[2]	lay	lain
*light	lit	lit
lose	lost	lost
make	made	made
mean	meant	meant
meet	met	met
mistake	mistook	mistaken
*mow	mowed	mown
pay	paid	paid
*plead	pled	pled
put	put	put
quit	quit	quit
read [rid]	read [red]	read [red]
rend	rent	rent
*rid	rid	rid
ride	rode	ridden
ring	rang	rung
rise	rose	risen
run	ran	run
*saw	sawed	sawn
say	said	said
see	saw	seen
seek	sought	sought

1. Es regular cuando significa 'ahorcar'.
2. Es regular cuando significa 'mentir'.

Presente	Pretérito	Participio pasivo
sell	sold	sold
send	sent	sent
set	set	set
*sew	sewed	sewn
shake	shook	shaken
*shave	shaved	shaven
*shear	sheared	shorn
shed	shed	shed
shine[3]	shone	shone
shoe	shod	shod
shoot	shot	shot
*show	showed	shown
*shred	shred	shred
shrink	shrank (shrunk)	shrunk (shrunken)
shut	shut	shut
sing	sang	sung
sink	sank	sunk
sit	sat	sat
slay	slew	slain
sleep	slept	slept
slide	slid	slid, slidden
sling	slung	slung
slink	slunk	slunk
slit	slit	slit
*smell	(smelt)	(smelt)
smite	smote	smitten
*sneak	snuck	snuck
*sow	sowed	sown
speak	spoke	spoken
*speed	sped	sped
*spell	(spelt)	(spelt)
spend	spent	spent
*spill	spilt	spilt
spin	spun	spun
spit	spat, spit	spat, spit
split	split	split
*spoil	(spoilt)	(spoilt)
spread	spread	spread
spring	sprang, sprung	sprung
stand	stood	stood
*stave	stove	stove
steal	stole	stolen
stick	stuck	stuck
sting	stung	stung
stink	stank	stunk

3. Suele ser regular cuando es transitivo, en el sentido 'pulir, dar brillo'.

Verbos irregulares

Presente	Pretérito	Participio pasivo
*strew	strewed	strewn
stride	strode	stridden
strike	struck	struck, stricken
string	strung	strung
*strive	strove	striven
swear	swore	sworn
*sweat	sweat	sweat
sweep	swept	swept
*swell	swelled	swollen
swim	swam	swum
swing	swung	swung
take	took	taken
teach	taught	taught
tear	tore	torn
tell	told	told
think	thought	thought
throw	threw	thrown
thrust	thrust	thrust
tread	trod	trodden
understand	understood	understood
undertake	undertook	undertaken
undo	undid	undone
uphold	upheld	upheld
upset	upset	upset
*wake	woke	woken
wear	wore	worn
weave	wove	woven
*wed	wed	wed
weep	wept	wept
*wet	wet	wet
win	won	won
wind	wound	wound
withdraw	withdrew	withdrawn
withhold	withheld	withheld
withstand	withstood	withstood
wring	wrung	wrung
write	wrote	written

Aa

a [ə, e] INDEF ART un *m*, una *f*; **what — fool!**
¡qué tonto! **such — fool** tan tonto; **I'm
— teacher / Catholic** soy maestro /
católico

aback [əbǽk] ADV **to be taken —** estar
desconcertado

abandon [əbǽndən] VT abandonar; N **with
wild —** desenfrenadamente

abandonment [əbǽndənmənt] N abandono
m, desamparo *m*

abashed [əbǽʃt] ADJ humillado, avergonzado

abate [əbét] VI/VT disminuir, mitigar(se);
(storm) calmarse, atenuarse

abbey [ǽbi] N abadía *f*

abbot [ǽbət] N abad *m*

abbreviate [əbríviet] VT abreviar

abbreviation [əbriviéʃən] N (act of
abbreviating) abreviación *f*; (short form)
abreviatura *f*

abdicate [ǽbdiket] VI/VT abdicar

abdomen [ǽbdəmən] N abdomen *m*, vientre
m

abdominal [æbdámənəł] ADJ abdominal

abduct [æbdʌ́kt] VT secuestrar, raptar

abduction [æbdʌ́kʃən] N rapto *m*, secuestro
m

aberration [æbəréʃən] N anomalía *f*,
aberración *f*

abet [əbét] VT instigar

abeyance [əbéəns] ADV LOC **in —** pendiente,
en suspenso

abhor [əbhɔ́r] VT aborrecer

abhorrence [əbhɔ́rəns] N aborrecimiento *m*

abhorrent [əbhɔ́rənt] ADJ aborrecible

abide [əbáid] VT (tolerate) soportar; VI (dwell)
morar, permanecer; **to — by** acatar,
atenerse a

ability [əbílɪdi] N (skill) habilidad *f*;
(aptitude) capacidad *f*

abject [ǽbdʒékt] ADJ abyecto; **in — poverty**
en extrema miseria

ablaze [əbléz] ADV en llamas

able [ébəł] ADJ hábil, capaz; **—-bodied** de
cuerpo sano; **to be — to** (be capable of)
poder; (have an acquired skill) saber

abnegate [ǽbnɪget] VT renunciar

abnormal [æbnɔ́rməł] ADJ anormal

aboard [əbɔ́rd] ADV a bordo; **all —!** (train)
¡viajeros al tren! (ship) ¡pasajeros a bordo!
to go — embarcarse

abode [əbód] N morada *f*; **place of —**
domicilio *m*

abolish [əbálɪʃ] VT abolir, suprimir

abolition [æbəlíʃən] N abolición *f*

abominable [əbámənəbəł] ADJ abominable

abomination [əbàmənéʃən] N (action)
abominación *f*; (condition, habit) horror
m

aboriginal [æbərídʒənəł] ADJ aborigen

aborigine [æbərídʒəni] N aborigen *mf*;
Australian — aborigen australiano -na
mf

abort [əbɔ́rt] VT (fetus) abortar; VI/VT
(mission) suspender

abortion [əbɔ́rʃən] N aborto *m*

abortionist [əbɔ́rʃənɪst] N abortador -ra *mf*,
abortero -ra *mf*

abortive [əbɔ́rdɪv] ADJ frustrado

abound [əbáund] VI abundar; **to — with**
abundar en

about [əbáut] PREP (concerning) acerca de,
tocante a; (near, surrounding) alrededor
de, por; **to be — one's business** atender
a su negocio; ADV más o menos, alrededor
de; **at — ten o'clock** a eso de las diez,
sobre las diez; **to be — to do something**
estar por / para hacer algo, estar a punto
de hacer algo

above [əbʌ́v] PREP **you could see the
towers — the buildings** se veían las
torres sobre los edificios; **everyone —
five years of age** todos los de más de
cinco años; **he's — me in the company**
es mi superior en la compañía; **to be —
suspicion** estar libre de toda sospecha; **I
thought you were — such things** no
pensaba que te rebajarías a eso; ADV **the
apartment —** el apartamento de arriba;
books of fifty pages and — libros de
cincuenta páginas y más; **the remark
quoted —** la observación anteriormente
citada; **— all** sobre todo; **—-mentioned**
susodicho, ya mencionado; **from — de**
arriba, del cielo, de Dios

abrasion [əbréʒən] N abrasión *f*

abrasive [əbrésɪv] ADJ (material) abrasivo;
(person, tone) irritante

abreast [əbrést] ADV al lado; **to keep —**
mantenerse al corriente; **four —** de cuatro
en fondo

abridge [əbrídʒ] VT abreviar

abroad [əbrɔ́d] ADV en el extranjero; **to go
—** ir al extranjero

abrupt [əbrʌ́pt] ADJ abrupto

ABS (antilock braking system) [ebiés] N
SFA *m*

abscess [ǽbses] N absceso *m*

abscond [æbskánd] VI fugarse

absence [ǽbsəns] N (nonpresence) ausencia *f*; (lack) falta *f*; **in the — of** a falta de

absent [ǽbsənt] ADJ ausente; **—-minded** distraído, despistado; **to be — from school** faltar a la escuela

absentee [æbsəntí] N ausente *mf*

absenteeism [æbsəntíizəm] N ausentismo *m*

absolute [ǽbsəlút] ADJ absoluto; (prohibition) terminante

absolutely [æbsəlútli] ADV **— not** en absoluto; INTERJ **—!** ¡sí, señor!

absolve [æbzátv] VT absolver

absorb [əbzórb] VT (emission) absorber; (shock) amortiguar; (people, information) asimilar

abstain [əbstén] VI abstenerse; **— from** abstenerse de

abstinence [ǽbstənəns] N abstinencia *f*

abstract [ǽbstrækt] ADJ abstracto; N resumen *m*, extracto *m*; **in the —** en abstracto

abstraction [æbstrǽkʃən] N abstracción *f*

absurd [əbsɜ́-d] ADJ absurdo, disparatado

absurdity [əbsɜ́-DIDi] N (quality) absurdo *m*; (action) disparate *m*

abundance [əbándəns] N abundancia *f*

abundant [əbándənt] ADJ abundante

abuse [əbjús] N (of privileges) abuso *m*; (of authority) desmán *m*; (physical) maltrato *m*; (verbal) injuria *f*; [əbjúz] VT (privileges) abusar de; (physically) maltratar; (verbally) injuriar

abusive [əbjúsiv] ADJ (physically) violento; (verbally) injurioso

abysmal [əbízməl] ADJ abismal; **— ignorance** ignorancia supina *f*; **— results** resultados desastrosos *m pl*

abyss [əbís] N abismo *m*

A/C (air conditioning) [esí] N aire acondicionado *m*

academic [ækədémɪk] ADJ (university) académico; (school) escolar; N profesor -ra universitario -ria *mf*

academy [əkǽdəmi] N academia *f*

accede [æksíd] VI acceder; **to — to** acceder a

accelerate [æksélərət] VI/VT acelerar

acceleration [ækseləréʃən] N aceleración *f*

accelerator [æksélərεDə▸] N acelerador *m*

accent [ǽksεnt] N (pronunciation) acento *m*; (written) tilde *f*, acento escrito *m*; [æksént] VT (stress, syllable) acentuar

accentuate [æksénʃuεt] VT (differences, facts) acentuar, recalcar; (beauty) realzar

accept [æksépt] VT aceptar

acceptable [ækséptəbəl] ADJ aceptable

acceptance [ækséptəns] N (action) aceptación *f*; (approval) aprobación *f*

access [ǽksεs] N acceso *m*

accessible [æksésəbəl] ADJ accesible

accessory [æksésəri] ADJ accesorio; N accesorio *m*; (to a crime) cómplice *mf*

accident [ǽksɪDənt] N accidente *m*; (mishap) percance *m*; **by —** por casualidad

accidental [æksɪdént] ADJ (injury) accidental; (discovery, meeting) casual, fortuito

acclaim [əklém] VT aclamar; N aclamación *f*, ovación *f*

acclamation [ækləméʃən] N aclamación *f*

acclimate [ǽkləmət] VI/VT (to physical conditions) aclimatar(se); (to an ambiance) acostumbrar(se)

accolade [ǽkəled] N elogio *m*

accommodate [əkámədet] VT (adjust) tener en cuenta; (lodge) hospedar, alojar; (contain) tener capacidad para; VI **to — oneself** adaptarse

accommodation [əkamədéʃən] N (adjustment) acomodación *f*, adaptación *f*; **—s** (lodging) alojamiento *m*; (facilities) comodidades *f pl*

accompaniment [əkámpənɪmənt] N acompañamiento *m*

accompanist [əkámpənɪst] N acompañante *mf*

accompany [əkámpəni] VI/VT acompañar

accomplice [əkámplɪs] N cómplice *mf*

accomplish [əkámplɪʃ] VT (objective) lograr; (mission) completar

accomplished [əkámplɪʃt] ADJ (actor, athlete) consumado; (musician) talentoso

accomplishment [əkámplɪʃmənt] N (achievement) logro *m*; (skill) habilidad *f*; (completion) realización *f*

accord [əkórd] N acuerdo *m*, convenio *m*; **of one's own —** voluntariamente; VT otorgar, conceder

accordance [əkórdns] ADV LOC **in — with** de acuerdo con, de conformidad con

according [əkórdɪŋ] ADV LOC **— to** según

accordingly [əkórdɪŋli] ADV (therefore) por consiguiente; (correspondingly) como corresponde

accordion [əkórdiən] N acordeón *m*

accost [əkóst] VT abordar

account [əkáunt] N (bill) cuenta *f*; (story) relato *m*, relación *f*; **to open (close) an —** abrir (cerrar) una cuenta; **on — of** a causa de, debido a; **on my —** por mí; **on one's own —** por cuenta propia; **on no —** de ninguna manera; **of no —** de ningún valor; **to take into —** tener en cuenta; VI **to — for** dar cuenta de; **how do you — for that?** ¿cómo se explica eso?

accountable [əkáuntəbəł] ADJ responsable

accountant [əkáuntṇt] N *Am* contador -ra *mf*; *Sp* contable *mf*

accounting [əkáuntiŋ] N contabilidad *f*; — **firm** empresa de contadores públicos *f*; — **period** ejercicio contable *m*

accredit [əkrɛ́dɪt] VT acreditar

acculturate [əkʌ́łtʃəret] VI/VT aculturar(se)

accumulate [əkjúmjəlet] VI/VT acumular(se)

accumulation [əkjumjəléfən] N acumulación *f*

accuracy [ǽkjə-əsi] N precisión *f*, exactitud *f*

accurate [ǽkjə-ɪt] ADJ (measure, instrument) preciso, exacto; (translation) fiel

accursed [əkɔ́-sɪd] ADJ maldito

accusation [ækjuzéfən] N acusación *f*

accuse [əkjúz] VT acusar

accused [əkjúzd] ADJ acusado; N acusado -da *mf*, reo -a *mf*, procesado -da *mf*

accuser [əkjúzə-] N acusador -ra *mf*

accustom [əkʌ́stəm] VT acostumbrar, habituar; **to — oneself** acostumbrarse, habituarse; **to be —ed to** tener la costumbre de, estar acostumbrado a

AC/DC (alternating current / direct current) [ésidísi] ADJ (electricity) alterna y continua; (sexuality) bisexual

ace [es] N (cards, athlete, aviator) as *m*; VT sacarse la máxima nota en

acetone [ǽsəton] N acetona *f*

ache [ek] N dolor *m*; **—s and pains** achaques *m pl*; VT doler; **my stomach —s** me duele el estómago

achieve [ətʃív] VT (a goal) conseguir, lograr; (a level) alcanzar

achievement [ətʃívmənt] N (attainment) consecución *f*; (success) logro *m*, realización *f*

achy [éki] ADJ dolorido

acid [ǽsɪd] ADJ ácido; N ácido *m*; (hallucinogen) LSD *m*; — **rain** lluvia ácida *f*; — **test** prueba de fuego *f*

acidic [əsídɪk] ADJ ácido

acidity [əsídɪdi] N acidez *f*

acknowledge [æknáłɪdʒ] VT (merits) reconocer; (faults) admitir, reconocer; **to — receipt** acusar recibo

acknowledgment [æknáłɪdʒmənt] N (of merits) reconocimiento *m*; (of merits, faults) reconocimiento *m*, admisión *f*; (gratefulness) agradecimiento *m*; — **of receipt** acuse de recibo *m*

acme [ǽkmi] N súmmum *m*

acne [ǽkni] N acné *m*

acorn [ékɔrn] N bellota *f*

acoustics [əkústɪks] N acústica *f*

acquaint [əkwént] VT informar, familiarizar; **to — oneself with** informarse de, familiarizarse con; **to be —ed with** (a person, city, country) conocer; (a piece of news) estar enterado de

acquaintance [əkwéntṇs] N (with facts) conocimiento *m*; (a person) conocido -a *mf*

acquiesce [ækwiés] VT asentir, condescender; (unwillingly) consentir

acquiescence [ækwiésəns] N asentimiento *m*, consentimiento *m*, condescendencia *f*

acquire [əkwáɪr] VT (knowledge, skill, purchase) adquirir; (fortune, information) obtener; (disease) contraer

acquisition [ækwəzífən] N (knowledge, skill, purchase) adquisición *f*; (fortune, information) obtención *f*

acquisitive [əkwízɪdɪv] ADJ codicioso

acquit [əkwít] VT absolver

acquittal [əkwídł] N absolución *f*

acre [éka-] N acre (0,405 hectáreas) *m*

acrid [ǽkrɪd] ADJ acre

acrimony [ǽkrəmoni] N acritud *f*

acrobat [ǽkrəbæt] N acróbata *mf*

acrobatic [ækrəbǽdɪk] ADJ acrobático; **—s** acrobacia *f*

acronym [ǽkrənɪm] N acrónimo *m*, sigla *f*

acrophobia [ækrəfóbiə] N acrofobia *f*

across [əkrɔ́s] PREP **to lay one stick — the other** poner dos palos cruzados; **there's a bridge — that river** hay un puente sobre ese río; **he came — his old love letters** encontró sus viejas cartas de amor; **the library is — the street** la biblioteca está al otro lado de la calle; ADV **cut the boards —** corta los tablones a lo ancho; **five hundred miles —** de quinientas millas de ancho; **the meaning doesn't come —** el significado no se entiende; **to come/ run —** encontrarse con, tropezar con

acrylic [əkrílɪk] ADJ & N acrílico *m*

act [ækt] N (deed, part of play) acto *m*; (part of show) número *m*; (law) ley *f*, decreto *m*; VI (behave) actuar, comportarse; (take measures) obrar; (play a part, chemical process) actuar; (on someone's behalf) representar; (mechanism) funcionar; **to — up** (child) portarse mal; (car) funcionar mal; **to — out** (event) representar; (feelings) exteriorizar

acting [ǽktiŋ] N actuación *f*; (in a drama) representación *f*; ADJ (interim) interino; (substitute) suplente

action [ǽkʃən] N (practical measure, plot of a play) acción *f*; (deed) acto *m*; (mechanism) funcionamiento *m*; **to take —** tomar

medidas
activate [ǽktıvet] VT activar
active [ǽktıv] ADJ activo
activism [ǽktıvızəm] N activismo *m*
activist [ǽktıvıst] N activista *mf*
activity [æktívıdi] N actividad *f*
actor [ǽktə-] N actor *m*
actress [ǽktrıs] N actriz *f*
actual [ǽktʃuəl] ADJ verdadero, real
actually [ǽktʃuəli] ADV en realidad
actuary [ǽktʃueri] N actuario -ria *mf*
acuity [əkjúıdi] N agudeza *f*
acumen [ǽkjəmən] N perspicacia *f*, agudeza *f*
acupuncture [ǽkjupʌŋktʃə] N acupuntura *f*
acupuncturist [ǽkjupʌ́ŋktʃə-ıst] N acupuntor -ra *mf*
acute [əkjút] ADJ (pain, illness) agudo; (observation) perspicaz, penetrante
A.D. [edí] ADV d.C.
adamant [ǽdəmənt] ADJ inflexible, firme
adapt [ədǽpt] VT adaptar; VI **to — to** adaptar(se) a, acomodar(se) a
adaptation [ædəptéʃən] N adaptación *f*
add [æd] VT añadir, agregar; (sum) sumar; **to — to** aumentar; **to — up** (sum) sumar; (make sense) cuadrar; N **—on** accesorio *m*
addict [ǽdıkt] N adicto -ta *mf*
addicted [ədíktıd] ADJ adicto
addiction [ədíkʃən] N adicción *f*
addition [ədíʃən] N (of numbers) suma *f*; (to a collection, staff) adición *f*, adquisición *f*; (to a building) anexo *m*; **in — (to)** además (de)
additional [ədíʃənəl] ADJ adicional
additive [ǽdıtıv] N aditivo *m*
address [ədrés] N (street) dirección *f*, domicilio *m*; (speech) discurso *m*; **form of —** tratamiento *m*; VT (write the address) dirigir; (speak to) dirigirse a; (deal with) vérselas con
addressee [ædresí] N destinatario -ria *mf*
adept [ədépt] ADJ hábil
adequacy [ǽdıkwəsi] N suficiencia *f*
adequate [ǽdıkwıt] ADJ (sufficient) suficiente; (acceptable) aceptable
adhere [ædhír] VI adherirse; **to — to** adherirse a
adherence [ædhírəns] N adhesión *f*
adhesion [ædhíʒən] N (thing or tissue that adheres) adherencia *f*; (act of sticking together) adhesión *f*
adhesive [ædhísıv] ADJ adhesivo; **— tape** cinta adhesiva *f*
adjacent [ədʒésənt] ADJ adyacente
adjective [ǽdʒıktıv] ADJ & N adjetivo *m*
adjoin [ədʒɔ́ın] VT lindar con, colindar con; VI estar contiguo a

adjourn [ədʒɜ́-n] VT **to — the meeting** levantar la sesión; **meeting —ed** se levanta la sesión
adjournment [ədʒɜ́-nmənt] N levantamiento de la sesión *m*
adjudge [ədʒʌ́dʒ] VT (declare) declarar; (deem) calificar
adjudicate [ədʒúdıket] VI arbitrar; VT declarar
adjunct [ǽdʒʌŋkt] ADJ adjunto; N agregado -da *mf*
adjust [ədʒʌ́st] VT (fix) ajustar, graduar; (adapt a machine) regular; VI ajustarse, adaptarse
adjustment [ədʒʌ́stmənt] N ajuste *m*; (on a machine) regulación *f*
ad lib [ædlíb] ADV improvisando
administer [ædmínıstə-] VT (control) administrar, gestionar; (punishment) aplicar; (oath) tomar
administration [ædmınıstréʃən] N administración *f*; (period in power) gestión *f*; (of punishment) aplicación *f*; (of an oath) toma *f*
administrative [ædmínıstredıv] ADJ administrativo
administrator [ædmínıstredə-] N administrador -ra *mf*
admirable [ǽdmə-əbəl] ADJ admirable
admiral [ǽdmə-əl] N almirante *m*
admiration [ædməréʃən] N admiración *f*
admire [ædmáır] VT admirar
admirer [ædmáırə-] N admirador -ra *mf*; (suitor) pretendiente *mf*
admissible [ædmísəbəl] ADJ admisible
admission [ædmíʃən] N (acceptance) admisión *f*; (access, ticket price) entrada *f*; (confession) confesión *f*
admit [ædmít] VT (allow entry) admitir; (to a hospital) internar; (acknowledge) reconocer, admitir
admittance [ædmítns] N entrada *f*; **no —** prohibida la entrada
admonish [ædmánıʃ] VT amonestar; **to — for** amonestar por
admonition [ædməníʃən] N (warning) amonestación *f*; (reproof) advertencia *f*
adobe [ədóbi] N (mud) adobe *m*; (house) casa de adobe *f*
adolescence [ædlésəns] N adolescencia *f*
adolescent [ædlésənt] ADJ & N adolescente *mf*
adopt [ədápt] VT (child, custom) adoptar; (suggestion) aprobar
adoption [ədápʃən] N (of a child, custom) adopción *f*; (of a suggestion) aprobación *f*
adoptive [ədáptıv] ADJ adoptivo
adorable [ədɔ́rəbəl] ADJ adorable, precioso
adoration [ædəréʃən] N adoración *f*

adore [ədɔ́r] VT adorar; **I — playing tennis**
me encanta jugar al tenis

adorn [ədɔ́rn] VT adornar, ornar

adornment [ədɔ́rnmənt] N adorno *m*

adrenal [ədrín]] ADJ **— gland** glándula
suprarrenal *f*

adrenalin [ədrénəlɪn] N adrenalina *f*

adrift [ədríft] ADJ & ADV a la deriva

adult [ədʌ́lt] ADJ & N adulto -ta *mf*

adulterate [ədʌ́ltərət] VT adulterar

adulterer [ədʌ́ltərə-] N adúltero -ra *mf*

adultery [ədʌ́ltəri] N adulterio *m*

advance [ædvǽns] VI (move forward)
avanzar; (make progress) avanzar,
progresar; (bring forward) adelantar; VT
(promote) promover; (propose) proponer;
(pay beforehand) adelantar, anticipar; N
(movement) avance *m*; (progress) adelanto
m; (loan) adelanto *m*, anticipo *m*; **—s**
(sexual) requiebros *m pl*; **in —** por
adelantado, con anticipación

advanced [ædvǽnst] ADJ (idea, stage)
avanzado; (country) adelantado

advancement [ædvǽnsmənt] N (movement)
avance *m*; (rank) ascenso *m*; (knowledge)
progreso *m*

advantage [ædvǽntɪdʒ] N ventaja *f*; **it
would be to your —** te convendría; **to
take — of** aprovecharse de

advantageous [ædvæntédʒəs] ADJ ventajoso,
provechoso

advent [ǽdvent] N advenimiento *m*

adventure [ædvéntʃə-] N aventura *f*

adventurer [ædvéntʃərə-] N aventurero -ra *mf*

adventuresome [ædvéntʃə-səm] ADJ osado

adventurous [ædvéntʃə-əs] ADJ (seeking
adventure) aventurero, intrépido; (daring)
atrevido, audaz

adverb [ǽdvə-b] N adverbio *m*

adversary [ǽdvə-seri] N adversario -ria *mf*

adverse [ǽdvə́-s] ADJ adverso

adversity [ædvə́-sɪdi] N adversidad *f*

advertise [ǽdvə-taɪz] VT anunciar, hacer
publicidad / propaganda para; VI hacer
propaganda / publicidad; **to — for a
cook** poner un anuncio buscando
cocinero

advertisement [ædvə-táɪzmənt] N anuncio
publicitario *m*, aviso *m*

advertiser [ǽdvə-taɪzə-] N anunciante *mf*

advertising [ǽdvə-taɪzɪŋ] N publicidad *f*

advice [ædváɪs] N consejo *m*; (expert)
asesoramiento *m*

advisable [ædváɪzəbəl] ADJ aconsejable,
recomendable

advise [ædváɪz] VI/VT (counsel) aconsejar,
advertir; VT (inform) avisar, informar;

(expertly) asesorar

adviser, advisor [ædváɪzə-] N consejero -ra
mf, asesor -ora *mf*

advocacy [ǽdvəkəsi] N defensa *f*

advocate [ǽdvəkɪt] N (promoter) partidario
-ria *mf*; (defender) defensor -ra *mf*,
intercesor -ra *mf*; (lawyer) abogado -da *mf*;
[ǽdvəket] VT abogar por, defender

aerial [ériəl] ADJ aéreo; N antena *f*

aerobic [eróbɪk] ADJ (exercise) aeróbico; (air-
breathing) aerobio; **—s** aeróbic *m*

aerodynamic [erodaɪnǽmɪk] ADJ
aerodinámico; **—s** aerodinámica *f*

aeronautics [erənɔ́dɪks] N aeronáutica *f*

aerosol [érəsaɪ] N aerosol *m*

aerospace [érospes] N espacio aéreo *m*; ADJ
aeroespacial

aesthetic [esθɛ́dɪk] ADJ estético; N **—s** estética
f

affable [ǽfəbəl] ADJ afable

affair [əfér] N (social) acontecimiento social
m; (business) asunto *m*, negocio *m*; (love)
aventura amorosa *f*, affaire *m*

affect [əfékt] VT (have effect on) afectar;
(move) conmover; (feign) fingir

affectation [æfektéʃən] N afectación *f*,
melindre *m*

affected [əféktɪd] ADJ (moved) afectado,
conmovido; (feigned) fingido, artificioso,
melindroso

affection [əfékʃən] N afecto *m*, cariño *m*

affectionate [əfékʃənɪt] ADJ afectuoso,
cariñoso

affidavit [æfɪdévɪt] N declaración jurada *f*

affiliate [əfíliet] VT afiliar; VI afiliarse,
asociarse; [əfíliɪt] N filial *f*

affinity [əfínɪdi] N afinidad *f*

affirm [əfə́-m] VT afirmar

affirmation [æfə-méʃən] N afirmación *f*

affirmative [əfə́-mədɪv] ADJ afirmativo; N **—
action** discriminación positiva *f*; **reply
in the —** dar una respuesta afirmativa

affix [əfíks] VT fijar; **to — one's signature**
poner su firma, firmar

afflict [əflíkt] VT aquejar; **to be —ed with**
padecer de, sufrir de

affliction [əflíkʃən] N (misery) aflicción *f*;
(ailment) achaque *m*, mal *m*

affluent [ǽfluənt] ADJ (society) opulento;
(person) rico

afford [əfɔ́rd] VT **I cannot — a car** no me
alcanza el dinero para un coche; **he
cannot — to waste time** no puede
darse el lujo de perder tiempo; **I cannot
— the risk** no me puedo permitir ese
riesgo; **we will — you every
opportunity** se te darán todas las

oportunidades

affordable [əfɔ́rdəbəl] ADJ asequible

affront [əfránt] N afrenta f

Afghan, Afghani [ǽfgæn / æfgǽni] ADJ & N afgano -na mf

Afghanistan [æfgǽnɪstæn] N Afganistán m

afire [əfáɪr] ADJ & ADV en llamas

afloat [əflót] ADJ & ADV flotando, a flote

afraid [əfréd] ADJ asustado; **to be — (of)** temer, tener miedo (de)

afresh [əfréʃ] ADV de nuevo, desde el principio

Africa [ǽfrɪkə] N África f

African [ǽfrɪkən] ADJ & N africano -na mf

African-American [ǽfrɪkənəmérɪkən] ADJ & N afroamericano -na mf

after [ǽftə] PREP (temporal) después de, tras; (spatial) detrás de; **— all** después de todo; ADV después; CONJ después (de) que

afterbirth [ǽftə-bɜ-θ] N placenta f

afterlife [ǽftə-laɪf] N el más allá

aftermath [ǽftə-mæθ] N secuelas f pl

afternoon [æftə-nún] N tarde f; INTERJ **good — buenas tardes**

aftershave [ǽftə-ʃev] N loción para después del afeitado f

aftershock [ǽftə-ʃak] N réplica f

aftertaste [ǽftə-test] N (in the mouth) dejo m; (bad memory) resabio m

aftertax [ǽftə-tæks] ADJ **— profit** ganancia neta f

afterthought [ǽftə-θɔt] N **it was just an —** se nos ocurrió después

afterward, afterwards [ǽftə-wə-d(z)] ADV después, luego

again [əgén] ADV otra vez, de nuevo; (on the other hand) por otra parte; **— and —** repetidas veces; **to fall —** volver a caerse

against [əgénst] PREP contra; **— the grain** a contrapelo; **— all odds** a pesar de todo

age [edʒ] N (of a person) edad f; (era) era f, época f; **— of —** mayor de edad; **old —** vejez f; **to come of —** llegar a la mayoría de edad; **under —** menor de edad; VI/VT envejecer

aged [edʒd] ADJ (wine) añejo; **— forty** de cuarenta años; [édʒɪd] anciano

ageless [édʒlɪs] ADJ (everlasting) eterno; (not showing age) siempre joven; (classic) clásico

agency [édʒənsi] N agencia f; **through the — of** por mediación de

agenda [ədʒéndə] N temario m, orden del día f

agent [édʒənt] N agente mf; (commercial) representante mf; (legal) apoderado -da mf

aggrandize [əgrǽndaɪz] VT engrandecer

aggravate [ǽgrəvet] VT (worsen) exacerbar, agravar; (annoy) irritar, exasperar, exacerbar

aggregate [ǽgrɪgɪt] N conjunto m; (rock) agregado m; ADJ total, global

aggression [əgréʃən] N agresión f

aggressive [əgrésɪv] ADJ (violent) agresivo; (dynamic) emprendedor

aggressor [əgrésə] N agresor -ra mf

aghast [əgǽst] ADJ horrorizado

agile [ǽdʒəl] ADJ ágil

agility [ədʒílɪti] N agilidad f

agitate [ǽdʒɪtet] VT (shake) agitar; (perturb) turbar; (campaign) alborotar

agitation [ædʒɪtéʃən] N agitación f

agitator [ǽdʒɪtedə] N agitador -ra mf

agnostic [ægnástɪk] ADJ & N agnóstico -ca mf

ago [əgó] ADV **many years —** hace muchos años; **long —** hace mucho tiempo

agog [əgág] ADJ pasmado, boquiabierto

agonize [ǽgənaɪz] VI sufrir angustiosamente; **to — over** atormentarse por

agony [ǽgəni] N (pain) dolor m, tormento m; (anguish) angustia f

agoraphobia [ægə-əfóbiə] N agorafobia f

agrarian [əgrériən] ADJ agrario

agree [əgrí] VI (be in agreement) estar de acuerdo; (in grammar, mathematics) concordar; (color, food) sentarle bien a uno; **they —d to buy the car** quedaron en comprar el coche

agreeable [əgríəbəl] ADJ (nice) agradable; (willing) conforme

agreement [əgrímənt] N (concord, document) acuerdo m, convenio m; (grammatical) concordancia f; **to be in —** estar de acuerdo; **to come to an —** ponerse de acuerdo

agricultural [ægrɪkʌ́ltʃə-əl] ADJ (related to crops) agrícola; (related to crops and cattle) agropecuario

agriculture [ǽgrɪkʌltʃə-] N agricultura f

aground [əgráund] ADV **to run —** encallar, varar

ahead [əhéd] ADV delante; **— of time** adelantado, antes de tiempo; **to go —** ir adelante, adelantarse; **to get —** prosperar; **our team is —** nuestro equipo va primero; **the years —** los años venideros

aid [ed] N (help) asistencia f; (assistant) ayudante mf; VT ayudar; **to — and abet** instigar

AIDS (acquired immune deficiency syndrome) [edz] N SIDA m

ail [el] VI/VT **what —s you?** ¿qué tienes? ¿qué te aflige? **he's —ing** está enfermo

aileron [élərɑn] N alerón m

ailment [éłmənt] N achaque *m*, dolencia *f*

aim [em] N (with a weapon) puntería *f*; (objective) objetivo *m*; VT (a weapon) apuntar; (a question, blow) dirigir; **to — to please** tratar de agradar

aimless [émlɪs] ADJ (purposeless) sin propósito; (directionless) sin rumbo

air [er] N aire *m*; **up in the —** en el aire, incierto; **in the open —** al aire libre; **to be on the —** estar en el aire, emitirse; **to put on —s** presumir, darse ínfulas; **to vanish into thin —** evaporarse; ADJ aéreo; **—bag** airbag *m*, bolsa de aire *f*; **—borne** (troops) aerotransportado; (particles) transportado por el aire; **—brake** freno neumático *m*; **— conditioned** con aire acondicionado; **— conditioner** acondicionador de aire *m*; **— conditioning** aire acondicionado *m*, climatización *f*; **—craft** aeronave *f*; **—craft carrier** portaaviones *m sg*; **—field** aeródromo *m*; **— Force** Fuerza Aérea *f*; **—head** cabeza de chorlito *mf*; **—lift** puente aéreo *m*; **—line** línea aérea *f*; **— mail** correo aéreo *m*; **—plane** avión *m*; **— piracy** piratería aérea *f*; **—port** aeropuerto *m*; **— power** fuerza aérea *f*; **— pressure** presión de aire *f*; **— raid** ataque aéreo *m*; **— rifle** escopeta de aire comprimido *f*; **—ship** dirigible *m*; **— strike** bombardeo aéreo *m*; **—strip** pista de aterrizaje *f*; **—tight** hermético; **—to—** aire-aire; **— traffic control** control del tráfico aéreo *m*; VT (an opinion) manifestar; **to —lift** aerotransportar; **to — out** orear, ventilar

aisle [aɪł] N pasillo *m*; (of a church) nave lateral *f*

ajar [ədʒár] ADJ entornado, entreabierto

akin [əkín] ADJ (related) emparentado; (similar) semejante

à la mode [ɑlɑmód] ADV con helado

alarm [əlárm] N (warning) alarma *f*; (worry) inquietud *f*; **— clock** despertador *m*; **to sound an —** tocar a rebato; VT (worry) alarmar; (frighten) asustar

Albania [ælbénɪə] N Albania *f*

Albanian [ælbénɪən] ADJ & N albanés -esa *mf*

albatross [ǽłbətrɑs] N albatros *m*

albino [ælbáɪno] N albino -na *mf*

album [ǽłbəm] N álbum *m*

alcohol [ǽłkəhɔl] N alcohol *m*

alcoholic [ælkəhɔ́lɪk] ADJ & N alcohólico -ca *mf*

alcoholism [ǽłkəhɔlɪzəm] N alcoholismo *m*

alcove [ǽłkov] N rincón *m*

ale [eł] N cerveza inglesa *f*

alert [ələ́-t] ADJ (vigilant) alerta; (awake) despierto; **to be —** (on guard) estar alerta; (lively) ser despierto; N alerta *f*; VT alertar, avisar

alfalfa [ælfǽłfə] N alfalfa *f*

algae [ǽłdʒi] N algas *f pl*

algebra [ǽłdʒəbrə] N álgebra *f*

Algeria [ældʒírɪə] N Argelia *f*

Algerian [ældʒírɪən] ADJ & N argelino -na *mf*

algorithm [ǽłgərɪðəm] N algoritmo *m*

alias [élɪəs] N alias *m sg*

alibi [ǽləbaɪ] N coartada *f*

alien [élɪən] N (visitor from space) extraterrestre *mf*; (foreigner) extranjero -ra *mf*; ADJ ajeno

alienate [élɪənet] VT (people) ofender, ganarse la antipatía de; (property) enajenar

alight [əláɪt] VI (rider) apearse; (bird, insect) posarse

align [əláɪn] VI/VT alinear(se)

alignment [əláɪnmənt] N alineación *f*

alike [əláɪk] ADJ parecido, igual; **to be —** parecerse, ser iguales; ADV del mismo modo

alimony [ǽləmoni] N pensión alimenticia *f*

alive [əláɪv] ADJ (living) vivo; **— with** lleno de; **the symphony came — under his direction** la sinfonía cobró vida bajo su dirección

alkali [ǽłkəlaɪ] N álcali *m*

alkaline [ǽłkəlɪn] ADJ alcalino

all [ɔł] ADJ todo; **— the time** todo el tiempo; N todo *m*; **he gave his —** dio todo de sí; PRON todo; **is that —?** ¿eso es todo? ADV completamente, todo; **— at once** (uninterrupted) de una vez; (sudden) de repente; **— told** en conjunto; **he's — dirty** está todo sucio; **it is — over** se acabó; **not at —** de ninguna manera; **nothing at —** nada en absoluto; **once (and) for —** de una vez por todas; **she's — right** está bien; INTERJ **— right** bueno

allay [əlé] VT (fear, doubt) calmar, disipar; (anger) aplacar

allegation [æləgéʃən] N acusación *f*

allege [əlédʒ] VT afirmar

allegiance [əlídʒəns] N lealtad *f*, fidelidad *f*; **to pledge — to the flag** jurar la bandera

allegory [ǽləgɔri] N alegoría *f*

allergic [ələ́-dʒɪk] ADJ alérgico

allergist [ǽlə-dʒɪst] N alergólogo -ga *mf*

allergy [ǽlə-dʒi] N alergia *f*

alleviate [əlíviet] VT (suffering) aliviar; (hunger) paliar

alley [ǽli] N callejón *m*; **right up her —** ideal para ella

alliance [əláɪəns] N alianza *f*

allied [əláɪd, ǽlaɪd] ADJ aliado

alligator [ǽlɪgeɪɾə] N caimán *m*; *Am* lagarto *m*

alliterate [əlíɾəret] VI hacer aliteración

allocate [ǽləket] VT asignar

allot [əlát] VT asignar

allow [əláʊ] VI/VT (permit) permitir; (admit) admitir; — **an hour to change trains** date una hora para cambiar de trenes; **to — for** tener en cuenta

allowable [əláʊəbəl] ADJ admisible, permisible

allowance [əláʊəns] N (regular payment) asignación *f*, pensión *f*; (monthly payment) mensualidad *f*; (for a child) paga *f*, mesada *f*; (payment for a particular purpose) pago *m*; (food) ración *f*; **to make — for** tener en cuenta

alloy [ǽlɔɪ] N aleación *f*; [əlɔɪ] VT alear

allude [əlúd] VI aludir; **to — to** aludir a

allure [əlúr] VI/VT seducir, atraer; N atractivo *m*

alluring [əlúrɪŋ] ADJ seductivo, atractivo

allusion [əlúʒən] N alusión *f*

ally [ǽlaɪ] N aliado -da *mf*; [əláɪ] VT **to — oneself with** aliarse con

almanac [ɔ́lmənæk] N almanaque *m*

almighty [ɔlmáɪdi] ADJ todopoderoso

almond [ɔ́mənd] N almendra *f*; — **tree** almendro *m*

almost [ɔ́lmost] ADV casi; **I — fell down** por poco me caigo

alms [ɔmz] N limosna *f*

aloe vera [ǽlovíɾə] N áloe *m*

alone [əlón] ADJ solo; — **among his contemporaries** único entre sus contemporáneos; ADV sólo, solamente; **she — knew that** sólo ella sabía eso; **all — a** solas; **to leave —** no tocar, dejar en paz

along [əlɔ́ŋ] PREP **he was walking — the street** andaba por la calle; **all — the coast** a lo largo de toda la costa; **— with** junto con; **all —** desde el principio; **to carry — with oneself** llevar consigo; **to go — with** acceder a; **to get — with** llevarse bien con

alongside [əlɔ́ŋsaɪd] PREP al lado de; **— the boat** al lado del bote; ADV al lado, al costado; **the dog ran —** el perro corría al costado

aloof [əlúf] ADJ reservado, esquivo; ADV apartado

aloud [əláʊd] ADV en voz alta

alphabet [ǽlfəbet] N alfabeto *m*, abecedario *m*

alphanumeric [ǽlfənumérɪk] ADJ alfanumérico

alpine [ǽlpaɪn] ADJ alpino

already [ɔlrɛ́di] ADV ya

also [ɔ́lso] ADV también, además; **—-ran** (horse, candidate) candidato / candidato vencido *m*; (loser) nulidad *f*, segundón -ona *mf*

altar [ɔ́ltə] N altar *m*; **—piece** retablo *m*

alter [ɔ́ltə] VI/VT (change) alterar; (neuter) capar, castrar

alteration [ɔltəréʃən] N (change) alteración *f*, cambio *m*; **—s** arreglos *m pl*, reformas *f pl*

altercation [ɔltəkéʃən] N altercado *m*

alternate [ɔ́ltənɪt] ADJ alternativo, alterno; **— route** ruta alternativa *f*; **— spelling** ortografía alterna *f*; **he visits us on — Mondays** nos visita un lunes sí y otro no; N suplente *mf*; [ɔ́ltə-net] VI/VT alternar

alternative [ɔltɜ́-nəDɪv] ADJ alternativo; N alternativa *f*

alternator [ɔ́ltə-neDə] N alternador *m*

although [ɔlðó] CONJ aunque, si bien

altimeter [æltímɪDə] N altímetro *m*

altitude [ǽltɪtjud] N altura *f*, altitud *f*; **— sickness** mal de altura *m*

alto [ǽlto] N contralto *mf*; ADJ alto

altogether [ɔltəgéðə] ADV (completely) completamente; (all included) en total

altruism [ǽltruɪzəm] N altruismo *m*

aluminum [əlúmənəm] N aluminio *m*; **— foil** papel de aluminio *m*

always [ɔ́lwez] ADV siempre

a.m. [eém] ADV de la mañana

amalgamate [əmǽlgəmet] VI/VT (metals) amalgamar(se); (companies) fusionar(se)

amass [əmǽs] VT acumular, amasar

amateur [ǽmətʃɜ-] ADJ amateur; N aficionado -da *mf*

amaze [əméz] VT maravillar, asombrar

amazement [əmézmənt] N asombro *m*

amazing [əmézɪŋ] ADJ asombroso, increíble

Amazon [ǽməzɑn] N (region) Amazonia *f*; (river) Amazonas *m sg*

ambassador [æmbǽsəɒə] N embajador -ra *mf*

amber [ǽmbə] N ámbar *m*; ADJ (quality) ambarino; (material) de ámbar; (color) (de) color ámbar

ambiance [ǽmbiəns] N ambiente *m*

ambidextrous [æmbɪdékstrəs] ADJ ambidiestro

ambient [ǽmbiənt] ADJ ambiental; **— temperature** temperatura ambiente *f*

ambiguity [æmbɪgjúɪDi] N ambigüedad *f*

ambiguous [æmbígjuəs] ADJ ambiguo

ambition [æmbíʃən] N ambición *f*,

aspiración f
ambitious [æmbíʃəs] ADJ ambicioso
ambivalent [æmbívələnt] ADJ ambivalente
amble [æmbəl] VI deambular
ambulance [æmbjələns] N ambulancia f
ambush [æmbuʃ] N emboscada f, celada f; **to
lie in** — acechar; VT emboscar
ameliorate [əmíliəret] VI/VT mejorar
amen [ámén] INTERJ amén
amenable [əménəbəl] ADJ bien dispuesto
amend [əménd] VT enmendar; **to make —s
(for)** compensar (por)
amendment [əméndmənt] N enmienda f
amenities [əménidiz] N PL comodidades f pl
America [əmérikə] N América f
American [əmérikən] ADJ & N (continental)
americano -na mf; (USA) americano -na
mf, norteamericano -na mf,
estadounidense mf
amethyst [æməθɪst] N amatista f
amiable [émiəbəl] ADJ amable
amicable [æmɪkəbəl] ADJ amistoso
amid [əmíd] PREP en medio de
amino acid [əmínoæsɪd] N aminoácido m
amiss [əmís] ADV **something is** — algo anda
mal
ammonia [əmónjə] N amoníaco m
ammunition [æmjəníʃən] N munición f
amnesia [æmníʒə] N amnesia f
amnesty [æmnɪsti] N amnistía f
amniocentesis [æmniosəntísɪs] N
amniocentesis f
amoeba [əmíbə] N ameba f
among [əmáŋ] PREP entre
amoral [emórəl] ADJ amoral
amorous [æmərəs] ADJ (sexually aroused)
excitado; (loving) amoroso
amorphous [əmórfəs] ADJ amorfo
amortize [æmə-taɪz] VT amortizar
amount [əmáunt] N cantidad f; (of money)
suma f, importe m; VI ascender (a); **that
—s to stealing** eso equivale a robar
ampere [æmpír] N amperio m
amphetamine [æmféɾəmin] N anfetamina f
amphibian [æmfíbiən] N anfibio m
amphibious [æmfíbiəs] ADJ anfibio
amphitheater [æmfəθiədə-] N anfiteatro m
ampicillin [æmpɪsílɪn] N ampicilina f
ample [æmpəl] ADJ (in quantity) suficiente;
(in size) amplio
amplifier [æmpləfaɪə-] N amplificador m
amplify [æmpləfaɪ] VT (an explanation)
ampliar; (a sound) amplificar
amplitude [æmplɪtud] N amplitud f
amputate [æmpjətet] VT amputar
amuck, amok [əmák] ADV **to run** — (kill
people) perpetrar un ataque homicida; (go

crazy) volverse loco
amulet [æmjəlɪt] N amuleto m
amuse [əmjúz] VT (make laugh) divertir;
(help pass time) entretener; **to — oneself**
divertirse, entretenerse, recrearse
amusement [əmjúzmənt] N diversión f,
entretenimiento m
amusing [əmjúzɪŋ] ADJ (entertaining)
divertido; (funny) gracioso, chistoso
an [ən, æn] INDEF ART un m, una f
anachronism [ənækrənɪzəm] N anacronismo
m
anaerobic [ænəróbɪk] ADJ anaerobio
anal [énəl] ADJ anal
analgesic [ænəldʒízɪk] N & ADJ analgésico m
analog [ænələg] ADJ analógico
analogical [ænəládʒɪkəl] ADJ analógico
analogous [ənæləgəs] ADJ análogo
analogy [ənælədʒi] N analogía f
analysis [ənælɪsɪs] N análisis f
analytic [ænəlídɪk] ADJ analítico
analytical [ænəlídɪkəl] ADJ analítico
analyze [ænəlaɪz] VT analizar
anarchist [ænə-kɪst] N anarquista f
anarchy [ænə-ki] N anarquía f
anathema [ənæθəmə] N anatema f
anatomical [ænətámɪkəl] ADJ anatómico
anatomy [ənæɾəmi] N anatomía f
ancestor [ænsestə-] N antepasado -da mf,
ascendiente mf
ancestral [ænséstrəl] ADJ de los antepasados;
— home casa solariega f
ancestry [ænsestri] N linaje m, ascendencia f,
abolengo m
anchor [æŋkə-] N ancla f; **— man**
presentador m; **—woman** presentadora f;
to drop — anclar, echar anclas; VT (a
boat) anclar; (an argument) basar; VI echar
anclas, fondear
anchovy [æntʃovi] N anchoa f
ancient [énʃənt] ADJ antiguo; pej vetusto
and [ænd] CONJ y; (before i, hi) e; **— so
forth** etcétera, y así sucesivamente; **more
— more** cada vez más
Andalusia [ændəlúʒə] N Andalucía f
Andalusian [ændəlúʒən] ADJ & N andaluz -za
mf
Andes [ændiz] N Andes m pl
Andorra [ændórə] N Andorra f
Andorran [ændórən] ADJ & N andorrano -na
mf
androgynous [ændrádʒənəs] ADJ andrógino
anecdote [ænɪkdot] N anécdota f
anemia [əními̯ə] N anemia f
anemic [əními̯k] ADJ anémico
anesthesia [ænɪsθíʒə] N anestesia f
anesthesiology [ænɪsθiziálədʒi] N

anestesiología f

anesthetic [ænɪsθɛ́ɾɪk] ADJ anestésico; N (substance) anestesia f

aneurysm [ǽnjərɪzəm] N aneurisma m

anew [ənjú] ADV otra vez

angel [éndʒəl] N ángel m

angelic [ændʒɛ́lɪk] ADJ angélico, angelical

anger [ǽŋgɚ] N enojo m, enfado m; VT enojar, enfadar

angina [ændʒáɪnə] N — **pectoris** angina de pecho f

angioplasty [ǽndʒiəplæsti] N angioplastia f

angle [ǽŋgəl] N (geometrical) ángulo m; (point of view) punto de vista m, perspectiva f; VI pescar

Anglo-Saxon [ǽŋglosǽksən] ADJ & N anglosajón -na mf

Angola [æŋgólə] N Angola f

Angolan [æŋgólən] ADJ angolano -na mf, angoleño -ña mf

angry [ǽŋgri] ADJ enojado, enfadado

angst [áŋkst] N angustia f

anguish [ǽŋgwɪʃ] N angustia f, ansia f, congoja f

angular [ǽŋgjələ] ADJ angular; (face) anguloso

animal [ǽnəməl] ADJ & N animal m; — **rights** derechos de los animales m pl

animate [ǽnəmɪt] ADJ animado; [ǽnəmet] VT (enliven) animar; (encourage) alentar; —**d cartoon** dibujo animado m

animation [ænəméʃən] N animación f

animosity [ænəmósɪɾi] N animosidad f, ojeriza f, encono m

anise [ǽnɪs] N anís m

ankle [ǽŋkəl] N tobillo m

annals [ǽnlz] N anales m pl

annex [ǽnɛks] N anexo m; [ənɛ́ks] VT anexar

annexation [ænɛkséʃən] N anexión f

annihilate [ənáɪəlet] VT aniquilar

anniversary [ænəvɚ́səri] N aniversario m

annotate [ǽnətet] VT anotar

annotation [ænətéʃən] N (action, result) anotación f; (result) nota f

announce [ənáʊns] VT anunciar; (an engagement, birth) participar

announcement [ənáʊnsmənt] N anuncio m; (of an engagement, birth) participación f

announcer [ənáʊnsɚ] N anunciador -ra mf; (on radio) locutor -ra mf

annoy [ənɔ́ɪ] VI/VT fastidiar, contrariar

annoyance [ənɔ́ɪəns] N fastidio m, contrariedad f

annual [ǽnjuəl] ADJ anual; N (book) anuario m; (plant) planta anual f

annuity [ənjúɪɾi] N anualidad f, renta anual f

annul [ənʌ́l] VT anular

annulment [ənʌ́lmənt] N anulación f

anomalous [ənáməlʌs] ADJ anómalo

anomaly [ənáməli] N anomalía f

anonymous [ənánəməs] ADJ anónimo

anorak [ǽnəræk] N anorak m

anorexia [ænəréksiə] N anorexia f

anorexic [ænəréksɪk] ADJ anoréxico

another [ənʌ́ðɚ] ADJ otro; — **day** otro día; PRON otro; **I want** — quiero otro; **one** — el uno al otro, los unos a los otros

answer [ǽnsɚ] N (to a question) respuesta f, contestación f; (to a problem) solución f; VI contestar, responder; **to** — **for** ser responsable de / por; VT contestar

answering [ǽnsɚɪŋ] ADJ — **machine** contestador automático m; — **service** servicio telefónico contratado m

ant [ænt] N hormiga f; —**eater** oso hormiguero m; —**hill** hormiguero m

antacid [æntǽsɪd] N & ADJ antiácido m

antagonism [æntǽgənɪzəm] N antagonismo m

antagonist [æntǽgənɪst] N antagonista mf

antagonize [æntǽgənaɪz] VT antagonizar

antarctic [æntárktɪk] ADJ antártico

Antarctica [æntárktɪkə] N Antártida f

antecedent [æntəsídn̩t] ADJ & N antecedente m

antelope [ǽntəlop] N antílope m

antenna [ænténə] N antena f

anterior [æntíriɚ] ADJ anterior

anthem [ǽnθəm] N himno m

anthology [ænθálədʒi] N antología f

anthracite [ǽnθrəsaɪt] N antracita f

anthrax [ǽnθræks] N ántrax m

anthropologist [ænθrəpálədʒɪst] N antropólogo -ga mf

anthropology [ænθrəpálədʒi] N antropología f

anthropomorphize [ænθrəpəmɔ́rfaɪz] VI/VT antropomorfizar

antiabortion [æntiəbɔ́rʃən] ADJ antiaborto inv

antiaircraft [æntiérkræft] ADJ antiaéreo

antibacterial [æntibæktíriəl] ADJ antibacteriano

antiballistic [æntibəlístɪk] ADJ antibalístico

antibiotic [æntibaɪáɾɪk] N & ADJ antibiótico m

antibody [ǽntibɑɾi] N anticuerpo m

anticipate [æntísəpet] VI/VT prever, calcular

anticipation [æntɪsəpéʃən] N previsión f; **with great** — con gran expectación

anticlimactic [æntiklɪmǽktɪk] ADJ decepcionante

antics [ǽntɪks] N payasadas f pl, monerías f

pl, monadas *f pl*

antidepressant [æntidɪprésənt] ADJ & N antidepresivo *m*

antidote [ǽntɪdot] N antídoto *m*

antifreeze [ǽntifriz] N anticongelante *m*

Antigua and Barbuda [æntígəændbɑrbúdə] N Antigua y Barbuda *f*

Antiguan [æntígən] ADJ & N antiguano -ana *mf*

antihistamine [æntihístəmin] N antihistamínico *m*

anti-inflammatory [æntiɪnflǽmətɔri] ADJ & N antiinflamatorio *m*

antilock [ǽntilɑk] ADJ antibloqueo

antimony [ǽntəmoni] N antimonio *m*

antioxidant [æntiáksɪdənt] N antioxidante *m*

antipathy [æntípəθi] N antipatía *f*

antiperspirant [æntipɝ́spəənt] N antitranspirante *m*

antiquated [ǽntɪkweDɪd] ADJ anticuado; (words) desusado

antique [æntík] ADJ antiguo; N antigüedad *f*

antiquity [æntíkwɪDi] N antigüedad *f*

anti-Semitism [æntisémɪtɪzəm] N antisemitismo *m*

antiseptic [æntɪséptɪk] ADJ & N antiséptico *m*

antisocial [æntisóʃəɬ] ADJ antisocial

antithesis [æntíθəsɪs] N antítesis *f*

antitrust [æntitrʌ́st] ADJ antimonopolio, antitrust

antler [ǽntlɚ] N asta *f*, cuerno *m*

antonym [ǽntənɪm] N antónimo *m*

antsy [ǽntsi] ADJ (impatient) impaciente; (anxious) ansioso

anus [énəs] N ano *m*

anvil [ǽnvəɬ] N yunque *m*

anxiety [æŋzáɪɪDi] N ansiedad *f*, angustia *f*

anxious [ǽŋkʃəs] ADJ (worried) ansioso, preocupado; (desirous) ansioso, deseoso

any [éni] ADJ & PRON cualquier(a), cualesquier(a); — **woman** cualquier mujer, una mujer cualquiera; — **man** cualquier hombre, un hombre cualquiera; — **houses** unas casas cualesquiera; *lit* cualesquiera casas; **in** — **case** en todo caso; **do you have** — **money?** ¿tienes dinero? **I don't have** — no tengo

anybody [énibɑDi] PRON alguien, cualquiera; — **could do that** cualquiera podría hacer eso; **is** — **here?** ¿hay alguien aquí? **he does not know** — no conoce a nadie

anyhow [énihaʊ] ADV de todos modos

anymore [énimɔ́r] ADV **he doesn't work** — ya no trabaja, no trabaja más

anyone [éniwʌn] PRON alguien, cualquiera; — **could do that** cualquiera podría hacer

eso; **is** — **here?** ¿hay alguien aquí? **he does not know** — no conoce a nadie

anyplace [éniples] ADV en cualquier parte/lugar; **you can buy it** — se puede comprar en cualquier lugar; **he's not going** — no va a ninguna parte

anything [éniθɪŋ] PRON cualquier cosa, algo; — **is fine** cualquier cosa me viene bien; — **you wish** todo lo que quieras; **do you have** — **for a cough?** ¿tienes algo para la tos? **I don't know** — no sé nada

anytime [énitaɪm] ADV en cualquier momento

anyway [éniwe] ADV de todos modos, de cualquier manera

anywhere [énihwɛr] ADV en cualquier parte/lugar; **you can buy it** — se puede comprar en cualquier lugar; **he's not going** — no va a ninguna parte

aorta [eɔ́rDə] N aorta *f*

apart [əpɑ́rt] ADV **they are three miles** — están a tres millas de distancia; **they kept him** — **from the group** lo apartaron del grupo; **each factor viewed** — cada factor visto por separado; **to take** — desarmar, desmontar; **to tear** — despedazar, hacer pedazos; **to tell** — distinguir

apartment [əpɑ́rtmənt] N apartamento *m*; *Sp* piso *m*

apathetic [æpəθéDɪk] ADJ apático

apathy [ǽpəθi] N apatía *f*, abulia *f*

ape [ep] N simio *m*; VT remedar

aperture [ǽpɚtʃɚ] N abertura *f*; (of a pipe) luz *f*

apex [épeks] N (of tongue) ápice *m*; (of a mountain) cumbre *f*

aphasia [əféʒə] N afasia *f*

aphrodisiac [æfrədíziæk] N afrodisíaco *m*

apiece [əpís] ADV cada uno

apnea [ǽpnia] N apnea *f*

apocalypse [əpákəlɪps] N apocalipsis *m*

apogee [ǽpədʒi] N apogeo *m*

apologetic [əpɑləɖʒéDɪk] ADJ lleno de disculpas

apologize [əpálədʒaɪz] VI disculparse

apology [əpálədʒi] N disculpa(s) *f (pl)*; (justification) apología *f*

apostle [əpásəɬ] N apóstol *m*

apostrophe [əpástrəfi] N (punctuation) apóstrofo *m*; (invocation) apóstrofe *m*

appall [əpɔ́ɬ] VT horrorizar

appalling [əpálɪŋ] ADJ horroroso

apparatus [æpəǽDəs] N (single) aparato *m*; (group) maquinaria *f*

apparel [əpǽrəɬ] N indumentaria *f*, ropa *f*; (fine) ropaje *m*

apparent [əpǽrənt] ADJ (visible) visible; (clear) obvio, evidente; (seeming) aparente

apparition [æpəríʃən] N aparición f, fantasma m

appeal [əpíł] N (legal) apelación f, recurso m; (request) ruego m, llamamiento m; (attraction) atractivo m; VT apelar, recurrir (contra); VI **to — to** atraer

appear [əpír] VI (show up) aparecer(se); (seem) parecer, aparentar; (a publication) salir; (before a judge) comparecer

appearance [əpírəns] N (looks) apariencia f, traza f, estampa f; (act of appearing) aparición f

appease [əpíz] VT aplacar, apaciguar

appeasement [əpízmənt] N aplacamiento m, apaciguamiento m

appellate [əpélɪt] N — **court** tribunal de apelaciones m

append [əpénd] VT adjuntar

appendage [əpéndɪdʒ] N apéndice m

appendectomy [æpɪndéktəmi] N apendicectomía f

appendicitis [əpendəsáɪdɪs] N apendicitis f

appendix [əpéndɪks] N apéndice m

appetite [ǽpɪtaɪt] N apetito m

appetizer [ǽpɪtaɪzɚ] N aperitivo m

appetizing [ǽpɪtaɪzɪŋ] ADJ apetecible, apetitoso

applaud [əplɔ́d] VI/VT aplaudir

applause [əplɔ́z] N aplauso(s) m (pl)

apple [ǽpəł] N manzana f; — **grove** manzanar m; — **of my eye** niña de mis ojos f; —**sauce** compota de manzana f; — **tree** manzano m; **Adam's** — nuez de Adán f

appliance [əpláɪəns] N aparato m; (electric) (aparato) electrodoméstico m

applicable [ǽplɪkəbəł] ADJ aplicable

applicant [ǽplɪkənt] N aspirante mf, solicitante mf

application [æplɪkéʃən] N (act of applying) aplicación f; (form) solicitud f, formulario f

apply [əpláɪ] VT aplicar; **to — for** solicitar, pedir; **are you —ing for the scholarship?** ¿te presentas para la beca? ¿estás solicitando la beca? **to — oneself** aplicarse, dedicarse

appoint [əpɔ́ɪnt] VT (designate) nombrar, designar; (furnish) amueblar, equipar; **a well —ed house** una casa bien amueblada

appointee [əpɔɪntí] N persona nombrada f

appointment [əpɔ́ɪntmənt] N (designation) nombramiento m, designación f; (engagement) cita f; **doctor's** — cita /

hora con el médico f; —**s** mobiliario m sg, accesorios m pl

apportion [əpɔ́rʃən] VT repartir proporcionalmente

apportionment [əpɔ́rʃənmənt] N reparto proporcional m

appraisal [əprézəł] N tasación f, valuación f

appraise [əpréz] VT avaluar, valorar, tasar

appreciable [əpríʃəbəł] ADJ apreciable

appreciate [əpríʃiet] VT (value) apreciar, estimar; (recognize) darse cuenta, percibir; (thank) agradecer; **to — in value** apreciarse

appreciation [əpriʃiéʃən] N (esteem) aprecio m; (thanks) agradecimiento m; (monetary value) apreciación f, alza f

apprehend [æprɪhénd] VT (arrest) aprehender; (understand) comprender

apprehension [æprɪhénʃən] N (arrest) aprehensión f; (worry) aprensión f

apprehensive [æprɪhénsɪv] ADJ aprensivo

apprentice [əpréntɪs] N aprendiz -iza mf; VT poner de aprendiz

apprenticeship [əpréntɪʃɪp] N aprendizaje m

apprise [əpráɪz] VT informar

approach [əprótʃ] N (act of approaching) aproximación f; (method) enfoque m, aproximación f, acercamiento m; (means of access) acceso m, entrada f; VI acercarse, aproximarse; VT (a problem) abordar, enfocar; **to — someone about a problem** plantearle a alguien un problema

approachable [əprótʃəbəł] ADJ tratable

approbation [æprəbéʃən] N aprobación f

appropriate [əprópriɪt] ADJ apropiado, adecuado; [əprópriet] VT apropiarse; (funds) asignar

appropriation [əpropriéʃən] N (act of appropriation) apropiación f; (assignment of funds) asignación f; (assigned funds) partida f

approval [əprúvəł] N aprobación f

approve [əprúv] VI/VT aprobar

approximate [əpráksəmɪt] ADJ aproximado; [əpráksəmet] VT aproximarse a

apricot [ǽprɪkat] N albaricoque m; Am damasco m; Mex chabacano m

April [éprəł] N abril m

apron [éprən] N (for a cook) delantal m; (for a workman) mandil m

apropos [æprəpó] ADV a propósito; ADJ oportuno, pertinente; — **of** a propósito de

apt [æpt] ADJ (prone, able) capaz; (suited) pertinente; **is he — to be at home?** ¿estará en casa?

aptitude [ǽptɪtud] N aptitud f, capacidad f

aquamarine [ɑkwəmərín] N aguamarina f
aquarium [əkwériəm] N (tank) acuario m, pecera f; (building) acuario m
aquatic [əkwɑ́dɪk] ADJ acuático
aqueduct [ǽkwɪdʌkt] N acueducto m
Arab [ǽrəb] ADJ & N árabe mf
Arabic [ǽrəbɪk] ADJ árabe, arábigo; N (language) árabe m
Aragonese [ærəgəníz] ADJ & N aragonés -esa mf
arbiter [árbɪdə] N árbitro -ra mf
arbitrary [árbɪtreri] ADJ arbitrario
arbitrate [árbɪtret] VI/VT (mediate) arbitrar (en), terciar (en); (submit to mediation) someter al arbitraje
arbitration [ɑrbɪtréʃən] N arbitraje m
arbitrator [árbɪtredə] N árbitro mf
arbor [árbə] N pérgola f, glorieta f
arboreal [arbóriəl] ADJ arbóreo
arc [ɑrk] N arco m
arcade [ɑrkéd] N (series of arcs) arcada f; (shops) galería f; (of video games) sala de juegos electrónicos f
arcane [ɑrkén] ADJ arcano
arch [ɑrtʃ] N arco m; (curved roof) bóveda f; —way arcada f; VI/VT arquear(se)
archaeology [ɑrkiáləʤi] N arqueología f
archaic [ɑrkéɪk] ADJ arcaico
archaism [árkeɪzəm] N arcaísmo m
archbishop [ɑrtʃbíʃəp] N arzobispo m
archenemy [ártʃénəmi] N archienemigo -ga mf
archery [ártʃəri] N tiro al arco m
archetype [árkɪtaɪp] N arquetipo m
archipelago [ɑrkəpéləgo] N archipiélago m
architect [árkɪtekt] N arquitecto -ta mf; (creator) artífice mf
architectural [ɑrkɪtéktʃəəl] ADJ arquitectónico
architecture [árkɪtektʃə] N arquitectura f
archive [árkaɪv] N archivo m
arctic [árktɪk] ADJ ártico
ardent [árdn̩t] ADJ ardiente
ardor [árdə] N ardor m, fervor m
arduous [árdʒuəs] ADJ arduo
area [ériə] N área f; (region) zona f; (of a geometric figure) superficie f, área f
arena [ərínə] N estadio m; (in circus) pista f
Argentina [ɑrʤəntínə] N Argentina f
Argentinian [ɑrʤəntíniən] ADJ & N argentino -na mf
argon [árgɑn] N argón m
argue [árgju] VT (reason) argüir, argumentar; VI (bicker) discutir, reñir
argument [árgjəmənt] N (reason) argumento m; (altercation) disputa f, discusión f
arid [ǽrɪd] ADJ árido

arise [əráɪz] VI (get up) levantarse; (appear) surgir; (result) provenir, resultar
aristocracy [ærɪstákrəsi] N aristocracia f
aristocrat [ərístəkræt] N aristócrata mf
aristocratic [ərɪstəkrǽdɪk] ADJ aristocrático
arithmetic [əríθmətɪk] N aritmética f; ADJ aritmético
ark [ɑrk] N arca f; **Noah's** — arca de Noé f
arm [ɑrm] N brazo m; **—chair** sillón m, butaca f; **—pit** sobaco m, axila f; **—rest** (in a car) apoyabrazos m sg; (on a sofa) brazo m; — **in** — del brazo; **at** —'s **length** a distancia; **with open** —s con los brazos abiertos; **—s** armas f pl
armada [ɑrmádə] N armada f, flota f
armament [árməmənt] N armamento m
Armenia [ɑrmíniə] N Armenia f
Armenian [ɑrmíniən] ADJ & N armenio -nia mf
armful [ármfʊl] N brazada f
armistice [ármɪstɪs] N armisticio m
armoire [ɑrmwár] N armario m
armor [ármə] N (of a knight) armadura f; (on a vehicle) blindaje m; (on insects) coraza f; VT (a car) blindar; (a tank) acorazar
armored [árməd] ADJ (van) blindado; (tank) acorazado
armory [árməri] N armería f
army [ármi] N ejército m; (multitude) muchedumbre f
aroma [ərómə] N aroma m
aromatic [ærəmǽdɪk] ADJ aromático
around [əráʊnd] ADV **there were books all** — había libros por todos lados; **there is a supermarket** — **here** hay un supermercado por aquí; **it was the only farm for miles** — era la única granja en millas a la redonda; **the tree is forty centimeters** — el árbol tiene cuarenta centímetros de circunferencia; **we drove** — **the block** dimos vuelta a la manzana; **I'll show you** — te enseño el lugar; **the wheels turned** — las ruedas giraban; **turn** — date la vuelta; **she finally came** — al final la convencimos; **he hasn't been** — no ha estado por aquí; **a town with mountains** — **it** un pueblo rodeado de montañas; **we walked** — **town** dimos una vuelta por el pueblo; — **five o'clock** a eso de las cinco; PREP **a ribbon** — **her wrist** una cinta alrededor de su muñeca; **tie a string** — **your finger** átate un hilo al dedo; **stay** — **the house** quédate cerca de la casa; **he wandered** — **the park** deambuló por el parque; **the church** — **the corner** la

iglesia a la vuelta de la esquina; **motion — its axis** movimiento en torno a su eje; **—-the-clock** veinticuatro horas al día

arouse [əráuz] VI despertar; VT (suspicion) despertar; (sexual response) excitar

arraign [ərén] VT hacer comparecer ante un juez

arrange [ərénʤ] VT arreglar

arrangement [ərénʤmənt] N arreglo *m*; (of objects) disposición *f*; (agreement) acuerdo *m*; **to make —s (for)** hacer arreglos (para)

array [əré] N (arrangement) abanico *m*, selección *f*; (of troops) orden *m*; (attire) gala *f*; VT (troops) formar; (attire) ataviar

arrears [ərírz] ADV LOC in — atrasado

arrest [ərést] N arresto *m*, detención *f*; VI/VT arrestar, detener

arrhythmia [əríθmiə] N arritmia *f*

arrival [əráivəl] N llegada *f*; lit arribo *m*; **the new —s** los recién llegados

arrive [əráiv] VI llegar; lit arribar

arrogance [ǽrəgəns] N arrogancia *f*

arrogant [ǽrəgənt] ADJ arrogante

arrow [ǽro] N flecha *f*; lit saeta *f*; **—head** punta de flecha *f*

arsenal [ársən] N arsenal *m*

arsenic [ársənɪk] N arsénico *m*

arson [ársən] N incendio doloso *m*

art [ɑrt] N arte *m* (*sg*) *f* (*pl*); (works) obras *f pl*; (skill) destreza *f*; **fine —s** bellas artes *f pl*; **master of —s** maestría en humanidades *f*; **— deco** art déco *m*

arteriosclerosis [ɑrtiriosklərósɪs] N arteriosclerosis *f*

artery [ártəri] N arteria *f*

artful [ártfəl] ADJ (esthetic) artístico; (deceitful) artero, ladino

arthritis [ɑrθráidɪs] N artritis *f*

arthroscopic [ɑrθrəskápɪk] ADJ artroscópico

artichoke [ártɪʧok] N alcachofa *f*

article [ártɪkəl] N artículo *m*; **— of clothing** prenda de vestir *f*

articulate [artíkjəlɪt] ADJ (clear) claro; (eloquent) elocuente; **he's very —** se expresa muy bien; [artíkjəlet] VI/VT (pronounce, join) articular; (express) enunciar

articulation [artɪkjəléʃən] N articulación *f*

artifact [ártəfækt] N artefacto *m*, ingenio *m*

artifice [ártəfɪs] N artificio *m*

artificial [ɑrdəfíʃəl] ADJ artificial; (affected) afectado; **— insemination** inseminación artificial *f*; **— intelligence** inteligencia artificial *f*

artillery [artíləri] N artillería *f*

artisan [árdɪzən] N artesano -na *mf*,

artífice *mf*

artist [árdɪst] N artista *mf*; (performer) intérprete *mf*

artistic [artístɪk] ADJ artístico

Aruba [ərúbə] N Aruba *f*

as [æz] CONJ **— for me** en lo que a mí respecta; **— if** como si; **— it were** por decirlo así; **— large** tan grande como; **— long — you wish** todo el tiempo que quieras; **— much** — tanto como; **— of a** partir de; **— per** según; **— well** también; **— the illness worsened** a medida que empeoraba la enfermedad; **— yet** hasta ahora, todavía; **the same —** lo mismo que; **it broke — I was using it** se rompió cuando lo usaba; **she knitted — we talked** tejía mientras conversábamos; **he played — never before** jugó como nunca; PREP **— a child, I always felt loved** de niño, siempre me sentí querido; **— a teacher, I must be tough** como maestro, tengo que ser estricto; ADV tan, tanto; **it's not — important** no es tan importante

asbestos [æzbéstəs] N asbesto *m*, amianto *m*

ascend [əsénd] VI ascender

ascent [əsént] N ascenso *m*

ascertain [æsəʳtén] VT averiguar, establecer

ascetic [əsédɪk] ADJ ascético; N asceta *mf*

ascorbic [əskórbɪk] ADJ ascórbico

ascribe [əskráib] VT atribuir, imputar

asexual [esékʃuəl] ADJ asexual

ash [æʃ] N (residue, remains) ceniza *f*; (species of tree) fresno *m*; **—tray** cenicero *m*; **— Wednesday** miércoles de ceniza *m*

ashamed [əʃémd] ADJ avergonzado; **to be —** tener vergüenza, avergonzarse

ashen [ǽʃən] ADJ ceniciento

ashore [əʃór] ADV (movement) a tierra; (location) en tierra; **to go —** desembarcar

Asia [éʒə] N Asia *f*

Asian [éʒən] ADJ & N asiático -ca *mf*

aside [əsáid] ADV **all kidding —** bromas aparte; **his father took him —** su padre lo llamó aparte; **he threw his coat —** tiró su saco a un lado; PREP **— from** aparte de, además; N (theater) aparte *m*

asinine [ǽsənain] ADJ necio

ask [æsk] VT (inquire) preguntar; (request) pedir; **to — a question** hacer una pregunta; **to — about** preguntar por; **to — for** pedir; **to — for someone** pedir para hablar con alguien; **to — out** invitar a salir; **what's your —ing price?** ¿cuánto pides? **you —ed for it** te lo has buscado

askance [əskǽns] ADV **to look —** (obliquely)

mirar de soslayo/través/reojo;
(suspiciously) mirar con recelo

askew [əskjú] ADJ ladeado

asleep [əslíp] ADJ dormido; **to fall —**
dormirse; **my arm is —** se me ha
dormido/entumecido el brazo

asparagus [əspérəgəs] N espárrago *m*

aspect [éspɛkt] N aspecto *m*

aspen [éspən] N álamo temblón *m*

asphalt [ésfɑlt] N asfalto *m*

aspiration [æspəréʃən] N aspiración *f*

aspire [əspáɪr] VI aspirar

aspirin [ésprɪn] N aspirina *f*

ass [æs] N (animal) asno *m*, burro *m*, borrico
m; (fool) *fam, pej* borrico -ca *mf*, idiota *mf*;
(body part) *vulg* culo *m*; **—hole** *vulg* hijo
de puta *m*; **to bust one's —** *vulg*
romperse el culo

assail [əsél] VT (physically) asaltar, atacar;
(verbally) atacar

assailant [əsélənt] N atacante *mf*, agresor -ra
mf

assassin [əsésɪn] N asesino -na *mf*

assassinate [əsésənet] VT asesinar

assassination [əsæsənéʃən] N asesinato *m*

assault [əsɔ́lt] N asalto *m*, agresión *f*; **— rifle**
rifle de asalto *m*; **— and battery** agresión
con lesiones *f*; VT asaltar, agredir;
(sexually) violar

assay [æsé] VT (situation) examinar, analizar;
(metal) ensayar; [æsé] N ensayo *m*

assemble [əsémbəl] VI/VT (call together)
reunir(se), congregar(se); VT (put together)
armar, montar

assembly [əsémbli] N (meeting) asamblea *f*,
reunión *f*; (putting together) montaje *m*,
armado *m*; **— language** lenguaje
ensamblador *m*; **— line** cadena de
producción *f*, línea de montaje *f*

assent [əsént] N asentimiento *m*; VI asentir

assert [əsɚ́t] VT (declare) aseverar; **to —
one's rights** hacer valer los derechos de
uno; **to — oneself** obrar con firmeza

assertion [əsɚ́ʃən] N (declaration)
aseveración *f*, afirmación *f*, aserto *m*; **an
— of ownership** una afirmación de los
derechos de propiedad

assess [əsés] VT (evaluate for tax purposes)
tasar; (impose tax) gravar, imponer

assessment [əsésmənt] N (estimate) avalúo *m*,
tasación *f*; (tax) imposición *f*, gravamen
m; (testing) evaluación *f*

asset [éset] N (useful thing) ventaja *f*; (useful
quality) virtud *f*; **—s** activo *m*, bienes *m pl*;
(on balance sheet) haber *m*, activo *m*;
personal —s bienes muebles *m pl*; **real
—s** bienes inmuebles *m pl*

assiduous [əsídʒuəs] ADJ (constant) asiduo;
(industrious) diligente

assign [əsáɪn] VT (give out) asignar; (appoint,
designate) designar; (transfer property)
ceder

assignment [əsáɪnmənt] N (act of assigning)
asignación *f*; (task) encargo *m*; (mission)
misión *f*; (transfer of property) cesión (de
bienes) *f*; (homework) tarea *f*; (lesson)
lección *f*

assimilate [əsíməlet] VI/VT asimilar(se)

assist [əsíst] VI/VT ayudar, asistir

assistance [əsístəns] N ayuda *f*, asistencia *f*

assistant [əsístənt] N ayudante *mf*, asistente
mf; ADJ auxiliar

assistantship [əsístəntʃɪp] N ayudantía *f*

associate [əsóʃit] ADJ asociado; N
(acquaintance) compañero -ra *mf*; (co-
worker) colega *mf*; (employee) empleado
-da *mf*; [əsóʃiet] VI/VT asociar(se)

association [əsosiéʃən] N asociación *f*

assonance [ésənəns] N asonancia *f*

assorted [əsɔ́rdɪd] ADJ variado, surtido

assortment [əsɔ́rtmənt] N (act of assorting)
clasificación *f*; (of wares) surtido *m*; (of
tools, etc.) colección *f*

assume [əsúm] VT (responsibility, role)
asumir; (right) arrogarse; (suppose) dar por
sentado, suponer

assumption [əsámpʃən] N (premise)
suposición *f*; (unstated belief)
sobreentendido *m*; (seizure) toma *f*

assurance [əʃúrəns] N (promise) promesa *f*,
palabra *f*; (reassurance) palabras de apoyo
f pl; (certainty) certeza *f*; (confidence)
confianza *f*

assure [əʃúr] VT asegurar; (encourage)
infundir confianza

assuredly [əʃúrdli] ADV seguramente, sin
duda

asterisk [éstərɪsk] N asterisco *m*

asteroid [éstərɔɪd] N asteroide *m*

asthma [æzmə] N asma *f*

asthmatic [æzmédɪk] ADJ asmático

astigmatism [əstígmətɪzəm] N astigmatismo
m

astonish [əstánɪʃ] VT asombrar, pasmar

astonishing [əstánɪʃɪŋ] ADJ asombroso,
pasmoso

astonishment [əstánɪʃmənt] M asombro *m*,
pasmo *m*

astound [əstáund] VT pasmar, asombrar

astraddle [əstrédl] ADV a horcajadas

astray [əstré] ADV **to go —** perderse,
extraviarse; **to lead —** (seduce) llevar por
mal camino, seducir; (perplex) confundir

astride [əstráɪd] ADV a horcajadas

astringent [əstríndʒənt] ADJ & N astringente *m*

astrology [əstrálədʒi] N astrología *f*

astronaut [ǽstrənɔt] M astronauta *mf*

astronautics [æstrənɔ́dɪks] N astronáutica *f*

astronomer [əstránəmə] N astrónomo -ma *mf*

astronomy [əstránəmi] N astronomía *f*

astrophysics [æstrofízɪks] N astrofísica *f*

Asturian [æstúriən] ADJ & N asturiano -na *mf*

Asturias [æstúriəs] N Asturias *f sg*

astute [əstút] ADJ astuto, sagaz

asylum [əsáɪləm] N asilo *m*

asymmetric [esɪmétrɪk] ADJ asimétrico

at [æt] PREP — **the end of the story** al final de la historia; — **five o'clock** a las cinco; — **high altitude** a grandes alturas; — **the table** a/en la mesa; — **five dollars a kilo** a cinco dólares el kilo; — **Easter** en Pascua; — **home** en casa; — **war** en guerra; **wait** — **the door** espera en la puerta; **he is** — **peace with himself** está en paz consigo mismo; **the children are** — **play** los niños están jugando; **look** — **that** mira eso; **amazed** — pasmado por; **he laughed** — **me** se rió de mí; — **last** por fin, al fin

atheism [éθiɪzəm] N ateísmo *m*

atheist [éθiɪst] N ateo -a *mf*

athlete [ǽθlit] N deportista *mf*; (track and field) atleta *mf*; — **'s foot** pie de atleta *m*

athletic [æθlédɪk] ADJ deportivo; (concerning track and field; well-built) atlético

athletics [æθlédɪks] N deporte *m*; (track and field) atletismo *m*

Atlantic [ætlǽntɪk] ADJ atlántico; N — **Ocean** Océano Atlántico *m*

atlas [ǽtləs] N atlas *m*

atmosphere [ǽtməsfɪr] N (air) atmósfera *f*; (mood) ambiente *m*

atmospheric [ætməsfírk] ADJ atmosférico

atom [ǽdəm] N átomo *m*; — **bomb** bomba atómica *f*

atomic [ətámɪk] ADJ atómico; — **age** era atómica *f*; — **energy** energía atómica *f*; — **number** número atómico *m*; — **weight** peso atómico *m*

atomize [ǽdəmaɪz] VT atomizar

atone [ətón] VI **to** — **for** expiar, purgar

atonement [ətónmənt] N expiación *f*, purgación *f*

atrium [étriəm] N (of office building, hotel) vestíbulo *m*, patio central *m*; (of church) atrio *m*

atrocious [ətróʃəs] ADJ atroz

atrocity [ətrásɪdi] N atrocidad *f*, barbaridad *f*

atrophy [ǽtrəfi] N atrofia *f*; VI/VT atrofiar(se)

attach [ətǽtʃ] VI/VT (pipe, cable) unir(se), juntar; (paper) sujetar; (wages) retener; (significance) atribuir; **to be** —**ed to someone** estar apegado a alguien

attaché [ætəʃé] N agregado -da *mf*

attachment [ətǽtʃmənt] N (act of attaching) unión *f*; (pipe, cable) conexión *f*; (affection) apego *m*, cariño *m*; (of wages) retención *f*; (significance) atribución *f*; (accessory) accesorio *m*

attack [ətǽk] N ataque *m*, acometida *f*; VI/VT atacar, acometer

attain [ətén] VT alcanzar; VI llegar a

attainment [əténmənt] N (act) alcance *m*; (accomplishment) logro *m*, consecución *f*

attempt [ətémpt] N tentativa *f*, intento *m*; (murder) atentado *m*; VT tratar (de), intentar

attend [əténd] VT (meeting) asistir a, acudir a; VI **to** — **to** (a sick person) atender, cuidar; (a speaker) prestar atención

attendance [əténdəns] N asistencia *f*

attendant [əténdənt] N (at a gas station) encargado -da *mf*; (servant) sirviente -ta *mf*; ADJ concomitante

attention [əténʃən] N atención *f*; (courtesy) atenciones *f pl*; **to pay** — prestar atención; **to pay** — **to** atender a; **to call** — llamar la atención; INTERJ —! ¡firmes!

attentive [əténtɪv] ADJ (focused) atento; (courteous) cortés

attenuate [əténjuet] VT atenuar

attest [ətést] VT (bear witness to) atestiguar; (manifest) demostrar; VI certificar, dar fe, atestar

attic [ǽdɪk] N desván *m*, altillo *m*

attire [ətáɪr] N atavío *m*, vestidura *f*; VT ataviar

attitude [ǽdɪtud] N (mental) actitud *f*; (physical) postura *f*; (insolence) insolencia *f*, descaro *m*

attorney [ətɜ́-ni] N abogado -da *mf*; — **General** Ministro -tra de Justicia *mf*

attract [ətrǽkt] VT atraer; **to** — **attention** llamar la atención

attraction [ətrǽkʃən] N (act, power) atracción *f*; (charm) atractivo *m*

attractive [ətrǽktɪv] ADJ atractivo; (beautiful) atractivo, agraciado

attractiveness [ətrǽktɪvnɪs] N atractivo *m*

attribute [ǽtrəbjut] N atributo *m*; [ətríbjut] VT atribuir

attribution [ætrəbjúʃən] N atribución *f*

attrition [ətríʃən] N (wearing out) desgaste *m*; (casualties) bajas *f pl*; **war of** — guerra de agotamiento *f*

auburn [ɔ́bə-n] N & ADJ castaño rojizo *m*

auction [ɔ́kʃən] N subasta f, remate m; VI/VT subastar, rematar
auctioneer [ɔkʃənɪ́r] N subastador -ra mf, rematador -ra mf
audacious [ɔdéʃəs] ADJ audaz, atrevido
audacity [ɔdǽsɪdɪ] N desfachatez f, atrevimiento m
audible [ɔ́dəbəł] ADJ audible
audience [ɔ́diəns] N público m, auditorio m; (TV, radio) audiencia f
audio [ɔ́dɪo] ADJ de audio; **— book** audiolibro m; **— frequency** audiofrecuencia f; **—visual** audiovisual; **—visuals** audiovisuales m pl; N audio m
audiology [ɔdɪálədʒi] N audiología f
audit [ɔ́dɪt] VI/VT (class) asistir de oyente; (accounts) auditar; N auditoría f
audition [ɔdíʃən] N audición f
auditor [ɔ́dɪdɚ] N (of accounts) auditor -ra mf, censor -ora mf; (of a class) oyente mf
auditorium [ɔdɪt́riəm] N auditorio m, paraninfo m
auditory [ɔ́dɪtɔri] ADJ auditivo
augment [ɔgmént] VT incrementar, aumentar
August [ɔ́gəst] N agosto m
aunt [ænt] N tía f
aura [ɔ́rə] N aura f
aurora [ərɔ́rə] N aurora f; **— borealis** aurora boreal f
auspices [ɔ́spɪsɪz] N auspicios m pl
auspicious [ɔspíʃəs] ADJ propicio
austere [ɔstír] ADJ austero
austerity [ɔstérɪdi] N austeridad f
Australia [ɔstréljə] N Australia f
Australian [ɔstréljən] ADJ & N australiano -na mf
Austria [ɔ́striə] N Austria f
Austrian [ɔ́striən] ADJ & N austríaco -ca mf
authentic [ɔθéntɪk] ADJ auténtico
authenticate [ɔθéntɪket] VT autenticar
author [ɔ́θɚ] N (professional) escritor -ra mf; (creator) autor -ra mf
authoritarian [əθɔntériən] ADJ autoritario
authoritative [əθɔ́rɪtedɪv] ADJ (official) autorizado; (dictatorial) autoritario
authority [əθɔ́rɪdi] N autoridad f; (permission) autorización f; **to have on good —** saber de buena fuente; **it's not within your —** no está dentro de tus facultades
authorization [ɔθɚɪzéʃən] N autorización f
authorize [ɔ́θəraɪz] VT autorizar, habilitar
autism [ɔ́tɪzəm] N autismo m
autobiography [ɔdobaɪágrəfi] N autobiografía f
autocrat [ɔ́dəkræt] N autócrata mf
autograph [ɔ́dəgræf] N autógrafo m

autoimmune [ɔdoɪmjún] ADJ autoinmune
automated [ɔ́dəmedɪd] ADJ automatizado
automatic [ɔdəmǽdɪk] ADJ automático; (response) maquinal; **— pilot** piloto automático m; **— transmission** transmisión automática f
automation [ɔdəméʃən] N automatización f
automobile [ɔ́dəməbił] N automóvil m
automotive [ɔdəmódɪv] ADJ (sport) automovilístico; (industry) automotor -ra, automotriz
autonomy [ɔtánəmi] N autonomía f
autopilot [ɔ́dopaɪlət] N piloto automático m
autopsy [ɔ́tɑpsi] N autopsia f
autumn [ɔ́dəm] N otoño m
autumnal [ɔtámnəł] ADJ otoñal
auxiliary [ɔgzíləri] ADJ & N auxiliar mf
avail [əvéł] VI/VT servir; **to — oneself of** aprovechar; N **of no —** de ninguna utilidad; **to no —** en vano
available [əvéləbəł] ADJ disponible, asequible
avalanche [ǽvəlæntʃ] N avalancha f, alud m
avarice [ǽvərɪs] N avaricia f
avaricious [ævəríʃəs] ADJ avaro, avariento
avenge [əvéndʒ] VT vengar
avenger [əvéndʒɚ] N vengador -ra mf
avenue [ǽvənu] N avenida f; (means of access) vía f
aver [əvɚ́] VT afirmar
average [ǽvrɪdʒ] N promedio m; **on —** de promedio; ADJ medio, mediano; **just —** (person) del montón; (thing) nada del otro mundo; VT promediar; **he —s 20 miles an hour** hace un promedio de 20 millas por hora
averse [əvɚ́s] ADJ reacio; **he's not — to a glass of wine** no se opone a una copa de vino
aversion [əvɚ́ʒən] N aversión f
avert [əvɚ́t] VT (eyes) desviar; (danger) evitar
aviation [eviéʃən] N aviación f
aviator [éviedɚ] N aviador -ra mf
avid [ǽvɪd] ADJ ávido
avocado [ævəkádo] N aguacate m; RP palta f
avocation [ævəkéʃən] N pasatiempo m
avoid [əvɔ́ɪd] VI/VT (stay away from) evitar; (dodge) esquivar
avow [əváu] VT confesar
avowal [əváuəł] N confesión f
avuncular [əváɲkjələ] ADJ propio de un tío; **— attitude** actitud paternal y amistosa
await [əwét] VT aguardar
awake [əwék] ADJ despierto; VI/VT despertar(se)
awaken [əwékən] VI/VT despertar(se)
award [əwɔ́rd] N premio m, galardón m; (judicial) adjudicación f; VT otorgar

aware [əwér] ADJ consciente, enterado; **I'm — of that** eso me consta

away [əwé] ADV far — lejos; **— from his family** lejos de su familia; **she looked** — apartó la vista; **she's** — no está; **he's been painting — all day** se ha pasado todo el día pintando; **right** — ahora mismo, ahorita; **ten miles** — a diez millas de distancia; **to give** — regalar; **to go** — irse; **to take** — quitar; **to blow** — (hacer) volar

awe [ɔ] N sobrecogimiento m; **to be in** — sobrecogerse; VT sobrecoger

awesome [ɔ́səm] ADJ (awe-inspiring) sobrecogedor; (impressive) fabuloso

awestruck [ɔ́strʌk] ADJ pasmado

awful [ɔ́fəl] ADJ terrible, horroroso; ADV espantoso; **it's — hot here** hace un calor horrible

awhile [əhwáɪl] ADV un rato

awkward [ɔ́kwəd] ADJ (clumsy) torpe, desmañado; (embarrassing) embarazoso; (unwieldy) incómodo

awl [ɔl] N punzón m

awning [ɔ́nɪŋ] N toldo m

awry [ərái] ADJ (clothes) mal puesto; (hat) ladeado; **my plans went** — mis planes fracasaron rotundamente

ax, axe [æks] N hacha f; VT eliminar

axis [æksɪs] N eje m

axle [æksəl] N eje m

Azerbaijan [æzə-baɪdʒán] N Azerbaiyán m

Azerbaijani, Azerbaijanian [æzə-baɪdʒáni(ən)] ADJ & N azerbaijano -na mf, azerbaiyano -na mf

azure [æʒə] ADJ (azul) celeste; N azul celeste m

Bb

babble [bǽbəl] N (baby talk) balbuceo m; (chatter) parloteo m; (murmur) murmullo m; VI (to talk like a baby) balbucear; (to chatter) parlotear; (to murmur) murmurar

baboon [bæbún] N babuino m

baby [bébi] N bebé mf; **who's the — in your family?** ¿quién es el menor/benjamín en tu familia? **— blue** celeste m; **— boomer** persona nacida entre 1946 y 1965 f; **— carriage** cochecito de bebé m; **— food** comida para bebés f; **— girl** nena f; **— sister** hermanita f; **— sitter** niñera f; **— talk** habla infantil f; **—**

tooth diente de leche m; **to —sit** cuidar niños; **she had a** — dio a luz; VT mimar

baccalaureate [bækəlɔ́riət] N bachillerato m

bachelor [bǽtʃələ] N soltero m; **—'s degree** licenciatura f; **— of Arts** (degree) licenciatura en filosofía y letras f; (person) licenciado -da en filosofía y letras mf

bacillus [bəsíləs] N bacilo m

back [bæk] N (human body part) espalda f; (animal body part) lomo m; (opposite side) dorso m; (of chair) respaldo m, espaldar m; **—ache** dolor de espalda m; **—bone** columna vertebral f, espinazo m; **—pack** mochila f; **behind one's** — a espaldas de uno; **he has no —bone** no tiene carácter; **in — of** detrás de, tras; **in the — of the house** atrás de la casa; **to fall on one's** — caer de espaldas; **to turn one's** — volver las espaldas; ADJ; **— door** puerta trasera f; **— issues** números atrasados m pl; **on the — burner** en suspenso; VT respaldar, apoyar; VI dar marcha atrás; **to — down** echarse (para) atrás, recular, cejar; ADV (look) atrás/para atrás; (fall) de espaldas; **— and forth** de aquí para allá; **—-and-forth movement** movimiento de vaivén m; **he ran — to the house** volvió corriendo a la casa; **he's — from work** está de vuelta del trabajo

backbite [bǽkbaɪt] VI/VT difamar

backer [bǽkə] N (financial) fiador -ra mf; (political) partidario -ria mf

backfire [bǽkfaɪr] VI (automobile) petardear, hacer detonaciones; (plan) ser contraproducente; N petardeo m

backgammon [bǽkgæmən] N backgammon m

background [bǽkgraʊnd] N (of a picture) fondo m; (experience) antecedentes m pl; **I have a — in computers** tengo conocimientos de informática; **I know what goes on in the** — sé lo que pasa entre bastidores; **a humble** — orígenes humildes m pl

backhand [bǽkhænd] N revés m

backing [bǽkɪŋ] N respaldo m, apoyo m; (fabric) refuerzo m

backlash [bǽklæʃ] N reacción violenta f

backlog [bǽklɑg] N atraso m

backseat [bǽksit] N asiento trasero m

backslide [bǽkslaɪd] VI volver a las andadas, reincidir

backspace [bǽkspes] N retroceso m; VI retroceder

backstage [bækstédʒ] ADV entre bastidores

backtrack [bǽktræk] VI retroceder, dar

marcha atrás

backup [bǽkʌp] N (support) respaldo *m*; (software) copia de seguridad *f*

backward [bǽkwə-d] ADV hacia atrás, para atrás; **to go —** recular; ADJ (underdeveloped) atrasado; (reactionary) retrógrado

backwardness [bǽkwə-dnɪs] N (underdevelopment) atraso *m*; (conservatism) retrogradismo *m*; (timidity) timidez *f*

backyard [bǽkjórd] N patio trasero *m*

bacon [békən] N tocino *m*, *Sp* beicon *m*

bacteria [bæktíriə] N bacteria(s) *f (pl)*

bacteriology [bæktiriáləʤi] N bacteriología *f*

bad [bæd] ADJ malo; (man) perverso; (teeth) feo; (drug) dañoso; (flood) grave; (fruit) podrido; (very good) *vulg* de puta madre; **— blood** enemistad *f*; **to go from — to worse** ir de mal en peor; **he has a — heart** está enfermo del corazón; **to —mouth** difamar (a); **to look —** tener mal aspecto; *fam* quedar mal; ADV mal; **not —** no está nada mal; **too —** ¡qué pena!

badge [bæʤ] N insignia *f*, chapa *f*

badger [bǽʤ] N tejón *m*; VT acosar

baffle [bǽfəl] VT (confuse) confundir; (frustrate) desconcertar; N deflector *m*

bag [bæg] N bolsa *f*, bolso *m*; (baggage) maleta *f*; **— lady** vagabunda *f*; **—pipe** gaita *f*; VT empacar, embolsar; (hunting) cazar

baggage [bǽgɪʤ] N (suitcases) equipaje *m*; (impediments) bagaje *m*; **— car** vagón de equipajes *m*; **— check** contraseña de equipajes *f*; **— tag** etiqueta *f*; **— inspection** revisión de equipaje *f*

baggy [bǽgi] ADJ flojo, holgado

Bahamas [bəháməz] N Bahamas *f pl*

Bahamian [bəhémiən] ADJ & N bahameño -ña *mf*

Bahrain [barén] N Bahréin *m*

Bahraini [baréni] ADJ & N bahreiní *mf*

bail [beɫ] N fianza *f*; **to let out on —** poner en libertad bajo fianza; VT pagar la fianza; **to — someone out** pagarle la fianza a alguien; **to — someone out of a predicament** sacar a alguien de un apuro; **to — out water** achicar, vaciar; VI **to — out** (of a plane) tirarse con paracaídas de un avión; (of a situation) abandonar

bailiff [béɫɪf] N ujier *m*

bait [bet] N cebo *m*; VT (prepare hook) cebar; (attract customers) seducir; (harass) acosar

bake [bek] VI/VT hornear; (sun) calcinar;

abrasar; **I'm baking in this heat** me estoy asando, me muero de calor

baker [békə-] N panadero -ra *mf*; **— 's dozen** la docena del fraile *f*

bakery [békəri] N panadería *f*

baking [békɪŋ] N (act of baking) horneado *m*; (activity) repostería *f*; **— powder** polvo de hornear *m*; **— soda** bicarbonato de sodio *m*

balance [bǽləns] N (instrument) balanza *f*; (equilibrium) equilibrio *m*; (debit, credit) saldo *m*, balance *m*; **— of payments** balanza de pagos *f*; **— of trade** balanza comercial *f*; **— sheet** balance *m*; **to lose one's —** perder el equilibrio; VT equilibrar, hacer equilibrio con; **to — the risks with the benefits** sopesar los riesgos y los beneficios; VI cuadrar

balcony [bǽɫkani] N balcón *m*; (in a theater) palco *m*, entresuelo *m*

bald [bɔɫd] ADJ (person) calvo, pelón; (mountain) pelón; (tire) liso; **— eagle** águila americana de cabeza blanca *f*; **—headed** calvo; **— spot** calva *f*; **he went —** se quedó calvo

bale [beɫ] N paca *f*, fardo *m*; VT empacar, enfardar

balk [bɔk] VI oponerse, rehusarse a

ball [bɔɫ] N (tennis, baseball, golf) pelota *f*; (basketball, football, soccer) balón *m*; (of string, thread) ovillo *m*; (cannon) bala (de cañón) *f*; (dance) baile *m*; **— and chain** grillete *m*; **— bearing** cojinete de bolas *m*; **— game** juego de pelota *m*; (baseball) partido de béisbol *m*; **—s** (testicles) *vulg* pelotas *f pl*, *vulg* huevos *m pl*; *Sp vulg* cojones *m pl*; VT (string) ovillar; (have sex) *Sp vulg* follar; *Am vulg* coger, culear

ballad [bǽləd] N balada *f*; (historical) romance *m*

ballast [bǽləst] N lastre *m*; (railroad) balasto *m*; VT lastrar

ballerina [bælərínə] N bailarina de ballet *f*

ballet [bælé] N ballet *m*

ballistic [bəlístɪk] ADJ balístico; **— missile** misil balístico *m*; N **—s** balística *f*

balloon [bəlún] N globo *m*; VI (travel in a balloon) pasear en globo; VI/VT (grow) inflar(se)

ballot [bǽlət] N (system of voting) votación *f*; (paper) papeleta *f*; *Mex* boleta *f*; **— box** urna *f*

balm [bam] N bálsamo *m*

balmy [bámi] ADJ templado

baloney [bəlóni] N pamplinas *f pl*, paparruchas *f pl*

balsa [bɔ́ɫsə] N (wood) madera balsa *f*; (raft)

balsa *f*

balsam [bɔ́lsəm] N (resin) bálsamo *m*; (tree) especie de abeto *m*

bamboo [bæmbú] N bambú *m*

ban [bæn] N prohibición *f*; (church) excomunión *f*; VT prohibir

banal [bénəl] ADJ banal

banana [bənǽnə] N plátano *m*, banana *f*; — **grove** platanar *m*; — **split** banana split *m*; — **tree** plátano *m*, banano *m*

band [bænd] N (group) banda *f*, pandilla *f*; (musicians) banda *f*, conjunto *m*; (cloth) banda *f*; (ribbon) cinta *f*; (leather) tira *f*; **to join the —wagon** subirse al carro/ tren; **—width** amplitud de banda *f*; VI/VT **to — together** unirse, juntarse

bandage [bǽndɪdʒ] N venda *f*, vendaje *m*; VT vendar

bandit [bǽndɪt] N bandido -da *mf*, bandolero -ra *mf*, salteador -ora *mf*

bang [bæŋ] N (blow) golpe *m*, golpazo *m*; (sound) estampido *m*, estallido *m*; —**s** fleco *m*, flequillo *m*; **I get a — out of seeing my grandkids** me emociona ver a mis nietos; VI/VT (hit) golpear; (make noise) hacer estrépito; (screw) *Sp vulg* follar; *Am vulg* coger, culear

Bangladesh [bæ̀ŋglədɛ́ʃ] N Bangladesh *m*

Bangladeshi [bæ̀ŋglədéʃi] ADJ & N bangladeshí *mf*

banish [bǽnɪʃ] VT desterrar

banishment [bǽnɪʃmənt] N destierro *m*, proscripción *f*

banister [bǽnɪstə˞] N barandal *m*, pasamano(s) *m*, balaustrada *f*

banjo [bǽndʒo] N banjo *m*

bank [bæŋk] N (financial institution) banco *m*; (in gambling) banca *f*; (of a body of water) orilla *f*, ribera *f*, margen *m*; (slope) escarpa *f*; — **statement** estado de cuenta *m*; — **vault** cámara *f*; ADJ bancario, de banco; VT (money) depositar en un banco; VI (snow, sand) amontonar; (airplane) ladear; **to — on** contar con; **to —roll** financiar

banker [bǽŋkə˞] N (bank owner) banquero -ra *mf*; (bank employee) bancario -ria *mf*

banking [bǽŋkɪŋ] N (activity) actividad bancaria *f*; (industry) banca *f*; ADJ bancario, de banco

banknote [bǽŋknot] N billete *m*

bankrupt [bǽŋkrʌpt] ADJ en bancarrota; VT arruinar, quebrar

bankruptcy [bǽŋkrʌptsi] N bancarrota *f*, quiebra *f*; **to go into** — declararse en quiebra

banner [bǽnə˞] N estandarte *m*, pendón *m*; ADJ sobresaliente

banquet [bǽŋkwɪt] N banquete *m*, gala *f*

baptism [bǽptɪzəm] N (sacrament) bautismo *m*; (action) bautizo *m*

baptize [bǽptaɪz] VT bautizar

bar [bɑr] N (of iron, sand, of a tavern) barra *f*; (of chocolate) barra *f*, tableta *f*; (vertical rod) barrote *m*; (obstacle) barrera *f*, obstáculo *m*; (in music) compás *m*; (saloon) bar *m*; —**bell** barra para pesas *f*; —**code** código de barras *m*; — **graph** gráfica de barras *f*; —**keeper** tabernero -ra *mf*, cantinero -ra *mf*; —**room** bar *m*; —**room brawl** pelea de borrachos *f*; —**tender** tabernero -ra *mf*, cantinero -ra *mf*; **behind** —**s** tras las rejas; **to be admitted to the** — recibirse de abogado; VT (door, exit) atrancar; (access) impedir; (from a group) excluir; — **none** sin excepción; —**ring a disaster** salvo en caso de desastre

barb [barb] N púa *f*; —**ed wire** alambre de púas *m*; *Sp* alambre de espino *m*

Barbadian [barbédiən] ADJ & N barbadense *mf*

Barbados [barbéɖos] N Barbados *m*

barbarian [barbériən] ADJ & N bárbaro -ra *mf*

barbaric [barbérɪk] ADJ bárbaro

barbarous [bárbə˞əs] ADJ bárbaro

barbecue [bárbɪkju] N (meat dish) barbacoa *f*, asado *m*, parrillada *f*; — **sauce** adobo de barbacoa *m*; VI/VT asar con adobo

barber [bárbə˞] N peluquero *m*, barbero *m*; —**shop** peluquería *f*, barbería *f*

barbiturate [barbɪtʃə˞ɪt] N barbitúrico *m*

bard [bard] N bardo *m*

bare [ber] ADJ (legs, walls) desnudo; (cabinet) vacío; —**back** a pelo; —**faced** descarado; —**foot** descalzo; **the** — **necessities** lo imprescindible; —**headed** con la cabeza descubierta; —**legged** con las piernas desnudas; — **majority** escasa mayoría *f*; **to lay** — poner al descubierto; **with his** — **hands** con las propias manos

barely [bérli] ADV apenas

bargain [bárgɪn] N (agreement) trato *m*; (inexpensive purchase) ganga *f*, ocasión *f*; — **basement** sección de ofertas *f*; **into the** — por añadidura; **to strike a** — cerrar un trato; VI (haggle) regatear; (expect) contar con

barge [bardʒ] N barcaza *f*; VI **to — in** interrumpir; **to — into** irrumpir en

baritone [bérɪton] N & ADJ barítono *m*

barium [bériəm] N bario *m*

bark [bark] N (of a dog) ladrido *m*; (on a tree) corteza *f*; VI/VT ladrar; **to — out an**

order gritar una orden

barley [bárli] N cebada f

barn [barn] N (for animals) establo m; (for grain) granero m; **— owl** lechuza f; **—yard** corral m

barnacle [bárnəkəł] N percebe m

barometer [bərúmɪdə⋅] N barómetro m

baron [bǽrən] N barón m

baroque [bərók] ADJ & N barroco m

barracks [bǽrəks] N cuartel m

barracuda [bǽrəkúdə] N barracuda f

barrage [bərá3] N (of artillery fire) barrera de fuego f; (of questions) lluvia f, aluvión m

barrel [bǽrəł] N barril m, tonel m; (gun) cañón m, caño m; **he's a — of laughs** es un payaso; **he is scraping the bottom of the —** está desesperado; **to — along** ir disparado

barren [bǽrən] ADJ (land) árido, yermo; (female) estéril

barrette [bərét] N broche m

barricade [bǽrɪkéd] N barricada f; VT cerrar con barricadas; VI atrincherarse

barrier [bǽriə⋅] N barrera f; **— reef** barrera de coral f

barrio [bário] N barrio hispano m

barter [bárɾə⋅] VI hacer trueque; VT trocar; N trueque m

basal cell carcinoma [bésəłsełkɑrsɪnómə] N carcinoma de célula basal m

basalt [bésɔłt] N basalto m

base [bes] N base f; **— pay** salario base m; **—ball** béisbol m; **—board** zócalo m; ADJ bajo, vil; (metal) de baja ley; VI/VT basar, fundar; **to be —d on** fundamentarse en; **the general is —d in Berlin** el general está estacionado en Berlín

baseless [béslɪs] ADJ sin fundamento

basement [bésmənt] N sótano m

baseness [bésnɪs] N bajeza f, vileza f

bash [bæʃ] VT golpear

bashful [bǽʃfəł] ADJ tímido, vergonzoso

bashfulness [bǽʃfəłnɪs] N timidez f

basic [bésɪk] ADJ básico

basin [bésɪn] N (bowl) palangana f, jofaina f; (of a fountain) pilón m; (geographical formation) cuenca f; (pond) estanque m

basis [bésɪs] N fundamento m, base f; **on the — of** en base a, con base en; **on a regular —** regularmente

bask [bæsk] VI (in the sun) asolearse; (in praise) deleitarse

basket [bǽskɪt] N canasta f, cesta f, cesto m; **—ball** baloncesto m, básquetbol m

basketful [bǽskɪtfʌł] N (contents of a basket) canasto m; (large amount) montón m

basketry [bǽskɪtri] N cestería f

Basque [bæsk] ADJ & N (person) vasco -ca mf; (language) vascuence m, vasco m

bass [bes] N (voice, bass guitar) bajo m; (double bass) contrabajo m; **— clef** clave de fa f; **— drum** bombo m; **— horn** tuba f; [bæs] (marine fish) lubina f; (freshwater fish) perca f

bassoon [bæsún] N fagot m

bastard [bǽstə⋅d] N & ADJ (illegitimate) bastardo -da mf; N (mean person) offensive hijo de puta m, cabrón m

baste [best] VT (fabric) hilvanar; (meat) rociar

bat [bæt] N (baseball, cricket) bate m; (animal) murciélago m; VT golpear; **not to — an eye** no pestañear; VI (baseball) batear

batch [bætʃ] N (of cookies) hornada f; (of cement) tanda f; (of data) colección f

bath [bæθ] N baño m; **—robe** bata (de baño) f; Sp albornoz m; **—room** (in a house) baño m, cuarto de baño m; (public) Sp aseo m; Am servicio m, baño m; **—tub** bañera f

bathe [beð] VI/VT bañar(se); **bathing beauty** muchacha en traje de baño f; **bathing suit** traje de baño m

bather [béðə⋅] N bañista mf

baton [bətún] N batuta f

battalion [bətǽljən] N batallón m

batter [bǽɾə⋅] N pasta f, masa f; (baseball) bateador m; VT golpear

battery [bǽɾəri] N (of car, artillery) batería f; (of electronic devices) pila f; (of tests) serie f; (assault) asalto m

battle [bǽdł] N batalla f; **—ax(e)** (weapon) hacha de guerra f; (woman) sargenta f; **— cry** grito de guerra m; **—field** campo de batalla m; **—ship** acorazado m; VI batallar; **to — cancer** luchar contra el cáncer

bawl [bɔł] VI berrear; **to — somebody out** echarle bronca a uno; **to — out orders** bramar órdenes

bay [be] N (body of water) bahía f; (howl) aullido m; **— leaf** hoja de laurel f; **— window** ventana saliente f; **to hold at —** tener a raya; ADJ bayo; VI aullar

bayonet [beənét] N bayoneta f

bazaar [bəzár] N (market place) bazar m; (benefit) kermés f

bazooka [bəzúka] N bazuca f

be [bi] VI **I am from Uruguay** soy de Uruguay; **there were four of us** éramos cuatro; **he is a doctor** es médico; **it's her** es ella; **sugar is sweet** el azúcar es dulce; **London is in England** Londres está en Inglaterra; **this water is cold** esta agua está fría; **the windows were**

open las ventanas estaban abiertas; **there is a problem** hay un problema; **to — cold/warm/hungry/right/in a hurry** tener frío/calor/hambre/razón/prisa; **it is cold/hot/windy** hace frío/calor/viento

beach [bitʃ] N playa f; **—comber** vagabundo -da mf; **—head** cabeza de playa f; VT varar, encallar

beacon [bíkən] N faro m

bead [bid] N cuenta f; (of sweat) gota f, perla f; **to get a — on somebody** apuntarle a alguien; **to tell one's —s** rezar el rosario; VT (string) enhebrar/ensartar cuentas; (decorate) adornar con cuentas

beagle [bígəɫ] N beagle m

beak [bik] N pico m

beaker [bíkɚ] N vaso de precipitados m

beam [bim] N (of light) rayo m, haz m; (in a building) viga f; (of a scale) brazo m; **broad in the —** ancho de caderas; VI/VT (light, radio) emitir; (smile) estar radiante

bean [bin] N judía f, habichuela f; Sp alubia f; Am frijol m, Am poroto m; **Lima —** haba f; **—stalk** tallo de habas/frijol m; **Jack and the —stalk** Juanito y las habichuelas; **I don't know —s about that** no sé ni papa/jota de eso

bear [bɛr] N oso m; **— hug** abrazo fuerte m; **— market** mercado bajista m; VT (hold up, tolerate) soportar, aguantar; (suffer) sobrellevar; (have a child) dar a luz; (produce young) parir; (produce fruit) producir; **to — down** (mash) apretar; (push) pujar; **to — a grudge** guardar rencor; **to — in mind** tener en cuenta; **to — oneself with dignity** portarse con dignidad; **to — out** confirmar; **to — testimony** dar testimonio; **to — interest** devengar interés; **to — gifts** traer regalos; **to — a resemblance** parecerse; **to — the cost of something** asumir el costo de algo; **it doesn't — repeating** no merece repetirse

bearable [bérəbəɫ] ADJ llevadero

beard [bird] N (on a man) barba f; (of wheat) aristas f pl

bearded [bírDɪd] ADJ barbado, barbudo

bearer [bérɚ] N portador -ra mf

bearing [bérɪŋ] N porte m; **to lose one's —s** perder el rumbo, desorientarse; **it has no — on our situation** no tiene relación con nuestra situación

bearish [bérɪʃ] ADJ (of bears) osuno; (of stock market) bajista

beast [bist] N bestia f

beat [bit] VT (wings, eggs) batir; (a person) golpear; (a drum) tocar; (an opponent) vencer; (tempo) marcar; VI (heart) latir; (drum) sonar; **to — around the bush** andarse por las ramas; **to — off** (repulse) rechazar; (masturbate) vulg hacerse una paja; **to — up** dar una paliza; **—s me!** ¡ni idea! N (blow) golpe m; (drum) toque m; (heart) latido m; (tempo) compás m; (policeman's territory) ronda f

beaten [bítn] ADJ (mixed) batido; (defeated) vencido; (tired) fatigado; **— path** camino trillado m

beater [bíDɚ] N batidor m

beating [bíDɪŋ] N (whipping) paliza f; (pulsation) latido m

beau [bo] N pretendiente m

beautiful [bjúDəfəɫ] ADJ hermoso; **— people** jet set mf

beautify [bjúDəfaɪ] VT embellecer, hermosear

beauty [bjúɾi] N belleza f, hermosura f; (woman) beldad f; **— contest** concurso/certamen de belleza m; **— pageant** concurso/certamen de belleza m; **— parlor** salón de belleza m

beaver [bívɚ] N (animal) castor m; (vagina) vulg chichi m, conejo m

because [bɪkɔ́z] CONJ porque; **— of** por, a causa de

beckon [békən] VT llamar por señas

become [bɪkʌ́m] VT (through effort) hacerse; **he became rich** se hizo rico; (emotional or physical condition) ponerse; **she became ill** se puso enferma; (long process) llegar a ser; **he became a doctor** llegó a ser médico; (turn into) convertirse en; **the water became ice** el agua se convirtió en hielo; (drastic change) volverse; **he became crazy** se volvió loco; (suit) sentar bien; **to — angry** enojarse; **to — frightened** asustarse; **to — old** envejecer(se); **what has — of him?** ¿qué ha sido de él?

becoming [bɪkʌ́mɪŋ] ADJ (appropriate) propio; **that dress is — to you** te sienta bien ese vestido

bed [bed] N (furniture) cama f; lit lecho m; (of a river) cauce m; (of the sea) fondo m; (in a garden) cuadro m; **—bug** chinche mf; **—clothes** ropa de cama f; **—pan** cuña f, chata f; **—ridden** postrado en cama; **—rest** reposo m; **—rock** lecho de roca m; **—room** alcoba f, dormitorio m; Mex recámara f; **at the —side** al lado de la cama; **—side table** mesita de noche f; **—side manner** manera agradable de tratar a los pacientes f; **—sore** llaga f;

—spread colcha *f*; **—spring** resorte del colchón *m*; **—time** hora de dormir *f*; **—wetting** enuresis nocturna *f*; **to go to —** acostarse; **to put to —** acostar

bedding [bédɪŋ] N ropa de cama *f*

bee [bi] N (insect) abeja *f*; (social gathering) tertulia *f*; **to have a — in one's bonnet** tener una idea metida en la cabeza; **—hive** colmena *f*; **— sting** picadura de abeja *f*

beech [bip̌] N haya *f*; **—nut** hayuco *m*

beef [bif] N (meat) carne de vaca/res *f*; (complaint) queja *f*; **— jerky** cecina *f*; **—steak** bistec *m*; VI quejarse; **to — up** reforzar

beep [bip] N pitazo *m*; VI/VT **the alarm is —ing** la alarma está sonando; **he —ed his horn** tocó el claxon

beeper [bípɚ] N buscapersonas *m sg*

beer [bir] N cerveza *f*

beet [bit] N remolacha *f*

beetle [bídl] N escarabajo *m*

befall [bɪfɔ́l] VT acontecerle a

befit [bɪfít] VT convenir

before [bɪfɔ́r] ADV (temporal) antes; (spatial) delante; PREP (temporal) antes de; (spatial) delante de; *lit* ante; CONJ antes (de) que, antes de; **— beginning** antes de que comiences, antes de comenzar

beforehand [bɪfɔ́rhænd] ADV de antemano

befriend [bɪfrénd] VT hacerse amigo de

beg [beg] VT **to — for mercy** implorar misericordia; **she —ged me to do it** me rogó que lo hiciera; **to — the question** dar por sentado lo mismo que se arguye; VI mendigar, pedir limosna

beget [bɪgét] VT engendrar; **money —s money** la plata llama a la plata

beggar [bégɚ] N mendigo -ga *mf*

begin [bɪgín] VI/VT comenzar, empezar; **the ten dollars won't — to cover the expense** los diez dólares ni siquiera cubren los gastos

beginner [bɪgínɚ] N principiante *mf*

beginning [bɪgínɪŋ] N principio *m*; (temporal only) comienzo *m*; **— with** comenzando con/por; **at the —** al/por el principio

begrudge [bɪgrʌ́ʤ] VT aceptar de mala gana

behalf [bɪhǽf] PREP LOC **in/on — of** (in place of) por, en nombre de; (in favor of) a favor de

behave [bɪhév] VI portarse, comportarse; **— yourself!** ¡pórtate bien!

behavior [bɪhévjɚ] N comportamiento *m*, conducta *f*

behead [bɪhéd] VT decapitar, descabezar

behind [bɪháɪnd] ADV detrás; (in payments,

schedule) atrasado; **he fell — his competitors** quedó a la zaga de sus competidores; **an hour —** una hora de retraso; **from —** desde atrás; **to fall —** atrasarse; **to leave something —** dejar atrás algo; PREP detrás de, tras; **we're all — you** todos te apoyamos; **who's — this evil plot?** ¿quién está detrás de este plan macabro? **— one's back** a espaldas de uno

behold [bɪhóld] VT contemplar; **— the future king!** ¡he aquí el futuro rey!

behoove [bɪhúv] VI corresponderle a uno

beige [beʒ] ADJ & N beige *m*

being [bíɪŋ] N ser *m*; **for the time —** por ahora

Belarus [belərús] N Bielorrusia *f*

belated [bɪléɪtɪd] ADJ atrasado

belch [belʧ] VI eructar, repetir; **to — from** salir de; N eructo *m*

belfry [bélfri] N campanario *m*

Belgian [bélʤən] ADJ & N belga *mf*

Belgium [bélʤəm] N Bélgica *f*

belief [bɪlíf] N creencia *f*; (strong opinion) convicción *f*

believable [bɪlívəbəl] ADJ creíble

believe [bɪlív] VI/VT creer

believer [bɪlívɚ] N creyente *mf*; (proponent) partidario -ria *mf*

belittle [bɪlídl] VT (a person) menospreciar, disminuir; (a situation) minimizar

Belize [bəlíz] N Belice *m*

Belizean [bəlízɪən] ADJ & N beliceño -ña *mf*

bell [bel] N campana *f*; (small) campanilla *f*; **—boy** botones *m sg*; **—flower** campanilla *f*, campánula *f*; **—hop** botones *m sg*; **— jar** campana de cristal *f*; **— pepper** pimiento *m*, morrón *m*; **— tower** campanario *m*; **with all the —s and whistles** con todos los accesorios

bellicose [bélɪkos] ADJ belicoso

belligerent [bəlíʤɚənt] ADJ & N beligerante *mf*

bellow [bélo] VI/VT bramar, berrear; N bramido *m*; **—s** fuelle *m*

belly [béli] N barriga *f*, vientre *m*; **—ache** dolor de barriga *m*; **— button** ombligo *m*; **— dance** danza del vientre *f*; **— laugh** carcajada *f*

belong [bɪlɔ́ŋ] VI (ownership) pertenecer; **this car —s to me** este coche me pertenece; (correspondence) corresponder; **this key —s to this door** esta llave corresponde a esta puerta; (placement) ir; **this —s on the shelf** esto va en el estante

belongings [bɪlɔ́ŋɪŋz] N pertenencias *f pl*

beloved [bɪlávɪd] ADJ querido; N amado -da *mf*

below [bɪló] ADV abajo; **five — (zero)** cinco bajo cero; PREP bajo, debajo de, abajo de

belt [bɛlt] N (for the waist) cinturón *m*, cinto *m*; (for a machine) correa *f*; (region) zona *f*; **— line** cintura *f*; VT pegar; **to — out a song** cantar una canción a voz en cuello

bemoan [bɪmón] VT lamentarse de, quejarse de

bench [bɛntʃ] N banco *m*; (without a back) banqueta *f*; (in sports) banquillo *m*; (in court) estrado *m*; **—mark** (upper limit) cota *f*; (parameter) punto de referencia *m*; **opinion of the —** opinión del tribunal *f*

bend [bɛnd] VI/VT (make curved) doblar(se); (force) someter; **to — over** inclinarse; **to — over backward** desvivirse; **to — the rules** hacer una excepción; N (road) curva *f*, recodo *m*; **—s** enfermedad de los buzos *f*

beneath [bɪníθ] ADV abajo; PREP debajo de, bajo; (in rank) inferior a; **— contempt** totalmente despreciable; **that's — me** no es digno de mí

benediction [bɛnɪdíkʃən] N bendición *f*

benefactor [bɛ́nəfæktɚ] N benefactor -ra *mf*; *lit* bienhechor -ra *mf*

beneficent [bənéfɪsənt] ADJ benéfico

beneficial [bɛnəfíʃəl] ADJ beneficioso

beneficiary [bɛnəfíʃieri] N beneficiario -ria *mf*

benefit [bɛ́nəfɪt] N beneficio *m*; **— performance** función de beneficencia *f*; VI/VT beneficiar(se), sacar provecho; **he —ed by the medicine** le hizo bien la medicina

benevolence [bənévələns] N benevolencia *f*

benevolent [bənévələnt] ADJ benévolo

benign [bɪnáɪn] ADJ benigno

Benin [bɛnín] N Benín *m*

Beninese [bɛnɪníz] ADJ & N beninés -esa *mf*

bent [bɛnt] N inclinación *f*; **to be — on** estar resuelto a

benzine [bɛ́nzin] N bencina *f*

bequeath [bɪkwíð] VT legar, heredar

bequest [bɪkwɛ́st] N legado *m*

berate [bɪrét] VT reprender

bereaved [bɪrívd] ADJ de luto

beret [bəré] N boina *f*

berry [bɛ́ri] N baya *f*

berserk [bɚɹzɝk] ADJ fuera de sí; **he went — se puso hecho una fiera, se enfureció

berth [bɚθ] N litera *f*; **to give a wide — to** mantener una distancia prudencial de

beseech [bɪsítʃ] VT suplicar, rogar

beset [bɪsɛ́t] VT (attack) acosar; (surround) rodear

beside [bɪsáɪd] PREP al lado de; **sit down —**

me siéntate a mi lado; **to be — oneself** estar fuera de sí; **that is — the point** eso no viene al caso; ADV al lado

besides [bɪsáɪdz] ADV además; **they have a table but not much** — tienen una mesa pero poca cosa más; PREP además de, aparte de

besiege [bɪsíʤ] VT (lay siege) sitiar, cercar; (importune) importunar, asediar

best [bɛst] ADJ mejor; **—-case scenario** la mejor situación; **— man** padrino de boda *m*; **— seller** bestseller *m*; **she's the —** ella es la mejor; ADV mejor; **at —** a lo más, en el mejor de los casos; N **the — is still to come** lo mejor está por venir; **to do one's —** hacer lo mejor posible; **to get the — of a person** ganarle a una persona; **to make the — of** sacar el mejor partido de

bestial [bɛ́stʃəl] ADJ bestial

bestow [bɪstó] VT conferir; **to — gifts upon** dar regalos a

bet [bɛt] N apuesta *f*; VI/VT apostar

betray [bɪtré] VT (a person) traicionar; (a secret) revelar; (a feeling) traslucir, delatar; **to — one's ignorance** hacer patente su ignorancia

betrayal [bɪtréəl] N traición *f*

betrayer [bɪtréɚ] N traidor -ra *mf*

betrothal [bɪtróðəl] N compromiso *m*, esponsales *f pl*

better, bettor [bɛ́dɚ] ADJ mejor; **— half** media naranja *f*; **the — part of a year** la mayor parte de un año; ADV mejor; **he lives — than a mile away** vive a más de una milla; **so much the —** tanto mejor; **—-off** en mejor posición económica; **to be — off** estar mejor así; **to change for the —** cambiar para bien; **to get —** mejorar(se), aliviarse; VT mejorar; **to — oneself** mejorarse, mejorar de situación; N **the — of the two** el / la mejor de los dos; **don't contradict your —s** no contradigas a tus superiores

better, bettor [bɛ́dɚ] N apostador -ra *mf*

between [bɪtwín] PREP entre; ADV en medio

bevel [bévəl] N bisel *m*; VT biselar

beverage [bévrɪʤ] N bebida *f*

bevy [bévi] N (of birds, people) bandada *f*; (of deer) manada *f*

beware [bɪwɛ́r] VI cuidarse (de); **— of the dog** cuidado con el perro

bewilder [bɪwíldɚ] VT dejar perplejo, ofuscar, aturdir; **to be —ed** estar perplejo

bewilderment [bɪwíldɚmənt] N perplejidad *f*, aturdimiento *m*

bewitch [bɪwítʃ] VT hechizar, embrujar

beyond [bɪjánd] ADV más allá; PREP más allá de; — **my reach** fuera de mi alcance; N **the great** — el más allá

Bhutan [bután] N Bután m

Bhutanese [butʃníz] ADJ & N butanés -esa mf

bias [báɪəs] N (prejudice) prejuicio m; (in fabric) sesgo m; ADJ sesgado, oblicuo; VT predisponer

bib [bɪb] N babero m; (of an apron) pechera f

Bible [báɪbəl] N Biblia f

biblical [bíblɪkəl] ADJ bíblico

bibliography [bɪblɪágrəfi] N bibliografía f

bicarbonate [baɪkárbənɪt] N bicarbonato m

bicep, biceps [báɪsep(s)] N bíceps m sg

bicker [bíkə] VI reñir

bicycle [báɪsɪkəl] N bicicleta f; VI andar en bicicleta

bid [bɪd] N (in an auction, contest) licitación f, puja f; (in card games) apuesta f; (attempt) tentativa f; VI/VT (offer) ofrecer; (command) mandar; (invite) rogar; (enter a bid in cards) apostar; **to — good-bye** despedirse; **to — up** pujar el precio

bidding [bídɪŋ] N (in auction) puja f; **at someone's** — por orden de alguien; **to do someone's** — cumplir con los deseos de alguien

bide [baɪd] VI/VT **to — one's time** esperar una oportunidad

biennium [baénɪəm] N bienio m

bifurcate [báɪfəket] VI/VT bifurcar(se)

big [bɪg] ADJ grande; — **Bang theory** teoría del Big Bang f; — **brother** hermano mayor m; — **bucks** mucha plata f; — **business** el gran capital; — **deal** asunto importante m; — **deal!** ¡no es para tanto! — **Dipper** Osa Mayor f; —**-headed** cabezón, cabezudo; —**-hearted** magnánimo; — **house** fam gayola f; — **name** personalidad prominente f; — **picture** panorama general m; — **shot** pez gordo m; — **sister** hermana mayor f; —**-ticket** caro; —**-wig** pez gordo m; — **with child** embarazada; **jazz was — in the 1920s** el jazz era popular en los años veinte; **she's a — deal** es una persona importante; **a — problem** un gran problema; ADV —**time** un montón; **she wants to go —time** se muere por ir; **to talk** — jactarse; Am lucirse; **to go over** — tener éxito; **to be — on** ser entusiasta de

bigamy [bígami] N bigamia f

bigot [bígət] N intolerante mf

bigotry [bígətri] N intolerancia f

bike [baɪk] N bici f

biker [báɪkə] N motociclista mf

bikini [bɪkíni] N bikini m

bilateral [baɪlǽtəɫ] ADJ bilateral

bile [baɪl] N (secretion) bilis f; (ill temper) mal genio m; — **duct** conducto biliar m

bilingual [baɪlíŋgwəl] ADJ & N bilingüe mf

bilingualism [baɪlíŋgwəlɪzəm] N bilingüismo m

bill [bɪl] N (statement) factura f; (in a restaurant) cuenta f; (poster) cartel m; (bank note) billete m; (for movies, theater) programa m; (of a bird) pico m; (legislative) proyecto de ley m; —**board** cartelera f; —**fold** cartera f, billetera f; — **of exchange** letra de cambio f; — **of lading** conocimiento de embarque m; — **of rights** declaración de derechos f; — **of sale** escritura de venta f; —**s payable** efectos a pagar m pl; VT cobrar, mandar la factura a

billable [bíləbəl] ADJ facturable

billiards [bíljədz] N billar m

billing [bílɪŋ] N (of theater) orden de importancia en espectáculos m; (business) facturación f

billion [bíljən] NUM mil millones m pl

billow [bílo] N (of smoke) nube f; (of water) ola f; VI ondular, hacer olas

bimbo [bímbo] N gachí f; pej putilla f, pej putón m

bin [bɪn] N (for clothes, food) cajón m, recipiente m; (on an airplane) portaequipajes m sg; (for coal) carbonera f; (for grain) granero m

binary [báɪneri] ADJ binario; — **star** estrella binaria f

bind [baɪnd] VI/VT (unite) unir; (connect) ligar; (tie) atar; (put a cover on a book) encuadernar; (press tightly) apretar; (oblige by contract) obligar

binding [báɪndɪŋ] N (of a book) encuadernación f; (on a rug) ribete m; ADJ obligatorio

binge [bɪndʒ] N (alcoholic) juerga f, parranda f; (food) comilona f; VI (on alcohol) emborracharse; (on food) atiborrarse

bingo [bíŋgo] N bingo m

binoculars [bənákjələz] N gemelos m pl, prismáticos m pl

binomial [baɪnómɪəl] N binomio m; ADJ binomial

biochemistry [baɪokémɪstri] N bioquímica f

biodegradable [baɪodɪgrédəbəl] ADJ biodegradable

bioengineering [baɪoɛndʒɪnírɪŋ] N bioingeniería f

biofeedback [baɪofídbæk] N biofeedback m, retroalimentación biológica f

biography [baɪágrəfi] N biografía f

biology [baɪúlədʒi] N biología f

biopsy [báɪɑpsi] N biopsia f

biorhythm [báɪorɪðəm] N biorritmo m

biotechnology [baɪoteknálədʒi] N biotecnología f

bipartisan [baɪpárɪzən] ADJ bipartidista

bipolar [baɪpólə] ADJ bipolar; — **disorder** trastorno bipolar m

birch [bɜ·tʃ] N abedul m

bird [bɜ·d] N ave f; (small) pájaro m; — **of prey** ave de rapiña f; — **seed** alpiste m; **odd** — persona peculiar f

birth [bɜ·θ] N (act of being born) nacimiento m; (act of giving birth) parto m; (lineage) linaje m; (origin) origen m; — **certificate** certificado de nacimiento m, fe / acta de nacimiento f; — **control** (policy) control de la natalidad m; (devices) anticonceptivos m pl; —**day** cumpleaños m sg; **in his / her** —**day suit** como Dios lo / la trajo al mundo; —**mark** antojo m; —**place** lugar de nacimiento m; —**rate** tasa de natalidad f; —**right** derechos de nacimiento m pl; (of oldest child) primogenitura f; **to give** — dar a luz, parir, alumbrar; **by** — de nacimiento

biscuit [bískɪt] N panecillo m

bisect [báɪsɛkt] VT bisecar

bisexual [baɪsɛkʃuəl] ADJ bisexual

bishop [bíʃəp] N obispo m; (in chess) alfil m

bison [báɪsən] N bisonte m, búfalo m

bit [bɪt] N (small piece) pedacito m, trocito m; (some) poquito m; (of a bridle) bocado m, freno m; (of a drill) broca f, barrena f; (computer) bit m; **I don't care a** — no me importa en absoluto

bitch [bɪtʃ] N (dog) perra f; (woman) *offensive* hija de puta f, cabrona f; (situation) plomazo m; *Sp vulg* coñazo m

bite [baɪt] VI/VT morder; (be duped) dejarse engañar; (insect, fish, snake) picar; **to** — **off** arrancar de un mordisco; N (act, wound) mordedura f, dentellada f; (morsel, small meal) bocado m, bocadito m; (of an insect) picadura f, roncha f

bitter [bíɾə] ADJ (taste) amargo; (cold) glacial; (enemy) acérrimo; —**sweet** dulceamargo, agridulce; **to fight to the** — **end** luchar hasta morir; N —**s** cerveza amarga f

bitterness [bíɾə·nɪs] N (taste) amargor m; (feelings) amargura f; (anger) rencor m, resentimiento m

bizarre [bɪzár] ADJ (event) extraño; (appearance) estrafalario

blab [blæb] VI parlotear; VT descubrir el pastel

black [blæk] ADJ (color, ethnicity) negro; (night) oscuro; —**-and-blue** lleno de moretones, amoratado; — **bean** frijol negro m; —**berry** zarzamora f, mora f; —**bird** mirlo m; —**board** pizarrón m, pizarra f; — **death** peste negra f; — **eye** ojo amoratado / morado m; —**head** espinilla f; — **hole** agujero negro m; —**jack** (weapon) cachiporra f; (card game) black-jack m, veintiuno m; — **magic** magia negra f; —**mail** chantaje m; — **mark** mancha f; — **market** mercado negro m; —**out** apagón m; — **pepper** pimienta negra f; — **pudding** morcilla f; — **sheep** oveja negra f; —**smith** herrero m; —**smith's shop** herrería f, forja f; —**top** asfalto m; — **widow spider** viuda negra f; N negro -a mf; **to put down in** — **and white** poner por escrito; VT —**mail** chantajear; VI **to** — **out** desmayarse

blacken [blǽkən] VT ennegrecer, negrear; VI (sky) oscurecerse

blackness [blǽknɪs] N negrura f

bladder [blǽɾə] N vejiga f

blade [bled] N (of a knife) hoja f; (of grass) brizna f; (of a sword) espada f; (of an oar) pala f, paleta f; (of a propeller) aspa f

blame [blem] VT culpar, echar la culpa a, achacar la culpa a; **to be to** — tener la culpa; N (responsibility) culpa f; (reproof) reproche m

blameless [blémlɪs] ADJ intachable

blanch [blæntʃ] VI palidecer; VT (whiten) blanquear; (scald) escaldar

bland [blænd] ADJ insulso

blank [blæŋk] ADJ (not written on) en blanco; (not recorded on) virgen; (unadorned, expressionless) vacío; (confused) desconcertado; — **cartridge** cartucho de fogueo m; — **check** cheque en blanco m; — **verse** verso libre m; N (place to be filled in on a form) espacio (en blanco) m; (gap) vacío m; VI **to** — **out** quedarse en blanco

blanket [blǽŋkɪt] N manta f, frazada f; *Am* cobija f; ADJ global; VT cubrir

blare [bler] VI hacer un ruido estruendoso; N estruendo m; (of a trumpet) toque m

blaspheme [blæsfím] VI/VT blasfemar (contra)

blasphemy [blǽsfəmi] N blasfemia f

blast [blæst] N (of wind) ráfaga f; (of criticism) lluvia f; (of a trumpet) trompetazo m; (explosive charge) carga f; (explosion) explosión f; — **furnace** alto horno m; —**off** despegue m; **we had a** — lo pasamos bomba; **at full** — a todo volumen; VI/VT (blow horn) pitar, tocar; (shatter) volar; (criticize) criticar duramente; (blow hard) azotar; **to — off** despegar

blatant [blétn̩t] ADJ descarado

blaze [blez] N (flame) llamarada f; (fire) incendio m; (glow) resplandor m; (mark) señal f; **— of anger** arranque de ira m; VI (burn) arder; (shine) resplandecer; **to — a trail** marcar una senda

blazer [bléz>] N blazer m, saco m

bleach [blitʃ] VI/VT (intentional) blanquear(se); (accidental) desteñir(se); N blanqueador m; Sp lejía f

bleachers [blítʃ>z] N gradas f pl

bleak [blik] ADJ (terrain) yermo, desolado; (winter) crudo; (wind) helado; (future) negro

bleary [blíri] ADJ nublado

bleat [blit] N balido m; VI balar

bleed [blid] VI (lose blood) sangrar; (run, as in colors) correrse, desteñir(se); **my heart —s for the poor** los pobres me dan lástima; VT (let blood) desangrar; (extort) extorsionar; (clean brakes) purgar

blemish [blémiʃ] N mancha f, tacha f; VT manchar

blend [blend] VI/VT (intermix) mezclar, entremezclar; (have no separation) fundirse; (harmonize voices) armonizar; N mezcla f

blender [blénd>] N licuadora f

bless [bles] VT bendecir; INTERJ **— you!** ¡salud!

blessed [blésid] ADJ (beatified) beato; (happy) bienaventurado, feliz; **— event** feliz acontecimiento m; **the whole — day** todo el santo día; **not a — drop of rain** ni una bendita gota de agua; [blest] **— with** dotado de

blessing [blésiŋ] N bendición f; **to say the — dar** gracias

blight [blait] N (plant disease) quemadura f, añublo m; (scourge) lacra f; VT (cause to wither) marchitar; (ruin) arruinar

blimp [blimp] N zepelín m

blind [blaind] ADJ ciego; **— alley** callejón sin salida m; **— date** cita a ciegas f; **—fold** venda para los ojos f; **to —fold** vendar los ojos a; **— man's bluff** juego de la gallina ciega m; **— spot** ángulo muerto m; **to fly —** volar a ciegas; **to go —** quedarse ciego; N (shade) persiana f; (hunter's hiding place) escondite m; VT (make blind) cegar; (darken) oscurecer

blinder [bláind>] N anteojera f

blindly [bláindli] ADV a ciegas

blindness [bláindnis] N ceguera f

blink [bliŋk] VI/VT (move eyelids) pestañear, parpadear; (go on and off, as of a light) parpadear; (ignore) pasar por alto; (flee a challenge) rajarse; N parpadeo m, pestañeo m; **on the —** averiado

blip [blip] N (on radar) punto m; (of a movie) interrupción f; (moment) bache m

bliss [blis] N dicha f, felicidad absoluta f

blister [blíst>] N ampolla f; (small) vejiga f; VT sacar ampollas; VI ampollarse

blitz [blits] N ataque relámpago m

blizzard [blíz>d] N ventisca f

bloat [blot] VI hinchar(se), abotagar(se)

blob [blab] N pedazo de algo sin forma m

block [blak] N (piece of stone, cement) bloque m; (piece of wood) trozo de madera m; (toy) cubo m; (sports play) bloqueo m; (length from one street to the next) cuadra f; (square block) manzana f; (obstacle) obstáculo m; (group of tickets) sección f; **—buster** éxito de taquilla m; **—head** tarugo -ga mf, alcornoque m; VT (obstruct) bloquear, tapar; (stop a pass) parar; **to — out** (an essay) esbozar, bosquejar; (the sun) ocultar

blockade [blakéd] N bloqueo m; VT bloquear

blockage [blákidʒ] N obstrucción f

blond [bland] ADJ & N rubio -a mf

blood [blʌd] N sangre f; **—bank** banco de sangre m; **—bath** carnicería f, baño de sangre m; **— count** recuento sanguíneo m; **— group** grupo sanguíneo m; **—hound** sabueso m; **— plasma** plasma sanguíneo m; **— poisoning** septicemia f; **— pressure** presión arterial f; **— relative** pariente consanguíneo mf; **—shed** derramamiento de sangre m; **— vessel** vaso sanguíneo m; **in cold — a** sangre fría; ADJ **—shot** inyectado de sangre; **—thirsty** sanguinario, sangriento

bloody [blʌ́di] ADJ (violent) sangriento; (smeared) ensangrentado

bloom [blum] N (flower) flor f; (flowering) floración f; (youthfulness) lozanía f; (flush) rubor m; **in —** en flor; VI florecer

blooming [blúmiŋ] ADJ (flowering) floreciente; (thriving) lozano

blooper [blúp>] N perla f

blossom [blósəm] N (flower) flor f; (flowering) floración f; VI florecer

blot [blat] N (on paper) mancha f, borrón m; (on honor) tacha f; VI/VT manchar(se), emborronar(se); **to — out** (obscure) borrar, tachar; (obliterate) destruir

blotch [blatʃ] VT borronear, manchar, cubrir con manchas; N mancha f, borrón m

blouse [blaus] N blusa f

blow [blo] VI (wind) soplar; (leaf) volar; (siren) sonar; (horse) resoplar; VT (play a horn) sonar; **to — a fuse** quemar un fusible; **to — away** dejar atónito; **to — down** tirar abajo; **to —-dry** secar con secador; **to — one's nose** sonarse las narices/la nariz; **to — on the soup** soplar la sopa; **to — one's brains out** levantarse la tapa de los sesos; **to — out** reventar(se); **to — over** (knock down) derribar; (dissipate) disiparse; **to — up** (a balloon) inflar, hinchar; (a bridge) volar; N (stroke, shock) golpe m; (wind) tempestad f; (breath) soplo m; — **job** vulg mamada f; **—out** (tire failure) reventón m; (party) fiestón m; **—pipe** cerbatana f; **—torch** soplete m; **—up** (fight) pelea f, riña f; (photo) ampliación f; **to come to —s** irse a las manos

blower [blóə] N (artisan) soplador m; (machine) aventadora f

blue [blu] ADJ azul; (sad) triste, melancólico; (from cold) amoratado; **—bell** campanilla f; **—bird** pájaro azul m; **—blood** sangre azul f; **— book** lista de precios de mercado f; **—chip** de primera línea; **—-collar** de clase obrera; **—jay** arrendajo m; **— jeans** vaqueros m pl; **—print** (of a building) cianotipo m; (of a project) plan m, trazado m; **—-ribbon** distinguido; **— whale** ballena azul f; N azul m; **light —** (azul) celeste m; **the —s** (sadness) melancolía f, murria f; (genre of music) blues m pl; VI ponerse azul, azulear; VT azular, teñir de azul; **to —print** trazar

bluff [blʌf] N (cliff) acantilado m, risco m; (false boast) bluff m; (in poker) farol m; VT hacer un bluff; **to call a —** poner en evidencia

bluffer [blʌfə] N bluff m

bluing [blúɪŋ] N añil m

bluish [blúɪʃ] ADJ azulado

blunder [blʌndə] N disparate m, patochada f; VI meter la pata; **to — upon/into** tropezar con

blunt [blʌnt] ADJ (not sharp) romo; (frank) directo, franco; VT despuntar

blur [blɚ] VT (to obscure) emborronar, desvanecer; (to make vision blurry) nublar; VI empañarse, nublarse; N (indistinct sight) mancha f; **it's a — in my mind** sólo tengo un recuerdo vago de eso

blurry [blɚ-i] ADJ borroso

blurt [blɚt] VT **to — (out)** espetar

blush [blʌʃ] VI sonrojarse, ponerse colorado, ruborizarse; N (act of blushing) sonrojo m; (effect of blushing) rubor m; **at first —** a primera vista

bluster [blʌstə] VI (blow hard) soplar fuerte, rugir; (boast) fanfarronear; N (noise) ventarrón m; (attitude) fanfarronería f

blustering [blʌstəɪŋ] ADJ fanfarrón, jactancioso; **— wind** ventarrón m

boa constrictor [bóəkənstríktə] N boa f

boar [bɔr] N jabalí m

board [bɔrd] N (wood) tabla f, listón m; (game) tablero m; (of directors) directorio m, mesa f; (for bulletins) cartelera f; **—ing school** pensionado m, internado m; **—inghouse** pensión f; **— of trustees** patronato m; **—room** sala de directorio f; **on — a** bordo; **to go by the —** irse por la borda; VI (lodge) alojarse; **to — up** tapiar, cerrar con tablas; VT (boat, plane, train) abordar; (provide lodging) alojar

boarder [bórdə] N pensionista mf

boast [bost] N alarde m; VI jactarse, vanagloriarse, blasonar; VT **the town —s two new schools** el pueblo ostenta dos escuelas nuevas

boastful [bóstfəl] ADJ jactancioso, vanaglorioso

boastfulness [bóstfəlnɪs] N jactancia f, vanagloria f

boat [bot] N (any water vessel) embarcación f; (open and small) bote m, lancha f; (closed, larger) barco m; **—house** cobertizo para botes m; **—man** barquero m, botero m

boating [bóɪŋ] N navegación f; **to go —** navegar

bob [bab] N (of horsetail) cola cortada f; (of the head) sacudida f; (haircut) melena corta f; (of a pendulum) pesa f, plomada f; **—tail** rabón m; VI sacudirse; (a ship) cabecear; VT **to — one's hair** cortarse el pelo en melena

bobbin [bábɪn] N carrete m, bobina f

bobcat [bábkæt] N lince rojo m

bode [bod] VI **that doesn't — well** eso no augura nada bueno

bodice [bádɪs] N corpiño m

bodily [bádli] ADJ corporal; **— harm** daño físico m

body [bádi] N (of a person, animal, wine, fabric) cuerpo m; (torso) tronco m; (corpse) cadáver m; (of a text, army, etc.) parte principal f; (of water) masa f; (of a car) carrocería f; (of an airplane) fuselaje m; **— bag** bolsa para cadáveres f; **—-building** culturismo m; **— count** número de muertos m; **—guard** guardaespaldas m sg; **— language**

lenguaje corporal m; — **temperature** temperatura f; **to —search** cachear; — **shop** taller de carrocería m

bog [bag] N pantano m; VI hundir(se); **to get —ged down** atascarse

bogeyman [búgimæn] N coco m; RP cuco m

bogus [bógəs] ADJ falso

Bohemian [bohímiən] ADJ & N bohemio -a mf

boil [bɔɪl] VI/VT (water) hervir; (eggs) cocer; (ocean) bullir; (angry person) echar chispas; **to — down** reducirse a; **to — over** derramarse; **—ing point** punto de ebullición m; N (inflammation) forúnculo m, divieso m; (act of boiling) hervor m; **to come to a** — soltar / romper el hervor

boiler [bɔ́ɪlə] N caldera f

boisterous [bɔ́ɪstə-əs] ADJ bullicioso

bold [bold] ADJ (not fearful) atrevido, osado; (unconventional) audaz; (visually striking) llamativo; **—faced** descarado; **—face type** negrita f

boldness [bóldnɪs] N (courage) atrevimiento m, osadía f, arrojo m; (unconventional attitude) audacia f

Bolivia [bəlívia] N Bolivia f

Bolivian [bəlívian] ADJ & N boliviano -na mf

bolster [bólstə] N cojín cilíndrico m; VT reforzar; **to — someone's courage** alentar a alguien

bolt [bolt] N (door lock) pestillo m, cerrojo m; (crossbar) aldaba f; (pin) perno m, tornillo grande m; (of cloth) rollo m; **it came as a — from the blue** cayó como bomba; VT (fasten) atornillar; (lock door) cerrar con tranca, atrancar; (devour) engullir; (break with) romper con; VI echarse a correr

bomb [bam] N bomba f; **—shell** bomba f; **—shelter** refugio antiaéreo m; VT (attack with bombs) bombardear; VI (fail) fracasar

bombard [bambárd] VT bombardear

bombardier [bambə-dír] N bombardero -ra mf

bombardment [bambárdmənt] N bombardeo m

bombastic [bambǽstɪk] ADJ grandilocuente, ampuloso

bomber [bámə-] N bombardero m, avión de bombardeo m

bona fide [bónəfaɪd] ADJ genuino; **— offer** oferta seria f

bonbon [bánban] N caramelo m; (chocolate) bombón m

bond [band] N (tie) lazo m; (fetter) cadenas f pl; (financial instrument) bono m, obligación f; (adhesion) adherencia f;

(chemical) enlace m; VI/VT (stick to) adherirse; (connect) establecer vínculos

bondage [bándɪdʒ] N (slavery) servidumbre f, esclavitud f; (sexual practice) prácticas sadomasoquistas f pl

bonding [bándɪŋ] N (mother-child) lazos afectivos m pl; (male) compenetración f

bondsman [bándzmən] N fiador -ra mf

bone [bon] N hueso m; (of fish) espina f; **— china** porcelana fina f; **—head** estúpido -da mf; **—yard** cementerio m; **— of contention** manzana de discordia f; **to make no —s about it** no andarse con rodeos; VT deshuesar; (fish) quitar las espinas; **to — up on something** estudiar algo

bonfire [bánfaɪr] N hoguera f, fogata f

bonnet [bánɪt] N gorro m

bonus [bónəs] N (extra salary) gratificación f, prima f; (at Christmas) aguinaldo m

bony [bóni] ADJ (with large bones) huesudo; (made of bones) óseo

boo [bu] VI/VT abuchear, rechiflar; INTERJ ¡bu! N rechifla f, abucheo m

boob [bub] N fam teta f; Am fam chiche m; Mex fam chichi f; RP fam lola f

boo-boo [búbu] N lastimadura f; Sp fam pupa f; Am nana f; **to make a** — meter la pata

booby [búbi] N (fool) bobo -a mf; (bird) bobo m; **— hatch** fam loquería f; **— prize** premio al peor competidor m; **— trap** trampa explosiva f

book [bʊk] N libro m; **—binding** encuadernación f; **—case** estante m, estantería f, biblioteca f; **—end** sujetalibros m sg; **—keeper** tenedor -ra de libros mf; Sp contable mf; **—keeping** teneduría de libros f, contabilidad f; **—mark** marcador de libros m; **—mobile** biblioteca móvil f; **— review** reseña f; **—seller** librero -ra mf; **—shelf** estante m; **—store** librería f; **— value** valor contable m; **by the** — según las reglas; **on the —s** registrado en los libros; **to keep —s** llevar los libros; VT (reserve) reservar; (hire) contratar; (record charges against) fichar

bookish [bʊkɪʃ] ADJ (person) estudioso; (allusion) libresco

booklet [bʊklɪt] N cartilla f

boom [bum] VI (resound) resonar; (prosper) prosperar; N (noise) explosión f; (increase) auge m

boon [bun] N (blessing) bendición f; (favor) favor m

boondocks [búndaks] ADV LOC **(out) in the — fam** en los quintos infiernos, en el quinto pino

boondoggle [búndɑgəł] N despilfarro *m*

boor [bur] N patán -ana *mf*

boorish [búrʃ] ADJ grosero, zafio

boost [bust] VT (to shove) empujar (desde abajo o detrás); (to promote) estimular, impulsar; N (shove) empujón (desde abajo) *m*; (aid) estímulo *m*, impulso *m*; — **in prices** alza de precios *f*

booster [bústɚ] N (person) animador -ra *mf*; (rocket) acelerador *m*; (electronic device) amplificador *m*; (vaccination) refuerzo *m*

boot [but] N (shoe) bota *f*; (trunk of a car) cajuela *f*; (clamp for cars) cepo *m*; —**black** limpiabotas *m sg*; —**legger** contrabandista de licores *m*; —**licker** *vulg* lameculos *mf*; **to — por** añadidura; **to give the —** poner de patitas en la calle; VT dar una patada a; **to — (out)** echar a patadas

booth [buθ] N (telephone) cabina *f*; (stand) puesto *m*; (ticket) taquilla *f*

booty [búti] N botín *m*

booze [buz] N *fam* bebercio *m*, bebida alcohólica *f*

borax [bóræks] N bórax *m*

border [bórdɚ] N (line between countries) frontera *f*; (edge, brink) borde *m*; (bed of flowers) ariete *m*; (design) ribete *m*; —**line** (on a border) fronterizo; (not up to standards) dudoso; VI/VT (make a design) ribetear; **to — on** colindar con; **it —s on madness** raya en la locura

bordering [bórdɚŋ] ADJ limítrofe

bore [bor] N (hole) agujero *m*; (of a gun, cylinder) calibre *m*; (uninteresting person) aburrido -da *mf*, pesado -da *mf*; (uninteresting thing) lata *f*; VT (make a hole) taladrar, horadar; (fail to interest) aburrir; **to — a hole** hacer un agujero

bored [bord] ADJ aburrido; **I'm —** estoy aburrido

boredom [bórdəm] N aburrimiento *m*, tedio *m*

boric acid [bórk ǽsd] N ácido bórico *m*

boring [bórŋ] ADJ aburrido; **he's —** es aburrido

born [born] ADJ nacido; **he's a — dancer** es un bailarín nato; **she's a — liar** es una mentirosa de nacimiento; **to be —** nacer

boron [bóran] N boro *m*

borrow [báro] VT pedir prestado; **I —ed money from Fred** le pedí dinero prestado a Fred; **may I — your car?** ¿me prestas tu coche? **I —ed these books from the library** saqué estos libros de la biblioteca

borrower [bároɚ] N (money) prestatario -ria *mf*; (books) usuario -ria *mf*

Bosnia and Herzegovina [bázniæændhɚrtsəgəvínə] N Bosnia-Herzegovina *f*

Bosnian [báznian] ADJ & N bosnio -nia *mf*

bosom [búzəm] N pecho *m*, seno *m*; **in the — of the family** en el seno de la familia; **— buddy** amigo -ga íntimo -ma *mf*

boss [bɔs] N jefe -fa *mf*; (on a plantation) mayoral *m*, capataz *m*; (political) dirigente *m*; (mafia) capo *m*; VT **to — around** mandonear

bossy [bósi] ADJ mandón

botanical [bətǽnıkəł] ADJ botánico

botany [bátni] N botánica *f*

botch [bátʃ] VT chapucear, estropear; N chapucería *f*, chapuza *f*

both [boθ] ADJ & PRON ambos, los dos

bother [báðɚ] VT molestar, fastidiar; VI molestarse, tomarse la molestia; N molestia *f*

bothersome [báðɚsəm] ADJ (activity) molesto, enojoso; (person) enfadoso, molesto

Botswana [batswánə] N Botsuana *f*

bottle [bádł] N botella *f*; (for medicine, perfume) frasco *m*; —**neck** atascadero *m*, embotellamiento *m*; — **top** chapa de botella *f*; VT embotellar; **to — up** atascar, embotellar

bottom [bádəm] N (of a hole) fondo *m*; (of a hall, pile, page, bed) pie *m*; (lower part) base *f*, parte de abajo *f*; (buttocks) trasero *m*; **to be at the — of the class** ser el último de la clase; **to hit —** tocar fondo; **to — out** tocar fondo; **who is at the — of all this?** ¿quién está detrás de todo esto? ADJ de abajo; — **line** (business) balance final *m*; (essential element) lo esencial

bottomless [bádəmlıs] ADJ sin fondo; — **supply** recursos ilimitados *m pl*; — **accusation** acusación infundada *f*; **he's a — pit** es un barril sin fondo

boudoir [búdwar] N tocador *m*

bough [baʊ] N rama *f*

bouillon [búljan] N caldo *m*

boulder [bółdɚ] N peña *f*, pedrusco *m*

boulevard [búləvard] N bulevar *m*

bounce [baʊns] N (of a ball) bote *m*, rebote *m*; (vitality) vitalidad *f*; VT echar, botar; **to — a check** rebotar un cheque; VI rebotar; **to — back** recuperarse

bouncer [baʊnsɚ] N gorila *m*

bound [baʊnd] N (jump) salto *m*; —**s** límite *m*, confín *m*; ADJ (tied up) atado; (confined) confinado; (obliged) obligado;

(as a book) encuadernado; **to be — for** ir
rumbo a; **to be — up in one's work**
estar absorto en su trabajo; **it is — to
happen** es seguro que pasará; **I am — to
do it** estoy resuelto a hacerlo; vi (jump)
saltar; (be contiguous) lindar

boundary [báundri] n (of a country, city)
límite m, término m; (of a property) linde
mf, lindero m

boundless [báundlɪs] adj ilimitado, sin
límites

bountiful [báuntɨfɨl] adj abundante

bounty [báunti] n (abundance) abundancia f;
(reward) recompensa f

bouquet [buké] n (flowers) ramo m; (small)
ramillete m; (of wine) aroma m, bouquet
m

bourgeois [burʒwá] adj & n burgués -sa mf

bout [baut] n encuentro m; **a — of flu** una
gripe

boutique [butík] n boutique f

bow [bau] n (gesture) reverencia f; (prow)
proa f; vi (bend at the waist) hacer una
reverencia; (yield) someterse; **to — out**
retirarse; vt inclinar; [bo] n (for arrows,
violin) arco m; (curve) curva f;
(decoration) moño m; **—knot** lazada f;
—-legged patizambo; **—-string** cuerda
de arco f; vi/vt (bend) arquear(se); (play
with a bow) tocar con arco

bowel [báuɨl] n **—s** intestinos m pl; **—s of
the earth** entrañas de la tierra f pl; **—
movement** evacuación del vientre f

bower [báuɚ] n enramada f

bowl [boɫ] n (container) bol m, tazón m;
(dish) plato hondo m; (depression) cuenco
m; (of a toilet) taza f; (of a pipe) cazoleta f;
vt **to — over** apabullar, deslumbrar

bowling [bólɪŋ] n boliche m, bowling m;
let's go — vamos al boliche; **— alley**
boliche m, bolera f

box [baks] n caja f; (for jewelry) estuche m;
(in the theater) palco de teatro m; (for the
jury) tribuna f; (on a page) cuadro m; **—
car** vagón de carga m; **— office** taquilla f;
— seat asiento de palco m; vt (put in a
box) meter en una caja; (hit) abofetear;
(engage in sport) boxear

boxer [báksɚ] n boxeador -ra mf, pugilista
mf; (breed of dog) bóxer m; **— shorts**
calzoncillo m

boxing [báksɪŋ] n boxeo m, pugilato m; **—
glove** guante de boxeo m; **— ring** ring
m, cuadrilátero m

boy [bɔɪ] n (baby) niño m; (young man)
muchacho m, chico m; **— scout** boy
scout m; **—friend** novio m

boycott [bóɪkat] vt boicotear; n boicoteo m,
boicot m

boyhood [bóɪhud] n niñez f, juventud f

boyish [bóɪʃ] adj de muchacho

brace [bres] n (in construction) tirante m;
(pair) par m; (printed character) corchete
m; (of a carpenter) berbiquí m; **—s** (for
teeth) aparato ortodóntico m; (for a leg)
aparato ortopédico m; vt (against a shock)
agarrarse; (support) asegurar; (with
alcohol) animarse

bracelet [bréslɪt] n brazalete m, pulsera f

bracket [brǽkɪt] n (support) soporte m,
sostén m; (typographic sign) paréntesis
recto m, corchete m; (division) banda f; vt
(fix with brackets) fijar con soportes;
(write in brackets) colocar entre paréntesis
rectos; (associate) agrupar

brag [bræg] vi jactarse (de), hacer alarde (de)

braggart [brǽgɚt] adj & n fanfarrón -na mf

braid [bred] n trenza f; vt trenzar

brain [bren] n cerebro m; (food) seso m; **she
blew out his —s** le levantó la tapa de los
sesos; **he's short on —s** es corto de
inteligencia; **he is the —s in this
operation** él es el cerebro en esta
operación; **to rack one's —s** devanarse
los sesos, romperse la cabeza; **— drain**
fuga de cerebros f; **— trust** grupo de
expertos m; **—storming** brainstorming m;
vt **to — someone** romperle la crisma a
alguien; **to —wash** lavarle el cerebro a;
—-dead clínicamente muerto, en estado
vegetativo

brainy [bréni] adj sesudo

brake [brek] n freno m; **— drum** tambor del
freno m; **— fluid** líquido para frenos m;
—man guardafrenos m sg; **— shoe** zapata
f; **to apply the —s** frenar; vi/vt frenar

bramble [brǽmbɨl] n zarza f

bran [bræn] n salvado m; (for birds) afrecho
m

branch [bræntʃ] n (of a plant, of a family)
rama f; (of a train) ramal m; (of antlers)
brazo m; (of a science) ramo m; (of a
business) sucursal f; (of the armed forces)
arma f; (in a computer program)
bifurcación f; (of a river) tributario m; vi/
vt ramificar(se)

brand [brænd] n (make, mark) marca f; (of
humor, etc.) tipo m; (mark of disgrace)
estigma m; **— name** marca f; **—-new**
flamante, recién comprado; vt (burn)
herrar, marcar; (stigmatize) estigmatizar;
to — as tildar de, tachar de

brandish [brǽndɪʃ] vt blandir, esgrimir

brandy [brǽndi] n (fine) brandy m; (cheap)

aguardiente m

brash [bræʃ] ADJ (impudent) descarado; (impetuous) impetuoso

brass [bræs] N (metal) latón m; (attitude) descaro m; (high-ranking officers) la plana mayor; — **instrument** instrumento de metal m; **to get down to — tacks** ir al grano; ADJ de latón

brassiere [brəzír] N sostén m

brat [bræt] N mocoso -sa mf

bravado [brəvÁDo] N alarde m

brave [brev] ADJ valiente, gallardo; N guerrero indio m; VT desafiar

bravery [brévəri] N valentía f, gallardía f

brawl [brɔl] N reyerta f, riña f, pelotera f; VI reñir

bray [bre] N rebuzno m; VI rebuznar

brazen [brézən] ADJ (impudent) descarado; (made of brass) de latón

brazier [bréʒə] N brasero m

Brazil [brəzíl] N Brasil m

Brazilian [brəzíljən] ADJ & N brasileño -ña mf, brasilero -ra mf

breach [britʃ] N (opening) brecha f; (infraction) infracción f; (severance) ruptura f; — **of contract** incumplimiento de contrato m; — **of faith** abuso de confianza m; VT abrir una brecha; (violate a law) violar, infringir

bread [brɛd] N pan m; — **basket** panera f; — **box** panera f; —**winner** sostén de la familia m; ADJ —**-and-butter** básico; VT empanar

breadth [brɛdθ] N anchura f, ancho m; (size) extensión f; (perspective) amplitud f

break [brek] VI (fracture) romperse; (pause) parar; VT (a record) batir; (a code) descifrar; (a law) violar; (news) dar, divulgar; (a bone) fracturar; (a horse) domar, desbravar; (a habit) quitar(se) (una costumbre); (one's spirit) quebrar, doblegar; (cause to go bankrupt) arruinar; **to — a promise** romper una promesa, faltar a la palabra; **to — a ten-dollar bill** conseguir cambio para un billete de diez dólares; **to — away** escaparse; **to — down** (a person) descomponerse; (a car) averiarse; (resistance) vencer; (continuity) interrumpir; **to — even** quedar a mano; **to — into** violentar; **to — loose** liberarse; **to — out** (war) estallar; (one's face) brotarse; (from prison) escaparse; **to — up** (into pieces) quebrarse; (a relationship) romper con; — **in** hurto con escalo m; —**down** (analysis) análisis m; (automotive) avería f; —**through** adelanto m; (military) penetración f;

—**water** rompeolas m sg; N (weather) cambio m; (from work) descanso m; (with tradition) quiebre m, rompimiento m; (of a bone) fractura f; (from prison) fuga f; (opportunity) oportunidad f; **give me a** —! vulg ¡déjate de joder! **lucky** — golpe de suerte m

breakable [brékəbəl] ADJ quebradizo, rompible

breaker [brékə] N rompiente f

breakfast [brékfəst] N desayuno m; VI desayunar

breast [brɛst] N seno m, pecho m; fam teta f; (bird) pechuga f; — **cancer** cáncer de mama m; —**stroke** (estilo) pecho m; VI/VT **to —-feed** amamantar, dar de mamar

breath [brɛθ] N aliento m; lit hálito m; (current of air) soplo m; —**taking** impresionante; **in the same** — al mismo tiempo; **out of** — sin aliento; **to catch one's** — recobrar el aliento; **to hold one's** — aguantar la respiración; **to take a** — inhalar; **to take a deep** — respirar hondo; **under one's** — entre dientes, por lo bajo

breathe [brið] VI/VT respirar; **to — in** inspirar, aspirar; **to — into** infundir; **to — out** exhalar, espirar; **he did not — a word** no dijo palabra

breathing [bríðɪŋ] N respiración f

breathless [brɛθlɪs] ADJ sin aliento

breed [brid] VT (mate) criar; (bring up) educar; (give rise to) engendrar; VI reproducirse, multiplicarse; N (species) raza f; (type) clase f

breeder [brídə] N (person who breeds) criador -ra mf; (animal used for breeding) (animal) reproductor m

breeding [brídɪŋ] N (of animals) cría f; (people) educación f, modales m pl

breeze [briz] N brisa f

breezy [brízi] ADJ (windy) ventoso; (jaunty) ameno

brevity [brévɪDi] N brevedad f

brew [bru] VT (coffee) hacer; (mischief) fomentar, tramar; (beer) fabricar; VI (storm) armarse una tormenta; **let the tea** — deja reposar el té; N (mixture) mezcla f; (beer) cerveza f

brewery [brúəri] N cervecera f, fábrica de cerveza f

briar [bráɚ] N zarza f

bribe [braɪb] N soborno m, cohecho m; Mex mordida f; VT sobornar

bribery [bráɪbəri] N soborno m

brick [brɪk] N ladrillo m; —**bat** (piece of brick) pedazo de ladrillo m; (insult) insulto

m; —**layer** albañil *m;* —**laying**
albañilería *f;* VT (adorn with bricks)
revestir de ladrillo; (pave with bricks)
enladrillar
bridal [bráɪdl] ADJ nupcial; — **dress** vestido
de novia *m*
bride [braɪd] N novia *f;* —**groom** novio *m;*
—**smaid** dama de honor *f*
bridge [brɪdʒ] N puente *m;* (of the nose)
caballete *m;* (card game) bridge *m;* VT
tender un puente sobre; **to — a gap**
llenar un vacío, salvar un obstáculo
bridle [bráɪdl] N (harness) brida *f;* (restraint)
freno *m;* VT (put on a bridle) embridar;
(restrain) frenar; VI (be insulted) ofenderse
brief [brif] ADJ (short) breve, escueto;
(concise) conciso, escueto; (curt) seco; N
sumario *m,* resumen *m;* (report)
expediente *m;* —**case** portafolio(s) *m sg,*
maletín *m;* —**s** calzoncillos *m pl;* **in —** en
suma; VT informar
briefing [brífɪŋ] N reunión para dar
instrucciones *f*
brigade [brɪgéd] N brigada *f*
bright [braɪt] ADJ (shining) brillante; (full
with light) iluminado; (smart) inteligente;
(future) venturoso, prometedor; (smile)
radiante; (color) subido
brighten [bráɪtn] VT (a room) iluminar; VI **to
— up** (become cheerful) animar(se); (sky)
despejarse
brightness [bráɪtnɪs] N (light) claridad *f;*
(cheerfulness) viveza *f;* (intelligence)
inteligencia *f*
brilliance [bríljəns] N (of hair, of a historical
period) brillantez *f;* (intelligence) genio *m*
brilliant [bríljənt] ADJ (shining) brillante;
(intelligent) genial; (splendid) espléndido;
N brillante *m,* diamante *m*
brim [brɪm] N borde *m;* (hat) ala *f;* **to fill to
the —** llenar hasta el borde; **to be filled
to the —** estar de bote en bote; **to be
—ming with** estar rebosante de; VI **to —
over** rebosar
brine [braɪn] N salmuera *f*
bring [brɪŋ] VT traer; (cause) ocasionar,
causar; **to — about** producir, ocasionar;
to — down (kill) bajar; (depress)
deprimir; **to — forth** (give birth) dar a
luz; (produce) producir; **to — to a stop**
parar; **to — together** reunir, juntar; **—
oneself to do something** poder hacer
algo; **to — a good price** redituar una
buena ganancia; **to — up** (raise children)
criar, educar; (mention) mencionar
brink [brɪŋk] N borde *m;* **on the — of** al
borde de

brisk [brɪsk] ADJ (walk) rápido; (weather)
fresco; (trading) activo
bristle [brɪsəl] N cerda *f;* VI erizar(se); **to —
with** estar erizado de
bristly [brísli] ADJ (with bristles) erizado,
cerdoso; (irascible) irascible
Britain [brítn] N Gran Bretaña *f*
British [brídɪʃ] ADJ británico
brittle [brídl] ADJ quebradizo, frágil
brittleness [brídnɪs] N fragilidad *f*
broach [brotʃ] VT sacar a colación
broad [brɔd] ADJ (wide) ancho; (vast) vasto;
(ample) amplio; —**cast** emisión *f;* —**cast
station** emisora *f;* —**casting** (radio)
radiodifusión *f;* (TV) transmisión por
televisión *f;* **to —cast** (communicate
electronically) transmitir, emitir, radiar; —
hint insinuación clara *f;* — **jump** salto
de longitud *m;* —**minded** tolerante;
—**side** andanada *f;* **in — daylight** en
pleno día; N *pej* tipa *f*
brocade [brokéd] N brocado *m*
broccoli [brákəli] N brócoli *m,* brécol *m*
brochure [broʃúr] N folleto *m*
broil [brɔɪl] VI/VT asar(se) (a la parrilla)
broiler [brɔ́ɪlɚ] N (oven) parrilla *f;* (chicken)
pollo (para asar) *m*
broke [brok] ADJ **to be —** estar limpio, estar
pelado; **to go —** irse a la quiebra
broken [brókən] ADJ (fragmented) roto,
quebrado; (tamed) domado; (not
functioning) descompuesto; (not
continuous) interrumpido; —**-down**
averiado, descompuesto; — **English**
inglés chapurrado/chapurreado *m;*
—**hearted** deshecho, con el corazón
destrozado
broker [brókɚ] N (intermediary) agente *mf;*
(stock salesman) corredor -ra de bolsa *mf*
brokerage [brókɚɪdʒ] N agencia de
corredores de bolsa *f*
bromide [brómaɪd] N bromuro *m*
bromine [brómin] N bromo *m*
bronchial [bránkiəl] ADJ bronquial; — **tube**
bronquio *m*
bronchitis [braŋkáɪdɪs] N bronquitis *f*
bronco [bráŋko] N caballo no domado *m*
bronze [branz] N bronce *m;* VT broncear
brooch [brutʃ] N broche *m,* prendedor *m*
brood [brud] N pollada *f,* nidada *f;* VI/VT
empollar; **to — over** rumiar
brook [bruk] N riachuelo *m,* cañada *f;* VT
tolerar
broom [brum] N (tool) escoba *f;* (plant)
retama *f;* —**stick** palo de escoba *m*
broth [brɔθ] N caldo *m*
brothel [bráθəl] N burdel *m*

brother [bráðɚ] N hermano m; —-**in-law** cuñado m; **Oh —!** ¡caray!

brotherhood [bráðɚhʊd] N hermandad f

brotherly [bráðɚli] ADJ fraternal

brow [braʊ] N (ridge of eye) arco superciliar m; (eyebrow) ceja f; (forehead) frente f

brown [braʊn] ADJ (skin) moreno; (eyes, shoes, clothes) café, marrón; (hair) castaño; (dun) pardo; (tanned) bronceado; VI/VT dorar(se); **to —-nose** vulg lamer culos; —-**noser** vulg lameculos mf pl, adulón -ona mf; N (color) café m, castaño m, moreno m, pardo m; — **bear** oso pardo m; — **rice** arroz integral m; — **sugar** azúcar moreno -na mf

brownie [bráʊni] N bizcocho de chocolate m

browse [braʊz] VT (leaf through) hojear; VI (graze) pacer, pastar; (surf the web) Sp navegar (la web); Am navegar (en la red)

browser [bráʊzɚ] N navegador m

bruise [bruz] N (skin) moretón m, cardenal m, contusión f; (fruit) magulladura f, cardenal m; VI/VT magullar(se), machucar(se)

brunch [brʌntʃ] N brunch m, desayuno tardío m

Brunei [brunái] N Brunéi m

Bruneian [brunáiən] ADJ & N bruneano -na mf

brunet, brunette [brunét] ADJ & N moreno -na mf, morocho -cha mf; Cuba trigueño -ña mf

brunt [brʌnt] N impacto m

brush [brʌʃ] N (tooth, clothes) cepillo m; (paint, shaving) brocha f; (artist's) pincel m; (vegetation) maleza f; (contact) roce m; —-**off** despedida brusca f; —-**wood** (dead) broza f; (live) maleza f; VT (clean with a brush) cepillar; (touch lightly) rozar; **to — aside** echar a un lado; **to — up on** repasar; **to — off** (clean) quitar con cepillo; (reject) despedir bruscamente a alguien

brusque [brʌsk] ADJ brusco

Brussels sprouts [brásəlsprauts] N coles de Bruselas f pl, repollitos de Bruselas m pl

brutal [brúdl] ADJ brutal

brutality [brutǽlɪɾi] N brutalidad f

brute [brut] N (animal) bestia f; (person) bruto -ta mf; ADJ bruto

bubble [bʌ́bl] N burbuja f; (in soap) pompa f; (in boiling water) borbollón m; (illusion) encanto m; — **bath** baño de burbujas m; —**gum** chicle de globo m; VI (make bubbles) borbotar, borbollar; (boil) bullir, hervir; **to — over with joy** rebosar de alegría

bubonic plague [bubánɪkplég] N plaga bubónica f

buck [bʌk] N (goat) macho cabrío m; (deer) gamo m; (male of other animals) macho m; (leap of horse) respingo m; — **private** soldado raso m; —**shot** posta f, perdigón m; —**skin** gamuza f; —**toothed** de dientes salidos; —**wheat** trigo sarraceno m; **to pass the —** echarle el muerto a uno; VI (horse) respingar, corcovear; **to — a trend** oponerse; **to — up** cobrar ánimo

bucket [bʌ́kɪt] N cubo m, balde m; (of a loader) cuchara f; — **seat** asiento delantero individual m

buckle [bʌ́kl] N (clasp) hebilla f; (kink in a board) torcedura f; VT (to clasp) abrocharse; (to bend) torcerse, pandearse; **to — down** esforzarse; **to — up** abrocharse

bud [bʌd] N botón m, retoño m; VI (make buds) echar retoños

buddy [bʌ́di] N camarada mf

budge [bʌ́dʒ] VI moverse

budget [bʌ́dʒɪt] N presupuesto m; VT (money) presupuestar; (time, personal resources) administrar

buff [bʌf] N (leather) gamuza f; (tan color) color beige m; (wheel for polishing) pulidor m; (devotee) aficionado m; **in the —** en cueros; ADJ (beige) de color beige; (muscular) musculoso; VT pulir

buffalo [bʌ́falo] N bisonte m, búfalo m; — **wings** alitas f pl

buffer [bʌ́fɚ] N (in a computer) memoria intermedia f; (shock absorber) amortiguador m; (polishing device) pulidor -ra mf; — **zone** zona tampón f

buffet [bʌfít] N (blow) golpe m, puñetazo m; (shock) azote m; VT (hit) golpear; (hit repeatedly) azotar; [bəfé] N (cabinet) aparador m; (meal) buffet m

buffoon [bəfún] N payaso -a mf, bufón -ona mf

bug [bʌg] N bicho m; (disease-causing) microbio m, virus m; (for eavesdropping) micrófono oculto m; (in a computer program) fallo m, bicho m; VT (bother) molestar; (install microphones) colocar micrófonos ocultos; **his eyes —ged out** se le saltaron los ojos

buggy [bʌ́gi] N (cart) calesa f; (baby carriage) cochecillo m

bugle [bjúgəl] N clarín m; VI tocar el clarín

build [bɪld] VT (construct) construir, edificar; (manufacture) fabricar; **to — into** incorporar; **to — up** (make stronger) fortalecer; (accumulate) acumular;

(enhance) desarrollar; (urbanize) urbanizar; —**-up** (of military forces) concentración f; (of substance) acumulación f; (of anticipation) aumento m; N (of human body) complexión f

builder [bíldə] N contratista mf

building [bíldɪŋ] N (thing built) edificio m, construcción f, edificación f; (act of building) construcción f, edificación f; (unit in a housing complex) bloque m; — **block** (solid mass) bloque (de construcción) m; (toy) cubo m; (essential element) elemento fundamental m

built [bɪlt] ADJ —**in** (furniture appliance) empotrado; (feature) incorporado; —**-up** urbanizado

bulb [bʌlb] N (plant) bulbo m; (light) bombilla f; Am foco m

bulbous [bʌ́lbəs] ADJ bulboso

Bulgaria [bʌlgériə] N Bulgaria f

Bulgarian [bʌlgériən] ADJ & N búlgaro -ra mf

bulge [bʌldʒ] N bulto m, protuberancia f; VI abultar, hincharse

bulgy [bʌ́ldʒi] ADJ abultado

bulk [bʌlk] N (mass) cantidad f, volumen m; (greater part) mayor parte f; **in** — a granel; VI **to** — **up** echar músculos

bulky [bʌ́lki] ADJ voluminoso

bull [bʊl] N toro m; —**dog** buldog m; —**dozer** bulldozer m; —**fight** corrida de toros f; —**fighter** torero m; —**fighting** tauromaquia f; —**frog** rana grande f; — **market** mercado alcista m; —**shit** disparates m pl, mentiras f pl; **that's** —**shit** y una polla (como una olla); —**'s eye** diana f; **to hit the** —**'s-eye** dar en el blanco; ADJ —**headed** terco, obstinado

bullet [bʊ́lɪt] N bala f; ADJ —**proof** antibalas inv

bulletin [bʊ́lɪtn̩] N boletín m; — **board** tablero m, cartelera f

bullion [bʊ́ljən] N oro en lingotes m

bully [bʊ́li] N matón -ona mf, bravucón -ona mf; VT intimidar

bulwark [bʊ́lwək] N baluarte m

bum [bʌm] N (lazy person) holgazán -ana mf; (hobo) vagabundo -da mf; (sports fan) fanático -ca mf; ADJ (accusation) falso; **my** — **knee** vulg mi rodilla jodida; VI holgazanear; VT gorronear

bumblebee [bʌ́mbəlbi] N abejorro m, abejón m

bummer [bʌ́mə] N vulg cagada f

bump [bʌmp] VT chocar; **to** — **along** ir dando tumbos; **to** — **off** despachar; **to** — **into** toparse con; N (blow) choque m, trastazo m; (lump) protuberancia f; (lump

on a person) chichón m

bumper [bʌ́mpə] N parachoques m sg, tope m; — **car** coche de choque m, autito chocador m; — **crop** cosecha abundante f; —**-to-— traffic** caravana de autos f; — **sticker** autoadhesivo m

bumpy [bʌ́mpi] ADJ bacheado, lleno de baches

bun [bʌn] N (bread) bollo m; (in hair) moño m; —**s** fam nalgas f pl

bunch [bʌntʃ] N (group of things) manojo m; (group of people) montón m, grupo m; (of grapes, bananas) racimo m; (of flowers) ramillete m; VI/VT juntar(se), agrupar(se)

bundle [bʌ́ndl] N paquete m, fardo m, envoltorio m; (of clothes) lío m, atado m; (of belongings) hato m, petate m; (of firewood) haz m; VT (tie together) liar, atar; **to** — **up** abrigarse; **to** — **off** despachar

bungalow [bʌ́ŋgəlo] N bungaló m

bungee jumping [bʌ́ndʒidʒʌmpɪŋ] N bungee m, puénting m

bungle [bʌ́ŋgəl] VT estropear; VI chapucear

bunion [bʌ́njən] N juanete m

bunk [bʌŋk] N (place to sleep) litera f; (nonsense) tonterías f pl; — **bed** litera f; VI dormir en una litera

bunker [bʌ́ŋkə] N búnker m

bunny [bʌ́ni] N conejito m

buoy [búi] N boya f; VI boyar; **to** — **up** mantener a flote, animar

buoyant [bɔ́iənt] ADJ (floating) boyante, flotante; (mood) optimista

bur [bə] N abrojo m

burden [bə́dn̩] N (load) carga f; (responsibility) peso m; — **of proof** carga de la prueba f; VT (heavily) recargar; (oppressively) agobiar

burdensome [bə́dn̩səm] ADJ agobiante, gravoso

bureau [bjúro] N (government department) oficina f, agencia f; (chest of drawers) cómoda f

bureaucracy [bjʊrákrəsi] N burocracia f

bureaucrat [bjúrəkræt] N burócrata mf

burglar [bə́glə] N ladrón -ona mf; — **alarm** alarma antirrobo f; — **proof** a prueba de robos

burglary [bə́gləri] N robo con allanamiento m

burial [bériəl] N entierro m; — **place** lugar de sepultura m

Burkina Faso [bəkínəfáso] N Burkina Faso m

burlap [bə́læp] N arpillera f

burlesque [bəlésk] ADJ burlesco; N

espectáculo de variedades *m*

burly [bɜ́-li] ADJ corpulento

Burma [bɜ́-mə] N Birmania *f*

Burmese [bə-míz] ADJ & N birmano -na *mf*

burn [bɜ-n] N quemadura *f*; **—out** surmenage *m*; VI/VT quemar(se), abrasar(se); (a house) incendiar(se); (food) quemar(se), requemar(se); **he got —ed in the transaction** lo estafaron en el negocio; **the bulb is still —ing** la bombilla sigue prendida; **the house is —ing** la casa se está quemando; **the iodine —ed his skin** el yodo le quemó la piel; **to — a hole** hacer un agujero con algo; VI (by heat, passion) arder, abrasar; **my skin —s** me arde la piel; **he's —ing with desire** arde en deseos; **to — down** incendiarse; **to — off** (fog) disiparse; **to — out** (to fuse) fundirse; (to be exhausted) agotarse; **to — up** quemarse completamente

burner [bɜ́-nə] N (person or thing that burns something) quemador -ra *mf*; (on stove) hornilla *f*; **Bunsen —** mechero Bunsen *m*

burning [bɜ́-nɪŋ] ADJ (desire) ardiente, abrasador; (question) urgente

burnish [bɜ́-nɪʃ] VT bruñir

burp [bɜ-p] N eructo *m*; VI eructar, repetir

burrow [bɜ́-o] N madriguera *f*; VI (dig) hacer madrigueras; (live) vivir en una madriguera

burst [bɜ-st] VI reventar(se); **to — into** irrumpir en; **to — into tears** romper en llanto; **to — out** salir disparado; **to — with laughter** estallar/reventar de risa; N **— of activity** explosión de actividad *f*; **— of laughter** carcajada *f*; **— of machine-gun fire** ráfaga de ametralladora *f*; **— of speed** aceleración *f*

Burundi [buɾúndi] N Burundi *m*

Burundian [buɾúndiən] ADJ & N burundés -esa *mf*

bury [béɾi] VT enterrar; (in sand) hundir; (corpse only) sepultar; **to be buried in thought** estar absorto/meditabundo

bus [bʌs] N autobús *m*, ómnibus *m*; *Mex* camión *m*; *RP* colectivo *m*; *Chile* micro *m*; *Cuba* guagua *f*; (in a computer) bus *m*; VT transportar en autobús

bush [bʊʃ] N (plant) arbusto *m*, mata *f*; (region) matorral *m*; **to beat around the — andarse por las ramas**

bushed [bʊʃt] ADJ fatigado

bushel [bʊ́ʃəl] N fanega *f*

bushing [bʊ́ʃɪŋ] N buje *m*, cojinete *m*

bushy [bʊ́ʃi] ADJ (whiskers) espeso; (plants) poblado de arbustos

business [bíznɪs] N (trade, store) negocio *m*;

(occupation) ocupación *f*; (commercial activity) comercio *m*; **— card** tarjeta comercial *f*; **— day** día hábil *m*; **— hours** horas hábiles *f pl*, horario de atención al público *m*; **— is booming** el negocio florece; **—man** hombre de negocios *m*, negociante *m*; **— suit** traje *m*; **— transaction** negocio *m*, transacción comercial *f*; **—woman** mujer de negocios *f*, negociante *f*; **I'm tired of the whole —** este asunto me tiene harto; **I mean —** hablo en serio; **to do — with** comerciar con; **he has no — doing it** no tiene derecho a hacerlo; **it's none of your —** no es asunto tuyo; **mind your own —** no te metas en lo que no te importa

businesslike [bíznɪslaɪk] ADJ (efficient) eficiente; (cold) impersonal

bust [bʌst] N (statue, body part) busto *m*; VI/VT (burst, hit, break) reventar; (force into bankruptcy) hacer quebrar; (lower in rank) degradar

bustle [bʌ́səl] N (noise) bullicio *m*; (movement) ajetreo *m*, tráfago *m*; VI (move busily) ajetrear(se); (be crowded) bullir

busy [bízi] ADJ ocupado, atareado; (overdecorated) recargado; **—body** entrometido -da *mf*; **— signal** señal de ocupado *f*; VI **to — oneself** ocuparse

but [bʌt] CONJ (on the contrary) pero; (excepting) sino; PREP menos; **any day — today** cualquier día menos hoy; **he's nothing — trouble** sólo da problemas; ADV **— for you** si no fuera por ti

butane [bjútén] N butano *m*

butch [bʊtʃ] ADJ (of a woman) marimacha, camionera; (of a man) machote

butcher [bʊtʃɚ] N carnicero -ra *mf*; **—'s shop** carnicería *f*; VT (cattle) matar; (people) masacrar; (performance) estropear

butchery [bʊ́tʃəɾi] N carnicería *f*

butler [bʌ́tlɚ] N mayordomo *m*

butt [bʌt] N (body part) *fam* culo *m*; (rifle part) culata *f*; (of a cigarette) colilla *f*; (blow with head) topetazo *m*, cabezada *f*, cabezazo *m*; **the — of ridicule** el blanco de las burlas; VT embestir, topar; **to — in** entrometerse; **to — into a conversation** meter baza; *Am* meter la cuchara

butter [bʌ́dɚ] N mantequilla *f*; VT (bread) untar con mantequilla; (a cakepan) enmantecar; **—cup** botón de oro *m*; **—dish** mantequera *f*; **—fingers** manos de mantequilla *mf sg*; **—milk** suero de leche *m*; **—scotch** dulce de azúcar y mantequilla *m*

butterfly [bʌ́də-flaɪ] N mariposa *f*; **— stroke**
   estilo mariposa *m*
buttery [bʌ́dəri] ADJ mantecoso
buttocks [bʌ́dəks] N nalgas *f pl*, asentaderas *f
   pl*, cachas *f pl*
button [bʌ́tn̩] N botón *m*; **—hole** ojal *m*; VI/
   VT abotonar(se); VT **to —hole** hacer ojales;
   to —hole someone detener a alguien
buttress [bʌ́trɪs] N apoyo *m*, sostén *m*; (of a
   building) contrafuerte *m*; VT apoyar,
   reforzar
buxom [bʌ́ksəm] ADJ (full-bosomed)
   pechugona; (fat and cheerful) frescachona,
   jamona
buy [baɪ] VT comprar; **to — into** dejarse
   convencer; **I don't — that** no me lo
   trago; **to — on credit** comprar a crédito;
   to — off sobornar; **to — in
   installments** comprar a plazos; **to —
   out** comprar la parte de; **to — up**
   acaparar; N (purchase) compra *f*; (bargain)
   ganga *f*
buyer [báɪə] N comprador -ra *mf*
buzz [bʌz] N zumbido *m*; (feeling of
   intoxication) borrachera *f*; (phone call)
   telefonazo *m*; **to give someone a —**
   pegarle / echarle un telefonazo a alguien;
   — saw sierra circular *f*; VI zumbar; (group)
   murmurar; VT hacer zumbar; **to — the
   bell** tocar el timbre; **to — off** largarse
buzzard [bʌ́zə-d] N buitre *m*
buzzer [bʌ́zə-] N timbre *m*, chicharra *f*
by [baɪ] PREP por; **we drove — the church**
   pasamos por la iglesia; **a 4 — 3 room** un
   cuarto de 4 por 3; **multiply 2 — 2**
   multiplica 2 por 2; **— the liter** por litro;
   we live — the church vivimos al lado
   de la iglesia; **she had a son — him** tuvo
   un hijo con él; **— and —** a la larga; **—
   dint of** a fuerza de; **— far** con mucho;
   — night de noche; **— the way** a
   propósito; **— chance** por casualidad;
   piece — piece pedazo a / por pedazo; **—
   this time tomorrow** mañana a esta
   hora; **— two o'clock** para las dos; ADV
   the factory is close — la fábrica está
   cerca; **the bus drove —** pasó el autobús
bye-bye [báɪbáɪ] INTERJ ¡adiós! ¡chaucito!
bygones [báɪɡɔnz] N **let — be —** lo pasado
   pisado
bylaw [báɪlɔ] N estatuto *m*
by-line [báɪlaɪn] N pie de autor *m*
bypass [báɪpæs] VT evitar; N desvío *m*; **—
   operation** bypass *m*
by-product [báɪprɑdəkt] N subproducto *m*;
   (chemical) derivado *m*
bystander [báɪstændə-] N persona presente *f*

byte [baɪt] N byte *m*, octeto *m*

Cc

cab [kæb] N (taxi) taxi *m*; (of a truck) cabina
   f; **— driver** taxista *mf*
cabaret [kæbəɾé] N cabaret *m*
cabbage [kǽbɪdʒ] N col *f*, repollo *m*, berza *f*
cabin [kǽbɪn] N (hut) cabaña *f*; (in an
   airplane) cabina *f*; (in a ship) camarote *m*
cabinet [kǽbnɪt] N (for dishes) armario *m*;
   (for medicines) botiquín *m*; (for display)
   vitrina *f*; (department heads) gabinete *m*;
   —maker ebanista *mf*
cable [kébəɫ] N cable *m*; (on ships) amarra *f*;
   (telegram) telegrama *m*; (talk) parloteo *m*;
   cacareo *m*; (talk) parloteo *m*
cachet [kæʃé] N caché *m*
cackle [kǽkəɫ] VI cacarear; (talk) parlotear; N
   cacareo *m*; (talk) parloteo *m*
cacophony [kəkɑ́fəni] N cacofonía *f*
cactus [kǽktəs] N cacto *m*, cactus *m*
cad [kæd] N *pej* canalla *m*
cadaver [kədǽvə] N cadáver *m*
caddie [kǽdi] N caddy *m*, caddie *m*
cadence [kédṇs] N cadencia *f*
cadet [kədét] N cadete *m*
cadmium [kǽdmiəm] N cadmio *m*
Caesarian section [sɪzériənsékʃən] N cesárea
   f
café [kæfé] N (coffee only) café *m*; (coffee and
   food) cafetería *f*
cafeteria [kæfɪtíriə] N cafetería *f*; (in school,
   factory) cantina *f*
caffeine [kæfín] N cafeína *f*
cage [kedʒ] N jaula *f*; VT enjaular
cahoots [kəhúts] ADV LOC **in —** arreglados
cajole [kədʒóɫ] VI/VT engatusar, persuadir con
   halagos
cake [kek] N pastel *m*, torta *f*; (sponge)
   bizcocho *m*; (soap) pastilla *f*; **a piece of
   — pan comido; to take the —** ser el
   colmo; VI/VT apelmazar(se)
calamine [kǽləmaɪn] N calamina *f*
calamity [kəlǽmɪDi] N calamidad *f*
calcium [kǽlsiəm] N calcio *m*
calculate [kǽlkjəlet] VI/VT calcular; **his
   actions were —d to fool us** con sus
   acciones trataba de engañarnos

calculating [kǽɪkjəleɪɪŋ] ADJ calculador

calculation [kæɪkjəléʃən] N cálculo *m*

calculator [kǽɪkjəleɪɾɚ] N calculadora *f.*

calculus [kǽɪkjələs] N cálculo *m*

calendar [kǽlɪndɚ] N calendario *m*,
almanaque *m*; **— year** año civil *m*

calf [kæf] N (animal) ternero -ra *mf*, becerro
-rra *mf*; (of leg) pantorrilla *f*, canilla *f*;
— skin piel de becerro *f*

caliber [kǽləbɚ] N calibre *m*

calibrate [kǽləbret] VT calibrar, graduar

calico [kǽlɪko] N calicó *m*

caliper [kǽləpɚ] N (on brakes) calibrador *m*;
(for measuring) calibre *m*

call [kɔl] N (bird call, device for calling birds)
reclamo *m*; (telephone call) llamada *f*;
(summons) llamamiento *m*; (to the
ministry) vocación *f*; **— girl** prostituta de
cita *f*; **there's no — for panic** no hay
motivo de alarma; **it's your —** tú decides;
within — al alcance de la voz; VT
(summon, by telephone, a name, a strike)
llamar; (cry out) gritar; (a meeting)
convocar; **she —ed me a liar** me llamó
mentiroso; **— me back** llámame tú; **to —
a meeting to order** abrir la sesión; VI/VT
(birds) reclamar; **to — roll** pasar lista; VI
(call out) gritar; **to — at a port** hacer
escala en un puerto; **to — for** pedir; **to —
off** cancelar; **to — on** (visit) visitar;
(depend on) acudir a; **to — together**
convocar; **to — up** llamar por teléfono

caller [kɔ́lɚ] N visita *f*, visitante *mf*; (by
telephone) persona que llama *f*; **— ID**
identificador de llamadas *m*

calligraphy [kəlígrəfi] N caligrafía *f*

calling [kɔ́lɪŋ] N vocación *f*

callous [kǽləs] ADJ (having calluses) calloso;
(insensitive) insensible

callus [kǽləs] N callo *m*

calm [kɑm] ADJ tranquilo, reposado, calmo; N
calma *f*, tranquilidad *f*, sosiego *m*; VT
calmar, tranquilizar, sosegar; **to — down**
calmar(se)

calmness [kɑ́mnɪs] N calma *f*, tranquilidad *f*

calorie [kǽləri] N caloría *f*

calumny [kǽləmni] N calumnia *f*

cam [kæm] N leva *f*

Cambodia [kæmbóɾiə] N Camboya *f*

Cambodian [kæmbóɾiən] ADJ & N
camboyano -na *mf*

camel [kǽməl] N camello *m*

cameo [kǽmio] N camafeo *m*; **—
appearance** actuación especial *f*

camera [kǽmrə] N cámara fotográfica *f*;
—man cámara *m*, camarógrafo *m*;
—woman cámara *f*, camarógrafa *f*

Cameroon [kæmərún] N Camerún *m*

Cameroonian [kæmərúniən] ADJ & N
camerunés -esa

camouflage [kǽməflɑʒ] N camuflaje *m*; VT
camuflar

camp [kæmp] N (campsite) campamento *m*;
(faction) bando *m*; **—fire** fogata *f*,
hoguera *f*; **—ground** campamento *m*,
cámping *m*; **—site** campamento *m*; **the
Republican —** el campo republicano; VI/
VT acampar

campaign [kæmpén] N campaña *f*; VI hacer
campaña

camper [kǽmpɚ] N acampante *mf*, campista
mf

camphor [kǽmfɚ] N alcanfor *m*

camping [kǽmpɪŋ] N cámping *m*, acampada
f; **let's go —** vamos de camping/
acampada

campus [kǽmpəs] N campus *m*

can [kæn] N lata *f*, bote *m*; **— of worms** caja
de Pandora *f*; **— opener** abrelatas *m sg*; VT
enlatar; V AUX **— you come tomorrow?**
¿puedes venir mañana? **— you see me?**
¿me ves? **I — ride a bicycle** sé andar en
bicicleta; **a —-do attitude** un espíritu
emprendedor

Canada [kǽnədə] N Canadá *m*

Canadian [kənéɾiən] ADJ & N canadiense *mf*

canal [kənǽl] N canal *m*

canary [kənéri] N canario *m*

Canary Islands [kənériaíləns] N Islas
Canarias *f pl*

cancel [kǽnsəl] VT cancelar; (a stamp)
matasellar; (an order) anular; (writing)
tachar

cancellation [kænsəléʃən] N cancelación *f*;
(of an order) anulación *f*

cancer [kǽnsɚ] N cáncer *m*; **— patient**
canceroso -sa *mf*; ADJ **— causing**
cancerígeno

candelabrum, candelabra [kændəlúbrəm
-brə] N candelabro *m*

candid [kǽndɪd] ADJ franco, sincero

candidacy [kǽndɪɾəsi] N candidatura *f*

candidate [kǽndɪdɪt] N (for office) candidato
-ta *mf*; (for a job) aspirante *mf*, postulante
mf

candle [kǽndl] N vela *f*, candela *f*; (on the
altar) cirio *m*; **—stick** candelero *m*

candor [kǽndɚ] N franqueza *f*

candy [kǽndi] N dulce *m*, caramelo *m*,
confite *m*; (with chocolate) bombón *m*; **—
store** bombonería *f*; VT confitar,
acaramelar; (nuts) garapiñar; VI (syrup)
cristalizarse

cane [ken] N (sugar) caña *f*; (walking) bastón

_m;_ — **chair** silla de mimbre _f;_ **to beat
with a** — bastonear, apalear
canine [kénaɪn] ADJ canino, perruno; N
(canid) can _m;_ (tooth) canino _m_
canister [kǽnɪstə] N lata _f_
canker [kǽŋkə] N úlcera _f_
cannery [kǽnəri] N fábrica de conservas _f_
cannibal [kǽnəbəl] N caníbal _m_
cannon [kǽnən] N cañón _m;_ — **fodder**
carne de cañón _f_
canny [kǽni] ADJ sagaz, astuto
canoe [kənú] N canoa _f_
canon [kǽnən] N (rule, melody) canon _m;_
(priest) canónigo _m_
canopy [kǽnəpi] N (of a bed) dosel _m;_ (of a
building) toldo _m_
cantaloupe [kǽntlop] N melón _m_
canteen [kæntín] N (snack bar) cantina _f;_
(container) cantimplora _f_
canvas [kǽnvəs] N (fabric) lona _f;_ (for
painting) lienzo _m_
canvass [kǽnvəs] VI/VT (poll) encuestar;
(solicit votes) solicitar votos en; (solicit
sales) buscar pedidos comerciales en; N
solicitud _f_
canyon [kǽnjən] N cañón _m_
cap [kæp] N (head covering without visor)
gorro _m;_ (head covering with visor) gorra
_f;_ (of a bottle) tapa _f;_ (of a pen) capucha _f;_
contera _f;_ (limit) tope _m;_ (for capgun)
fulminante _m,_ pistón _m;_ VT (to cover, put
a cap on) tapar; (to complete) rematar; (to
limit) limitar
capability [kepəbílɪdi] N capacidad _f_
capable [képəbəl] ADJ capaz
capacious [kəpéʃəs] ADJ amplio
capacity [kəpǽsɪdi] N capacidad _f_
cape [kep] N (clothing) capa _f;_ (promontory)
cabo _m_
caper [képə] N (skipping) cabriola _f;_ (prank)
treta _f,_ triquiñuela _f;_ (crime) delito _m;_
(food) alcaparra _f;_ VI retozar
Cape Verde [kepvɜ́-d] N Cabo Verde _m_
Cape Verdean [kepvɜ́-dian] ADJ & N
caboverdiano -na _mf_
capillary [kǽpəleri] N & ADJ (vaso) capilar _m_
capital [kǽpɪdl] N (city) capital _f;_ (wealth)
capital _m;_ (of a column) capitel _m;_ (letter)
mayúscula _f;_ **to make** — **of** sacar partido
de, aprovecharse de; ADJ (city) capital;
(financial) de capital; — **gains** ganancias
en bienes de capital _f pl;_ — **investment**
inversión de capital _f;_ — **punishment**
pena de muerte _f_
capitalism [kǽpɪdlɪzəm] N capitalismo _m_
capitalist [kǽpɪdlɪst] N capitalista _mf_
capitalistic [kǽpɪdlístɪk] ADJ capitalista

capitalization [kǽpɪdlɪzéʃən] N
capitalización _f_
capitalize [kǽpɪdlaɪz] VT (finance) capitalizar;
(write) escribir con mayúscula; **to** — **on**
sacar provecho de
capitol [kǽpɪdl] N capitolio _m_
capitulate [kəpítʃəlet] VI capitular
cappuccino [kæpətʃíno] N capuchino _m_
caprice [kəprís] N capricho _m_
capricious [kəpríʃəs] ADJ caprichoso
capsize [kǽpsaɪz] VI/VT volcar(se)
capsule [kǽpsəl] N cápsula _f_
captain [kǽptɪn] N capitán _m;_ VT capitanear
caption [kǽpʃən] N (with illustration) pie _m;_
(subtitle) subtítulo _m_
captivate [kǽptəvet] VT cautivar
captive [kǽptɪv] ADJ & N cautivo -va _mf;_ —
animals animales en cautiverio _m pl_
captivity [kæptívɪdi] N cautiverio _m_
captor [kǽptə] N captor -ra _mf_
capture [kǽptʃə] VT (apprehend, record data)
capturar; (attract) cautivar; (conquer)
tomar; N captura _f_
car [kɑr] N (automobile) coche _m,_ automóvil
_m; Am_ carro _m,_ auto _m;_ (railroad) vagón
_m,_ coche _m;_ (elevator) cabina _f; Am_
elevador _m;_ — **bomb** coche bomba _m;_
—**fare** pasaje _m;_ —**jacking** secuestro de
vehículo _m;_ —**load** carga de un coche _f;_
—**port** cochera _f;_ —**sick** mareado; **he got
—sick** se mareó en el coche; — **wash**
túnel de lavado _m_
caramel [kǽrəmət] N caramelo _m_
carat [kǽrət] N quilate _m_
caravan [kǽrəvæn] N caravana _f_
carbohydrate [kɑrbəháɪdret] N carbohidrato
_m,_ hidrato de carbono _m_
carbon [kɑ́rbən] N carbono _m;_ — **copy** copia
en papel carbón _f;_ — **dioxide** dióxido de
carbono _m;_ — **monoxide** monóxido de
carbono _m;_ — **paper** papel carbón _m_
carburetor [kɑ́rbəredə] N carburador _m_
carcass [kɑ́rkəs] N (of an animal) cuerpo
muerto _m;_ (human) cadáver _m;_ (of a ship)
casco _m_
carcinogen [kɑrsínədʒən] N cancerígeno _m,_
carcinógeno _m_
carcinoma [kɑrsənómə] N carcinoma _m_
card [kɑrd] N (piece of stiff paper) tarjeta _f;_
(playing) naipe _m,_ carta _f;_ (for boxing
events) programa _m;_ (for textiles) carda _f;_
(witty person) gracioso -sa _mf;_ (in a
computer) tarjeta _f,_ placa _f;_ —**board**
(thick) cartón _m;_ (thin) cartulina _f;_ —
sharp fullero -ra _mf;_ **pack of** —**s** baraja
_f;_ **to play** —**s** jugar a la baraja, jugar a los
naipes; **he's holding all the** —**s** tiene

todas las ventajas; VT (comb) cardar; (ask
for identification) pedir identificación
cardiac [kárɒɪæk] ADJ cardiaco, cardíaco
cardinal [kárdn̩l] ADJ (number, main)
cardinal; (colored red) rojo, bermellón; N
(bishop, bird) cardenal *m*
cardiology [karɒɪálǝdʒi] N cardiología *f*
cardiovascular [karɒlováeskjǝlǝ] ADJ
cardiovascular
care [ker] N (worry) preocupación *f*;
(attention) cuidado *m*, atención *f*, tiento
m; (extreme attention) esmero *m*, primor
m; —**free** despreocupado; —**giver**
cuidador -ra *mf*; **to take — of** cuidar de,
atender; (of a house) casero -ra *mf*; VI (be
concerned, object) importarle a uno; **to —
about** interesarle a uno, importarle a
uno; **to — for** (look after) cuidar de;
(love) tenerle cariño a; **to — to** tener
ganas de; **I couldn't — less** me importa
un rábano; **what does he —?** ¿a él qué
le importa? **would you — for a drink?**
¿te puedo ofrecer algo?
careen [kǝrín] VI ladearse a toda velocidad
career [kǝrír] N carrera *f*, trayectoria *f*
careful [kérfǝl] ADJ (cautious) cuidadoso,
cauteloso; (painstaking) esmerado; **to be
— tener cuidado**
carefulness [kérfǝlnɪs] N cuidado *m*
careless [kérlɪs] ADJ descuidado
caress [kɑrés] N caricia *f*; VT acariciar
cargo [kárgo] N cargamento *m*
Caribbean [kærǝbíǝn] N Caribe *m*; ADJ
caribeño
caricature [kǽrɪkǝtʃǝ] N caricatura *f*; VT
caricaturizar
caries [kériz] N caries *f*
carnage [kárnɪdʒ] N carnicería *f*
carnal [kárnl̩] ADJ carnal
carnation [karnéʃǝn] N (flower) clavel *m*;
(color) rosado *m*
carnival [kárnǝvǝl] N carnaval *m*; (traveling)
feria *f*
carnivorous [karnívǝ-ǝs] ADJ carnívoro,
carnicero
carol [kérǝl] N villancico *m*; VI cantar
villancicos
carom [kǽrǝm] N carambola *f*; VI rebotar
carotid artery [kǝrɑ́ɒɪdártǝri] N (arteria)
carótida *f*
carouse [kɑráuz] VI andar de parranda
carp [karp] N carpa *f*; VI (complain) quejarse
carpenter [kárpǝntǝ] N carpintero -ra *mf*
carpentry [kárpǝntri] N carpintería *f*
carpet [kárpɪt] N alfombra *f*; **—bagger**
político -ca oportunista *mf*; VT alfombrar
carriage [kǽrɪdʒ] N (wheeled vehicle) carruaje

m, coche *m*; (posture) porte *m*
carrier [kériǝ-] N (one who carries) portador
-ra *mf*; (postal worker) cartero -ra *mf*;
(transport company) mensajería *f*
carrion [kériǝn] N carroña *f*
carrot [kérǝt] N zanahoria *f*
carry [kéri] VT llevar; **do you — Italian
wine?** ¿venden vino italiano? **the bill
carried** se aprobó el proyecto de ley; **you
— yourself well** te comportas bien; **he
can't — a tune** no puede seguir una
tonada; **this suitcase carries a lot** esta
maleta es espaciosa; **to — away** llevarse;
he got carried away se le fue la mano;
to — on continuar; **to — out** (complete)
llevar a cabo, ejecutar; (take out) sacar;
—on de mano
cart [kart] N carro *m*; VT acarrear
cartilage [kárdlɪdʒ] N cartílago *m*
carton [kártn̩] N caja de cartón *f*
cartoon [kartún] N (drawing) caricatura *f*;
(strip) tira cómica *f*; (film) dibujo animado
m
cartoonist [kartúnɪst] N caricaturista *mf*
cartridge [kártrɪdʒ] N cartucho *m*; **— belt**
cartuchera *f*, canana *f*
carve [karv] VI/VT (piece of wood) tallar; (a
career) labrarse; (turkey) trinchar
carving [kárvɪŋ] N (action) tallado *m*; (figure)
talla *f*; **— knife** trinchante *m*
cascade [kæskéd] N cascada *f*
case [kes] N caso *m*; (box) caja *f*; (of a pillow)
funda *f*; **in — (that)** en caso de que; **in
— it rains** por si llueve; **in any —** en
todo caso; **just in —** por si acaso; **get off
my —!** ¡déjame en paz!
cash [kæʃ] N efectivo *m*; **— advance** anticipo
en efectivo *m*; **— and carry** al contado y
sin entrega a domicilio; **— flow** corriente
en efectivo *f*; **— on delivery** entrega
contra reembolso *f*; **— payment** pago en
efectivo *m*; **— register** caja registradora *f*;
to pay — pagar al contado; VT cobrar
cashew [kǽʃu] N marañón *m*, castaña de cajú
f, Sp anacardo *m*
cashier [kæʃír] N cajero -ra *mf*; **—'s check**
cheque de caja *m*
casino [kɑsíno] N casino *m*
cask [kæsk] N tonel grande *m*
casket [kǽskɪt] N ataúd *m*
casserole [kǽsǝrol] N (container) cazuela *f*;
(food) guiso *m*
cassette [kɑsét] N cassette *mf*, casete *mf*
cast [kæst] VT (throw) tirar, echar; (adapt)
adaptar; (form an object) moldear, vaciar;
(give out dramatic roles) repartir papeles;
to — a ballot votar; **to — about** buscar;

to — a glance echar un vistazo; to — aside desechar; to — doubt poner en duda; to — light on aclarar; to — lots echar suertes; to — off (a ship) soltar amarras; (something rejected) deshacerse de; to — out exiliar; to be — down estar abatido; N (form) molde m; (in theater) reparto m, elenco m; — iron hierro fundido m

castanet [kǽstənɛt] N castañuela f

caste [kæst] N casta f

castigate [kǽstɪget] VT (criticize) criticar, reprender; (punish) castigar

Castile [kæstíl] N Castilla f

Castilian [kæstíljən] N & ADJ castellano -na mf

casting [kǽstɪŋ] N (throwing) tiro m; (piece of metal) pieza fundida f; (selection of actors) cásting m

castle [kǽsəl] N castillo m; (chess piece) torre f, roque m

castor oil [kǽstə-ɔɪl] N aceite de ricino m

castrate [kǽstret] VT castrar; (animals) capar

casual [kǽʒuəl] ADJ (informal) informal; (offhand) al pasar

casualty [kǽʒuəlti] N (of war) baja f; (in an accident) víctima f

cat [kæt] N (domestic) gato -ta mf; (others) felino m; —'s meow súmmum m; —fish siluro m; —house burdel m

Catalan [kǽdlæn] ADJ & N catalán -ana mf; (language) catalán m

catalog, catalogue [kǽdlɔg] N catálogo m; VT catalogar

Catalonia [kædlónɪə] N Cataluña f

Catalonian [kædlónɪən] ADJ catalán

catalyst [kǽdlɪst] N catalizador m

cataract [kǽdərækt] N catarata f

catastrophe [kətǽstrəfi] N catástrofe f

catch [kætʃ] VT (a criminal, ball) atrapar; *Sp, Cuba* coger; (a fish) pescar, capturar; (someone in an act) pillar; (a bus) agarrar; (what someone said) comprender, agarrar; to — a glimpse of vislumbrar; to — cold resfriarse; to — fire prenderse fuego; to — on (understand) caer en cuenta; (become popular) ponerse de moda; to — oneself contenerse; to — one's eye llamarle a uno la atención; to — sight of avistar; to — unawares sorprender; to — up (with a person) alcanzar; (on work) ponerse al día; VI (get entangled) enredarse; (snap into place) agarrar; N (act of catching prey, quantity caught) captura f, redada f, pesca f; (prey) presa f; (device) pestillo m; (act of catching a ball) atrapada f; —phrase eslogan m; **he is a good —**

es un buen partido; **to play** — jugar a la pelota; **what's the —?** ¿cuál es la treta?

catching [kǽtʃɪŋ] ADJ contagioso

catchy [kǽtʃi] ADJ pegadizo

catechism [kǽdɪkɪzəm] N catecismo m

category [kǽdɪgɔri] N categoría f

cater [kédə-] VI/VT abastecer de alimentos (banquetes, fiestas, etc.); to — to atender a

caterpillar [kǽdəpɪlə-] N (insect) oruga f; (tractor) tractor oruga m, caterpillar m

cathedral [kəθídrəl] N catedral f

catheter [kǽθɪdə-] N catéter m, sonda f

cathode [kǽθod] N cátodo m; — **rays** rayos catódicos m pl

Catholic [kǽθlɪk] N & ADJ católico -ca mf

Catholicism [kəθálɪsɪzəm] N catolicismo m

CAT scan [kǽtskæn] N TAC f, tomografía axial computadorizada f

catsup [kǽtʃəp] N cátsup m, ketchup m

cattle [kǽdl] N ganado (vacuno) m; —**man** ganadero m; — **rustler** cuatrero m; — **rustling** abigeato m

catty [kǽbi] ADJ hiriente

cauliflower [kɔ́lɪflauə-] N coliflor f

cause [kɔz] N causa f; — **for celebration** motivo de celebración m; **the democratic** — la causa democrática; **without** — sin motivo; VT causar, ocasionar; (involving volition) motivar; to — to flee hacer huir; **the heat —d her to faint** el calor la hizo desmayar

caustic [kɔ́stɪk] ADJ cáustico

cauterize [kɔ́dəraɪz] VT cauterizar

caution [kɔ́ʃən] N (prudence) cautela f, recato m; (warning) advertencia f; —! ¡cuidado! ¡atención! VT advertir; to — against desaconsejar

cautious [kɔ́ʃəs] ADJ cauto, cauteloso, precavido

cavalier [kævəlír] N caballero m, galán m; ADJ (disdainful) desdeñoso; (overly casual) displicente

cavalry [kǽvəlri] N caballería f

cave [kev] N cueva f, caverna f; —**man** hombre de las cavernas m; VI to — in ceder, derrumbarse, desplomarse

cavern [kǽvə-n] N caverna f, gruta f

cavity [kǽvɪdi] N cavidad f; (in a tooth) caries f; (nasal) fosa f

cavort [kəvɔ́rt] VI cabriolar, retozar

caw [kɔ] N graznido m; VI graznar

CD (compact disc) [sidí] N CD m, disco compacto m; — **player** reproductor de discos compactos m; —**ROM** CD-ROM m

cease [sis] VI cesar; VT interrumpir; —**fire** alto el fuego m; *Am* cese el fuego m

ceaseless [síslɪs] ADJ incesante
cedar [síɾə] N cedro *m*
cede [sid] VT ceder
ceiling [sílɪŋ] N techo *m*, cielo raso *m*; (cap)
    tope *m*; (sky) altura máxima *f*
celebrate [séləbret] VI/VT celebrar, festejar
celebrated [séləbreɾɪd] ADJ célebre
celebration [seləbréʃən] N (action)
    celebración *f*, festejo *m*; (festivities) fiesta *f*
celebrity [səlébrɪɾi] N celebridad *f*
celery [séləri] N apio *m*
celestial [səléstʃəl] ADJ celeste; (heavenly)
    celestial; **— body** astro *m*
celibate [séləbɪt] ADJ célibe
cell [sɛl] N (room) celda *f*; (structural) célula *f*
cellar [sélə] N sótano *m*; (for wine) bodega *f*
cello [tʃélo] N violonchelo *m*
cellophane [séləfen] N celofán *m*
cellular [séljələ] ADJ celular; **— phone**
    celular *m*; *Sp* móvil *m*
cellulite [séljəlaɪt] N celulitis *f*
celluloid [séljələɪd] N celuloide *m*
cellulose [séljəlos] N celulosa *f*
cement [sɪmént] N cemento *m*; (glue)
    adhesivo *m*; **— mixer** hormigonera *f*; VI/
    VT cementar
cemetery [sémɪteri] N cementerio *m*
censor [sénsə] N censor -ora *mf*; VT censurar
censorship [sénsəʃɪp] N censura *f*
censure [sénʃə] N censura *f*; VT censurar
census [sénsəs] N censo *m*; **to take a —**
    censar
cent [sent] N centavo *m*, céntimo *m*
centennial [senténɪəl] ADJ & N centenario *m*
center [séntə] N centro *m*; **— of gravity**
    centro de gravedad *m*; VI/VT centrar(se)
centigrade [séntɪgred] ADJ centígrado
centimeter [séntəmiɾə] N centímetro *m*
centipede [séntəpid] N ciempiés *m*
central [séntrəl] ADJ central; (downtown)
    céntrico; N central de teléfonos *f*; **—
    heating** calefacción central *f*; **— nervous
    system** sistema nervioso central *m*; **—
    processing unit** unidad central de
    proceso *f*
Central [séntrəl] ADJ **— African Republic**
    República Centroafricana *f*; **— America**
    Centroamérica *f*
centralize [séntrəlaɪz] VI/VT centralizar(se)
centrifugal [sentrífəgəl] ADJ centrífugo
centripetal [sentrípɪɾl] ADJ centrípeto
century [séntʃəri] N siglo *m*
ceramic [sərǽmɪk] ADJ cerámico; N **—s**
    cerámica *f*
cereal [síriəl] N (breakfast food) cereal *m*;
    (the grain itself) grano *m*; ADJ cereal
cerebral [səríbrəl] ADJ cerebral; **— cortex**

    corteza cerebral *f*
ceremonial [serəmóniəl] ADJ & M ceremonial
ceremonious [serəmóniəs] ADJ ceremonioso
ceremony [sérəmoni] N ceremonia *f*
certain [sɜ́-tn̩] ADJ seguro; **— rules are
    inviolable** ciertas reglas son inviolables;
    death are taxes are — lo único seguro
    son los impuestos y la muerte; **he's — to
    come** seguro que viene; **it is — that it
    rained** es cierto que llovió
certainly [sɜ́-tn̩li] ADV (without doubt) sin
    duda; **she — gets her way** no cabe duda
    de que se sale con la suya; INTERJ ¡cómo
    no!
certainty [sɜ́-tn̩ti] N certeza *f*, certidumbre *f*
certificate [sə-tífɪkɪt] N certificado *m*; **— of
    baptism** fe de bautismo *f*; **— of deposit**
    certificado de depósito *m*
certification [sɜ-ɾəfɪkéʃən] N certificación *f*
certify [sɜ́-ɾəfaɪ] VT certificar; **certified
    check** cheque certificado *m*; **certified
    mail** correo certificado *m*; **certified
    public accountant** contador -ora
    público -ca *mf*
cervix [sɜ́-vɪks] N (neck) cerviz *f*; (uterine)
    cérvix *m*, cuello uterino *m*
cessation [seséʃən] N cese *m*
cesspool [séspul] N pozo séptico *m*, fosa
    séptica *f*
Chad [tʃæd] N Chad *m*
Chadian [tʃǽdiən] ADJ & N chadiano -na *mf*
chafe [tʃef] VI/VT rozar(se); N rozadura *f*
chaff [tʃæf] N ahechaduras *f pl*
chagrin [ʃəgrín] N mortificación *f*; VT
    mortificar
chain [tʃen] N cadena *f*; **— reaction**
    reacción en cadena *f*; **— saw** sierra *f*; **—
    smoker** persona que fuma como una
    chimenea *f*; **— store** tienda de cadena *f*;
    VI/VT encadenar(se)
chair [tʃer] N silla *f*; (academic) cátedra *f*; (of
    a meeting) presidente -ta *mf*; (of a
    department) jefe -fa *mf*; **—man** presidente
    m, director *m*, jefe *m*; **—manship**
    dirección *f*; **—person** presidente -ta *mf*,
    jefe -fa *mf*; **—woman** presidenta *f*, jefa *f*
chalk [tʃɔk] N (substance) caliza *f*; (piece) tiza
    f; **—board** pizarrón *m*, pizarra *f*; VT
    marcar con tiza; **to — up** (attribute)
    atribuir; (score) marcar
chalky [tʃɔ́ki] ADJ de/con/como tiza
challenge [tʃǽlɪndʒ] N desafío *m*, reto *m*; (of
    a jury) recusación *f*; VT (defy) desafiar,
    retar; (take exception) cuestionar, disputar;
    (recuse) recusar; **to be vertically —d** ser
    muy bajito
chamber [tʃémbə] N (legislative) cámara *f*;

(in a palace) aposento *m*; (of a cannon) recámara *f*; **—maid** camarera *f*, mucama *f*; **— music** música de cámara *f*; **— of commerce** cámara de comercio *f*; **— pot** orinal *m*; **—s** (of a judge) despacho *m*

chameleon [kəmíljən] N camaleón *m*

chamois [ʃǽmi] N gamuza *f*

champagne [ʃæmpén] N champán *m*, champaña *mf*

champion [tʃǽmpiən] N campeón -ona *mf*; (of a cause) defensor -ra *mf*, paladín *m*; VT defender

championship [tʃǽmpiənʃɪp] N campeonato *m*

chance [tʃæns] N (opportunity) oportunidad *f*; (probability) probabilidad *f*; (unpredictable element) casualidad *f*, azar *m*; **by —** por casualidad; **game of —** juego de azar *m*; **to take a —** correr riesgo, arriesgarse; ADJ casual; VI arriesgarse; **we —d to meet him at the bar** nos encontramos con él en el bar por casualidad

chancellor [tʃǽnsələ] N (chief minister) canciller *m*; (of a university) rector -ora de universidad *mf*

chandelier [ʃændəlír] N araña de luces *f*

change [tʃendʒ] VT cambiar; **to — clothes** cambiarse de ropa; **to — into** transformar; **to — trains** cambiar de tren; N cambio *m*; (money returned) vuelta *f*; Am vuelto *m*; (fresh clothes) muda de ropa *f*; **— of heart** cambio de opinión *m*

changeable [tʃéndʒəbəl] ADJ (variable) cambiante, variable; (fickle) inconstante, tornadizo; **— silk** seda tornasolada *f*

channel [tʃǽnəl] N canal *m*; (bed of stream) cauce *m*; VT canalizar, encauzar

chant [tʃænt] N (plain song) canto llano *m*; (hymn) cántico *m*; (repeated slogan) cantinela *f*; VI/VT (sing) cantar; (repeat a slogan) corear

chaos [kéɑs] N caos *m*

chaotic [keɑ́ɾɪk] ADJ caótico

chap [tʃæp] VI/VT cuartear(se), agrietar(se); N tipo *m*

chapel [tʃǽpəl] N capilla *f*

chaperon, chaperone [ʃǽpəron] N chaperón -ona *f*; VI ir de chaperón -ona

chaplain [tʃǽplɪn] N capellán *m*

chapter [tʃǽptə] N capítulo *m*

char [tʃɑr] VI/VT (reduce to ashes) carbonizar(se); (scorch) chamuscar(se)

character [kǽrɪktə] N carácter *m*; (of a novel) personaje *m*; **— actor** actor de carácter *m*; **Chinese —s** caracteres chinos

m pl; **he's quite a —** es todo un personaje; **that's out of — for him** eso no es característico de él

characteristic [kærɪktərístɪk] ADJ característico; N característica *f*; (genetic) carácter *m*

characterize [kǽrɪktəraɪz] VT (describe) caracterizar; (attribute) calificar

charade [ʃəréd] N farsa *f*; **—s** charada *f*

charcoal [tʃɑ́rkol] N carbón de leña *m*; **— drawing** dibujo al carbón *m*

charge [tʃɑrdʒ] VT (ask price) cobrar; (load) cargar; (buy on credit) cargar a cuenta; (attack) embestir; **to — off a loss** restar una pérdida; **to — with a task** encargarle a alguien una tarea; **to — with murder** acusar de homicidio; N (mission) misión *f*, encargo *m*; (accusation) cargo *m*, acusación *f*; (charge in account) cargo *m*, débito *m*; (explosives, electricity) carga *f*; (attack) embestida *f*; **— account** cuenta de crédito *f*; **— card** tarjeta de crédito *f*; **there will be a — for delivery** se cobra entrega a domicilio; **to be in — of** estar a cargo de; **under my —** a mi cargo

charger [tʃɑ́rdʒə] N (for a battery) cargador *m*; (horse) corcel *m*

chariot [tʃǽriət] N carro de guerra *m*

charisma [kərízmə] N carisma *m*

charitable [tʃǽrɪɾəbəl] ADJ caritativo

charity [tʃǽrɪɾi] N (virtue, aid to the poor) caridad *f*; (institution) institución benéfica *f*, institución de beneficencia *f*; **to give to —** dar dinero a las instituciones benéficas; **to live on —** vivir de la caridad

charlatan [ʃɑ́rlətən] N charlatán -ana *mf*

charm [tʃɑrm] N (attractiveness) encanto *m*, salero *m*; (trinket) dije *m*; (spell) sortilegio *m*, hechizo *m*; (amulet) talismán *m*, amuleto *m*; VT (delight) encantar; (influence) hechizar, subyugar

charming [tʃɑ́rmɪŋ] ADJ encantador, salero; *Sp* majo

chart [tʃɑrt] N (table) tabla *f*; (graph) gráfica *f*; (marine map) carta *f*; (of musical hits) lista de éxitos *f*; VT (in a table) tabular; (in a graph) graficar; (a region) cartografiar; **to — a course** trazar una ruta

charter [tʃɑ́rɾə] N (of a city) fuero *m*; (of an organization) estatuto *m*; (document granting rights) constitución *f*, carta *f*; (hire) flete *m*; **— flight** (vuelo) chárter *m*; **— member** socio fundador *mf*; VT (a corporation) aprobar los estatutos; (a flight) fletar

chase [tʃes] VT (hunt) cazar; (follow rapidly) perseguir; **to — after** correr tras; **to —**

away ahuyentar; N caza f, persecución f

chasm [kǽzəm] N sima f

chassis [tʃǽsi] N chasis m, bastidor m

chaste [tʃest] ADJ casto, honesto

chastise [tʃǽstaɪz] VT (punish) castigar; (criticize) criticar

chastisement [tʃæstáɪzmənt] N (punishment) castigo m; (criticism) crítica f

chastity [tʃǽstɪti] N castidad f, honestidad f

chat [tʃæt] N charla f; Mex plática f; **— room** chat m; VI charlar; Mex platicar

chattel [tʃǽdl] N (movable property) bien mueble m; (slave) esclavo -va mf

chatter [tʃǽdɚ] VI (jabber) cotorrear, parlotear; VT (click rapidly) castañetear; N (of speech) cotorreo m, parloteo m; (of teeth) castañeteo m; **—box** charlatán -ana mf, cotorra f

chauffeur [ʃofɚ] N chófer m

chauvinism [ʃóvənɪzəm] N (nationalist) chovinismo m; (sexist) machismo m

cheap [tʃip] ADJ (costs little) barato; (stingy) avaro; **life is — there** la vida no vale nada allí; **talk is —** hablar no cuesta nada; **to feel —** sentirse despreciable; **— shot** golpe bajo m; **—skate** tacaño -ña mf

cheapen [tʃípən] VI/VT (lower in price) abaratar(se); VT (lower in esteem) desvalorizar

cheapness [tʃípnɪs] N (low price) baratura f (stinginess) avaricia f

cheat [tʃit] N tramposo -sa mf, fullero -ra mf; VT engañar; **to — at cards** hacer trampa en/a las cartas, trampear; **to — on a test** copiar; **to — on one's spouse** engañar a la pareja de uno

check [tʃɛk] VT (stop) refrenar; (restrain) reprimir; (hand over luggage) facturar; (hand over coat) dejar; (verify) verificar; Am chequear; (in chess) dar jaque; **to — against** cotejar con; **to — into a hotel** registrarse; **to — into something** averiguar algo; **to — off** puntear; **to — out a book** sacar (prestado) un libro; **to — up on** controlar; **—-up** examen / control médico m; **—out counter** caja f; **—point** control m; **—room** guardarropa m; **that —s out** lo hemos comprobado; N (bank) cheque m; (means of restraint) control m; (ticket) ficha f; (mark) marca f; (in a restaurant) cuenta f; (in fabric) cuadro m; (checked fabric) tela a cuadros f; (examination) comprobación f; (in chess) jaque m; **—book** chequera f, talonario m; **—ing account** cuenta corriente f; **—list** lista de control f; **—mate** jaque mate m; **— stub** talón m

checker [tʃɛkɚ] N (on a fabric) cuadro m; (on a checkerboard) casilla f; (game piece) ficha f; (cashier) cajero -ra mf; (person who checks) verificador -ra mf; **— board** tablero m; **—s** juego de damas m; VT cuadricular; **—ed cloth** tela a cuadros f; **—ed past** pasado oscuro m

cheek [tʃik] N (on face) mejilla f; Am cachete m; (impudence) descaro m; (of buttocks) nalga f; **— bone** pómulo m

cheer [tʃir] N (shout) viva m, vítor m; (applause) aplausos m pl; (encouragement) ánimo m; (joy) alegría f; **—leader** animador -ra mf; Am porrista mf; INTERJ **—s!** ¡salud! VI/VT vitorear; **to — on** dar ánimo; **to — up** animar(se)

cheerful [tʃírfəl] ADJ (person) risueño, alegre; (room, etc.) alegre

cheerfulness [tʃírfəlnɪs] N alegría f

cheerless [tʃírlɪs] ADJ triste, sombrío

cheese [tʃiz] N queso m; **—burger** hamburguesa con queso f; **—cake** tarta de queso f

cheesy [tʃízi] ADJ (of cheese) de queso; (cheap) barato; (uncool) Sp hortera

cheetah [tʃídə] N guepardo m

chef [ʃɛf] N chef mf

chemical [kɛ́mɪkəl] ADJ químico; **— engineering** ingeniería química f; **— warfare** guerra química f; N producto químico m

chemist [kɛ́mɪst] N químico -ca f

chemistry [kɛ́mɪstri] N química f

chemotheraphy [kimoθɛ́rəpi] N quimioterapia f

cherish [tʃɛ́rɪʃ] VT apreciar; **I — the memory of him** tengo muy buenos recuerdos de él

cherry [tʃɛ́ri] N cereza f; **— tree** cerezo m

chess [tʃɛs] N ajedrez m; **—board** tablero de ajedrez m

chest [tʃɛst] N (box) arca f; (body part) pecho m; **— of drawers** cómoda f

chestnut [tʃɛ́snʌt] N castaña f; **— tree** castaño m; ADJ castaño; (horse) zaino

chew [tʃu] VT (food) masticar; (non-food) mascar; **—ing gum** goma de mascar f; Am chicle m; **to — a hole** hacer un agujero a mordiscones; **to — out** reprender; **to — over** meditar sobre; **to — up** romper a mordiscones; N mascada f, bocado m

chewy [tʃúi] ADJ correoso

chic [ʃik] ADJ & N chic m

chick [tʃik] N (young chicken) pollito m; (young bird) pichón m; (young woman) fam chavala f; **—pea** garbanzo m

chicken [tʃíkɪn] N gallina f; (flesh) pollo m;
— **coop** gallinero m; —-**hearted** cobarde;
— **pox** varicela f
chicory [tʃíkəri] N achicoria f
chide [tʃaɪd] VT regañar
chief [tʃif] N jefe m; (of a tribe) cacique m;
ADJ principal; — **justice** presidente de la
Suprema Corte de los Estados Unidos m;
— **of staff** (military) jefe del estado
mayor m; (of a division) secretario -ria
general mf
chieftain [tʃíftən] N cacique m
chiffon [ʃifán] N chifón m
chigger [tʃígɚ] N nigua f
chilblain [tʃílblen] N sabañón m
child [tʃaɪld] N (young person) niño -ña mf;
(offspring) hijo -ja mf; —**bearing** en edad
de procrear; —**birth** parto m,
alumbramiento m; —**like** infantil,
aniñado; —**proof** a prueba de niños; —'s
play cosa de niños f; **to be with** — estar
embarazada
childhood [tʃáɪldhʊd] N niñez f, infancia f
childish [tʃáɪldɪʃ] ADJ infantil, pueril
childless [tʃáɪldlɪs] ADJ sin hijos
Chile [tʃíli] N Chile m
Chilean [tʃílɪən] ADJ & N chileno -na mf
chili, chile [tʃíli] N (pepper) chile m, ají m;
(meat dish) chile con carne m
chill [tʃɪl] N (coldness) frío m; (fear, cold with
shivering) escalofrío m; **it had a —ing
effect on the group** le cayó al grupo
como un baldazo de agua fría; VI/VT
enfriar(se); **to — out** tranquilizarse
chilly [tʃíli] ADJ frío
chime [tʃaɪm] N (sound) repique m;
(instrument) carillón m, carillón m; VI
repicar; VT tañer; **to — in** intervenir (en
una conversación)
chimney [tʃímni] N chimenea f
chimpanzee [tʃɪmpænzí] N chimpancé m
chin [tʃɪn] N barbilla f, mentón m
china [tʃáɪnə] N (material) porcelana f, china
f; (dishes) vajilla de porcelana f, china f;
—**ware** vajilla de porcelana f
China [tʃáɪnə] N China f
Chinese [tʃaɪníz] ADJ chino; N (inhabitant of
China) chino -na mf; (language) chino m
chink [tʃɪŋk] N grieta f
chip [tʃɪp] N (of wood) astilla f; (in glass)
desportilladura f; (in gambling) ficha f; (in
computers) chip m; **he's a — off the old
block** de tal palo, tal astilla; **he has a —
on his shoulder** guarda resentimientos;
VI/VT (wood) astillar(se); (glass, plaster)
desportillarse, desconchar(se); (paint)
descascarar(se); **to — in** contribuir; **to —**

a tooth romperse un diente
chipmunk [tʃípmʌŋk] N ardilla listada f
chiropractic [kaɪrəpræktɪk] ADJ
quiropráctico; N quiropráctica f
chiropractor [káɪrəpræktɚ] N quiropráctico
-ca mf
chirp [tʃɚp] N gorjeo m; VI/VT piar, gorjear
chisel [tʃízəl] N escoplo m; (for stone) cincel
m; (for wood) formón m; VT cincelar;
(swindle) estafar
chiseler [tʃízlɚ] N estafador -ra mf
chit-chat [tʃíttʃæt] N palique m; VI charlar
chivalrous [ʃívəlrəs] ADJ (of knights)
caballeresco; (courteous to women)
caballeroso
chivalry [ʃívəlri] N caballerosidad f
chloride [klóraɪd] N cloruro m
chlorine [klórin] N cloro m
chloroform [klórəfɔrm] N cloroformo m
chlorophyl, chlorophyll [klórəfɪl] N
clorofila f
chocolate [tʃáklɪt] N chocolate m; (piece)
chocolatina f; — **pot** chocolatera f
choice [tʃɔɪs] N (act of selecting, thing
selected) selección f; (alternative) opción f;
to have no other — no tener más
remedio; ADJ selecto
choir [kwaɪr] N coro m
choke [tʃok] VI/VT (suffocate) ahogar(se);
(strangle) estrangular(se); (on food)
atragantarse, atorarse; (obstruct) tapar(se);
VI (in sports) bloquearse; **I'm all —d up**
estoy muy conmovido; **to — back /
down** contener; N (act of choking on
something) atragantamiento m; (act of
choking someone) estrangulación f;
(device in cars) obturador m; (in sports)
bloqueo m
cholera [kálə] N cólera f
cholesterol [kaléstərɔl] N colesterol m
choose [tʃuz] VI/VT elegir, seleccionar,
escoger; **to — to** optar por
choosy [tʃúzi] ADJ quisquilloso
chop [tʃap] VI/VT cortar; **to — down** talar;
to — off mochar, tronchar; **to — up**
picar; N (act of chopping) golpe m; (cut of
meat) chuleta f; —**s** morro m; —**stick**
palillo m
choppy [tʃápi] ADJ picado, agitado
choral [kórəl] ADJ coral
chord [kɔrd] N (mathematical) cuerda f;
(musical) acorde m; **it struck a — in me**
me conmovió
chore [tʃɔr] N tarea f, faena f, quehacer m;
it's such a — es un trabajo asqueroso
choreography [kɔriágrafi] N coreografía f
chorus [kórəs] N coro m

chosen [tʃóːzən] ADJ **my — profession** la profesión de mi preferencia; **the — one** el elegido, la elegida
christen [krísən] VT bautizar
Christendom [krísəndəm] N cristianismo m
christening [krísənɪŋ] N bautizo m, bautismo m
Christian [krístʃən] ADJ & N cristiano -na mf; **— name** nombre de pila m
Christianity [krɪstʃiǽnɪɾi] N cristianismo m
Christmas [krísməs] N Navidad f, Pascua de Navidad f; ADJ navideño; **— card** tarjeta de Navidad f; **— Eve** Nochebuena f; **— gift** regalo de Navidad m; **— tree** árbol de Navidad m
chrome [krom] N cromo m; ADJ cromado
chromium [krómiəm] N cromo m
chromosome [króməsom] N cromosoma m
chronic [kránɪk] ADJ crónico
chronicle [kránɪkəl] N crónica f; VT registrar
chronological [kɑnəládʒɪkəl] ADJ cronológico
chronology [krənálədʒi] N cronología f
chronometer [krənámɪɾɚ] N cronómetro m
chrysalis [krísəlɪs] N crisálida f
chrysanthemum [krɪsǽnθəməm] N crisantemo m
chubby [tʃʌ́bi] ADJ rechoncho, gordito
chuck [tʃʌk] N (cut of meat) paletilla f; VT (to throw) lanzar; (to discard) tirar, botar
chuckle [tʃʌ́kəl] N risita f; VI reírse levemente
chum [tʃʌm] N compinche mf
chunk [tʃʌŋk] N trozo m, pedazo m; **a — of cash** un montón de plata
church [tʃɚtʃ] N iglesia f; **—man** clérigo m
churn [tʃɚn] N mantequera f; VI/VT (make butter) batir; (agitate) agitar, revolver
CIA (Central Intelligence Agency) [siaé] N CIA f
cicada [sɪkéɾə] N chicharra f
cider [sáɪɾɚ] N (alcoholic) sidra f; (non-alcoholic) Am jugo de manzana m; Sp zumo de manzana m
cigar [sɪgár] N puro m, habano m; **— store** tabaquería f; **close, but no —** bien, pero te quedaste corto
cigarette [sɪgərét] N cigarrillo m; Sp pitillo m; Am cigarro m; **— case** cigarrera f; Sp pitillera f; **— holder** boquilla f; **— lighter** encendedor m
cinch [sɪntʃ] N (for a saddle) cincha f; (something easy) pan comido m; (favorite) favorito -ta mf; VT cinchar
cinder [síndɚ] N ceniza f, rescoldo m
cinema [sínəmə] N cine m
cinnamon [sínəmən] N canela f; **— tree** canelo f

cipher [sáɪfɚ] N cifra f, guarismo m; VI/VT cifrar(se)
circle [sɚ́kəl] N círculo m; (literary) ámbito m, círculo m; VT (draw a circle) encerrar en un círculo; VI (go around) dar una vuelta
circuit [sɚ́kɪt] N circuito m; **— board** circuito impreso m; **— breaker** cortacircuitos m
circuitry [sɚ́kɪtri] N circuitería f
circular [sɚ́kjələ] ADJ circular; **— saw** sierra circular f; N circular f
circulate [sɚ́kjəlet] VI circular; VT (to pass around) poner en circulación
circulation [sɚkjəléʃən] N circulación f
circulatory system [sɚ́kjələtɔːrɪsɪstəm] N aparato circulatorio m
circumcise [sɚ́kəmsaɪz] VT circuncidar
circumference [sɚkʌ́mfəəns] N circunferencia f
circumlocution [sɚkəmlokjúʃən] N circunlocución f, rodeo m
circumscribe [sɚkəmskráɪb] VT circunscribir
circumspect [sɚ́kəmspekt] ADJ circunspecto
circumstance [sɚ́kəmstæns] N circunstancia f; **—s** condiciones financieras f pl
circumstantial [sɚkəmstǽnʃəl] ADJ circunstancial; **— evidence** pruebas circunstanciales f pl
circumvent [sɚkəmvént] VT evitar, obviar
circus [sɚ́kəs] N circo m
cirrhosis [sɪrósɪs] N cirrosis f
cirrus [sírəs] N cirro m
cistern [sístɚn] N cisterna f, aljibe m
citadel [síɾədəl] N ciudadela f
citation [saɪtéʃən] N (summons) citación f; (quote, quotation) cita f; (commendation for bravery) mención f
cite [saɪt] VT (quote, summon) citar; (comment on) mencionar
citizen [síɾɪzən] N (of a nation) ciudadano -na mf; (of a city or region) habitante mf
citizenship [síɾɪzənʃɪp] N ciudadanía f
citrus [sítrəs] ADJ & N cítrico m
city [síɾi] N ciudad f; ADJ municipal, urbano; **— council** concejo m; **— hall** ayuntamiento m; **— planning** urbanismo m
civic [sívɪk] ADJ cívico; N **—s** educación cívica f
civil [sívəl] ADJ (civilian) civil; (polite) cortés; **— disobedience** desobediencia civil f; **— engineer** ingeniero -ra civil mf; **— rights** derechos civiles m pl; **— service** administración pública f; **— war** guerra civil f
civilian [sɪvíljən] ADJ & N civil mf
civility [sɪvílɪɾi] N civilidad f, cortesía f

civilization [sɪvəlɪzéʃən] N civilización f
civilize [sívəlaɪz] VT civilizar
clad [klæd] ADJ vestido
claim [klem] VT (demand) reclamar,
reivindicar; (assert) sostener, pretender;
(notify of the existence of) denunciar; **to
— to be** pretender ser; N (demand)
reclamación f, reclamo m; (assertion)
afirmación f; (right) derecho m, título m;
(on insurance) demanda f, denuncia f
claimant [klémənt] N demandante mf,
reclamante mf; (to the throne)
pretendiente mf
clairvoyant [klervóɪənt] ADJ & N clarividente
mf
clam [klæm] N almeja f; VI **to — up** callarse
clamber [klémbə] VI/VT (climb with effort)
trepar con dificultad; (climb on all fours)
subir gateando
clammy [klémi] ADJ frío y húmedo
clamor [klémə] N clamor m, vocerío m; VI
clamar, vociferar
clamorous [kléməəs] ADJ clamoroso
clamp [klæmp] N (support) grapa f; (vice)
tornillo m; (wrap-around) abrazadera f; VT
sujetar; **to — down on** reprimir
clan [klæn] N clan m
clandestine [klændéstɪn] ADJ clandestino
clang [klæŋ] VI sonar; N sonido metálico m
clap [klæp] N (tap) palmada f; (blow) golpe
seco m; (gonorrhea) gonorrea f; **— of
thunder** trueno m; VT (on the back)
palmear; (in approval) aplaudir; (a book)
cerrar de golpe; **to — in jail** meter en la
cárcel
clapper [klépə] N badajo m
clarification [klærəfɪkéʃən] N aclaración f
clarify [klérəfaɪ] VT aclarar, clarificar
clarinet [klærənét] N clarinete m
clarity [klérɪɾi] N claridad f
clash [klæʃ] N (noise) estruendo metálico m;
(collision) choque m; (conflict) conflicto
m, enfrentamiento m; VI/VT (collide)
chocar; (oppose, fight) enfrentarse a; (not
go with) no combinar, no pegar
clasp [klæsp] N (fastener) broche m, cierre m;
(grip) apretón m; VT (fasten) abrochar;
(grip) apretar; (embrace) abrazar, prender
class [klæs] N clase f; (graduation class)
promoción f, graduación f; **in a — by
itself** único; **—mate** compañero -ra de
clase mf, condiscípulo -la mf; **—room**
salón de clase m, aula f; **—struggle**
lucha de clases f; VI/VT clasificar(se)
classic [klésɪk] ADJ & N clásico -ca mf
classical [klésɪkəl] ADJ clásico
classicism [klésəsɪzəm] N clasicismo m

classification [klæsəfɪkéʃən] N clasificación f
classify [klésəfaɪ] VT clasificar; N **classified
ad** anuncio clasificado m
clatter [klérə] N (noise) estrépito m;
(movement) traqueteo m; VI (make noise)
causar estrépito; (move) traquetear
clause [klɔz] N cláusula f
claustrophobia [klɔstrəfóbiə] N claustrofobia
f
claustrophobic [klɔstrəfóbɪk] ADJ
claustrofóbico
clavicle [klévɪkəl] N clavícula f
claw [klɔ] N (of a bear) garra f, zarpa f; (of a
cat) uña f; (of a crab) pinza f; (of a
hammer) orejas f pl; VI/VT arañar; **they
—ed their way through** se abrieron
paso con las uñas
clay [kle] N arcilla f; (for ceramics) greda f
clean [klin] ADJ limpio; (free from impurities,
not ornate) puro; (honorable) decente;
—cut (person) acicalado; (concept) bien
definido; **— joke** broma inocente f;
—shaven afeitado; **—up** limpieza f; **he
has a — record** no tiene antecedentes;
you'd better come — deberías confesar;
VI/VT limpiar; **he —ed me out** me limpió,
me desvalijó; **to — out something**
vaciar algo; **to — up** (a room) limpiar,
asear; (a document) pasar en limpio; (get
rich) forrarse
cleaner [klínə] N limpiador -ra mf; **—s**
tintorería f
cleanliness [klénlɪnɪs] N limpieza f;
(personal) aseo m
cleanse [klenz] VT limpiar
cleanser [klénzə] N limpiador m
clear [klir] ADJ claro; (skin, conscience)
limpio; (sky) despejado; (path) libre;
—cut (clearly defined) bien definido;
(obvious) claro; **—headed** lúcido; **—
profit** ganancia neta f; **to be in the —**
estar libre de culpa; **to keep — of
someone** evitar a alguien; **to pass —
through** pasar de lado a lado; VT (the
mind, confusion, voice) aclarar(se); (a
road, one's reputation, computer screen)
limpiar; (of criminal charges) absolver; (of
suspicion) eximir; (liquid) clarificar; (a
legislative bill, plan) aprobar, obtener
autorización para; (land for farming)
desmontar; (a hurdle) salvar; (a net gain)
sacar; **to — the air** sincerarse; **to — the
table** levantar la mesa; **to — up** (a
mystery) aclarar(se); (the sky) despejar(se)
clearance [klírəns] N (space) espacio libre m;
(vertical) margen de altura m; (permission)
autorización f; **— sale** liquidación f

clearing [klíríŋ] N (terrain) claro m; (of checks) clearing m; — **house** banco de compensación m

cleavage [klívɪdʒ] N (cut) hendidura f; (in dress) escote m

cleave [kliv] VT hender(se); **to — to** adherirse a

cleaver [klívə-] N cuchilla f

clef [klef] N clave f

cleft [kleft] N hendidura f; ADJ hendido, partido; — **palate** paladar hendido m

clemency [klémənsi] N clemencia f

clench [klentʃ] VT agarrar, asir; (teeth, fist) apretar

clergy [klɜ́-dʒi] N clero m, clerecía f; —**man** clérigo m, pastor m; —**woman** pastora f

clerical [klérɪkəl] ADJ (of the clergy) clerical, eclesiástico; (of office personnel) de oficina; — **error** error de copia m; — **work** trabajo de escritorio m

clerk [klɜ-k] N (sales) dependiente -ta mf; (office) empleado -da de oficina mf; (court) escribiente mf, actuario -ria mf; VI trabajar como actuario -ria

clever [klévə-] ADJ (ingenious) ingenioso; (smart) listo, vivo; (dexterous) habilidoso

cleverness [klévə-nɪs] N (intelligence) inteligencia f, viveza f; (ingenuity) ingenio m; (dexterity) habilidad f

cliché [klíʃé] N cliché m, muletilla f; Sp tópico m

click [klɪk] N clic m, chasquido m; (sound of heels) taconeo m; VI chascar; (on a computer) hacer clic; (heels) taconear; VT chascar, chasquear

client [kláɪənt] N (of professional or store) cliente -ta mf; (of social service) beneficiario -ria mf

clientele [klaɪəntél] N clientela f

cliff [klɪf] N precipicio m, despeñadero m; (by the sea) acantilado m

climate [kláɪmɪt] N clima m

climax [kláɪmæks] N clímax m; VI culminar, alcanzar el clímax

climb [klaɪm] N (ascent) subida f; (in alpinism) escalada f; VI/VT (ascend) subir; (ascend with effort) trepar(se) (a), encaramar(se) (a); VT (a mountain, wall) escalar; **to — down** bajar

climber [kláɪmə-] N (in alpinism) escalador -ora mf; (plant) trepadora f

clinch [klɪntʃ] VT (resolve) rematar; (hammer down) remachar; (hug, in boxing) trabar; (secure) sujetar; (finalize) cerrar; N (nail) remache m; (embrace) abrazo m; (in boxing) clinch m

cling [klɪŋ] VI (to stick to) pegarse; (to hold onto) aferrarse

clinic [klínɪk] N clínica f; (workshop) taller m

clink [klɪŋk] N tintín m; VI tintinear

clip [klɪp] VT (cut) cortar; (trim) recortar; (shear) esquilar; (shorten) acortar; (hit) tocar; (fasten) abrochar; (attach paper) sujetar con un clip; N (fastener) gancho m; (for paper) clip m; (of cartridge) cargador m; (brooch) broche m

clipper [klípə-] N (shearer) esquilador -ra mf; —**s** (scissors) tijeras f pl; (hair trimmer) maquinilla f

clipping [klípɪŋ] N recorte m

clique [klɪk] N (political) camarilla f; (in school) pandilla f

clitoris [klítə-ɪs] N clítoris m

cloak [klok] N capa f; (military) capote m; —**room** guardarropa m; VT (put a cloak on) vestirse con una capa; (hide) encubrir

clock [klɑk] N reloj m; —**making** relojería f; — **radio** radio reloj f; —**work** maquinaria de reloj f; **like** —**work** con precisión, sin falta; VT **you swim and I'll — you** tú nadas y yo te tomo el tiempo; **the police —ed him at 90 mph** la policía lo pescó haciendo noventa millas por hora

clockwise [klákwaɪz] ADV en el sentido de las manecillas de reloj

clod [klɑd] N (piece of dirt) terrón m, pelotón m; (dolt) tonto -ta mf, necio -cia mf

clog [klɑg] VI/VT obstruir(se), tapar(se); N (shoe) zueco m; — **dance** baile zapateado m

cloister [klɔ́ɪstə-] N claustro m; (monastery) monasterio m; VT enclaustrar

clone [klon] N clon m; VT clonar

cloning [klónɪŋ] N clonaje m, clonación f

close [kloz] VI/VT cerrar(se); VT (a hole) tapar; **to — an account** cerrar una cuenta; **to — a meeting** levantar una sesión; **to — in upon** (oppress) oprimir; (approach) cercar a uno; **to — out** liquidar; N fin m; (act of closing) cierre m; —**out** saldo m; [klos] ADJ (near) cercano; (dense) tupido; (intimate) íntimo; — **attention** mucha atención f; —**fought** reñido; —**knit** muy unido; — **questioning** interrogatorio minucioso m; — **translation** traducción fiel f; —**up** primer plano m; **at — range** de cerca; **that was a — call** nos salvamos por poco; ADV cerca

closed [klozd] ADJ cerrado; — **circuit** circuito cerrado m; —**minded** cerrado; —**mindedness** cerrazón f

closeness [klósnɪs] N cercanía f; (friendship)

intimidad *f*; (correctness) fidelidad *f*

closet [klázɪt] N ropero *m*, armario *m*; VI enclaustrarse; ADJ a escondidas

closure [klóʒɚ] N (conclusion) cierre *m*; (sense of completeness) clausura *f*

clot [klɑt] VI/VT coagular(se); N coágulo *m*, cuajarón *m*

cloth [klɔθ] N tela *f*, tejido *m*; (wool) paño *m*; ADJ de tela; **— bound** encuadernado en tela; **man of the —** clérigo *m*

clothe [kloð] VT vestir; N **—s** ropa *f*; **—sline** tendedero *m*; **—spin** pinza *f*

clothier [klóðjɚ] N comerciante en ropa o paño *mf*

clothing [klóðɪŋ] N ropa *f*

cloud [klaʊd] N nube *f*; **—burst** chaparrón *m*, aguacero *m*; VT nublar, anublar; (make indistinct, place under suspicion) enturbiar; **to — up** nublarse, anublarse; **to be on — nine** estar en el séptimo cielo; **under a —** bajo sospecha

cloudless [kláʊdlɪs] ADJ despejado

cloudy [kláʊdi] ADJ nublado; *Sp* nuboso; (gloomy) sombrío

clout [klaʊt] N influencia *f*

clove [klov] N clavo *m*; **— of garlic** diente de ajo *m*

cloven [klóvən] ADJ hendido; **—-hoofed** patihendido

clover [klóvɚ] N trébol *m*; **—leaf** trébol *m*; **to be in —** vivir en el lujo

clown [klaʊn] N payaso *m*; VI payasear, bufonear

cloy [klɔɪ] VI/VT (to satiate) hastiar; (to be too sweet for) repugnar

club [klʌb] N (society, nightclub) club *m*; (stick) porra *f*, garrote *m*; (suit of cards) basto *m*; **—house** casa de club *f*; VT aporrear

cluck [klʌk] VI cloquear; N cloqueo *m*

clue [klu] N pista *f*, indicio *m*; **to have no —** no tener ni noción

clueless [klúlɪs] ADJ (absent-minded) despistado; (uninformed) en ayunas

clump [klʌmp] N (of bushes) matorral *m*; (of trees) arboleda *f*; VI/VT apiñar(se)

clumsiness [klʌ́mzinɪs] N torpeza *f*

clumsy [klʌ́mzi] ADJ torpe, desmañado, chambón; *Sp* patoso

clunker [klʌ́ŋkɚ] N cacharro *m*

cluster [klʌ́stɚ] N grupo *m*; (of grapes) racimo *m*; VI/VT agrupar(se), arracimar(se)

clutch [klʌtʃ] N (in a car) embrague *m*; **—pedal** pedal del embrague *m*; **to step on the —** pisar el embrague; **—es** garras *f pl*; VT (seize) asir; (hold) apretar

clutter [klʌ́dɚ] VT **books —ed her desk** tenía libros desparramados por todo el escritorio; N desparramo *m*, desorden *m*, confusión *f*

coach [kotʃ] N (carriage) coche *m*, carruaje *m*, carroza *f*; (bus) autobús *m*; (trainer) entrenador -ra *mf*; (in air travel) clase turista *f*; (tutor) profesor -ra particular *mf*; **—man** cochero *m*; VI/VT entrenar

coagulate [koǽgjəlet] VI/VT coagular(se)

coal [kol] N carbón *m*; **— bin** carbonera *f*; **— tar** alquitrán *m*

coalition [koəlíʃən] N coalición *f*

coarse [kɔrs] ADJ (fabric) burdo, basto; (sand) grueso; (manners, language) grosero, tosco, rudo

coarseness [kɔ́rsnɪs] N (fabric) bastedad *f*; (language, manners) tosquedad *f*, rudeza *f*; (of a joke) chocarrería *f*

coast [kost] N costa *f*; **— Guard** Guardia Costera *f*; **—line** costa *f*; **—-to—** de costa a costa; VI (on a sled) deslizar(se); (in a car, on a bike) tirarse por una bajada; **he —ed through medical school** la Facultad de Medicina le resultó muy fácil

coastal [kóstəl] ADJ costero

coat [kot] N abrigo *m*; (of paint) capa *f*, mano *f*; (on animals) pelaje *m*; **— of arms** escudo de armas *m*, blasón *m*; **— rack** percha *f*, perchero *m*; **—tail** faldón *m*; VT cubrir; (with paint) dar una mano a; (with grease) engrasar; (with soap) enjabonar; (with sugar) bañar

coax [koks] VT persuadir con halagos, engatusar

cob [kɑb] N mazorca *f*, panoja *f*; **—web** telaraña *f*

cobalt [kóbɔlt] N cobalto *m*

cobbler [kɑ́blɚ] N (person who repairs shoes) zapatero -ra *mf*, remendón -ona *mf*; (dessert) budín de bizcocho y fruta *m*

cobblestone [kɑ́bəlston] N adoquín *m*

cobra [kóbrə] N cobra *f*

cocaine [kokén] N cocaína *f*

cock [kɑk] N (rooster) gallo *m*; (male bird) macho de ave de corral *m*; (faucet) llave *f*; (gun part) martillo *m*; (penis) *vulg* polla *f*, pija *f*; **—fight** riña de gallos *f*; **—pit** (for cockfights) gallera *f*; (in an airplane) cabina *f*; **—scomb** cresta de gallo *f*; **—sure** gallito *m*; VT (a gun) amartillar; (one's head) ladear

cock-a-doodle-doo [kákədudldú] INTERJ quiquiriquí

cockatoo [kákətu] N cacatúa *f*

cocker spaniel [kákɚspǽnjəl] N cócker *m*

cockroach [kákrotʃ] N cucaracha *f*

cocktail [káktel] N cóctel *m*; **— party**

cóctel *m*

cocky [káki] ADJ gallito, valentón

cocoa [kóko] N (powder) cacao *m*; (drink) chocolate *m*

coconut [kókʌnʌt] N coco *m*

cocoon [kəkún] N capullo *m*

cod [kad] N *Sp* abadejo *m*; *Am* bacalao *m*; —**-liver oil** aceite de hígado de bacalao *m*

coddle [kádl] VT mimar

code [kod] N código *m*; — **switching** alternancia de códigos *f*

codeine [kódin] N codeína *f*

codger [kádʒə] N vejete *m*, vejancón *m*

codify [kádəfaɪ] VT codificar

coed [kóed] ADJ mixto; N alumna universitaria *f*

coefficient [koəfíʃənt] N coeficiente *m*

coerce [koɚs] VT forzar, obligar

coercion [koɚʒən] N coacción *f*

coexistence [koɪgzístəns] N coexistencia *f*

coffee [kɔ́fi] N café *m*; — **bean** grano de café *m*; — **break** descanso para tomar el café *m*; — **bush** cafeto *m*; — **maker** máquina de café *f*, cafetera *f*; —**pot** cafetera *f*; — **shop** (for coffee) café *m*; (for coffee and light meals) cafetería *f*; — **table** mesa baja *f*

coffer [kɔ́fə] N cofre *m*

coffin [kɔ́fɪn] N ataúd *m*, féretro *m*

cog [kag] N diente *m*; —**wheel** rueda dentada *f*

cogent [kódʒənt] ADJ convincente

cognac [kánjæk] N coñac *m*

cognate [kágnet] ADJ & N cognado *m*

cognitive [kágnɪtɪv] ADJ cognitivo

cohabitate [kohǽbɪtet] VI cohabitar

coherent [kohírənt] ADJ coherente; (sticking together) cohesivo

cohesion [kohíʒən] N cohesión *f*

coiffure [kwafjúr] N peinado *m*

coil [kɔɪl] VI/VT arrollar(se), enrollar(se); (snake) enroscar(se); N (roll) rollo *m*; (spiral) tirabuzón *m*; (electric) bobina *f*; — **spring** muelle en espiral *m*

coin [kɔɪn] N moneda *f*; —**-operated** de monedas; VT acuñar (also words)

coinage [kɔ́ɪnɪdʒ] N acuñación *f* (also of words)

coincide [koɪnsáɪd] VI coincidir

coincidence [koínsɪdəns] N coincidencia *f*, casualidad *f*

coitus [kóɪtəs] N coito *m*

coke [kok] N (coal) cok *m*, coque *m*; (cocaine) *fam* coca *f*

cola [kólə] N gaseosa *f*

colander [káləndə] N colador *m*

cold [koɫd] ADJ frío; — **cream** cold cream *m*;

— **cuts** fiambres *m pl*; — **fish** *fam* témpano *m*; — **snap** ola de frío *f*; — **sore** herpes *m sg*; — **war** guerra fría *f*; **to be** — tener frío; **to be out** — quedar seco; **it is** — **today** hace frío hoy; **he gave me the** — **shoulder** me hizo el vacío; **he quit** — **turkey** dejó de un día para otro; **he got** — **feet** se acobardó; N frío *m*; (illness) resfrío *m*, resfriado *m*, catarro *m*; **to catch a** — resfriarse

coldness [kóɫdnɪs] N frialdad *f*

colic [kálɪk] N cólico *m*

coliseum [kalɪsíəm] N coliseo *m*

collaborate [kəlǽbəret] VI colaborar

collaboration [kəlæbəréʃən] N colaboración *f*

collaborator [kəlǽbəretə] N colaborador -ora *f*

collage [kəláʒ] N collage *m*

collagen [kálədʒən] N colágeno *m*

collapse [kəlǽps] VI (fold into sections) plegarse; (cave in) hundirse, derrumbarse; (fail) fracasar; (faint) desmayarse; (empty of air, decline in value) colapsar(se); N (falling in) derrumbe *m*, derrumbamiento *m*, desplome *m*; (breakdown) colapso *m*

collar [kálə] N (for restraining dogs, marking on an animal, necklace) collar *m*; (of a shirt) cuello *m*; —**bone** clavícula *f*; VT acollarar; (grab by the neck) agarrar por el cuello; **I was —ed by the boss** el jefe me agarró de charla

collate [kólet] VT (put in order) colacionar; (compare) cotejar

collateral [kəlǽDəəɫ] ADJ (on the side) colateral; (auxiliary) subsidiario; N garantía subsidiaria *f*

colleague [kálig] N colega *mf*

collect [kəlékt] VT (gather) recoger; (make a collection) coleccionar; (receive taxes) recaudar; VI/VT (receive payment) cobrar, percibir; (assemble) reunir(se); (accumulate) acumular(se); **to — oneself** calmarse; **on delivery** pago contra reembolso *m*; — **call** llamada de cobro revertido *f*, llamada por / a cobrar *f*

collection [kəlékʃən] N (set of collectibles, clothes) colección *f*; (for charity) colecta *f*; (of taxes) recaudación *f*, cobranza *f*, cobro *m*; (of data, fruit) recolección *f*

collective [kəléktɪv] N & ADJ colectivo *m*; — **bargaining** convenio colectivo *m*

collector [kəléktə] N (of taxes) recaudador -ra *mf*; (of collectibles) coleccionista *mf*; (of other things) colector -ora *mf*

college [kálɪdʒ] N (institution) universidad *f*; (division) facultad *f*; (association) colegio *m*; **let's give it the old — try** vamos a

hacer un esfuerzo supremo
collegial [kəlíʤəɫ] ADJ cooperador
collegiate [kəlíʤɪt] ADJ universitario
collide [kəláɪd] VI/VT chocar
collie [káli] N collie *m*
collision [kəlíʒən] N colisión *f*, choque *m*
colloid [kál.ɪd] N coloide *m*
colloquial [kəlókwɪəɫ] ADJ coloquial; —
  expression frase familiar *f*
colloquium [kəlókwɪəm] N coloquio *m*,
  jornada *f*
collusion [kəlúʒən] N confabulación *f*
cologne [kəlón] N colonia *f*
Colombia [kəlámbɪə] N Colombia *f*
Colombian [kəlámbɪən] ADJ & N colombiano
  -na *m*
colon [kólən] N (punctuation) dos puntos *m*
  pl; (bowels) colon *m*; [kəlón] (currency of
  El Salvador and Costa Rica) colón *m*
colonel [kɝnəɫ] N coronel *m*
colonial [kəlóniəɫ] ADJ colonial
colonist [kálənɪst] N (settler) colono *m*;
  (colonizer) colonizador -ra *mf*
colonization [kalənɪzéʃən] N colonización *f*
colonize [kálənaɪz] VT colonizar
colony [káləni] N colonia *f*
color [kálɚ] N color *m*; (colorfulness) colorido
  m; **the —s** la bandera; **he showed his
  true —s** se mostró tal cual era; **persons
  of —** gente de color *f*; **a — TV** un
  televisor en/a color; ADJ **—-blind**
  daltónico; **—fast** de colores firmes; VT
  (give color) colorear; (make colorful) dar
  colorido; (taint) teñir; (blush) ruborizarse
colored [kálɚd] ADJ coloreado; (biased)
  sesgado
colorful [kálɚfəɫ] ADJ (full of color) colorido;
  (eccentric) pintoresco
coloring [kálɚɪŋ] N (tone) colorido *m*;
  (action) coloración *f*; (substance) colorante
  m
colorless [kálɚlɪs] ADJ (without color)
  incoloro; (bleached) descolorido
colossal [kəlásəɫ] ADJ colosal
colt [koɫt] N potro *m*
column [káləm] N columna *f*
columnist [káləmnɪst] N columnista *mf*
coma [kómə] N coma *m*
comatose [kámətos] ADJ comatoso
comb [kom] N (for hair) peine *m*; (of a
  rooster) cresta *f*; (for wool) carda *f*; (for
  horses) almohaza *f*; (of honey) panal *m*;
  VT (hair) peinar; (wool) cardar; (search an
  area) peinar, batir; **to — one's hair**
  peinarse
combat [kámbæt] VI/VT combatir; N combate
  m

combatant [kəmbǽtn̩t] ADJ & N combatiente
  mf
combative [kəmbǽDɪv] ADJ combativo
combination [kambənéʃən] N combinación
  f; **— lock** cerradura de combinación *f*
combine [kəmbáɪn] VI/VT combinar(se);
  [kámbaɪn] N cosechadora *f*
combo [kámbo] N combo *m*
combustible [kəmbástəbəɫ] ADJ & N
  combustible *m*
combustion [kəmbástʃən] N combustión *f*
come [kʌm] VI venir; (have an orgasm) *fam*
  venirse; *Sp fam* correrse; **an idea came to
  me** se me ocurrió una idea; **Christmas is
  coming** llega la Navidad; **milk —s from
  cows** la leche se saca de las vacas; **no
  harm will — to you** no te va a pasar
  nada; **the dress —s to her knees** el
  vestido le llega a las rodillas; **to — about**
  suceder; **to — across** (find) encontrar;
  (make an impression) parecer; **to —
  along** (accompany) acompañar; (appear)
  surgir; **how's your paper coming
  along?** ¿cómo va tu trabajo? **to — again**
  volver, volver a venir; **to — at** venirse
  encima; **to — back** volver; **to make a
  —back** resurgir; (in sports) recuperarse; **to
  — down with a cold** coger un
  resfriado; **to — downstairs** bajar; **to —
  from** ser de; **to — in** entrar; **to — off**
  salir(se); **to — out** salir; **to — over** venir
  para acá; **to — to** volver en sí; **to —
  together** (meet) juntarse, unirse; (reach
  agreement) ponerse de acuerdo; **to — up**
  subir; **your name came up** tu nombre
  vino a colación; N (semen) *vulg* leche *f*;
  —back (reply) réplica *f*; (in sports)
  recuperación *f*
comedian [kəmídɪən] N cómico -ca *mf*,
  comediante *mf*
comedy [káməDi] N (genre) comedia *f*;
  (profession) humorismo *m*
comet [kámɪt] N cometa *m*
comfort [kámfɚt] VT reconfortar; N (feeling
  of ease) comodidad *f*, confort *m*, holgura
  f; (solace) consuelo *f*
comfortable [kámfɚ-Dəbəɫ] ADJ cómodo,
  confortable; **— income** buen pasar *m*; **—
  life** vida holgada/desahogada *f*
comforter [kámfɚ-Dɚ] N edredón *m*
comic [kámɪk] ADJ cómico, chistoso, gracioso;
  — book revista de historietas *f*, comic *m*;
  —s tiras cómicas *f pl*, historietas *f pl*; **—
  strip** tira cómica *f*
comical [kámɪkəɫ] ADJ cómico, gracioso
coming [kámɪŋ] N venida *f*; **— of Christ**
  advenimiento de Cristo *m*; **—s and**

goings idas y venidas *f pl*; ADJ que viene, próximo
comma [kámə] N coma *f*
command [kəmǽnd] VT (order) mandar; (have authority over) comandar; **to — respect** inspirar respeto, imponerse; N (order) mandato *m*, orden *f*; (post) comandancia *f*; (dominance) dominio *m*; (on a computer) comando *m*; **he has a good — of English** domina bien el inglés; **to be in — of** estar al mando de; **to be under the — of** estar al mando de; **at your —** a sus órdenes
commandeer [kamandír] VT apoderarse de; (for the military) requisar
commander [kəmǽndə-] N (leader) jefe -fa *mf*; (army officer) comandante *mf*; (navy officer) capitán de fragata *m*; **— in chief** comandante en jefe *mf*
commandment [kəmǽndmənt] N mandamiento *m*
commemorate [kəmémərat] VT conmemorar
commence [kəméns] VI/VT comenzar, principiar
commencement [kəménsmənt] N (beginning) comienzo *m*; (graduation) graduación *f*, colación *f*
commend [kəménd] VT (praise) alabar; (entrust) encomendar
commendation [kamandéʃən] N (praise) alabanza *f*; (mention) mención de honor *f*
commensurate [kəménsə-ɪt] ADJ proporcional, acorde
comment [kámɛnt] N comentario *m*; **no —** sin comentarios; VI/VT comentar
commentary [kámənteri] N comentario *m*
commentator [kámənteɪə-] N (person who describes) comentador -ra *mf*; (on radio, etc.) comentarista *mf*
commerce [káməs] N comercio *m*
commercial [kəmə́-ʃəl] ADJ comercial; N (on radio or television) anuncio *m*
commercialize [kəmə́-ʃəlaɪz] VT comercializar
commiserate [kəmízəret] VI/VT compadecerse de
commiseration [kəmɪzəréʃən] N conmiseración *f*
commissary [kámɪseri] N economato *m*
commission [kəmíʃən] N (act, committee, payment) comisión *f*; (of a broker) corretaje *m*; (charge) encargo *m*; (mission) misión *f*; (title) nombramiento *m*; **to be in —** estar en servicio; **to be out of —** estar fuera de servicio; **to put out of —** (object) inutilizar; (person) retirar de servicio; VT (authorize) comisionar; (order)

encargar; (appoint) nombrar; (get ready) poner en servicio; **—ed officer** oficial *m*
commissioner [kəmíʃənə-] N comisario -ria *mf*
commit [kəmít] VT (perpetrate) cometer; (entrust) encargar; (direct) destinar; **to — to an asylum** internar; **to — to memory** aprender de memoria; **to — to paper** poner por escrito; **to — to prison** encarcelar
commitment [kəmítmənt] N compromiso *m*
committee [kəmídi] N comité *m*, comisión *f*
commode [kəmód] N wáter *m*, inodoro *m*
commodity [kəmádɪdi] N (product) mercancía *f*, artículo *m*, producto *m*; (raw material) materia prima *f*
common [kámən] ADJ (shared, frequent) común; (general) general; (vulgar) ordinario; (unremarkable) simple; **— cold** resfriado *m*; **— denominator** denominador común *m*; **— law** derecho consuetudinario *m*; **—place** trivial; **— sense** sentido común *m*, sensatez *f*; **— soldier** soldado raso *m*; **— stock** acciones ordinarias *f pl*; **— wealth** (state) estado *m*; (republic) república *f*; N **—s** (land) ejido *m*
commotion [kəmóʃən] N conmoción *f*, revuelo *m*
commune [kəmjún] VI (communicate) comunicarse, departir; (take communion) comulgar; [kámjun] N comuna *f*
communicable [kəmjúnɪkabəl] ADJ comunicable; (disease) transmisible
communicate [kəmjúnɪket] VI/VT comunicar(se); (disease) transmitir(se)
communication [kəmjunikéʃən] N comunicación *f*
communicative [kəmjúnɪkədɪv] ADJ comunicativo
communion [kəmjúnjən] N comunión *f*
communism [kámjənɪzəm] N comunismo *m*
communist [kámjənɪst] N & ADJ comunista *mf*
community [kəmjúnɪdi] N comunidad *f*
commute [kəmjút] VT (reduce a sentence) conmutar; VI viajar diariamente al trabajo
commuter [kəmjúdə-] N persona que viaja diariamente al trabajo *f*
Comoros [káməroz] N Comoras *f pl*
compact [kəmpǽkt] ADJ compacto; (dense) tupido, apretado; (concise) conciso; **— disk** disco compacto *m*; VT compactar; (make denser) tupir; [kámpækt] N (agreement) pacto *m*; (case for powder) polvera *f*
compactness [kəmpǽktnɪs] N densidad *f*; (conciseness) concisión *f*

companion [kəmpǽnjən] N (comrade, partner) compañero -ra *mf;* (caregiver) acompañante *mf*

companionship [kəmpǽnjənʃip] N compañía *f*

company [kʌ́mpəni] N compañía *f;* **to keep — with** codearse con, frecuentar

comparable [kʌ́mpəəbəł] ADJ comparable

comparative [kəmpǽrədiv] ADJ comparativo

compare [kəmpɛ́r] VI/VT comparar(se); **beyond —** incomparable, sin parangón

comparison [kəmpǽrisən] N comparación *f;* **in — with** comparado con

compartment [kəmpʌ́rtmənt] N compartimiento *m*

compass [kʌ́mpəs] N (for drawing) compás *m;* (for directions) brújula *f*

compassion [kəmpǽʃən] N compasión *f*

compassionate [kəmpǽʃənit] ADJ compasivo

compatible [kəmpǽɾəbəł] ADJ compatible (also computer term)

compatriot [kəmpétriət] N compatriota *mf*

compel [kəmpɛ́ł] VT (force) obligar; (demand) exigir

compelling [kəmpɛ́liŋ] ADJ (argument) convincente; (story) emocionante

compensate [kʌ́mpənset] VT (make up for) compensar, resarcir; (pay) remunerar

compensation [kampənséʃən] N (making up for) compensación *f;* (remuneration) remuneración *f*

compete [kəmpít] VI/VT competir

competence [kʌ́mpidəns] N competencia *f*

competent [kʌ́mpidənt] ADJ competente

competition [kampitíʃən] N competencia *f;* (sports match) competición *f,* contienda *f*

competitive [kəmpédidiv] ADJ competitivo; **— examination** *Sp* oposición *f; Am* concurso *m;* **— sports** deportes de competición *m pl*

competitor [kəmpédidəˑ] N competidor -ra *mf*

compile [kəmpáł] VT recopilar, compilar

compiler [kəmpáłəˑ] N compilador *m*

complacency [kəmplésənsi] N confianza infundada *f*

complacent [kəmplésənt] ADJ confiado

complain [kəmplén] VI quejarse

complaint [kəmplént] N queja *f;* (civil charge) demanda *f;* (ailment) dolencia *f*

complement [kʌ́mpləmənt] N complemento *m;* (of staff) dotación *f;* [kʌ́mpləmənt] VT complementar

complete [kəmplít] ADJ completo, pleno; **a — stranger** un perfecto desconocido; VT completar

completion [kəmplíʃən] N finalización *f,*

terminación *f;* **she brought the project to —** completó el proyecto

complex [kəmplɛ́ks] ADJ complejo; [kʌ́mplɛks] N complejo *m*

complexion [kəmplɛ́kʃən] N (skin) cutis *m;* (color) tez *f;* (perspective) cariz *m*

complexity [kamplɛ́ksidi] N complejidad *f*

compliance [kəmpláiəns] N (obedience) conformidad *f,* acatamiento *m;* (meek agreement) pleitesía *f;* **in — with** en conformidad con

complicate [kʌ́mpliket] VT complicar

complicated [kʌ́mplikedid] ADJ complicado

complication [kamplikéʃən] N complicación *f*

complicity [kəmplísidi] N complicidad *f*

compliment [kʌ́mpləmənt] N cumplido *m;* (on looks) piropo *m;* (from a suitor) galantería *f;* **to pay someone a —** hacerle un cumplido a alguien; **to send one's —s** enviar saludos; [kʌ́mpləmənt] VI/VT elogiar

comply [kəmplái] VI obedecer; **to — with** cumplir con, acatar

component [kəmpónənt] ADJ & N componente *m*

compose [kəmpóz] VI/VT componer; **to — oneself** sosegarse

composed [kəmpózd] ADJ sosegado; **to be — of** estar compuesto de, componerse de, constar de

composer [kəmpózəˑ] N compositor -ra *mf*

composite [kəmpázit] ADJ compuesto; N amalgama *f*

composition [kampəzíʃən] N (make-up, musical piece) composición *f;* (aggregate material) compuesto *m;* (school essay) composición *f,* redacción *f*

composure [kəmpóʒəˑ] N compostura *f*

compound [kʌ́mpaund] ADJ & N compuesto *m;* **— fracture** fractura expuesta *f;* **— interest** interés compuesto *m;* [kampáund] VT (combine) combinar; (worsen) empeorar

comprehend [kamprihénd] VT comprender

comprehensible [kamprihénsəbəł] ADJ comprensible

comprehension [kamprihénʃən] N comprensión *f*

comprehensive [kamprihénsiv] ADJ exhaustivo; **— insurance** seguro contra todo riesgo *m*

compress [kəmprés] VT comprimir; [kʌ́mprɛs] N compresa *f*

compression [kəmpréʃən] N compresión *f*

comprise [kəmpráiz] VT comprender, incluir; **to be —d of** comprender, incluir

compromise [kámprəmaız] N (arrangement) arreglo por concesiones mutuas *m*, compromiso *m*; (intermediate thing) cruce *m*, término medio *m*; VI/VT (make agreement) transigir; *Am* transar; (jeopardize) comprometer

comptroller [kəntrólə] N controlador -ra *mf*; *Am* contralor -ora *mf*

compulsion [kəmpʌ́lʃən] N (impulse) compulsión *f*, coacción *f*; (coercion) coerción *f*

compulsive [kəmpʌ́lsıv] ADJ compulsivo

compulsory [kəmpʌ́lsəri] ADJ obligatorio

computation [kampjʊtéʃən] N cómputo *m*, cálculo *m*

compute [kəmpjút] VI/VT computar, calcular

computer [kəmpjúdə] N *Am* computadora *f*; *Sp* ordenador *m*; **— graphics** gráficos por computadora/ordenador *m pl*; **— science** informática *f*; **— virus** virus de computadora/ordenador *m*

computerize [kəmpjúpəraız] VI/VT informatizar, computarizar

comrade [kámræd] N camarada *mf*

concave [kánkev] ADJ cóncavo

conceal [kənsíl] VT encubrir, ocultar, disimular

concealment [kənsílmənt] N encubrimiento *m*, disimulo *m*

concede [kənsíd] VI/VT (recognize) conceder; (yield) otorgar

conceit [kənsít] N (vanity) vanidad *f*; (literary device) concepto *m*

conceited [kənsídıd] ADJ engreído, presumido

conceivable [kənsívəbəl] ADJ imaginable, concebible

conceive [kənsív] VI/VT concebir; (a plan) concebir, idear

concentrate [kánsəntret] VI/VT concentrar(se)

concentration [kansəntréʃən] N concentración *f*; **— camp** campo de concentración *m*

concept [kánsept] N concepto *m*

conception [kənsépʃən] N concepción *f*

concern [kənsɜ́-n] N (interest) interés *m*; (affair) asunto *m*; (worry) preocupación *f*; (company) compañía *f*; **to be of no —** no tener consecuencia; VT (be of interest) concernir, atañer; (worry) preocupar; **to — oneself with** ocuparse de; **to whom it may —** a quien corresponda

concerned [kənsɜ́-nd] ADJ (involved) involucrado; (anxious) preocupado; **as far as I am —** en lo que a mí respecta; **to be — about** preocuparse por

concerning [kənsɜ́-nɪŋ] PREP tocante a, respecto a

concert [kánsɜ-t] N concierto *m*; [kənsɜ́-t] VT concertar

concession [kənséʃən] N concesión *f*

conciliate [kənsíliet] VI/VT (make compatible) conciliar; (appease) aplacar

concise [kənsáıs] ADJ conciso, sucinto

conciseness [kənsáısnıs] N concisión *f*

conclude [kənklúd] VI/VT concluir, terminar; (deduce) deducir

conclusion [kənklúʒən] N conclusión *f*

conclusive [kənklúsıv] ADJ concluyente

concoct [kənkákt] VT (contrive) fabricar, urdir; (prepare by cooking) preparar

concoction [kənkákʃən] N menjurje *m*

concord [kánkɔrd] N (peace) concordia *f*; (agreement) convenio *m*, acuerdo *m*

concrete [kankrít] ADJ concreto; (made of concrete) de hormigón; [kánkrit] N hormigón *m*

concubine [káŋkjəbaın] N concubina *f*

concur [kənkɜ́-] VI estar de acuerdo

concussion [kənkʌ́ʃən] N (brain injury) conmoción cerebral *f*; (shock) concusión *f*

condemn [kəndém] VT condenar; (acquire public ownership) expropiar; (declare unsafe) declarar ruinoso

condemnation [kandəmnéʃən] N condenación *f*, condena *f*

condensation [kandenséʃən] N condensación *f*; (of a book) compendio *m*

condense [kəndéns] VI/VT condensar(se)

condescend [kandəsénd] VI condescender a

condescension [kandəsénʃən] N condescendencia *f*

condiment [kándəmənt] N condimento *m*, aliño *m*

condition [kəndíʃən] N condición *f*; **he's got a heart —** sufre del corazón, tiene una afección cardíaca; **he's in good physical —** está en buen estado físico; **the patient is in critical —** el paciente está en estado crítico; **on — that** a condición de que; VT (restrict on a condition, establish a conditioned response) condicionar; (accustom oneself) acostumbrarse

conditional [kəndíʃənəl] ADJ & N condicional *m*

conditioning [kəndíʃənɪŋ] N condicionamiento *m*

condolences [kəndólənsız] N pésame *m*, condolencias *f*; **to express one's —** dar las condolencias

condom [kándəm] N condón *m*, preservativo *m*

condominium [kandəmíniəm] N

condominio *m*
condone [kəndón] VT tolerar
conducive [kəndúsɪv] ADJ conducente
conduct [kándʌkt] N conducta *f*,
comportamiento *m*; [kəndʌ́kt] VI/VT
(behave) conducirse, comportarse; (carry
out) llevar a cabo; (direct, lead) dirigir;
(serve as channel for) conducir
conductor [kəndʌ́ktɚ] N (substance that
conducts) conductor *m*; (of an orchestra)
director -ra *mf*; (of a train) revisor -ra *mf*
conduit [kánduɪt] N conducto *m*
cone [kon] N cono *m*; (container) cucurucho
m
confection [kənfékʃən] N (of clothes)
confección *f*; (of candy) confitura *f*
confectionery [kənfékʃəneri] N confitería *f*;
(shop) dulcería *f*; (candies) dulces *m pl*
confederacy [kənfédɚəsi] N confederación *f*
confederate [kənfédɚət] ADJ & N
confederado -da *mf*; [kənfédɚet] VI/VT
confederar(se)
confederation [kənfedəréʃən] N
confederación *f*
confer [kənfɚ́] VT (grant) conferir; (consult)
consultar; (negotiate) conferenciar
conference [kánfɚəns] N (consultation)
consulta *f*; (professional meeting) congreso
m; (legislative) asamblea general *f*; (sports
league) liga *f*; **— call** llamada en
conferencia *f*
confess [kənfés] VI/VT confesar(se)
confession [kənféʃən] N confesión *f*
confessional [kənféʃənəl] N confesionario *m*
confessor [kənfésɚ] N confesor *m*
confidant [kánfɪdant] N confidente *mf*
confide [kənfáɪd] VI/VT (entrust) confiar; VI
(tell secrets to) hacer confidencias a
confidence [kánfɪdəns] N confianza *f*;
(certainty) seguridad *f*; (secret
communication) confidencia *f*; **— game**
timo *m*; **— man** timador *m*, embaucador
m; **in —** en confianza
confident [kánfɪdənt] ADJ seguro; **he's a —
person** tiene mucha confianza
confidential [kɑnfɪdénʃəl] ADJ confidencial;
(secretary, etc.) de confianza
configuration [kənfɪgjɚéʃən] N
configuración *f* (also computer term)
confine [kənfáɪn] VT confinar, recluir; **to —
oneself to** limitarse a; [kánfaɪn] N confín
m
confinement [kənfáɪnmənt] N
confinamiento *m*
confirm [kənfɚ́m] VT confirmar
confirmation [kɑnfɚméʃən] N confirmación
f

confiscate [kánfɪsket] VT confiscar
confiscation [kɑnfɪskéʃən] N confiscación *f*
conflagration [kɑnfləgréʃən] N incendio *m*
conflict [kánflɪkt] N conflicto *m*, contienda *f*;
— of interest conflicto de intereses *m*;
[kənflíkt] VI oponerse
confluence [kánfluəns] N confluencia *f*
conform [kənfɔ́rm] VI/VT conformar(se)
conformity [kənfɔ́rmɪɖi] N (agreement)
conformidad *f*; (passive acquiescence)
conformismo *m*
confound [kənfáʊnd] VT (bewilder)
desconcertar; (mix) confundir; **— it!** *fam*
¡caramba!
confront [kənfránt] VT (set face to face,
fight) confrontar; (face up to) enfrentarse
a
confuse [kənfjúz] VT confundir
confused [kənfjúzd] ADJ (person)
confundido; (situation) confuso; **to
become —** confundirse
confusing [kənfjúzɪŋ] ADJ confuso
confusion [kənfjúʒən] N confusión *f*
congeal [kəndʒíl] VI/VT cuajar(se)
congenial [kəndʒínjəl] ADJ agradable,
simpático; **to be — with** congeniar con
congenital [kəndʒénɪdl] ADJ congénito
congestion [kəndʒéstʃən] N congestión *f*
conglomeration [kənglamɚéʃən] N (unit)
conglomeración *f*; (mass) conglomerado *m*
Congo [káŋgo] N Congo *m*
Congolese [kaŋgəlíz] ADJ & N congoleño -ña
mf
congratulate [kəngrǽtʃəlet] VI/VT felicitar(se)
congratulation [kəngratʃəléʃən] N
felicitación *f*, parabién *m*; **—s!**
¡enhorabuena! ¡albricias!
congregate [káŋgriget] VI/VT congregar(se)
congregation [kaŋgrigéʃən] N (worshippers)
fieles *m pl*, feligreses *m pl*; (act of
congregating, committee of cardinals)
congregación *f*
congress [káŋgrɪs] N (professional) congreso
m; (political) asamblea legislativa *f*; (US)
congreso *m*
congressional [kəngréʃənəl] ADJ congresual
congressman [káŋgrɪsmən] N representante
m; (US) congresista *m*
congresswoman [káŋgrɪswʊmən] N
representante *f*; (US) congresista *f*
congruence [kaŋgrúəns] N congruencia *f*
conifer [kánəfɚ] N conífera *f*
conjecture [kəndʒéktʃɚ] N conjetura *f*; VI
conjeturar
conjugal [kándʒəgəl] ADJ conyugal
conjugate [kándʒəget] VI/VT conjugar(se)
conjugation [kandʒəgéʃən] N conjugación *f*

conjunction [kəndʒʌ́ŋkʃən] N conjunción *f*

conjunctivitis [kəndʒʌ̀ŋktəváɪdɪs] N conjuntivitis *f*

conjure [kándʒɚ] VT invocar; **to — up** evocar; VI hacer hechizos

connect [kənékt] VI/VT (join) conectar(se), enlazar(se); (buildings, callers) comunicar(se); (concepts) relacionar(se); (pipes) acoplar(se); **—ing rod** biela *f*

connection [kənékʃən] N (act of connecting, electrical device) conexión *f*; (of telephone) comunicación *f*, enganche *m*; (of concepts) relación *f*; (of pipes) acople *m*; (affinity) afinidad *f*; (supplier) contacto *m*; **—s** contactos *m pl*, enchufe *m*

connive [kənáɪv] VI conspirar

connoisseur [kɑnəsɚ́] N conocedor -ra *f*

connotation [kɑnətéʃən] N connotación *f*

conquer [kɑ́ŋkɚ] VT (win) conquistar; (overcome) vencer

conqueror [kɑ́ŋkɚɚ] N conquistador -ra *mf*; (one who overcomes) vencedor -ra *mf*

conquest [kɑ́ŋkwɛst] N conquista *f*

conscience [kɑ́nʃəns] N conciencia *f*

conscientious [kɑnʃiénʃəs] ADJ concienzudo

conscious [kɑ́nʃəs] ADJ consciente

consciousness [kɑ́nʃəsnɪs] N conciencia *f*; **to lose —** perder el conocimiento

conscript [kənskrípt] VT reclutar; [kɑ́nskrɪpt] N recluta *mf*

conscription [kənskrípʃən] N reclutamiento *m*

consecrate [kɑ́nsɪkret] VT consagrar

consecration [kɑnsɪkréʃən] N consagración *f*

consecutive [kənsékjədɪv] ADJ consecutivo

consensus [kənsénsəs] N consenso *m*

consent [kənsént] N consentimiento *m*; VI consentir

consequence [kɑ́nsɪkwɛns] N consecuencia *f*; (negative) secuela *f*

consequent [kɑ́nsɪkwənt] ADJ consiguiente, resultante; N (in mathematics) consecuente *m*; (in logic) consiguiente *m*

consequently [kɑ́nsɪkwəntli] ADV por consiguiente, en consecuencia

conservation [kɑnsɚvéʃən] N conservación *f*, preservación *f*

conservatism [kənsɚ́vətɪzəm] N conservadurismo *m*

conservative [kənsɚ́vədɪv] ADJ & N conservador -ra *mf*

conservatory [kənsɚ́vətɔri] N conservatorio *m*

conserve [kənsɚ́v] VT conservar, preservar; [kɑ́nsɚv] N dulce *m*

consider [kənsídɚ] VT considerar

considerable [kənsídɚəbəł] ADJ considerable

considerate [kənsídɚɪt] ADJ considerado

consideration [kənsɪdɚéʃən] N consideración *f*; (tolerance) miramiento *m*; (payment) remuneración *f*

considering [kənsídɚɪŋ] PREP en vista de, teniendo en cuenta; **she cooks well, —** para ser ella, cocina bien

consign [kənsáɪn] VT consignar

consignee [kɑnsaɪní] N consignatario -ria *mf*

consignment [kənsáɪnmənt] N consignación *f*; **on —** a consignación

consist [kənsíst] VI consistir (en)

consistency [kənsístənsi] N (adherence to principles) coherencia *f*, consecuencia *f*; (density) consistencia *f*

consistent [kənsístənt] ADJ (adherent to principles) consecuente, coherente; (cohering) consistente

consolation [kɑnsəléʃən] N consuelo *m*, consolación *f*

console [kənsóɫ] VT consolar; [kɑ́nsoɫ] N consola *f*

consolidate [kənsálɪdet] VI/VT consolidar(se)

consonant [kɑ́nsənənt] N consonante *f*; ADJ consonante, conforme

consort [kɑ́nsɔrt] N consorte *mf*; [kənsɔ́rt] VI **to — with** asociarse con

consortium [kənsɔ́rʃiəm] N consorcio *m*

conspicuous [kənspíkjuəs] ADJ evidente

conspiracy [kənspírəsi] N conspiración *f*, conjura *f*

conspirator [kənspírədɚ] N conspirador -ora *mf*, conjurado -da *mf*

conspire [kənspáɪr] VI conspirar, conjurar

constable [kɑ́nstəbəɫ] N oficial de policía *mf*; (keeper of fortress) condestable *m*

constancy [kɑ́nstənsi] N constancia *f*

constant [kɑ́nstənt] ADJ & N constante *f*

constellation [kɑnstəléʃən] N constelación *f*

consternation [kɑnstɚnéʃən] N consternación *f*

constipate [kɑ́nstəpet] VT estreñir

constipated [kɑ́nstəpeɪdɪd] ADJ estreñido

constipation [kɑnstəpéʃən] N estreñimiento *m*

constituent [kənstítʃuənt] ADJ componente, constitutivo; N (component) componente *m*; (voter) votante *mf*; (part of a sentence) constituyente *m*

constitute [kɑ́nstɪtut] VT constituir

constitution [kɑnstɪtúʃən] N constitución *f*

constitutional [kɑnstɪtúʃənəɫ] ADJ constitucional; N caminata *f*

constrain [kənstrén] VT constreñir

constraint [kənstrént] N constreñimiento *m*

constrict [kənstríkt] VT constreñir

constriction [kənstríkʃən] N (action)

constricción *f*; (place) estrechamiento *m*

construct [kənstrʌ́kt] VT construir; [kánstrʌkt] N invención *f*

construction [kənstrʌ́kʃən] N construcción *f*

constructive [kənstrʌ́ktɪv] ADJ constructivo

construe [kənstrú] VT interpretar

consul [kánsəł] N cónsul *mf*

consulate [kánsəlɪt] N consulado *m*

consult [kənsʌ́lt] VI/VT consultar; VI (serve as a consultant) asesorar

consultant [kənsʌ́ltənt] N asesor -ra *mf*

consultation [kansəłtéʃən] N consulta *f*

consulting [kənsʌ́ltɪŋ] N asesoramiento *m*, consultoría *f*

consume [kənsúm] VI/VT consumir

consumer [kənsúmə] N consumidor -ra *mf*

consumerism [kənsúmənzəm] N consumismo *m*

consuming [kənsúmɪŋ] ADJ **a — need** una necesidad imperiosa; **a — drive** un deseo abrasador

consummate [kánsəmet] VT consumar; [kánsəmɪt] ADJ consumado

consumption [kənsʌ́mpʃən] N (using up) consumo *m*; (wasting of the body) consunción *f*; (tuberculosis) tisis *f*

consumptive [kənsʌ́mptɪv] ADJ tísico

contact [kántækt] N contacto *m*; **— lens** lente de contacto *mf*; VI/VT (touch) tocar; (communicate with) contactar

contagion [kəntédʒən] N (spread) contagio *m*; (disease spread) enfermedad contagiosa *f*

contagious [kəntédʒəs] ADJ contagioso

contain [kəntén] VI/VT contener

container [kənténə] N recipiente *m*; (on a ship) contenedor *m*; **—ship** buque portacontenedores *m*

contaminate [kəntémənet] VT contaminar

contamination [kəntæmənéʃən] N contaminación *f*

contemplate [kántəmplet] VT (observe) contemplar; (consider) considerar

contemplation [kantəmpléʃən] N (observation) contemplación *f*; (consideration) consideración *f*

contemporary [kəntémpəreri] ADJ contemporáneo

contempt [kəntémpt] N desprecio *m*, menosprecio *m*; **— of court** desacato al tribunal *m*

contemptible [kəntémptəbəł] ADJ despreciable, rastrero

contemptuous [kəntémptʃuəs] ADJ desdeñoso

contend [kənténd] VI (struggle) contender, lidiar; (argue) disputar; VT afirmar

content, contents [kántent(s)] N contenido *m*

content [kəntént] ADJ (happy) contento; (resigned) conforme; N **to one's heart's — a** discreción

contented [kənténtɪd] ADJ contento, satisfecho

contention [kənténʃən] N (opinion) opinión *f*; **in —** (disputed) en discusión; (with possibilities) con posibilidades

contentment [kənténtmənt] N contento *m*

contest [kántest] N (competition) concurso *m*, certamen *m*; (struggle) contienda *f*; [kəntést] VT (compete) contender; (dispute) disputar; (challenge) impugnar

contestant [kəntéstənt] N concursante *mf*, participante *mf*

context [kántekst] N contexto *m*

contiguous [kəntígjuəs] ADJ contiguo

continent [kántənənt] N continente *m*; ADJ (sexually) continente; (of bodily functions) capaz de controlar los esfínteres

continental [kantənéntł] ADJ continental

contingency [kəntíndʒənsi] N contingencia *f*

contingent [kəntíndʒənt] ADJ & N contingente *m*

continual [kəntínjuəł] ADJ continuo

continuance [kəntínjuəns] N continuación *f*; (delay) aplazamiento *m*

continuation [kəntɪnjuéʃən] N continuación *f*

continue [kəntínju] VI/VT continuar

continuity [kantŋúɪɾi] N continuidad *f*

continuous [kəntínjuəs] ADJ (uninterrupted in time) continuo; (uninterrupted in space) ininterrumpido

contortion [kəntórʃən] N contorsión *f*

contour [kántur] N contorno *m*

contraband [kántrəbænd] N contrabando *m*

contraception [kantrəsépʃən] N anticoncepción *f*

contraceptive [kantrəséptɪv] ADJ & N anticonceptivo *m*

contract [kántrækt] N contrato *m*; **— killer** asesino -na a sueldo *mf*; [kəntrǽkt] VI/VT contraer(se); (assign by contract) contratar

contraction [kəntrǽkʃən] N contracción *f*; (in childbirth) contracción *f*, pujo *m*

contractor [kántræktə] N contratista *mf*

contractual [kəntrǽktʃuəł] ADJ contractual

contradict [kantrədíkt] VI/VT contradecir

contradiction [kantrədíkʃən] N contradicción *f*

contradictory [kantrədíktəri] ADJ contradictorio

contraption [kəntrǽpʃən] N chisme *m*, coso *m*

contrary [kántreri] ADJ contrario, opuesto; (obstinate) testarudo; N lo contrario; **on the —** al contrario

contrast [kántræst] N contraste *m*; [kəntræst] VI/VT contrastar

contravene [kɑntrəvín] VT contravenir

contribute [kəntríbjut] VI contribuir; (to a newspaper) colaborar; VT contribuir con, aportar

contribution [kɑntrəbjúʃən] N (donation, article) contribución *f*; (scientific) aporte *m*, aportación *f*

contributor [kəntríbjədəˑ] N colaborador -ra *mf*

contrite [kəntráit] ADJ contrito

contrivance [kəntráivəns] N artefacto *m*

contrive [kəntráiv] VI/VT ingeniar; **he —d to get their money** se las ingenió para sacarles el dinero

contrived [kəntráivd] ADJ artificioso

control [kəntrót] VI/VT controlar; N control *m*; (of a machine) mando *m*; **who's in —?** ¿quién manda? **under —** bajo control; **— freak** mandón -ona *mf*; **— key** tecla de control / mando *f*; **— tower** torre de control *f*

controller [kəntrólər] N (comptroller) controlador -ora *mf*; *Am* contralor -ora *mf*; (device) regulador *m*

controversy [kántrəvɚsi] N controversia *f*, polémica *f*

conundrum [kənándrəm] N (riddle) adivinanza *f*, acertijo *m*; (mystery) enigma *m*

convalesce [kɑnvəlés] VI convalecer

convection [kənvékʃən] N convección *f*

convene [kənvín] VT convocar; VI reunirse

convenience [kənvínjəns] N (practicality) conveniencia *f*; (appliance) comodidad *f*; **— store** autoservicio *m*; **at your —** cuando le venga bien

convenient [kənvínjənt] ADJ conveniente, oportuno; (at hand) accesible

convent [kánvent] N convento *m*

convention [kənvénʃən] N (political assembly) convención *f*; (professional assembly) congreso *m*; (pact) convenio *m*; (international agreement, acceptable usage) convención *f*

conventional [kənvénʃənəɫ] ADJ (not original) convencional; (traditional) clásico

conventioneer [kənvenʃənír] N congresista *mf*

converge [kənvɚ́dʒ] VI converger

conversant [kánvɚsənt] ADJ **— with** versado en

conversation [kɑnvɚséʃən] N conversación *f*; **— piece** tema de conversación *m*

converse [kɑnvɚ́s] VI conversar

conversion [kənvɚ́ʒən] N conversión *f*

convert [kənvɚ́t] VI/VT convertir(se); [kánvɚt] N converso -sa *mf*

converter [kənvɚ́dəˑ] N convertidor *m*

convertible [kənvɚ́dəbəɫ] ADJ convertible; (car) descapotable; N descapotable *m*

convex [kánveks] ADJ convexo

convey [kənvé] VT (carry) llevar; (transfer a title) transferir; (transmit) transmitir; (communicate) comunicar; **to — thanks** expresar agradecimiento

conveyance [kənvéəns] N (vehicle) vehículo *m*; (transfer of property) transferencia *f*; (document) escritura de traspaso *f*

conveyer, conveyor [kənvéəˑ] N transmisor -ra *mf*; **— belt** cinta transportadora *f*

convict [kánvikt] N convicto -ta *mf*; [kənvíkt] VI/VT declarar culpable

conviction [kənvíkʃən] N (belief) convicción *f*, convencimiento *m*; (act of convicting) declaración de culpabilidad *f*; (on one's record) condena *f*

convince [kənvíns] VT convencer

convincing [kənvínsɪŋ] ADJ convincente

convocation [kɑnvəkéʃən] N (act) convocación *f*; (group of people) asamblea *f*

convoke [kənvók] VT convocar

convoluted [kɑnvəlúdɪd] ADJ retorcido

convoy [kánvɔɪ] N convoy *m*; VT convoyar

convulse [kənváts] VI/VT convulsionar(se)

convulsion [kənvátʃən] N convulsión *f*

coo [ku] VI arrullar; N arrullo *m*

cook [kʊk] N cocinero -ra *mf*; VT cocinar, guisar; **—book** libro de cocina *m*; **to — up a plan** urdir un plan

cookery [kúkəri] N cocina *f*

cookie [kúki] N galletita dulce *f*

cool [kuɫ] ADJ (not hot) fresco; (indifferent) frío, indiferente; (calm) tranquilo; (good) excelente; *Caribbean* chévere; *RP* macanudo; *Sp* guay; *Sp vulg* cojonudo; **that's not —** eso no se hace; N (cold) fresco *m*; (composure) tranquilidad *f*; VT (make cooler) enfriar; (air condition) refrigerar; **to — off** (get cold) enfriarse; (get cooler) refrescar(se); (calm down) calmarse; **—ing-off period** tregua *f*

coolant [kúlənt] N refrigerante *m*

cooler [kúləˑ] N (room) cámara frigorífica *f*; (container) nevera portátil *f*

coolness [kútnɪs] N (cold weather) fresco *m*, frescor *m*; (indifference) frialdad *f*, indiferencia *f*

coon [kun] N (raccoon) mapache *m;* **a —'s age** una eternidad

co-op [kóap] N cooperativa *f*

coop [kup] N jaula *f;* (for chickens) gallinero *m;* VT enjaular; **to — up** encerrar

cooperate [koápəret] VI cooperar

cooperation [koapəréʃən] N cooperación *f*

cooperative [koápə-ədɪv] ADJ cooperativo; N cooperativa *f*

coordinate [koórdɪnt] ADJ coordinado; N coordenada *f;* **—s** conjunto *m;* [koórdɪnet] VI/VT coordinar

coordination [koordɪnéʃən] N coordinación *f*

cop [kap] N *fam* poli *mf,* polizonte *m;* VI **to — out** zafarse

cope [kop] VI **to — with** arreglárselas con; **I cannot — with this** no puedo con esto

copious [kópiəs] ADJ copioso

copper [kápə-] N cobre *m;* (cop) *fam* poli *mf;* ADJ de cobre

copulate [kápjələt] VI copular

copy [kápi] N (reproduction) copia *f;* (specimen, example) ejemplar *m;* (news story) texto *m;* **—cat** copión -ona *mf;* **—machine** copiadora *f;* **—right** copyright *m,* derechos de autor *m pl;* **this material is —righted** reservados todos los derechos; VT copiar; **to —right** registrar los derechos

coquette [kokét] N coqueta *f*

coral [kórəl] N coral *m;* ADJ (related to coral) coralino; (made of coral) de coral; **— reef** arrecife de coral *m*

cord [kord] N (thread) cuerda *f;* (for shoes) cordón *m;* (firewood measure) medida de leña *f;* **—s** pantalones de pana *m pl*

cordial [kórdʒəl] ADJ cordial; N licor *m*

cordless [kórdlɪs] ADJ inalámbrico

corduroy [kórdərɔɪ] N pana *f;* **—s** pantalones de pana *m pl*

core [kor] N (of fruit) corazón *m;* (of a problem) meollo *m;* (of a magnet, reactor) núcleo *m;* VT despepitar

cork [kork] N (woody material) corcho *m;* (stopper, buoy) tapón *m;* **—screw** sacacorchos *m sg,* tirabuzón *m;* **— tree** alcornoque *m;* VT tapar con un corcho

corn [korn] N (plant) maíz *m;* (painful growth) callo *m;* **—bread** pan de maíz *m;* **—cob** mazorca *f; Sp* zuro *m;* **— on the cob** choclo *m; Mex* elote *m;* **—ed beef** corned beef *m;* **—field** maizal *m; Mex* milpa *f;* **—flakes** copos de maíz *m pl;* **—meal** harina de maíz *f;* **—starch** maicena® *f*

corner [kórnə-] N (angle) ángulo *m;* (of a room, of a country) rincón *m;* (of two streets) esquina *f;* (monopoly) monopolio *m;* **—stone** piedra angular *f;* **— table** mesa rinconera *f;* VT (trap) arrinconar, acorralar; (monopolize) monopolizar; VI doblar; *Sp* girar

cornered [kórnə-d] ADJ (animal) acorralado; (person) arrinconado

cornet [kornét] N corneta *f*

cornice [kórnɪs] N cornisa *f*

corny [kórni] ADJ sensiblero; (joke) viejo

corollary [kórələri] N corolario *m*

coronation [korənéʃən] N coronación *f*

coroner [kórənə-] N médico -ca forense *mf*

corporal [kórpə-əł] ADJ corporal; N (rank) cabo *m*

corporation [korpəréʃən] N sociedad anónima *f*

corps [kor] N cuerpo *m*

corpse [korps] N cadáver *m*

corpulent [kórpjələnt] ADJ corpulento

corpus [kórpəs] N corpus *m*

corpuscle [kórpʌsəł] N corpúsculo *m;* (of blood) glóbulo *m*

corral [kərǽł] N corral *m;* VT acorralar

correct [kərékt] VT corregir; ADJ correcto; **that is —** es cierto

correction [kərékʃən] N corrección *f;* (for glasses) graduación *f*

correctness [kəréktnɪs] N corrección *f*

corrector [kəréktə-] N corrector -ra *mf*

correlate [kórəlet] VI/VT correlacionar; [kórəlɪt] N correlato *m*

correspond [kɔrəspánd] VI (be in agreement) corresponder, responder; (exchange letters) cartearse, escribirse

correspondence [kɔrəspándəns] N correspondencia *f*

correspondent [kɔrəspándənt] ADJ correspondiente; N (writer of letters) correspondiente *mf;* (news gatherer) corresponsal *mf,* enviado -da *mf*

corresponding [kɔrəspándɪŋ] ADJ correspondiente; (secretary, etc.) encargado de la correspondencia

corridor [kórɪdɔr] N corredor *m,* pasillo *m*

corroborate [kərábəret] VT corroborar

corrode [kəród] VI/VT corroer(se)

corrosion [kəróʒən] N corrosión *f*

corrupt [kərápt] ADJ (dishonest) corrupto; (rotten) corrompido; **to become —** corromperse; VT corromper, viciar

corruption [kərápʃən] N corrupción *f*

corset [kórsɪt] N corsé *m*

cortex [kórteks] N córtex *m,* corteza cerebral *f*

cortisone [kórtɪzon] N cortisona *f*

cosigner [kósaɪnə-] N cosignatario -ria *mf*

cosmetic [kɑzmétɪk] ADJ & N cosmético *m*

cosmic [kázmɪk] ADJ cósmico

cosmology [kazmáləʤi] N cosmología f

cosmonaut [kázmənɔt] N cosmonauta mf

cosmopolitan [kazməpálɪtn] ADJ cosmopolita

cosmos [kázmos] N cosmos m

cost [kɔst] N costo m; Sp coste m; **—s** (court costs) costas f pl; **at all —s** a toda costa; **— effective** económico; **— of living** costo/coste de vida m; **to sell at —** vender al costo/al coste; VT costar; **how much does this —?** ¿cuánto vale/cuesta esto?

co-star [kóstar] N coprotagonista mf

Costa Rica [kóstəríkə] N Costa Rica f

Costa Rican [kóstəríkən] ADJ & N costarricense mf

costly [kɔ́stli] ADJ costoso, caro

costume [kástum] N (style of clothing) vestimenta f; (in the theater) vestuario m; (disguise) disfraz m; **— jewelry** bisutería f

cot [kat] N catre m

cottage [kádɪʤ] N (small house) casita f; (vacation house) cabaña f, chalé m; **— cheese** requesón m

cotter pin [kúdəpɪn] N chaveta f

cotton [katn] N algodón m; **— candy** algodón de azúcar m; **— gin** desmotadora de algodón f; **—seed** semilla de algodón f; **—wood** álamo (de Virginia) m; **— wool** algodón en rama m

couch [kautʃ] N sofá m; (psychiatrist's) diván m; **— potato** telebobo -ba mf; VT expresar

cougar [kúgə] N puma f

cough [kɔf] VI toser; **to — up** (spit) expectorar; (hand over) soltar, largar; N tos f; **— drop** pastilla para la tos f; **— syrup** jarabe para la tos m

could [kʊd] V AUX **I — do it if I wanted** podría hacerlo si quisiera; **— you arrive early?** ¿podrías llegar temprano? **— I leave early?** ¿puedo salir temprano? **you — be right** quizá tengas razón

council [káunsəł] N (religious) concilio m; (advisory) consejo m, junta f; (provincial) diputación f; (municipal) concejo m; **—man** concejal m; **—woman** concejal f, concejala f

councilor [káunsələ] N concejal mf

counsel [káunsəł] N (advice) consejo m; (lawyer) abogado -da mf; VI/VT (give advice) aconsejar

counselor [káunsələ] N consejero -ra mf; (lawyer) abogado -da mf

count [kaunt] VI/VT contar; **to — in** incluir; **to — on** contar con; **to — oneself lucky** considerarse dichoso; **to — out** excluir; **—down** cuenta regresiva f; N (reckoning) cuenta f; (charge) cargo m; (noble) conde m

countenance [káuntnəns] N (expression) semblante m; (face) cara f; VT (tolerate) tolerar; (approve) aprobar

counter [káuntə] N (in a kitchen) Sp encimera f; Am mostrador m; (in a store) mostrador m; (in a bar) barra f; (in board games) tablero m; (counting device) contador m; (in a shoe) contrafuerte m; **over the —** sin receta; ADJ contrario, opuesto; ADV **— to** contra; **to run — to** ser contrario a; VT (an argument) retrucar; (a blow) devolver; VI/VT replicar

counteract [kauntəǽkt] VT contrarrestar

counterattack [káuntəətæk] N contraataque m; VI/VT contraatacar

counterbalance [kauntəbéləns] VI/VT contrapesar; [káuntəbæləns] N contrapeso m

counterculture [káuntəkʌltʃə] N contracultura f

counterespionage [kauntəéspiənaʒ] N contraespionaje m

counterexample [káuntəɪgzæmpəł] N contraejemplo m

counterfeit [káuntəfit] N falsificación f; ADJ falso; **— money** moneda falsa f; VT falsificar

countermand [kauntəmǽnd] VT contramandar; [káuntəmænd] N contraorden f

counteroffer [káuntəɔfə] N contraoferta f

counterpart [káuntəpart] N homólogo -ga mf

counterproductive [kauntəprədáktɪv] ADJ contraproducente

counterrevolution [kauntərevəlúʃən] N contrarrevolución f

countersign [káuntəsaɪn] N contraseña f; VT refrendar

countess [káuntɪs] N condesa f

countless [káuntlɪs] ADJ incontables, innumerables

country [kántri] N (nation) país m; (territory) territorio m; (homeland) patria f; (rural area) campo m; ADJ (of the countryside) rural; (uncouth) rústico; **— club** club campestre m; **—man** compatriota m; **— music** música country f; **—side** campo m; (scenery) paisaje m; **—woman** compatriota f

county [káunti] N condado m; **— fair** feria (de ganado) f; **— seat** capital de condado f

coup [ku] N (success) golpe maestro m;

(putsch) golpe de estado *m*; **— d'état** golpe de estado *m*

coupe [kup] N cupé *m*

couple [kápəł] N (of times, of forces, of people) par *m*; (romantic) pareja *f*; VI/VT (pair up) formar parejas; VT (connect) acoplar; VI (copulate) copular

couplet [kápłɪt] N pareado *m*

coupling [kápłɪŋ] N (action) acoplamiento *m*, enganche *m*; (device) acople *m*, enganche *m*

coupon [kjúpɑn] N cupón *m*

courage [kɜ́·ɪʤ] N valentía *f*, valor *m*, coraje *m*

courageous [kərédʒəs] ADJ valiente

courier [kúriə·] N mensajero -ra *mf*

course [kɔrs] N (of a river, of study, of a disease) curso *m*; (of a road, route) trayecto *m*; (of a ship, plane) derrotero *m*; (progression of time) marcha *f*; (dish) plato *m*; **— of action** línea de conducta *f*, proceder *m*; **in the — of a year** en el transcurso de un año; **in due —** a la larga; INTERJ **of —** claro, por supuesto, naturalmente; VI correr, fluir

court [kɔrt] N (courtyard) patio *m*; (atrium) patio interior *m*; (in sports) cancha, pista *f*; (in a city) plazuela *f*, plazoleta *f*; (tribunal) juzgado *m*, tribunal *m*; (session) audiencia *f*; (royal residence, retinue) corte *f*; **—-martial** consejo de guerra *m*; **— of law** tribunal de justicia *m*; **— reporter** estenotipista *mf*; **—yard** patio *m*; **to settle out of —** llegar a un arreglo extrajudicial; **to pay — to** cortejar; VT cortejar, galantear; **to — danger** tentar a la suerte; **to —-martial** someter a consejo de guerra; VI estar de novios

courteous [kɜ́·Diəs] ADJ cortés

courtesy [kɜ́·DIsi] N (attitude) cortesía *f*; (act) fineza *f*, atención *f*

courtier [kɔ́rDiƏ·] N (member of the court) cortesano -na *mf*; (sycophant) adulador -ra *mf*

courtship [kɔ́rtʃɪp] N cortejo *m*

cousin [kázən] N primo -ma *mf*; **first —** primo -ma hermano -na *mf*

counterclockwise [kaʊntə·klákwaɪz] ADV en el sentido opuesto al de las manecillas del reloj

cove [kov] N ensenada *f*

covenant [kávənənt] N pacto *m*; (religious) alianza *f*

cover [kávə·] VI/VT cubrir; (with lid, screen) tapar; (replace) sustituir; (include, deal with) comprender; (traverse) recorrer; (sing) hacer una versión; **to — one's ass** cuidarse la retaguardia; **to — up** (wrap up) tapar bien; (hide) ocultar; **—all** mono *m*; **—-up** encubrimiento *m*; N (lid) tapa *f*; (blanket) manta *f*; (for appliances, furniture) funda *f*; (front for activity) tapadera *f*, pantalla *f*; (shelter) resguardo *m*, abrigo *m*; **— charge** entrada *f*; **—girl** modelo de portada *f*; **to send under separate —** enviar por separado; **to take —** resguardarse; **under —** de incógnito; **under — of dark** bajo el manto de la noche

coverage [kávə·ɪʤ] N cobertura *f*; (of a cell phone) alcance *m*

covering [kávə·ɪŋ] N cubierta *f*

covert [kovɜ́·t] ADJ encubierto

covet [kávɪt] VT (desire wrongfully) codiciar; (want) ansiar

covetous [kávɪDəs] ADJ codicioso

cow [kaʊ] N (bovine female) vaca *f*; (female of other animals) hembra *f*; **—bell** cencerro *m*, esquila *f*; **—boy** vaquero *m*; **—hide** cuero de vaca *m*, vaqueta *f*; **—lick** remolino *m*; **—shed** vaquería *f*, vaqueriza *f*; **to have a —** tener una pataleta; VT intimidar

coward [káʊə·d] N cobarde *mf*

cowardice [káʊə·DIs] N cobardía *f*

cowardly [káʊə·dli] ADJ cobarde

cower [káʊə·] VI achicarse

cowl [kaʊł] N capucha *f*

coy [kɔɪ] ADJ (coquettish) remilgado; (evasive) esquivo

coyote [kaɪóDi, káɪot] N coyote *m*

cozy [kózi] ADJ (warm) acogedor; (beneficial) conveniente; **to — up to** adular

CPU (central processing unit) [sipijú] N UCP *f*

crab [kræb] N cangrejo *m*; (mechanism) carro corredizo *m*; (grouch) cascarrabias *mf*; **— apple** manzana silvestre *f*; **—s** ladillas *f pl*; VI (fish) pescar cangrejos; (complain) quejarse

crack [kræk] VI (single fissure) rajarse; (multiple fissures) resquebrajarse, agrietarse; (psychological breakdown) sufrir un ataque de nervios; (of voice) quebrarse; VT (knuckles) hacer un chasquido con, chascar, chasquear; (nuts) cascar; (jokes) contar; (a prisoner) quebrar; (a case) resolver; (a code) descifrar; (a door) entreabrir; **to — down on** reprimir; **that —s me up** esto me hace desternillar de risa; N (fissure) rajadura *f*, grieta *f*, resquebrajadura *f*; (sound) chasquido *m*; (joke) pulla *f*, chanza *f*; (of the butt) *vulg* raja *f*; **— cocaine** crack *m*; **—down**

represión f; **—house** fumadero m; **—pot** excéntrico -ca mf; **at the — of dawn** al romper el alba; **I'd like a — at the championship** me gustaría poder participar en el campeonato

cracked [krækt] ADJ rajado, quebrado; (crazy) chiflado; **it's not all it's — up to be** no es para tanto

cracker [krǽkɚ] N galleta f

crackle [krǽkəɫ] N (of paper) crujido m; (of fire) crepitación f; VI crujir, crepitar

cradle [krédɫ] N cuna f

craft [kræft] N (skill) destreza f; (cunning) astucia f; (occupation) arte m, oficio m; (boat) embarcación f; **—sman** artesano m; **—swoman** artesana f; VT fabricar

crafty [krǽfti] ADJ astuto, taimado

crag [kræg] N risco m, peñasco m, peñón m

craggy [krǽgi] ADJ peñascoso

cram [kræm] VT (pack in) embutir; VI (study intensely) memorizar; Sp empollar; **the bar was —med with people** el bar estaba atestado

cramp [kræmp] N (spasm) calambre m; (staple) grapa f; VI/VT (to suffer a spasm) acalambrar(se); VT (to staple) engrapar; **you're —ing my style** me estorbas

cranberry [krǽnberi] N arándano agrio m

crane [kren] N (bird) grulla f; (machine) grúa f; VT **to — one's neck** estirar el cuello

cranium [kréniəm] N cráneo m

crank [kræŋk] N (mechanism) manivela f; (grouch) cascarrabias mf sg; (overzealous advocate) fanático -ca mf; **—case** cárter superior del aceite m; **—shaft** cigüeñal m; VI/VT arrancar con manivela

cranky [krǽŋki] ADJ (irritable) irritable; (eccentric) excéntrico

cranny [krǽni] N (crevice) rendija f; (corner) recoveco m

crap [kræp] N (excrement) vulg mierda f; (nonsense) estupideces f pl; **to take a —** vulg cagar; **—s** dados m pl; VI vulg cagar

crappy [krǽpi] ADJ vulg de mierda

crash [kræʃ] VI (collide) estrellarse; (market) quebrar; (overnight with someone) quedarse a dormir; (hang up, as with a computer) colgarse; (sleep) dormir; VT **to — a car** chocar un coche; **to — a party** colarse en una fiesta; N (noise) estallido m; (collision) choque m; (financial) quiebra f; **— landing** aterrizaje forzoso m

crass [kræs] ADJ craso

crate [kret] N cajón m, guacal m; VT poner en cajones

crater [krédɚ] N cráter m

cravat [krəvǽt] N corbata f

crave [krev] VT anhelar; **I — chocolate** me muero por un chocolate

craving [krévɪŋ] N antojo m

crawl [krɔɫ] VI (on hands and knees) gatear; (on the belly) arrastrarse, reptar; (proceed slowly) avanzar a paso de tortuga; **to be —ing with** hormiguear de; N (swimming stroke) crol m; **traffic is going at a —** el tráfico va a paso de tortuga

crayon [kréan] N lápiz de color m, crayola™ f

craze [krez] N (vogue) moda f; VI/VT enloquecer(se)

craziness [krézinɪs] N locura f, chifladura f

crazy [krézi] ADJ & N loco -ca mf; **I'm — about you** estoy loco por ti; **that's —!** ¡qué locura! **to go —** volverse loco, enloquecerse

creak [krik] N (of wooden floor) crujido m; (of a hinge) rechinamiento m; VI (a wooden floor) crujir; (a hinge) rechinar

cream [krim] N (milk product) crema f; Sp nata f; (medicament) crema f; **— cheese** queso de untar m; **— of tomato soup** sopa crema de tomate f; **the — of the crop** la flor y nata; VT (decream) desnatar; (butter, sugar) batir; (vegetables) preparar con salsa blanca; (defeat) aplastar

creamy [krími] ADJ cremoso

crease [kris] N (in trousers) raya f, repliegue m; (wrinkle) arruga f; VT (trousers) planchar la raya; (wrinkle) arrugar

create [kriét] VI/VT crear

creation [kriéʃən] N creación f

creationism [kriéʃənɪzəm] N creacionismo m

creative [kriédɪv] ADJ creativo

creator [kriédɚ] N creador -ra mf

creature [krítʃɚ] N (being) ser m; (animal) animal m; **a — of your imagination** un producto de tu imaginación

credence [krídn̩s] N crédito m

credentials [krɪdɛntʃəlz] N credenciales f pl

credible [krɛ́dəbəɫ] ADJ creíble

credit [krɛ́dɪt] N crédito m; (commendation) reconocimiento m; **— card** tarjeta de crédito f; **— line** línea de crédito f; **—s** créditos m pl; **— underwriters** aseguradores de crédito m pl; **— union** banco cooperativo m; **on —** a crédito; **to give — to** (believe) dar crédito; (ascribe) acreditar; VT (believe) creer; (enter as credit) acreditar; (attribute) atribuir

creditor [krɛ́dɪdɚ] N acreedor -ra mf

credulous [krɛ́dʒələs] ADJ crédulo

creed [krid] N credo m

creek [krik] N arroyo m

creep [krip] VI (crawl on belly) arrastrarse;

(crawl on all fours) gatear; (grow upward) trepar; (go slowly) andar a paso de tortuga; **to — up on** acercarse furtivamente a; N (obnoxious person) *pej* repulsivo -va *mf*, sinvergüenza *mf*; **that gives me the —s** eso me da asco; *Sp* eso me da grima

creeper [krípə] N enredadera *f*, planta trepadora *f*

creepy [krípi] ADJ repulsivo

cremate [krímet] VT cremar

Creole [kríɫol] ADJ & N criollo -lla *mf*

creosote [kríəsot] N creosota *f*

crepe [krep] N (fabric) crespón *m*; (band of fabric) crespón negro *m*

crescent [krésənt] N media luna *f*; ADJ creciente

crest [krest] N (of a wave, rooster) cresta *f*; (of feathers) penacho *m*, copete *m*; (of mountain) cima *f*, cumbre *f*; (of heraldic arms) timbre *m*; **—fallen** alicaído, cabizbajo; VI **the river —ed at two meters above flood-level** el río creció hasta dos metros por encima de lo normal

crevice [krévɪs] N grieta *f*

crew [kru] N (for ships, etc.) tripulación *f*; (of workers) cuadrilla *f*

crib [krɪb] N (bed) cuna *f*; (manger) pesebre *m*; (bin for grain) granero *m*; (cheat notes) hoja para copiar *f*; VI copiar

cricket [kríkɪt] N (insect) grillo *m*; (game) criquet *m*

crime [kraɪm] N (illegal act) delito *m*; (act of violence against people) crimen *m*; (criminal activity) delincuencia *f*, criminalidad *f*

criminal [krímənəɫ] ADJ & N delincuente *mf*, malhechor -ora *mf*; (violent crimes) criminal *mf*

crimp [krɪmp] VT rizar; N rizo *m*

crimson [krímzən] ADJ & N carmesí *m*, carmín *m*

cringe [krɪndʒ] VI **he makes me —** me da asco

cripple [krípəɫ] N *offensive* tullido -da *mf*; (in the legs) *offensive* cojo -ja *mf*; (in the arms) *offensive* manco -ca *mf*; VT tullir

crisis [kráɪsɪs] N crisis *f*

crisp [krɪsp] ADJ (apple, bacon, etc.) crocante, crujiente; (weather) fresco y despejado; (hair) crespo; VI/VT volver crujiente

crispy [kríspi] ADJ crocante, crujiente

criterion [kraɪtíriən] N criterio *m*

critic [krídɪk] N crítico -ca *mf*

critical [krídɪkəɫ] ADJ crítico

criticism [krídɪsɪzəm] N crítica *f*

criticize [krídɪsaɪz] VT criticar

croak [krok] VI (make the sound of a frog) croar; (make the sound of a crow) graznar; (die) *fam* espichar; N (sound made by frogs) canto de ranas *m*; (sound made by crows) graznido *m*

Croatia [kroéʃə] N Croacia *f*

Croatian [kroéʃən] ADJ & N croata *mf*

crochet [kroʃé] N ganchillo *m*, croché *m*, crochet *m*; **— hook** aguja de croché *f*; VI hacer ganchillo, hacer croché

crock [krɑk] N (pot) vasija *f*; (lies) pamplinas *f pl*

crockery [krákəri] N loza *f*

crocodile [krákədaɪɫ] N cocodrilo *m*

croissant [krɔsánt] N cruasán *m*, croissant *m*

crony [króni] N compinche *mf*, compadre *m*, comadre *f*

crook [krʊk] N (criminal) delincuente *mf*; (curve) curva *f*; (hook) gancho *m*; (staff) cayado *m*

crooked [krúkɪd] ADJ (bent) torcido; *Am* chueco; (dishonest) deshonesto

crop [krɑp] N (harvest) cosecha *f*; (group of contemporaries) promoción *f*; (of a bird) buche *m*; (horse whip) fusta *f*; **— rotation** rotación de cultivos *f*; VT (graze) pastar, pacer; (trim) recortar; **to — up** surgir

croquet [kroké] N cróquet *m*

cross [krɔs] N (symbol) cruz *f*; (street intersection) cruce *m*; (act of mixing) cruzamiento *m*; (in boxing) cruzado *m*; **—bar** (soccer) travesaño *m*; (gymnastics) barra *f*; (high jump) listón *m*; (of a door) tranca *f*; **—check** verificación *f*; **—piece** cruceta *f*; **to bear one's —** cargar la cruz; VI/VT (intersect, form a cross, breed, meet) cruzar(se); (make sign of the cross) santiguarse; **to —-dress** transvestir(se); VT (betray) traicionar; (pass) cruzar, franquear; **to — out** tachar; **to — over** (change allegiance) cambiar de bando; (go to the other side) traspasar; **you've —ed the line** se te fue la mano; **to —-check** verificar; ADJ (transverse) transversal; (angry) enojado; **—-country** a campo traviesa; **—-cultural** transcultural; **—-dresser** travesti *mf*, travestí *mf*; **to —-examine** interrogar; **—-eyed** bizco; **to be —-eyed** bizquear; **—-fertilization** fecundación cruzada *f*; **—-reference** referencia cruzada *f*; **to —-reference** hacer una referencia cruzada; **—road** encrucijada *f*; **— section** corte transversal *m*; **—walk** cruce peatonal *m*, cebra *f*; **—word puzzle** crucigrama *m*

crossing [krósɪŋ] N (street or railroad

intersection, pedestrian path) cruce *m*;
(hybridization, act of mixing) cruzamiento
m; (of ocean) travesía *f*; (of a border) paso
m; (of a river) vado *m*

crotch [krɑtʃ] N entrepierna *f*

crotchety [krɑ́tʃɪdɪ] ADJ cascarrabias

crouch [krautʃ] VI (stoop) agacharse; (prepare
to spring) agazaparse

croup [krup] N tos *f*, croup *m*

crow [kro] N (bird) cuervo *m*; (sound of
rooster) canto del gallo *m*; **—bar**
alzaprima *f*; **—'s-foot** pata de gallo *f*; **to
eat —** comerse sus propias palabras; VI
cantar; (gloat, brag) jactarse

crowd [kraud] N (group of people)
muchedumbre *f*, gentío *m*, aglomeración *f*;
(at a performance) público *m*; (clique)
pandilla *f*; VI (push forward) agolparse; VI/
VT (gather in large numbers) apiñar(se),
amontonar(se), aglomerar(se); (gather in a
confined space) hacinar(se)

crowded [kráudɪd] ADJ **it is — in here** hay
demasiada gente aquí; **the restaurant is
—** el restaurante está lleno

crown [kraun] N corona *f*; (of head) coronilla
f, crisma *f*; (of a hat) copa *f*; **— jewels**
joyas de la corona *f pl*; VT coronar; (hit on
head) dar un coscorrón

crucial [krúʃəl] ADJ (element) fundamental;
(moment) crucial

crucible [krúsəbəl] N crisol *m*

crucifix [krúsəfɪks] N crucifijo *m*

crucify [krúsəfaɪ] VT crucificar

crud [krʌd] N (filth) mugre *f*; (worthless
thing, sickness, despicable person) *fam*
porquería *f*

crude [krud] ADJ (vulgar, unpolished) basto,
tosco; **— oil** petróleo crudo *m*; **— sugar**
azúcar sin refinar *mf*

cruel [krúəl] ADJ cruel

cruelty [krúəlti] N crueldad *f*

cruise [kruz] VI (take a cruise) tomar un
crucero; (patrol) patrullar; (seek sexual
partners) salir a buscar plan; **— missile**
misil crucero *m*; **cruising speed**
velocidad de crucero *f*; N crucero *m*; **—
control** control de crucero *m*

cruiser [krúzə] N crucero *m*

crumb [krʌm] N (small) miga *f*, migaja *f*;
(large) mendrugo *m*; VT (break into
crumbs) desmigajar; (remove crumbs)
sacar las migas

crumble [krʌ́mbəl] VI/VT (bread)
desmigajar(se); (clods of dirt)
desmenuzar(se); (house) desmoronar(se)

crummy [krʌ́mi] ADJ (place) *fam* de mala
muerte; (object) *fam* de porquería; (show)

flojo

crumple [krʌ́mpəl] VI/VT (crush) arrugar(se);
VI (collapse) aplastarse

crunch [krʌntʃ] VI/VT (eat noisily) mascar; N
(sound) crujido *m*; (shortage) crisis *f*; **—es**
abdominales *m pl*

crunchy [krʌ́ntʃi] ADJ crocante, crujiente

crusade [kruséd] N cruzada *f*; VI (engage in a
campaign) hacer una campaña

crusader [krusédə] N cruzado -da *mf*; **a —
for human rights** un paladín de los
derechos humanos

crush [krʌʃ] VI/VT aplastar, machacar; (stone)
demoler; N (act of crushing) aplastamiento
m; (crowd) tumulto *m*; (infatuation)
enamoramiento *m*

crust [krʌst] N (of bread, earth) corteza *f*; (of
bread) costra *f*; (of pie) tapa *f*

crusty [krʌ́sti] ADJ (with a crust) costroso;
(grouchy) irascible

crutch [krʌtʃ] N muleta *f*

cry [kraɪ] N (shout) grito *m*; (weeping) llanto
m; (call of an animal) reclamo *m*; **a far —
from** muy distante de, muy lejos de; VI
(shout) gritar; (weep) llorar; **—baby** llorón
-ona *mf*; **to — over spilt milk** hacer
como la lechera; **to — for attention**
reclamar atención; **to — for help** pedir
socorro; **to — out** vocear

crystal [krístl] N cristal *m*; **— ball** bola de
cristal *f*; **— clear** cristalino

crystalline [krístlɪn] ADJ cristalino

crystallize [krístlaɪz] VI/VT cristalizar(se)

cub [kʌb] N (lion) cachorro *m*; (bear) osezno
m; (whale) ballenato *m*; (wolf) lobato *m*,
lobezno *m*; **— reporter** reportero -ra
novato -ta *mf*

Cuba [kjúbə] N Cuba *f*

Cuban [kjúbən] ADJ & N cubano -na *mf*

cubbyhole [kʌ́bihol] N casilla *f*

cube [kjúb] N cubo *m*; **— root** raíz cúbica *f*;
VT (cut) cortar en cubos; (raise to the third
power) elevar al cubo

cubic [kjúbɪk] ADJ cúbico

cubicle [kjúbɪkəl] N cubículo *m*

cubism [kúbɪzəm] N cubismo *m*

cuckold [kʌ́kəld] N cornudo *m*, cabrón *m*; VT
poner los cuernos a

cuckoo [kúku] N cuco *m*, cuclillo *m*; **—
clock** reloj de cucú *m*; ADJ & N chiflado
-da *mf*; INTERJ cucú

cucumber [kjúkʌmbə] N pepino *m*

cud [kʌd] N **to chew the —** rumiar

cuddle [kʌ́dl] VI/VT hacer(se) mimos; N mimo
m

cuddly [kʌ́dli] ADJ mimoso

cudgel [kʌ́dʒəl] N porra *f*; VT aporrear

cue [kju] N (in theater) pie m; (stimulus) estímulo m; **— ball** bola blanca f; **— stick** taco de billar m; VT dar pie, dar la señal

cuff [kʌf] N (of sleeve, glove) puño m; (of pants) bajo m; (handcuffs) esposas f pl; (blow) bofetada f; VT (pants) hacer los bajos; (with handcuffs) esposar; (hit) abofetear

cuisine [kwɪzín] N cocina f

cul-de-sac [kʌ́ldəsæk] N callejón sin salida m

culinary [kjúlǝneri] ADJ culinario

cull [kʌl] VT (choose) seleccionar, entresacar; (collect) recoger

culminate [kʌ́lmǝnet] VI/VT culminar

culprit [kʌ́lprɪt] N culpable mf

cult [kʌlt] N (sect) secta religiosa f; (worship) culto m

cultivate [kʌ́ltǝvet] VT cultivar

cultivated [kʌ́ltǝveɪd] ADJ (land) cultivado; (plant) de cultivo; (educated) culto

cultivation [kʌltǝvéʃǝn] N (tillage) cultivo m; (education) cultura f

cultivator [kʌ́ltǝvedɚ] N (person) cultivador -ra mf; (implement) cultivadora f

cultural [kʌ́ltʃǝˑl] ADJ cultural

culture [kʌ́ltʃɚ] N cultura f; (microorganisms) cultivo m; **— shock** choque cultural m; VT (microorganisms) cultivar

cultured [kʌ́ltʃɚd] ADJ (person) culto; (pearl) cultivado, de cultivo

cumbersome [kʌ́mbɚsǝm] ADJ (bulky) voluminoso; (unwieldy) incómodo

cumulative [kjúmjǝlǝdɪv] ADJ acumulativo

cumulus [kjúmjǝlǝs] N cúmulo m

cunning [kʌ́nɪŋ] ADJ (sly) astuto, zorro; N astucia f, maña f

cunt [kʌnt] N Sp vulg coño m; Mex vulg chocho m; RP vulg concha f

cup [kʌp] N (with handle) taza f, pocillo m; (without handle) vaso m; (measure) taza f; (trophy, brassiere part) copa f; **—board** armario m, aparador m

cur [kɝ] N (dog) perro m; (villain) pej villano -na mf

curable [kjúrǝbǝl] ADJ curable

curator [kjúredɚ] N conservador -ra mf

curb [kɝb] N (of a street) Sp bordillo m; Mex borde m; RP cordón m; (of a well) brocal m; (restraint) freno m, restricción f; VT (emotions) refrenar; (spending) limitar

curd [kɝd] N cuajada f; VI/VT cuajar(se), coagular(se)

curdle [kɝ́dl] VI/VT cuajar(se), coagular(se); **my blood —d** se me heló la sangre

cure [kjur] N (healing, preserving meat) cura

f, curación f; (method) tratamiento m; VI/VT curar(se); **—all** sanalotodo m

curfew [kɝ́fju] N toque de queda m, queda f

curio [kjúrio] N curiosidad f

curiosity [kjuriásɪdi] N curiosidad f

curious [kjúriǝs] ADJ curioso

curl [kɝl] VI/VT (form ringlets) rizar(se), ensortijar(se); (coil) enroscar(se); (smoke) alzarse en espirales; **to — up** ovillar(se); N (of hair) rizo m, bucle m; (of smoke) espiral f

curler [kɝ́lɚ] N Sp rulo m; Mex tubo m; RP rulero m

curly [kɝ́li] ADJ rizado

currant [kɝ́ǝnt] N (fruit) grosella f; (tree) grosellero m

currency [kɝ́ǝnsi] N (money) moneda f, divisa f; (acceptance) aceptación f

current [kɝ́ǝnt] ADJ (commonly used) corriente; (prevalent) actual; **the — issue of a magazine** el último número de una revista; **the — month** el corriente mes; N corriente f

curriculum [kǝríkjǝlǝm] N plan de estudios m

curry [kɝ́ri] N curry m

curse [kɝs] N (ill wish) maldición f; (swear word) palabrota f; VI/VT (wish ill) maldecir; (swear) decir palabrotas

cursive [kɝ́sɪv] ADJ cursivo; N cursiva f

cursor [kɝ́sɚ] N cursor m

curt [kɝt] ADJ (abrupt) seco, brusco; (brief) breve

curtail [kǝtéɪ] VT restringir, cercenar

curtain [kɝ́tn] N cortina f; (theater) telón m; VT ponerle cortinas a

curvature [kɝ́vǝtʃur] N curvatura f; (of the spine) desviación f

curve [kɝv] N curva f; **he threw me a —** me agarró desprevenido; VI/VT encorvar(se); (road) torcer(se), desviar(se); VI **the ball —s** la pelota tiene efecto

curved [kɝvd] ADJ curvo

cushion [kúʃǝn] N (pad) almohadilla f; (emergency resources, pad of air) colchón m; (pillow) almohadón m; (decorative pillow) cojín m; VT (put pads) poner almohadones; (soften a blow) amortiguar

cuss [kʌs] VI decir palabrotas; N **—word** fam palabrota f; **strange old —** fam bicho raro m

custard [kʌ́stɚd] N flan m, natillas f pl

custodian [kʌstódiǝn] N (caretaker) cuidador -ra mf; (guardian) custodio -dia mf

custody [kʌ́stǝdi] N custodia f; **to take into —** detener

custom [kʌ́stǝm] N costumbre f, uso m;

—-**built** construido por encargo;
—-**made** hecho a medida; **—s**
(government department) aduana f;
(taxes) derechos de aduana m pl;
—(s)**house** aduana f
customary [kástəmeri] ADJ acostumbrado
customer [kástəmə-] N cliente -ta mf
customize [kástəmaɪz] VT adaptar por
encargo
cut [kʌt] VI/VT cortar; (shorten) acortar; (trees)
talar; (prices) rebajar; —! ¡corte(n)! **to — a**
deal llegar a un arreglo; **to — across**
(take a shortcut) cortar por; (transcend)
trascender; **to — back** reducir; **to —**
class faltar a clase; **to — down on**
reducir; **to — in** (interrupt) interrumpir;
(in traffic) atravesarse; **may I — in?** ¿me
permite? **to — off** (interrupt) interrumpir;
(intercept) interceptar; **to — out** omitir;
to be — out for estar hecho para; **to —**
up (divide) trozar; (misbehave) portarse
mal; —-**and-dried** predeterminado;
—**back** reducción f; **— glass** cristal
labrado m; —**off date** fecha límite f;
—-**rate** de rebajas; —**throat** despiadado;
N corte m; (in salary) recorte m; (of prices)
rebaja f; (of a suit) hechura f, corte m;
(insult) desaire f
cute [kjut] ADJ mono, rico; **to act —** ser
afectado, ser melindroso
cuticle [kjúːɪkəɫ] N cutícula f
cutlery [kátləri] N (knives, knife store)
cuchillería f; (eating utensils) cubiertos m
pl
cutlet [kátlɪt] N filete m
cutter [kádə-] N (person) cortador -ra mf;
(device) cortadora f; (sleigh) trineo m;
Coast Guard — guardacostas m sg
cutting [kádɪŋ] ADJ (sharp) cortante; (cold)
penetrante; (sarcastic) mordaz, sarcástico;
— board tabla de cortar f; **— edge** filo m
cyanide [sáɪənaɪd] N cianuro m
cybernetics [saɪbə-nédɪks] N cibernética f
cyberpunk [sáɪbə-pʌŋk] N ciberpunk m
cyberspace [sáɪbə-spes] N ciberespacio m
cyborg [sáɪbɔrg] N cyborg m
cycle [sáɪkəɫ] N ciclo m
cyclical [síklɪkəɫ] ADJ cíclico
cyclone [sáɪklon] N ciclón m
cyclotron [sáɪklətrɑn] N ciclotrón m
cylinder [sílɪndə-] N cilindro m; (of a gun)
tambor m; **— head** culata f
cylindrical [sɪlíndrɪkəɫ] ADJ cilíndrico
cymbal [símbəɫ] N címbalo m, platillo m
cynic [sínɪk] N cínico -ca mf
cynical [sínɪkəɫ] ADJ cínico
cynicism [sínɪsɪzəm] N cinismo m

cypress [sáɪprɪs] N ciprés m
Cypriot, Cypriote [sípriət] ADJ & N chipriota
mf
Cyprus [sáɪprəs] N Chipre m
cyst [sɪst] N quiste m
czar [zɑr] N zar m
Czech [tʃɛk] ADJ & N checo -ca mf
Czech Republic [tʃɛ́krɪpʌ́blɪk] N República
Checa f

Dd

dab [dæb] VT (pat) dar toques; (apply) aplicar
con golpecitos; N toque m
dabble [dǽbəɫ] VI (splash) chapotear; (be
interested superficially) ser aficionado a
dachshund [dáksənd] N perro salchicha m
dad [dæd] N papá m
daddy [dǽdi] N papaíto m, papito m,
papacito m
daffodil [dǽfədɪɫ] N narciso m
dagger [dǽgə-] N daga f, puñal m; **to look**
—s at traspasar con la mirada
dahlia [dǽljə] N dalia f
daily [déli] ADJ diario; **— wage** jornal m,
salario m; N diario m
dainty [dénti] ADJ (delicate) delicado,
exquisito; (finicky) remilgado
dairy [déri] N (milk) lechería f; (cheese)
quesería f; ADJ (industry) lechero;
(product) lácteo
daisy [dézi] N margarita f; **to be pushing**
up daisies fam estar criando malvas
dale [deɫ] N valle m
dally [dǽli] VI (risk danger) jugar con fuego;
(waste time) remolonear
dam [dæm] N presa f, represa f; VT represar
damage [dǽmɪʤ] N daño m, destrozo m; **—s**
daños y perjuicios m pl; **to pay —s**
indemnizar m; VI/VT dañar(se)
damaging [dǽmɪʤɪŋ] ADJ perjudicial
dame [dem] N (noblewoman) dama f;
(woman) pej tipa f
damn [dæm] VT condenar; **it's not worth a**
— no vale un comino; INTERJ vulg ¡maldito
sea!
damnation [dæmnéʃən] N condenación f,
perdición f
damp [dæmp] ADJ húmedo; N humedad f; VT
(wet) humedecer; (deaden) amortiguar;
(extinguish) apagar
dampen [dǽmpən] VT (wet) humedecer;
(depress) deprimir; (deaden) amortiguar

dampness [dǽmpnɪs] N humedad f

damsel [dǽmzəl] N damisela f

dance [dæns] N (act of dancing, party, activity) baile m; (artistic activity, animal courtship movements) danza f; — **music** música bailable f; VI/VT (at a party) bailar; (in ballet, of animals) danzar; **she —d her way to stardom** llegó al estrellato bailando

dancer [dǽnsə] N bailarín -ina mf, danzante f

dancercise [dǽnsə-saɪz] N baile aeróbico m

dandelion [dǽndlaɪən] N diente de león m

dandruff [dǽndrəf] N caspa f

dandy [dǽndi] N (affected man) dandi m, señorito m; ADJ estupendo

Dane [den] N danés -esa mf

danger [dénʤə] N peligro m

dangerous [dénʤəəs] ADJ peligroso

dangle [dǽŋgəl] VI/VT (hang) colgar; (sway) bambolear(se); (tempt) tentar con; **her legs were dangling off the bench** sus piernas pendían del banco

Danish [dénɪʃ] ADJ danés; N bollo dulce m

dapple, dappled [dǽpəl(d)] ADJ pinto, moteado

dare [dɛr] VI/VT (be brave) atreverse (a), osar; (challenge) desafiar; **how — you?** ¿cómo te atreves? N desafío m; **— devil** temerario -ria mf

daring [dérɪŋ] N atrevimiento m, osadía f; ADJ atrevido, osado, arriesgado

dark [dark] ADJ (in color) oscuro; (of hair) moreno, morocho, trigueño; (gloomy) sombrío, tenebroso; (evil, ignorant) oscuro; (hidden) turbio; — **Ages** (Alta) Edad Media f; **—room** cuarto oscuro m; **-skinned** moreno; N oscuridad f; **after —** después de que oscurece

darken [dárkən] VI/VT oscurecer(se)

darkness [dárknɪs] N (complete) oscuridad f, tinieblas f pl; (partial) penumbra f

darling [dárlɪŋ] ADJ & N amado -da mf, querido -da mf; **my —** vida mía, amor mío

darn [darn] VT zurcir, remendar; **—ing needle** aguja de zurcir f; N zurcido m; **it is not worth a —** no vale un comino; INTERJ ¡caramba! ¡caracoles!

dart [dart] N (missile) dardo m; (tuck) pinza f; (swift movement) movimiento rápido m; **—board** diana f; **to play —s** jugar a los dardos; VI disparar; **to — out** salir disparado

dash [dæʃ] VI/VT (of waves, porcelain) estrellar(se); VT (plans) frustrar; VI (hopes) desplomarse; **to — by** pasar corriendo; **to**

— off / out salir disparado; **to — off a letter** escribir de prisa una carta; N (line) raya f; (run) corrida f; (race) carrera f; (small amount) pizca f; (splash) salpicadura f; **the one-hundred-meter —** la carrera de los cien metros llanos/planos; **—board** tablero m, salpicadero m

data [dépə,dǽpə] N datos m pl; **—base** base de datos f; **—bank** banco de datos m; **— processing** procesamiento de datos m

date [det] N (time) fecha f; (appointment) cita f; (person) acompañante mf; (fruit) dátil m; **out of —** anticuado; **to —** hasta ahora; **up to —** al día; VI (be dated) estar fechado; (go out socially) salir; VT (write the date) fechar; (show to be old-fashioned) delatar la edad; (go out socially) salir con; **to — from** datar de, remontarse a

dated [dépɪd] ADJ (having a date) fechado; (old-fashioned) anticuado

daub [dɔb] VT (smear) embarrar, embadurnar; (apply unskillfully) pintarrajear

daughter [dópə] N hija f; **-in-law** nuera f

daunt [dɔnt] VT (intimidate) intimidar; (dishearten) desanimar

dauntless [dóntlɪs] ADJ intrépido

davenport [dǽvənport] N sofá grande m

dawn [dɔn] N alba f, amanecer m, aurora f; **the — of civilization** los albores de la civilización; VI amanecer, aclarar; **it just —ed on me that** caí en (la) cuenta de que

day [de] N día m; **— after tomorrow** pasado mañana m; **— before yesterday** anteayer m; **—break** amanecer m; **at —break** al amanecer; **—care** guardería f; **—dream** fantasía f; **to —dream** soñar despierto; **— laborer** jornalero -ra mf; **—light** luz del día f; **—time** día m; **—time activity** actividad diurna f; **-to-** día a día; **by —** de día; **by the —** por día; **eight-hour —** jornada de ocho horas f; **in my —** en mis tiempos; **in the old —s** antaño; **make my —** dame el gusto; **New Year's —** Año Nuevo m; ADJ diurno

daze [dez] VT aturdir; N **to be in a —** estar aturdido

dazzle [dǽzəl] VI/VT deslumbrar

deacon [díkən] N diácono m

deactivate [diǽktəvet] VI/VT desactivar

dead [ded] ADJ muerto; **—beat** moroso -sa mf; **—bolt** pestillo m; **he's a — duck** está muerto; **— end** callejón sin salida m; **—end job** puesto sin perspectivas m; **— letter** letra muerta f; **—line** fecha límite f; **—lock** punto muerto m; **to —lock** trancarse; **—pan** de palo; **— ringer** fiel retrato m; **— sure** completamente seguro; **— tired** muerto de cansancio; **—wood** (person) persona inútil f; (thing) cosa inútil f; N **the —** los muertos; **in the — of the night** en el silencio de la noche; **in the — of winter** en pleno invierno

deaden [dέdn] VT amortiguar

deadly [dέdli] ADJ (enemy) mortal; (poison) letal; (weapon) mortífero; ADV mortalmente; **— dull** sumamente aburrido

deaf [dεf] ADJ sordo; **—-mute** sordomudo -da mf

deafen [dέfən] VT (make deaf) ensordecer; (deaden) amortiguar

deafening [dέfənɪŋ] ADJ ensordecedor, atronador

deafness [dέfnɪs] N sordera f

deal [diɫ] VT (cards) dar, repartir; (drugs) vender; (a blow) dar, asestar; **to — in** comerciar en; **biology —s with the study of life** la biología se ocupa del estudio de la vida; **I have to — with all kinds of people** tengo que vérmelas con todo tipo de gente; N (business transaction) trato m, negocio m; (shady transaction) componenda f; (act of dealing) reparto m; **a great — of** una gran cantidad de; **it's a —** ¡trato hecho! **I got a raw —** me clavaron

dealer [dílə-] N (in cars, antiques) comerciante mf; (in drugs, arms) traficante mf; (of cards) el / la que reparte mf

dealings [dílɪŋz] N trato m, relaciones f pl; (business) negocios m pl

dean [din] N (of university, professional group) decano -na mf; (in church) deán m

dear [dɪr] ADJ (beloved) querido; (expensive) caro; (cherished) apreciado; **— Sir / Madam** Estimado señor / Estimada señora; **my —est wish** mi deseo más ferviente; N **he's such a —!** ¡es un amor! **my —** querido mío m / querida mía f; ADV caro; **that cost me —** eso me costó caro; **— me!** ¡Dios mío! **oh —!** ¡Dios mío!

dearth [dɜ-θ] N escasez f

death [dεθ] N muerte f; **—bed** lecho de muerte m; **— certificate** partida de defunción f; **— penalty** pena de muerte f; **— rate** tasa de mortalidad f; **— row** pabellón de los condenados a muerte m; **— squad** escuadrón de la muerte m; **— toll** mortandad f; **—trap** trampa mortal f; **— wish** instinto suicida m; **to put to —** ejecutar; **we have discussed this to —** hemos discutido esto hasta el hartazgo; **I'm sick to — of this job** estoy harto de este trabajo

debacle [dɪbákəɫ] N debacle f

debase [dɪbés] VT degradar, envilecer

debatable [dɪbéɖəbəɫ] ADJ discutible

debate [dɪbét] N debate m; VI/VT (discuss) debatir, discutir; (weigh a decision) considerar

debilitate [dɪbílɪtet] VT debilitar

debit [dέbɪt] N débito m, adeudo m; (column in an account) debe m; (total sum owed) pasivo m; **— card** tarjeta de cobro automático f; VT adeudar, cargar a la cuenta

debriefing [dibrífɪŋ] N informe m

debris [dəbrí] N (ruins) escombros m pl; (detritus) detritus m (pl)

debt [dεt] N deuda f; **bad —** cuenta incobrable f; **to get into —** endeudarse

debtor [dέɖə-] N deudor -ra mf

debug [dibág] VT depurar

debugging [dibágɪŋ] N depuración f

debunk [dibáŋk] VT (ideas, beliefs) desacreditar; (myths) desmitificar

debut [debjú] N (of a play or film) estreno m; (in society) presentación en sociedad f; **to make a —** (an actor) debutar; (in society) presentarse en sociedad; VI/VT (a film) estrenar(se); (a product) lanzar(se) al mercado

decade [dέked] N década f, decenio m

decadence [dέkədəns] N decadencia f

decadent [dέkədənt] ADJ decadente

decaffeinated [dɪkǽfɪneɪd] ADJ descafeinado

decal [díkæɫ] N calcomanía f, autoadhesivo m

decanter [dɪkǽntə-] N garrafa f

decapitate [dɪkǽpɪtet] VT decapitar

decathlon [dɪkǽθlɑn] N decatlón m

decay [dɪké] VI/VT (biological matter) descomponer(se); (teeth) cariar(se); VI (health) deteriorarse; (radioactive matter) desintegrarse; (of morals) decadencia f; (of biological matter) descomposición f; (nuclear) desintegración f; (tooth) caries f

decease [dɪsís] N muerte f, fallecimiento m; VI morir, fallecer

deceased [dɪsíst] ADJ & N difunto -ta mf

deceit [dɪsít] N engaño m, trampa f

deceitful [dɪsítfəɫ] ADJ tramposo, engañoso

deceive [dɪsív] VI/VT engañar

decelerate [disέləret] VI desacelerar

December [dɪsέmbə-] N diciembre m

decency [dísənsi] N decencia f

decent [dísənt] ADJ decente

deception [dɪsépʃən] N engaño *m*

decibel [désəbəl] N decibelio *m*

decide [dɪsáɪd] VT (make a decision) decidir; (award victory) fallar; **what —d you to come?** ¿qué te motivó a venir?

decided [dɪsáɪdɪd] ADJ (resolute) decidido; (clear) claro

deciduous [dɪsíʤuəs] ADJ deciduo, caduco; **— tooth** diente de la primera dentición *m*

decimal [désəməł] ADJ decimal

decimate [désəmet] VT diezmar

decipher [dɪsáɪfɚ] VT descifrar

decision [dɪsíʒən] N decisión *f*; (in court) fallo *m*

decisive [dɪsáɪsɪv] ADJ decisivo

deck [dɛk] N (of a boat) cubierta *f*; (of a house) terraza *f*; (of playing cards) baraja *f*; VT (knock down) tumbar; (decorate) decorar; **to — oneself out** emperifollarse; **hit the —!** ¡cuerpo a tierra!

declaration [dɛkləréʃən] N declaración *f*

declare [dɪklɛ́r] VI/VT declarar, afirmar

decline [dɪkláɪn] N (deterioration) decadencia *f*; (slope) declive *m*; (reduction in prices) baja *f*; VI/VT declinar; (an offer) rechazar; **to — to do something** negarse a hacer algo

decode [dikód] VT descodificar

decompose [dikəmpóz] VI/VT descomponer(se)

decongestant [dikənʤéstənt] N descongestionante *m*

decorate [dékəret] VT decorar; (award medals) condecorar

decoration [dɛkəréʃən] N (embellishment) adorno *m*; (interior decorating) decoración *f*; (medal of honor) condecoración *f*

decorative [dékəɹɑDɪv] ADJ decorativo

decorous [dékəəs] ADJ decoroso

decorum [dɪkɔ́rəm] N decoro *m*

decoy [díkɔɪ] N (artifact) señuelo *m*, reclamo *m*; (live animal or person) cimbel *m*; VT atraer con señuelo / cimbel

decrease [díkris] N disminución *f*, merma *f*; [dɪkrís] VI/VT disminuir, mermar

decree [dɪkrí] N decreto *m*; VI/VT decretar

decrepit [dɪkrépɪt] ADJ decrépito

decry [dɪkráɪ] VT condenar

dedicate [déDɪket] VI/VT dedicar(se); VT (mark opening of a highway, etc.) inaugurar

dedication [dɛDɪkéʃən] N (act of dedicating) dedicación *f*; (in a book) dedicatoria *f*; (of a highway, etc.) inauguración *f*

deduce [dɪdús] VT deducir

deduct [dɪdʌ́kt] VT deducir

deductible [dɪdʌ́ktəbəł] ADJ deducible, desgravable; N deducible *m*

deduction [dɪdʌ́kʃən] N deducción *f*

deed [did] N (action) acción *f*; (exploit) hazaña *f*; (certificate of ownership) escritura *f*

deem [dim] VT considerar

deep [dip] ADJ (extending down) hondo, profundo; (dark) oscuro; (of a voice) grave; **— freeze** congelador *m*; **— in debt** cargado de deudas; **— in thought** absorto; **—sea** de altura; **he's got — pockets** es un ricachón; **he went off the — end with his hobby** se le fue la mano con el pasatiempo; **ten meters —** de diez metros de profundidad; **to —six** hacer desaparecer; N **the —** el piélago, el abismo; ADV **to dive —** bucear en las profundidades

deepen [dípən] VI/VT ahondar, profundizar

deer [dir] N ciervo *m*, venado *m*; **—skin** gamuza *f*

deface [dɪfés] VT (disfigure) desfigurar; (smear with paint) pintarrajear; (mutilate) mutilar

defame [dɪfém] VT difamar

default [dɪfɔ́łt] N (negligence) negligencia *f*; (failure to appear in court) rebeldía *f*; (computer setting) opción por defecto *f*; **in —** en mora; **by —** en ausencia de alternativa; (in sports) por abandono de los contrincantes; VI (on a loan) no pagar; (in a sports match) no comparecer

defeat [dɪfít] VT vencer, derrotar; N derrota *f*

defecate [défɪket] VI defecar

defect [dífɛkt] N defecto *m*; [dɪfɛ́kt] VI desertar

defection [dɪfɛ́kʃən] N defección *f*

defective [dɪfɛ́ktɪv] ADJ defectuoso

defend [dɪfɛ́nd] VI/VT defender

defendant [dɪfɛ́ndənt] N (criminal) acusado -da *mf*, reo -a *mf*; (civil) demandado -da *mf*

defender [dɪfɛ́ndɚ] N defensor -ora *mf*

defense [dɪfɛ́ns] N defensa *f*

defenseless [dɪfɛ́nslɪs] ADJ indefenso

defensible [dɪfɛ́nsəbəł] ADJ defendible

defensive [dɪfɛ́nsɪv] ADJ defensivo; **on the —** a la defensiva

defer [dɪfɚ́] VT (a meeting) diferir, posponer; (a payment) prorrogar; (an appointment) dilatar; (from military service) eximir; **to — to another's opinion** remitirse a la opinión de otro

deference [défəəns] N deferencia *f*

defiance [dɪfáɪəns] N (challenge) desafío *m*; (resistance to authority) rebeldía *f*; **in — of** en abierta oposición a

defibrillate [difíbɹəlet] VT desfibrilar

deficiency [dɪfíʃənsi] N deficiencia *f*

deficient [dɪfíʃənt] ADJ deficiente
deficit [défɪsɪt] N déficit *m*; **— spending** gastos deficitarios *m pl*
defile [dɪfáɪl] VT (violate) mancillar; (desecrate) profanar; (to make dirty) ensuciar
define [dɪfáɪn] VI/VT definir
defining [dɪfáɪnɪŋ] ADJ decisivo
definite [défənɪt] ADJ (clearly defined) definido; (certain) seguro; **she was — in her demands** ella fue terminante es sus exigencias; **— article** artículo definido *m*
definitely [défənɪtli] ADV sin duda
definition [defənɪʃən] N definición *f*
definitive [dɪfínɪtɪv] ADJ (final) definitivo; (authoritative) de mayor autoridad
deflate [dɪflét] VI/VT desinflar(se)
deflation [dɪfléʃən] N deflación *f*
deflect [dɪflékt] VI/VT desviar(se)
deforestation [difɔrɪstéʃən] N deforestación *f*
deform [dɪfɔrm] VI/VT deformar(se)
deformed [dɪfɔrmd] ADJ deforme
deformity [dɪfɔrmɪDi] N (body part) deformidad *f*; (act or result of deforming) deformación *f*
defraud [dɪfrɔ́d] VT defraudar
defray [dɪfré] VT sufragar, costear
defrost [difróst] VI/VT descongelar(se)
deft [deft] ADJ diestro, habilidoso
defunct [dɪfʌ́ŋkt] ADJ caduco; **the Whig party is now —** el partido de los whigs se disolvió
defuse [difjúz] VT (bomb) desactivar; (situation) distender
defy [dɪfáɪ] VT (challenge) desafiar; (resist) resistir
degenerate [dɪdʒénə-ɪt] ADJ & N degenerado -da *mf*; [dɪdʒénəret] VI degenerar(se)
degradation [degrədéʃən] N degradación *f*
degrade [dɪgréd] VI/VT degradar(se)
degree [dɪgrí] N (stage) grado *m*; (academic) título *m*; **by —s** gradualmente; **to a —** hasta cierto punto; **to get a —** graduarse
dehumanize [dihjúmənaɪz] VI/VT deshumanizar
dehydrate [diháɪdret] VI/VT deshidratar(se)
deign [den] VI dignarse
deity [díɪDi] N deidad *f*
déjà vu [deʒɑvú] N deja vu *m*
dejected [dɪdʒéktɪd] ADJ abatido, desconsolado
dejection [dɪdʒékʃən] N abatimiento *m*, desconsuelo *m*
delay [dɪlé] N demora *f*, retraso *m*; VT demorar, retrasar; VI demorar, retrasarse
delectable [dɪléktəbəl] ADJ delicioso; N delicia *f*

delegate [délɪgɪt] N delegado -da *mf*; [délɪget] VT delegar
delegation [delɪgéʃən] N delegación *f*, representación *f*
delete [dɪlít] VT (omit) suprimir; (cross out) tachar
deletion [dɪlíʃən] N supresión *f*
deliberate [dɪlíbə-ɪt] ADJ (intentional) deliberado; (careful) cuidadoso; [dɪlíbəret] VI/VT deliberar
deliberation [dɪlɪbəréʃən] N deliberación *f*
delicacy [délɪkəsi] N (fineness, precision, sensitivity) delicadeza *f*; (food) manjar *m*, delicatessen *f pl*, golletía *f*; (breakability) fragilidad *f*
delicate [délɪkɪt] ADJ delicado, tenue; (breakable) frágil; (acute) fino
delicatessen [delɪkətésən] N (store) tienda de fiambres *f*, charcutería *f*; *RP* rotisería *f*; (foods) delicatessen *f pl*
delicious [dɪlíʃəs] ADJ delicioso, rico
delight [dɪláɪt] N (pleasure) deleite *m*, regalo *m*; (source of pleasure) delicia *f*; VI/VT deleitar(se)
delighted [dɪláɪtɪd] ADJ encantado; **to be — to** alegrarse de; **I'm — to meet you** me alegro de conocerla; **I'd be — to dance with you** me encantaría bailar contigo
delightful [dɪláɪtfəl] ADJ encantador
delimit [dɪlímɪt] VT delimitar
delineate [dɪlíniet] VT delinear
delinquent [dɪlíŋkwənt] ADJ & N (debtor) moroso -sa *mf*; (wrong-doer) delincuente *mf*; (juvenile) delincuente juvenil *mf*
delirious [dɪlíriəs] ADJ delirante; (happy) contentísimo; **to be —** delirar
delirium [dɪlíriəm] N delirio *m*
deliver [dɪlívə-] VT (hand over) entregar; (hand out) repartir; (liberate) liberar; (pronounce a speech) pronunciar; (administer a blow) dar; (have a baby) dar a luz; (assist a birth) atender en un parto; **— the goods** cumplir
deliverance [dɪlívə-əns] N liberación *f*
delivery [dɪlívəri] N (handing out) entrega *f*, expedición *f*; (things to be delivered) pedido *m*; (birth) parto *m*; (speaking) ejecución *f*, expresión oral *f*; **— service** servicio de entrega *m*; **— truck** camión de reparto *m*
dell [del] N hondonada *f*
delude [dɪlúd] VT engañar
deluge [déljudʒ] N diluvio *m*; VT abrumar
delusion [dɪlúʒən] N (act of deluding, state of being deluded) engaño *m*; **—s of grandeur** delirios de grandeza *m pl*
deluxe [dɪlʌ́ks] ADJ de lujo

demagog, demagogue [déməgɑg] N
demagogo -ga *mf*

demand [dɪmǽnd] VT (ask for) exigir;
(require) requerir, exigir; N demanda *f*,
exigencia *f*; **on — por demanda

demanding [dɪmǽndɪŋ] ADJ exigente

demarcate [dɪmárket] VT demarcar

demean [dɪmín] VT menospreciar

demeanor [dɪmínə] N conducta *f*,
comportamiento *m*

demented [dɪméntɪd] ADJ demente

demijohn [démɪdʒɑn] N damajuana *f*

demise [dɪmáɪz] N fallecimiento *m*,
desaparición *f*

demobilize [dimóbəlaɪz] VT desmovilizar

democracy [dɪmákrəsi] N democracia *f*

democrat [déməkræt] N demócrata *mf*

democratic [deməkrǽdɪk] ADJ democrático

demographics [deməgrǽfɪks] N demografía *f*

demolish [dɪmálɪʃ] VT demoler, derrumbar

demon [dímən] N demonio *m*

demonstrate [démənstret] VT (prove)
demostrar; (show a product) hacer una
demostración; VI manifestar

demonstration [demənstréʃən] N (proof,
exhibition) demostración *f*; (protest)
manifestación *f*, concentración *f*

demonstrative [dɪmánstrədɪv] ADJ
demostrativo

demoralize [dɪmɔ́rəlaɪz] VT desmoralizar

demote [dɪmót] VT degradar, bajar de
categoría

den [dɛn] N (of an animal) guarida *f*; (room
in a house) cuarto de estar *m*; (cave) cueva
f; **— of iniquity** antro de perdición *m*

denial [dɪnáɪəł] N (refusal to recognize)
negación *f*; (act of denying) negativa *f*,
rechazo *m*; (assertion that an allegation is
false) desmentido *m*; **he is in —** no lo
quiere aceptar

denigrate [dénɪgret] VT denigrar

denim [dénɪm] N tela de vaquero *f*

Denmark [dénmark] N Dinamarca *f*

denomination [dɪnɑmənéʃən] N (name,
monetary value) denominación *f*; (sect)
secta religiosa *f*

denotation [dinotéʃən] N denotación *f*

denote [dɪnót] VT denotar

denounce [dɪnáuns] VT denunciar

dense [dɛns] ADJ (compacted) denso, tupido,
cerrado; (stupid) *fam* burro, duro de
entenderas

density [dénsɪdi] N densidad *f*

dent [dɛnt] N abolladura *f*; **to make a — in
a task** hacer mella en una tarea; VI/VT
abollar(se)

dental [dént] ADJ dental; **— floss** hilo dental

m; **— hygienist** higienista dental *mf*

dentifrice [déntəfrɪs] N dentífrico *m*, pasta
dental *f*

dentist [déntɪst] N dentista *mf*

dentistry [déntɪstri] N odontología *f*

dentures [déntʃəz] N dientes postizos *m pl*

denunciation [dɪnʌnsiéʃən] N denuncia *f*,
acusación *f*

deny [dɪnáɪ] VT (state that something is false)
negar, desmentir; (refuse to approve)
rechazar; **to — oneself** abstenerse

deodorant [diódəənt] N desodorante *m*

deoxidize [diáksɪdaɪz] VT desoxidar

depart [dɪpárt] VI (leave) salir, partir;
(deviate) desviarse, apartarse; (die) dejar de
existir

departed [dɪpárdɪd] ADJ & N difunto -ta *mf*

department [dɪpártmənt] N (of company,
school, country) departamento *m*; (of
government) ministerio *m*; (of a store)
sección *f*; (of knowledge, expertise)
especialidad *f*; **— store** gran almacén *m*

departure [dɪpártʃə] N (scheduled) salida *f*;
(not scheduled) partida *f*; (deviation)
desviación *f*

depend [dɪpénd] VI depender; **to — on** (be
conditioned by) depender de; (rely on)
contar con

dependable [dɪpéndəbł] ADJ confiable,
fiable

dependence [dɪpéndəns] N dependencia *f*

dependency [dɪpéndənsi] N dependencia *f*

dependent [dɪpéndənt] ADJ dependiente;
success is — on perseverance el éxito
depende de la perseverancia; N familiar a
cargo *mf*

depict [dɪpíkt] VT (verbally) describir;
(visually) representar

depilate [dépəlet] VT depilar(se)

depilatory [dɪpílətɔri] ADJ & N depilatorio *m*

deplane [diplén] VI desembarcar

deplete [dɪplít] VT agotar

depletion [dɪplíʃən] N agotamiento *m*

deplorable [dɪplɔ́rəbł] ADJ deplorable

deplore [dɪplɔ́r] VT deplorar

deploy [dɪplɔ́ɪ] VT desplegar

deport [dɪpɔ́rt] VT deportar; VI comportarse

deportment [dɪpɔ́rtmənt] N comportamiento
m, conducta *f*

depose [dɪpóz] VT (overthrow) deponer,
derrocar; (testify) declarar; (take
testimony) tomar declaración

deposit [dɪpázɪt] VT (add to an account)
depositar; *Sp* ingresar; (place) colocar; N
(amount added to an account) depósito *m*;
Sp ingreso *m*; (of a mineral) yacimiento *m*;
(earnest money) señal *f*, anticipo *m*

deposition [dɛpəzíʃən] N (removal from office) deposición f; (testimony) declaración f

depositor [dɪpázɪðə-] N depositante mf

depot [dípo] N (of trains) estación f; (of buses) terminal mf; (for storage) almacén m, depósito m; (for military training) cuartel m

depraved [dɪprévd] ADJ depravado

deprecate [déprɪket] VT despreciar

depreciate [dɪpríʃiet] VT (currency) depreciar(se); (goods) desvalorizar(se), amortizar(se)

depress [dɪprés] VT deprimir

depressed [dɪprést] ADJ deprimido

depressing [dɪprésɪŋ] ADJ deprimente

depression [dɪpréʃən] N depresión f

deprive [dɪpráɪv] VT privar

depth [dépθ] N (of hole, feeling) profundidad f, hondura f; (of the voice) gravedad f; **in the —s** en las profundidades; **in — a** fondo; **what is the — of that bookshelf?** ¿cuánto miden estos estantes de fondo? **he has sunk to such —s** ha caído muy bajo; **in the — of the night** bien entrada la noche; **in the — of winter** en lo más crudo del invierno

deputation [depjətéʃən] N delegación f

deputy [dépjədi] N (elected official) diputado -da mf; (substitute) suplente mf

derail [dɪréɪl] VI/VT descarrilar(se)

deranged [dɪréndʒd] ADJ trastornado, demente

derby [dɝbi] N (hat) sombrero hongo m; (race) derby m

deregulate [dɪrégjəlet] VT desregular

derelict [dérəlɪkt] ADJ (deserted) abandonado; (negligent) negligente; N (ship) buque abandonado m; (person) vagabundo -da mf

deride [dɪráɪd] VT escarnecer, ridiculizar

derision [dɪríʒən] N escarnio m

derivation [dɛrəvéʃən] N derivación f

derivative [dɪrívəDɪv] ADJ & N derivado m

derive [dɪráɪv] VI/VT derivar(se); **to — pleasure from** disfrutar de

dermatology [dɝmətálədʒi] N dermatología f

derogatory [dɪrágətɔri] ADJ despectivo

derrick [dérɪk] N torre de perforación f

descend [dɪsénd] VI/VT descender; **to — upon** caer sobre

descendant [dɪséndənt] ADJ & N descendiente mf

descent [dɪsént] N (act of descending, decline) descenso m; (slope) bajada f; (lineage) descendencia f

describe [dɪskráɪb] VT describir

description [dɪskrípʃən] N descripción f; **of all —s** de todas clases

descriptive [dɪskríptɪv] ADJ descriptivo

desecrate [désɪkret] VT profanar

desecration [desɪkréʃən] N profanación f

desegregate [diségrɪget] VI/VT eliminar la segregación racial

desensitize [disénsɪtaɪz] VT insensibilizar

desert [dézɝt] ADJ (barren, empty) desierto; (of the desert) desértico; N desierto m; [dɪzɝt] VI/VT (a person, place) abandonar; (military service) desertar

deserter [dɪzɝDə-] N desertor -ra mf

desertion [dɪzɝʃən] N (of a person or place) abandono m; (from the military) deserción f

deserve [dɪzɝv] VT merecer

deserving [dɪzɝvɪŋ] ADJ merecedor

design [dɪzáɪn] VI/VT (prepare a sketch of) diseñar, trazar; (plan) planear, idear; N (model, pattern) diseño m; (sketch) esbozo m; **he has —s on her** le ha echado el ojo

designate [dézɪgnet] VT designar, denominar

designation [dezɪgnéʃən] N denominación f, designación f

designer [dɪzáɪnə-] N diseñador -ra mf; **— drugs** drogas de diseño f pl

desirability [dɪzaɪrəbílɪDi] N deseabilidad f, conveniencia f

desirable [dɪzáɪrəbəl] ADJ deseable

desire [dɪzáɪr] VT desear; **I — your cooperation** requiero tu cooperación; N deseo m

desirous [dɪzáɪrəs] ADJ deseoso

desist [dɪsíst] VI desistir

desk [desk] N escritorio m; (school) pupitre m; **—top publishing** edición de sobremesa f

desolate [désəlɪt] ADJ (barren) desolado; [désəlet] VT desolar, asolar

desolation [desəléʃən] N desolación f, asolamiento m

despair [dɪspér] N desesperanza f; VI desesperarse, perder la esperanza

despairing [dɪspérɪŋ] ADJ de desesperación

desperate [déspəɪt] ADJ desesperado; **— illness** enfermedad gravísima

desperation [despəréʃən] N desesperación f

despicable [dɪspíkəbəl] ADJ despreciable, deleznable

despise [dɪspáɪz] VT despreciar, menospreciar

despite [dɪspáɪt] N despecho m; PREP a pesar de

despoil [dɪspɔ́ɪl] VT despojar

despondency [dɪspándənsi] N abatimiento m, desaliento m

despondent [dɪspándənt] ADJ abatido, desalentado

despot [déspət] N déspota *mf*

despotic [dɪspádɪk] ADJ despótico

despotism [déspətɪzəm] N despotismo *m*

dessert [dɪzɔ́-t] N postre *m*

destabilize [distébəlaɪz] VT desestabilizar

destination [destənéʃən] N destino *m*

destine [déstɪn] VT destinar; **she's —d for greatness** promete grandes cosas

destiny [déstəni] N destino *m*

destitute [déstɪtut] ADJ menesteroso, indigente; **— of** falto de, desprovisto de

destroy [dɪstrɔ́ɪ] VT (demolish) destruir, deshacer; (kill) sacrificar; (ruin a reputation) arruinar

destroyer [dɪstrɔ́ɪə] N (person who destroys) destructor -ra *mf*; (ship) destructor *m*

destructible [dɪstrʌ́ktəbəl] ADJ destructible

destruction [dɪstrʌ́kʃən] N (act of demolishing) destrucción *f*; (act of killing) matanza *f*; (act of ruining a reputation) ruina *f*

destructive [dɪstrʌ́ktɪv] ADJ destructivo, destructor

detach [dɪtǽtʃ] VT separar, desprender; (troops) destacar

detachment [dɪtǽtʃmənt] N (physical) separación *f*; (emotional) desapego *m*; (of troops) destacamento *m*; (of the retina) desprendimiento *m*

detail [dítel] N detalle *m*, pormenor *m*; (military) destacamento *m*; **to go into —** detallar, pormenorizar; [dɪtél] VT detallar, pormenorizar; (assign duties) destacar

detain [dɪtén] VT detener

detect [dɪtékt] VT detectar

detective [dɪtéktɪv] N detective *mf*

detector [dɪtéktə] N detector *m*

detention [dɪténʃən] N detención *f*

deter [dɪtɔ́-] VT (dissuade) disuadir; (prevent) prevenir

detergent [dɪtɔ́-dʒənt] N detergente *m*

deteriorate [dɪtíriəret] VI deteriorar(se)

deterioration [dɪtiriəréʃən] N deterioro *m*

determination [dɪtɔ-mənéʃən] N determinación *f*; (resolution) resolución *f*; (persistence) tesón *m*, perseverancia *f*

determine [dɪtɔ́-mɪn] VT determinar; **to — to do something** decidirse a hacer algo

determined [dɪtɔ́-mɪnd] ADJ decidido, resuelto; (persistent) tesonero

detest [dɪtést] VT detestar, abominar de

detestable [dɪtéstəbəl] ADJ detestable

dethrone [diθrón] VT destronar

detonate [détnet] VI/VT detonar

detonation [detnéʃən] N detonación *f*

detour [dítur] N desvío *m*; VI/VT desviar(se)

detoxification [ditɑksəfɪkéʃən] N

destoxificación *f*

detract [dɪtrékt] VT distraer; VI **to — from** disminuir

detrimental [detrəmént]] ADJ perjudicial

devaluation [divæljuéʃən] N devaluación *f*

devastate [dévəstet] VT devastar, asolar

develop [dɪvéləp] VI/VT (mature, elaborate) desarrollar(se); (build houses on) construir, edificar; (treat film) revelar; **she —ed an allergy** le vino una alergia; **—ing countries** países en desarrollo *m pl*

development [dɪvéləpmənt] N (evolution) desarrollo *m*; (buildings) urbanización *f*, colonia *f*; (of a photograph) revelado *m*

deviate [díviet] VI/VT desviar(se)

deviation [diviéʃən] N desviación *f*

device [dɪváɪs] N (gadget) artefacto *m*; (literary convention) recurso *m*; (emblem) divisa *f*; **they left me to my own —s** me dejaron que me las arreglara sola

devil [dévəl] N diablo *m*; **lucky —!** ¡suertudo! **what the — are you saying?** ¿qué diablos dices? **—'s advocate** abogado del diablo *m*

devilish [dévəlɪʃ] ADJ (evil) diabólico; (large, extreme) endiablado, endemoniado

deviltry [dévəltri] N (mischief) diablura *f*; (witchcraft) brujería *f*

devious [dívias] ADJ (roundabout) sinuoso, tortuoso; (crafty) taimado, retorcido

devise [dɪváɪz] VT idear, urdir

devoid [dɪvɔ́ɪd] ADJ **— of** falto de, desprovisto de

devote [dɪvót] VT dedicar; (consecrate) consagrar

devoted [dɪvódɪd] ADJ (friend) leal; (parent) dedicado; (worshipper) devoto

devotion [dɪvóʃən] N devoción *f*

devour [dɪváur] VT devorar

devout [dɪváut] ADJ devoto

dew [dju] N rocío *m*; **—drop** gota de rocío *f*; **—point** punto de condensación *m*

dexterity [dekstérɪDi] N destreza *f*

dextrose [dékstros] N dextrosa *f*

diabetes [daɪəbíDiz] N diabetes *f*

diabolic [daɪəbálɪk] ADJ diabólico

diacritic [daɪəkrídɪk] ADJ & N diacrítico *m*

diagnose [daɪəgnós] VT diagnosticar

diagonal [daɪǽgənəl] ADJ & N diagonal *f*

diagram [dáɪəgræm] N diagrama *m*

dial [dáɪəl] N (of a watch, clock) esfera *f*; (of radio) dial *m*; VI/VT (telephone number) *Sp* marcar; *Am* discar; **— tone** *Sp* señal de marcar *f*; *Am* tono de discar *m*

dialect [dáɪəlekt] N dialecto *m*

dialectic [daɪəléktɪk] ADJ dialéctico; N dialéctica *f*

dialectology [daɪəlektɑ́lədʒi] N dialectología *f*

dialog, dialogue [dáɪəlɑg] N diálogo *m*; VI dialogar

dialysis [daɪǽlɪsɪs] N diálisis *f*

diameter [daɪǽmɪdɚ] N diámetro *m*

diamond [dáɪəmənd] N (stone) diamante *m*; (shape) rombo *m*

diaper [dáɪpɚ] N pañal *m*; VT poner pañales

diaphragm [dáɪəfræm] N diafragma *m*

diarrhea [daɪəríə] N diarrea *f*

diary [dáɪəri] N diario *m*

diatribe [dáɪətraɪb] N diatriba *f*

dice [daɪs] N PL dados *m pl*; VT cortar en cubos; VI jugar a los dados; **no —!** (impossibility) no hay forma; *Mex* ¡ni modo! (refusal) de ninguna manera

dichotomy [daɪkɑ́dəmi] N dicotomía *f*

dick [dɪk] N (penis) *vulg* polla *f*, pija *f*, verga *f*, rabo *m*; (detective) sabueso -sa *mf*; **—head** *offensive* capullo *m*; VI **to — somebody around** fastidiar a alguien

dicker [dɪ́kɚ] VI regatear

dictate [dɪ́ktet] VI/VT dictar; N dictado *m*, precepto *m*

dictation [dɪktéʃən] N dictado *m*; **to take —** escribir al dictado

dictator [dɪ́ktedɚ] N dictador -ra *mf*

dictatorship [dɪktédɚʃɪp] N dictadura *f*

diction [dɪ́kʃən] N dicción *f*

dictionary [dɪ́kʃəneri] N diccionario *m*

didactic [daɪdǽktɪk] ADJ didáctico

die [daɪ] VI morir(se); **—hard** intransigente *mf*; **to — down / away** disminuir; **to — off** irse muriendo; **to — out** morirse, extinguirse; **my car —d** se me murió el coche; N (game piece) dado *m*; (press) molde *m*; (stamp) cuño *m*, troquel *m*

diesel [dízəl] N diesel *m*; **— engine** motor diesel *m*

diet [dáɪt] N (food) dieta *f*; (controlled intake of food) dieta *f*, régimen *m*; **to be / go on a —** estar a dieta / régimen; **to put on a —** poner a dieta; VI estar a dieta

differ [dɪ́fɚ] VI diferir; **to — with** disentir, no estar de acuerdo con; **to — from** ser diferente de

difference [dɪ́fɚəns] N diferencia *f*; **it makes no —** no importa, da igual

different [dɪ́fɚənt] ADJ diferente, distinto

differential [dɪfɚénʃəl] ADJ & N (difference, car part) diferencial *m*; **— equation** diferencial *f*

differentiate [dɪfɚénʃiet] VI/VT diferenciar(se), distinguir(se)

difficult [dɪ́fɪkəlt] ADJ difícil

difficulty [dɪ́fɪkəlti] N dificultad *f*

diffident [dɪ́fɪdənt] ADJ tímido

diffuse [dɪfjúz] VI/VT difundir; [dɪfjús] ADJ difuso

diffusion [dɪfjúʒən] N difusión *f*

dig [dɪg] VI/VT cavar; (by machine) excavar; (superficially) escarbar; **to — in the files** escarbar en los archivos; **to — under** socavar; **to — up** desenterrar; **he dug his heels into the ground** clavó los talones en el suelo; **I — your new shoes** están muy buenos tus zapatos nuevos; N (archaeological site) excavación *f*; (sarcastic remark) pulla *f*; **a — in the ribs** un codazo

digest [dɪdʒést] VI/VT digerir; [dáɪdʒest] N (summary) compendio *m*; (legal) digesto *m*

digestible [dɪdʒéstəbəl] ADJ digerible, digestible

digestion [dɪdʒéstʃən] N digestión *f*

digestive [dɪdʒéstɪv] ADJ digestivo

digit [dɪ́dʒɪt] N dígito *m*

digital [dɪ́dʒɪd̩l] ADJ digital

dignified [dɪ́gnəfaɪd] ADJ digno

dignitary [dɪ́gnɪteri] N dignatario -ria *mf*

dignity [dɪ́gnɪdi] N dignidad *f*

digress [dɪgrés] VI divagar

digression [dɪgréʃən] N digresión *f*

dike [daɪk] N dique *m*

dilapidated [dɪlǽpɪdeɪd] ADJ (machine) destartalado; (furniture) desvencijado; (house) derruido, venido abajo

dilate [dáɪlet] VI/VT dilatar(se)

dilation [daɪléʃən] N dilatación *f*

dilemma [dɪlémə] N dilema *m*

dilettante [dɪ́lɪtɑnt] N diletante *mf*

diligence [dɪ́lədʒəns] N diligencia *f*

diligent [dɪ́lədʒənt] ADJ diligente, hacendoso

dill [dɪl] N eneldo *m*; **— pickle** pepinillo en vinagre con eneldo *m*

dilute [dɪlút] VI/VT diluir(se); ADJ diluido

dim [dɪm] ADJ (light) tenue; (outline) difuso; (room) oscuro, en penumbras; (person) *fam* de pocas luces; **—wit** *fam* tonto, bobo; VI/VT (make less bright) atenuar; VT (switch to low beam) bajar

dime [daɪm] N moneda de diez centavos *f*; **English teachers are a — a dozen** sobran los profesores de inglés

dimension [dɪménʃən] N dimensión *f*

diminish [dɪmɪ́nɪʃ] VI/VT disminuir, menguar; **the law of —ing returns** la ley de los rendimientos decrecientes

diminution [dɪmənúʃən] N disminución *f*, mengua *f*

diminutive [dɪmɪ́nʝətɪv] ADJ (small) diminuto; N diminutivo *m*

dimmer [dɪ́mɚ] N regulador de voltaje *m*

dimness [dímnɪs] N oscuridad f, penumbra f

dimple [dímpəł] N hoyuelo m; VT formar hoyuelos

din [dɪn] N estruendo m, estrépito m

dine [daɪn] VI cenar; **to — out** cenar afuera

diner [dáɪnə] N (restaurant) cafetería f; (on a train) coche-comedor m; (person) comensal mf

ding-a-ling [díŋəlɪŋ] N (silly person) ganso -sa mf; (eccentric person) excéntrico -ca mf; (sound) tilín m

dingy [díndʒi] ADJ deslucido

dining [dáɪnɪŋ] ADJ **— car** coche-comedor m; **— room** comedor m

dinner [dínə] N (main meal) comida f; (at midday) almuerzo m; (in the evening) cena f; **— jacket** smoking m; **—time** hora de la comida f

dinosaur [dáɪnəsɔr] N dinosaurio m

dint [dɪnt] ADV LOC **by — of** a fuerza de

dip [dɪp] VT (make wet) mojar; (scoop) sacar; (immerse) sumergir; (in insecticide) bañar; (in sauce, coffee) pringar, mojar; VI (sun) hundirse; (stocks) bajar; (road) hacer una bajada; (airplane) descender súbitamente; N (act of wetting) mojada f; (of ice-cream) bola f, cucharada f; (sauce) mojo m; (decrease) bajada f; (in a road) declive m; (in the land) hondonada f; (swim) baño m; (air travel) descenso rápido m; (irritating person) pej pesado -da mf

diphtheria [dɪpθíriə] N difteria f

diphthong [dífθɔŋ] N diptongo m

diploma [dɪplómə] N diploma m

diplomacy [dɪplóməsi] N diplomacia f

diplomat [dípləmæt] N diplomático -ca mf

diplomatic [dɪpləmǽdɪk] ADJ diplomático -ca

dipper [dípə] N cucharón m, cazo m

dire [daɪr] ADJ terrible, espantoso; **— need** necesidad acuciante f; **— predictions** predicciones funestas f pl; **— situation** situación extrema f

direct [dɪrékt] ADJ directo; **— current** corriente continua f; **— object** complemento directo m; **— quotation** cita textual f; ADV directo, directamente; VI/VT dirigir; **he —ed me to leave** me mandó irme

direction [dɪrékʃən] N dirección f; **—s** indicaciones f pl; **I'm thinking in that — me** inclino por eso

directive [dɪréktɪv] ADJ directivo; N directiva f

director [dɪréktə] N director -ra mf

directory [dɪréktəri] N directorio m (also computer term)

dirigible [dərídʒəbəł] ADJ & N dirigible m

dirt [dɜt] N (filth) suciedad f; (foul

substance) mugre f; (vile person) offensive mierda f; (earth) tierra f; **—bag** offensive porquería f; **— cheap** baratísimo; **—-poor** pobrísimo; **I've got some — on him** le conozco los trapos sucios

dirty [dɜdi] ADJ sucio, mugriento; **— joke** chiste verde m; **— look** mirada asesina f; **— money** dinero sucio m; **— shame** pena horrible f; **— trick** trampa f; **— word** palabrota f; Sp taco m; **— work** trabajo sucio m; VI/VT ensuciar; ADV **to talk —** decir cosas obscenas

disability [dɪsəbílɪdi] N incapacidad f

disable [dɪsébəł] VT (person) incapacitar; (device) desactivar

disabled [dɪsébəłd] ADJ minusválido

disabuse [dɪsəbjúz] VT desengañar

disadvantage [dɪsɪdvǽntɪdʒ] N desventaja f; **to be at a —** estar en desventaja

disadvantaged [dɪsɪdvǽntɪdʒd] ADJ carenciado

disagree [dɪsəgrí] VI (differ) diferir; (differ in opinion) disentir, no estar de acuerdo; **pizza —s with me** no me cae bien la pizza

disagreeable [dɪsəgríəbəł] ADJ desagradable

disagreement [dɪsəgrímənt] N (lack of agreement, argument) desacuerdo m; (discrepancy) discrepancia f

disallow [dɪsəláu] VT desaprobar; (in sports) anular

disappear [dɪsəpír] VI desaparecer

disappearance [dɪsəpírəns] N desaparición f

disappoint [dɪsəpɔ́ɪnt] VI/VT decepcionar, desilusionar; **to be —ed** estar desilusionado

disappointing [dɪsəpɔ́ɪntɪŋ] ADJ decepcionante

disappointment [dɪsəpɔ́ɪntmənt] N decepción f, desilusión f

disapproval [dɪsəprúvəł] N desaprobación f

disapprove [dɪsəprúv] VI/VT desaprobar

disarm [dɪsárm] VI/VT desarmar(se)

disarmament [dɪsárməmənt] N desarme m

disarray [dɪsəré] VT desordenar; N confusión f, desorden m; **in —** en desorden

disaster [dɪzǽstə] N desastre m

disastrous [dɪzǽstrəs] ADJ desastroso

disavow [dɪsəváu] VT negar

disband [dɪsbǽnd] VT disolver; VI desbandarse

disbelief [dɪsbɪlíf] N incredulidad f

disbelieve [dɪsbɪlív] VI/VT descreer de

disburse [dɪsbɜs] VT desembolsar

disbursement [dɪsbɜsmənt] N desembolso m

discard [dɪskárd] VT (a card) descartar; (garbage) desechar; [dískard] N (card) descarte *m*; (garbage) desecho *m*

discern [dɪsɔ́·n] VT (distinguish mentally) discernir; (perceive) percibir

discernment [dɪsɔ́·nmənt] N discernimiento *m*

discharge [dɪstʃárʤ] VI/VT (battery, load, firearm) descargar(se); (obligation) cumplir; (prisoner) poner en libertad, soltar; (odor) despedir; (soldier) dar de baja; (patient) dar de alta; (a debt) pagar; (pus) supurar; [dístʃarʤ] N (of a battery, load, firearm) descarga *f*; (of an obligation) cumplimiento *m*; (from a job) despido *m*; (of a soldier) baja *f*; (of a patient) alta *f*; (of a debt) pago *m*; (of an odor) emisión *f*; (of a prisoner) puesta en libertad *f*; (of oil) pérdida *f*; (of pus) supuración *f*; (uterine, vaginal) flujo *m*

disciple [dɪsáɪpəl] N discípulo -la *mf*

discipline [dísəplɪn] N disciplina *f*; VT disciplinar

disclaimer [dɪskléma·] N descargo de responsabilidad *m*

disclose [dɪsklóz] VT revelar

disco [dísko] N discoteca *f*

discolor [dɪskɔ́lə·] VI/VT descolorar(se)

discomfort [dɪskʌ́mfə·t] N malestar *m*

disconcert [dɪskansɔ́·t] VT desconcertar

disconnect [dɪskənékt] VI/VT desconectar; N desconexión *f*

disconnected [dɪskənéktɪd] ADJ (broken) desconectado; (incoherent) inconexo

disconsolate [dɪskánsəlɪt] ADJ desconsolado

discontent [dɪskəntént] N descontento *m*

discontinue [dɪskəntínju] VT suspender, interrumpir; VI abandonar

discontinuous [dɪskəntínjuəs] ADJ discontinuo

discord [dískɔrd] N (lack of concord) discordia *f*, desavenencia *f*; (dissonance) disonancia *f*, discordancia *f*

discotheque [dískotɛk] N discoteca *f*

discount [dískaunt] VT (deduct from a charge, take into account in advance) descontar; (sell at a reduced price) rebajar; (disregard) ignorar; N descuento *m*

discourage [dɪskɔ́·ɪʤ] VT desanimar, desalentar; **to — from** disuadir de

discouragement [dɪskɔ́·ɪʤmənt] N desánimo *m*, desaliento *m*

discourse [dískɔrs] N (conversation, talk) discurso *m*; (treatise) disertación *f*; [dɪskɔ́rs] VI (talk) discurrir; (treat a subject) disertar

discourteous [dɪskɔ́·ɪdiəs] ADJ descortés

discourtesy [dɪskɔ́·ɪdɪsi] N descortesía *f*

discover [dɪskʌ́və·] VT descubrir

discoverer [dɪskʌ́vərə·] N descubridor -ra *mf*

discovery [dɪskʌ́vəri] N descubrimiento *m*

discredit [dɪskrédɪt] VT (injure the reputation of) desacreditar; (give no credence to) no creer; N descrédito *m*

discreet [dɪskrít] ADJ discreto

discrepancy [dɪskrépənsi] N discrepancia *f*

discrete [dɪskrít] ADJ discreto

discretion [dɪskréʃən] N discreción *f*; **at your own —** a discreción; **at the judge's —** al arbitrio del juez

discriminate [dɪskrímənet] VI/VT distinguir; **to — against** discriminar a

discuss [dɪskás] VT discutir

discussion [dɪskáʃən] N discusión *f*

disdain [dɪsdén] N desdén *m*, desprecio *m*; VT (treat with contempt) desdeñar; (think unworthy of a response) no dignarse a

disdainful [dɪsdénfəl] ADJ desdeñoso

disease [dɪzíz] N enfermedad *f*

diseased [dɪzízd] ADJ enfermo

disembark [dɪsɪmbárk] VI/VT desembarcar

disenfranchise [dɪsɪnfrǽntʃaɪz] VT (politician) proscribir; (minorities) privar de derechos, desheredar

disengage [dɪsɪngéʤ] VI/VT (a clutch) soltar(se); (from a situation) distanciar(se)

disentangle [dɪsɪnténgəl] VT desenredar, desenmarañar

disfavor [dɪsfévə·] N **to fall into —** (a person) caer en desgracia; (a fashion) caer en desuso; VT mirar con malos ojos

disfigure [dɪsfígjə·] VT desfigurar

disgrace [dɪsgrés] N (dishonor) deshonra *f*; (shame) vergüenza *f*; **to fall into —** caer en desgracia; VT deshonrar

disgraceful [dɪsgrésfəl] ADJ vergonzoso

disgruntled [dɪsgrántld] ADJ descontento, resentido

disguise [dɪsgáɪz] VT disfrazar(se); N disfraz *m*

disgust [dɪsgást] VT (repel) asquear, repugnar; (displease) disgustar; N asco *m*, repugnancia *f*

disgusted [dɪsgástɪd] ADJ asqueado, repugnado

disgusting [dɪsgástɪŋ] ADJ asqueroso, repugnante

dish [dɪʃ] N (plate, food, quantity) plato *m*; (serving container) fuente *f*; (attractive person) *fam* bombón *m*; **—es** vajilla *f*; **—cloth / towel** paño de cocina *m*, repasador *m*; **—washer** lavaplatos *m sg*, lavavajillas *m sg*; **—water** agua de fregar *f*; VI/VT (serve food) servir; **to — out** repartir

dishearten [dɪshártn] VT desanimar, descorazonar, desalentar

disheartening [dɪshártnɪŋ] ADJ desalentador

dishevel [dɪʃévəl] VT desgreñar
disheveled [dɪʃévəld] ADJ (hair) desgreñado, revuelto; (clothes) desaliñado
dishonest [dɪsánɪst] ADJ deshonesto
dishonesty [dɪsánɪsti] N deshonestidad f
dishonor [dɪsánə] N deshonra f; VT deshonrar; (a check) no pagar
dishonorable [dɪsánə-əbəl] ADJ deshonroso
disillusion [dɪsɪlúʒən] N desilusión f, desencanto m; VT desilusionar, desencantar
disinfect [dɪsɪnfékt] VT desinfectar
disinfectant [dɪsɪnféktənt] N desinfectante m
disinformation [dɪsɪnfə-méʃən] N desinformación f
disinherit [dɪsɪnhérɪt] VT desheredar
disintegrate [dɪsíntɪgret] VI/VT desintegrar(se)
disintegration [dɪsɪntɪgréʃən] N desintegración f
disinterested [dɪsíntrɪstɪd] ADJ desinteresado
disjointed [dɪsdʒóɪntɪd] ADJ desarticulado
disk, disc [dɪsk] N disco m; (in certain games) tejo m; (in a computer) disco m, disquete m; — **brake** freno de disco m; — **drive** disquetera f; — **jockey** pinchadiscos mf sg
diskette [dɪskét] N disquete m
dislike [dɪsláɪk] N aversión f, tirria f; VT **I** — **parties** no me gustan las fiestas
dislocate [dɪslóket] VT dislocar, descoyuntar
dislodge [dɪsládʒ] VT (force out) desatascar; (displace) desprender
disloyal [dɪslóɪəl] ADJ desleal
dismal [dízməl] ADJ pésimo; **a** — **failure** un fracaso rotundo
dismantle [dɪsmæntl] VT (a factory) desmantelar; (a car, watch, etc.) desmontar
dismay [dɪsmé] VT (disappoint) consternar; (daunt) desalentar; (alarm) alarmar; N (disappointment) consternación f; (loss of courage) desaliento m; (alarm) alarma f
dismember [dɪsmémbə] VT desmembrar
dismiss [dɪsmís] VT (fire a private employee) despedir; (fire a public employee) destituir, cesar; (reject a possibility) desechar, descartar; (discharge from military service) dar de baja; (reject a claim) desestimar; **class —ed!** ¡pueden retirarse!
dismissal [dɪsmísəl] N (firing) destitución f, despido m; (of a possibility) rechazo m; (from military service) baja f; (of a claim) desestimación f
dismount [dɪsmáunt] VI (get off a horse) desmontarse, apearse; (take apart) desarmar; N bajada f
disobedience [dɪsəbídɪəns] N desobediencia f

disobedient [dɪsəbídɪənt] ADJ desobediente
disobey [dɪsəbé] VI/VT desobedecer
disorder [dɪsɔ́rdə] N (confusion) desorden m; (public disturbance) desorden público m; (illness) trastorno m, desarreglo m
disorderly [dɪsɔ́rdə-li] ADJ (untidy) desordenado; (unruly) revoltoso; — **conduct** alteración del orden público f
disorganization [dɪsɔrgənɪzéʃən] N desorganización f
disorganized [dɪsɔ́rgənaɪzd] ADJ desorganizado
disown [dɪsón] VT repudiar
disparage [dɪspærɪdʒ] VT denigrar
disparate [díspə-ɪt] ADJ dispar
dispassionate [dɪspǽʃənɪt] ADJ desapasionado
dispatch [dɪspǽtʃ] VT despachar; N (sending off) envío m; (putting to death) ejecución f; (news story, official communication) despacho m
dispel [dɪspél] VT disipar
dispensable [dɪspénsəbəl] ADJ prescindible
dispensary [dɪspénsəri] N dispensario m
dispensation [dɪspɛnséʃən] N (relaxation of law) dispensa f; (act of handing out) dispensación f
dispense [dɪspéns] VT (goods) dispensar; (justice) administrar; **to** — **from an obligation** eximir de una obligación; **to** — **with** prescindir de
dispersal [dɪspə́-səl] N dispersión f
disperse [dɪspə́-s] VI/VT dispersar(se)
displace [dɪsplés] VT (evict) desalojar; (take up space, remove from office) desplazar; **—d person** expatriado -da mf
display [dɪsplé] VT (exhibit) exhibir, exponer; (unfold, flaunt) desplegar, ostentar; (show on a computer screen) visualizar; N (of wares, etc.) exhibición f, despliegue m; (advertisement) cartel m; (flaunting) ostentación f; (computer) visualizador m, display m
displease [dɪsplíz] VT contrariar, desagradar, descontentar; VI molestar
displeasure [dɪspléʒə] N disgusto m, desagrado m
disposal [dɪspózəl] N (arrangement) disposición f; (disposing of) eliminación f
dispose [dɪspóz] VT (give inclination) predisponer; (set in order, make ready) disponer; **to** — **of** descartar, eliminar
disposition [dɪspəzíʃən] N (attitude) temperamento m; (inclination) inclinación f, tendencia f; (arrangement, disposal) disposición f
dispossess [dɪspəzés] VT desposeer

disproportionate [dɪsprəpórʃənɪt] ADJ desproporcionado

disprove [dɪsprúv] VT refutar

dispute [dɪspjút] N disputa f; VI disputar; VT discutir, impugnar

disqualify [dɪskwálɪfaɪ] VT (deprive of rights) inhabilitar; (exclude from a sport event) descalificar

disregard [dɪsrɪgárd] VT hacer caso omiso de, ignorar; N (neglect) descuido m; (disrespect) falta de respeto f

disrepair [dɪsrɪpér] N mal estado m; **to fall into** — caer en ruina

disreputable [dɪsrépjəbəbəł] ADJ (of bad reputation) de mala reputación; (shabby) de mala muerte

disrespect [dɪsrɪspékt] N desacato m, falta de respeto f; VT faltar el respeto

disrespectful [dɪsrɪspéktfəł] ADJ irrespetuoso

disrobe [dɪsrób] VI/VT desvestir(se)

disrupt [dɪsrápt] VT (cause disorder) trastornar, trastocar; (interrupt) interrumpir

dissatisfied [dɪsséɪɪsfaɪd] ADJ insatisfecho, disconforme

dissatisfy [dɪssǽtɪsfaɪ] VT no satisfacer

dissect [daɪsékt] VT (cut apart) disecar; (analyze argument) analizar minuciosamente

dissemble [dɪsémbəł] VI/VT (hide) disimular; (feign) fingir

disseminate [dɪsémənet] VT (spread out) diseminar; (publicize) divulgar

dissemination [dɪsemənéʃən] N diseminación f

dissension [dɪsénʃən] N disensión f, disenso m

dissent [dɪsént] VI disentir; N disenso m

dissertation [dɪsətéʃən] N (formal discourse) disertación f; (doctoral treatise) tesis de doctorado f

dissident [dísɪdənt] N disidente mf

dissimilar [dɪssímələ] ADJ diferente

dissimulation [dɪsɪmjəléʃən] N disimulo m

dissipate [dísəpet] VI/VT disipar(se)

dissipation [dɪsəpéʃən] N disipación f

dissolute [dísəlut] ADJ disoluto

dissolution [dɪsəlúʃən] N disolución f

dissolve [dɪzálv] VI/VT disolver(se)

dissuade [dɪswéd] VT disuadir

distance [dístəns] N distancia f, recorrido m; — **learning** educación a distancia f; **in the** — a lo lejos, en la lejanía; VT distanciarse de, distanciar

distant [dístənt] ADJ (far away, aloof) distante; (remote) lejano, remoto; **to be** — **from** distar de

distaste [dɪstést] N aversión f

distasteful [dɪstéstfəł] ADJ desagradable

distemper [dɪstémpə] N moquillo m

distend [dɪsténd] VI/VT distender(se)

distill [dɪstíł] VI/VT destilar(se)

distillation [dɪstəléʃən] N destilación f

distillery [dɪstíləri] N destilería f

distinct [dɪstíŋkt] ADJ (different) distinto; (clear) bien delineado, neto

distinction [dɪstíŋkʃən] N distinción f; **he passed with** — aprobó con sobresaliente

distinctive [dɪstíŋktɪv] ADJ distintivo

distinguish [dɪstíŋgwɪʃ] VI/VT distinguir

distinguished [dɪstíŋgwɪʃt] ADJ distinguido

distinguishing [dɪstíŋgwɪʃɪŋ] ADJ distintivo

distort [dɪstórt] VT (an object) deformar; (reports, sound) distorsionar

distortion [dɪstórʃən] N (object) deformación f; (image, sound) distorsión f; (of a statement) tergiversación f

distract [dɪstrǽkt] VT distraer, entretener

distraction [dɪstrǽkʃən] N distracción f; **to drive to** — volver loco

distraught [dɪstrót] ADJ angustiado

distress [dɪstrés] N (anxiety) angustia f; (pain) dolor m, congoja f; **to be in** — (a person) estar en apuros; (a ship, plane) estar en peligro; VT (cause anxiety) angustiar, atribular; (cause pain) acongojar, afligir

distribute [dɪstríbjut] VT distribuir, repartir

distribution [dɪstrəbjúʃən] N distribución f, reparto m

distributor [dɪstríbjəɾə] N distribuidor m

district [dístrɪkt] N distrito m, comarca f; — **attorney** fiscal de distrito mf

District of Columbia [dístrɪktəvkəlámbiə] N Distrito de Columbia m

distrust [dɪstrást] N desconfianza f; VT desconfiar de

distrustful [dɪstrástfəł] ADJ desconfiado

disturb [dɪstə́b] VI/VT (interrupt, interfere, perplex) perturbar; (trouble) turbar; (alter mentally) trastornar; (mess up) desarreglar; **do not** — se ruega no molestar

disturbance [dɪstə́bəns] N disturbio m; (weather) perturbación f

disuse [dɪsjús] N desuso m; **to fall into** — caer en desuso

ditch [dɪtʃ] N (trench) zanja f; (roadside) cuneta f; (for irrigation) acequia f; VT (make ditches) abrir zanjas; (get rid of) deshacerse de; (crash-land an airplane on water) hacer un amarizaje; **to** — **someone** dejar a alguien

dither [díðə] VI (hesitate) titubear; N **it threw her into a** — se puso muy nerviosa

ditsy [dítsi] ADJ atolondrado, cabeza de chorlito

ditto [dído] PRON & ADV ídem *m*

diuretic [daɪəɾédɪk] ADJ & N diurético *m*

diurnal [daɪᵊnəl] ADJ diurno

divan [dɪvǽn] N diván *m*, canapé *m*

dive [daɪv] VI (into water) zambullirse, chapuzar; (into an activity) zambullirse; (with scuba equipment) bucear; (airplane) bajar en picada; (submarine) sumergirse; N (of a person) zambullida *f*, chapuz *m*; (of an airplane) picada *f*; (cheap bar) antro *m*

diver [dáɪvᵊ] N saltador -ra *mf*; (high-dive) clavadista *mf*; (scuba) buzo *mf*

diverge [dɪvᵊdʒ] VI (branch off, differ in opinion) divergir; VI/VT (deviate) desviar

divergence [dɪvᵊdʒəns] N (separation, difference in opinion) divergencia *f*; (deviation) desviación *f*

diverse [dɪvᵊs] ADJ (of various kinds) diverso; (different) diferente

diversify [dɪvᵊsəfaɪ] VI/VT diversificar(se)

diversion [dɪvᵊʒən] N (entertainment) entretenimiento *m*; (distraction) distracción *f*; (military) diversión *f*; (turning aside) desvío *m*, desviación *f*

diversity [dɪvᵊsɪdi] N diversidad *f*

divert [dɪvᵊt] VI/VT (turn aside) desviar, distraer; (distract) entretener

divest [dɪvést] VT (strip) despojar; (get rid of) deshacerse de

divide [dɪváɪd] VI/VT dividir(se); (classify) clasificar(se); N línea divisoria *f*

dividend [dívɪdɛnd] N dividendo *m*

divine [dɪváɪn] ADJ divino; VI/VT adivinar

divinity [dɪvínɪdi] N divinidad *f*; (theology) teología *f*

division [dɪvíʒən] N división *f*

divorce [dɪvɔ́rs] N divorcio *m*; VI/VT divorciar(se)

divulge [dɪváɫdʒ] VT divulgar, publicar

dizziness [dízɪnɪs] N mareo *m*

dizzy [dízi] ADJ (person) mareado; (height) vertigoso; (speed) vertiginoso; — **spell** vahído *m*

DJ (disc jockey) [díʤe] N pinchadiscos *mf sg*

Djibouti [ʤɪbúti] N Yibuti *m*

Djiboutian [ʤɪbúɖiən] ADJ & N yibutiano -na *mf*

DNA (deoxyribonucleic acid) [dɪené] N ADN *m*

do [du] VI/VT hacer; **to — away with** eliminar; **to — one's hair** arreglarse el pelo; **to — the dishes** lavar los platos; **to — drugs** tomar drogas; **to — in** matar; **to — time** cumplir una condena; **we were —ing 100 kph** íbamos a cien kph;

to — well prosperar; **to — without** prescindir de; **to have nothing to — with** no tener nada que ver con; **that will — basta**; **that won't — eso no** sirve; **I'm —ing well** estoy bien; **I did her last night** *fam* me la tiré anoche; **this will have to —** habrá que conformarse con; **—-it-yourself** hágalo usted mismo; V AUX **I feel as you —** pienso igual que tú; **how — you —?** ¿cómo estás? — **you hear me?** ¿me oyes? **yes, I —** sí; **— come again** vuelve por favor; N (hairstyle) peinado *m*; (party) fiesta *f*

DOA (dead on arrival) [dioé] ADJ muerto -ta antes de ingresar al hospital *mf*

docile [dásəɫ] ADJ dócil

dock [dɑk] N (pier) muelle *m*; (for landing) desembarcadero *m*, atracadero *m*; (water between piers) dique *m*, dársena *f*; **dry —** dique seco *m*; VI/VT (a boat) atracar; (a space ship) acoplar(se); (wages) descontar

doctor [dáktᵊ] N (physician) médico -ca *mf*; (Ph.D., scholar) doctor -ra *mf*; (expert) especialista *mf*; VT (treat) atender; (cure) curar; (restore) restaurar; (counterfeit) alterar; **I —ed up this recipe** le hice unos retoques a esta receta

doctorate [dáktᵊɪt] N doctorado *m*

doctrine [dáktrɪn] N doctrina *f*

document [dákjəmənt] N documento *m*; [dákjəmənt] VT documentar

documentary [dɑkjəméntəri] N documental *m*

dodder [dádᵊ] VI (stumble along) tambalearse, titubear; (shake) temblequear

dodge [dɑʤ] VT esquivar, sortear; VI (be evasive) dar rodeos; (move sideways) apartarse, echarse a un lado; N evasiva *f*

doe [do] N cierva *f*; (female of various animals) hembra *f*

dog [dɔg] N perro -rra *mf*; **—catcher** perrero -ra *mf*; **— collar** collar de perro *m*; **—-eared** sobado, muy gastado; **—-fight** (dogs) pelea *f* de perros; (aircraft) combate aéreo *m*; (people) reyerta *f*; **—gone** maldito -ta *mf*; **—house** casilla de perro *f*; *Sp* caseta *f*; **to be in the —house** haber caído en desgracia, estar en capilla; **—. paddle** nado estilo perrito *m*; **to —-paddle** nadar estilo perrito; **—sled** trineo para perros *m*; **— tag** placa de identificación *f*; **—wood** cornejo *m*; **to go to the —s** venirse abajo; VT (follow) seguir la pista de; (harass) hostigar

doggy [dɔ́gi] N perrito -ta *mf*; **— bag** bolsa para las sobras *f*

dogma [dɔ́gmə] N dogma *m*

dogmatic [dɔgmǽdɪk] ADJ dogmático

doily [dɔ́ɪli] N mantelito *m*

doings [dúɪŋz] N acciones *f pl*

dole [doł] N (alms) limosna *f*; **to be on the
— **estar cobrando el seguro de desempleo/
paro; **to — out** repartir

doleful [dóɫfəł] ADJ apesadumbrado, triste

doll [dɑł] N (toy) muñeco -ca *mf*; (attractive
female) muñeca *f*; **—house** casa de
muñecas *f*; VI **to get —ed up**
empérifollarse, empaquetarse

dollar [dálə] N dólar *m*; **— diplomacy**
diplomacia del dólar *f*; **— sign** signo del
dólar *m*

dolly [dáli] N (doll) muñeca *f*; (cart) carretilla
f

dolphin [dɔ́łfɪn] N (mammal) delfín *m*; (fish)
dorado *m*

dolt [doɫt] N zopenco -ca *mf*

domain [domén] N dominio *m*

dome [dom] N (roof) cúpula *f*, domo *m*;
(head) coco *m*, pelada *f*; **the — of the
sky** la bóveda celeste

domestic [dəméstɪk] ADJ (appliance, pet,
chore) doméstico; (devoted to
homemaking) hogareño; (home-loving)
casero; (of a country) interno, nacional; **—
violence** violencia doméstica *f*; N
doméstico -ca *mf*

domesticate [dəméstɪket] VI/VT (animals)
domesticar; (plants) aclimatar

domicile [dáməsaɪł] N domicilio *m*

dominant [dámənənt] ADJ dominante

dominate [dámanet] VI/VT dominar; VI
señorear

domination [damənéʃən] N (act of
dominating) dominación *f*; (rule) dominio
m

domineer [damənɪ́r] VI/VT dominar,
mandonear

domineering [damənɪ́rɪŋ] ADJ tiránico,
mandón

Dominica [dəmíníkə] N Dominica *f*

Dominican [dəmínɪkən] ADJ & N (of
Dominica) dominiqués -esa *mf*; (of the
Dominican Republic) dominicano -na *mf*

Dominican Republic [dəmínɪkənrɪpábłɪk] N
República Dominicana *f*

dominion [dəmínjən] N dominio *m*, señorío
m

domino [dáməno] N (game, costume)
dominó *m*; (piece) ficha *f*

don [dɑn] N (title, form of address, mafia
boss) don *m*; (lecturer) profesor -ra
universitario -ria *mf*; VT ponerse, vestirse

donate [dónet] VI/VT donar

donation [donéʃən] N donación *f*

done [dʌn] ADJ terminado, acabado; **when
you are —** cuando termines; **to be all —
in** estar muerto de cansancio; **the meat
is well —** está bien asada la carne; **that
sort of thing just isn't —** eso no se
hace

donkey [dáŋki] N burro *m*, asno *m*, borrico
m

donor [dónə] N donante *mf*, donador -ora *mf*

doodad [dúdæd] N (trinket) chuchería *f*;
(device) chisme *m*, coso *m*

doohickey [dúhɪki] N chisme *m*, coso *m*

doom [dum] N perdición *f*; **—sday** día del
juicio final *m*; VT condenar; **to be —ed to
failure** estar condenado al fracaso

door [dɔr] N puerta *f*; **—to-—** de puerta a
puerta; **—bell** timbre *m*; **—keeper**
portero -ra *mf*; **—knob** pomo *m*; **—man**
portero *m*; **—mat** felpudo *m*; **—step**
umbral *m*; **—way** puerta *f*, portal *m*; **I
showed him the —** lo eché

dope [dop] N (narcotic) droga *f*; (stimulant)
estimulante *m*; (information) chismes *m
pl*; **he is a —** fam es un zopenco; VT
dopar; **to — oneself up** medicarse en
exceso

dork [dɔrk] N fam idiota *mf*, tarambana *mf*

dorky [dɔ́rki] ADJ **that's a — dress** fam
pareces una idiota con ese vestido

dormant [dɔ́rmənt] ADJ latente

dormitory [dɔ́rmɪtɔri] N residencia
estudiantil *f*

DOS (Disk Operating System) [dɑs] N DOS
m

dose [dos] N dosis *f*; VT dosificar

dossier [dósie] N expediente *m*

dot [dɑt] N punto *m*; (on a tie) pinta *f*;
—-com punto com; **—matrix printer**
impresora de matriz de puntos *f*; **—ted
eighth note** corchea con puntillo *f*; **on
the —** en punto; VT marcar con puntos

dotage [dódɪdʒ] N chochez *f*, chochera *f*; **to
be in one's —** chochear, estar chocho

dote [dot] VI **to — on** estar chocho con

double [dábəł] ADJ doble; **— agent** doble
agente *mf*; **—-barreled** de doble caño; **—
bass** contrabajo *m*; **— bed** cama doble *f*;
— bind dilema *m*; **— boiler** baño de
María *m*; **—-breasted** cruzado; **— chin**
papada *f*; **—-click** hacer doble clic; **—
cross** traición *f*; **to —-cross** traicionar; **to
—-date** salir dos parejas juntas; **—
dealing** duplicidad *f*; **— entry** entrada
por partida doble *f*; **— sided** de dos caras;
— shift turno doble *m*; **— standard**
trato discriminatorio *m*; **— vision** doble

visión f; **to do a — take** quedar atónito; N doble m; **—s** juego de dobles m; ADV **to sleep —** dormir de a dos; **to —-check** verificar; **to —-talk** salirse con evasivas; VI/VT duplicar(se); (an effort) redoblar(se); (fold, be twice as old, challenge a bid) doblar(se); **to — up** (bend over) doblarse; (crowd) amontonarse; **this sofa —s as a bed** este sofá sirve también de cama

doubt [daʊt] VI/VT dudar; (not trust) desconfiar; N duda f; **beyond a —** indudablemente; **in —** en duda; **no —!** ¡sin duda!

doubtful [dáʊtfəł] ADJ dudoso

doubtless [dáʊtlɪs] ADV (certainly) sin duda; (probably) probablemente

douche [duʃ] N ducha vaginal f; **—bag** offensive porquería f

dough [do] N pasta f, masa f; (money) pasta f, mosca f; **—nut** rosquilla f; Mex dona f; Sp donut m

douse [daʊs] VI/VT empapar; (a flame) apagar (con agua)

dove [dʌv] N paloma f

dowdy [dáʊdi] ADJ (article of clothing) pasado de moda; (person) sin gracia

dowel [dáʊəł] N clavija f

down [daʊn] ADV abajo; **two blocks —** dos calles más abajo; **to turn — the volume** bajar el volumen; **to water — a drink** rebajar una bebida con agua; **to get — to work** aplicarse al trabajo; **to fall —** caerse; **to go / come —** bajar; **to come — with a cold** caer con gripe; Sp cogerse un resfriado; **to lie —** tumbarse, echarse; **to write —** anotar; **to put — someone** denigrar a alguien; **slow —!** ¡anda más despacio! **the wind died —** amainó el viento; PREP **— the street** calle abajo; ADJ (depressed) abatido; **one — and two to go** hicimos uno y nos quedan dos por hacer; **prices are —** han bajado los precios; **they're — on me** están mal conmigo; N (turn for the worse) revés m; (feathers) plumón m; VT (knock down, shoot down) derribar; (drink quickly) despachar de un solo trago; (defeat) vencer

down-and-dirty [dáʊnɪndɚ́di] ADJ sucio

down-and-out [dáʊnɪnáʊt] ADJ tirado

downcast [dáʊnkæst] ADJ abatido, cabizbajo

downfall [dáʊnfɔ̱ł] N ruina f

downgrade [dáʊngred] N declive m, pendiente f; VT quitarle importancia a

downhill [dáʊnhɪ̱ł] ADV cuesta abajo; **his health is going —** su salud se deteriora; [dáʊnhɪ̱ł] ADJ **a — slope** una pendiente; N

bajada contra-reloj f

download [dáʊnlod] VT descargar

down payment [dáʊnpémənt] N entrega inicial f, entrada f

downplay [dáʊnple] VT quitar la importancia a

downpour [dáʊnpɔr] N aguacero m

downright [dáʊnraɪt] ADJ absoluto; **— foolishness** reverenda tontería f; **he was — angry** echaba chispas

downshift [dáʊnʃɪft] VI rebajar (el cambio)

downside [dáʊnsaɪd] N inconveniente m

downsize [dáʊnsaɪz] VI (cut back) hacer reducción de personal; VT (make smaller) reducir el tamaño de; **he got —d** perdió el trabajo cuando hicieron reducción de personal

downstairs [dáʊnstérz] ADV abajo; (in the apartment one floor lower) en el piso de abajo; [dáʊnsterz] ADJ de abajo; N planta baja f

downstream [dáʊnstrím] ADV río abajo

downtime [dáʊntaɪm] N (of a machine) tiempo de inactividad m; (of a person) horas de ocio f pl

down-to-earth [dáʊntəɚ́θ] ADJ sensato, práctico

downtown [dáʊntáʊn] ADV (toward) al centro; (in) en el centro; ADJ del centro, céntrico; N centro m

downturn [dáʊntɚn] N tendencia a la baja f

down under [dáʊnándɚ] ADV en / a Australia

downward [dáʊnwɚd] ADJ descendente; **— mobility** descenso social m; **—s** hacia abajo

downwind [dáʊnwínd] ADV en la dirección del viento

downy [dáʊni] ADJ sedoso, suave

dowry [dáʊri] N dote f

doze [doz] VI dormitar; N siesta f

dozen [dázən] N docena f

drab [dræb] ADJ triste; N pardo m

draft [dræft] N (of air) corriente f; (drink) trago m; (bank) giro m; (outline) esbozo m; (military) conscripción f, quinta f; (of a ship) calado m; **— beer** cerveza de barril f; **— horse** caballo de tiro m; **—sman** dibujante m; VT (to sketch) esbozar; (to compose) redactar; (to select for military service) reclutar

drag [dræg] VI/VT (haul slowly) arrastrar(se); (search a body of water) dragar; **don't — me into this** no me metas en esto; **to — on and on** eternizarse; **to — out** estirar; N (dredge) draga f; (boring person) pesado -da mf; (hassle) lata f; (counterforce)

resistencia *f*; (on a cigarette) pitada *f*; —
race carrera de dragsters *f*; — **strip** pista
de dragsters *f*; **in** — vestido de mujer

dragon [drǽgən] N dragón *m*; —**fly** libélula *f*

drain [dren] N (channel) desagüe *m*,
sumidero *m*; (depletion of resources)
sangría *f*, fuga *f*; — **pipe** desaguadero *m*,
desagüe *m*; **to go down the** — irse por la
borda; VT (empty a sink) desagotar(se),
desaguar(se); (exhaust) agotar(se); VT
(wetlands) drenar, sanear; VI (a battery)
descargarse

drainage [drénɪʤ] N (act of draining)
desagüe *m*, drenaje *m*; (system) drenaje *m*;
—**pipe** tubo de desagüe *m*

drake [drek] N pato (macho) *m*

drama [drámə] N drama *m*

dramatic [drəmǽɪk] ADJ dramático

dramatist [drámətɪst] N dramaturgo -ga *mf*

dramatize [drámətaɪz] VI/VT dramatizar

drape [drep] VI (hang in folds) colgar,
drapear; VT (cover) cubrir; N cortina *f*

drapery [drépəri] N cortinado *m*, colgadura *f*

drastic [drǽstɪk] ADJ drástico

draw [drɔ] VT (a picture) dibujar; (lines,
shapes) trazar; (a cart) tirar de; (a curtain)
correr; (cards, blood, water, conclusion,
strength) sacar; (a crowd) atraer;
(withdraw money) retirar, sacar; (receive
money) cobrar; (comparison, distinction)
hacer; (sword) desenvainar; VI (of a boat)
tener calado; (of a fireplace) tirar; (in
sports, have the same score) empatar; **to
— aside** apartar(se); **to — away**
separar(se); **to — a breath** aspirar, tomar
aliento; **to — a blank** quedarse en
blanco; **to — in** involucrar; **to — lots /
straws** echar a la suerte, sortear; **to —
near** acercarse; **to — off** irse, retirarse; **to
— on** (be based on) basarse en; (have
recourse to) recurrir a; **to — out** (remove)
sacar; (prolong) alargar, prolongar; **to —
up** (approach) acercar(se); (write) redactar;
(shrink) encoger; N (tie) empate *m*; (lot)
número sorteado *m*; (attraction) atracción
f; —**back** inconveniente *m*; —**bridge**
puente levadizo *m*

drawer [drɔə] N cajón *m*; (small) gaveta *f*;
—**s** calzones *m pl*

drawing [drɔ́ɪŋ] N (picture) dibujo *m*; (raffle)
sorteo *m*; — **room** sala (de recibo) *f*

drawn [drɔn] ADJ demacrado; —**-out**
interminable

dread [drɛd] N pavor *m*, terror *m*, espanto *m*;
VT temer; **I** — **going to the dentist** me aterra ir
al dentista

dreadful [drédfəl] ADJ horrendo, espantoso,

temible

dream [drim] N sueño *m* (also aspiration);
(reverie) ensueño *m*, ensoñación *f*; (fancy)
ilusión *f*; —**land** tierra del ensueño *f*; VI/
VT soñar; **to** — **of** soñar con; **I wouldn't
— of stealing** no se me ocurriría robar;
to — **that** soñar que; **to** — **up** imaginar;
ADJ **a** — **holiday** unas vacaciones
perfectas; — **team** dream team *m*, equipo
de estrellas *m*; — **world** mundo de
ensueño *m*

dreamer [drímə] N (impractical person)
soñador -ora *mf*; (visionary) visionario -ria
mf

dreary [dríri] ADJ sombrío, deprimente

dredge [drɛʤ] N draga *f*; VT dragar

dregs [drɛgz] N heces *f pl*, poso *m*; — **of
society** escoria de la sociedad *f*

drench [drɛntʃ] VT empapar, calar; —**ed in
blood** bañado en sangre

dress [drɛs] N (article of clothing for women)
vestido *m*; (attire) ropa *f*; (formal) traje de
etiqueta *m*, ropa de etiqueta *f*; (costume)
vestimenta *f*; —**maker** modista *mf*; —
rehearsal ensayo general *m*; — **shirt**
camisa para traje *f*; VI/VT vestir(se); VT
(store window) arreglar; (slaughtered
animals) limpiar; (salad) aderezar; (hides)
adobar; (a wound) vendar; **to — down**
(scold) regañar; (wear casual clothes)
ponerse ropa informal; **to — up** (wear
fine clothes) vestirse de gala; (make more
appealing) embellecer

dresser [drésə] N cómoda *f*; **she is a good**
— se viste con elegancia

dressing [drésɪŋ] N (act, result) vestir(se) *m*;
(for salad) aderezo *m*; (for fowl) relleno *m*;
(for wounds) gasa *f*, vendaje *m*; —**down**
regaño *m*; — **gown** bata *f*; — **room** (in a
theater) camerino *m*; (in a store) probador
m; — **table** tocador *m*

dribble [dríbəl] VI (trickle) gotear; (sliver)
babear; VT (a ball) driblar; (liquid) rociar; N
(trickle) goteo *m*; (small quantity) chorrito
m; (of a ball) dribbling *m*

dried [draɪd] ADJ seco; — **fig** higo paso / seco
m; —**-up** (without water) seco; (wizened)
arrugado

drift [drɪft] N (direction) deriva *f*; (current)
corriente *f*; (meaning) sentido *m*, tenor *m*;
(pile) montón *m*, acumulación *f*; **do you
get my** —**?** ¿me captas la onda? VI (float)
flotar; (be adrift) ir a la deriva; (wander)
errar; **he** —**ed off** se durmió; VI/VT
(deviate) desviar(se); (accumulate)
amontonar(se), acumular(se); —**wood**
madera flotante *f*

drifter [dríftə-] N (wanderer) vagabundo -da mf; (of a worker) itinerante mf

drill [drɪł] N (tool) taladro m; (training) ejercicios m pl; (procedure) procedimiento m; (rehearsal) simulacro m; (cloth) dril m; VI/VT (make a hole) taladrar, perforar, barrenar; (train) entrenar(se), adiestrar(se); VI (train) hacer ejercicios; (practice) practicar; VT hacer practicar

drink [drɪŋk] VI/VT (person) beber; (animal) abrevar; (absorb, take in) absorber; **to — up** apurar el trago; **to — to someone's health** brindar por alguien; N bebida f (also alcoholic); (a measure of beverage) trago m

drinkable [dríŋkəbəł] ADJ potable

drip [drɪp] N goteo m; (a bore) plasta mf; VI gotear; VT dejar caer gotas

drive [draɪv] VI/VT (a car) conducir, manejar; VI (go in a vehicle) ir en coche; VT (move forth) impulsar, impeler; (an animal) arrear; (convey) llevar (en coche); (force labor) forzar a trabajar; (a nail) clavar; (a ball) tirar, golpear; **to — a hard bargain** regatear mucho; **to — away** ahuyentar; **to — someone mad** volver loco a alguien; **what are you driving at?** ¿qué quieres decir con eso? **—by shooting** tiroteo desde un coche m; **—in** drive-in m, establecimiento en que el cliente es atendido en el coche m; **—in movie theater** autocine m; **—way** camino de entrada m, entrada de coches f; N (ride) paseo (en coche) m; (of an animal) arreo m; (urge) impulso m; (military offensive) ofensiva f; (road) carretera f; (driveway) camino m; (campaign) campaña f; (energy) empuje m; (propulsion system) propulsión f; (of a ball) tiro m; (in tennis and golf) drive m; **front wheel —** tracción delantera f

drivel [drívəł] N (saliva) baba f; (idiocy) tontería f; VI babearse

driveling [drívəlɪŋ] ADJ baboso; **he's a — idiot** es un oligofrénico

driver [dráɪvə-] N (chauffeur) chofer mf, conductor -ra mf; (of animals) arriero -ra mf; (golf club) driver m

drizzle [drízəł] VI lloviznar; N llovizna f

drone [dron] N (male bee; idler) zángano m; (remote-controlled vehicle) nave teledirigida f; (drudge) esclavo m; (sound) zumbido m; VI/VT (make a sound) zumbar; (talk) hablar monótonamente

drool [druł] N baba f; VI babearse

droop [drup] VI doblarse; (sag) colgarse; (flag) languidecer; (wither) marchitarse; **his**

shoulders — tiene los hombros caídos; **—ing ears** orejas gachas f pl

drop [drɑp] N (liquid quantity) gota f; (descent) caída f; (incline) declive m; (in value) baja f; (lozenge) pastilla f; (of mail, etc.) buzón m, punto de recolección m; (of supplies) lanzamiento m; VI caer; (let fall) dejar caer, descargar; **to — a line** mandar unas líneas; **to — from sight** desaparecer; **to — in** caer de sorpresa; **to — out** (sports) retirarse; (school) abandonar; **—out** (student) estudiante que abandona mf; (marginalized person) marginado -da mf; **to — the curtain** bajar el telón; **why don't you — by?** ¿por qué no pasas por aquí? **—-dead beautiful** hermosísima

dropper [drɑpə-] N gotero m

drought [draut] N sequía f

drove [drov] N tropel m

drown [draun] VI/VT ahogar(se)

drowse [drauz] VI (be half-asleep) dormitar; (feel drowsy) estar amodorrado

drowsiness [dráuzɪnɪs] N modorra f, somnolencia f

drowsy [dráuzi] ADJ amodorrado, somnoliento; **to become —** amodorrarse

drudge [drʌdʒ] N esclavo del trabajo m, fregona f; VI trabajar como un esclavo

drug [drʌg] N (chemical substance, narcotic) droga f; (medicine) medicamento m; **to be a — on the market** ser invendible; **— addict** drogadicto -a mf; **—store** (drugs) farmacia f; (non-drug items) droguería f; perfumería f; VT (stupefy with drugs) drogar; (mix with a drug) adulterar con droga

druggist [drʌgɪst] N farmacéutico -ca mf, droguero -ra mf

drum [drʌm] N (musical instrument) tambor m; (eardrum) tímpano m; (receptacle for storing liquids) barril m; **—head** parche m; **—stick** (music) palillo de tambor m; (fowl) pata f; VI (play a drum) tocar el tambor; (beat rhythmically) tamborilear; **to — out** expulsar; **to — up** fomentar; **I'm trying to — this idea into his head** le estoy repitiendo esta idea con insistencia

drummer [drʌmə-] N (classical) tambor m; (folk) tamborilero -ra mf; (rock & roll) baterista mf; (sales person) viajante de comercio mf

drunk [drʌŋk] ADJ & N borracho -cha mf; fam mamado -da mf; **to get —** emborracharse

drunkard [drʌŋkə-d] N borracho -cha mf, borrachín -ina mf

drunken [dráŋkən] ADJ borracho, embriagado

drunkenness [dráŋkənnıs] N borrachera f, embriaguez f

dry [draı] ADJ seco; (sober) sobrio; (topic, book) árido, aburrido; **— land** tierra firme f; **— cleaner** (business) tintorería f; (owner of business) tintorero -ra mf; **— cleaning** limpieza en seco f; **— county** condado seco m; **— wit** humor agudo m; **— goods** géneros m pl; **— measure** medida para áridos f; **— run** prueba f; **— ice** hielo seco m; **— dock** dique seco m, varadero m; VI/VT (wet clothes) secar(se); (leather) resecar(se); **to — up** secarse, resecarse; **to — out** desintoxicar(se)

dryer [dráıə·] N (hair) secador m; (clothes) secadora f

dryness [dráınıs] N (skin, etc.) sequedad f; (land, lecture) aridez f

dual [dúəl] ADJ (function) doble; (ownership) compartido

dub [dʌb] VT doblar

dubious [dúbıəs] ADJ dudoso

duchess [dátʃıs] N duquesa f

duck [dʌk] N (species) pato m; (downward dodge) agachada f; VI/VT (plunge under water) hundir(se); (bend down) agachar(se); VT (avoid) esquivar

duckling [dákliŋ] N patito m

duct [dʌkt] N conducto m; **— tape** cinta aislante f

ductile [dákt!] ADJ dúctil

dud [dʌd] N (disappointing thing) chasco m; (unexploded bomb) bomba que no estalla f; **—s** (clothes) ropa f, fam trapos m pl; (belongings) pertenencias f pl

dude [dud] N (dandy) chulo m; (fellow) tipo m

due [du] ADJ (payable) pagadero; (immediately owed) vencido; (fitting, rightful) debido; (adequate) suficiente; **in — time / course** a su debido tiempo; **the train is — at two o'clock** se supone que el tren llega a las dos; ADV **— east** hacia el este; N (punishment) merecido m; **give Mary her —; she's honest** tienes que reconocer que María es honrada; **—s** cuota f

duel [dúəl] N duelo m; VI/VT batirse en / a duelo (con alguien)

duet [duét] N (played) dúo m; (sung) dueto m

dugout [dágaut] N (canoe) piragua f; (underground refuge) trinchera f

DUI (driving under the influence) [dijuáı] N conducir en estado de ebriedad m

duke [duk] N duque m; **to put up one's —s**

levantar los puños; VT **to — it out** arreglarlo con los puños

dukedom [dúkdəm] N ducado m

dull [dʌl] ADJ (lackluster) opaco; (listless, muted) apagado; (boring) aburrido, soso, desanimado; (blunt) romo, desafilado; (sluggish, stupid) lento; (pain) sordo; VI/VT (a knife) desafilar(se); (color) opacar(se); (sound, impact) amortiguar(se); (pain) aliviar(se); (senses) embotar(se), entorpecer(se)

duly [dúli] ADV debidamente

dumb [dʌm] ADJ (mute) mudo; (dull) tonto; **—bell** (handweight) mancuerna f; (stupid person) bobo -ba mf; **—founded** patitieso, atónito; VT **to — down** simplificar demasiado

dumbness [dámnıs] N (muteness) mudez f; (foolishness) estupidez f

dummy [dámi] N (figure) muñeco m; (fool) tonto -ta mf; offensive pendejo -ja mf; (front) hombre de paja m; ADJ (fake) falso; **a — president** un títere

dump [dʌmp] VT (unload) descargar; (empty) botar; (dismiss) echar, despedir; (discard) tirar la basura, descargar desechos; (flood a market) hacer dumping; (abandon) plantar; **to — on** (criticize) criticar; (unload problems) descargarse; N (place for waste) vertedero m, basural m, basurero m; (of weapons) depósito m; (act of discarding) vertido m; (act or effect of defecating) vulg cagada f; **—truck** camión volteador m, volquete m; **to be in the —s** estar deprimido, estar depre; **to take a —** vulg cagar

dunce [dʌns] N burro -rra mf, tonto -ta de capirote mf

dune [dun] N duna f, médano m

dung [dʌŋ] N boñiga f, bosta f; **—hill** estercolero m

dungeon [dándʒən] N mazmorra f

dupe [dup] N (gullible person) ingenuo -nua mf, inocente mf; Sp primo -ma mf; (manipulated person) títere m; VT embaucar

duplex [dúpleks] N & ADJ dúplex m

duplicate [dúplıkıt] ADJ & N duplicado m; **in — por** duplicado; [dúplıket] VT duplicar(se)

duplicity [duplísıdi] N duplicidad f

durability [dʊrəbílıdi] N durabilidad f

durable [dúrəbəl] ADJ (long-lasting) duradero; (serviceable) sufrido

duration [dʊréʃən] N duración f

duress [dʊrés] N coacción f

during [dúrıŋ] PREP durante

dusk [dʌsk] N atardecer m, anochecer m; **at**

— al atardecer

dusky [dʌ́ski] ADJ (dark) oscuro; (gloomy) sombrío

dust [dʌst] N polvo m; **—pan** pala f; **to bite the —** (die) fam espichar; (lose) morder el polvo de la derrota; **cloud of —** polvareda f; VI/VT (remove dust) quitar/ sacudir el polvo (a); VT (sprinkle with powder) espolvorear; VI (become dusty) empolvarse; **to — off** no desempolvar

duster [dʌ́stə] N plumero m

dusty [dʌ́sti] ADJ polvoriento

Dutch [dʌtʃ] ADJ & N holandés -esa mf; **to go —** pagar a escote

Dutchman [dʌ́tʃmən] N holandés m

duty [dúɾi] N deber m, obligación f; (tax on imports) derechos aduaneros m pl; (any tax) impuesto m; **to be on —** estar de guardia; **to be off —** no estar de guardia; **—free** libre de impuestos

DVD (digital versatile disc) [dívídí] N DVD m

dwarf [dwɔrf] ADJ & N enano -na mf; VT hacer parecer pequeño

dwell [dwɛl] VI morar, habitar; **to — on a subject** dilatarse en un asunto

dweller [dwɛ́lə] N habitante mf, morador -ra mf

dwelling [dwɛ́lɪŋ] N vivienda f, domicilio m

DWI (driving while intoxicated) [didʌbəljuái] N conducir en estado de ebriedad m

dwindle [dwíndl] VI/VT menguar, mermar

dye [daɪ] N tinte m, tintura f; VT teñir

dying [dáɪŋ] ADJ moribundo

dyke [daɪk] N offensive tortillera f

dynamic [daɪnǽmɪk] ADJ dinámico; N **—s** dinámica f

dynamite [dáɪnəmaɪt] N dinamita f; VT dinamitar; ADJ fabuloso

dynamo [dáɪnəmo] N dínamo m

dynasty [dáɪnəsti] N dinastía f

dysentery [dísnteri] N disentería f

dysfunction [dɪsfʌ́ŋkʃən] N disfunción f

Ee

each [itʃ] ADJ cada; **— person** cada persona; PRON cada uno; **— receives a prize** cada uno recibe un premio; **they looked at — other** se miraron el uno al otro

eager [ígə] ADJ (enthusiastic) ansioso; (avid) ávido

eagerness [ígənɪs] N (enthusiasm) ansia f, afán m; (strong desire) avidez f

eagle [ígəl] N águila f; **—-eye** ojo de lince m

eaglet [íglɪt] N aguilucho m

ear [ir] N (outer organ) oreja f; (inner organ, sense of hearing, musical aptitude) oído m; (of corn) mazorca f; Am elote m; **—ache** dolor de oídos m; **—drops** gotas para los oídos f pl; **—drum** tímpano m; **—lobe** lóbulo de la oreja m; **— muff** orejera f; **— of wheat** espiga f; **—phone** audífono m; **—ring** pendiente m, zarcillo m; **by —** de oído; **within —shot** al alcance del oído; **he has the — of the governor** el gobernador le presta mucha atención

earful [írfʊl] N **I got an —** (scolding) me echó un rapapolvo; (gossip) me dio la lata

early [ə́li] ADJ temprano; **— detection** diagnóstico precoz m; **— man** hombre primitivo m; **— reply** respuesta rápida f; **— riser / bird** madrugador -ra m, mañanero -ra mf; **the — bird gets the worm** al que madruga, Dios lo ayuda

earn [ɚn] VT (money, admiration, etc.) ganar; (salary) cobrar, ganar; (interest) devengar; N **to — a living** ganarse la vida

earnest [ə́nɪst] ADJ (sincere) serio, formal; (grave) grave; **in —** en serio; **— money** señal f; Mex enganche m

earnestness [ə́nɪstnɪs] N (sincerity) seriedad f, formalidad f; (gravity) gravedad f; **in all —** con toda sinceridad

earnings [ə́nɪŋz] N (of a person) ingresos m pl, haberes m pl; (of a business) ganancias f pl

earth [ɚθ] N tierra f; **—mover** excavadora f; **—quake** terremoto m, temblor de tierra m; **—shaking** revolucionario; **—worm** lombriz f; **the —** la Tierra

earthen [ə́θən] ADJ (wall) de tierra; (pot) de barro; **—ware** vajilla de barro f, cerámica f

earthly [ə́θli] ADJ terrenal; **— possessions** bienes terrenales m pl; **to be of no — use** no servir para nada

earthy [ə́θi] ADJ natural; (person) campechano; (sense of humor, joke) basto; **— smell** olor a tierra m

ease [iz] N (facility) facilidad f; (unaffectedness) soltura f, desparpajo m; (comfort) comodidad f; (lack of worry) tranquilidad f; (fullness of a garment) holgura f; **at —** (military) en descanso; (comfortable) tranquilo, a gusto; **a life of —** una vida desahogada; **ill at —** incómodo; VT (make easier) facilitar; VI/VT (relieve pain) aliviar(se); (release from tension) aflojar(se); (relieve anxiety) tranquilizar(se); **to — up** aflojar

easel [ízł] N caballete *m*

east [ist] N este *m*, oriente *m*; ADJ del este, oriental; ADV **— of here** al este (de aquí); **to go** — ir al/hacia el este; **back** — en el este

Easter [ístə-] N Pascua *f*; **— egg** huevo de Pascua *m*; **— Sunday** Domingo de Pascua *m*

eastern [ístə-n] ADJ oriental, del este

eastward [ístwə-d] ADV & ADJ hacia el este

easy [ízi] ADJ (simple) fácil, sencillo; (compliant) fácil; (comfortable) cómodo; (informal) desenvuelto; (unworried) tranquilo; **— chair** poltrona *f*; **—-going** calmoso; **— terms** facilidades de pago *f pl*; **at an — pace** a paso moderado; **within — reach** al alcance de la mano; **go — on me** sea bueno; **he's on — street** vive en la abundancia

eat [it] VI/VI comer(se); VT (costs) absorber; **to — away** corroer, comer; **to — breakfast** desayunar(se); **to — dinner** (midday) comer; (evening) cenar; **to — lunch** comer, almorzar; **to — one's heart out** morirse de envidia; **to — one's words** tragarse las palabras; **to — supper** cenar; **to — up** comerse todo; **what's —ing you?** ¿qué bicho te picó?

eating [íDɪŋ] N (act) comer *m*; (food) comida *f*; **— utensils** cubiertos *m pl*; **— apples** manzanas para comer *f pl*

eaves [ivz] N PL alero *m*

eavesdrop [ívzdrɑp] VI escuchar sin ser visto

ebb [ɛb] N (flowing back) reflujo *m*; (decay) decadencia *f*; **— tide** reflujo *m*; **to be at a low —** estar en un punto bajo; VI (tide) bajar; (energy) decaer

ebony [ébəni] N ébano *m*

eccentric [ɛkséntrɪk] ADJ & N excéntrico -ca *mf*

ecclesiastic [ɪkliziǽstɪk] ADJ & N eclesiástico *m*

echelon [éʃəlɑn] N (military formation) escalón *m*; (rank) nivel *m*, estrato *m*

echo [éko] N eco *m*; VI hacer eco; **the gym —ed with laughter** el gimnasio resonó de risas; VT repetir

eclectic [ɪkléktɪk] ADJ ecléctico

eclipse [ɪklíps] N eclipse *m*; VT eclipsar

ecology [ɪkálɑʤi] N ecología *f*

e-commerce [íkɑmə-s] N comercio electrónico *m*

economic [ɛkənámɪk] ADJ económico; **—s** economía *f*

economical [ɛkənámɪkəl] ADJ económico

economist [ɪkánəmɪst] N economista *mf*

economize [ɪkánəmaɪz] VI economizar

economy [ɪkánəmi] N economía *f* (also thrift); ADJ **— car** coche económico *m*; **— class** clase turista *f*

ecosystem [íkosɪstəm] N ecosistema *m*

ecstasy [ékstəsi] N éxtasis *m* (also drug)

Ecuador [ékwədɔr] N Ecuador *m*

Ecuadorian [ekwədɔ́rian] ADJ & N ecuatoriano -na *mf*

ecumenical [ɛkjəménɪkəl] ADJ ecuménico

eczema [égzəmə] N eccema *m*

eddy [édi] N remolino *m*; VI arremolinarse

edge [ɛʤ] N borde *m*, canto *m*; (of a knife) filo *m*; (of a cube) arista *f*; **to be on —** estar nervioso; **her voice has an — to it** tiene la voz penetrante; **a competitive —** una ventaja sobre la competencia; VT (make an edge) hacerle el borde; (sharpen) afilar; (move sideways) meterse de costado; **to — out** ganar por un pelito; **to — up** aproximarse; ADV **—wise** de costado

edgy [éʤi] ADJ nervioso

edible [édəbəl] ADJ & N comestible *m*

edict [ídɪkt] N edicto *m*, bando *m*

edifice [édəfɪs] N edificio *m*

edify [édəfaɪ] VT edificar

edit [édɪt] VT (revise, correct) corregir; (serve as editor) editar; (film) montar; **to — out** eliminar; **— correción** *f*

edition [ɪdíʃən] N edición *f*

editor [éDɪtə-] N (director of a publication) redactor -ra *mf*; (compiler, radio or film worker) editor -ra *mf*; (proofreader) corrector -ra *mf*

editorial [ɛDɪtɔ́riəl] ADJ editorial; N editorial *f*

editorialize [ɛDɪtɔ́riəlaɪz] VI editorializar

educate [éʤəket] VT educar

education [ɛʤəkéʃən] N educación *f*, enseñanza *f*; (academic subject) pedagogía *f*; **school of —** escuela normal *f*

educational [ɛʤəkéʃənət] ADJ educativo

educator [éʤəketə-] N educador -ra *mf*

eel [it] N anguila *f*

eerie [íri] ADJ misterioso

effect [ɪfékt] N efecto *m*; **—s** efectos *m pl*; **to go into —** entrar en vigencia, ponerse en operación; **I wrote a letter to that —** le escribí una carta en ese sentido; VT efectuar

effective [ɪféktɪv] ADJ efectivo, eficaz; (a law) vigente; **— date** fecha de vigencia *f*

effectively [ɪféktɪvli] ADV (well) eficazmente; (in fact) de hecho, en efecto

effectual [ɪféktʃuət] ADJ eficaz

effeminate [ɪfémənət] ADJ afeminado

efficacy [éfɪkəsi] N eficacia f
efficiency [ɪfíʃənsi] N eficiencia f; —
  apartment estudio m
efficient [ɪfíʃənt] ADJ eficiente; (motor)
  económico
effigy [éfəʤi] N efigie f; **to burn in** —
  quemar en efigie
effort [éfɚt] N (exertion) esfuerzo m; (work of
  art) obra f; (campaign) campaña f
effrontery [ɪfrántəri] N descaro m
effusive [ɪfjúsɪv] ADJ efusivo
egg [ɛg] N huevo m; (female gamete) óvulo m;
  (fellow) tipo m; **—beater** batidor de
  huevos m; **—head** empollón -na mf;
  —nog rompoco m, rompope m, ponche
  de huevo m; **—plant** berenjena f; **—shell**
  cáscara de huevo f; **to have** — **on one's
  face** estar avergonzado, quedar mal; **to
  lay an** — (of a hen) poner un huevo;
  (fail) fracasar; **to walk on —shells** ir
  pisando huevos; VT **to** — **on** incitar
ego [ígo] N (self) yo m, ego m; (vanity) ego m;
  (self-esteem) amor propio m; **winning
  the prize was an** — **trip for him**
  ganar el premio le aceitó el ego
egocentric [igoséntrɪk] ADJ egocéntrico
egotism [ígətɪzəm] N egotismo m
Egypt [íʤɪpt] N Egipto m
Egyptian [iʤípʃən] ADJ & N egipcio -cia mf
eight [et] NUM ocho
eighteen [ettín] NUM dieciocho
eighth [etθ] ADJ, N & ADV octavo m; — **note**
  corchea f
eighty [éDi] NUM ochenta
either [íðɚ] ADJ & PRON — **will do**
  cualquiera de los dos está bien; **choose** —
  suit elige uno de los dos trajes; **choose** —
  elige uno (u otro) de los dos; **there were
  flowers on** — **side of the road** había
  flores a ambos lados de la carretera; ADV **if
  you don't, I won't** — si tú no lo haces,
  yo tampoco; **I'll** — **go by bus or by car**
  voy (o) en autobús o en auto
ejaculate [ɪʤækjəlæt] VI/VT eyacular;
  (exclaim) exclamar
eject [ɪʤékt] VT (throw out) echar, expulsar;
  VI/VT (from a plane) eyectar(se)
ejection [ɪʤékʃən] N expulsión f
elaborate [ɪlǽbɚɪt] ADJ (ornate) elaborado;
  (detailed) detallado; [ɪlǽbəret] VI/VT
  (create) elaborar; (develop) desarrollar
elapse [ɪlǽps] VI transcurrir, pasar
elastic [ɪlǽstɪk] ADJ elástico; N elástico m;
  (rubber band) goma elástica f
elasticity [ɪlæstísɪdi] N elasticidad f
elated [ɪléDɪd] ADJ encantado
elbow [éɫbo] N codo m; **to be within** —

reach estar a la mano; VI/VT codear, dar
  codazos; **to** — **one's way through**
  abrirse paso a codazos
elder [éɫdɚ] ADJ (older) mayor; N (older
  person) mayor mf; (old person) anciano
  -na mf; (in a church) miembro del consejo
  de una iglesia m; **our —s** nuestros
  mayores m pl
elderly [éɫdɚli] ADJ anciano
elect [ɪlékt] ADJ (elected) electo; (chosen by
  God) elegido -da mf; VI/VT elegir
election [ɪlékʃən] N elección f
elector [ɪléktɚ] N elector -ra mf
electoral [ɪléktɚəɫ] ADJ electoral
electric [ɪléktrɪk] ADJ eléctrico; (exciting)
  electrizante; (excited) electrizado; — **chair**
  silla eléctrica f; — **eel** anguila eléctrica f;
  — **eye** célula fotoeléctrica f; — **meter**
  contador eléctrico m; — **storm** tormenta
  eléctrica f
electrical [ɪléktrɪkəɫ] ADJ eléctrico; —
  engineer ingeniero electricista mf; —
  engineering ingeniería eléctrica f; —
  tape cinta aislante f
electrician [ɪlɛktríʃən] N electricista mf
electricity [ɪlɛktrísɪdi] N electricidad f
electrify [ɪléktrəfaɪ] VT (apply electricity)
  electrificar; (thrill) electrizar
electrocardiogram [ɪlɛktrokárDiəgræm] N
  electrocardiograma m
electrocute [ɪléktrəkjut] VT electrocutar
electrode [ɪléktrod] N electrodo m
electroencephalogram [ɪlɛktroɛnséfələgræm]
  N electroencefalograma m
electrolysis [ɪlɛktrálɪsɪs] N electrólisis f
electromagnet [ɪlɛktromǽgnɪt] N
  electroimán m
electromagnetic [ɪlɛktromægnéDɪk] ADJ
  electromagnético
electron [ɪléktrɑn] N electrón m; —
  microscope microscopio electrónico m
electronic [ɪlɛktránɪk] ADJ electrónico; —
  banking banca electrónica f; — **mail**
  correo electrónico m; **—s** electrónica f; —
  signature firma electrónica f
elegance [élɪgəns] N elegancia f, gallardía f
elegant [élɪgənt] ADJ elegante, gallardo; (gift)
  de lujo
element [éləmənt] N elemento m;
  (component part) componente m, pieza f;
  (for heating) resistencia f; **the —s** los
  elementos
elemental [ɛləméntɫ] ADJ elemental; —
  forces fuerzas de la naturaleza f pl
elementary [ɛləméntri] ADJ elemental; —
  school escuela primaria f
elephant [éləfənt] N elefante -ta mf

elevate [éləvet] VT elevar

elevation [eləvéʃən] N elevación f; (altitude) altura f

elevator [éləveDə-] N ascensor m; Am elevador m; (for grain) elevador m

eleven [ɪlévən] NUM once

elf [etf] N elfo m; (child) pillo -lla mf

elicit [ɪlísɪt] VT provocar; **to — admiration** despertar admiración; **to — applause** suscitar el aplauso

eligible [éliʤəbəł] ADJ elegible; **an — bachelor** un buen partido; **you are — for a scholarship** tienes derecho a solicitar una beca

eliminate [ɪlímənet] VT eliminar

elimination [ɪlɪmənéʃən] N eliminación f

elite [ɪlít] N elite f, élite f

elitist [ɪlíDɪst] ADJ & N elitista mf

elk [etk] N alce m

elliptical [ɪlíptɪkəł] ADJ elíptico

elm [ɛłm] N olmo m

elongate [ɪlɔ́ŋget] VI/VT alargar(se)

elope [ɪlóp] VI fugarse para casarse a escondidas

eloquence [éləkwəns] N elocuencia f

eloquent [éləkwənt] ADJ elocuente

El Salvador [etsǽłvədɚ] N El Salvador m

else [ɛłs] ADJ & ADV **who — was there?** ¿quién más estaba? **someone —'s son** el hijo de otro; **somebody —** (algún) otro; **or —** si no; **leave town or —** vete del pueblo o sufre las consecuencias / o verás lo que es bueno; **nobody —** nadie más; **nothing —** nada más; **how —?** ¿de qué otra forma? ADV **—where** (location) en otra parte / en otro lado; (movement) a otra parte / a otro sitio

elucidate [ɪlúsɪdet] VI/VT dilucidar, esclarecer

elucidation [ɪlusɪdéʃən] N elucidación f

elude [ɪlúd] VT eludir

elusive [ɪlúsɪv] ADJ (slippery) escurridizo; (evasive) esquivo; (difficult to understand) difícil de entender

emaciated [ɪméʃieDɪd] ADJ escuálido, descarnado

e-mail, E-mail [ímeł] N correo electrónico m

emanate [émənet] VI/VT emanar

emanation [emənéʃən] N emanación f

emancipate [ɪmǽnsəpet] VT emancipar

emancipation [ɪmænsəpéʃən] N emancipación f

emasculate [ɪmǽskjəlet] VT castrar; (remove testicles) castrar, emascular

embalm [ɪmbám] VT embalsamar

embankment [ɪmbǽŋkmənt] N terraplén m

embargo [ɪmbárgo] N embargo m; VT imponer un embargo

embark [ɪmbárk] VI/VT embarcar(se)

embarrass [ɪmbǽrəs] VT (shame) hacerle pasar vergüenza a; (discomfit, financial difficulties) poner en aprietos; VI avergonzarse

embarrassing [ɪmbǽrəsɪŋ] ADJ (shameful) vergonzoso; (impeding) embarazoso

embarrassment [ɪmbǽrəsmənt] N (shame) vergüenza f, bochorno m; (act of embarrassing) vergüenza f; (financial difficulty) aprieto m; **he's an — to the company** siempre deja mal a la compañía; **we have an — of riches** nadamos en la abundancia

embassy [émbəsi] N embajada f

embattled [ɪmbǽd]d] ADJ hostigado, agobiado

embed [ɪmbéd] VT incrustar

embedded [ɪmbéDɪd] ADJ incrustado

embellish [ɪmbélɪʃ] VT adornar, ornamentar

ember [émbə-] N ascua f, brasa f

embezzle [ɪmbézəł] VT desfalcar, malversar

embezzlement [ɪmbézəłmənt] N desfalco m, peculado m

embitter [ɪmbíDə-] VT amargar

emblem [émbləm] N emblema m, divisa f

embody [ɪmbádi] VT (personify) personificar; (to provide with a body) encarnar

embolism [émbəlɪzəm] N embolia f

embrace [ɪmbrés] VI/VT (hug, adopt) abrazar(se); (include) abarcar; N abrazo m

embroider [ɪmbrɔ́ɪdə-] VI/VT bordar, recamar

embroidery [ɪmbrɔ́ɪdəri] N bordado m

embroil [ɪmbrɔ́ɪł] VT (involve in a conflict) meterse en un lío; (throw into confusion) embrollar

embryo [émbrio] N embrión m

emerald [émə-əłd] N esmeralda f

emerge [ɪmɚ́ʤ] VI (come into view) emerger; (arise, as a question, problem) surgir

emergency [ɪmɚ́ʤənsi] N emergencia f; **— brake** freno de emergencia m; **— exit** salida de emergencia f; **— room** urgencias f pl

emigrant [émɪgrənt] ADJ & N emigrante mf

emigrate [émɪgret] VI emigrar

emigration [emɪgréʃən] N emigración f

eminence [émənəns] N eminencia f

eminent [émənənt] ADJ eminente

emissary [émɪseri] N emisario -ria mf

emission [ɪmíʃən] N emisión f

emit [ɪmít] VT (light, sound, etc.) emitir; (smells) despedir; (sparks) echar

emotion [ɪmóʃən] N emoción f

emotional [ɪmóʃənəł] ADJ (of the emotions) emocional; (arousing or expressing emotions) emotivo; (easily moved) sensible

empathy [émpəθi] N empatía f

emperor [émpərə] N emperador m; —
penguin pingüino emperador m

emphasis [émfəsɪs] N énfasis m, hincapié m

emphasize [émfəsaɪz] VT enfatizar, hacer
hincapié en, subrayar

emphatic [ɪmfǽdɪk] ADJ enfático

emphysema [emfɪsímə] N enfisema m

empire [émpaɪr] N imperio m

empirical [empírɪkəɫ] ADJ empírico

employ [ɪmplɔ́i] VT emplear; (hire) emplear,
ocupar; N empleo m; **to be in someone's**
— trabajar a las órdenes de alguien

employee [ɪmplɔ́i] N empleado -da mf

employer [ɪmplɔ́iə] N patrón -na mf

employment [ɪmplɔ́imənt] N empleo m;
(occupation) ocupación f; —
opportunities oportunidades laborales f
pl; **place of** — lugar de trabajo m

empower [ɪmpáuə] VT (authorize) autorizar;
(give strength) dar poder

empress [émprɪs] N emperatriz f

emptiness [émptɪnɪs] N vacío m

empty [émpti] ADJ vacío; (devoid of activity)
desocupado; VI/VT vaciar(se), volcar(se);
(debouch) desembocar; —**-handed** con
las manos vacías; **to run on** — (of a car,
person) quedarse sin combustible

emulate [émjəlet] VT emular (also computer
term)

enable [ɪnébəɫ] VT permitir

enact [ɪnǽkt] VT (a law) promulgar; (a role)
desempeñar

enamel [ɪnǽməɫ] N esmalte m; VT esmaltar

enamor [ɪnǽmə] VT enamorar; **to be —ed
of** estar enamorado de

encamp [ɪnkǽmp] VI acampar

enchant [ɪntʃǽnt] VT (bewitch) hechizar;
(delight) encantar

enchanting [ɪntʃǽntɪŋ] ADJ encantador

enchantment [ɪntʃǽntmənt] N
encantamiento m, encanto m, hechicería f

encircle [ɪnsɚkəɫ] VT cercar, ceñir

enclave [ánklev] N enclave m

enclose [ɪnklóz] VT (confine someone or
something) encerrar; (fence in) cercar; (put
in the same envelope) adjuntar, anexar

enclosure [ɪnklóʒə] N (wall or fence) cerca f;
(enclosed area) cercado m, recinto m;
(enclosed document) documento adjunto
m; (act of enclosing) encierro m

encompass [ɪnkámpəs] VT (include) abarcar,
englobar; (surround) circundar

encore [ánkɔr] N bis m; INTERJ ¡otra!

encounter [ɪnkáuntə] VI/VT encontrar(se);
they —ed the enemy army se

enfrentaron con el ejército enemigo; N
(meeting) encuentro m (also sports);
(battle) enfrentamiento m

encourage [ɪnkɚ́-ɪdʒ] VT (inspire with
confidence) alentar, animar; (promote)
fomentar, estimular

encouragement [ɪnkɚ́-ɪdʒmənt] N aliento m;
(inspiration) ánimo m; (promotion)
estímulo m, fomento m

encroach [ɪnkrótʃ] VT **to — upon** (liberties)
cercenar; (territory) usurpar; (time) quitar

encrypt [ɪnkrípt] VT codificar

encumber [ɪnkámbə] VT (block) impedir;
(burden) agobiar

encyclopedia [ɪnsaɪkləpídiə] N enciclopedia f

end [end] N (temporal) fin m, término m;
(limit, boundary) final m, extremo m; (tip)
cabo m; (aim) fin m; — **to** — uno tras
otro; — **table** mesa pequeña f; **at the** —
of the movie al final de la película; **the
north** — **of town** el barrio norte; **no** —
of things un sinfín de cosas; **at the** —
of the day al fin y al cabo; **on** — de
punta; **for days on** — día tras día; **to
put an** — **to** poner fin a; VI/VT terminar;
(a street) morir; **he** —**ed his life** puso fin
a su vida; **a prayer** —**s the class** la clase
termina con una oración; **a war to — all
wars** una guerra que supera a todas las
anteriores

endanger [ɪndéndʒə] VT poner en peligro;
—**ed species** especie en peligro de
extinción f

endear [ɪndír] VI **to — oneself** congraciarse;
his humor —**ed him to her** se ganó la
simpatía de ella gracias a su humor

endeavor [ɪndévə] VT (try) tratar de,
intentar, procurar; VI (strive) esforzarse
por; N esfuerzo m

endemic [ɪndémɪk] ADJ endémico

ending [éndɪŋ] N final m; (derivational,
inflectional) terminación f; (inflectional)
desinencia f

endless [éndlɪs] ADJ interminable;
(continuous) sin fin; (infinite) eterno

endocrine [éndəkrɪn] ADJ endócrino

endorphin [ɪndɔ́rfɪn] N endorfina f

endorse [ɪndɔ́rs] VT (sign a check) endosar;
(support) respaldar; (authorize a
document) refrendar, visar

endorsement [ɪndɔ́rsmənt] N (signature)
endoso m; (backing) respaldo m;
(authorization) refrendo m

endorser [ɪndɔ́rsə] N (check signer)
endosante mf; (supporter) partidario -ria
mf; (authorizer) refrendario -ria mf

endow [ɪndáu] VT (grant funds) hacer un

legado; (furnish powers) dotar

endowment [ɪndáumənt] N (funds granted) legado *m*, dotación *f*; (power) dote *f*; **— annuity** anualidad dotal *f*; **— fund** fondo de un legado *m*

endurance [ɪndúrəns] N (stamina) resistencia *f*, fondo *m*; (power of bearing pain) aguante *m*

endure [ɪndúr] VT (undergo) sobrellevar, soportar, pasar; VI (live on) durar; (bear up) aguantar

enema [énəmə] N enema *m*, lavativa *f*

enemy [énəmi] N enemigo -ga *mf*

energetic [enədʒétɪk] ADJ enérgico

energy [énədʒi] N energía *f*; **— policy** política energética *f*

enervate [énə-vet] VT enervar, debilitar

enforce [ɪnfɔ́rs] VT hacer cumplir

enforcement [ɪnfɔ́rsmənt] N **law —** autoridades *f pl*; **the sheriff is responsible for the — of the law** el alguacil es responsable de hacer cumplir la ley

engage [ɪngédʒ] VT (hire) contratar; (attract) captar, atraer; (interlock) engranar; **to — the brake** poner el freno; **to — someone in conversation** trabar conversación con alguien; **to — in battle** trabar batalla; **to be —d in something** estar ocupado en algo; **to be —d to be married** estar comprometido (para casarse), estar prometido

engagement [ɪngédʒmənt] N (commitment) compromiso *m*; (betrothal) compromiso *m*, noviazgo *m*; (employment) empleo *m*; (battle) batalla *f*; (gear interlocking) engranaje *m*

engender [ɪndʒéndə-] VT engendrar

engine [éndʒɪn] N (machine) máquina *f*; (in a vehicle) motor *m*; (locomotive) locomotora *f*; **— block** bloque del motor *m*

engineer [endʒənír] N ingeniero -ra *mf*; (of locomotive) maquinista *mf*; VT (create) idear; (plot) maquinar

engineering [endʒəníriŋ] N ingeniería *f*

English [íŋglɪʃ] ADJ inglés; N (spin) efecto *m*; **the —** los ingleses; **—man, —woman** inglés -esa *mf*

engrave [ɪngrév] VI/VT grabar

engraver [ɪngrévə-] N grabador -ora *mf*

engraving [ɪngrévɪŋ] N grabado *m*

engross [ɪngrós] VT absorber

engrossed [ɪngróst] ADJ absorto

engulf [ɪngʌ́lf] VT (swallow) tragar; (overwhelm) abrumar

enhance [ɪnhǽns] VT (intensify) realzar;

(improve) mejorar

enigma [ɪnígmə] N enigma *m*

enjoin [ɪndʒɔ́ɪn] VT instar; **to — from** prohibir

enjoy [ɪndʒɔ́ɪ] VI/VT (take pleasure) disfrutar (de), gozar (de); (benefit from) gozar (de); **—!** ¡Que lo disfrutes! **to — oneself** divertirse; **to — the use of** usufructuar

enjoyable [ɪndʒɔ́ɪəbəł] ADJ (pleasant) agradable, gozoso; (fun) ameno

enjoyment [ɪndʒɔ́ɪmənt] N (act of enjoying) goce *m*, disfrute *m*; (right of use) usufructo *m*; (pleasure) placer *m*, gozo *m*

enlarge [ɪnlárdʒ] VI/VT agrandar(se); VT (blow up a photo) ampliar; VI **to — upon** explayarse sobre, extenderse sobre

enlargement [ɪnlárdʒmənt] N (photo, building) ampliación *f*; (act of enlarging) agrandamiento *m*; (temporary swelling) dilatación *f*

enlighten [ɪnláɪtn̩] VT (morally) iluminar; (intellectually) explicar, ilustrar

enlightenment [ɪnláɪtn̩mənt] N (moral) iluminación *f*; (intellectual) explicación *f*; **The —** La Ilustración

enlist [ɪnlíst] VI/VT (for the army) alistar(se); (for a campaign) conseguir el apoyo

enlistment [ɪnlístmənt] N alistamiento *m*

enliven [ɪnláɪvən] VT animar, avivar

enmity [énmɪdi] N enemistad *f*

ennoble [ɪnnóbəł] VT ennoblecer

enormous [ɪnɔ́rməs] ADJ enorme, descomunal

enough [ɪnʌ́f] ADJ suficiente; ADV **he's tall —** tiene altura suficiente; N lo suficiente; **we have — to live comfortably** tenemos lo suficiente como para vivir cómodamente; **that is —** con eso basta; **more than —** bastante; INTERJ ¡basta!

enrage [ɪnrédʒ] VT enfurecer

enrapture [ɪnrǽptʃə-] VT embelesar

enrich [ɪnrítʃ] VT enriquecer

enroll [ɪnrół] VI/VT matricular(se), inscribir(se); (in army) alistar(se)

enrollment [ɪnrółmənt] N matrícula *f*, inscripción *f*; **what is your —?** ¿Cuántos alumnos tienes matriculados?

ensemble [ɑnsámbəł] N conjunto *m*

ensign [énsɪn] N (naval rank) alférez de fragata *mf*; (flag) enseña *f*; (badge) insignia *f*

enslave [ɪnslév] VT esclavizar

ensnare [ɪnsnér] VT atrapar, coger en una trampa

ensue [ɪnsú] VI (follow) ocurrir después, suceder; (result from) resultar; **the ensuing events** los sucesos subsiguientes

ensure [ɪnʃúr] vt asegurar

entail [ɪntél] vt implicar, traer aparejado; (an inheritance) vincular

entangle [ɪntǽŋgəł] vt enredar

enter [éntə] vt entrar en/a; (join) ingresar en/a; (write) escribir; (put data in a computer) dar entrada a; (put data in account books) asentar; vi/vt (register for a competition) inscribir(se); **to — into** (make an agreement) concertar; (form part of) figurar; vi salir/entrar a escena

enterprise [éntə-praiz] n empresa f

enterprising [éntə-praiziŋ] adj emprendedor

entertain [entə-tén] vi/vt (amuse) divertir, recrear; (host) invitar; **we — a lot** tenemos invitados muy a menudo; (consider) contemplar; (harbor) abrigar

entertainer [entə-ténə] n artista mf

entertaining [entə-téniŋ] adj (fun) divertido; (serving as pastime) entretenido; (pleasant) ameno

entertainment [entə-ténmənt] n (source of fun) diversión f; (pastime) entretenimiento m; (of guests) agasajo m

enthrall [ɪnθrɔ́ł] vt (captivate) cautivar, hechizar; (make a slave of) esclavizar

enthusiasm [ɪnθúziæzəm] n entusiasmo m

enthusiast [ɪnθúzist] n entusiasta mf

enthusiastic [ɪnθuziǽstɪk] adj entusiasta inv; **I'm very — about the trip** estoy muy entusiasmado con el viaje

entice [ɪntáis] vi/vt (attract) atraer; (lure) tentar; (seduce) seducir

entire [ɪntáɪr] adj (unbroken) entero; (complete) completo; **the — crew** toda la tripulación, la tripulación entera

entirety [ɪntáɪrɪɾi] n totalidad f

entitle [ɪntáɪɾł] vt (give a title) titular, intitular; (give a right) dar derecho

entitlement [ɪntáɪɾłmənt] n derecho m

entity [éntɪɾi] n (institution) entidad f; (being) ente m, ser m

entomology [entəmáləʤi] n entomología f

entourage [ánturaʤ] n séquito m, cortejo m

entrails [éntrełz] n entrañas f pl

entrance [éntrəns] n (act, point of entering) entrada f; (permission to enter) ingreso m; **— examination** examen de ingreso m; [ɪntréns] vt embelesar

entrant [éntrənt] n participante mf; **—s in the law profession** abogados recién recibidos m pl

entrap [ɪntrǽp] vt (ensnare) coger con una trampa; (deceive) embaucar

entreaty [ɪntríɾi] n súplica f, ruego m

entrench [ɪntréntʃ] vt (establish) afianzar(se); (dig trenches) atrincherar; **a deeply —ed**

habit un hábito muy arraigado

entrepreneur [antrəprənúr] n empresario -ria mf

entropy [éntrəpi] n entropía f

entrust [ɪntrást] vt confiar, encomendar

entry [éntri] n (act, point of entry) entrada f; (permission to enter) ingreso m; (record) anotación f; (contestant) participante mf; (dictionary definition) entrada f, artículo m; (computer) entrada f; (in bookkeeping) asiento m; **double —** contabilidad por partida doble f

enumerate [ɪnúmə-ret] vt enumerar

enunciate [ɪnánsiet] vi/vt articular; (state a theory) enunciar; (proclaim) proclamar

envelop [ɪnvéləp] vt envolver

envelope [énvəlop] n sobre m

enviable [énviəbəł] adj envidiable

envious [énviəs] adj envidioso

environment [ɪnváɪə-nmənt] n ambiente m, medio ambiente m; (biological) medio ambiente m, ecología f; adj ambiental; (biological) medioambiental, ecológico

environmental [ɪnvaɪə-nmɛ́ntł] adj ambiental; (biological) medioambiental, ecológico

environmentalist [ɪnvaɪə-nmɛ́ntłɪst] n ecologista mf

envisage [ɪnvízɪʤ] vt anticipar, prever

envision [ɪnvíʒən] vt imaginar

envoy [ánvɔɪ] n enviado -da mf

envy [énvi] n envidia f; vi/vt envidiar

enzyme [énzaɪm] n enzima f

ephemeral [ɪfémə-əł] adj efímero

epic [épɪk] n (poem) epopeya f; (genre) épica f; adj épico

epicenter [épɪsɛntə-] n epicentro m

epidemic [ɛpɪdémɪk] adj epidémico; n epidemia f

epidermis [ɛpɪdɔ́-mɪs] n epidermis f

epilepsy [épələpsi] n epilepsia f

epilog, epilogue [épəlɔg] n epílogo m

epiphany [ɪpífəni] n epifanía f

episode [épɪsod] n episodio m

episodic [ɛpɪsádɪk] adj (sporadic) episódico; (serial) en episodios

epitaph [épɪtæf] n epitafio m

epitome [ɪpíɾəmi] n epítome m

epoch [épək] n época f; **—-making** trascendental

equal [íkwəł] adj igual; **— rights** igualdad de derechos f; **an — contest** una competición pareja; **to be — to a task** capaz de cumplir una tarea; n igual m; **— sign** signo de igual m; vt igualar

equality [ɪkwálɪɾi] n igualdad f

equalize [íkwəlaɪz] vt igualar; (electronically)

ecualizar
equate [ɪkwét] VT equiparar
equation [ɪkwéʒən] N ecuación *f*
equator [ɪkwédə] N ecuador *m*
Equatorial Guinea [ekwətóriəłgíni] N Guinea Ecuatorial *f*
equidistant [ikwɪdístənt] ADJ equidistante
equilibrium [ikwəlíbriəm] N equilibrio *m*
equine [íkwaɪn] ADJ & N equino *m*
equinox [íkwənaks] N equinoccio *m*
equip [ɪkwíp] VT equipar
equipment [ɪkwípmənt] N (supplies) equipo *m*; (act of equipping) equipamiento *m*
equitable [ékwɪɾəbəł] ADJ equitativo, justo
equity [ékwɪɾi] N equidad *f*, valor libre de hipoteca de una propiedad *m*; **equities** acciones *f pl*
equivalent [ɪkwívələnt] ADJ & N equivalente *m*
equivocal [ɪkwívəkəł] ADJ equívoco
era [írə] N era *f*
eradicate [ɪrǽdɪket] VT (extirpate) erradicar; (pull up by roots) arrancar
erase [ɪrés] VI/VT borrar(se)
eraser [ɪrésə] N (pencil) goma de borrar *f*; (blackboard) borrador *m*
erasure [ɪréʃə] N (act of erasing) borrado *m*; (smudge) borrón *m*
erect [ɪrékt] ADJ (of an organ) erecto; (posture) erguido; VT erigir
erection [ɪrékʃən] N erección *f*
Eritrea [ɛrɪtríə] N Eritrea *f*
Eritrean [ɛrɪtríən] ADJ & N eritreo -a *mf*
ermine [ɝ́mɪn] N armiño *m*
erode [ɪród] VI/VT erosionar(se)
erogenous [ɪrádʒənəs] ADJ erógeno
erosion [ɪróʒən] N erosión *f*
erotic [ɪrádɪk] ADJ erótico
err [ɛr] VI errar
errand [ɛrənd] N mandado *m*, recado *m*; — **boy** mandadero *m*
errant [ɛrənt] ADJ errante
erratic [ɪrǽdɪk] ADJ (unpredictable) irregular, errático; (eccentric) excéntrico; (wandering) errante
erroneous [ɪróniəs] ADJ erróneo, errado
error [ɛrə] N error *m*; **to be in —** estar errado
erudite [ɛ́rjədaɪt] ADJ erudito
erupt [ɪrápt] VI (volcano) hacer erupción; (anger) estallar; (pimples) salir
eruption [ɪrápʃən] N erupción *f*
escalate [éskəlet] VI (prices) aumentar; (violence) intensificarse, aumentar
escalator [éskəlɛdə] N escalera mecánica *f*
escapade [éskəped] N (adventure) aventura *f*; (prank) travesura *f*

escape [ɪskép] N (of gas) escape *m* (also computer term); (from reality) escape *m*, evasión *f*; (of prisoners) fuga *f*, evasión *f*; (means of escaping) escapatoria *f*; VI escapar(se), evadirse; VT (elude) eludir; **his name —s me** no me acuerdo de su nombre
escort [éskɔrt] N (people who accompany) escolta *mf*; (male companion) acompañante *m*; (paid female companion) señorita de compañía *f*; [ɪskɔrt] VT (protect) escoltar; (accompany) acompañar
escrow [éskro] ADV LOC **in —** en custodia
escudo [ɪskúdo] N escudo *m*
Eskimo [éskəmo] N esquimal *mf*
esophagus [ɪsáfəgəs] N esófago *m*
esoteric [ɛsətérɪk] ADJ esotérico
especial [ɪspéʃəł] ADJ especial
espionage [éspiɑnɑʒ] N espionaje *m*
espouse [ɪspáuz] VT abrazar
essay [ése] N ensayo *m*; [ɛsé] VT ensayar
essence [ésəns] N esencia *f*; **time is of the —** el tiempo apremia
essential [ɪsénʃəł] ADJ esencial
establish [ɪstǽblɪʃ] VT establecer; (a university) fundar
establishment [ɪstǽblɪʃmənt] N establecimiento *m*; (authority) establishment *m*
estate [ɪstét] N (piece of land) hacienda *f*; (possessions) bienes *m pl*; (property) propiedades *f pl*; (of a dead person) testamentaría *f*; **— tax** impuesto de sucesión *m*
esteem [ɪstím] VT (regard highly) estimar; (consider) considerar; N estima *f*
estimate [éstəmet] VT estimar, evaluar; VI hacer una estimación; [éstəmɪt] N (calculation) estimación *f*; (approximate charge) presupuesto *m*
estimation [ɛstəméʃən] N (opinion) juicio *m*; (esteem) estima *f*; (estimate) estimación *f*; **in my —** a mi juicio
Estonia [ɛstóniə] N Estonia *f*
Estonian [ɛstóniən] ADJ & N estonio -nia *mf*
estrange [ɪstrénʤ] VT (alienate) enajenar; **to become —d** separarse
estrogen [éstrədʒən] N estrógeno *m*
estuary [éstʃueri] N estuario *m*
etcetera [ɛtsétrə] ADV etcétera
etch [ɛtʃ] VI/VT (engrave) grabar; (outline) perfilar(se)
etching [étʃɪŋ] N grabado *m*
eternal [ɪtɝ́nəł] ADJ eterno
eternity [ɪtɝ́nɪɾi] N eternidad *f*
ether [íθə] N éter *m*
ethical [éθɪkəł] ADJ ético

ethics [éθɪks] N ética *f*
Ethiopia [iθiópiə] N Etiopía *f*
Ethiopian [iθiópiən] ADJ & N etíope *mf*
ethnic [éθnɪk] ADJ étnico; (dances, clothes) tradicional; — **Chinese** de ascendencia china; — **cleansing** limpieza étnica *f*
ethnicity [εθnísɪDi] N etnicidad *f*; (group) grupo étnico *m*
ethnography [εθnágrəfi] N etnografía *f*
ethnology [εθnáləʤi] N etnología *f*
ethyl alcohol [éθəlǽlkəhɑl] N alcohol etílico *m*
etiquette [éɾɪkɪt] N etiqueta *f*
etymology [εɾəmáləʤi] N etimología *f*
eucalyptus [jukəlíptəs] N eucalipto *m*
eulogy [júləʤi] N (praise) elogio *m*; (at a funeral) panegírico *m*
eunuch [júnək] N eunuco *m*
euphemism [júfəmɪzəm] N eufemismo *m*
euphoria [jufɔ́riə] N euforia *f*
euro [júro] N euro *m*
Europe [júrəp] N Europa *f*
European [jurəpíən] ADJ & N europeo -a *mf*
euthanasia [juθənéʒə] N eutanasia *f*
evacuate [ɪvǽkjuet] VI/VT (remove due to danger, defecate) evacuar; (empty a building) desalojar
evade [ɪvéd] VT (taxes, responsibilities) evadir, burlar; (questions) eludir
evaluate [ɪvǽljuet] VT (assess) evaluar; (appraise) avaluar, tasar
evangelical [ɪvænʤέlɪkəl] ADJ evangélico
evaporate [ɪvǽpəret] VI/VT evaporar(se); VI (vanish) esfumarse
evaporation [ɪvæpəréʃən] N evaporación *f*
evasion [ɪvéʒən] N (escape) evasión *f*; (subterfuge) evasiva *f*
evasive [ɪvésɪv] ADJ evasivo
eve [iv] N (day before) víspera *f*; (evening) atardecer *m*; **on the — of** en vísperas de
even [ívən] ADJ (flat) plano, llano; (smooth) liso; (parallel) paralelo; (without fluctuation) parejo; (equal) igual; (divisible by two) par; (placid) tranquilo; —**handed** imparcial; —**-tempered** apacible; **an — dozen** una docena exacta; **to be — with someone** estar a mano con alguien; **to get — with someone** desquitarse de alguien; ADV (still, yet) aun; (for extreme case) hasta, inclusive, incluso; — **if / though** aun cuando; — **my mother went** hasta mi madre fue; — **so** aun así; **it's — more expensive** es aun más caro; **not** — ni siquiera; VI/VT (make a surface even) nivelar(se); (make accounts even) emparejar
evening [ívnɪŋ] N tarde *f*, velada *f*; (dusk)

atardecer *m*; — **gown** vestido de fiesta *m*, vestido de noche *m*; — **party** velada *f*; — **star** lucero de la tarde *m*; **good —!** ¡buenas noches!
event [ɪvέnt] N (happening) hecho *m*, evento *m*; (of importance) acontecimiento *m*, suceso *m*; **in any** — en todo caso; **in the — of** en caso de
eventful [ɪvέntfəl] ADJ agitado, movido
eventual [ɪvέntʃuəl] ADJ (later) posterior; (final) final
eventuality [ɪvεntʃuǽlɪDi] N eventualidad *f*
eventually [ɪvέntʃuəli] ADV a la larga
ever [έvə] ADV alguna vez; —**green** (planta de hoja) perenne *f*; —**lasting** eterno; —**more** para siempre; — **since** desde entonces; **have you — studied French?** ¿alguna vez has estudiado francés? **how did you — do this?** ¿cómo pudiste hacer esto? **for — and —** por / para siempre jamás; **hardly —** casi nunca; **if —** si alguna vez; **more than —** más que nunca; **the best friend I — had** el mejor amigo que he tenido jamás; **for—more** para / por siempre jamás
every [έvri] ADJ (each) cada; — **child is different** cada niño es diferente; (all) todo(s); **we go — Friday** vamos todos los viernes; —**body** todos -das *mf pl*, todo el mundo *m*; — **day** todos los días; —**day** (of clothes) de diario, de todos los días; (of occurrences) cotidiano; — **once in a while** de vez en cuando; —**one** todos -das *mf pl*, todo el mundo *m*; — **other day** cada dos días, un día sí y otro no; —**thing** todo; **you are —thing to me** eres todo para mí; —**where** (location) por / en todas partes; (direction) a todas partes
evict [ɪvíkt] VT desalojar
evidence [έvɪdəns] N evidencia *f*; (data in court) prueba *f*; **to be in —** ser evidente; VI/VT evidenciar(se), demostrar(se)
evident [έvɪdənt] ADJ evidente
evil [ívəl] ADJ (wicked) malo, malvado; (harmful) maligno; —**doer** malhechor -ora *mf*; — **eye** mal de ojo *m*; N (force of nature) mal *m*; (wickedness) maldad *f*; **the lesser of two —s** el mal menor
evoke [ɪvók] VT (call up) evocar; (elicit) provocar
evolution [εvəlúʃən] N evolución *f*
evolve [ɪváʧv] VI/VT desarrollar(se); VI evolucionar
ewe [ju] N oveja *f*
ex [εks] N ex *mf*
exacerbate [ɪgzǽsə-bet] VI/VT exacerbar

exact [ɪgzǽkt] ADJ exacto; VT exigir

exacting [ɪgzǽktɪŋ] ADJ exigente

exaggerate [ɪgzǽdʒəret] VT exagerar

exalt [ɪgzɔ́lt] VT exaltar

exam [ɪgzǽm] N examen m

examination [ɪgzæmənéʃən] N examen m (also medical)

examine [ɪgzǽmɪn] VT (inspect) examinar; (analyze) analizar

example [ɪgzǽmpəl] N ejemplo m

exasperate [ɪgzǽspəret] VT exasperar

excavate [ékskavet] VT excavar

excavator [ékskaveɖɚ] N (person) excavador -ora mf; (machine) excavadora f

exceed [ɪksíd] VT (go beyond) exceder, rebasar; (be superior) superar, sobrepasar

exceedingly [ɪksídɪŋli] ADV sumamente, extremadamente

excel [ɪksél] VI sobresalir, lucirse, descollar

excellence [éksələns] N excelencia f

excellent [éksələnt] ADJ excelente

except [ɪksépt] PREP excepto, menos; **all the students — Pam** todos los estudiantes menos Pam; CONJ excepto, salvo; **the cars are identical — that one is older** los coches son idénticos salvo que uno es más viejo; **we would go to the beach, — for the inclement weather** iríamos a la playa si no fuera por el mal tiempo; VT exceptuar

excepting [ɪkséptɪŋ] PREP exceptuando

exception [ɪksépʃən] N excepción f; **with the — of** con/a excepción de; **to take — (object)** objetar; (resent) ofenderse

exceptional [ɪksépʃənəl] ADJ (unusual) excepcional; (gifted) superdotado; (handicapped) con necesidades especiales

excerpt [éksɚpt] N fragmento m; VT seleccionar fragmentos

excess [ɪksɛs] N exceso m, hartazgo m; **— baggage** exceso de equipaje m; **— profits tax** impuesto sobre ganancias excesivas m; **— weight** exceso de peso m; **in — of twenty pounds** más de veinte libras; **to drink to —** beber en exceso

excessive [ɪksésɪv] ADJ excesivo, desmedido

exchange [ɪkstʃéndʒ] VT (replace with something similar) cambiar; (give mutually) intercambiar; (trade political prisoners, books, CDs) canjear; (barter) permutar; **to — greetings** saludarse; N (replacement) cambio m; (interchange) intercambio m; (barter) permuta f; (of prisoners, books, etc.) canje m; (for stock trading) bolsa f; (for commodity trading) lonja f; (telephone) central de teléfonos f; **— student** estudiante de intercambio mf;

rate of — tipo de cambio m

excise [éksaɪz] N impuesto sobre bienes de consumo m

excite [ɪksáɪt] VT excitar, alborotar; (enthuse) entusiasmar

excited [ɪksáɪɖɪd] ADJ (agitated, aroused) excitado; (enthusiastic) entusiasmado; **to get —** (enthused) entusiasmarse; (aroused) excitarse

excitement [ɪksáɪtmənt] N (arousal) excitación f; (enthusiasm) entusiasmo m

exciting [ɪksáɪɖɪŋ] ADJ (stimulating) excitante; (thrilling) emocionante

exclaim [ɪksklém] VI exclamar

exclamation [ɛkskləméʃən] N exclamación f; **— point** signo de admiración m

exclude [ɪksklúd] VT excluir

exclusion [ɪksklúʒən] N exclusión f

exclusive [ɪksklúsɪv] ADJ exclusivo; **— of** sin incluir

excommunicate [ɛkskəmjúnɪket] VT excomulgar

excrement [ékskrəmənt] N excremento m

excrete [ɪkskrít] VI/VT excretar

excruciating [ɪkskrúʃieɖɪŋ] ADJ insoportable, atroz

excursion [ɪkskɚ́ʒən] N excursión f

excusable [ɪkskjúzəbəl] ADJ excusable, disculpable

excuse [ɪkskjúz] VT (release from a duty, seek exemption) excusar, eximir; (forgive) disculpar, perdonar; **— me!** (forgive me) disculpe; (let me pass) con permiso; [ɪkskjús] N excusa f, disculpa f; **it's a poor — for a car** no merece llamarse un coche

execute [éksɪkjut] VT ejecutar (also computer term); (by firing squad) fusilar

execution [eksɪkjúʃən] N ejecución f; **— wall** paredón m

executioner [eksɪkjúʃənɚ] N verdugo mf

executive [ɪgzékjəɖɪv] ADJ ejecutivo; N (person) ejecutivo -va mf; (branch of government) poder ejecutivo m

executor [ɪgzékjəɖɚ] N albacea mf

exemplary [ɪgzémpləri] ADJ ejemplar

exemplify [ɪgzémpləfaɪ] VT ejemplificar

exempt [ɪgzémpt] VT eximir, dispensar; ADJ exento, libre

exemption [ɪgzémpʃən] N exención f, franquicia f

exercise [éksɚsaɪz] N ejercicio m; **—s** ceremonia f; VT ejercer; VI hacer ejercicio; **to be —d about something** estar disgustado por algo

exert [ɪgzɚ́t] VT ejercer; **to — oneself** esforzarse, empeñarse

exertion [ɪgzɚ́ʃən] N (use of powers,

faculties) ejercicio *m*; (vigorous action) esfuerzo *m*, empeño *m*

exhale [ekshéł] VT exhalar; VI espirar

exhaust [ɪgzɔ́st] VT agotar, desmadejar; (a topic) tratar exhaustivamente; N (from a car) escape *m*

exhausted [ɪgzɔ́stɪd] ADJ rendido, agotado

exhaustion [ɪgzɔ́stʃən] N (act or process of exhausting) agotamiento *m*; (weakness, tiredness) fatiga *f*

exhaustive [ɪgzɔ́stɪv] ADJ exhaustivo

exhibit [ɪgzíbɪt] VI/VT (manifest) exhibir; (put on view) exponer; N exposición *f*

exhibition [eksəbíʃən] N (manifestation, show of skills) exhibición *f*; (public display of objects) exposición *f*

exhilarated [ɪgzílərɛɪd] ADJ exultante

exhort [ɪgzɔ́rt] VT exhortar

exile [égzaɪł] N exilio *m*, destierro *m*; (person exiled) exiliado -da *mf*, desterrado -da *mf*; VT exiliar

exist [ɪgzíst] VI existir

existence [ɪgzístəns] N existencia *f*

exit [égzɪt] N salida *f*; VI/VT salir (de); (theater) hacer mutis; **he —ed the building** salió del edificio

exodus [éksədəs] N éxodo *m*

exonerate [ɪgzánərɛt] VT exonerar

exorbitant [ɪgzɔ́rbɪdənt] ADJ exorbitante

exorcise [éksɔrsaɪz] VT exorcisar

exorcism [éksɔrsɪzəm] N exorcismo *m*

exotic [ɪgzɑ́dɪk] ADJ exótico

expand [ɪkspǽnd] VI/VT expandir(se), ampliar(se); (an equation, an idea) desarrollar(se); (through heat) dilatar(se)

expanse [ɪkspǽns] N extensión *f*

expansion [ɪkspǽnʃən] N expansión *f*; (of an equation, of an idea) desarrollo *m*; (through heat) dilatación *f*

expansive [ɪkspǽnsɪv] ADJ expansivo

expatriate [ekspétriet] VI/VT expatriar(se); [ekspétrɪt] N expatriado -da *mf*

expect [ɪkspékt] VT esperar; **we — guests** esperamos visita(s); **I — you to be on time** cuento con que vengas puntualmente; **I'm —ed to work fifty hours a week** tengo que trabajar cincuenta horas por semana; **I — you're tired** estarás cansado; **she's —ing** está embarazada / encinta

expectation [ɛkspɛktéʃən] N (anticipation) expectación *f*; (expected thing) expectativa *f*; **he has great —s** tiene grandes expectativas

expectorate [ɪkspéktərɛt] VI/VT expectorar

expedient [ɪkspídiənt] ADJ conveniente, expeditivo

expedite [ékspɪdaɪt] VT (speed up) acelerar; (deal with promptly) despachar

expedition [ekspɪdíʃən] N expedición *f*

expeditionary [ekspɪdíʃəneri] ADJ expedicionario

expel [ɪkspéł] VT (discharge) expeler; (throw out) expulsar

expend [ɪkspénd] VT gastar, agotar

expenditure [ɪkspéndɪtʃɚ] N gasto *m*

expense [ɪkspéns] N gasto *m*; **— account** cuenta de gastos *f*; **they had fun at my —** se divirtieron a mi costa

expensive [ɪkspénsɪv] ADJ caro

experience [ɪkspíriəns] N experiencia *f*; VT experimentar; **—d** experimentado

experiment [ɪkspérəmənt] N experimento *m*; VI experimentar

experimental [ɪkspɛrəmɛ́ntł] ADJ experimental

expert [ékspɚt] N experto -ta *mf*; ADJ experto, idóneo, perito; **— system** sistema experto *m*

expertise [ekspɚtíz] N pericia *f*

expiration [ekspəréʃən] N (of a contract) vencimiento *m*, caducidad *f*; (breathing out) espiración *f*

expire [ɪkspáɪr] VI (die, terminate) expirar; (breathe out) espirar; (lapse) vencer, caducar

explain [ɪksplén] VT explicar; **he tried to — away his absence** trató de justificar su ausencia

explainable [ɪksplénəbəł] ADJ explicable

explanation [eksplənéʃən] N explicación *f*

explanatory [ɪksplǽnətɔri] ADJ explicativo

expletive [ɪksplídɪv] N palabrota *f*

explicable [ɪksplíkəbəł] ADJ explicable

explicit [ɪksplísɪt] ADJ explícito

explode [ɪksplód] VI/VT estallar, hacer explosión, explotar; VT (a theory) hacer añicos; VI (population) dispararse

exploit [ékspłɔɪt] N hazaña *f*, proeza *f*; [ɪkspłɔ́ɪt] VT explotar

exploitation [ekspłɔɪtéʃən] N explotación *f*

exploration [ekspłəréʃən] N exploración *f*

explore [ɪkspłɔ́r] VI/VT explorar; (a topic) bucear

explorer [ɪkspłɔ́rɚ] N explorador -ra *mf*

explosion [ɪkspłóʒən] N explosión *f*, estallido *m*

explosive [ɪkspłósɪv] ADJ & N explosivo *m*

exponent [ɪkspónənt] N exponente *m*

export [ɪkspɔ́rt] VI/VT exportar; [ékspɔrt] N exportación *f*

exportation [ekspɔrtéʃən] N exportación *f*

expose [ɪkspóz] VT (to lay open to danger, exhibit, subject to light) exponer; (to

make known) revelar; (to unmask)
desenmascarar

exposition [ɛkspəzíʃən] N exposición f

exposure [ɪkspóʒɚ] N (to danger, to light, act
of exposing) exposición f; (disclosure)
revelación f; **to die of** — morir de frío

expound [ɪkspáund] VI/VT exponer, explicar

express [ɪksprɛ́s] VT expresar; (send by mail)
enviar por correo expreso; (squeeze out)
exprimir; ADJ (clearly indicated) expreso;
— **train** tren expreso m; ADV por expreso;
N expreso m

expression [ɪksprɛ́ʃən] N expresión f

expressive [ɪksprɛ́sɪv] ADJ expresivo

expropriate [ɛksprópriet] VT expropiar

expulsion [ɪkspʌ́lʃən] N expulsión f

exquisite [ɛkskwízɪt] ADJ exquisito,
primoroso; (pain) penetrante

extant [ɛ́kstənt] ADJ existente

extemporaneous [ɪkstɛmpəréniəs] ADJ
improvisado

extend [ɪkstɛ́nd] VI/VT extender(se); (a street)
ampliar(se); **he —ed his hand to her** le
tendió la mano

extended [ɪkstɛ́ndɪd] ADJ (extensive) extenso;
(prolonged) prolongado; (folded out)
extendido

extension [ɪkstɛ́nʃən] N extensión f; (of a
deadline) prórroga f; (phone line)
extensión f; (addition) anexo m,
ampliación f; — **cord** extensión f

extensive [ɪkstɛ́nsɪv] ADJ extenso;
(agriculture) extensivo

extent [ɪkstɛ́nt] N extensión f; **to a great —**
en alto grado; **to such an — that** a tal
grado que; **to the — that you are able**
en la medida en que seas capaz; **up to a
certain —** hasta cierto punto

extenuate [ɪkstɛ́njuet] VT atenuar

exterior [ɪkstíriɚ] ADJ exterior; N exterior m

exterminate [ɪkstɝ́mənet] VT exterminar

extermination [ɪkstɝmənéʃən] N exterminio
m, exterminación f

external [ɪkstɝ́nəl] ADJ externo; (concerned
with foreign countries) exterior; N exterior m

extinct [ɪkstíŋkt] ADJ extinto

extinguish [ɪkstíŋgwɪʃ] VT apagar, extinguir

extol [ɪkstól] VT ensalzar, enaltecer

extort [ɪkstɔ́rt] VT extorsionar

extortion [ɪkstɔ́rʃən] N extorsión f

extra [ɛ́kstrə] ADJ de más, adicional; **make
some — cakes** haz unos pasteles de más/
adicionales/extras; ADV extra; N extra m
(including newspaper, actor); —**marital**
extramarital; —**ordinary** extraordinario;
—**sensory** extrasensorial

extract [ɛ́kstrækt] N (something extracted)

extracto m; (passage from a book)
fragmento m; [ɪkstrǽkt] VT extraer; (a
secret) sonsacar

extradite [ɛ́kstrədaɪt] VT extraditar

extraneous [ɪkstréniəs] ADJ superfluo

extrapolate [ɪkstrǽpəlet] VI/VT extrapolar

extravagance [ɪkstrǽvəgəns] N (unnecessary
expense) despilfarro m, derroche m;
(excess) exceso m; (oddity) extravagancia f

extravagant [ɪkstrǽvəgənt] ADJ (shopper)
gastador, derrochador; (price) exorbitante;
(praise, demand) excesivo

extreme [ɪkstrím] ADJ extremo; N extremo m;
to go to —s exagerar, llegar a extremos;
to the — sumamente, extremadamente

extremity [ɪkstrɛ́mɪɾi] N extremidad f

extricate [ɛ́kstrɪket] VT sacar; VI **to —
oneself from** conseguir salir de

extrovert [ɛ́kstrəvɚt] N extrovertido -da mf

extroverted [ɛ́kstrəvɚɾɪd] ADJ extrovertido

exuberant [ɪgzúbɚənt] ADJ exuberante

exude [ɪgzúd] VI/VT (liquid) exudar;
(cheerfulness, confidence) emanar

exult [ɪgzʌ́lt] VI exultar

eye [aɪ] N ojo m (also of hurricane, needle,
tools); (look) mirada f; —**ball** globo ocular
m; —**brow** ceja f; —**dropper** cuentagotas
m sg; —**glass** (of a telescope, microscope)
ocular m; —**glasses** anteojos m pl, lentes
m pl; —**lash** pestaña f; —**lid** párpado m;
—**liner** delineador m; —**opener**
revelación f; —**piece** ocular m; —**sight**
vista f; —**sore** monstruosidad f; —
shadow sombra para ojos f; —**socket**
órbita f; —**tooth** colmillo m; —**witness**
testigo ocular mf; **my —s are bad** tengo
mala vista; **in the twinkling of an —**
en un abrir y cerrar de ojos; **her dress
caught his —** su vestido le llamó la
atención; **to keep an — on** cuidar,
vigilar; **to see — to —** estar de acuerdo;
in the —s of the law ante la ley; **to
give someone the —** hacerle ojito a
alguien; **to have —s for someone** estar
prendado de alguien; **to keep one's —
open** tener cuidado; VT mirar

eyeful [áɪfʊl] N **we got an —** vimos más
que suficiente

e-zine [ízin] N revista electrónica f

Ff

fable [fébəl] N fábula f

fabric [fǽbrɪk] N tela f, tejido m; (wool) paño

m; (of society) estructura *f;* — **softener** suavizante *m*
fabricate [fǽbrɪket] vt (goods) fabricar; (a story) inventar
fabulous [fǽbjələs] ADJ fabuloso
façade [fəsád] N fachada *f*
face [fes] N (front part of head, coin, cube, facial expression) cara *f;* (of a building) frente *m;* (of a watch) esfera *f;* (of the Earth) faz *f;* **—cloth** toalla para la cara *f;* **—lift** lifting *m;* **—-to-—** cara a cara; — **value** valor nominal *m;* **in the — of** ante, frente a; **on the — of** aparentemente; **she put on a brave —** se comportó con entereza; **to make —s** hacer muecas; **to lose —** quedar mal; **to save —** quedar bien; **to show one's —** aparecerse; vt (stand opposite to) encarar; (meet defiantly) enfrentar, enfrentarse con, afrontar; (look forward) mirar a / hacia; (to have the front toward) dar a / hacia; (to put on facing) ribetear; **about —!** ¡media vuelta! **left —!** ¡a la izquierda! **to — down** intimidar; **to — the music** dar la cara; **to — with marble** revestir de mármol
faceless [féslɪs] ADJ (anonymous) anónimo; (without a face) sin cara
facet [fǽsɪt] N faceta *f*
facetious [fəsíʃəs] ADJ gracioso
facial [féʃəl] ADJ facial; N limpieza de cutis *f*
facilitate [fəsílɪtet] vt facilitar
facility [fəsílɪDi] N (skill) facilidad *f;* **facilities** (of a building) instalación *f;* (restroom) aseo *m,* servicio *m*
fact [fækt] N hecho *m;* **hard —s** datos concretos *m pl;* **is that a —!** ¡no me digas! **as a matter of —** de hecho; **in —** de hecho; **it's a — of life** así son las cosas
faction [fǽkʃən] N facción *f*
factor [fǽktə] N factor *m;* vt descomponer en factores; vi **to — in** tener en cuenta
factory [fǽktəri] N fábrica *f*
factual [fǽktʃuəl] ADJ (of facts) fáctico; (based on facts) objetivo
faculty [fǽkəlti] N (ability) facultad *f;* (in a college) profesorado *m,* cuerpo docente *m,* claustro *m*
fad [fæd] N moda pasajera *f*
fade [fed] vi/vt (cloth) decolorar(se), desteñir(se); (color) deslavar(se); vi (strength) disminuir; (lights) apagarse; (feelings, colors) desvanecerse
fag [fæg] N *offensive* marica *m,* maricón *m*
faggot [fǽgət] N (male homosexual) *offensive* marica *m,* maricón *m;* (bundle) haz *m*

fail [fel] vi (faculties, organs, machinery, structure) fallar; (experiment, plan) fracasar, frustrarse; (health) decaer; (business) quebrar, hacer bancarrota; vi/vt (exam, student) suspender, reprobar; **he —ed to remember their anniversary** no se acordó de su aniversario; **don't — to come** no dejes de venir; **without —** sin falta
failure [féljə] N (of a plan, a person) fracaso *m;* (of organs) insuficiencia *f;* (of faculties) deterioro *m;* (of machinery) falla *f; Sp* fallo *m;* (of business) quiebra *f,* bancarrota *f;* (in an exam) suspenso *m;* **her — to respond puzzled me** su falta de respuesta me confundió
faint [fent] ADJ (sound) débil; (light) tenue; (image) vago; **to feel —** sentirse mareado; **—-hearted** timorato, cobarde; N desmayo *m,* desfallecimiento *m;* vi desmayarse, desfallecer
faintness [féntnɪs] N (of sound) debilidad *f;* (of light) tenuidad *f;* (of an image) vaguedad *f*
fair [fer] ADJ (just) justo; (by the rules) limpio; (large) considerable; (of weather) bueno; (of sky) despejado; (of wind) propicio; (of complexion) blanco; — **play** juego limpio *m;* — **chance of success** buena probabilidad de éxito *f;* **the — sex** el sexo bello; **that's not —!** ¡no vale! ¡no es justo! ADV **to play —** jugar limpio; N feria *f;* **—ground** real de la feria *m;* **—way** calle *f,* fairway *m*
fairly [férli] ADV (justly) justamente; (moderately) medianamente; — **difficult** bastante difícil
fairness [férnɪs] N (justice) justicia *f;* (whiteness) blancura *f*
fairy [féri] N hada *f;* (male homosexual) *offensive* maricón *m;* — **godmother** hada madrina *f;* **—land** país de las hadas *m;* — **tale** cuento de hadas *m*
faith [feθ] N fe *f;* (fidelity) fidelidad *f;* — **healing** cura por la fe *f;* **in good —** de buena fe; **to have — in someone** tener confianza en alguien; **to keep —** cumplir con la palabra
faithful [féθfəl] ADJ fiel
faithfulness [féθfəlnɪs] N fidelidad *f*
faithless [féθlɪs] ADJ (disloyal) desleal, falso; (lacking in faith, fidelity) infiel
fake [fek] N (object) objeto falso *m;* (person who fakes) farsante *mf;* ADJ falso; — **pearls** perlas de fantasía *f pl;* vt (render false, counterfeit) falsificar; vi/vt (feign) fingir

falcon [fǽɫkən] N halcón *m*

Falkland Islands [fɔ́klǝndáɪlǝndz] N Islas Malvinas *f pl*

fall [fɔ́ɫ] VI (drop) caer(se); (light upon) detenerse; (slope downward) bajar; (be assigned to) tocar a, recaer sobre; **—ing out** desavenencia *f*, pique *m*; **—ing star** estrella fugaz *f*; **to — asleep** dormirse; **to — back** retroceder; **to — back on** recurrir a; **to — behind** atrasarse, retrasarse; **to — down** (drop) caerse; (fail) fallar; **to — in love** enamorarse; **to — off** disminuir; **he —s for blondes** se enamora de las rubias; **to — out with** reñir con; **to — through** quedar en la nada; **you — for it** te dejas engañar; N (drop) caída *f*; (of a terrain) declive *m*; (season) otoño *m*; **— guy** cabeza de turco *mf*; **—s** catarata *f*, salto de agua *m*

fallacious [fǝléʃəs] ADJ falaz

fallacy [fǽləsi] N (false notion) falacia *f*; (false argument) sofisma *m*

fallible [fǽlǝbəɫ] ADJ falible

fallout [fɔ́laʊt] N (particle-settling) precipitación radiactiva *f*; (consequences) repercusiones *f pl*

fallow [fǽlo] ADJ baldío, en barbecho; N barbecho *m*; VT dejar en barbecho

false [fɔ́ls] ADJ falso; **to bear — witness** jurar en falso; **— alarm** falsa alarma *f*; **— arrest** detención ilegal *f*; **— pretense** estafa *f*; **— start** salida en falso *f*; **— step** paso en falso *m*; **— teeth** postizo *m*

falsehood [fɔ́lshud] N falsedad *f*, mentira *f*

falseness [fɔ́lsnɪs] N falsedad *f*

falsify [fɔ́lsəfaɪ] VT falsificar, falsear

falter [fɔ́ltə] VI (hesitate) vacilar, entrecortarse; (stutter) titubear

fame [fem] N fama *f*

famed [femd] ADJ afamado

familiar [fəmíljə] ADJ (generally known) familiar, conocido; (informal) familiar; (too friendly) confianzudo; (closely personal) íntimo; **to be — with a subject** conocer bien un tema

familiarity [fəmiljǽɪti] N familiaridad *f*

family [fǽmli] N familia *f*; **— doctor** médico general *m*; **— jewels** *vulg* cojones *m pl*; **— man** hombre de familia *m*; **— name** apellido *m*; **— planning** planificación familiar *f*; **— room** cuarto de estar *m*; **— tree** árbol genealógico *m*; **— values** valores tradicionales *m pl*

famine [fǽmɪn] N (lack of food) hambruna *f*, hambre *f*; (scarcity) escasez *f*

famished [fǽmɪʃt] ADJ hambriento, muerto de hambre; **to be —** morirse de hambre

famous [fémǝs] ADJ famoso

fan [fæn] N (handheld) abanico *m*; (electrical) ventilador *m*; (for cleaning grain) aventadora *f*; (of sports) aficionado -da *mf*; (of a person) admirador -ra *mf*; VT (blow air) abanicar; (enliven) avivar; **to — out** abrirse en abanico; **— belt** correa del ventilador *f*; **— mail** correo de admiradores *m*

fanatic [fǝnǽɪk] ADJ & N fanático -ca *mf*

fanaticism [fǝnǽɪsɪzəm] N fanatismo *m*

fanciful [fǽnsɪfəl] ADJ (whimsical) caprichoso; (imaginary) imaginario; (led by fancy) fantasioso

fancy [fǽnsi] N fantasía *f*; (whim) capricho *m*; **to strike one's —** gustarle a alguien; **to take a — to** aficionarse a; **he took a — to his teacher** se enamoró de su maestra; ADJ (luxurious) de lujo; (elaborate) elaborado; (strange) estrafalario; **— free** despreocupado; **— work** bordado fino *m*; VT imaginar(se); **he fancies himself an artist** se cree artista; **just — the idea!** ¡figúrate!

fanfare [fǽnfer] N fanfarria *f*; **with great —** con bombo y platillo

fang [fæŋ] N colmillo *m*

fantasize [fǽntǝsaɪz] VI fantasear

fantastic [fæntǽstɪk] ADJ fantástico

fantasy [fǽntǝsi] N fantasía *f*

far [fɑr] ADV lejos; **— and away** sin duda; **— and wide** por todas partes; **— away / off** lejos, lejano; **—fetched** (implausible) inverosímil, peregrino; (forced) traído por los cabellos; **-flung** remoto; **—off** distante; **—out** radical, poco convencional; **—reaching** de gran alcance; **—sighted** (with defective vision) présbita, hipermétrope; (seeing the future) con visión de futuro; **— be it from me to complain** no es mi intención quejarme; **— more money** mucho más dinero; **— off we could see land** a lo lejos divisábamos tierra; **as — as I know** que yo sepa; **as — as I'm concerned** en lo que a mí respecta; **by —** con mucho; **how — do I need to walk?** ¿cuánto tengo que caminar? **how — is the church?** ¿a cuánto queda la iglesia? **so —** hasta ahora; **we talked — into the night** hablamos hasta entrada la noche; **we traveled as — as Chicago** viajamos hasta Chicago; ADJ lejano; **the — corner** la esquina de más allá; **it is a — cry from what you said** dista mucho de lo que dijiste

farce [fɑrs] N farsa *f*

fare [fer] N (ticket) billete *m*; (price of transport) tarifa *f*; (food) comida *f*; VI I **—d well in the course** me fue bien en el curso; **—well** despedida *f*; **to bid —well to** despedirse de; **—well!** ¡adiós!

farm [farm] N (large) hacienda *f*; (small) granja *f*; **—hand** peón *m*; **—house** alquería *f*, caserío *m*; **— produce** productos agrícolas *m pl*; **—yard** (enclosed) corral *m*; (open) patio *m*; VI/VT cultivar; **to — out** (lease) dar en arriendo; (distribute) repartir; (subcontract) subcontratar; (exhaust) agotar

farmer [fármɚ] N agricultor -ra *mf*; (small) granjero -ra *mf*; (large) hacendado -da *mf*

farming [fármɪŋ] N agricultura *f*; ADJ agrícola *mf*

fart [fart] N *vulg* pedo *m*; **old —** *fam, pej* viejo pesado *m*; VI *vulg* tirarse pedos; **to — around** *vulg* rascarse el culo

farther [fárðɚ] ADV más lejos; **it's an even — distance** es una distancia mayor todavía; **the concept was extended —** el concepto se extendió más; **— on** más adelante; ADJ más lejano

farthest [fárðɪst] ADJ el más lejano; ADV lo más lejos

fascinate [fǽsənet] VI/VT fascinar, alucinar

fascination [fæsənéʃən] N fascinación *f*

fascism [fǽʃɪzəm] N fascismo *m*

fascist [fǽʃɪst] N fascista *mf*

fashion [fǽʃən] N (style) moda *f*; (way) manera *f*, modo *m*; **— plate** figurín *m*; **after a —** más o menos; **to be in —** estar de moda; VT hacer; (metal) forjar; (character) formar; (putty, etc.) moldear

fashionable [fǽʃənəbəl] ADJ de moda

fast [fæst] ADJ (quick) rápido, veloz; (ahead, of a watch) adelantado; (firm, permanent) firme; (closed) atrancado; (loyal) fiel; (dissolute) disipado; **— food** comida rápida *f*; **to —-forward** avanzar; **life in the —** lane vida loca *f*; **— money** dinero mal habido *m*; **— woman** mujer ligera de cascos *f*; ADV (quickly) rápido; (firmly) firmemente; **— asleep** profundamente dormido; N ayuno *m*; VI ayunar

fasten [fǽsən] VT (with buckles, buttons, hooks) abrochar(se), prender; (with ribbon, thread) atar; (door) atrancar

fastener [fǽsənɚ] N cierre *m*

fastidious [fæstídiəs] ADJ (hard to please) maniático; (painstaking) minucioso

fat [fæt] ADJ gordo; **— cat** pez gordo *m*; **— cell** célula adiposa *f*; **— chance** ¡ni soñar! **—head** idiota *mf*; **— job** trabajo lucrativo *m*; **— profits** pingües ganancias *f pl*; **to get —** engordar; N (oily substance) grasa *f*; (animal tissue) gordura *f*, sebo *m*; **the — of the land** la abundancia de la tierra

fatal [fédl] ADJ fatal

fatality [fatǽlɪɾi] N víctima fatal *f*

fate [fet] N (lot) destino *m*, fatalidad *f*, hado *m*; (outcome) suerte *f*; VT destinar

father [fáðɚ] N padre *m*; **— figure** figura paterna *f*; **—-in-law** suegro *m*; **—land** patria *f*

fatherhood [fáðɚhud] N paternidad *f*

fatherly [fáðɚli] ADV paternal

fathom [fǽðəm] N braza *f*; VT (measure) sondear; (understand) comprender

fatigue [fatíg] N fatiga *f*; **—s** ropa de faena *f*; VI/VT fatigar(se), rendir(se)

fatness [fǽtnɪs] N gordura *f*

fatso [fǽtso] N *pej* gordinflón *m*, tonel *m*

fatten [fǽtn̩] VT engordar, cebar

fatty [fǽɾi] ADJ adiposo; N (insult for fat people) *pej* gordito -ta *mf*

faucet [fɔ́sɪt] N grifo *m*, llave *f*

fault [fɔlt] N (defect, misdeed) falta *f*; (responsibility) culpa *f*; (geological) falla *f*; **—finder** criticón -ona *mf*; **to a —** demasiado cuidadoso; **to be at —** ser culpable; **to find — with** criticar a

faultless [fɔ́ltlɪs] ADJ perfecto

faulty [fɔ́lti] ADJ defectuoso; (grammar) vicioso

faux pas [fopá] N gaffe *f*, metedura de pata *f*

favor [févɚ] N (kind act, goodwill) favor *m*, gracia *f*; (popularity) popularidad *f*; (party gift) sorpresa *f*; VT (give help, show preference) favorecer; (foster) propiciar; (approve of) estar a favor de; **they are —ed to win** son los favoritos; **she —s her mother** se parece a su madre

favorite [févɚɪt] ADJ & N preferido -da *mf*, favorito -ta *mf*, predilecto -ta *mf*

favoritism [févɚɪtɪzəm] N favoritismo *m*

fawn [fɔn] N cervatillo *m*; VI **to — (over)** adular

fax [fæks] N fax *m*, facsímil *m*; VT faxear

FBI (Federal Bureau of Investigation) [εfbiái] N FBI *m*

fear [fɪr] N miedo *m*, temor *m*; **— of God** temor de Dios *m*; VI/VT (be afraid of) temer, tenerle miedo a; (suspect) temerse; **to — for** temer por

fearful [fírfəl] ADJ (causing fear) terrible, espantoso; (showing fear) temeroso, miedoso, medroso

fearless [fírlɪs] ADJ intrépido

fearlessness [fírlɪsnɪs] N intrepidez *f*

feasible [fízəbəl] ADJ factible

feast [fist] N (party, religious celebration)

fiesta *f*; (abundant meal) festín *m*,
banquete *m*; VI **to — on** darse un festín
de; **to — one's eyes on** deleitarse la vista
con

feat [fit] N (heroic act) hazaña *f*; (trick) logro
m

feather [féðɚ] N pluma *f*; **a — in one's cap**
un triunfo personal; **—weight** peso
pluma *m*; **birds of a — flock together**
Dios los cría y ellos se juntan; VI/VT (grow
feathers, cover with feathers) emplumar;
(change blade angle) poner horizontal

feature [fítʃɚ] N (characteristic) aspecto *m*,
característica *f*; (newspaper article)
reportaje *m*; (facial) facción *f*, fisonomía *f*,
rasgo *m*; **— article** artículo principal *m*;
— film largometraje *m*; VT (give
prominence to) destacar; (depict) mostrar;
this film —s John Smith esta película
cuenta con la actuación de John Smith; **—
that!** ¡imagínate! VI figurar

February [fébjueri] N febrero *m*

feces [físiz] N PL heces *f pl*

federal [féðɚəł] ADJ federal

federation [fɛɖəréʃən] N federación *f*

fee [fi] N (professional) honorarios *m pl*;
(artist) cachet *m*; (admission) derecho de
admisión *m*; **—s** (university) matrícula *f*

feeble [fíbəł] ADJ (person) débil, endeble;
(sound, light) tenue; **—-minded**
(retarded) *pej* retrasado; (stupid) tonto

feed [fid] VI/VT (supply with food, materials)
alimentar(se); (prompt lines) apuntar;
(broadcast) transmitir; **he —s sugar
cubes to his horse** le da terrones de
azúcar a su caballo; **I fed him a lie** le
dije una mentira; **to be fed up** estar
harto, estar hasta la coronilla; VI **—
into** desembocar en; **—back**
retroalimentación *f*; (response) respuesta *f*,
reacción *f*; **—ing frenzy** (of the press)
escándalo periodístico *m*; (of sharks, etc.)
carnicería *f*; N (fodder) pienso *m*, cebo *m*;
(transmission) transmisión *f*

feel [fił] VI/VT (perceive, experience)
sentir(se); (examine with the hands)
palpar, manosear; (suffer) sufrir; (have an
opinion) creer; VI (grope, check out)
tantear; (seem) parecer; **to — one's way**
tantear el camino, andar a tientas; **I —
for you** te compadezco; **to — up/off**
toquetear, manosear; **it —s soft** está
suave al tacto; **I — like a coffee** tengo
ganas de tomar un café; **to — up to
something** sentirse capaz de algo; N
(feeling) sensación *f*; (sense) tacto *m*;
(ability) don *m*; (groping) manoseo *m*,

toqueteo *m*

feeler [fílɚ] N (of insects) antena *f*; (of snails)
cuerno *m*; (person who feels) persona
emotiva *f*; **to put out —s** tantear el
terreno

feeling [fíłɪŋ] N (sense of touch) tacto *m*;
(instance of physical perception) sensación
f; (emotion) sentimiento *m*; (opinion)
opinión *f*; (compassion) compasión *f*; **a —
of sadness** un sentimiento de tristeza;
with — con sentimiento; **to hurt
someone's —s** herirle los sentimientos a
alguien; ADJ sensible

feign [fen] VI/VT fingir, simular, aparentar

feisty [fáisti] ADJ (aggressive) pugnaz,
belicoso; (energetic) vivaz

feline [fílaɪn] ADJ felino

fell [fɛł] VT (an animal) derribar; (a tree) talar;
N (pelt) piel de animal *f*; **in one —
swoop** de un golpe

fellow [félo] N (member) miembro *m*;
(scholar) becario -ria *mf*; (man or boy) tipo
m; **— citizen** conciudadano -na *mf*; **—
man** prójimo *m*; **— student** compañero
-ra de clase *mf*

fellowship [féloʃip] N (friendly relations)
amistad *f*; (community of interest)
confraternidad *f*; (scholarship) beca *f*

felony [féłəni] N delito grave *m*

felt [fɛłt] N fieltro *m*; ADJ de fieltro

female [fímeł] N (animal) hembra *f*; (person)
mujer *f*; ADJ (animal, fastener) hembra;
(person) femenino

feminine [fémənɪn] ADJ femenino

femininity [fémənínɪti] N feminidad *f*

feminism [fémənɪzəm] N feminismo *m*

femur [fímɚ] N fémur *m*

fence [fɛns] N (barrier) cerca *f*, cerco *m*, valla
f; (person who deals in stolen goods)
vendedor -ra de artículos robados *mf*;
(store for stolen goods) tienda de artículos
robados *f*; **to be sitting on the —** estar
indeciso; VT (enclose) cercar, vallar; **to —
in** cercar; **to — off** dividir con una cerca;
VI (sport) practicar esgrima

fencing [fénsɪŋ] N (barrier) cerca *f*; (sport)
esgrima *f*

fender [féndɚ] N guardabarro(s) *m*,
guardafango *m*; **— bender** choquecito *m*

ferment [fɚˈment] N fermento *m*; [fɚˈmént]
VI/VT fermentar(se)

fermentation [fɚmentéʃən] N fermentación
f

fern [fɚn] N helecho *m*

ferocious [fəróʃəs] ADJ feroz, fiero

ferocity [fərásɪdi] N ferocidad *f*, fiereza *f*

ferret [férɪt] N hurón *m*; VI **to — out**

huronear

Ferris wheel [férɪshwiɫ] N rueda gigante *f*

ferry [féri] N ferry *m*; **— boat** ferry *m*; VT transportar de una orilla a otra; VI viajar en ferry

fertile [fɝ́dl] ADJ fértil, fecundo

fertility [fɝtíliɾi] N fertilidad *f*

fertilize [fɝ́dlaɪz] VT fertilizar; (female, egg) fecundar; (land) abonar

fertilizer [fɝ́dlaɪzɚ] N fertilizante *m*, abono *m*

fervent [fɝ́vənt] ADJ ferviente

fervor [fɝ́vɚ] N fervor *m*

fester [féstɚ] VI (form pus) supurar; (rankle) enconarse

festival [féstəvəɫ] N festival *m*

festive [féstɪv] ADJ festivo

festivity [festívɪɾi] N festividad *f*

fetal [fidl] ADJ fetal; **— position** posición fetal *f*

fetch [fetʃ] VT *Sp* ir a por; *Am* ir a buscar; **the ring —ed a fancy price** nos dieron una buena suma por el anillo; VI/VT (dog) buscar

fetish [fédɪʃ] N fetiche *m*

fetter [fédɚ] N grillete *m*; VT engrillar

fetus [fíɾəs] N feto *m*

feud [fjud] N enemistad hereditaria *f*; VI pelear

feudal [fjúdl] ADJ feudal

fever [fívɚ] N fiebre *f*, calentura *f*; **— pitch** punto álgido *m*

feverish [fívɚɪʃ] ADJ (related to fever) febril; (having a fever) afiebrado, destemplado

few [fju] ADJ & PRON pocos; **a —** unos pocos, algunos; **the —** una minoría

fiancé [fiɑnsé] N novio *m*, prometido *m*; **—e** novia *f*, prometida *f*

fiasco [fiǽsko] N fiasco *m*

fib [fɪb] N mentirilla *f*; VI decir mentirillas

fiber [fáɪbɚ] N (textile) fibra *f*; (animal, vegetable) hebra *f*; **—-optic** de fibra óptica; **—glass** fibra de vidrio *f*

fibrous [fáɪbrəs] ADJ fibroso

fickle [fíkəɫ] ADJ veleidoso, mudable

fiction [fíkʃən] N ficción *f*

fictional [fíkʃənəɫ] ADJ novelesco

fictitious [fɪktíʃəs] ADJ ficticio

fiddle [fídl] N violín *m*; VI (play the violin) tocar el violín; **to — around** perder el tiempo; **to — with** juguetear con; **stop fiddling with the computer** deja de juguetear con la computadora

fidelity [fɪdélɪɾi] N fidelidad *f*; **high —** alta fidelidad *f*

fidget [fídʒɪt] VI estar inquieto; **stop —ing!** ¡deja de moverte!

fiduciary [fɪdúʃieri] ADJ & N fiduciario -ria *mf*

field [fiɫd] N (land) campo *m* (also in computers, heraldry, optics); (in sports) campo *m*; *Am* cancha *f*; (of oil) yacimiento *m*; (group of competitors) participantes *mf pl*; (of knowledge) campo *m*, terreno *m*; **— artillery** artillería de campaña *f*; **— day** (day for outdoor activity) día de campo *m*; (for military maneuvers) día de maniobras *m*; (unrestrained enjoyment) festín *m*; **— glasses** binoculares *m pl*; **— mouse** ratón de campo *m*; **— trip** (in school) paseo escolar *m*; (in science) viaje de estudio *m*; **—work** trabajo de campo *m*; VT (catch) atrapar; (answer) contestar

fiend [find] N (devil) demonio *m*, diablo *m*; (fanatic) fanático -ca *mf*

fierce [firs] ADJ (animals) feroz, fiero; (illness) espantoso; (storms, etc.) furioso, espantoso; (competition, debate) intenso, encarnizado; (a look) torvo

fierceness [fírsnɪs] N ferocidad *f*, bravura *f*

fiery [fáɪəri] ADJ (passionate) fogoso; (hot, causing burning sensation) ardiente

fife [faɪf] N pífano *m*

fifteen [fɪftín] NUM quince

fifth [fɪfθ] ADJ & N quinto *m*; (measure of liquor) tres cuartos de un litro *m pl*

fifty [fɪfti] NUM cincuenta; **to go —— on something** ir a medias; **a —— chance** un cincuenta por ciento de probabilidades

fig [fɪg] N higo *m*; **— leaf** hoja de higuera *f*; **— tree** higuera *f*; **it's not worth a —** no vale ni un pepino / pito

fight [faɪt] N (combat) lucha *f*, pelea *f*; **the — against AIDS** la lucha contra el SIDA; (argument) pelea *f*, riña *f*; VI/VT (combat) luchar (con), pelear (con); VI (argue) pelear, reñir; **to — a duel** batirse a duelo; **to — back** (to hold back) contener; (resist) resistir; **to — it out** arreglarlo a los golpes; **to — off** rechazar; **to — one's way through** abrirse camino a la fuerza

fighter [fáɪɾɚ] N (boxer) boxeador -ra *mf*; (someone who fights) luchador -ra *mf*; (dog, cock) animal de pelea / riña *m*; **— airplane** avión caza *m*

fighting [fáɪɾɪŋ] N (fight) lucha *f*; ADJ combativo; **— chance** posibilidad remota *f*; **— words** palabras incendiarias *f pl*

figurative [fígjəɚdɪv] ADJ (art) figurativo; (language) figurado

figure [fígjɚ] N (number, amount) cifra *f*; (form, bodily shape, representation, dance move, syllogism) figura *f*; (character) personaje *m*; **—head** figurón de proa *m*;

— **of speech** figura retórica *f*; —**s** (written symbols) números *m pl*; — **skating** patinaje artístico *m*; **to be good at** —**s** ser bueno con los números; **to cut a poor** — dar una mala impresión; VI (appear) figurar; VI/VT (think) imaginar(se), figurar(se); **to** — **in** tener en cuenta; **to** — **on** contar con; **to** — **out** (solve) resolver; (calculate) calcular; **it** —**s!** no me extraña, era de esperar; VT calcular

Fijian [fíʤiən] N fijiano -na *mf*

Fiji Islands [fíʤiáiləndz] N Islas Fiji *f pl*

filament [fíləmənt] N filamento *m*

file [faɪł] N (documents) archivo *m*; (for computers) archivo *m*, fichero *m*; (official report) expediente *m*, legajo *m*; (line) fila *f*; (tool) lima *f*; —**name** nombre de archivo *m*; — **server** servidor *m*; **filing cabinet** fichero *m*, archivador *m*; VT (papers) archivar; (news story) entregar; (tax return, claim, etc.) presentar; **to** — **a suit** entablar una demanda, querellarse; VI (for a job) presentarse; (walk in a line) desfilar; VI/VT (smooth) limar

filial [fíliəł] ADJ filial

filibuster [fíləbʌstɚ] VI/VT practicar obstrucción parlamentaria; N filibusterismo *m*, obstrucción *f*

filigree [fíligri] N filigrana *f*

fill [fɪł] VI/VT (glass, container) llenar(se); (a hole, a pastry, land) rellenar; **the smell** —**ed the room** la habitación se llenó del olor; **the airline** —**ed the position** la compañía aérea llenó el cargo; **the new employee** —**ed the vacancy** el nuevo empleado ocupó el cargo vacante; VT (a tooth) empastar; (prescription, order) despachar; (a need) satisfacer; VI (sails) hinchar; **to** — **out** llenar; **to** — **in** (inform) informar; (fill out) llenar; (replace) sustituir; **to** — **up** llenarse hasta el tope

fillet [fílé] N filete *m*; VT filetear; [fílɪt] N cinta *f*; (on a book) filete *m*

filling [fílɪŋ] N (act) rellenado *m*; (filler) relleno *m*; (of a tooth) empaste *m*; — **station** estación de servicio *f*, gasolinera *f*

filly [fíli] N potranca *f*

film [fɪłm] N película *f* (also thin coating); (material) película *f*, cinta *f*; — **industry** industria cinematográfica *f*; VI/VT filmar, cinematografiar

filter [fíltɚ] N filtro *m*; VI/VT filtrar(se)

filth [fɪłθ] N (dirt, despicable person) mugre *f*, suciedad *f*; (moral impurity) porquería *f*; (vulgar material) obscenidades *f pl*

filthiness [fíłθinɪs] N suciedad *f*

filthy [fíłθi] ADJ (dirty) cochino, mugriento; (obscene, vile) puerco, cochino; *Sp* guarro; — **rich** riquísimo

filtration [fɪłtréʃən] N filtración *f*

fin [fɪn] N aleta *f*

final [fáɪnəł] ADJ (result, conclusion) final; (last) último; (conclusive) definitivo; N (in sports) final *f*; (exam) examen final *m*

finalist [fáɪnəlɪst] N finalista *mf*

finalize [fáɪnəlaɪz] VT completar, ultimar

finance [fáɪnæns] N finanza *f*; —**s** finanzas *f pl*; VI/VT (to fund) financiar; (to purchase on credit) comprar financiado

financial [fɪnǽnʃəł] ADJ financiero

financier [fɪnænsír] N financiero -ra *mf*

financing [fáɪnænsɪŋ] N financiamiento *m*; *Am* financiación *f*

find [faɪnd] VT hallar, encontrar; (discover) descubrir; (determine innocence or guilt) declarar; VI (determine officially) fallar; **to** — **fault with** criticar a, censurar a; **to** — **out** (discover) descubrir; (verify) averiguar; N hallazgo *m*

finding [fáɪndɪŋ] N fallo *m*; —**s** resultados *m pl*

fine [faɪn] ADJ (wine, sand, hair, precious metal) fino; (thread) delgado; (cloth) delicado; (artist, athlete) consumado; (manners) refinado; (good-looking) atractivo, guapo; (weather) bueno; (distinction) sutil; — **arts** bellas artes *f pl*; — **print** letra pequeña *f*, letra chica *f*; **to** —**tune** (a receiver) sintonizar; (an engine) ajustar; (a plan) afinar; **I'm** — estoy bien; **to feel** — sentirse muy bien de salud; **to have a** — **time** pasarlo bien; N multa *f*; VT multar

finery [fáɪnəri] N galas *f pl*

finesse [fɪnés] N (subtlety) sutileza *f*; (tact) diplomacia *f*; VI usar artimañas; VT conseguir por artimañas

finger [fíŋgɚ] N dedo *m*; —**food** canapé *m*, aperitivo *m*; —**nail** uña *f*; —**print** huella dactilar/ digital *f*; —**tip** punta del dedo *f*; **at one's** —**tips** al alcance de la mano; **little** — dedo meñique *m*; **middle** — dedo del corazón *m*; VI/VT toquetear, manosear; VT (guitar) tañer; (squeal on) delatar; **to give someone the** — hacerle un gesto obsceno a alguien; **I'll keep my** —**s crossed** cruzo los dedos; **to wrap someone around one's** — meterse a alguien en el bolsillo; **I can't put my** — **on it** no se me ocurre una solución

finicky [fíniki] ADJ melindroso, dengoso

finish [fíniʃ] VI/VT (end) terminar(se), finalizar(se); VT (polish) pulir; (varnish)

barnizar; (kill) liquidar; — **line** meta *f*; **to
— off** acabar con, rematar; **to — up**
terminar; N (ending) final *m*; (decisive
end) fin *m*; (polish, treatment) acabado *m*;
(varnish) barniz *m*; (coat of paint) última
mano *f*; **with a rough** — sin pulir
finished [fíniʃt] ADJ (doomed) acabado;
(polished) pulido
finite [fáɪnaɪt] ADJ finito
Finland [fɪnlənd] N Finlandia *f*
Finn [fɪn] N finlandés -esa *mf*, finés -esa *mf*
Finnish [fíniʃ] ADJ finlandés, finés
fir [fɜ·] N abeto *m*
fire [faɪr] N (flame) fuego *m*; (conflagration)
incendio *m*; (passion) ardor *m*; (for
cigarettes, hearths) lumbre *f*; — **alarm**
alarma contra incendios *f*; —**cracker**
triquitraque *m*; — **drill** simulacro de
incendio *m*; — **department** cuerpo de
bomberos *m*; — **engine** coche de
bomberos *m*, autobomba *f*; — **escape**
escalera de incendios *f*; — **extinguisher**
extinguidor (de incendios) *m*, extintor *m*;
—**fly** luciérnaga *f*; — **hydrant** boca de
incendio *f*; — **insurance** seguro contra
incendios *m*; —**man** (who extinguishes)
bombero *m*; (stoker) fogonero *m*; —**place**
hogar *m*, chimenea *f*; —**proof**
ininflamable, a prueba de incendio; **to
—proof** hacer incombustible, ignifugar;
—**side** hogar *m*; — **station** estación de
bomberos *f*; — **trap** edificio sin medios de
escape en caso de incendio *m*; —**wood**
leña *f*; —**works** fuegos artificiales *m pl*;
**when he finds out, there will be
—works** cuando se entere, se va a armar
la gorda; **to be on** — estar quemándose;
to catch — incendiarse, prenderse fuego;
to set — **to** prender fuego a, incendiar;
under — bajo fuego; **to play with** —
jugar con fuego; **firing pin** percutor *m*;
firing squad pelotón de fusilamiento *m*;
VT (pottery) cocer; (an employee) despedir;
(a projectile) lanzar; VI/VT (a gun) disparar;
VI **to — off** (gun)
disparar; (letter) despachar
firm [fɜ·m] ADJ (solid, unwavering) firme;
(fixed) fijo; (not fluctuating, as prices)
estable; VI/VT **to — up** (finalize) concretar;
(harden) endurecer; N firma *f*
firmness [fɜ·mnɪs] N firmeza *f*
first [fɜ·st] ADJ primero; — **aid** primeros
auxilios *m pl*; — **base** primera base *f*; **to
get to** — **base** comenzar con éxito;
—**born** primogénito -ta *mf*; — **chapter**
capítulo primero *m*, primer capítulo *m*; —
class primera clase *f*; —**-class** de primera

clase; — **cousin** primo hermano;
—**degree** (burn) de primer grado;
(murder) en primer grado; — **floor**
(ground floor) planta baja *f*; **for the —
time** por primera vez; —**hand** de
primera mano; — **lady** primera dama *f*;
— **name** nombre de pila *m*; — **person**
primera persona *f*; —**-rate** de primera
clase; ADV (before anything else) primero;
I'd die — antes la muerte; **at** — al
principio; — **off** al principio; N (first in
series) primero -ra *mf*; (low gear) primera *f*
fiscal [fískəl] ADJ fiscal; — **period** año fiscal
m
fish [fɪʃ] N (in water) pez *m*; (out of water)
pescado *m*; —**hook** anzuelo *m*; —
market pescadería *f*; — **story** patraña *f*;
like a — out of water como sapo de
otro pozo; **neither — nor fowl** ni
chicha ni limonada; **I have other — to
fry** tengo otras cosas mejores que hacer;
VI/VT pescar; **to — out** sacar, rebuscar; **to
— for compliments** buscar cumplidos;
to —tail colear
fisherman [fíʃə·mən] N pescador *m*
fishery [fíʃəri] N (for breeding) piscifactoría *f*;
(for fishing) pesquería *f*; (industry)
industria pesquera *f*
fishing [fíʃɪŋ] N pesca *f*; — **pole / rod** caña
de pescar *f*; — **tackle** aparejos de pescar
m pl; **to go** — ir de pesca
fishy [fíʃi] ADJ (of smell, taste) a pescado;
(suspicious) sospechoso
fissure [fíʃə·] N fisura *f*
fist [fɪst] N puño *m*; —**fight** pelea a
puñetazos *f*
fit [fɪt] ADJ (suited) apto; (healthy) en buen
estado físico; **are you — for driving?**
¿estás en condiciones de manejar? **he was
— to be tied** estaba que trincha; **he
didn't see — to greet her** no se le
antojó saludarla; N (process of fitting)
prueba *f*; (mechanical union) encaje *m*;
(attack of a disease) ataque *m*; (sudden
outburst) rapto *m*; (of anger, coughing)
acceso *m*; **to throw a** — tener una
pataleta; **by —s and starts** a
trompicones; **that suit is a good** — ese
traje le queda bien; VT (be suitable for)
adecuarse a; (be in agreement with)
cuadrar con, ajustarse a; (measure for
clothes) tomarle las medidas a; (make
suitable) capacitar, preparar; **to — in
with** acomodarse a; **I tried to — you in**
traté de incluirte; VI (conform to contours
of a person) quedarle bien a alguien;
(conform to the contours of a mechanism)

encajar

fitness [fítnıs] N (suitability) aptitud *f*; (health) buen estado físico *m*

fitting [fídɪŋ] ADJ apropiado; N ajuste *m*; (trying on) prueba *f*

five [faɪv] NUM cinco

fix [fıks] VT (repair, arrange) arreglar, aviar; **he —ed his eyes on me** me miró fijamente; (place permanently, determine) fijar; (prepare food) preparar; **to — up** arreglar, aviar; **to get an animal —ed** castrar a un animal; **I was —ing to call** estaba a punto de llamar; **I'll — you!** ¡ya te arreglo! N (predicament) apuro *m*, aprieto *m*; (temporary repair) arreglo provisorio *m*; (narcotic injection) chute *m*; **to get a — on** localizar

fixed [fıkst] ADJ (stationary) fijo; (arranged in advance) arreglado

fixture [fıkstʃə-] N (thing) artefacto *m*; **she's a permanent — in this office** está siempre en la oficina

fizzle [fízəl] VI (fail) fracasar; **to — (out)** (make a noise) apagarse chisporroteando

flabby [fǽbi] ADJ flácido

flag [flæg] N bandera *f*; **—pole** mástil *m*; **—staff** mástil *m*; **—stone** losa *f*, baldosa *f*; VT (adorn with flags) embanderar; (mark) marcar con banderas; **to — (down)** hacer parar; VI (diminish) menguar

flagrant [flégrənt] ADV flagrante

flair [flɛr] N (aptitude) aptitud *f*, facilidad *f*; (style) estilo *m*

flak [flæk] N (anti-artillery fire) fuego antiaéreo *m*; (criticism) crítica *f*

flake [flek] N (snow) copo *m*; (small thin piece) escama *f*; (eccentric person) chiflado -da *mf*; VI descascararse

flamboyant [flæmbɔ́ıənt] ADJ (clothes) llamativo; (behavior) extravagante

flame [flem] N llama *f*; **— thrower** lanzallamas *m sg*; **old —** viejo amor *m*; VI llamear, flamear, encenderse

flaming [flémıŋ] ADJ (emitting flames) llameante; (like a flame) flamígero; (ardent) ardiente; **— red** rojo encendido

flammable [flǽməbəl] ADJ inflamable

flank [flæŋk] N (of a bastion or army) flanco *m*; (of an animal) ijar *m*; VT flanquear

flannel [flǽnəl] N franela *f*, lanilla *f*

flap [flæp] VI (wings) aletear; (flag) flamear; VT (wings) batir; (arms) sacudir; N (of a jacket, pocket) cartera *f*; (of a saddle, table) hoja *f*; (of an airplane) alerón *m*; (action of flapping) aleteo *m*

flare [flɛr] VI (burn unsteadily) llamear; (skirt)

ensancharse; **to — up** (fire) avivarse; (activity) recrudecer; **the illness —d up** recudeció la enfermedad; VT (a skirt) levantar; (a flame) avivar; (a pipe) abocinar; (signal by flare) señalar con bengala; N (flaring light, burst of flame) llamarada *f*; (signal light) bengala *f*; (sudden emotional outburst) arranque *m*; (outward curvature) vuelo *m*; **—up** recrudecimiento *m*

flash [flæʃ] N (of light) destello *m*, ráfaga *f*; (of explosion) fogonazo *m*; (news, camera, vision) flash *m*; **— of hope** rayo de esperanza *m*; **— of lightning** relampagueo *m*, rayo *m*; **in a —** en un instante; VI/VT (shine) destellar (sobre); (expose) exhibir(se); VI (gleam) relucir, fulgurar, relampaguear; (appear) aparecer; VT (display) ostentar; **—back** flashback *m*, escena retrospectiva *f*; **—bulb** flash *m*; **— flood** riada *f*; **—light** linterna *f*; **to — by** pasar como un relámpago

flashing [flǽʃıŋ] ADJ destellante

flashy [flǽʃi] ADJ (colorful) llamativo; (ostentatious) ostentoso; (tasteless) *Am* charro

flask [flæsk] N (glass container) frasco *m*; (in a laboratory) matraz *m*, redoma *f*; (for alcoholic beverages) petaca *f*

flat [flæt] ADJ (of surfaces) plano; (of land) llano; (smooth) liso; (horizontal) horizontal, acostado; (flattened) arrasado, aplastado; (of shoes, nose) chato; (deflated) desinflado, pinchado; (dull of color) apagado; (without effervescence) sin gas; (lifeless) soso; (without gloss) mate; (absolute) terminante; (of a photo) sin contraste; (of a painting) sin volumen; (too low in pitch) demasiado grave; (of a musical note) bemol; **—footed** con pie plano; **— rate** tarifa fija *f*; **trading was — hubo poco movimiento económico; to be — broke** estar completamente pelado; **to fall —** (of a body) caer de plano / redondo; (of a joke) caer mal; (of a plan) fracasar; N (shoe) zapato sin tacón *m*; (flat tire) desinflado *m*, pinchadura *f*, pinchazo *m*; (wooden box) caja para plantas *f*; (musical note) bemol *m*; **—iron** plancha *f*; ADV **—out** (directly) absolutamente; (at full speed) a toda velocidad; **in two minutes —** en dos minutos exactos

flatten [flǽtn̩] VI/VT (make flat) achatar(se), aplanar(se); VT (knock down) tumbar, voltear; (raze) arrasar

flatter [flǽdə-] VI/VT lisonjear, adular, halagar; **this picture —s you** esta foto te favorece; **I was —ed by his attentions** me halagaron sus atenciones

flatterer [flǽɒərɚ] N lisonjero -ra *mf*, adulador -ora *mf*

flattering [flǽɒərɪŋ] ADJ (comment) lisonjero, halagüeño; (person) adulón

flattery [flǽɒəri] N lisonja *f*, adulación *f*, halago *m*

flatulence [flǽtʃələns] N flatulencia *f*

flaunt [flɔnt] VI/VT ostentar, lucir(se)

flavor [flévɚ] N (taste, quality) sabor *m*; (flavoring) condimento *m*; VT sazonar

flavorless [flévɚlɪs] ADJ insípido

flaw [flɔ] N (in character, in construction) defecto *m*; (in an argument) falla *f*

flawless [flɔlɪs] ADJ (logic) impecable; (behavior) intachable, irreprochable; (appearance) perfecto

flax [flæks] N lino *m*

flea [fli] N pulga *f*; **— collar** collar antipulgas *m*; **— market** *Sp* rastro *m*; *Am* mercado de (las) pulgas *m*

flee [fli] VI huir; VT huir de

fleece [flis] N vellón *m*; VT (shear) trasquilar, esquilar; (defraud) estafar; (in card games) pelar, desplumar

fleet [flit] N (of boats, buses) flota *f*; (of cars) parque *m*; ADJ veloz

fleeting [flíɒɪŋ] ADJ fugaz, efímero, pasajero

Flemish [flémɪʃ] ADJ & N flamenco -ca *mf*

flesh [fleʃ] N carne *f*; (of a fruit) pulpa *f*; **— and blood** carne y hueso; **of my own — and blood** de mi propria sangre; **in the —** en persona; VI/VT **to — out** (a character) dar cuerpo a; (an argument) desarrollar

fleshy [fléʃi] ADJ (succulent) carnoso; (fat) metido en carnes

flexibility [fleksəbíliɒi] N flexibilidad *f*

flexible [fléksəbəl] ADJ flexible

flicker [flíkɚ] VI (stars) titilar; (candle) parpadear; (of wings, etc.) temblar; N (of light) parpadeo *m*, titilación *f*; (of hope) rayo *m*

flier [flái ɚ] N (one who flies) volador -ra *mf*; (aviator) aviador -ra *mf*; (leaflet) volante *m*

flight [flaɪt] N (act of flying, trip) vuelo *m*; (trajectory) trayectoria *f*; (flock of birds) bandada *f*; (group of military aircraft) escuadrilla *f*; (escape) fuga *f*, huida *f*; **— attendant** azafata -ta *mf*; **— plan** plan de vuelo *m*; **— school** escuela de aviación *f*; **a — of fancy** una fantasía; **— of stairs** tramo de escalera *m*; **to put to —** poner en fuga; **to take —** darse a la fuga

flimsy [flímzi] ADJ (structure, argument) endeble; (excuse) flojo, pobre

flinch [flɪntʃ] VI pestañear

fling [flɪŋ] VT (a coin) tirar, lanzar; **she flung herself at the attacker** se le tiró arriba al atacante; **he flung himself into his work** se dedicó de lleno a su trabajo; **he flung open the door** abrió la puerta de golpe; N (act of flinging) lanzamiento *m*; (sexual affair) aventura *f*; **he had a — at selling cars** intentó vender coches

flint [flɪnt] N pedernal *m*

flip [flɪp] VT (a coin) tirar; (a switch) (up) levantar, (down) bajar; (a pancake) dar vuelta; VI (head over heels) dar una voltereta; (get excited, go crazy) volverse loco; **to — through** hojear; **—-flop** (reversal of opinion) giro de 180 grados *m*; (backward somersault) voltereta para atrás *f*; (slipper) chancleta *f*; **— side** la otra cara de la moneda

flippant [flípənt] ADJ (frivolous) frívolo, displicente; (impudent) impertinente

flipper [flípɚ] N aleta *f*

flirt [flɚt] VI coquetear; N coqueto -ta *mf*

flirtation [flɚtéʃən] N coquetería *f*, coqueteo *m*

flit [flɪt] VI revolotear; **a smile —s across her face** una sonrisa le cruza la cara

float [flot] VI (rest on water, air, etc., fluctuate freely) flotar; (in soup) sobrenadar; (drift) errar, ir a la deriva; **she —ed down the stairs** se deslizó por la escalera; VT (set afloat) poner a flote; (start a company, scheme) lanzar; (emit shares) emitir; (let fluctuate) dejar flotar; (try out an idea) proponer; N (thing that floats) flotador *m*; (on a line) corcho *m*, boya *f*; (in a parade) carro alegórico *m*, carroza *f*; (with soda) gaseosa con helado *f*

flock [flak] N (birds, children) bandada *f*; (sheep) rebaño *m*; (worshipers) grey *f*; (people) muchedumbre *f*; VI acudir en masa, afluir; **to — around someone** rodear a alguien; **to — together** andar juntos

flog [flɑg] VT azotar

flood [flʌd] N inundación *f*; **— of tears** torrente de lágrimas *m*; **the —** El Diluvio Universal; (of tides) creciente *f*; **—gate** (of a dam) compuerta *f*; (of a canal lock) esclusa *f*; **—light** reflector *m*; VI/VT inundar(se), anegar(se); (car) ahogar(se), emborrachar(se)

floor [flɔr] N (surface of a room, vehicle) suelo *m*, piso *m*; (story) piso *m*; (of sea) fondo *m*; (dance) pista *f*; (minimum level) mínimo *m*; **to have the —** tener la palabra; VT (topple over) tumbar, derribar;

(stun, surprise) asombrar; — **it!** ¡acelera! *Sp* ¡mete caña!

flop [flɑp] VI (flail) zarandearse; (fish) dar coletazos; (drop) dejarse caer; (fail) fracasar; **to — down** dejarse caer, desplomarse; **to — over** voltear(se) flojamente; N (failure) fracaso *m*; (sound) ruido sordo *m*

floppy [flɑpi] ADJ caído; **— disk** disquete *m*, floppy *m*

florist [flɔrɪst] N florista *mf*; **—'s (shop)** florería *f*

floss [flɔs] N (silk) seda floja *f*; (for embroidery) hilo de seda *m*; (dental) hilo dental *m*; VI/VT pasar hilo dental (por)

flounder [flɑʊndɚ] VI (in mud, etc.) andar/moverse con dificultades; (for an answer) quedarse sin saber qué decir, perder pie; N platija *f*

flour [flaʊr] N harina *f*

flourish [flɝɪʃ] VI (prosper) florecer, prosperar; VT (brandish) blandir; N (ornament, florid language, brandishing) floreo *m*; (of music) floritura *f*; (of a signature) rúbrica *f*; **in full —** en plena eclosión

flow [flo] VI (run) fluir, correr; (issue forth) surgir, brotar; (come and go) circular; (fall loosely) caer; (abound) abundar; (rise) crecer; **to — into** desembocar en, afluir a; N (liquid) flujo *m*; (electricity) corriente *f*; (of traffic, blood, air) circulación *f*; **—chart** diagrama de flujo *m*; **— of words** torrente de palabras *m*

flower [flɑʊɚ] N flor *f*; (paragon) flor y nata *f*; **in —** en flor; **— bed** *Mex, Sp* arriate *m*; *RP* cantero *m*; **—pot** maceta *f*, tiesto *m*; **— vase** florero *m*; VI florecer

flowery [flɑʊɚri] ADJ (of a garden, language) florido; (of a pattern) floreado; (of a fragrance) floral

flowing [floɪŋ] ADJ (liquid) fluyente; (clothing) suelto

flu [flu] N gripe *f*

fluctuate [flʌktʃuet] VI fluctuar

fluctuation [flʌktʃuéʃən] N fluctuación *f*

fluency [flúənsi] N fluidez *f*

fluent [flúənt] ADJ fluido; **he is — in French** habla francés con fluidez/soltura

fluff [flʌf] VT mullir; (blunder) pifiar; N pelusa *f*; (blunder) pifia *f*; **this book is pure —** este libro es insustancial

fluffy [flʌfi] ADJ (airy) mullido; (covered with fluff) peludo

fluid [flúɪd] ADJ & N fluido *m*; **— ounce** onza líquida (29,42 mililitros) *f*

fluke [fluk] N (of whale) aleta *f*; (chance)

chiripa *f*; **by a —** por chiripa

flunk [flʌŋk] VI/VT reprobar, suspender; VI **to — out** abandonar

flunky [flʌŋki] N (lackey, servant) lacayo *m*; (yes-man) adulón *m*

fluorescent [flurésənt] ADJ fluorescente; **— light** tubo fluorescente *m*

fluoride [flɔraɪd] N (chemical) fluoruro *m*; (dental aid) flúor *m*

fluorine [flɔrin] N flúor *m*

flurry [flɝi] N (of snow) nevisca *f*; (of activity) frenesí *m*

flush [flʌʃ] N (rosy glow, heat) rubor *m*; (of anger) arranque *m*; (of youth, color) resplandor *m*; (of embarrassment) sonrojo *m*; (in poker) color *m*; **did you hear the — of the toilet?** ¿oíste el sonido de la cisterna? ADJ (well supplied, rich) forrado; (ruddy, reddish) rubicundo; (full) rebosante; **— with** a(l) ras de; **— against** pegado a; VI/VT (make or turn red) sonrojar(se), ruborizar(se); (activate toilet) tirar la cadena; (rinse) baldear; VT **to — out** levantar

fluster [flʌstɚ] VI/VT agitar(se), poner(se) nervioso

flute [flut] N (musical instrument) flauta *f*; (of a column) estría *f*; VT estriar

flutter [flʌdɚ] VI (wings) aletear; (butterfly) revolotear; (flag) tremolar; (heart) palpitar; VT (agitate) agitar; N (of wings) aleteo *m*; (of excitement) agitación *f*; (of a fly) tremolar *m*; (of the heart) palpitación *f*

flux [flʌks] N flujo *m*; **a state of —** un estado de cambio continuo

fly [flaɪ] VI (through air) volar; (from danger) huir; (flag) ondear; (kite) remontar; VT (aircraft) pilotar; (air cargo) transportar en avión; **to — at** abalanzarse sobre; **to — away** volarse; **to — into a rage** montar en cólera; **to — off the handle** perder los estribos; **to — open (shut)** abrirse (cerrarse) de un golpe; **to — out of a room** salir disparado de un cuarto; **that idea won't —** esa idea no va a ser aceptada; **he flew the coop** se escapó; N (insect) mosca *f*; (over a zipper) bragueta *f*; **—catcher** papamoscas *m sg*; **—leaf** solapa *f*; **—swatter** matamoscas *m sg*; **—wheel** volante *m*; **on the —** al vuelo

flying [flaɪŋ] ADJ (passing through the air) volador; (fluttering) ondeante; **with — colors** con distinción; **— saucer** platillo volador *m*; **I hate —** no me gusta viajar en avión

foam [fom] N (suds, padding) espuma *f*; **— rubber** goma espuma *f*; VI hacer espuma;

to — at the mouth echar espuma por la boca

focus [fókəs] N foco *m*; VI/VT (bring into or be in focus) enfocar(se); (concentrate) centrarse; **to — on** fijarse en

fodder [fádə-] N forraje *m*

foe [fo] N enemigo -ga *mf*

fog [fɑg] N niebla *f*; **to be in a —** estar confundido; **—horn** sirena de niebla *f*; VI/VT (confuse) ofuscar; (spray with insecticide) fumigar; (film) velar(se); **to — up** (window) empañar(se); (one's sight) nublar(se); **the airport was —ged in** el aeropuerto estaba cerrado por niebla

foggy [fági] ADJ (weather) brumoso, nebuloso; (window) empañado; (confused) confuso; (blurred, as a photograph) velado

foil [fɔɪl] N (any metal) hoja de metal *f*; (aluminum) papel de aluminio *m*; (on mirrors) azogue *m*; (rapier) florete *m*; (thing contrasted) contraste *m*; VT frustrar

fold [foɪd] VI/VT (sheets) doblar(se); (paper, folding chairs) plegar(se); (wings, flag) replegar(se); (in cards) abandonar; (close a business) cerrar(se); (performance) bajar de cartel; **to — in** (in cooking) incorporar; **to — one's arms** cruzarse de brazos; N (pleat, hollow) pliegue *m*; (crease) doblez *m*; (enclosure) redil *m*, aprisco *m*; (sheep) rebaño *m*; (congregation) grey *f*; **to rejoin the —** volver al redil; **three—** tres veces

folder [fóɪdə-] N (file) carpeta *f*; (instrument for folding) plegadera *f*

folding [fóɪdɪŋ] ADJ plegadizo, plegable; **— chair** silla plegadiza *f*; **— screen** biombo *m*

foliage [fólɪʤ] N follaje *m*, fronda *f*, ramaje *m*

folic acid [fólɪkǽsɪd] N ácido fólico *m*

folio [fólɪo] N (page) folio *m*; (book) libro en folio *m*

folk [fok] N (people) gente *f*; (nation) pueblo *m*; ADJ popular; **— dance** baile folclórico *m*; **—lore** folclore *m*; (traditional stories) leyendas tradicionales *f pl*; **— medicine** medicina tradicional *f*; **— music** música folclórica *f*; **old —s** los viejos; **—s** (relatives) parientes *m pl*; (parents) padres *m pl*, viejos *m pl*; **— song** canción tradicional *f*

follow [fálo] VI/VT seguir; VI (be a consequence) seguirse; (come next) ir a continuación; **to — suit** seguir el ejemplo, secundar; **to — through** llevar a cabo; **—-through** continuación del movimiento; **to — up (on)** (pursue) obtener más detalles sobre; (develop) desarrollar; **—-up** seguimiento *m*

follower [fáloə-] N seguidor -ra *mf*

following [fáloɪŋ] N seguidores -ras *mf pl*; **the —** lo siguiente; ADJ siguiente

foment [fomɛ́nt] VT fomentar

fond [fɑnd] ADJ **I'm — of strolls** soy amigo de los paseos, soy gustoso de los paseos; **I'm — of Chinese food** me gusta la comida china; **I'm — of John** le tengo cariño a Juan; **— hopes** ilusión *f*; **to become — of** encariñarse de

fondle [fɑ́ndl] VI/VT (touch affectionately) acariciar; (grope) manosear, sobar

fondness [fɑ́ndnɪs] N (affection) cariño *m*, afecto *m*; (liking or weakness) afición *f*

font [fɑnt] N (of water) pila *f*; (of characters) fuente *f*

food [fud] N comida *f*, alimento *m*; **— chain** cadena alimenticia *f*; **— poisoning** intoxicación por alimentos *f*; **—stuff** producto alimenticio *m*; **— for thought** algo para reflexionar

fool [ful] N (foolish person) tonto -ta *mf*, bobo -ba *mf*, necio -cia *mf*; (jester) bufón *m*; **to make a — of someone** hacer quedar como un tonto; **to play the —** hacer el tonto; **I'm a card-playing —** soy loco por los naipes; VI bromear; **to — around** tontear; VT engañar; ADJ **—proof** (plan) infalible; (device) a prueba de tontos

foolish [fúlɪʃ] ADJ tonto, necio

foolishness [fúlɪʃnɪs] N tontería *f*, bobería *f*, sandez *f*

foot [fut] N pie *m*; (of an animal) pata *f*; **on — a pie; to put one's — in it** meter la pata; **—-and-mouth disease** fiebre aftosa *f*; **—ball** (American) fútbol americano *m*; (soccer) fútbol *m*; (ball) balón de fútbol *m*, pelota (de fútbol) *f*; **—hill** pie de la montaña *m*; **—hold** punto de apoyo *m*; **he has a —hold in the computer business** ha logrado establecerse en el negocio de la informática; **—lights** candilejas *f pl*; **—man** lacayo *m*; **—note** nota al pie de página *f*, llamada *f*; **—path** senda *f*; **—print** huella *f*, pisada *f*; **—race** carrera a pie *f*; **— soldier** soldado de infantería *m*; **—step** pisada *f*, paso *m*; (footprint) huella *f*, pisada *f*; **to follow in the —steps of** seguir los pasos de; **—stool** taburete *m*; **—wear** calzado *m*; **—work** (in sports) juego de piernas *m*; **it'll take some pretty fancy —work to get out of this** va a ser difícil zafar de esto; VI **to — it** andar a pie; VT **to — the bill** pagar la cuenta

footing [fÚDıŋ] N (basis) base f; (foothold) punto de apoyo m; **to be on a friendly — with** tener relaciones amistosas con; **to lose one's —** perder pie

for [fɔr] PREP para; **this gift is — John** este regalo es para John; **we're headed — the beach** vamos para la playa; **this is a device — sorting letters** este es un aparato para clasificar cartas; **they gave me enough food — three people** me dieron comida (como) para tres personas; **she's studying — the bar** está estudiando para el examen de abogación; **the party is planned — Saturday** la fiesta está organizada para el sábado; **he has a good eye — talent** tiene buen ojo para descubrir talento; **he works — IBM** trabaja para IBM; **smoking is bad — your health** fumar es perjudicial para la salud; **he's mature — his age** es maduro para su edad; por; **I've come — the money** he venido por el dinero; **she asked — you** pidió por ti; **I walk to work — the exercise** voy al trabajo andando por el ejercicio; **we went to Spain — a month** fuimos a España por un mes; **she did it — the first time** lo hizo por primera vez; **my wife signed — me** mi esposa firmó por mí; **mothers feel love — their children** las madres sienten amor por sus hijos; **they fired him — arriving late** lo echaron por llegar tarde; **run — your life!** ¡corre por tu vida! **she took me — a fool** me tomó por tonto; **thanks — the help** gracias por la ayuda; **I paid ten dollars — the book** pagué diez dólares por el libro; **I'm — gun control** estoy por el control de armas; **— all her intelligence** a pesar de su inteligencia; **that's not — you to decide** a ti no te toca decidir esto; **as — him** en cuanto a él; **it's time — me to go** es hora de que me vaya; **to know — a fact** saber a ciencia cierta; CONJ porque, pues; **I wish to eat, — I'm hungry** quiero comer, pues tengo hambre

forage [fɔ́rıʤ] N (feed) forraje m; (searching) recolección f; VI (gather food) forrajear; VT (feed) dar forraje a; (collect) recolectar

foray [fɔ́re] N incursión f, correría f; VI (explore) incursionar; (maraud) saquear

forbear [fɔrbɛ́r] VT abstenerse de; VI contenerse; [fɔ́rbɛr] N antepasado -da mf

forbid [fəbíd] VT prohibir

forbidden [fəbídn̩] ADJ prohibido

forbidding [fəbídıŋ] ADJ (strict) severo; (daunting) imponente

force [fɔrs] N fuerza f; **in —** (effective) en vigor, vigente; (in large numbers) en masa; **armed —s** fuerzas armadas f pl; VT (oblige, compel) obligar; (rape, break open) forzar; **she —d a laugh** soltó una risa forzada; **to — upon** imponer; **to — one's way** abrirse paso a la fuerza; **to — out** echar a la fuerza

forced [fɔrst] ADJ forzado; (of a landing) forzoso

forceful [fɔ́rsfəɫ] ADJ (of personality) fuerte; (of arguments) convincente; (of behavior) enérgico

forceps [fɔ́rsəps] N (in obstetrics) fórceps m; (in dentistry) tenazas f pl, gatillo m

forcible [fɔ́rsəbəɫ] ADJ (done by force) forzoso; (effective) convincente; (by force) violento; **— entry** allanamiento de morada m

ford [fɔrd] N vado m; VT vadear

fore [fɔr] ADJ delantero; (of a ship) de proa; N frente m; **to come to the —** ponerse en evidencia; INTERJ ¡cuidado!

forearm [fɔ́rɑrm] N antebrazo m

forebode [fɔrbód] VT (foretell) presagiar; (have a presentiment) presentir

foreboding [fɔrbódıŋ] N (omen) presagio m; (presentiment) presentimiento m

forecast [fɔ́rkæst] N pronóstico m; VI/VT pronosticar

foreclose [fɔrklóz] VI ejecutar una hipoteca

foreclosure [fɔrklóʒə] N ejecución f

forefather [fɔ́rfɑðə] N antepasado m

forefront [fɔ́rfrʌnt] ADV LOC **at the —** a la cabeza, a la vanguardia

forego [fɔrgó] VT abstenerse de

foregone [fɔ́rgɔn] ADJ **it's a — conclusion** eso es de cajón

foreground [fɔ́rgraund] N primer plano m

forehead [fɔ́rıd] N frente f

foreign [fɔ́rın] ADJ extranjero; (not local) foráneo; (alien) ajeno; **— affairs** relaciones exteriores f pl; **— aid** ayuda exterior f; **—born** nacido en el extranjero; **— currency** divisa f; **— debt** deuda exterior f; **— exchange** cambio de divisas m; **— matter** materia extraña f; **— policy** política exterior f; **— trade** comercio exterior m

foreigner [fɔ́rənə] N extranjero -ra mf

foreman [fɔ́rmən] N (in a factory) capataz m, sobrestante m; (of a jury) presidente m

foremost [fɔ́rmost] ADJ principal, preeminente

forensic [fərénzık] ADJ forense

forerunner [fɔ́rrʌnə] N (precursor) precursor -ora mf; (omen) presagio m; (harbinger) mensajero -ra *mf*

foresee [fɔrsí] VT prever, prevenir

foresight [fɔ́rsaɪt] N previsión *f*

foreskin [fɔ́rskɪn] N prepucio *m*

forest [fɔ́rɪst] N (temperate) bosque *m*; (tropical) selva *f*; **— fire** incendio forestal *m*; **— ranger** guardabosques *m sg*

forestall [fɔrstɔ́l] VT bloquear

forester [fɔ́rɪstɚ] N (forest ranger) guardabosques *m sg*; (forest animal) animal silvícola *m*

forestry [fɔ́rɪstri] N silvicultura *f*

foretell [fɔrtɛ́l] VT predecir, vaticinar

forever [bréva] ADV para siempre; **I'm — having to pick up after him** siempre tengo que estar juntando sus cosas; **we can't go on like this** — no podemos seguir así por toda la vida

foreword [fɔ́rwəd] N prólogo *m*

forfeit [fɔ́rfɪt] VT perder; N (fine) multa *f*; (loss) pérdida *f*

forge [fɔrdʒ] N fragua *f*, forja *f*; VT (plans) fraguar; (metal, agreement) forjar; VI/VT (signature, legal document) falsificar; **to — ahead** abrirse paso

forgery [fɔ́rdʒəri] N falsificación *f*

forget [fɚgɛ́t] VI/VT olvidar, olvidarse de; **I forgot my keys** se me olvidaron las llaves; **to — oneself** meter la pata; N **—-me-not** nomeolvides *mf*

forgetful [fɚgɛ́tfəl] ADJ olvidadizo; **— of** negligente de

forgetfulness [fɚgɛ́tfəlnɪs] N falta de memoria *f*

forgive [fɚgív] VI/VT perdonar (also a debt), disculpar

forgiveness [fɚgívnɪs] N perdón *m*

forgiving [fɚgívɪŋ] ADJ clemente

fork [fɔrk] N (for eating) tenedor *m*; (for hay) horca *f*, trinche *m*; (for tuning) diapasón *m*; (in a road) bifurcación *f*; **—lift** montacargas de horquilla *m sg*; VI bifurcarse; **to — over** soltar

forlorn [fɔrlɔ́rn] ADJ desamparado, abandonado

form [fɔrm] N forma *f*; (physical condition) condiciones físicas *f pl*; (document to be filled in) formulario *m*; VI/VT formar(se)

formal [fɔ́rməl] ADJ formal; **— attire** ropa de etiqueta *f*; **— dance** baile de etiqueta *m*

formality [fɔrmǽlɪɾi] N (conventionality) formalidad *f*; (rigidity) formalismo *m*; (legal step) trámite *m*

format [fɔ́rmæt] N formato *m*; VT formatear

formation [fɔrméʃən] N formación *f*

formative [fɔ́rmədɪv] ADJ formativo

formatting [fɔ́rmædɪŋ] N formateo *m*

former [fɔ́rmə] ADJ **the — capital** la antigua capital; **my — husband** mi ex-marido; **the — president** el ex-presidente; **in — times** antiguamente; PRON aquel (aquella, etc.), ese (esa, etc.)

formidable [fɔ́rmɪdəbət] ADJ formidable

formula [fɔ́rmjələ] N fórmula *f*; (for babies) preparado para biberón *m*

formulate [fɔ́rmjəlet] VT formular

fornicate [fɔ́rnɪket] VI fornicar

forsake [fɔrsék] VT abandonar, desamparar

fort [fɔrt] N fuerte *m*, fortaleza *f*; **to hold (down) the** — quedarse cuidando

forth [fɔrθ] ADV (time) en adelante; (space) hacia adelante; **to go —** irse; **and so —** etcétera, y así sucesivamente

forthcoming [fɔrθkámɪŋ] ADJ (approaching) venidero, próximo; (available) disponible; **help wasn't —** no había ayuda disponible; (frank, friendly) abierto; (soon to be published) de próxima aparición

forthright [fɔ́rθraɪt] ADJ directo

forthwith [fɔrθwíθ] ADV en seguida, al punto

fortification [fɔrtəfɪkéʃən] N fortificación *f*

fortify [fɔ́rtəfaɪ] VT (building, body) fortificar; (food) enriquecer; (hair, mind) fortalecer; (argument) reforzar

fortitude [fɔ́rtɪtud] N fortaleza *f*, entereza *f*

fortress [fɔ́rtrɪs] N fortaleza *f*

fortuitous [fɔrtúɪɾəs] ADJ (coincidental) fortuito; (lucky) afortunado

fortunate [fɔ́rtʃənɪt] ADJ afortunado

fortune [fɔ́rtʃən] N fortuna *f*; **— teller** adivino -na *mf*; **it cost me a —** me costó un dineral; **to tell someone's —** decirle la buenaventura a alguien

forty [fɔ́rɾi] NUM cuarenta

forum [fɔ́rəm] N foro *m*

forward [fɔ́rwəd] ADJ (toward the front) hacia adelante; (leading, in the front) delantero; (pushy) descarado; ADV adelante, en adelante; **to bring —** presentar; VT reexpedir; N delantero -ra *mf*

fossil [fásət] N fósil *m*; (old fogey) carcamal *m*, carca *mf*; **— fuel** combustible fósil *m*

foster [fɔ́stə] VT (promote) fomentar, promover; (bring up) criar; ADJ adoptivo

foul [faʊl] ADJ (dirty, illicit) sucio; (disgusting) asqueroso; (of a smell) fétido; (of weather) inclemente; (of winds) adverso; (morally offensive) vil; (of air) viciado; **—mouthed** mal hablado; **the police suspect — play** la policía sospecha que fue un crimen; N falta *f*, foul *m*; **—-up** desastre *m*; VT (make dirty)

ensuciar; (pollute) viciar; (tarnish)
manchar; VI cometer una falta; **to — up**
estropear

found [faʊnd] VT (establish) fundar; (build)
cimentar

foundation [faʊndéʃən] N (establishment,
institution) fundación f; (of a building)
cimiento m; (of an argument) fundamento
m; (cosmetic) base f

founder [fáʊndɚ] N (establisher) fundador
-ra mf; (smith) fundidor -ra mf; VI (sink)
zozobrar, irse a pique; (fail) fracasar

foundry [fáʊndri] N fundición f

fountain [fáʊntn̩] N fuente f; **— pen** pluma
fuente f

four [fɔr] NUM cuatro; **—-eyes** fam cuatro
ojos m sg; **—-letter word** palabrota f;
—score ochenta; **—some** grupo de cuatro
m

fourteen [fɔrtín] NUM catorce

fourth [fɔrθ] ADJ cuarto; N cuarta parte f; **the
Fourth of July** el cuatro de julio

fowl [faʊl] N (domestic) ave de corral m;
(wild) ave m

fox [fɑks] N zorro -rra mf; (crafty person)
persona astuta f; (attractive person)
guapetón -na mf; **—hole** madriguera f;
(military) trinchera f

foxy [fáksi] ADJ (crafty) zorro; (attractive) sexy

foyer [fɔ́ɪɚ] N vestíbulo m

fraction [frǽkʃən] N fracción f, quebrado m

fracture [frǽktʃɚ] N fractura f; VI/VT
fracturar(se)

fragile [frǽdʒəl] ADJ frágil

fragment [frǽgmənt] N fragmento m;
[frǽgmént] VI/VT fragmentar(se)

fragrance [frégrəns] N fragancia f

fragrant [frégrənt] ADJ fragante

frail [frel] ADJ frágil, débil

frailty [fréti] N fragilidad f, debilidad f

frame [frem] N (of a building, airplane,
furniture) armazón m; (of eyeglasses)
montura f, armadura f; (of a car) chasis m;
(of a person's body) estatura f; (of a
picture, door) marco m; (for embroidery)
bastidor m; (on a strip of film) imagen f;
— of mind disposición f; **—work** (of a
house, structure) armazón m; (of
reference) marco m, esquema m; VT (a
document) forjar; (a question, plan)
formular; (a picture) enmarcar; (a person)
tenderle una trampa

franc [fræŋk] N franco m

France [fræns] N Francia f

franchise [frǽntʃaɪz] N (license) concesión f,
franquicia f; (voting privilege) derecho al
voto m; VT conceder en franquicia, dar la

concesión

frank [fræŋk] ADJ franco, abierto; VT
franquear; N salchicha alemana f

frankfurter [frǽŋkfɚDɚ] N salchicha
alemana f

frankness [frǽŋknɪs] N franqueza f

frantic [frǽntɪk] ADJ (wild) frenético;
(desperate) desesperado

fraternal [frətɚ́nəl] ADJ fraternal, fraterno

fraternity [frətɚ́nɪdi] N (relationship)
fraternidad f, confraternidad f; (student
association) asociación estudiantil f

fraternize [frǽDɚnaɪz] VI confraternizar,
fraternizar

fraud [frɔd] N (deceit) fraude m; (impostor)
farsante mf, impostor -ra mf

fraudulent [frɔ́dʒələnt] ADJ (of a business,
etc.) fraudulento; (of a person) engañoso

fray [fre] N (fight) reyerta f, riña f; (harsh
debate) refriega f; VI/VT (rub, wear out)
desgastar(se); (strain) crispar(se)

freak [frik] N (anomaly) anomalía f;
(monster) monstruo m, anormal mf;
(enthusiast) fanático -ca mf; (pervert)
pervertido -da mf; ADJ (unusual) insólito;
VT chiflar, flipar; **to — out** chiflar(se),
flipar(se)

freakish [fríkɪʃ] ADJ insólito

freckle [frékəl] N peca f; VI/VT cubrir(se) de
pecas

freckled [frékəld] ADJ pecoso

free [fri] ADJ (having liberty, unrestricted,
loose, uncombined chemically,
independent) libre; (unobstructed,
unoccupied) libre, despejado; (without
charge) gratis, gratuito; (generous)
generoso; (unstinted) sin límites,
descontrolado; (frank) franco, abierto; **—
and easy** despreocupado; **— enterprise**
empresa libre f; **— fall** caída libre f;
—-for-all rifirrafe m; **— lance** freelance
m; **— lunch / ride** algo gratis m; **—
market** mercado libre m; **— radical**
radical libre m; **— speech** libertad de
expresión f; **— spirit** espíritu fuerte m;
—style estilo libre m; **— thinker** libre
pensador -ra mf; **— trade** libre cambio m;
— verse verso libre m; **—way** autopista f,
autovía f; **— will** libre albedrío m; **to
give someone a — hand** dar rienda
suelta a alguien; **to set —** poner en
libertad; **for —** gratis; **sugar-—** sin
azúcar; ADV libremente; **—lance** por
cuenta propia; VT (liberate) liberar;
(deliver, rid) librar; (untie a knot)
desenredar; (drain) desatascar; **to —load**
gorronear; **to — up** (time) dejar libre

freedom [fríðəm] N libertad *f*; **— of speech** libertad de expresión *f*; **we all want — from fear** todos queremos vivir libres de miedo; **I want — from having to go to work every day** no quiero tener que ir a trabajar todos los días

freeze [friz] VI/VT (of food, water) congelar(se); (of accounts) bloquear(se), congelar(se); **he froze to death** murió congelado; **my computer froze up** se me colgó la computadora / el ordenador; VI (of temperature) helar; N (action or state of being frozen) congelación *f*; (cold snap) helada *f*

freezer [frízə] N congelador *m*

freezing [frízɪŋ] ADJ helado; **— cold** frío glacial *m*; **— point** punto de congelación *m*

freight [fret] N (load) carga *f*; (charge) flete *m*, porte *m*; **— train** tren de carga *m*, tren de mercancías *m*; **by —** por carga

French [frɛntʃ] ADJ francés; **— dressing** salsa francesa *f*; **— fries** *Am* papas fritas *f pl*; *Sp* patatas fritas *f pl*; **— horn** corno francés *m*; **— kiss** beso francés *m*; **(to) —kiss** besar en la boca; **—man** francés *m*; **—woman** francesa *f*; N **the —** los franceses

frenzy [frénzi] N frenesí *m*; **he worked himself into a —** se puso histérico

frequency [fríkwənsi] N frecuencia *f*

frequent [fríkwənt] ADJ frecuente; VT frecuentar

fresh [frɛʃ] ADJ (pure, cool, not stale, not frozen, not tired) fresco; (new) nuevo; (bold) impertinente, atrevido; (healthy) lozano; **— out of school** recién salido de la escuela; **— paint** pintura fresca *f*; **— water** agua dulce *f*; **we're — out of ideas** se nos acabaron las ideas

freshen [fréʃən] VI/VT refrescar(se); **to — up** arreglarse, lavarse

freshman [fréʃmən] N (student) estudiante de primer año *mf*; (novice) novato -ta *mf*

freshness [fréʃnɪs] N (of food, of temperature) frescor *m*, frescura *f*; (of skin, flowers, youth) lozanía *f*; (of an idea) originalidad *f*; (impudence) descaro *m*

fret [frɛt] VI/VT (worry) preocupar(se); (irritate) irritar(se); N traste *m*

fretful [frétfəl] ADJ preocupado

friar [fráɚ] N fraile *m*

friction [fríkʃən] N fricción *f*, rozamiento *m*

Friday [fráɪde] N viernes *m*

fried [fraɪd] ADJ frito

friend [frɛnd] N amigo -ga *mf*

friendliness [fréndlinɪs] N afabilidad *f*,

simpatía *f*

friendly [fréndli] ADJ amistoso, simpático, amigable; **— advice** consejo de amigo *m*; **user-—** fácil de usar

friendship [fréndʃɪp] N amistad *f*

frigate [frígɪt] N fragata *f*

fright [fraɪt] N (fear) espanto *m*, susto *m*; (grotesque thing or person) espantajo *m*, esperpento *m*; **to take —** asustarse

frighten [fráɪtn] VI/VT espantar(se), asustar(se); **to — away** ahuyentar, espantar; **to get —ed** espantarse

frightened [fráɪtnd] ADJ asustado, espantado

frightful [fráɪtfəl] ADJ espantoso, pavoroso; **we had a — time** lo pasamos horrible; **he's a — flatterer** es un adulón espantoso

frigid [frídʒɪd] ADJ (of weather) gélido; (of sexual response) frígida; (of personal relations) frío

frill [frɪl] N (trimming) volante *m*; (something superfluous) adorno *m*; **with no —s** sin lujos, sencillo

fringe [frɪndʒ] N (of a rug, etc.) fleco *m*, orla *f*; (of a city) periferia *f*; (of a political party) extremo *m*; (of society) margen *m*; **— benefits** prestaciones *f pl*, complementos *m pl*; VT orlar, poner un fleco

frisk [frɪsk] VI/VT (frolic) retozar, triscar; (search) cachear

frisky [fríski] ADJ retozón

fritter [frítɚ] VI/VT desmenuzar(se); VT **to — away** malgastar; VI irse gastando de poco a poco; N buñuelo *m*, churro *m*

frivolity [frɪválɪɾi] N frivolidad *f*

frivolous [frívələs] ADJ frívolo

fro [fro] ADV **to and —** de aquí para allá

frock [frɑk] N (dress) vestido *m*; (habit) hábito *m*

frog [frɑg] N (animal) rana *f*; (fastener) alamar *m*; (of a hoof) ranilla *f*; (French person) *pej* franchute -ta *mf*; **to have a — in one's throat** tener gallos en la garganta; **—man** hombre rana *m*

frolic [frálɪk] N retozo *m*; VI retozar

from [frʌm] PREP desde; **— here to there** desde aquí hasta allá; **— two to four** de las dos a las cuatro; **— what I can tell** por lo que yo veo; **four hours — now** de aquí a cuatro horas, dentro de cuatro horas; **different — the other one** diferente del otro; **to come — Minnesota** ser de Minesota; **death — starvation** muerte por inanición *f*

front [frʌnt] N frente *m*; (cover for illegal activity) pantalla *f*; **in — of** en frente de,

delante de; **—-runner** favorito -ta *mf*;
—-wheel drive tracción delantera *f*; ADJ
delantero; VT/VT (face) dar a; (cover up)
servir de pantalla

frontier [frʌntír] N frontera *f*; ADJ fronterizo;
— spirit espíritu pionero *m*; **— town**
pueblo fronterizo *m*

frost [frɔst] N helada *f*, escarcha *f*; VI/VT helar,
escarchar; VT (a cake) bañar; (glass)
esmerilar; (hair) hacer rayitos/reflejos;
—bite necrosis por congelación *f*

frosting [frɔstɪŋ] N (of a cake) baño *m*; (for
glass) esmerilado *m*; (of hair) rayos *m* pl,
reflejos *m* pl

frosty [frɔsti] ADJ (cold, unfriendly) helado;
(covered with frost) escarchado

froth [frɔθ] N espuma *f*; VI echar espuma; VT
batir

frown [fraun] VI fruncir el ceño; **to — on**
desaprobar; N ceño *m*

frozen [frózən] ADJ congelado

fructose [frúktos] N fructosa *f*

frugal [frúgəl] ADJ (economical) económico,
ahorrativo; (meager) frugal

fruit [frut] N (food) fruta *f*; (plant part,
product of labor) fruto *m*; (male
homosexual) *offensive* maricón *m*; **—cake**
(food) torta de frutas secas *f*; (crazy
person) *fam* chiflado -da *mf*

fruitful [frútfəl] ADJ fructífero

fruitless [frútlɪs] ADJ infructuoso

frumpy [frʌmpi] ADJ matrona

frustrate [frʌstret] VT frustrar; **to get —d**
frustrar(se)

frustration [frʌstréʃən] N frustración *f*

fry [fraɪ] VI/VT (cook, also execute by
electrocution) freír(se); **—ing pan** sartén
f; N (fried potato) papa/patata frita *f*;
(gathering of fried food) fiesta con
comida frita *f*; (young fish) alevín *m*;
small — gente menuda *f*

fuck [fʌk] VI/VT (have intercourse) *Sp vulg*
follar; *Am vulg* coger, culear; (treat
harshly) *vulg* joder; **—!** *vulg* ¡mierda!
¡coño! **— off!** *vulg* ¡vete a la mierda! **—
you!** *vulg* ¡vete a la mierda! **to — around**
(be idle) *vulg* rascarse las bolas; (be
promiscuous) *vulg* coger/follar con todo el
mundo; **to — up** *vulg* cagar, joder; **she's
—ed up** (mentally ill, in trouble) *vulg* está
jodida; (under the influence) está
colocada; (confused) está confundida;
—up *offensive* pendejo -ja *mf*; N (sexual
act) *fam* polvo *m*; **he's a good —** *vulg*
folla/coge muy bien; **what the — do
you want?** *vulg* ¿qué carajo quieres? ¿qué
demonios quieres?

fucker [fʌkɚ] N (person who fucks) *vulg*
follador -ra *mf*; (annoying person) *offensive*
hijo -ja de puta *mf*

fucking [fʌkɪŋ] ADJ *vulg* jodido, de mierda;
the whole — day *fam* todo el maldito
día

fudge [fʌdʒ] N turrón blando de chocolate *m*;
VI (cheat) hacer trampa; (avoid an issue)
dar rodeos

fuel [fjúəl] N (combustible) combustible *m*;
(topic) tema *m*; **— injection** inyección *f*;
— oil fuel-oil *m*; VT (a vehicle) llenar el
tanque, cargar de combustible; (fire,
debate) avivar

fugitive [fjúdʒɪdɪv] ADJ (fleeing) fugitivo;
(transitory) fugaz; N fugitivo -va *mf*,
prófugo -ga *mf*

fulfill [fʊɫfíɫ] VT (promise, order) cumplir;
(need) satisfacer; **she doesn't feel —ed**
no se siente realizada

fulfillment [fʊɫfíɫmənt] N (of a promise,
order) cumplimiento *m*; (of a need)
satisfacción *f*; (of a person) realización *f*

full [fʊɫ] ADJ (completely filled) lleno;
(complete) completo; (a dress) amplio; (a
person's figure) relleno; (sated) harto;
—-blooded de raza; **—-blown** (of
disease) declarado; (complete) auténtico;
—-bodied con cuerpo; **—-fledged**
verdadero; **—-grown** adulto; **— house**
full *m*; **—-length** (movie) de
largometraje; (mirror) de cuerpo entero; **—
moon** luna llena *f*; **—-scale** (model, etc.)
de tamaño natural; (war) total;
(investigation) exhaustivo; **—-service** de
servicio completo; **—-size** (bed) de
matrimonio; (model, etc.) de tamaño
natural; **— time** tiempo completo *m*, de
tiempo completo; **to pay in —** pagar el
total de la deuda; ADV **you know — well**
sabes perfectamente; **it hit him — in
the chest** le pegó en pleno pecho

fully [fúli] ADV (entirely) completamente; (at
least) al menos

fumble [fʌmbəl] VI (search for) buscar a
tientas; (move clumsily) andar a tientas;
(blunder) meter la pata; **he —d his way
into the living room** entró a tientas a
la sala

fume [fjum] VI (be angry) rabiar; (emit
vapors, smoke) emitir humo; N **—s** gases
m pl, vapores *m* pl, tufo *m*

fumigate [fjúmɪget] VT fumigar

fun [fʌn] N diversión *f*; **for —** por gusto; **to
make —** of burlarse de; **to have —**
divertirse; ADJ divertido

function [fʌŋkʃən] N (systems, computers,

etc.) función *f*; vi (work) funcionar; (serve) oficiar

fund [fʌnd] N (of money) fondo *m*; (of knowledge) acervo *m*; **—-raising** recaudación de fondos *f*; vt financiar

fundamental [fʌndəmɛ́ntl̩] ADJ fundamental; N fundamento *m*

fundamentalism [fʌndəmɛ́ntl̩ɪzəm] N fundamentalismo *m*

funding [fʌ́ndɪŋ] N financiamiento *m*, financiación *f*

funeral [fjúnəɹəl̩] N funeral *m*, entierro *m*, exequias *f pl*; **— director** director -ora de pompas fúnebres *mf*; **— home** casa de pompas fúnebres *f*, funeraria *f*; **— service** funeral *m*; **it's your —** te estás cavando tu propia tumba; ADJ (march, procession) fúnebre; (pyre) funerario; (expenses) de entierro

fungus [fʌ́ŋgəs] N hongo *m*

funky [fʌ́ŋki] ADJ (of music) funky; (strange) estrafalario, raro; (smelly) hediondo

funnel [fʌ́nl̩] N (for liquids) embudo *m*; (in a chimney) humero *m*; vt canalizar, encauzar

funny [fʌ́ni] ADJ (amusing) cómico, chistoso, gracioso; (strange) raro; **— farm** *fam* loquero *m*, loquería *f*; **that's not —** eso no tiene gracia; **don't get — with me** no te pases de listo; N **funnies** historietas *f pl*, tiras cómicas *f pl*; ADV raro

fur [fɝ] N (hair) pelo *m*; (coat) pelaje *m*; (hide) piel *f*; **— store** peletería *f*; vt forrar de piel

furious [fjúɹiəs] ADJ (angry) furioso, sañudo, rabioso; (fight, storm) feroz; (activity) febril

furlough [fɝ́lo] N licencia *f*, permiso *m*; vt dar licencia

furnace [fɝ́nɪs] N (for heating) caldera *f*; (in industry) horno *m*

furnish [fɝ́nɪʃ] vt (put in furniture) amueblar; (equip) equipar; (provide) proporcionar, suministrar, facilitar

furniture [fɝ́nɪtʃɚ] N muebles *m pl*, mobiliario *m*; **— store** mueblería *f*

furrow [fɝ́o] N surco *m*; vt (soil) arar; (face) fruncir

furry [fɝ́i] ADJ peludo

further [fɝ́ðɚ] ADV **we want to go —** queremos ir más lejos; **I refuse to discuss this —** me niego a seguir discutiendo esto; (furthermore) (lo que) es más; ADJ (more distant) más lejano; (additional) adicional; vt (promote) promover; ADV **—more** además

furthest [fɝ́ðɪst] ADJ (el) más lejano, (el) más remoto; ADV más lejos

furtive [fɝ́dɪv] ADJ furtivo; (shifty) sospechoso

fury [fjúɾi] N furia *f*, furor *m*, saña *f*

fuse [fjuz] N (in an explosive) mecha *f*; (in a circuit) fusible *m*; **he has a short —** tiene pocas pulgas; **he blew a —** estalló; vt (to join) fusionar; vi/vt (to merge) fusionar(se); (to blend metals) fundir(se)

fuselage [fjúsəlɑʒ] N fuselaje *m*

fusion [fjúʒən] N fusión *f*

fuss [fʌs] N (bustle) alboroto *m*, bulla *f*; (uproar) escándalo *m*, alharaca *f*; (argument) discusión *f*; vi (worry about trifles) preocuparse por naderías; (complain) quejarse

fussiness [fʌ́sɪnɪs] N remilgo *m*, ñoñería *f*

fussy [fʌ́si] ADJ (particular) quisquilloso, remilgado; (overdecorated) recargado; (whiny) quejica, cargoso

futile [fjúdl̩] ADJ inútil

futility [fjutɪ́lɪdi] N inutilidad *f*

future [fjútʃɚ] N futuro *m*, porvenir *m*; **—s** futuros *m pl*; ADJ futuro

fuzz [fʌz] N (fluff) pelusa *f*; (fine hair) vello fino *m*; (on the lip) bozo *m*

fuzzy [fʌ́zi] ADJ (fluffy) cubierto de pelusa; (hairy) velloso; (blurred) borroso; (muddled) confuso

Gg

gab [gæb] vi parlotear, charlar; N parloteo *m*, charla *f*; **gift of —** labia *f*, facundia *f*

gable [gébəl̩] N hastial *m*; **— roof** tejado de dos aguas *m*; **— window** buhardilla *f*

Gabon, Gabun [gəbón] N Gabón *m*

Gabonese [gæbəníz] ADJ & N gabonés -esa *mf*

gad [gæd] vi **to — about** callejear

gadget [gǽdʒɪt] N adminículo *m*

gaffe [gæf] N gaffe *f*, metedura de pata *f*

gag [gæg] vt (stop up mouth, silence) amordazar; (cause to choke) dar arcadas; vi tener arcadas; N (thing stuffed into mouth) mordaza *f*; (joke) gag *m*, burla *f*; **— order** orden de supresión de la libertad de expresión *f*

gaiety [géɪdi] N alegría *f*; **gaieties** festejos *m pl*

gain [gen] vt ganar; vi **to — on** irse acercando a; vi/vt (watch) adelantar; N (profit, act of gaining) ganancia *f*; (in weight) aumento *m*

gainful [génfəł] ADJ remunerado

gait [get] N marcha f, paso m

galaxy [gǽləksi] N galaxia f

gale [geł] N ventarrón m, vendaval m; **—force winds** vientos huracanados m pl; **— of laughter** risotada f

Galicia [gəlíʃə] N Galicia f

Galician [gəlíʃən] ADJ & N gallego -ga mf

gall [gɔł] N (bile, bitterness) hiel f; (impudence) morro m; (of a plant) agalla f; **— bladder** vesícula (biliar) f; **—nut** agalla f; **—stone** cálculo biliar m; VT (irritate) irritar

gallant [gǽlənt] ADJ (brave) valiente; (attentive to women) galante; [gəlánt] N galán m

gallantry [gǽləntri] N (courage) valentía f, bizarría f; (chivalrous attention) galantería f

gallery [gǽləri] N (art, shopping) galería f; (theater) paraíso m, gallinero m; (golf) público m

galley [gǽli] N (kitchen) cocina f; (boat) galera f; **— proof** galerada f

gallium [gǽliəm] N galio m

gallon [gǽlən] N galón m (3.7853 liters) m

gallop [gǽləp] VI galopar; N galope m

gallows [gǽloz] N horca f, cadalso m

galore [gəlɔ́r] ADV en abundancia

galoshes [gəlɔ́ʃiz] N chanclos m pl

galvanize [gǽlvənaiz] VT (metals) galvanizar; (a crowd) electrizar

Gambia [gǽmbiə] N Gambia f

Gambian [gǽmbiən] ADJ & N gambiano -na mf

gamble [gǽmbəł] VI jugar; VT jugarse; **I'll — my whole fortune on this venture** voy a jugarme todo en este negocio; **to — away** perder en el juego; N (risk) riesgo m; (bet) apuesta f

gambler [gǽmblə] N apostador -ora mf, tahúr m

game [gem] N juego m; (match of chess, etc.) partida f; (sports match) partido m; (wild animals and their meat) caza f; **— show** programa concurso m; **to be fair —** ser blanco legítimo; ADJ **I'm — for some tennis** me apunto para jugar al tenis; **he has a — knee from years of rugby** tiene la rodilla lisiada después de años de jugar al rugby

gamut [gǽmət] N gama f

gander [gǽndə] N ganso (macho) m; **to take a — at** echarle un vistazo a

gang [gǽŋ] N (of youths, thieves, etc.) pandilla f, gavilla f, banda f; (group of friends) grupo m; **—plank** pasarela f;

—way (passage way) pasillo m; (on a ship) pasamano m; **—way!** ¡abran cancha! VI **to — up on** conspirar contra, conspirar en masa

gangrene [gǽŋgrin] N gangrena f; VI/VT gangrenar(se)

gangster [gǽŋstə] N gángster m, maleante m

gap [gǽp] N (breach) brecha f, hueco m; (of memory) laguna f; (of time) intervalo m; **she has a — between her teeth** tiene los dientes separados; VT espaciar (correctamente)

gape [gep] VI mirar boquiabierto

garage [gəráʒ] N (for parking) garaje m; (for repairing) taller mecánico m; **— sale** venta de garaje f; VT estacionar en un garaje

garb [gɑrb] N vestimenta f, atavío m; VT vestir, ataviar

garbage [gɑ́rbidʒ] N basura f; **— can** bote de basura m; **— disposal unit** trituradora f; **—man** basurero m; **— truck** camión de la basura m; **what a lot of —!** ¡qué montón de mentiras!

garden [gɑ́rdn] N jardín m; **— of Eden** jardín del Edén m; VI cultivar un jardín

gardener [gɑ́rdnə] N jardinero -ra mf

gargle [gɑ́rgəł] VI hacer gárgaras; VT hacer gárgaras con; N (liquid) gargarismo m; (sound) gárgara f

garland [gɑ́rlənd] N guirnalda f

garlic [gɑ́rlɪk] N ajo m

garment [gɑ́rmənt] N prenda f

garner [gɑ́rnə] VT cosechar

garnet [gɑ́rnɪt] N granate m

garnish [gɑ́rnɪʃ] VT (decorate) decorar; (decorate food) aderezar, guarnecer; (withhold wages) retener; N (decoration) adorno m, decoración f

garret [gǽrt] N desván m, buhardilla f

garrison [gǽrɪsən] N guarnición f; VT guarnecer

garrulous [gǽrələs] ADJ locuaz, gárrulo

garter [gɑ́rtə] N liga f; **— belt** liguero m, portaligas m sg; **— snake** culebra de jaretas f; VT sujetar con ligas

gas [gǽs] N (vapor) gas m; (fuel) gasolina f; (flatulence) gases m pl; **— chamber** cámara de gas f; **— mask** máscara de gas f; **— pedal** acelerador m; **— station** gasolinera f; **we had a —** lo pasamos bomba; VT asfixiar con gas, matar en la cámara de gas; **to step on the —** acelerar; **to — up** llenar el tanque

gaseous [gǽʃəs] ADJ gaseoso

gash [gǽʃ] N tajo m; VT hacer un tajo en

gasket [gǽskɪt] N junta (de culata) f

gasoline [gǽsəlin] N gasolina f, nafta f
gasp [gæsp] N (cry) grito sofocado m; (pant) jadeo m, boqueada f; VI (cry out) dar un grito sofocado; (in surprise) quedar boquiabierto; (for breath) jadear, boquear
gastric [gǽstrɪk] ADJ gástrico; — **ulcer** úlcera gástrica f
gastritis [gæstrɑ́ɪDɪs] N gastritis f
gastroenteritis [gæstroɛntəɾɑ́ɪDɪs] N gastroenteritis f
gastrointestinal [gæstroɪntɛ́stɪnəł] ADJ gastrointestinal
gastronomy [gæstrúnəmi] N gastronomía f
gate [get] N (to a garden) portón m; (to a city) puerta f; (at an airport) puerta de embarque f; —**way** (entrance, access) puerta (de entrada) f; (in computers) portal m
gather [gǽðɚ] VT (bring together) reunir, allegar; (pick) recolectar; (pick up, sort out) juntar; (deduce) deducir, colegir; (sew) fruncir; VI (come together) reunirse; (collect) juntarse; (contract into folds) fruncirse; **to** — **dust** juntar polvo / tierra; **to** — **speed** acelerar; N frunce m
gathering [gǽðɚɪŋ] N (meeting) asamblea f; (social) tertulia f; (assemblage of people) concurrencia f, reunión f; (act of gathering fruit, etc.) recolección f
gaudy [gɔ́di] ADJ (of bright color) chillón; (ostentatious) llamativo
gauge [geʤ] VT (measure) medir; (estimate) estimar; (calibrate) calibrar; N (measurement standard) medida f; (caliber) calibre m; (measuring device) medidor m; (track width) entrevía f
gaunt [gɔnt] ADJ demacrado
gauntlet [gɔ́ntlɪt] N (glove) guante m; (mailed glove) guantelete m; **to throw down the** — retar, desafiar; **to run the** — sufrir acosos
gauze [gɔz] N gasa f
gavel [gǽvəł] N martillo m
gawk [gɔk] VT mirar boquiabierto
gawky [gɔ́ki] ADJ torpe, desgarbado
gay [ge] ADJ (happy) alegre, festivo; (homosexual) homosexual; N fam homosexual m
gaze [gez] VI mirar fijamente, contemplar; N mirada fija f
gazelle [gəzɛ́ł] N gacela f
gazette [gəzɛ́t] N gaceta f
gear [gir] N (equipment) equipo m; (cog) rueda dentada f; (assembly of cogs) engranaje m; (speed) marcha f, cambio m; (personal property) pertenencias f pl; —**box** caja de cambios f; —**shift lever**

palanca de cambios f; **to be in** — estar engranado; **to change** —s cambiar de marcha, poner el cambio; **to put into** — engranar; **to put out of** — desengranar; **to** — **up** prepararse
gearing [gírɪŋ] N engranaje m
gecko [gɛ́ko] N geco m
Geiger counter [gáɪgɚ-káʊntɚ] N contador Geiger m
gel [ʤɛł] VI/VT cuajar(se)
gelatin [ʤɛ́lətɪn] N gelatina f
gem [ʤɛm] N (precious stone) gema f; (valuable person) joya f; —**stone** piedra preciosa f
gender [ʤɛ́ndɚ] N género m; — **gap** diferencias entre los sexos f pl; —**specific** propio de un solo sexo
gene [ʤin] N gen m; — **marker** marcador genético m; — **pool** conjunto de genes de una población m; — **splicing** empalme genético m; — **therapy** terapia genética f
genealogy [ʤiniálɑʤi] N genealogía f
general [ʤɛ́nɚəł] ADJ & N general mf; **in** — por lo general; — **practitioner** médico -ca general mf
generality [ʤɛnɚǽlɪDi] N generalidad f
generalize [ʤɛ́nɚəlaɪz] VI/VT generalizar
generate [ʤɛ́nɚet] VT generar
generation [ʤɛnɚéʃən] N generación f; — **gap** brecha generacional f, abismo generacional m
generator [ʤɛ́nɚeDɚ] N generador m
generic [ʤɚnɛ́rɪk] ADJ genérico
generosity [ʤɛnɚúsɪDi] N generosidad f, largueza f
generous [ʤɛ́nɚəs] ADJ generoso
genetic [ʤɚnɛ́Dɪk] ADJ genético; — **code** código genético m; — **engineering** ingeniería genética f; — **fingerprinting** identificación genética f; — **marker** marcador genético m; —**s** genética f
genial [ʤínjəł] ADJ afable, de buen genio
genital [ʤɛ́nɪdł] ADJ genital; — **herpes** herpes genital m; — **wart** verruga genital f; —**s** genitales m pl, sexo m
genius [ʤínjəs] N genio m
genocide [ʤɛ́nɚsaɪd] N genocidio m
genome [ʤínom] N genoma m
genre [ʒánrə] N género m
genteel [ʤɛntíł] ADJ refinado
gentile [ʤɛntaɪł] ADJ & N gentil m
gentle [ʤɛ́ntł] ADJ (kindly) amable; (mild, slow, gradual) suave; (tame) manso
gentleman [ʤɛ́ntłmən] N caballero m
gentlemanly [ʤɛ́ntłmənli] ADJ caballeroso
gentleness [ʤɛ́ntłnɪs] N (kindness) amabilidad f; (mildness) suavidad f;

(tameness) mansedumbre *f*
genuine [dʒénjuin] ADJ genuino
genus [dʒínəs] N género *m*
geocentric [dʒioséntrɪk] ADJ geocéntrico
geographical [dʒiəgræfɪkəl] ADJ geográfico
geography [dʒiágrəfi] N geografía *f*
geological [dʒiəládʒikəl] ADJ geológico
geology [dʒiálədʒi] N geología *f*
geometric [dʒiəmétrɪk] ADJ geométrico
geometry [dʒiámɪtri] N geometría *f*
geophysics [dʒiofízɪks] N geofísica *f*
Georgia [dʒórdʒə] N Georgia *f*
Georgian [dʒórdʒən] ADJ & N georgiano -na *mf*
geostationary [dʒiostéʃəneri] ADJ geoestacionario
geothermal [dʒioθə́rməl] ADJ geotérmico
geranium [dʒəréniəm] N geranio *m*
geriatric [dʒeriátrɪk] ADJ geriátrico
germ [dʒə́rm] N (microorganism) microbio *m*, germen *m*; (bud, embryo, rudiment) germen *m*; — **warfare** guerra biológica *f*
German [dʒə́r-mən] ADJ & N alemán -na *mf*; — **measles** rubeola, rubéola *f*; — **shepherd** pastor alemán *m*
germane [dʒə-mén] ADJ pertinente, relacionado
Germany [dʒə́r-məni] N Alemania *f*
germinate [dʒə́r-mənet] VI germinar; VT hacer germinar
gerund [dʒérənd] N gerundio *m*
gestate [dʒéstet] VI/VT gestar(se)
gestation [dʒestéʃən] N gestación *f*
gesticulate [dʒestíkjəlet] VI gesticular
gesture [dʒéstʃər] N gesto *m*, además *m*; (token) muestra *f*; VI gesticular
gesundheit [gəzúnthait] INTERJ ¡salud! *Sp* ¡Jesús!
get [get] VT (receive, earn) recibir; (obtain) obtener; (reach by phone, etc.) comunicarse con; (hear, understand) entender; (seize) agarrar; *Sp* coger; (prevail) conseguir, lograr; (affect) afectar; (strike) pegar, dar; (catch disease) pescar; *Sp* coger; **to — across** comunicar; **to — ahead** prosperar; **to — along (with)** llevarse bien (con); **to — angry** enojarse; **to — around** (skirt) esquivar, evitar; (go out) salir mucho; **to — away** escapar(se); **to — away with** quedar impune; —**away** (escape) escape *m*; (vacation) escapada *f*; **to — back** (return) volver; (recover) recuperar; **to — back at** vengarse de; **to be** —**ting on in years** ponerse viejo; **to — by** (go past) pasar; (survive) ir tirando; **to — down** (lower oneself) bajar; (depress) deprimir; (swallow) tragar; **to —**

down to business / brass tacks ir al grano; **from the** —**go** desde el principio; **to — going** ponerse en marcha; **to — in** (enter) entrar; (arrive) llegar; (a vehicle) subir a; **to — it** captar, entender; **to — married** casarse; **to — nowhere** no llegar a ningún lado; **to — off** (dismount, get down) bajar; (not receive punishment) salir impune; (leave work) salir; **to — off on** enloquecerse por; **to — off someone's back** dejar de fastidiar; **to — old** envejecer; **to — on** montarse a; **to — out** (take out) sacar; (exit) salir; **to — over** (recuperate) recuperarse, sobreponerse a; (forgive) olvidar; **to — ready** preparar(se); **to — rich** enriquecerse; **to — rid of** deshacerse de; **to — sick** enfermarse; **to — somewhere** tener resultado; **to — through** (survive an ordeal) sobrevivir; (reach by phone, be understood) comunicarse; (complete) lograr terminar; **to — to someone** afectar a alguien; **to — together** reunirse; —-**together** reunión *f*; **to — up** (arise) levantarse; (prepare) montar; —**up** disfraz *m*, atuendo *m*; **I got him to do it** conseguí / logré que lo hiciera; **I have got to do it** tengo que hacerlo; **we got our house painted** pintamos la casa; **he got a year in jail** le dieron un año de cárcel; **we — to stay up late in summer** en el verano nos dejan quedarnos despiertos hasta tarde; **that —s my goat** eso me fastidia
geyser [gáɪzə-] N géiser *m*
Ghana [gánə] N Ghana *f*
Ghanaian [gánəjən] ADJ & N ghanés -esa *mf*
ghastly [gǽstli] ADJ (horrible) horrendo, espantoso; (cadaverous) cadavérico
ghetto [gédo] N gueto *m*
ghost [gost] N fantasma *m*; **not a — of a chance** ni la menor posibilidad; — **town** pueblo fantasma *m*; —**writer** colaborador -ora anónimo -ma *mf*
ghostly [góstli] ADJ fantasmagórico
ghoul [guł] N fantasma *m*
giant [dʒáɪənt] N & ADJ gigante -ta *mf*
gibberish [dʒíbə-ɪʃ] N jerigonza *f*
gibbon [gíbən] N gibón *m*
Gibraltar [dʒɪbróltə] N Gibraltar *m*
Gibraltarian [dʒɪbrɔltériən] ADJ & N gibraltareño -ña *mf*
giddy [gídi] ADJ (dizzy) mareado; (of heights) vertigoso; (of speed) vertiginoso
gift [gɪft] N (thing given, act of giving) regalo *m*, presente *m*; (special ability) don *m*; — **certificate** vale por un regalo *m*;

—-**wrap** envolver para regalo; VT regalar

gifted [gíftɪd] ADJ (artist) talentoso; (child) superdotado

gigabyte [gígəbaɪt] N gigabyte *m*

gigantic [dʒaɪgǽntɪk] ADJ gigantesco, gigante

giggle [gígəł] VI reír tontamente; N risita tonta *f*

gild [gɪld] VT dorar

gill [gɪł] N agalla *f*

gilt [gɪłt] ADJ & N dorado *m*

gimmick [gímɪk] N treta *f*, estratagema *f*

gin [dʒɪn] N (liquor) ginebra *f*; — **rummy** gin rummy *m*

ginger [dʒíndʒɚ] N jengibre *m*; — **ale** ginger ale *m*; —**bread** pan de jengibre *m*

gingham [gíŋəm] N guingán *m*

gingivitis [dʒɪndʒəváɪdɪs] N gingivitis *f*

giraffe [dʒərǽf] N jirafa *f*

gird [gɝd] VT ceñir; **to — oneself** prepararse

girder [gɝ́dɚ] N viga *f*

girdle [gɝ́dł] N faja *f*; VT rodear

girl [gɝł] N (female child) niña *f*; (young female) muchacha *f*, joven *f*, chica *f*; (servant) muchacha *f*, chacha *f*; —**friend** novia *f*

girlhood [gɝ́łhud] N niñez *f*

girlish [gɝ́łɪʃ] ADJ de niña

girth [gɝθ] N (of things) circunferencia *f*; (of persons) contorno *m*; (of horses) cincha *f*; VT cinchar

gist [dʒɪst] N esencia *f*, lo esencial

give [gɪv] VT dar; (present as a gift) regalar; (organize a party) organizar; (assign a name) poner; (donate) donar; **I don't — a hoot** me importa un comino; VI dar; (yield) ceder; (break) romperse; **to — away** (a gift) regalar, donar; (the bride) entregar; (the truth) revelar; **to — back** devolver; **to — in** (acknowledge defeat) rendirse; (hand in) entregar; **to — off** emitir, despedir, desprender; **to — out** (announce) anunciar; (distribute) repartir; (become exhausted) rendirse; (run out) acabarse; **to — over** entregar; **to — up** (surrender) darse por vencido; (stop) dejar (de); **we'll work on this two years, — or take a month** vamos a trabajar en esto dos años, un mes más, un mes menos; N elasticidad *f*; — **and take** toma y daca *m*

given [gívən] ADJ (stated, fixed) dado; (bestowed) regalado; — **name** nombre de pila *m*; — **that she's not here** dado que ella no está; — **to** propenso a; N premisa *f*

giver [gívɚ] N dador -ora *mf*, donador -ora *mf*

gizmo [gízmo] N coso *m*, chisme *m*

glacial [gléʃəł] ADJ glacial

glacier [gléʃɚ] N glaciar *m*

glad [glæd] ADJ contento; **I'm — to see you** me alegro de verte; **I'd be — to help** sería un placer ayudarte

gladden [glǽdn̩] VT alegrar, regocijar, alborozar

gladiator [glǽDieDɚ] N gladiador *m*

glamorous [glǽmɚəs] ADJ glamoroso, encantador

glamour [glǽmɚ] N (charm) glamour *f*, encanto *m*; (excitement) atractivo *m*

glance [glæns] VI echar un vistazo; **to — off** rebotar con efecto; N (look) vistazo *m*; (bounce) rebote oblicuo *m*

gland [glænd] N glándula *f*

glandular [glǽndʒələ-] ADJ glandular

glare [gler] N (bright light) relumbre *m*; (stare) mirada furiosa *f*; VI (shine) relumbrar; (stare fiercely) lanzar una mirada hostil

glaring [glérɪŋ] ADJ (blinding) deslumbrante; (obvious) evidente; (hostile) hostil

glass [glæs] N (substance) vidrio *m*; (window pane) vidrio *m*, cristal *m*; (tumbler) vaso (de vidrio) *m*; (mirror) espejo *m*; (glassware) cristalería *f*; (magnifier) lupa *f*; —**blowing** soplado de vidrio *m*; — **cutter** cortavidrio *m*; —**es** anteojos *m pl*, lentes *m pl*, gafas *f pl*; — **eye** ojo de vidrio *m*; —**maker** vidriero -ra *mf*; —**ware** cristalería *f*

glassy [glǽsi] ADJ vidrioso

glaucoma [glɔkómə] N glaucoma *m*

glaze [glez] VT (a window) poner vidrios a; (ceramic) vidriar; (food) glasear; (varnish) barnizar; VI vidriarse; N (pottery) vidriado *m*, barniz *m*; (food) glaseado *m*

glazier [gléʒɚ] N vidriero -ra *mf*

gleam [glim] N reflejo *m*, brillo *m*; **a — of hope** un rayo de esperanza; VI brillar, relucir

glean [glin] VT (grain) espigar; (information) extraer, deducir

glee [gli] N regocijo *m*, júbilo *m*; — **club** coro *m*

glib [glɪb] ADJ (fluent) de mucha labia; (superficial) simplista, superficial

glide [glaɪd] VI (slide) deslizarse; (fly) planear; N (sliding movement) deslizamiento *m*; (flight) planeo *m*

glider [gláɪDɚ] N planeador *m*

glimmer [glímɚ] N luz trémula *f*; **a — of hope** un destello de esperanza; **the — of an idea** el atisbo de una idea; VI guiñar, emitir una luz trémula

glimpse [glɪmps] N (look) ojeada *f*, vistazo *m*; (hint) atisbo *m*; VT ojear

glint [glɪnt] N destello *m*; VI destellar

glisten [glísən] VI brillar, relucir

glitch [glɪtʃ] N problema técnico *m*

glitter [glídə] VI destellar; N (light) destello *m*; (showiness) brillo *m*; (sparkling powder) brillantina *f*

gloat [glot] VI regodearse; N regodeo *m*

glob [glɑb] N pegote *m*

global [glóbəł] ADJ global, mundial; — **positioning system** sistema mundial de posicionamiento *m*; — **warming** calentamiento global *m*

globe [glob] N globo *m*; (map of the Earth) globo terráqueo *m*

globule [glóbjuł] N glóbulo *m*

gloom [glum] N (darkness) oscuridad *f*; (melancholy) melancolía *f*, tristeza *f*

gloomy [glúmi] ADJ (dark, depressing) sombrío, lúgubre, tenebroso; (melancholic) melancólico, deprimido

glorify [glɔ́rəfaɪ] VT glorificar

glorious [glɔ́riəs] ADJ (wonderful) magnífico, excelente; (related to glory) glorioso

glory [glɔ́ri] N gloria *f*; VI **to — in** regocijarse con

gloss [glɔs] N (shine) brillo *m* (also cosmetics); (marginal note) glosa *f*; (in a dictionary) acepción *f*; VT (polish) lustrar, dar brillo a; (explain) glosar; **to — over** disfrazar, encubrir

glossary [glɔ́səri] N glosario *m*

glossy [glɔ́si] ADJ lustroso; (paper) glaseado

glove [glʌv] N guante *m*; — **compartment** guantera *f*

glow [glo] N incandescencia *f*; (of cheeks) rubor *m*; (of emotion) calor *m*; VI resplandecer; (of metal) estar al rojo vivo; (of cheeks) ruborizarse; **to — with health** estar rebosante de salud; —**worm** luciérnaga *f*

glowing [glóɪŋ] ADJ (with light) incandescente; (colors) vivo; (with health) rebosante; (report, etc.) favorable

glucose [glúkos] N glucosa *f*

glue [glu] N cola *f*, pegamento *m*; VT (put glue on) engomar; (stick together) pegar; (stick wood together) encolar

glum [glʌm] ADJ tristón

glut [glʌt] VI/VT (with food) hartar(se); VT (with products) saturar; N exceso *m*

glutton [glʌ́tn̩] N glotón -ona *mf*

gluttonous [glʌ́tnəs] ADJ glotón

gluttony [glʌ́tn̩i] N glotonería *f*, gula *f*

glycerin [glísə·ɪn] N glicerina *f*

gnarled [nɑrłd] ADJ (knotty) nudoso, sarmentoso; (twisted) retorcido

gnash [næʃ] VI/VT rechinar

gnat [næt] N jején *m*

gnaw [nɔ] VI/VT (bite, corrode) roer; (torment) remorder; **to — a hole** hacer un agujero a mordiscos

GNP (gross national product) [ʤienpí] N PNB *m*

gnu [nu] N ñu *m*

go [go] VI (move) ir; (function) andar, marchar; **to — against** oponerse a; **to — ahead** seguir adelante; —-**ahead** visto bueno *m*; **to — all out** dar todo de sí; **to — along** estar de acuerdo; **to — around** (circumvent) dar la vuelta a; (circulate) circular; (be sufficient) alcanzar; **to — around with** andar con; **to — away** irse; **to — back** volver; **to — back on one's word** faltar a la palabra; —-**between** intermediario -ria *mf*; **to — beyond** traspasar; **to — by** (pass) pasar; (be guided by) guiarse por; **to — by another name** usar otro nombre; **to — crazy** enloquecerse; —-**cart** kart *m*; **to — down** (descend) bajar; (fall) caer, estrellarse; (lose) perder; (be accepted) gustar; **to — down on** practicar sexo oral; **to — for** (attack) atacar; **pizza to — for** pizza para llevar; **to — in with** participar; **to — it alone** tirarse solo; **to — off** (explode) estallar; (happen) suceder; (leave) irse; **to — on** (happen) pasar; (continue) seguir; **to — out** (extinguish) apagarse; (socialize) salir; **to — over** (review) repasar, revisar; (be accepted) gustar; (read) leer; (cross) cruzar; **to — through** (suffer) sufrir; (examine) examinar; (be approved) ser aprobado; (spend) gastar; **to — through with** llevar a cabo; **to — to sleep** dormirse; **to — under** (go bankrupt) quebrar; (sink) hundirse; **to — up** (building) levantarse; (prices) subir; **to let — soltar(se); **the car went for a good price** el coche se vendió a un buen precio; **he's smart, as dogs —** para ser perro, es inteligente; **that old couch has got to —** hay que deshacernos de ese sofá viejo; **cows — "moo"** las vacas hacen "mu"; **she went straight for the pizza** se fue derechito a la pizza; **she's —ing to buy a house** va a comprar una casa; **anything —es** todo vale; **what I say —es** lo que yo digo, vale; **don't — to any trouble** no te molestes; **— figure!** ¡vaya a saber uno! **I've got to — (to the bathroom)** tengo que ir al baño; N (energy) energía *f*; (attempt) intento *m*; **in one —** de una vez; **on the —** a las corridas; **at the first**

— de primera; **they made a — of it** tuvieron éxito; **it's a —** ¡trato hecho! **from the word —** desde el vamos

goad [god] N aguijada f; VT aguijonear

goal [goł] N (objective) meta f; (score) gol m; **—keeper** portero -ra mf

goalie [góli] N guardameta mf

goat [got] N cabra f; **—herd** cabrero -ra mf; **he gets my —** me saca de quicio

goatee [goti] N perilla f

gobble [gábəł] VI/VT (devour) engullir; VI (turkey) gluglutear; **to — up** engullir

gobbledygook [gábəłdiguk] N jerigonza f

gobbler [gáblə-] N pavo m

goblet [gáblɪt] N copa f

goblin [gáblɪn] N duende m

god, God [gad] N dios m, Dios m; **God bless you!** ¡que Dios te bendiga! (after a sneeze) ¡salud! ¡Jesús! **—child** ahijado -da mf; **—damned** vulg maldito; **—father** padrino m; **—forsaken** de mala muerte; **—given** divino; **—mother** madrina f; **—send** bendición f; **God willing** si Dios quiere; **by God** por Dios; **my God!** ¡Dios mío!

goddess [gádɪs] N diosa f

godless [gádlɪs] ADJ impío

godly [gádli] ADJ piadoso

goggles [gágəłz] N gafas protectoras f pl, antiparras f pl

going [góɪŋ] ADJ que marcha bien; **—s-on** tejemaneje m

gold [gołd] N oro m; **a heart of —** un corazón de oro; **— digger** mujer cazafortunas f; **—finch** jilguero m; **—fish** pez dorado m; **— medal** medalla de oro f; **—smith** orfebre m

golden [gółdən] ADJ (made of gold) de oro, áureo; (of gold color) dorado; **— eagle** águila dorada f; **— retriever** golden retriever m; **— rule** regla de oro f

golf [galf] N golf m; **— ball** pelota de golf f; **— club** (stick) palo de golf m; (place) club de golf m; **— course** campo de golf m

gondola [gándələ] N (boat, basket under a balloon) góndola f; (cable car) cabina f

gone [gɔn] ADJ **my computer is —** desapareció mi computadora; **the candy is all —** se acabaron los dulces

gong [gaŋ] N batintín m, gong m

gonorrhea [ganərÍə] N gonorrea f

good [gud] ADJ bueno; (valid) válido; **—-for-nothing** inútil, zanguango; **—-looking** guapo, apuesto; **—-natured** apacible, bonachón; **for — para** siempre; **a — hour** una hora larga; **a — many** muchos; **to have a — time** divertirse; **to**

make — cumplir; **to smell —** oler bien; N (moral act, benefit) bien m; **— for two burritos** vale por dos burritos; **—s** mercancías f pl; **—s and services** bienes y servicios m pl; **for your own —** por tu propio bien; **to deliver the —s** cumplir lo prometido; INTERJ ¡bien! **— afternoon** buenas tardes; **—bye** adiós; **— day** buenos días; **— evening** buenas noches; **— morning** buenos días; **— night** buenas noches

goodly [gúdli] ADJ (considerable) considerable; (of fine appearance) de buen aspecto

goodness [gúdnɪs] N bondad f; (of food) calidad f; INTERJ ¡Dios mío!

goody [gúdi] N golosina f; **——** santurrón -ona mf; INTERJ ¡qué bien!

goof [guf] VI pifiar; **to — off** perder el tiempo; **to — up** pifiarla; N pifia f

goofy [gúfi] ADJ (person) bobalicón; (idea) tonto

goose [gus] N ganso -sa mf (also fool); VT sorprender a alguien tocándole entre las nalgas; **—berry** (berry) grosella espinosa f; (bush) grosellero m; **—bumps** carne de gallina f; **— egg** cero m

GOP (Grand Old Party) [ʤiopí] N Partido Republicano m

gopher [gófə-] N ardilla de tierra f

gore [gɔr] N sangre derramada f; VT cornear

gorge [gɔrʤ] N (body part) garganta f; (ravine) garganta f, tajo m; VI **to — one's self (on)** atracarse (de), darse un atracón (de)

gorgeous [górʤəs] ADJ (woman, outfit) precioso; (weather) espléndido

gorilla [gərÍlə] N gorila mf; (thug) matón m

gory [góri] ADJ (of a battle) sangriento; (of a surface) ensangrentado

gospel [gáspəł] N evangelio m; (music) gospel m; **— truth** pura verdad f

gossip [gásəp] N (rumor) chismorreo m, murmuración f, habladurías f pl; (person) chismoso -sa mf; (woman) comadre f; **a piece of —** us chisme; VI chismear, murmurar

gossipy [gásəpi] ADJ chismoso, lenguaraz

Gothic [gáθɪk] ADJ gótico (also literature); N (language) gótico m; (style) estilo gótico m

gouge [gauʤ] N gubia f; VT (scoop) sacar con gubia; (overcharge) cobrar de más; **to — someone's eyes out** arrancarle los ojos a alguien

gourd [gɔrd] N calabaza f

gourmet [gɔrmé] N & ADJ gourmet mf; **— cheese** queso fino m

gout [gaut] N gota *f*

govern [gávə-n] VI/VT gobernar, regir; VT (in grammar) regir

governess [gávə-nɪs] N institutriz *f*

government [gávə-nmənt] N gobierno *m*; (in grammar) rección *f*

governmental [gavə-nmént]] ADJ gubernamental, gubernativo

governor [gávə-nə-] N (leader) gobernador -ora *mf*; (of an engine) regulador *m*

gown [gaun] N (woman's dress) vestido *m*; (for sleeping) camisón *m*; (in hospital) bata *f*; (for graduation) toga *f*

grab [græb] VT agarrar, prender; **how does that idea — you?** ¿qué te parece esa idea? VI **to — at** tratar de agarrar; N agarrón *m*; **up for —s** a la rebatiña

grace [gres] N gracia *f*; (of movement) garbo *m*; (of expression) donaire *m*; **to say —** decir la oración; **to be in the good —s of someone** gozar del favor de alguien, disfrutar de la gracia de alguien; VT (adorn) adornar; (honor) honrar, agraciar

graceful [grésfəl] ADJ (of movement) grácil, garboso; (of behavior) donoso

gracefulness [grésfə-lnɪs] N gracia *f*, donaire *m*

gracious [gréʃəs] ADJ (kind) gentil, cortés; (elegant) elegante; (merciful) misericordioso; —! ¡válgame Dios!

graciousness [gréʃəsnɪs] N gentileza *f*

gradation [gredéʃən] N gradación *f*

grade [gred] N (degree) grado *m*; (category) calidad *f*; (year in school) año *m*, curso *m*; (marks) nota *f*, calificación *f*; (slope) declive *m*; **to make the —** alcanzar el nivel deseado; — **point average** promedio de notas *m*; VT (classify) clasificar; (assign grades) calificar, corregir; (level) nivelar

gradual [grédʒuəl] ADJ gradual

graduate [grédʒuɪt] N (advanced student) estudiante de posgrado *mf*; (degree-holder) graduado -da *mf*, egresado -da *mf*; ADJ de posgrado; — **school** programa de posgrado *m*; [grédʒuet] VI graduarse, titularse; VT (confer a degree) dar un diploma a; (mark a scale) graduar

graduation [grædʒuéʃən] N graduación *f*

graffiti [grəfíɾi] N graffiti *m*

graft [græft] N (of plant, tissue) injerto *m*; (corruption) concusión *f*, corrupción *f*; VI/VT injertar(se)

grain [gren] N (cereal, seed) grano *m*, mies *f*; (photographic texture) grano *m*; (of gold) pepita *f*; (of wood, meat, stone) veta *f*; (texture) textura *f*; (small amount) pizca *f*;

against the — a / al redopelo, a contrapelo

gram [græm] N gramo *m*

grammar [græmə-] N gramática *f*

grammatical [grəmǽɾɪkəl] ADJ gramatical

granary [grénəri] N granero *m*, troje *m*

grand [grænd] ADJ (splendid) grandioso, espléndido; (lofty) elevado; (impressive) impresionante; —**child** nieto -ta *mf*; —**children** nietos *m pl*; —**daughter** nieta *f*; —**father** abuelo *m*; — **jury** jurado de acusación *m*; —**mother** abuela *f*; —**ma** abuelita *f*; —**pa** abuelito *m*; —**parent** abuelo *m*; —**parents** abuelos *m pl*; — **piano** piano de cola *m*; —**son** nieto *m*; —**stand** tribuna *f*; **a — old man** un gran señor; **the — total** el total

grandeur [grǽndʒə-] N grandiosidad *f*

grandiose [grǽndios] ADJ (complex) complejo; (of speech) grandilocuente, rimbombante; (imposing) grandioso

granite [grǽnɪt] N granito *m*

grant [grænt] VT (give) conceder, otorgar, dispensar; (accept) admitir; (transfer) ceder; **to take for —ed** (an assumption) dar por sentado; (a person) no valorar; N (something granted) concesión *f*; (act of granting) concesión *f*, otorgamiento *m*; (subsidy) subvención *f*

granulate [grǽnjəlet] VI/VT granular(se)

grape [grep] N uva *f*; —**fruit** pomelo *m*, toronja *f*; —**vine** vid *f*; (ornamental) parra *f*; **I heard it through the —vine** me lo contó un pajarito

graph [græf] N (curve) gráfica *f*; VT grafiar; — **paper** papel cuadriculado *m*

graphic [grǽfɪk] ADJ gráfico; — **design** diseño gráfico *m*; N gráfico *m*; —**s** gráfica *f*

graphite [grǽfaɪt] N grafito *m*

grapple [grǽpəl] VI/VT (hold) aferrar; (struggle) luchar, lidiar

grasp [græsp] VT (seize) agarrar, asir, aferrar; (understand) comprender; VI **to — at / for** tratar de agarrar; N (hold) agarre *m*, asidero *m*; (comprehension) comprensión *f*; **within one's —** al alcance; **to have a good — of a subject** dominar una materia

grass [græs] N (plant) hierba *f*; (lawn) césped *m*; (pasture) pasto *m*; (marijuana) marihuana *f*, maría *f*; —**hopper** saltamontes *m sg*, saltón *m*; —**land** pradera *f*, pastizal *m*; — **roots** las bases *f pl*

grassy [grǽsi] ADJ herboso

grate [gret] N (of a fireplace) parrilla *f*; (partition, guard) reja *f*, verja *f*; VT (install a grate) enrejar; (mince) rallar; (rub teeth together) crujir, rechinar; VI **to — on** rechinar

grateful [grétfəł] ADJ agradecido

grater [gréɖə] N rallador *m*

gratification [græɖəfikéʃən] N gratificación *f*

gratify [græɖəfaɪ] VT complacer, gratificar

grating [gréɖɪŋ] N reja *f*, enrejado *m*, rejilla *f*; ADJ (discordant) rechinante; (irritating) irritante

gratitude [græɖɪtud] N gratitud *f*

gratuitous [grətúɪɖəs] ADJ gratuito

gratuity [grətúɪɖi] N propina *f*

grave [grev] ADJ grave; N fosa *f*, sepultura *f*; **—digger** sepulturero *m*; **—stone** lápida *f*; **—yard** cementerio *m*; **—yard shift** turno de la noche *m*; **to have one foot in the —** *fam* estar por reventar

gravel [grǽvəl] N grava *f*; VT cubrir con grava

gravitation [grævɪtéʃən] N gravitación *f*

gravity [grǽvɪɖi] N gravedad *f* (also seriousness)

gravy [grévi] N jugo de carne *m*; **the rest is —** el resto es fácil

gray [gre] ADJ gris; (hair) canoso; (horses) rucio; **— area** zona gris *f*; **—haired** cano, canoso; **— matter** materia gris *f*; N gris *m*; VI/VT agrisar; (hair) encanecer

grayish [gréɪʃ] ADJ grisáceo

graze [grez] VI/VT (feed) pacer, pastar, apacentar; (brush) rozar; N roce *m*

grease [gris] N grasa *f*; VT engrasar; **to — someone's palm** untarle la mano a alguien, engrasar a alguien

greasy [grísi, grízi] ADJ grasiento, grasoso

great [gret] ADJ (large, numerous) grande; **a — tree blocked the path** un árbol grande bloqueaba el camino; (good, excellent, considerable) gran; **she's a — friend** es una gran amiga; (long) largo; **a — while** un largo rato; (skillful) excelente; **she's — at tennis** juega muy bien al tenis; **a — deal of** mucho; ADV muy bien, excelente; **she did —** le fue muy bien; **the —s** los/las grandes *mf*; **—-grandchild** bisnieto -ta *mf*; **—-grandfather** bisabuelo *m*; **—-grandmother** bisabuela *f*; **—-grandchild** tataranieto -ta *mf*; INTERJ ¡qué bien!

greatness [grétnɪs] N grandeza *f*

Greece [gris] N Grecia *f*

greed [grid] N codicia *f*

greedy [grídi] ADJ (covetous) codicioso; (voracious) voraz; (eager) ávido

Greek [grik] ADJ & N griego -ga *mf*; **that's — to me** eso es chino

green [grin] ADJ verde; (verdant, unripe, inexperienced, nauseated, environmentally conscious) verde; N (color) verde *m*; (lawn) césped *m*; (pasture) prado *m*; (in golf) green *m*; (commons) ejido *m*; **—back** dólar *m*; **— bean** *Sp* judía verde *f*; *Mex* ejote *m*; *RP* chaucha *f*; **— card** tarjeta verde *f*; **—horn** novato -ta *mf*; **—house** invernadero *m*; **—house effect** efecto invernadero *m*; **— light** luz verde *f*; **— pepper** pimiento verde *m*; **—s** verduras de hoja verde *f pl*

greenish [grínɪʃ] ADJ verdoso

greenness [grínnɪs] N verdor *m*

greet [grit] VT (say hello) saludar; (welcome) dar la bienvenida; (receive) recibir

greeting [grídɪŋ] N saludo *m*; **— card** tarjeta de felicitación *f*; **—s!** ¡saludos!

gregarious [grɪgɛ́riəs] ADJ (animal) gregario; (person) sociable

gremlin [grémlɪn] N duende *m*

Grenada [grənédə] N Granada *f*

grenade [grənéd] N granada *f*

Grenadian [grənédiən] ADJ & N granadino -na *mf*

greyhound [gréhaʊnd] N galgo *m*

griddle [gríd] N plancha *f*

gridlock [grídlɑk] N paralización *f*; VI paralizarse

grief [grif] N congoja *f*, pesar *m*, pesadumbre *f*; **to come to —** sufrir una desgracia; **to give someone —** meterse con alguien, jorobar a alguien; **good —!** ¡caramba!

grievance [grívəns] N (complaint) queja *f*; (cause for complaint) motivo de queja *m*

grieve [griv] VI estar de duelo; **to — for/over** llorar (la muerte de alguien); **he's grieving over the loss of his dog** lamenta la muerte de su perro; VT **that —s me** eso me apena

grieved [grivd] ADJ apenado

grievous [grívəs] ADJ (painful) doloroso, penoso; (atrocious) grave, atroz; (sorrowful) dolido

grill [grɪl] N (metal grid, restaurant fixture) parrilla *f*; (dish) parrillada *f*; VI/VT asar a la parrilla; (interrogate) interrogar

grille [grɪł] N parrilla *f*

grim [grɪm] ADJ (news, situation) desalentador; (war) cruento; (joke) macabro

grimace [grímɪs] N mueca *f*, mohín *m*; VI hacer muecas

grime [graɪm] N mugre *f*, suciedad *f*

grimy [gráɪmi] ADJ mugriento, sucio; **to make —** percudir; **to get —** percudirse

grin [grɪn] VI sonreír; N sonrisa *f*; **wipe that**

— **off your face** deja de reírte

grind [graınd] VI/VT (mill finely) moler; (mill coarsely) triturar; (make shiny) pulir; (rub harshly) rechinar; (study hard) estudiar mucho; *Sp* empollar; **to — to a halt** pararse con un chirrido; N (drudgery) trabajo pesado *m*; (overzealous student) empollón -ona *mf*; **the daily —** la lucha diaria; **—stone** muela *f*; **to keep one's nose to the —stone** matarse trabajando / estudiando

grinder [graındə] N (for coffee, pepper) molinillo *m*; (for meat) picadora *f*; (for sharpening tools) afilador *m*

grip [grıp] N (hold) agarre *m*; (control) control *m*; (handle) mango *m*; **he had a firm — on the tool** tenía bien agarrada la herramienta; **get a — on yourself** contrólate, cálmate; VT (seize) agarrar, asir; (take hold, interest) atrapar

gripe [graıp] VI quejarse, rezongar, renegar; N queja *f*

grisly [grízli] ADJ cruento, espantoso

gristle [grísəl] N cartílago *m*

grit [grıt] N (sand) arena *f*; (pluck) firmeza *f*, *fam* cojones *m pl*; **—s** sémola de maíz *f*; VT apretar

gritty [gríɾi] ADJ (sandy) arenoso; (plucky) resuelto, *fam* cojonudo

grizzly [grízli] ADJ (grayish) grisáceo; **— bear** oso pardo *m*

groan [gron] N quejido *m*, gemido *m*; VI quejarse, gemir; (creak) crujir

grocer [grósə] N tendero -ra *mf*; *Mex* abarrotero -ra *mf*; *Caribbean* bodeguero -ra *mf*; *RP* almacenero -ra *mf*

grocery [grósəri] N tienda de comestibles *f*; *Mex* tienda de abarrotes *f*; *Caribbean* bodega *f*; *RP* almacén *m*; **groceries** comestibles *m pl*

groin [grɔın] N ingle *f*

groom [grum] N (in a wedding) novio *m*; (in a stable) mozo de cuadra *m*, caballerizo *m*; VT (a horse) almohazar; (prepare for a position) preparar; **to — oneself** arreglarse; **well-—ed** bien arreglado

groove [gruv] N (narrow cut) estría *f*, ranura *f*; (on a record, road) surco *m*; (routine) rutina *f*; VT estriar, acanalar

grope [grop] VI (feel one's way) andar a tientas; (search) buscar a tientas; VT manosear, toquetear; N manoseo *m*, toqueteo *m*

gross [gros] ADJ (before deductions) bruto; (flagrant) flagrante; (indecent) grosero; (overall) general; (disgusting) asqueroso; **— domestic product** producto interno

bruto *m*; N gruesa *f*; VT recaudar en bruto; **to — out** dar asco, asquear

grotesque [grotésk] ADJ grotesco

grotto [gráɾo] N gruta *f*

grouch [grautʃ] N cascarrabias *mf sg*, refunfuñón -ona *mf*, rezongón -ona *mf*; VI refunfuñar

grouchy [gráutʃi] ADJ cascarrabias, refunfuñón

ground [graund] N (land) tierra *f* (also electrical); (soil) suelo *m*; (basis) fundamento *m*; **—s** (reason) motivo *m*; (dregs) borra *f*, poso *m*; (tract of land) terreno *m*; **— floor** planta baja *f*; **—hog** marmota *f*; **to gain / lose —** ganar / perder terreno; **to stand one's —** ponerse firme; **from the — up** de piso a techo; VT (a wire) conectar a tierra; (a ship) hacer encallar; (punish) poner en penitencia; **the 747 was —ed** se prohibió volar en el 747

groundless [gráundlıs] ADJ infundado

group [grup] N grupo *m*; **— therapy** terapia de grupo *f*; VI/VT agrupar(se)

grouper [grúpə] N mero *m*

groupie [grúpi] N admirador -ra *mf*

grove [grov] N arboleda *f*, plantío *m*; **orange —** naranjal *m*

grovel [grávəl] VI arrastrarse, humillarse

grow [gro] VI (naturally increase in size) crecer; (increase) aumentar, acrecentarse; (expand) desarrollarse; VT (crops) cultivar; (beard) dejarse crecer; **to — old** envejecer; **to — up** madurar; **Thai food —s on you** la comida tailandesa acaba gustándote

growl [graul] VI gruñir; (of thunder) retumbar; (of stomach) rugir; N gruñido *m*

grown [gron] ADJ adulto; **— man** hombre hecho y derecho *m*; **— up** adulto *m*; **—-up** para adultos

growth [groθ] N (increase in size) crecimiento *m*; (increase in number) aumento *m*, acrecentamiento *m*; (tumor) bulto *m*; (expansion) desarrollo *m*; **a — industry** una industria en expansión

grudge [grʌdʒ] N resentimiento *m*

grueling [grúəlıŋ] ADJ arduo

gruesome [grúsəm] ADJ cruento, truculento

gruff [grʌf] ADJ (manner) bronco; (voice) ronco

grumble [grámbəl] VI/VT refunfuñar, rezongar; N refunfuño *m*, gruñido *m*

grumpy [grámpi] ADJ refunfuñón, gruñón, rezongón

grunt [grʌnt] VI/VT gruñir; N gruñido *m*

guarantee [gærəntí] N (promise, pledge)

garantía *f*; (guaranty) fianza *f*; VT (promise, pledge) garantizar; (warrant) dar fianza, avalar

guarantor [gǽrəntɔr] N fiador -ora *mf*

guaranty [gǽrəntì] N (guarantee) garantía *f*; (thing taken as security) fianza *f*; (guarantor) fiador -ora *mf*

guard [gɑrd] VT custodiar; (watch over) vigilar; (protect) proteger; VI protegerse; **to — against** guardarse de; N (person that guards) guardia *mf*, guarda *mf*; (of a machine) dispositivo protector *m*; **to be on** — estar alerta / estar en guardia; —**dog** perro guardián *m*; —**rail** baranda *f*, pasamano *m*

guardian [gɑ́rdiən] N guardián -ana *mf*; (legal) tutor -ora *mf*; — **angel** ángel de la guarda *m*

guardianship [gɑ́rdiənʃip] N tutela *f*

Guatemala [gwɑDəmɑ́lə] N Guatemala *f*

Guatemalan [gwɑDəmɑ́lən] ADJ & N guatemalteco -ca *mf*

guava [gwɑ́və] N guayaba *f*

guess [gɛs] VT (hazard, conjecture) adivinar; (suppose) suponer; N (conjecture) conjetura *f*; (supposition) suposición *f*; **I'll give you three —es** te doy tres oportunidades para adivinar

guest [gɛst] N (to a party, function) invitado -da *mf*; (to a restaurant) cliente *mf*; (overnight) huésped *mf*

guffaw [gʌfɔ́] N carcajada *f*, risotada *f*

guidance [gɑ́idns] N (act of guiding) dirección *f*; (counsel) orientación *f*; (in a missile) teledirección *f*

guide [gɑid] VT guiar; (force to move) dirigir; (counsel) orientar; N (person) guía *mf*; (publication, mechanism) guía *f*; —**book** guía *f*; —**dog** perro guía *m*; —**d missile** misil guiado *m*; —**lines** directivas *f pl*, pautas *f pl*

guild [gɪld] N gremio *m*, corporación *f*

guile [gɑil] N astucia *f*

guilt [gɪlt] N culpa *f*; — **trip** manipulación por acusaciones falsas *f*

guiltless [gɪ́ltlɪs] ADJ inocente

guilty [gɪ́lti] ADJ culpable; **we find the defendant not** — hallamos al acusado inocente

Guinea [gɪ́ni] N Guinea *f*; — **pig** conejillo de Indias *m*; —-**Bissau** Guinea-Bissau *f*

Guinean [gɪ́niən] ADJ & N guineano -na *mf*

guise [gɑiz] ADV LOC **under the** — **of** so / bajo pretexto de; **in the** — **of** a manera de

guitar [gɪtɑ́r] N guitarra *f*

gulf [gʌlf] N (body of water) golfo *m*; (abyss,

gap) abismo *m*; — **Stream** corriente del Golfo *f*

gull [gʌl] N (bird) gaviota *f*; (dupe) crédulo -la *mf*; *Sp* primo -ma *mf*

gullet [gʌ́lɪt] N gaznate *m*

gullible [gʌ́ləbəl] ADJ crédulo, ingenuo

gully [gʌ́li] N barranco *m*, barranca *f*; (gutter) alcantarilla *f*

gulp [gʌlp] VT tragar saliva; N trago *m*

gum [gʌm] N goma *f*; (for chewing) chicle *m*; —**s** encías *f pl*; VT **to — up** (ruin) jorobar; (stick) pegotear

gumption [gʌ́mpʃən] N (initiative) iniciativa *f*, arranque *m*; (courage) agallas *f pl*

gun [gʌn] N (firearm) arma de fuego *f*; (revolver) revólver *m*; (rifle) rifle *m*; (shotgun) escopeta *f*; (cannon) cañón *m*; (for painting, nailing) pistola *f*; VT (an engine) acelerar; **to — down** matar a tiros; **to — for** andar a la caza de; **to stick to one's —s** mantenerse firme; **don't jump the** — no te precipites; **to be under the** — estar bajo mucha presión; —**boat** cañonero *m*; —**fire** tiroteo *m*; —**man** pistolero *m*; **at —point** a mano armada; —**powder** pólvora *f*; —**shot** disparo *m*

gung-ho [gʌ́ŋhó] ADJ fanático, entusiasta

gunner [gʌ́nə] N (shooting artillery) artillero -ra *mf*; (shooting a machine gun) ametrallador -ora *mf*

gurgle [gɝ́gəl] VI (water) borbotar; (baby) gorjear; N (of water) borboteo *m*; (of a baby) gorjeo *m*

gush [gʌʃ] VI (liquids) chorrear, brotar; (talk effusively) hablar con efusividad

gust [gʌst] N ráfaga *f*; — **of wind** racha / ráfaga de viento *f*, ventolera *f*; VI soplar en ráfagas

gusto [gʌ́sto] N (pleasure) placer *m*; (enthusiasm) entusiasmo *m*

gut [gʌt] N tripa *f*; (belly) barriga *f*; — **feeling** corazonada *f*; —**s** (intestines) entrañas *f pl*; (courage) *fam* cojones *m pl*; VT (eviscerate) destripar; (destroy the insides of) destrozar el interior de; (strip) desarmar

gutsy [gʌ́tsi] ADJ *fam* cojonudo

gutter [gʌ́Də] N (in the street) alcantarilla *f*; (on the roof) canaleta *f*, desagüe *m*; (squalor) miseria *f*

guy [gɑi] N (man) tipo *m*; *Sp* tío *m*; **you —s** *Sp* vosotros / vosotras, ustedes; — **wire** cable *m*

Guyana [gɑiɑ́nə] N Guyana *f*

Guyanese [gɑiəníz] ADJ & N guyanés -esa *mf*

gym [dʒɪm] N gimnasio *m*

gymnasium [dʒɪmnéziəm] N gimnasio *m*
gymnastics [dʒɪmnǽstɪks] N gimnasia *f*
gynecology [gaɪnəkúlədʒi] N ginecología *f*
gyp [dʒɪp] VT estafar, timar; N estafa *f*, timo *m*
gypsum [dʒípsəm] N yeso *m*
gypsy [dʒípsi] N & ADJ gitano -na *mf*
gyrate [dʒáiret] VI girar
gyroscope [dʒáirəskop] N giroscopio *m*

Hh

habit [hǽbɪt] N (custom) hábito *m*, costumbre *f*; (clerical dress) hábito *m*; (vice) vicio *m*; **—-forming** que genera dependencia
habitat [hǽbɪtæt] N hábitat *m*
habitual [həbítʃuəł] ADJ habitual
hack [hæk] N (cut) tajo *m*, machetazo *m*; (cough) tos seca *f*; (horse for hire) caballo de alquiler *m*; (nag) jamelgo *m*; (writer) escritor -a mercenario -ria *mf*; VI/VT tajar, cortar a machetazos; VI toser con tos seca; **—saw** sierra para metales *f*
hag [hæg] N (witch) bruja *f*; (ugly old woman) vieja fea *f*
haggard [hǽgəd] ADJ demacrado
haggle [hǽgəl] VI regatear
hail [heł] N (precipitation) granizo *m*; (greeting) saludo *m*; (shout) llamada *f*; **— Mary** Ave María *f*; **—storm** granizada *f*; VI (precipitate) granizar; VT (greet) saludar; (call out) llamar; (acclaim) aclamar; **to — from** ser oriundo de
hair [her] N pelo *m*; (of the head only) cabello *m*; (of the body only) vello *m*; (on plants) pelusa *f*; **—brush** cepillo para el cabello *m*; **—cut** corte de pelo *m*; **to get a —cut** cortarse el pelo; **—do** peinado *m*; **—dresser** peluquero -ra *mf*, peinador -ora *mf*; **— follicle** folículo capilar *m*; **—piece** postizo *m*; **—pin** horquilla *f*; **—raising** horripilante, espeluznante; **—spray** fijador *m*
hairless [hérlɪs] ADJ (deprived of hair) pelado; (growing no hair) lampiño
hairy [héri] ADJ (including head) peludo; (body only) velludo
Haiti [hédi] N Haití *m*
Haitian [héʃən] ADJ & N haitiano -na *mf*
hake [hek] N merluza *f*
half [hæf] N mitad *f*; **— an apple** media manzana *f*; ADJ medio; **—-baked** (not fully cooked) a medio cocer; (not fully

developed) mal concebido; **—-breed** mestizo -za *mf*; **— brother** hermano medio hermano *m*; **—-cocked** mal preparado; **he went off half-cocked** actuó precipitadamente; **—-cooked** a medio cocer; **—-dozen** media docena *f*; **—-hearted** desganado; **—-hour** media hora *f*; **—-moon** media luna *f*; **— note** blanca *f*; **—-open** entreabierto, entornado; **— past one** la una y media; **—time** medio tiempo *m*; **—way** a medio camino; **—way measures** medidas parciales *f pl*; **—way point** punto medio *m*; **—-wit** *pej* imbécil *mf*, papamoscas *mf*; **at —-mast** a media asta; **to do something —way** hacer algo a medias; **to go halves** ir a medias
halibut [hǽləbət] N hipogloso *m*
hall [hɔl] N (corridor) corredor *m*, pasillo *m*; (large room) salón *m*; (building) edificio *m*; **—mark** distintivo *m*; **—way** (corridor) corredor *m*, pasillo *m*; (entrance) zaguán *m*, vestíbulo *m*
Halloween [hæləwín] N víspera del día de Todos los Santos *f*, noche de brujas *f*
hallucinate [həlúsənet] VI alucinar
halo [hélo] N halo *m*, aureola *f*
halogen [hǽlədʒən] ADJ halógeno
halt [hɔlt] N **to come to a —** detenerse; VI/VT parar, detener(se); **—!** ¡alto!
halter [hɔ́łtə] N cabestro *m*
halting [hɔ́łtɪŋ] ADJ vacilante
halve [hæv] VT partir por la mitad
ham [hæm] N (meat) jamón *m*; (attention getter) payaso *m*; **—string** (human) ligamento de la corva *m*; (horse) tendón del jarrete *m*; **to — it up** sobreactuar, exagerar
hamburger [hǽmbɚgɚ] N (meat) carne picada de vaca *f*; (sandwich or patty) hamburguesa *f*
hamlet [hǽmlɪt] N aldea *f*, poblado *m*, caserío *m*
hammer [hǽmɚ] N martillo *m*; VI/VT martillar, amartillar; **to — out** (an agreement) forjar; (differences) negociar
hammock [hǽmək] N hamaca *f*
hamper [hǽmpɚ] N canasto *m*, cesto *m*; VT impedir, embarazar
hamster [hǽmstɚ] N hámster *m*
hand [hænd] N mano *f*; (of a clock) aguja *f*, manecilla *f*; (farm helper) peón *m*; **—bag** (purse) bolsa *f*, cartera *f*; (valise) maletín *m*; **—ball** (American) pelota *f*, frontón *m*; (European) balonmano *m*; **—bill** volante *m*; **—cuffs** esposas *f pl*; **— grenade** granada de mano *f*, bomba de piña *f*;

—**gun** revólver *m*; —**held** de mano; — **in** — (cogidos) de la mano; —**kerchief** pañuelo *m*; —**made** hecho a mano; —**out** (notes) repartido *m*, notas *f pl*; (alms) limosna *f*; —**saw** serrucho *m*; —**shake** apretón de manos *m*; —**s-on** práctico; —**stand** pino *m*, paro de manos *m*; —**work** trabajo manual *m*; —**writing** letra *f*; **at** — (within reach) al alcance; (about to happen) cerca; **on** — disponible, a mano; **on the other** — en cambio, por otra parte; **to have one's** —**s full** estar ocupadísimo; VT entregar, dar; **to** —**cuff** esposar; **to** — **down** (a thing) pasar; (a judgment) pronunciar; **to** — **in** entregar; **to** — **over** entregar

handful [hǽndfʊl] N manojo *m*, puñado *m*

handicap [hǽndikæp] N (physical disability) impedimento *m*; (mental disability) retardo *m*; (disadvantage) desventaja *f*; **physically** —**ped** minusválido físico; — **race** carrera de hándicap *f*; VT (hinder) perjudicar, handicapar; (injure) lisiar

handiwork [hǽndiwɚk] N labor *f*

handle [hǽndl] N (straight) mango *m*; (curved) asa *f*; (of a drawer) manija *f*; (of a sword) empuñadura *f*, puño *m*; —**bar** manubrio *m*; VT (manage) manejar; (touch) manipular, tocar; (deal in) comerciar en; **the car** —**s easily** el coche tiene buena maniobrabilidad

handling [hǽndlɪŋ] N (dealing) manejo *m*; (touching) manipulación *f*; (charge) porte *m*; (of a car) maniobrabilidad *f*

handsome [hǽnsəm] ADJ guapo, bien parecido; **a — sum** una suma considerable

handy [hǽndi] ADJ (near) a (la) mano; (practical) práctico; (skillful) hábil, diestro; —**man** hombre habilidoso *m*

hang [hæŋ] VI/VT colgar, suspender; — **glider** ala delta *f*; —**man** verdugo *m*; —**nail** padrastro *m*; —**out** sitio frecuentado *m*; —**over** resaca *f*; —**up** complejo *m*; VT (door) colocar; (one's head) inclinar; VI pender; — **in there!** ¡ánimo! **to** — **around** quedarse por ahí, rondar; **to** — **on** (hold tight) agarrarse bien; (persevere) aguantar; (wait) esperar; **to** — **out** (be outside) estar fuera; (hang around with) andar (con); **to** — **over** sobresalir; **to** — **paper on a wall** empapelar una pared; **to** — **up** colgar; **sentenced to** — condenado a la horca; N caída *f*; **to get the** — **of something** agarrarle la onda a algo

hangar [hǽŋɚ] N hangar *m*

hanger [hǽŋɚ] N colgadero *m*; (for clothes) percha *f*

hanging [hǽŋɪŋ] N muerte en la horca *f*; —**s** colgaduras *f pl*, tapiz *m*; ADJ colgante

hanky-panky [hǽŋkipǽŋki] N (deceit) tejemaneje *m*; (illicit sexual activity) aventuras *f pl*

haphazard [hæphǽzɚd] ADV a la buena de Dios; ADJ irregular

happen [hǽpən] VI suceder, pasar, acontecer; **I — to know** da la casualidad de que sé; **to — to pass by** acertar a pasar; **to — upon** encontrarse con, toparse con

happening [hǽpənɪŋ] N acontecimiento *m*, suceso *m*

happiness [hǽpinɪs] N felicidad *f*, dicha *f*

happy [hǽpi] ADJ (satisfied) feliz, dichoso; (pleased) contento; (lucky) afortunado; — **ending** final feliz *m*; **to be — to** hacer algo de buena gana

harangue [hərǽŋ] N arenga *f*; VT arengar

harass [hərǽs] VT acosar, hostigar

harbor [hárbɚ] N (for ships) puerto *m*; (refuge) refugio *m*; VT (refugees, suspicions) albergar; (hopes) abrigar

hard [hɑrd] ADJ (firm) duro; (erect) tieso; (difficult) difícil; (arduous) arduo; **to play** —**ball** ser despiadado; — **cash** dinero contante y sonante *m*; — **coal** antracita *f*; — **copy** copia *f*; — **core** núcleo resistente *m*; —**-core** (pornography) duro; (politics) radical; — **disk** disco duro *m*; — **hat** casco *m*; —**headed** testarudo; —**hearted** duro de corazón; — **liquor** bebida alcohólica fuerte *f*; — **luck** mala suerte *f*; — **of hearing** medio sordo; —**-on** erección *f*; **he had a** —**on** la tenía dura; —**pressed** en aprietos; —**ware** (metal articles) ferretería *f*; (computer) hardware *m*; —**ware store** ferretería *f*; —**wood** madera noble *f*; — **water** agua dura *f*; — **winter** invierno crudo *m*; —**-wired** programado; —**working** trabajador; ADV (fall, push) con fuerza; (work) duro, con ahinco

harden [hárdn] VI/VT (make or become hard) endurecer(se); (make or become experienced) curtir(se)

hardening [hárdnɪŋ] N endurecimiento *m*

hardly [hárdli] ADV (scarcely) apenas; (at all) en absoluto; — **anyone** casi nadie; — **surprising** nada sorprendente

hardness [hárdnɪs] N dureza *f*

hardship [hárdʃɪp] N penuria *f*, penalidad *f*

hardy [hárdi] ADJ robusto

hare [hɛr] N liebre *f*; —**brained** descabellado; —**lip** labio leporino *m*

harem [hérəm] N harén m

harm [hɑrm] N daño m, mal m, perjuicio m; vt (object) dañar; (person) hacer daño; (chances) perjudicar

harmful [hɑ́rmfəł] ADJ perjudicial, dañino, nocivo

harmless [hɑ́rmlɪs] ADJ inocuo, inofensivo

harmonic [hɑrmɑ́nɪk] ADJ & N armónico m

harmonious [hɑrmóniəs] ADJ armonioso

harmonize [hɑ́rmənaɪz] vi/vt armonizar

harmony [hɑ́rməni] N armonía f

harness [hɑ́rnɪs] N arnés m, jaez m, guarnición f; vt (put on a harness) enjaezar; (utilize) aprovechar

harp [hɑrp] N arpa f; vi (play the harp) tocar el arpa; (insist) machacar; **to — on** insistir sobre

harpoon [hɑrpún] N arpón m; vt arponear

harpsichord [hɑ́rpsɪkɔrd] N clavicémbalo m

harrowing [hǽroɪŋ] ADJ angustioso; **— adventure** aventura espeluznante f

harry [hǽri] vt acosar, hostigar

harsh [hɑrʃ] ADJ (words) duro; (surface) áspero; (discipline) severo, férreo; (winter) crudo, riguroso

harshness [hɑ́rʃnɪs] N (of words) dureza f; (of a surface) aspereza f; (of character) severidad f; (of a winter) rigor m

harvest [hɑ́rvɪst] N cosecha f; (of sugar) zafra f; vt cosechar

hash [hæʃ] N guisado m, picadillo m

hashish [hæʃíʃ] N hachís m

hassle [hǽsəł] N rollo m, lío m; vt jorobar

haste [hest] N prisa f; **in —** de prisa; **to make —** darse prisa, apresurarse; *Am* apurarse

hasten [hésən] vi apresurarse; *Am* apurarse; vt acelerar, adelantar

hasty [hésti] ADJ apresurado, precipitado, presuroso; *Am* apurado; **to be —** precipitarse, apresurarse

hat [hæt] N sombrero m

hatch [hætʃ] vi/vt (chicks) empollar; (plot, scheme) fraguar, maquinar; N (chicks) nidada f; (opening) escotilla f; **— way** escotilla f

hatchet [hǽtʃɪt] N hacha f; **— job** crítica feroz f; **— man** sicario m; **to bury the —** hacer las paces

hate [het] N odio m; vi/vt odiar; **I — to admit it** me molesta admitirlo; **I — eating leftovers** detesto comer restos

hateful [hétfəł] ADJ odioso, aborrecible

hatred [hétrɪd] N odio m

haughtiness [hɔ́dɪnɪs] N altivez f, altanería f, soberbia f

haughty [hɔ́di] ADJ altivo, altanero, soberbio

haul [hɔl] vt (transport) transportar; (drag) arrastrar; vi (pull) jalar (de), tirar (de); N (quantity transported) carga f; (tug) tirón m; (catch of fish) redada f; (stolen goods) botín m; **long — distancia larga f

haunch [hɔntʃ] N anca f

haunt [hɔnt] vi/vt (frequent) frecuentar; (enchant) rondar; **that idea —s me** me obsesiona esa idea; **—ed house** casa embrujada f; N (of animals, criminals) guarida f; (of people socializing) sitio frecuentado m

have [hæv] v AUX haber; vt tener; **to — to** tener que; **to — a baby** dar a luz; **to — a look at** echar una mirada a; **to — a suit made** mandarse hacer un traje; **— him come later** dile que venga más tarde; **what did she — on?** ¿qué tenía puesto? **we've been had** nos estafaron

haven [hévən] N abrigo m, refugio m

havoc [hǽvək] N estrago m; **to wreak —** hacer estragos

hawk [hɔk] N gavilán m; vt pregonar

hay [he] N heno m; **— fever** alergia al polen f; **— loft** henil m; **—seed** paleto -ta mf; **—stack** almiar m; **to look for a needle in a —** buscar una aguja en un pajar

hazard [hǽzəd] N (chance) azar m; (danger) peligro m; vt arriesgar, aventurar

hazardous [hǽzədəs] ADJ peligroso

haze [hez] N neblina f, calina f; vt atormentar (como parte de un rito de iniciación)

hazel [hézəł] N avellano m; **—nut** avellana f; ADJ de avellano

hazy [hézi] ADJ (weather) brumoso; (idea) confuso, vago

he [hi] PRON él; **—-goat** macho cabrío m; **— who** el que, quien

head [hed] N (of body) cabeza f; (of bed) cabecera f; (chief) jefe -fa mf; **—ache** dolor de cabeza m; **— cold** resfrío m; **—dress** tocado m, adorno para la cabeza m; **—gear** (hat) sombrero m; (helmet) casco m; (for a horse) cabezada f; **—land** cabo m, promontorio m; **—light** faro delantero m; **—line** titular m; **—long** (head first) de cabeza; (hastily) precipitadamente; **— of hair** cabellera f; **—on** de frente; **—phone** audífono m, auricular m; **—quarters** (military) cuartel general m; (police) jefatura f; (corporation) oficina central f; **—rest** reposacabezas m sg; **—set** auriculares m pl; **—s or tails** cara o cruz; **I can't make —s or tails of it** esto no tiene ni pies ni cabeza; **— start** ventaja f; **— stone** lápida f; **—strong**

testarudo; —**way** avance *m*; —**word** voz
f; **to make** —**way** avanzar, progresar; **to
be out of one's** — desvariar; **to come to
a** — (a crisis) precipitarse; (an abscess)
supurar; **to keep one's** — mantener la
calma; VT (lead) encabezar; (steer) dirigir;
VI dirigirse; **to** — **off** atajar; **it went to
his** — se le fue a la cabeza

heading [hέdɪŋ] N encabezamiento *m*

heal [hil] VT curar; VI (get well) sanar,
curarse; (form a scar) cicatrizarse

health [hɛlθ] N salud *f*; — **care** asistencia
médica *f*; — **food** comida macrobiótica *f*;
— **insurance** seguro de salud *m*

healthful [hέlθfəl] ADJ saludable, sano

healthy [hέlθi] ADJ sano, saludable

heap [hip] N montón *m*, pila *f*; VT
amontonar; VI apilar; **to** — **up**
amontonarse

hear [hir] VI/VT (perceive) oír; VT (listen)
escuchar; **to** — **about** / **of someone** /
something oír hablar de alguien / algo;
to — **from someone** tener noticias de
alguien; **I won't** — **of your leaving** no
quiero saber de que te vayas

hearer [hírə] N oyente *mf*

hearing [hírɪŋ] N (sense) oído *m*; (trial)
audiencia *f*; **within** — al alcance del
oído; — **aid** audífono *m*; —-**impaired**
sordo

hearsay [hírse] N testimonio de oídas *m*; **by**
— de oídas

hearse [hɜ-s] N coche fúnebre *m*, carroza *f*

heart [hɑrt] N (organ) corazón *m*; (spirit)
ánimo *m*; —**ache** angustia *f*; — **attack**
ataque cardíaco *m*; —**beat** latido *m*; **I
would do it in a** —**beat** lo haría sin
pestañear; —**broken** inconsolable;
—**burn** acidez de estómago *f*; — **disease**
enfermedad coronaria *f*; —**felt** sincero,
sentido; — **murmur** soplo cardíaco *m*;
my —**felt sympathy** mi más sentido
pésame; —-**warming** reconfortante; **at**
— en realidad, en el fondo; **from the
bottom of one's** — de corazón, con toda
el alma; **to learn by** — aprender de
memoria; **to take** — cobrar ánimo; **to
take to** — tomar a pecho

hearten [hártn̩] VT animar

hearth [hɑrθ] N hogar *m*

heartless [hártlɪs] ADJ despiadado, desalmado

hearty [hárdi] ADJ (cordial) cordial; (strong)
fuerte; — **appetite** apetito saludable *m*; **a**
— **laugh** una risa desbordante; — **meal**
una comida abundante

heat [hit] N (warmth) calor *m*; (passion) ardor
m; (estrus) celo *m*; (source of heat)

calefacción *f*; (preliminary race)
eliminatoria *f*; —**stroke** insolación *f*; VI/VT
calentar(se); **to** — **up** acalorarse

heater [híɾə] N calentador *m*

heating [híɾɪŋ] N calefacción *f*

heave [hiv] VT (raise) levantar; (throw)
arrojar, lanzar; (sigh) exhalar; (pull) jalar;
VI (pant) jadear; (vomit) hacer arcadas; N
(throw) lanzamiento *m*; (pull) tirón *m*

heaven [hέvən] N cielo *m*

heavenly [hέvənli] ADJ celestial; — **bodies**
cuerpos celestes *m pl*; **it was** — estuvo
divino

heaviness [hέvɪnɪs] N pesadez *f*

heavy [hέvi] ADJ (weighty) pesado; (thick)
grueso, pesado; (dense) denso; (oppressive)
opresivo; — **artillery** artillería pesada *f*;
— **breathing** jadeos *m pl*; —-**duty** para
uso industrial; —-**handed** severo,
autoritario; **with a** — **heart** abatido; —
rain lluvia fuerte *f*; — **schedule** agenda
cargada *f*, —**weight** peso pesado *m*; N
villano -na *mf*

Hebrew [híbru] N & ADJ hebreo -a *mf*;
(language) hebreo *m*

heck [hɛk] INTERJ ¡caramba! **what the** — **are
you doing?** ¿qué demonios haces? **that
was a** — **of a good game** fue un
partidazo

hectare [hέktɛr] N hectárea *f*

hectic [hέktɪk] ADJ febril, agitado

hedge [hɛdʒ] N (row of bushes) seto *m*;
(precaution) precaución *f*; VI/VT (a bet)
cubrir(se); VT (a question) evadir

hedgehog [hέdʒhɑg] N erizo *m*

hedonism [hídnɪzəm] N hedonismo *m*

heebie-jeebies [híbidʒíbiz] N **it gives me
the** — me pone los pelos de punta

heed [hid] VT atender; N atención *f*, cuidado
m; **to pay** — **to** prestar atención a

heel [hil] N (of foot or sock) talón *m*; (of
shoe) tacón *m*; **kick up one's** —**s** tirar la
chancleta, soltarse el pelo; VT poner tacón
a; VI/VT seguir de cerca

hegemony [hɪdʒέməni] N hegemonía *f*

heifer [hέfə] N novilla *f*, vaquilla *f*

height [haɪt] N (of a building, mountain)
altura *f*; (of a person) estatura *f*; (utmost
point) colmo *m*

heighten [háɪtn̩] VI/VT (increase)
aumentar(se); (intensify) realzar

heinous [hénəs] ADJ aborrecible

heir [ɛr] N heredero -ra *mf*; — **apparent**
presunto heredero *m*, presunta heredera *f*

heiress [έrɪs] N heredera *f*

helicopter [hέlɪkɑptə] N helicóptero *m*

helium [híliəm] N helio *m*

helix [hílɪks] N hélice f

hell [hɛł] N infierno m; **—-raiser** camorrista mf

hello [heló] INTERJ ¡hola! (on the telephone) hola; Sp diga; Mex bueno; RP olá

helm [hɛłm] N timón m

helmet [hɛ́łmɪt] N (for bikes, etc.) casco m; (armor) yelmo m

help [hɛłp] N (aid) ayuda f; (rescue) auxilio m; (remedy) remedio m; (employee) empleado -da mf; INTERJ ¡auxilio! ¡socorro! VI/VT (aid) ayudar, asistir; (rescue) auxiliar, socorrer; **— yourself** sírvete; **he cannot — it** no puede evitarlo; **he cannot — but come** no puede menos que venir; **may I — you?** ¿en qué le puedo servir?

helper [hɛ́łpɚ] N ayudante mf, asistente mf

helpful [hɛ́łpfəł] ADJ (useful) útil; (willing to help) servicial

helping [hɛ́łpɪŋ] N porción f

helpless [hɛ́łpłɪs] ADJ desamparado, desvalido

helplessness [hɛ́łpłɪsnɪs] N desamparo m, desvalimiento m

hem [hɛm] N dobladillo m, orillo m; (of a skirt) ruedo m; VT hacer dobladillos en, orillar; **to — in** arrinconar; **to — and haw** vacilar

hematoma [himətómə] N hematoma m

hemisphere [hɛ́mɪsfɪr] N hemisferio m

hemlock [hɛ́mlɑk] N cicuta f

hemoglobin [hímǝglobɪn] N hemoglobina f

hemophilia [himǝfíliǝ] N hemofilia f

hemorrhage [hɛ́mǝrɪdʒ] N hemorragia f

hemorrhoids [hɛ́mǝrɔɪdz] N hemorroides f pl

hemp [hɛmp] N cáñamo m

hen [hɛn] N (chicken) gallina f; (female bird) ave hembra f; **—-pecked** dominado por su mujer

hence [hɛns] ADV de ahí; **a week —** de aquí a una semana

henceforth [hɛ́nsfɔrθ] ADV de aquí en adelante, de hoy en adelante

hepatitis [hɛpǝtáɪtɪs] N hepatitis f

her [hɚ] PRON **I see —** la veo; **I talk to —** le hablo (a ella); **I went with —** fui con ella; POSS ADJ **this is — dog** este es su perro, este es el perro de ella

herald [hɛ́rǝłd] N heraldo m; VT anunciar, proclamar

herb [ɝb] N hierba f

herbal [ɝ́bǝł] ADJ de hierbas; **— tea** tisana f

herbicide [ɝ́bɪsaɪd] N herbicida m

herbivore [ɝ́bǝvɔr] N herbívoro m

herbivorous [hɝbívǝrǝs] ADJ herbívoro

herd [hɝd] N (of animals) manada f; (of goats) hato m; (of sheep) rebaño m; (of horses, donkeys) recua f; **the common —** el populacho, la chusma; **—sman** pastor m; VT arrear; VI ir en manada

here [hir] ADV aquí, acá; **— it is** aquí está; **that is neither — nor there** eso no viene al caso; **—after** en adelante; **the —after** el más allá; **—by** (in writing) por la presente; **I —by pronounce you husband and wife** los declaro marido y mujer; **—in** en el presente; **—'s to you!** ¡a tu salud! **—tofore** hasta ahora; **—with** (hereby) por la presente; (attached) adjunto; **the — and now** el presente

hereditary [hǝrɛ́DɪtɛrI] ADJ hereditario

heredity [hǝrɛ́DɪtI] N herencia f

heresy [hɛ́rɪsi] N herejía f

heretic [hɛ́rɪtɪk] N hereje mf

heritage [hɛ́rɪtɪdʒ] N herencia f, patrimonio m

hermetic [hɝmɛ́Dɪk] ADJ hermético

hermit [hɝ́mɪt] N ermitaño -ña mf; **— crab** ermitaño m

hernia [hɝ́niǝ] N hernia f; **—ted** herniado; **—ted disk** hernia de disco f

hero [híro] N (brave man) héroe m; (main character) protagonista mf

heroic [hɪróɪk] ADJ heroico

heroin [hɛ́roɪn] N heroína f

heroine [hɛ́roɪn] N heroína f

heroism [hɛ́roɪzǝm] N heroísmo m

heron [hɛ́rǝn] N garza f

herpes [hɝ́piz] N herpes m

herring [hɛ́rɪŋ] N arenque m

hers [hɝz] PRON **this book is —** este libro es suyo/de ella; **these things are —** estas cosas son suyas; **— is bigger** el suyo/la suya es más grande; **a friend of —** un amigo suyo/de ella

herself [hɝsɛ́łf] PRON ella misma; **she — wrote the letter** ella misma escribió la carta; **she's not — today** hoy no es la misma de siempre; **she was sitting by —** estaba sentada sola; **she — did it** lo hizo sola, lo hizo ella misma; **she talks to —** ella habla para sí, habla sola; **she looked at — in the mirror** se miró en el espejo; **she bought — a house** se compró una casa

hesitant [hɛ́zɪtǝnt] ADJ vacilante

hesitate [hɛ́zɪtet] VI (pause) vacilar; (stutter) titubear; (doubt) dudar

hesitating [hɛ́zɪteDɪŋ] ADJ vacilante

hesitation [hɛzɪtéʃǝn] N (pause) vacilación f; (stammer) titubeo m; (doubt) duda f

heterogeneous [hɛDǝrǝdʒínɪǝs] ADJ heterogéneo

heterosexual [hɛDǝrosɛ́kʃuǝł] ADJ heterosexual

hexagon [héksəgɑn] N hexágono *m*
hey [he] INTERJ ¡oiga!
heyday [héde] N auge *m*
hiatus [haiéɒəs] N hiato *m*
hibernate [háibə-net] VI hibernar
hiccup, hiccough [híkʌp] N hipo *m*; VI hipar, tener hipo
hick [hɪk] N & ADJ paleto -ta *mf*
hickory [híkəri] N nogal americano *m*
hide [haɪd] VI/VT ocultar(se), esconder(se); — **and seek** *Sp* escondite *m*; *Am* escondidas *f pl*; —**out** escondite *m*; N cuero *m*, piel *f*, pellejo *m*
hideous [hídɪəs] ADJ horrendo, espantoso
hierarchy [háɪərɑrki] N jerarquía *f*
hieroglyphic [haɪrəglífɪk] ADJ & N jeroglífico *m*
high [haɪ] ADJ alto; (intoxicated) ebrio; (on drugs) volado; — **and dry** (ship) en seco; (person) colgado; — **blood pressure** hipertensión *f*; —**brow** culto; —**class** de clase; —**er-up** superior; — **explosive** explosivo de alta potencia *m*; — **fever** fiebre elevada *f*; — **fidelity** alta fidelidad *f*; —**grade** de calidad superior; —**handed** arbitrario; — **jump** salto alto *m*; —**lands** tierras altas *f pl*; —**lights** lo más destacado *m*, —**lights** claritos *m pl*, mechas *f pl*; **to** —**light** resaltar; —**minded** idealista; —**pitched** agudo; —**powered** de alta potencia; —**priced** caro; —**rise** de muchos pisos; — **school** escuela secundaria *f*; *Sp* instituto *m*; — **seas** alta mar *f*, —**sounding** altisonante; —**speed** de alta velocidad; — **spirits** buen ánimo *m*; —**strung** nervioso; —**tech** alta tecnología *f*; — **temperature** temperatura máxima *f*; — **tide** pleamar *f*; —**way** carretera *f*, ruta *f*; — **wind** ventarrón *m*; **in** — **gear** a toda marcha; **two feet** — dos pies de altura; **it is** — **time that** ya era hora de que; **to look** — **and low** buscar por todas partes; N flash *m*, subida *f*
highly [háɪli] ADV — **amusing** sumamente divertido; — **paid** muy bien pagado; **he spoke** — **of her** habló muy bien de ella
highness [háɪnɪs] N alteza *f*
hijack [háɪdʒæk] VT secuestrar (un vehículo)
hike [haɪk] N caminata *f*; VI salir a caminar; **take a** —! ¡ve a freír espárragos!
hilarious [hɪlérɪəs] ADJ graciosísimo, para morirse de risa
hill [hɪl] N (elevated area) colina *f*, cerro *m*; (pile) montón *m*; —**billy** paleto -ta *mf*; —**side** ladera *f*, —**top** cumbre *f*, cima *f*
hillock [hílək] N otero *m*

hilly [híli] ADJ accidentado
hilt [hɪlt] N empuñadura *f*; **to the** — al máximo
him [hɪm] PRON **I see** — lo veo; *Sp* le veo; **I talk to** — le hablo; **I went with** — fui con él
himself [hɪmsélf] PRON él mismo; **he** — **wrote the letter** el mismo escribió la carta; **he's not** — **today** hoy no es el mismo de siempre; **he was sitting by** — estaba sentado solo; **he talks to** — el habla para sí/solo; **he looked at** — **in the mirror** se miró en el espejo; **he bought** — **a house** se compró una casa
hind [haɪnd] ADJ trasero; —**most** último; **in** —**sight** a posteriori; N cierva *f*
hinder [híndə-] VT impedir, entorpecer, estorbar
Hindi [híndi] N hindi *m*
hindrance [híndrəns] N obstáculo *m*, impedimento *m*, traba *f*
Hindu [híndu] ADJ & N hindú *mf*
hinge [hɪndʒ] N gozne *m*, quicio *m*; VT engoznar, poner goznes; VI **to** — **on** depender de
hint [hɪnt] N (clue) indirecta *f*, pista *f*; (trace) dejo *m*; **to take the** — darse por enterado; VT insinuar
hip [hɪp] N cadera *f*
hippopotamus [hɪpəpáɒəməs] N hipopótamo *m*
hire [haɪr] VT (engage for work) contratar; VI/VT (rent) alquilar(se); **to** — **out** dar en alquiler, alquilar; N (engagement) contratación *f*; (employee) nuevo -va empleado -da *mf*; (rent) alquiler *m*
his [hɪz] POSS ADJ **this is** — **dog** este es su perro/el perro de él; PRON **these things are** — estas cosas son suyas; — **is right here** el suyo/la suya está aquí; **a friend of** — un amigo suyo/una amiga suya
Hispanic [hɪspǽnɪk] ADJ hispánico, hispano; N hispano -na *mf*
hiss [hɪs] VI sisear; (to boo) silbar; N siseo *m*
histamine [hístəmin] N histamina *f*
historian [hɪstɔ́rian] N historiador -ra *mf*
historic [hɪstɔ́rɪk] ADJ histórico
historical [hɪstɔ́rɪkəl] ADJ histórico
history [hístəri] N historia *f*
histrionics [hɪstriɑ́nɪks] N histrionismo *m*
hit [hɪt] VT (a target) dar en; (a car) chocar con; (a key) pulsar, tocar; **they** — **it off well** se llevaron bien desde el principio; **to** — **the mark** acertar, dar en el blanco; **to** — **upon** dar con; **to** — **on** ligar (con); N (blow) golpe *m*; (success) éxito *m*; (dose) dosis *f*; **that was a** — **with me** me

encantó; —**and-run** que se da a la fuga
después de atropellar a alguien; —**man**
sicario *m*; —**or-miss** al azar

hitch [hɪtʃ] VT atar, amarrar; (pants) levantar;
(yoke) uncir, enganchar; **to get —ed**
casarse; **to —hike** *Sp* hacer autostop; *Am*
hacer dedo; N (knot) nudo *m*; (difficulty)
dificultad *f*; (period) período *m*

hither [híðɚ] ADV acá; — **and thither** acá y
allá; —**to** hasta ahora

HIV (human immunodeficiency virus)
[etʃaɪví] N VIH *m*

hive [haɪv] N (shelter for bees) colmena *f*;
(colony of bees) enjambre *m*; —**s** urticaria
f

hoard [hɔrd] N reserva *f*; VI/VT acaparar

hoarse [hɔrs] ADJ ronco; (of alcoholics)
aguardentoso

hoarseness [hɔ́rsnɪs] N ronquera *f*

hoax [hoks] N engaño *m*

hobble [hábəł] VI (limp) cojear; VT (tie to
impede walking) manear; (hinder) trabar;
N cojera *f*; (rope) traba *f*, manea *f*

hobby [hábi] N hobby *m*

hobo [hóbo] N vagabundo *m*

hockey [háki] N hockey *m*

hodgepodge [hádʒpadʒ] N mezcolanza *f*,
batiburrillo *m*

hoe [ho] N azada *f*, azadón *m*; VI/VT limpiar
con azadón

hog [hɑg] N puerco *m*, cerdo *m*, marrano *m*;
Am chancho *m*; —**wash** pamplinas *f pl*;
to live high on the — vivir en la
abundancia; VT acaparar, adueñarse de

hoist [hɔɪst] VT izar; N torno *m*, guinche *m*

hokey [hóki] ADJ sensiblero

hold [hołd] VT (bear) llevar, sujetar; (contain)
contener; (detain) detener; (decide legally,
sustain a note) sostener; (opine) opinar; VI
(remain fast) aguantar, resistir; (occupy a
position) ocupar; (be valid) ser válido; **to
— back** detener; **to — down** sujetar; **to
— forth** perorar; **to — hands** tomarse de
la mano; **to — in place** sujetar; **to — a
meeting** celebrar una reunión; **to — off**
mantener(se) a distancia; **to — on** (not let
go) agarrar(se), sujetar(se); (stop) esperar;
(persist) persistir; — **the pickles on that
burger!** una hamburguesa sin pepinillos,
por favor; **to — someone responsible**
hacerle a uno responsable; **to —
someone to his word** obligar a uno a
cumplir con su palabra; **to — oneself
erect** ponerse derecho; **to — one's own**
defenderse; **to — one's tongue** callarse,
morderse la lengua; **to — out** tender; **to
— still** quedarse/estarse quieto; **to —**

tight agarrarse; **to — to one's promise**
cumplir con la palabra; **to — up** (raise)
alzar; (detain) detener; (rob) atracar,
asaltar; (persevere) aguantar; **how much
does it —** ? ¿Qué capacidad tiene? N
(grip) agarro *m*; (thing to grasp) asidero *m*;
(dominion) dominio *m*; (wrestling move)
llave *f*; (in music) calderón *m*; (of a ship)
bodega *f*; —**up** golpe *m*, atraco *m*; **to get
—** of agarrar; **to take — of** *Sp* coger,
agarrar; **to have a good — on
something** agarrarse bien de algo

holder [hółdɚ] N (person) tenedor -ra *mf*,
poseedor -ra *mf*; (device) receptáculo *m*

holding [hółdɪŋ] N propiedad *f*; —
company holding *m*; —**s** (financial)
valores en cartera *m pl*; (of a library)
fondos *m pl*

hole [hoł] N agujero *m*; (in a wall) boquete
m; (of an animal) madriguera *f*; (in
ground only, golf included) hoyo *m*; **to
be in a —** hallarse/estar en un apuro/
aprieto

holiday [hálɪde] N día de fiesta *m*; —**s**
vacaciones *f pl*

holiness [hólɪnɪs] N santidad *f*

holistic [holístɪk] ADJ holístico

Holland [hálənd] N Holanda *f*

hollow [hálo] ADJ (empty) hueco; (concave)
cóncavo; (sunken) hundido; (insincere)
falso; N (cavity) hueco *m*, concavidad *f*;
(valley) hondonada *f*, hondo *m*; VT **to —
out** ahuecar, vaciar

holly [háli] N acebo *m*

holocaust [háləkɔst] N holocausto *m*

holster [hółstɚ] N pistolera *f*, funda de
pistola *f*

holy [hóli] ADJ santo, sagrado; — **Bible** Santa
Biblia *f*; — **cow/Moses/mackerel!**
¡jobar! — **Ghost** Espíritu Santo *m*; —
Spirit Espíritu Santo *m*; — **war** guerra
santa *f*; — **water** agua bendita *f*

homage [hámɪdʒ] N homenaje *m*; **to pay —**
rendir homenaje, honrar

home [hom] N casa *f*, hogar *m*; (for old
people, orphans) asilo *m*, hogar *m*; **at —**
en casa; ADJ doméstico; — **economics**
economía doméstica *f*; — **game** partido
en casa *m*; —**land** patria *f*; —**less** sin
techo; —**made** casero; — **office** oficina
central *f*; —**owner** propietario -ria de un
bien inmueble *mf*; — **page** página de
inicio *f*; — **rule** autonomía *f*; — **run**
jonrón *m*; **to be —sick** echar de menos/
extrañar (a la familia); —**sickness**
morriña *f*, añoranza *f*; — **stretch** último
trecho *m*; —**work** tarea domiciliaria *f*,

deber *m*; ADV (direction) a casa; (location) en casa; **to strike** — dar en el blanco

homely [hómlɪ] ADJ (ugly) feo; (familiar) familiar, doméstico

homeopathic [homiopǽθɪk] ADJ homeopático

homeopathy [homiápəθi] N homeopatía *f*

homestead [hómstɛd] N heredad *f*, casa de la familia *f*

homeward [hómwəd] ADV a casa; **— bound** camino a casa

homicide [hámɪsaɪd] N homicidio *m*

homogeneous [homədʒínɪəs] ADJ homogéneo

homogenize [həmádʒənaɪz] VT homogeneizar

homonym [hámənɪm] N homónimo *m*

homosexual [homosɛ́kʃuəł] ADJ & N homosexual *mf*

Honduran [handúrən] ADJ & N hondureño -ña *mf*

Honduras [handúrəs] N Honduras *f*

hone [hon] VT afilar; **to —** one's skills desarrollar las destrezas; N piedra de afilar *f*

honest [ánɪst] ADJ honrado, honesto; **I'll be — with you** voy a ser franco contigo; **—!** ¡de veras!

honesty [ánɪsti] N (integrity) honradez *f*, honestidad *f*; (sincerity) franqueza *f*

honey [háni] N (sweet substance) miel *f*; (endearment) querido -da *mf*; **—bee** abeja *f*; **—comb** panal *m*; **—suckle** madreselva *f*

honeymoon [hánimun] N luna de miel *f*; VI pasar la luna de miel

honk [haŋk] N (car) bocinazo *m*, pitazo *m*; (goose) graznido *m*; VI/VT tocar la bocina; VI graznar

honor [ánə] N (respect, privilege) honor *m*; (good reputation) honra *f*; (title) señoría *f*; **with —s** con honores; VT (revere) honrar; (accept invitation, check) aceptar

honorable [ánərəbəł] ADJ honorable

honorary [ánəreri] ADJ honorario

hood [hud] N (of a coat) capucha *f*, caperuza *f*; (of a car) capó *m*; *Am* tapa *f*; VT encapuchar

hoodlum [húdləm] N maleante *mf*, gamberro -rra *mf*

hoof [huf] N casco *m*, pezuña *f*; VI **to — it** ir andando

hook [huk] N (for lifting) gancho *m*, garfio *m*; (for fishing) anzuelo *m*; **— and eye** alamar *m*, macho y hembra *m*; **by — or by crook** por las buenas o por las malas; **—up** conexión *f*, enganche *m*; VT (snag) enganchar; (a dress) abrochar; **to — up**

conectar, enganchar

hooked [hukt] ADJ (shaped like a hook) ganchudo; (addicted) enganchado

hooky [húki] N **to play** — hacer novillos

hoop [hup] N aro *m*

hoot [hut] VI/VT (of owl) ulular; (in derision) abuchear; N (of an owl) ululato *m*; (cry of derision) abucheo *m*; **I don't give a —** no me importa un comino; **it's a —** es para morirse de risa

hop [hap] VI saltar, brincar; **to — on** subirse a montar; N (short jump) saltito *m*, brinco *m*; (dance) bailongo *m*; **—s** lúpulo *m*

hope [hop] N esperanza *f*; VI/VT esperar; **to — for** esperar; **to — against** esperar lo imposible

hopeful [hópfəł] ADJ (having hopes) esperanzado; (giving hopes) esperanzador, alentador

hopefully [hópfəli] ADV **she'll come** ojalá (que) venga

hopeless [hóplɪs] ADJ (without hope) desesperanzado; (with no solution) irremediable; (unattainable) inalcanzable; **— cause** causa perdida *f*; **it is —** no tiene remedio; **the new secretary is — with numbers** el nuevo secretario es un desastre con los números

hopelessness [hóplɪsnɪs] N desesperanza *f*

horde [hɔrd] N (of people) horda *f*; (of animals) plaga *f*

horizon [həráɪzən] N horizonte *m*

horizontal [hɔrɪzántł] ADJ horizontal

hormone [hɔ́rmon] N hormona *f*

horn [hɔrn] N (of an animal, substance) cuerno *m*, asta *f*; (of an automobile) bocina *f*, claxon *m*; (musical) corno *m*, trompa *f*; **— of plenty** cuerno de la abundancia *m*; **to toot one's own —** darse autobombo; VI **to — in** entremeterse

hornet [hɔ́rnɪt] N avispón *m*; **—'s nest** avispero *m*

horny [hɔ́rni] ADJ (with hard skin) calloso; (sexually excited) *Sp fam* cachondo; *Am fam* caliente

horoscope [hɔ́rəskop] N horóscopo *m*

horrendous [hərɛ́ndəs] ADJ horrendo

horrible [hɔ́rəbəł] ADJ horrible

horrid [hɔ́rɪd] ADJ horrendo

horrify [hɔ́rəfaɪ] VT horrorizar

horror [hɔ́rə] N horror *m*

hors d'oeuvre [ɔrdɔ́-v] N entremés *m*

horse [hɔrs] N caballo *m*; **—back** lomo de caballo *m*; **to ride —back** montar a caballo, cabalgar; **—fly** tábano *m*; **—laugh** carcajada *f*; **—man** jinete *m*;

—manship equitación *f*; **—play** payasadas *f pl*; **—power** caballo de fuerza *m*; **— race** carrera de caballos *f*; **—radish** rábano picante *m*; **— sense** sentido común *m*; **—shoe** herradura *f*; hold your **—s!** ¡para el carro! vi to **— around** payasear

horticulture [hórɪkʌltʃ*ə*] N horticultura *f*

hose [hoz] N (for legs) medias *f pl*; (for irrigation) manguera *f*, manga *f*

hosiery [hóȝəri] N (stockings) medias *f pl*; (shop for stockings) calcetería *f*

hospice [háspɪs] N (inn) hospicio *m*; (hospital) hospital para enfermos terminales *m*

hospitable [haspíɾəbəł] ADJ hospitalario, acogedor

hospital [háspɪd] N hospital *m*

hospitality [haspɪtǽlɪɾi] N hospitalidad *f*

host [host] N anfitrión *m*; (at home, also for a parasite) huésped *m*; (on television) presentador -ra *mf*; (army) hueste *f*; (multitude) multitud *f*, cúmulo *m*; (wafer) hostia *f*

hostage [hástɪʤ] N rehén *m*

hostel [hástəł] N hostal *m*

hostelry [hástəłri] N hostería *f*

hostess [hóstɪs] N (at home) anfitriona *f*; (on airplanes) azafata *f*

hostile [hástəł] ADJ hostil

hostility [hastíłɪɾi] N hostilidad *f*

hot [hat] ADJ (at high temperature) caliente; (sweltry) caluroso; (spicy) picante; (sexy) bueno; (sexually aroused) *Sp* cachondo; *Am* caliente; (stolen) robado; (recent) de último momento; (popular) popular; **— and heavy** apasionadamente; **—bed** semillero *m*; **— dog** perro caliente *m*; **—headed** impetuoso, exaltado; **—house** invernadero *m*; **— potato** patata caliente *f*; **— seat** situación embarazosa *f*; **—shot** estrella *f*; **— tub** jacuzzi *m*; (to) **—wire** hacerle un puente a; **it is — today** hace calor hoy; **— under the collar** enojado

hotel [hotéł] N hotel *m*; **—keeper** hotelero -ra *mf*

hound [haund] N perro de caza *m*, sabueso *m*; vt acosar, perseguir

hour [aur] N hora *f*; **— hand** horario *m*; **his finest —** su mejor momento *m*

hourly [áurli] ADV (by the hour) por horas; (on the hour) cada hora; **— wages** salario por hora *m*

house [haus] N (residence) casa *f*; (legislature) cámara legislativa *f*; **— arrest** detención domiciliaria *f*; **—boat** casa flotante *f*; **—cleaning** limpieza de la casa *f*; **—hold**

casa *f*, familia *f*; **—keeper** (in a house) ama de llaves *f*; (in a home) encargado -da de limpieza *mf*; **—keeping** mantenimiento del hogar *m*; **—to—** puerta a puerta; **—top** techo *m*, tejado *m*; **—wife** ama de casa *f*; **—work** trabajo de casa *m*, quehaceres domésticos *m pl*; **on the —** la casa paga; **to keep —** cuidar la casa; [hauz] vi/vt alojar

housing [háuzɪŋ] N (place to live) vivienda *f*; (protective covering) caja *f*

hovel [hávəł] N (hut) choza *f*, cabaña *f*, tugurio *m*; (open shed) cobertizo *m*

hover [hávə] vi (bird) cernerse; (hang in air) estar suspendido; (linger) rondar; **—craft** aerodeslizador *m*

how [hau] ADV cómo; **— about your mom?** ¿y tu mamá? **— beautiful!** ¡qué hermoso! **— come?** ¿por qué? **— early (late, soon)?** ¿cuándo? ¿a qué hora? **— far is it?** ¿a qué distancia está? ¿cuánto dista de aquí? **— long?** ¿cuánto tiempo? **— many?** ¿cuántos? **— much is it?** ¿cuánto vale? **— old are you?** ¿cuántos años tienes? **no matter —** much it rains por mucho que llueva; **he knows — difficult it is** él sabe lo difícil que es

however [hauévə] CONJ sin embargo, no obstante; ADV como quieras; **— difficult it may be** por muy difícil que sea; **— much it rains** por mucho que llueva

howl [haul] vi aullar; (wind) ulular; (with laughter) reír a carcajadas; N aullido *m*, alarido *m*

HTML (HyperText Markup Language) [etʃtiemét] N HTML *m*

hub [hʌb] N (center of wheel) cubo *m*; (center of activity) núcleo *m*; **—cap** tapacubos *m sg*

hubbub [hábʌb] N alboroto *m*, barullo *m*

huckster [hákstə] N (peddler) vendedor ambulante *m*; (promoter) mercachifle *m*

huddle [hádł] vi/vt (a group) apiñar(se); (curl up) acurrucar(se); (consult) conferenciar; N tropel *m*; (group meeting for consultation) reunión *f*; **to be in a —** estar agrupados; **to get in a —** agruparse

hue [hju] N matiz *m*

huff [hʌf] N **to get into a —** enojarse; **to — and puff** resoplar

hug [hʌg] vi/vt abrazar(se); **to — the coast** costear; N abrazo *m*

huge [hjuʤ] ADJ enorme, fiero

hull [hʌł] N (of a ship, airplane) casco *m*; (of beans, peas) vaina *f*; (of fruits, nuts) cáscara *f*; vt (beans, peas) desvainar; (nuts) cascar

hum [hʌm] VI/VT (person) tararear; (insect, machine) zumbar; (place of activity) hervir; **to —** to sleep arrullar; N (of voice) tarareo m; (of insect, machine) zumbido m

human [hjúmən] ADJ & N humano m; **— being** ser humano m

humane [hjumén] ADJ humano, humanitario

humanism [hjúmənɪzəm] N humanismo m

humanitarian [hjumænɪtériən] ADJ humanitario

humanity [hjumǽnɪdi] N humanidad f; **humanities** humanidades f pl

humble [hʌ́mbəl] ADJ humilde; VT humillar

humid [hjúmɪd] ADJ húmedo

humidify [hjumídəfaɪ] VT humidificar

humidity [hjumídɪdi] N humedad f

humiliate [hjumíliet] VT humillar, vejar

humiliation [hjumìliéʃən] N humillación f

humility [hjumílɪdi] N humildad f

hummingbird [hʌ́mɪŋbɚd] N colibrí m

humor [hjúmɚ] N humor m, humorismo m; **out of —** de mal humor, malhumorado; VT complacer a

humorous [hjúmɚəs] ADJ gracioso, chistoso

hump [hʌmp] N joroba f, giba f, corcova f; **we're over the —** ya pasamos lo peor; VI/VT Sp vulg follar; Am coger, culear

humpback [hʌ́mpbæk] N jorobado -da mf; **— whale** ballena jorobada f, yubarta f

hunch [hʌntʃ] N presentimiento m, corazonada f; **— back** (person) jorobado -da mf; (hump) corcova f; VI encorvar

hundred [hʌ́ndrɪd] NUM cien(to); **a — people** cien personas; **a — and fifty people** ciento cincuenta personas; N cien / ciento m; **—s** centenares m pl, cientos m pl

hundredth [hʌ́ndrɪdθ] ADJ centésimo

Hungarian [hʌŋgériən] ADJ & N húngaro -ra mf

Hungary [hʌ́ŋgəri] N Hungría f

hunger [hʌ́ŋgɚ] N hambre f; VI pasar hambre; **to — for** ansiar, anhelar

hungry [hʌ́ŋgri] ADJ hambriento; **to be —** tener hambre

hunk [hʌŋk] N pedazo m, cacho m; **he's a real —** es un cacho de hombre

hunt [hʌnt] VI/VT (seek prey) cazar; **to — down** dar caza a; **to — for** buscar; N (activity of hunting) caza f; (instance of hunting) cacería f; (search) búsqueda f

hunter [hʌ́ntɚ] N (who captures game) cazador -ra mf; (seeker) buscador -ra mf; (dog) perro de caza m

hunting [hʌ́ntɪŋ] N caza f; **— knife** cuchillo de caza m

huntsman [hʌ́ntsmən] N cazador m

hurdle [hɚ́dl] N (impediment) obstáculo m; (in races) valla f; VT saltar

hurl [hɚl] VI/VT arrojar, lanzar, precipitar

hurrah [hərá] INTERJ ¡hurra!

hurricane [hɚ́ɪken] N huracán m

hurried [hɚ́id] ADJ apresurado; Am apurado

hurry [hɚ́i] VI darse prisa, apresurarse; Am apurarse; VT apresurar; Am apurar; **to — in (out)** entrar (salir) de prisa; **to — up** apresurar(se), dar(se) prisa; Am apurar(se); N prisa f; Am apuro m; **to be in a —** tener prisa; Am estar apurado

hurt [hɚt] VI/VT (to injure) lastimar(se), hacer(se) daño; (damage) dañar(se); (harm) perjudicar(se); VI (suffer pain) doler; **to get —** lastimarse; **to — someone's feelings** lastimar a uno; **my tooth —s** me duele la muela / el diente; N (damage) daño m; (wound) herida f, lastimadura f

hurtful [hɚ́tfəl] ADJ hiriente

husband [hʌ́zbənd] N marido m, esposo m; VT administrar

hush [hʌʃ] VI/VT acquietar(se), callar(se); **—!** ¡chitón! ¡silencio! **to — up a scandal** encubrir un escándalo; N silencio m

husk [hʌsk] N (shell) cáscara f; (pod) vaina f; (of corn) chala f; Sp farfolla f; N (corn) quitar la chala / farfolla a; (beans, peas) desvainar

husky [hʌ́ski] ADJ (voice) ronco; (strong) recio; N husky m, perro esquimal m

hustle [hʌ́səl] VI (work energetically) afanarse; (swindle) estafar; VT (hurry along) empujar; N (bustle) ajetreo m; (scheme) timo m; **— and bustle** ajetreo m, trajín m

hut [hʌt] N choza f, cabaña f

hyacinth [háɪəsɪnθ] N jacinto m

hybrid [háɪbrɪd] ADJ híbrido

hydrate [háɪdret] N hidrato m; VI/VT hidratar(se)

hydraulic [haɪdrɔ́lɪk] ADJ hidráulico

hydrocarbon [háɪdrəkɑrbən] N hidrocarburo m

hydroelectric [haɪdroɪléktrɪk] ADJ hidroeléctrico

hydrogen [háɪdrədʒən] N hidrógeno m; **— bomb** bomba de hidrógeno f; **— peroxide** peróxido de hidrógeno m, agua oxigenada f

hydrophobia [haɪdrəfóbiə] N hidrofobia f

hydroplane [háɪdrəplen] N hidroavión m

hyena [haɪínə] N hiena f

hygiene [háɪdʒin] N higiene f

hymn [hɪm] N himno m

hype [haɪp] N exageración f; VT promocionar (exageradamente)

hyper [háɪpɚ] ADJ hiperactivo

hyperactive [haɪpə-ǽktɪv] ADJ hiperactivo

hypersensitive [haɪpə-sénsɪDɪv] ADJ hipersensible

hyperventilate [haɪpə-vént|et] VI hiperventilar

hyphen [háɪfən] N guión m

hypnosis [hɪpnósɪs] N hipnosis f

hypnotize [hípnətaɪz] VT hipnotizar

hypoallergenic [haɪpoæləɽénɪk] ADJ hipoalérgico

hypochondriac [haɪpokándriæk] N hipocondríaco mf, hipocondriaco mf

hypocrisy [hɪpákrɪsi] N hipocresía f

hypocrite [hípəkrɪt] N hipócrita mf

hypocritical [hɪpəkrídɪkəl] ADJ hipócrita

hypoglycemia [haɪpoglaɪsímiə] N hipoglucemia f

hypothesis [haɪpáθɪsɪs] N hipótesis f

hysterectomy [hɪstəréktəmi] N histerectomía f

hysterical [hɪstérɪkəl] ADJ (out of control) histérico; (funny) desternillante

Ii

I [aɪ] PRON yo

I-beam [áɪbim] N viga doble f

Iberian [aɪbíriən] ADJ ibérico

ice [aɪs] N hielo m; — age periodo glaciar m; —berg iceberg m; —box Sp nevera f; Am refrigerador m; — cream helado m; — cream cone cucurucho de helado m; —-cream parlor heladería f; — hockey hockey sobre hielo m; — skates patines de cuchilla m pl; —d tea té helado m; — water agua helada f; to break the — romper el hielo; on — en suspenso; VI/VT (freeze) helar(se); (cover with ice) cubrir(se) de hielo; VT (cover with icing) bañar; (insure a deal) cerrar; to —-skate patinar sobre hielo

Iceland [áɪslænd] N Islandia f

Icelander [áɪslændə] N islandés -esa mf

Icelandic [aɪslǽndɪk] ADJ islandés

icicle [áɪsɪkəl] N carámbano m

icing [áɪsɪŋ] N (frosting) baño m; (formation of ice) formación de hielo f

icon [áɪkən] N icono m, ícono m (also computer term)

icy [áɪsi] ADJ helado

idea [aɪdíə] N idea f

ideal [aɪdíəl] N ideal m; ADJ ideal, idóneo

idealism [aɪdíəlɪzəm] N idealismo m

idealist [aɪdíəlɪst] N idealista mf

idealistic [aɪdiəlístɪk] ADJ idealista

identical [aɪdéntɪkəl] ADJ idéntico

identification [aɪdɛntəfɪkéʃən] N identificación f; — card carnet de identidad m, cédula de identidad f

identify [aɪdéntəfaɪ] VI/VT identificar(se)

identity [aɪdéntɪDi] N identidad f

ideology [aɪdiáləʤi] N ideología f

idiocy [ídiəsi] N idiotez f

idiom [ídiəm] N modismo m

idiosyncrasy [ɪDiosínkrəsi] N idiosincrasia f

idiot [ídiət] N idiota mf, gilipollas mf sg

idiotic [ɪDiádɪk] ADJ idiota

idle [áɪdl] ADJ (not active) ocioso; (lazy) perezoso, holgazán; (of a machine, worker) parado; (of an engine) en ralentí; (meaningless) vacío; VI (person) holgazanear; (motor) girar en vacío; VT (cause to be idle) dejar parado / desocupado

idleness [áɪdl|nɪs] N (inactivity) ociosidad f, ocio m, holganza f; (sloth) pereza f

idler [áɪdlə] N holgazán -ana mf, zanguango -ga mf

idol [áɪdl] N ídolo m

idolatry [aɪdálətri] N idolatría f

idolize [áɪdl|aɪz] VT idolatrar

idyll [áɪdl] N idilio m

if [ɪf] CONJ si; — I were you en tu lugar/yo que tú; — only I had known de haber sabido/ojalá hubiera sabido; he's tall, — a bit stooped es alto, aunque un poco encorvado; N —s condiciones f pl; no —s, ands, or buts no hay pero que valga

igloo [íglu] N iglú m

ignite [ɪgnáɪt] VI/VT encender(se), prender fuego (a)

ignition [ɪgníʃən] N ignición f, encendido m; — switch llave de contacto f

ignoble [ɪgnóbəl] ADJ innoble

ignorance [ígnərəns] N ignorancia f

ignorant [ígnərənt] ADJ ignorante

ignore [ɪgnór] VT ignorar

ilk [ɪlk] N ralea f, calaña f

ill [ɪl] ADJ enfermo, malo; — fortune mala suerte f; — nature mal genio m, mala índole f; — repute mala fama f; — will mala voluntad f; N (unfavorable statement) mal m; (sickness) enfermedad f; (calamity) calamidad f; ADV — at ease incómodo; —-bred maleducado; —-fated fatídico, funesto, desastrado; —-gotten mal adquirido; —-humored malhumorado; —-mannered maleducado, grosero; —-natured de mal genio; we can — afford to stop now de ninguna manera podemos detenernos ahora; **you would be —-advised to invest** sería desaconsejable que invirtieras

illegal [ɪlígəł] ADJ ilegal

illegitimate [ɪlɪʤ́ɪɾəmɪt] ADJ ilegítimo

illicit [ɪlísɪt] ADJ ilícito

illiteracy [ɪlíɾərəsi] N analfabetismo *m*

illiterate [ɪlíɾɪt] ADJ & N analfabeto -ta *mf*

illness [íłnɪs] N enfermedad *f*

illuminate [ɪlúmɪnet] VI/VT iluminar(se)

illumination [ɪlumənéʃən] N iluminación *f*

illusion [ɪlúʒən] N ilusión *f*

illusory [ɪlúzɑɾi] ADJ ilusorio

illustrate [íləstret] VI/VT ilustrar

illustration [ɪləstréʃən] N ilustración *f*, estampa *f*

illustrator [íləstreɾɚ] N ilustrador -ra *mf*, dibujante *mf*

illustrious [ɪlástriəs] ADJ ilustre, eximio

image [ímɪʤ] N imagen *f*

imagery [ímɪʤri] N conjunto de imágenes *m*

imaginary [ɪmǽʤəneri] ADJ imaginario, fabuloso

imagination [ɪmæʤənéʃən] N imaginación *f*, fantasía *f*

imaginative [ɪmǽʤənəɾɪv] ADJ imaginativo, fantasioso

imagine [ɪmǽʤɪn] VI/VT imaginar(se); — **that!** ¡figúrate!

imbalance [ɪmbǽləns] N desequilibrio *m*

imbecile [ímbəsəł] N imbécil *mf*

imbibe [ɪmbáɪb] VI/VT beber

imbue [ɪmbjú] VT imbuir, infundir

imitate [ímɪtet] VT imitar

imitation [ɪmɪtéʃən] N imitación *f*; ADJ — **leather** imitación de cuero *f*

imitator [ímɪteɾɚ] N imitador -ra *mf*

immaculate [ɪmǽkjəłɪt] ADJ inmaculado

immaterial [ɪmətíriəł] ADJ inmaterial; **it is — to me** me es indiferente

immature [ɪmətʃúr] ADJ inmaduro

immediate [ɪmídɪɪt] ADJ inmediato

immense [ɪméns] ADJ inmenso

immensity [ɪménsɪɾi] N inmensidad *f*

immerse [ɪmɚ́s] VT (submerge) sumergir; (absorb) sumir

immigrant [ímɪɡrənt] ADJ & N inmigrante *mf*

immigrate [ímɪɡret] VI inmigrar

immigration [ɪmɪɡréʃən] N inmigración *f*

imminent [ímənənt] ADJ inminente

immobile [ɪmóbəł] ADJ inmóvil

immobilize [ɪmóbəlaɪz] VT inmovilizar

immodest [ɪmádɪst] ADJ impúdico, deshonesto

immodesty [ɪmádɪsti] N deshonestidad *f*

immoral [ɪmɔ́rəł] ADJ inmoral

immorality [ɪmɔrǽlɪɾi] N inmoralidad *f*

immortal [ɪmɔ́rdł] ADJ & N inmortal *mf*

immortality [ɪmɔrtǽlɪɾi] N inmortalidad *f*

immovable [ɪmúvəbəł] ADJ inamovible

immune [ɪmjún] ADJ inmune; — **system** sistema inmune *m*

immunity [ɪmjúnɪɾi] N inmunidad *f*

immutable [ɪmjúɾəbəł] ADJ inmutable

impact [ímpækt] N impacto *m*; VI/VT impactar

impair [ɪmpér] VT dañar, deteriorar, menoscabar

impairment [ɪmpérmənt] N daño *m*, deterioro *m*, menoscabo *m*

impala [ɪmpálə] N impala *m*

impale [ɪmpéł] VT empalar

impart [ɪmpárt] VT (bestow knowledge) impartir; (reveal) revelar

impartial [ɪmpárʃəł] ADJ imparcial

impartiality [ɪmparʃiǽlɪɾi] N imparcialidad *f*

impasse [ímpæs] N impasse *m*

impassioned [ɪmpǽʃənd] ADJ apasionado

impassive [ɪmpǽsɪv] ADJ impasible

impatience [ɪmpéʃəns] N impaciencia *f*

impatient [ɪmpéʃənt] ADJ impaciente

impeach [ɪmpítʃ] VT acusar formalmente; **to — a person's honor** poner en tela de juicio el honor de uno

impeachment [ɪmpítʃmənt] N impeachment *m*

impede [ɪmpíd] VT obstaculizar, estorbar, trabar

impediment [ɪmpédəmənt] N impedimento *m*, obstáculo *m*; (of speech) defecto *m*

impel [ɪmpéł] VT impeler

impending [ɪmpéndɪŋ] ADJ inminente

impenetrable [ɪmpénɪtrəbəł] ADJ impenetrable

imperative [ɪmpéraɾɪv] ADJ (like a command) imperativo; (necessary) imperioso; N (command, grammatical mood) imperativo *m*; (obligation) obligación *f*

imperceptible [ɪmpɚséptəbəł] ADJ imperceptible

imperfect [ɪmpɚ́fɪkt] ADJ & N imperfecto *m*

imperial [ɪmpíriəł] ADJ imperial

imperialism [ɪmpíriəlɪzəm] N imperialismo *m*

imperil [ɪmpérəł] VT poner en peligro

imperious [ɪmpíriəs] ADJ imperioso

impersonal [ɪmpɚ́sənəł] ADJ impersonal

impersonate [ɪmpɚ́sənet] VT (assume traits of) hacerse pasar por; (mimic) imitar

impertinence [ɪmpɚ́tnəns] N impertinencia *f*

impertinent [ɪmpɚ́tnənt] ADJ impertinente

impervious [impə́·viəs] ADJ impermeable; (to reason) refractario

impetuous [impétʃuəs] ADJ impetuoso

impetus [ímpədəs] N ímpetu *m*, empuje *m*

impious [ímpiəs] ADJ impío

implacable [implǽkəbəl] ADJ implacable

implant [implǽnt] VT implantar; [ímplænt] N implante *m*

implement [ímpləmənt] N implemento *m*, utensilio *m*; [ímpləmənt] VT implementar, instrumentar

implicate [ímplɪket] VT implicar, involucrar

implicit [implísɪt] ADJ implícito

implore [implɔ́r] VI/VT implorar

imply [implái] VT dar a entender

impolite [impəláit] ADJ descortés

import [impɔ́rt] VT (bring in) importar; [ímpɔrt] N (act of importing, thing imported) importación *f*; (significance) significado *m*

importance [impɔ́rtn̩s] N importancia *f*

important [impɔ́rtn̩t] ADJ importante

impose [impóz] VT imponer; **to — (upon)** abusar (de)

imposing [impózɪŋ] ADJ imponente, impresionante

imposition [impəzíʃən] N (act of imposing, burden) imposición *f*; (abuse) abuso *m*

impossibility [impəsəbílɪDi] N imposibilidad *f*

impossible [impásəbəl] ADJ (not possible) imposible; (unbearable) insoportable; **to make —** imposibilitar

impostor [impástə·] N impostor -ra *mf*

impotence [ímpətəns] N impotencia *f*

impotent [ímpətənt] ADJ impotente

impoverish [impávə·ıʃ] VT empobrecer

impregnate [imprégnet] VT (cause to be permeated) impregnar; (make pregnant) fecundar

impress [imprés] VT (make a mark by pressing) estampar; VI/VT (affect deeply) impresionar

impression [impréʃən] N impresión *f*; (feeling) impresión *f*, sensación *f*

impressive [imprésiv] ADJ impresionante

imprint [ímprɪnt] N (indentation) impresión *f*, marca *f*; (printer's mark) pie de imprenta *m*; [imprínt] VT (impress on) imprimir; (fix firmly in mind) grabar

imprison [imprízən] VT (in jail) encarcelar; (anywhere) apresar

imprisonment [imprízənmənt] N encarcelamiento *m*

improbable [imprábəbəl] ADJ improbable

impromptu [imprámptu] ADJ improvisado; **he gave the speech —** improvisó el discurso; N impromptu *m*

improper [imprápə·] ADJ indecoroso, inconveniente

improve [imprúv] VI/VT mejorar(se); **to — upon** mejorar

improvement [imprúvmənt] N (act & effect of improving) mejora *f*; (in health) mejoría *f*

improvisation [imprɑvɪzéʃən] N improvisación *f*

improvise [ímprəvaiz] VI/VT improvisar

imprudent [imprúdn̩t] ADJ imprudente, desatinado

impudence [ímpjədəns] N impertinencia *f*, descaro *m*, desparpajo *m*

impudent [ímpjədənt] ADJ impertinente, descarado

impulse [ímpʌls] N impulso *m*; **to act on —** obrar impulsivamente

impulsive [impʌ́lsiv] ADJ impulsivo

impunity [impjúnɪDi] N impunidad *f*

impure [impjúr] ADJ impuro

impurity [impjúrɪDi] N impureza *f*

in [ɪn] PREP en; **— London** en Londres; **— haste** de prisa; **— the morning** por / en la mañana; **— writing** por escrito; **she was walking — the street** andaba por la calle; **to arrive — London** llegar a Londres; **the books — the box** los libros de la caja; **at two — the morning** a las dos de la mañana; **dressed — white** vestido de blanco; **the tallest — his class** el más alto de su clase; **to come — a week** venir dentro de una semana; ADV adentro, dentro; **is she — or out?** ¿está adentro o afuera? **to be all —** estar rendido; **to be — with someone** estar bien con alguien; **to come —** entrar; **to have it — for someone** tenerle ojeriza a una persona; **to put —** meter; **the doctor is —** el doctor está; **hats are —** los sombreros están de moda; **—patient** paciente internado -da *mf*; **—seam** entrepierna *f*; **—step** empeine *m*; ADJ **the — place to eat** el restaurante de moda; **an — joke** una broma para un grupo selecto

inability [ɪnəbílɪDi] N inhabilidad *f*, incapacidad *f*

inaccessible [ɪnæksésəbəl] ADJ inaccesible, inasequible

inaccurate [ɪnǽkjə·ɪt] ADJ (not precise) inexacto, impreciso; (wrong) incorrecto

inactive [ɪnǽktiv] ADJ inactivo

inactivity [ɪnæktívɪDi] N inactividad *f*

inadequate [ɪnǽDɪkwɪt] ADJ (insufficient) insuficiente; (unacceptable) inaceptable

inadvertent [ɪnədvə́ːtn̩t] ADJ (unintentional) involuntario; (careless) descuidado, negligente

inadvisable [ɪnədváɪzəbəl] ADJ desaconsejable

inane [ɪnén] ADJ necio

inanimate [ɪnǽnəmɪt] ADJ inanimado

inasmuch as [ɪnəzmátʃæz] CONJ puesto que

inattentive [ɪnətɛ́ntɪv] ADJ desatento

inaudible [ɪnɔ́ːdəbəl] ADJ inaudible

inaugurate [ɪnɔ́gjəret] VT (initiate) inaugurar; (induct into office) investir de un cargo

inauguration [ɪnɔgjəréʃən] N (initiation) inauguración f; (induction) investidura f

inboard [ɪnbɔrd] ADJ dentro del casco

inborn [ɪnbɔ́rn] ADJ innato

incandescence [ɪnkændésəns] N incandescencia f

incandescent [ɪnkændésənt] ADJ incandescente

incantation [ɪnkæntéʃən] N conjuro m

incapable [ɪnképəbəl] ADJ incapaz

incapacitate [ɪnkəpǽsɪtet] VT incapacitar

incarcerate [ɪnkɑ́rsəret] VT encarcelar

incendiary [ɪnséndɪɛri] ADJ & N incendiario -ria mf; **— bomb** bomba incendiaria f

incense [ɪnséns] N incienso m; [ɪnséns] VT encolerizar

incentive [ɪnséntɪv] N incentivo m, acicate m

inception [ɪnsépʃən] N comienzo m

incessant [ɪnsésənt] ADJ incesante

incest [ɪnsɛst] N incesto m

inch [ɪntʃ] N pulgada (2.54 centímetros) f; **to be within an — of** estar a un punto de; VI avanzar poco a poco

incidence [ɪnsɪdəns] N incidencia f

incident [ɪnsɪdənt] N incidente m, lance m; (crime, accident) suceso m

incidental [ɪnsɪdɛ́ntl] ADJ (happening in accordance with) accesorio; N **— music** música incidental f; **—s** gastos imprevistos m pl

incidentally [ɪnsɪdɛ́ntli] ADV a propósito

incinerate [ɪnsínəret] VT incinerar

incipient [ɪnsípiənt] ADJ incipiente, naciente

incision [ɪnsíʒən] N incisión f

incisive [ɪnsáɪsɪv] ADJ incisivo

incite [ɪnsáɪt] VT incitar

inclement [ɪnklémənt] ADJ inclemente

inclination [ɪnklənéʃən] N (slope) inclinación f; (tendency) afición f, inclinación f

incline [ɪnkláɪn] VI/VT inclinar(se); [ɪnkláɪn] N declive m, pendiente f

include [ɪnklúd] VT incluir

inclusive [ɪnklúsɪv] ADJ inclusivo; **from Monday to Friday —** de lunes a viernes inclusive

incoherent [ɪnkohírənt] ADJ incoherente

income [ɪ́nkʌm] N Sp renta f; Am ingreso m; **— tax** Sp impuesto sobre la renta m; Am impuesto sobre ingresos m

incoming [ɪ́nkʌmɪŋ] ADJ entrante

incomparable [ɪnkámpə·əbəl] ADJ incomparable, sin parangón

incompatible [ɪnkəmpǽɾəbəl] ADJ incompatible

incompetent [ɪnkámpɪtənt] ADJ incompetente

incomplete [ɪnkəmplít] ADJ incompleto

incomprehensible [ɪnkɑmprɪhɛnsəbəl] ADJ incomprensible

inconceivable [ɪnkənsívəbəl] ADJ inconcebible

inconclusive [ɪnkənklúsɪv] ADJ no concluyente

inconsiderate [ɪnkənsíɾə·ɪt] ADJ desconsiderado

inconsistency [ɪnkənsístənsi] N (condition) inconsecuencia f; (instance) incoherencia f

inconsistent [ɪnkənsístənt] ADJ inconsecuente

inconspicuous [ɪnkənspíkjuəs] ADJ poco llamativo; **to be —** pasar inadvertido

inconstancy [ɪnkánstənsi] N inconstancia f

inconstant [ɪnkánstənt] ADJ inconstante

incontinent [ɪnkántənənt] ADJ incontinente

incontrovertible [ɪnkantrəvə́ːɾəbəl] ADJ incontrovertible

inconvenience [ɪnkənvínjəns] N (state of being inconvenient) inconveniencia f; (thing that is inconvenient) molestia f, inconveniente m; VT incomodar, molestar

inconvenient [ɪnkənvínjənt] ADJ (bothersome) incómodo; (untimely) inoportuno

incorporate [ɪnkɔ́rpəret] VI/VT (include) incorporar(se); (form a corporation) constituir(se) en sociedad

incorrect [ɪnkərɛ́kt] ADJ incorrecto

incorrigible [ɪnkɔ́rɪdʒəbəl] ADJ incorregible

increase [ɪnkrís] VI/VT aumentar(se), incrementar(se); [ɪnkris] N aumento m, incremento m

increasingly [ɪnkrísɪŋli] ADV cada vez más

incredible [ɪnkrɛ́ɾəbəl] ADJ increíble

incredulous [ɪnkrɛ́dʒələs] ADJ incrédulo

increment [ɪ́nkrəmənt] N incremento m

incriminate [ɪnkrímənet] VT incriminar

incubator [ɪ́ŋkjəbeɾə·] N incubadora f

inculcate [ɪnkʌ́fket] VT inculcar

incumbent [ɪnkʌ́mbənt] ADJ **a duty — upon me** un deber que me incumbe; N titular *m*

incur [ɪnkɝ] VT incurrir en

incurable [ɪnkjúrəbəl] ADJ incurable

indebted [ɪndéɾɪd] ADJ endeudado; **I'm — to you for your kindness** estoy en deuda contigo por tu amabilidad

indebtedness [ɪndéɾɪdɪns] N endeudamiento *m*, adeudo *m*

indecency [ɪndísənsi] N indecencia *f*

indecent [ɪndísənt] ADJ indecente; **— exposure** delito de exhibicionismo *m*

indecision [ɪndɪsíʒən] N indecisión *f*

indeed [ɪndíd] ADV de verdad; INTERJ (ironically) ¡no me digas! (sincerely) ¡tienes razón!

indefensible [ɪndɪfénsəbəl] ADJ indefendible

indefinite [ɪndéfənɪt] ADJ indefinido

indelible [ɪndéləbəl] ADJ indeleble

indelicate [ɪndélɪkɪt] ADJ (tactless) indelicado; (offensive) indecoroso

indemnify [ɪndémnəfaɪ] VT indemnizar

indemnity [ɪndémnɪɾi] N indemnización *f*

indent [ɪndént] VI/VT sangrar

indentation [ɪndɛntéʃən] N (notch) muesca *f*; (blank space) sangría *f*

independence [ɪndɪpéndəns] N independencia *f*

independent [ɪndɪpéndənt] ADJ independiente

indestructible [ɪndɪstráktəbəl] ADJ indestructible

indeterminate [ɪndɪtɝmənɪt] ADJ indeterminado

index [índɛks] N índice *m*; **— card** ficha *f*; **finger** índice *m*; VT (incorporate into an index) poner en el índice; (make the index) poner un índice; (adjust wages) indexar

India [índiə] N India *f*

Indian [índiən] ADJ & N indio -a *mf*; **— Ocean** Océano Indico *m*

indicate [índɪket] VT indicar

indication [ɪndɪkéʃən] N indicación *f*

indicative [ɪndíkəɾɪv] ADJ & N indicativo *m*

indict [ɪndáɪt] VT acusar

indictment [ɪndáɪtmənt] N acusación *f*

indifference [ɪndífrəns] N indiferencia *f*

indifferent [ɪndífrənt] ADJ indiferente

indigenous [ɪndíʤənəs] ADJ (person) indígena; (plant, animal) autóctono

indigent [índɪʤənt] ADJ & N indigente *mf*

indigestion [ɪndɪʤéstʃən] N indigestión *f*

indignant [ɪndígnənt] ADJ indignado

indignation [ɪndɪgnéʃən] N indignación *f*

indignity [ɪndígnɪɾi] N ultraje *m*, afrenta *f*

indigo [índɪgo] N índigo *m*, añil *m*; **— blue** azul añil *m*

indirect [ɪndɪrékt] ADJ indirecto; **— object** complemento / objeto indirecto *m*

indiscreet [ɪndɪskrít] ADJ indiscreto

indiscretion [ɪndɪskréʃən] N indiscreción *f*

indispensable [ɪndɪspénsəbəl] ADJ indispensable, imprescindible

indispose [ɪndɪspóz] VT indisponer

indisposed [ɪndɪspózd] ADJ indispuesto; **to become —** indisponerse

indistinct [ɪndɪstíŋkt] ADJ indistinto

individual [ɪndəvíʤuəl] ADJ individual; N individuo *m*, persona *f*; *pej* sujeto *m*, individuo *m*

individualism [ɪndəvíʤuəlɪzəm] N individualismo *m*

individualist [ɪndəvíʤuəlɪst] N individualista *mf*

individuality [ɪndəvɪʤuælɪɾi] N individualidad *f*

indivisible [ɪndəvízəbəl] ADJ indivisible

indoctrinate [ɪndáktrɪnet] VT adoctrinar

indolence [índələns] N indolencia *f*, desidia *f*

indolent [índələnt] ADJ indolente, haragán

indomitable [ɪndámɪɾəbəl] ADJ indomable

Indonesia [ɪndəníʒə] N Indonesia *f*

Indonesian [ɪndəníʒən] ADJ & N indonesio -sia *mf*

indoor [índɔr] ADJ interior; [ɪndɔrz] ADV **—s** dentro; **to go —s** entrar, ir para adentro

induce [ɪndús] VT inducir

inducement [ɪndúsmənt] N aliciente *m*, incentivo *m*

induct [ɪndákt] VT (initiate) admitir, iniciar; (draft) reclutar

induction [ɪndákʃən] N (philosophical, electrical) inducción *f*; (into an organization) admisión *f*, iniciación *f*

indulge [ɪndálʤ] VT mimar, consentir; VI **to — in** darse a, entregarse a; **to — oneself (in)** darse el gusto (de)

indulgence [ɪndálʤəns] N (act or state of indulging, religious) indulgencia *f*; (thing indulged in) exceso *m*, lujo *m*

indulgent [ɪndálʤənt] ADJ indulgente; (toward a child) complaciente

industrial [ɪndástriəl] ADJ industrial

industrialist [ɪndástriəlɪst] N industrial *mf*

industrious [ɪndástriəs] ADJ (student) aplicado, diligente; (worker) industrioso

industry [índəstri] N (manufacturing) industria *f*; (hard work) diligencia *f*

inebriated [iníbrietɪd] ADJ ebrio

inedible [ɪnédəbəl] ADJ incomestible, incomible

ineffable [ɪnéfəbəl] ADJ inefable

ineffective [ɪnɪféktɪv] ADJ (measure) ineficaz; (person) ineficiente

ineffectual [ɪnɪféktʃuəł] ADJ ineficaz
inefficient [ɪnɪfíʃənt] ADJ ineficiente
ineligible [ɪnélɪʤəbəł] ADJ inelegible
inept [ɪnépt] ADJ inepto
inequality [ɪnɪkwáłɪɾi] N desigualdad f
inert [ɪnɜ́ɾt] ADJ inerte
inertia [ɪnɜ́ɾʃə] N inercia f
inescapable [ɪnéskápəbəł] ADJ inevitable
inestimable [ɪnéstəməbəł] ADJ inestimable
inevitable [ɪnévɪɖəbəł] ADJ inevitable
inexcusable [ɪnɪkskjúzəbəł] ADJ inexcusable
inexhaustible [ɪnɪgzɔ́stəbəł] ADJ inagotable
inexorable [ɪnéksə-əbəł] ADJ inexorable
inexpensive [ɪnɪkspénsɪv] ADJ económico,
    barato
inexperienced [ɪnɪkspíɾiənst] ADJ inexperto
inexplicable [ɪnɪksplíkəbəł] ADJ inexplicable
infallible [ɪnfǽłəbəł] ADJ infalible
infamous [ínfəməs] ADJ infame, de mala
    fama
infamy [ínfəmi] N infamia f
infancy [ínfənsi] N primera infancia f
infant [ínfənt] N bebé m
infantile [ínfəntaɪł] ADJ infantil
infantry [ínfəntri] N infantería f; **—man**
    infante m
infatuated [ɪnfǽtʃuedɪd] ADJ enamorado
infect [ɪnfékt] VT (cause disease) infectar;
    (spread a mood) contagiar
infection [ɪnfékʃən] N infección f
infectious [ɪnfékʃəs] ADJ (disease) infeccioso,
    contagioso; (mood) contagioso
infer [ɪnfɜ́-] VT inferir, deducir
inference [ínfə-əns] N inferencia f, deducción
    f
inferior [ɪnfíɾiə-] ADJ & N inferior
inferiority [ɪnfɪɾiɔ́ɾɪɖi] N inferioridad f; **—**
    complex complejo de inferioridad m
infernal [ɪnfɜ́-nəł] ADJ infernal
inferno [ɪnfɜ́-no] N (fire) incendio m; (hot
    place) infierno m
infest [ɪnfést] VT infestar, plagar
infiltrate [ɪnfíltret] VI/VT infiltrar(se); **to —**
    an organization infiltrarse en una
    organización
infinite [ínfənɪt] ADJ & N infinito m
infinitive [ɪnfínɪɖɪv] ADJ & N infinitivo m
infinity [ɪnfínɪɖi] N (large number) infinidad
    f; (space) infinito m
infirm [ɪnfɜ́-m] ADJ enfermizo, achacoso
infirmary [ɪnfɜ́-məri] N enfermería f
infirmity [ɪnfɜ́-mɪɖi] N enfermedad f,
    achaque m
inflame [ɪnflém] VT (with infection)
    inflamar(se); (with passion) enardecer(se);
    (with fire) encender(se)
inflammation [ɪnfləméʃən] N inflamación f

inflate [ɪnflét] VI/VT (fill with air) inflar(se),
    hincharse; (exaggerate) exagerar
inflation [ɪnfléʃən] N (rise in prices) inflación
    f; (introduction of air) inflado m
inflexible [ɪnfléksəbəł] ADJ inflexible
inflict [ɪnflíkt] VT (impose on) infligir; **to —**
    a blow asestar un golpe
influence [ínfluəns] N influencia f, influjo m;
    VT influir en / sobre; **— peddling** tráfico
    de influencias m
influential [ɪnfluénʃəł] ADJ influyente
influenza [ɪnfluénzə] N gripe f
influx [ínflʌks] N (of fluid, goods) entrada f;
    (of people) afluencia f
infomercial [ínfomɚ-ʃəł] N infomercial m
inform [ɪnfɔ́rm] VI/VT (give knowledge)
    informar(se); VT (inspire) inspirar; **to —**
    against / on delatar a, denunciar a
informal [ɪnfɔ́rməł] ADJ informal
informant [ɪnfɔ́rmənt] N informante mf
information [ɪnfə-méʃən] N (service)
    información f; (details) informes m pl
informer [ɪnfɔ́rmə-] N informante mf, delator
    -ora mf, pej soplón -ona mf
infraction [ɪnfrǽkʃən] N infracción f
infrared [ɪnfrəréd] ADJ & N infrarrojo m
infrastructure [ínfrəstrʌktʃə-] N
    infraestructura f
infringe [ɪnfrínʤ] VT infringir; VI **to —**
    upon violar
infuriate [ɪnfjúriet] VT enfurecer, sublevar
infuse [ɪnfjúz] VT infundir
ingenious [ɪnʤínjəs] ADJ ingenioso
ingenuity [ɪnʤənúɪɖi] N ingenio m,
    inventiva f
ingest [ɪnʤést] VI/VT ingerir
ingrate [íngret] N ingrato -ta mf
ingratitude [ɪngrǽɖɪtud] N ingratitud f
ingredient [ɪngrídiənt] N ingrediente m
ingrown [íngron] ADJ encarnado
inhabit [ɪnhǽbɪt] VT habitar
inhabitant [ɪnhǽbɪtənt] N habitante mf
inhale [ɪnhél] VI/VT inhalar, aspirar
inherent [ɪnhérənt] ADJ inherente
inherit [ɪnhérɪt] VI/VT heredar
inheritance [ɪnhérɪ́nəns] N herencia f
inhibit [ɪnhíbɪt] VT inhibir, cohibir
inhibition [ɪnhɪbíʃən] N inhibición f,
    cohibición f
inhospitable [ɪnhɑspíɾəbəł] ADJ (person)
    inhospitalario; (place) inhóspito
inhuman [ɪnhjúmən] ADJ inhumano
inimitable [ɪnímɪɖəbəł] ADJ inimitable
initial [ɪníʃəł] ADJ & N inicial f; VT firmar las
    iniciales
initialize [ɪníʃəlaɪz] VT inicializar
initiate [ɪníʃiet] VT iniciar

initiative [ɪníʃəbɪv] N iniciativa *f*

inject [ɪndʒékt] VI/VT inyectar(se), pinchar(se)

injection [ɪndʒékʃən] N inyección *f*

injunction [ɪndʒʌ́ŋkʃən] N mandato judicial *m*, orden judicial *f*

injure [índʒɚ] VI/VT herir(se); (sports) lesionar(se)

injurious [ɪndʒúriəs] ADJ (harmful) perjudicial; (defamatory) injurioso

injury [índʒəri] N herida *f*, lesión *f*

injustice [ɪndʒʌ́stɪs] N injusticia *f*

ink [ɪŋk] N tinta *f*; VT (mark with ink) entintar; (sign) firmar; **—jet printer** impresora de inyección de tinta *f*; **—pad** almohadilla *f*; **—well** tintero *m*

inkling [íŋklɪŋ] N idea *f*

inlaid [ínled] ADJ incrustado; **— work** incrustación *f*

inland [ínlənd] ADJ interior; ADV tierra adentro

inlay [ɪnlé] VT incrustar; [ínle] N incrustación *f*

inmate [ínmet] N (in a prison) preso -sa *mf*, recluso -sa *mf*; (in an asylum) internado -da *mf*; (in a hospital) paciente *mf*

inn [ɪn] N posada *f*, fonda *f*; **—keeper** posadero -ra *mf*, fondista *mf*

innate [ɪnét] ADJ innato

inner [ínɚ] ADJ (inside) interior; (intimate) íntimo; **— city** zona céntrica empobrecida *f*; **— ear** oído interno *m*; **—most** más recóndito; **— tube** cámara *f*

inning [íniŋ] N entrada *f*

innocence [ínəsəns] N (absence of guilt) inocencia *f*; (naivety) candidez *f*, candor *m*

innocent [ínəsənt] ADJ & N inocente *mf*

innocuous [ɪnákjuəs] ADJ innocuo

innovation [ɪnəvéʃən] N innovación *f*

innuendo [ɪnjuéndo] N insinuación *f*

innumerable [ɪnúmərəbəł] ADJ innumerables

inoculate [ɪnákjəlet] VI/VT inocular(se)

inoffensive [ɪnəfénsɪv] ADJ inofensivo

inoperable [ɪnápə-əbəł] ADJ inoperable

inopportune [ɪnapə-tún] ADJ inoportuno

inordinate [ɪnɔ́rdnɪt] ADJ desmesurado

inorganic [ɪnɔrgǽnɪk] ADJ inorgánico; **— chemistry** química inorgánica *f*

input [ínput] N (electric, computer) entrada *f*; (opinion) opinión *f*; VT ingresar / entrar datos

inquire [ɪnkwáɪr] VI/VT inquirir, preguntar; **to — about / after** preguntar por; **to — into** indagar, investigar

inquiry [íŋkwəri] N (scientific) investigación *f*; (police) pesquisa *f*; **we made — about hotels** hicimos averiguaciones acerca de hoteles

inquisition [ɪnkwɪzíʃən] N inquisición *f*

inquisitive [ɪnkwízɪdɪv] ADJ (curious) inquisitivo, curioso; (asking many questions) preguntón

insane [ɪnsén] ADJ demente, loco; **— asylum** manicomio *m*

insanity [ɪnsǽnɪdi] N locura *f*, demencia *f*

insatiable [ɪnséʃəbəł] ADJ insaciable

inscribe [ɪnskráɪb] VT (mark) inscribir; (engrave) grabar; (dedicate) dedicar

inscription [ɪnskrípʃən] N (marks, engraving) inscripción *f*; (dedication) dedicatoria *f*

inscrutable [ɪnskrúdəbəł] ADJ inescrutable

insect [ínsekt] N insecto *m*

insecticide [ɪnséktɪsaɪd] N insecticida *m*

insectivorous [ɪnsektívə-əs] ADJ insectívoro

insecure [ɪnsɪkjúr] ADJ inseguro

insensible [ɪnsénsəbəł] ADJ insensible

insensitive [ɪnsénsɪdɪv] ADJ insensible

inseparable [ɪnsépə-əbəł] ADJ inseparable

insert [ɪnsɚ́t] VT insertar, introducir; (into a text) intercalar; [ínsɚt] N encarte *m*

insertion [ɪnsɚ́ʃən] N inserción *f*; (into a text) intercalación *f*

inside [ɪnsáɪd] PREP dentro de; ADV dentro, adentro; [ínsaɪd] N interior *m*; **to turn — out** volver del revés; **—s** entrañas *f pl*; **he passed me on the —** me pasó por la derecha; ADJ (interior) interior; **— job** delito cometido por un empleado *m*; **— track** pista interior *f*

insider [ɪnsáɪdɚ] N privilegiado -da *mf*; **— trading** abuso de información privilegiada *m*

insidious [ɪnsídiəs] ADJ insidioso

insight [ínsaɪt] N (intuition) perspicacia *f*; (discernment) discernimiento *m*

insignia [ɪnsígniə] N insignia *f*

insignificant [ɪnsɪgnífɪkənt] ADJ insignificante, menudo, nimio

insincere [ɪnsɪnsír] ADJ insincero

insinuate [ɪnsínjuet] VT insinuar

insinuation [ɪnsɪnjuéʃən] N insinuación *f*

insipid [ɪnsípɪd] ADJ insípido, soso

insist [ɪnsíst] VI/VT insistir; **to — on** insistir en

insistence [ɪnsístəns] N insistencia *f*

insistent [ɪnsístənt] ADJ insistente

insole [ínsoł] N plantilla *f*

insolence [ínsələns] N insolencia *f*

insolent [ínsələnt] ADJ insolente, atrevido

insoluble [ɪnsáljəbəł] ADJ insoluble

insolvent [ɪnsáłvənt] ADJ insolvente

inspect [ɪnspékt] VT inspeccionar; **to — the troops** pasar revista a la tropa, revistar la tropa

inspection [ɪnspékʃən] N inspección f; (of troops) revista f

inspector [ɪnspéktə] N inspector -ra mf

inspiration [ɪnspəréʃən] N inspiración f

inspire [ɪnspáɪr] VI/VT inspirar

instability [ɪnstəbíliɖi] N inestabilidad f

install [ɪnstɔ́l] VT instalar (also computer term)

installation [ɪnstəléʃən] N instalación f (also computer term)

installment [ɪnstɔ́lmənt] N (payment of debt) cuota f; (of a book) entrega f, fascículo m; **to pay in** —s pagar a plazos

instance [ínstəns] N ejemplo m; **for** — por ejemplo; **court of first** — tribunal de primera instancia m

instant [ínstənt] N instante m; **this** — ahora mismo; ADJ inmediato; — **coffee** café instantáneo m

instantaneous [ɪnstənténiəs] ADJ instantáneo

instead [ɪnstéd] ADV **she didn't want a sandwich, so she ordered a hamburger** — no quería un bocadillo, así que pidió una hamburguesa en su lugar; — **of** en lugar de, en vez de

instigate [ínstɪget] VT instigar

instill [ɪnstíl] VT inculcar

instinct [ínstɪŋkt] N instinto m

instinctive [ɪnstíŋktɪv] ADJ instintivo

institute [ínstɪtut] N instituto m; VT instituir

institution [ɪnstɪtúʃən] N institución f

instruct [ɪnstrʌ́kt] VT (teach) instruir; (command, advise) dar instrucciones; (command) mandar

instruction [ɪnstrʌ́kʃən] N instrucción f (also computer term); —s (orders) órdenes f pl; (information) instrucciones f pl, indicaciones f pl

instructive [ɪnstrʌ́ktɪv] ADJ instructivo

instructor [ɪnstrʌ́ktə] N (of skills) instructor -ra mf; (of knowledge) profesor -ra mf

instrument [ínstrəmənt] N instrumento m; — **panel** salpicadero m, tablero m

instrumental [ɪnstrəméntl] ADJ instrumental; **to be** — **in** ser fundamental para

insubordinate [ɪnsəbɔ́rdɲɪt] ADJ insubordinado

insufferable [ɪnsʌ́fəbəl] ADJ insufrible

insufficiency [ɪnsəfíʃənsi] N insuficiencia f

insufficient [ɪnsəfíʃənt] ADJ insuficiente

insulate [ínsəlet] VT aislar

insulation [ɪnsəléʃən] N aislamiento m

insulator [ínsəletə] N (material) aislante m; (device) aislador m

insulin [ínsəlɪn] N insulina f

insult [ínsʌlt] N insulto m, injuria f; [ɪnsʌ́lt] VT insultar, injuriar

insulting [ɪnsʌ́ltɪŋ] ADJ insultante, injurioso

insuperable [ɪnsúpəəbəl] ADJ insuperable

insurance [ɪnʃúrəns] N seguro m; — **agent** agente de seguros mf; — **company** compañía de seguros f; — **policy** póliza de seguro f

insure [ɪnʃúr] VI/VT asegurar(se)

insurmountable [ɪnsəmáuntəbəl] ADJ insuperable

insurrection [ɪnsərékʃən] N insurrección f

intact [ɪntækt] ADJ intacto

intangible [ɪntǽndʒəbəl] ADJ intangible

integer [íntɪdʒə] N (número) entero m

integral [íntɪgrəl] ADJ (complete) integral; (forming part of) integrante; N integral f; — **calculus** cálculo integral m

integrate [íntɪgret] VT integrar; VI integrarse a

integrity [ɪntégrɪɖi] N integridad f

intellect [íntlekt] N intelecto m

intellectual [ɪnt]éktʃuəl] ADJ & N intelectual mf

intelligence [ɪntélɪdʒəns] N inteligencia f (also secret information); — **quotient** coeficiente intelectual / de inteligencia m

intelligent [ɪntélɪdʒənt] ADJ inteligente

intelligible [ɪntélɪdʒəbəl] ADJ inteligible

intend [ɪnténd] VT pensar; **to** — **to do something** pensar hacer algo; **a book** —**ed for children** un libro destinado / dirigido a los niños

intense [ɪnténs] ADJ intenso

intensify [ɪnténsɪfaɪ] VI/VT intensificar(se)

intensity [ɪnténsɪɖi] N intensidad f

intensive [ɪnténsɪv] ADJ intensivo

intent [ɪntént] N intención f, propósito m; **to / for all** —**s and purposes** en la práctica; ADJ atento; — **on** resuelto a

intention [ɪnténʃən] N intención f

intentional [ɪnténʃənəl] ADJ intencional

intentionally [ɪnténʃənəli] ADV a propósito

inter [ɪntə́] VT sepultar

interact [ɪntəǽkt] VI interactuar

interactive [ɪntəǽktɪv] ADJ interactivo

intercede [ɪntəsíd] VI interceder

intercept [ɪntəsépt] VT interceptar

interception [ɪntəsépʃən] N interceptación f

intercession [ɪntəséʃən] N intercesión f

interchange [ɪntətʃéndʒ] N cambio m; (on road) enlace m; Sp intercambiador m; [ɪntətʃéndʒ] VI/VT cambiar, intercambiar

intercourse [ɪntəkɔrs] N (sexual) relación sexual f; (social) comunicación f, trato f

interest [íntrɪst] N interés m; (financial) interés m, rédito m; (share in a business) participación f; **mining** —s los negocios mineros; — **rate** tasa de interés f; VT interesar; **may I — you in a cookie?** ¿te puedo ofrecer una galleta?

interested [íntrɪstɪd] ADJ interesado; **to be / become — in** interesarse en / por

interesting [íntrɪstɪŋ] ADJ interesante

interface [íntə-fes] N interface mf, interfaz f

interfere [ɪntə-fír] VI interferir; (meddle) entrometerse; **to — with** interferir en

interference [ɪntə-fírəns] N interferencia f

interim [íntə-ɪm] N ínterin m; ADJ (person) interino; (decision) provisional

interior [ɪntíriə-] ADJ & N interior m; — **decoration** decoración de interiores f; — **design** diseño de interiores m

interjection [ɪntə-dʒékʃən] N interjección f, exclamación f

interlace [ɪntə-lés] VI/VT entrelazar(se)

interlinear [ɪntə-líniə-] ADJ interlineal

interlock [ɪntə-lák] VI/VT (gears) engranar(se); (branches, etc.) entrelazar(se); N interlock m

interlocking [ɪntə-lákɪŋ] ADJ (gears) engranado; (branches) entrelazado

interlude [íntə-lud] N (interval) intervalo m; (musical) interludio m; (theatrical) entremés m

intermediate [ɪntə-mídiɪt] ADJ intermedio

interment [ɪntɚ-mənt] N entierro m

interminable [ɪntɚ-mənəbəl] ADJ interminable

intermingle [ɪntə-míŋgəl] VI/VT entremezclar(se)

intermission [ɪntə-míʃən] N entreacto m, intervalo m

intermittent [ɪntə-mítṇt] ADJ intermitente

intern [íntɚ-n] VT internar, confinar; N (prisoner, doctor) interno -na mf

internal [ɪntɚ-nəl] ADJ interno, interior; —**combustion engine** motor de combustión interna m; — **revenue** rentas internas f pl; — **Revenue Service** Hacienda f

internalize [ɪntɚ-nəlaɪz] VT interiorizar, internalizar

international [ɪntə-næʃənəl] ADJ internacional; — **law** derecho internacional m

Internet [íntə-net] N internet m

internist [íntɚ-nɪst] N internista mf

internship [íntə-nʃɪp] N (medical) internado m; (student) práctica f

interpersonal [ɪntə-pɚ́-sənəl] ADJ interpersonal

interpose [ɪntə-póz] VI/VT interponer(se)

interpret [ɪntɚ́-prɪt] VI/VT interpretar

interpretation [ɪntə-prɪtéʃən] N interpretación f

interpreter [ɪntɚ́-prɪtə-] N intérprete mf

interracial [ɪntə-réʃəl] ADJ interracial

interrelated [ɪntə-nlédɪd] ADJ interrelacionado

interrogate [ɪntéraget] VI/VT interrogar

interrogation [ɪntəragéʃən] N interrogación f, interrogatorio m

interrogative [ɪntərúgədɪv] ADJ interrogativo; N palabra / oración interrogativa f

interrupt [ɪntərápt] VI/VT interrumpir

interruption [ɪntərápʃən] N interrupción f

intersect [ɪntə-sékt] VI/VT (math) intersecar(se); (road) cruzar(se)

intersection [íntə-sekʃən] N (math) intersección f; (street) cruce m, intersección f

intersperse [ɪntə-spɚ́-s] VT (scatter) esparcir; (intermingle) entremezclar, entreverar; (spice up) salpicar

interstate [ɪntə-stet] ADJ interestatal; N — **highway** autopista interestatal f

interstellar [ɪntə-stélə-] ADJ interestelar

interstice [ɪntɚ́-stɪs] N intersticio m

intertwine [ɪntə-twáɪn] VI/VT entrelazar(se)

interval [íntə-vəl] N intervalo m

intervene [ɪntə-vín] VI intervenir; (mediate) interponerse, mediar

intervention [ɪntə-vénʃən] N intervención f; (mediation) mediación f

interview [íntə-vju] N entrevista f; (for entertainment) Sp interviú f; VT entrevistar; VI entrevistarse

intestine [ɪntéstɪn] ADJ & N intestino m; **small —** intestino delgado m; **large —** intestino grueso m

intimacy [íntəməsi] N intimidad f

intimate [íntəmɪt] ADJ íntimo; (knowledge) profundo; [íntəmet] VT insinuar, dar a entender

intimation [ɪntəméʃən] N insinuación f

intimidate [ɪntímɪdet] VT intimidar, acobardar

into [íntu] PREP **she came — the room** entró en la habitación; **he put it — the box** lo metió en la caja; **he translated it — German** lo tradujo al alemán; **he ran — a tree** chocó contra un árbol; **it fell — oblivion** cayó en el olvido; **he went — medicine** entró a medicina; **I'm really — pop music** me ha dado por la música pop

intolerable [ɪntálə-əbəl] ADJ intolerable

intolerance [ɪntálə-əns] N intolerancia f

intolerant [ɪntálə-ənt] ADJ intolerante

intonation [ɪntənéʃən] N entonación f
intoxicate [ɪntáksɪket] VI/VT embriagar (also exhilarate); (poison) intoxicar
intoxication [ɪntɑksɪkéʃən] N (drunkenness) embriaguez f; (poisoning) intoxicación f
intransigent [ɪntrǽnzɪdʒənt] ADJ intransigente
intransitive [ɪntrǽnzɪdɪv] ADJ intransitivo
intrauterine device [ɪntrəjúvərɪndɪváɪs] N dispositivo intrauterino m
intravenous [ɪntrəvínəs] ADJ intravenoso
intrepid [ɪntrépɪd] ADJ intrépido
intricate [ɪntrɪkɪt] ADJ intrincado
intrigue [ɪntríg] VI/VT intrigar; [íntrɪg] N intriga f
intrinsic [ɪntrínzɪk] ADJ intrínseco
introduce [ɪntrədús] VT (put in, bring) introducir; (to a person) presentar
introduction [ɪntrədÁkʃən] N (putting in, preface) introducción f; (to a person) presentación f
introspection [ɪntrəspékʃən] N introspección f
introvert [íntrəvɚt] N introvertido -da mf
introverted [ɪntrəvɚ-dɪd] ADJ introvertido
intrude [ɪntrúd] VI/VT interrumpir; (penetrate, of rock) penetrar
intruder [ɪntrúdɚ] N intruso -sa mf
intrusion [ɪntrúʒən] N (interruption) interrupción f; (penetration) intrusión f
intrusive [ɪntrúsɪv] ADJ (rock) intrusivo; (people) entrometido
intuition [ɪntuíʃən] N intuición f
intuitive [ɪntúɪdɪv] ADJ intuitivo
inundate [ínəndet] VT inundar
invade [ɪnvéd] VI/VT invadir
invader [ɪnvédɚ] N invasor -ra mf
invalid [ínvəlɪd] ADJ & N (infirm) inválido -da mf; [ɪnvǽlɪd] ADJ (not valid) nulo
invaluable [ɪnvǽljuəbəl] ADJ invalorable, inestimable
invariable [ɪnvériəbəl] ADJ invariable
invariably [ɪnvériəbli] ADV siempre
invasion [ɪnvéʒən] N invasión f
invent [ɪnvént] VT inventar
invention [ɪnvénʃən] N (act of inventing, thing invented) invención f, invento m; (falsehood) invención f
inventive [ɪnvéntɪv] ADJ inventivo
inventor [ɪnvéntɚ] N inventor -ra mf
inventory [ínvəntɔri] N inventario m; VT inventariar
inverse [ɪnvɚ́s] ADJ & N inverso m
inversion [ɪnvɚ́ʒən] N inversión f
invert [ɪnvɚ́t] VT invertir
invest [ɪnvést] VI/VT (money) invertir; (a rank upon someone) investir

investigate [ɪnvéstɪget] VI/VT investigar, indagar
investigation [ɪnvestɪɡéʃən] N investigación f
investigator [ɪnvéstɪɡedɚ] N investigador -ra mf
investment [ɪnvéstmənt] N (of money) inversión f; (of rank) investidura f; — **broker** corredor -ra de bolsa mf
investor [ɪnvéstɚ] N inversionista mf, inversor -ra mf
invigorate [ɪnvíɡəret] VT vigorizar
invincible [ɪnvínsəbəl] ADJ invencible
invisible [ɪnvízəbəl] ADJ invisible
invitation [ɪnvɪtéʃən] N invitación f
invite [ɪnváɪt] VI/VT invitar; **to — trouble** buscarse problemas; [ínvaɪt] N fam invitación f
inviting [ɪnváɪdɪŋ] ADJ atractivo, seductor
in vitro fertilization [ɪnvítrofɚdʒɪzéʃən] N fertilización in vitro f
invocation [ɪnvəkéʃən] N invocación f
invoice [ínvɔɪs] N factura f; VT facturar
invoke [ɪnvók] VT invocar
involuntary [ɪnválənteri] ADJ involuntario
involve [ɪnválv] VT (take, last) suponer; **how much time will this —?** ¿cuánto tiempo supone esto? (consist of, entail) consistir en, involucrar; **what does your work —?** ¿en qué consiste tu trabajo? (be in question) ser cuestión de; **national security is —d!** ¡es una cuestión de seguridad nacional! (implicate) implicar; **they tried to — her** trataron de implicarla; (wrapped up in) estar metido; **he's very —d in the family business** está muy metido en el negocio familiar; (have a liaison) enredarse; **she got —d with a married man** se enredó con un hombre casado
involved [ɪnválvd] ADJ complicado, enrevesado
inward [ínwɚd] ADV hacia dentro; ADJ interior
iodide [áɪdaɪd] N yoduro m
iodine [áɪədaɪn] N yodo m
ion [áɪɑn] N ión m
ionize [áɪənaɪz] VT ionizar
IQ (intelligence quotient) [aɪkjú] N coeficiente de inteligencia m
Iran [ɪrán] N Irán m
Iranian [ɪréniən] ADJ & N iraní mf
Iraq [ɪrǽk] N Irak m
Iraqi [ɪrǽki] ADJ & N iraquí mf
irascible [ɪrǽsəbəl] ADJ irascible
irate [aɪrét] ADJ airado
ire [aɪr] N ira f
Ireland [áɪrlənd] N Irlanda f

iridescent [ɪrɪdésənt] ADJ iridiscente, tornasolado

iridium [ɪrídiəm] N iridio *m*

iris [áɪrɪs] N (of eye) iris *m*; (plant, flower) lirio *m*; (rainbow) arco iris *m*

Irish [áɪrɪʃ] ADJ irlandés; N (language) irlandés *m*; **the** — los irlandeses

irk [ɚk] VT fastidiar; **—ed** fastidiado

irksome [ɚ́ksəm] ADJ engorroso, molesto

iron [áɪrən] N (element, golf club) hierro *m*; (appliance) plancha *f*; **in —s** en grilletes; ADJ férreo, de hierro; **—work** herrajes *m* pl; **—works** fundición *f*; VI/VT planchar; **to — out a difficulty** allanar una dificultad

ironic [aɪránɪk] ADJ irónico

ironing [áɪɚnɪŋ] N planchado *m*

irony [áɪrəni] N ironía *f*; (mockery) ironía *f*, sorna *f*

irradiate [ɪrédiet] VT irradiar

irrational [ɪrǽʃənəl] ADJ irracional

irrefutable [ɪrɪfjúðəbəl] ADJ irrefutable

irregular [ɪrégjələ] ADJ irregular

irrelevant [ɪréləvənt] ADJ no pertinente; **your age is —** tu edad no viene al caso

irreparable [ɪrépəəbəl] ADJ irreparable

irreplaceable [ɪrɪplésəbəl] ADJ irreemplazable

irreproachable [ɪrɪprótʃəbəl] ADJ irreprochable

irresistible [ɪrɪzístəbəl] ADJ irresistible

irresponsible [ɪrɪspúnsəbəl] ADJ irresponsable

irretrievable [ɪrɪtrívəbəl] ADJ irrecuperable

irreverent [ɪrévəənt] ADJ irreverente

irrevocable [ɪrévəkəbəl] ADJ irrevocable

irrigate [írɪget] VI/VT (a garden) irrigar, regar; (the eyes) irrigar

irrigation [ɪrɪgéʃən] N riego *m*, irrigación *f*; **— ditch** acequia *f*

irritable [írɪtəbəl] ADJ irritable, colérico

irritate [írɪtet] VT irritar

irritating [írɪtetɪŋ] ADJ irritante

irritation [ɪrɪtéʃən] N irritación *f*

IRS (Internal Revenue Service) [aɪɑrés] N Hacienda *f*

Islam [ízlɑm] N islamismo *m*, islam *m*

Islamic [ɪzlǽmɪk] ADJ islámico

island [áɪlənd] N isla *f*

islander [áɪləndə] N isleño -ña *mf*

isle [aɪl] N isla *f*

isobar [áɪsəbɑr] N isobara *f*

isolate [áɪsəlet] VT aislar

isolation [aɪsəléʃən] N aislamiento *m*

isolationism [aɪsəléʃənɪzəm] N aislacionismo *m*

isometric [aɪsəmétrɪk] ADJ isométrico

isotope [áɪsətop] N isótopo *m*

Israel [ízriəl] N Israel *m*

Israeli [ɪzréli] ADJ & N israelí *mf*

issue [íʃu] N (of printed matter) tirada *f*; (of stock, bonds) emisión *f*; (copy of a magazine) número *m*, entrega *f*; (of a fluid) flujo *m*; (problem) problema *m*, tema *m*; (progeny) descendencia *f*; **he's got —s** es muy acomplejado; **to take — with** discrepar de; VT (written material) publicar; (a decree) promulgar; (a permit, document) expedir; (shares) emitir; (to flow) brotar; (to come out of) salir de; (to descend from) descender de

isthmus [ísməs] N istmo *m*

it [ɪt] PRON **— all started yesterday** todo empezó ayer; **— is necessary** es necesario; **— is raining** llueve, está lloviendo; **— is said that** se dice que; **— is two o'clock** son las dos; **— was broken** estaba roto; **who is —?** ¿quién es? if **— weren't five o'clock** si no fueran las cinco; **I saw —** lo / la vi; **he talked about —** habló de eso; **what time is — ?** ¿qué hora es? **how is — going?** ¿qué tal? **I don't get —** no entiendo; **you're —!** ¡tú te / la quedas! / ¡tú la traes!

Italian [ɪtǽljən] ADJ & N italiano -na *mf*

italic [ɪtǽlɪk] ADJ itálico; N **—s** letra bastardilla / cursiva *f*

italicize [ɪtǽlɪsaɪz] VT poner en bastardilla / cursiva

Italy [ɪdji] N Italia *f*

itch [ɪtʃ] VI/VT picar; **to be —ing to** tener ganas de; N comezón *f*, picazón *f*; (longing) ansia *f*

itchy [ítʃi] ADJ que pica; **it feels — to me** me pica

item [áɪdəm] N (piece of news) artículo *m*; (topic of gossip) tema de conversación *m*; (unit) ítem *m*; (couple) pareja *f*

itemize [áɪdəmaɪz] VT (list) enumerar; (break down) desglosar

itinerant [aɪtínəənt] ADJ itinerante, ambulante

itinerary [aɪtínəreri] N (schedule) itinerario *m*; (guidebook) guía de viajeros *f*

its [ɪts] POSS ADJ su / sus, de él, de ella, de ello

itself [ɪtsɛ́lf] PRON **this story wrote —** esta historia se escribió sola; **the bike was standing by —** la bici estaba parada sola; **the dog bit —** el perro se mordió (a sí mismo); **the fox found — a hole** la zorra se encontró una guarida

Ivorian [aɪvɔ́riən] ADJ & N marfileño -ña *mf*

ivory [áɪvri] N marfil *m*; **— tower** torre de marfil *f*

Ivory Coast [áivrikóst] N Costa de Marfil f

ivy [áivi] N hiedra f

Jj

jab [dʒæb] VI/VT (hit) golpear; (hit with elbow) codear; N (blow) golpe m; (blow with elbow) codazo m; (in boxing) jab m, puñetazo directo m

jabber [dʒǽbə] VI (unintelligibly) farfullar; (incessantly) charlotear; N (unintelligible) farfulla f; (incessant) charloteo m

jack [dʒæk] N (tool) gato m; (card) sota f; (plug-in) hembra f, toma f; (flag) bandera de proa f; **—ass** asno m, burro m (also person); **—hammer** martillo neumático m; **—knife** navaja f; **— of all trades** hombre orquesta m; **—pot** premio gordo m; **—rabbit** liebre americana f; **you don't know** — no sabes ni un comino; VI/VT **to — off** vulg hacer(se) una paja; VT **to — up** (a car) alzar con gato; (prices) subir

jackal [dʒǽkəl] N chacal m

jacket [dʒǽkɪt] N (clothing) chaqueta f; (of a book) forro m; (of a potato) piel f

jade [dʒed] N jade m

jaded [dʒédɪd] ADJ (disenchanted) de vuelta; (sated) hastiado

jagged [dʒǽgɪd] ADJ recortado, desigual

jaguar [dʒǽgwar] N jaguar m

jail [dʒel] N cárcel f; **—break** fuga f; VT encarcelar

jailer [dʒélə] N carcelero -ra mf

jalopy [dʒəlápi] N cacharro m

jam [dʒæm] VT (stuff) embutir; (block) atestar; (immobilize) trabar; (make unworkable) obstruir, atascar, atorar; (stop radio signals) interferir; VI (become stuck or unworkable) atascarse; (crowd in) apiñarse; **to — on the brakes** frenar de golpe; **to — one's fingers** pillarse los dedos; N (jelly) mermelada f, dulce m; (difficult situation) aprieto m; (traffic) embotellamiento m; **— session** jam m

Jamaica [dʒəméka] N Jamaica f

Jamaican [dʒəmékan] ADJ & N jamaicano -na mf, jamaiquino -na mf

janitor [dʒǽnɪtə] N conserje m

January [dʒǽnjueri] N enero m

Japan [dʒəpǽn] N Japón m

Japanese [dʒæpəníz] ADJ & N japonés -esa mf

jar [dʒar] VI/VT (shake) sacudir(se); (clash) chocar; **to — one's nerves** ponerle a uno los nervios de punta; N (container) tarro m, frasco m, pote m; (large earthen container) tinaja f; (collision) choque m; (shake) sacudida f

jargon [dʒárgən] N jerga f

jasmine [dʒǽzmɪn] N jazmín m

jasper [dʒǽspə] N jaspe m

jaundice [dʒɔ́ndɪs] N ictericia f

jaunt [dʒɔnt] N excursión f; VI pasear

javelin [dʒǽvlɪn] N jabalina f

jaw [dʒɔ] N (of animal) quijada f; (of human) mandíbula f; (of carnivores) fauces f pl; **—bone** mandíbula f, maxilar m

jay [dʒe] N arrendajo m

jazz [dʒæz] N jazz m; VI **to — up** animar

jealous [dʒélas] ADJ (possessive) celoso; (envious) envidioso; (protective) protector

jealousy [dʒélasi] N celos m pl

jeans [dʒinz] N jeans m pl, vaqueros m pl

jeer [dʒir] VI/VT (mock) mofarse (de), burlarse (de); (boo) abuchear; N (act of mockery) mofa f, burla f; (boos) abucheo m, befa f

jelly [dʒéli] N jalea f; **—fish** medusa f

jeopardize [dʒépə·daɪz] VT comprometer, poner en peligro

jeopardy [dʒépə·di] ADV LOC **in** — en peligro

jerk [dʒə·k] N (quick pull) tirón m; (muscular contraction) espasmo m; (idiot) pej pelmazo m; VI/VT tironear; **to — around** manipular, vulg joder; **to — off** vulg hacerse una paja; **—water** de mala muerte

jerky [dʒə́·ki] ADJ espasmódico; N tasajo m

jersey [dʒə́·zi] N jersey m

jest [dʒest] N broma f, chanza f; **in** — en broma; VI bromear

jester [dʒéstə] N bufón m

Jesuit [dʒézuɪt] N jesuita m

jet [dʒet] N (stream) chorro m; (spout) surtidor m; (stone) azabache m; **— (air)plane** avión a reacción m; **— engine** motor a reacción m; **— lag** jet lag m; **—liner** avión a reacción de pasajero m; **— propulsion** propulsión a chorro f; **— set** jet-set m; **— stream** (of air) corriente en chorro f; (of a jet) chorro m; ADJ **—black** negro como el azabache; VI (stream out) salir a chorros; (travel) volar en avión a reacción; VT (spew out) lanzar a chorros; (transport) transportar en avión a reacción

jettison [dʒɛ́DɪsƏn] VT echar por la borda

Jew [dʒu] N judío -día mf

jewel [dʒúəl] N (ornament, prized person) joya f, alhaja f; (stone) gema f; (watch jewel) rubí m; **— box** joyero m

jeweler [ʤúələ] N joyero -ra *mf;* **—'s shop** joyería *f*

jewelry [ʤúəlri] N joyas *f pl,* alhajas *f pl;* **— box** alhajero *m;* **— store** joyería *f*

Jewish [ʤúʃ] ADJ judío

jiffy [ʤifi] ADV LOC **in a —** en un santiamén

jig [ʤig] N giga *f;* **—saw** sierra de vaivén *f;* **—saw puzzle** rompecabezas *m sg;* VI (dance) bailotear; **to — up and down** zangolotearse

jiggle [ʤigəł] VI/VT zangolotear(se), zarandear(se); N zangoloteo *m,* zarandeo *m*

jilt [ʤiłt] VT dejar plantado

jingle [ʤiŋgəł] VI tintinear; VT agitar; N retintín *m;* (short song) jingle *m*

jinx [ʤiŋks] N gafe *m;* VT gafar

job [ʤab] N (task) tarea *f;* (position) trabajo *m,* empleo *m;* (theft) golpe *m;* **to be out of a —** estar sin trabajo; *Sp* estar en (el) paro; **by the —** a destajo; **to do a good —** hacer buen trabajo; VI trabajar a destajo

jobber [ʤábə] N (day-worker) trabajador -ra a destajo *mf;* (wholesaler) vendedor -ra mayorista *mf*

jobless [ʤáblɪs] ADJ sin trabajo; *Sp* en paro

jock [ʤak] N deportista *mf;* **— (strap)** suspensorio *m*

jockey [ʤáki] N jockey *m;* VI **to — for position** disputarse la posición

jocular [ʤákjələ] ADJ jocoso

jog [ʤag] VI (run) correr; VT (refresh) refrescar; N trote *m;* **to go for a —** salir a correr

john [ʤan] N (urinal) *fam* meadero *m;* (customer of a prostitute) *fam* putañero *m*

join [ʤɔɪn] VI/VT juntar(se); (pipes) acoplar(se), unir(se); (bones) articular(se); (a club) asociarse (a); (the navy, etc.) alistarse (en)

joint [ʤɔɪnt] N (point of contact) juntura *f,* junta *f;* (connection between bones) articulación *f,* coyuntura *f;* (nodule on a plant) nudo *m;* (marijuana cigarette) porro *m;* (public place) antro *m;* **out of —** descoyuntado; ADJ (shared) común; **— account** cuenta conjunta *f;* **— action** acción colectiva *f;* **— owner** copropietario -ria *mf;* **— session** sesión plena *f;* **— venture** joint venture *m*

joke [ʤok] N broma *f,* chiste *m;* VI bromear

joker [ʤókə] N (person who jokes) bromista *mf,* guasón -ona *mf;* (card) comodín *m*

jokingly [ʤókɪŋli] ADV en broma

jolly [ʤáli] ADJ jovial

jolt [ʤołt] N sacudida *f;* VT sacudir; **to — along** avanzar a los tumbos

Jordan [ʤórdṇ] N Jordania *f*

Jordanian [ʤɔrdéniən] ADJ & N jordano -na *mf*

jostle [ʤásəł] VI/VT codear(se), dar empujones (a); N empujón *m*

jot [ʤat] VT **to — down** apuntar; N pizca *f*

journal [ʤɜ́nəł] N (diary) diario *m;* (periodical) revista *f;* (logbook) cuaderno de bitácora *m*

journalism [ʤɜ́nəlɪzəm] N periodismo *m*

journalist [ʤɜ́nəlɪst] N periodista *mf*

journalistic [ʤɜnəlɪ́stɪk] ADJ periodístico

journey [ʤɜ́ni] N viaje *m;* VI viajar

joust [ʤaust] N justa *f*

joy [ʤɔɪ] N (delight) alegría *f,* regocijo *m,* alborozo *m;* (source of delight) deleite *m;* **—ride** paseo en coche robado *m;* **—stick** joystick *m,* palanca de juegos *f*

joyful [ʤɔ́ɪfəł] ADJ alborozado

joyous [ʤɔ́ɪəs] ADJ jubiloso, alegre

jubilant [ʤúbələnt] ADJ jubiloso

jubilee [ʤubəlí] N jubileo *m*

judge [ʤʌʤ] N juez -za *mf;* **to be a good — of character** saber juzgar a la gente; VI/VT juzgar; (estimate) calcular

judgment [ʤʌ́ʤmənt] N juicio *m;* (in court) fallo *m;* **— day** día del juicio final *m*

judicial [ʤudíʃəł] ADJ judicial

judicious [ʤudíʃəs] ADJ juicioso, sensato

judo [ʤúdo] N judo *m*

jug [ʤʌg] N (pitcher) jarro *m,* jarra *f;* (storage jar) pote *m;* **—s** *vulg* tetas *f pl*

juggle [ʤʌ́gəł] VI/VT hacer juegos malabares (con), hacer malabarismo (con); **to — the accounts** manipular las cuentas

juggler [ʤʌ́glə] N malabarista *m*

jugular [ʤʌ́gjələ] N yugular *f*

juice [ʤus] N jugo *m;* (fruit only) *Sp* zumo *m*

juicer [ʤúsə] N exprimidor *m*

juicy [ʤúsi] ADJ jugoso; **a — story** un cuento sabroso

jukebox [ʤúkbaks] N juke-box *m*

July [ʤulái] N julio *m*

jumble [ʤʌ́mbəł] VI/VT revolver(se) *m;* N revoltijo *m*

jumbo [ʤʌ́mbo] ADJ jumbo, gigantesco; **— jet** jumbo *m*

jump [ʤʌmp] VI (spring) saltar; (increase, as temperature, prices) dar un salto; VT (capture in checkers) comer; (ride a horse over barrier) hacer saltar; (mug) asaltar; (cross a river, mountains, etc.) salvar; **to — at** abalanzarse sobre; **to — over** saltar; **to — the track** descarrilarse; **to — to conclusions** hacer deducciones precipitadas; N salto *m;* (in prices) subida repentina *f;* **— rope** cuerda de saltar *f;* **to —start** hacer un puente; **—suit** mono *m*

jumper [dʒámpə] N (person who jumps) saltador -ra *mf*; (dress) jumper *m*; *Sp* pichi *m*; — **cable** puente *m*

jumpy [dʒámpi] ADJ nervioso, asustadizo

junction [dʒáŋkʃən] N (act or state of joining) unión *f*; (joining of two rivers) confluencia *f*; (of two railways) empalme *m*; (of roads) entronque *m*

juncture [dʒáŋktʃə] N (point where joined) juntura *f*; **at this** — en esta coyuntura

June [dʒun] N junio *m*

jungle [dʒáŋgəł] N selva *f*, jungla *f*; **the law of the** — la ley de la selva

junior [dʒúnjə] ADJ (younger) menor; (more recent) más nuevo, de menos antigüedad; — **college** institución para los dos primeros años de la licenciatura *f*; **John Smith,** — John Smith, hijo; N estudiante del tercer año *mf*

juniper [dʒúnəpə] N enebro *m*

junk [dʒʌŋk] N (useless articles) trastos viejos *m pl*; (metal) chatarra *f*; (Chinese boat) junco *m*; — **dealer** chatarrero -ra *mf*; — **food** comida basura *f*, porquerías *f pl*; — **mail** publicidad por correo *f*; —**yard** chatarrería *f*; VT desechar, echar a la basura

junkie [dʒáŋki] N *fam* drogata *mf*, drogota *mf*

jurisdiction [dʒurɪsdíkʃən] N jurisdicción *f*

jurisprudence [dʒurɪsprúdn̩s] N jurisprudencia *f*

juror [dʒúrə] N miembro de un jurado *m*, jurado -da *mf*

jury [dʒúri] N jurado *m*; — **box** banco de jurado *m*; **to** —**rig** chapucear

just [dʒʌst] ADJ justo; ADV (exactly) exactamente; (only) sólo; **he** — **left** acaba de salir; **she is** — **a little girl** no es más que una niña; **you'll** — **have to wait** tendrás que esperar; — **barely** apenas; **the meeting is** — **starting** la reunión está empezando

justice [dʒástɪs] N (fairness) justicia *f*; (judge) juez -za *mf*; **to bring to** — enjuiciar; **the painting doesn't do him** — el retrato no le favorece

justification [dʒʌstəfɪkéʃən] N justificación *f*

justify [dʒástəfai] VT justificar

jut [dʒʌt] VI sobresalir, proyectarse

juvenile [dʒúvənaɪł] ADJ juvenil; — **delinquent** delincuente juvenil *mf*

juxtapose [dʒákstəpoz] VT yuxtaponer

Kk

kangaroo [kæŋgərú] N canguro *m*

karat, carat [kǽrət] N quilate *m*

kayak [káɪæk] N kayak *m*

Kazak, Kazakh [kəzǽk] ADJ & N kazako -ka *mf*

Kazakhstan [kəzákstɑn] N Kazajstán *m*

keel [kił] N quilla *f*; VI/VT volcar(se); **to** — **over** (ship) volcar(se); (person) caer de cabeza, desplomarse

keen [kin] ADJ (sharp) afilado; (ear) fino; (mind) agudo, penetrante

keenness [kínnɪs] N agudeza *f*

keep [kip] VI (continue) seguir; (not spoil) aguantar; VT (retain) guardar; (maintain) mantener; (employ) tener; (look after) cuidar; **to** — **a diary** llevar un diario; **to** — **a secret** guardar un secreto; **to** — **at it** persistir; **to** — **away** mantener(se) alejado; **to** — **back** (stay away) tener a raya; (restrain) contener; **to** — **bad company** andar en mala compañía; **to** — **from** (prevent) impedir; (protect) proteger; **to** — **(on) talking** seguir hablando; **to** — **the door open** mantener la puerta abierta; **to** — **off the grass** no pisar el cesped; **to** — **up** (perform as well) seguir el tren; (stay informed) mantenerse al tanto; **to** — **one's hands off** no tocar; **to** — **someone posted** mantener al corriente a alguien; **to** — **quiet** estarse callado; **to** — **to the right** mantenerse a la derecha; **to** — **track of** (do accounts) llevar la cuenta de; (consider) no perder de vista; **to** — **watch** vigilar; **he** —**s a maid** tiene una criada; **she kept me on the phone** me (re)tuvo en el teléfono; N **for** —**s** (forever) para siempre; (for real) en serio

keeper [kípə] N (of people) guardián *m*; (of things) custodio *m*

keeping [kípɪŋ] N custodia *f*; **in** — **with** en armonía con

keepsake [kípsek] N recuerdo *m*

keg [keg] N barril *m*

kennel [kénəł] N residencia de perros *f*

Kenya [kénjə] N Kenia *f*

Kenyan [kénjən] ADJ & N keniata *mf*

kernel [kɜ́-nəł] N (seed) semilla *f*, grano *m*; (essence) meollo *m*

kerosene [kérəsin] N queroseno *m*

kestrel [késtrəł] N cernícalo *m*

ketchup [kétʃəp] N salsa de tomate *f*, cátsup *m*

kettle [kédl] N caldera *f*, hervidor *m*; (for tea) tetera *f*; — **drum** tímpano / timbal *m*; **that's another — of fish** es harina de otro costal

key [ki] N (for locks) llave *f*; (secret, book of answers) clave *f*; (for winding) clavija *f*; (for keyboard) tecla *f*; (island) cayo *m*; (music) clave *f*; —**board** teclado *m*; —**hole** ojo de la cerradura *m*; —**note** tónica *f*; —**note address** discurso de apertura *m*; —**pad** teclado numérico *m*; —**ring** llavero *m*; — **signature** armadura *f*; —**stone** piedra angular *f*; —**stroke** pulsación (de la tecla) *f*; — **word** palabra clave *f*; **to sing on** — cantar a tono; ADJ clave; VT (scratch) rayar; **to be —ed up** estar sobreexcitado

khaki [kǽki] N kaki *m*, caqui *m*

kick [kɪk] VI/VT (person) patear; (horse) dar coces (a), cocear; VI (gun) dar un culatazo, retroceder; **to — around** (discuss) discutir; (to mistreat) dar por la cabeza; **to — at** dar patadas; **to — out** echar a patadas; **to — the bucket** estirar la pata; **to — up a lot of dust** levantar una polvareda; **to — a habit** dejar un vício; N patada *f*, puntapié *m*; (of a horse) coz *f*; *Am* patada *f*; (of a gun) culatazo *m*; (in the air) pataleo *m*; **this whisky has a** — este whisky es fuerte; **I get a — out of swimming** me encanta nadar; —**back** comisión ilegal *f*; *Mex* mordida *f*; —**stand** soporte *m*; **to —start** arrancar

kid [kɪd] N (young goat) cabrito *m*, chivo *m*; (leather) cabritilla *f*; (child) niño -ña *mf*, chico -ca *mf*; — **stuff** juego de niños *m*; VI bromear, embromar, tomar el pelo

kidnap [kídnæp] VT secuestrar, raptar

kidnapper [kídnæpɚ] N secuestrador -ra *mf*

kidnapping [kídnæpɪŋ] N secuestro *m*, rapto *m*

kidney [kídni] N riñón *m*; — **bean** judía *f*; — **stone** cálculo renal *m*

kill [kɪl] VI/VT matar; (drink completely) terminar; (turn off) apagar; **that comedian —s me** ese cómico me mata de risa; N (animal killed) caza *f*; (slaughter) matanza *f*; —**joy** aguafiestas *mf sg*

killer [kílɚ] N asesino -na *mf*; **a — game** un partidazo; — **bee** abeja asesina *f*; — **whale** orca *f*

killing [kílɪŋ] N (slaughter) matanza *f*; (murder) asesinato *m*; (game killed) caza *f*; **to make a —** llenarse de oro

kilo [kílo] N kilo *m*

kilobyte [kíləbaɪt] N kilobyte *m*

kilometer [kɪlámɪdɚ] N kilómetro *m*

kilowatt [kíləwɑt] N kilovatio *m*; —**-hour** kilovatio-hora *f*

kin [kɪn] N parentela *f*, parientes *m pl*; —**sman** pariente *m*; —**swoman** parienta *f*; **to notify the next of** — avisar a los deudos

kind [kaɪnd] ADJ (benevolent) bondadoso, bueno; (words) amable; **to be — to animals** ser cariñoso con los animales; —**hearted** de buen corazón; — **of tired** algo cansado; N clase *f*, tipo *m*, género *m*; **to pay in** — (without money) pagar en especie; (retaliate) pagar con la misma moneda

kindergarten [kíndɚgɑrtn̩] N jardín de niños *m*; *Sp* parvulario *m*

kindle [kíndl] VT (fire) prender; (interest) despertar, provocar; VI encenderse

kindling [kíndlɪŋ] N leña ligera *f*, astillas *f pl*

kindly [kándli] ADJ bondadoso, bueno; ADV (with kindness) amablemente; (please) por favor; **we thank you —** le agradecemos mucho; **not to take — to criticism** no aceptar de buen grado las críticas

kindness [kándnɪs] N (state) bondad *f*, amabilidad *f*; (act) favor *m*

kindred [kíndrɪd] ADJ emparentado; — **spirits** espíritus afines *m pl*, almas gemelas *f pl*

king [kɪŋ] N rey *m* (also chess, cards); (in checkers) dama *f*; —**fisher** martín pescador *m*; —**pin** (in a mechanism) pivote central *m*; (in bowling) bolo central *m*; (person) figura central *f*; —**-sized** extra grande

kingdom [kíndəm] N reino *m*

kingly [kíŋli] ADJ real

kink [kɪŋk] N (bend) doblez *m*; (pain) tortícolis *f*

kinky [kɪŋki] ADJ crespo; (sex) pervertido, *Sp* morboso

kinship [kínʃɪp] N parentesco *m*; (likeness) afinidad *f*

kiosk [kíɑsk] N quiosco *m*

Kiribati [kɪrəbáʊi] N Kiribati *m*

kiss [kɪs] VI/VT besar(se); N beso *m*

kit [kɪt] N (of tools) caja *f*; (of first aid) botiquín *m*; (of sewing notions) costurero *m*

kitchen [kítʃɪn] N cocina *f*; —**ware** utensilios de cocina *m pl*

kite [kaɪt] N (toy) cometa *f*; (bird) milano *m*

kitten [kítn̩] N gatito *m*

kitty [kídi] N (young cat) gatito *m*, minino *m*; (petty cash) caja chica *f*, fondo *m*

knack [næk] N buena mano f, maña f; **once you get the —** una vez que le agarras la vuelta/onda

knapsack [nǽpsæk] N mochila f

knave [nev] N pícaro m; (in cards) sota f

knead [nid] VT amasar, sobar

knee [ni] N rodilla f; **—cap** rótula f; **—-deep** hasta las rodillas; **—-jerk liberal** liberal fanático m; **—-jerk reaction** reacción visceral f; VT dar un rodillazo

kneel [nil] VI arrodillarse

knell [nɛl] N doble m; VI doblar

knickknack [níknæk] N chuchería f, baratija f

knife [naɪf] N cuchillo m; (big) cuchilla f; (folding) navaja f; (for carving) trinchante m; VT acuchillar; **at —point** a punta de cuchillo

knight [naɪt] N caballero m; (in chess) caballo m; **— errant** caballero andante m; VT armar caballero

knighthood [náɪthʊd] N (all knights) caballería f; (title) orden de la caballería f

knit [nɪt] VI/VT tejer; **to — one's brow** fruncir el entrecejo/el ceño

knitting [nídɪŋ] N tejido m; **— needle** aguja de punto f

knob [nɑb] N (on a door) pomo m, perilla f, tirador m; (protuberance) protuberancia f

knock [nɑk] VI (pound) golpear; (of motors) golpetear; (call at the door) llamar; VT (criticize) criticar; **to — a hole in the wall** hacer un agujero en la pared a golpes; **to — down** derribar, echar abajo, tumbar; **to — off** (stop working) terminar; (reduce) rebajar; (make fall) tirar; (kill) liquidar; **— it off!** ¡basta! **to — into** golpearse contra; **to — out** noquear; **to — over** voltear, revolcar; **to — up** vulg preñar; N (pounding) golpe m, toque m; (criticism) crítica f; (in a motor) golpeteo m; **—-kneed** patizambo, zambo; **—out** (boxing) nócaut m; (attractive person) bomba f

knocker [nákɚ] N (handle on door) llamador m, aldaba f; (breast) vulg teta f

knoll [nol] N morro m, loma f

knot [nɑt] N nudo m (also in wood, unit of speed); (of people) grupo m; (swelling) chichón m; VI/VT anudar(se)

knotty [nápi] ADJ (full of knots) nudoso; (difficult) dificultoso, enredado

know [no] VI/VT (to have knowledge of; to know how to) saber; VT (to be acquainted with, have sexual intercourse with) conocer; (to recognize) reconocer; (distinguish) distinguir; **to — how to**

swim saber nadar; **to — of** estar enterado de; N **to be in the —** estar al tanto; **—-how** conocimiento m; **—-it-all** sabelotodo mf

knowing [nóɪŋ] ADJ (complicitous) cómplice; (astute) astuto

knowingly [nóɪŋli] ADV a sabiendas

knowledge [nálɪdʒ] N (awareness) conocimiento m; (information known) saber m, conocimientos m pl; **not to my —** no que yo sepa

knuckle [nákəl] N nudillo m; **—head** tarambana mf; VI **to — down** arremangarse, aplicarse con empeño; **to — under** someterse

Korean [kɔrían] ADJ & N coreano -na mf

kosher [kóʃɚ] ADJ kosher

Kuwait [kuwét] N Kuwait m

Kuwaiti [kuwépi] ADJ & N kuwaití mf

Kyrgyzstan [kɚgistán] N Kirguistán m

Ll

label [lébəl] N etiqueta f, rótulo m; (brand) marca f; (of recording companies) sello m; VT etiquetar, rotular

labor [lébɚ] N trabajo m, labor f; (body of workers) mano de obra f; (working class) clase obrera f; (uterine contractions) trabajo de parto m; **—-intensive** que requiere mucha mano de obra; **— union** sindicato m; **to be in —** estar de parto; ADJ laboral; VI (work) trabajar; (dedicate oneself) afanarse; **to — under a disadvantage** sufrir una desventaja

laboratory [lǽbrətɔri] N laboratorio m

laborer [lébarɚ] N jornalero -ra mf; (unskilled) peón -ona mf

laborious [labórias] ADJ (industrious) laborioso; (difficult) trabajoso

labyrinth [lǽbənɪnθ] N laberinto m

lace [les] N (cloth) encaje m; (cord) cordón m; VT (to adorn with lace) bordar con encaje; (to insert laces into) poner cordones a; (to spike) echar alcohol; VI atarse

lack [læk] N falta f, carencia f; VI/VT carecer de, faltarle a uno; **he —s courage** le falta valentía; **—luster** mediocre

lackey [lǽki] N lacayo m

lacking [lǽkɪŋ] ADJ (deficient) deficiente; **good maids are — in this town** faltan buenas criadas en este pueblo; **— in** falto de, carente de

laconic [ləkánɪk] ADJ lacónico

lacquer [lǽkə·] N laca f; VT lacar, laquear

lactic acid [lǽktɪkǽsɪd] N ácido láctico m

ladder [lǽɾə·] N escalera f

laden [lédn̩] ADJ cargado

ladle [lédl̩] N cucharón m, cazo m; VT servir con cucharón

lady [lédi] N señora f, dama f; **—bug** mariquita f; **—like** muy fina; **—love** amada f; **ladies' room** Sp aseo/servicio de damas m

lag [læg] VI (fall behind) quedarse atrás, rezagarse; (flag) disminuir; N retardo m, retraso m

lagoon [ləgún] N laguna f

lair [lɛr] N guarida f

lake [lek] N lago m

lamb [læm] N cordero m; (yearling) borrego m

lame [lem] ADJ cojo; Am rengo; **—brained** idiota; **— duck** funcionario -ria cesante mf; **— excuse** pretexto tonto m; VT dejar cojo

lament [ləmént] N lamento m; VI lamentar(se); VT llorar

lamentable [ləméntəbəl] ADJ lamentable

lamentation [læməntéʃən] N lamentación f, lamento m

laminate [lǽmənet] VT laminar

lamp [læmp] N lámpara f; (on a street) farol m; **—post** farol m; **—shade** pantalla f

lance [læns] N lanza f; (lancet) lanceta f; VT lancear; (a wound) abrir con una lanceta

lancet [lǽnsɪt] N lanceta f

land [lænd] N tierra f; (lot) terreno m; (country) país m, tierra f; **—fill** vertedero m; **— grant** con terrenos concedidos por el estado; **—lady** casera f, propietaria f; **—lord** casero m, propietario m; **—mark** hito m (also historical), mojón m; **—mine** mina f; **—owner** hacendado -da mf; **—scape** paisaje m; **—scape architecture** paisajismo m; **—slide** derrumbe m, desprendimiento m; (election) victoria aplastante f; VI/VT (a ship) atracar; (an airplane) aterrizar; VT (a fish) Sp coger; Am pescar; (a job) conseguir; **you'll — in jail** terminarás en la cárcel

landing [lǽndɪŋ] N (of a ship) desembarco m; (of cargo) desembarque m; (of an airplane) aterrizaje m; (place) desembarcadero m; (on stairs) descanso m; **— field** campo de aterrizaje m; **— gear** tren de aterrizaje m; **— strip** pista de aterrizaje f

lane [len] N (country road) sendero m; (road division) carril m; (for ships) ruta f

language [lǽŋgwɪʤ] N lengua f, idioma m; (faculty, computer) lenguaje m

languid [lǽŋgwɪd] ADJ lánguido

languish [lǽŋgwɪʃ] VI languidecer

languor [lǽŋgə·] N languidez f

lanky [lǽŋki] ADJ larguirucho, zancudo

lanolin [lǽnəlɪn] N lanolina f

lantern [lǽntə·n] N farol m; (of a lighthouse) faro m, linterna f

Laos [léas] N Laos m

Laotian [leóʃən] ADJ & N laosiano -na mf

lap [læp] N (part of body) regazo m; (part of a race) vuelta f; **—dog** perro faldero m; **—top** laptop m; **to live in the — of luxury** vivir en la abundancia; VI/VT lamer

lapel [ləpɛ́l] N solapa f

lapidary [lǽpɪdɛri] ADJ & N lapidario -ria mf

lapse [læps] N (period of time) lapso m; (linguistic error) lapsus m; (defect in memory) fallo m; (fall) caída f; (termination) caducidad f; VI (fall) caer; (decline) decaer; (end) caducar, vencer

larceny [lársəni] N latrocinio m, hurto m

lard [lard] N manteca f; VT enmantecar; (with bacon) mechar

large [larʤ] ADJ grande; **—-scale** de gran escala; **a — company** una gran compañía/una compañía grande; **at —** (not in jail) suelto, libre; (in general) en general; N tamaño grande m

lariat [lǽrɪət] N reata f

lark [lark] N (bird) alondra f; (bit of fun) diversión f; **to go on a —** ir de jarana

larva [lárvə] N larva f

laryngitis [lærənʤáɪdɪs] N laringitis f

larynx [lǽrɪŋks] N laringe f

lascivious [ləsɪ́vɪəs] ADJ lascivo

laser [lézə·] N láser m; **— printer** impresora láser f

lash [læʃ] N (blow with a whip, tail, etc.) azote m, latigazo m; (blow of waves) embate m; (part of eye) pestaña f; VT azotar; (tie) amarrar; **to — out at** fustigar

lasso [lǽso] N lazo m, reata f; VT lazar; Am enlazar

last [læst] ADJ (in a series) último; (definitive) final; **—-ditch** desesperado; **— minute** de último momento; **— name** apellido m; **— night** anoche; **— rites** extrema unción f, viático m; **— straw** colmo m; **— word** última palabra f; **— year** el año pasado; **next to the —** penúltimo; ADV último; **to arrive —** llegar al último; **when — seen** cuando se lo vio por última vez; **at —** finalmente; N el último;

(of a shoe) horma *f*; vi durar; (live on)
perdurar

lasting [lǽstɪŋ] ADJ duradero, perdurable

lastly [lǽstli] ADV por último

latch [lætʃ] N pestillo *m*, picaporte *m*, cierre
m; vi cerrar con el pestillo; **to — on**
agarrarse de; **to — onto** pegarse a

late [let] ADJ (tardy) tardío; (hour) avanzada;
(recent) reciente, último; (recently
deceased) finado; **—comer** rezagado -da
mf; **— afternoon** atardecer *m*; ADV tarde;
— in the night a una hora avanzada de
la noche; **— into the night** hasta
cualquier hora de la noche; **— in the
week** a finales de la semana; **it is —** ya
es tarde; **of —** últimamente; **to be —**
llegar tarde; **to work —** trabajar hasta
tarde; **the train was ten minutes —** el
tren llegó con diez minutos de retraso

lately [létli] ADV últimamente

lateness [létnɪs] N tardanza *f*

latent [létn̩t] ADJ latente

later [lédə·] ADJ posterior; **see you —** hasta
luego; **— on** más tarde

lateral [lǽdə·əl] ADJ lateral

latest [lédɪst] ADJ último; **the — fashion** la
última moda; **the — news** las últimas
novedades; **at the —** a más tardar; N la
última

latex [léteks] N látex *m*

lathe [leð] N torno *m*

lather [lǽðə·] N (foam) espuma *f*; (sweat)
sudor *m*; **he got into a —** se puso
histérico; vt enjabonar; vi hacer espuma

Latin [lǽtn̩] ADJ latino; N latín *m*; **—
America** América Latina *f*, Latinoamérica
f; **— American** latinoamericano -na *mf*

latitude [lǽdɪtud] N latitud *f*; (freedom)
flexibilidad *f*

latrine [lətrín] N letrina *f*

latter [lǽdə·] ADJ último; **in the — days of
the Roman Republic** en los últimos
días de la República Romana; **toward
the — part of the week** a finales de la
semana; **the —** este *m*, esta *f*

lattice [lǽdɪs] N enrejado *m*, entramado *m*;
(of a window) celosía *f*

Latvia [lǽtviə] N Letonia *f*

Latvian [lǽtviən] ADJ & N letón -ona *mf*

laud [lɔd] vt loar

laudable [lɔ́dəbəl] ADJ laudable, loable

laugh [læf] vi reír(se); **to — at** reírse de; **to
— loudly** reírse a carcajadas; **to — up /
in one's sleeve** reírse para sus adentros;
she —ed in his face se rió en su cara; N
risa *f*; **we did it for —s** lo hicimos por
diversión

laughable [lǽfəbəl] ADJ risible

laughingstock [lǽfɪŋstak] N hazmerreír *m*

laughter [lǽftə·] N risa *f*

launch [lɔntʃ] vt (put into water) botar; (a
rocket, new product) lanzar; **to — forth /
out** lanzarse; N lancha *f*; (act of launching
a boat) botadura *f*; (act of launching a
rocket) lanzamiento *m*

launder [lɔ́ndə·] vi/vt (wash) lavar; (money)
blanquear, lavar; (wash and iron) lavar y
planchar

laundry [lɔ́ndri] N (business establishment)
lavandería *f*, lavadero *m*; (room in house)
cuarto de lavado *m*, lavadero *m*; (clothes
to be washed) ropa sucia *f*; (washed
clothes) ropa limpia *f*

laurel [lɔ́rəl] N laurel *m* (also honor); **to rest
on one's —s** dormirse sobre los laureles

lava [lávə] N lava *f*

lavatory [lǽvətɔri] N (basin) lavabo *m*;
(bathroom) baño *m*, retrete *m*

lavender [lǽvəndə·] N espliego *m*, lavanda *f*;
ADJ lavanda

lavish [lǽvɪʃ] ADJ INV (generous) pródigo,
espléndido; (abundant) abundante,
copioso; vt prodigar; **to — praise upon**
colmar de alabanzas a

law [lɔ] N (discipline) derecho *m*,
jurisprudencia *f*; (police) policía *f*; **— and
order** orden público *m*; **—breaker**
infractor -ora *mf*, transgresor -ora *mf*;
—maker legislador -ra *mf*; **— student**
estudiante de derecho *mf*; **—suit** pleito *m*,
litigio *m*; **to practice —** ejercer la
abogacía; **to take the — into one's
hands** hacer justicia por mano propia; ADJ
—abiding respetuoso de las leyes

lawful [lɔ́fəl] ADJ (in accordance with the
law) legal; (allowed by law) lícito;
(recognized by law) legítimo

lawless [lɔ́lɪs] ADJ (anarchic) anárquico;
(illegal) ilegal

lawn [lɔn] N césped *m*, grama *f*; **— mower**
cortadora de césped *f*

lawyer [lɔ́jə·] N abogado -da *mf*

lax [læks] ADJ laxo

laxative [lǽksədɪv] ADJ & N laxante *m*,
purgante *m*

laxity [lǽksɪdi] N flojedad *f*, laxitud *f*

lay [le] vt colocar; (eggs) poner; (a cable)
tender; (to have sexual intercourse with)
fam tirarse a; **to — aside** (abandon) dejar
de lado; (save) guardar; **to — a wager**
apostar; **to — bare** poner al descubierto;
to — bricks poner ladrillos; **to — down
arms** rendir las armas; **to — down the
law** imponerse; **to — hold of** asir,

agarrar; **to — into** atacar; **to — off a workman** despedir temporalmente a un obrero; **to — one's head on a pillow** recostar la cabeza sobre una almohada; **to — open** exponer; **to — out a plan** trazar un plan; **to — up** almacenar; **to be laid up** estar en cama; **to — waste** asolar; N situación f, orientación f; **she's an easy — fam** es una mujer fácil; **—man** (nonexpert) lego m; (clergy) laico m; **—out** trazado m; ADJ lego, laico

layer [léə⋅] N capa f; (geological) estrato m; (hen) gallina ponedora f; **— cake** tarta de capas f

laziness [lézɪnɪs] N pereza f, holgazanería f, flojera f

lazy [lézi] ADJ perezoso, holgazán, flojo

lead [led] N (metal) plomo m; (graphite) mina f; [lid] VT (guide) guiar; (guide a horse) llevar de la rienda; (induce, take) llevar, inducir; (be in charge, be first) encabezar; (direct) dirigir; (be superior to) estar a la cabeza de; **to — a life of ease** llevar una vida fácil; **to — astray** llevar por mal camino; **to — the way** mostrar el camino; VI (afford passage to, result in) llevar a; (be first) estar a la cabeza; N (first position) delantera f, primer lugar m; (clue) indicio m; (most important role) papel principal m; **— story** noticia principal f

leaden [lédn̩] ADJ (of lead) de plomo; (color) plomizo; (oppressive, slow) pesado

leader [lídə⋅] N (in politics) líder mf, caudillo m; (in a race) líder mf; (in music) director -ora mf; (as a guide) guía mf

leadership [lídə⋅ʃɪp] N dirección f, liderazgo m

leading [lídɪŋ] ADJ (most important) principal; (arriving first) delantero; **— man** primer actor m

leadoff [lídɔf] ADJ comienzo

leaf [lif] N hoja f; VI echar hojas; **to — through a book** hojear un libro

leafless [líflɪs] ADJ sin hojas, deshojado

leaflet [líflɪt] N (small leaf) folíolo m; (printed matter) volante m; (folded printed matter) pliego m

leafy [lífi] ADJ (with foliage) frondoso; (in the form of leaves) de hoja

league [lig] N (alliance) liga f; (unit of distance) legua f; VI/VT aliar(se)

leak [lik] N (in a roof) gotera f; (in a boat, bucket, etc.) agujero m; (of information) filtración f; (of gas, steam, electricity) escape m, fuga f; VI (roof) gotear(se); (boat) hacer agua; (gas) salirse, escaparse; (information) filtrarse; VT pasar información

leaky [líki] ADJ (roof) que tiene goteras; (boat) que hace agua; (gas, electricity) que pierde

lean [lin] VI/VT (incline) inclinar(se); (support) apoyar(se), reclinar(se), recostar(se); **to — on** presionar; ADJ magro; **— year** mal año m

leap [lip] VI/VT saltar; **to — at** aprovechar; **to — to mind** ocurrírsele a uno; N salto m; **—frog** pídola f; **— year** año bisiesto m

learn [lɚn] VI/VT aprender; (find out) enterarse de

learned [lɚ́nɪd] ADJ erudito, letrado

learner [lɚ́nə⋅] N estudiante mf; (driver) aprendiz -za mf

learning [lɚ́nɪŋ] N (result) erudición f, saber m; (process) aprendizaje m; **— disability** problema de aprendizaje m

lease [lis] N (action) arrendamiento m; (contract) contrato de arrendamiento m; (period) período de arrendamiento m; **to have a new — on life** nacer de nuevo; VI/VT arrendar

leash [liʃ] N traílla f, correa f

least [list] ADJ **he doesn't have the — chance** no tiene la más mínima posibilidad; **the — amount of money** la menor cantidad de dinero; **— common denominator** mínimo común denominador m; ADV menos; **the — important** lo menos importante; **at — al** menos, por lo menos; N **I received the — of anyone** yo fui el que recibió menos de todos

leather [léðə⋅] N cuero m; ADJ de cuero; **— strap** correa f

leave [liv] VT (a person, thing) dejar; (a place) salir de, irse de; VI salir, partir; **to — off** (stop) parar de; (omit) omitir; **to — out** omitir; **I have two books left** me quedan dos libros; N permiso m; **to be on — estar de licencia; **to take — of** despedirse de

leaven [lévən] N levadura f; VT leudar

leavings [lívɪŋz] N (leftovers) sobras f pl; (refuse) desperdicios m pl; (act of leaving) partida f

Lebanese [lebəníz] ADJ & N libanés -esa mf

Lebanon [lébənan] N Líbano m

lecherous [létʃə⋅əs] ADJ lujurioso

lecture [léktʃə⋅] N (presentation) conferencia f, disertación f; (sermon) sermón m; (longwinded speech) perorata f; VI (present) dar una conferencia, disertar; VT (scold) sermonear

lecturer [léktʃərə] N conferenciante *mf*; (academic rank) profesor -ra *mf*

LED (light-emitting diode) [elidí] N LED *m*

ledge [ledʒ] N cornisa *f*

ledger [lédʒə] N libro mayor *m*

leech [litʃ] N sanguijuela *f*

leer [lir] VT (sideways) mirar de soslayo; (lecherously) mirar con lujuria; N (sideways) mirada de soslayo *f*; (lecherous) mirada lujuriosa *f*

leeway [líwe] N margen de maniobra *m*; (of a ship) deriva *f*

left [left] ADJ izquierdo; —-**handed** zurdo, con la mano izquierda; —-**handed compliment** alabanza irónica *f*; —-**handed tool** herramienta para zurdos *f*; —-**wing** de izquierdas; N izquierda *f*; **at / on / to / toward the** — a / hacia la izquierda; **make a** — dobla / gira a la izquierda

leftist [léftɪst] N & ADJ izquierdista *mf*

leg [leg] N (human) pierna *f*; (animal, furniture) pata *f*; (wading bird) zanca *f*; (furniture) pie *m*; (of a trip) etapa *f*; **to be on one's last** —**s** estar en las últimas; **to pull someone's** — tomarle el pelo a alguien; **to stretch one's** —**s** estirar las piernas

legacy [légəsi] N legado *m*

legal [lígəɫ] ADJ (in accordance with the law) legal; (permitted by law) lícito; (recognized by law) legítimo; — **age** mayoría de edad *f*; — **fees** honorarios del abogado *m pl*; — **holiday** día feriado *m*; — **procedure** procedimiento jurídico *m*; — **tender** moneda de curso legal *f*

legalize [lígəlaɪz] VT legalizar

legation [lɪgéʃən] N legación *f*

legend [lédʒənd] N leyenda *f* (also inscription); (of a map) clave *f*

legendary [lédʒənderi] ADJ legendario

leggings [légɪŋz] N (ankle to knee) polainas *f pl*; (trousers) leggings *m pl*

legible [lédʒəbəɫ] ADJ legible

legion [lídʒən] N legión *f*

legislate [lédʒɪslet] VI/VT legislar

legislation [ledʒɪsléʃən] N legislación *f*

legislative [lédʒɪslɛdɪv] ADJ legislativo

legislator [lédʒɪslɛdə] N legislador -ra *mf*

legislature [lédʒɪsletʃə] N legislatura *f*

legitimate [lədʒínəmɪt] ADJ legítimo

legitimize [lədʒínəmaɪz] VT legitimar

legume [légjum] N legumbre *f*

leisure [líʒə] N ocio *m*, holgura *f*; — **hours** horas de ocio *f pl*, tiempo libre *m*; **to be at** — estar desocupado; **do it at your** —

hazlo cuando te convenga

leisurely [líʒəli] ADJ lento, deliberado; ADV sin prisa

lemon [lémən] N limón *m*; ADJ de limón; — **tree** limonero *m*

lemonade [lemənéd] N limonada *f*

lend [lend] VI/VT prestar; **to** — **a hand** dar una mano

lender [léndə] N (person who lends) prestador -ora *mf*; (professional) prestamista *f*

length [leŋkθ] N largo *m*, largura *f*, longitud *f*; (of movie) duración *f*; (of a book) extensión *f*; **at** — (in detail) pormenorizadamente; (finally) finalmente; **by two** —**s** por dos cuerpos; **two meters in** — dos metros de largo; **to go to any** —**s** hacer lo imposible

lengthen [léŋkθən] VI/VT alargar(se)

lengthwise [léŋkθwaɪz] ADV & ADJ a lo largo

lengthy [léŋkθi] ADJ largo, prolongado

lenient [líniənt] ADJ indulgente

lens [lenz] N lente *m*; (of the eye) cristalino *m*

Lent [lent] N Cuaresma *f*

lentil [léntɫ] N lenteja *f*

Leon [león] N León *m*

Leonese [liəníz] ADJ leonés

leopard [lépəd] N leopardo *m*

leprosy [léprəsi] N lepra *f*

lesbian [lézbiən] ADJ lesbiano; N lesbiana *f*

lesion [líʒən] N lesión *f*

Lesotho [ləsóto] N Lesoto *m*

less [les] ADJ, ADV & PREP menos; **I have** — **than you do** tengo menos que tú; — **and** — cada vez menos

lessen [lésən] VI/VT disminuir, aminorar

lesser [lésə] ADJ menor

lesson [lésən] N lección *f*

lest [lest] CONJ no sea que; — **you should think I'm teasing** para que no vayas a creer que estoy bromeando

let [let] VT (permit) dejar, permitir; (rent) alquilar; — **him come** que venga; —**'s do it** hagámoslo; **to** — **be** dejar en paz; **to** — **down** (lower) bajar; (disappoint) decepcionar; **to** — **go** soltar; **to** — **in** dejar entrar; **to** — **know** hacer saber; **to** — **off** dejar ir; **to** — **through** dejar pasar; **to** — **up** (permit to stand) dejar incorporarse; (cease) disminuir; N —**down** desilusión *f*; —**up** tregua *f*

lethal [líθəɫ] ADJ letal

lethargy [léθədʒi] N letargo *m*, sopor *m*; **to fall into a** — aletargarse

letter [lédə] N (of alphabet) letra *f*; (missive) carta *f*; — **box** buzón *m*; — **carrier** cartero -ra *mf*; —**head** membrete *m*;

—head paper papel membretado m; **—s letras** f pl; **the — of the law** la letra de la ley; **to the —** al pie de la letra; vt escribir

lettuce [lɛ́ɾɪs] N lechuga f

leukemia [lukímiǝ] N leucemia f

levee [lévi] N dique m

level [lévǝl] ADJ llano, plano; N nivel m (also tool); vt (make level) nivelar, igualar; (to demolish) arrasar, allanar; (to knock down a person) tumbar; (to aim criticism) dirigir; (to aim a gun) apuntar; **—-headed** sensato; **— with** a nivel de; **a — teaspoon** una cucharada al ras; **to be on the —** ser serio; **to — off** quedar paralelo al suelo; **to — with** hablar en serio con/a

lever [lévǝ] N palanca f

leverage [lévǝɪʤ] N (influence) palanca f; (physical) apalancamiento m

levity [lévɪɾi] N ligereza f

levy [lévi] N (of taxes) recaudación f; (of troops) leva f; vt (taxes) recaudar; (troops) reclutar, hacer una leva de

lewd [lud] ADJ lascivo

lewdness [lúdnɪs] N lascivia f

lexical [léksɪkǝl] ADJ léxico

lexicography [leksɪkúgrǝfi] N lexicografía f

lexicon [léksɪkɑn] N léxico m

liability [laɪǝbílɪɾi] N (disadvantage) desventaja f; (debits) pasivo m; (debts) deudas f pl; (responsibility) responsabilidad legal f; **— insurance** seguro contra daños a terceros m; **liabilities** obligaciones f pl

liable [láɪǝbǝl] ADJ responsable; **— to** propenso a; **she's — to get angry** es probable que se enoje

liaison [liézɑn] N enlace m; (illicit love affair) aventura f

liar [láɪǝ] N mentiroso -sa mf, embustero -ra mf

libel [láɪbǝl] N libelo m, difamación f; vt difamar

liberal [líbǝǝ] ADJ & N liberal mf

liberalism [líbǝǝlɪzǝm] N liberalismo m

liberality [lɪbǝrǽlɪɾi] N (generosity) liberalidad f; (tolerance) tolerancia f

liberalize [líbǝ-ǝlaɪz] vi/vt liberalizar(se)

liberate [líbǝret] vt (give freedom to) libertar, liberar; (release from obligation) librar; (give off) desprender

liberation [lɪbǝréʃǝn] N liberación f

liberator [líbǝreɾǝ] N libertador -ra mf

Liberia [laɪbíriǝ] N Liberia f

Liberian [laɪbíriǝn] ADJ & N liberiano -na mf

libertine [líbǝ-tin] ADJ & N libertino -na mf, calavera m

liberty [líbǝ-ɾi] N libertad f; **at —** autorizado

libido [lɪbído] N libido f

librarian [laɪbríriǝn] N bibliotecario -ria mf

library [láɪbreri] N biblioteca f

libretto [lɪbréɾo] N libreto m

Libya [líbjǝ] N Libia f

Libyan [líbjǝn] ADJ & N libio -bia mf

license [láɪsǝns] N permiso m; (driver's permit, poetic freedom) licencia f; **— plate** placa f, matrícula f; vt (issue license to) otorgar una licencia; (give permission) autorizar

licentious [laɪsénʃǝs] ADJ licencioso

lick [lɪk] vt (touch with tongue) lamer (also waves); (thrash) dar una paliza; (defeat) derrotar; N lamida f, lengüetazo m; (blow) golpe m; **not to do a — of work** no mover un dedo

lickety-split [lɪkɪɾisplít] ADV en un santiamén

licking [líkɪŋ] N paliza f

licorice [líkǝɪʃ] N regaliz m

lid [lɪd] N tapadera f, tapa f; (of eye) párpado m; (on prices) tope m

lie [laɪ] N (falsehood) mentira f, embuste m; (orientation of an object) orientación f; **— detector** detector de mentiras m; **to give the —** desmentir; vi mentir; **to — one's way out of a situation** salirse de una situación a mentiras; (be buried) yacer; (to be on a flat surface) estar; (to be situated) estar situado; (be horizontal) tumbarse, acostarse; **he's lying in bed** está acostado en la cama; **to — back** recostarse; **to — down** acostarse, tumbarse; **to — in wait** acechar

Liechtenstein [líktǝnstaɪn] N Liechtenstein m

Liechtensteiner [líktǝnstaɪnǝ] N liechtensteiniano -na mf

lien [lin] N gravamen m, carga f

lieutenant [luténǝnt] N teniente mf; **— colonel** teniente coronel mf; **— governor** vicegobernador -ora mf

life [laɪf] N vida f; **—-and-death** de vida o muerte; **—boat** bote de salvamento m; **— cycle** ciclo vital m; **— expectancy** expectativa de vida f; **—guard** salvavidas mf sg; **— imprisonment** prisión perpetua f; **— insurance** seguro de vida m; **— jacket** salvavidas m sg; **—like** natural, que parece vivo; **—long** de toda la vida; **— of the party** alma de la fiesta f; **— preserver** salvavidas m sg; **— raft** balsa salvavidas f; **—-support system** (in space) equipo de vida m; (in a hospital) máquina corazón-pulmón f; **—style** estilo de vida *m*; **—time** vida *f*; ADJ (relative to life) vital; (for duration of life) vitalicio; **-—sized** de tamaño natural

lifeless [láɪflɪs] ADJ (without living things) sin vida; (dead) muerto, sin vida; (fainted) desfallecido; (without liveliness) sin animación

lifer [láɪfɚ] N (prisoner) condenado -da a cadena perpetua *mf*; (soldier) militar de carrera *m*

lift [lɪft] VT levantar; (steal) robar; (plagiarize) copiar; VI (disperse) disiparse; (go up) elevarse; N (upward force) empuje *m*; (feeling) mejoría de ánimo *f*; (device for lifting) montacargas *m sg*; **to give someone a** — llevar en coche; *Mex* dar un aventón; **—off** despegue *m*

ligament [lígəmənt] N ligamento *m*

ligature [lígətfɚ] N ligadura *f*

light [laɪt] N luz *f*; (device) luz *f*, lámpara *f*; (for traffic) semáforo *m*; (perspective) perspectiva *f*; (for cigarettes) fuego *m*; **—house** faro *m*; ADJ (well-lighted) claro; (of little weight) ligero, leve; (of clothes) fresco; *Am* liviano; **— blue** azul claro *m*; **-—emitting diode** diodo electroiluminiscente *m*; **-—headed** mareado; **-—hearted** alegre; **— rain** lluvia fina *f*; **-—skinned** de tez blanca; **— touch** mano delicada *f*; **—weight** de peso ligero; **-—year** año luz *m*; **to make — of** restar importancia a; VI/VT (turn on, ignite) encender(se), prender(se); (provide light, brighten) iluminar(se); (land on) posarse en; **to — up** prender, encender, alumbrar; **to — upon** caer sobre

lighten [láɪtn] VI/VT (make/become lighter) aligerar(se), alivianar(se); (brighten) iluminar(se); **— up!** ¡No tomes las cosas a la tremenda!

lighter [láɪtɚ] N encendedor *m*

lighting [láɪtɪŋ] N iluminación *f*; (in the street) alumbrado *m*

lightness [láɪtnɪs] N (little weight) ligereza *f*, levedad *f*; (brightness) claridad *f*

lightning [láɪtnɪŋ] N relámpago *m*; **— bug** luciérnaga *f*; **— rod** pararrayos *m sg*; **it happened at — speed** pasó como rayo; VI relampaguear

likable [láɪkəbəɫ] ADJ agradable, simpático

like [laɪk] ADV & PREP como; ADJ semejante, parecido; **in — manner** del mismo modo; **to feel — going** tener ganas de ir; **to look — someone** parecerse a alguien; **it looks — rain** parece que va a llover; **-—minded** del mismo parecer; N **—s** gustos *m pl*, preferencias *f pl*; VT gustarle a

uno; **he —s dogs** le gustan los perros; **do whatever you —** haz lo que quieras; CONJ **he talked —** he was crazy hablaba como si estuviera loco; **she came — you predicted** she would vino, tal como tú pronosticaste; **I'm —, "you're crazy"** yo pensé / dije, "estás loco"; INTERJ **he was, like, way too old** era como que demasiado viejo

likely [láɪkli] ADJ (probable) probable; (believable) creíble; (promising) prometedor; **John is — to win** es probable que gane Juan; ADV probablemente

liken [láɪkən] VT comparar, asimilar

likeness [láɪknɪs] N (similarity) parecido *m*; (portrait) retrato *m*

likewise [láɪkwaɪz] ADV (the same thing) lo mismo; **we did —** hicimos lo mismo; (similarly) asimismo; (also) también

liking [láɪkɪŋ] N preferencia *f*, gusto *m*

lilac [láɪlək] N lila *f*; ADJ lila *inv*

lily [lɪli] N lirio *m*, azucena *f*; ADJ **-—white** (very white) blanquísimo; (pure) puro; (for whites only) exclusivamente para blancos

limb [lɪm] N (branch) rama *f*; (appendage) miembro *m*

limber [límbɚ] ADJ flexible; VT hacer flexible; VI **to — up** estirarse

lime [laɪm] N (mineral) cal *f*; (fruit, color) lima *f*; **—light** candilejas *f pl*; **in the —light** en el candelero; **-—stone** piedra caliza *f*; **— tree** limero *m*, lima *f*

limit [límɪt] N límite *m*; **to the —** al máximo; VT limitar

limitation [lɪmɪtéʃən] N limitación *f*

limitless [límɪtlɪs] ADJ ilimitado

limousine [líməzin] N limusina *f*

limp [lɪmp] N cojera *f*, renguera *f*; VI cojear, renguear, renquear; ADJ (body) flácido; (plants) mustio

limpid [límpɪd] ADJ límpido

line [laɪn] N (bus route, telephone connection) línea *f*; (of words) renglón *m*, línea *f*; (row) raya *f*, hilera *f*; (cord) cuerda *f*; (persons waiting) cola *f*, fila *f*; (business) ramo *m*; (wrinkle) arruga *f*; (boundary) límite *m*; **— of credit** línea de crédito *f*; **—s** (in a play) parte *f*; **—up** hilera de personas *f*; (sports) alineación *f*; **drop me a —** escríbeme unas líneas; **off-—** fuera de línea; **on-—** en línea; **out of —** irrespetuoso; **to get in —** hacer cola; VI/VT (border) alinear, bordear; (put in a lining) forrar; **to — up** alinear(se)

lineage [líniɪʤ] N linaje *m*, estirpe *f*

linear [líniɚ] ADJ lineal

lined [laɪnd] ADJ (with lines) rayado; (with a lining) forrado

linen [línɪn] N (fabric) lino *m*; (bedclothes, etc.) ropa blanca *f*

liner [láɪnə] N (ocean) transatlántico *m*; (air) avión comercial *m*; (eye) delineador *m*

linger [língə] VI (stay) quedarse, demorarse; (persist) persistir; (saunter) rezagarse; (contemplate) detenerse; (delay death) aguantar

lingerie [lɑnʒəré] N lencería *f*

linguist [língwɪst] N lingüista *mf*

linguistics [lɪngwístɪks] N lingüística *f*

liniment [línəmənt] N linimento *m*

lining [láɪnɪŋ] N forro *m*; **every cloud has a silver —** no hay mal que por bien no venga

link [lɪŋk] N (of a chain) eslabón *m*; (bond, tie) vínculo *m*; (computer, rail, radio connection) enlace *m*; VI/VT enlazar(se), conectar(se), vincular(se)

linnet [línɪt] N pardillo *m*

linoleum [lɪnóliəm] N linóleo *m*

linseed [línsid] N linaza *f*; **— oil** aceite de linaza *m*

lint [lɪnt] N pelusa *f*

lion [láɪən] N león *m*; **—'s share** la parte del león

lioness [láɪənɪs] N leona *f*

lip [lɪp] N labio *m*; (of a pitcher) borde *m*; **—stick** lápiz de labios *m*; **to —read** leer los labios; **don't give me no —**! no me contestes

liposuction [láɪposʌkʃən] N liposucción *f*

liqueur [lɪkɛ́] N licor *m*

liquid [líkwɪd] ADJ líquido; **— assets** activo líquido *m*; **— measure** medida para líquidos *f*; N líquido *m*

liquidate [líkwɪdet] VI/VT liquidar

liquidation [lɪkwɪdéʃən] N liquidación *f*

liquidity [lɪkwídɪDi] N liquidez *f*

liquor [líkə] N bebida espirituosa *f*

lira [lírə] N lira *f*

lisp [lɪsp] N ceceo *m*; VI cecear

list [lɪst] N lista *f*; (of a ship) escora *f*; **— price** precio de lista *m*; **— server** servidor de lista *m*; VT (make a list) hacer una lista de; VI (lean) escorar; **this chair —s for two hundred dollars** esta silla está a doscientos dólares

listen [lísən] VI/VT (hear) escuchar, oír; (heed) escuchar, prestar atención; **to — in** (on radio) sintonizar; (eavesdrop) escuchar a hurtadillas

listener [lísənə] N oyente *mf*; **radio —** radioescucha *mf*, oyente *mf*

listing [lístɪŋ] N listado *m*

listless [lístlɪs] ADJ lánguido

lit [lɪt] ADJ (provided with light) iluminado; (tipsy) alegre, alumbrado

literacy [lírəsi] N (action of making literate) alfabetización *f*; (rate) alfabetismo *m*

literal [lírəɫ] ADJ literal

literary [lírəreri] ADJ literario

literate [lírət] ADJ (who can read and write) alfabeto; (erudite) erudito, letrado; **he's barely —** apenas sabe leer y escribir

literature [lírətʃə] N literatura *f*; (handbills) impresos *m pl*, folletos *m pl*; **the scientific —** la literatura científica

lithium [líθiəm] N litio *m*

Lithuania [lɪθuéniə] N Lituania *f*

Lithuanian [lɪθuéniən] ADJ & N lituano -na *mf*

litigation [lɪdɪgéʃən] N litigio *m*, pleito *m*

litter [lírə] N (young animals) camada *f*, cría *f*; (stretcher) camilla *f*; (straw) cama de paja para animales *f*; (trash) basura *f*; (for cats) arena higiénica *f*; VI/VT (dirty) ensuciar; (strew) esparcir; VI (give birth) parir

little [lídl] ADJ (small) pequeño, chico; (not much) poco; **— brother** hermano menor *m*, hermanito *m*; **— finger** (dedo) meñique *m*; **— pig** puerquito *m*; **a — coffee** un poco de café; **a — while** un ratito, un poco; ADV & N poco; **— by —** poco a poco

live [lɪv] VI/VT vivir; **to — up to** cumplir; **to — it up** tirar la casa por la ventana; **all the —long day** todo el santo día; [laɪv] ADJ vivo; (ammunition) cargado; **— coal** ascua encendida *f*; **— oak** roble de Virginia *m*; **—stock** ganado *m*; **— wire** (electric) cable cargado *m*; (person) persona vivaz *f*; **before a — audience** en vivo; **—in** con cama; ADV en vivo y en directo

livelihood [láɪvlihud] N sustento *m*

liveliness [láɪvlinɪs] N viveza *f*, animación *f*

lively [láɪvli] ADJ (party) animado; (person) vivaz, avispado; ADV con animación

liver [lívə] N hígado *m*

livid [lívɪd] ADJ (bluish) lívido; (angry) furibundo

living [lívɪŋ] N (life) vida *f*; **to earn / make a —** ganarse la vida; ADJ vivo, viviente; **— room** sala *f*, living *m*; **— wage** sueldo suficiente para vivir *m*; **the —** los vivos

lizard [lízəd] N lagartija *f*

llama [lámə] N llama *f*

load [lod] N carga *f*; (weight) peso *m*; (of a ship) cargamento *m*; **—s of** montones de;

VI/VT cargar; **to — down** colmar; **to — oneself down** agobiarse

loaf [lof] N hogaza de pan f, pan m; VI holgar, holgazanear, haraganear

loafer [lófə˞] N (idler) holgazán -ana mf, haragán -na mf, gandul -la mf; (shoe) mocasín m

loan [lon] N préstamo m; (to a government) empréstito m; **— shark** usurero -ra mf; **—word** préstamo m; VI/VT prestar

loath [loθ] ADJ renuente; **to be — to** ser renuente a

loathe [loð] VT aborrecer

loathsome [lóðsəm] ADJ repugnante, abominable

lob [lɑb] VT tirar por lo alto; N (tennis) globo m

lobby [lábi] N (vestibule) vestíbulo m; (special interest) grupo de presión m, lobby m; VI/VT (influence) presionar

lobbyist [lábiıst] N lobbista mf, lobista mf

lobe [lob] N lóbulo m

lobotomy [ləbádəmi] N lobotomía f

lobster [lábstə˞] N langosta f

local [lókəl] ADJ local; **— train** tren de cercanías m

localize [lókəlaız] VT localizar

locate [lóket] VI/VT (establish in a place) situar, ubicar; (find) localizar; VI (settle) radicarse, establecerse

location [lokéʃən] N (position) ubicación f; (finding) localización f; **on —** en exteriores

lock [lɑk] N (door) cerradura f; (canal) esclusa f; (firearms, wrestling) llave f; (of hair) mechón m; **to have a — on the award** tener asegurado el premio; **—out** cierre patronal m; **—smith** cerrajero -ra mf; VI/VT cerrar con llave; (make immovable) trabar(se); **to — in** encerrar; **to — out** dejar afuera; **to — up** (door) cerrar con llave; (animal) encerrar; (prisoner) encarcelar; (valuables) poner bajo llave

locker [lákə˞] N (for athletic equipment) casillero m; (for frozen food) cámara frigorífica f; **— room** vestuario m

locket [lákıt] N relicario m, guardapelo m

locomotive [lokəmódıv] N locomotora f

locust [lókəst] N langosta f; **— tree** algarrobo m

lodge [lɑdʒ] N (of fraternal organization) logia f; (cabin) cabaña f; (hotel) posada f, mesón m; VI/VT alojar(se), hospedar(se); **to — a complaint** presentar una queja

lodger [ládʒə˞] N inquilino -na mf

lodging [ládʒıŋ] N alojamiento m, hospedaje m

loft [lɔft] N (attic) desván m; (for choir) coro m; (for hay) pajar m; VT tirar por lo alto

lofty [lɔ́fti] ADJ elevado, encumbrado

log [lɑg] N leño m, madero m, rollizo m; (ship record) cuaderno de bitácora m; (record of activity) diario m; **— cabin** cabaña de troncos f; VI/VT (cut trees) cortar; VT (write down) anotar; **to — off / out** salir (del sistema)

logarithm [lágərıðəm] N logaritmo m

logic [ládʒık] N lógica f

logical [ládʒıkəl] ADJ lógico

logistics [lədʒístıks] N logística f

loin [lɔın] N ijada f; (in animals) ijar m; (cut of meat) lomo m; **—s** entrañas f pl

loiter [lɔ́ıdə˞] VI (idly) holgazanear; (with intent) merodear; **to — behind** rezagarse

loll [lɑl] VI arrellanarse

lollipop [lálıpɑp] N Sp pirulí m; Mex paleta f; RP chupetín m

lone [lon] ADJ (solitary) solitario; (only) único

loneliness [lónlinıs] N soledad f

lonely [lónli] ADJ solo

lonesome [lónsəm] ADJ solo

long [lɔŋ] ADJ largo; **a — way home** lejos de casa; **to work — hours** trabajar muchas horas; **— distance** de larga distancia; **— division** división de más de una cifra f; **—hand** letra manuscrita f; **— johns** calzoncillos largos m pl; **— jump** salto largo m; **—lasting** duradero, perdurable; **—lived** (batteries) duradero; (people) longevo; **—range** de largo alcance; **—shoreman** estibador m; **—term** a largo plazo; **— underwear** calzoncillo largo m; **—winded** verborrágico, palabrero; **it's a — shot** es muy improbable; ADV mucho, mucho tiempo; **— ago** hace mucho tiempo; **— before** mucho antes; **— live . . . !** ¡viva . . . ! **—suffering** sufrido; **all winter —** todo el invierno; **how — did he stay?** ¿cuánto tiempo se quedó ? **not for — no** por mucho tiempo; **so — !** ¡hasta luego! **to be — in coming** tardar en venir; **three meters —** tres metros de largo; **will you be —?** ¿tardarás mucho? **the whole day —** todo el santo día; VI **to — for** anhelar

longer [lɔ́ŋgə˞] ADJ más largo; ADV más; **no — ya** no; **how much —?** ¿hasta cuándo?

longevity [lɑndʒévıdi] N longevidad f

longing [lɔ́ŋıŋ] N anhelo m; ADJ anhelante

longitude [lándʒıtud] N longitud f

look [lʊk] VI (see) mirar; (seem) parecer; **it —s good on you** te queda bien, te luce; **to — after** atender, cuidar; **to — alike**

parecerse; **to — down on someone** despreciar a alguien; **to — for** (search for) buscar; (anticipate) esperar; **I — forward to it** lo espero con ansia, me da mucha ilusión; **to — into** investigar; **she —'s her age** aparenta la edad que tiene; **to — out on** dar a, tener vista a; **to — out of** asomarse a; **— out!** ¡cuidado! **to — over** dar un vistazo a; **to — up** (upwards) levantar la vista; (in a directory) buscar; **to — up to** admirar; N (gaze) mirada f; (examination) vistazo m; **—alike** doble mf; **—out** (person) vigía mf; (place) mirador m, vigía f; **to be on the —out** estar alerta; **—s** aspecto m, pinta f; **good —s** belleza f

looking glass [lúkıŋglæs] N espejo m

loom [lum] N telar m; VI (appear indistinctly) dibujarse; (threaten) cernerse

loony [lúni] ADJ chiflado

loop [lup] N (for fastening) presilla f; (in a rope) lazo m; (of a flight) rizo m; (electric) circuito cerrado m; (computer programming, ice-skating) bucle m; **—hole** resquicio m, agujero m; VI (make a loop) hacer un lazo; (curve around) serpentear; (loop the loop) rizar el rizo; VT enlazar

loose [lus] ADJ (free) suelto; (not tight) flojo; (approximate) libre; (unfettered) desatado; (immoral) disoluto; (promiscuous) fácil; **— cannon** mono con una metralleta m; **— change** suelto m, cambio m; **— end** cabo suelto m; **—-fitting** holgado; **—-jointed** de articulaciones flexibles; **—leaf** (de) hojas sueltas; **to let —** soltar; VT desatar, soltar

loosen [lúsən] VI/VT (untie) soltar(se), desatar; (make/become less tight/dense/strict) aflojar(se)

looseness [lúsnıs] N (of skin) flojedad f; (of morals) relajamiento m; (of clothing) holgura f; (of soil) friabilidad f; (of translation) lo libre

loot [lut] N botín m; VI/VT saquear

lop [lap] VT (cut) cortar; (eliminate) eliminar; VI caer(se); ADJ **—sided** (leaning to one side) ladeado; (unbalanced) desequilibrado; (listing) escorado

lope [lop] VI correr a pasos largos

loquacious [lokwéʃəs] ADJ locuaz

loquat [lókwat] N níspero m

lord [lɔrd] N señor m; (God) Señor m; (British title) lord m; **—'s Prayer** Padrenuestro m; **my —!** ¡Dios mío! VI **to — it over someone** tratarle a alguien con arrogancia

lordly [lɔ́rdli] ADJ (kingly) señorial; (haughty) altivo

lordship [lɔ́rdʃıp] N (title) señoría f; (power) señorío m

lore [lɔr] N saber m

lose [luz] VI/VT perder; (a pursuer) dejar atrás; **to — sight of** perder de vista; **to — oneself in thought** ensimismarse

loser [lúzə-] N perdedor -ra mf

loss [lɔs] N (destruction) pérdida f; (misplacement) pérdida f, extravío m; (sports) derrota f; **to be at a —** no saber qué hacer; **to sell at a —** vender con pérdida; **—es** bajas f pl

lost [lɔst] ADJ perdido; **— in thought** absorto; **to get —** perderse, extraviarse

lot [lat] N (parcel) lote m; (luck) suerte f, destino m; (piece of land) solar m, terreno m; **the —** todo; **a — of / —s of** mucho(s); **a — of money** mucho dinero; **by —** al azar; **to draw —s** echar suertes; **to fall to one's —** caerle en suerte a uno; ADV **a — better** mucho mejor

lotion [lóʃən] N loción f

lottery [látəri] N lotería f

loud [laud] ADJ (noisy) ruidoso; (strong) fuerte; (ostentatious) chillón; ADV fuerte, alto; **—speaker** altavoz m, altoparlante m; **—mouth** bocazas mf sg

lounge [laundʒ] VI repantigarse, arrellanarse; **to — away** pasar holgazaneando; N (waiting-room) sala de espera f; (room in bar) salón m; (divan) diván m; **— chair** diván m

louse [laus] N piojo m

lousy [láuzi] ADJ (infested with lice) piojoso; (contemptible) despreciable; (poorly done) pésimo

lout [laut] N bruto m

lovable [lávəbəl] ADJ adorable

love [lʌv] N (affection) amor m; (fondness) afición f; (in tennis) nada f; **— affair** aventura f, amorío m; **— at first sight** amor a primera vista m, flechazo m; **— life** vida sentimental f; **— seat** confidente m; **books were her great —** los libros fueron su gran pasión; **to be in —** estar enamorado; **to fall in — with** enamorarse de; **to make — to** hacerle el amor a; VI/VT amar, querer; **I — to eat apples** me encanta comer manzanas

loveliness [lávlınıs] N (beauty) hermosura f; (charm) encanto m

lovely [lávli] ADJ (beautiful) hermoso; (charming) encantador; (pleasant) ameno

lover [lávə-] N (sexually involved) amante mf; (in love) enamorado -da mf, amante mf;

(interested in) aficionado -da *mf*

loving [lávɪŋ] ADJ cariñoso, afectuoso

low [lo] ADJ (not high) bajo; (base) vil; (humble) humilde; (downcast) abatido; (deep in pitch) grave; **— beam** luces cortas *f pl*; **—brow** poco culto; **—cal** de bajas calorías; **—down** verdad *f*; **—end** barato; **— gear** primera marcha *f*; **—grade** (inferior) inferior; (low) bajo; **—key** tranquilo; **—land** tierra baja *f*; **—level** de bajo nivel; **—life** canalla *f*; **—tech** sencillo; **— tide** bajamar *f*, marea baja *f*; **dress with a — neck** vestido escotado *m*; **to be — on something** estar escaso de algo; **to be in — spirits** estar abatido / desanimado; ADV bajo; **to buy —** comprar barato; N (sound of a cow) mugido *m*; VI mugir

lower [lóə] VI/VT bajar; (prices) rebajar; (flag, sail) arriar; ADJ más bajo, inferior; **—case** minúscula *f*; **— house** cámara de diputados *f*

lowliness [lólɪnɪs] N humildad *f*

lowly [lóli] ADJ humilde

loyal [lɔ́ɪəl] ADJ leal

loyalty [lɔ́ɪəlti] N lealtad *f*

LSD (lysergic acid diethylamide) [elesdí] N LSD *m*

lubricant [lúbrɪkənt] ADJ & N lubricante *m*

lubricate [lúbrɪket] VI/VT lubricar

lucid [lúsɪd] ADJ lúcido

luck [lʌk] N suerte *f*; **in —** de suerte; **to be out of —** estar de mala suerte; **to — into** conseguir por un golpe de suerte; **to — out** tener suerte

lucky [lʌ́ki] ADJ afortunado; **— charm** amuleto de la suerte *m*; **to be —** tener suerte

lucrative [lúkrədɪv] ADJ lucrativo

ludicrous [lúdɪkrəs] ADJ ridículo

lug [lʌg] VT acarrear

luggage [lágɪʤ] N equipaje *m*; **— rack** rejilla *f*

lukewarm [lúkwɔ́rm] ADJ (not warm or cold) tibio; (indifferent) indiferente

lull [lʌł] VT (put to sleep) arrullar; VI/VT (soothe) calmar(se); N (calm) calma *f*, tregua *f*; (sound) arrullo *m*

lullaby [lʌ́ləbaɪ] N canción de cuna *f*, nana *f*

lumber [lámbə] N madera *f*; **—jack** leñador *m*; **—man** maderero *m*; **— mill** aserradero *m*; **—yard** almacén de maderas *m*; VI/VT (cut trees) talar; (move heavily) moverse pesadamente; (make a low noise) tronar

luminous [lúmənəs] ADJ luminoso

lump [lʌmp] N (in breast) bulto *m*; (in sauce) grumo *m*; (in throat) nudo *m*; (of coal)

trozo *m*; (of rice) plasta *f*; (on head) chichón *m*; (of sugar) terrón *m*; **to take one's —s** recibir palos; **— sum** pago global *m*; VT juntar; VI agruparse

lumpy [lámpi] ADJ grumoso

lunar [lúnə] ADJ lunar; **— eclipse** eclipse lunar *m*

lunatic [lúnətɪk] ADJ & N lunático -ca *mf*, loco -ca *mf*; **— fringe** extremistas *mf pl*

lunch [lʌntʃ] N comida *f*, almuerzo *m*; **—time** hora de almorzar / comer *f*; **out to —** (crazy) en la luna; VI comer, almorzar

lung [lʌŋ] N pulmón *m*

lunge [lʌnʤ] N arremetida *f*; VI arremeter, abalanzarse; **to — at** arremeter contra, abalanzarse sobre

lurch [lɜtʃ] N tambaleo *m*; **to give a —** tambalearse; **to leave someone in the —** dejar a alguien en la estacada; VI tambalearse, dar barquinazos

lure [lur] N (thing that attracts) atractivo *m*, gancho *m*; (in hunting) señuelo *m*; (in fishing) cebo *m*; VT atraer, seducir

lurid [lúrɪd] ADJ (gruesome) sangriento; (shocking) escabroso

lurk [lɜk] VI (lie in wait) estar en acecho, acechar; (move furtively) moverse furtivamente

luscious [lʌ́ʃəs] ADJ (delicious) exquisito, delicioso; (sexy) voluptuoso

lust [lʌst] N (sexual desire) lujuria *f*, lascivia *f*; (craving) deseo *m*, ansia *f*; VI desear; **to — after** codiciar

luster [lʌ́stə] N lustre *m*, brillo *m*

lustful [lʌ́stfəl] ADJ lujurioso

lusty [lʌ́sti] ADJ (robust) robusto; (full of lust) lujurioso

Luxembourg [láksəmbəg] N Luxemburgo *m*

Luxembourger [láksəmbəgə] N luxemburgués -esa *mf*

Luxembourgian [lʌksəmbɜ́giən] ADJ luxemburgués

luxurious [lʌgʒúriəs] ADJ (characterized by luxury) lujoso; (luxuriant) exuberante

luxury [lágʒəri] N lujo *m*; **— tax** impuesto suntuario *m*; ADJ de lujo

lye [laɪ] N lejía *f*

lying [láɪŋ] ADJ mentiroso

lymph [lɪmf] N linfa *f*; **— node** nodo linfático *m*

lynch [lɪntʃ] VT linchar

lynx [lɪŋks] N lince *m*

lyric [lírɪk] N poema lírico *m*; **—s** letra *f*; ADJ lírico

lyrical [lírɪkəl] ADJ lírico

lyricism [lírɪsɪzəm] N lirismo *m*

Mm

ma'am [mæm] N señora f
Macao [məkáú] N Macao m
macaroni [mækəróni] N macarrones m pl
Macedonia [mæsɪdóniə] N Macedonia f
Macedonian [mæsɪdóniən] ADJ & N macedonio -nia mf
machine [məʃín] N máquina f; (of government) maquinaria f, aparato m; — **gun** (not portable) ametralladora f; (portable) metralleta f; — **language** lenguaje de máquina m; —**made** hecho a máquina; VT trabajar a máquina
machinery [məʃínəri] N maquinaria f
machinist [məʃínɪst] N maquinista mf, operario -ria mf
mackerel [mækəɹɪ] N caballa f
mad [mæd] ADJ (crazy) loco; (angry) rabioso, enojado; (hydrophobic) rabioso; **to be — about someone** estar loco por alguien; **to drive —** enloquecer, volver loco; **to get —** enojarse; **to go —** volverse loco, enloquecerse; **like —** como loco; —**man** loco m
Madagascan [mædəgǽskən] ADJ & N malgache mf
Madagascar [mædəgǽskɑr] N Madagascar m
madam [mǽdəm] N señora f; (woman who runs a brothel) madama f
maddening [mǽdɪŋɪŋ] ADJ enloquecedor
made [med] ADJ —**to-measure** hecho a la medida; —**to-order** hecho por encargo; —**up** (invented) inventado, falso; (wearing make-up) maquillado; **to be — of** ser de; **to have something —** mandar hacer algo; **I'm a — man** estoy hecho; **to have it —** estar hecho
madness [mǽdnɪs] N (insanity) locura f; (anger) rabia f
Mafia [mɑ́fiə] N mafia f
mafioso [mɑfióso] N mafioso m
magazine [mǽɡəzin] N (publication) revista f; (room for ammunition) polvorín m; (part of gun) cargador m
magic [mǽdʒɪk] N magia f; ADJ mágico; — **bullet** panacea f; — **wand** varita mágica f
magical [mǽdʒɪkəɹ] ADJ mágico
magician [mədʒíʃən] N mago -ga mf
magistrate [mǽdʒɪstret] N magistrado -da mf
magma [mǽɡmə] N magma m
magnanimous [mæɡnǽnəməs] ADJ

magnánimo
magnate [mǽɡnet] N magnate m
magnesia [mæɡnízə] N magnesia f
magnesium [mæɡnízɪəm] N magnesio m
magnet [mǽɡnɪt] N imán m
magnetic [mæɡnɛ́DɪK] ADJ magnético; — **pole** polo magnético m; — **resonance imaging** imagen por resonancia magnética f; — **tape** cinta magnetofónica f
magnetism [mǽɡnɪtɪzəm] N magnetismo m
magnetize [mǽɡnɪtaɪz] VT magnetizar, imantar
magnificence [mæɡnífɪsəns] N magnificencia f
magnificent [mæɡnífɪsənt] ADJ magnífico
magnify [mǽɡnɪfaɪ] VT (to make larger) aumentar; (to make louder) amplificar; (to exaggerate) exagerar, magnificar
magnitude [mǽɡnɪtud] N magnitud f
magnolia [mæɡnóljə] N (flower) magnolia f; (tree) magnolio m
magpie [mǽɡpaɪ] N urraca f (also hoarder)
mahogany [məhɑ́ɡəni] N caoba f
maid [med] N criada f, sirvienta f; (in hotel) camarera f; — **of honor** dama de honor f
maiden [médn] N lit doncella f, virgen f; — **voyage** primer viaje m; — **name** nombre de soltera m
mail [mel] N correo m; (electronic) mensaje m; (of metal) malla f; —**bag** cartera f; —**box** buzón m; —**man** cartero m; — **order** pedido por correo m; VT echar al correo
maim [mem] VT mutilar
main [men] ADJ principal; — **office** oficina central f; N (pipe) cañería principal f; (sea) alta mar f; —**frame** Sp ordenador central m, Am computadora central f; —**land** continente m; —**spring** muelle real m; —**stream** tendencia mayoritaria f; —**stay** pilar m, puntal m; — **street** calle principal f
maintain [mentén] VT mantener (also support); (assert) afirmar
maintenance [méntnəns] N (repairs) mantenimiento m; (monetary support) manutención f
maize [mez] N maíz m
majestic [mədʒéstɪk] ADJ majestuoso
majesty [mǽdʒɪsti] N majestad f; **Your —** Su Majestad
major [médʒɚ] ADJ (greater) mayor, más grande; (large) grande; — **key** mayor m; N (military rank) comandante m; (field of study) especialidad f; — **league** liga mayor f; VI especializarse

majority [məʤɔ́rɪdi] N mayoría f; **the —** el grueso; (age) mayoría de edad f

make [mek] VT (do) hacer; (create) fabricar; (cause) causar; (earn) ganar; (a speech) pronunciar; **to — a clean breast of** sacarse del pecho; **to — a decision** tomar una decisión; **to — a living** ganarse la vida; **to — a train** llegar a tiempo para tomar un tren; **to — a turn** girar, doblar; **to — away with** fugarse con; **two plus two —s four** dos y dos son cuatro; **to — believe** hacer de cuenta que; **to — out** (see) vislumbrar, divisar; (read) descifrar; (kiss) Sp morrear; Am besuquearse; **to — too much of** exagerar; **what do you — of that?** ¿cómo interpretas eso? **to — up** (a story) inventar un cuento; (after a quarrel) hacer las paces; (for a loss) recuperar; (one's face) maquillarse; (one's mind) decidirse; **to — up for** suplir; **you'll — a good teacher** vas a ser un buen profesor; N marca f; **—up** (composition) composición f; (character) carácter m; (cosmetics) maquillaje m; ADJ **—shift** provisional

maker [mékə] N (creator) creador mf, hacedor -ora mf; (manufacturer) fabricante m

makings [mékɪŋz] N (potential) potencial m; (ingredients) ingredientes m pl

maladjusted [mæləʤʌ́stɪd] ADJ inadaptado

malady [mǽlədi] N mal m

malaise [məléz] N malestar m

malaria [məléria] N malaria f, paludismo m

Malawi [məláwi] N Malawi m

Malawian [məláwiən] ADJ & N malawiano -na mf

Malaysia [məléʒə] N Malasia f

Malaysian [məléʒən] ADJ & N malasio -sia mf

malcontent [mǽlkantent] ADJ & N descontento -ta mf

Maldives [mɔ́ldaɪvz] N Maldivas f pl

Maldivian [mɔ́ldíviən] ADJ & N maldivo -va mf

male [mel] ADJ (animal, plant) macho; (person) varón; (trait) masculino; N (animal, plant) macho m; (person) varón m

malevolent [məlévələnt] ADJ malévolo

malfunction [mælfʌ́ŋkʃən] N funcionamiento defectuoso m; VI funcionar mal

Mali [máli] N Malí m

Malian [málian] ADJ & N malí mf

malice [mǽlɪs] N malicia f; **with — aforethought** con premeditación y alevosía

malicious [məlíʃəs] ADJ malicioso

malign [məláɪn] VT calumniar, difamar

malignant [məlígnənt] ADJ maligno

mall [mɔl] N (closed street) paseo m; (enclosed shopping area) galería f, centro comercial m

mallet [mǽlɪt] N mazo m

malnourished [mælnɔ́-rɪʃt] ADJ desnutrido

malnutrition [mælnutríʃən] N desnutrición f

malpractice [mælprǽktɪs] N negligencia f, mala práctica f

malt [mɔlt] N malta f; **—ed milk** leche malteada f

Malta [mɔ́ltə] N Malta f

Maltese [mɔltíz] ADJ & N maltés -esa mf

mama, mamma [mámə] N mamá f; **—'s boy** nene de mamá m

mammal [mǽməl] N mamífero m

mammography [mæmágrəfi] N mamografía f

mammoth [mǽməθ] ADJ enorme; N mamut m

man [mæn] N hombre m; (servant) criado m; (in games) pieza f, ficha f; **— and wife** marido y mujer; **—hunt** persecución f; **—kind** humanidad f; **—of-war** (ship) buque de guerra m; (jellyfish) medusa f; **—power** (for work) mano de obra f; (for war) soldados m pl; **every — for himself** cada cual para sí; **to a —** unánimemente; ADJ **—eating** que come carne humana; **—made** (fiber) sintético; (lake) artificial; INTERJ ¡hombre! VT (a fort) guarnecer; (a ship) tripular; **to —handle** violentar

manage [mǽnɪʤ] VT (succeed in) conseguir, lograr; (direct) dirigir, administrar; (maneuver) manejar; VI **to — without help** arreglárselas sin ayuda; **—d care** asociación mutualista de salud f

manageable [mǽnɪʤəbəl] ADJ manejable; (hair) dócil

management [mǽnɪʤmənt] N (act of managing) manejo m, dirección f; (persons controlling a business) gerencia f, gestión f

manager [mǽnɪʤə] N (of a store) gerente -ta mf; (of a company) director -ra mf

mandate [mǽndet] N mandáto m; VT decretar

mandatory [mǽndətɔri] ADJ obligatorio

mandolin [mǽndəlɪn] N mandolina f

mane [men] N (of a lion) melena f; (of a horse) crin f

maneuver [mənúvə] N maniobra f; VI/VT maniobrar

manganese [mǽŋgəniz] N manganeso m

mange [mendʒ] N sarna f, roña f

manger [méndʒə-] N pesebre m

mangle [mǽŋgəł] VT (mutilate) magullar, mutilar; (ruin) estropear

mango [mǽŋgo] N mango m

mangrove [mǽŋgrov] N mangle m

mangy [méndʒi] ADJ sarnoso

manhood [mǽnhʊd] N virilidad f; (male genitals) miembro viril m; (men collectively) hombres m pl; (adult age) edad adulta f

mania [ménìə] N manía f

maniac [méniæk] N maníaco -ca mf, maniaco -ca mf

maniacal [mənáiəkəł] ADJ maníaco

manic-depressive [mǽnɪkdɪprésɪv] ADJ maniaco-depresivo

manicure [mǽnɪkjʊr] N manicura f; VT manicurar

manifest [mǽnəfest] ADJ manifiesto; N (list of cargo) manifiesto m, hoja de ruta f; VT (show) manifestar, poner de manifiesto; (express) declarar

manifestation [mǽnəfestéʃən] N manifestación f

manifesto [mænɪfésto] N manifiesto m

manifold [mǽnəfołd] ADJ diverso; N colector m

manila [mənílə] N abacá m; — **envelope** sobre manila m

manioc [mǽniɑk] N mandioca f, yuca f

manipulate [mənípjəlet] VT manipular

manipulation [mənɪpjəléʃən] N manipulación f

manlike [mǽnlaɪk] ADJ (manly) varonil; (mannish) hombruna; (resembling a human) de hombre

manly [mǽnli] ADJ varonil, viril

manner [mǽnə-] N (way) manera f, modo m, forma f; (type) tipo m; (air) aire m, ademán m; (outward bearing) porte m; —**s** modales m pl, crianza f; **in the — of** a la manera de

mannerism [mǽnərɪzəm] N peculiaridad f

mannish [mǽnɪʃ] ADJ hombruno, varonil

manor [mǽnə-] N feudo m, solar m; — **house** casa solariega f

mansion [mǽnʃən] N mansión f

mantel [mǽntl] N repisa de chimenea f

mantle [mǽntl] N manto m

mantra [mǽntrə] N mantra f

manual [mǽnjuəł] ADJ & N manual m

manufacture [mænjəfǽktʃə-] VT fabricar, manufacturar; (clothes, shoes) confeccionar; N fabricación f, manufactura f; (of clothes, shoes) confección f

manufacturer [mænjəfǽktʃərə-] N fabricante m

manufacturing [mænjəfǽktʃə-ɪŋ] N fabricación f, manufactura f; ADJ fabril, manufacturero

manure [mənúr] N estiércol m; VT estercolar, abonar

manuscript [mǽnjəskrɪpt] ADJ & N manuscrito m

many [méni] ADJ muchos; — **apples** muchas manzanas; — **came** vinieron muchos; — **a time** muchas veces; **a great** — muchísimos; **as — as** tantos como; **as — as five** hasta cinco; **how** — ¿cuántos? **three books too** — tres libros de más; **too** — demasiados

map [mæp] N (geographical) mapa m; (of streets) plano m; VT trazar un mapa de; **to — out** planear

maple [mépəł] N Sp arce m; Am maple m; — **syrup** miel de arce / maple m

mar [mɑr] VT estropear

marathon [mǽrəθɑn] N maratón mf

marble [mɑ́rbəł] N mármol m; (toy) canica f, bola f; **to play** —**s** jugar a las canicas; ADJ de mármol, marmóreo

march [mɑrtʃ] N marcha f; VI marchar; (leave) marcharse; **to — in** entrar; **to — out** marcharse; VT hacer marchar

March [mɑrtʃ] N marzo m

mare [mer] N yegua f

margarine [mɑ́rdʒə-ɪn] N margarina f

margin [mɑ́rdʒɪn] N margen m

marginal [mɑ́rdʒənəł] ADJ marginal

marginalize [mɑ́rdʒənəlaɪz] VT marginar

marigold [mǽrɪgołd] N caléndula f, maravilla f

marijuana, marihuana [mærəwɑ́nə] N marihuana f

marinate [mǽrənet] VT marinar

marine [mərín] ADJ (of the sea) marino; (maritime) marítimo; — **corps** infantería de marina f; N soldado de infantería de marina m

marionette [mæriənét] N marioneta f

marital [mǽrɪdł] ADJ conyugal

maritime [mǽrɪtaɪm] ADJ marítimo

mark [mɑrk] N marca f, seña f; (token) señal f; (indication) seña f; (grade) nota f, calificación f; (former German currency) marco m; —**sman** tirador m; **he's a good** —**sman** tiene muy buena puntería / muy buen tino; **the halfway** — el punto medio, la mitad; **to hit the** — dar en el blanco; **on your** —, **set, go!** ¡en sus marcas, listos y ya! ¡en sus marcas, listos, fuera! **to make one's** — distinguirse; **to miss the** — errar el tiro; **easy** — blanco

fácil *m*; VT marcar; (indicate) señalar;
(observe) observar, notar; (grade) calificar;
—ed for greatness destinado a la
grandeza; **— my words!** ¡ya verás! **to —
down prices** rebajar los precios; **to —
off** acotar, deslindar; **to — up prices**
subir los precios

markdown [márkdaʊn] N rebaja *f*

marker [márkɚ] N marcador *m*

market [márkɪt] N mercado *m*; **—place**
mercado *m*; **— price** precio de mercado
m; **— share** sector del mercado *m*; **I'm in
the — for** estoy buscando; VT
comercializar, mercadear

marketable [márkɪɾəbəl] ADJ vendible

marketing [márkɪɾɪŋ] N (field of study)
mercadotecnia *f*, marketing *m*; (selling)
comercialización *f*

marmalade [mármɛlɛd] N mermelada de
naranja *f*

maroon [mərún] ADJ & N bordó / bordeaux
m; VT abandonar

marriage [mǽrɪʤ] N matrimonio *m*;
(combination) combinación *f*; **— license**
licencia de matrimonio *f*

marriageable [mǽrɪʤəbəl] ADJ casadero

married [mǽrid] ADJ (united in marriage)
casado; (relation to marriage) conyugal; **—
couple** matrimonio *m*; **to get —** casarse

marrow [mǽro] N (in the bones) médula *f*;
(food) tuétano *m*; (essential part) meollo
m

marry [mǽri] VT (to marry off) casar; (to get
married) casarse con; VI casarse

marsh [mɑrʃ] N pantano *m*, ciénaga *f*

marshal [márʃəl] N (military) mariscal *m*;
(police chief) alguacil *m*; (of a parade)
maestro de ceremonia *m*; VT (facts, forces)
reunir; (troops) formar

Marshallese [mɑrʃəlíz] ADJ & N marshalés
-esa *mf*

Marshall Islands [márʃəláɪləndz] N Islas
Marshall *f pl*

marshmallow [márʃmɛlo] N caramelo de
azúcar y gelatina *m*

marshy [márʃi] ADJ pantanoso, cenagoso

martial [márʃəl] ADJ marcial; **— arts** artes
marciales *f pl*; **— law** ley marcial *f*

martin [mártɪn] N avión *m*

martini [mɑrtíni] N martini *m*

martyr [márdɚ] N mártir *m*; VT martirizar

martyrdom [márdɚdəm] N martirio *m*

marvel [márvəl] N maravilla *f*; VI
maravillarse

marvelous [márvələs] ADV maravilloso

Marxism [márksɪzəm] N marxismo *m*

mascara [mæskǽrə] N rímel *m*

mascot [mǽskɑt] N mascota *f*

masculine [mǽskjəlɪn] ADJ masculino

mash [mæʃ] VT aplastar, pisar; N (pulpy mass)
puré *m*; (food for livestock) afrecho *m*;
(malt) malta remojada *f*; **—ed potatoes**
puré de papas / patatas *m*

mask [mæsk] N máscara *f*, careta *f*; VT
enmascarar; **—ed ball** baile de máscaras
m

masochism [mǽsəkɪzəm] N masoquismo *m*

mason [mésən] N (builder) albañil *m*;
(freemason) masón *m*

masonry [mésənri] N (bricklaying) albañilería
f; (fraternal order) masonería *f*

masquerade [mæskəréd] N mascarada *f*; VI
to — as hacerse pasar por

mass [mæs] N masa *f*; (in church) misa *f*; **—
communication** comunicación de masas
f; **—marketing** comercialización masiva
f; **— media** medios de comunicación (de
masas) *m pl*; **— production** fabricación
en masa *f*; **— unemployment**
desempleo / paro masivo *m*; **— transit**
transporte público *m*; **the —es** las masas
pl; VI/VT juntar(se) en masa; (troops)
concentrar(se)

massacre [mǽsəkɚ] N masacre *m*; VT
masacrar

massage [məsáʒ] N masaje *m*; **— parlor**
salón de masajes *m*; VT (give a massage)
masajear; (change data) manipular

masseur [məsɚ] N masajista *m*

masseuse [məsús] N masajista *f*

massive [mǽsɪv] ADJ (severe) masivo; (solid)
macizo; (large) enorme

mast [mæst] N mástil *m*, árbol *m*

mastectomy [mæstéktəmi] N mastectomía *f*

master [mǽstɚ] N (person in control) amo -a
mf, señor -ora *mf*; (owner of slave or
animal) amo -a *mf*; (best representative,
skilled laborer) maestro *m*; (young boy)
señorito *m*; (tape or disk) original *m*; **—'s
degree** maestría *f*; ADJ (dominant)
dominante; **— bedroom** dormitorio
principal *m*; **— key** llave maestra *f*;
—piece obra maestra *f*; VT dominar

masterful [mǽstɚfəl] ADJ magistral

masterly [mǽstɚli] ADJ magistral

mastery [mǽstɚi] N dominio *m*

mastiff [mǽstɪf] N mastín *m*, alano *m*

masturbate [mǽstɚbet] VI/VT masturbar

mat [mæt] N (floor covering) estera *f*; (for
wiping feet) felpudo *m*; (in gymnastics)
colchoneta *f*; (of hair) maraña *f*; VI
enmarañarse

match [mæʧ] N (pair) pareja *f*; (chess game)
partida *f*; (tennis game) partido *m*; (boxing

encounter) combate *m*; (device for fire) fósforo *m*, cerilla *f*; **—box** cajita de fósforos *f*; **—maker** casamentero -ra *mf*; **he has no** — no tiene igual; **he is a good** — es un buen partido; **the hat and coat are a good** — el abrigo y el sombrero hacen juego; VI/VT hacer juego (con); VI (to correspond) estar de acuerdo; **the colors don't** — los colores no combinan; VT (equal) igualar; (come to correspond) poner de acuerdo; (form pairs) parear

matchless [mǽtʃlɪs] ADJ sin par

mate [met] N (one of a pair) pareja *f*; (friend) compañero -ra *mf*; (on a ship) oficial *m*; (in chess) mate *m*; VI/VT aparear(se)

material [mətíriəl] ADJ material; (pertinent) pertinente; N (substance) material *m*; (fabric) tejido *m*, género *m*

materialize [mətíriəlaɪz] VI/VT materializar(se)

maternal [mətɚ́nəl] ADJ (motherly) maternal; (on mother's side of family) materno

maternity [mətɚ́nɪdɪ] N maternidad *f*

math [mæθ] N matemática(s) *f (pl)*

mathematical [mæθəmǽDɪkəl] ADJ matemático

mathematician [mæθəmətíʃən] N matemático -ca *mf*

mathematics [mæθəmǽDɪks] N matemática(s) *f (pl)*

matinée [mætɪné] N matiné *f*

matriarch [métriɑrk] N matriarca *f*

matriculate [mətríkjəlet] VI/VT matricular(se)

matriculation [mətrɪkjəléʃən] N matriculación *f*, matrícula *f*

matrimony [mǽtrəmoni] N matrimonio *m*

matrix [métrɪks] N matriz *f*

matron [métrən] N matrona *f*; (in a hospital) jefa de enfermeras *f*

matter [mǽDɚ] N (substance, pus) materia *f*; (affair) asunto *m*; (printed) impreso *m*; (reading) material de lectura *m*; **— for complaint** motivo de queja *m*; **a — of two minutes** cosa de dos minutos *f*; **as a — of fact** de hecho; **it is of no** — no tiene importancia; **no — what you say** no importa lo que digas; **to do something as a — of course** hacer algo por rutina; **what is the** — **?** ¿qué pasa? VI importar; **it doesn't** — no importa

mattress [mǽtrɪs] N colchón *m*

mature [mətʃúr] ADJ maduro; **a — note** un pagaré vencido / pagadero; **for — audiences** para adultos; VI/VT madurar(se); (a savings bond) vencer(se)

maturity [mətúrɪdɪ] N madurez *f*; (of a debt) vencimiento *m*

maul [mɔl] VT atacar, herir gravemente

Mauritania [mɔrɪténiə] N Mauritania *f*

Mauritanian [mɔrɪténiən] ADJ & N mauritano -na *mf*

Mauritian [mɔríʃən] ADJ & N mauriciano -na *mf*

Mauritius [mɔríʃəs] N Mauricio *m*

maverick [mǽvɚ-ɪk] N cimarrón *m* (also person); (person) inconformista *mf*

maxim [mǽksɪm] N máxima *f*, sentencia *f*

maximum [mǽksəməm] ADJ & N máximo *m*

may [me] V AUX **— I sit down?** ¿puedo sentarme? **— you have a merry Christmas** que pases una feliz Navidad; **it — be that** puede ser que; **it — rain** puede (ser) que llueva, tal vez llueva; **she — have been late** puede (ser) que haya llegado tarde; **be that as it —** sea como fuere

May [me] N mayo *m*; **— Day** primero de mayo *m*; **—pole** mayo *m*

maybe [mébi] ADV quizá(s), tal vez

mayonnaise [méənez] N mayonesa *f*, mahonesa *f*

mayor [méɚ] N alcalde *m*

maze [mez] N laberinto *m*

me [mi] PRON **she sees** — me ve; **he talks to** — me habla; **he comes with** — viene conmigo; **he did it for** — lo hizo para mí

meadow [méDo] N pradera *f*, prado *m*; **—lark** alondra *f*

meager [mígɚ] ADJ escaso, exiguo

meal [mil] N comida *f*; (flour) harina *f*; **—time** hora de comer *f*

mean [min] ADJ (unkind) cruel; (petty) vil; (humble) humilde; (stingy) mezquino; (difficult) de mal genio; (middle) medio; **—-spirited** mezquino; **I make a — lasagna** me sale muy rica la lasagna; N (average) media *f*, promedio *m*; **—s** medios *m pl*; **the ends justify the —s** el fin justifica los medios; **a man of —s** un hombre adinerado; **by —s of** por medio de; **by all —s** (of course) por supuesto; (using all resources) por todos los medios; **by no —s** de ningún modo; VT (intend) querer, tener intenciones; (signify) querer decir, significar; **he — s well** tiene buenas intenciones; **winning —s everything to them** lo que más les importa es ganar; **they are meant for each other** son el uno para el otro

meander [miǽndɚ] VI (be winding) serpentear; (to wander) vagar

meaning [mínɪŋ] N (sense) significado *m*, sentido *m*; (purpose) sentido *m*; ADJ **well-—** bien intencionado

meaningless [mínɪŋlɪs] ADJ sin sentido

meanness [mínnɪs] N (cruelty) crueldad *f*; (pettiness) mezquindad *f*

meantime [míntaɪm] ADV LOC **in the —** mientras tanto

meanwhile [mínhwaɪl] ADV mientras tanto

measles [mízəlz] N sarampión *m*

measurable [méʒ-əbəl] ADJ medible, mensurable

measure [méʒ-] N (dimension) medida *f*; (criterion) criterio *m*; (in musical bar) compás *m*; (bill) proyecto de ley *m*; **—s** medidas *f pl*; **beyond —** sobremanera; **dry —** medida de áridos *f*; **in large —** en gran parte; VI/VT medir; **to — up** compararse con; **measuring tape** cinta de medir *f*, metro *m*

measured [méʒə-d] ADJ (rhythmical) acompasado; (moderate) moderado, mesurado

measurement [méʒə-mənt] N (act of measuring) medición *f*; (dimension) medida *f*, dimensión *f*

meat [mit] N carne *f*; (essential point) meollo *m*; **—ball** albóndiga *f*; **— loaf** pan/pastel de carne *m*

meaty [mídi] ADJ (with meat) con mucha carne; (substantial) sustancioso

mechanic [mɪkénɪk] ADJ & N mecánico *m*; **—s** mecánica *f*

mechanical [mɪkénɪkəl] ADJ mecánico

mechanism [mékənɪzəm] N mecanismo *m*

medal [médl] N medalla *f*; VI ganar una medalla

meddle [médl] VI entrometerse, inmiscuirse

meddler [médlə-] N entrometido -da *mf*

meddlesome [médlsəm] ADJ entrometido

media [mídiə] N media *m pl*, medios de comunicación (de masas) *m pl*

median [mídiən] ADJ mediano; N (middle value, line) mediana *f*

mediate [mídiet] VI/VT mediar

mediation [midiéʃən] N mediación *f*

mediator [mídieDə-] N mediador -ra *mf*

medical [médɪkəl] ADJ médico; **— school** facultad de medicina *f*

medication [meDɪkéʃən] N medicación *f*

medicine [médɪsɪn] N medicina *f*, medicamento *m*; **— ball** balón medicinal *m*; **— cabinet** botiquín *m*; **— man** curandero *m*

medieval [mɪdívəl] ADJ medieval

mediocre [miDióka-] ADJ mediocre

mediocrity [miDiákrɪDi] N mediocridad *f*

meditate [méDɪtet] VI meditar

meditation [meDɪtéʃən] N meditación *f*, recogimiento *m*

medium [mídiəm] N medio *m*; (person who contacts spirits) médium *mf*; ADJ mediano; ADV término medio; **— of exchange** medio de cambio *m*

medley [médli] N (music) popurrí *m*; (mixture) mezcla *f*

meek [mik] ADJ manso

meet [mit] VT (encounter) encontrarse con; (make acquaintance) conocer; (face in conflict) enfrentar; (satisfy) satisfacer; (pay) pagar; **to — a deadline** cumplir el plazo; **to — the expenses** sufragar los gastos; **to — halfway** partir la diferencia; **to — a train** esperar un tren; **I will — you at the station** nos encontramos/vemos en la estación; **have you met my brother?** ¿conoces a mi hermano? **we were met with disapproval** se nos recibió con desaprobación; VI (encounter) encontrarse; (make acquaintance) conocerse; (have a meeting) reunirse; (cross) cruzarse; **to — in battle** trabar batalla; **to — with** (intentional) reunirse con; (unintentional) tropezar con; N encuentro deportivo *m*, competición *f*

meeting [mídɪŋ] N reunión *f*, junta *f*; (political) mitin *m*; (crossing of roads) cruce *m*

megabyte [mégəbaɪt] N megabyte *m*

megahertz [mégəhɚtz] N megahertz *m*, megahercio *m*

megaphone [mégəfon] N megáfono *m*, bocina *f*

melancholy [mélənkɑli] N melancolía *f*; ADJ melancólico

melanoma [melənómə] N melanoma *m*

meld [meld] VT fusionar

melee [méle] N reyerta *f*, tumulto *m*

mellow [mélo] ADJ (soft) dulce, suave; (gentle) tranquilo; VI/VT suavizar(se)

melodious [məlódiəs] ADJ melodioso

melodrama [mélodramə] N melodrama *m*

melody [méləDi] N melodía *f*

melon [mélən] N melón *m*

melt [mɛlt] VI/VT (liquefy) derretir(se); (dissolve) disolver(se); **—down** (fusion) catástrofe por fusión nuclear incontrolada *f*; (any developing disaster) catástrofe *f*

melting pot [méltɪŋpɑt] M crisol *m*

member [mémbə-] N miembro *m* (also body part)

membership [mémbə-ʃɪp] N (number) número de miembros/socios *m*; (state) calidad de miembro/socio *f*

membrane [mémbren] N membrana *f*
memento [məméntо] N recuerdo *m*
memoir [mémwɑr] N memoria *f*; **—s**
memorias *f pl*, autobiografía *f*
memorable [mémə‑əbəł] ADJ memorable
memorandum [memərǽndəm] N
memorándum *m*
memorial [məmɔ́riəł] N (monument)
monumento conmemorativo *m*; (petition)
memorial *m*; ADJ conmemorativo
memorize [mémərɑɪz] VI/VT memorizar
memory [méməri] N (faculty) memoria *f*;
(recollection) recuerdo *m*
menace [ménɪs] N amenaza *f*; VI/VT amenazar
mend [mend] VT remendar; **to — matters**
enmendar la situación; **to — one's ways**
enmendarse, reformarse; VI (sick person)
mejorarse; (bones) soldarse; N remiendo *m*;
to be on the — ir mejorando
menial [mínɪəł] ADJ bajo; (job) servil; N
criado ‑da *mf*
meningitis [menɪndʒɑɪDɪs] N meningitis *f*
menopause [ménəpɔz] N menopausia *f*
menstruation [menstruéʃən] N
menstruación *f*
mental [méntł] ADJ mental; (insane) *fam*
chiflado; **— health** salud mental *f*; **—
illness** enfermedad mental *f*; **—
retardation** retraso mental *m*
mentality [mentǽlɪDi] N mentalidad *f*
mention [ménʃən] VT mencionar; **don't —
it** no hay de qué; N mención *f*
mentor [méntɔr] N mentor ‑ra *mf*
menu [ménju] N (list of dishes) carta *f*, menú
m; (computer) menú *m*
meow [mjɑU] INTERJ miau
mercantile [mɝ́kɑntił] ADJ mercantil
mercenary [mɝ́səneri] ADJ mercenario
merchandise [mɝ́tʃəndɑɪs] N mercancía *f*,
mercadería *f*
merchandising [mɝ́tʃəndɑɪzɪŋ] N mercadeo
m, comercialización *f*
merchant [mɝ́tʃənt] N (trader) comerciante
m, mercader *m*; ADJ mercante; **— marine**
marina mercante *f*
merciful [mɝ́sɪfəł] ADJ misericordioso
merciless [mɝ́sɪlɪs] ADJ despiadado
mercury [mɝ́kjɔri] N mercurio *m*; (on a
mirror) azogue *m*
mercy [mɝ́si] N (compassion) misericordia *f*,
clemencia *f*, piedad *f*; **to be at the — of**
estar a merced de; **— killing** eutanasia *f*
mere [mir] ADJ mero, simple; **a — trifle** una
nonada
merge [mɝdʒ] VI/VT (join) unir(se); (colors)
fundir(se); (companies) fusionar(se)
merger [mɝ́dʒɚ] N fusión *f*

meridian [mərídiən] ADJ & N meridiano *m*
merit [mérɪt] N mérito *m*; VT merecer
meritorious [mérɪtɔ́riəs] ADJ meritorio
mermaid [mɝ́med] N sirena *f*
merriment [mérɪmənt] N alegría *f*, algazara *f*
merry [méri] ADJ alegre; **—go-round**
tiovivo *m*; **—maker** fiestero *mf*, juerguista
mf; **—making** fiesta *f*, juerga *f*; **to make
—** divertirse; INTERJ **— Christmas** Feliz
Navidad *f*, Felices Pascuas
mesa [mésə] N mesa *f*
mesh [meʃ] N (of metal) malla *f*; (of fiber) red
f; (of gears) engranaje *m*; VI engranar
mesmerize [mézmərɑɪz] VI/VT hipnotizar
mess [mes] N (state of confusion) desorden *m*,
desarreglo *m*; (disorderly person)
desordenado ‑da *mf*, mugriento ‑ta *mf*;
(confused person) desastre *m*; (difficult
situation) lío *m*, jaleo *m*; (food for
soldiers) rancho *m*; (cafeteria) cantina *f*; **—
hall** cantina *f*; **— of fish** plato de
pescado *m*; **to make a — of** (a room)
ensuciar, desordenar; (a project) estropear;
VI/VT **to — around** (waste time) perder el
tiempo; (get involved with) meterse con;
(philander) correr detrás de las mujeres; **to
— up** (a room) alborotar, desordenar;
(clothes, hair) desarreglar; (a project)
estropear; (make a muddle of) *vulg* cagarla;
to — with meterse con
message [mésɪdʒ] N mensaje *m*, recado *m*; **I
get the —** ya caí en cuenta
messenger [mésəndʒɚ] N mensajero ‑ra *mf*
messy [mési] ADJ (chaotic) desordenado;
(embarrassing) embarazoso
metabolism [mətǽbəlɪzəm] N metabolismo
m
metal [méDł] N metal *m*; ADJ de metal,
metálico
metallic [mətǽlɪk] ADJ metálico
metallurgy [méDlɚdʒi] N metalurgia *f*
metamorphosis [meDəmɔ́rfəsɪs] N
metamorfosis *f*
metaphor [méDəfɔr] N metáfora *f*
metaphysics [meDəfízɪks] N metafísica *f*
metastasis [mətǽstəsɪs] N metástasis *f*
meteor [mídiɔr] N meteoro *m*; **— shower**
lluvia de meteoritos *f*
meteorite [mídiərɑɪt] N meteorito *m*
meteorology [miDiərálədʒi] N meteorología *f*
meter [mídɚ] N (unit of length) metro *m*;
(measuring device) contador *m*, medidor
m
methane [méθen] N metano *m*
method [méθəd] N método *m*
methodical [məθɑ́Dɪkəł] ADJ metódico
methodology [meθədáRədʒi] N metodología *f*

meticulous [mətíkjələs] ADJ detallista

metric [métrɪk] ADJ métrico

metronome [métrənom] N metrónomo *m*

metropolis [mətrápəlɪs] N metrópoli *f*, urbe *f*

metropolitan [metrəpálɪɪən] ADJ metropolitano

mettle [médl] N temple *m*, valor *m*

mew [mju] N maullido *m*; VI maullar

Mexican [méksɪkən] ADJ & N mexicano -na *mf*

Mexico [méksɪko] N México *m*

mezzanine [mézənin] N entrepiso *m*, entresuelo *m*

mickey mouse [míkimáus] ADJ poco serio, informal

microbe [máɪkrob] N microbio *m*

microcomputer [maɪkrokəmpjúɪə] N *Am* microcomputadora *f*; *Sp* microordenador *m*

microeconomics [maɪkroekənámɪks] N microeconomía *f*

microfiche [máɪkrofiʃ] N microficha *f*

microfilm [máɪkrofɪlm] N microfilm *m*

micromanage [maɪkromǽnɪʤ] VI/VT administrar con excesivo control

micron [máɪkran] N micrón *m*, micra *f*

Micronesia [maɪkroníʒə] N Micronesia *f*

Micronesian [maɪkroníʒən] ADJ & N micronesio -sia *mf*

microorganism [maɪkroórgənɪzəm] N microorganismo *m*

microphone [máɪkrəfon] N micrófono *m*

microprocessor [maɪkroprásesə] N microprocesador *m*

microscope [máɪkrəskop] N microscopio *m*

microscopic [maɪkrəskápɪk] ADJ microscópico

microsurgery [maɪkrosə́ʤəri] N microcirugía *f*

microwave [máɪkrowev] N microonda *f*; **— oven** (horno) microondas *m sg*

mid [mɪd] ADJ medio; **—air** en el aire; **—day** (del) mediodía *m*; **—life** madurez *f*; **—night** (de) medianoche *f*; **—shipman** guardiamarina *m*; **in —stream** (of a river) en medio del río; (of a task) en plena actividad; **—summer** pleno verano *m*; **—term examination** examen a mitad del curso *m*; **—way** a medio camino, a mitad del camino; **—wife** partera *f*, comadre *f*

middle [mídl] ADJ (average) medio, mediano; (intermediate) intermedio; (central) central; **— aged** de mediana edad; **— Ages** Edad Media *f*; **— ear** oído medio *m*; **— finger** dedo mayor *m*, dedo del corazón *m*; **—man** intermediario *m*,

revendedor *m*; **— management** mandos medios *m pl*; **— name** segundo nombre *m*; **—sized** (de) tamaño mediano; N medio *m*; (waist) cintura *f*; **in the — of** en el medio de; **I'm in the — of something** estoy ocupado haciendo algo; **—-of-the-road** moderado; **toward the — of the month** a mediados del mes

midget [míʤɪt] N enano -na *mf*

midst [mɪdst] N medio *m*, centro *m*; **in the — of** en medio de, entre; **in our —** entre nosotros

mien [min] N porte *m*

might [maɪt] V AUX **it — be that** podría ser que; **he said it — rain tomorrow** dijo que tal vez lloviera mañana; **she — have been late** puede ser que haya llegado tarde; N poder *m*, poderío *m*

mighty [máɪɪi] ADJ (strong) poderoso, potente; (large) imponente; ADV muy

migraine [máɪgren] N migraña *f*, jaqueca *f*

migrant [máɪgrənt] ADJ migratorio, migrante; N trabajador -ra itinerante *mf*, bracero -ra *mf*

migrate [máɪgret] VI emigrar

migration [maɪgréʃən] N migración *f*

mild [maɪld] ADJ (gentle) suave; (moderate) moderado; (not serious) leve

mildew [míldu] N moho *m*

mildness [máɪldnɪs] N (gentleness) suavidad *f*; (lack of gravity) levedad *f*

mile [maɪl] N milla *f*; **—stone** hito *m*

mileage [máɪlɪʤ] N (distance, odometer reading) millaje *m*, kilometraje *m*; **this car gets good —** este coche es económico; **what kind of — are you getting?** ¿cuántos kilómetros por litro hace tu coche?

milieu [mɪljú] N ambiente *m*

militant [mílɪtənt] ADJ & N (fanatic) militante *mf*; (combatant) combatiente *mf*

military [mílɪteri] ADJ militar; N **the —** (armed forces) el ejército; (military personnel) los militares

militia [məlíʃə] N milicia *f*

milk [mɪlk] N leche *f*; **— chocolate** chocolate con leche *m*; **—maid** lechera *f*; **—man** lechero *m*; **— shake** batido *m*; VT ordeñar; (exploit) exprimir; **he's —ing it for all it's worth** le está sacando todo el jugo

milky [mílki] ADJ (consistency) lechoso; (product) lácteo; **— Way** Vía Láctea *f*

mill [mɪl] N (building) molino *m*; (factory) fábrica *f*; (for sugar) trapiche *m*, ingenio *m*; (rotating tool) fresa *f*; (small grinder) molinillo *m*; **—stone** muela de molino *f*;

a —stone around your neck una piedra al cuello; VT (grind grain) moler; (cut wood) aserrar; (cut grooves on coins) acordonar; (machine) fresar; **to — around** dar vueltas

millennium [məlíniəm] N milenio m

miller [mílə] N (person who mills) molinero m; (machine for milling) fresadora f; (moth) mariposa nocturna f

milligram [mílɪɡræm] N miligramo m

milliliter [mílɪlidə] N mililitro m

millimeter [mílɪmidə] N milímetro m

milliner [mílɪnə] N sombrerero -ra mf

millinery [mílɪnɛri] N (shop) sombrerería f; (hats) sombreros de señora m pl

million [míljən] N millón m; **a — dollars** un millón de dólares

millionaire [mɪljənér] N millonario -ria mf

millionth [míljənθ] ADJ & N millonésimo m

mime [maɪm] N (actor) mimo m; (technique, performance) pantomima f; VI hacer la mímica

mimic [mímɪk] VT imitar, remedar; N mono -na mf, remedador -ra mf

mince [mɪns] VT picar, desmenuzar; **—meat** picadillo m; **not to — words** no tener pelos en la lengua; **I'm going to make —meat of you** te voy a hacer picadillo

mind [maɪnd] N (thinking process) mente f; (person of intellect) inteligencia f; (opinion) parecer m, opinión f; **—-altering** alucinógeno; **— games** manipulación psicológica f; **— over matter** el espíritu sobre la materia; **—set** actitud f; **to be out of one's —** estar loco; **to change one's —** cambiar de parecer/opinión; **to give someone a piece of one's —** cantarle a alguien las cuarenta; **I have a — to** me dan ganas de; **to make up one's —** decidirse; **to my —** a mi modo de ver; **to speak one's — freely** hablar con toda franqueza; **what do you have in —?** ¿qué tienes en mente? **to call to —** recordar; **to keep one's — on one's work** concentrarse en el trabajo; VT (take care of) cuidar; (pay attention to) atender a; (obey) obedecer; **I don't —** no tengo inconveniente en ello; **— what you say** cuidado con lo que dices; **to — one's own business** no meterse en lo ajeno

mindful [máɪndfəl] ADJ atento (a)

mine [maɪn] PRON **this book is —** este libro es mío; **these things are —** estas cosas son mías; **— is bigger** el mío/la mía es más grande; **a friend of —** un amigo mío/una amiga mía; N mina f (also

explosive device); **—field** campo minado m; **— sweeper** dragaminas m sg, barreminas m sg; VT (plant explosives) minar; (dig out minerals) extraer; (exploit an area for minerals) explotar; VI (lay mines) sembrar minas; (dig a mine) cavar una mina; **to — for** extraer

miner [máɪnə] N minero -ra mf

mineral [mínəɹəl] ADJ & N mineral m; **— water** agua mineral f

mingle [míŋɡəl] VI mezclarse; (sounds) confundirse; VT mezclar

miniature [mínɪətʃə] N miniatura f; ADJ en miniatura

minicomputer [mɪnɪkəmpjúdə] N Am minicomputadora f; Sp miniordenador m

minimal [mínəməl] ADJ mínimo

minimize [mínəmaɪz] VT minimizar

minimum [mínəməm] ADJ & N mínimo m; **— wage** salario mínimo m

mining [máɪnɪŋ] N (of minerals) minería f; (with explosives) minado m; ADJ minero; **— engineer** ingeniero -ra de minas mf

miniskirt [mínɪskət] N minifalda f

minister [mínɪstə] N (official) ministro -tra mf; (pastor) pastor -ora mf, clérigo m; VI **to — to** atender a

ministry [mínɪstri] N (government agency) ministerio m; (functions of pastor) clerecía f

minivan [mínɪvæn] N camioneta f

mink [mɪŋk] N visón m

minnow [míno] N pececillo m

minor [máɪnə] ADJ (smaller) menor, más pequeño; (of secondary importance) menor; **— key** tono menor m; **— league** liga menor f; N (young person) menor de edad mf; (musical interval) tono menor m; (subfield) asignatura secundaria f; VI tener como segunda especialización

minority [mənɔ́ɾɪdi] N (smaller part or group) minoría f; (state of being underage) minoridad f; (member of a minority) miembro de una minoría m; ADJ minoritario

mint [mɪnt] N (flavor) menta f, hierbabuena f; (candy) pastilla de menta f; (money) casa de la moneda f; VT acuñar

minus [máɪnəs] PREP **seven — four** siete menos cuatro; **we came — my brother** vinimos sin mi hermano; N signo de menos m; ADJ negativo

minuscule [mínəskjul] ADJ minúsculo

minute [mínɪt] N minuto m; **— hand** minutero m; **—s** actas f pl; [mənjút] ADJ (small) diminuto; (detailed) detallado, minucioso

miracle [mírəkəł] N milagro *m*

miraculous [mɪrǽkjələs] ADJ milagroso

mirage [mɪrɔ́ʒ] N espejismo *m*

mire [maɪr] N (mud) cieno *m*, fango *m*; (muddy place) ciénaga *f*; VI/VT (bog down) atascar(se) en el fango; (be or get covered with mud) enlodar(se)

mirror [mírɚ] N espejo *m*; (large) luna *f*; — **image** imagen especular *f*; VT reflejar

mirth [mɝθ] N risa *f*, hilaridad *f*

mirthful [mɝ́θfəł] ADJ risueño

miry [máɪri] ADJ cenagoso, fangoso

misappropriation [mɪsəproupriéʃən] N malversación *f*

misbehave [mɪsbɪhév] VI portarse mal

miscarriage [mískæɾɪdʒ] N aborto espontáneo *m*, malparto *m*; — **of justice** injusticia *f*

miscarry [mɪskǽri] VI (abort) abortar espontáneamente; (fail) malograrse, frustrarse

miscellaneous [mɪsəléniəs] ADJ diverso; (of texts) misceláneo; — **expenses** gastos varios *mf*

mischief [místʃɪf] N travesura *f*, diablura *f*, picardía *f*; (serious prank) barrabasada *f*, bellaquería *f*; **this will come to** — va a suceder una desgracia

mischievous [místʃəvəs] ADJ travieso, pícaro

misconception [mɪskənsépʃən] N concepto erróneo *m*

misconduct [mɪskándʌkt] N (bad behavior) mala conducta *f*; (malfeasance) mala administración *f*; [mɪskəndákt] VT administrar mal; **to** — **oneself** portarse mal

miscue [mɪskjú] N pifia *f*; VI/VT pifiar

misdeed [mɪsdíd] N fechoría *f*

misdemeanor [mɪsdɪmínɚ] N delito menor *m*

miser [máɪzɚ] N avaro -ra *mf*, tacaño -ña *mf*

miserable [mízɚəbəł] ADJ infeliz, desdichado, mísero; **a** — **day** un día asqueroso; **a** — **failure** un fracaso rotundo

miserly [máɪzɚli] ADJ avariento, tacaño

misery [mízari] N (wretchedness) desgracia *f*; (poverty) miseria *f*; (unhappiness) infelicidad *f*

misfit [mísfɪt] N inadaptado -da *mf*

misfortune [mɪsfɔ́rtʃən] N desgracia *f*, desdicha *f*, desventura *f*

misgivings [mɪsgívɪŋz] N aprensión *f*, recelo *m*

misguided [mɪsgáɪdɪd] ADJ mal aconsejado, poco feliz

mishap [míshæp] N contratiempo *m*, percance *m*

misinform [mɪsɪnfɔ́rm] VT desinformar, dar información errónea

misjudge [mɪsdʒʌ́dʒ] VT juzgar mal

mislay [mɪslé] VT (lose keys, etc.) extraviar, perder; (lose a document) traspapelar; (lay wrong) colocar mal

mislead [mɪslíd] VT (lead in wrong direction) guiar por mal camino; (lead into error) engañar, confundir

mismanage [mɪsmǽnɪdʒ] VT administrar mal

misogyny [mɪsádʒəni] N misoginia *f*

misplace [mɪsplés] VT (lose keys, etc.) extraviar; (lose a document) traspapelar; (place wrong) colocar mal; **she** —**d her trust** confió en la persona equivocada

misprint [mísprɪnt] N errata *f*, error de imprenta *m*

misrepresent [mɪsrɛprɪzént] VT distorsionar, tergiversar

misrepresentation [mɪsrɛprɪzɛntéʃən] N distorsión *f*, tergiversación *f*

miss [mɪs] VI (fail to hit) errar; (misfire) fallar; VT (fail to hit) errar, no acertar; (fail to be on time for) perder; (fail to attend) faltar a; (feel absence of) echar de menos; *Am* extrañar; **he just** —**ed being killed** por poco se mata; N (of a target) tiro errado *m*; (in a motor) falla *f*; (from class) falta *f*; (young woman) señorita *f*; — **Smith** la señorita Smith

missile [mísəł] N (projectile) proyectil *m*; (guided weapon) misil *m*

missing [mísɪŋ] ADJ (not present) ausente; (lost) perdido; — **link** eslabón perdido *m*; **one book is** — falta un libro

mission [míʃən] N misión *f*

missionary [míʃəneri] ADJ & N misionero -ra *mf*; — **position** posición del misionero *f*

misspell [mɪsspéł] VT (written) escribir mal; (oral) deletrear mal

misstep [místep] N paso en falso *m*

mist [mɪst] N (of water droplets) neblina *f*, bruma *f*; (of perfume) rocío *m*; VI llovizbar; VT rociar

mistake [mɪsték] N error *m*, equivocación *f*; (orthographical) falta *f*; **to make a** — equivocarse; VI/VT equivocar(se); **I mistook my sister for my mother** confundí a mi hermana con mi madre

mistaken [mɪstékən] ADJ equivocado; **to be** — estar equivocado, equivocarse; **unless I'm** — si no me equivoco

mister [místɚ] N señor *m*

mistletoe [mísəłto] N muérdago *m*

mistreat [mɪstrít] VT maltratar

mistreatment [mɪstrítmənt] N maltrato *m*

mistress [místrıs] N (of a household) señora *f*; (employing servants, animal owner) ama *f*; (lover) amante *f*

mistrial [místrəł] N proceso viciado de nulidad *m*

mistrust [mıstrást] N desconfianza *f*; VT desconfiar de

mistrustful [mıstrástfəł] ADJ desconfiado, receloso

misty [místi] ADJ (foggy) neblinoso, brumoso; (in tears) nublado; (blurry) empañado

misunderstand [mısandə‑stǽnd] VT comprender mal, malinterpretar

misunderstanding [mısandə‑stǽndıŋ] N (confusion) malentendido *m*; (failure to understand) equivocación *f*, mala inteligencia *f*; (argument) desavenencia *f*

misuse [mısjús] N (of drugs) abuso *m*; (of a word) mal uso *m*; (of funds) malversación *f*; [mısjúz] VT (drugs) abusar de; (a friend) maltratar; (a word) emplear mal; (funds) malversar

mite [maıt] N ácaro *m*; **a — greedy** un poquito codicioso

mitigate [mítıget] VT mitigar

mitten [mítŋ] N manopla *f*

mix [mıks] VI/VT mezclar(se); **to — up** confundir; N mezcla *f*; (for baking) preparado *m*; **—-up** (confusion) confusión *f*; (fight) pelea *f*; **—ed bag** grupo heterogéneo *m*; **—ed drink** cóctel *m*; **—ed-up** confundido

mixed [mıkst] ADJ mixto

mixer [míksə‑] N (appliance) batidora *f*; (party) fiesta *f*; (soda) refresco *m*; (sound technician) mezclador -ra *mf*; (sound device) mezcladora *f*

mixture [míkstʃə‑] N mezcla *f*

moan [mon] N quejido *m*, gemido *m*; VI gemir, quejarse; VI/VT lamentar

moat [mot] N foso *m*

mob [mɑb] N (disorderly crowd) tumulto *m*, turba *f*; (crowd) muchedumbre *f*, populacho *m*; (Mafia) mafia *f*; VT (attack) asaltar; (crowd) atestar

mobile [móbəł] ADJ móvil; (personnel) que tiene movilidad; **— home** casa prefabricada *f*; **— phone** (teléfono) móvil *m*, (teléfono) celular *m*

mobilize [móbəlaız] VI/VT movilizar(se)

moccasin [mákəsın] N mocasín *m* (also snake)

mock [mɑk] VI (ridicule) burlar(se); VT (imitate) remedar; **to — at** burlarse de; ADJ de práctica; **— battle** simulacro de batalla *m*; **—-up** maqueta *f*, modelo *m*

mockery [mákəri] N (ridicule) burla *f*;

(imitation) remedo *m*; (travesty) farsa *f*

mockingbird [mákıŋbə‑d] N sinsonte *m*

mode [mod] N modo *m*

model [mádł] N (guide) modelo *m*; (person) modelo *mf*, maniquí *mf*; ADJ modelo, ejemplar; **— school** escuela modelo *f*; VI/VT modelar; (display clothes) lucir

modem [módəm] N módem *m*

moderate [mádə‑ıt] ADJ (not excessive) moderado, mesurado; (person) comedido; (weather) templado; (price) módico; N moderado -da *mf*; [mádəret] VI/VT moderar(se) (also preside at meetings)

moderation [mɑdəréʃən] N moderación *f*, mesura *f*

modern [mádə‑n] ADJ moderno

modernize [mádə‑naız] VI/VT modernizar(se)

modest [mádıst] ADJ (humble) modesto; (chaste) recatado, honesto

modesty [mádısti] N (humility) modestia *f*; (chastity) recato *m*, pudor *m*

modification [mɑdəfıkéʃən] N modificación *f*

modify [mádəfaı] VT modificar

modulate [mádʒəlet] VI/VT modular(se)

mohair [móher] N mohair *m*

moist [mɔıst] ADJ húmedo

moisten [mɔ́ısən] VI/VT humedecer(se)

moisture [mɔ́ıstʃə‑] N humedad *f*

moisturizer [mɔ́ıstʃəráızə‑] N (crema) hidrante / humectante *f*

molar [mólə‑] ADJ molar; N muela *f*, molar *m*

molasses [məlǽsız] N melaza *f*

mold [mołd] N (form) molde *m*; (fungi) moho *m*; (mettle) temple *m*; VT (shape) moldear; (adapt) amoldar; (fuse) fundir; VI/VT (become moldy) enmohecer(se)

molder [móldə‑] VI/VT descomponerse; (paper) enmohecerse

molding [mółdıŋ] N (adornment) moldura *f*; (action of molding) moldeado *m*

Moldova [mołdóvə] N Moldavia *f*

Moldovan [mołdóvən] ADJ & N moldavo -va *mf*

moldy [móldi] ADJ mohoso

mole [mol] N (blemish) lunar *m*; (animal, spy) topo *m*; (breakwater) rompeolas *m sg*

molecule [málıkjuł] N molécula *f*

molest [məlést] VT abusar sexualmente de

mollify [máləfaı] VT apaciguar, aplacar

mollusk [máləsk] N molusco *m*

molt [mołt] VI (birds) mudar la pluma; (snakes) mudar la piel; N muda *f*

molten [mółtŋ] ADJ fundido

molybdenum [məlíbdənəm] N molibdeno *m*

mom [mɑm] N mamá *f*; **— and pop store** tienda familiar *f*

moment [mómənt] N momento *m*; **being a parent has its —s** ser padre/madre tiene sus momentos de recompensa

momentary [mómənteri] ADJ momentáneo

momentous [moméntəs] ADJ importante, trascendental

momentum [moméntəm] N (in physics) momento *m*; (in politics, sports) empuje *m*

mommy [mámi] N mami *f*

Monaco [mánəko] N Mónaco *m*

monarch [mánɑrk] N monarca *mf*

monarchy [mánə·ki] N monarquía *f*

monastery [mánəsteri] N monasterio *m*

Monday [mánde] N lunes *m*

Monegasque [mɑnɪgásk] ADJ & N monegasco -ca *mf*

monetary [mánɪteri] ADJ monetario

money [máni] N dinero *m*; **— belt** faltriquera en forma de cinturón *f*; **— changer** cambista *mf*; **— machine** cajero automático *m*; **—-making** lucrativo, rentable; **— market** mercado de valores *m*; **— order** giro postal *m*; **to get one's —'s worth** sacar jugo al dinero

Mongolia [mɑŋgóliə] N Mongolia *f*

Mongolian [mɑŋgóliən] ADJ & N mongol -la *mf*

mongoose [mángus] N mangosta *f*

mongrel [máŋgrəl] ADJ & N mestizo *m*

monitor [mánɪtə·] N monitor *m*; (in a school) celador -ora *mf*; **— lizard** varano *m*

monk [mʌŋk] N monje *m*, religioso *m*

monkey [máŋki] N mono *m*, mico *m* (also child); **— bars** jaula de los monos *f*; **— business** (mischief) picardía *f*; (trickery) chanchullo *m*; **— wrench** llave inglesa *f*; **to have a — on one's back** estar adicto; VI **to — around** bobear, payasear; **to — with** bobear con

monogamy [mənágəmi] N monogamia *f*

monolog, monologue [mánəlɔg] N monólogo *m*

mononucleosis [mɑnonukliósɪs] N mononucleosis *f*

monopolize [mənápəlaɪz] VT monopolizar

monopoly [mənápəli] N monopolio *m*

monotonous [mənátnəs] ADJ monótono

monotony [mənátn̩i] N monotonía *f*

monster [mánstə·] N monstruo *m*; ADJ enorme, monstruo *inv*

monstrosity [mɑnstrásɪdi] N monstruosidad *f*

monstrous [mánstrəs] ADJ monstruoso

month [mʌnθ] N mes *m*

monthly [mánθli] ADJ mensual; **— installment** mensualidad *f*; N

publicación mensual *f*, mensuario *m*; ADV mensualmente

monument [mánjəmənt] N monumento *m*

monumental [mɑnjəméntl̩] ADJ monumental

moo [mu] N mugido *m*; VI mugir

mooch [mutʃ] VI/VT gorronear

mood [mud] N (emotional state) humor *m*, vena *f*, ánimo *m*; (grammatical category) modo *m*; **to be in a good —** estar de buen humor; **to be in the — to** tener ganas de

moody [múdi] ADJ (sullen) malhumorado; (changing) voluble

moon [mun] N luna *f*; **—beam** rayo de luna *m*; **—light** claro de la luna *m*, luz de la luna *f*; **—shine** bebida alcohólica destilada sin licencia *f*; **once in a blue —** de Pascuas a Ramos; VT *fam* mostrar el culo

moor [mʊr] VI/VT amarrar; N páramo *m*

Moor [mʊr] N moro -ra *mf*

Moorish [mʊrɪʃ] ADJ morisco, moro

moose [mus] N alce *m*

moot [mut] ADJ **it became a — point** dejó de tener importancia

mop [mɑp] N *Sp* fregona *f*, *Sp* mopa *f*; *Mex* trapeador *m*; (for dust) plumero *m*; (of hair) greña *f*; **—-up** (of an enemy) limpieza *f*; (of a task) remate *m*; VI/VT pasar la mopa (sobre); *Am* trapear; **to — one's brow** enjugarse la frente; **to — up** (a spill) limpiar; (an enemy) acabar con; (a task) rematar

mope [mop] VI andar abatido

moped [móped] N ciclomotor *m*, scooter *m*

moral [mɔ́rəl] ADJ moral; N moraleja *f*; **—s** moral *f*

morale [mərǽl] N moral *f*

moralist [mɔ́rəlɪst] N moralista *mf*

morality [mɔrǽlɪdi] N moralidad *f*

moralize [mɔ́rəlaɪz] VI/VT moralizar

morbid [mɔ́rbɪd] ADJ mórbido, morboso

more [mɔr] ADJ & ADV más; **— and —** cada vez más; **— or less** más o menos; **there is no —** no hay más; **—over** además

morgue [mɔrg] N depósito de cadáveres *m*, morgue *f*

moribund [mɔ́rəbʌnd] ADJ moribundo

morning [mɔ́rnɪŋ] N mañana *f*; **good —!** ¡buenos días! **tomorrow —** mañana por la mañana; ADJ de la mañana, matutino; **— glory** dondiego de día *m*; **— sickness** náuseas *f pl*; **— star** lucero del alba *m*

Moroccan [mərákən] ADJ & N marroquí *mf*

Morocco [məráko] N Marruecos *m*

moron [mɔ́rɑn] N imbécil *m*

morphine [mɔ́rfin] N morfina f

morsel [mɔ́rsəł] N bocado m

mortal [mɔ́rdl] ADJ & N mortal mf; — **sin** pecado mortal m

mortality [mɔrtǽlɪɾi] N (rate) mortalidad f; (toll) mortandad f

mortar [mɔ́rɾəʳ] N (for pounding) mortero m (also ballistics); (for bricks) argamasa f, mezcla f; —**board** birrete m

mortgage [mɔ́rgɪʤ] N hipoteca f; VT hipotecar; ADJ hipotecario

mortgagor [mɔ́rgɪʤəʳ] N deudor -ra hipotecario -ria mf

mortify [mɔ́rɾəfaɪ] VI/VT mortificar(se)

mosaic [mozéɪk] N mosaico m

Moslem [mázləm] ADJ & N musulmán -ana mf

mosque [mɔsk] N mezquita f

mosquito [məskíɾo] N mosquito m; — **net** mosquitero m

moss [mɔs] N musgo m

mossy [mɔ́si] ADJ musgoso

most [most] ADJ — **children are good** la mayoría de los niños son buenos; — **people** la mayoría de la gente; the — **money** más dinero m; the — **votes** el mayor número de votos; for the — **part** generalmente; PRON the — **that I can do** lo más que puedo hacer; **we ate the** — comimos más que nadie; — **of the guests are here** ha llegado la mayoría de los invitados; ADV the — **ambitious** el más ambicioso; a — **pleasant day** un día de lo más agradable

mostly [mɔ́stli] ADV generalmente

motel [motéł] N motel m

moth [mɔθ] N (pest) polilla f; (nocturnal insect) mariposa nocturna f; —**ball** bolita de naftalina f; —-**eaten** apolillado

mother [mʌ́ðəʳ] N madre f; —**board** plaqueta madre f; — **country** madre patria f; —**fucker** offensive hijo de puta m; —-**in-law** suegra f; —-**of-pearl** madreperla f; — **tongue** lengua materna f; VT mimar a, cuidar de/a

motherhood [mʌ́ðəʳhud] N maternidad f

motherly [mʌ́ðəʳli] ADJ maternal

motif [motíf] N motivo m

motion [móʃən] N (movement) movimiento m; (signal) ademán m; (proposal) moción f; — **picture** película de cine f; —-**picture industry** industria cinematográfica f; — **sickness** mareo m; VI/VT hacer un ademán

motionless [móʃənlɪs] ADJ inmóvil

motivate [móɾəvet] VT motivar

motivation [moɾəvéʃən] N motivación f

motive [móɾɪv] N motivo m; ADJ motriz

motley [mátli] ADJ abigarrado

motor [móɾəʳ] N motor m; —**bike** motocicleta pequeña f; —**boat** lancha a motor f; —**cycle** motocicleta f; —**cyclist** motociclista mf; — **home** casa rodante f, caravana f; — **scooter** scooter m; — **vehicle** vehículo motorizado m; VI pasear en coche

motorist [móɾəʳɪst] N automovilista mf

motto [máɾo] N lema f

mound [maund] N montículo m; **burial** — túmulo m; — **of laundry** pila de ropa f

mount [maunt] VI/VT montar; (increase) subir; VT (assemble) armar; N (mountain) monte m; (getting on a horse) monta f; (animal for riding) montura f

mountain [maʊntn̩] N montaña f; ADJ (animal, person) montañés; (thing) de montaña; — **bike** bicicleta de montaña f; — **climber** alpinista mf; — **climbing** alpinismo m, montañismo m; — **goat** cabra montés f; — **lion** puma f, gato montés m; — **range** (large) cordillera f; (small) sierra f; — **side** ladera (de una montaña) f; —**top** cumbre (de una montaña) f

mountaineer [maʊntn̩íʳ] N alpinista mf

mountainous [máʊntn̩əs] ADJ montañoso

mourn [mɔrn] VI estar de duelo/luto; VT llorar; **to** — **for** llorar a

mourner [mɔ́rnəʳ] N doliente mf

mournful [mɔ́rnfəł] ADJ lúgubre, triste

mourning [mɔ́rnɪŋ] N luto m, duelo m; **to be in** — estar de luto/duelo; ADJ de luto

mouse [maus] N ratón m (also computer); — **pad** bandeja del ratón f; —**trap** ratonera f

mouth [mauθ] N boca f; (of a cave) abertura f; (of a river) desembocadura f; —**piece** (part of a trumpet) boquilla f; (spokesman) portavoz mf; —-**to-mouth resuscitation** respiración boca a boca f; —**wash** enjuague bucal m; —-**watering** delicioso; [mauð] VT articular silenciosamente una palabra; VI **to** — **off** contestar

mouthful [máʊθfʊł] N (of food) bocado m; (of liquid) bocanada f, buche m

movable [múvəbəł] ADJ movible, móvil

move [muv] VI (change position) mover(se) (also board games); (change residence) mudar(se) de casa; (sell) venderse; **to** — **away** (distance oneself) apartarse; (change residence) irse; **to** — **forward** avanzar; **to** — **on** seguir adelante; **to** — **out** mudarse de casa; **to** — **up** anticipar; VT (propose) proponer; (affect emotionally) conmover; N (act of moving) movimiento m; (change of residence) mudanza f; (action toward a goal) paso m; (play, in games) jugada f; **get a — on there!** ¡date prisa! **he made the first —** dio el primer paso

movement [múvmənt] N (motion, part of a watch) movimiento m; **to have a bowel —** mover el vientre

mover [múvə-] N compañía de mudanzas f; **—s and shakers** la plana mayor

movie [múvi] N película f; **—s** cine m

moving [múviŋ] ADJ (target) móvil; (car) en movimiento; (company) de mudanzas; (story) conmovedor; **— picture** película f; **— van** camión de mudanzas m; N **I hate —** no me gusta mudarme de casa

mow [mo] VT cortar; (harvest) segar

mower [móə-] N (for lawns) cortadora de césped f, cortacésped m; (farm implement) segadora f; (farm worker) segador -ra mf

Mozambican [mozæmbíkən] ADJ & N mozambiqueño -ña mf

Mozambique [mozæmbík] N Mozambique m

Mozarabic [mozérəbɪk] ADJ mozárabe

Mr. [místə-] N Sr. m

Mrs. [mísɪz] N Sra. f

Ms. [mɪz] N Sra. f

much [mʌtʃ] ADJ & ADV mucho; **— the same** casi lo mismo; **— like the others** muy parecido a los demás; **as — as** tanto como; **how — ?** ¿cuánto? **too —** demasiado; **very —** muchísimo; **to make — of** dar mucha importancia a; **— as I'd like, I won't do it** aunque me gustaría, no lo voy a hacer; **that's not — of a book** ese libro no es gran cosa; **she cried so — that her eyes turned red** lloró tanto que se le enrojecieron los ojos; **they need water, — as they need sun** necesitan agua, del mismo modo que necesitan sol

muck [mʌk] N (manure) estiércol m; (mire) cieno m, lodo m; (filth) porquería f; **to — up** vulg cagarla

mucous [mjúkəs] ADJ mucoso

mucus [mjúkəs] N mucosidad f

mud [mʌd] N lodo m, barro m; **—slinging** difamación f

muddle [mʌdl] VT (confuse) confundir; (make turbid) enturbiar; VI **to — along** ir tirando; **to — through** salir del paso; N (confusion) confusión f; (confused situation) embrollo m

muddy [mʌdi] ADJ (path) lodoso, barroso; (shoes) embarrado; (vague) confuso; VT

(cover with mud) enlodar, embarrar; (make unclear) enturbiar

muff [mʌf] N manguito m; VT estropear

muffin [mʌfɪn] N mollete m

muffle [mʌfəl] VT amortiguar

muffler [mʌflə-] N (scarf) bufanda f; (exhaust device) silenciador m

mug [mʌg] N (ceramic) tazón m; (glass) jarra f; (face) jeta f; VT atracar

mugger [mʌgə-] N asaltante mf; atracador -ora mf

muggy [mʌgi] ADJ bochornoso

mulatto [mulÁɗo] ADJ & N mulato -ta mf

mulberry [mʌlbɛri] N mora f; **— tree** moral m

mule [mjul] N mulo -la mf (also in drug trafficking)

mull [mʌl] VI/VT rumiar

multicultural [mʌltikʌltʃə-əl] ADJ multicultural

multiple [mʌltəpəl] N múltiplo m; ADJ múltiple; **—-choice** de opción múltiple; **— personality disorder** trastorno de personalidad múltiple m; **— sclerosis** esclerosis múltiple f

multiplication [mʌltəplɪkéʃən] N multiplicación f; **— sign** signo de multiplicación m; **— table** tabla de multiplicar f

multiplicity [mʌltəplísɪɗi] N multiplicidad f

multiply [mʌltəplaɪ] VI/VT multiplicar(se)

multitasking [mʌltitæskɪŋ] N multitarea f

multitude [mʌltitud] N multitud f

multi-user [mʌltijúzə-] N multiusuario -ria mf

mum [mʌm] ADJ callado; **to keep —** callarse la boca

mumble [mʌmbəl] VI/VT mascullar; N refunfuño m

mumbo jumbo [mámbodʒámbo] N jerigonza f

mummy [mámi] N momia f

mumps [mʌmps] N paperas f pl

munch [mʌntʃ] VT mascar

mundane [mʌndén] ADJ mundano

municipal [mjunísəpəl] ADJ municipal; **— council** concejo m

municipality [mjunɪsəpélɪɗi] N municipio m, municipalidad m

munition [mjuníʃən] N munición f

mural [mjúrəl] ADJ & N mural m

murder [mɜ́-ɗə-] N asesinato m, homicidio m; **to get away with —** salirse con la suya; **that exam was —** ese examen fue matador; VI/VT asesinar

murderer [mɜ́-ɗərə-] N asesino mf, homicida mf

murderous [mɜ́·Dɚ·əs] ADJ asesino, homicida

murky [mɜ́·ki] ADJ (of water, matter) turbio; (of sky) oscuro

murmur [mɜ́·mɚ] N (noise) murmullo *m*, susurro *m*; (complaint) queja *f*; VI/VT (make noise) murmurar, susurrar; (complain) quejarse

muscle [mʌ́səł] N músculo *m*

muscular [mʌ́skjələ·] ADJ (relative to muscles) muscular; (endowed with muscles) musculoso

muse [mjuz] VI meditar; VT cavilar; N musa *f*

museum [mjuzíəm] N museo *m*

mushroom [mʌ́ʃrum] N seta *f*, hongo *m*, champiñón *m*

mushy [mʌ́ʃi] ADJ (soft) fofo; (sentimental) sensiblero

music [mjúzɪk] N música *f*; — **stand** atril *m*; — **video** *Am* video musical *m*; *Sp* vídeo musical *m*

musical [mjúzɪkəł] ADJ (pertaining to music) musical; (fond of music) aficionado a la música, melómano; — **comedy** comedia musical *f*

musician [mjuzíʃən] N músico -ca *mf*

muskrat [mʌ́skræt] N ratón almizclero *m*

Muslim [mʌ́zləm] ADJ & N musulmán -ana *mf*

muslin [mʌ́zlɪn] N muselina *f*

muss [mʌs] VT revolver, alborotar; N revoltijo *m*

mussel [mʌ́səł] N mejillón *m*

must [mʌst] V AUX **you — arrive before nine** debes llegar antes de las nueve; **you really — eat at that restaurant** tienes que comer en ese restaurante; **you — be his son** debes (de) / has de ser su hijo; **they — have seen me** deben (de) haberme visto

mustache, moustache [mʌ́stæʃ] N bigote *m*; (large) mostacho *m*

mustard [mʌ́stɚd] N mostaza *f*; — **gas** gas mostaza *m*

muster [mʌ́stɚ] VT (troops) formar; (courage) juntar, reunir; VI (assemble for inspection) formar; (come together) reunirse; **to — out** dar de baja; **to — up one's courage** juntar valor; N revista *f*; **to pass —** ser aceptable

musty [mʌ́sti] ADJ (stale smelling) con olor a encierro / humedad; (antiquated) anticuado

mutant [mjútn̩t] ADJ & N mutante *mf*

mutation [mjutéʃən] N mutación *f*

mute [mjut] ADJ mudo; N (mute person) mudo -da *mf*; (for musical instruments) sordina *f*

mutilate [mjúdl̩et] VT mutilar

mutiny [mjútn̩i] N motín *m*; VI amotinarse

mutter [mʌ́dɚ] VI/VT refunfuñar, musitar; N refunfuño *m*

mutton [mʌ́tn̩] N carne de cordero *f*

mutual [mjútʃuəł] ADJ mutuo; — **fund** fondo mutuo / mutual *m*

muzzle [mʌ́zəł] N (snout) hocico *m*; (mouthguard) bozal *m*; (gun opening) boca *f*; VT (a dog) abozalar, poner bozal a; (critics) amordazar, silenciar

my [maɪ] POSS ADJ mi; **these are — friends** estos son mis amigos; **oh —!** ¡Dios mío! — **foot!** ¡ni lo pienses!

Myanmar [mjɑnmár] N Myanmar *m*

myopia [maɪópiə] N miopía *f*

myriad [mírɪəd] N miríada *f*, sinfín *m*; — **problems** un sinfín de problemas

myrtle [mɜ́·dl̩] N mirto *m*, arrayán *m*

myself [maɪséłf] PRON **I — wrote the letters** yo mismo escribí las cartas; **I'm not — today** hoy no soy la misma de siempre; **I was sitting by —** estaba sentado solo; **I talk to —** hablo solo; **I looked at — in the mirror** me miré en el espejo; **I bought — a house** me compré una casa

mysterious [mɪstírɪəs] ADJ misterioso

mystery [místəri] N misterio *m*

mystic [místɪk] ADJ & N místico -ca *mf*

mystical [místɪkəł] ADJ místico

myth [mɪθ] N mito *m*

mythology [mɪθálədʒi] N mitología *f*

Nn

nab [næb] VT pescar; *Sp* coger

nag [næg] N (horse) jaca *f*, rocín *m*, penco *m*; (complainer) quejica *mf*; VI/VT regañar, criticar

nail [neł] N (for nailing) clavo *m*; (of finger, toe) uña *f*; —**biter** situación angustiante *f*; — **file** lima *f*; — **polish** esmalte para uñas *m*; **to hit the — on the head** dar en el clavo; VT (fasten) clavar; (nab) pescar; *Sp* coger

naïve [naív] ADJ ingenuo, cándido, bonachón

naked [nékɪd] ADJ desnudo

nakedness [nékɪdnɪs] N desnudez *f*

name [nem] N nombre *m*; —**brand** marca *f*; —**plate** placa *f*; —**sake** tocayo *m*; —**tag** etiqueta de identificación *f*; — **of the game** lo esencial *m*; **to call someone**

—s motejar a alguien; **to make a —** for oneself hacerse un nombre; **what is your —?** ¿cómo te llamas? VT nombrar; **— your price** haz una oferta

namely [némli] ADV a saber, en concreto

Namibia [nəmíbiə] N Namibia f

Namibian [nəmíbiən] ADJ & N namibio -bia mf

nanny [næni] N niñera f

nanosecond [nǽnosekand] N nanosegundo m

nap [næp] N (sleep) siesta f; (fibers) pelo m; **to take a —** echar/dormir una siesta; VI echar/dormir una siesta

napalm [népalm] N napalm m

nape [nep] N nuca f

napkin [nǽpkɪn] N servilleta f

narcissism [nársɪsɪzəm] N narcisismo m

narcissus [narsísəs] N narciso m

narcolepsy [nárkəlepsi] N narcolepsia f

narcotic [narkádɪk] ADJ & N narcótico m, estupefaciente m

narco-trafficking [narkotrǽfɪkɪŋ] N narcotráfico m

narrate [néret] VI/VT narrar

narration [næréʃən] N narración f

narrative [nǽrəDɪV] ADJ narrativo; N narrativa f

narrator [nǽreDə] N narrador -ora mf

narrow [nǽro] ADJ (of little width) estrecho, angosto; (exhaustive) exhaustivo; (limited in scope) limitado; (intolerant) intolerante; **to have a — escape** salvarse por poco; **— gauge** de vía angosta/estrecha; **—-minded** intolerante; N **—s** desfiladero m, estrecho m, angostura f; VI/VT angostar(se), estrechar(se); **to — down** reducir

narrowness [nǽronɪs] N (quality of being narrow) estrechez f, angostura f; (intolerance) estrechez f

nasal [nézəl] ADJ nasal

nastiness [nǽstinɪs] N (filth) suciedad f; (stinkiness) asquerosidad f; (rudeness, obscenity) grosería f

nasturtium [nəstɚ-ʃəm] N capuchina f

nasty [nǽsti] ADJ (mess) sucio; (smell) asqueroso; (comment) hiriente; (accident) feo; (word) grosero; (disposition) malo

natal [nédl] ADJ natal

nation [néʃən] N nación f; **—wide** a escala nacional

national [nǽʃənəl] ADJ nacional; **— park** parque nacional m; N ciudadano -na mf, nacional mf

nationalism [nǽʃənəlɪzəm] N nacionalismo m

nationality [næʃənǽlɪDi] N nacionalidad f; **adjective of —** gentilicio m

nationalize [nǽʃənəlaɪz] VT nacionalizar

native [nédɪv] ADJ nativo; **— language** lengua nativa f; **— plants** flora nativa f; **my — Italy** mi Italia natal f; (innate) innato; N (person born in a place) natural m; (member of a tribal group) indígena mf, nativo -va mf

nativity [nətívɪDi] N nacimiento m; **— scene** pesebre m; **the —** la Natividad

NATO (North Atlantic Treaty Organization) [nédo] N OTAN f

natural [nǽtʃərəl] ADJ natural; (inborn) innato; **— childbirth** parto natural m; **— gas** gas natural m; **— resources** recursos naturales m pl; **— selection** selección natural f; N (musical sign) becuadro m; **he is a — for that job** tiene aptitud natural para ese puesto

naturalist [nǽtʃərəlɪst] N naturalista mf

naturalization [nætʃərəlɪzéʃən] N naturalización f

naturalize [nǽtʃərəlaɪz] VI/VT naturalizar(se)

naturally [nǽtʃərəli] ADV (of course) naturalmente; **I have — curly hair** tengo rizos naturales

naturalness [nǽtʃərəlnɪs] N naturalidad f

nature [nétʃə] N naturaleza f; (disposition) genio m, natural m

naught [nɔt] N (zero) cero m; (nothing) nada f

naughty [nɔ́Di] ADJ (child) travieso, pícaro, pillo; **— word** picardía f

Nauru [naúru] N Nauru f

Nauruan [naúruən] ADJ & N nauruano -na mf

nausea [nɔ́ziə] N náusea f, mareo m

nauseate [nɔ́ziet] VT dar náuseas; **to be —d** tener náuseas

nauseating [nɔ́zieDɪŋ] ADJ nauseabundo

nauseous [nɔ́ʃəs] ADJ (feeling nausea) mareado; (causing nausea) nauseabundo

nautical [nɔ́Dɪkəl] ADJ náutico

naval [névəl] ADJ naval; **— officer** oficial de marina m

nave [nev] N nave f

navel [névəl] N ombligo m; **— orange** naranja de ombligo f

navigable [nǽvɪgəbəl] ADJ navegable

navigate [nǽvɪget] VI/VT navegar

navigation [nævɪgéʃən] N navegación f; (science) náutica f

navigator [nǽvɪgeDə] N navegante mf

navy [névi] N marina (de guerra) f, armada f; **— bean** judía blanca f; **— blue** azul marino m

nay [ne] N (refusal) no *m*; (negative vote) voto negativo *m*

near [nir] ADV cerca; **— at hand** cerca, a la mano; **to come / go / draw —** acercarse; **—sighted** miope; PREP cerca de; **— the end of the month** hacia fines del mes; **to be — death** estar a punto de morir; ADJ cercano, próximo; **— East** Cercano Oriente *m*, Oriente Próximo *m*; **I had a — miss** por poco me sucede un accidente; VI/VT acercarse (a)

nearby [nírbái] ADV cerca; ADJ cercano, próximo

nearly [nírli] ADV casi, cerca de; **I — did it** casi lo hago

nearness [nírnis] N cercanía *f*, proximidad *f*

neat [nit] ADJ (clean) limpio, pulcro; (ordered) ordenado; (great) bueno

neatness [nítnis] N (cleanness) limpieza *f*, pulcritud *f*; (order) orden *m*

nebulous [nébjələs] ADJ nebuloso

necessary [nésɪsɛri] ADJ (needed) necesario; (involuntary) forzoso

necessitate [nəsésɪtet] VT requerir

necessity [nəsésɪdi] N necesidad *f*

neck [nɛk] N (of a human) cuello *m*; (of an animal) pescuezo *m*; (of clothes) escote *m*; (throat) garganta *f*; **— and —** parejos; **—lace** collar *m*; **—line** escote *m*; **— of land** istmo *m*; **—tie** corbata *f*

necrology [nəkrálədʒi] N necrología *f*

nectar [nɛ́ktɚ] N néctar *m*

nectarine [nɛktərín] N nectarina *f*

need [nid] N (lack) necesidad *f*; (poverty) carencia *f*; **in —** en aprietos; **if — be** en caso de necesidad; VT necesitar, precisar; **you — to come at four** tienes que venir a las cuatro

needle [nídl̩] N aguja *f*; **—point** bordado *m*; **—work** (embroidery) bordado *m*; (sewing) costura *f*; VT pinchar

needless [nídlɪs] ADJ innecesario; **— to say** huelga decir

needy [nídi] ADJ necesitado, menesteroso

ne'er-do-well [nérduwɛɫ] N inútil *mf*

negate [nɪgét] VT negar

negation [nɪgéʃən] N negación *f*

negative [négəðɪv] ADJ negativo; **the search proved —** la búsqueda no dio resultado; N negativa *f*; (photographic) negativo *m*; **this plan has one —** este plan tiene una contra; INTERJ ¡negativo!

neglect [nɪglékt] VT postergar; (children) descuidar; (chores) desatender; **you're —ing your friends** tienes abandonados a tus amigos; **to — to** olvidarse de; N negligencia *f*, descuido *m*

neglectful [nɪgléktfəl] ADJ negligente, descuidado

negligence [néglɪdʒəns] N negligencia *f*

negligent [néglɪdʒənt] ADJ negligente, descuidado

negligible [néglɪdʒəbəl] ADJ despreciable

negotiate [nɪgóʃiet] VI/VT (a contract) negociar, gestionar; (an obstacle) salvar

negotiation [nɪgoʃiéʃən] N negociación *f*, gestión *f*

Negro [nígro] ADJ & N negro -gra *mf*

neigh [ne] N relincho *m*; VI relinchar

neighbor [nébɚ] N (person who lives near) vecino -na *mf*; (fellow human) prójimo -ma *mf*; ADJ vecino; VI **to — with** lindar con

neighborhood [nébɚhud] N vecindario *m*, barrio *m*; **in the — of a hundred dollars** alrededor de cien dólares

neighboring [nébərɪŋ] ADJ vecino, colindante

neither [níðɚ] PRON ninguno de los dos, ni (el) uno ni (el) otro; **— of the two** ninguno de los dos; ADJ ninguno de los dos; **— one of us** ninguno de nosotros dos; CONJ ni; **— hot nor cold** ni caliente ni frío; **— will I** yo tampoco

nemesis [némɪsɪs] N némesis *f*

neologism [niálədʒɪzəm] N neologismo *m*

neon [nían] N neón *m*

Nepal [nəpɔ́l] N Nepal *m*

Nepalese [nepalíz] ADJ & N nepalés -esa *mf*, nepalí *mf*

nephew [néfju] N sobrino *m*

nephritis [nəfráɪdɪs] N nefritis *f*

nepotism [népətɪzəm] N nepotismo *m*

nerd [nɚd] N (technological adept) persona aficionada a las computadoras / los ordenadores *f*; (socially inept person) persona socialmente inepta *f*

nerve [nɚv] N (anatomy) nervio *m*; (courage) presencia de ánimo *f*; (impertinence) descaro *m*, morro *m*; **— cell** neurona *f*; **— gas** gas nervioso *m*; **-(w)racking** angustiante; **he gets on my —s** me saca de quicio

nervous [nɚ́vəs] ADJ nervioso; **— breakdown** ataque de nervios *m*

nervousness [nɚ́vəsnɪs] N nerviosismo *m*

nest [nɛst] N nido *m*; (brood) nidada *f*; **— egg** ahorros *m pl*; **— of thieves** guarida de ladrones *f*; VI/VT anidar; (fit together) encajarse

nestle [nésəɫ] VI acurrucarse; VT apoyar, recostar

net [nɛt] N red *f* (also network); (in hair) redecilla *f*; VT (catch a fish) pescar con red;

(cover with a net) cubrir con una red; (catch a criminal) atrapar; (hit the tennis net) dar en la red; (make money after expenses) producir / ganar neto; ADJ neto; — **price** precio neto *m*; — **profit** ganancia neta *f*; — **assets** activo neto *m*; — **income** ingreso neto *m*; —**work** red *f*; —**working** (social) relaciones profesionales *f pl*; (computer) diseño de redes y comunicaciones *m*

Netherlander [néðə-ləndə-] N holandés -esa *mf*

Netherlands [néðə-ləndz] N Países Bajos *m pl*

nettle [nédl] N ortiga *f*

neural [núrəl] ADJ neural

neuron [núran] N neurona *f*

neurosis [nurósɪs] N neurosis *f*

neurotic [nurádɪk] ADJ & N neurótico -ca *mf*

neuter [núdə-] ADJ neutro; VT castrar

neutral [nútrəl] ADJ neutral; (of colors) neutro; N punto muerto *m*

neutrality [nutrǽlɪɾi] N neutralidad *f*

neutralize [nútrəlaɪz] VI/VT neutralizar(se)

neutron [nútran] N neutrón *m*; — **bomb** bomba de neutrones *f*

never [névə-] ADV nunca, jamás; — **mind** no te preocupes; **this will — do** esto no va a funcionar; —**ending** interminable

nevertheless [nevə-ðəlés] ADV & CONJ sin embargo, no obstante

new [nu] ADJ (not old) nuevo; (fresh) otro; **a — sheet of paper** otra hoja de papel; — **Age** (music) new age *f*; —**born baby** recién nacido -da *mf*; —**comer** recién llegado -da *mf*; —**fangled** moderno, recién inventado; —**found** nuevo; — **year** año nuevo *m*; — **Year's Eve** fin de año *m*; *Sp* nochevieja *f*

newly [núli] ADV recientemente; —**arrived** recién llegado; —**wed** recién casado

newness [núnɪs] N novedad *f*

news [nuz] N noticias *f pl*; (latest gossip) novedades *f pl*; (newspaper) periódico *m*; **it is — to me** recién me entero; **piece of** — noticia *f*; — **broadcast / bulletin** noticiero *m*, noticiario *m*; —**cast** noticiero *m*, noticiario *m*; — **clipping** recorte de diario *m*; —**letter** boletín informativo *m*; —**paper** periódico *m*, diario *m*; —**print** papel de periódico *m*; —**room** sala de redacción *f*; —**stand** quiosco *m*; —**worthy** de interés periodístico

newt [nut] N tritón *m*

New Zealand [nuzíland] N Nueva Zelanda *f*

New Zealander [nuzíləndə-] N neozelandés -esa *mf*

next [nɛkst] ADJ (future) próximo, entrante;

(following) siguiente; (contiguous) contiguo, de al lado; **who's —?** ¿quién sigue? ADV después, luego; — **best** segundo en calidad; **when — we meet** cuando nos volvamos a ver; PREP —-**door** de al lado; — **of kin** familiares *m pl*; — **to** junto a, al lado de

nibble [níbəl] VI/VT (bite) mordiscar, mordisquear; (eat) picotear; (of fish) picar; N (bite) mordisco *m*; (act of nibbling) mordisqueo *m*

Nicaragua [nɪkɑrágwə] N Nicaragua *f*

Nicaraguan [nɪkɑrágwən] ADJ & N nicaragüense *mf*

nice [naɪs] ADJ (kind) amable, simpático; (agreeable) *Am* majo, *Sp* majo; **it's — and hot** está bien calentito

nicety [náɪsɪɾi] N (subtlety) sutileza *f*; (detail) exactitud *f*, precisión *f*

niche [nɪtʃ] N nicho *m* (also environmental); **I've found my —** he encontrado mi lugar

nick [nɪk] N (chip) muesca *f*; (cut) corte *m*; **in the — of time** justo a tiempo; VT (chip) hacer muescas; (cut) cortar

nickel [níkəl] N (metal) níquel *m*; (coin) moneda de cinco centavos *f*; —-**plated** niquelado

nickname [níknem] N apodo *m*, mote *m*, sobrenombre *m*; VT apodar

nicotine [níkətin] N nicotina *f*

niece [nis] N sobrina *f*

Niger [náɪdʒə-] N Níger *m*

Nigeria [naɪdʒíriə] N Nigeria *f*

Nigerian [naɪdʒíriən] ADJ & N nigeriano -na *mf*

Nigerien [naɪdʒíriɛn] ADJ & N nigerino -na *mf*

niggardly [nígə-dli] ADJ mezquino

night [naɪt] N noche *f*; ADJ nocturno, de noche; —**club** club nocturno *m*; —**fall** anochecer *m*, atardecer *m*; —**gown** camisón *m*; —**life** vida nocturna *f*; *Sp* marcha *f*; —-**light** lamparilla *f*; —**mare** pesadilla *f*; — **owl** trasnochador -ora *mf*; — **shift** turno de la noche *m*; —**stand** veladora *f*, mesilla de noche *f*; —**time** noche *f*; — **watchman** sereno *m*

nightingale [náɪtɪŋgel] N ruiseñor *m*

nightly [náɪtli] ADV todas las noches; ADJ nocturno

nihilism [náɪəlɪzəm] N nihilismo *m*

nil [nɪl] ADJ **your chances are —** tus probabilidades son nulas

nimble [nímbəl] ADJ ágil

nincompoop [nínkəmpup] N *fam* tarambana *mf*, bobalicón -ona *mf*

nine [naɪn] NUM nueve

nineteen [naɪntín] NUM diecinueve

ninety [náɪnti] NUM noventa

ninth [náɪnθ] ADJ & N noveno *m*

nip [nɪp] VT (pinch) pellizcar; (bite) mordiscar, mordisquear; (cause frostbite) helar; **to — in the bud** cortar de raíz; **to — off** despuntar; VI (drink in sips) dar sorbitos; N (pinch) pellizco *m*; (bite) mordisco *m*; (sip) traguito *m*, sorbito *m*; (cold) frío *m*; **it's going to be — and tuck** va a ser muy reñido

nipple [nípəl] N (on female breast) pezón *m*; (on male breast) tetilla *f*; (on bottle) tetina *f*

nitpick [nítpɪk] VI criticar detalles insignificantes

nitrate [náɪtret] N nitrato *m*

nitric acid [náɪtrɪkǽsɪd] N ácido nítrico *m*

nitrogen [náɪtrədʒən] N nitrógeno *m*

nitroglycerin [naɪtroɡlísə-ɪn] N nitroglicerina *f*

nitty-gritty [nídɪɡrídi] N **to get down to the —** ir al grano

no [no] ADV no; **— longer** ya no; **he was a —-show** no se presentó; **a —-win situation** una situación insoluble; **there is — more** no hay más; ADJ ningun(o); **—man's land** tierra de nadie *f*; **— matter how much** por mucho que; **— one** ninguno, nadie; **— smoking** se prohíbe fumar; **—where** (location) en ninguna parte/ningún lado; (direction) a ninguna parte/ningún lado; **I have — friends** no tengo amigos; **it's a —-brainer** la respuesta es obvia; **— friend of mine will go hungry** ningún amigo mío pasará hambre; **of — use** inútil; N (refusal) no *m*; (negative vote) voto negativo *m*

nobility [nobílɪɖi] N nobleza *f*, hidalguía *f*

noble [nóbəl] ADJ & N noble *mf*

nobody [nóbadi] PRON nadie, ninguno; N un don nadie, pelagatos *mf sg*

nocturnal [nakt-nəl] ADJ nocturno

nod [nad] VI/VT (signal affirmation) asentir con la cabeza; VI (doze) cabecear, dar cabezadas; **to — off** dormirse; N (as signal) inclinación de cabeza *f*, saludo con la cabeza *m*; (from sleepiness) cabezada *f*

node [nod] N (of cells) nódulo *m*; (in plants) nudo *m*; (in physics) nodo *m*

noise [nɔɪz] N ruido *m*; VI **it is being —d about that** corre el rumor que

noiseless [nɔ́ɪzlɪs] ADJ silencioso

noisy [nɔ́ɪzi] ADJ ruidoso

nomad [nómæd] N nómada *mf*

nomenclature [nómɪnkletʃə-] N nomenclatura *f*

nominal [námənəl] ADJ nominal

nominate [námənet] VT nominar

nomination [namənéʃən] N nominación *f*

nominee [naməní] N candidato *-ta mf*

nonchalant [nanʃəlánt] ADJ despreocupado

nonconformist [nankənfɔ́rmɪst] ADJ & N inconformista *mf*

none [nʌn] PRON ninguno; **I want — of that** no me quiero meter en eso; **that is — of your business** no es asunto tuyo; ADV **— too soon** al último momento; **—theless** sin embargo

nonentity [nanéntɪɖi] N nulidad *f*

nonfiction [nanfíkʃən] N no ficción *f*

nonpartisan [nanpárɖɪzən] ADJ imparcial

nonproductive [nanprədáktɪv] ADJ improductivo

nonprofit [nanpráfɪt] ADJ sin fines de lucro

nonresident [nanrézɪdənt] ADJ & N no residente *mf*

nonsense [nánsɛns] N tonterías *f pl*, monsergas *f pl*, estupideces *f pl*; **to talk —** decir barbaridades/disparates

nonstop [nánstáp] ADJ sin escala, directo; ADV sin parar

noodle [núdl] N fideo *m*, tallarín *m*

nook [nuk] N rincón *m*

noon [nun] N mediodía *m*; **—time** mediodía *m*

noose [nus] N soga *f*, lazo *m*; **with a — around his neck** con la soga al cuello; VT (catch with a rope) enlazar; (make a loop in) hacer un lazo corredizo en

nope [nop] ADV no

nor [nɔr] CONJ ni; **we have neither eggs — flour** no tenemos ni huevos ni harina

Nordic [nɔ́rdɪk] ADJ nórdico

norm [nɔrm] N norma *f*

normal [nɔ́rməl] ADJ normal; N (line) normal *f*; **to return to —** volver a la normalidad; (perpendicular line) línea perpendicular *f*

normalize [nɔ́rməlaɪz] VI/VT normalizar(se)

north [nɔrθ] N norte *m*; ADJ (in the north) norte, norteño; **the — entrance** la entrada norte; (from the north) del norte; **— America** América del Norte *f*; **— American** norteamericano *-na mf*; **—east** noreste, hacia el noreste; **—eastern** del noreste; **— Korea** Corea del Norte *f*; **— Korean** norcoreano *-na*; **— Pole** Polo Norte *m*; **—west** noroeste *m*, hacia el noroeste; **— wind** cierzo *m*, viento norte *m*; ADV al norte, hacia el norte

northern [nɔ́rðə-n] ADJ del norte; (from the north) norteño; (in the north) septentrional; **— lights** aurora boreal *f*

465

northerner [nɔ́rðə·nə·] N norteño -ña *mf*

northward [nɔ́rθwə·d] ADV hacia el norte

Norway [nɔ́rwe] N Noruega *f*

Norwegian [nɔrwíd͡ʒən] ADJ & N noruego -ga *mf*

nose [noz] N nariz *f*; (of an airplane) morro *m*; (of an animal) hocico *m*; (perspicacity) olfato *m*; **—bleed** hemorragia nasal *f*; **—dive** picado *m*; **— job** rinoplastia *f*; **keep your — clean** no te metas en líos; **on the —** exactamente; **look down one's — at** desdeñar; VI/VT (move forward) entrar de punta; (muzzle) hocicar; **to — around** husmear

nostalgia [nɑstǽld͡ʒə] N nostalgia *f*

nostalgic [nɑstǽld͡ʒɪk] ADJ nostálgico

nostrils [nɑ́strəɫz] N narices *f pl*, ventanillas de la nariz *f pl*

nosy, nosey [nózi] ADJ entrometido

not [nɑt] ADV no; **I'm — your friend** no soy tu amigo; **— at all** (no way) de ningún modo; (you're welcome) de nada; **— at all sure** nada seguro; **— even a word** ni una palabra

notable [nódəbəɫ] ADJ notable, granado

notarize [nódəraɪz] VT notariar

notary [nódəri] N notario -ria *mf*; **— public** notario -ria público -ca *mf*

notation [notéʃən] N (system of signs) notación *f*; (act of writing) anotación *f*; (short note) anotación *f*, apunte *m*

notch [nɑtʃ] N (nick) muesca *f*, mella *f*; (degree) grado *m*; **a — above the rest** mejor que los demás; VT hacer una muesca; **he —ed another win** se anotó otra victoria

note [not] N nota *f*; (touch) toque *m*; **—book** cuaderno *m*; (small) libreta *f*; **—s** apuntes *m pl*; **—worthy** notable; **of — de** renombre / de nota; **to take — of** notar; VT (notice) notar; (write down) anotar, apuntar

noted [nódɪd] ADJ célebre

nothing [nʌ́θɪŋ] PRON nada; (score) cero, nada; N (insignificant person) don nadie *m*; (insignificant thing) nadería *f*; **— to it** no tiene ciencia; ADV **it was — like that** no fue así para nada; **we did it for —** (free) lo hicimos gratis; (fruitlessly) lo hicimos en balde

notice [nódɪs] N (information) aviso *m*; (warning) advertencia *f*; (attention) atención *f*; **a week's —** una semana de plazo; **to give —** renunciar; **to take —** hacer caso; VT (perceive) notar, advertir; (pay attention to) fijarse (en), reparar (en)

noticeable [nódɪsəbəɫ] ADJ perceptible,

apreciable

notification [nodəfɪkéʃən] N notificación *f*

notify [nódəfaɪ] VT notificar

notion [nóʃən] N noción *f*, idea *f*; (whim) capricho *m*; **—s** mercería *f*

notorious [notɔ́riəs] ADJ de mala fama; **he's a — liar** tiene fama de mentiroso

nougat [núgət] N turrón *m*

noun [naun] N sustantivo *m*

nourish [nɝ́ɪʃ] VT (a person) nutrir, alimentar; (a hope) abrigar

nourishing [nɝ́ɪʃɪŋ] ADJ nutritivo

nourishment [nɝ́ɪʃmənt] N (food) alimento *m*; (act of nourishing) alimentación *f*

novel [návəɫ] N novela *f*; ADJ novedoso

novelist [návəlɪst] N novelista *mf*

novelty [návəɫti] N novedad *f*; **the — soon wore off** se pasó la novedad; **novelties** chucherías *f pl*

November [novémbə·] N noviembre *m*

novice [návɪs] N novato -ta *mf*, pipiolo -la *mf*; (religious) novicio -cia *mf*

now [nau] ADV ahora; **— and then** de vez en cuando; **— that** ahora que; **he left just —** salió hace poco, recién salió; **—, — calm down!** bueno, bueno, ¡cálmate!

nowadays [náuədez] ADV hoy (en) día

noxious [nákʃəs] ADJ nocivo

nuance [núans] N matiz *m*

nuclear [núkliə·] ADJ nuclear; **— energy** energía nuclear *f*; **— family** familia nuclear *f*; **— fission** fisión nuclear *f*; **— fusion** fusión nuclear *f*; **— physics** física nuclear *f*; **— weapon** arma nuclear *f*

nucleus [núkliəs] N núcleo *m*

nude [nud] ADJ & N desnudo *m*

nudge [nʌd͡ʒ] VI/VT codear; N golpe suave con el codo *m*

nugget [nʌ́gɪt] N (gold) pepita *f*; (chicken) pedacito *m*; (wisdom) perla *f*

nuisance [núsəns] N molestia *f*; *Sp* pesadez *f*; (legal) perjuicio *m*; **you're such a —!** ¡qué pesado eres tú! **— tax** impuesto de consumo *m*

nuke [nuk] N arma nuclear *f*; VT (bomb) bombardear con armas nucleares; (cook) calentar en microondas

null [nʌɫ] ADJ nulo; **— and void** nulo

nullify [nʌ́ləfaɪ] VT anular

numb [nʌm] ADJ entumecido; **to get —** entumecerse; VT entumecer

number [nʌ́mbə·] N número *m*; **— one** uno mismo *m*; **—crunching** procesamiento de datos numéricos complejos *m*; VT numerar; VI (total) ascender a; **I — him among my friends** lo cuento entre mis amigos

numberless [nʌ́mbəlɪs] ADJ sin número
numbskull, numskull [nʌ́mskʌl] N
zopenco -ca *mf*
numeral [núməəl] N número *m*; ADJ
numeral
numerical [numérɪkəl] ADJ numérico
numerous [núməəs] ADJ numeroso
nun [nʌn] N monja *f*, religiosa *f*
nuptial [nʌ́pʃəl] ADJ nupcial; N —s nupcias *f*
pl
nurse [nɝs] N (for the sick) enfermero -a *mf*;
(for children) niñera *f*; VT (give milk)
amamantar, lactar; (tend to a sick person)
cuidar; **to — a grudge** guardar rencor; **to
— a cup of coffee** tomar una taza de
café a sorbitos; **to — a cold** cuidarse
durante un resfrío; VI (drink milk) mamar
nursery [nɝ́sri] N (children's room) cuarto
para niños *m*; (day-care center) guardería
f; (place for growing plants) almáciga *f*,
vivero *m*, plantel *m*; **— rhyme** canción
infantil *f*, ronda *f*; **— school** pre-escolar
m; *Sp* parvulario *m*; *Am* jardín infantil *m*
nursing [nɝ́sɪŋ] N (profession) enfermería *f*;
(care) cuidado *m*; **— home** (for old
people) hogar de ancianos *m*; (for sick
people) casa de salud *f*
nurture [nɝ́tʃə] VT (rear) criar; (feed) nutrir,
alimentar; (encourage) fomentar; N
(rearing) crianza *f*; (feeding) alimentación
f
nut [nʌt] N (fruit) fruto seco *m*; (device)
tuerca *f*; (person) excéntrico -ca *mf*;
—cracker cascanueces *m sg*; **—meg** nuez
moscada *f*; **—s** *vulg* cojones *m pl*; **he's —s**
está loco; **—s and bolts** los fundamentos;
—shell cáscara de fruto seco *f*; **in a
—shell** en pocas palabras
nutrient [nútriənt] N nutriente *m*
nutrition [nutríʃən] N nutrición *f*,
alimentación *f*
nutritious [nutríʃəs] ADJ nutritivo,
alimenticio
nylon [náɪlɑn] N nilón *m*, nailon *m*

Oo

oak [ok] N roble *m*, encina *f*; **— grove**
robledal *m*
oar [ɔr] N remo *m*; VI/VT remar, bogar; **—lock**
tolete *m*
OAS (Organization of American States)
[oeś] N OEA *f*

oasis [oésɪs] N oasis *m*
oat [ot] N avena *f*; **—meal** (flour) harina de
avena *f*; (breakfast food) gachas de avena *f*
pl; **—s** avena *f*
oath [oθ] N (pledge) juramento *m*; (curse)
maldición *f*; (swear word) palabrota *f*, taco
m; **to take an —** prestar juramento
obedience [obídiəns] N obediencia *f*
obedient [obídiənt] ADJ obediente
obese [obís] ADJ obeso
obesity [obísɪdi] N obesidad *f*
obey [obé] VI/VT obedecer
obituary [obítʃueri] N nota necrológica *f*,
obituario *m*
object [ábdʒɪkt] N objeto *m*; (of a verb)
complemento *m*; [əbdʒékt] VI/VT objetar
objection [əbdʒékʃən] N objeción *f*
objective [əbdʒéktɪv] ADJ objetivo; N objetivo
m
obligate [ábləget] VT obligar
obligation [abləgéʃən] N obligación *f*; **under
no — to buy** sin compromiso de compra
obligatory [əblígətɔri] ADJ obligatorio
oblige [əbláɪdʒ] VT (make obliged) obligar; VI/
VT (do a favor for) complacer; VI (obey an
order) obedecer; **much —d!** ¡muchas
gracias! ¡muy agradecido!
obliging [əbláɪdʒɪŋ] ADJ complaciente; *Am*
comedido
oblique [oblík] ADJ oblicuo
obliterate [əblídəret] VT (blot out) tachar;
(destroy) arrasar, destruir
oblivion [əblíviən] N olvido *m*
oblivious [əblíviəs] ADJ inconsciente; **— to
the danger** ajeno al peligro
obnoxious [əbnákʃəs] ADJ (remark, behavior)
ofensivo; (person) molesto
oboe [óbo] N oboe *m*
obscene [əbsín] ADJ obsceno; **his salary is
—** lo que gana es escandaloso
obscenity [əbsénɪdi] N obscenidad *f*
obscure [əbskjúr] ADJ oscuro; VT oscurecer
obscurity [əbskjúrɪdi] N oscuridad *f*
obsequious [əbsíkwiəs] ADJ obsequioso
observance [əbzɝ́vəns] N observancia *f*
observant [əbzɝ́vənt] ADJ observador
observation [abzɝvéʃən] N observación *f*
observatory [əbzɝ́vətɔri] N observatorio *m*
observe [əbzɝ́v] VT observar; (holidays,
rituals) guardar
observer [əbzɝ́və] N observador -ra *mf*
obsess [əbsés] VI/VT obsesionar(se); **he's
—ing over it** está obsesionado
obsession [əbséʃən] N obsesión *f*
obsessive-compulsive [əbsésɪvkəmpʌ́lsɪv]
ADJ obsesivo-compulsivo
obsolescence [absəlésəns] N desuso *m*

obsolete [ɑbsəlít] ADJ anticuado, desusado

obstacle [ábstəkəł] N obstáculo *m*

obstetrics [abstétriks] N obstetricia *f*

obstinacy [ábstənəsi] N obstinación *f*, terquedad *f*, porfía *f*

obstinate [ábstənɪt] ADJ obstinado, terco, recalcitrante; **to be** — obstinarse

obstruct [əbstrÁkt] VI/VT obstruir; (traffic) atascar, obstruir

obstruction [əbstrÁkʃən] N obstrucción *f*

obtain [əbtén] VT obtener, procurar; VI prevalecer

obtainable [əbténəbəł] ADJ conseguible

obviate [ábviet] VT hacer innecesario

obvious [ábviəs] ADJ obvio, evidente

occasion [əkéʒən] N (moment) ocasión *f*; (chance) oportunidad *f*, ocasión *f*; (cause) motivo *m*; (event) acontecimiento *m*, ocasión *f*; VT ocasionar

occasional [əkéʒənəł] ADJ ocasional

occasionally [əkéʒənəli] ADV de vez en cuando, ocasionalmente

occidental [aksidéntł] ADJ & N occidental *mf*

occult [əkÁłt] ADJ oculto; N ocultismo *m*, ciencias ocultas *f pl*; VT ocultar

occupant [ákjəpənt] N ocupante *mf*

occupation [akjəpéʃən] N ocupación *f*

occupy [ákjəpai] VI/VT ocupar

occur [əkɚ] VI ocurrir, suceder; **it —red to me** se me ocurrió

occurrence [əkɚəns] N suceso *m*, acontecimiento *m*

ocean [óʃən] N océano *m*

oceanography [oʃənágrəfi] N oceanografía *f*

ocelot [ásəlɑt] N ocelote *m*

o'clock [əklák] ADV **it is one** — es la una; **it is two** — son las dos

octagon [áktəgən] N octágono *m*, octógono *m*

octane [ákten] N octano *m*

octave [áktɪv] N octava *f*

October [aktóbɚ] N octubre *m*

octopus [áktəpəs] N pulpo *m*

OD (overdose) [odí] N sobredosis *f*; VI tomar una sobredosis

odd [ad] ADJ (unusual) extraño; (not even) impar, non; **—ball** excéntrico -ca *mf*; **— change** suelto *m*, cambio *m*; **— job** trabajo ocasional *m*; **— shoe** zapato sin compañero *m*; **thirty-—** treinta y tantos

oddity [áɒiti] N rareza *f*; (person) excéntrico -ca *mf*

odds [adz] N (probabilities) probabilidades *f pl*; **— and ends** cachivaches *m pl*; **—on favorite** favorito *m*; **the — are against me** llevo las de perder; **to be at** — estar en desacuerdo

ode [od] N oda *f*

odious [óɒiəs] ADJ odioso

odor [óɒɚ] N olor *m*; (bad) hedor *m*

odorless [óɒɚlɪs] ADJ inodoro

odorous [óɒɚəs] ADJ oloroso

of [ʌv] PREP de; **— course** por supuesto, desde luego; **a quarter — five** las cinco menos cuarto; **doctor — medicine** doctor -ra en medicina *mf*; **the smell — paint** el olor a pintura; **a friend — mine** un amigo mío

off [ɔf] ADV **— and on** de vez en cuando; **— the record** extraoficialmente; **ten cents —** rebaja de diez centavos *f*; **ten miles —** a diez millas de distancia; **to take a day —** tomarse un día libre; ADJ **— chance** posibilidad remota *f*; **—color** verde; **— season** temporada baja *f*; **— year** de producción decreciente; **our deal is —** se canceló nuestro plan; **prices are —** los precios han caído; **you're — by a mile** estás equivocadísimo; **he's a little —** está tocadito; **with his hat —** sin el sombrero; **the electricity is —** está apagada la electricidad; **to be — to war** haberse ido a la guerra; **to be well —** tener mucho dinero; PREP **— course** fuera de curso; **he drove — the road** se salió de la carretera; **I bought it — a gypsy** se lo compré a un gitano; **he's — playing golf** se fue a jugar al golf; VT liquidar

off-duty [ɔfdúɒi] ADJ **to be** — no estar de turno

offend [əfénd] VI/VT (insult) ofender, afrentar; (affect disagreeably) desagradar

offender [əféndɚ] N delincuente *mf*

offense [əféns] N (sin, insult) ofensa *f*; (misdemeanor) delito *m*; **no — was meant** no te lo tomes a mal; [áfens] (in sports) ofensiva *f*

offensive [əfénsɪv] ADJ ofensivo; N ofensiva *f*

offer [ɔfɚ] VT ofrecer; **to — to** ofrecerse a; N oferta *f*

offering [ɔfɚɪŋ] N (thing given in worship) ofrenda *f*; (thing presented for sale) oferta *f*; (action of offering) ofrecimiento *m*

offhand [ɔfhǽnd] ADV **he remarked —** mencionó al descuido; ADJ **an — remark** un comentario descuidado

office [ɔfɪs] N (function) cargo *m*, función *f*; (place) oficina *f*, despacho *m*; (headquarters) oficinas *f pl*; **— boy** mandadero de oficina *m*; **— building** edificio para oficinas *m*; **through the —s of** por la intervención de

officer [ɔfɪsɚ] N (military) oficial *m*; (police) agente de policía *mf*; (of an organization) directivo -va *mf*

official [əfíʃəł] ADJ oficial; N funcionario -ria *mf*

officiate [əfíʃiet] VI oficiar; (in sports) arbitrar

officious [əfíʃəs] ADJ oficioso

off-key [ɔfkí] ADJ desafinado

off-limits [ɔflímɪts] ADJ vedado

off-season [ɔfsízən] ADJ de temporada baja

offset [ɔfsɛt] N offset *m*; VT compensar

offshore [ɔfʃɔr] ADJ & ADV cerca de la costa; — **drilling** explotación petrolífera en el fondo del mar *f*

offspring [ɔfsprɪŋ] N prole *m*

offstage [ɔfstédʒ] ADV & ADJ entre bastidores, fuera de escena

often [ɔfən] ADV a menudo; **how** — ? ¿con qué frecuencia? ¿cada cuánto?

ogre [óɡɚ] N ogro *m*

ohm [om] N ohmio *m*

oil [ɔɪl] N (for cars, cooking) aceite *m*; (crude) petróleo *m*; —**can** alcuza *f*, aceitera *f*; —**cloth** hule *m*, tela de hule *f*; — **field** yacimiento petrolífero *m*; — **lamp** quinqué *m*; — **painting** pintura al óleo *f*, óleo *m*; — **pan** cárter *m*; — **rig** plataforma petrolífera *f*; — **slick** mancha de petróleo *f*; — **well** pozo de petróleo *m*; VT (apply oil) aceitar; (bribe) untar

oily [ɔɪli] ADJ aceitoso, oleoso; (unctuous) untuoso

oink [ɔɪŋk] VI gruñir; N gruñido *m*

ointment [ɔɪntmənt] N ungüento *m*

OK [oké] ADJ bueno; ADV bien; **he's an** — **guy** es un buen tipo; **it's** — (fine) está bien; (adequate) es regular; **to give one's** — dar el visto bueno; VT dar el visto bueno, aprobar

okra [ókrə] N quingombó *m*

old [oɫd] ADJ viejo; (objects only) antiguo; (wine) añejo; — **age** vejez *f*, ancianidad *f*; —**fashioned** (unfashionable) pasado de moda; (antiquated) anticuado; (morally prudish) chapado a la antigua; — **fogey** carcamal *m*, carca *m*; — **hat** pasado de moda; — **maid** solterona *f*; —**time** antiguo, viejo; —**timer** (long-time member) miembro de la vieja guardia *m*; (oldster) viejo *m*; — **wives' tale** superstición *f*; — **world** viejo mundo *m*; **days of** — antaño; **how** — **are you?** ¿cuántos años tienes? — **man** (husband) marido *m*; (father) *fam* viejo *m*; **I'm not** — **enough to drive** soy muy joven para conducir; **to be an** — **hand at** ser ducho en

olden [óɫdən] ADJ **in** — **days** antaño

oldie [óɫdi] N viejo éxito *m*

oleander [óliændɚ] N adelfa *f*

olfactory [ɔɫfæktəri] ADJ olfatorio

olive [áɫɪv] N (tree) olivo *m*; (fruit) aceituna *f*, oliva *f*; — **branch** ramo de olivo *m*; — **grove** olivar *m*; — **oil** aceite de oliva *m*; — **wood** madera de olivo *m*; ADJ verde oliva

Olympiad [olímpiæd] N olimpiada *f*

Olympic [olímpɪk] ADJ olímpico; — **Games** Olimpiadas *f pl*, Juegos Olímpicos *m pl*

Oman [omán] N Omán *m*

Omani [ománi] ADJ & N omaní *mf*

omelet [áɱlɪt] N tortilla francesa *f*

omen [ómən] N agüero *m*, presagio *m*

ominous [ámənəs] ADJ (threatening) amenazador; (like an omen) agorero

omission [omíʃən] N omisión *f*

omit [omít] VT omitir

omnipotence [amnípətəns] N omnipotencia *f*

omnipotent [amnípətənt] ADJ omnipotente

omniscience [amníʃəns] N omnisciencia *f*

omniscient [amníʃənt] ADJ omnisciente

omnivorous [amnívɚəs] ADJ omnívoro

on [ɑn] PREP en, sobre, encima de; — **the table** en/sobre/encima de la mesa; — **all sides** por todos lados; — **arriving** al llegar; — **call** de guardia; — **credit** al fiado; — **drugs** drogado; — **horseback** a caballo; —**line** en linea; — **Monday** el lunes; — **purpose** a propósito; — **screen** en la pantalla; — **the house** la casa paga; — **time** a tiempo; **a book** — **stamps** un libro sobre sellos; **do you have any cigarettes** — **you?** ¿tienes cigarros? **drunk** — **beer** borracho de cerveza; **to talk** — **the phone** hablar por teléfono; ADV — **and** — dale que dale; ADJ **his hat is** — lleva puesto el sombrero; **the light is** — está encendida la luz; **there's a war** — estamos en guerra; **you're** — (broadcasting) estás en el aire

once [wʌns] ADV (in the past, a single time) una vez; (if ever) si alguna vez; — **and for all** una vez por todas; — **in a while** de vez en cuando; — **upon a time** érase una vez; **at** — de inmediato; **just this** — sólo por esta vez; — **removed** primo segundo *m*; CONJ una vez que, cuando; N una vez

oncology [ankálədʒi] N oncología *f*

one [wʌn] ADJ uno; — **book** un libro; — **thousand** mil; —**armed** manco; —**armed bandit** tragaperras *mf sg*; —**eyed** tuerto; — **John Smith** un tal John Smith; —**man band** hombre orquesta *m*; — **on** — mano a mano;

—-sided fight pelea desigual f; **—-upmanship** competitividad f; **—-way street** calle de sentido único f; **his — chance** su única oportunidad; **the — and only** el único; **this is — smart dog** es un perro muy listo; N & PRON uno m; **— at a time** de a uno; **— by —** uno por uno; **love — another** amaos los unos a los otros; **the — who** el/la que; **the green —** el verde; **this —** este/esta

oneself [wʌnsélf] PRON **to be —** ser uno mismo; **to sit by —** estar sentado solo; **to talk to —** hablar para sí; **to look at — in the mirror** mirarse en el espejo; **to buy — a house** comprarse una casa

ongoing [ángoɪŋ] ADJ continuo

onion [ánjən] N cebolla f; **— patch** cebollar m

onlooker [ánlʊkə-] N espectador -ra mf, mirón -ona mf

only [ónli] ADJ único; ADV sólo, solamente; **I — just caught the train** por poco pierdo el tren; CONJ sólo que, pero

onomatopoeia [anəmɑɒəpíə] N onomatopeya f

onset [ánset] N comienzo m

onto [ɑntu] PREP en, sobre, encima de; **he placed it — the top of the refrigerator** lo colocó encima de la nevera; **I'm — your plot** conozco tu plan

onward [ánwə-d] ADV hacia adelante

onyx [ánɪks] N ónix m

oops [ʊps] INTERJ ¡huy!

ooze [uz] VI/VT rezumar(se); N cieno m

opal [ópəł] N ópalo m

opaque [opék] ADJ opaco

OPEC (Organization of Petroleum Exporting Countries) [ópɛk] N OPEP f

open [ópən] VI/VT abrir(se); **to — into** comunicarse con; **to — one's way** abrirse paso; **to — onto** dar a; **to — up** abrirse; ADJ abierto; **— and shut** claro, evidente; **— door policy** política de acceso libre f; **—-ended** abierto; **—-heart surgery** cirujía de corazón abierto f; **—-minded** de amplias miras; **—-mouthed** boquiabierto; **— question** cuestión discutible f; **— season** temporada de caza f; **— to criticism** expuesto a la crítica; N (outdoors) aire libre m; (tournament) abierto m

opener [ópənə-] N abridor m; (in sports) primer partido m; **for —s** para empezar

opening [ópənɪŋ] N (open space) abertura f; (act of making or becoming open, ceremony) apertura f; (beginning)

comienzo m; (clearing) claro m; (vacancy) vacante m; (pretext) oportunidad f; **— night** estreno m

opera [ápərə] N ópera f; **— glasses** gemelos m pl; **— house** ópera f

operable [ápə-əbəł] ADJ operable

operate [ápəret] VI (function) funcionar; (intervene surgically) operar; **to — on a person** operar a una persona; VT (run a machine) manejar; (administrate) dirigir; (make function) accionar

operating room [ápəreɒɪŋrum] N sala de operaciones f, quirófano m

operation [apəréʃən] N (surgical intervention, mission, math function) operación f; (function) funcionamiento m; (use of a machine) manejo m; **to be in —** (law) estar vigente; (machine) estar funcionando

operative [ápə-əɒɪv] ADJ (law) vigente; (contract provision) pertinente; (word) clave; N (machine worker) operario -ria mf; (spy) agente mf

operator [ápə-eɒə-] N (telephone, math) operador -ra mf; (machine) operario -ria mf; (stock) especulador -ra mf; **he's a smooth —** es un astuto

opinion [əpínjən] N opinión f

opium [ópiəm] N opio m

opossum [əpásəm] N zarigüeya f

opponent [əpónənt] N opositor -ora mf, contrincante mf, adversario -ria mf

opportune [apə-tún] ADJ oportuno

opportunistic [apə-tunístɪk] ADJ oportunista, aprovechado

opportunity [apə-túnɪɒi] N oportunidad f, ocasión f

oppose [əpóz] VI/VT oponer(se)

opposing [əpózɪŋ] ADJ opuesto, contrario; **— thumb** pulgar oponible m

opposite [ápəzɪt] ADJ (contrary) opuesto, contrario; **— to** frente a; PREP frente a, en frente de; N contrario m, opuesto m; ADV en frente

opposition [apəzíʃən] N oposición f; **they met with little —** encontraron poca resistencia

oppress [əprés] VT oprimir

oppression [əpréʃən] N opresión f

oppressive [əprésɪv] ADJ (harsh) opresivo; (heat) bochornoso, sofocante

oppressor [əprésə-] N opresor -ra mf

optic [áptɪk] ADJ óptico; N **—s** óptica f

optical [áptɪkəł] ADJ óptico; **— fiber** fibra óptica f; **— illusion** ilusión óptica f

optician [aptíʃən] N óptico -ca mf

optimism [áptəmɪzəm] N optimismo m

optimist [áptəmɪst] N optimista *mf*
optimistic [aptəmístɪk] ADJ optimista
option [ápʃən] N opción *f* (also financial);
(feature) extra *m*; **to leave one's —s
open** no descartar posibilidades
optional [ápʃənəł] ADJ opcional, optativo
optometry [aptámɪtri] N optometría *f*
opulence [ápjələns] N opulencia *f*
opulent [ápjələnt] ADJ opulento
or [ɔr] CONJ o; **seven — eight** siete u ocho
oracle [ɔ́rəkəł] N oráculo *m*
oral [ɔ́rəł] ADJ oral; (hygiene) bucal
orange [ɔ́rɪndʒ] N naranja *f*; **— blossom**
azahar *m*; **— grove** naranjal *m*; **— tree**
naranjo *m*; ADJ anaranjado
orangutan [ərǽŋətæn] N orangután *m*
orator [ɔ́rəɖə-] N orador -ra *mf*
oratory [ɔ́rətɔri] N (skill in speaking) oratoria
f; (place for prayer) oratorio *m*
orbit [ɔ́rbɪt] N órbita *f*; VI/VT orbitar
orbital [ɔ́rbɪɖəł] ADJ orbital
orbiter [ɔ́rbɪɖə-] N orbitador *m*
orchard [ɔ́rtʃə-d] N huerto *m*; (large) huerta *f*
orchestra [ɔ́rkɪstrə] N orquesta *f*
orchestrate [ɔ́rkɪstret] VT orquestar
orchid [ɔ́rkɪd] N orquídea *f*
ordain [ɔrdén] VT (as minister) ordenar;
(with an edict) decretar
ordeal [ɔrdíł] N suplicio *m*, tortura *f*; **— by
fire** ordalía de fuego *f*
order [ɔ́rɖə-] N (command) orden *f*, mandato
m; (request, commission) pedido *m*;
(obedience to law, sequence, regime)
orden *m*; **holy —s** órdenes sagradas *f pl*;
an apology is in — corresponde una
disculpa; **in — to** para; **in working —**
en buen estado; **in — that** para que, a fin
de que; **to the — of** a la orden de; **out
of —** no funciona; **to put in —** ordenar;
VI/VT (command, arrange) ordenar,
mandar; (ask for) pedir
orderly [ɔ́rɖə-li] ADJ ordenado; N (military)
ordenanza *m*; (hospital) camillero *m*
ordinal [ɔ́rdnəł] ADJ ordinal
ordinance [ɔ́rdnəns] N ordenanza *f*
ordinary [ɔ́rdneri] ADJ común, corriente,
ordinario; **do it the — way** hazlo de la
forma habitual
ore [ɔr] N mineral *m*
oregano [ərégano] N orégano *m*
organ [ɔ́rgan] N órgano *m* (also musical
instrument)
organic [ɔrgǽnɪk] ADJ orgánico; **—
chemistry** química orgánica *f*
organism [ɔ́rgənɪzəm] N organismo *m*
organist [ɔ́rgənɪst] N organista *mf*
organization [ɔrgənɪzéʃən] N organización *f*

organize [ɔ́rgənaɪz] VI/VT organizar(se)
organizer [ɔ́rgənaɪzə-] N organizador -ra *mf*
orgasm [ɔ́rgæzəm] N orgasmo *m*
orgy [ɔ́rdʒi] N orgía *f*
orient [ɔ́riənt] N oriente *m*; [ɔ́riɛnt] VT
orientar
oriental [ɔriɛ́ntł] ADJ & N oriental *mf*
orientate [ɔ́riɛntet] VT orientar
orientation [ɔriɛntéʃən] N (guidance)
orientación *f*; (tendency, leaning)
tendencia *f*
orifice [ɔ́rəfɪs] N orificio *m*
origin [ɔ́rədʒɪn] N origen *m*; (of a river)
naciente *f*, nacimiento *m*
original [ərídʒənəł] ADJ & N original *m*
originality [ərɪdʒənǽlɪɖi] N originalidad *f*
originate [ərídʒənet] VI/VT originar(se)
oriole [ɔ́rioł] N oropéndola *f*
Orlonᵀᴹ [ɔ́rlɑn] N orlón *m*
ornament [ɔ́rnəmənt] N adorno *m*,
ornamento *m*; [ɔ́rnəment] VT adornar,
ornamentar
ornamental [ɔrnəméntł] ADJ ornamental
ornate [ɔrnét] ADJ adornado en exceso; **—
style** estilo rebuscado *m*
ornithology [ɔrnəθάlədʒi] N ornitología *f*
orphan [ɔ́rfən] ADJ & N huérfano -na *mf*; VT
dejar huérfano a
orphanage [ɔ́rfənɪdʒ] N orfanato *m*, hospicio
m
orthodontics [ɔrθədántɪks] N ortodoncia *f*
orthodox [ɔ́rθədaks] ADJ ortodoxo
orthography [ɔrθάgrəfi] N ortografía *f*
oscillate [ásəlet] VI oscilar; VT hacer oscilar
oscillation [asəléʃən] N oscilación *f*
osmosis [azmósɪs] N ósmosis *f*
osprey [áspre] N águila pescadora *f*
ostensible [asténsəbəł] ADJ aparente
ostentation [astentéʃən] N ostentación *f*
ostentatious [astentéʃəs] ADJ ostentoso
osteoporosis [astiopərósɪs] N osteoporosis *f*
ostracize [ástrəsaɪz] VT aislar
ostrich [ástrɪtʃ] N avestruz *m*
other [Áðə-] ADJ, PRON & N otro -tra *mf*; **—
than Bob** salvo Bob; **every — day** cada
dos días, un día sí y otro no; **—wise** de
otro modo; **—worldly** fantástico
otter [áɖə-] N nutria *f*
ouch [autʃ] INTERJ ¡ay!
ought [ɔt] V AUX **you — to sit down**
deberías sentarte; **we — to get up early**
deberíamos levantarnos más temprano
ounce [auns] N onza *f*
our [aur] POSS ADJ nuestro
ours [aurz] ADJ nuestro; **this book is —** este
libro es nuestro; **these things are —**
estas cosas son nuestras; PRON el nuestro;

— is bigger el nuestro/la nuestra es más grande; **a friend of —** un amigo nuestro

ourselves [aʊrsélvz] PRON **we made the cake —** nosotros mismos hicimos la torta; **we were sitting by —** estábamos sentados solos; **we look at — in the mirror** nos miramos en el espejo; **we bought — a house** nos compramos una casa

oust [aʊst] VT echar, expulsar

out [aʊt] ADV (outside) fuera; ADJ (turned off, extinguished) apagado; INTERJ ¡fuera! N escape m; VT (expel) expulsar; (expose) descubrir; VI **the truth will —** se descubrirá la verdad; PREP **she ran — the door** salió corriendo por la puerta; **they locked me — and** me dejaron fuera; **— and — criminal** criminal empedernido f; **— and — refusal** una negativa rotunda; **— of commission/order** fuera de servicio; **—-of-date** pasado de moda, anticuado; **— of fashion** pasado de moda; **— of fear** por miedo; **— of joint** dislocado; **— of money** sin dinero; **— of print/stock** agotado; **— of touch with** desconectado de; **— of tune** desentonado; **— of work** desempleado; **made — of** hecho de; **miniskirts are on the way —** las minifaldas se están dejando de usar; **I had it — with him** me peleé con él; **you were —** no estabas; **before the week is —** antes de que termine la semana; **the book is just —** acaba de publicarse el libro; **the secret is —** se ha divulgado el secreto; **we had some, but now we're —** teníamos, pero se nos acabó; **I'm — $10** perdí $10

outage [áʊdɪʤ] N apagón m

outbreak [áʊtbrek] N (of pimples) erupción f; (of war) comienzo m; (of disease) brote m

outburst [áʊtbɚst] N (emotional) arrebato m; (of tears) ataque m; (of violence) motín m, explosión f

outcast [áʊtkæst] ADJ & N marginado -da mf

outcome [áʊtkʌm] N resultado m

outcry [áʊtkraɪ] N clamor m, protesta f

outdated [aʊtdéɪɾɪd] ADJ anticuado

outdoor [áʊtdɔr] ADJ al aire libre; [aʊtdɔ́rz] ADV **-s** al aire libre, afuera

outer [áʊdɚ] ADJ exterior; **— ear** oído externo m; **— space** espacio exterior m

outfit [áʊtfɪt] N (gear) equipo m; (clothes) conjunto m; (soldiers) unidad f; VI/VT equipar, habilitar

outfox [aʊtfáks] VT ser más listo que

outgoing [áʊtɡoɪŋ] ADJ (leaving) saliente; [aʊtɡóɪŋ] (extrovert) extrovertido

outgrow [aʊtɡró] VT **she will — her clothes** le quedará la ropa pequeña; **she will — her epilepsy** la epilepsia se le irá con la edad

outing [áʊdɪŋ] N excursión f, paseo m

outlandish [aʊtlǽndɪʃ] ADJ estrafalario

outlast [aʊtlǽst] VT (last longer than) durar más que; (live longer than) sobrevivir a

outlaw [áʊtlɔ] N bandido -da mf, forajido -da mf; VT prohibir

outlay [áʊtle] N gasto m, desembolso m; [aʊtlé] VT gastar, desembolsar

outlet [áʊtlɪt] N (exit) salida f; (stream) desagüe m, emisario m; (store) tienda f; (electric connection) toma de corriente f; **she needs an — for her talent** necesita canalizar su talento

outline [áʊtlaɪn] N (abstract) bosquejo m, esbozo m, trazado m; (boundary) contorno m; VT (summarize) bosquejar, esbozar; (draw) delinear; (plan) trazar

outlook [áʊtlʊk] N perspectiva f, panorama m

outlying [áʊtlaɪŋ] ADJ (marginal) periférico; (distant) remoto

output [áʊtpʊt] N (production) rendimiento m; (computer information) salida f

outrage [áʊtreʤ] N (offense) ultraje m, agravio m, atropello m; (indignation) indignación f; VT (offend) ultrajar, agraviar; (enrage) indignar

outrageous [aʊtréʤəs] ADJ (offensive) ultrajante; (exorbitant) exorbitante; (extravagant) extravagante

outreach [áʊtritʃ] N extensión f; [aʊtrítʃ] VT exceder

outright [aʊtráɪt] ADV completamente; **he bought it —** lo compró al contado; **he rejected it —** lo rechazó categóricamente; [áʊtraɪt] ADJ **— denial** negativa rotunda f; **— lie** mentira descarada f

outset [áʊtset] N comienzo m, principio m

outshine [aʊtʃáɪn] VT eclipsar

outside [aʊtsáɪd] ADV fuera, afuera; PREP fuera de; [áʊtsaɪd] ADJ (external) exterior; (foreign) foráneo; N exterior m; **— chance** posibilidad remota f; **in a week, at the —** en una semana, a lo sumo; **to close on the —** cerrar por fuera

outsider [aʊtsáɪdɚ] N forastero -ra mf

outskirts [áʊtskɚts] N alrededores m pl, afueras f pl

outspoken [aʊtspókən] ADJ franco

outstanding [aʊtstǽndɪŋ] ADJ (excellent) sobresaliente, destacado; (pending) pendiente

outstretched [autstrétʃt] ADJ extendido

outward [áutwə·d] ADJ exterior, externo; — **appearances** apariencias f pl; ADV hacia fuera; — **bound** que sale

outweigh [autwé] VT (weigh more) pesar más que; (be more important) sobreponerse a, valer más que

outwit [autwít] VT ser más listo que

oval [óvəł] ADJ oval, ovalado; N óvalo m

ovary [óvəri] N ovario m

ovation [ovéʃən] N ovación f

oven [ávən] N horno m

over [óvə·] PREP — **here** acá; — **in Japan** allá en Japón; — **many years** durante muchos años; — **the sea** al otro lado del mar; — **the hill** viejo; — **there** allá; **an umbrella** — **his head** un paraguas sobre la cabeza; **I heard it** — **the radio** lo oí por la radio; **he jumped** — **the fence** saltó por encima de la cerca; **he is** — **her in the hierarchy** él está por encima de ella en la jerarquía; **not** — **one year** no más de un año; **he hit him** — **the head with a rock** le golpeó en la cabeza con una piedra; **all** — **the city** por toda la ciudad; ADV — **again** de nuevo, otra vez; — **against** en contraste con; — **and** — una y otra vez; —**generous** demasiado generoso; **do it** — hazlo de nuevo, hazlo otra vez; **the world** — por todo el mundo; **it is** — **with** se acabó; INTERJ — **and out** cambio y fuera

overactive [ovə·ǽktɪv] ADJ hiperactivo, demasiado activo

overall [ovə·ɔ́ł] ADJ global, total; —**s** mono m, overol m

overbearing [ovə·bérɪŋ] ADJ mandón -ona, dominante

overboard [óvə·bɔrd] ADV (into the water) al agua; **she went** — **on her project** se le fue la mano con su proyecto

overcast [óvə·kæst] ADJ nublado, encapotado; **to become** — nublarse, encapotarse

overcharge [ovə·tʃárʤ] VI/VT cobrar demasiado

overcoat [óvə·kot] N sobretodo m, gabán m

overcome [ovə·kám] VI/VT (to get the better of) superar; (to overwhelm) embargar; **to be** — **by weariness** estar agobiado

overdose [óvə·dos] N sobredosis f; VI tomar una sobredosis

overdraft [óvə·dræft] N sobregiro m, descubierto m

overdraw [ovə·drɔ́] VI/VT sobregirar(se)

overdrawn [ovə·drɔ́n] ADJ en descubierto, sobregirado

overdrive [óvə·draɪv] N superdirecta f

overdue [ovə·dú] ADJ (borrowed item) atrasado; (bill) vencido

overeat [ovə·ít] VI comer en exceso

overexcite [ovə·ɪksáɪt] VT sobreexcitar

overflow [ovə·fló] VI desbordarse, rebosar; [óvə·flo] N desborde m

overgrown [ovə·grón] ADJ cubierto, crecido; — **boy** muchacho demasiado crecido para su edad m

overhang [ovə·hǽŋ] VI (jut) proyectarse; (hang over) estar suspendido; [óvə·hæŋ] N saliente m

overhaul [ovə·hɔ́ł] VT revisar; [óvə·hɔł] N revisión f

overhead [óvə·hed] N gastos generales mf; ADJ elevado; — **projector** retroproyector m; [ovə·héd] ADV en lo alto

overhear [ovə·hír] VT oír por casualidad

overkill [óvə·kɪł] N exageración f

overland [óvə·lænd] ADV & ADJ por tierra

overlap [ovə·lǽp] VI/VT solapar(se), superponer(se); [óvə·læp] N traslapo m

overlay [ovə·lé] VT cubrir; (with gold, etc.) incrustar; [óvə·le] N cubierta f; (with metal, wood) revestimiento m, chapa f

overload [ovə·lód] VT sobrecargar, recargar, saturar; [óvə·lod] N sobrecarga f

overlook [ovə·lúk] VT (fail to mention) pasar por alto, omitir; (pardon) perdonar; (look from above) mirar desde arriba; (afford a view of) dar a, tener vista a; [óvə·luk] N mirador m

overly [óvə·li] ADV excesivamente

overnight [óvə·naɪt] ADJ — **delivery** entrega al otro día f; — **guest** invitado -da a dormir mf; [ovə·náɪt] ADV **he succeeded** — tuvo éxito de la noche a la mañana

overpass [óvə·pæs] N paso elevado m

overpower [ovə·páυə·] VT vencer

overqualified [ovə·kwálə·faɪd] ADJ sobrecalificado

overreach [ovə·rítʃ] VI **to** — **oneself** abarcar demasiado

overreact [ovə·riǽkt] VI reaccionar exageradamente

override [ovə·ráɪd] VT anular

overrule [ovə·rúł] VT anular

overrun [ovə·rán] VT (overflow) desbordarse; (exceed) exceder; (invade) infestar; [óvə·rʌn] N exceso m

overseas [ovə·síz] ADV (beyond the sea) en ultramar; (abroad) en el extranjero

oversee [ovə·sí] VI dirigir, supervisar

overseer [óvə·sir] N capataz -za mf, supervisor -ra mf

overshadow [ovə·ʃǽdo] VT eclipsar, opacar

overshoe [óvəʃu] N chanclo *m*
oversight [óvəsaɪt] N (mistake) descuido *m*; (act of overseeing) supervisión *f*
overstep [ovəstép] VT excederse en
overt [ovə́t] ADJ evidente
overtake [ovəték] VT (pass someone) pasar, rebasar; (befall) abatirse sobre
overtax [ovətǽks] VT (tax too much) gravar excesivamente; (demand too much) exigir demasiado
overthrow [ovəθró] VT derrocar, derribar; [óvəθro] N derrocamiento *m*
overtime [óvətaɪm] N (at work) horas extras *f pl*; (in a game) prórroga *f*; **to work —** hacer horas extras
overture [óvətʃə] N (musical composition) obertura *f*; (initial move) propuesta *f*
overturn [ovətə́n] VI/VT volcar(se); VT (a decision) anular; (a government) derrocar
overview [óvəvju] N vista global *f*, panorama *m*
overweight [ovəwét] ADJ **he's —** pesa demasiado; [óvəwet] N sobrepeso *m*
overwhelm [ovəhwélm] VT abrumar, agobiar
overwhelming [ovəhwélmɪŋ] ADJ (responsibility, task) abrumador, agobiante; (victory) arrollador
overwork [ovəwə́k] VI trabajar demasiado; VT hacer trabajar demasiado; [óvəwɜk] N exceso de trabajo *m*
ovulate [ávjəlet] VI ovular
owe [o] VI/VT deber; (a sum) adeudar, deber
owing [óɪŋ] ADJ debido a; **— to** debido a
owl [auɬ] N lechuza *f*, búho *m*
own [on] ADJ & PRON propio; **a house of his —** una casa suya; **to be on one's —** ser independiente; **to come into one's —** conseguir lo que uno se merece; **to hold one's —** mantenerse firme; VT poseer; **to — up (to)** confesar
owner [ónə] N dueño -ña *mf*, propietario -ria *mf*
ownership [ónəʃɪp] N propiedad *f*
ox [aks] N buey *m*
oxidize [áksɪdaɪz] VI/VT oxidar(se)
oxygen [áksɪdʒən] N oxígeno *m*; **— tent** cámara de oxígeno *f*
oyster [5istə] N ostra *f*; (large) ostión *m*
ozone [ózon] N ozono *m*; **— layer** capa de ozono *f*

Pp

pace [pes] N paso *m*; VT (traverse) ir y venir por; (set the pace) marcar al paso; (measure) medir a pasos; **—maker** marcapasos *m sg*
pacific [pəsífɪk] ADJ pacífico; **— Ocean** Océano Pacífico *m*
pacifier [pǽsəfaɪə] N chupete *m*
pacifism [pǽsəfɪzəm] N pacifismo *m*
pacify [pǽsəfaɪ] VT (a country) pacificar; (a person) apaciguar
pack [pæk] N (of wolves) manada *f*; (of dogs) jauría *f*; (of cigarettes) cajilla *f*, cajetilla *f*; (of cloth) compresa *f*; (of cards) baraja *f*; (of cyclists) pelotón *m*; **— animal** acémila *f*, bestia de carga *f*; **a — of lies** una sarta de mentiras; VT empacar, empaquetar; (carry a gun) portar; (crowd) atestar; (load) cargar; **to — off** despachar; **to — one's bags** hacer las maletas; **to — rat** rata urraca *f*; (person who saves everything) urraca *f*
package [pǽkɪdʒ] N paquete *m* (also organized vacation); VT (gift) empaquetar; (food) envasar; (in advertising) presentar
packer [pǽkə] N empacador -ra *mf*, embalador -ra *mf*
packet [pǽkɪt] N paquete *m*; (of soup) sobre *m*
packing [pǽkɪŋ] N embalaje *m* (also cushioning material)
pact [pækt] N pacto *m*
pad [pæd] N (cushion) almohadilla *f* (also for ink); (block of paper) bloc *m*; (for aircraft) pista *f*; (for spacecraft) plataforma de lanzamiento *f*; VT (stuff with padding) acolchar; (add to dishonestly) rellenar
padding [pǽdɪŋ] N relleno *m*; (cotton) guata *f*; (of a speech) ripio *m*
paddle [pǽdl] N (for rowing) pala *f*, remo *m*; (for mixing, beating, ping-pong) paleta *f*; **— wheel** rueda de paleta *f*; VI remar; VT hacer avanzar remando; (hit) dar una paletada
paddock [pǽdɔk] N (field) prado *m*; (enclosure at racetrack) paddock *m*
padlock [pǽdlɑk] N candado *m*; VT cerrar con candado
pagan [pégən] ADJ & N pagano -na *mf*
paganism [pégənɪzəm] N paganismo *m*
page [pedʒ] N (sheet) hoja *f*, página *f*; (boy servant) paje *m*; (hotel employee) botones *m sg*; VT (number pages) paginar; (call)

llamar por altavoz; *Mex* vocear; **to —
through** hojear

pageant [pǽdʒənt] N (parade) desfile *m*;
(show) espectáculo *m*

pail [peł] N balde *m*, cubeta *f*

pain [pen] N dolor *m*; (suffering) sufrimiento
m; **—killer** analgésico *m*; **—staking**
esmerado; **on — of** so pena de; **to take
—s** esmerarse; **he's a —** es un chinche; VT
(physical) doler; (mental) apenar

painful [pénfəł] ADJ (hurting) doloroso;
(distressing) penoso; (difficult) arduo

painless [pénlɪs] ADJ sin dolor, indoloro

paint [pent] N (substance) pintura *f*; (spotted
horse) pinto *m*; **—brush** (for art) pincel
m; (for a house) brocha *f*; VI/VT pintar; **to
— the town red** irse de juerga

painter [péntɚ] N pintor -ra *mf*

painting [péntɪŋ] N pintura *f*

pair [per] N par *m*; (married couple) pareja *f*;
(span) yunta *f*; **a — of scissors** unas
tijeras, una tijera; VI/VT aparear(se),
emparejar(se); **to — off** aparearse

pajamas [pədʒámǝz] N pijama / piyama *mf*

Pakistan [pǽkɪstæn] N Paquistán *m*

Pakistani [pækɪstǽni] ADJ & N paquistano
-na *mf*

pal [pæł] N compañero -ra *mf*, compadre *m*,
comadre *f*

palace [pǽlɪs] N palacio *m*

palate [pǽlɪt] N paladar *m*

palatial [pǝléʃǝł] ADJ suntuoso

Palau [pɑláu] N Paláu *m*

pale [peł] ADJ pálido, macilento; **beyond the
—** grosero; VI palidecer

paleness [pélnɪs] N palidez *f*

paleontology [peliəntálǝdʒi] N paleontología
f

palette [pǽlɪt] N paleta *f*

palisade [pælɪséd] N empalizada *f*; **—s**
acantilados *m pl*

pall [pɔł] VT (cover with a cloth) cubrir con
un paño mortuorio; (satiate) hartar; VI
cansar; N paño mortuorio; **—bearer**
portador del féretro *m*; **to cast a — on**
empañar

pallid [pǽlɪd] ADJ pálido

pallor [pǽlɚ] N palidez *f*

palm [pɑm] N (part of hand) palma *f*; (tree)
palmera *f*, palma *f*; **— Sunday** Domingo
de Ramos *m*; VT (hide in palm)
escamotear; **to — something off on
someone** encajar algo a alguien

palpable [pǽłpǝbǝł] ADJ (perceptible)
palpable; (tangible) tangible

palpitate [pǽłpɪtet] VI palpitar

palpitation [pæłpɪtéʃǝn] N palpitación *f*

paltry [półtri] ADJ miserable, despreciable

pamper [pǽmpɚ] VT mimar, consentir

pamphlet [pǽmflɪt] N (informative) folleto
m; (political) panfleto *m*

pan [pæn] N (for boiling) cazuela *f*, cacerola *f*;
(for frying) sartén *f*; (for baking) molde *m*;
—handle mango de sartén *m*; **—handler**
pordiosero -ra *mf*; VT criticar duramente; VI
to — for gold extraer oro; **to — out** dar
buen resultado; **to —handle** mendigar,
pordiosear

panacea [pænǝsíǝ] N panacea *f*

Panama [pǽnǝmǝ] N Panamá *f*

Panamanian [pænǝméniǝn] ADJ & N
panameño -ña *mf*

Pan-American [pænǝmérɪkǝn] ADJ
panamericano

pancake [pǽnkek] N panqueque *m*; **flat as a
—** chato como una tabla

pancreas [pǽnkriǝs] N páncreas *m*

panda [pǽndǝ] N panda *m*

pander [pǽndɚ] N proxeneta *mf*; VI consentir

pane [pen] N vidrio *m*, cristal *m*

panel [pǽnǝł] N (wall, group of persons)
panel *m*; (of instruments) tablero *m*; VT
revestir con paneles

pang [pæŋ] N (sharp pain, hunger) punzada
f; (anguish) remordimientos *m pl*

panic [pǽnɪk] ADJ & N pánico *m*;
—-stricken sobrecogido de pánico

panorama [pænǝrǽmǝ] N panorama *m*

panoramic [pænǝrǽmɪk] ADJ panorámico

pansy [pǽnzi] N (flower) pensamiento *m*;
(sissy) *offensive* marica *m*

pant [pænt] VI jadear; **to — out** decir
jadeando

panther [pǽnθɚ] N pantera *f*

panties [pǽntiz] N *Sp* bragas *f pl*; *Mex*
pantaletas *f pl*; *RP* bombacha *f*

pantomime [pǽntǝmaɪm] N pantomima *f*

pantry [pǽntri] N despensa *f*, alacena *f*

pants [pænts] N pantalones *m pl*, pantalón *m*

pantyhose [pǽntihoz] N panty *m*

papa [pápǝ] N papá *m*

papacy [pépǝsi] N papado *m*

papaya [pǝpáɪǝ] N papaya *f*; *Cuba* fruta
bomba *f*

paper [pépɚ] N (material) papel *m*;
(newspaper) periódico *m*; (assignment)
trabajo *m*; (oral learned contribution)
comunicación *f*; (written learned
contribution) artículo *m*; **—back** libro en
rústica *m*; **— clip** clip *m*, sujetapapeles *m
sg*; **— cutter** guillotina *f*; **— money** papel
moneda *m*; **—s** papeles *m pl*; **— shredder**
trituradora *f*; **—weight** pisapapeles *m sg*;
—work trámites *m pl*; **on —** por escrito;

vi/vt empapelar

paprika [pæpríka] N pimentón *m*, páprika *f*

Papua New Guinea [pǽpjuənugíni] N Papúa
Nueva Guinea *f*

Papua New Guinean [pǽpjuənugíniən] ADJ
& N papú *mf*

par [par] N (financial) paridad *f*; (in golf) par
m; **at —** a la par; **below —** bajo par; **to
be on a — with** estar en pie de igualdad
con; **to feel above —** sentirse mejor que
lo normal; vt hacer el par

parachute [pǽrəʃut] N paracaídas *m sg*

parachutist [pǽrəʃutist] N paracaidista *mf*

parade [pəréd] N (procession) desfile *m*;
(military review) parada *f*; **— ground**
campo de maniobras *m*; **to make a — of**
ostentar, hacer ostentación de; vi desfilar;
vt hacer ostentación de

paradigm [pǽrədaɪm] N paradigma *m*

paradise [pǽrədaɪs] N paraíso *m*

paradox [pǽrədaks] N paradoja *f*

paradoxical [pærədáksɪkəl] ADJ paradójico

paraffin [pǽrəfɪn] N parafina *f*

paragraph [pǽrəgræf] N párrafo *m*; vt dividir
en párrafos

Paraguay [pǽrəgwaɪ] N Paraguay *m*

Paraguayan [pærəgwáiən] ADJ & N
paraguayo -ya *mf*

parakeet [pǽrəkit] N perico *m*, periquito *m*

parallel [pǽrəlɛl] ADJ & N paralelo *m*;
(geometry) paralela *f*; vt (run equidistant
from) correr paralelo a; (compare)
comparar

paralysis [pərǽləsɪs] N (of the body) parálisis
f; (of a transportation system) paralización
f

paralyze [pǽrəlaɪz] vt paralizar

paramedic [pærəmɛ́dɪk] ADJ & N paramédico
-ca *mf*

parameter [pərǽmɪdə] N parámetro *m*

paramilitary [pærəmílɪteri] ADJ & N
paramilitar *mf*

paramount [pǽrəmaunt] ADJ supremo, sumo

paranoia [pærənɔ́iə] N paranoia *f*

paranoid [pǽrənɔid] ADJ & N paranoico -ca
mf; **— delusion** delirio paranoico *m*

paranormal [pærənɔ́rməl] ADJ paranormal

paraphernalia [pærəfənéljə] N parafernalia *f*

paraphrase [pǽrəfrez] N paráfrasis *f*; vi/vt
parafrasear

parapsychology [pærəsaɪkáləʤi] N
parapsicología *f*

parasite [pǽrəsaɪt] N parásito *m*

parasol [pǽrəsɔl] N parasol *m*, sombrilla *f*

paratroops [pǽrətrups] N tropas
paracaidistas *f pl*

parcel [pársəl] N (package) paquete *m*; (lot)

partida *f*; (land) parcela *f*; **— post** paquete
postal *m*; vt (land) parcelar; **to — out**
repartir

parch [partʃ] vt secar; **I'm —ed** estoy
muerto de sed

parchment [pártʃmənt] N pergamino *m*

pardon [párdn] N perdón *m*, gracia *f*; (legal)
indulto *m*; **I beg your —** perdone; vt
perdonar, disculpar; (legally) indultar

pare [per] vt mondar, pelar; **to — down
expenditures** reducir gastos

parent [pérənt] N padre *m*, madre *f*; **—s**
padres *m pl*

parental [pərɛ́nt] ADJ parental

parenthesis [pərɛ́nθəsɪs] N paréntesis *m*

pariah [pəráiə] N paria *m*

parish [pǽrɪʃ] N parroquia *f*; **— priest** (cura)
párroco *m*

parishioner [pəríʃənə] N feligrés -esa *mf*,
parroquiano -na *mf*

parity [pǽrɪdi] N paridad *f*

park [park] N parque *m*; (for baseball) estadio
de béisbol *m*; vi/vt estacionar, aparcar

parking [párkɪŋ] N estacionamiento *m*,
aparcamiento *m*; **— lot** estacionamiento
m, aparcamiento *m*; **— place** lugar de
estacionamiento / aparcamiento *m*

parlance [párləns] N habla *f*

parley [párli] N (peace negotiation)
parlamento *m*; (discussion) discusión *f*; vi
parlamentar

parliament [párləmənt] N parlamento *m*

parliamentary [parləmɛ́ntri] ADJ
parlamentario

parlor [párlə] N sala *f*, salón *m*; **— game**
juego de salón *m*; **beauty —** salón de
belleza *m*

parochial [pərókiəl] ADJ (of a parish)
parroquial; (provincial) pueblerino

parody [pǽrədi] N parodia *f*; vt parodiar

parole [pəról] N libertad condicional *f*; vt
poner en libertad condicional

parrot [pǽrət] N loro *m*, papagayo *m*; vt
repetir como loro

parry [pǽri] vt (a blow) parar; (a remark)
eludir; N parada *f*

parsley [pársli] N perejil *m*

parsnip [pársnɪp] N chirivía *f*

parson [pársən] N pastor *m*

part [part] N (component) parte *f*; (role)
papel *m*; (in hair) raya *f*; **— and parcel**
parte esencial *f*; **—-time** a tiempo parcial;
in foreign —s en el extranjero; **spare
—s** piezas de repuesto *f pl*, repuestos *m pl*;
vi/vt (cut into parts) partir(se); (divide
into parts) dividir(se); (separate, leave)
separar(se); (apportion) repartir(se); **to —**

company separararse; **to — one's hair** hacerse la raya; **to — with** desprenderse de

partake [pɑrtékʼ] VI **to — in** participar; **to — of** (share) compartir; (eat) comer

partial [pɑ́rʃəł] ADJ parcial

participant [pɑrtísəpənt] ADJ & N participante mf, partícipe mf

participate [pɑrtísəpet] VI participar

participation [pɑrtɪsəpéʃən] N participación f

participle [pɑ́rDɪsɪpəł] N participio m

particle [pɑ́rDɪkəł] N partícula f; **— board** aglomerado m

particular [pəʼtíkjələʼ] ADJ particular; (fussy) quisquilloso; N **—s** particulares m pl; **in —** en particular

parting [pɑ́rDɪŋ] N (farewell) despedida f; (separation) separación f; **— of the ways** encrucijada f

partisan [pɑ́rDɪzən] N (supporter) partidario -ria m; (guerrilla) partisano -na m; ADJ (of supporters) partidario; (of guerrillas) de partisanos

partition [pɑrtíʃən] N (distribution) reparto m; (division) división f; (wall) tabique m, mampara f; VT (distribute) repartir; (divide) dividir; (divide with a wall) tabicar

partly [pɑ́rtli] ADV en parte

partner [pɑ́rtnəʼ] N (in business) socio -cia mf; (in an activity) compañero -ra mf; (in dancing, sports, marriage) pareja f

partnership [pɑ́rtnəʼʃíp] N (business) sociedad f; (relationship) asociación f

partridge [pɑ́rtrɪdʒ] N perdiz f

party [pɑ́rDi] N (get-together) fiesta f; (political group) partido m; (group of people) partida f; (litigant) parte f; **— of four** mesa para cuatro f; **— animal** fiestero -ra mf, parrandero -ra mf

pass [pæs] VI/VT pasar; (a law) aprobar; (an exam, test) aprobar, superar; **to — away** fallecer; **to — for** pasar por; **to — in review** pasar revista; **to — judgment** juzgar; **to — on** (die) fallecer; (approve) aceptar; (refuse) no querer; **to — oneself off as** hacerse pasar por; **to — out** desmayarse; **to — over** no tener en cuenta; **to — up an opportunity** perderse una oportunidad; **he —ed a kidney stone** expulsó un cálculo renal; **— me the salt** pásame la sal, alcánzame la sal; N (road through mountains) paso m; (motion, permission) pase m; (for transportation) abono m; (over a surface) pasada f; (on an exam) aprobación f;

(difficult event) trance m; **—key** llave maestra f; **—port** pasaporte m; **—word** contraseña f, clave de seguridad f; **he made a — at her** trató de ligar con ella

passable [pǽsəbəł] ADJ (penetrable) transitable; (mediocre) pasable

passage [pǽsɪdʒ] N (fare, musical or textual phrase, alley) pasaje m; (passing of time) paso m, transcurso m; (hallway in a house) pasillo m; (secret pathway) pasadizo m; (crossing) travesía f; (approval of a bill) aprobación f; **—way** (corridor) corredor m, pasillo m; (alley) pasaje m

passenger [pǽsəndʒəʼ] N pasajero -ra mf

passerby [pǽsəʼbaɪ] N transeúnte mf, viandante mf

passing [pǽsɪŋ] ADJ **each — day** cada día que pasa; **a — grade** una nota de aprobado; **a — fancy** un capricho pasajero; **a — mention** una mención al pasar

passion [pǽʃən] N pasión f

passionate [pǽʃənɪt] ADJ apasionado

passive [pǽsɪv] ADJ pasivo; N pasiva f

past [pæst] ADJ pasado; **— participle** participio pasado m; **— perfect** pluscuamperfecto m; **— precedents** precedentes anteriores m pl; **— tense** tiempo pretérito m; **the — president** el expresidente; PREP **— hope** más allá de toda esperanza; **— noon** después de mediodía; **the house — the store** la casa pasando la tienda; **we went — the tower** pasamos al lado de la torre; **half — two** las dos y media; **a woman — forty** una mujer de más de cuarenta años; ADV **for some time** — desde hace algún tiempo; **they drove —** pasaron en coche; N (time) pasado m; (tense) pretérito m

pasta [pɑ́stə] N pasta f

paste [pest] N (soft material, purée) pasta f; (glue) engrudo m; **—board** cartón m; VT pegar

pastel [pæstéł] ADJ & N pastel m

pasteurize [pǽstʃəraɪz] VT pasterizar / pasteurizar

pastime [pǽstaɪm] N pasatiempo m

pastor [pǽstəʼ] N pastor -ra f

pastoral [pǽstəʼəł] ADJ (literary) pastoril; (ecclesiastical) pastoral; N pastoral f; (literary work) égloga f

pastry [péstri] N (in general) pastelería f; (specific) pastel m; **— cook** pastelero -ra mf, repostero -ra mf; **— shop** pastelería f, repostería f

pasture [pǽstʃəʼ] N (grassland) prado m;

(grass) pasto *m;* (for horses) potrero *m;* vi/
vt pastar, pacer, apacentar

pasty [pésti] ADJ pastoso

pat [pæt] ADJ banal; **(down)** — al dedillo; **to
stand** — mantenerse firme; vi/vt dar
palmaditas (a); N palmadita *f;* — **of
butter** porción de mantequilla *f*

patch [pætʃ] N (piece of cloth to repair
clothes) remiendo *m,* parche *m* (also for
eye); (spot or area, as of ice) tramo (con
hielo) *m;* (plot) parcela *f;* vt (repair)
remendar; **to — up a quarrel** hacer las
paces

patent [pætṇt] ADJ (evident) patente;
(protected by patent) patentado; —
leather charol *m;* N patente *f;* —
pending patente en trámite; vt patentar

paternal [pətɔ́-nəl] ADJ (fatherly) paternal;
(of the father's lineage) paterno

paternity [pətɔ́-nɪɾi] N paternidad *f*

path [pæθ] N senda *f,* sendero *m;* (of a
projectile, storm) trayectoria *f;* **—way**
senda *f,* sendero *m*

pathetic [pəθɛ́ɾɪk] ADJ (moving) patético;
(contemptible) lamentable

pathogen [pǽθədʒən] N patógeno *m*

pathology [pæθɑ́ləd͡ʒi] N patología *f*

pathos [péθɑs] N patetismo *m*

patience [péʃəns] N paciencia *f*

patient [péʃənt] ADJ & N paciente *mf*

patriarch [pétriɑrk] N patriarca *m*

patriarchal [petriɑ́rkəl] ADJ patriarcal

patrimony [pætrəmoni] N patrimonio *m*

patriot [pétriət] N patriota *mf*

patriotic [petriɑ́ɾɪk] ADJ patriótico

patriotism [pétriətɪzəm] N patriotismo *m*

patrol [pətróɫ] vi/vt patrullar, rondar; N
patrulla *f,* ronda *f;* **— car, — man**
patrullero *m*

patron [pétrən] N (customer) cliente -ta *mf;*
(benefactor) benefactor -ra *mf,* mecenas
mf; (saint) patrono *m*

patronage [pétrənɪdʒ] N (support of an artist)
mecenazgo *m;* (clientele) clientela *f;*
(political) clientelismo *m;* **we appreciate
your** — agradecemos su preferencia

patronize [pétrənaɪz] vt (be condescending)
tratar con condescendencia; (do business
with) frecuentar

patter [pǽɾɚ] vi (strike lightly) golpetear;
(chatter) parlotear; N (small blows)
golpeteo *m;* (chatter) parloteo *m*

pattern [pǽɾɚn] N (for sewing) molde *m;*
(for drawing) plantilla *f;* (of behavior)
patrón *m;* vi/vt **to — something after**
modelar algo a imitación de, basarse en el
modelo de; **to — oneself after** seguir el

ejemplo de

paucity [pɔ́sɪɾi] N escasez *f*

paunch [pɔntʃ] N panza *f,* barriga *f*

pause [pɔz] N pausa *f;* vi (while talking) hacer
pausa; (while moving) detenerse

pave [pev] vt (with asphalt) pavimentar;
(with bricks) enladrillar; (with flagstones)
enlosar; **to — the way for** preparar el
camino para

pavement [pévmənt] N (asphalt) calzada *f;* (of asphalt)
pavimento *m;* (of bricks) enladrillado *m;*
(of flagstones) enlosado *m*

pavilion [pəvíljən] N pabellón *m*

paw [pɔ] N (with claws) pata *f;* (with claws) garra *f;* vt
(touch with paw) tocar con la pata; (touch
with claws) dar zarpazos; (grope)
manosear

pawn [pɔn] N (object left in deposit) prenda
f; (chess piece) peón *m;* (puppet) títere *m;*
—broker prestamista *mf;* **—shop** casa de
empeños *f,* monte de piedad *m;* **in** — en
prenda; vt empeñar, dejar en prenda

pay [pe] vt (remit) pagar; vi (be profitable)
ser provechoso, convenir; (be worthwhile)
valer la pena; **to — attention** prestar
atención, fijarse en; **to — back** (return)
restituir; (retaliate) vengarse; **to — a
compliment** hacer un cumplido; **to —
homage** rendir homenaje; **to — one's
respects** saludar; **to — off a debt**
cancelar una deuda; **to — a visit** hacer
una visita; **to — through the nose**
pagar demasiado; **I will — for your
meal** te pago la comida; N (payment)
pago *m;* (wages) paga *f,* salario *m;* **—back**
venganza *f;* **—check** cheque del sueldo *m;*
—day día de pago *m;* **—load** carga útil *f;*
—off (pay) pago *m;* (reward) recompensa
f; (bribe) soborno *m;* **— phone** teléfono
público *m;* **—roll** nómina *f,* planilla *f;* **to
hit — dirt** encontrar una mina de oro

payable [péəbəl] ADJ pagadero

payee [peí] N tenedor -ra *mf,* beneficiario -ria
mf

payment [pémənt] N pago *m;* **— in full**
liquidación *f*

PC [pisí] N (personal computer) PC *m;*
(political correctness) lo políticamente
correcto; ADJ (politically correct)
políticamente correcto

pea [pi] N guisante *m; Am* arveja *f;* **—nut** *Sp*
cacahuete *m; Mex* cacahuate *m; Am* maní
m; **—nut butter** *Sp* crema de cacahuete *f;
Mex* crema de cacahuate *f; Am* manteca /
mantequilla de maní *f*

peace [pis] N paz *f;* **— officer** oficial de
policía *m;* **at** — en paz; **to keep the** —

mantener el orden público; **to hold one's —** callar

peaceful [písfəł] ADJ pacífico, tranquilo

peach [pitʃ] N durazno *m*; *Sp* melocotón *m*; (nice thing or person) delicia *f*, monada *f*; **— tree** durazno *m*, duraznero *m*, *Sp* melocotonero *m*

peacock [píkak] N pavo real *m*, pavón *m*

peak [pik] N pico *m*, cumbre *f*; (of production, of one's abilities) punto máximo *m*; — **load** carga máxima *f*; — **season** temporada alta *f*; — **time** hora punta *f*

peal [pił] N (of bells) repique *m*; (of laughter) carcajada *f*; VI/VT repicar

pear [per] N pera *f*; — **tree** peral *m*

pearl [pɝł] N perla *f*; — **necklace** collar de perlas *m*

pearly [pɝ́li] ADJ (color) nacarado, perlado; (with pearls) perlado; **the — Gates** las puertas del cielo

peasant [pɛ́zənt] ADJ & N campesino -na *mf*

peat [pit] N turba *f*

pebble [pɛ́bəł] N guijarro *m*, piedrecilla *f*; (smooth) canto *m*

pecan [pɪkán] N pacana *f*

peccary [pɛ́kəri] N pecarí / pécari *m*

peck [pɛk] VI/VT (strike with beak) picar; (eat bit by bit) picotear; (kiss) dar un besito; **to — a hole** agujerear a picotazos; N (quick stroke) picotazo *m*; (kiss) besito *m*; (measure) medida de áridos (9 litros) *f*; **you're in a — of trouble** estás metido en un lío

pecking order [pɛ́kɪŋɔrdə] N jerarquía *f*

pectoral [pɛ́ktəəł] ADJ & N pectoral *m*

peculiar [pɪkjúljə] ADJ peculiar, particular

peculiarity [pɪkjuljǽrɪti] N peculiaridad *f*

pedagogue [pɛ́dəgag] N pedagogo -ga *mf*

pedagogy [pɛ́dəgadʒi] N pedagogía *f*

pedal [pɛ́dł] N pedal *m*; VI/VT pedalear

pedant [pɛ́dn̩t] N pedante *mf*

pedantic [pədǽntɪk] ADJ pedante

peddle [pɛ́dł] VI/VT ir vendiendo de puerta en puerta; **to — gossip** repartir chismes

peddler [pɛ́dlə] N buhonero -ra *mf*, mercachifle *m*

pedestal [pɛ́dɪstəł] N pedestal *m*

pedestrian [pədɛ́striən] N peatón -ona *mf*; ADJ pedestre

pediatrician [pidiətríʃən] N pediatra *mf*

pediatrics [pidiǽtrɪks] N pediatría *f*

pedigree [pɛ́dəgri] N (of persons) linaje *m*; (of animals) pedigrí *m*

pee [pi] VI *fam* mear, hacer pipí; N *fam* pipí *m*

peek [pik] VI atisbar; N atisbo *m*

peel [pił] VI/VT (fruit, tree) pelar(se),

descortezar(se); (paint) descascarar(se); **to keep one's eyes —ed** mantener los ojos abiertos; N cáscara *f*

peeler [pílə] N pelador *m*

peep [pip] VI/VT (begin to appear) asomar(se); VI (make sound of chicks) piar; **to — at** atisbar; N (look) atisbo *m*; (sound of chicks) pío *m*; **—hole** mirilla *f*; **— show** espectáculo de striptease *m*

peer [pir] N par *m* (also nobleman); **— group** grupo paritario *m*; VI (look attentively) escudriñar; (peep out) asomar

peerless [pírlɪs] ADJ incomparable, sin par

peeve [piv] VT irritar; **to get —d** ponerse de mal humor; N cosa que irrita *f*

peevish [pívɪʃ] ADJ malhumorado

peg [pɛg] N percha *f*; (on violin) clavija *f*; **to take a person down a —** bajarle los humos a alguien; VT clavar, clavetear; (price) estabilizar

pejorative [pɪdʒɔ́rəDɪv] ADJ peyorativo, despectivo

pelican [pɛ́lɪkən] N pelícano *m*

pellet [pɛ́lɪt] N (ball) bola *f*, bolita *f*; (shot) perdigón *m*

pell-mell [pɛ́lmɛ́l] ADJ confuso, tumultuoso; ADV a troche y moche

pelt [pɛlt] N piel *f*, pellejo *m*; VI/VT acribillar; **to — with stones** apedrear

pelvis [pɛ́lvɪs] N pelvis *f*

pen [pɛn] N (fountain) pluma *f*; (ballpoint) bolígrafo *m*; (for pigs) pocilga *f*; (for sheep) redil *m*; (for cows) corral *m*; **— holder** mango de pluma *m*, portaplumas *m sg*; **— name** seudónimo *m*; VT (write) escribir; (shut in) acorralar, encerrar

penal [pínəł] ADJ penal

penalize [pínəlaɪz] VT penar; (in sports) penalizar

penalty [pɛ́nəłti] N (punishment) pena *f*, castigo *m*; (forfeiture) multa *f*; (in sports) penalidad *f*; **— kick** tiro de penalidad *f*, penalty *m*

penance [pɛ́nəns] N penitencia *f*

pencil [pɛ́nsəł] N (writing instrument) lápiz *m*; (beam of light) haz *m*; **— sharpener** sacapuntas *m sg*

pendant [pɛ́ndənt] N colgante *m*; ADJ pendiente

pending [pɛ́ndɪŋ] ADJ pendiente; PREP **— his arrival** hasta que llegue, mientras no llegue

pendulum [pɛ́ndʒələm] N péndulo *m*

penetrate [pɛ́nɪtret] VT penetrar

penetrating [pɛ́nɪtreDɪŋ] ADJ penetrante

penetration [pɛnɪtréʃən] N penetración *f*

penguin [pɛ́ŋgwɪn] N pingüino *m*

penicillin [penisílin] N penicilina *f*

peninsula [pənínsələ] N península *f*

penis [pínis] N pene *m*

penitent [pénitənt] ADJ & N penitente *mf*

penitentiary [peniténʃəri] N penitenciaría *f*, penal *m*

penmanship [pénmənʃip] N escritura *f*, caligrafía *f*

pennant [pénənt] N banderín *m*, gallardete *m*

penniless [pénilɪs] ADJ pobre, sin dinero

penny [péni] N centavo *m*; **—pincher** avaro -ra *mf*; **to cost a pretty —** costar un dineral

pension [pénʃən] N (paid to a worker) jubilación *f*; (paid to a worker's survivors) pensión *f*; **— fund** caja de jubilaciones *f*; VT jubilar, pensionar

pensioner [pénʃənə] N pensionista *mf*

pensive [pénsiv] ADJ pensativo

pent [pent] ADJ encerrado; **—up** reprimido

pentagon [péntəgən] N pentágono *m*

penthouse [pénthaus] N penthouse *m*

penultimate [pɪnʌltəmit] ADJ penúltimo

people [pípəl] N gente *f*; (national group) pueblo *m*; VT poblar

pep [pep] N energía *f*; VI **to — up** animar

pepper [pépə] N (black) pimienta *f*; (green) pimiento *m*; (plant, shaker) pimentero *m*; **—mint** menta *f*; VT pimentar; **to — with bullets** acribillar a balazos

peptic [péptik] ADJ —; **— ulcer** úlcera péptica *f*

per [pɚ] PREP (for each) por; (according to) según; **— capita** per capita; **—cent** por ciento; **— diem** viático *m*

percale [pəkél] N percal *m*

perceive [pəsív] VT percibir

percentage [pəséntɪdʒ] N porcentaje *m*

percentile [pəséntaɪl] N percentil *m*

perceptible [pəséptəbəl] ADJ perceptible

perception [pəsépʃən] N percepción *f*

perceptive [pəséptɪv] ADJ (pertaining to perception) perceptivo; (having keen perception) perspicaz

perch [pɚtʃ] N (rod for birds) percha *f*; (type of fish) perca *f*; VT (alight) posarse; VI/VT (set) encaramar(se)

percolate [pɚkəlet] VI/VT filtrar(se)

percussion [pəkʌ́ʃən] N percusión *f*

perdition [pədíʃən] N perdición *f*

perennial [pəréniəl] ADJ perenne; N **— plant** planta perenne *f*

perfect [pɚ́fɪkt] ADJ perfecto; **a — stranger** un completo desconocido; [pəfékt] VT perfeccionar

perfection [pəfékʃən] N perfección *f*

perforate [pɚ́fəret] VI/VT perforar(se); VT calar

perforation [pɚfəréʃən] N perforación *f*

perform [pəfɔ́rm] VT (a task) ejecutar, realizar; (a rite, ceremony) celebrar; (a contract) cumplir; (a play) representar; VI (give a performance) actuar; (play music) interpretar; (function) funcionar; (do well) rendir

performance [pəfɔ́rmens] N (of a task) ejecución *f*; (of a ceremony) celebración *f*; (of a contract) cumplimiento *m*; (of a motor) desempeño *m*, rendimiento *m*; (of a play) representación *f*; (of an actor) actuación *f*; (of music) interpretación *f*

perfume [pɚ́fjum] N perfume *m*; [pəfjúm] VT perfumar

perfumery [pəfjúməri] N (store) perfumería *f*; (collection) perfumes *m pl*

perhaps [pəhǽps] ADV tal vez, quizá(s), acaso

peril [pérəl] N peligro *m*; VT poner en peligro

perilous [pérələs] ADJ peligroso

perimeter [pərímɪdə] N perímetro *m*

period [pɪ́riəd] N período *m*; (historical) época *f*; (punctuation) punto *m*; (menstruation) período *m*, regla *f*; **you can't go, —!** no puedes ir, y sanseacabó; **within a — of ten days** en el término de diez días

periodic [pɪriádɪk] ADJ periódico; **— table** tabla periódica *f*

periodical [pɪriádɪkəl] ADJ periódico; N revista *f*

peripheral [pərífəəl] ADJ & N periférico *m*; **— vision** visión periférica *f*

periphery [pərífəri] N periferia *f*

periscope [pɪ́rɪskop] N periscopio *m*

perish [pérɪʃ] VI perecer

perishable [pérɪʃəbəl] ADJ perecedero

peritonitis [peritɲáɪdɪs] N peritonitis *f*

perjure [pɚ́dʒə] VI **to — oneself** perjurarse, jurar en falso

perjury [pɚ́dʒəri] N perjurio *m*

permanence [pɚ́mənəns] N permanencia *f*

permanent [pɚ́mənənt] ADJ permanente; (of a position) titular

permeable [pɚ́miəbəl] ADJ permeable

permeate [pɚ́miet] VI/VT permear

permissible [pəmísəbəl] ADJ permisible, lícito

permission [pəmíʃən] N permiso *m*

permissive [pəmísɪv] ADJ permisivo

permit [pəmít] VI/VT permitir; [pɚ́mɪt] N permiso *m*

permutation [pɚmjutéʃən] N permutación *f*

pernicious [pəníʃəs] ADJ pernicioso

peroxide [pəɹáksaɪd] N peróxido *m*

perpendicular [pɚpɪndíkjələ] ADJ & N perpendicular *f*

perpetrate [pɜ́-pɪtret] VT perpetrar
perpetual [pə-pétʃuəɬ] ADJ perpetuo
perpetuate [pə-pétʃuet] VT perpetuar
perplex [pə-pléks] VT confundir, dejar perplejo; **—ed** perplejo
perplexity [pə-pléksɪdi] N perplejidad f
persecute [pɜ́-sɪkjut] VT perseguir
persecution [pə-sɪkjúʃən] N persecución f
persecutor [pɜ́-sɪkjudə-] N perseguidor -ra mf
perseverance [pə-səvírəns] N perseverancia f
persevere [pə-səvír] VI perseverar, persistir
Persian [pɜ́-ʒən] ADJ & N persa mf
persist [pə-síst] VI (continue, endure) persistir; (to be insistent) insistir
persistence [pə-sístəns] N (endurance) persistencia f; (insistence) insistencia f
persistent [pə-sístənt] ADJ (lasting) persistente; (insisting) insistente, machacón
person [pɜ́-sən] N persona f
personable [pɜ́-sənəbəɬ] ADJ agradable
personage [pɜ́-sənɪʤ] N personaje m
personal [pɜ́-sənəɬ] ADJ personal; **— computer** Sp ordenador personal m; Am computadora personal f; **— effects** efectos personales m pl; **— identification number** número de identificación personal m; **— pronoun** pronombre personal m; **— property** bienes muebles m pl; **to make a — appearance** presentarse en persona
personality [pə-sənálɪdi] N personalidad f
personify [pə-sánəfaɪ] VT personificar
personnel [pə-sənéɬ] N personal m
perspective [pə-spéktɪv] N perspectiva f
perspicacious [pə-spɪkéʃəs] ADJ perspicaz
perspiration [pə-spəréʃən] N transpiración f
perspire [pə-spáɪr] VI transpirar
persuade [pə-swéd] VT persuadir, convencer
persuasion [pə-swéʒən] N persuasión f; (belief) convicción f
persuasive [pə-swésɪv] ADJ persuasivo, convincente
pert [pɜ́t] ADJ (insolent) insolente; (lively) vivaz
pertain [pə-tén] VI atañer, corresponder
pertinent [pɜ́-tnənt] ADJ pertinente
perturb [pə-tɜ́-b] VT perturbar
Peru [pərú] N Perú m
perusal [pərúzəɬ] N lectura f
peruse [pərúz] VT (read carefully) leer con cuidado; (read carelessly) hojear
Peruvian [pərúviən] ADJ & N peruano -na mf
pervade [pə-véd] VT difundirse por
perverse [pə-vɜ́-s] ADJ perverso
perversion [pə-vɜ́-ʒən] N perversión f
perversity [pə-vɜ́-sɪdi] N perversidad f

pervert [pə-vɜ́-t] VT pervertir; (misconstrue) desvirtuar; [pɜ́-vɜ-t] N pervertido -da mf
peso [péso] N peso m
pessimism [pésəmɪzəm] N pesimismo m
pessimist [pésəmɪst] N pesimista mf
pest [pest] N (insect, disease) peste f, plaga f; (person) pesado -da mf
pester [péstə-] VT molestar
pesticide [péstɪsaɪd] N pesticida m
pestilence [péstələns] N pestilencia f
pet [pet] N (animal) mascota f; (favorite) favorito -ta mf, preferido -da mf; ADJ predilecto; **— name** apodo cariñoso m; VT (caress) acariciar; (pat) dar palmaditas a
petal [pédɬ] N pétalo m
petition [pətíʃən] N petición f, solicitud f; VI/VT peticionar, solicitar
petrify [pétrəfaɪ] VI/VT petrificar(se)
petroleum [pətróliəm] N petróleo m; **— products** productos petrolíferos m pl; **— jelly** vaselina f
petticoat [pédɪkot] N enaguas f pl
petty [pédi] ADJ (trivial) trivial; (mean) mezquino; **— cash** caja chica f; **— larceny** ratería f; **— officer** suboficial de marina m
petunia [pɪtúnjə] N petunia f
pew [pju] N banco de iglesia m
pewter [pjúðə-] N peltre m
peyote [peóði] N peyote m
phallus [féləs] N falo m
phantom [féntəm] N fantasma m
pharmaceutical [farməsúːtɪkəɬ] ADJ farmacéutico; N producto farmacéutico m
pharmacist [fármɪst] N farmacéutico -ca mf
pharmacology [farməkáləʤi] N farmacología f
pharmacy [fárməsi] N farmacia f
pharynx [férɪŋks] N faringe f
phase [fez] N fase f; VI **to — out** retirar por etapas; **to — in** incorporar paulatinamente
pheasant [fézənt] N faisán m
phenomenon [fɪnámənən] N fenómeno m
philanthropy [fɪlánθrəpi] N filantropía f
philharmonic [fɪɬharmánɪk] ADJ filarmónico; N filarmónica f
Philippine [fíləpɪn] ADJ & N filipino -na mf
Philippines [fíləpɪnz] N Filipinas f pl
philosopher [fɪlásəfə-] N filósofo -fa mf
philosophical [fɪləsáfɪkəɬ] ADJ filosófico
philosophy [fɪlásəfi] N filosofía f
phlegm [flem] N flema f
phobia [fóbiə] N fobia f
phone [fon] N teléfono m; VI/VT telefonear; **— card** tarjeta telefónica f

phonetics [fənéɒɪks] N fonética f
phonograph [fónəgræf] N fonógrafo m
phonology [fənúlədʒi] N fonología f
phony [fóni] ADJ falso
phosphate [fásfet] N fosfato m
phosphorus [fásfərəs] N fósforo m
photo [fóɒo] N foto f; — **finish** final muy reñido m
photocopier [fóɒəkɑpiə] N fotocopiadora f
photocopy [fóɒəkɑpi] N fotocopia f; VI/VT fotocopiar
photoelectric [foɒoɪléktrɪk] ADJ fotoeléctrico
photogenic [foɒədʒénɪk] ADJ fotogénico
photograph [fóɒəgræf] N fotografía f; VT fotografiar
photographer [fətágrəfə] N fotógrafo -fa mf
photography [fətágrəfi] N fotografía f
photon [fótɑn] N fotón m
photosynthesis [foɒosínθəsɪs] N fotosíntesis f
phrase [frez] N frase f; VI/VT expresar; (musical) frasear
phylum [fáiləm] N filo m
physical [fízɪkəl] ADJ físico; — **education** educación física f; — **geography** geografía física f; — **science** ciencia física f
physician [fɪzíʃən] N médico -ca mf; —'**s assistant** ayudante médico -ca sanitario -ria mf
physicist [fízɪsɪst] N físico -ca mf
physics [fízɪks] N física f
physiological [fɪzɪəládʒɪkəl] ADJ fisiológico
physiology [fɪzɪálədʒi] N fisiología f
physique [fɪzík] N físico m
piano [piǽno] N piano m; — **bench** banqueta de piano f; — **hammer** martinete m; — **stool** taburete de piano m
picaresque [pɪkərésk] ADJ picaresco
piccolo [píkəlo] N flautín m, pícolo m
pick [pɪk] VT (choose) escoger, elegir; (gather flowers) juntar; (play a guitar) puntear; (clean teeth) mondarse; (eat with the bill) picotear; (provoke a fight) armar, entablar; VI picar; **to — at** picotear; **to — apart** criticar; **to — a lock** violar una cerradura con ganzúa; **to — on** meterse con; **to — out** (choose) escoger; (distinguish) distinguir; **to — pockets** ratear; **to — up** (gather) recoger; (lift) levantar; (learn) aprender; (order) ordenar; (improve) mejorar; (contact in hope of sex) ligar con; **to — up speed** acelerar la marcha; —**proof** a prueba de ladrones; N (tool) pico m; (of a guitar) púa f; (act of selecting) selección f; (thing or person selected) elección f; (the best) lo selecto, lo

mejor; —**ax(e)** zapapico m; —**lock** ganzúa f; —**pocket** ratero -ra mf, carterista mf; —**up** (taking on freight) recolección f; (improvement in business) recuperación f; (casual sexual acquaintance) ligue m, plan m; (acceleration) aceleración f; —**up truck** camioneta f
picket [píkɪt] N piquete m (also union worker); — **fence** cerca de piquetes f; VT (fence) vallar; (block with workers) bloquear
pickle [píkəl] N pepinillo en vinagre m, curtido m; **to be in a** — hallarse en un aprieto; VT encurtir, escabechar; —**d fish** pescado al/en escabeche m, pescado adobado m
picnic [píknɪk] N picnic m; — **area** merendero m; VI hacer un picnic
picture [píktʃə] N (image) imagen f; (drawing) dibujo m; (photo) fotografía f; (situation) panorama m; (movie) película f; — **frame** marco m; — **gallery** galería de pinturas f; — **tube** tubo de imagen m; **she is the — of unhappiness** es la imagen de la infelicidad; VT (describe) describir; (imagine) imaginar
picturesque [pɪktʃərésk] ADJ pintoresco
pie [paɪ] N pastel m, tarta f; — **chart** gráfica circular f; — **in the sky** castillos en el aire m pl; **it's as easy as** — es pan comido
piece [pis] N (of music, in a board game, of furniture) pieza f; (of wood, rock, pie) pedazo m, trozo m; —**meal** por partes; — **of advice** consejo m; — **of cake** pan comido m; — **of land** parcela f, terreno m; — **of one's mind** regaño m; — **of news** noticia f; — **of shit** vulg mierda f; —**work** trabajo a destajo m; **to go to** —**s** descomponerse; VI remendar; **to** — **together** (assemble) armar; (make sense of) atar cabos
pier [pir] N muelle m, embarcadero m; (breakwater) rompeolas m sg
pierce [pirs] VI/VT (make a hole in) agujerear; (penetrate) penetrar; (cause a sharp pain) punzar; (make a sharp sound) quebrar
piercing [pírsɪŋ] ADJ (glance, sound) penetrante; (pain) punzante
piety [páɪɒi] N piedad f
pig [pɪg] N puerco m, cerdo m, cochino m; Sp guarro m; —**headed** testarudo, cabezón; —**iron** hierro en lingotes m; — **Latin** jerigonza f; —**pen** pocilga f; —**tail** coleta f
pigeon [pídʒən] N paloma f; (young) pichón

m; **—hole** casilla *f;* **to —hole** encasillar; **— loft** palomar *m*

piggy [pígi] N cerdito *m;* **—bank** alcancía *f; Sp* hucha *f;* **—back** a hombros, a cuestas

pigment [pígmənt] N pigmento *m*

pike [paɪk] N (weapon) pica *f;* (fish) lucio *m*

pile [paɪl] N (ordered stack) pila *f;* (chaotic group) montón *m*, amontonamiento *m;* (surface of a carpet) pelo *m;* (post) pilote *m;* **— driver** martinete *m;* **—s** almorranas *f pl;* **—-up** accidente múltiple *m;* VI/VT apilar(se), amontonar(se)

pilfer [pílfɚ] VI/VT ratear, sisar

pilgrim [pílgrəm] N peregrino -na *mf,* romero -ra *mf*

pilgrimage [pílɬgrəmɪdʒ] N peregrinación *f,* romería *f*

pill [pɪl] N píldora *f* (also birth control), pastilla *f;* (naughty child) pesado -da *mf*

pillage [pílɪdʒ] N pillaje *m*, saqueo *m*, rapiña *f;* VI/VT pillar, saquear

pillar [pílɚ] N pilar *m*, columna *f*

pillow [pílo] N almohada *f;* **—case** funda *f*

pilot [páɪlət] N piloto *mf* (also test, light); (of a boat) timonel *m*, piloto *mf;* VT pilotar, comandar

pimp [pɪmp] N proxeneta *mf*, rufián *m*

pimple [pímpəɬ] N grano *m*, barro *m*

pin [pɪn] N alfiler *m;* (ornament) prendedor *m;* (rod) pasador *m*, perno *m;* (bowling) bolo *m;* (electric) pata *f*, clavija *f;* **—cushion** acerico *m;* **—wheel** molinete *m*, remolino *m;* VT (affix with pins) prender; (in wrestling) inmovilizar; **to be on —s and needles** estar en ascuas; **to — someone down** (hold down) inmovilizar; (force to act) hacer que concrete detalles; **to — one's hopes on** poner sus esperanzas en; **to —point** localizar con precisión; **to — up** sujetar con alfileres

PIN (personal identification number) [pɪn] N PIN *m*

pincers [pínsɚz] N (of lobsters) pinzas *f pl;* (tool) tenazas *f pl*

pinch [pɪntʃ] VT (squeeze with fingers) pellizcar; (squeeze tightly, hamper) apretar; (steal) birlar; (arrest) prender; VI (be too tight) apretar; (economize) economizar; N (act of pinching) pellizco *m;* (small amount) pizca *f;* (trying circumstances) aprieto *m*, apuro *f*

pine [paɪn] N pino *m;* **—apple** piña *f,* ananá(s) *m;* **— cone** piña *f;* **— grove** pinar *m;* **— nut** piñón *m;* VI **to — away** languidecer; **to — for** anhelar, suspirar por

ping-pong [píŋpaŋ] N ping-pong *m*, tenis de mesa *m*

pinion [pínjən] N piñón *m*

pink [pɪŋk] N rosado *m*, rosa *m;* **in the —** rebosante de salud; ADJ rosado, rosa *inv*

pinnacle [pínəkəɬ] N pináculo *m*

pint [paɪnt] N pinta *f;* **—-sized** diminuto

pinto bean [píntobɪn] N judía pinta *f*

pioneer [paɪənír] N pionero -ra *mf;* VI ser el primero en hacer algo; VT promover

pious [páɪəs] ADJ (religious) pío, piadoso; (hypocritical) beato

pipe [paɪp] N (for smoking) pipa *f;* (for water) tubo *m*, caño *m;* (of an organ) tubo *m;* (for playing music) caramillo *m*, flauta *f;* **— dream** ilusiones *f pl;* **—line** (for oil) oleoducto *m;* (for gas) gasoducto *m;* (for water) tubería *f;* **in the —line** en trámite; **— wrench** llave inglesa *f;* VT (convey water) conducir por cañerías; (make music) tocar la flauta; VI chillar; **to — down** callarse

piping [páɪpɪŋ] N (many pipes) cañería *f,* tubería *f;* (border on clothes) ribete *m;* (sound of pipes) sonido de la gaita / flauta *m;* **— hot** hirviendo

pipsqueak [pípskwik] N chisgarabís *m*, mequetrefe *m*

pirate [páɪrət] N pirata *mf;* VT piratear

piss [pɪs] VI/VT *fam* mear

pistol [pístəɬ] N pistola *f,* revólver *m;* **to —-whip** dar culatazos

piston [pístən] N pistón *m*, émbolo *m;* **— ring** segmento de compresión *m;* **— rod** eje del pistón *m*

pit [pɪt] N (hole) hoyo *m*, pozo *m;* (in a garage, theater) foso *m;* (trap) trampa *f;* (seed) hueso *m;* (part of a racetrack) box *m*, paddock *m;* (part of the stomach) boca *f;* **—fall** (trap) trampa *f;* (difficulty) dificultad *f;* **this is the —s** esto es lo peor; VI/VT (make holes) picarse; VT (set against) oponer, enfrentar

pitch [pɪtʃ] VT (throw) tirar, lanzar; (try to sell) pregonar; **to — a tent** armar una tienda de campaña; VI (plane, ship) cabecear; **to — in** colaborar; N (throw) tiro *m*, lanzamiento *m;* (in music) tono *m;* (in printing) espaciado *m;* (slope) grado de inclinación *m;* (tar) brea *f*, pez *f;* **— dark** oscuro como boca del lobo; **—fork** horca *f*, horquilla *f*

pitcher [pítʃɚ] N (vessel) cántaro *m*, jarro *m*, jarra *f;* (in baseball) lanzador *m*

pith [pɪθ] N (in plants, feathers) médula *f;* (essence) meollo *m*

pithy [píθi] ADJ sustancial

pitiful [pídɪfəl] ADJ (deserving pity) lastimoso; (deserving contempt) despreciable

pitiless [pídɪlɪs] ADJ despiadado

pituitary [ptúɪteri] ADJ pituitario; — **gland** glándula pituitaria f

pity [pídi] N compasión f, lástima f; **what a** —! ¡qué lástima! VT compadecerse (de)

pivot [pívət] N pivote m; VI pivotar

pixel [píksəl] N píxel m

pizza [pítsə] N pizza f

placard [plǽkəd] N cartel m

placate [pléket] VT apaciguar

place [ples] N (site) lugar m, sitio m; (position) puesto m; (passage in text) pasaje m; — **mat** mantel individual m; — **of business** oficina f; — **setting** cubierto para una persona m; — **of worship** templo m; **in** — **of** en lugar de; **it is not my** — **to do it** no me corresponde a mí hacerlo m; VT colocar; (identify) situar, ubicar; VI clasificarse; **to** — **an order** hacer un pedido; **to** — **an ad** poner un anuncio

placebo [pləsíbo] N placebo m

placement [plésmənt] N colocación f

placenta [pləséntə] N placenta f

placid [plǽsɪd] ADJ plácido

plagiarism [pléd͡ʒərɪzəm] N plagio m

plague [pleg] N plaga f, peste f; VT atormentar, apestar

plaid [plæd] N tela escocesa f

plain [plen] ADJ (without embellishment) sencillo, llano; (clear) claro; (downright, unadulterated) puro; (ordinary) común; (unattractive) poco atractivo; — **fool** tonto de capirote; **in** — **sight** en plena vista; —-**clothesman** policía en traje de civil m; —-**Jane** sencillo; ADV completamente; N llano m, llanura f

plaintiff [pléntɪf] N demandante mf, querellante mf

plan [plæn] N plan m; (drawing, sketch, map, outline) plano m; VI/VT planear, planificar; (diagram) hacer el plano de

plane [plen] N (airplane) avión m; (surface) plano m; (tool) cepillo m; ADJ plano; — **geometry** geometría plana f; — **tree** plátano m; VI (glide, hover) planear; VT (smooth) cepillar, planear

planet [plǽnɪt] N planeta m

planetarium [plænɪtériəm] N planetario m

plank [plæŋk] N (board) tabla f, tablón m; (tenet) principio m, base f; VT entarimar

plankton [plǽŋktən] N plancton m

plant [plænt] N (vegetation) planta f; (industrial installation) fábrica f, planta f;

(mole, spy) topo m; VT (plants) plantar; (ideas) sembrar; (a spy, evidence) colocar

plantation [plæntéʃən] N plantación f

plaque [plæk] N placa f; (on teeth) sarro m, placa f

plasma [plǽzmə] N plasma m

plaster [plǽstə-] N (substance) yeso m; (preparation applied to body) emplasto m; — **of Paris** yeso m; VT (cover with plaster) revocar; (apply a preparation) emplastar; (cover with posters) cubrir, empapelar; (defeat) aplastar; **to** — **down one's hair** achatarse el pelo; **he got** —**ed** se emborrachó

plastic [plǽstɪk] ADJ plástico; — **surgery** cirugía plástica/estética f

plate [plet] N (for food) plato m; (for collections) bandeja f; (metal) plancha f, lámina f; (license) placa f; — **glass** vidrio cilindrado m; — **tectonics** tectónica de placas f; VT (apply metal covering) chapar, enchapar; (apply armor) blindar

plateau [plætó] N meseta f, macizo m

platform [plǽtfɔrm] N plataforma f (also political); (railway) andén m; (mobile) tarima f, tinglado m

platinum [plǽtnəm] N platino m

platitude [plǽdɪtud] N lugar común m, perogrullada f

platter [plǽDə-] N fuente f

plausible [plɔ́zəbəl] ADJ plausible

play [ple] VT (game) jugar; (an opponent) jugar contra; (an instrument) tocar; (a drama) representar; (a role) desempeñar; (bet on) apostar; VI divert oneself, gamble) jugar; (kid) bromear; (make music) tocar; **to** — **a joke** gastar una broma; **to** — **along** seguir la corriente; **to** — **cards** jugar a los naipes; **to** — **down** minimizar; **to** — **havoc** hacer estragos; **to** — **tennis** jugar al tenis; **to** — **the fool** hacerse el tonto; **to be all** —**ed out** estar agotado; N (recreational activity, looseness) juego m; (instance of playing) jugada f; (theater work) obra de teatro f; — **on words** juego de palabras m; —**boy** playboy m; —**ground** recreo m, patio m; —**ing card** naipe m; —**mate** compañero -ra de juego mf; —**thing** juguete m

player [pléə-] N (one who plays, gambler) jugador -ra mf; (musician) músico -ca m; (actor) actor m, actriz f; (participant) participante mf; — **piano** pianola f

playful [pléfəl] ADJ juguetón

playwright [plérart] N dramaturgo -ga mf

plea [pli] N (entreaty) súplica f, ruego m; (allegation) alegato m; **to enter a** — **of**

guilty declararse culpable

plead [plid] vi/vt (entreat) suplicar, rogar; (defend) abogar, defender; **to — guilty** declararse culpable

pleasant [plézənt] ADJ agradable, grato, placentero

pleasantry [plézəntri] N cortesía f

please [pliz] ADV por favor; vi/vt agradar, complacer; **as you —** como quieras; **to be —d to** tener el gusto de, tener gusto en; **to be —d with** estar satisfecho con

pleasing [plízıŋ] ADJ agradable

pleasure [pléʒɚ] N placer m, gusto m, agrado m; **— trip** viaje de placer m

pleat [plit] N pliegue m, tabla f; (wide) tabla f; vt plisar; (wide) tablear

pledge [plɛdʒ] N (promise) promesa f; (security deposit) prenda f; (in a fraternity) miembro provisorio m; **as a — of** en prenda de; vi/vt (promise) prometer; vt (give as a deposit) empeñar; **to — one's word** dar la palabra; **to — to secrecy** exigir promesa de discreción

plenary [plénəri] ADJ & N plenario m

plentiful [pléntıfəł] ADJ abundante, copioso

plenty [plénti] N abundancia f; **— of time** suficiente tiempo m; **that's —** con eso basta

pliable [pláıəbəł] ADJ (flexible) flexible; (docile) dócil

pliant [plaıənt] ADJ (flexible) flexible; (docile) dócil

pliers [pláıɚz] N alicates m pl, tenazas f pl

plight [plaıt] N aprieto m

plod [plad] vi (walk) caminar trabajosamente; (work) trabajar laboriosamente

plop [plap] vi hacer plaf; vt dejar caer; N plaf m

plot [plat] N (storyline) trama f, argumento m; (conspiracy) complot m, conspiración f; (land) parcela f, era f; (floor plan) plano m; vi/vt (plan secretly) tramar, conspirar, maquinar; vt (make a graph) hacer un gráfico; **to — a course** trazar un curso

plotter [pládɚ] N (one who plots) conspirador -ora mf; (device) trazador de gráficos m

plover [plóvɚ] N chorlito m

plow [plau] N arado m; **—share** reja de arado f; vi/vt arar; (fresh soil) roturar; **to — through** abrirse paso

plowing [pláuıŋ] N labranza f

pluck [plʌk] vt (a feather, flower) arrancar; (bird) desplumar; (guitar) puntear, pulsar; **to — at** tirar de; **to — out/off** desprender; **to — up courage** animarse, cobrar ánimo; N (act of plucking) tirón m;

(courage) valor m

plug [plʌg] N (stopper) tapón m; (horse) pej penco m; (electric) enchufe m; (advertisement) mención favorable f; (tobacco) rollo m; **—in** enchufe m; vt tapar; (advertise) hacer una mención favorable de; vi **to — along** afanarse; **to — in** enchufar; **to — up** tapar

plum [plʌm] N (fruit) ciruela f; **— tree** ciruelo m; **that job is a real —** ese trabajo es estupendo

plumage [plúmıdʒ] N plumaje m

plumb [plʌm] N (lead weight) plomada f; **to be out of —** no estar a plomo; ADJ (perpendicular) a plomo; **— bob** plomada f; ADV (in a vertical direction) a plomo; (completely) completamente; vt (measure depth) sondear; (test for verticality) aplomar; (examine) examinar

plumber [plámɚ] N plomero -ra mf; Sp fontanero -ra mf

plumbing [plámıŋ] N (work and trade) plomería f; Sp fontanería f; (system of pipes) cañerías f pl

plume [plum] N penacho m; vt adornar con plumas

plummet [plámıt] vi precipitarse; N plomada f

plump [plʌmp] ADJ rechoncho, regordete, rollizo; ADV a plomo; vi/vt **to — down** dejar(se) caer

plunder [plándɚ] N (act of plundering) pillaje m, saqueo m; (loot) botín m; vi/vt pillar, saquear

plunge [plʌndʒ] vi/vt (into water) zambullir(se), sumergir(se); (into something solid) hundir(se); vi (fall) precipitarse; (slope downward) bajar repentinamente; **to — headlong** echarse de cabeza; N zambullida f; (rush) salto m

plunger [plándʒɚ] N (for a toilet) desatascador m; (of a pump) émbolo m

pluperfect [plupɚ́fıkt] N pluscuamperfecto m

plural [plúrəł] ADJ & N plural m

plurality [plʊrǽlıti] N pluralidad f

plus [plʌs] PREP más; N signo más m; (advantage) ventaja f; **two — three** dos más tres m; **on the — side** en el lado positivo; **— sign** signo de más m

plush [plʌʃ] N felpa f; ADJ (fabric) afelpado; (hotel) lujoso

plutonium [plutóniəm] N plutonio m

ply [plaı] vt (use) manejar; (assail with questions) acosar; (navigate a body of water) surcar; vi (travel regularly) recorrer con regularidad; (work steadily) aplicarse; **to — a trade** ejercer un oficio; N (layer of

cloth, rubber) capa *f*; (layer of plywood)
chapa *f*; **—wood** madera compensada *f*,
contrachapado *m*

pneumatic [numǽdɪk] ADJ neumático

pneumonia [numónjə] N pulmonía *f*

poach [potʃ] VT (eggs) escalfar; VI/VT (game)
cazar furtivamente

pocket [pákɪt] N bolsillo *m*; (vein of ore)
filón *m*; (on a pool table) tronera *f*; (of air)
bache *m*; (of poverty) bolsa *f*; **—book**
cartera *f*, *Sp* bolso *m*; **— book** libro de
bolsillo *m*; **—knife** navaja *f*; **— of
resistance** foco de resistencia *m*; VT
meterse en el bolsillo; (appropriate)
embolsar; (knock in a billiard ball) meter
en la tronera

pod [pad] N (seed vessel) vaina *f*; (herd of
cetaceans) manada *f*

podium [pódiəm] N podio *m*

poem [póəm] N poema *m*, poesía *f*

poet [póɪt] N poeta *mf*

poetic [poédɪk] ADJ poético; **—s** poética *f*; **—
justice** justicia divina *f*

poetry [póɪtri] N poesía *f*

poignant [pɔ́injənt] ADJ conmovedor

poinsettia [pɔɪnsédə] N flor de Pascua *f*

point [pɔɪnt] N (place) punto *m*; (sharp end)
punta *f*; **— of view** punto de vista *m*;
—blank a quemarropa; **it is not to the
—** no viene al caso; **I don't see the —**
no le veo el sentido; **on the —** of a
punto de; VT (direct finger at) apuntar
con, señalar con; (indicate) señalar; **to —
out** señalar, indicar; **to — up** enfatizar

pointed [pɔ́ɪntɪd] ADJ (having a point)
puntiagudo; (piercing) agudo; (aimed) a
propósito; **— arch** arco ojival *m*

pointer [pɔ́ɪntə] N (stick) puntero *m*; (on a
scale) indicador *m*; (dog) perro de muestra
m; (advice) consejo *m*

pointless [pɔ́ɪntlɪs] ADJ inútil

poise [pɔɪz] N (balance, steadiness) equilibrio
m; (dignified bearing) aplomo *m*; VI/VT
equilibrar(se); VT (ready) preparar; VI
(hover) cernerse

poison [pɔ́ɪzən] N veneno *m*, ponzoña *f*; **—
ivy** hiedra venenosa *f*; VT envenenar,
emponzoñar

poisoning [pɔ́ɪzənɪŋ] N intoxicación *f*

poisonous [pɔ́ɪzənəs] ADJ venenoso,
ponzoñoso

poke [pok] VT (jab) clavar, pinchar; (stir a
fire) atizar; (thrust out, as one's head)
asomar; **to — out an eye** sacar un ojo; VI
to — along andar perezosamente; **to —
around** husmear; **to — fun at** burlarse
de; **to — into** meterse en; **to — out**

(project) sobresalir; N pinchazo *m*

Poland [pólənd] N Polonia *f*

polar [pólə] ADJ polar; **— bear** oso polar *m*

polarity [polǽrɪdi] N polaridad *f*

polarization [polərɪzéʃən] N polarización *f*

polarize [póləraɪz] VI/VT polarizar(se)

pole [pol] N (long piece of wood, metal)
poste *m*; (for a flag) asta *f*; (for vaulting)
pértiga *f*, garrocha *f*; (earth's axis) polo *m*;
(for skiing) bastón *m*; **— vault** salto con
pértiga *m*

Pole [pol] N polaco -ca *mf*

polemic [pəlémɪk] ADJ polémico *m*; N
polémica *f*

police [polís] N policía *f*; **— car** patrullero *m*;
— dog perro policía *m*; **— force** cuerpo
de policía *m*; **—man** policía *m*; **— officer**
oficial de policía *mf*; **— state** estado
policíaco *m*; **— station** comisaría de
policía *f*; **—woman** policía *f*; VT patrullar

policy [pálɪsi] N (procedure) política *f*; (for
insurance) póliza *f*

polio [pólio] N polio *f*

Polish [pólɪʃ] ADJ & N polaco -ca *mf*

polish [pálɪʃ] N (sheen) lustre *m*,
refinamiento *m*; (refinement) urbanidad *f*,
cultura *f*; (substance for furniture) cera *f*;
(substance for shoes) betún *m*; VT (a
speech) pulir; (a metal) sacar brillo; (a car)
encerar; (shoes) lustrar, embetunar; VI
lustrarse; **to — off** despachar; **to — up**
(metal) sacar brillo; (speech) pulir

polite [pəláɪt] ADJ cortés

politeness [pəláɪtnɪs] N cortesía *f*

politic [pálɪtɪk] ADJ diplomático, político

political [pəlídɪkəl] ADJ político; **—
prisoner** preso -sa político -ca *mf*; **—
science** ciencias políticas *f pl*

politically correct [pəlídɪklikɔ́rékt] ADJ
políticamente correcto

politician [pɑlɪtíʃən] N político -ca *mf*

politics [pálɪtɪks] N política *f*

polka [pótkə] N polca *f*; **— dot** lunar *m*

poll [pol] N (survey) encuesta *f*; **—s**
(elections) comicios *m pl*; (voting place)
urna *f*; VT (survey) encuestar; (receive
votes) obtener; (record vote of) registrar

pollen [pálən] N polen *m*

pollinate [pálənet] VT polinizar

pollute [pəlút] VI/VT contaminar

pollution [pəlúʃən] N contaminación *f*

polo [pólo] N polo *m*

polyester [pɑliéstə] N poliéster *m*

polygamy [pəlígəmi] N poligamia *f*

polyglot [páliglat] ADJ & N políglota *mf*

polygraph [páligræf] N polígrafo *m*

polymer [páləmə] N polímero *m*

polyp [pálɪp] N pólipo *m*

polyunsaturated [palɪʌnsǽtʃəreɪdɪd] ADJ poliinsaturado

polyurethane [palijúrəθen] N poliuretano *m*

pomegranate [pámɪgrænɪt] N granada *f*; — **tree** granado *m*

pomp [pamp] N pompa *f*, boato *m*, aparato *m*

pompous [pámpəs] ADJ pomposo, aparatoso

pond [pand] N (natural) charca *f*; (artificial) estanque *m*; (for irrigation) balsa *f*

ponder [pándə] VI meditar; VT considerar

ponderous [pándəəs] ADJ enorme

pontoon [pantún] N (on a bridge) pontón *m*; (on an airplane) flotador *m*

pony [póni] N póney *m*; —**tail** colita *f*, cola de caballo *f*; VI **to — up** soltar

poodle [púdl] N caniche *m*

pool [puł] N (puddle of water, blood, etc.) charco *m*; (swimming place) piscina *f*, *Mex* alberca *f*; (association of competitors) pool *m*; (game) pool *m*, billar *m*; (bets) pozo *m*; — **table** billar *m*; — **hall** billar *m*; VI acumularse; VT combinar fondos

poop [pup] N (part of ship) popa *f*; (excrement) *fam* caca *f*; VI *fam* hacer caca

poor [pur] ADJ (lacking money) pobre; (deficient) malo; **I'm a — cook** no sé cocinar; —**house** asilo para los pobres *m*; — **little thing** pobrecito -ta *mf*; **the —** los pobres

pop [pap] VI reventar, estallar; (eyes, cork) saltar; **to — in** entrar de paso; VT (make explode) hacer reventar; (take out cork) hacer saltar; (put) meter; (take, as pills) tomar (píldoras); **to — a question** espetar una pregunta; **to — corn** hacer palomitas; N estallido *m*, detonación *f*; —**corn** palomitas *f pl*; — **music** música popular *f*; — **quiz** prueba sorpresa *f*; — **of a cork** taponazo *m*

Pope [pop] N Papa *m*

poplar [páplə] N álamo *m*, chopo *m*; — **grove** alameda *f*

poppy [pápi] N amapola *f*

popular [pápjələ] ADJ popular; **he's very — with the ladies** tiene mucho éxito con las mujeres

popularity [papjəlǽrɪɾi] N popularidad *f*

populate [pápjəlet] VT poblar

population [papjəléʃən] N población *f*

populous [pápjələs] ADJ populoso

porcelain [pórsəlɪn] N porcelana *f*

porch [pórtʃ] N porche *m*

porcupine [pórkjəpaɪn] N puercoespín *m*

pore [pɔr] N poro *m*; VI **to — over a book** estudiar detenidamente

pork [pɔrk] N carne de cerdo *f*; — **chop** chuleta de cerdo *f*

pornography [pɔrnágrəfi] N pornografía *f*

porous [pórəs] ADJ poroso

porpoise [pórpəs] N marsopa *f*

port [pɔrt] N (harbor, computer) puerto *m*; (wine) oporto *m*; (left side of ship) babor *m*; —**hole** ojo de buey *m*

portable [pórɾəbəł] ADJ portátil

portal [pórɾł] N portal *m* (also of Internet)

portent [pórtɛnt] N (omen) presagio *m*, agüero *m*; (marvel, prodigy) portento *m*

portentous [pɔrtɛntəs] ADJ (ominous) de mal agüero; (prodigious) portentoso

porter [pórɾə] N mozo -za *mf*

portfolio [pɔrtfólio] N cartera *f*; (flat case for papers) carpeta *f*

portion [pórʃən] N porción *f*; VI **to — out** repartir

portly [pórtli] ADJ grueso

portrait [pórtrnt] N retrato *m*

portray [pɔrtré] VT (draw, describe) retratar; (in a drama) representar

portrayal [pɔrtréəł] N (portrait) retrato *m*; (act of portraying) representación *f*

Portugal [pórtʃəgəł] N Portugal *m*

Portuguese [pórtʃəgiz] ADJ & N portugués -esa *mf*

pose [poz] N (posture) pose *f*, postura *f*; (affected attitude) afectación *f*; VI (sit as a model) posar; (act affectedly) afectar una actitud; VT (to make sit as model) hacer posar; (to present) plantear; **to — as** hacerse pasar por

position [pəzíʃən] N (place) posición *f*; (job) puesto *m*, colocación *f*

positive [pázɪɾɪv] ADJ positivo; — **proof** prueba certera *f*; **I am —** estoy seguro

possess [pəzés] VT poseer

possession [pəzéʃən] N posesión *f*

possessive [pəzésɪv] ADJ & N posesivo *m*

possessor [pəzésə] N poseedor -ra *f*

possibility [pasəbílɪɾi] N posibilidad *f*

possible [pásəbəł] ADJ posible

post [post] N (pole) poste *m*; (position) puesto *m*; (mail) correo *m*; —**card** tarjeta postal *f*; — **haste** a la brevedad; —**man** cartero *m*; —**mark** matasellos *m*; —**master** director de correos *m*; — **office** oficina de correos *f*, casa de correos *f*; —-**office box** apartado postal *m*; — **paid** porte pagado; VT (affix) fijar; (announce) anunciar; (list) poner en lista; (place) apostar, situar; (mail) echar al correo; **keep me —ed** manténme al tanto

postage [póstɪdʒ] N franqueo *m*; — **meter** franqueadora *f*; — **stamp** *Sp* sello *m*; *Am* estampilla *f*; *Mex* timbre *m*

postal [póstəł] ADJ postal; **to go —** perpetrar un ataque homicida, volverse loco

poster [póstə-] N cartel *m*, póster *m*, afiche *m*; **— child** modelo *m*

posterior [pastíriə-] ADJ posterior; N trasero *m*

posterity [pastériɖi] N posteridad *f*

postgraduate [postgrǽʤuɪt] ADJ de posgrado

posthumous [pástʃəməs] ADJ póstumo

postpone [postpón] VT posponer, aplazar

postponement [postpónmənt] N aplazamiento *m*

postscript [póstskrɪpt] N posdata *f*

postulate [pástʃəlet] VT postular; [pástʃələt] N postulado *m*

posture [pástʃə-] N (carriage, attitude) postura *f*; (affectation) afectación *f*; VI darse aires

posy [pózi] N ramillete *m*

pot [pɑt] N (vessel) olla *f*, marmita *f*; (marijuana) marihuana *f*; (hashish) *fam* chocolate *m*; **—bellied** panzudo, barrigón; **—hole** bache *m*

potable [pódəbəł] ADJ potable

potassium [pətǽsiəm] N potasio *m*

potato [pətéɖo] N *Sp* patata *f*; *Am* papa *f*; **— chip** patata/papa frita a la inglesa *f*, chip *m*

potency [pótṇsi] N potencia *f*

potent [pótṇt] ADJ potente

potentate [pótṇtet] N potentado -da *mf*

potential [pəténʃəł] ADJ & N potencial *m*

potion [póʃən] N poción *f*

potter [pádə-] N alfarero -ra *mf*

pottery [pádəri] N (craft, shop) alfarería *f*; (objects) cerámica *f*, objetos de alfarería *m pl*

pouch [pautʃ] N bolsa *f*; (for mail) valija *f*; (for tobacco) petaca *f*

poultry [póltri] N aves de corral *f pl*

pounce [pauns] VI saltar; **to — upon/on** abalanzarse sobre; **to — on an opportunity** no dejar pasar una oportunidad; N salto *m*

pound [paund] N (unit of weight, British currency) libra *f*; (blow) golpazo *m*; (place for stray dogs) perrera *f*; VT (a door) golpear; (seeds) machacar; (a military target) bombardear; VI (beat) latir con fuerza

pour [pɔr] VT verter; VI (leave en masse) salir en tropel; (rain) llover a cántaros; **to — out one's feelings** desahogarse

pout [paut] VI hacer pucheros; N puchero *m*

poverty [pávə-ɖi] N pobreza *f*, penuria *f*; **—stricken** indigente

powder [páuɖə-] N polvo *m*; (for the face) polvos *m pl*; (for guns) pólvora *f*; **— compact** polvera *f*; **— puff** borla *f*; **to**

take a — poner pies en polvorosa; VI/VT (use powder) empolvar(se); (pulverize) pulverizar(se)

power [páuə-] N (control) poder *m*, poderío *m*; (might, in physics, in math) potencia *f*; (physical strength) fuerza *f*; (energy) energía *f*; **— of attorney** poder *m*; **— plant** central eléctrica *f*; **— steering** dirección asistida *f*; **legislative —s** atribuciones legislativas *f pl*

powerful [páuə-fəł] ADJ poderoso, potente

powerless [páuə-lɪs] ADJ impotente

practical [prǽktɪkəł] ADJ práctico; **— joke** broma pesada *f*; **— nurse** enfermero -ra sin título *mf*

practice [prǽktɪs] N práctica *f*; (habit) costumbre *f*; (doctor's office) consultorio *m*; (lawyer's office) bufete *m*; VI/VT practicar; VT (a profession) ejercer

practiced [prǽktɪst] ADJ experto, perito

practitioner [prǽktɪʃənə-] N practicante *mf*; **general —** médico -ca general *mf*

pragmatic [prægmǽɖɪk] ADJ pragmático

prairie [préri] N pradera *f*, llanura *f*

praise [prez] N alabanza *f*, elogio *m*; VT alabar, elogiar; **—worthy** loable, encomiable

prance [præns] VI cabriolar, hacer cabriolas; N cabriola *f*

prank [præŋk] N travesura *f*, chasco *m*; **to play —s** hacer travesuras

prawn [prɔn] N langostino *m*; *Sp* gamba pequeña *f*

pray [pre] VI/VT (religious) rezar, orar; (beg) rogar, suplicar

prayer [prer] N (devout petition to God) oración *f*, rezo *m*; (entreaty) ruego *m*, súplica *f*

praying mantis [préɪŋmǽntɪs] N mantis religiosa *f*

preach [pritʃ] VI/VT predicar; (moralize) sermonear

preacher [prítʃə-] N predicador -ra *mf*

preamble [príæmbəł] N preámbulo *m*

precarious [prɪkériəs] ADJ precario

precaution [prɪkɔ́ʃən] N precaución *f*

precede [prɪsíd] VI/VT preceder

precedence [présɪɖəns] N precedencia *f*, prioridad *f*

preceding [prɪsíɖɪŋ] ADJ precedente, anterior

precept [prísɛpt] N precepto *m*

precinct [prísɪŋkt] N distrito *m*; (police station) comisaría *f*; **—s** límites *m pl*

precious [préʃəs] ADJ precioso; (overly refined) preciosista; **— little** muy poco; **— metal** metal precioso *m*; **— stone** piedra preciosa *f*

precipice [présəpɪs] N precipicio *m*, derrumbadero *m*

precipitate [prɪsípɪtet] VI/VT precipitar(se); [prɪsípɪtət] ADJ & N precipitado *m*

precipitation [prɪsɪpɪtéʃən] N precipitación *f*

precipitous [prɪsípɪɖəs] ADJ (steep) escarpado; (hasty) precipitado

precise [prɪsáɪs] ADJ preciso, exacto

precision [prɪsíʒən] N precisión *f*, exactitud *f*; (of expression) propiedad *f*

preclude [prɪklúd] VT excluir; **that doesn't — our considering your application** esto no obsta para que tengamos en cuenta su solicitud

precocious [prɪkóʃəs] ADJ precoz

precursor [prɪkɝ́sə-] N precursor *m*

predator [prédəɖə-] N depredador *m*

predatory [prédəɔtri] ADJ (animal) depredador; (persona) rapaz

predecessor [prédɪsɛsə-] N predecesor -ra *mf*, antecesor -ra *mf*

predestine [pridéstɪn] VT predestinar

predicament [prɪdíkəmənt] N aprieto *m*

predicate [prédɪkɪt] ADJ & N predicado *m*; [prédɪket] VT basar

predict [prɪdíkt] VT predecir

prediction [prɪdíkʃən] N predicción *f*, vaticinio *m*

predilection [predlékʃən] N predilección *f*

predispose [pridɪspóz] VI/VT predisponer

predominance [prɪdámənəns] N predominio *m*

predominant [prɪdámənənt] ADJ predominante

predominate [prɪdámənet] VI/VT predominar, preponderar

preface [préfɪs] N prefacio *m*, prólogo *m*; VT hacer una introducción; (a book) prologar

prefer [prɪfɝ́-] VT preferir; **to — a claim** presentar una demanda

preferable [préfə-əbəl] ADJ preferible

preference [préfə-əns] N preferencia *f*

preferential [prefə-rénʃəl] ADJ preferente

preferred [prɪfɝ́-d] ADJ preferido; **— stocks** acciones preferentes *f pl*

prefix [prífɪks] N prefijo *m*; VT poner un prefijo

pregnancy [prégnənsi] N embarazo *m*; (of an animal) preñez *f*

pregnant [prégnənt] ADJ (person) embarazada, encinta; (animal) preñada; (full of meaning, rain) preñado, cargado

prehensile [prihénsəl] ADJ prensil

prehistoric [prihɪstɔ́rɪk] ADJ prehistórico

prejudge [pridʒʌ́dʒ] VT prejuzgar

prejudice [prédʒədɪs] N (bias) prejuicio *m*; (harm) perjuicio *m*; VT (cause bias against)

predisponer en contra; (harm) perjudicar

preliminary [prɪlímənɛri] ADJ & N preliminar *m*

prelude [prélud] N preludio *m*; VI/VT preludiar

premarital [primǽrɪɖəl] ADJ prematrimonial

premature [primətʃúr] ADJ prematuro

premeditated [priméditeɖɪd] ADJ premeditado

premier [prɪmír] N primer ministro / primera ministra *mf*; ADJ principal

premiere [prɪmír] N estreno *m*, première *f*

premise [prémɪs] N premisa *f*; **—s** local *m*

premium [prímiəm] N (bonus) premio *m*; (insurance) prima *f*; (surcharge) recargo *m*; **at a —** muy escaso; ADJ superior

premonition [prɛmənɪ́ʃən] N premonición *f*

prenatal [prinéɖəl] ADJ prenatal

prenuptial [prinʌ́pʃəl] ADJ prenupcial

preoccupy [priákjəpaɪ] VT absorber

prepaid [pripéd] ADJ pagado de antemano; **to send —** enviar porte pagado

preparation [prɛpəréʃən] N (act of preparing) preparación *f*; (substance) preparado *m*; (for a trip) preparativos *m pl*

preparatory [prépə-ətɔri] ADJ preparatorio, preparativo

prepare [prɪpér] VI/VT preparar(se)

preponderance [prɪpándə-əns] N preponderancia *f*

preponderant [prɪpándə-ənt] ADJ preponderante

preposition [prɛpəzíʃən] N preposición *f*

preposterous [prɪpástə-əs] ADJ absurdo

prerequisite [prirékwəzɪt] N prerequisito *m*

prerogative [prɪrágəɖɪv] N prerrogativa *f*

prescribe [prɪskráɪb] VT (order) prescribir; (medicine) recetar

prescription [prɪskrípʃən] N (order) prescripción *f*; (of medicine) receta *f*

presence [prézəns] N presencia *f*; **— of mind** aplomo *m*, presencia de ánimo *f*

present [prézənt] N (time) presente *m*; (gift) regalo *m*, presente *m*; **at —** ahora; **for the —** por ahora; ADJ (at a place) presente; (at this time) actual; **— company excepted** con perdón de los presentes; **—day** actual; **— participle** gerundio *m*; **— perfect** pretérito perfecto *m*; [prɪzént] VT presentar, entregar

presentable [pnzéntəbəl] ADJ presentable

presentation [prɛzəntéʃən] N presentación *f*, entrega *f*; (talk) ponencia *f*

presentiment [prɪzéntəmənt] N presentimiento *m*

presently [prézəntli] ADV (soon) pronto; (now) actualmente

preservation [prɛzɚ-véʃən] N preservación f,
conservación f

preservative [prɪzɚ́-vədɪv] N conservante m

preserve [prɪzɚ́-v] VI/VT (protect) preservar;
(keep food fresh) conservar; N (for game)
coto m; (for animals) reserva f; **—s**
mermelada f, dulce m

preside [prɪzáɪd] VI presidir; **to — over a
meeting** presidir una reunión

presidency [prézɪdənsi] N presidencia f

president [prézɪdənt] N presidente -ta mf

presidential [prɛzɪdénʃəl] ADJ presidencial

press [prɛs] VI/VT (bear down, squeeze)
apretar, oprimir; (iron) planchar; (force)
presionar; (extract juice) prensar; (put
under pressure) apremiar; **to — on**
avanzar; **to — one's point** insistir en un
argumento; **to — through** abrirse paso; N
(newspapers) prensa f; (printing machine)
imprenta f; (crowding) empuje m; **—
conference** conferencia de prensa f; **—
corps** cuerpo de prensa m; **— release**
comunicado de prensa m

pressing [présɪŋ] ADJ apremiante, urgente

pressure [préʃɚ] N presión f; **— cooker** olla
a presión f; **— gauge** manómetro m; **—
group** grupo de presión m; VT apremiar,
presionar

prestige [prɛstíʒ] N prestigio m

prestigious [prɛstíʤəs] ADJ prestigioso

presume [prɪzúm] VI (be presumptuous)
presumir; VT (suppose) suponer; (dare)
atreverse a

presumption [prɪzámpʃən] N presunción f

presumptuous [prɪzámptʃuəs] ADJ
presuntuoso, presumido

presuppose [prisəpóz] VT presuponer

preteen [pritín] ADJ & N preadolescente mf

pretend [prɪténd] VI/VT (make believe) hacer
de cuenta que; (feign) fingir; VT (claim)
pretender; **to — to the throne** pretender
el trono

pretense [prítɛns] N (faked action or belief)
engaño m; (false show) apariencia f;
under — of so pretexto de

pretension [prɪténʃən] N pretensión f;
(pretext) pretexto m

pretentious [prɪténʃəs] ADJ (full of
pretension) pretencioso; (showy) ostentoso

pretext [prítɛkst] N pretexto m

pretrial [pritráɪl] ADJ anterior al juicio

pretty [prídi] ADJ bonito; (human only) Sp
guapo; ADV bastante; VI/VT **to — up**
embellecer

prevail [prɪvél] VI (win) prevalecer; (be
widespread, dominant) preponderar,
imperar; **to — on (upon)** persuadir

prevailing [prɪvélɪŋ] ADJ (dominant)
predominante; (existing) reinante

prevalent [prévələnt] ADJ prevaleciente,
preponderante

prevent [prɪvént] VT (keep from occurring)
prevenir; VI/VT (impede) impedir

prevention [prɪvénʃən] N prevención f; (of a
disease) prevención f, profilaxis f

preventive [prɪvéntɪv] ADJ preventivo

preview [prívju] N preestreno m

previous [prívias] ADJ previo, anterior

prey [pre] N (animal) presa f; VI **to — on**
alimentarse de cazar; **it —s upon my
mind** me tiene preocupado

price [praɪs] N precio m; **at any — a** toda
costa; **— control** control de precios m; **—
fixing** fijación de precios f; **— index**
índice de precios m; **— tag** etiqueta de
precio f; VT (set price) poner precio a; (ask
price) averiguar el precio de

priceless [práɪslɪs] ADJ (without price)
invalorable; (amusing) divertidísimo

prick [prɪk] N (puncture) pinchazo m; (sharp
point) púa f; (penis) vulg pija f; (creep)
offensive hijo de puta m; VT pinchar,
punzar; **to — up one's ears** parar las
orejas

prickly [príkli] ADJ espinoso; **— heat**
sarpullido causado por el calor m; **— pear**
tuna f, nopal m

pride [praɪd] N orgullo m; (excessive) soberbia
f; VI **to — oneself on** enorgullecerse de

priest [prist] N sacerdote m; (Catholic only)
cura m; **—hood** sacerdocio m

prim [prɪm] ADJ remilgado

primary [práɪmɛri] ADJ primario; (main)
fundamental, principal; **— colors** colores
primarios m pl; **— election** elección
primaria f; **— school** escuela primaria f

primate [práɪmet] N primate m

prime [praɪm] ADJ (principal) fundamental;
(of a number) primo; (select) de primera;
— minister primer ministro m, primera
ministra f; N (stage) flor f; (number)
número primo m; **to be in one's — estar
en la flor de la edad, estar en la plenitud
de la vida; **— rate** tasa prima f; VT
preparar; (a pump) cebar

primer [prímɚ] N (first book) manual
elemental m; (pump part) cebador m

primitive [prímɪtɪv] ADJ & N primitivo -va
mf

prince [prɪns] N príncipe m

princely [prínsli] ADJ noble, principesco; **a —
sum** una suma muy grande

princess [prínsɛs] N princesa f

principal [prínsəpəl] ADJ principal; N

(money invested) capital *m*; (giver of power of attorney) poderdante *mf*, mandante *mf*; (head of a school) director -ora *mf*

principle [prínsəpəl] N principio *m*

print [prɪnt] VI/VT imprimir; (write in block letters) escribir en letra de molde; **to — out** imprimir; N (type) letra de imprenta *f*; (of art) lámina *f*; (of photographs) copia *f*; (of fingers) huella digital *f*; (on cloth) estampado *m*; **—out** listado *m*; **in —** publicado, en venta; **out of —** agotado

printer [príntə] N (person) impresor -ra *mf*, gráfico -ca *mf*; (machine) impresora *f*

printing [príntɪŋ] N (art, trade) imprenta *f*; (process) impresión *f*, tipografía *f*; (block letters) letra de molde *f*, letra de imprenta *f*; **— press** imprenta *f*; **this book is in its second —** este libro está en su segunda edición

prior [práɪə] ADJ previo; **— to** anterior a

priority [praɪɔ́rɪɾi] N prioridad *f*

prism [prízəm] N prisma *m*

prison [prízən] N prisión *f*, cárcel *f*, presidio *m*

prisoner [prízənə] N (captive) prisionero -ra *mf*; (in jail) preso -sa *mf*, presidiario -ria *mf*; **— of war** prisionero -ra de guerra *mf*

pristine [prɪstín] ADJ (immaculate) puro; (perfect) perfecto

privacy [práɪvəsi] N privacidad *f*

private [práɪvɪt] ADJ (not public) privado; (individual) particular; **— enterprise** empresa privada *f*; **— eye** detective privado -da *mf*; **— parts** partes pudendas *f pl*; **— school** escuela privada *f*; **— sector** sector privado *m*; **a — citizen** un particular; **in —** en privado; N soldado raso *m*

privation [praɪvéʃən] N privación *f*

privilege [prívəlɪdʒ] N privilegio *m*

privileged [prívəlɪdʒd] ADJ privilegiado

privy [prívi] ADJ **to be — to** estar enterado de; N retrete *m*

prize [praɪz] N (reward) premio *m*; (booty) botín *m*; **— fight** pelea de boxeo profesional *f*; **— fighter** boxeador -ora *mf*, pugilista *mf*; VT apreciar

pro [pro] N profesional *mf*

probability [prabəbílɪɾi] N probabilidad *f*

probable [prábəbəl] ADJ probable

probation [probéʃən] N libertad condicional *f*

probe [prob] VI/VT (explore with a probe) sondear; (examine) examinar; N sonda *f* (also space); (investigation) indagación *f*

problem [prábləm] N problema *m*

procedure [prəsíʤə] N procedimiento *m*; (legal) trámite *m*

proceed [prəsíd] VI (originate) proceder; (continue) proseguir, continuar; **to — against** demandar a; **to — to** proceder a; N **—s** ganancia *f*, lo recaudado

proceedings [prəsídɪŋz] N (events) acontecimientos *m pl*; (record of a conference) actas *f pl*, memoria *f*; (legal action) procedimiento *m*

process [práses] N proceso *m*; **in the — of** en vías de

procession [prəséʃən] N procesión *f*

pro-choice [protʃɔ́ɪs] ADJ proaborto

proclaim [prəklém] VT proclamar

proclamation [prakləméʃən] N proclamación *f*, proclama *f*

procrastinate [prəkræstənet] VI/VT dejar para último momento

procreate [prókriet] VI/VT procrear, engendrar

procure [prəkjúr] VT procurar, obtener; VI ser proxeneta

prod [prad] VT aguijonear; **they —ded me into going / to go** insistieron en que fuera

prodigal [prádɪgəl] ADJ & N pródigo -ga *mf*

prodigious [prədíʤəs] ADJ prodigioso

prodigy [prádəʤi] N prodigio *m*

produce [pródus] N (vegetables) verduras *f pl*, hortalizas *f pl*; [prədús] VI/VT producir; VT (present) presentar

producer [prədúsə] N productor -ora *mf*

product [prádəkt] N producto *m*

production [prədákʃən] N producción *f*; (TV, radio) producción *f*, realización *f*; (exaggerated situation) teatro *m*

productive [prədáktɪv] ADJ productivo

profane [profén] ADJ profano; (vulgar) grosero; VT profanar

profanity [prəfǽnɪɾi] N groserías *f pl*, palabrotas *f pl*

profess [prəfés] VI/VT (publicly accept, take vows) profesar; VT (express) expresar

profession [prəféʃən] N profesión *f*

professional [prəféʃənəl] ADJ & N profesional *mf*

professor [prəfésə] N profesor -ra universitario -ria *mf*; (full) catedrático -ca *mf*

proffer [práfə] VT ofrecer; N oferta *f*

proficiency [prəfíʃənsi] N competencia *f*

proficient [prəfíʃənt] ADJ competente

profile [prófaɪl] N (contour) perfil *m*; **a high-— case** un caso muy sonado

profit [práfɪt] N (gain) ganancia *f*; **— and loss** ganancias y pérdidas *f pl*; **— sharing**

participación en las ganancias de una empresa *f*; **at a —** con ganancia; **to turn a —** dar ganancia; **not for —** sin fines de lucro; VI salir ganando; **to — from** (benefit) aprovechar, sacar provecho de; (use to get an advantage) aprovecharse de; VT servir

profitable [práfɪṭəbəł] ADJ (beneficial) provechoso; (lucrative) lucrativo, rentable

profound [prəfáund] ADJ profundo

profundity [prəfʌ́ndɪṭi] N profundidad *f*

profuse [prəfjús] ADJ profuso, pródigo

progesterone [proʤéstəron] N progesterona *f*

prognosis [prɑgnósɪs] N pronóstico *m*

program [prógræm] N programa *m*; VI/VT programar

programmer [prógræmə] N programador -ora *mf*

programming [prógræmɪŋ] N programación *f*

progress [prágres] N progreso *m*; [prəgrés] VI progresar

progressive [prəgrésɪv] ADJ (advancing) progresivo; ADJ & N (liberal) progresista *mf*, progresivo -va *mf*

prohibit [prohíbɪt] VT prohibir, vedar

prohibition [proəbíʃən] N prohibición *f*

project [práʤekt] N proyecto *m*; [prəʤékt] VI/VT proyectar(se); VI (jut out) sobresalir

projectile [prəʤéktaɪł] N proyectil *m*; ADJ arrojadizo

projection [prəʤékʃən] N proyección *f*; (jut) saliente *f*

projector [prəʤéktə] N proyector *m*

proletariat [prolɪtériət] N proletariado *m*

pro-life [prolaíf] ADJ antiaborto

prolific [prəlífɪk] ADJ prolífico

prologue [prólɔg] N prólogo *m*

prolong [prəlɔ́ŋ] VT prolongar

prolongation [prolɔŋgéʃən] N prolongación *f*

promenade [prɑmənéd] N paseo *m*; (prom) baile *m*; VI/VT pasear(se)

prominent [prámənənt] ADJ prominente

promiscuous [prəmískjuəs] ADJ promiscuo, liviano

promise [prámɪs] N promesa *f*; **he showed —** prometía mucho; VI/VT prometer

promising [prámɪsɪŋ] ADJ prometedor, halagüeño

promissory [prámɪsɔri] ADJ promisorio; **— note** pagaré *m*

promontory [práməntɔri] N promontorio *m*

promote [prəmót] VT (foster) promover, fomentar; (advance in rank) ascender; (in school) pasar de año, promover; (advertise) promocionar

promoter [prəmóṭə] N (fomenter) propulsor -ora *mf*; (organizer) promotor -ora *mf*

promotion [prəmóʃən] N (act of promoting) promoción *f*; (advance in rank) ascenso *m*

prompt [prɑmpt] ADJ (quick) rápido; (punctual) puntual; VT (cause) inducir; (in theater) apuntar; **to give someone a —** apuntarle a alguien

promptly [prámptli] ADV (soon) pronto; (punctually) puntualmente

promulgate [práməłget] VT promulgar

prone [pron] ADJ (disposed) propenso, proclive; (face down) boca abajo; (prostrate) postrado

prong [prɔŋ] N púa *f*, diente *m*

pronoun [prónaun] N pronombre *m*

pronounce [prənáuns] VT (enunciate) pronunciar; (declare) declarar

pronounced [prənáunst] ADJ pronunciado

pronunciation [prənʌnsiéʃən] N pronunciación *f*

proof [pruf] N (evidence, test, trial printing) prueba *f*; (of alcohol) graduación *f*, grado *m*; **— of purchase** comprobante de compra *m*; **—reader** corrector -ra de pruebas *mf*; **fifty —** veinticinco por ciento de graduación alcohólica; ADJ **fire—** a prueba de incendios; **water—** impermeable; **bullet—** a prueba de balas

prop [prɑp] N (pole) puntal *m*; (in theater) accesorio *m*; (propeller) hélice *f*; (support) sostén *m*, apoyo *m*; (of a plant) tutor *m*; VT **to — against** apoyar en, sostener en; **to — up** apuntalar, sostener

propaganda [prɑpəgǽndə] N propaganda *f*

propagate [prápəget] VI/VT propagar(se)

propagation [prɑpəgéʃən] N propagación *f*

propane [própen] N propano *m*

propel [prəpéł] VT propulsar, impulsar

propeller [prəpélə] N hélice *f*

propensity [prəpénsɪṭi] N propensión *f*

proper [prápə] ADJ (appropriate) apropiado; (decorous) decoroso; (genuine) como Dios manda; (correct) correcto; (in math, grammar) propio; **to be — to** ser propio de

property [prápə·ṭi] N (characteristic) propiedad *f*; (real estate) propiedad *f*, finca *f*; (assets) bienes *m pl*

prophecy [práfɪsi] N profecía *f*

prophesy [práfɪsaɪ] VI/VT profetizar

prophet [práfɪt] N profeta -tisa *mf*

prophetic [prəfédɪk] ADJ profético

propitious [prəpíʃəs] ADJ propicio

proponent [prəpónənt] N (person who proposes) proponente *mf*; (adherent) defensor -ra *mf*

proportion [prəpórʃən] N proporción f; **out of** — desproporcionado; VT proporcionar; **well** —**ed** bien proporcionado

proposal [prəpózəł] N (suggestion) propuesta f; (of marriage, dishonest) proposición f

propose [prəpóz] VI/VT (suggest) proponer; VI (ask in marriage) declararse, hacer una proposición de matrimonio; **to** — **to do something** proponerse hacer algo

proposition [prɑpəzíʃən] N proposición f; VT hacer proposiciones deshonestas

proprietor [prəpráiɪɾɚ] N propietario -ria mf

propriety [prəpráiɪɾi] N decoro m

propulsion [prəpʌ́łʃən] N propulsión f

prorate [prorét] VT prorratear

prosaic [prozéɪk] ADJ prosaico

prose [proz] N prosa f

prosecute [prásɪkjut] VI/VT (take to court) procesar, enjuiciar; VT (pursue) llevar adelante

prosecution [prɑsɪkjúʃən] N (act of prosecuting) procesamiento m; (officials who prosecute) ministerio público m, fiscalía f

prosecutor [prásɪkjuɾɚ] N fiscal mf

proselytize [prásəlɪtaɪz] VT convertir; VI ganar prosélitos

prospect [práspɛkt] N (outlook, possibility) perspectiva f, expectativa f; (candidate) candidato -ta mf; (possible client) posible cliente -ta mf; VT prospectar; VI **to** — **for** buscar

prospective [prəspɛ́ktɪv] ADJ posible, potencial

prospector [práspɛktɚ] N prospector -ora mf

prosper [práspɚ] VI prosperar

prosperity [prɑspɛ́rɪɾi] N prosperidad f, bonanza f

prosperous [práspərəs] ADJ próspero

prostate [prástet] N próstata f; — **gland** próstata f

prosthesis [prɑsθísɪs] N prótesis f

prostitute [prástɪtut] N prostituto -ta mf; VT prostituir

prostrate [prástret] VT postrar; ADJ (lying flat, overcome) postrado; (lying face down) boca abajo

protagonist [protǽɡənɪst] N protagonista mf

protect [prətɛ́kt] VI/VT proteger, amparar

protection [prətɛ́kʃen] N protección f

protectionist [prətɛ́kʃənɪst] ADJ & N proteccionista mf

protective [prətɛ́ktɪv] ADJ protector

protector [prətɛ́ktɚ] N protector -ra mf

protectorate [prətɛ́ktərɪt] N protectorado m

protégé, protégée [próɾəʒe] N protegido -da mf

protein [prótin] N proteína f

protest [prótɛst] N protesta f, reclamación f; [prətɛ́st] VI/VT protestar, reclamar

Protestant [práɾɪstənt] ADJ & N protestante mf

protestation [protɛstéʃən] N declaración f

protocol [próɾəkɔł] N protocolo m

proton [prótɑn] N protón m

protoplasm [próɾəplæzəm] N protoplasma m

prototype [próɾətaɪp] N prototipo m

protozoan [proɾəzóən] N protozoario m

protract [protrǽkt] VT prolongar

protrude [protrúd] VI sobresalir, proyectarse

protuberance [prətúbərəns] N protuberancia f

proud [praʊd] ADJ orgulloso; (haughty) soberbio; **to be** — **of** enorgullecerse de, ufanarse de

prove [pruv] VT (demonstrate) probar, demostrar; (verify) resultar; VI resultar; **events have** —**d me right** los hechos me han dado la razón

proverb [právɚb] N proverbio m, refrán m

provide [prəváɪd] VT (furnish) proveer, proporcionar; (supply) abastecer, aportar; (stipulate) estipular, prevenir; VI **to** — **for** (support) mantener; (stipulate) estipular; **to** — **with** proveer de, proporcionar

provided [prəváɪdɪd] CONJ (that) con tal (de) que, siempre que

providence [právɪdəns] N providencia f

provider [prəváɪdɚ] N (supplier) proveedor -ra mf; (breadwinner) sostén m

province [právɪns] N (area) provincia f; (competence) competencia f

provincial [prəvínʃəł] ADJ (of a province) provincial; (rustic) provinciano, pueblerino; N provinciano -na mf

provision [prəvíʒən] N (act of providing, thing provided) provisión f, prestación f; (precaution) medida f, precaución f; (clause) estipulación f, prevención f; —**s** provisiones f pl, víveres m pl, bastimentos m pl

provisional [prəvíʒənəł] ADJ provisional

proviso [prəváizo] N condición f, estipulación f

provocation [prɑvəkéʃən] N provocación f

provoke [prəvók] VT provocar

provost [próvost] N vicerrector -ora f

prow [praʊ] N proa f

prowess [práʊɪs] N valentía f

prowl [praʊł] VI/VT rondar en acecho

proximity [prɑksímɪɾi] N proximidad f

proxy [práksi] N (person) apoderado -da mf; (power of attorney) poder m; **by** — por poder

prude [prud] N mojigato -ta *mf*, gazmoño -ña *mf*

prudence [prúdn̩s] N prudencia *f*

prudent [prúdn̩t] ADJ prudente

prudery [prúpəri] N mojigatería *f*, gazmoñería *f*

prudish [prúdɪʃ] ADJ mojigato, gazmoño

prune [prun] N ciruela pasa *f*; VI/VT podar

pry [praɪ] VT curiosear; **to — into** entrometerse; **to — open** abrir por la fuerza; **to — a secret out** extraer / arrancar un secreto

pseudonym [súdn̩ɪm] N seudónimo *m*

psoriasis [sɔráɪəsɪs] N psoriasis *f*

psychedelic [saɪkədélɪk] ADJ psicodélico

psychiatrist [saɪkáɪətrɪst] N psiquiatra *mf*

psychiatry [saɪkáɪətri] N psiquiatría *f*

psychic [sáɪkɪk] ADJ psíquico; N médium *mf*, psíquico -ca *mf*

psychological [saɪkəládʒɪkəl] ADJ psicológico

psychologist [saɪkáləʤɪst] N psicólogo -ga *mf*

psychology [saɪkáləʤi] N psicología *f*

psychopath [sáɪkəpæθ] N psicópata *mf*

psychosis [saɪkósɪs] N psicosis *f*

psychosomatic [saɪkosəmǽDɪk] ADJ psicosomático

psychotherapy [saɪkoθérəpi] N psicoterapia *f*

psychotic [saɪkáDɪk] ADJ psicótico

puberty [pjúbəɾi] N pubertad *f*

public [páblɪk] ADJ público; **— domain** dominio público *m*; **— relations** relaciones públicas *f pl*; **— school** escuela pública *f*; **— service** servicio público *m*; N público *m*

publication [pʌblɪkéʃən] N publicación *f*

publicity [pʌblísɪDi] N publicidad *f*, propaganda *f*

publish [páblɪʃ] VI/VT publicar, editar; **—ing house** editorial *f*

publisher [páblɪʃə] N editor -ra *mf*

puck [pʌk] N puck *m*

pucker [pákə] VI/VT fruncir(se); N frunce *m*

pudding [púdɪŋ] N budín *m*

puddle [pádl̩] N charco *m*

Puerto Rican [pɔrɾəríkən] ADJ & N puertorriqueño -ña *mf*

Puerto Rico [pɔrɾəríko] N Puerto Rico *m*

puff [pʌf] N (air) resoplido *m*, soplo *m*; (smoke) bocanada *f*; (on a cigarette) pitada *f*, chupada *f*; (of a sleeve) bullón *m*; **— pastry** masa de hojaldre *f*; VI (blow) resoplar; (breathe hard) jadear; (smoke a cigarette) echar bocanadas; **to — up** hincharse; **to — up with pride** henchirse de orgullo

pug [pʌg] N dogo *m*; **— nose** nariz chata *f*

puke [pjuk] VI/VT vomitar, lanzar; N vómito *m*

pull [pʊl] VI/VT (tug) tirar, jalar; (extract) arrancar, extraer; (stretch) estirar; (injure) desgarrarse; **to — apart** destrozar; **to — down** (demolish) demoler; (earn) sacar; **to — for** hinchar; **to — off** conseguir; **to — oneself together** calmarse; **to — over** parar; **to — up** parar; **to — through** salvarse; **to — strings** mover palancas; **to — out** (leave a place) salir; (back out) retirarse; **the train —ed into the station** el tren entró a la estación; N (act of pulling) tirón *m*; (force) fuerza *f*; (influence) influencia *f*; (injury) desgarro *m*

pullet [pʊlɪt] N polla *f*

pulley [pʊli] N polea *f*, carrucha *f*

pulp [pʌłp] N (of paper, wood, fruit) pulpa *f*; (residue of grape, sugarcane, olive, etc.) bagazo *m*

pulpit [pʊłpɪt] N púlpito *m*

pulsar [pʌłsar] N púlsar *m*

pulsate [pʌłset] VI latir

pulse [pʌłs] N pulso *m*; (single pulsation, act of pulsing) pulsación *f*

pulverize [pálvəraɪz] VT pulverizar(se)

pumice [pámɪs] N piedra pómez *f*

pump [pʌmp] N bomba *f*; (shoe) zapatilla *f*, zapato escotado *m*; (for gasoline) surtidor *m*; VI/VT bombear; (inflate) inflar; **to — someone for information** sonsacar (información) a alguien

pumpkin [pámpkɪn] N calabaza *f*

pun [pʌn] N juego de palabras *m*, retruécano *m*; VI hacer juegos de palabras

punch [pʌntʃ] N (blow) puñetazo *m*; (drink) ponche *m*; (drill) sacabocados *m sg*; (force) fuerza *f*, empuje *m*; **— bowl** ponchera *f*; **— line** remate de un chiste *m*; VI/VT (hit) dar un puñetazo; VT (drive cattle) arriar; (make a hole) agujerear; **to — in / out** marcar tarjeta

punctual [páŋktʃuəł] ADJ puntual

punctuality [pʌŋktʃuǽlɪDi] N puntualidad *f*

punctuate [páŋktʃuet] VI/VT puntuar; (interrupt) interrumpir; (accentuate) salpicar

punctuation [pʌŋktʃuéʃən] N puntuación *f*

puncture [páŋktʃə] VI/VT pinchar(se); **—d tire** neumático pinchado *m*; N (action of perforating) perforación *f*; (hole) pinchazo *m*

pundit [pándɪt] N experto -ta *mf*

pungent [pándʒənt] ADJ (acrid) acre; (sarcastic) mordaz

punish [pánɪʃ] VT castigar, penar

punishment [pánɪʃmənt] N castigo *m*

punitive [pjúnɪdɪv] ADJ punitivo; —
damages daños punitivos *m pl*

punk [pʌŋk] N (inexperienced boy) mocoso
m; (hoodlum) gamberro *m*; (rock) punk *m*;
(punker) punkero -ra *mf*

punt [pʌnt] N (kick) patada de despeje *f*;
(boat) balsa *f*; VI/VT despejar; VI andar en
balsa

puny [pjúni] ADJ endeble, ruin

pupil [pjúpəl] N escolar *mf*; — **of the eye**
pupila *f*, niña *f*

puppet [pápɪt] N títere *m*, monigote *m*; —
show teatro de títeres *m*

puppy [pápi] N cachorro *m*

purchase [pə́ːtʃəs] VI/VT comprar, adquirir; N
compra *f*; (hold) asidero *m*

purchaser [pə́ːtʃəsə] N comprador *mf*

pure [pjur] ADJ puro; ADJ & N —**bred**
purasangre *m*

puree [pjuré] N puré *m*

purgative [pə́ːgədɪv] ADJ & N purgante *m*

purgatory [pə́ːgətəri] N purgatorio *m*

purge [pə́ːdʒ] VI/VT purgar(se); N purga *f*

purify [pjúrəfaɪ] VI/VT purificar(se),
depurar(se)

purist [pjúrɪst] N purista *mf*

puritanical [pjurɪtǽnɪkəl] ADJ puritano

purity [pjúrɪti] N pureza *f*

purple [pə́ːpəl] N morado *m*, púrpura *f*; ADJ
púrpura *inv*, morado

purport [pə́ːpɔrt] N (meaning) significado *m*;
(purpose) propósito *m*; [pə-pórt] VT
pretender

purpose [pə́ːpəs] N propósito *m*, objetivo *m*;
on — adrede, a propósito

purr [pə] N ronroneo *m* (also motors); VI
ronronear

purse [pə́ːs] N bolso *m*, cartera *f*; VT **to** —
one's lips fruncir los labios

pursuant [pə-súənt] ADV LOC — **to** conforme
a, de acuerdo con

pursue [pə-sú] VT (follow) perseguir; (strive)
dedicarse a; (continue) continuar con;
(practice a profession) ejercer

pursuer [pə-súə] N perseguidor -ora *mf*

pursuit [pə-sút] N (chase) persecución *f*,
seguimiento *m*; (striving for) búsqueda *f*;
(pastime) pasatiempo *m*; (practice)
ejercicio *m*; **in** — **of** (chasing) detrás de;
(striving for) en busca de

pus [pʌs] N pus *m*

push [puʃ] VI/VT (shove) empujar; VT
(pressure) presionar, promover; (sell drugs)
camellear; VI (in childbirth) pujar; **to** —
aside / away apartar; **to** — **forward**
abrirse paso, avanzar; **to** — **open** abrir de
un empujón; **to** — **through** hacer pasar;

to — **a button** apretar un botón; N
empujón *m*; (military) ofensiva *f*;
—**-button** de botones; —**-up** lagartija *f*

pusher [púʃə] N camello *mf*

pushy [púʃi] ADJ insistente

pussy [púsi] N (cat) minino *m*, gatito *m*;
(female genitalia) *vulg* coño *m*; *Am vulg*
concha *f*; —**-whipped man** *vulg*
calzonazos *m sg*; — **willow** sauce *m*

put [pʊt] VT poner, colocar; **to** — **a**
question plantear una pregunta; **to** —
across expresar; **to** — **away** guardar; **to**
— **down** (write down) apuntar; (suppress)
sofocar; (attribute) atribuir; (humiliate)
humillar; (make a deposit) hacer un
depósito; **to** — **into** meter; **to** — **into**
words expresar, decir; **to** — **in writing**
poner por escrito; **to** — **off** (postpone)
aplazar, posponer; (perturb) desagradar; **to**
— **on** ponerse; **to** — **on airs** darse tono;
to — **on weight** engordar; **to** — **out**
(extinguish) apagar, extinguir; (annoy)
molestar; **to** — **the blame** echar la culpa;
to — **to sea** echar al mar; **to** — **up**
(construct) levantar; (lodge) alojar; **to** —
up for sale poner a la venta; **to** — **up**
with aguantar; —**-down** insulto *m*; **I**
felt —**-upon** sentí que se habían
aprovechado de mí

putrid [pjútrɪd] ADJ putrefacto

putter [pádə] VI entretenerse; N putter *m*

putty [pádi] N masilla *f*; VT rellenar con
masilla

puzzle [pázəl] N (jigsaw) rompecabezas *m sg*;
(riddle) acertijo *m*; (problem) enigma *m*;
(crossword) crucigrama *m*; VT dejar
perplejo, desconcertar; VI **to** — **out**
desentrañar; **to** — **over** meditar sobre; **to**
be —**d** estar perplejo

pygmy [pígmi] N pigmeo -a *mf*

pylon [páɪlən] N pilón *m*

pyramid [pírəmɪd] N pirámide *f*

pyromaniac [paɪroméniæk] N pirómano -na
mf

pyrotechnics [paɪrətékniks] N pirotecnia *f*

python [páɪθən] N pitón *mf*

Qq

Qatar [katár] N Qatar *m*

Qatari [kətári] ADJ & N catarí *mf*

quack [kwæk] N (sound of duck) graznido *m*;
(charlatan) matasanos *mf*, charlatán -ana

mf; ADJ charlatán; VI graznar

quadrilateral [kwadrəlǽɾəɹt] ADJ & N cuadrilátero *m*

quadriplegic [kwadrəplíʤɪk] ADJ & N tetrapléjico -ca *mf*

quadruped [kwádrəped] ADJ & N cuadrúpedo *m*

quadruplet [kwɑdrúplɪt] N cuatrillizo -za *mf*

quagmire [kwǽgmaɪr] N (bog) cenagal *m*, atascadero *m*; (crisis) atolladero *m*, atascadero *m*

quail [kweł] N codorniz *f*

quaint [kwent] ADJ pintoresco

quake [kwek] N (instance of quaking) temblor *m*; (earthquake) terremoto *m*; VI temblar

qualification [kwaləfɪkéʃən] N (for a race) clasificación *f*; (requirement) requisito *m*; **without —** sin reservas

qualify [kwáləfaɪ] VT (characterize) calificar; (moderate) moderar; (provide with credentials) capacitar; VI (for a race) clasificarse; (for a position) estar capacitado

quality [kwálɪɖi] N (characteristic) cualidad *f*; (excellence) calidad *f*

qualm [kwɔm] N escrúpulo *m*

quantify [kwántəfaɪ] VT cuantificar

quantity [kwántɪɖi] N cantidad *f*

quantum mechanics [kwántəmmməkénɪks] N mecánica cuántica *f*

quarantine [kwɔ́rəntin] N cuarentena *f*; VT poner en cuarentena

quarrel [kwɔ́rəł] N riña *f*, rencilla *f*; VI reñir, pelear

quarrelsome [kwɔ́rəłsəm] ADJ pendenciero

quarry [kwɔ́ri] N (stone) cantera *f*; (game) presa *f*; VT explotar

quart [kwɔrt] N cuarto de galón (0.9463 litros) *m*

quarter [kwɔ́rɖə] N (one-fourth) cuarto *m*, cuarta parte *f*; (coin) moneda de 25 centavos *f*; (of a sporting match) tiempo *m*; (of a calendar or school year) trimestre *m*; (district) barrio *m*; **— note** negra *f*; **—s** alojamiento *m*; **from all —s** de todas partes; **to give no — to the enemy** no dar cuartel al enemigo; ADJ cuarto; VT (divide) cuartear, dividir en cuartos; (execute) descuartizar; (lodge troops) acuartelar, acantonar

quarterly [kwɔ́rɖəli] ADV trimestralmente; ADJ trimestral; N publicación trimestral *f*

quartet [kwɔrtét] N cuarteto *m*

quartz [kwɔrts] N cuarzo *m*

quasar [kwézar] N cuásar *m*, quásar *m*

quash [kwaʃ] VT (a rebellion) sofocar; (a decision) anular

quaver [kwévə] VI temblar; N temblor *m*; (in music) trémolo *m*

queasy [kwízi] ADJ nauseoso

queen [kwin] N reina *f*; (effeminate male homosexual) *offensive* loca *f*; *offensive* reinona *f*

queer [kwir] ADJ (strange) raro; (eccentric) excéntrico; (homosexual) *offensive* maricón; **to feel —** sentirse raro; N (homosexual) *offensive* marica *m*, maricón *m*; VT comprometer

quell [kweł] VT (suppress) reprimir, sofocar; (calm) calmar

quench [kwentʃ] VT (flames, thirst) apagar; (passions) aplacar, apagar

query [kwíri] N (question) pregunta *f*; (question mark) signo de interrogación *m*; (doubt) duda *f*; VT (ask) preguntar; (question) expresar dudas; (mark with a question mark) marcar con signo de interrogación

quest [kwest] N búsqueda *f*

question [kwéstʃən] N (thing asked) pregunta *f*; (issue) cuestión *f*; **— mark** signo de interrogación *m*; **beyond —** fuera de duda; **that is out of the —** ¡ni pensarlo! VT (ask) preguntar; (interrogate) interrogar; (call into doubt) dudar, cuestionar

questionable [kwéstʃənəbəł] ADJ (doubtful) cuestionable, discutible; (morally dubious) equívoco

questioner [kwéstʃənə] N interrogador -ra *mf*

questioning [kwéstʃənɪŋ] N interrogatorio *m*; ADJ (asking) interrogador; (doubting) cuestionador

questionnaire [kwestʃənér] N cuestionario *m*

quibble [kwíbəł] VI (split hairs) sutilizar; (evade) evadir; (argue) andar en dimes y diretes; N (hairsplitting) sutileza *f*; (evasion) evasiva *f*

quiche [kiʃ] N quiche *f*

quick [kwɪk] ADJ rápido, pronto; **—-tempered** irascible, geniudo; **—-witted** agudo; ADV rápido; N (flesh under nails) carne viva *f*; (the living) los vivos; **to cut to the —** herir en lo vivo; **—sand** arena movediza *f*; **—silver** mercurio *m*, azogue *m*

quicken [kwíkən] VI/VT (speed up) acelerar(se), aligerar(se); (liven) avivar(se)

quickly [kwíkli] ADV rápido, deprisa

quickness [kwíknɪs] N (speed) rapidez *f*; (of wit) agudeza *f*

quiet [kwáɪt] ADJ (not noisy) silencioso; (not talking) callado; (restrained) tranquilo; (peaceful, still) reposado; **be —!** ¡silencio!

¡cállate! N (freedom from noise) silencio *m*; (tranquility) tranquilidad *f*, sosiego *m*; VT (make quiet) acallar; (make tranquil) sosegar, tranquilizar, serenar; VI **to — down** calmarse

quill [kwɪɫ] N (feather) pluma *f*; (hollow base of feather) cañón *m*; (spine on a porcupine) púa *f*

quilt [kwɪɫt] N edredón *m*; VI/VT acolchar

quip [kwɪp] N ocurrencia *f*; VI decir ocurrencias

quirk [kwɝk] N excentricidad *f*

quit [kwɪt] VT (a competition) abandonar; (a place) irse de, salir de; (a job) dejar; **to call it —s** abandonar; **to — smoking** dejar de fumar; VI (withdraw) abandonar; (stop) parar; (resign) renunciar

quite [kwaɪt] ADV (very) bastante; (entirely) del todo, enteramente; **— a person** una persona admirable *f*; **— a lot** bastante; **it's — the fashion** está muy de moda

quiver [kwívɚ] VI temblar; N (shake) temblor *m*; (sheath for arrows) carcaj *m*, aljaba *f*

quiz [kwɪz] N (test) prueba *f*; (show) concurso *m*; VI (give a quiz) examinar, poner una prueba; (interrogate) interrogar

quota [kwóɾə] N cuota *f*

quotation [kwotéʃən] N cita *f*; (of a price) cotización *f*; **— marks** comillas *f pl*

quote [kwot] VI/VT citar; (prices) cotizar; **to — from** citar a; N cita *f*; (of a price) cotización *f*; **in —s** entre comillas

quotient [kwóʃənt] N cociente *m*

Rr

rabbi [ræbaɪ] N rabino -na *mf*

rabbit [ræbɪt] N conejo *m*

rabble [ræbəɫ] N chusma *f*, plebe *f*, gentuza *f*

rabid [ræbɪd] ADJ rabioso

rabies [rébiz] N rabia *f*

raccoon [rækún] N mapache *m*

race [res] N (lineage) raza *f*; (competition) carrera *f*; **—horse** caballo de carreras *m*; **—track** (for runners) pista *f*; (for horses) hipódromo *m*; VI (participate in competition) correr, competir en una carrera; (hurry) ir corriendo; (of heart) latir rápido; (of a motor) acelerar; VT (a horse) hacer correr; (an engine) acelerar; **I'll — you** te echo una carrera

racer [résɚ] N corredor -ra *mf*; (horse) caballo de carreras *m*

racial [réʃəɫ] ADJ racial

racism [résɪzəm] N racismo *m*

rack [ræk] N (for clothes) perchero *m*; (on a vehicle) baca *f*; (for spices) especiero *m*; (for towels) toallero *m*; (torture) potro de tormento *m*; **— and pinion** cremallera *f* y piñón *m*; VT **to be —ed with pain** estar transido de dolor; **to — one's brain** devanarse los sesos; **to — up** acumular

racket [rækɪt] N (sports) raqueta *f*; (noise of an impact) estrépito *m*, estruendo *m*; (noise of voices and movement) barahúnda *f*, batahola *f*; (swindle) estafa *f*; (extortion) extorsión *f*

racketeer [rækɪtír] N trapacero -ra *mf*; (swindler) estafador -ra *mf*; (extortionist) extorsionista *mf*; VI (swindle) estafar; (extort) extorsionar

radar [réɖɑr] N radar *m*

radial [rédiəɫ] ADJ radial

radiance [rédiəns] N resplandor *m*, fulgor *m*

radiant [rédiənt] ADJ radiante, resplandeciente

radiate [rédiet] VI/VT irradiar, radiar; (health) derrochar

radiation [rediéʃən] N radiación *f*

radiator [rédietɚ] N radiador *m*

radical [rædɪkəɫ] ADJ & N radical *mf*

radicalism [rædɪkəlɪzəm] N radicalismo *m*

radio [rédio] ADJ **—active** radiactivo, radioactivo; N (device, system of communication) radio *f*; **— announcer** locutor -ra *mf*; **— listener** radioescucha *mf*; **— station** radiodifusora *f*; **— telescope** radiotelescopio *m*; **— transmitter** radiotransmisor *m*; **by —** por radio; VT (broadcast) transmitir por radio; VI/VT (call) llamar por radio

radiology [rediáləʤi] N radiología *f*

radish [rædɪʃ] N rábano *m*

radium [rédiəm] N radio *m*

radius [rédiəs] N radio *m*

radon [rédan] N radón *m*

raffle [ræfəɫ] N rifa *f*, sorteo *m*; VI rifar, sortear

raft [ræft] N balsa *f*

rafter [ræftɚ] N viga *f*, cabrio *m*

rag [ræg] N (piece of cloth) trapo *m*, guiñapo *m*; (clothes) harapo *m*, andrajo *m*; **— doll** muñeca de trapo *f*

rage [reʤ] N ira *f*, rabia *f*, cólera *f*; **to be all the —** estar de moda; VI enfurecerse; **to — with anger** bramar de ira

ragged [rægɪd] ADJ (ill-clothed) andrajoso, harapiento, desharrapado; (voice) ronco, roto; (on an edge) irregular, desigual; **to be on the — edge** estar al borde

raid [red] N (military) incursión f; (by police) allanamiento m, redada f; (by air) bombardeo aéreo m; VI/VT hacer una incursión; VT (attack) atacar; (rob) asaltar; (by the police) allanar

rail [reł] N (of a railroad track) riel m, carril m; (railing) baranda f, barandilla f; — **fence** barrera f; —**road** ferrocarril m; —**road company** empresa ferroviaria f; —**road crossing** cruce de ferrocarril m; —**road employee** ferroviario -a mf; **to** —**road** (goods) transportar por ferrocarril; (laws) hacer aprobar apresuradamente; (a person) condenar injustamente; —**way** ferrocarril m; **by** — por ferrocarril

railing [réłɪŋ] N (barrier) baranda f; (on a bridge) pretil m; (on a stairway) pasamano m

rain [ren] N lluvia f; —**bow** arco iris m; —**coat** impermeable m; —**drop** gota de lluvia f; —**fall** precipitación f; — **forest** selva tropical f; — **gauge** pluviómetro f; —**storm** temporal de lluvia f; — **water** agua llovediza f; VI/VT llover; — **or shine** llueva o truene; **to** — **cats and dogs** llover a cántaros

rainy [réni] ADJ lluvioso

raise [rez] VI/VT (voice, hand, a house, spirits) levantar(se); VT (prices) subir; (an alarm) dar; (a flag) izar; (crops) cultivar; (animals, children) criar; (money) recabar, recaudar; **to** — **a question** plantear una pregunta; **to** — **a racket** armar un alboroto; N aumento m

raisin [rézn] N pasa (de uva) f

rake [rek] N rastrillo m; VI/VT rastrillar; **to** — **in money** amasar dinero

rally [réłi] VI/VT (reorganize troops) reunir(se), juntar(se); (inspire) reanimar; VI (demonstrate) concentrarse; (recuperate) recuperarse; (reinvigorate) recobrar ánimo; (rise in value) repuntar; **to** — **around someone** apoyar a alguien; N (demonstration) concentración f; (recovery) recuperación f; (rise in prices) subida f

RAM (random-access memory) [ræm] N RAM m

ram [ræm] N (male sheep) carnero m; (tool for battering) ariete m; (part of a ship) espolón m; VT chocar contra; **to** — **a boat** embestir un buque con el espolón

ramble [rémbəł] VI vagar; **to** — **on** divagar; N paseo m

ramp [ræmp] N rampa f

rampage [rémpeʤ] N **to go on a** — andar destrozando todo; VI andar destrozando todo

rampant [rémpənt] ADJ desenfrenado

ranch [rænʧ] N hacienda f; Mex rancho m

rancid [rénsɪd] ADJ rancio

rancor [rénkɚ] N rencor m

random [réndəm] ADJ aleatorio, azaroso; **at** — al azar; — **access memory** memoria de acceso directo f

range [renʤ] N (gamut) gama f; (of a gun) alcance m; (amplitude of variation) fluctuación f; (of mountains) cadena f; (for shooting) campo de tiro m; (of an aircraft) autonomía f; (grazing place) campo abierto m; (stove) cocina f; Mex estufa f; — **finder** telémetro m; VT alcance visual m; VT (align) alinear; (of a gun) tener alcance; VI (vary) oscilar; (be found in an area) extenderse; **his children** — **in age between 2 and 10** sus hijos van en edad entre 2 y 10

ranger [rénʤɚ] N (in a park) guardabosques mf; (soldier) guardia de asalto m

rank [ræŋk] N (in a hierarchy) rango m, grado m; (line) fila f; — **and file** (of an army) tropa f sg; **the** —**s** (soldiers) la tropa; (union members) bases f pl; **a sculptor of the first** — un escultor de primer orden; VT (arrange) poner en orden de importancia; VI (rate) figurar; **to** — **high** tener alto rango; **to** — **second** estar clasificado en el segundo lugar; ADJ (smelly) hediondo; (growing vigorously) exuberante

ransack [rénsæk] VT saquear, desvalijar

ransom [rénsəm] N rescate m; VT rescatar

rant [rænt] VI/VT despotricar

rap [ræp] VI/VT (strike) golpear; (chat) charlar; VI rapear, cantar rap; N (blow) golpe m; (accusation) cargo m; **to take the** — ser el cabeza de turco; — **music** música rap f

rapacious [rəpéʃəs] ADJ rapaz

rape [rep] N (violation) violación f; (statutory) estupro m; (plant) colza f; (grape pulp) orujo m; VT violar

rapid [répɪd] ADJ rápido; N —**s** rápidos m pl

rapidity [rəpídɪti] N rapidez f

rapport [rəpór] N relación f

rapt [ræpt] ADJ extasiado

rapture [répʧɚ] N éxtasis m, embeleso m; **to go into a** — arrobarse

rare [rer] ADJ (infrequent) raro, poco frecuente, extraño; (of gas, earth) raro; (thin, of air) enrarecido; (excellent) excepcional; (not well-done) crudo; — **earths** tierras raras f pl

rarity [rérɪti] N rareza f; (of air) enrarecimiento m

rascal [ɹǽskəl] N bribón *m*, bellaco *m*, pícaro *m*; *Sp* golfo *m*; **you little —!** ¡bandido! ¡sinvergüenza!

rash [ɹæʃ] ADJ (thoughtless) precipitado, temerario; N sarpullido *m*

raspberry [ɹǽzberi] N frambuesa *f*; **— bush** frambueso *m*

raspy [ɹǽspi] ADJ ronco, áspero

rat [ɹæt] N rata *f*; **I smell a —** aquí hay gato encerrado; VI (one's hair) cardar; **to — on** chivar, delatar

ratchet [ɹǽtʃit] N trinquete *m*

rate [ret] N (amount of interest) tasa *f*; (charge) tarifa *f*; (unit charge for insurance) prima *f*; (pace) paso *m*, ritmo *m*; **— of exchange** tipo de cambio *m*; **at any —** en todo caso; **at this —** a este ritmo; **at the — of** a razón de; VT (estimate) valorar, estimar; (esteem) considerar; **he —s as the best** se le considera como el mejor; **he —s high** se le tiene en alta estima

rather [ɹǽðɚ] ADV (somewhat) bastante; (more precisely) más bien; **— than** en vez de; **I would — die than** antes la muerte que; **I would — not go** prefiero no ir

ratify [ɹǽdəfaɪ] VT ratificar

rating [ɹédɪŋ] N (act of adjudging) calificación *f*; (for credit) clasificación *f*; (TV quotient) rating televisivo *m*, índice de audiencia *m*

ratio [ɹéʃio] N razón *f*, proporción *f*

ration [ɹǽʃən] N ración *f*; VT racionar

rational [ɹǽʃənəl] ADJ racional

rationale [ɹæʃənǽl] N motivo *m*

rationalize [ɹǽʃənəlaɪz] VI/VT racionalizar

rationing [ɹǽʃənɪŋ] N racionamiento *m*

rattle [ɹǽdl] VI (bang) golpetear; (move noisily) traquetear; **to — on** parlotear; VT hacer sonar, sacudir; **to — off** recitar; N (banging) golpeteo *m*; (movement) traqueteo *m*; (toy) sonaja *f*, sonajero *m*; (of a rattlesnake) cascabel *m*; (of death) estertor *m*, **—snake** víbora de cascabel *f*

raucous [ɹɔ́kəs] ADJ (loud) estridente; (rowdy) escandaloso

ravage [ɹǽvɪdʒ] VI/VT asolar, arruinar; N estrago *m*

rave [ɹev] VI (rant) desvariar, delirar; VI/VT (roar) bramar; **to — about** deshacerse en elogios; N crítica muy favorable *f*

raven [ɹévən] N cuervo *m*; ADJ azabache

ravenous [ɹǽvənəs] ADJ voraz, famélico; **to be —** tener un hambre canina

ravine [ɹəvín] N quebrada *f*, barranco *m*, cañada *f*

raving [ɹévɪŋ] ADJ delirante; (extraordinary)

extraordinario; **— mad** loco de remate; N desvarío *m*

ravish [ɹǽvɪʃ] VT (kidnap) raptar, secuestrar; (rape) violar

raw [ɹɔ] ADJ (uncooked, unprocessed, damp and cold) crudo; (of vegetables) fresco, crudo; (unadorned) descarnado; **— flesh** carne viva *f*; **— material** materia prima *f*; **— sugar** azúcar bruto *m*; N **—hide** cuero crudo *m*

ray [ɹe] N (beam) rayo *m*; (stingray) raya *f*

rayon [ɹéɑn] N rayón *m*

raze [ɹez] VT arrasar, asolar

razor [ɹézɚ] N (device with blade) maquinilla de afeitar *f*, rasuradora *f*; (barber's tool) navaja *f*; (electric) rasuradora electrica *f*; **— blade** hoja de afeitar *f*; **safety —** navaja de seguridad *f*

reach [ɹitʃ] VI/VT (extend) alcanzar; VT (arrive at) llegar a; (contact) ponerse en contacto con; **to — for** tratar de agarrar; *Sp* tratar de coger; **to — into** meter la mano en; **to — out one's hand** alargar la mano; N alcance *m*; **beyond his —** fuera de su alcance; **within his —** a su alcance; **far —es** zona remota *f*

react [ɹiǽkt] VI reaccionar

reaction [ɹiǽkʃən] N reacción *f*

reactionary [ɹiǽkʃəneɹi] ADJ & N reaccionario -ria *mf*

reactor [ɹiǽktɚ] N reactor *m*

read [ɹid] VI/VT leer; VT (interpret) interpretar; (give as a reading) decir; (indicate) indicar, marcar; **it —s easily** es fácil de leer; N lectura *f*

reader [ɹídɚ] N (person who reads) lector -ra *mf*; (schoolbook) libro de lectura *m*, cartilla *f*; (anthology) antología *f*

readily [ɹédli] ADV fácilmente

readiness [ɹédɪnɪs] N estado de preparación *m*; (willingness) buena disposición *f*; **to be in —** estar preparado, estar listo

reading [ɹídɪŋ] N lectura *f*; (interpretation) interpretación *f*; **— room** sala de lectura *f*

readjust [ɹiədʒʌ́st] VI/VT (improve fit) reajustar; (acclimate) readaptar

readjustment [ɹiədʒʌ́stmənt] N (fitting) reajuste *m*; (acclimation) readaptación *f*

ready [ɹédi] ADJ (prepared) listo, preparado, pronto; (willing) dispuesto; (available) disponible; (quick) rápido; **—-made** de confección

reagent [ɹiédʒənt] ADJ & N reactivo *m*

real [ɹil] ADJ real, verdadero; **— estate** bienes raíces *m pl*, bienes inmuebles *m pl*

realism [ɹíəlɪzəm] N realismo *m*

realist [ɹíəlɪst] N realista *mf*

realistic [rɪəlístɪk] ADJ realista

reality [rɪǽlɪDi] N realidad f; — **check** ajuste de perspectiva m

realization [rɪəlɪzéʃən] N (making real) realización f; (understanding) comprensión f

realize [ríəlaɪz] VT (achieve) realizar; (comprehend) darse cuenta de, comprobar

realm [rɛlm] N (kingdom) reino m; (domain) terreno m, esfera f

realtorᵐ [ríəltɚ] N agente inmobiliario -ria mf

reap [rip] VI/VT (cut with sickle) segar; (harvest) cosechar; **to — a benefit** obtener, sacar

reaper [rípɚ] N (person) segador -ora mf; (machine) segadora f; (death) la Parca, la Muerte

reappear [riəpír] VI reaparecer

rear [rir] ADJ trasero, posterior; **—guard** retaguardia f; N (space at the back) parte de atrás f, fondo m; (backside) trasero m, posaderas f pl; — **end** trasero m; **—view mirror** espejo retrovisor m; VT (raise) criar; VI (rise on back legs) encabritarse, empinarse

reason [rízən] N (faculty) razón f; (cause) motivo m, razón f; **by — of** por causa de; **it stands to** — es lógico; VI razonar; **to — out** resolver por medio de la razón; **to — with** hacer entrar en razón

reasonable [rízənəbəl] ADJ razonable; (in price) módico, moderado

reasoning [rízənɪŋ] N razonamiento m, raciocinio m; ADJ racional

reassure [riəʃúr] VT tranquilizar

rebate [ríbet] N reembolso m, reintegro m; VT reembolsar, reintegrar

rebel [rɛbəl] ADJ & N rebelde mf, insurrecto -ta mf; [rɪbɛl] VI rebelarse

rebellion [rɪbéljən] N rebelión f

rebellious [rɪbéljəs] ADJ rebelde, insurrecto

rebelliousness [rɪbéljəsnɪs] N rebeldía f

rebound [rɪbáʊnd] VI (bounce) rebotar; (recover) recuperarse; [ríbaʊnd] N rebote m; **on the —** de rebote

rebuff [rɪbʌ́f] N desaire m, repulsa f; VT desairar, rechazar

rebuild [ribíld] VI/VT reconstruir, reedificar; (auto engine) reacondicionar

rebuke [rɪbjúk] VT reprender, reprochar; N reproche m, reprimenda f

recall [rɪkɔ́l] VT (remember) recordar; (call back) retirar; (remove from office) destituir; [ríkɔl] N (memory) memoria f; (of a diplomat, product) retirada f; (from office) destitución f

recapitulate [rikəpítʃəlet] VI/VT recapitular

recast [rikǽst] VT refundir

recede [rɪsíd] VI retroceder; (of hairline) tener entradas

receipt [rɪsít] N recibo m; **upon — of** al recibo de; **—s** entradas f pl, ingresos m pl

receive [rɪsív] VI/VT recibir; (suggestions) acoger, recibir; (a broadcast) captar, recibir

receiver [rɪsívɚ] N recibidor -ora mf; (of a telephone) auricular m; (of a television or radio, in sports) receptor m; (of a business) síndico m

recent [rísənt] ADJ reciente

receptacle [rɪséptəkəl] N receptáculo m

reception [rɪsépʃən] N (hotel, social event, TV) recepción f; (act of receiving) recibimiento m, acogida f; — **room** recibidor m

recess [ríses] N (niche) nicho m, entrante m; (pause) descanso m; (playtime) recreo m; **in the —es** en lo más recóndito de; VI/VT (a meeting) interrumpir; VT (a wall) hacer un nicho en

recession [rɪséʃən] N (act of receding) retroceso m; (economic) recesión f

recipe [résəpi] N receta f

recipient [rɪsípiənt] N destinatario -ria mf

reciprocal [rɪsíprəkəl] ADJ recíproco

reciprocate [rɪsíprəket] VI/VT corresponder (a)

recital [rɪsáɪdl] N recital m

recitation [resɪtéʃən] N recitación f

recite [rɪsáɪt] VI/VT recitar

reckless [réklɪs] ADJ (driver) temerario, imprudente; (speed) desenfrenado

recklessness [réklɪsnɪs] N temeridad f, imprudencia f

reckon [rékən] VI/VT calcular; (consider) considerar; (think) suponer

reckoning [rékənɪŋ] N (computation) cálculo m; (settlement of accounts) ajuste de cuentas m; **the day of —** el día del juicio final

reclaim [rɪklém] VT (win back, recover) recuperar; (make land usable) ganar, sanear

recline [rɪkláɪn] VI/VT reclinar(se), recostar(se)

recluse [réklus] ADJ & N solitario -ria mf, ermitaño -ña mf

recognition [rekəgníʃən] N reconocimiento m

recognize [rékəgnaɪz] VT reconocer

recoil [rɪkɔ́ɪl] VI (firearm) dar un culatazo; (move back) retroceder; [ríkɔɪl] N (of a gun) culatazo m; (move back) retroceso m

recollect [rekəlékt] VI/VT recordar

recollection [rekəlékʃən] N recuerdo m

recommend [rɛkəménd] VI/VT recomendar

recommendation [rɛkəmendéʃən] N recomendación f

recompense [rékəmpɛns] VI/VT recompensar; N recompensa f

reconcile [rékənsaɪt] VT (persons) reconciliar; (statements) conciliar; **to — oneself to** resignarse a, conformarse con

reconciliation [rɛkənsɪliéʃən] N reconciliación f

reconnoiter [rikənɔ́ɪdə] VT reconocer; VI hacer un reconocimiento

reconsider [rikənsídə] VI/VT reconsiderar

reconstruct [rikənstrʌ́kt] VT reconstruir

reconstruction [rikənstrʌ́kʃən] N reconstrucción f

record [rékə·d] N (account) registro m, asiento m; (account of a meeting) acta f; (of criminal acts) antecedentes m pl; (of past activities) historial m, hoja de servicios f; (phonographic) disco m; (best performance) récord m, marca f; — **player** tocadiscos m sg; **off the** — extraoficialmente; [rɪkɔ́rd] VI/VT (write down) registrar, apuntar; (cut a recording) grabar

recorder [rɪkɔ́rdə] N (archivist) archivero -ra mf; (sound device) grabadora f; (musical instrument) flauta dulce f

recording [rɪkɔ́rdɪŋ] N grabación f; — **company** grabadora f

recount [rɪkáunt] VT (tell) narrar, relatar; [ríkaunt] (count again) recontar

recourse [ríkɔrs] N recurso m; **to have — to** recurrir a

recover [rɪkʌ́və] VI/VT recobrar(se), recuperar(se); VI (lost health) restablecerse; VT (lost time, property) recuperar; (damages) obtener indemnización

recovery [rɪkʌ́vəri] N recuperación f, recobro m; (from a lawsuit) indemnización f

recreation [rɛkriéʃən] N recreación f, recreo m, esparcimiento m

recreational [rɛkriéʃənəł] ADJ de recreo; — **drug** droga de recreo f; — **vehicle** caravana f

recriminate [rɪkrímənet] VI/VT recriminar

recruit [rɪkrút] N recluta mf; VI/VT reclutar

recruitment [rɪkrútmənt] N reclutamiento m, recluta f

rectangle [réktæŋgəł] N rectángulo m

rectify [réktəfaɪ] VT rectificar

rector [réktə·] N rector -ra mf

rectum [réktəm] N recto m

recuperate [nkúpəret] VI/VT recuperar(se), recobrar(se)

recur [nkɚ́] VI volver a ocurrir, repetirse

recycle [risáɪkəł] VI/VT reciclar

red [rɛd] ADJ & N rojo m, colorado m; — **blood cell** glóbulo rojo m; —-**handed** fam in fraganti; —-**headed** pelirrojo; —-**hot** candente, al rojo vivo; — **light** luz roja f; —-**neck** granjero -ra blanco -ca pobre mf; — **pepper** pimienta de cayena f; — **snapper** pargo m; — **tape** trámites m pl; — **wine** vino tinto m; —-**wood** secoya / secuoya f; **in the** — en números rojos; **to see** — enfurecerse

redden [rédn] VI/VT enrojecer, ruborizar(se)

reddish [rédɪʃ] ADJ rojizo, bermejo

redeem [rɪdím] VT (deliver from sin) redimir; (pay off a mortgage) cancelar; (buy back) desempeñar; (exchange) canjear; (fulfill) cumplir

redemption [rɪdémpʃən] N redención f; (of something pawned) desempeño m

redness [rédnɪs] N rojez f; (inflammation) inflamación f

redress [rídrɛs] N reparación f, desagravio m; [rɪdrés] VT reparar, desagraviar

reduce [rɪdús] VI/VT reducir(se); **she was —d to tears** se echó a llorar

reduction [rɪdʌ́kʃən] N reducción f

redundant [rɪdʌ́ndənt] ADJ (repetitive) redundante; (superfluous) superfluo

reed [rid] N caña f, junco m, carrizo m; (of a musical instrument) lengüeta f

reef [rif] N (underwater ridge) escollo m; (of coral) arrecife m

reek [rik] VI heder, apestar; N hedor m

reel [rił] N carrete m, bobina f; VT (on a spool) bobinar; VI tambalearse; **to — off** recitar; **to — in a fish** sacar un pez del agua

reelect [riɪlékt] VT reelegir

reelection [riɪlékʃən] N reelección f

reestablish [riɪstǽblɪʃ] VT restablecer

refer [rɪfɚ́] VI referir; (direct to a source of information) remitir; (direct to a doctor) mandar; (mention) referirse a, aludir; (look up in) consultar

referee [rɛfərí] N árbitro m; VT (a game) arbitrar; (a submission) hacer el referato

reference [réfərəns] N (mention) referencia f; — **book** libro de consulta m; **with — to** con respecto a, respecto de

referendum [rɛfəréndəm] N referéndum m

referral [rɪfɚ́əł] N **he gave me a — to a specialist** me mandó con un especialista

refill [rifɪ́ł] VI/VT rellenar; [rífɪł] N (for a pen) repuesto m; (for a lighter) carga f; **may I have a —?** ¿me sirve más?

refine [nfáɪn] VT (purify) refinar; (polish) refinar, pulir

refined [rɪfáɪnd] ADJ refinado

refinement [rɪfáɪnmənt] N (of manners) refinamiento *m*, pulimento *m*; (of oil) refinación *f*

refinery [rɪfáɪnəri] N refinería *f*; (of sugar) ingenio *m*

reflect [rɪflékt] VI/VT (mirror) reflejar; VI (ponder) reflexionar; **to — poorly on** desacreditar

reflection [rɪflékʃən] N (image) reflejo *m*; (consideration) reflexión *f*; (unfavorable observation) tacha *f*; **on —** pensándolo bien

reflector [rɪfléktə] N reflector *m*

reflex [rɪfleks] ADJ & N reflejo *m*

reflexive [rɪfléksɪv] ADJ reflexivo

reform [rɪfɔrm] VI/VT reformar(se); N reforma *f*

reformation [refəméʃən] N reforma *f*

reformatory [rɪfɔrmətɔri] N reformatorio *m*

reformer [rɪfɔrmə] N reformador -ra *mf*, reformista *mf*

refraction [rɪfrǽkʃən] N refracción *f*

refractory [rɪfrǽktɔri] ADJ (not malleable) refractario; (rebellious) rebelde

refrain [rɪfrén] VI abstenerse; N estribillo *m*

refresh [rɪfréʃ] VI/VT refrescar(se)

refreshing [rɪfréʃɪŋ] ADJ (drink) refrescante; (sleep) reparador; (honesty) agradable

refreshment [rɪfréʃmənt] N (drink) refresco *m*; (food) refrigerio *m*

refrigerate [rɪfrídʒəret] VT refrigerar

refrigeration [rɪfrɪdʒəréʃən] N refrigeración *f*

refrigerator [rɪfrídʒəretə] N *Sp* frigorífico *m*, nevera *f*; *Am* refrigerador *m*; *RP* heladera *f*

refuge [réfjudʒ] N refugio *m*

refugee [refjudʒí] N refugiado -da *mf*

refund [rífʌnd] N reembolso *m*; [rɪfʌnd] VT reembolsar

refurbish [rɪfɜ́bɪʃ] VT restaurar

refusal [rɪfjúzəl] N negativa *f*, rechazo *m*; **first —** opción *f*

refuse [rɪfjúz] VI/VT (deny a request) rehusarse (a); (decline to accept) negarse (a); VT (reject) rechazar, desechar; **to — to** rehusarse a, negarse a; [réfjus] N desechos *m pl*, desperdicios *m pl*

refute [rɪfjút] VT refutar, rebatir

regain [rɪgén] VT (recover) recobrar; (get back to) volver a

regal [rígəl] ADJ regio, real

regard [rɪgárd] VT (consider) considerar; (esteem) estimar; **as —s** en cuanto a; N (consideration) consideración *f*; (esteem) respeto *m*, estima *f*; **—s** recuerdos *m pl*, saludos *m pl*; **with — to** con respecto a

regarding [rɪgárdɪŋ] PREP con respecto a

regardless [rɪgárdlɪs] ADV LOC **— of** independientemente de

regenerate [rɪdʒénəret] VI/VT regenerar(se)

regent [rídʒənt] N regente -ta *mf*

reggae [régé] N reggae *m*

regime [rɪʒím] N régimen *m*

regiment [rédʒəmənt] N regimiento *m*

region [rídʒən] N región *f*

register [rédʒɪstə] N (recording, range of voice) registro *m*; (entry) asiento *m*; VI/VT (enter into a list) registrar(se); (enroll) matricular(se), inscribir(se); VT (indicate) indicar, registrar; (a letter) certificar; VI (appear) aparecer; **that didn't —** no cayó en la cuenta

registered [rédʒɪstə-d] ADJ registrado; **— mail** correo certificado *m*; **— nurse** enfermero -ra titulado -da *mf*; **— trademark** marca registrada *f*

registrar [rédʒɪstrɑr] N secretario -ria de admisiones *mf*

registration [redʒɪstréʃən] N registro *m*; (of a car) matrícula *f*; (of a student) inscripción *f*

regret [rɪgrét] VT (feel sorry) lamentar; (feel rueful) arrepentirse de; N arrepentimiento *m*; **to send —s** enviar sus excusas

regretful [rɪgrétfəl] ADJ lleno de remordimientos

regrettable [rɪgrédəbəl] ADJ lamentable

regroup [rigrúp] VT reagrupar; VI reorganizarse

regular [régjələ] ADJ (symmetrical, uniform) regular; (normal) normal; (habitual) habitual; **a — fool** un verdadero necio; **a — guy** un buen tipo; (habitual customer) parroquiano -na *mf*; (soldier) soldado de línea *m*

regularity [regjəlǽrɪdi] N regularidad *f*

regulate [régjəlet] VT (control) regular; (make regular) regularizar

regulation [regjəléʃən] N regulación *f*; **—s** reglamento *m*

regulator [régjəledə] N regulador *m*

regurgitate [rigɜ́dʒɪtet] VI/VT regurgitar

rehabilitate [rihəbílɪtet] VI/VT rehabilitar(se)

rehearsal [rɪhɜ́səl] N ensayo *m*

rehearse [rɪhɜ́s] VI/VT ensayar

reign [ren] N reino *m*, reinado *m*; VI reinar

reimburse [riɪmbɜ́s] VI/VT reembolsar

reimbursement [riɪmbɜ́smənt] N reembolso *m*

rein [ren] N rienda *f* (also control); VI **to — in** dominar, refrenar

reincarnation [riɪnkarnéʃən] N reencarnación *f*

reindeer [réndɪr] N reno *m*

reinforce [riɪnfɔ́rs] VT reforzar

reinforcement [riɪnfɔ́rsmənt] N refuerzo *m*

reiterate [riʃɾəret] VT reiterar

reject [rɪʤékt] VT rechazar; [rɪʤekt] N (thing) cosa rechazada *f*, desecho *m*; (person) rechazado -da *mf*

rejoice [rɪʤɔ́ɪs] VI regocijarse

rejoicing [rɪʤɔ́ɪsɪŋ] N regocijo *m*

rejoin [rɪʤɔ́ɪn] VT (come again into group) reincorporarse a; VI/VT (reunite) volver a unir(se); [riʤɔ́ɪn] VI/VT replicar

rejuvenate [rɪʤúvənet] VI/VT rejuvenecer

relapse [rɪlǽps] VI (into bad health) recaer; (into crime) reincidir; [rílæps] N (into bad health) recaída *f*; (into crime) reincidencia *f*

relate [rɪlét] VT (tell) relatar, narrar; (connect) relacionar; VI **to —** relacionarse con

related [rɪlédɪd] ADJ (connected) relacionado; (kin) emparentado

relation [rɪléʃən] N (association) relación *f*; (act of narrating) narración *f*; (kinship) parentesco *m*; (relative) pariente -ta *mf*; **with —** con respecto a

relationship [rɪléʃənʃɪp] N relación *f*

relative [rélədɪv] ADJ relativo; N pariente -ta *mf*, allegado -da *mf*; **— to** relativo a, referente a

relax [rɪlǽks] VI/VT relajar(se), distender(se); VT (grip) aflojar

relaxation [rɪlækséʃən] N (recreation) esparcimiento *m*, recreo *m*; (loosening) relajamiento *m*, relajación *f*

relay [ríle] N relevo *m*, posta *f*; (electrical) relé *m*; **— race** carrera de relevos/postas *f*; [rɪlé] VT transmitir; **to — a broadcast** transmitir un programa

release [rɪlís] VT (let go) soltar; (free prisoners) librar, poner en libertad; (energy) liberar; (news) divulgar; (discharge from hospital) dar de alta; N (liberation) liberación *f*; (permission) permiso *m*; (of film) estreno *m*; (of gas) escape *m*; (of energy) desprendimiento *m*

relegate [rélɪget] VT relegar

relent [rɪlént] VI aplacarse

relentless [rɪléntlɪs] ADJ implacable

relevant [réləvənt] ADJ pertinente

reliability [rɪlaɪəbílɪdi] N fiabilidad *f*, confiabilidad *f*

reliable [rɪláɪəbəl] ADJ fiable, confiable; (a person) formal

reliance [rɪláɪəns] N (dependency) dependencia *f*; (trust) confianza *f*

relic [rélɪk] N reliquia *f*

relief [rɪlíf] N (ease) alivio *m*; (aid) ayuda *f*; (projection) relieve *m*; (soldier) relevo *m*;

in — en relieve; **— map** mapa en relieve *m*

relieve [rɪlív] VT (alleviate) aliviar; (free) liberar; (replace) relevar; VI **to — oneself** orinar

religion [rɪlíʤən] N religión *f*

religious [rɪlíʤəs] ADJ religioso

relinquish [rɪlíŋkwɪʃ] VT (give up) renunciar; (let go) soltar

relish [rélɪʃ] VT (to like the taste) saborear, paladear; (enjoy) disfrutar; N (enjoyment) gusto *m*; (condiment) condimento de pepinillos en vinagre *m*

relocate [rilóket] VI/VT trasladar(se)

reluctance [rɪláktəns] N renuencia *f*

reluctant [rɪláktənt] ADJ renuente, reacio

rely [rɪláɪ] VI **to — on** (trust) confiar en; (depend on) depender de

REM (rapid eye movement) [ɑriém] N REM *m*

remain [rɪmén] VI (continue to be) seguir siendo; (stay) quedar(se), permanecer; (to be left) quedar, restar; (to be left over) sobrar; VI **—s** restos *m pl*

remainder [rɪméndə] N resto *m*, remanente *m*

remake [rimék] VT rehacer; (film) hacer de nuevo; [rímek] N nueva versión *f*

remark [rɪmárk] VT (comment) comentar, observar; (notice) notar, observar; **to — on** comentar; N observación *f*, comentario *m*

remarkable [rɪmárkəbəl] ADJ notable

remedial [rɪmídiəl] ADJ (rehabilitative) rehabilitador; (to improve skills) de recuperación

remedy [rémɪdi] N (solution) remedio *m*; (cure) cura *f*; VT (solve) remediar, subsanar; (heal) curar

remember [rɪmémbə] VI/VT recordar, acordarse (de); **— me to him** mándale saludos míos

remind [rɪmáɪnd] VT recordar

reminder [rɪmáɪndə] N (of a date, deadline) recordatorio *m*; (warning) advertencia *f*

reminiscence [rɛmənísəns] N reminiscencia *f*, recuerdo *m*

remiss [rɪmís] ADJ negligente

remission [rɪmíʃən] N remisión *f*

remit [rɪmít] VI/VT remitir

remittance [rɪmítns] N remesa *f*, giro *m*

remnant [rémnənt] N (remainder) resto *m*; (of fabric) retazo *m*, retal *m*; (vestige) vestigio *m*

remodel [rimádl] VI/VT remodelar

remorse [rɪmɔ́rs] N remordimiento *m*

remote [rɪmót] ADJ (far away) remoto,

refined [rɪfáɪnd] ADJ refinado

refinement [rɪfáɪnmənt] N (of manners) refinamiento *m*, pulimento *m*; (of oil) refinación *f*

refinery [rɪfáɪnəri] N refinería *f*; (of sugar) ingenio *m*

reflect [rɪflékt] VI/VT (mirror) reflejar; VI (ponder) reflexionar; **to — poorly on** desacreditar

reflection [rɪflékʃən] N (image) reflejo *m*; (consideration) reflexión *f*; (unfavorable observation) tacha *f*; **on —** pensándolo bien

reflector [rɪfléktɚ] N reflector *m*

reflex [rɪfléks] ADJ & N reflejo *m*

reflexive [rɪfléksɪv] ADJ reflexivo

reform [rɪfɔ́rm] VI/VT reformar(se); N reforma *f*

reformation [rɛfɚméʃən] N reforma *f*

reformatory [rɪfɔ́rmətɔri] N reformatorio *m*

reformer [rɪfɔ́rmɚ] N reformador -ra *mf*, reformista *mf*

refraction [rɪfrǽkʃən] N refracción *f*

refractory [rɪfrǽktɔri] ADJ (not malleable) refractario; (rebellious) rebelde

refrain [rɪfrén] VI abstenerse; N estribillo *m*

refresh [rɪfréʃ] VI/VT refrescar(se)

refreshing [rɪfréʃɪŋ] ADJ (drink) refrescante; (sleep) reparador; (honesty) agradable

refreshment [rɪfréʃmənt] N (drink) refresco *m*; (food) refrigerio *m*

refrigerate [rɪfrídʒəret] VT refrigerar

refrigeration [rɪfrɪdʒɚéʃən] N refrigeración *f*

refrigerator [rɪfrídʒəredɚ] N *Sp* frigorífico *m*, nevera *f*; *Am* refrigerador *m*; *RP* heladera *f*

refuge [réfjudʒ] N refugio *m*

refugee [refjudʒí] N refugiado -da *mf*

refund [rífʌnd] N reembolso *m*; [rɪfʌ́nd] VT reembolsar

refurbish [rɪfɚ́bɪʃ] VT restaurar

refusal [rɪfjúzəɫ] N negativa *f*, rechazo *m*; **first —** opción *f*

refuse [rɪfjúz] VI/VT (deny a request) rehusarse (a); (decline to accept) negarse (a); VT (reject) rechazar, desechar; **to — to** rehusarse a, negarse a; [réfjus] N desechos *m pl*, desperdicios *m pl*

refute [rɪfjút] VT refutar, rebatir

regain [rɪgén] VT (recover) recobrar; (get back to) volver a

regal [rígəɫ] ADJ regio, real

regard [rɪgárd] VT (consider) considerar; (esteem) estimar; **as —s** en cuanto a; N (consideration) consideración *f*; (esteem) respeto *m*, estima *f*; **—s** recuerdos *m pl*, saludos *m pl*; **with — to** con respecto a

regarding [rɪgárdɪŋ] PREP con respecto a

regardless [rɪgárdlɪs] ADV LOC **— of** independientemente de

regenerate [rɪdʒénəret] VI/VT regenerar(se)

regent [rídʒənt] N regente -ta *mf*

reggae [régé] N reggae *m*

regime [rɪʒím] N régimen *m*

regiment [rédʒəmənt] N regimiento *m*

region [rídʒən] N región *f*

register [rédʒɪstɚ] N (recording, range of voice) registro *m*; (entry) asiento *m*; VI/VT (enter into a list) registrar(se); (enroll) matricular(se), inscribir(se); VT (indicate) indicar, registrar; (a letter) certificar; VI (appear) aparecer; **that didn't —** no cayó en la cuenta

registered [rédʒɪstɚd] ADJ registrado; **— mail** correo certificado *m*; **— nurse** enfermero -ra titulado -da *mf*; **— trademark** marca registrada *f*

registrar [rédʒɪstrɑr] N secretario -ria de admisiones *mf*

registration [redʒɪstréʃən] N registro *m*; (of a car) matrícula *f*; (of a student) inscripción *f*

regret [rɪgrét] VT (feel sorry) lamentar; (feel rueful) arrepentirse de; N arrepentimiento *m*; **to send —s** enviar sus excusas

regretful [rɪgrétfəɫ] ADJ lleno de remordimientos

regrettable [rɪgrédəbəɫ] ADJ lamentable

regroup [rigrúp] VT reagrupar; VI reorganizarse

regular [régjəlɚ] ADJ (symmetrical, uniform) regular; (normal) normal; (habitual) habitual; **a — fool** un verdadero necio; **a — guy** un buen tipo; (habitual customer) parroquiano -na *mf*; (soldier) soldado de línea *m*

regularity [regjəlǽrɪdi] N regularidad *f*

regulate [régjəlet] VT (control) regular; (make regular) regularizar

regulation [regjəléʃən] N regulación *f*; **—s** reglamento *m*

regulator [régjəledɚ] N regulador *m*

regurgitate [rigɚ́dʒɪtet] VI/VT regurgitar

rehabilitate [rihəbílɪtet] VI/VT rehabilitar(se)

rehearsal [rɪhɚ́səɫ] N ensayo *m*

rehearse [rɪhɚ́s] VI/VT ensayar

reign [ren] N reino *m*, reinado *m*; VI reinar

reimburse [riɪmbɚ́s] VI/VT reembolsar

reimbursement [riɪmbɚ́smənt] N reembolso *m*

rein [ren] N rienda *f* (also control); VI **to — in** dominar, refrenar

reincarnation [rɪnkɑrnéʃən] N reencarnación *f*

reindeer [réndɪr] N reno *m*

reinforce [riinfɔ́rs] VT reforzar

reinforcement [riinfɔ́rsmənt] N refuerzo *m*

reiterate [riítəret] VT reiterar

reject [ridʒékt] VT rechazar; [rídʒekt] N (thing) cosa rechazada *f*, desecho *m*; (person) rechazado -da *mf*

rejoice [ridʒɔ́is] VI regocijarse

rejoicing [ridʒɔ́isiŋ] N regocijo *m*

rejoin [ridʒɔ́in] VT (come again into group) reincorporarse a; VI/VT (reunite) volver a unir(se); [ridʒɔ́in] VI/VT replicar

rejuvenate [ridʒúvənet] VI/VT rejuvenecer

relapse [rílæps] VI (into bad health) recaer; (into crime) reincidir; [rílæps] N (into bad health) recaída *f*; (into crime) reincidencia *f*

relate [rilét] VT (tell) relatar, narrar; (connect) relacionar; VI to — to relacionarse con

related [rilétid] ADJ (connected) relacionado; (kin) emparentado

relation [riléʃən] N (association) relación *f*; (act of narrating) narración *f*; (kinship) parentesco *m*; (relative) pariente -ta *mf*; with — to con respecto a

relationship [riléʃənʃip] N relación *f*

relative [rélətiv] ADJ relativo; N pariente -ta *mf*, allegado -da *mf*; — to relativo a, referente a

relax [riléks] VI/VT relajar(se), distender(se); VT (grip) aflojar

relaxation [rilækséʃən] N (recreation) esparcimiento *m*, recreo *m*; (loosening) relajamiento *m*, relajación *f*

relay [ríle] N relevo *m*, posta *f*; (electrical) relé *m*; — race carrera de relevos / postas *f*; [rílé] VT transmitir; to — a broadcast transmitir un programa

release [rilís] VT (let go) soltar; (free prisoners) librar, poner en libertad; (energy) liberar; (news) divulgar; (discharge from hospital) dar de alta; N (liberation) liberación *f*; (permission) permiso *m*; (of film) estreno *m*; (of gas) escape *m*; (of energy) desprendimiento *m*

relegate [réliget] VT relegar

relent [rilént] VI aplacarse

relentless [riléntləs] ADJ implacable

relevant [rélavant] ADJ pertinente

reliability [rilaiəbíliDi] N fiabilidad *f*, confiabilidad *f*

reliable [riláiəbəł] ADJ fiable, confiable; (a person) formal

reliance [rilái.əns] N (dependency) dependencia *f*; (trust) confianza *f*

relic [rélik] N reliquia *f*

relief [rilíf] N (ease) alivio *m*; (aid) ayuda *f*; (projection) relieve *m*; (soldier) relevo *m*;

in — en relieve; — map mapa en relieve *m*

relieve [rilív] VT (alleviate) aliviar; (free) liberar; (replace) relevar; VI to — oneself orinar

religion [rilídʒən] N religión *f*

religious [rilídʒəs] ADJ religioso

relinquish [rilíŋkwiʃ] VT (give up) renunciar; (let go) soltar

relish [réliʃ] VT (to like the taste) saborear, paladear; (enjoy) disfrutar; N (enjoyment) gusto *m*; (condiment) condimento de pepinillos en vinagre *m*

relocate [rilóket] VI/VT trasladar(se)

reluctance [riláktəns] N renuencia *f*

reluctant [riláktənt] ADJ renuente, reacio

rely [rilái] VI to — on (trust) confiar en; (depend on) depender de

REM (rapid eye movement) [ɑriém] N REM *m*

remain [rimén] VI (continue to be) seguir siendo; (stay) quedar(se), permanecer; (to be left) quedar, restar; (to be left over) sobrar; — s restos *m pl*

remainder [riméndɚ] N resto *m*, remanente *m*

remake [rimék] VT rehacer; (film) hacer de nuevo; [rímek] N nueva versión *f*

remark [rimárk] VT (comment) comentar, observar; (notice) notar, observar; to — on comentar; N observación *f*, comentario *m*

remarkable [rimárkəbəł] ADJ notable

remedial [rimídiəł] ADJ (rehabilitative) rehabilitador; (to improve skills) de recuperación

remedy [rémiDi] N (solution) remedio *m*; (cure) cura *f*; VT (solve) remediar, subsanar; (heal) curar

remember [rimémbɚ] VI/VT recordar, acordarse (de); — me to him mándale saludos míos

remind [rimáind] VT recordar

reminder [rimáindɚ] N (of a date, deadline) recordatorio *m*; (warning) advertencia *f*

reminiscence [remənísəns] N reminiscencia *f*, recuerdo *m*

remiss [rimís] ADJ negligente

remission [rimíʃən] N remisión *f*

remit [rimít] VT remitir

remittance [rimítn̩s] N remesa *f*, giro *m*

remnant [rémnənt] N (remainder) resto *m*; (of fabric) retazo *m*, retal *m*; (vestige) vestigio *m*

remodel [rimódl̩] VI/VT remodelar

remorse [rimɔ́rs] N remordimiento *m*

remote [rimót] ADJ (far away) remoto,

recóndito; (aloof) distante; (in kinship)
lejano; N **— control** control remoto *m*,
mando a distancia *m*
removal [rɪmúvəł] N (dismissal) deposición *f*;
(elimination) eliminación *f*; (extirpation)
extirpación *f*
remove [rɪmúv] VT (an obstacle) remover;
(take away, take off) quitar; (dismiss)
deponer; (eliminate) eliminar; (extirpate)
extirpar; **to — from office** separar /
apartar del cargo
renaissance [rénɪsɑns] N renacimiento *m*
rend [rɛnd] VI/VT desgarrar(se), rajar(se)
render [réndɚ] VT (give) dar; (cause to
become) dejar; (depict) representar;
(translate) traducir; (homage, account)
rendir; (services, assistance) prestar; (fat)
derretir; (a verdict) pronunciar; **to —
useless** inutilizar
rendition [rɛndíʃən] N (translation)
traducción *f*; (interpretation)
interpretación *f*, versión *f*
renegade [rénɪged] N renegado -da *mf*
renew [rɪnú] VT (vows, contract) renovar;
(furniture) restaurar; (friendship, effort)
reanudar; (a loan) prorrogar
renewal [rɪnúəł] N (of vows, contract)
renovación *f*; (of furniture) restauración *f*;
(of friendship, effort) reanudación *f*; (of
loan) prórroga *f*
renounce [rɪnáuns] VT (give up) renunciar a;
(repudiate) repudiar, renegar de
renovate [rénəvet] VT renovar
renown [rɪnáun] N renombre *m*
renowned [rɪnáund] ADJ renombrado
rent [rɛnt] N (monthly payment) alquiler *m*,
arrendamiento *m*; **for —** se alquila, se
arrienda; (fissure) rajadura *f*, hendidura *f*;
(tear) rasgadura *f*; (schism) escisión *f*; VI/VT
(lease) alquilar, arrendar
rental [rɛ́ntł] ADJ de alquiler; N alquiler *m*,
arrendamiento *m*
renter [réntɚ] N inquilino -na *mf*
renunciation [rɪnʌnsiéʃən] N renuncia *f*
reopen [riópən] VI/VT (doors) reabrir(se);
(negotiations) reanudar(se)
reorganize [riɔ́rgənaɪz] VI/VT reorganizar(se)
repair [rɪpér] VT (fix) reparar, arreglar,
componer; (shoes) remendar; **to — to**
acudir a; N (fixing) reparación *f*; (of shoes)
remiendo *m*, compostura *f*; **in —** en buen
estado; **—man** técnico -ca en reparaciones
mf
reparation [rɛpəréʃən] N reparación *f*,
indemnización *f*
repay [rɪpé] VT (return money, favor)
devolver; (pay off) pagar

repayment [rɪpémənt] N (of an object)
devolución *f*; (of a sum) reembolso *m*; (of
a loan) pago *m*
repeal [rɪpíł] VT derogar, revocar, abrogar; N
derogación *f*, revocación *f*, abrogación *f*
repeat [rɪpít] VI/VT repetir; N repetición *f*
repeated [rɪpíɾɪd] ADJ repetido
repel [rɪpéł] VI/VT repeler; (an attack)
rechazar
repellent [rɪpélənt] ADJ & N repelente *m*
repent [rɪpént] VI/VT arrepentirse (de)
repentance [rɪpéntəns] N arrepentimiento *m*
repentant [rɪpéntənt] ADJ arrepentido,
pesaroso
repercussion [rɛpɚkáʃən] N repercusión *f*; **to
have —s** repercutir
repertoire [rɛ́pɚtwɑr] N repertorio *m*
repetition [rɛpɪtíʃən] N repetición *f*
replace [rɪplés] VT (place again) volver a
colocar; (substitute for) reemplazar;
(provide a substitute for) reponer
replaceable [rɪplésəbəł] ADJ reemplazable,
sustituible
replacement [rɪplésmənt] N (substitute,
substitution) reemplazo *m*; (making up
for) reposición *f*
replenish [rɪplénɪʃ] VI/VT (supply) reabastecer;
(fill again) rellenar
replete [rɪplít] ADJ repleto
replica [réplɪkə] N réplica *f*
replicate [réplɪket] VT reproducir
reply [rɪpláɪ] VI replicar, contestar; N réplica *f*,
contestación *f*
report [rɪpɔ́rt] VT (recount) relatar; (make a
crime known, denounce) denunciar;
(make an accident known) dar parte de; VI
hacer un informe, informar; **to — for
duty** presentarse; **to — on** hacer un
informe sobre; **to — sick** dar parte de
enfermo, reportarse enfermo; **it is —ed
that** se dice que; N informe *m*; (rumor)
rumor *m*; (loud noise) estallido *m*; **— card**
boletín de calificaciones *m*
reporter [rɪpɔ́rɾɚ] N reportero -ra *mf*
repose [rɪpóz] VI/VT reposar, descansar; N
reposo *m*, descanso *m*
repository [rɪpázɪtɔri] N (object) depósito *m*;
(person) depositario -ria *mf*
repossess [ripəzés] VT retomar posesión de
represent [rɛprɪzént] VT representar
representation [rɛprɪzɛntéʃən] N
representación *f*
representative [rɛprɪzéntəɾɪv] ADJ
representativo; N representante *mf*
repress [rɪprés] VI/VT reprimir
repression [rɪpréʃən] N represión *f*
reprieve [rɪprív] VT (pardon) indultar;

(commute) conmutar; (delay) aplazar; N
(pardon) indulto m; (commutation)
conmutación f; (delay) aplazamiento m

reprimand [réprəmænd] N reprimenda f,
regaño m; VT reprender, regañar

reprint [ríprɪnt] N reimpresión f; (offprint)
separata f

reprisal [rɪpráɪzəl] N represalia f

reproach [rɪprótʃ] VT reprochar; N reproche
m

reproduce [riprədús] VI/VT reproducir(se)

reproduction [riprədákʃən] N reproducción f

reproof [rɪprúf] N reprobación f

reprove [rɪprúv] VT reprobar

reptile [réptaɪl] N reptil m

republic [rɪpáblɪk] N república f

republican [rɪpáblɪkən] ADJ & N republicano
-na mf

repudiate [rɪpjúdiet] VT repudiar

repugnance [rɪpágnəns] N repugnancia f

repugnant [rɪpágnənt] ADJ repugnante

repulse [rɪpáls] VT repeler, rechazar; N
repulsa f, rechazo m

repulsive [rɪpálsɪv] ADJ repulsivo

reputable [répjətəbəl] ADJ reputado

reputation [repjətéʃən] N reputación f, fama
f

request [rɪkwést] N solicitud f, petición f,
requerimiento m; **at the — of** a solicitud
de, a instancias de; VT solicitar, pedir

require [rɪkwáɪr] VI/VT (need) requerir;
(demand) exigir

requirement [rɪkwáɪrmənt] N (demand)
requisito m; (need) necesidad f

requisite [rékwɪzɪt] ADJ requerido, necesario;
N requisito m

requisition [rekwɪzíʃən] N (taking over)
requisa f; (order) pedido m; VT (take over)
requisar; (order) pedir

rerun [rírʌn] N refrito m

rescind [rɪsínd] VT rescindir

rescue [réskju] VT rescatar, salvar; N rescate m,
salvamento m; **to go to the — of** acudir
al socorro de, salir al quite de

research [rísɚtʃ] N investigación f; [rɪsɚ́tʃ] VI/
VT investigar

researcher [rɪsɚ́tʃɚ] N investigador -ora mf

resell [risél] VT revender

resemblance [rɪzémbləns] N semejanza f,
parecido m

resemble [rɪzémbəl] VT semejar, asemejarse a,
parecerse a

resent [rɪzént] VT resentirse de

resentful [rɪzéntfəl] ADJ resentido, rencoroso

resentment [rɪzéntmənt] N resentimiento m

reservation [rezɚvéʃən] N reserva f; Am
reservación f; **to have one's —s** tener

reservas

reserve [rɪzɚ́v] VT reservar; N reserva f;
(shyness) pudor m

reserved [rɪzɚ́vd] ADJ reservado

reservoir [rézɚvwar] N (tank) depósito m,
alberca f; (artificial lake) embalse m,
represa f

reside [rɪzáɪd] VI residir

residence [rézɪdəns] N residencia f

resident [rézɪdənt] ADJ & N residente mf; (of
a neighborhood) vecino -na mf

residential [rezɪdéntʃəl] ADJ residencial

residue [rézɪdu] N residuo m

resign [rɪzáɪn] VI/VT renunciar (a), dimitir
(de); **to — oneself to** resignarse a

resignation [rezɪgnéʃən] N (act of resigning
an office) renuncia f, dimisión f;
(accepting attitude) resignación f

resilience [rɪzíljans] N (elasticity) elasticidad
f; (adaptability) adaptabilidad f

resilient [rɪzíljant] ADJ (elastic) elástico;
(adaptable) adaptable

resin [rézɪn] N resina f

resist [rɪzíst] VT (a temptation) resistir; VI/VT
(tyranny) resistirse (a)

resistance [rɪzístəns] N resistencia f

resistant [rɪzístənt] ADJ resistente

resolute [rézəlut] ADJ resuelto, decidido

resolution [rezəlúʃən] N resolución f

resolve [rɪzálv] VT resolver(se); **to — into**
convertirse en; **to — to** decidir, resolver;
N resolución f

resonance [rézənəns] N resonancia f

resonate [rézənet] VI/VT resonar

resort [rɪzɔ́rt] VI **to — to** recurrir; N (seaside)
centro de veraneo m; (for skiing) estación
de esquí f; **as a last —** como último
recurso; **to have — to** recurrir a

resound [rɪzáʊnd] VI/VT resonar

resource [rísɔrs] N recurso m

resourceful [rɪsɔ́rsfəl] ADJ ingenioso

respect [rɪspékt] N (esteem) respeto m; (detail)
aspecto m; **with — to** (con) respecto a,
respecto de; VT respetar; **as —s** por lo que
respecta a

respectable [rɪspéktəbəl] ADJ respetable

respectful [rɪspéktfəl] ADJ respetuoso

respective [rɪspéktɪv] ADJ respectivo

respiration [respəréʃən] N respiración f

respite [réspɪt] N (pause) respiro f, tregua m;
(postponement) prórroga f

resplendent [rɪspléndənt] ADJ
resplandeciente, refulgente

respond [rɪspánd] VI/VT responder

response [rɪspáns] N respuesta f

responsibility [rɪspansəbílɪdi] N
responsabilidad f

responsible [rɪspánsəbəł] ADJ responsable

rest [rest] N (repose) descanso *m*, reposo *m*; (musical) pausa *f*; (support) apoyo *m*; (remainder) resto *m*; **an object at —** un objeto en reposo; **he's at —** descansa en paz; **— home** (for convalescents) casa de reposo *f*; (for the aged) casa de ancianos *f*; **— room** servicio *m*; *Sp* aseo *m*; VI/VT descansar, reposar; VT (one's gaze) posar; (against a wall) reclinar; VI parar; **to — on** depender de; **let it —** déjalo en paz

restaurant [réstərant] N restaurante *m*; *Am* restorán *m*

restitution [restɪtúʃən] N restitución *f*

restless [réstlɪs] ADJ (worried) inquieto; (fidgety) movedizo, revuelto

restlessness [réstlɪsnɪs] N inquietud *f*, desasosiego *m*

restoration [restəréʃən] N restauración *f*

restore [rɪstɔ́r] VT restaurar

restrain [rɪstrén] VT (hold back) refrenar, contener, moderar; (bring under control) reducir

restraint [rɪstrént] N (self-control) compostura *f*, moderación *f*; (device) seguro *m*; **under —** bajo control

restrict [rɪstríkt] VT restringir; (someone's liberty) coartar

restriction [rɪstríkʃən] N restricción *f*

result [rɪzʌ́lt] VI resultar; **to — from** resultar de; **to — in** dar por resultado; N resultado *m*; **as a —** de resultas, como resultado

resume [rɪzúm] VI/VT (take up again) reasumir, volver a asumir; (continue) reanudar

résumé [rézume] N currículum *m*, historial personal *m*

resurrection [rezərékʃən] N resurrección *f*

resuscitate [rɪsʌ́sɪtet] VI/VT resucitar

resuscitation [rɪsʌsɪtéʃən] N resucitación *f*

retail [rítel] N venta al por menor *f*; **at —** al por menor, al menudeo; **— trade** comercio minorista *m*; VI/VT vender al por menor

retailer [rítelə] N minorista *mf*, detallista *mf*

retain [rɪtén] VT (recall, confine, detain) retener; (keep) conservar, quedarse con; (hire) contratar

retainer [rɪténə] N (device that holds back) retén *m*; (payment) honorarios pagados por adelantado *m pl*

retaliate [rɪtǽliet] VI vengarse

retaliation [rɪtæliéʃən] N venganza *f*

retard [rɪtárd] VI/VT retardar

retarded [rɪtárdɪd] ADJ retrasado

retention [rɪténʃən] N retención *f*

reticence [rɛ́dɪsəns] N reserva *f*

retina [rétnə] N retina *f*

retinue [rétnu] N séquito *m*, comitiva *f*

retire [rɪtáɪr] VI/VT (stop working) retirar(se), jubilar(se); (withdraw) retirar(se); (to bed) acostarse; (money, troops, machines) retirar

retirement [rɪtáɪrmənt] N retiro *m*, jubilación *f*

retort [rɪtɔ́rt] N (reply) réplica *f*; (vessel) retorta *f*

retouch [ritátʃ] VT retocar; N retoque *m*

retrace [ritrés] VT (mental steps) repasar; (one's route) volver sobre

retract [rɪtrǽkt] VT retractar; (claws) retraer(se); VI desdecirse, retractarse

retreat [rɪtrít] N (place of refuge, period of meditation) retiro *m*, refugio *m*; (military) retirada *f*, repliegue *m*; (bugle call) retreta *f*; VI batirse en retirada, retroceder, replegarse

retrench [rɪtréntʃ] VI economizar

retrieve [rɪtrív] VT (game) cobrar; (something lost) recuperar

retriever [rɪtrívə] N perro cobrador *m*

retroactive [retroǽktɪv] ADJ retroactivo

retrospect [rétrəspekt] ADV LOC **in —** mirando para atrás

retrovirus [rétrovaɪrəs] N retrovirus *m*

return [rɪtə́n] VI (come back) volver, regresar; VT (put back) devolver, retornar; (a verdict) fallar; N (to a place) vuelta *f*, regreso *m*; (thing bought, of a thing) devolución *f*; (profit) ganancia *f*; (electoral) resultados *m pl*; **— address** señas del remitente *f pl*; **— game** revancha *f*; **— ticket** billete de vuelta *m*; **by — mail** a vuelta de correo; **election —s** resultados electorales *m pl*; **in — a** cambio; **in — for** a cambio de; **income tax —** *Sp* declaración de la renta *f*; *Am* declaración de impuestos *f*

reunion [rijúnjən] N reunión *f*

reunite [rijunáɪt] VI/VT reunir(se)

rev [rev] VI/VT acelerar en vacío

reveal [rɪvíł] VT revelar

revealing [rɪvílɪŋ] ADJ revelador; (neckline) atrevido

revel [révəł] VI (enjoy) deleitarse, gozar; (party) parrandear; N parranda *f*

revelation [revəléʃən] N revelación *f*; **—s** Apocalipsis *m sg*

revelry [révətri] N parranda *f*, jarana *f*

revenge [rɪvéndʒ] N venganza *f*, revancha *f*

revengeful [rɪvéndʒfəł] ADJ vengativo

revenue [révənu] N (of a government) rentas públicas *f pl*; (of a person) ingresos *m pl*; **— stamp** sello fiscal *m*

reverberate [rɪvə́·bəret] VI reverberar; VT hacer reverberar

revere [rɪvír] VT reverenciar

reverence [révə·əns] N reverencia f, veneración f; VT venerar

reverend [révə·ənd] ADJ & N reverendo -da mf

reverent [révə·ənt] ADJ reverente

reverie, revery [révəri] N ensueño m, ensoñación f

reverse [rɪvə́·s] ADJ inverso, opuesto; **the — side** el revés; N (opposite) lo opuesto; (back of clothing, mishap) revés m; (back of a coin, medal) reverso m; (gear) marcha atrás f; (back of a piece of paper) dorso m; VI/VT invertir(se); VT (a policy, a vehicle) dar marcha atrás; (a verdict) revocar

revert [rɪvə́·t] VI revertir

review [rɪvjú] N (inspection of a military unit, periodical publication) revista f; (repetition of studied material) repaso m; (critique of a book, drama) reseña f, crítica f; (examination of a judicial case) revisión f; VI/VT (examine) repasar, revisar; VT (reexamine) revisar, examinar; (inspect troops) pasar revista a; (write a critique of) reseñar

revile [rɪváɪl] VT vilipendiar, denostar

revise [rɪváɪz] VT corregir, enmendar

revision [rɪvíʒən] N (action of revising) corrección f; (revised version) versión corregida f

revival [rɪváivəl] N (of customs) retorno m; (of religious feeling) resurgimiento m, despertar m; (from unconsciousness) resucitación f; (of a play) reposición f, revisión f; (evangelical meeting) asamblea evangelista f

revive [rɪváiv] VT (an unconscious person) reavivar, reanimar; (an apparently dead person) resucitar; (an old play) reponer; (a custom) restablecer; VI revivir, reanimarse; (be reestablished) restablecerse

revocation [revəkéʃən] N revocación f

revoke [rɪvók] VT revocar

revolt [rɪvólt] N revuelta f, sublevación f; VI rebelarse, sublevarse; **it —s me** me da asco

revolting [rɪvóltɪŋ] ADJ repugnante, asqueroso

revolution [revəlúʃən] N revolución f

revolutionary [revəlúʃəneri] ADJ & N revolucionario -ria mf

revolve [rɪváɪv] VI/VT girar

revolver [rɪváɪvə·] N revólver m

revue [rɪvjú] N revista f

revulsion [rɪváʃən] N repugnancia f, asco m

reward [rɪwɔ́rd] N recompensa f; VT recompensar

rewind [riwáɪnd] VI/VT rebobinar

rewrite [riráɪt] VI/VT reescribir; [ríraɪt] N corrección f

rhea [ríə] N ñandú m

rhetoric [rédə·ɪk] N retórica f

rheumatism [rúmətɪzəm] N reumatismo m, reuma m

Rh factor [ɑrétʃfæktə·] N factor Rh m

rhinoceros [raɪnásərəs] N rinoceronte m

rhinovirus [ráɪnováɪrəs] N rinovirus m

rhododendron [rodədéndrən] N rododendro m

rhubarb [rúbɑrb] N (vegetable) ruibarbo m; (brawl) reyerta f

rhyme [raɪm] N rima f; **without — or reason** sin ton ni son; VI/VT rimar

rhythm [ríðəm] N ritmo m

rhythmical [ríðmɪkəl] ADJ rítmico; (breathing) acompasado

rib [rɪb] N (of person, animal) costilla f; (of umbrella) varilla f; (in garment) canalé m, cordoncillo m; **— cage** caja torácica f; VT burlarse de

ribbon [ríbən] N (of cloth) cinta f; (of land) franja f, faja f

rice [raɪs] N arroz m; **— field** arrozal m

rich [rɪtʃ] ADJ rico; (tasty) sabroso; (buttery) mantecoso; (colorful) vivo; N **—es** riquezas f pl

rickety [ríkɪdi] ADJ (shaky) desvencijado; (affected with rickets) raquítico

ricochet [ríkəʃe] N rebote m; VI rebotar

rid [rɪd] VT librar, desembarazar; **to get — of** librarse de, deshacerse de

riddle [rídl] N (puzzle) acertijo m, adivinanza f; (puzzling person) enigma m; VI hablar en enigmas; VT acribillar, perforar; **to be —d with graft** estar plagado de corrupción

ride [raɪd] VI (on a horse) cabalgar, jinetear; (on a bicycle) montar; (in a vehicle) andar, viajar / ir en; **this car —s well** este coche anda bien; **his hopes are riding on that** tiene las esperanzas puestas en eso; **just let it —** déjalo tranquilo; VT (travel on horse, bicycle) montar; (travel on bus) andar en; (harass) hostigar; **to — away** irse; **to — by** pasar; **to — out** capear; **to — up** subirse; N paseo m, viaje m; **to give someone a —** acercar en coche; **to go on a —** dar un paseo

rider [ráɪdə·] N (on a horse) jinete m; (on a bicycle) ciclista mf; (on an insurance policy) cláusula añadida f; (law) anexo m

ridge [rɪdʒ] N (back of an animal) espinazo *m*, lomo *m*; (chain of hills) cadena *f*; (of a roof) caballete *m*; (of cloth) cordoncillo *m*

ridicule [rídɪkjuɫ] N burla *f*, mofa *f*; VT ridiculizar, poner en ridículo

ridiculous [rɪdíkjələs] ADJ ridículo

riffraff [rífræf] N *pej* gentuza *f*, chusma *f*

rifle [ráɪfəɫ] N rifle *m*, fusil *m*; VT robar; **to — through** revolver

rift [rɪft] N (opening) grieta *f*, hendidura *f*; (disagreement) desavenencia *f*

rig [rɪg] VT (sails) aparejar, equipar; (an election) amañar; **to — up** armar; N (on a ship) aparejo *m*, equipo *m*; (apparatus) aparato *m*; (truck) camión *m*

rigging [rígɪŋ] N jarcia *f*

right [raɪt] ADJ (not left) derecho; (not wrong) correcto, acertado; (suitable) adecuado; **— angle** ángulo recto *m*; **—-hand** derecho; **—-hand man** brazo derecho *m*; **—-handed** diestro; **—-to-life** antiaborto, pro vida; **— triangle** triángulo recto *m*; **—-wing** derechista, de derecha; **at the — moment** en el momento justo; **the — people** la gente indicada; **to be —** tener razón; **to be all — estar bien; he's not in his — mind** no está en sus cabales; **to turn out —** salir bien; ADV (straight) derecho, directamente; (correctly) correctamente; (to the right) a la derecha; **— after** justo después de; **—-face** media vuelta a la derecha; **— now** ahora mismo; **— there** allí mismo; **it is — where you left it** está exactamente donde lo dejaste; **to hit — in the eye** darle de lleno en el ojo; N (just claim) derecho *m*; (moral good) bien *m*; (direction, political persuasion) derecha *f*; **— of way** prioridad *f*, preferencia *f*; **make a — at the corner** gira / dobla a la derecha; **to the —** a la derecha; **to be in the —** tener razón; VI/VT (make upright) enderezar(se); VT (correct) corregir

righteous [ráɪtʃəs] ADJ recto, justo; **— rage** rabia justificada *f*

righteousness [ráɪtʃəsnɪs] N rectitud *f*, superioridad moral *f*

rightful [ráɪtfəɫ] ADJ legítimo

rightist [ráɪdɪst] N derechista *mf*

rightly [ráɪtli] ADV con razón

rigid [rídʒɪd] ADJ rígido

rigidity [rɪdʒídɪti] N rigidez *f*

rigor [rígɚ] N rigor *m*

rigorous [rígɚəs] ADJ riguroso

rim [rɪm] N (edge) borde *m*; (on a car) llanta *f*; *Am* rin *m*; (on a bicycle) aro *m*; (on a plate) filete *m*; (of glasses) montura *f*

rind [raɪnd] N (cheese) corteza *f*; (fruit) cáscara *f*

ring [rɪŋ] N (on finger, of smoke) anillo *m*; (for women only) sortija *f*; (under the eyes) ojeras *f pl*; (in the nose) argolla *f*; (circle) círculo *m*, redondel *m*, ruedo *m*; (in a circus) pista *f*; (for bullfights) plaza de toros *f*; (for boxing) cuadrilátero *m*; (for gymnastics) anillas *f pl*; (of criminals) banda *f*; (undertone) tono *m*; (sound of telephone) timbrazo *m*, telefonazo *m*; (sound of bells) retintín *m*, repique *m*; **— finger** anular *m*; **—leader** cabecilla *mf*; **—worm** tiña *f*; VT (surround) cercar; (make doorbell sound) tocar; (make bell sound) tañer; VI (of ears) zumbar; (make sound, doorbell) sonar; (make sound, bell) repicar, repiquetear; **to — the nose of an animal** ponerle una argolla en la nariz a un animal; **to — the hour** dar la hora; **to — true** parecer verdad; **to — up the sale** marcar la venta

ringlet [ríŋlɪt] N (curl) rizo *m*, bucle *m*, sortija *f*; (small ring) pequeña sortija *f*

rink [rɪŋk] N pista de patinaje *f*

rinkydink [ríŋkidɪŋk] ADJ de pacotilla

rinse [rɪns] VI/VT enjuagar, aclarar; N enjuague *m*, aclarado *m*

riot [ráɪət] N (uprising) motín *m*, tumulto *m*; (excess) exceso *m*; **he's a —** es un cómico; VI amotinarse

riotous [ráɪədəs] ADJ (wanton) desenfrenado; (funny) graciosísimo

rip [rɪp] VI/VT rasgar(se), rajar(se); VT (something sewn) descoser; **to — away** desprender; **to — into** asaltar; **to — off** robar; **to — out a seam** descoser una costura; N rasgadura *f*, rajadura *f*; **— cord** cordón de apertura *m*; **—off** robo *m*

ripe [raɪp] ADJ maduro; **to be — for** estar preparado para, listo para; **— old age** edad avanzada *f*

ripen [ráɪpən] VI/VT madurar(se), sazonar(se)

ripeness [ráɪpnɪs] N madurez *f*

ripple [rípəɫ] VI/VT (water) rizar(se); (grass) agitar(se); N ondulación *f*, rizo *m*

rise [raɪz] VI (go up) subir; (increase) aumentar; (get up, stand up) levantarse; (slope up) elevarse; (arise) surgir; (of mist) levantarse; (of the sun, moon) salir; (of dough) crecer, leudar; **to — up in rebellion** sublevarse, alzarse; **to — above** superar; **to — to the challenge** aceptar el desafío; N (of prices, volume) subida *f*, aumento *m*; (of an empire, talent) surgimiento *m*; (slope upward) elevación *f*; **to get a — out of someone**

provocar a alguien; **to give — to**
ocasionar

risk [rɪsk] N riesgo *m*; VT arriesgar, aventurar;
to — defeat correr el riesgo de perder,
exponerse a perder

risky [ríski] ADJ arriesgado, aventurado,
azaroso

risqué [rɪské] ADJ subido de tono, atrevido,
picante

rite [raɪt] N rito *m*

ritual [rítʃuəl] ADJ & N ritual *m*

ritzy [rítsi] ADJ elegante

rival [ráɪvəl] ADJ & N rival *mf*; VT rivalizar
con, competir con

rivalry [ráɪvəlri] N rivalidad *f*

river [rívə-] N río *m*; **—bank** orilla *f*, ribera *f*

rivet [rívɪt] N remache *m*; VT (put rivets)
remachar; (fix) fijar, clavar

RNA (ribonucleic acid) [ɑrɪné] N ARN *m*

roach [rotʃ] N cucaracha *f*

road [rod] N (in the country) camino *m*;
(highway) carretera *f*; **on the — to
recovery** en vías de recuperación; **—
map** mapa carretero *m*; **— rage** ira
caminera *f*; **—side** borde del camino *m*;
—way camino *m*

roam [rom] VI/VT vagar (por), errar (por),
rodar (por); VI vagabundear

roar [rɔr] VI/VT rugir, bramar; **to — with
laughter** reír a carcajadas; N rugido *m*,
bramido *m*; **— of laughter** risotada *f*,
carcajada *f*

roast [rost] VI/VT (meat, potatoes) asar(se);
(coffee, nuts) tostar, torrar; (criticize)
criticar; N (meat) asado *m*; (party)
barbacoa *f*; **— beef** rosbif *m*

rob [rɑb] VI/VT robar; **to — someone of
something** robarle algo a alguien

robber [rábə-] N ladrón -ona *mf*

robbery [rábəri] N robo *m*

robe [rob] N manto *m*, traje talar *m*, túnica *f*;
(ceremonial dress) toga *f*; (bath wrap) bata
f

robin [rábɪn] N petirrojo *m*

robot [róbɑt] N robot *m*

robotics [robɑ́ɾɪks] N robótica *f*

robust [robást] ADJ (strong) robusto; (hearty)
saludable; (solid) sólido

rock [rɑk] N roca *f*; (crag) peñasco *m*, peñón
m; (diamond) diamante *m*; (music style)
rock *m*; **— crystal** cristal de roca *m*; **—
salt** sal de piedra *f*, sal gema/mineral *f*;
to go on the —s tropezar en un escollo;
Am escollar; **he hit —-bottom** tocó
fondo; VI/VT (move to and fro) mecer(se);
(stagger) sacudir, estremecer; **to — to
sleep** arrullar

rocker [rákə-] N mecedora *f*

rocket [rákɪt] N cohete *m*

rocketry [rákɪtri] N cohetería *f*

rocking [rákɪŋ] N **— chair** mecedora *f*; **—
horse** caballito de madera *m*, caballito
mecedor *m*

rocky [ráki] ADJ (with rocks) rocoso;
(difficult) difícil

rod [rɑd] N vara *f*, varilla *f*; (in engine)
vástago *m*; medida de longitud *f*
(aproximadamente 5 metros)

rodent [ródənt] N roedor *m*

rodeo [ródio] N rodeo *m*

rogue [rog] N pícaro -ra *mf*, bribón -ona *mf*;
ADJ solitario y bravo

roguish [rógɪʃ] ADJ (rascally) pícaro, bribón;
(mischievous) travieso

role [rol] N papel *m*, rol *m*; **— model**
modelo ejemplar *m*; **—-playing**
improvisación *f*

roll [rol] VI (move on wheels, rotate) rodar;
(rotate one's eyes) revolear; (sway)
balancearse, bambolearse; (reverberate)
retumbar; (flow as waves) ondular; VT
(steel) aplanar; (cigarettes) liar; (a drum)
redoblar; (one's r's) pronunciar la erre; **to
— over in the snow** revolcarse en la
nieve; **to — up** arrollar, enrollar; **to —
around** llegar; **to — back** reducir,
rebajar; **to — by** pasar; **to — over** volcar,
darse vuelta; **to get —ing** ponerse en
marcha; N (of paper, fabric, etc.) rollo *m*;
(of coins) cartucho *m*; (of a ship) balanceo
m; (of thunder) retumbo *m*; (of a drum)
redoble *m*; (catalog of members) lista *f*; (of
waves) ondulación *f*; (of a typewriter)
carro *m*; (piece of bread) bollo *m*,
panecillo *m*; (of dice) tiro *m*; ADJ **—-on** de
bolita

roller [rólə-] N (for painting, moving things)
rodillo *m*; (hair) rulo *m*, rulero *m*; **—
coaster** montaña rusa *f*; **— skate** patín
de ruedas *m*

rolling pin [rólɪŋ pɪn] N rodillo *m*, palote *m*

roly-poly [rólipóli] ADJ rechoncho

ROM (read-only memory) [rɑm] N ROM *f*

Roman [rómən] ADJ & N romano -na *mf*; **—
numeral** número romano *m*

romance [rómæns] N (love affair, story)
romance *m*; (romantic atmosphere)
romanticismo *m*; VT cortejar; ADJ romance,
románico

romanesque [romənésk] ADJ románico

Romania [roménia] N Rumania *f*

Romanian [roméniən] ADJ & N rumano -na
mf

romantic [romǽntik] ADJ romántico

romanticism [romántəsızəm] N
romanticismo *m*

romp [rɑmp] VI retozar, brincar; (win easily)
arrasar con; N (frolic) retozo *m*; (victory)
victoria fácil *f*

roof [ruf] N (ceiling) techo *m*, tejado *m*; (flat
roof) azotea *f*; — **of the mouth** paladar
m; **to hit the** — poner el grito en el
cielo; VT techar

rookie [rúki] N novato -ta *mf*

room [rum] N (in building) cuarto *m*; (large)
sala *f*; (in a hotel) habitación *f*; (space)
lugar *m*, sitio *m*; — **and board** pensión
completa *f*; —**mate** compañero -ra de
cuarto *mf*; — **service** servicio a la
habitación *f*; **to take up** — ocupar
espacio; **the whole** — **laughed** todos los
presentes se rieron; VI hospedarse, alojarse

roomy [rúmi] ADJ espacioso, amplio

roost [rust] N vara *f*; VI posarse (para dormir)

rooster [rústə] N gallo *m*

root [rut] N raíz *f*; **to take** — (a plant) echar
raíces, prender; (an idea) arraigar(se); —
canal tratamiento de conducto *m*; VI
(grow roots) arraigar(se), echar raíces; (dig)
hozar; **to** — **for** animar; **to** — **out / up**
(uproot) arrancar de raíz; (eradicate)
erradicar

rope [rop] N (cord) soga *f*, cuerda *f*; (lasso)
reata *f*, lazo *m*; (on a ship) cabo *m*; (thick)
maroma *f*; **to be at the end of one's** —
no dar más; **to know the** —**s** conocer el
paño, sabérselas todas; VT enlazar; **to** —
off acordonar; **to** — **someone in** agarrar
a alguien

rosary [rózəri] N rosario *m*

rose [roz] N rosa *f*; (color) rosa *m*; —**bud**
capullo de rosa *m*, pimpollo de rosa *m*;
—**bush** rosal *m*; —**colored** de color rosa

rosemary [rózməri] N romero *m*

roster [rústə] N lista *f*

rostrum [rústrəm] N tribuna *f*

rosy [rózi] ADJ (pink) rosado, color de rosa;
(of cheeks) sonrosado; — **future** porvenir
halagüeño *m*

rot [rat] VI/VT pudrir(se); N podredumbre *f*

rotary [ródəri] ADJ rotatorio, rotativo

rotate [rótet] VI/VT rotar

rotation [rotéʃən] N rotación *f*, giro *m*

rotor [ródə] N rotor *m*

rotten [rátṇ] ADJ (decomposing) podrido;
(stinking) hediondo; (morally corrupt)
corrupto; (despicable) odioso

rotund [roténd] ADJ rollizo

rouge [ruʒ] N colorete *m*

rough [rʌf] ADJ (coarse) áspero, rugoso;
(violent) violento; (rude) tosco;
(approximate) aproximado; (road)
desigual, irregular; (terrain) agreste,
bronco; (sea) picado, revuelto; —
diamond diamante en bruto *m*; — **draft**
borrador *m*; — **weather** mal tiempo *m*;
he had a — **time** le fue mal; ADV con
violencia; VI ponerse áspero; **to** — **it** vivir
sin lujos ni comodidades

roughly [rʌfli] ADV (not smoothly)
ásperamente; (rudely) groseramente,
rudamente; (approximately)
aproximadamente; **to estimate** — tantear

roughness [rʌfnɪs] N (lack of smoothness)
aspereza *f*; (rudeness) rudeza *f*;
(unevenness) desigualdad *f*; **the** — **of the
sea** lo picado del mar

roulette [rulét] N ruleta *f*

round [raund] ADJ redondo; — **trip** viaje de
ida y vuelta *m*; N (of talks, drinks, dance)
ronda *f*; (of cheese) rodaja *f*; (in cards,
sports) vuelta *f*; (in boxing) round *m*,
asalto *m*; (of golf) partido *m*; (canon)
canon *m*; — **number** número redondo *m*;
— **of ammunition** carga de municiones
f; — **of applause** aplauso *m*; **to make
the** —**s** hacer la ronda; PREP & ADV
—**about** indirecto; —**the-clock**
veinticuatro horas al día; —**up** (of cattle)
rodeo *m*; (of criminals) redada *f*; **all year**
— todo el año; **to come** — pasar; **to go**
— **a corner** doblar una esquina; VT (a
corner) doblar; (an edge, a number)
redondear; **to** — **off / out** redondear; **to**
— **up** juntar, reunir; **to** — **up cattle**
juntar el ganado

roundness [ráundnɪs] N redondez *f*

rouse [rauz] VI/VT (wake) despertar(se); VT
(instigate) incitar

rout [raut] N (defeat) derrota aplastante *f*;
(flight) huida en desbandada *f*; VT (defeat)
derrotar, destrozar; (cause to flee) poner en
fuga

route [raut, rut] N ruta *f*, trayecto *m*; (of
newspaper delivery) reparto *m*; VT dirigir

routine [rutín] N rutina *f*

rove [rov] VI/VT vagar (por), errar (por)

rover [róvə] N vagabundo -da *mf*

row [rau] N (fight) riña *f*, pelea *f*, bronca *f*;
[ro] N (line) fila *f*, hilera *f*, ringlera *f*; **four
times in a** — cuatro veces seguidas; VI/VT
(propel with oars) remar, bogar; —**boat**
bote de remos *m*, barca *f*, chinchorro *m*

rowdy [ráudi] ADJ (person) alborotador;
(party) bullicioso; N camorrista *mf*

rower [róə] N remero -ra *mf*

royal [rɔ́ıəl] ADJ real; — **blue** azul marino *m*;
— **flush** escalera real *f*

royalty [rɔ́ɪəlti] N realeza *f*; (person) miembro de la realeza *m*; **royalties** derechos *m pl*, regalías *f pl*

RSVP (répondez s'il vous plaît) [ɑresvipí] LOC S.R.C.

rub [rʌb] VI/VT (apply friction) frotar(se); (massage) friccionar; (spread on) aplicar frotando; (make sore) rozar; **to — off** quitar(se) frotando; **to — out** borrar; **to — shoulders with** codearse con; **to — someone the wrong way** peinar a contrapelo; **don't — it in!** ¡no me lo refriegues por la cara! N (act of rubbing) fricción *f*; (difficulty) dificultad *f*; (abraded area) roce *m*, frote *m*

rubber [rʌ́bə] N caucho *m*, goma *f*; (condom) *fam* condón *m*; **— band** goma elástica *f*; **—s** chanclos *m pl*; **— stamp** sello de goma *m*; **— tree** gomero *m*

rubbish [rʌ́bɪʃ] N (trash) basura *f*; (nonsense) pamplinas *f pl*

rubble [rʌ́bəɫ] N (debris) escombros *m pl*; (stone fragments) ripios *m pl*, cascote *m*

rubric [rúbrɪk] N rúbrica *f*

ruby [rúbi] N rubí *m*

ruckus [rʌ́kəs] N barahúnda *f*, jaleo *m*

rudder [rʌ́də] N timón *m*

ruddy [rʌ́di] ADJ rubicundo

rude [rud] ADJ (impolite) grosero; (uncouth, crude, simple) tosco; (harsh) rudo

rudeness [rúdnɪs] N (impoliteness) grosería *f*; (harshness) rudeza *f*; (crudeness) tosquedad *f*

rueful [rúfəɫ] ADJ (sad) triste; (repentant) arrepentido

ruffian [rʌ́fiən] N rufián *m*

ruffle [rʌ́fəɫ] VI/VT (gather cloth) fruncir(se); (raise feathers) erizar(se); (water) agitar(se), rizar(se); (hair) desgreñar(se); (bother) molestar(se), fastidiar(se); N (frill on clothes) volante *m*; (gathering in cloth) frunce *m*, pliegue *m*; (ripples in water) ondulación *f*, rizo *m*

rug [rʌg] N alfombra *f*; (hairpiece) peluquín *m*

rugby [rʌ́gbi] N rugby *m*

rugged [rʌ́gɪd] ADJ (terrain) escarpado, áspero, fragoso; (face) recio; (manners) tosco; (way of life) duro; (man) robusto

ruin [rúɪn] N ruina *f*; **to go to —** arruinarse, venirse abajo; VI/VT arruinar(se), estropear(se); (spoil) echar(se) a perder

ruinous [rúɪnəs] ADJ ruinoso

rule [ruɫ] N (principle) regla *f*; (line separating newspaper columns) filete *m*; (government) mando *m*, gobierno *m*; **the — of law** el imperio de la ley; **as a — of thumb** por regla general, a ojo de buen

cubero; VI/VT (govern) reinar, gobernar; (decree) fallar, dictaminar, sentenciar; (put lines on paper) rayar, poner renglones; **to — out** excluir; **to — over** reinar, gobernar

ruler [rúlə] N (governor) gobernante *mf*; (instrument) regla *f*

ruling [rúlɪŋ] N (decision) fallo *m*, sentencia *f*, dictamen *m*; (line on paper) renglón *m*; ADJ (governing) gobernante

rum [rʌm] N ron *m*

rumble [rʌ́mbəɫ] VI (roar) retumbar; (of stomach) hacer ruido; (fight) pelear; N (roar) retumbo *m*; (of stomach) ruido *m*; (fight) pelea *f*

ruminate [rúmənet] VI rumiar

rummage [rʌ́mɪʤ] VI/VT rebuscar, hurgar; N cachivaches *m pl*; **— sale** venta de beneficencia *f*

rumor [rúmə] N rumor *m*; VT murmurar; **it is —ed that** se rumorea que, corre la voz que

rump [rʌmp] N (of quadruped) anca *f*, grupa *f*; (of bird) rabadilla *f*; (of person) trasero *m*

run [rʌn] VI (person, tears, water) correr; (stockings, dyes) correrse; (function) funcionar; (travel briefly) hacer una escapadita; (circulate) circular, hacer el recorrido; (drip) chorrear; (be a candidate) presentarse como candidato; (suppurate) supurar; VT (a mile, a risk) correr; (one object through another) pasar; (a business) manejar, dirigir; (a red light) comerse; (a news story) publicar; (a sum of money) costar; (a computer program) ejecutar; (a fever) tener; **— along now!** ¡vete! **to — across someone** encontrarse con alguien; **to — after** perseguir; **to — around with** andar con; **to — away** fugarse, escaparse; **to — down** (stop working) dejar de funcionar; (capture) aprehender; (criticize) hablar mal de; (run over) atropellar; (tire) cansar; **to — dry** secarse; **to — into** (encounter) tropezar con, encontrarse con; (collide) chocar con; **to — out** salir corriendo; **to — out of money** quedarse sin dinero; **to — over** (spill) derramarse; (run down) atropellar, arrollar; (move along a surface) deslizar por; **to — through** (stab) atravesar; (squander) despilfarrar; (repeat) repetir; **the play ran for three months** la obra estuvo en cartel durante tres meses; **it —s in the family** es un rasgo de familia; N (act of running) carrera *f*, corrida *f*; (defect in stockings) carrera *f*, corrida *f*; (routine trip) recorrido *m*; (of newspapers) tirada *f*; (of a play) temporada en cartel *f*; (on a bank) pánico *m*, corrida *f*; **—away** fugitivo -va *mf*; **—away horse** caballo desbocado *m*; **—down** desvencijado; **— of good luck** racha de buena suerte *f*; **— of performances** temporada en cartel *f*; **— of the mill** del montón; **—way** (for planes) pista *f*; (for models) pasarela *f*; **to be on the —** estar huyendo; **in the long — a** la larga; **the —s** *vulg* cagalera *f*; **he gave me the —around** contestó con evasivas

rung [rʌŋ] N (of a chair) barrote *m*; (of a ladder) peldaño *m*

runner [ránə-] N (one who runs) corredor -ora *mf*; (on a table) tapete *m*; (on a sled) patín *m*; (on a skate) cuchilla *f*; (on a plant) estolón *m*; (of drugs, contraband) contrabandista *mf*; **—up** segundo -da *mf*

running [ránɪŋ] N (race) corrida *f*, carrera *f*; (direction) manejo *m*, dirección *f*; (flow) flujo *m*; (of machines) funcionamiento *m*; (of a car) rodaje *m*; **to be out of the —** estar fuera de combate; **— board** estribo *m*; ADJ (of horses) de carrera; (of plants) trepador; (of sores) supurante; **— water** agua corriente *f*; **in — condition** en buen estado; **for ten days —** durante diez días seguidos

runt [rʌnt] N (animal) animal más pequeño de la camada *m*; (person) *pej* mequetrefe *m*

rupture [ráptʃə-] N (of relations, internal organ) ruptura *f*; (of a tire) rotura *f*; (hernia) hernia *f*; VI/VT romper(se), reventar(se)

rural [rúrəl] ADJ rural

rush [rʌʃ] VI/VT (hurry) apresurar(se); *Am* apurar(se); VT (to dispatch) llevar con prisa, llevar rápido; (to attack) precipitarse, abalanzarse sobre; **to — by / past** pasar corriendo; **to — out** salir corriendo; N (haste) prisa *f*; *Am* apuro *m*; (attack) acometida *f*; (hurried activity) bullicio *m*; (plant) junco *m*; **— of air** ráfaga *f*; **— of people** tumulto *m*; **— of water** torrente *m*; **— order** pedido urgente *m*

Russia [ráʃə] N Rusia *f*

Russian [ráʃən] ADJ & N ruso -sa *mf*

rust [rʌst] N (oxidation) herrumbre *f*, orín *m*; (disease) tizón *m*; **—colored** color herrumbre; **—proof** inoxidable; VI/VT herrumbrar(se)

rustic [rástɪk] ADJ rústico; N campesino -na *mf*, paleto -ta *mf*

rustle [rásəl] VI susurrar, crujir; VT hacer susurrar, hacer crujir; **to — cattle** robar

ganado; N susurro *m*, crujido *m*

rusty [rásti] ADJ (oxidized) herrumbrado, oxidado; (rust-colored) color herrumbre; (out of practice) falto de práctica; **my German is —** se me ha olvidado el alemán

rut [rʌt] N (furrow) surco *m*; (of a wheel) rodada *f*; (routine) rutina *f*; (heat) celo *m*; **to be in a —** ser esclavo de la rutina; VI estar en celo

ruthless [rúθlɪs] ADJ despiadado

ruthlessness [rúθlɪsnɪs] N crueldad *f*

Rwanda [ruándə] N Ruanda *f*

Rwandan [ruándən] ADJ & N ruandés -esa *mf*

rye [raɪ] N centeno *m*; **— bread** pan de centeno *m*

Ss

saber [sébə-] N sable *m*

sabotage [sǽbətɑʒ] N sabotaje *m*; VT sabotear

saccharine [sǽkərɪn] ADJ empalagoso; N sacarina *f*

sack [sæk] N (bag) saco *m*, bolso *m*; (looting) saqueo *m*; **in the —** en la cama; VT (bag) embolsar, ensacar; (loot) saquear; (fire) despedir

sacrament [sǽkrəmənt] N sacramento *m*

sacred [sékrɪd] ADJ sagrado

sacrifice [sǽkrəfaɪs] N sacrificio *m*; **at a —** con pérdida; VT sacrificar

sacrilege [sǽkrəlɪdʒ] N sacrilegio *m*

sacrilegious [sækrəlídʒəs] ADJ sacrílego

sad [sæd] ADJ triste

sadden [sǽdn̩] VI/VT entristecer(se); VT pesar

saddle [sǽdl̩] N (for horse) silla de montar *f*, montura *f*; (for bicycle) sillín *m*; **—bag** alforja *f*; **— horse** caballo de silla *m*; **— pad** carona *f*; **— tree** arzón *m*; VT ensillar; **to — up** ensillar; **to — someone with responsibilities** cargar a alguien de responsabilidades

sadism [sédɪzəm] N sadismo *m*

sadistic [sədístɪk] ADJ sádico

sadness [sǽdnɪs] N tristeza *f*

sadomasochism [sedomǽsəkɪzəm] N sadomasoquismo *m*

safari [səfári] N safari *m*

safe [sef] ADJ (secure) seguro, salvo; (trustworthy) digno de confianza; (careful) precavido, prudente; **— and sound** sano y salvo; **—conduct** salvoconducto *m*; **—guard** salvaguarda *f*; **to — guard**

salvaguardar; — **in jail** confinado;
—keeping custodia f; — **sex** sexo seguro
m; N caja fuerte f

safety [séfti] N seguridad f; — **belt** cinturón
de seguridad m; — **device** mecanismo de
seguridad m, seguro m; — **glass** vidrio
inastillable m; — **net** red f; — **pin**
imperdible m

saffron [sǽfrən] N (spice) azafrán m; (color)
color azafrán m

sag [sæg] VI/VT (wall) combar(se), pandear(se);
VI (stock market, breast) caer; (spirits)
decaer; (rope) aflojarse; (pants) abolsarse;
his shoulders — tiene las espaldas
caídas; N (of a wall) pandeo m, comba f;
(in prices) caída f

sage [sedʒ] ADJ sabio; N (wise person) sabio
-bia mf; (plant) salvia f

sail [sel] N (part of a boat) vela f; (trip) viaje
en barco m; —**boat** velero m; —**fish** pez
vela m; **under full** — a toda vela; **to set**
— zarpar; VI/VT (travel by boat) navegar;
(set sail) zarpar; **to — along** deslizarse,
navegar; **to — along the coast** costear;
to — through an exam aprobar un
examen con facilidad

sailor [séla-] N marinero -ra mf

saint [sent] N santo -ta mf; — **John** San Juan

saintly [séntli] ADJ santo, piadoso

sake [sek] N **for the — of** por; **for my —**
por mí; **for pity's** — por el amor de Dios;
for brevity's — para ser breve; **for the**
— **of argument** por vía de argumento;
art for art's — el arte por el arte

salad [sǽləd] N ensalada f; — **dressing**
aderezo m

salamander [sǽləmændə-] N salamandra f

salary [sǽləri] N sueldo m; — **bracket**
categoría salarial f

sale [sel] N (act of selling) venta f; (special
sales event) liquidación f, saldo m; —**s
force** personal de ventas m; —**sperson**
vendedor -ora mf; (in a store) dependiente
-ta mf; —**s tax** impuesto sobre las ventas
m; **for** — en venta

salient [sélient] ADJ & N saliente m

saline [sélin] ADJ salino

saliva [səláivə] N saliva f

sally [sǽli] N (sortie) salida f; (excursion)
excursión f; VI salir, hacer una salida; **to**
— **forth** salir

salmon [sǽmən] N salmón m

salmonella [sælmənélə] N salmonela f

salon [səlán] N salón m; (beauty parlor) salón
de belleza m, peluquería f

saloon [səlún] N salón m, taberna f, bar m

salt [sɔlt] N sal f; (for smelling) sales f pl; **the**

— **of the earth** la sal de la tierra; **old —**
lobo de mar m; —**cellar** salero m; — **lick**
salegar m; — **mine** salina f; —**shaker**
salero m; —**water** agua salada f; VT salar;
to — **away** ahorrar

salty [sɔ́lti] ADJ salado; (land) salobre

salutation [sæljətéʃən] N saludo m

salute [səlút] N saludo m; (of guns) salva f;
VI/VT (greet) saludar; (acknowledge)
reconocer

Salvadoran, Salvadorian [sælvədór(i)ən]
ADJ & N salvadoreño -ña mf

salvage [sǽlvɪdʒ] N (recovery) salvamento m;
(objects recovered) objetos salvados m pl;
VT salvar

salvation [sælvéʃən] N salvación f

salve [sæv] N ungüento m, pomada f

salvo [sǽlvo] N salva f

same [sem] ADJ (identical) mismo; (similar)
igual; **it is all the — to me** me da igual,
me da lo mismo; **all the —** de todos
modos; —**sex marriage** matrimonio
homosexual m

Samoa [səmóə] N Samoa f

Samoan [səmóən] ADJ & N samoano -na mf

sample [sǽmpəl] N muestra f; VT (try) probar;
(take samples) muestrear

sampling [sǽmplɪŋ] N muestreo m

sanctify [sǽŋktəfaɪ] VT santificar

sanction [sǽŋkʃən] N sanción f; VT sancionar

sanctity [sǽŋktɪDi] N santidad f

sanctuary [sǽŋktʃueri] N (church
auditorium, place of refuge) santuario m;
(game preserve) reserva f

sand [sænd] N arena f; —**box** arenero m; —
dollar erizo de mar plano m; —**paper**
papel de lija m; **to** —**paper** lijar; —**stone**
arenisca f; —**storm** tormenta de arena f;
VT lijar, pulir

sandal [sǽndl] N sandalia f

sandwich [sǽndwɪtʃ] N bocadillo m,
emparedado m; VT intercalar; **to be** —**ed
between** quedar apretado entre

sandy [sǽndi] ADJ (full of sand) arenoso,
arenisco; (yellowish red) rubio

sane [sen] ADJ cuerdo

sanitarium [sænítériəm] N sanatorio m

sanitary [sǽnɪteri] ADJ sanitario; — **napkin**
paño higiénico m

sanitation [sænɪtéʃən] N (sewers)
saneamiento m; (hygiene) salubridad f

sanity [sǽnɪDi] N cordura f

San Marinese [sænmærəníz] ADJ & N
sanmarinense mf, sanmarinés -esa mf

San Marino [sænmaríno] N San Marino m

Sanskrit [sǽnskrɪt] N sánscrito f

Santa Claus [sǽntəklɔz] N Papá Noel m,

Santa Claus *m*

São Tomean [sautoméən] ADJ & N santotomense *mf*

São Tome and Principe [sautoméændprínsipe] N Santo Tomé y Príncipe *m*

sap [sæp] N (juice) savia *f*; (fool) tonto -ta *mf*; VT (exhaust) agotar

sapling [sǽpliŋ] N (tree) árbol joven *m*; (person) jovenzuelo -la *mf*

sapphire [sǽfair] N zafiro *m*

sarcasm [sárkæzəm] N sarcasmo *m*, socarronería *f*

sarcastic [sarkǽstik] ADJ sarcástico, socarrón

sarcoma [sarkómə] N sarcoma *m*

sarcophagus [sarkófəgəs] N sarcófago *m*

sardine [sardín] N sardina *f*

sardonic [sardónik] ADJ sardónico

sash [sæʃ] N (around waist) faja *f*; (around shoulder) banda *f*; (on window) marco *m*, bastidor *m*

sassy [sǽsi] ADJ insolente

satanic [sətǽnik] ADJ satánico

satchel [sǽtʃəl] N cartera *f*

satellite [sǽdlait] N satélite *m*; **— dish** (antena) parabólica *f*

satiate [séʃiet] VT saciar, hartar

satin [sǽtn] N raso *m*, satén *m*

satire [sǽtair] N sátira *f*

satirical [sətírikəl] ADJ satírico

satirize [sǽdəraiz] VT satirizar

satisfaction [sædisfǽkʃən] N satisfacción *f*

satisfactory [sædisfǽktəri] ADJ satisfactorio

satisfied [sǽdisfaid] ADJ satisfecho

satisfy [sǽdisfai] VI/VT satisfacer

saturate [sǽtʃəret] VI/VT (impregnate) saturar(se); (soak) empapar(se); **—d fat** grasa saturada *f*

Saturday [sǽdə-De] N sábado *m*

sauce [sɔs] N salsa *f*; **—pan** cacerola *f*; VT aderezar con salsa

saucer [sɔ́sə-] N platillo *m*

saucy [sɔ́si] ADJ descarado, insolente; (who talks back) respondón

Saudi Arabia [sɔ́diərébiə] N Arabia Saudí *f*, Arabia Saudita *f*

Saudi Arabian [sɔ́diərébiən] ADJ & N saudí *mf*, saudita *mf*

saunter [sɔ́ntə-] VI pasearse, deambular

sausage [sɔ́sidʒ] N (thick) chorizo *m*; (thin) salchicha *f*; (cured) longaniza *f*; **—-making** charcutería *f*

savage [sǽvidʒ] ADJ salvaje; (furious) rabioso; (rugged) agreste; N salvaje *m*; VT hacer trizas

savagery [sǽvidʒri] N salvajismo *m*, barbarie *f*

save [sev] VT (a sinner, a person in danger)

salvar; (furniture) salvaguardar, proteger; (money, time, energy) ahorrar, economizar; (data) guardar; VI (lay up money, be economical) ahorrar; (protect) salvaguardar; **to — from** librar de; **to — one's eyes** cuidarse la vista; PREP salvo, menos

savings [séviŋz] N ahorros *m pl*; **— account** cuenta de ahorros *f*; **— bank** caja de ahorros *f*

savior [sévjə-] N salvador -ora *mf*

savor [sévə-] N (taste) sabor *m*; (trace) dejo *m*; VT saborear

savory [sévəri] ADJ sabroso

savvy [sǽvi] N astucia *f*; ADJ astuto

saw [sɔ] N sierra *f*; **—horse** caballete *m*; VI/VT aserrar(se); **—dust** aserrín *m*, serrín *m*; **—mill** aserradero *m*

saxophone [sǽksəfon] N saxofón *m*

say [se] VI/VT decir; VT (a clock) marcar; (a sign) rezar, decir; (a prayer) rezar; **—!** ¡oye! **that is to —** es decir; **— I bought it** supongamos que yo lo comprara; **it goes without —ing** huelga decirlo; **there's a lot to be said for** es muy recomendable; **when all is said and done** al fin y al cabo; **you can — that again** tú no has dicho; N **the final —** la última palabra; **to have one's —** dar su opinión; ADV **you could earn, —, 1 million dollars** podrías ganar pongamos un millón de dólares

saying [séŋ] N dicho *m*, refrán *m*

scab [skæb] N (of a wound) costra *f*; (on plants) roña *f*; (strikebreaker) esquirol *m*, amarillo -lla *mf*; VI (wound) encostrarse; (break a strike) ser esquirol

scabby [skǽbi] ADJ (of wounds) costroso; (of plants) roñoso; (of scalp) tiñoso

scaffold [skǽfəld] N (in construction) andamio *m*; (of a gallows) patíbulo *m*

scald [skɔld] VI/VT escaldar(se); N escaldadura *f*

scale [skeł] N (progression) escala *f*; (for weighing) balanza *f*; (for heavy weights) báscula *f*; (on fish, reptiles, human skin) escama *f*; **pair of —s** balanza *f*; VT (climb) escalar; (remove scales) escamar; VI/VT (adjust proportionately) graduar; **to — down** rebajar proporcionalmente

scallion [skǽljən] N cebollino *m*

scallop [skǽləp] N (mollusk) vieira *f*; (of beef) escalope *m*; (of fabric) festón *m*; VT festonear

scalp [skætp] N cuero cabelludo *m*; VT (to skin) arrancar la cabellera; (to resell) revender

scalpel [skǽlpəɫ] N bisturí *m*

scalper [skǽlpɚ] N revendedor -ra *mf*

scam [skæm] N timo *m*, estafa *f*

scamp [skæmp] N pícaro -ra *mf*, tunante -ta *mf*, pillo -lla *mf*

scamper [skǽmpɚ] VI (run) escabullirse, escaparse; (caper) cabriolar

scan [skæn] VT (horizon) escudriñar, escrutar; (with radar) explorar; (brain) hacer una tomografía; (page) echar un vistazo a; (verse) escandir; (digitalize for computer) escanear; N tomografía *f*

scandal [skǽndɫ] N escándalo *m*

scandalize [skǽndɫaɪz] VT escandalizar

scandalous [skǽndɫəs] ADJ escandaloso

scanner [skǽnɚ] N escáner *m*

scant [skænt] ADJ escaso

scanty [skǽnti] ADJ (scant) escaso; (of a skirt) muy corto; (of a bikini) breve

scapegoat [skégot] N chivo expiatorio *m*, cabeza de turco *m*

scar [skɑr] N cicatriz *f*, lacra *f*; VT dejar una cicatriz

scarce [skɛrs] ADJ escaso; **to be —** escasear

scarcely [skɛrsli] ADV (barely) apenas; **he's — a genius** no es un genio ni mucho menos

scarcity [skɛ́rsɪDi] N escasez *f*, pobreza *f*, carestía *f*

scare [skɛr] VI/VT espantar(se), asustar(se); **to — away** ahuyentar; **to — up** reunir; N susto *m*, sobresalto *m*; (of war) amago *m*; **—crow** espantapájaros *m sg*

scarf [skɑrf] N (woolen) bufanda *f*; (silk, cotton) pañuelo *m*; VI **to — up** engullir

scarlet [skɑ́rlɪt] N escarlata *m*, grana *f*; **— fever** escarlatina *f*

scary [skɛ́ri] ADJ (causing fright) de miedo; (easily frightened) asustadizo

scat [skæt] INTERJ ¡fuera!

scatter [skǽDɚ] VI/VT (seeds) esparcir(se), desparramar(se), desperdigar(se); (crowd) dispersar(se); N cabeza de chorlito *mf*; **—brained** atolondrado

scavenge [skǽvɪndʒ] VT recoger, rescatar; VI hurgar

scenario [sɪnério] N guión *m*; **worst-case —** el peor de los casos

scene [sin] N escena *f*; (sphere) ambiente *m*, ámbito *m*; **to make a —** montar una escena; **behind the —s** entre bastidores

scenery [sínəri] N paisaje *m*; (on a stage) decorado *m*

scenic [sínɪk] ADJ panorámico

scent [sɛnt] N (smell) olor *m*; (fragrance) perfume *m*; (trace) pista *f*, rastro *m*; (sense of smell) olfato *m*; VI/VT (perceive through smell) olfatear; (intuit) presentir; (give fragrance to) perfumar

schedule [skédʒuɫ] N (plan) calendario *m*; (timetable) horario *m*; (appendix) apéndice *m*; (list) lista *f*; **on —** en fecha; **ahead of —** adelantado; VT programar, fijar

scheme [skim] N (plan) plan *m*, proyecto *m*; (plot) ardid *m*, trama *f*; (of colors) combinación *f*; VI/VT maquinar, intrigar, tramar

schemer [skímɚ] N maquinador -ra *mf*, intrigante *mf*

scheming [skímɪŋ] ADJ intrigante; N maquinación *f*

schizophrenia [skɪtsəfréniə] N esquizofrenia *f*

schmuck [ʃmʌk] N *pej* pendejo -ja *mf*, gilipollas *mf sg*

scholar [skɑ́lɚ] N (student) alumno -na *mf*; (fellow) becario -ria *mf*; (erudite person) erudito -ta *mf*, estudioso -sa *mf*

scholarly [skɑ́lɚli] ADJ erudito

scholarship [skɑ́lɚʃɪp] N (erudition) erudición *f*; (award) beca *f*

school [skuɫ] N (primary) escuela *f*, colegio *m*; (secondary) secundaria *f*; Sp instituto *m*; (university) universidad *f*; (of law, etc.) facultad *f*; (of language, driving) academia *f*; (of thought) escuela *f*; (of fish) banco *m*, cardumen *m*; **—boy** escolar *m*; **—girl** escolar *f*; **—house** escuela *f*; **—master** maestro -tra *mf*; **—mate** compañero -ra de escuela *mf*; **—room** aula *f*, sala de clase *f*; **—teacher** maestro -tra *mf*; **—year** año lectivo *m*; VT instruir, entrenar

schooling [skúlɪŋ] N instrucción *f*

schooner [skúnɚ] N goleta *f*

sciatic nerve [saɪǽDɪknɚ́v] N nervio ciático *m*

science [sáɪəns] N ciencia *f*; **— fiction** ciencia ficción *f*

scientific [saɪəntífɪk] ADJ científico; **— method** método científico *m*

scientist [sáɪəntɪst] N científico -ca *mf*

scintillate [síntlet] VI (diamonds) centellear, destellar; (stars) titilar

scissors [sízɚz] N tijeras *f pl*

sclerosis [sklɚósɪs] N esclerosis *f*

scoff [skɑf] N mofa *f*, burla *f*; VI mofarse; **to — at** mofarse de, burlarse de

scold [skoɫd] VI/VT reprender, regañar, reñir; N regañón -ona *mf*

scolding [skóɫdɪŋ] N regaño *m*, reprimenda *f*

scoliosis [skolíosɪs] N escoliosis *f*

scoop [skup] N (ladle) cucharón *m*; (spoon for ice-cream) cuchara *f*; (shovel) pala *f*; (news

item) primicia *f*; VT sacar con cuchara;
(report first) adelantarse a; **to — in a
good profit** sacar buena ganancia; **to —
out** (water) achicar; (a hole) cavar; **to —
up** recoger

scoot [skut] VI (go fast) correr; (go away)
largarse

scooter [skúdɚ] N (with motor) scooter *m*;
(toy) monopatín *m*, patinete *m*

scope [skop] N (range) alcance *m*, ámbito *m*;
(sphere) esfera *f*; VT observar

scorch [skɔrtʃ] VI/VT chamuscar(se),
quemar(se); N chamuscadura *f*; *Am*
quemadura *f*

score [skor] N (partial result) tanteo *m*; (total
result) resultado *m*; (in a test) calificación
f; (scratch) arañazo *m*; (twenty) veintena *f*;
(of music) partitura *f*; **on that** — a ese
respecto; **to keep** — llevar la cuenta; **to
settle old** —s ajustar cuentas; VT (a test)
calificar; (to orchestrate) orquestar; (to
scratch) arañar; VI/VT (points) marcar,
tantear; (sexually) ligar

scorn [skɔrn] N desdén *m*, menosprecio *m*; VI/
VT desdeñar, menospreciar

scornful [skɔ́rnfəɫ] ADJ desdeñoso

scorpion [skɔ́rpiən] N escorpión *m*, alacrán *m*

Scotch [skɑtʃ] ADJ escocés; **— whisky** whisky
escocés *m*

Scotland [skɑ́tlənd] N Escocia *f*

Scotsman [skɑ́tsmən] N escocés *m*

Scotswoman [skɑ́tswumən] N escocesa *f*

Scottish [skɑ́dɪʃ] ADJ escocés

scoundrel [skɑ́undɹəɫ] N bellaco *m*, infame
m, truhán *m*

scour [skaur] VT (clean) fregar, restregar;
(search) recorrer

scourge [skɜ·ʤ] N azote *m*; VT azotar

scout [skaut] N (military) explorador -ra *mf*;
(child explorer) explorador -ra *mf*, scout
mf; (for talent) cazatalentos *mf sg*; **a good
—** una buena persona; VI/VT explorar; VI
to — for buscar

scowl [skaut] N ceño fruncido *m*; VI fruncir el
ceño

scram [skɹæm] VI largarse

scramble [skɹǽmbəɫ] VI (climb) subir a gatas;
VT (eggs) revolver; (numbers) mezclar; **to
— for** pelearse por; **to — up** subir a
gatas; **—d eggs** huevos revueltos *m pl*; N
(difficult climb) subida difícil *f*; (struggle
for possession) arrebatiña *f*

scrap [skɹæp] N (fragment) fragmento *m*,
pedacito *m*; (of truth) ápice *m*; (fight) riña
f, reyerta *f*; **—book** álbum de recortes *m*;
— iron chatarra *f*; **—s** sobras *f pl*,
desperdicios *m pl*; VT (break apart)

desguazar; (discard) desechar; VI pelearse,
reñir

scrape [skɹep] VI/VT (rub) raspar; (damage)
arañar; **to — along** ir tirando, ir
pasándola; **to — by** arreglárselas; **to —
together** reunir; **to bow and —** ser muy
servil; N (act of scraping) raspado *m*;
(injury) raspón *m*, raspadura *f*; (sound)
chirrido *m*; (fight) pelea *f*; (difficult
situation) aprieto *m*

scraper [skɹépɚ] N raspador *m*

scratch [skɹætʃ] VI/VT (mark) arañar,
rasguñar; (relieve itching) rascar(se);
(cancel from a race) retirar(se); (cause
itching) picar; VI (to dig, as a hen)
escarbar; **to — out** (words) tachar; (eyes)
sacar; N (injury) arañazo *m*, rasguño *m*;
(sound) chirrido *m*; **to start from —**
empezar de cero

scrawny [skɹɔ́ni] ADJ esmirriado

scream [skɹim] N grito *m*, alarido *m*; **he's a
—** es un payaso; VI/VT gritar

screech [skɹitʃ] N (of brakes) chirrido *m*; (of
voice) chillido *m*; **— owl** lechuza *f*; VI (of
brakes) chirriar; (of voice) chillar

screen [skɹin] N (movie, computer) pantalla *f*;
(divider) biombo *m*; (on window)
mosquitero *m*; (sifter) tamiz *m*; **— door**
puerta con mosquitero *f*; **—play** guión *m*;
—writer guionista *mf*; VT (conceal) tapar;
(sift) tamizar; (project) proyectar; (select)
seleccionar

screw [skɹu] N tornillo *m*; (one turn) vuelta *f*;
(propeller) hélice *f*; (sexual intercourse)
fam polvo *m*; **—driver** destornillador *m*
(also cocktail); VT (turn) atornillar; (have
intercourse) *Sp vulg* follar; *Am vulg* coger,
culear; **to — on** enroscar; **to — up one's
courage** cobrar ánimo; **to — around**
(waste time) perder tiempo; (be
promiscuous) ser promiscuo; **to —
something up** *vulg* chingar algo, joder
algo; **I —ed up** *vulg* la cagué; **to — with**
vulg chingar

scribble [skɹíbəɫ] VI/VT garabatear,
garrapatear; N garabato *m*

script [skɹɪpt] N (writing) escritura *f*;
(screenplay) guión *m*

scripture [skɹíptʃɚ] N escritura sagrada *f*

scroll [skɹoɫ] N (roll) rollo *m*; (adornment)
voluta *f*; VI **to — down** bajar el cursor

scrotum [skɹódəm] N escroto *m*

scrub [skɹʌb] VI/VT (rub) fregar, restregar; VT
(cancel) cancelar; **to — up** lavarse las
manos; N (cleaning) friega *f*, fregada *f*;
(bushes) maleza *f*; (rough terrain) breña *f*;
— pine pino achaparrado *m*; **— team**

equipo suplente *m*; **—woman** fregona *f*
scruple [skrúpəɫ] N escrúpulo *m*
scrupulous [skrúpjələs] ADJ escrupuloso
scrutinize [skrútṇaɪz] VI/VT escrutar
scrutiny [skrútṇi] N escrutinio *m*, examen minucioso *m*
scuba [skúbə] N escafandra *f*; VI **to —-dive** bucear
scuff [skʌf] VT (shoes) rayar; (floor) marcar; N (on shoes) raya *f*; (on floor) marca *f*
scuffle [skʌ́fəɫ] N refriega *f*, riña *f*; VI pelear, reñir; (shuffle) arrastrar los pies
sculptor [skʌ́ɫptɚ] N escultor -ra *mf*
sculpture [skʌ́ɫptʃɚ] N escultura *f*; VI/VT esculpir
scum [skʌm] N (in a glass) capa de suciedad *f*; (in a pond) verdín *m*; (people) escoria *f*; (vile person) pej canalla *mf*; **—bag** pej canalla *mf*; VI cubrirse de espuma; VT espumar
scurrilous [skɚ́ələs] ADJ (coarse) grosero; (injurious) injurioso
scurry [skɚ́i] VI correr; **to — away / off** escabullirse; N carrera *f*
scuttle [skʌ́dɫ] VI (run) correr; **to — away / off** escabullirse; VT (sink a ship) hundir; (abandon a plane) abandonar
scythe [saɪð] N guadaña *f*
sea [si] N mar *mf*; **at** — en el mar; **by** — por barco; **to put to** — hacerse a la mar; **on the high —s** en alta mar; ADJ marino; **— battle** batalla naval *f*; **—board** costa *f*, litoral *m*; **—coast** costa *f*, litoral *m*; **— cow** vaca marina *f*; **— current** corriente marina *f*; **—faring** marinero; **—food** frutos del mar *m pl*; **— green** verdemar *m*; **—gull** gaviota *f*; **— horse** caballito de mar *m*; **— level** nivel del mar *m*; **— lion** léon marino *m*; **—man** marino *m*, marinero *m*; **—plane** hidroavión *m*; **—port** puerto de mar *m*; **— power** potencia naval *f*; **—shore** costa *f*; **—sick** mareado; **to get —sick** marearse; **—sickness** mareo *m*; **—side** costa *f*, litoral *m*; **— turtle** tortuga marina *f*; **— urchin** erizo de mar *m*; **—weed** alga (marina) *f*; **—worthy** marinero
seal [siɫ] N (stamp) sello *m*; (on a jar) precinto *m*; (animal) foca *f*; **to set one's — to** sellar; **—ing wax** lacre *m*; VT (put a seal on) sellar; (close with a seal) precintar; **to — one's fate** determinar el destino de uno; **to — off** acordonar; **to — in** cerrar herméticamente; **to — with sealing wax** lacrar
seam [sim] N (sewing) costura *f*; (in rock) grieta *f*; (in ore deposits) veta *f*; VT coser

seamstress [símstɪs] N costurera *f*
seamy [sími] ADJ sórdido
sear [sɪr] VT chamuscar
search [sɝtʃ] VI/VT (an area) rastrear, requisar; (a suitcase) registrar; (a person) cachear; **— me!** ¡a mí que me registren! ¡yo que sé! **to — for** buscar; N (for something) búsqueda *f*; (of baggage, ships) registro *m*; (of an area) rastreo *m*; **— engine** motor de búsqueda *m*, máquina de búsqueda *f*; **—light** reflector *m*; **— warrant** orden de registro *m*; **in — of** en busca de
season [sízən] N (of the year) estación *f*; (period of time) temporada *f*, época *f*; **in** — en temporada/época; **— ticket** billete de abono *m*; **open** — temporada de caza/pesca *f*; **out of** — fuera de temporada/época; VT (to spice) sazonar, aderezar; VI (wood) secarse; **a —ed pilot** un piloto experimentado
seasoning [sízənɪŋ] N condimento *m*, aliño *m*
seat [sit] N (furniture) asiento *m*; (of bicycle) sillín *m*; (in parliament) escaño *m*; (of government) sede *f*; (in the theater) localidad *f*; (buttocks) asentaderas *f pl*; (of clothes) fondillos *m pl*; **to take a** — sentarse, tomar asiento; **— belt** cinturón de seguridad *m*; VT (cause to sit) sentar; (accommodate with seats) tener capacidad para; (place) colocar; **to — oneself** sentarse
seclude [sɪklúd] VT aislar; **to — oneself from** recluirse de, aislarse de
secluded [sɪklúdɪd] ADJ apartado, aislado
seclusion [sɪklúʒən] N recogimiento *m*, aislamiento *m*
second [sékənd] ADJ & N segundo -da *mf*; **— fiddle** segundón -ona *mf*; **— floor** primer piso *m*; **—hand** de segunda mano; **— lieutenant** subteniente *m*; **on — thought** pensándolo bien; **—-rate** mediocre, de segunda; N (part of a minute) segundo *m*; (helper in a duel) padrino *m*; **— child** segundón -ona *mf*; **— cousin** primo -ma segundo -da *mf*; **— nature** automático; **—s** artículos de segunda *m pl*; **may I have —s?** ¿puedo repetir? **to —-guess** cuestionar; VT (support) secundar, apoyar; (assist in duels) apadrinar; (support a motion) apoyar
secondary [sékəndeɾi] ADJ secundario; **— school** escuela secundaria *f*
secondly [sékəndli] ADV en segundo lugar
secrecy [síkɾɪsi] N secreto *m*
secret [síkɾɪt] ADJ & N secreto *m*

secretariat [sɛkrɪtǽriət] N secretaría *f*
secretary [sɛ́krɪteri] N (assistant) secretario
  -ria *mf*; (government) ministro -tra *mf*;
  (furniture) escritorio *m*
secrete [sɪkrít] VT (discharge) secretar,
  segregar; (hide) ocultar
secretion [sɪkríʃən] N secreción *f*
secretive [síkrɪtɪv] ADJ hermético
sect [sɛkt] N secta *f*
section [sɛ́kʃən] N sección *f*; (of a chapter)
  apartado *m*; (passage) trozo *m*; (of a city)
  sector *m*; (incision) corte *m*; (of orange)
  gajo *m*; VT seccionar
sector [sɛ́ktə] N sector *m*
secular [sɛ́kjələ] ADJ secular; N seglar *mf*, lego
  -ga *mf*
secure [sɪkjúr] ADJ (certain, safe) seguro;
  (firm) firme; VT (make certain, guarantee)
  asegurar, afianzar; (make firm) afirmar,
  cimentar; (obtain) obtener; (protect)
  proteger; (lock) cerrar con llave; (capture)
  capturar; (tie) amarrar
security [sɪkjúrɪti] N (safety, freedom from
  worry) seguridad *f*; (guarantee) fianza *f*,
  garantía *f*; (guarantor) fiador -ora *mf*;
  securities valores *m pl*
sedan [sɪdǽn] N sedán *m*
sedate [sɪdét] ADJ sosegado, tranquilo; VT
  sedar
sedation [sɪdéʃən] N sedación *f*
sedative [sɛ́dətɪv] ADJ & N calmante *m*,
  sedante *m*
sedentary [sɛ́dnteri] ADJ sedentario
sediment [sɛ́dəmənt] N sedimento *m*; (dregs)
  heces *f pl*
sedition [sɪdíʃən] N sedición *f*
seduce [sɪdús] VI/VT seducir (a)
seduction [sɪdákʃən] N seducción *f*
see [si] VI/VT (perceive, find out, meet, visit)
  ver; (understand) entender; (make sure)
  fijarse, asegurarse; (date) salir con; (help)
  ayudar; (accompany) acompañar; **to — to**
  encargarse de, atender; **let me — a** ver;
  to — off despedir; **to — through**
  someone calar a alguien; **to — about**
  ocuparse de; **to — out** acompañar a la
  puerta; N sede *f*
seed [sid] N (grains) semilla *f*; (semen)
  simiente *f*; **to go to —** echarse a perder;
  — bed semillero *m*; VI/VT (sow) sembrar;
  VT despepitar, quitar las semillas; (player)
  clasificar; VI producir semillas
seedy [sídi] ADJ sórdido
seek [sik] VT (search for) buscar; (ask for)
  pedir; **to — after** buscar; **to — to** tratar
  de, esforzarse por
seem [sim] VI parecer; **they — to be here**

parece que están aquí; **it —s to me** me
  parece
seemingly [símɪŋli] ADV aparentemente
seep [sip] VI/VT rezumar(se)
seer [sir] N vidente *mf*
seesaw [sísɔ] N balancín *m*, subibaja *m*; VI
  oscilar
seethe [sið] VI bullir, hervir; **he was**
  seething hervía de rabia
segment [sɛ́gmənt] N segmento *m*
segregate [sɛ́grɪget] VI/VT segregar
seismic [sáɪzmɪk] ADJ sísmico
seize [siz] VT (grab) asir, agarrar; (take
  possession) apoderarse de; (take advantage
  of) aprovecharse de; (confiscate) embargar,
  incautarse de, secuestrar; **to — upon** asir;
  VI **to — (up)** agarrotarse; **to — upon**
  valerse de
seizure [síʒə] N (of power) toma *f*; (of
  property) confiscación *f*; (of drugs, guns)
  incautación *f*, secuestro *m*; (epileptic)
  ataque *m*
seldom [sɛ́ldəm] ADV rara vez, raramente
select [sɪlɛ́kt] ADJ selecto; VI/VT elegir,
  seleccionar
selection [sɪlɛ́kʃən] N selección *f*, elección *f*
selective [sɪlɛ́ktɪv] ADJ selectivo
self [sɛłf] N (ego) yo *m*; **—-assurance**
  desenvoltura *f*; **—-control** autocontrol *m*;
  —-defense defensa propia *f*; (juridical
  term) legítima defensa *f*; **—-denial**
  abnegación *f*; **—-discipline**
  autodisciplina *f*; **—-esteem** autoestima *f*;
  —-government autogobierno *m*;
  —-help autoayuda *f*; **—-image**
  autoimagen *f*; **—-improvement** mejora
  personal *f*; **—-interest** interés personal *m*;
  —-made man hombre que debe su éxito
  a sus propios esfuerzos *m*; **—-pity**
  autocompasión *f*; **—-reliance**
  independencia *f*; **—-respect** amor propio
  m; **—-sacrifice** sacrificio *m*;
  —-satisfaction autosatisfacción *f*; **his**
  better — su lado bueno *m*; **his former**
  — lo que era antes *m*; ADJ **—-assured**
  desenvuelto; **—-centered** egocéntrico;
  —-composed tranquilo; **—-confident**
  con confianza de sí mismo; **—-conscious**
  (shy) cohibido; (with complexes)
  acomplejado; **—-destructive**
  autodestructivo; **—-employed** que trabaja
  por cuenta propia; **—-evident** evidente;
  —-explanatory claro, fácil de entender;
  —-propelled autopropulsado;
  —-righteous que afecta superioridad
  moral; **—-satisfied** pagado de sí,
  satisfecho de sí; **—-service** autoservicio;

—**-serving** interesado; —**-sufficient** autosuficiente
selfish [sélfɪʃ] ADJ egoísta
selfishness [sélfɪʃnɪs] N egoísmo *m*
selfless [sélflɪs] ADJ desinteresado, generoso
sell [sɛl] VI/VT vender(se); **this book sold a thousand copies** se vendieron mil ejemplares de este libro; **to be sold on** estar entusiasmado con; **to — out** (dispose of) liquidar; (betray) traicionar, vender; (run out) agotarse; N **—off** (liquidation) liquidación *f*; (decline) baja *f*; **—out** traición *f*
seller [sɛlə·] N vendedor -ora *mf*
semantics [sɪmǽntɪks] N semántica *f*
semblance [sémbləns] N apariencia *f*
semen [símɪn] N semen *m*
semester [səméstə·] N semestre *m*
semicircle [sémɪsɚkəl] N semicírculo *m*
semicolon [sémɪkolən] N punto y coma *m*
semiconductor [semɪkəndʌ́ktə·] N semiconductor *m*
semifinal [sémɪfaɪnəl] ADJ & N semifinal *f*
seminar [sémənɑr] N seminario *m*
seminary [sémənɛri] N seminario *m*
Semitic [səmídɪk] ADJ semítico
senate [sénɪt] N senado *m*
senator [sénətə·] N senador -ora *mf*
send [sɛnd] VT enviar, mandar; **that sent chills down my spine** me dio escalofríos; **to — away** hacer salir; **to — for** mandar buscar a; **to — in** remitir; **to — out for** encargar; **to — word** mandar decir
sender [séndə·] N remitente *m*
Senegal [sénɪɡɔl] N Senegal *m*
Senegalese [senɪɡəlíz] ADJ & N senegalés -esa *mf*
senile [sínaɪl] ADJ senil, chocho
senility [sɪnílɪdi] N senilidad *f*, chochera *f*, chochez *f*
senior [sínjə·] ADJ (with more seniority) más antiguo; (in school) de cuarto año; (for the elderly) para ancianos; **John Smith — John Smith** padre; N (person of higher rank) superior *mf*; (fourth year student) estudiante de cuarto año *mf*; (elderly person) persona de la tercera edad *f*; **to be somebody's —** ser mayor que alguien; **— citizen** persona de la tercera edad *f*
seniority [sinjɔ́rɪdi] N antigüedad *f*
sensation [senséʃən] N sensación *f*
sensational [senséʃənəl] ADJ sensacional
sense [sɛns] N (of humor, honor, direction) sentido *m*; (of pain, insecurity) sensación *f*; (meaning) significado *m*, sentido *m*; **to make — tener sentido; to make — of**

something entender algo; **in a —** en cierto sentido; **to take leave of one's —s** volverse loco; **to come to one's —s** (wake up) volver en sí; (be reasonable) recobrar el juicio; VT (perceive) percibir, sentir; (intuit) intuir
senseless [sénslɪs] ADJ (meaningless) sin sentido; (unconscious) inconsciente
sensibility [sensəbílɪdi] N sensibilidad *f*
sensible [sénsəbəl] ADJ sensato, razonable
sensitive [sénsɪdɪv] ADJ (to emotions) sensible; (to stimuli) sensitivo
sensitivity [sensɪtívɪdi] N sensibilidad *f*
sensitize [sénsɪtaɪz] VT sensibilizar
sensor [sénsɔr] N sensor *m*
sensory [sénsəri] ADJ sensorial
sensual [sénʃuəl] ADJ sensual
sensuality [senʃuǽlɪdi] N sensualidad *f*
sensuous [sénʃuəs] ADJ sensual
sentence [séntəns] N (to prison) sentencia *f*, condena *f*; (phrase) oración *f*; VT condenar, sentenciar
sentiment [séntəmənt] N sentimiento *m*
sentimental [sentəméntl] ADJ sentimental; (excessively) sensiblero
sentimentality [sentəmentǽlɪdi] N sentimentalismo *m*; (excessive) sensiblería *f*
sentinel [séntənəl] N centinela *m*
sentry [séntri] N centinela *m*; **— box** garita *f*
separate [sépɪt] ADJ (apart) separado; [sépəret] VI/VT separar(se)
separation [sepəréʃən] N separación *f*
Sephardi [səfárdi] N sefardí *mf*, sefardita *mf*
September [septémbə·] N septiembre *m*
sequel [síkwəl] N continuación *f*
sequence [síkwəns] N secuencia *f*; (of events) serie *f*; **in —** en orden; VT secuenciar
serenade [serənéd] N serenata *f*, ronda *f*; VI/VT dar (una) serenata (a), rondar (a)
serene [sərín] ADJ sereno
serenity [sərénɪdi] N serenidad *f*
sergeant [sárdʒənt] N sargento *m*
serial [sírɪəl] N novela por entregas *f*; ADJ (published in installments) por entregas; (murder) en serie
series [síriz] N serie *f*
serious [síriəs] ADJ serio; (illness) grave
seriousness [síriəsnɪs] N seriedad *f*; (of an illness) gravedad *f*
sermon [sɚ́mən] N sermón *m*
serpent [sɚ́pənt] N sierpe *f*
serrated [sérétɪd] ADJ serrado
serum [sírəm] N suero *m*
servant [sɚ́vənt] N sirviente -ta *mf*, criado -da *mf*
serve [sɚv] VI/VT (in a restaurant, in a store)

servir, atender; (in tennis) sacar; **to — a
term in prison** cumplir una condena; **to
— a warrant** entregar una orden
judicial; **to — as** servir de; **to — notice**
advertir; **to — one's purpose** resultarle
útil a alguien; **it —s me right** me lo
merezco; N saque *m*

server [sɜ́·və·] N (one who serves) servidor -ra
mf; (in a restaurant) camarero -ra *mf*; (for
pie) utensilio para servir *m*; (computer)
servidor *m*

service [sɜ́·vis] N servicio *m*; (in tennis) saque
m; (of a warrant) entrega *f*; **at your — a**
su servicio; **— entrance** entrada de
servicio *f*; **— man** (soldier) militar *m*; (for
repairs) reparador *m*; **— station** estación
de servicio *f*; VT (a car) revisar; (an
industry) atender, servir; (a debt) pagar

serviceable [sɜ́·visəbəl] ADJ (practical)
práctico; (durable) duradero

servile [sɜ́·vaɪl] ADJ servil

servitude [sɜ́·vɪtud] N servidumbre *f*

sesame [sɛ́səmi] N sésamo *m*

session [sɛ́ʃən] N sesión *f*; (semester) semestre
m; (of Congress) período de sesiones *m*

set [set] VT (place) colocar; (fix) fijar,
establecer; (sic) azuzar; (print) componer;
VI (cement) fraguar; (jelly) cuajar; (sun)
ponerse; (glue) endurecerse; **to — a bone**
reducir un hueso dislocado; **to — a
diamond** engastar un diamante; **to —
an example** dar ejemplo; **to — a poem
to music** ponerle música a un poema; **to
— a precedent** establecer un precedente;
to — a trap tender una trampa; **to — a
watch** poner el reloj en hora; **to —
about** disponerse a; **to — aside** apartar;
(money) ahorrar; (a claim) rechazar; (a
verdict) anular; **to — back** (hinder, make
earlier) atrasar; (cost) costar; (a clock)
retrasar; **to — forth** exponer; **to —
forth on a journey** ponerse en camino;
to — free librar; **to — off** (make
explode) hacer estallar; (start on a
journey) ponerse en camino; (intensify)
resaltar; **to — one's heart on** tener la
esperanza puesta en; **to — one's mind
on** resolverse a; **to — out for** partir para;
to — out to proponerse; **to — right**
rectificar; **to — the table** poner la mesa;
to — up (assemble) armar; (set a trap for)
tender; (establish) establecer; **to — upon
someone** acometer a alguien; ADJ (fixed)
fijo; (ready) listo; (hard) duro; N
(ensemble) juego *m*; (group) conjunto *m*;
(TV) aparato *m*; (scenery) escenario *m*; (of
tennis) set *m*; **—back** revés *m*; **— of**

teeth dentadura *f*; **—up** (arrangement)
arreglo *m*; (assembly) montaje *m*; (trap)
tongo *m*, timo *m*

setter [sɛ́tə·] N sétter *m*

setting [sɛ́dɪŋ] N (act of putting down)
colocación *f*; (jewel) engaste *m*; (in
theater) escenario *m*; (of sun, moon)
puesta *f*; **— sun** sol poniente *m*

settle [sɛ́dl] VT (a territory) colonizar, poblar;
(affairs) arreglar; (argument) zanjar;
(lawsuit) arreglar; (an estate) liquidar; (a
bill) saldar, solventar; (one's nerves)
calmar; VI (end a dispute) llegar a un
arreglo; (take up residence) establecerse;
(alight) posarse; (sink to bottom)
depositarse; **to — down** (get married)
casarse; (mend one's ways) sentar cabeza;
(take up residence) instalarse; (become
calm) calmarse; **to — on a date** fijar /
señalar una fecha; **to — for** conformarse
con; **to — up** pagar

settlement [sɛ́dlmənt] N (community)
colonia *f*, población *f*; (agreement)
acuerdo *m*; (of a lawsuit) arreglo *m*; (of a
bill) pago *m*, finiquito *m*; (final
disposition) liquidación *f*

settler [sɛ́tlə·] N colono -na *mf*, poblador -ra
mf

seven [sɛ́vən] NUM siete

seventeen [sɛvəntín] NUM diecisiete

seventh [sɛ́vənθ] ADJ séptimo

seventy [sɛ́vənti] NUM setenta

sever [sɛ́və·] VT (an arm) cortar; (relations)
romper

several [sɛ́vərəl] ADJ varios

severe [səvír] ADJ (criticism, standards) severo;
(winter, test) duro; (storm, heat) intenso;
(illness) grave

severity [səvɛ́rɪdi] N (of criticism, standards)
severidad *f*; (of water, test) dureza *f*; (of
storm, heat) intensidad *f*; (of illness)
gravedad *f*

sew [so] VI/VT coser

sewage [súɪdʒ] N aguas negras *f pl*; **— system**
alcantarillado *m*

sewer [súə·] N alcantarilla *f*, cloaca *f*, colector
m

sewing [sóɪŋ] N costura *f*; **— machine**
máquina de coser *f*

sex [sɛks] N sexo *m*; **to have —** tener
relaciones (sexuales); **— appeal** atractivo
sexual *m*; **— symbol** símbolo sexual *m*; VT
sexar

sexism [sɛ́ksɪzəm] N sexismo *m*

sexton [sɛ́kstən] N sacristán *m*

sexual [sɛ́kʃuəl] ADJ sexual; **— assault**
violación *f*; **— harassment** acoso sexual

m; — **intercourse / relations** relaciones sexuales *f pl;* —**ly transmitted disease** enfermedad de transmisión sexual *f*

sexuality [sɛkʃuǽlɪɒi] N sexualidad *f*

sexy [sɛ́ksi] ADJ sexy

Seychelles [seʃɛ́l] N Seychelles *f pl*

shabby [ʃǽbi] ADJ (worn) gastado; (slovenly) andrajoso; (tawdry) sórdido; (mean) mezquino; **not too** — no está mal

shack [ʃæk] N casucha *f,* choza *f*

shackle [ʃǽkəl] N grillete *m;* —**s** cadenas *f pl,* grillos *m pl;* VT (put in chains) engrillar; (impede) estorbar

shad [ʃæd] N sábalo *m*

shade [ʃed] N (shadow) sombra *f;* (nuance) matiz *m;* (for windows) persiana *f;* (phantom) espectro *m;* (of a lamp) pantalla *f;* **a** — **longer** un poco más largo; **in the** — a la sombra; —**s** lentes negros / oscuros *m pl; Sp* gafas de sol *f pl;* VT (protect from sun) sombrear, dar sombra; (darken a picture) sombrear

shadow [ʃǽdo] N (dark image, shade) sombra *f;* (phantom) espectro *m;* **in the** — **of** a la sombra de; **without a** — **of doubt** sin sombra de duda; VT (darken) sombrear; (make gloomy) ensombrecer; **to** — **someone** seguirle la pista a alguien

shady [ʃédi] ADJ sombreado, umbrío; — **character** sospechoso *m;* — **dealings** negocios turbios *m pl*

shaft [ʃæft] N (of a mine) pozo *m;* (of a feather) cañón *m;* (of an elevator) hueco *m;* (of an arrow) asta *f*

shaggy [ʃǽgi] ADJ peludo, lanudo

shake [ʃek] VI (tremble) temblar; VI / VT (move back and forth) sacudir(se); (in order to mix) agitar(se); (elude) deshacerse de; **to** — **hands** darse la mano; **to** — **one's head** menear la cabeza; **to** — **with cold** tiritar; **to** — **with fear** temblar de miedo; **to** — **off** (a cold, disappointment, etc.) deshacerse de; (depression) librarse de; **to** — **up** (a liquid) agitar; (a person) trastornar; N (violent) sacudida *f;* (of milk) batido *m;* **hand**— apretón de manos *m;* **the** —**s** escalofríos *m pl;* —**-up** reorganización *f*

shaky [ʃéki] ADJ (hand) tembloroso; (start) vacilante

shall [ʃæl] V AUX **I** — **come** vendré; — **I help you?** ¿te ayudo? **thou shalt not steal** no robarás

shallow [ʃǽlo] ADJ (plate) llano; (water) poco profundo; (breathing) superficial; (explanation) superficial, somero

shallowness [ʃǽlonɪs] N (of plate) lo llano;

(of water) poca profundidad *f;* (of person) superficialidad *f*

sham [ʃæm] N (hoax) farsa *f;* (trickster) farsante *mf;* — **battle** simulacro de batalla *m*

shambles [ʃǽmbəlz] N desorden *m,* caos *m*

shame [ʃem] N (embarrassment) vergüenza *f;* (dishonor) deshonra *f;* (pity) lástima *f;* — **on you!** ¡qué vergüenza! **to bring** — **upon** deshonrar; VT avergonzar

shameful [ʃémfəl] ADJ vergonzoso

shameless [ʃémlɪs] ADJ desvergonzado, descarado

shamelessness [ʃémlsnɪs] N desvergüenza *f*

shampoo [ʃæmpú] N (product) champú *m;* (wash) lavado del cabello *m;* VI / VT lavar con champú

shamrock [ʃǽmrɑk] N trébol *m*

shank [ʃæŋk] N (part of leg) canilla *f,* espinilla *f;* (cut of meat) pierna *f,* pata *f*

shanty [ʃǽnti] N casucha *f; Sp* chabola *f;* —**town** suburbio *m*

shape [ʃep] N (form) forma *f;* (condition) condición *f;* (silhouette) bulto *m;* **to be in bad** — andar mal; **to get in** — ponerse en forma; VT dar forma a; **to** — **up** reformarse

shapeless [ʃéplɪs] ADJ informe

share [ʃer] N (portion) parte *f,* porción *f;* (stock) acción *f;* —**cropper** aparcero *m;* —**holder** accionista *mf;* VI / VT compartir; **to** — **in** participar en

shark [ʃɑrk] N (fish) tiburón *m;* (swindler) estafador -ra *mf*

sharp [ʃɑrp] ADJ (blade) afilado, filoso; (needle) puntiagudo; (curve) cerrado; (contrast) marcado, nítido; (smell) acre; (wind) cortante; (pain) punzante; (remark) mordaz, agudo; (mind) perspicaz; (musical note) sostenido; (dresser) elegante; (cheese) picante; (ear) fino; — **eye** vista aguzada *f;* —**-tongued** mordaz; —**-witted** agudo; —**shooter** tirador -ra de primera *mf;* N sostenido *m*

sharpen [ʃɑ́rpən] VI / VT (knife) afilar(se); VT (pencil) sacar punta a; (skill) afinar

sharpness [ʃɑ́rpnɪs] N (of a blade) lo afilado; (of a needle) lo puntiagudo; (of a curve) lo cerrado; (of a contrast) nitidez *f;* (of a smell) acritud *f;* (of pain) intensidad *f;* (of a remark) mordacidad *f;* (of a mind) perspicacia *f,* agudeza *f;* (of cheese) lo picante

shatter [ʃǽdɚ] VI / VT (glass) astillar(se), hacer(se) añicos; (nerves) destrozar(se); (health) quebrantar(se); (hopes) frustrar

shave [ʃev] VI / VT (beard, legs) afeitar(se),

rasurar(se); vt (wood) cepillar; (graze)
rozar; **to — off** rapar; n afeitado m,
rasurado m; **he had a close —** se salvó
por poco

shaver [shévɚ] n afeitadora f

shavings [ʃévɪŋz] n virutas f pl

shawl [ʃɔl] n mantón m, chal m

she [ʃi] PRON ella; **— who** la que, quien; n
—-bear osa f

sheaf [ʃif] n (of corn) gavilla f; (of arrows)
haz m; (of paper) fajo m

shear [ʃɪr] vt esquilar, trasquilar; n **—s** (for
sheep) tijeras para esquilar f pl; (for plants)
tijeras para podar f pl; (for metal) cizallas f
pl; (for hair) tijeras de peluquero f pl

shearing [ʃírɪŋ] n esquila f, esquileo m

sheath [ʃiθ] n (of sword, peas) vaina f; (of
knife, umbrella) funda f

sheathe [ʃið] vt (a sword) envainar; (a knife)
enfundar

shed [ʃɛd] n cobertizo m, galpón m, tinglado
m; vt (tears) derramar; (light) arrojar;
(leaves) perder; (skin, hair) mudar, perder;
vi (be waterproof) ser impermeable; (lose
hair) pelechar; (lose leaves) deshojarse;
(lose skin) mudar la piel

sheen [ʃin] n brillo m

sheep [ʃip] n oveja f; **—dog** perro pastor m,
ovejero m; **—skin** (hide) piel de oveja f;
(leather) badana f; (parchment) pergamino
m; (diploma) diploma m

sheepish [ʃipiʃ] ADJ vergonzoso, tímido

sheer [ʃɪr] ADJ (absolute) puro, total; (fine)
fino; (vertical) vertical, acantilado

sheet [ʃit] n (bedding) sábana f; (of ice) capa
f; (of paper) hoja f; (of glass) lámina f; (of
rain) cortina f; **— metal** chapa de metal f;
— music música en hojas de partitura f

shelf [ʃɛlf] n estante m, repisa f, anaquel m;
(of rock) saliente f

shell [ʃɛl] n (turtles, snail) caparazón f; (of
mollusk) concha f; (of egg, nut) cáscara f;
(of peas) vaina f; (of a ship) casco m; (of a
building) armazón m; (of artillery)
proyectil m; (of a rifle) cartucho m; **—fish**
mariscos m pl; vt (nuts, eggs) pelar; (peas)
desgranar; (military target) bombardear

shelter [ʃɛltɚ] n (refuge) refugio m, resguardo
m, abrigo m; **to take —** refugiarse,
guarecerse; vi/vt (take or give refuge)
refugiar(se), resguardar(se), abrigar(se)

shelve [ʃɛlv] vt (place on a shelf) colocar en
un estante; (defer) archivar

shepherd [ʃɛpɚd] n pastor m; (dog) perro
pastor m

sherbet [ʃɝbɪt] n sorbete m

sheriff [ʃɛrɪf] n alguacil m

sherry [ʃɛri] n jerez m

shield [ʃild] n escudo m; vi/vt (protect)
escudar(se); vt (conceal) ocultar

shift [ʃift] vt (gears) cambiar; **to — for
oneself** arreglárselas solo; **to — the
blame** echar la culpa a otro; n (of gears,
of wind) cambio m; (dress) vestido suelto
m; (of workers) turno m; **— key** tecla (de)
mayúscula f

shiftless [ʃiftlɪs] ADJ holgazán

shimmer [ʃimɚ] vi titilar; n titileo m

shin [ʃin] n espinilla f, canilla f; vi **to — up**
trepar

shine [ʃain] vi brillar, relucir; vt (shoes)
limpiar, lustrar; (furniture) lustrar; n brillo
m, resplandor m; (of shoes) lustre m

shingle [ʃiŋgɫ] n (on roof) teja f; (sign)
chapa f; **—s** culebrilla f, zona f; **to hang
out one's —** abrir un consultorio; vt
cubrir con tejas

shiny [ʃáini] ADJ (bright) brillante; (worn)
brilloso

ship [ʃip] n (on water) buque m, navío m; (in
air) avión m; **—builder** constructor -ra
naval mf; **—mate** camarada de a bordo
mf; **—wreck** naufragio m; **—yard**
astillero m; ADJ **—shape** ordenado; vt
transportar; **to —wreck** hacer naufragar;
to — off sacarse de encima; vi **to
—wreck** naufragar

shipment [ʃipmənt] n cargamento m, remesa
f

shipper [ʃipɚ] n (sender) expedidor -ra mf;
(carrier) transportista mf

shipping [ʃipiŋ] n envío m; **— charges**
gastos de envío m pl; **— and handling**
gastos de envío m pl

shirk [ʃɝk] vt evadir, esquivar, rehuir

shirt [ʃɝt] n camisa f; **in — sleeves** en
mangas de camisa; **—tail** faldón m

shit [ʃit] n (excrement) vulg mierda f; (stuff)
porquerías f pl; **the —s** fam cagalera;
that's a crock of — y una polla (como
una olla); **he doesn't know —** vulg no
sabe un carajo; vi/vt (defecate) vulg cagar;
(lie to) vulg joder; **to — bricks** vulg
cagarse de miedo; **he's on my —list**
estoy enojado con él; INTERJ vulg carajo; Sp
vulg joder

shitty [ʃidi] ADJ vulg de mierda

shiver [ʃivɚ] vi (from cold) tiritar; (from
cold, fear, etc.) temblar; n temblor m; **—s**
escalofríos m pl

shoal [ʃoʊl] n (sandbank) bajío m, banco de
arena m; (school of fish) banco m,
bandada f

shock [ʃɑk] n (impact, disturbance) choque

m; (of electricity) sacudida *f;* (of wheat) hacina *f;* (physical convulsion) shock *m,* choque *m;* — **absorber** amortiguador *m;* — **of hair** guedeja *f;* — **troops** tropas de choque *f pl;* — **wave** onda expansiva *f;* VT (bewilder) chocar, horrorizar, azorar; (discharge electricity) dar una descarga eléctrica; (make bundles of grain) hacinar, hacer gavillas de

shocking [ʃákɪŋ] ADJ chocante, escandaloso

shoddy [ʃádi] ADJ chapucero

shoe [ʃu] N zapato *m;* (for brakes) zapata *f;* (for horses) herradura *f;* —**horn** calzador *m;* —**lace** cordón *m;* —**maker** zapatero -ra *mf;* — **polish** betún *m;* — **repairman** zapatero -ra remendón -ona *mf;* —**store** zapatería *f;* —**string** cordón *m;* **to live on a** —**string** vivir con poco dinero; **to tie one's** —**s** atarse los zapatos; VT (a person) calzar; (a horse) herrar

shoo-in [ʃúɪn] N favorito -ta *mf*

shoot [ʃut] VT (wound with a bullet) pegar un tiro, abatir; (discharge a firearm) disparar; (film a movie) rodar; VI (discharge bullet, arrow) disparar, tirar; (be discharged) dispararse; (hunt with a gun) cazar; (germinate) brotar; (throw) lanzar; (take a photo) fotografiar; (film) filmar; (kick a ball) chutar; **to** — **at** disparar a, tirar a; **to** — **by** pasar rápidamente; **to** — **down** (plane) derribar; (argument) refutar; **to** — **forth** brotar; **to** — **up** (grow) crecer rápidamente; (damage by shooting) tirotear; (inject drugs) chutar; N (new growth) yema *f,* retoño *m,* vástago *m;* (filming) rodaje *m*

shooter [ʃúdə] N (of guns) tirador -ra *mf;* (of balls, soccer) goleador -ra *mf*

shooting [ʃúdɪŋ] N (discharge of a gun) tiro *m,* disparo *m;* (exchange of shots) tiroteo *m;* — **match** concurso de tiro *m;* — **pain** punzada *f;* — **star** estrella fugaz *f*

shop [ʃap] N (store) tienda *f;* (artisan's place of business, carpentry course) taller *m;* (business) planta *f;* —**keeper** tendero -ra *mf;* —**lifter** mechero -ra *mf;* **to** —**lift** mechar; — **window** escaparate *m,* vitrina *f;* **to talk** — hablar de negocios; VI ir de compras; **to** — **for** ir a comprar

shopper [ʃápə] N cliente -ta *mf,* comprador -ra *mf*

shopping [ʃápɪŋ] N **to go** — ir de compras; — **center** centro comercial *m*

shore [ʃɔr] N costa *f,* ribera *f;* (of a lake) orilla *f;* VT **to** — **up** apuntalar

short [ʃɔrt] ADJ (not long in duration) corto, breve; (not long in length) corto; (not tall)

bajo; (scanty) escaso; (curt) brusco; — **circuit** cortocircuito *m;* —**comings** limitaciones *f pl;* —**cut** atajo *m,* cortada *f;* —**fall** agujero *m;* —**hand** taquigrafía *f;* —**-handed** escaso de personal; —**-legged** pernicorto; —**sighted** miope, corto de vista; — **story** cuento *m;* —**wave** onda corta *f;* **in the** — **run** (haul, term) a corto plazo; **for** — para abreviar; **in** — en resumen, en suma; **in** — **order** rápidamente; **to be** — **on** estar escaso de, estar alcanzado de; **to be** — **on something** faltarle a uno algo; **to cut** — interrumpir; **I'm running** — **on sugar** se me está acabando el azúcar; ADV **to stop** — parar de repente, parar en seco; **to come up** — quedarse corto; N (circuit) cortocircuito *m;* —**s** short *m,* pantalón corto *m;* VI/VT (a circuit) cortocircuitar(se); (change) dar de menos; **to** —**change** dar de menos; **to** — **out** fundir

shortage [ʃɔrdɪdʒ] N escasez *f,* penuria *f*

shorten [ʃɔrtn] VI/VT acortar(se); VT recortar

shortening [ʃɔrtnɪŋ] N (lard) manteca *f;* (abbreviation) acortamiento *m*

shortly [ʃɔrtli] ADJ (soon) en breve, pronto; (curtly) bruscamente, secamente

shortness [ʃɔrtnɪs] N (of length, height) cortedad *f;* (of time) brevedad *f;* (of breath) falta *f;* (of a reply) brusquedad *f*

shot [ʃat] N (discharge) tiro *m,* disparo *m;* (photograph) foto *f;* (pellet) perdigón *m,* plomo *m;* (ball in shot-putting) bala *f;* (injection) inyección *f;* (swallow) trago *m;* (throw) tirada *f;* —**gun** escopeta *f;* —**put** lanzamiento de bala *m;* **not by a long** — ni con mucho; **he is a good** — tiene buena puntería; **to take a** — disparar; **to take a** — **at** intentar

should [ʃud] V AUX **I** — **think so** ya lo creo; **you** — **arrive before nine** deberías llegar antes de las nueve; **you** — **eat less** tendrías que comer menos; **you** — **have seen her** tendrías que haberla visto; **were he to come, I** — **be pleased** si viniera, me alegraría

shoulder [ʃóldə] N (of a person, coat) hombro *m;* (cut of meat) paletilla *f;* (of a road) arcén *m;* —**blade** (person) homóplato *m;* (animal) paletilla *f;* **to turn a cold** — **to** hacerle el vacío a; **the responsibility is on your** —**s** tú tienes la responsabilidad; VT (a load) cargar al hombro; (an expense) cargar con, asumir; (a door) empujar con el hombro

shout [ʃaut] VI/VT gritar; N grito *m*

shove [ʃʌv] VI/VT empujar; **to** — **aside** echar

a un lado; **to — off** (go away) largarse; (push off) desatracar; N empujón *m*, empellón *m*

shovel [ʃʌvəl] N pala *f*; VT echar con la pala

show [ʃo] VT (exhibit) mostrar, manifestar; (prove) demostrar; (indicate) indicar, marcar; (a film, a TV program) dar; VI (be visible) verse, asomar; (make an appearance) aparecerse; — **him in** hazle entrar; **to — a film** dar una película; **to — mercy** tener piedad; **to — off** hacer alarde, aparentar; **to — up** aparecer; **to — someone up** poner en evidencia; **to — the way** señalar el camino; N (exhibition) exposición *f*; (display) demostración *f*; (ostentation) ostentación *f*, alarde *m*; (performance) espectáculo *m*; (showing) función *f*; (on TV) programa *m*; (movie theater) cine *m*; — **business** farándula *f*; **—case** vitrina *f*; **to —case** presentar; **—down** confrontación *f*; **—-off** fanfarrón -ona *mf*; **to go to the —** ir al cine

shower [ʃáuɚ] N (rain) aguacero *m*, chubasco *m*; (bath) ducha *f*; (for brides) fiesta para novias *f*; (of sparks, blows) lluvia *f*; VI (bathe) ducharse; (rain) llover; VT (with gifts) inundar; (with praise) colmar

showy [ʃói] ADJ ostentoso; (attractive) vistoso

shred [ʃrɛd] N (of paper) tira *f*; (of evidence) pizca *f*; **to be in —s** estar hecho jirones; **to tear to —s** hacer trizas; VI/VT (documents) triturar; (vegetables) rallar

shrew [ʃru] N (animal) musaraña *f*; (woman) arpía *f*

shrewd [ʃrud] ADJ astuto, sagaz

shriek [ʃrik] VI/VT chillar; N chillido *m*

shrill [ʃrɪl] ADJ chillón

shrimp [ʃrɪmp] N (animal) camarón *m*; (small person) renacuajo *m*; VI pescar camarones

shrine [ʃraɪn] N (chapel) capilla *f*; (altar) altar *m*

shrink [ʃrɪŋk] VI/VT encoger; VI (value) reducirse; **to — from** retroceder; N *fam* loquero -ra *mf*

shrinkage [ʃrɪŋkɪdʒ] N (of clothes) encogimiento *m*; (of value) reducción *f*

shrivel [ʃrívəl] VI/VT secar(se), marchitar(se)

shroud [ʃraʊd] N mortaja *f*; VT (to wrap for burial) amortajar; (to hide) cubrir

shrub [ʃrʌb] N arbusto *m*

shrug [ʃrʌg] VI encogerse de hombros; VT encogerse de; **to — off** minimizar, ignorar; N encogimiento de hombros *m*

shudder [ʃʌdɚ] VI (from cold) tiritar; (from fear) temblar, estremecerse; N temblor *m*, estremecimiento *m*

shuffle [ʃʌfəl] VT (mix) mezclar; VI (walk) arrastrar los pies; (dance) bailar arrastrando los pies; VI/VT (cards) barajar; **to — along** ir arrastrando los pies; N (of cards) barajadura *f*; (of feet) arrastrapiés *m sg*

shun [ʃʌn] VT rehuir, evitar

shut [ʃʌt] VI/VT cerrar(se); **to — down** cerrar; **to — off** cortar; **to — out** impedir la entrada de; **to — up** (close) cerrar bien; (lock up) encerrar; (be quiet) callarse; **—-down** cese de actividades *m*; **—-eye** sueño *m*; **—-in** enfermo -ma confinado -da a la casa *mf*

shutter [ʃʌdɚ] N (of a window) postigo *m*, contraventana *f*; (of a camera) obturador *m*

shuttle [ʃʌdl] N (in loom) lanzadera *f*; (spaceship) transbordador espacial *m*; (airplane) puente aéreo *m*; (bus, train) servicio regular *m*; VI ir y venir; VT llevar y traer

shy [ʃaɪ] ADJ tímido, retraído; (wary) esquivo; (lacking) escaso; VI asustarse, respingar; **to — away** (start) asustarse, respingar; (avoid) esquivar

shyness [ʃáɪnɪs] N timidez *f*, retraimiento *m*

shyster [ʃáɪstɚ] N *fam* picapleitos *m sg*

sic [sɪk] VT azuzar

sick [sɪk] ADJ (ill) enfermo; (deranged) enfermizo, morboso; (at heart) angustiado; — **and tired** harto; **to be — of** estar harto de; **to be — to one's stomach** tener náuseas; **to make —** (disgust) dar asco; (anger) dar rabia, enfermar; — **leave** licencia por enfermedad *f*

sicken [síkən] VI/VT (with illness) enfermar(se), poner(se) enfermo; (to disgust) dar asco; (to anger) dar rabia, enfermar

sickening [síkənɪŋ] ADJ repugnante

sickle [síkəl] N hoz *f*; — **cell anemia** anemia falciforme *f*

sickly [síkli] ADJ enfermizo, enclenque

sickness [síknɪs] N enfermedad *f*

side [saɪd] N lado *m*; (of coin, piece of paper) cara *f*; (of a person) costado *m*; (of hill) ladera *f*; (of beef) media res *f*; (of boat) banda *f*; (team) equipo *m*; (garnish) acompañamiento *m*; — **by** — uno al lado del otro; **by his —** a su lado; **by the — of** al lado de; **on all —s** por todos lados; ADJ (on the side) lateral; (secondary) secundario; **—arm** arma de mano *f*; **—board** aparador *m*; **—burns** patillas *f pl*; **—-glance** mirada de soslayo/ reojo *f*; **—light** (illumination) luz lateral *f*; (detail) detalle incidental *m*; **—line** (in sports) línea de banda f; **to sit on the —lines** no intervenir; **to —step** evitar, esquivar; (in business) negocio suplementario m; **to —track** (a train) desviar; (attention) distraer; **—walk** acera f; Mex banqueta f; **—wall** flanco m; VI **to — with** ponerse del lado de

sideways [sáɪdwez] ADV (walk) de costado; (glance) de soslayo

siege [sidʒ] N sitio m, asedio m, cerco m; **to lay — to** sitiar

Sierra Leone [siéraliόn] N Sierra Leona f

sieve [sɪv] N tamiz m, cedazo m

sift [sɪft] VT cerner, tamizar; **to — through** revisar

sigh [saɪ] VI suspirar; N suspiro m

sight [saɪt] N (sense) vista f; (attraction) punto de interés m; (ridiculous thing or person) adefesio m, mamarracho m; (on a gun) mira f; **—seeing** turismo m; **in —** a la vista; **on —** en el acto; **he is out of —** ya no se ve; **at first —** a primera vista; **to catch —of** divisar; **to lose — of** perder de vista; **you're a — for sore eyes** dichosos los ojos que te ven; VT (a ship) avistar, divisar; (a gun) apuntar

sign [saɪn] N (gesture) seña f, señal f; (indication) muestra f, señal f, indicio m; (placard) letrero m; (omen) agüero m, presagio m; (astrological, mathematical) signo m; (on road) cartel m, letrero m; VI/VT (write name) firmar; (signal) hacer señas (de); VT (hire) contratar; (use sign language) hablar por señas; **— language** lenguaje de signos m; **to — over property** ceder una propiedad; **to — up** (in a club) anotarse; (in the army) alistarse

signal [sígnəł] N señal f; VI/VT señalar, hacer señas (a); ADJ notable

signature [sígnətʃɚ] N firma f

signer [sáɪnɚ] N firmante mf, signatario -ria mf

significance [sɪgnífɪkəns] N significación f

significant [sɪgnífɪkənt] ADJ significativo; **my — other** mi media naranja f

signify [sígnəfaɪ] VT significar

silence [sáɪləns] N silencio m; VT (child, fears) acallar; (criticism) silenciar, enmudecer

silencer [sáɪlənsɚ] N silenciador m

silent [sáɪlənt] ADJ (machine) silencioso; (person) callado, silencioso; **— agreement** acuerdo tácito m; **— film** película muda f

silhouette [sɪluét] N silueta f; VT **to be —d against** perfilarse contra

silicon [sílɪkən] N silicio m

silk [sɪłk] N seda f; **— industry** industria

sedera f; **—worm** gusano de seda m

silken [sɪłkən] ADJ (of silk) de seda; (like silk) sedoso

silky [sɪłki] ADJ sedoso

sill [sɪł] N alféizar m, antepecho m

silly [síli] ADJ necio, bobo, lelo

silo [sáɪlo] N silo m

silt [sɪłt] N cieno m, limo m

silver [sɪłvɚ] N (metal, color) plata f; (tableware) cubiertos de plata m pl; ADJ (of silver) de plata; (silver-colored) plateado; **— anniversary** las bodas de plata f pl; **—plated** bañado en plata; **—plating** plateado m; **—smith** platero -ra mf; **—ware** cubiertos de plata m pl; VT platear; (a mirror) azogar

similar [símələ] ADJ semejante, similar

similarity [sɪmələ́ɾɪDi] N semejanza f, parecido m

simile [síməli] N símil m

simmer [símə] VI/VT hervir a fuego lento; **to — down** calmarse

simple [símpəł] ADJ (uncomplicated) simple, sencillo; (naive) simple; **—minded** simple, simplón

simpleton [símpəłtən] N simplón -ona mf, mentecato -ta mf

simplicity [sɪmplísɪDi] N (lack of complication) sencillez f, simplicidad f; (naiveté) simpleza f

simplify [símpləfaɪ] VI/VT simplificar

simplistic [sɪmplístɪk] ADJ simplista

simulate [símjəlet] VI/VT simular

simultaneous [saɪməłténiəs] ADJ simultáneo

sin [sɪn] N pecado m; VI pecar

since [sɪns] CONJ (continuously) desde que; (inasmuch as) puesto que, ya que; PREP (continuously) desde; (from a past time) a partir de; ADV desde entonces; **ever — desde entonces; he died long —** murió hace mucho tiempo; **she has — agreed** después de eso consintió; **we have been here — five** estamos aquí desde las cinco

sincere [sɪnsír] ADJ sincero

sincerity [sɪnséɾɪDi] N sinceridad f

sinew [sínju] N tendón m

sinewy [sínjuwi] ADJ (full of tendons) nervudo; (vigorous) membrudo; (chewy) estropajoso

sinful [sínfəł] ADJ (act) pecaminoso; (person) pecador

sing [sɪŋ] VI/VT cantar; **—song** sonsonete m

Singapore [síŋəpɔr] N Singapur m

Singaporean [sɪŋəpɔ́riən] ADJ & N singapurense mf

singe [sɪndʒ] VT chamuscar, socarrar; N chamusquina f, socarrina f

singer [síŋə-] N cantante *mf*

single [síŋgəł] ADJ (only one) solo, único; (for one person) individual; (unmarried) soltero; **— bed** cama de una plaza *f*; **— entry bookkeeping** teneduría por partida simple *f*; **— file** fila india *f*; **—-handed** solo, sin ayuda; **—-minded** resuelto; **—-spacing** sencillo *m*; **every — one** cada uno; **not a — word** ni una sola palabra; N (bill) billete de uno *m*; (unmarried person) soltero -ra *mf*; (record) disco sencillo *m*; (in tennis) **—s single** *m*; VT **to — out** elegir

singular [síŋgjələ-] ADJ & N singular *m*

sinister [sínɪstə-] ADJ siniestro

sink [sɪŋk] VI/VT hundir(se); VT (invest) invertir; (dig) cavar; (put in ground) enterrar; **it finally sank in** finalmente nos dimos cuenta de eso; **to — one's teeth into** clavar los dientes en; **to — to one's knees** caer de rodillas; **sunk in thought** absorto; **my heart sank** se me fue el alma al piso; **the sun was —ing** se iba poniendo el sol; N (in the kitchen) fregadero *m*; (in bathroom) lavabo *m*; (pond for sewage) pozo negro *m*; **—hole** socavón *m*, sumidero *m*

sinner [sínə-] N pecador -ora *mf*

sinuous [sínjuəs] ADJ sinuoso

sinus [sáɪnəs] N seno *m*

sip [sɪp] VI/VT sorber; N sorbo *m*

siphon [sáɪfən] N sifón *m*; VI/VT (liquid) sacar con sifón; (money) desviar

sir [sɝ] N señor *m*

siren [sáɪrən] N sirena *f*

sirloin [sɝ́lɔɪn] N solomillo *m*

sissy [sísi] ADJ & N afeminado *m*; *offensive* marica *m*, maricón *m*

sister [sístə-] N hermana *f*; **—-in-law** cuñada *f*; **— Mary** Sor María *f*

sit [sɪt] VI sentar(se); (pose) posar; (be seated) estar sentado; (be located) estar situado; **to — down** sentarse; **to — in on a class** ir de oyente a una clase; **to — on** posponer; **to — out a dance** saltearse una pieza; **to — still** estarse quieto; **to — tight** mantenerse firme en su puesto; **to — up** incorporarse; **to — up all night** quedarse en vela; **to — well** caer bien; **—-in** sentada *f*; **—-up** abdominal *m*

sitcom [sítkɑm] N comedia de situación *f*

site [saɪt] N (for construction) terreno *m*, solar *m*; (on the Internet) sitio *m*

sitter [sítə-] N niñera *f*

sitting [sítɪŋ] N sesión *f*; **in one —** de una sentada, de un tirón; ADJ **— duck** blanco fácil *m*; **— room** cuarto de estar *m*

situated [sítʃuedɪd] ADJ situado, ubicado

situation [sɪtʃuéʃən] N situación *f*

six [sɪks] NUM seis; **—-pack** paquete de seis *m*; **—-shooter** revólver de seis tiros *m*

sixteen [sɪkstín] NUM dieciséis

sixth [sɪksθ] ADV & N sexto *m*

sixty [síksti] NUM sesenta

size [saɪz] N tamaño *m*; (clothing) talla *f*; VT clasificar según el tamaño; **to — up** juzgar

sizeable, sizable [sáɪzəbəł] ADJ de tamaño considerable

sizzle [sízəł] VI chisporrotear; N chisporroteo *m*

skate [sket] N patín *m*; VI/VT patinar; **—board** monopatín *m*

skein [sken] N madeja *f*

skeleton [skélɪtən] N esqueleto *m*, osamenta *f*; (of a building) armazón *m*; **— key** llave maestra *f*

skeptic, sceptic [sképtɪk] N escéptico -ca *mf*

skeptical [sképtɪkəł] ADJ escéptico

skepticism [sképtɪsɪzəm] N escepticismo *m*

sketch [sketʃ] N (of a drawing) boceto *m*, croquis *m*; (outline) esbozo *m*, bosquejo *m*; (skit) sketch *m*; VI/VT (outline) bosquejar; (draw) dibujar

skew [skju] VT (cloth) sesgar; (data) tergiversar

skewer [skjúə-] N brocheta *f*

ski [ski] N esquí *m*; VI/VT esquiar (en); **— jump** (sport) salto con esquís *m*; (course) pista de saltos *m*; **— lift** telesquí *m*

skid [skɪd] N patinazo *m*; VI patinar

skill [skɪł] N destreza *f*, habilidad *f*, maña *f*

skilled [skɪłd] ADJ diestro, habilidoso; **— worker** obrero -ra calificado -da *mf*

skillet [skílɪt] N sartén *f*

skillful, skilful [skíłfəł] ADJ diestro, habilidoso

skim [skɪm] VT (milk) desnatar; (a broth) espumar; (move near surface) rozar; VI/VT (read) leer por encima, repasar; **to — over** rozar; **— milk** *Sp* leche desnatada *f*; *Am* leche descremada *f*

skimp [skɪmp] VI escatimar; **to — on** escatimar

skimpy [skímpi] ADJ (funds) escaso; (dress) corto; (bikini) pequeño

skin [skɪn] N piel *f* (also of animal, sausage, potato); (of the face) cutis *m*, tez *f*; (for carrying wine) pellejo *m*; (of boiled milk) nata *f*; (of grapes) hollejo *m*; **—-deep** superficial; **—-diving** natación submarina *f*; **— flick** película pornográfica *f*; **— flint** roña *mf*; **—head** cabeza rapada *mf*; **to save one's —** salvar el pellejo; **to be saved by the — of one's teeth** salvarse por un pelo; VT (animal) despellejar, desollar; (fruit) pelar; (a person) quitarle a uno el dinero

skinny [skíni] ADJ flaco; **to —-dip** nadar desnudo

skip [skɪp] VI (jump) brincar, ir dando saltos en un pie; (omit) saltarse; (bounce) rebotar; VT (a page) saltar(se); (class) faltar a; (a stone) hacer rebotar; **to — out** escaparse; N salto *m*, brinco *m*

skipper [skípɚ] N (captain) patrón -ona *mf*, capitán -ana *mf*; (jumper) saltador -ora *mf*

skirmish [skɝ́mɪʃ] N escaramuza *f*; VI escaramuzar

skirt [skɝt] N falda *f*; VT bordear; **to — an issue** evitar un tema

skit [skɪt] N sketch *m*

skull [skʌl] N cráneo *m*, calavera *f*; **— and crossbones** calavera *f*

skunk [skʌŋk] N mofeta *f*; *Am* zorrillo *m*

sky [skaɪ] N cielo *m*; **— blue** azul celeste *m*; **—diving** paracaidismo *m*; **—-high** muy alto; **—lark** alondra *f*; **—light** claraboya *f*; **—line** horizonte *m*; **—scraper** rascacielos *m sg*; **to —rocket** subir vertiginosamente

slab [slæb] N (of wood) trozo *m*; (of stone) losa *f*, laja *f*; (of meat) tajada *f*

slack [slæk] ADJ (not taut) flojo; (careless) descuidado; (sluggish) lento; **— season** temporada baja *f*; **to take up the —** llenar el vacío; **—s** pantalones *m pl*; VI holgazanear; **to — off** aflojar

slag [slæg] N escoria *f*

slalom [sláləm] N slalom *m*

slam [slæm] VI/VT cerrar(se) de un golpe; VI (hit) chocar; VT (throw down) hacer golpear; (criticize) criticar; **to — on the brakes** dar un frenazo; **to — the door** dar un portazo; N (blow) golpazo *m*; (criticism) crítica *f*; (of a door) portazo *m*

slander [slǽndɚ] N calumnia *f*, difamación *f*; VT calumniar, difamar

slanderous [slǽndərəs] ADJ calumnioso, difamatorio

slang [slæŋ] N (jargon) jerga *f*; (argot) argot *m*

slant [slænt] N (orientation, bias) sesgo *m*; (of a roof) inclinación *f*; VI/VT (bias) sesgar; (slope) inclinar(se), ladear(se)

slap [slæp] N (to the body) palmada *f*; (to the face) bofetada *f*, torta *f*, cachetada *f*; (with a glove) guantada *f*; **—happy** aturdido; **—stick** de golpe y porrazo; **a — in the face** un desaire; **a — on the wrist** un tirón de orejas; **a — on the back** una palmadita en la espalda; VT abofetear; **to — down** reprimir

slash [slæʃ] VI/VT (cut) acuchillar; *Am* tajear; VT (whip) azotar; (reduce) reducir, rebajar; N (sweeping stroke, wound) cuchillada *f*, tajo *m*; (typographical sign) barra *f*

slat [slæt] N tablilla *f*

slate [slet] N (rock, roofing) pizarra *f*; (color) color pizarra *m*; (list of candidates) lista de candidatos *f*; VT empizarrar; **this building is —d for destruction** se ha programado la demolición de este edificio

slaughter [slɔ́ɾə] N matanza *f*; **—house** matadero *m*; VT (animals) matar; (people, opponents) masacrar

slave [slev] N esclavo -va *mf*; **— driver** capataz de esclavos *m*; **— labor** (workers) mano de obra esclava *f*; (work) trabajo de esclavos *m*; VI trabajar como esclavo -va

slavery [slévəri] N esclavitud *f*

Slavic [slávɪk] ADJ eslavo

sleazy [slízi] ADJ (squalid) sórdido; (contemptible) despreciable

sled [slɛd] N trineo *m*

sledgehammer [slɛ́ʤhæmə] N almádena *f*

sleek [slik] ADJ (hair) lustroso; (sports car) elegante

sleep [slip] VI/VT dormir; **it —s three** tiene espacio para que duerman tres personas; **to — around** ser promiscuo; **to — in** dormir hasta tarde; **to — it off** dormir la mona; **to — something off** dormir para que desaparezca algo; **to — over** dormir en casa ajena; **to — together** acostarse juntos; **to — with** acostarse con; **to — on it** consultarlo con la almohada; N sueño *m*; **—walker** sonámbulo -la *mf*; **to go to —** dormirse; **to put to —** (put to bed) dormir a; (euthanize) sacrificar

sleeper [slípɚ] N (one who sleeps) persona que duerme *f*; (beam) durmiente *m*; (on a train) coche cama *m*; (unexpected success) éxito inesperado *m*; (sofa bed) sofá-cama *m*

sleepily [slípɪli] ADV con somnolencia

sleepiness [slípɪnɪs] N sueño *m*, somnolencia *f*

sleeping [slípɪŋ] N sueño *m*; ADJ dormido; **— bag** saco de dormir *m*; **— pill** píldora para dormir *f*, somnífero *m*; **— sickness** enfermedad del sueño *f*

sleepless [slíplɪs] ADJ (person) desvelado; (night) en blanco

sleepy [slípi] ADJ somnoliento, adormilado; **to be —** tener sueño

sleet [slit] N cellisca *f*; VI caer cellisca

sleeve [sliv] N manga *f*; **to have something up one's —s** tener algo en la manga

sleigh [sle] N trineo *m*; **— bell** cascabel *m*; VI

pasear en trineo

sleight [slaɪt] N **— of hand** prestidigitación f

slender [sléndə-] ADJ delgado, esbelto

sleuth [sluθ] N sabueso m

slice [slaɪs] N (of bread, cheese) rebanada f; (of fruit) tajada f, raja f; (of meat) lonja f; VT cortar, rebanar, tajar

slick [slɪk] ADJ (unctuous) untuoso; (sly) astuto; (slippery) resbaladizo

slicker [slíkə-] N impermeable m

slide [slaɪd] VI/VT deslizar(se); **to — in** cerrar(se) deslizando; **to — out** abrirse deslizando; **to let something —** dejar pasar algo; N deslizamiento m; (playground equipment) tobogán m; (of a trombone) vara corredora f; (photographic) diapositiva f; (for microscopes) portaobjeto m

slight [slaɪt] N desaire m; VT (snub) desairar; (neglect) descuidar; ADJ (slim) delgado; (delicate) delicado, tenue; (small in degree) leve, ligero

slim [slɪm] ADJ delgado, esbelto; **a — chance** una posibilidad remota

slime [slaɪm] N (in rivers) limo m, fango m; (of snails) baba f; (despicable person) asqueroso -sa mf

slimy [slámi] ADJ (muddy) fangoso; (slobbery) baboso, gomoso; (despicable) asqueroso

sling [slɪŋ] N honda f; (for arm) cabestrillo m; **—shot** (toy) tirachinas m sg, tirador m; (weapon) honda f; VT lanzar; **to — a rifle over one's shoulder** ponerse el rifle en bandolera

slink [slɪŋk] VI (move furtively) andar furtivamente; (move provocatively) caminar provocativamente; **to — away** escurrirse

slip [slɪp] VI (slide) deslizarse; (slide accidentally) resbalar(se); (fail to engage) patinar; (deteriorate) empeorar; VT (make slip) hacer resbalar; (put) meter; **to — away** escaparse, escabullirse; **to — by** correr; **to — in** meter(se); **to — one's dress on** ponerse el vestido; **to — out** (leave) salir inadvertido; (say inadvertently) escapársele a uno algo; **to — up** meter la pata; **to let an opportunity — by** dejar pasar una oportunidad; **it —ped my mind** se me olvidó; **it —ped off** se zafó; N (act of slipping) resbalón m, traspié m; (mistake) equivocación f; (pillow cover) funda f; (underskirt) viso m; (piece of paper) papeleta f, tira de papel f; (space for boats) embarcadero m; **— of the tongue** lapsus

(linguae) m; **—knot** nudo corredizo m; **Freudian —** acto fallido m

slipper [slípə-] N zapatilla f, pantufla f

slippery [slípəri] ADJ resbaloso, resbaladizo; (evasive) evasivo, escurridizo

slipshod [slípʃɑd] ADJ chapucero

slit [slɪt] VT cortar a lo largo; **to — someone's throat** degollar a alguien; **to — into strips** cortar en tiras; N raja f

slither [slíðə-] VI serpentear, culebrear; N serpenteo m, culebreo m

sliver [slívə-] N astilla f; VI/VT astillar(se)

slob [slɑb] N (unkempt) dejado -da mf; (uncouth) bruto -ta mf

slobber [slábə-] N baba f; VI/VT babosear, babear(se)

slogan [slógən] N eslogan m, lema m

slop [slɑp] VT (splash) salpicar; (feed) dar de comer; N (pigswill) bazofia f; (mud) fango m

slope [slop] VI/VT inclinar(se); N vertiente f, declive m, cuesta f; (in math) pendiente f

sloppiness [slápinəs] N chapucería f

sloppy [slápi] ADJ (ground) fangoso; (splashed) salpicado; (slovenly) cochino; (poorly done) chapucero

slot [slɑt] N (for coins, letters) ranura f; (place in a series) casilla f; (job) puesto m; **— machine** tragamonedas mf sg, tragaperras mf sg; VT hacer una ranura

sloth [sloθ] N (vice) pereza f; (animal) perezoso m

slouch [slaʊtʃ] N (posture) encorvamiento m; (inept person) torpe mf; (lazy person) holgazán -ana mf; VI/VT (crouch) andar agachado, encorvar(se); (shuffle) andar caído de hombros

Slovakia [slovákiə] N Eslovaquia f

Slovakian [slovákiən] ADJ & N eslovaco -ca mf

Slovene [slóvin] ADJ & N esloveno -na mf

Slovenia [slovíniə] N Eslovenia f

slovenliness [slávənlinɪs] N (of a person) desaseo m, desaliño m; (of work) descuido m

slovenly [slávənli] ADJ (unclean) desaseado; (unkempt) desaliñado

slow [slo] ADJ (not fast) lento, tardo; (running behind) atrasado; (sluggish) lerdo, torpe, pesado; ADV lentamente, despacio; VI/VT **to — down / up** andar más despacio, frenar; **—down** (in business) disminución de actividades f; (in labor disputes) huelga de celo f; **in — motion** en cámara lenta

slowness [slónɪs] N (of speed) lentitud f; (of intelligence) torpeza f

slug [slʌg] N (bullet) bala f; (coin) moneda

falsa f; (animal) babosa f; (swallow) trago m; (blow with fist) puñetazo m; VT aporrear; **to — it out** agarrarse a puñetazos

sluggard [slágə-d] N holgazán -ana mf

sluggish [slágɪʃ] ADJ (slow) lento; (torpid) aletargado, torpe

sluggishness [slágɪʃnɪs] N torpeza f

sluice [slus] N (channel with a gate) esclusa f; (channel) canal m; **— gate** compuerta f

slum [slʌm] N barrio bajo m; **—s** tugurios m pl; **—lord** propietario de tugurio m; VI visitar los barrios bajos; **to — it** divertirse en lugares de poca categoría

slumber [slámbə-] VI dormitar; N sueño ligero m; **— party** fiesta de niñas que se quedan a dormir f

slump [slʌmp] VI (a person) desplomarse; (prices, markets) bajar repentinamente; N (in prices) baja repentina f; (in the economy) ralentización f; (in sports) mala racha f

slur [slɚ] VT (pronounce indistinctly) pronunciar mal; (connect notes) ligar; N (connection of notes) ligado m; (insult) insulto m

slush [slʌʃ] N (melted snow) nieve a medio derretir f; (sludge) nieve fangosa f; (mud) fango m; (refuse) desperdicios m pl; **— fund** (illicit fund) cuenta para fines ilícitos f; (petty cash) caja chica f

slut [slʌt] N (slovenly woman) pej puerca f; (loose woman) offensive mujerzuela f, puta f

sly [slaɪ] ADJ astuto, taimado; **on the — a** escondidas

smack [smæk] N (taste) dejo m; Sp deje m; (kiss) beso ruidoso m; (loud eating) chasquido m; (slap) palmada f, sopapo m; (heroin) fam caballo m; VT (kiss) dar un beso ruidoso; (eat loudly) chascar, chasquear; (slap) dar una palmada; **to — of** tener un dejo de

small [smɔl] ADJ (not large) pequeño, chico; (of build) menudo; (narrow) estrecho; (lower case) minúsculo; (petty) mezquino; N (size) pequeño m; **— change** cambio suelto m; **— fry** gente menuda f; **— intestine** intestino delgado m; **— of the back** baja espalda f; **—pox** viruela f; **— talk** cháchara f; **to feel —** avergonzarse

smallness [smɔlnɪs] N pequeñez f

smart [smart] ADJ (intelligent) listo, inteligente; (astute) astuto; (stylish) elegante; **— alec, aleck** sabihondo -da mf; **— ass** fam sabihondo -da mf; **— bomb** bomba inteligente f; **— money**

inversión inteligente f; **— remark** insolencia f; N escozor m; VI picar; **I'm —ing from his rude remarks** todavía me duelen sus groserías

smash [smæʃ] VT estrellar, destrozar; (a rebellion) aplastar; **to — into** estrellarse contra; N (sound) estrépito m; (blow) choque violento m; **a — hit** un exitazo

smear [smɪr] VT (daub) untar; (spot, vilify) manchar; (blur) correrse; (defeat) reventar; **to — with paint** pintorrear, pintarrajear; N (stain) mancha f; (culture) frotis m; **— campaign** campaña de difamación f

smell [smɛl] VI/VT oler; **to — of** oler a; **that —s** huele mal, apesta; **to — up** apestar; N (odor) olor m; (sense) olfato m; **— of** olor a

smelly [smέli] ADJ hediondo, apestoso

smile [smaɪl] VI sonreír(se); **to — approval** sonreír en aprobación; N sonrisa f

smiling [smáɪlɪŋ] ADJ risueño, sonriente

smirk [smɚk] N sonrisa suficiente f; VI sonreír con suficiencia

smith [smɪθ] N herrero -ra mf

smog [smɑg] N smog m

smoke [smok] N humo m; (cigarette) cigarro m, cigarrillo m; **— detector** detector de humo m, detector de incendios m; **— screen** cortina de humo f; **— stack** chimenea f; **to have a —** fumar; VI (put off smoke) echar humo; (go fast) volar; VT (tobacco) fumar; (ham, fish, glass) ahumar; **to — out** (drive out) ahuyentar con humo; (expose) poner al descubierto

smoker [smókə-] N fumador -ora mf; (train car) vagón de fumar m

smoking [smókɪŋ] ADJ humeante; **— car** vagón de fumar m; **— gun** prueba irrefutable f; **— room** cuarto de fumar m; N (use of tobacco) tabaquismo m

smoky [smóki] ADJ humoso

smolder, smoulder [smóldə-] VI arder

smooth [smuð] ADJ (surface) liso; (skin) suave, terso; (tire) gastado; (sea) sereno, tranquilo; (polished) agradable, fino; (ingratiating) zalamero; VT (make surface even) alisar; (make easy) allanar; **to — away** hacer desaparecer; **to — one's hair** atusarse el cabello; **to — over** limar asperezas

smoothness [smúðnɪs] N (evenness) lisura f; (of skin) tersura f, suavidad f; (of sea) tranquilidad f; (polish) fineza f; (suaveness) zalamería f

smother [smáðə-] VT (stifle) ahogar(se), sofocar(se), asfixiar(se); (envelop) cubrir; (overprotect) sobreproteger

smudge [smʌdʒ] N borrón *m*, mancha *f*; vi/vt borronear(se), manchar(se)

smug [smʌg] ADJ suficiente, petulante

smuggle [smʌ́gəl] vi/vt contrabandear, hacer contrabando; **to — in** entrar de contrabando; **to — out** sacar de contrabando

smuggler [smʌ́glə] N contrabandista *mf*

smut [smʌt] N (soot) hollín *m*; (obscenity) obscenidad *f*

snack [snæk] N tentempié *m*, bocadillo *m*; **— bar** cafetería *f*

snafu [snæfú] N relajo *m*

snag [snæg] N (a branch) gancho *m*; (in fabric) enganchón *m*; (any obstacle) pega *f*, obstáculo *m*, contrariedad *f*; **to hit a —** tropezar con un obstáculo; vi/vt enganchar(se); vt agarrar

snail [sneł] N caracol *m*; **— mail** correo regular *m*; **—'s pace** paso de tortuga *m*

snake [snek] N serpiente *f*; **—bite** mordedura de serpiente *f*; **— in the grass** víbora *f*; **—skin** piel de serpiente *f*; vi serpentear

snap [snæp] vi (make sound) chasquear, dar un chasquido; (lose control) estallar, perder los estribos; vt (a photograph) sacar; vi/vt (break) quebrar(se); **to — at** (try to bite) tirar un mordiscón; (speak harshly) ladrar; **to — one's fingers** chasquear los dedos, castañetear con los dedos; **to — out of** recuperarse de; **to — shut** cerrar(se) de golpe; **to — together** abrochar; **to — up** llevarse; N (sound) chasquido *m*; (fastener) broche *m*; (bite) tarascada *f*; **it's a —** es pan comido; **— judgment** decisión atolondrada *f*; **—dragon** dragón *m*; **—shot** instantánea, foto *f*

snappy [snǽpi] ADJ (that bites) mordedor; (elegant) elegante; **make it —!** ¡en seguida!

snare [snɛr] N (trap) trampa *f*; **— drum** tambor con bordón *m*; vt atrapar

snarl [snɑrł] vi/vt (growl) regañar; (tangle) enmarañar(se), enredar(se); N (growl) gruñido *m*; (tangle) maraña *f*, enredo *m*

snatch [snætʃ] vt (seize) arrebatar; (kidnap) secuestrar; vi **to — at** dar manotazos; N (act of snatching) arrebato *m*; (fragment) fragmento *m*

snazzy [snǽzi] ADJ llamativo

sneak [snik] vi andar furtivamente; vt (put away) meter a escondidas; **to — in** entrar a escondidas; **to — something in** meter a escondidas; **to — out** salir a hurtadillas; **to — something out** sacar a escondidas; **to — a cigarette** fumar a escondidas; N

persona solapada *f*

sneakers [sníkə-z] N zapatillas (deportivas) *f pl*, tenis *m pl*

sneer [snir] vi (smile) sonreír con sorna; **to — at** mofarse de; N expresión de sorna *f*

sneeze [sniz] vi estornudar; **that's nothing to — at** no es nada desdeñable; N estornudo *m*

snicker [sníkə-] vi reírse burlonamente; N risita burlona *f*

snide [snaid] ADJ malévolo

sniff [snif] vi/vt husmear, olfatear; **to — at** husmear; (ridicule) menospreciar; N (act of sniffing) husmeo *m*, olfateo *m*; (smell) bocanada *f*

sniffle [snífəł] vi (with a cold) sorberse los mocos; (when crying) gimotear; N (when crying) gimoteo *m*; **the —s** un resfrío

snip [snip] vt tijeretear; **to — off** cortar de un tijeretazo; N (act of snipping) tijeretada *f*, tijeretazo *m*; (piece cut off) pedacito *m*, recorte *m*; **— of conversation** retazo de conversación *m*

sniper [snáipə] N francotirador -ora *mf*

snitch [snitʃ] vi (tell on) chivar, chivatar; vt (rob) ratear; N soplón -ona *mf*, chivato -ta *mf*

snob [snab] N esnob *mf*

snoop [snup] vi fisgar, fisgonear; N fisgón -ona *mf*

snooze [snuz] vi dormitar; N siesta *f*; **to take a —** echar un sueñecito/ sueñito

snore [snɔr] vi roncar; N ronquido *m*

snorkel [snɔ́rkəł] N esnórquel *m*

snort [snɔrt] vi resoplar, bufar; vi/vt (drugs) esnifar; N resoplido *m*, bufido *m*; (drink) trago *m*

snot [snat] N (mucus) *fam, vulg* moco *m*; (person) *pej* mocoso -sa *mf*

snout [snaut] N hocico *m*, jeta *f*, morro *m*; (nose) napias *f pl*

snow [sno] N nieve *f* (also cocaine, heroin); **—ball** bola de nieve *f*; **to —ball** aumentar rápidamente; **—board** monopatín de nieve *m*; **—drift** ventisquero *m*; **—fall** nevada *f*; **—flake** copo de nieve *m*; **—man** muñeco de nieve *m*; **—mobile** motonieve *f*; **—plow** quitanieves *m sg*; **—shoe** raqueta *f*; **—storm** ventisca *f*; vi nevar; **the airport was —ed in** cerraron el aeropuerto por nieve; **to — under** (cover in snow) cubrir de nieve; (overwhelm) abrumar

snowy [snói] ADJ nevado; (white) níveo

snub [snʌb] vt volverle la cara a, desairar; (reject) despreciar; N desprecio *m*, desaire *m*; **—nosed** chato; *Am* ñato

snuff [snʌf] VI **to — out** apagar, extinguir; N rapé *m*; **to be up to —** dar la talla

snug [snʌg] ADJ (tight-fitting) ajustado; (comfortable) cómodo

so [so] ADV (in this way) así; (to this degree) tan; (so much) tanto; **— am I** yo también; **—and—** fulano (de tal); **—called** llamado; **— as to** para; **— far as I know** que yo sepa; **— many** tantos; **— much** tanto; **—·—** regular; **— much the better** tanto mejor; **— that** de modo que; **I was — a beauty queen!** ¡sí que fui reina de belleza! **— long!** ¡hasta luego! **and — forth** etcetera, y así sucesivamente; **I believe —** creo que sí; **is that — ?** ¿en serio? ¡no me digas! **ten minutes or —** unos diez minutos; INTERJ ajajá; CONJ (in order that) de modo que; (consequently) así que, entonces

soak [sok] VI/VT (immerse) remojar(se); (drench) empapar(se); **it finally —ed in on him that** por fin se dio cuenta de que; **to — through** colarse por; **to — up** absorber, embeber; **to be —ed through** estar empapado, estar calado hasta los huesos; N remojón *m*

soap [sop] N jabón *m*; (soap opera) telenovela *f*; **— bubble** pompa de jabón *f*; **— dish** jabonera *f*; VT enjabonar

soapy [sópi] ADJ jabonoso

soar [sɔr] VI/VI (airplane) elevar(se); (kite) remontar(se); (hopes) aumentar(se); (prices) disparar(se); (glider) planear(se); VI (bird) volar

sob [sɑb] VI sollozar, hipar; N sollozo *m*, hipo *m*

SOB (son of a bitch) [esobí] N *offensive* hijo de puta *m*, *offensive* hijo de perra *m*

sober [sóbɚ] ADJ (not drunk) sobrio; (temperate) moderado; (serious, subdued) serio, sobrio; VI **to — up** (get over drunkenness) despejarse; (become more serious) sentar cabeza

sobriety [səbráιιDi] N (not being drunk) sobriedad *f*; (moderation) moderación *f*; (seriousness) seriedad *f*

soccer [sákɚ] N fútbol *m*, balompié *m*

sociable [sóʃəbəɫ] ADJ sociable

social [sóʃəɫ] ADJ (of society) social; (friendly) sociable; N reunión social *f*; **— climber** arribista *mf*; **— science** ciencias sociales *f pl*; **— security** seguridad social *f*; **— welfare** asistencia social *f*; **— work** asistencia social *f*

socialism [sóʃəlɪzəm] N socialismo *m*

socialist [sóʃəlɪst] ADJ & N socialista *mf*

socialize [sóʃəlaɪz] VT socializar; VI salir, tener

trato social

society [səsáιιDi] N sociedad *f*; (companionship) compañía *f*

socioeconomic [sosioɛkənámɪk] ADJ socioeconómico

sociology [sosiálədʒi] N sociología *f*

sociopath [sósiəpæθ] N sociópata *mf*

sock [sɑk] N (garment) calcetín *m*; (blow) puñetazo *m*, zumbido *m*; VT pegar, zumbar; **to — away** ahorrar

socket [sákιt] N (of eye) cuenca *f*; (electrical outlet) enchufe *m*; (for bulb) portalámparas *m sg*, casquillo *m*

sod [sɑd] N (lawn) césped *m*; (piece) tepe *m*; VT cubrir de césped

soda [sóDə] N (drink) gaseosa *f*; (sodium hydroxide) soda *f*, sosa *f*; **— fountain** bar de bebidas sin alcohol *m*; **— pop** gaseosa *f*; **— water** agua con gas *f*

sodium [sóDiəm] N sodio *m*

sodomy [sáDəmi] N sodomía *f*

sofa [sófə] N sofá *m*; **— bed** sofá-cama *m*

soft [sɔft] ADJ (butter, bed, water, penalty) blando; (life) fácil, cómodo; (hair, skin) suave; (light) tenue; **—ball** softball *m*; **—boiled eggs** huevos pasados por agua *m pl*; **— coal** carbón bituminoso *m*; **— drink** gaseosa *f*; **— palate** velo del paladar *m*; **—ware** software *m*

soften [sɔfən] VI/VT (butter) ablandar(se); (skin) suavizar(se); VT (a blow) amortiguar; (voice) bajar

softness [sɔftnιs] N (of butter) blandura *f*; (of hair, skin) suavidad *f*; (of light) tenuidad *f*

soggy [sági] ADJ (clothes) empapado; (day) húmedo

soil [sɔιɫ] N suelo *m*, tierra *f*; VI/VT ensuciar(se), manchar(se)

solace [sálιs] N consuelo *m*; VT consolar

solar [sólɚ] ADJ solar; **— eclipse** eclipse de sol *m*; **— energy** energía solar *f*; **— plexus** plexo solar *m*; **— system** sistema solar *m*

solder [sáDɚ] VI/VT soldar(se); N soldadura *f*

soldering iron [sáDɚιŋaιrn] N soldador *m*

soldier [sótʤɚ] N (of low rank) soldado *m*; (of any rank) militar *m*

sole [soɫ] ADJ solo, único; N (of a foot) planta *f*; (of a shoe) suela *f*; (fish) lenguado *m*

solemn [sáləm] ADJ solemne

solemnity [səlémnιDi] N solemnidad *f*

solenoid [sólənɔιd] N solenoide *m*

solicit [səlísιt] VT (aid) pedir; (a prostitute) ofrecerse; VI (sell) vender, ofrecer productos

solicitor [səlísιtɚ] N abogado *m*; **— General** Subsecretario -ria de Justicia *mf*

solicitous [səlísɪtəs] ADJ solícito

solid [sálɪd] ADJ (firm) sólido; (dense) denso; — **blue** azul liso m; — **geometry** geometría del espacio f; — **gold** oro puro m; — **line** línea continua f; —**state** de estado sólido; **for one** — **hour** por una hora entera; N sólido m

solidarity [sálɪdǽɾɪtɪ] N solidaridad f

solidify [səlídəfaɪ] VI/VT solidificar(se)

solidity [səlídɪtɪ] N solidez f

solitary [sálɪtɛɾɪ] ADJ solitario; **to be in** — **confinement** estar incomunicado

solitude [sálɪtud] N soledad f

solo [sólo] N solo m

soloist [sóloɪst] N solista mf

Solomon Islander [sáləmənáɪləndɚ] N salomonense mf

Solomon Islands [sáləmənáɪləndz] N Islas Salomón f pl

solstice [sálstɪs] N solsticio m

soluble [sáljəbəɫ] ADJ soluble

solution [səlúʃən] N solución f

solve [salv] VT resolver, solucionar

solvent [sálvənt] N solvente m, disolvente m

Somalia [somália] N Somalia f

Somalian [somáljən] ADJ & N somalí mf

somber [sámbɚ] ADJ sombrío

some [sam] ADJ alguno; **I worked for** — **time** trabajé por un rato; **that is** — **dog!** ¡menudo perro! PRON algunos; **and then** — y más todavía; ADV — **twenty people** unas veinte personas; **I like it** — me gusta un poco

somebody [sámbadɪ] PRON alguien

someday [sámde] ADV algún día

somehow [sámhau] ADV de alguna manera; — **or other** de alguna manera u otra

someone [sámwan] PRON alguien

somersault [sámɚsɔɫt] N (on ground) voltereta f; (in air) salto mortal m; VI (on ground) dar una voltereta; (in air) dar un salto mortal

something [sámθɪŋ] N algo m; — **else** otra cosa; **thirty**— treinta y tantos

sometime [sámtaɪm] ADV algún día, en algún momento; —**s** a veces, de vez en cuando

somewhat [sámhwat] ADV algo

somewhere [sámhwɛɾ] ADV en alguna parte; — **else** en alguna otra parte

son [san] N hijo m; —**in-law** yerno m; — **of a bitch** offensive hijo de puta m; — **of a gun** fam hijo de su madre m

sonar [sónar] N sonar m

song [sɔŋ] N canción f; (of a bird) canto m; — **and dance** cuento chino m; —**writer** compositor -ora mf; —**bird** ave canora f, pájaro cantor m; **to buy something for**

a — comprar algo muy barato

sonic barrier [sánɪkbǽɾiɚ] N barrera del sonido f

sonnet [sánɪt] N soneto m

sonorous [sánɚəs] ADJ sonoro

soon [sun] ADV pronto; — **after nine** poco después de las nueve; **as** — **as** tan pronto como, en cuanto; **see you** — hasta pronto; **how** — **do you want it?** ¿para cuándo lo necesitas? —**er or later** tarde o temprano; **I'd** —**er stay here** prefiero quedarme aquí

soot [sut] N hollín m, tizne m

soothe [suð] VT calmar, aliviar

soothsayer [súθseɚ] N agorero -ra mf

sooty [súdɪ] ADJ tiznado

sop [sap] VT empapar; **to** — **up** absorber; **to be** —**ping wet** estar empapado; N sopa f

sophisticated [səfístɪkeɪdɪd] ADJ sofisticado

sophomore [sáfəmɔr] N estudiante de segundo año mf

soprano [səprǽno] N soprano m

sorcerer [sɔ́rsərɚ] N brujo m, hechicero m

sorceress [sɔ́rsəɪs] N hechicera f

sordid [sɔ́rdɪd] ADJ sórdido, escabroso

sore [sɔr] ADJ (painful) dolorido, doloroso; (grieved) dolorido; (angry) enojado; —**head** cascarrabias mf; **my arm is** — me duele el brazo; **to have a** — **throat** tener dolor de garganta; N llaga f, úlcera f

soreness [sɔ́rnɪs] N dolor m

sorority [sərɔ́rɪdɪ] N asociación femenina de estudiantes f

sorrow [sáro] N (sadness) pena f, pesar m, pesadumbre f; (cause of sadness) fuente de disgustos f

sorrowful [sárəfəɫ] ADJ triste, pesaroso

sorry [sárɪ] ADJ **I am** — lo siento; **I am** — **about that** lo lamento; **I am** — **for her** la compadezco; —**?** ¿Cómo? **a** — **SOB** pej un desgraciado; **you'll be** — te arrepentirás; **he was in** — **shape** estaba en un estado lamentable

sort [sɔrt] N clase f, tipo m; — **of tired** algo cansado; **all** —**s of** toda clase de; **out of** —**s** (depressed) de mal humor; (ill) indispuesto; VT (classify) clasificar; **to** — **out** separar, apartar; **to** — **out a problem** resolver un problema

SOS [ésoés] N SOS m

soul [soɫ] N alma f; — **music** música soul f; **not a** — nadie, ni un alma; **the** — **of tact** la imagen del tacto

sound [saund] N sonido m; (inlet) brazo de mar m; — **wave** onda sonora f; ADJ (healthy) sano; (sane) cuerdo; (well founded) bien fundado, lógico; — **advice**

buen consejo *m*; — **barrier** barrera del
sonido *f*; —**proof** a prueba de sonido; —
sleep sueño profundo *m*; —**track** banda
sonora *f*; **a — beating** una buena paliza;
of — mind en su sano juicio; **safe and
— sano y salvo**; VI sonar; VT (an alarm)
tocar; (a channel) sondar; (opinion)
sondear; **to — out** tantear, sondear

soup [sup] N sopa *f*; — **dish** plato sopero *m*;
—**spoon** cuchara sopera *f*; — **tureen**
sopera *f*

sour [saur] ADJ (acidic) agrio, ácido; (peevish)
agrio, avinagrado; **to go —** cortarse,
agriarse; — **cream** *Sp* nata agria *f*; *Am*
crema agria *f*; — **milk** leche cortada *f*;
—**puss** cascarrabias *mf*, avinagrado -da *mf*;
VI/VT agriar(se), avinagrar(se); (milk)
cortar(se)

source [sɔrs] N fuente *f*, origen *m*

sourness [sáurnɪs] N acidez *f*

souse [saus] VI/VT (plunge) zambullir(se);
(soak) empapar(se); N borracho -cha *mf*,
esponja *f*

south [sauθ] N sur *m*; ADJ meridional; —
Africa Sudáfrica *f*; — **African**
sudafricano -na *mf*; — **America** América
del Sur *f*, Sudamérica *f*; — **American**
sudamericano -na *mf*; —**bound** con
rumbo al sur; —**east** sureste, sudeste;
—**eastern** sureste, sudeste; — **Korea**
Corea del Sur *f*; — **Korean** surcoreano -na
mf; —**paw** zurdo -da *mf*; — **pole** polo sur
m; —**west** sudoeste, suroeste; —**western**
sudoeste, suroeste; ADV hacia el sur

southern [sáðən] ADJ meridional, sureño

southerner [sáðənə] N sureño -ña *mf*,
meridional del sur *mf*

southward [sáuθwəd] ADV hacia el sur,
rumbo al sur

souvenir [suvənír] N recuerdo *m*

sovereign [sávərɪn] ADJ & N soberano -na *mf*

sovereignty [sávərɪnti] N soberanía *f*

sow [sau] N puerca *f*; [so] VI/VT sembrar

soy [sɔi] N *Sp* soja *f*; *Am* soya *f*; —**bean** *Sp*
semilla de soja *f*; *Am* semilla de soya *f*; —
sauce *Sp* salsa de soja *f*; *Am* salsa de soya
f

spa [spɑ] N balneario *m*

space [spes] N espacio *m*; —**age** de la era
espacial; —**bar** barra espaciadora *f*;
—**craft** nave espacial *f*; —**ship** nave
espacial *f*; — **shuttle** transbordador
espacial *m*; — **station** estación espacial *f*;
— **suit** traje espacial *m*; VT espaciar

spacious [spéʃəs] ADJ espacioso, amplio

spade [sped] N pala *f*; (in cards) pica *f*; **to
call a — a —** al pan, pan y al vino, vino

Spain [spen] N España *f*

span [spæn] N (of hand) palmo *m*; (of time)
espacio *m*; (of attention) lapso *m*, período
m; (of bridge) tramo *m*; (of wing)
envergadura *f*; (of life) duración *f*; VT
(time) abarcar; (a river) atravesar, salvar

Spaniard [spénjəd] N español -ola *mf*

Spanish [spǽnɪʃ] ADJ (of Spain) español;
(Spanish-speaking) hispano; N (language)
español *m*

Spanish America [spǽnɪʃəménkə] N
Hispanoamérica *f*

spank [spæŋk] VT dar nalgadas; N palmada *f*,
nalgada *f*

spanking [spǽŋkɪŋ] N zurra en las nalgas *f*;
ADJ — **new** flamante

spare [sper] VT (embarrassment) ahorrar,
evitar; (money) prestar; (an enemy)
perdonar la vida a; (a worker) prescindir
de; — **me!** ¡ten piedad de mí! **to — no
expense** no escatimar gastos; **to have
time to —** tener tiempo de sobra; ADJ
(austere) austero; (extra) de sobra, de más;
— **cash** dinero disponible *m*; — **parts**
repuestos *m pl*; — **time** tiempo libre *m*; N
(part) repuesto *m*; (tire) neumático de
repuesto *m*

spark [spark] N chispa *f*; — **plug** bujía *f*; VI
chispear, echar chispas; VT (a riot)
desencadenar; (interest, criticism) provocar

sparkle [spárkəl] VI (diamond) centellear;
(sparkler) chispear; (eyes) brillar; N
(flashing) brillo *m*, centelleo *m*; (spirit)
viveza *f*, animación *f*

sparkling [spárklɪŋ] ADJ (diamond)
centelleante; (eyes) brillante; — **water**
agua con gas *f*; — **wine** vino espumoso *m*

sparrow [spǽro] N gorrión *m*

sparse [spɑrs] ADJ escaso; (hair) ralo

spasm [spǽzəm] N espasmo *m*

spastic [spǽstɪk] ADJ espástico

spat [spæt] N riña *f*

spatial [spéʃəl] ADJ espacial

spatter [spǽDə] VI/VT salpicar; N salpicadura
f

spatula [spǽtʃələ] N espátula *f*

spawn [spɔn] VI desovar; VT engendrar; N (of
fish) huevas *f pl*; (of frogs) huevos *m pl*

spay [spe] VT esterilizar, castrar

speak [spik] VI hablar; VT (language) hablar;
(truth, amusement) decir; (lines) recitar,
decir; **so to —** por decirlo así, valga la
expresión; **to — for** hablar en nombre
de / a favor de; **to — one's mind** hablar
sin rodeos; **to — out against** denunciar;
to — out for defender; **to — up** hablar
fuerte

speaker [spíkɚ] N orador -ra *mf*; (at a
  conference) conferenciante *mf*; **— of the
  House** presidente -ta de la cámara de
  representantes *mf*; **—phone** teléfono con
  parlante *m*
spear [spir] N lanza *f*; (for fishing) arpón *m*;
  (sprout) brote *m*; VT (wound with lance)
  alancear, herir con lanza; (fish with lance)
  arponear
spearmint [spírmɪnt] N mentaverde *f*
special [spéʃəł] ADJ especial; **— delivery**
  entrega inmediata *f*; **— education**
  educación especial *f*; **— effects** efectos
  especiales *m pl*; **— interest (group)**
  grupo de presión *m*; N (sale item)
  especialidad *f*; (TV program) especial *m*
specialist [spéʃəlɪst] N especialista *mf*
specialization [speʃəlɪzéʃən] N
  especialización *f*, especialidad *f*
specialize [spéʃəlaɪz] VI/VT especializar(se)
specialty [spéʃəłti] N especialidad *f*
species [spíʃiz] N especie *f*
specific [spɪsífɪk] ADJ específico; **— gravity**
  peso específico *m*; N **—s** detalles *m pl*
specify [spésəfaɪ] VI/VT especificar
specimen [spésəmən] N (representative)
  espécimen *m*, ejemplar *m*; (sample)
  muestra *f*
speck [spɛk] N (small dot) mota *f*, manchita *f*;
  (small amount) pizca *f*
speckle [spékəł] N manchita *f*, mota *f*; VT
  salpicar, motear; **—d** moteado
spectacle [spéktəkəł] N espectáculo *m*; **—s**
  gafas *f pl*, anteojos *m pl*; **to make a — of
  oneself** dar un espectáculo, ponerse en
  ridículo
spectacular [spɛktækjələ] ADJ espectacular
spectator [spékteɾɚ] N espectador -ra *mf*
spectrum [spéktrəm] N espectro *m*
speculate [spékjəlet] VI/VT especular
speculation [spɛkjəléʃən] N especulación *f*
speculator [spékjəleɾɚ] N especulador -ora
  mf
speech [spitʃ] N (faculty of speaking) habla *f*;
  (formal) discurso *m*; (in a play)
  parlamento *m*; **to make a —** pronunciar
  un discurso; **— defect** defecto de
  pronunciación *m*
speechless [spítʃlɪs] ADJ (dumb) mudo;
  (astonished) estupefacto
speed [spid] N velocidad *f* (also gear), rapidez
  f; (amphetamine) anfeta *f*; **— limit** límite
  de velocidad *m*; **at full —** a toda
  velocidad; VI (break speed limit) ir con
  exceso de velocidad; **to — by** pasar a toda
  velocidad; **to — off / away** irse a toda
  velocidad; **to — up** acelerar; VT (supplies)

hacer llegar a toda velocidad; (work)
  acelerar
speedometer [spɪdámɪɾɚ] N velocímetro *m*
speedy [spídi] ADJ veloz, rápido
spell [spɛł] N (charm) hechizo *m*, sortilegio
  m, conjuro *m*; (period) temporada *f*;
  (sickness) ataque *m*; **—bound** hechizado;
  to put under a — hechizar; VT (spoken)
  deletrear; (written) escribir; (represent)
  significar, representar; **to —check**
  comprobar el deletreo; **I —ed it out for
  him** se lo dije con todas las letras
spelling [spélɪŋ] N ortografía *f*; **— bee**
  concurso de ortografía *m*
spend [spɛnd] VT (money) gastar; (time)
  pasar; **—thrift** derrochador -ra *mf*,
  gastador -ra *mf*, pródigo -ga *mf*
sperm [spɚm] N esperma *mf*, semen *m*; **—
  bank** banco de semen / esperma *m*; **—
  whale** cachalote *m*
sphere [sfir] N esfera *f*
spherical [sférɪkəł] ADJ esférico
spice [spaɪs] N especia *f*; VT condimentar; **to
  — up** dar sal
spiciness [spáɪsɪnɪs] N lo picante
spick and span [spíkənspæn] ADJ impecable
spicy [spáɪsi] ADJ picante
spider [spáɪɾɚ] N araña *f*; **— monkey** mono
  araña *m*; **—'s web** telaraña *f*
spigot [spígət] N grifo *m*, espita *f*
spike [spaɪk] N (sprout) espiga *f*; (sharp
  object) púa *f*, pincho *m*; (on shoes) clavo
  m; **—s** zapatillas con clavos *f pl*; VT
  (impale) clavar; (add alcohol to) echar
  alcohol a; (hit a volleyball) picar
spill [spɪł] VI/VT volcar(se), derramar(se),
  verter(se); (a rider) hacer caer; **to —
  the beans** descubrir el pastel; VI **to —
  over** (a liquid) desbordarse; (a conflict)
  extenderse; N (of water) derrame *m*; (of
  blood) derramamiento *m*; (fall) caída *f*
spin [spɪn] VT (wool) hilar; (a top, one's
  partner) hacer girar; VI dar vueltas, girar;
  to — yarns contar cuentos; N (turning)
  giro *m*, vuelta *f*; (of an airplane) barrena *f*;
  (political) sesgo *m*; **to take a —** dar una
  vuelta
spinach [spínɪtʃ] N espinaca *f*
spinal [spáɪnəł] ADJ espinal, vertebral; **—
  column** columna vertebral *f*, espina
  dorsal *f*; **— cord** médula espinal *f*
spindle [spíndł] N (for weaving) huso *m*; (on
  machines) eje *m*
spine [spaɪn] N espina *f*, espinazo *m*
spinning [spínɪŋ] N (action) hilado *m*; (art)
  hilandería *f*; **— machine** máquina de
  hilar *f*; **— mill** hilandería *f*; **— top**

trompo *m*, peonza *f*; — **wheel** rueca *f*
spinster [spínstɚ] N solterona *f*
spiral [spáɪrəł] ADJ & N espiral *m*; —
notebook cuaderno de espiral *m*; —
staircase escalera de caracol *f*
spire [spaɪr] N aguja *f*, chapitel *m*
spirit [spírɪt] N (ghost) espíritu *m*;
(animation) ánimo *m*, brío *m*; (alcohol)
alcohol *m*; **low —s** abatimiento *m*; **to be
in good —s** estar de buen humor; VT **to
— away** llevar como por arte de magia
spirited [spírɪdɪd] ADJ fogoso, brioso
spiritual [spírɪtʃuəł] ADJ & N espiritual *m*
spit [spɪt] VI/VT escupir; N (saliva) escupitajo
m; (for roasting) asador *m*; (of sand) banco
m
spite [spaɪt] N despecho *m*, inquina *f*; **in —
of** a pesar de; **out of —** por despecho; VT
contrariar
spiteful [spáɪtfəł] ADJ malicioso
splash [splæʃ] VI/VT salpicar; VI chapotear,
chapalear; N salpicadura *f*, chapoteo *m*; **to
make a —** hacer olas
splatter [splǽDɚ] VI/VT salpicar; N
salpicadura *f*
spleen [splin] N bazo *m*; (ill humor) mal
humor *m*
splendid [spléndɪd] ADJ espléndido
splendor [spléndɚ] N esplendor *m*
splice [splaɪs] VT (tape, genes) empalmar,
unir; N empalme *m*, unión *f*
splint [splɪnt] N tablilla *f*; VT entablillar
splinter [splíntɚ] N astilla *f*; VI/VT astillar(se)
split [splɪt] VI/VT (stone, wood) hender(se),
rajar(se); (candy bar) partir(se), dividir(se);
to — hairs hilar fino; **to — one's sides
with laughter** desternillarse de risa; **to
— the difference** partir la diferencia; ADJ
(wood) partido, hendido; (a group)
dividido; **—-level** en desnivel; **—
personality** doble personalidad *f*; **—
screen** pantalla dividida *f*; **— second**
fracción de segundo *f*; N hendidura *f*,
grieta *f*; (in a group) escisión *f*, división *f*
spoil [spɔɪl] VI (milk) cortar(se); (food)
echarse a perder, averiarse; VT (vacation,
performance) estropear, arruinar; (plans)
desbaratar; (enjoyment) aguar; (child)
malcriar, mimar demasiado; N **—s** botín *m*
spoiler [spɔ́ɪlɚ] N alerón *m*
spoke [spok] N rayo *m*
spokesperson [spókspɚ-sən] N portavoz *mf*,
vocero -ra *mf*
sponge [spʌndʒ] N (animal, utensil) esponja *f*;
(parasite) gorrón -ona *mf*; **— cake** *Am*
bizcochuelo *m*; *Sp* bizcocho *m*; VI **to —
off** quitar con esponja; **to — off of**

gorronear; **to — up** absorber con una
esponja
sponger [spʌ́ndʒɚ] N gorrón -ona *mf*, parásito
m
spongy [spʌ́ndʒi] ADJ esponjoso, esponjado
sponsor [spʌ́nsɚ] N (of the arts) mecenas *mf*;
(of sports, TV program) patrocinador -ora
mf; (of a bill) proponente *mf*; VT (a child)
apadrinar; (arts, sports, TV show)
patrocinar; (bill) proponer
sponsorship [spʌ́nsɚ-ʃɪp] N patrocinio *m*
spontaneity [spɑntənéɪdɪ] N espontaneidad *f*
spontaneous [spɑnténiəs] ADJ espontáneo
spook [spuk] N (ghost) espectro *m*; (spy) espía
mf
spool [spuł] N carrete *m*, carretel *m*; VT (wool)
devanar; (tape) enrollar
spoon [spun] N cuchara *f*; VT cucharear,
poner con una cuchara; **to —-feed** dar de
comer en la boca
spoonful [spúnfuł] N cucharada *f*
spore [spɔr] N espora *f*
sport [spɔrt] N deporte *m*; **to be a good —**
tener espíritu deportivo; VT lucir; ADJ
deportivo; **— utility vehicle** vehículo
utilitario deportivo *m*; **—s car** coche
deportivo *m*; **—s jacket** saco de sport *m*,
americana *f*; **—sman** (hunter) cazador *m*;
(in sports) hombre de espíritu deportivo
m; **—smanship** espíritu deportivo *m*,
deportividad *f*; **—swriter** cronista
deportivo -va *m*
sporty [spɔ́rDi] ADJ deportivo
spot [spat] N (stain) mancha *f*, mota *f*;
(blemish) espinilla *f*; (insect bite) roncha *f*;
(place) lugar *m*, paraje *m*; (scrape) aprieto
m; **on the —** en el acto; **—-check**
inspección al azar *f*; **—light** (in theater)
foco *m*; (outdoors) reflector *m*; **to be in
the —light** ser el centro de atención; **—
remover** quitamanchas *m sg*; VI/VT (stain)
manchar, ensuciar; VT (see in the distance)
divisar; (notice) notar; (give advantage)
dar como ventaja
spotless [spátlɪs] ADJ inmaculado
spotted [spáDɪd] ADJ manchado, moteado
spouse [spaʊs] N cónyuge *mf*
spout [spaʊt] VT (throw) arrojar chorros de;
(talk) soltar tonterías; VI (flow out) salir a
chorros; (talk) perorar; N (of a fountain)
caño *m*; (of a gutter) canalón *m*; (of a
teapot) pico *m*
sprain [spren] VT torcerse; N torcedura *f*
sprawl [sprɔ́ł] VI (spread limbs) despatarrarse;
(extend) extenderse; (fall) tumbarse; N
postura despatarrada *f*
spray [spre] N (of liquid) rociada *f*; (foam)

espuma *f*; (of flowers) ramillete *m*; VI/VT
rociar(se); — **can** aerosol *m*; — **paint**
pintura en aerosol *f*

spread [sprɛd] VI/VT (arms, newspaper)
extender(se); (butter) untar(se); (map)
desdoblar(se); (legs) abrir(se); (seeds)
esparcir(se); (news) difundir(se),
diseminar(se); (rumor) propalar; (panic)
sembrar; VT (panic, news) sembrar; N (of
ideas) difusión *f*; (of opinion)
diseminación *f*; (of disease) propagación *f*;
(of nuclear weapons) proliferación *f*; (for a
bed) cubrecama *m*; (for bread) pasta *f*; (of
food) festín *m*; (ranch) hacienda *f*;
—**sheet** (paper) planilla de cálculo *f*;
(program) planilla electrónica *f*

spree [spri] N parranda *f*, farra *f*; **to go on a**
— ir de parranda / farra; **to go on a**
shopping — gastar dinero
desenfrenadamente

spring [sprɪŋ] VI saltar; **to** — **at** abalanzarse
sobre; **to** — **from** nacer de; **to** — **to**
mind venir a la mente; **to** — **up** surgir;
VT **to** — **a leak** (boat) hacer agua; (pipe)
comenzar a gotear; **to** — **news** dar una
noticia de sopetón; **to** — **open** abrir(se)
de golpe; N (season) primavera *f*; (coil)
muelle *m*, resorte *m*; (elasticity) elasticidad
f; (jump) salto *m*; (water) manantial *m*,
fuente *f*; —**board** trampolín *m*; — **fever**
fiebre de primavera *f*; — **mattress**
colchón de muelles *m*; —**time** primavera
f; — **water** agua de manantial *f*; **he's no**
— **chicken** no se cuece en el primer
hervor

sprinkle [sprɪ́ŋkəł] VT (with sugar)
espolvorear; (with droplets) salpicar,
rociar; (rain) gotear, chispear

sprint [sprɪnt] VI (run) echarse una carrera;
(run a competitive race) (e)sprintar; N
(run) corrida corta *f*; (race) (e)sprint *m*

sprocket [sprάkɪt] N piñón *m*, rueda dentada
f

sprout [spraʊt] VI (leaf) brotar, salir; (plants)
retoñar; (seeds) germinar; (houses) surgir;
VT echar; **he** —**ed horns** le salieron
cuernos; N retoño *m*, brote *m*, renuevo *m*

spruce [sprus] N picea *f*; VI **to** — **up**
arreglarse

spunk [spʌŋk] N agallas *f pl*, *vulg* cojones *m*
pl

spur [spɚ] N espuela *f*; (stimulus) aguijón *m*;
(of a rooster) espolón *m*; (of a mountain)
estribación *f*; (of a railroad track) ramal *m*;
on the — **of the moment**
espontáneamente; VT espolear; **to** — **on**
animar

spurious [spjʊ́riəs] ADJ espurio

spurn [spɚn] VT rechazar, desdeñar

spurt [spɚt] VI salir a chorros; N (of water)
chorro *m*; (of a runner) esfuerzo repentino
m; **in** —**s** por rachas

sputter [spʌ́dɚ] VI (fire) chisporrotear;
(person) refunfuñar; N (fire) chisporroteo
m

sputum [spjútəm] N esputo *m*

spy [spaɪ] N espía *mf*; VI espiar; **to** — **on**
espiar, avizorar; —**glass** catalejo *m*

squabble [skwάbəł] VI reñir; N reyerta *f*

squad [skwad] N (of police) patrulla *f*; (for
execution) pelotón *m*; (of athletes) equipo
m; (for guarding) retén *m*; — **car** (coche)
patrullero *m*

squadron [skwάdrən] N (in navy) escuadra *f*;
(in army) escuadrón *m*

squalid [skwάlɪd] ADJ escuálido

squall [skwɔł] N (rain) chubasco *m*, borrasca
f; (sound) berrido *m*; VI berrear

squalor [skwάlɚ] N miseria *f*, escualidez *f*

squander [skwάndɚ] VT despilfarrar,
derrochar, disipar

squanderer [skwάndərɚ] N derrochador -ora
mf

square [skwɛr] N (shape) cuadrado *m*; (on a
pattern) cuadro *m*; (plaza) plaza *f*; (tool in
carpentry) escuadra *f*; (on chessboard)
casilla *f*; **he is a** — es muy conservador;
VT (make square) cuadrar; (draw squares
on) cuadricular; (multiply by itself) elevar
al cuadrado; **to** — **one's shoulders**
erguirse; ADJ (in shape) cuadrado; (at
ninety degrees) en ángulo recto; (tied)
empatado; (frank) franco; — **dance**
cuadrilla *f*; — **knot** nudo de rizo *m*; —
meal comida completa *f*; — **root** raíz
cuadrada *f*; **to be** — **with someone** estar
a mano con alguien; ADV **right** —
between the eyes justo entre los ojos

squash [skwaʃ] N (gourd) calabaza *f*; (sport)
squash *m*; VT aplastar, despachurrar

squat [skwɑt] VI (sit low) acuclillarse;
(occupy) ocupar sin autorización; ADJ
(sitting low) acuclillado; (thick set)
rechoncho, achaparrado; N **in a** — en
cuclillas

squawk [skwɔk] VI (of chickens) cacarear;
(complain) quejarse; N (of chickens)
cacareo *m*; (complaint) quejido *m*

squeak [skwik] VI (door) rechinar, chirriar;
(shoe) rechinar; (mouse) chillar; N (of
door) rechinamiento *m*, chirrido *m*; (of
shoe) rechinamiento *m*; (of mouse)
chillido *m*

squeaky [skwíki] ADJ (door) chirriante;

(shoes) rechinante

squeal [skwiɫ] VI chillar; (complain) protestar; (snitch) chivatar, delatar; N chillido *m*

squeamish [skwímɪʃ] ADJ delicado

squeegee [skwíʤi] N escurridor de goma *m*, limpiavidrios *m sg*

squeeze [skwiz] VT apretar; (press very hard) estrujar; (an orange) exprimir; (hug) abrazar; **to — into** meter(se) con dificultad en, encajar(se) en; **to — out** (an orange) exprimir; (a towel) escurrir; **to — through a crowd** abrirse paso entre la multitud; N (of hands) apretón *m*; (excessive squeeze) estrujón *m*; (hug) abrazo *m*; (lack) restricción *f*

squelch [skwɛɫʧ] VT (revolt) aplastar, sofocar; (criticism) acallar

squid [skwɪd] N calamar *m*

squint [skwɪnt] VI (partially close eyes) entrecerrar los ojos; (look askance) mirar de soslayo; N (look with partially closed eyes) mirada con los ojos entrecerrados *f*; (side-glance) mirada de soslayo *f*

squirm [skwɜˑm] VI retorcerse; **to — out of a difficulty** zafarse de un aprieto

squirrel [skwɜˑəɫ] N ardilla *f*

squirt [skwɜˑt] VT echar un chisguete en; VI salir a chorritos; N chisguete *m*, chorrito *m*; **— gun** pistola lanzaagua *f*, pistola de agua *f*

Sri Lanka [srilájŋkə] N Sri Lanka *f*

Sri Lankan [srilájŋkən] ADJ & N cingalés -esa *mf*

stab [stæb] VI/VT apuñalar, acuchillar; **to — at** tirar puñaladas a; N (with a dagger) puñalada *f*; (with a knife) cuchillada *f*; (with a pocketknife) navajazo *m*; (of pain) punzada *f*, pinchazo *m*; **— wound** cuchillada *f*

stability [stəbílɪɾi] N estabilidad *f*

stable [stébəɫ] ADJ estable; N establo *m*, cuadra *f*; (for horses) caballeriza *f*; VT poner en el establo

stack [stæk] N pila *f*, montón *m*; (of a chimney) chimenea *f*; (in a library) estantería *f*; VT amontonar, apilar

stadium [stédiəm] N estadio *m*

staff [stæf] N (stick) cayado *m*; (of a flag) asta *f*; (personnel) personal *m*, plantel *m*; (of music) pentagrama *m*; **— of life** pan de cada día *m*; **— officer** oficial de estado mayor *m*; **editorial —** redacción *f*; **teaching —** cuerpo docente *m*; VT contratar personal

stag [stæg] N (of deer) venado *m*, ciervo *m*; (of other animals) macho *m*; **— beetle**

ciervo volante *m*; **— party** fiesta para hombres *f*

stage [steʤ] N (showplace) escenario *m*; (for popular entertainment) tablado *m*; (theater) teatro *m*, las tablas *f pl*; (period) etapa *f*, estadio *m*; (distance) etapa *f*; **—coach** diligencia *f*; **— fright** miedo al escenario *m*, fiebre de candilejas *f*; **—hand** tramoyista *mf*; **by —s** por etapas; VT (a play) poner en escena; (an attack) organizar

stagger [stǽgɚ] VI (totter) tambalearse, dar tumbos; VT (hit hard) hacer tambalear; (overwhelm) dejar azorado; (alternate) escalonar; N tambaleo *m*

stagnant [stǽgnənt] ADJ estancado

stagnate [stǽgnet] VI estancarse

staid [sted] ADJ serio

stain [sten] VI/VT (spot) manchar(se); (color) teñir(se); **—ed-glass window** vitral *m*; N (spot) mancha *f*; (color) tinte *m*, tintura *f*

stainless [sténlɪs] ADJ sin mancha; **— steel** acero inoxidable *m*

stair [ster] N peldaño *m*, escalón *m*; **—case** escalera *f*; **—s** escalera *f*; **—way** escalera *f*

stake [stek] N (pole) estaca *f*; (investment) interés *m*; (bet) apuesta *f*; **at —** en juego; **to die at the —** morir en la hoguera; VT estacar; **to — out** vigilar

stalactite [stəlǽktaɪt] N estalactita *f*

stalagmite [stəlǽgmaɪt] N estalagmita *f*

stale [steɫ] ADJ (bread) duro; (air) viciado; (joke) viejo; **—mate** punto muerto *m*

stalk [stɔk] N tallo *m*; VT acechar

stall [stɔɫ] N (at a market) puesto *m*; (at a fair) caseta *f*, barraca *f*; (in a stable) compartimiento *m*; VI (airplane) entrar en pérdida; (talks) llegar a un punto muerto; (motor) pararse; **he is —ing** está arrastrando los pies; VT (airplane) hacer entrar en pérdida; (talks) paralizar; (motor) parar

stallion [stǽljən] N semental *m*

stamina [stǽmənə] N resistencia *f*, aguante *m*

stammer [stǽmɚ] VI balbucear; N balbuceo *m*

stamp [stæmp] VT (a letter) sellar; *Mex* timbrar; *Am* estampillar; (an official document) sellar, timbrar; (a coin) acuñar; VI (with foot) pisotear, patalear; (horse) piafar; **to — out** eliminar; N (on a letter) *Sp* sello *m*; *Mex* timbre *m*; *Am* estampilla *f*; (on an official document) sello *m*, timbre *m*; (instrument, character) sello *m*; (on the ground) pisotón *m*; (sound) paso *m*

stampede [stæmpíd] N estampida *f*; VI huir en estampida; VT hacer huir en estampida

stance [stæns] N posición f, postura f

stanch, staunch [stɔntʃ] VT restañar; ADJ (strong) firme; (loyal) fiel

stand [stænd] VI (take a standing position) ponerse de pie, levantarse; *Am* parar(se); (to be in a standing position) estar de pie; *Am* estar parado; (stop) detenerse; (withstand, tolerate) aguantar, tolerar, soportar; (remain valid) mantenerse; **—by** recurso viejo m; **—by passenger** pasajero -ra en la lista de espera mf; **to — aside** apartarse; **to — back** retroceder; **to — behind** respaldar; **to — by** (be uninvolved) mantenerse al margen; (be alert) estar alerta; (support) respaldar; **to — for** (mean) significar; (tolerate) tolerar; **to — one's ground** mantenerse firme; **to — out** destacarse, sobresalir; **to — up for** defender; **it —s to reason** es razonable; **it —s one meter tall** mide un metro de alto; **to — a chance of** tener posibilidad de; **where do you — on this issue?** ¿qué opinas al respecto? N (at a market) puesto m; (at a fair) caseta f; (of trees) bosque m; (opinion) posición f; (for taxis) atril m; (for music) atril m; (for taxis) parada f; **—off** empate m; **—point** punto de vista m; **to come to a —still** pararse; **to be at a —still** estar parado

standard [stændərd] N (of behavior) norma f; (of living, performance) nivel m; (of weights) patrón m; (banner) estandarte m; **gold —** patrón oro m; **to be up to —** satisfacer los requisitos; **—bearer** portaestandarte mf; **— of living** nivel de vida m; ADJ (normal) normal; (standardized) estándar; **— deviation** desviación estándar f; **— time** hora oficial f

standardization [stændərdɪzéʃən] N estandarización f

standardize [stændərdaɪz] VT estandarizar, uniformar

standing [stændɪŋ] N (position) posición f; (rank) rango m; (reputation) reputación f; ADJ (not seated) derecho, en pie; (permanent) permanente; (stagnant) estancado; **— order** pedido fijo m; **— ovation** ovación de pie f

stanza [stænzə] N estrofa f

staple [stépəl] N (for paper) grapa f; (main product) producto principal m; (food) alimento básico m; ADJ (principal) principal; (basic) básico; VT engrapar

stapler [stéplə] N grapadora f

star [star] N estrella f (also actor); (asterisk) asterisco m; **— attraction** atracción principal f; **—fish** estrella de mar f; **—light** luz de las estrellas f; **—-spangled** salpicado de estrellas; **a — student** un(a) estudiante sobresaliente; VT (act in) protagonizar; VI (put asterisk on) marcar con asterisco; (cover with stars) estrellar

starboard [stárbərd] N estribor m; ADV a estribor

starch [startʃ] N almidón m (also food); VT almidonar

stardom [stárdəm] N estrellato m

stare [ster] VI/VT mirar fijamente; N mirada fija f

stark [stark] ADJ (landscape) yermo; (truth) descarnado, desnudo; (contrast) marcado; **— naked** en cueros; **— raving mad** loco de remate

starling [stárlɪŋ] N estornino m

starry [stári] ADJ estrellado

start [start] VI/VT (begin) comenzar, empezar; (a car) poner(se) en marcha, arrancar; VT (a fire) provocar; VI (jump) sobresaltarse; **to — off / out / up** empezar; N (beginning) comienzo m, principio m; (of a race) salida f; (nervous jump) sobresalto m; (nervous jump of a horse) respingo m

starter [stártə] N (on an automobile) arranque m; (for a race) juez de salida m; **for —s** para empezar

startle [stárdl] VI/VT asustar(se), sobresaltar(se)

startling [stárdlɪŋ] ADJ asombroso, sorprendente

starvation [starvéʃən] N inanición f

starve [starv] VI/VT hambrear; VI morirse de hambre; VT matar de hambre; (for affection) privar de cariño

starving [stárvɪŋ] ADJ hambriento, muerto de hambre

stash [stæʃ] VI **to — away** ir ahorrando; N alijo m

state [stet] N estado m; **— of the art** con los últimos avances; **—room** (on a ship) camarote m; (on a train) compartimiento m; **—sman** estadista m; **—swoman** estadista f; VT (declare) declarar, aseverar, manifestar; (describe) exponer

stately [stétli] ADJ majestuoso, imponente

statement [stétmənt] N (declaration) declaración f, aseveración f; (bill) estado de cuentas m

static [stætɪk] ADJ estático; N interferencia f; **— electricity** electricidad estática f; **don't give me any —** no me compliques la vida

station [stéʃən] N estación f; (of radio) emisora f; (of television) canal m; (social

rank) condición *f*; — **wagon** camioneta *f*;
VT (a sentry) apostar; (troops) estacionar

stationary [stéʃəneri] ADJ (not moving)
estacionario; (stopped) detenido; (fixed)
fijo

stationery [stéʃəneri] N (material) artículos
de papelería *m pl*; (paper) papel de carta *m*

statistics [stətístɪks] N (science) estadística *f*;
(data) estadísticas *f pl*

statue [stǽtʃu] N estatua *f*

stature [stǽtʃɚ] N estatura *f*; (moral) talla *f*

status [stǽɾəs] N (prestige, rank) status *m*;
(legal, financial) situación *f*; (marital)
estado *m*; — **symbol** símbolo de status *m*

statute [stǽtʃut] N (by-law) estatuto *m*; (law)
ley *f*; — **of limitations** ley de
prescripción *f*

statutory rape [stǽtʃətɔrirép] N estupro *m*

stave [stev] N (of a barrel) duela *f*; VI **to** —
off evitar

stay [ste] VI (remain) quedarse, permanecer;
to — **away** mantenerse alejado; **to** — **in**
quedarse en casa; **to** — **out of trouble**
no meterse en líos; **to** — **up** quedarse
levantado; VT **to** — **an execution** aplazar
una ejecución; N (time spent) estancia *f*,
estadía *f*, permanencia *f*; (support) sostén
m, soporte *m*

STD (sexually transmitted disease) [estidí]
N ETS *f*

stead [sted] N **in her** — en su lugar; **to
stand one in good** — ser de provecho
para uno

steadfast [stédfæst] ADJ fijo, firme

steadiness [stédɪnɪs] N (firmness) firmeza *f*;
(of the hand) pulso *m*; (constancy)
constancia *f*; (continuity) continuidad *f*

steady [stédi] ADJ (not shaky) firme;
(constant) constante; (continuous)
continuo; — **boyfriend** novio formal *m*;
— **customer** cliente -ta asiduo -dua *mf*;
— **income** ingreso fijo *m*; VI/VT (an
object) asegurar; (nerves) calmar

steak [stek] N bistec *m*, churrasco *m*

steal [stil] VI/VT (a thing) robar, hurtar; (a
girlfriend) soplar; VI **to** — **away / out**
escabullirse, escaparse; N ganga *f*

stealth [stɛlθ] M sigilo *m*; **by** — furtivamente

stealthy [stélθi] ADJ furtivo

steam [stim] N (evaporated water) vapor *m*;
(arising from an object) vaho *m*; —
engine máquina de vapor *f*; — **roller**
apisonadora *f*, aplanadora *f*; — **ship**
(buque de) vapor *m*; — **shovel** excavadora
f; VT (cook) cocer al vapor; VI (give off
steam) echar vapor; **to get** —**ed up**
(angry) indignarse; (covered with vapor)

empañarse

steamer [stímɚ] N buque de vapor *m*

steed [stid] N corcel *m*

steel [stil] N acero *m*; — **blue** azul acero *m*;
— **industry** siderurgia *f*; — **mill** acería *f*;
— **wool** lana de acero *f*; VT acerar; **to** —
oneself prepararse

steep [stip] ADJ (hill) empinado, escarpado,
acantilado; (decline) marcado; (price)
excesivo; VT infusionar; VI estar en
infusión, infusionarse

steeple [stípəl] N (spire) aguja *f*, chapitel *m*;
(bell tower) campanario *m*

steer [stir] N (young) novillo *m*; (grown) buey
m; VI/VT (a car) conducir, manejar; (a ship)
gobernar, timonear; VI (turn) girar, doblar;
to — **clear of** evitar; **to** — **a
conversation** desviar una conversación;
the car —**s easily** el coche es fácil de
conducir; —**ing** dirección *f*; —**ing wheel**
volante *m*

stellar [stélɚ] ADJ estelar

stem [stem] N (of a plant) tallo *m*; (of a leaf)
pedúnculo *m*, rabo *m*; (of a glass) pie *m*;
(of a pipe) cañón *m*; — **cell** célula
estaminal / embrional *f*; VT detener,
contener, estancar; **to** — **from** provenir
de

stench [stɛntʃ] N hedor *m*, hediondez *f*, tufo
m

stencil [sténsəl] N plantilla *f*, matriz *f*

stenographer [stənágrəfɚ] N taquígrafo -fa
mf

step [step] N (in walking, dancing) paso *m*;
(on stairs) peldaño *m*, escalón *m*; (in
music) tono *m*; **to take** —**s to** tramitar;
— **by** — paso a paso; —**ladder** escalera *f*;
in — **with the music** al compás de la
música; **to take** —**s** (walk) dar pasos; (act)
tomar medidas; VI dar un paso; — **this
way** pase por aquí; **to** — **aside** hacerse a
un lado; **to** — **back** retroceder; **to** —
down (descend) bajar; (resign) renunciar;
to — **off** bajar; **to** — **off a distance**
medir a pasos una distancia; **to** — **on**
pisar, pisotear; **to** — **on the gas** pisar el
acelerador; **to** — **out** salir; **to** — **up** subir

stepbrother [stépbrʌðɚ] N hermanastro *m*

stepdaughter [stépdɔdɚ] N hijastra *f*

stepfather [stépfaðɚ] N padrastro *m*

stepmother [stépmʌðɚ] N madrastra *f*

steppe [step] N estepa *f*

stepsister [stépsɪstɚ] N hermanastra *f*

stepson [stépsʌn] N hijastro *m*

stereo [stério] ADJ & N estéreo *m*

stereotype [stériətaɪp] N estereotipo *m*

sterile [stérəl] ADJ estéril

sterility [stərílɪDi] N esterilidad *f*

sterilize [stérəlaɪz] VT esterilizar

stern [stɜ˞n] ADJ austero, severo, adusto; N popa *f*

sternum [stɜ˞nəm] N esternón *m*

steroid [stérɔɪd] N esteroide *m*

stethoscope [stéθəskop] N estetoscopio *m*

stew [stu] VI/VT (cook) estofar(se), guisar(se); VI (worry) preocuparse; N estofado *m*, guiso *m*; **to be in a** — estar preocupado

steward [stúwə˞d] N (manager) administrador *m*; (on a ship) camarero *m*; (on an airplane) auxiliar de vuelo *m*

stewardess [stúwə˞DIS] N (on a ship) camarera *f*; (on an airplane) azafata *f*

stick [stɪk] N (of wood) palo *m*, vara *f*; (of firewood) raja *f*; (of dynamite) cartucho *m*; **— shift** palanca de cambios *f*; **—-up** atraco *m*, asalto *m*; VI/VT (adhere) pegar(se), adherir(se); VT (place) poner, meter; (stab) clavar, pinchar; VI (become jammed) atascarse; **— 'em up!** ¡arriba las manos! **to — out** salir, sobresalir; **to — out one's head** asomar la cabeza; **to — out one's tongue** sacar la lengua; **to — to a job** persistir en una tarea; **to — up** estar parado de punta; **to — up for** defender; **to — someone up** asaltar / atracar a alguien

sticker [stíkə˞] N (thistle) abrojo *m*; (adhesive) etiqueta adhesiva *f*

sticky [stíki] ADJ pegajoso

stiff [stɪf] ADJ (leather, cardboard) tieso, duro; (drink) fuerte, cargado; (shirt) almidonado; (back) entumecido; (test) difícil; (breeze) fuerte; (personality) envarado; (climb) arduo; (price) alto; **to get** — entumecerse; N (cadaver) *fam* fiambre *m*

stiffen [stífən] VI/VT (leather) atiesar(se); (back) entumecer(se); (shirt) almidonar(se); **to — up** agarrotar(se)

stiffness [stífnɪs] N (of leather) dureza *f*, tiesura *f*; (of one's back) entumecimiento *m*; (of one's personality) envaramiento *m*; (of resistance) firmeza *f*

stifle [stáɪfəl] VI/VT ahogar(se), sofocar(se); **to — a yawn** contener un bostezo

stigma [stígmə] N estigma *m*

stigmatize [stígmətaɪz] VI/VT estigmatizar

still [stɪl] ADJ (not moving) quieto; (quiet) silencioso; **—born** nacido muerto; **— life** naturaleza muerta *f*; VT acallar; ADV todavía, aún; CONJ de todos modos; N (for distilling) alambique *m*; (quiet) silencio *m*

stillness [stílnɪs] N quietud *f*, silencio *m*

stilt [stɪlt] N (for walking) zanco *m*; (support) pilote *m*

stilted [stíltɪd] ADJ (personality) envarado; (style) afectado

stimulant [stímjələnt] ADJ & N estimulante *m*

stimulate [stímjəlet] VT estimular

stimulation [stɪmjəléʃən] N estimulación *f*

stimulus [stímjələs] N estímulo *m*

sting [stɪŋ] VI/VT (insects, thorns) picar; (insects) aguijonear; VT (shampoo) hacer picar; (rain) azotar; (cheat) timar; N (pain) picadura *f*; (stinger) aguijón *m*; (confidence game) golpe *m*; **— of remorse** punzada de remordimiento *f*; **—ray** manta raya *f*

stinger [stíŋə˞] N aguijón *m*

stinginess [stínʤinɪs] N tacañería *f*, mezquindad *f*

stingy [stínʤi] ADJ mezquino, tacaño

stink [stɪŋk] VI (smell bad) heder, apestar; **to — of** heder a; **to — up** dar mal olor a; **your performance stank** tu actuación fue un desastre; N hedor *m*

stipend [stáɪpɛnd] N (fellowship) beca *f*; (salary) estipendio *m*

stipulate [stípjəlet] VT estipular

stipulation [stɪpjəléʃən] N estipulación *f*

stir [stɜ˞] VI/VT (move) bullir, rebullir; VT (mix) revolver; (move emotionally) conmover; (awake) despertar; (stoke) atizar; **to — up** (trouble) provocar, suscitar; (an old grudge) remover; N **to give something a** — revolver algo; **to cause a** — causar revuelo; **—-crazy** claustrofóbico; **to —-fry** saltear

stirring [stɜ˞ɪŋ] ADJ conmovedor

stirrup [stɜ˞rəp] N estribo *m*

stitch [stɪtʃ] N puntada *f*; (on a wound) punto *m*; **to be in —es** desternillarse de risa; VI/VT coser

St. Kitts and Nevis [sɛntkítsənnívɪs] N San Cristóbal y Nieves *m*

St. Lucia [sɛntlúʃə] N Santa Lucía *f*

St. Lucian [sɛntlúʃən] ADJ & N santalucense *mf*

stock [stɑk] N (selection) surtido *m*; (reserves) existencias *f pl*; (livestock) ganado *m*; (lineage) estirpe *f*; (shares) acciones *f pl*, valores *m pl*; (in grafting) patrón *m*; (broth) caldo *m*; **out of** — agotado; **in —** en existencia; ADJ (common) trillado; **—broker** corredor -ra de bolsa *mf*, bolsista *mf*; **— company** sociedad anónima *f*; **— exchange** bolsa de valores *f*; **—holder** accionista *mf*; **— market** mercado de valores *m*, bolsa de valores *f*; **— options** opciones *f pl*; **—pile** acopio *m*; **—room** depósito *m*; **— size** tamaño ordinario *m*; **—yard** corral *m*; VT (sell) vender; (fill shelves) abastecer; **to — up on** surtirse de, acumular; **to —pile** acopiar

stockade [stəkéd] N (fence) estacada *f*, empalizada *f*; (prison) prisión militar *f*

stocking [stákɪŋ] N (hose) media *f*; (sock) calcetín *m*

stocky [stáki] ADJ robusto

stoic [stóɪk] ADJ & N estoico -ca *mf*

stoke [stok] VT (fire) atizar; (engine) alimentar

stomach [stámək] N (organ) estómago *m*; (belly) panza *f*, barriga *f*; **he has a big —** es barrigón; **to lie on one's —** estar panza abajo; VT aguantar

stomp [stamp] VI pisar fuerte; VT (crush) pisotear; (defeat) aplastar

stone [ston] N (rock, gem) piedra *f*; (in fruit) hueso *m*; (in kidneys) cálculo *m*; **within a —'s throw** a tiro de piedra; **— Age** Edad de Piedra *f*; **—-deaf** sordo como una tapia; VT (a person) lapidar; (a fruit) deshuesar; **to get —d** *fam* volarse; *Sp fam* colocarse

stony [stóni] ADJ (made of stone) pétreo; (driveway) pedregoso; (silence) sepulcral

stool [stuł] N (furniture) taburete *m*, banqueta *f*; (excrement) materia fecal *f*; **—pigeon** soplón -ona *mf*, chivato -ta *mf*

stoop [stup] VI (bend over) agacharse; (have bad posture) encorvarse; **to — to** rebajarse a; N (posture) encorvamiento *m*; (porch) entrada *f*, porche *m*; **to walk with a —** andar encorvado; **—-shouldered** encorvado, cargado de espaldas

stop [stap] VI (halt) parar, detenerse; (malfunction) parar(se); VT (halt) parar, detener; (cancel) cancelar; (suspend) suspender; (plug) tapar; **to — at nothing** no tener escrúpulos; **to — by/in** visitar; **to — from** impedir; **to — over at** hacer escala en; **to — short** parar en seco; **to — up** tapar, atascar; **it —ped raining** paró/dejó de llover; N parada *f*, detención *f*; (on organ) registro *m*; **—gap** arreglo provisorio *m*; **—light** semáforo *m*; **—over** escala *f*; **— sign** *Sp* stop *m*; *Am* señal de pare *f*; *Mex* alto *m*; **—watch** cronómetro *m*; **to bring to a —** parar; **to make a —** parar

stoppage [stápɪʤ] N interrupción *f*; (strike) huelga *f*

stopper [stápə] N tapón *m*

storage [stórɪʤ] N almacenaje *m*, almacenamiento *m*; **— battery** acumulador *m*; **to keep in —** almacenar

store [stɔr] N (shop) tienda *f*, almacén *m*; (supply) reserva *f*, provisión *f*; **—house** (warehouse) almacén *m*, depósito *m*; (source) mina *f*, fuente *f*; **—keeper** tendero -ra *mf*, almacenista *mf*; **—room** almacén *m*, depósito *m*; **what is in — for us?** ¿Qué nos espera? VT (commercial goods) almacenar; (personal effects) guardar; **to — up** acumular

stork [stɔrk] N cigüeña *f*

storm [stɔrm] N tormenta *f*; (at sea) tempestad *f*, temporal *m*; (of protest) ola *f*; **— troops** tropas de asalto *f pl*; VT tomar por asalto; VI **to — in/out** entrar/salir en tromba

stormy [stɔ́rmi] ADJ tormentoso, tempestuoso

story [stɔ́ri] N (tale) cuento *m*, historia *f*; (newspaper article) artículo *m*; (lie) mentira *f*; (information) información *f*; (plot) argumento *m*, trama *f*; (floor) piso *m*

stout [staʊt] ADJ (fat) corpulento; (robust) robusto, fornido; (strong) fuerte; (courageous) valiente

stove [stov] N (for heating) estufa *f*; (for cooking) cocina *f*; *Mex* estufa *f*

stow [sto] VT (keep) guardar; (hide) esconder; (put in cargo hold) estibar; **to — away on a ship** viajar de polizón

stowaway [stóəwe] N polizón -ona *mf*

straddle [strǽdḷ] VI/VT estar a horcajadas; VT (a fence) ponerse a horcajadas; (one's legs) abrir; (not take sides) no comprometerse

strafe [stref] VT ametrallar

straggle [strǽgəl] VI **to — along/behind** rezagarse; **to — in** entrar de a pocos

straight [stret] ADJ (not curved) recto; (not tilted) derecho; (in succession) seguido; (hair) lacio, liso; (teeth) parejo; (frank) franco; (heterosexual) heterosexual; **— A's** sobresaliente en todo; **— face** cara seria *f*; **— flush** escalera de color *f*; **—forward** campechano; **—edge** regla *f*; ADV **— ahead** todo derecho, todo recto; **for two hours —** dos horas seguidas; **to come — home** volver derecho a casa; **to leave — after lunch** irse justo después de comer; **to set a person —** aclararle algo a alguien; **tell me —** dímelo francamente; **he can't think —** no puede pensar con claridad; **—forward** (honest) honesto; (simple) sencillo; (clear) claro

straighten [strétṇ] VI/VT enderezar(se); (situation) arreglar(se); VT (hair) alisar, *RP* laciar; **to — out a child** enderezar a un niño

straightness [strétnɪs] N derechura *f*

strain [stren] VI (pull) tironear; (try hard)

esforzarse; VT (exhaust) agotar; (hurt voice) forzar; (injure a joint) torcer; (injure a muscle) sufrir un tirón en; (hurt a relationship) crear una tirantez en; VI/VT (filter) colar(se); N (effort) esfuerzo *m*; (injury) torcedura *f*; (pressure) presión *f*; (trouble in a relationship) tirantez *f*; (lineage) cepa *f*; (style) veta *f*

strainer [strénə] N colador *m*

strait [stret] N estrecho *m*; **in dire —s** en aprietos; ADJ **—jacket** camisa de fuerza *f*, chaleco de fuerza *m*; **—laced** puritano

strand [strænd] VI/VT (a ship) encallar, varar; VT (a person) dejar plantado; **to be —ed** (boat) estar encallado; (person) quedar plantado; N (beach) costa *f*, playa *f*; (of rope) ramal *m*; (of thread) hebra *f*; (of hair) mechón *m*

strange [strendʒ] ADJ (bizarre) extraño, raro; (unknown) desconocido

strangeness [stréndʒnɪs] N (unusualness) lo extraño, rareza *f*; (unexpectedness) lo inesperado

stranger [stréndʒə] N (unknown person) extraño -ña *mf*, desconocido -da *mf*; (outsider) forastero -ra *mf*; **to be no — to something** saber bien lo que es algo

strangle [stræŋgəl] VI/VT estrangular(se); **—hold** (in wrestling) llave al cuello *f*; (in markets) monopolio *m*; VT (creativity) coartar

strap [stræp] N (leather band) correa *f*, tira *f*; (on a dress) tirante *m*; VT atar con correa; **to —** in amarrar(se)

stratagem [strétədʒəm] N estratagema *f*

strategic [strətídʒɪk] ADJ estratégico

strategy [strétədʒi] N estrategia *f*

stratosphere [strǽdəsfɪr] N estratosfera *f*

stratum [strǽdəm] N estrato *m*

straw [strɔ] N paja *f* (also for drinking); **—berry** fresa *f*; **—-colored** pajizo; **— man** testaferro *m*; **— vote** votación de prueba *f*

stray [stre] VI (deviate, digress) desviarse; (get lost) perderse; (wander) vagar; (morally) descarriarse, perderse; ADJ extraviado, perdido; N perro/gato mostrenco *m*

streak [strik] N (line) raya *f*; (vein) vena *f*; (of luck) racha *f*; (of light) rayo *m*; VI (run naked) correr desnudo; (get discolored) aclararse

stream [strim] N (jet) chorro *m*; (river) río *m*; (brook) arroyo *m*; VI (water) correr, fluir; (blood) derramar; **—lined** aerodinámico; **to — out** brotar, manar; **to — in** entrar a raudales

street [strit] N calle *f*; **—car** tranvía *f*;

—lamp/lamp farol *m*, poste de alumbrado *m*; **— sweeper** barrendero -ra *mf*; **—walker** prostituta *f*

strength [streŋθ] N fuerza *f*; (spiritual) firmeza *f*; **on the — of** en base a

strengthen [stréŋθən] VI/VT fortalecer(se), reforzar(se)

strenuous [strénjuəs] ADJ arduo

strep throat [strépθrót] N infección por estreptococo *f*

stress [stres] N (tension) tensión *f*; (strain) estrés *m*; (pressure) esfuerzo *m*; (emphasis) énfasis *m*; (accent) acento *m*; VT (emphasize) enfatizar; (accentuate) acentuar; (exert force) someter a un esfuerzo; (put under pressure) estresar; **to — out** estresar

stretch [stretʃ] VI/VT (make or become longer) estirar(se), alargar(se); (extend) extender(se); (exaggerate) exagerar; **to — oneself** estirarse, desperezarse; **to — out** (lengthen) extender(se); (lie) tumbarse, tenderse; N (act of stretching) desperezo *m*; (length) trecho *m*, tramo *m*, tirada *f*; (period) período *m*; (exaggeration) exageración *f*; **— mark** estría *f*

stretcher [strétʃə] N camilla *f*

strew [stru] VT esparcir

stricken [stríkən] ADJ (with disease) aquejado; (by a flood) afectado; (with fear) aterrado

strict [strɪkt] ADJ estricto; **in — confidence** en absoluta confianza

stride [straɪd] VI caminar a paso largo, dar zancadas; N (gait) paso *m*; (long step) zancada *f*, tranco *m*

strident [stráɪdənt] ADJ estridente

strife [straɪf] N conflictos *m pl*

strike [straɪk] VI/VT (hit) golpear, pegar; (stop work) hacer huelga (contra); VT (find) dar con, encontrar; (occur to) ocurrírsele a uno; (cross out) tachar; (mark by chimes) dar; (light) encender; (coin) acuñar; **to — a compromise** llegar a un acuerdo; **to — one's fancy** antojársele a uno; **to — out** (cross out) tachar; (set forth) encaminarse; (fail) fracasar; **to — up a conversation** entablar conversación; **to — up a friendship** trabar amistad; **how does she — you?** ¿qué tal te parece? N (work stoppage) huelga *f*; (attack) ataque *m*; (finding of oil) descubrimiento *m*; **—breaker** esquirol *m*, rompehuelgas *m sg*

striker [stráɪkə] N (person on strike) huelguista *mf*; (of a bell) badajo *m*

striking [stráɪkɪŋ] ADJ (unusual, conspicuous) notable; (attractive) llamativo; (on strike) en huelga

string [strɪŋ] N (cord) cuerda *f*, cordel *m*; (of pearls, lies) sarta *f*; (of questions) serie *f*; (of beans) fibra *f*; (of garlic) ristra *f*; — **bean** habichuela *f*, judía verde *f*; —**s** cuerdas *f pl*; VT (beads) ensartar; (a musical instrument) encordar; **to — along** tener en ascuas; **to — out** extender(se), prolongar(se); **to — up** colgar, ahorcar; **to be strung out** estar muy tenso

stringent [strínʤənt] ADJ (law, need) riguroso; (time limit) estrecho, ajustado

strip [strɪp] VI/VT (make/get naked) desnudar(se); VT (remove bark) descortezar; (remove leaves) deshojar; (remove sheets) deshacer; (remove varnish) quitar el barniz; (damage gears) estropear el engranaje; **to —-mine** explotar a cielo abierto; N tira *f*; (of land) faja *f*; — **mall** centro comercial *m*; —**tease** strip-tease *m*

stripe [straɪp] N (band) raya *f*, lista *f*, banda *f*; (military insignia) galón *m*; (type) tipo *m*

striped [straɪpt, stráɪpɪd] ADJ listado, rayado

stripper [strípɚ] N striptisero -ra *mf*

strive [straɪv] VI esforzarse por, luchar por

stroke [strok] N (in golf, tennis, of luck, of genius) golpe *m*; (cerebral hemorrhage) derrame cerebral *m*; (movement in swimming) brazada *f*; (style in swimming) estilo *m*; (of a piston) carrera *f*; (of a painter's brush) pincelada *f*; (of lightning) rayo *m*; **at the — of ten** al dar las diez; VT (pet) acariciar; (praise) halagar

stroll [strol] VI dar un paseo, pasearse; N paseo *m*, caminata *f*

stroller [strólɚ] N cochecito de bebé *m*

strong [strɔŋ] ADJ fuerte; (husky) recio; (eyesight, probability) bueno; (protest) enérgico; (views, faith, support) firme; (features, resemblance) marcado; (argument) sólido; —**hold** (fortress) fortaleza *f*; (center of activity) baluarte *m*; —**-willed** (resolute) resuelto, decidido; (stubborn) terco; **to —-arm** intimidar; ADV **to be going** — seguir activo

structural [strʌ́ktʃɚəl] ADJ estructural

structure [strʌ́ktʃɚ] N (manner of construction) estructura *f*; (thing constructed) construcción *f*

struggle [strʌ́gəl] VI (with difficulties) luchar, bregar; (with an assailant) forcejear; **she —s in math** la pasa mal en matemáticas; N lucha *f*; (of ideas) pugna *f*, lucha *f*; (fight) contienda *f*, forcejeo *m*; **it's a —** da mucho trabajo

strut [strʌt] VI pavonearse; N pavoneo *m*;

(support) tirante *m*, puntal *m*; (on a car) amortiguador *m*

strychnine [stríknaɪn] N estricnina *f*

stub [stʌb] N talón *m*; VT **to — one's toe** dar(se) un tropezón, reventarse el dedo

stubble [stʌ́bəl] N (of a crop) rastrojo *m*; (of a beard) barba de unos días *f*

stubborn [stʌ́bɚn] ADJ terco, testarudo

stubbornness [stʌ́bɚnnɪs] N terquedad *f*, testarudez *f*

stucco [stʌ́ko] N estuco *m*; VT estucar

stuck [stʌk] ADJ atascado; **to be — on someone** estar loco por alguien; —-**up** estirado, presumido

stud [stʌd] N (knob) tachuela *f*; (earring) arete *m*; (cufflink) gemelo *m*; (on shirtfront) botón *m*; (horse, man) semental *m*, garañón *m*; VT tachonar

student [stúdṇt] N alumno -na *mf*; (secondary, university) estudiante *mf*; — **body** alumnado *m*; ADJ estudiantil *m*

studio [stúdɪo] N estudio *m*, taller *m*; — **apartment** estudio *m*

studious [stúdɪəs] ADJ estudioso

study [stʌ́di] N estudio *m*; VT estudiar

stuff [stʌf] N (material) materia *f*, material *m*; (things) trastos *m pl*, bártulos *m pl*; (cloth) paño *m*, tela *f*; (affair) cosa *f*; (junk) cachivaches *m pl*; VT (mattress) rellenar; (dead animal) embalsamar, disecar; **to — into** meter en; **I'm —ed** estoy lleno

stuffing [stʌ́fɪŋ] N relleno *m*

stuffy [stʌ́fi] ADJ (person) envarado; (air) viciado

stumble [stʌ́mbəl] VI (trip) tropezar, trastabillar, dar un traspié; (stutter) balbucear; **to — out** salir a tropezones; **to — upon** tropezar con; N tropezón *m*, tropiezo *m*, traspié *m*; **stumbling block** obstáculo *m*

stump [stʌmp] N (of a tree) tocón *m*, cepa *f*; (of a tooth) raigón *m*; (of a limb) muñón *m*; **to be on the —** hacer una campaña electoral; VT (baffle) dejar perplejo; (remove stumps) arrancar los tocones de; **to — the country** recorrer el país haciendo campaña

stun [stʌn] VT (shock, surprise) dejar atónito, pasmar; (render unconscious) dejar sin sentido; — **gun** pistola tranquilizante *f*

stunning [stʌ́nɪŋ] ADJ (shocking) pasmoso; (beautiful) elegante, bellísimo

stunt [stʌnt] VT (stop growth) atrofiar; (do acrobatic tricks) hacer acrobacia; N (feat) acrobacia *f*; (for publicity) maniobra *f*; —**man** doble *m*; —**woman** doble *f*; **to pull a —** hacerse el listo

stupefy [stúpəfaɪ] VT (make lethargic) atontar, embrutecer; (astonish) dejar estupefacto, alelar

stupendous [stupéndəs] ADJ estupendo

stupid [stúpɪd] ADJ tonto, estúpido, majadero

stupidity [stupídɪti] N tontería f, estupidez f, majadería f

stupor [stúpɚ] N estupor m

sturdy [stɜ́ɾdi] ADJ (person) fornido, fuerte; (construction) sólido, robusto

stutter [stáɾɚ] VI tartamudear, tartajear; VT decir tartamudeando; N (act of stuttering) tartamudeo m; (speech defect) tartamudez f

stutterer [stáɾərɚ] N tartamudo -da mf

stuttering [stáɾərɪŋ] ADJ tartamudo; N (act of stuttering) tartamudeo m; (speech defect) tartamudez f

St. Vincent and the Grenadines [sentvínsəntənðəgrénədinz] N San Vicente y las Granadinas m

sty [staɪ] N (for pigs) pocilga f; (in eye) orzuelo m

style [staɪl] N estilo m; (type) modelo m; **out of —** fuera de moda; **like it's going out of —** como loco; VT (a book) intitular; (hair) peinar; **he —s himself Professor Smith** se hace llamar Profesor Smith

stylish [stáɪlɪʃ] ADJ elegante, de moda

stymie, stymy [stáɪmi] VT obstaculizar

Styrofoam[tm] [stáɪrəfom] N poliestireno m

suave [swɑv] ADJ urbano, educado

subconscious [sʌbkánʃəs] ADJ subconsciente

subcontract [sʌbkántrækt] VT subcontratar

subdivision [sʌbdɪvɪʒən] N subdivisión f; (of land) parcelación f

subdue [səbdú] VT (overcome, vanquish) sojuzgar, someter, rendir; (repress) reprimir; (attenuate) atenuar

subdued [səbdúd] ADJ (atmosphere) tranquilo; (mood) deprimido; (lighting, color) tenue

subject [sʌbʤkt] N (of a king) súbdito -ta mf; (of a sentence, in an experiment) sujeto m; (in school) asignatura f, materia f; **— matter** tema m; ADJ **— to** (changes, laws, conditions) sujeto a; (depression, earthquakes) propenso a; [səbʤékt] VT someter

subjection [səbʤékʃən] N sometimiento m

subjective [səbʤéktɪv] ADJ subjetivo

subjugate [sʌbʤəget] VT sojuzgar, avasallar

subjunctive [səbʤʌ́ŋktɪv] ADJ & N subjuntivo m

sublet [sʌblét] VI/VT subarrendar

sublime [səbláɪm] ADJ sublime

submarine [sʌbmərín] ADJ submarino; [sábmərin] N submarino m

submerge [səbmɜ́ʤ] VI/VT sumergir(se)

submission [səbmíʃən] N (humility) sumisión f; (subjugation) sometimiento m, sumisión f; (sending) entrega f, envío m

submissive [səbmísɪv] ADJ sumiso

submit [səbmít] VI/VT someter(se); (to a judge) elevar(se); **to — a report** presentar un informe

subordinate [səbórdṇɪt] ADJ & N subordinado -da mf, subalterno -na mf; [səbórdṇet] VT subordinar

subpoena [səpína] N citación f, orden de comparecencia f

subroutine [sábrutin] N subrutina f

subscribe [səbskráɪb] VI (underwrite, sign) suscribir; (receive a magazine) abonarse, suscribirse; (agree with) adherirse a

subscriber [səbskráɪbɚ] N (to shares) suscriptor -ora mf; (to services) abonado -da mf; (to a magazine) suscriptor -ora mf, abonado -da mf; (to an idea) partidario -ria mf

subscription [səbskrípʃən] N suscripción f, abono m

subsequent [sábsɪkwənt] ADJ subsiguiente

subservient [səbsɜ́·viənt] ADJ servil

subside [səbsáɪd] VI (sediment) hundirse; (water level) bajar; (volcano, storm, anger) calmarse, aquietarse

subsidiary [səbsídiɛri] ADJ subsidiario; N sucursal f

subsidize [sábsɪdaɪz] VT subvencionar

subsidy [sábsɪdi] N subvención f

substance [sábstəns] N sustancia f; **— abuse** abuso de sustancias m

substantial [səbstǽnʃəl] ADJ (changes) sustancial; (food, lecture) sustancioso; (furniture) sólido; (amount) considerable, importante; **to be in — agreement** estar básicamente de acuerdo

substantiate [səbstǽnʃiet] VT (verify) verificar; (prove) probar

substantive [sábstəntɪv] ADJ & N sustantivo m

substitute [sábstɪtut] VT **I —d water for milk** usé agua en vez de leche, sustituí/ reemplacé la leche por agua; VI **John —d for Mary** Juan sustituyó/reemplazó a María; N (one who substitutes) sustituto m, reemplazo m; (teacher, athlete) suplente -ta mf; (thing) sucedáneo m

substitution [sʌbstɪtúʃən] N sustitución f; **the — of water for milk** la sustitución de leche por agua

subterfuge [sábtɚfjuʤ] N subterfugio m

subterranean [sʌbtəréniən] ADJ subterráneo

subtitle [sábtaɪdl] N subtítulo *m*
subtle [sádl] ADJ sutil
subtlety [sádlti] N sutileza *f*
subtract [səbtrǽkt] VT (deduct) restar; (take away) sustraer
subtraction [səbtrǽkʃən] N sustracción *f*, resta *f*
suburb [sábɚb] N barrio residencial periférico *m*
suburban [səbɚbən] ADJ (residential) residencial; (on the outskirts) periférico
subversive [səbvɚsɪv] ADJ subversivo
subway [sábwe] N metropolitano *m*, metro *m*, subterráneo *m*
succeed [səksíd] VI (be successful) tener éxito; (manage) lograr; **to — to** heredar; VT (follow) suceder a
success [səksɛ́s] N éxito *m*
successful [səksɛ́sfəl] ADJ exitoso; **to be —** tener éxito
succession [səksɛ́ʃən] N sucesión *f*
successive [səksɛ́sɪv] ADJ sucesivo
successor [səksɛ́sɚ] N sucesor -ora *mf*
succinct [səksíŋkt] ADJ sucinto, escueto
succor [sákɚ] N socorro *m*; VT socorrer
succumb [səkám] VI sucumbir
such [sʌtʃ] ADJ tal; **he's — an idiot!** ¡es tan idiota! **in — a case** en tal caso/en semejante caso; **— as tal como; at — and — a place** en tal o cual lugar; **there's no — thing** eso no existe; PRON **hobbies, pastimes, and —** hobbies, pasatiempos y cosas por el estilo; **a car — as yours** un coche como el tuyo; ADV **— nice neighbors** vecinos tan simpáticos
suck [sʌk] VI/VT chupar; (suckle) mamar; (vacuum, pump) aspirar; (perform fellatio) *vulg* mamarla; **to be —ed into** ser arrastrado a; VI **this book —s!** *vulg* ¡este libro es una cagada! **to — in** (air) aspirar; (stomach) meter; (fools) timar; **to — up to someone** *vulg* lamerle el culo a alguien; N chupada *f*; (sexual) *vulg* mamada *f*
sucker [sákɚ] N (gullible person) primo -ma *mf*; (lollipop) *Sp* pirulí *m*; *Mex* paleta *f*; *RP* chupetín *m*
suction [sákʃən] N succión *f*, aspiración *f*
Sudan [sudǽn] N Sudán *m*
Sudanese [sudníz] ADJ & N sudanés -esa *mf*
sudden [sádn] ADJ súbito, repentino, brusco; **all of a —** de repente, de improviso
suddenness [sádnnɪs] N brusquedad *f*, lo repentino
suds [sʌdz] N espuma *f*
sue [su] VI/VT demandar, poner pleito; **to — for** pedir, suplicar; **to — for damages**

demandar por daños y perjuicios
suede [swed] N gamuza *f*, ante *m*
suffer [sáfɚ] VI/VT (feel pain) sufrir, padecer; VT (tolerate) tolerar
sufferer [sáfɚɚ] N paciente *mf*
suffering [sáfɚɪŋ] N sufrimiento *m*, padecimiento *m*
suffice [səfáɪs] VI/VT bastar, ser suficiente
sufficient [səfíʃənt] ADJ suficiente, bastante
suffix [sáfɪks] N sufijo *m*
suffocate [sáfəket] VI/VT ahogar(se), sofocar(se); (to die, kill) asfixiar(se)
suffocation [sʌfəkéʃən] N ahogo *m*, sofoco *m*
suffrage [sáfrɪʤ] N sufragio *m*
sugar [ʃúgɚ] N azúcar *m/f*; (endearment) cariño *m*; **— cane** caña de azúcar *f*; VT azucarar; **to — the pill** dorar la píldora
suggest [səgʤɛ́st] VT (propose) sugerir; (hint) insinuar
suggestion [səgʤɛ́stʃən] N (proposal) sugerencia *f*; (in hypnosis) sugestión *f*
suggestive [səgʤɛ́stɪv] ADJ insinuante; **to be — of** evocar
suicide [súɪsaɪd] N (act) suicidio *m*; (person) suicida *mf*; **to commit —** suicidarse
suit [sut] N traje *m*; (in cards) palo *m*, color *m*; (lawsuit) demanda *f*, pleito *m*, querella *f*; **—case** maleta *f*, valija *f*; VT (adapt) adaptar, ajustar; (satisfy) satisfacer; (look good) quedarle bien a, sentarle bien a; (be convenient, appropriate) convenir, venir bien; **— yourself** haz lo te parezca
suitable [súɪʤəbəl] ADJ (appropriate) apropiado; (apt) apto
suitably [súɪʤəbli] ADV como corresponde
suite [swit] N (series) serie *f*; (series of rooms, musical composition) suite *f*; (furniture) juego *m*
suitor [súɾɚ] N pretendiente *m*, galán *m*
sulk [sʌlk] VI enfurruñarse; N **to be in a —** estar enfurruñado
sulky [sálki] ADJ malhumorado, enfurruñado
sullen [sálən] ADJ hosco, huraño
sully [sáli] VT mancillar, ensuciar
sulphate, sulfate [sálfet] N sulfato *m*
sulphide, sulfide [sálfaɪd] N sulfuro *m*
sulphur, sulfur [sálfɚ] N azufre *m*
sulphuric, sulfuric [sʌlfjúrɪk] ADJ sulfúrico
sultry [sáltri] ADJ (hot) bochornoso, sofocante; (sensual) sensual
sum [sʌm] N suma *f*, adición *f*; **in —** en resumen; VI **to — up** resumir, recapitular
summarize [sámɚaɪz] VI/VT resumir
summary [sámɚi] N resumen *m*; ADJ sumario
summer [sámɚ] N verano *m*, estío *m*; **— resort** balneario *m*, lugar de veraneo *m*;

— school cursos de verano *m pl;* **—time** verano *m;* vi veranear

summit [sÁmɪt] N cumbre *f,* cima *f*

summon [sÁmən] vt (witness) citar; (employee, police) llamar; N **—s** citación judicial *f*

sumptuous [sÁmptʃuəs] ADJ suntuoso

sun [sʌn] N sol *m;* **to — bathe** tomar el sol; **—beam** rayo de sol *m;* **—block** protector solar *m;* **—burn** quemadura de sol *f;* **to —burn** quemar(se) al sol; **—dial** reloj de sol *m;* **—down** puesta de(l) sol *f;* **—flower** girasol *m;* **—glasses** gafas de sol *f pl,* anteojos de sol *m pl;* **— lamp** lámpara solar *f;* **—light** luz del sol *f;* **—rise** salida de(l) sol *f,* amanecer *m;* **—screen** protector solar *m;* **—set** puesta de(l) sol *f;* **—shine** luz (del sol) *f;* **—spot** mancha solar *f;* **—stroke** insolación *f;* **—tan** bronceado *m;* **—up** salida del sol *f;* vi **to — oneself** tomar el sol

Sunday [sándé] N domingo *m;* **— school** escuela dominical *f*

sundry [sándri] ADJ diversos

sunny [sáni] ADJ (day, patio) soleado; (disposition) alegre

super [súpɚ] N conserje *m;* ADJ súper, bárbaro

superb [supɚb] ADJ excelente

supercharger [súpɚtʃɑrdʒɚ] N sobrealimentador *m*

supercomputer [súpɚkəmpjudɚ] N *Am* supercomputadora *f; Sp* superordenador *m*

superego [supɚígo] N superego *m,* superyó *m*

superficial [supɚfíʃəl] ADJ superficial

superfluous [supɚ́fluəs] ADJ superfluo

superhuman [supɚhjúmən] ADJ sobrehumano

superimpose [supɚɪmpóz] vt superponer, sobreponer

superintendent [supɚɪnténdənt] N (of work) superintendente *mf,* supervisor -ora *mf;* (of building) portero -ra *mf,* conserje *mf*

superior [supíriɚ] ADJ & N superior *m*

superiority [supiriɔ́rɪdi] N superioridad *f*

superlative [supɚ́lədɪv] ADJ & N superlativo *m*

supermarket [súpɚmɑrkɪt] N supermercado *m*

supernatural [supɚnǽtʃɚəl] ADJ sobrenatural

superpower [súpɚpauɚ] N superpotencia *f*

superscript [súpɚskrɪpt] N número volado *m*

supersede [supɚsíd] vt reemplazar

supersonic [supɚsánɪk] ADJ supersónico

superstar [súpɚstɑr] N superestrella *f*

superstition [supɚstíʃən] N superstición *f*

superstitious [supɚstíʃəs] ADJ supersticioso

supervise [súpɚvaɪz] vi/vt supervisar

supervision [supɚvíʒən] N supervisión *f*

supervisor [súpɚvaɪzɚ] N supervisor -ra *mf*

supper [sápɚ] N cena *f*

supplant [səplǽnt] vt suplantar

supple [sápəl] ADJ (flexible) flexible, elástico; (agile) ágil, grácil

supplement [sápləmənt] N (of a newspaper) suplemento *m;* (of a book) apéndice *m;* (of one's diet) complemento *m;* [sápləmənt] vt complementar, suplementar

supply [səplái] vt abastecer, suministrar; N (act of supplying) abastecimiento *m;* **— and demand** oferta y demanda *f;* **supplies** suministros *m pl,* provisiones *f pl;* **office supplies** artículos de oficina *m pl;* **military supplies** pertrechos *m pl;* **in short —** escaso

support [səpórt] vt (keep from falling) sostener, soportar; (encourage) mantener, apoyar; (corroborate) corroborar; N (of a structure) sostén *m,* soporte *m;* (of a family) sustento *m;* (of a candidate, idea) apoyo *m;* (of a theory) respaldo *m;* **— group** grupo de apoyo *m*

supporter [səpórdɚ] N partidario -ria *mf;* (in sports) hincha *mf*

suppose [səpóz] vt suponer; **we are —d to go** tenemos que ir

supposition [sápəzíʃən] N suposición *f,* supuesto *m*

suppository [səpázɪtɔri] N supositorio *m*

suppress [səprés] vt (repress) reprimir; (eliminate) suprimir; (a revolt) sofocar

suppression [səpréʃən] N (repression) represión *f;* (elimination) supresión *f*

supremacy [suprémɘsi] N supremacía *f*

supreme [suprím] ADJ supremo

surcharge [sɚ́tʃɑrdʒ] N recargo *m,* prima *f*

sure [ʃur] ADJ seguro; (judgment) certero; (hand) firme; **to make — of** asegurarse de; ADV **he — drinks a lot** es una esponja; **may I sit here? —!** ¿me puedo sentar? ¡cómo no!

surely [ʃúrli] ADV seguramente, ciertamente; **— you jest** no hablarás en serio; **he will — come** seguramente vendrá

surf [sɚf] N (breaking waves) rompientes *mf pl;* (foam) espuma *f;* (undertow) resaca *f;* **—board** tabla de surf *f;* vi/vt (on water) hacer surfing (en), surfear; (on Internet) navegar, surfear

surface [sɚ́fɪs] N superficie *f;* (of a solid) cara *f;* vi (come to top) emerger; (turn up) salir a la luz; vt (a submarine) sacar a la superficie; (a road) revestir

surfeit [sɚ́fɪt] N (excess) exceso *m;* (feeling of

fullness) hartazgo *m*; VI/VT hartar(se)
surfing [sə́·fɪŋ] N surfing *m*
surge [sə·ʤ] N (of people, disgust) oleada *f*; (of waves) oleaje *m*; (of electricity) tensión *f*; VI (people) precipitarse; (current) subir; — **protector** protector de tensión *m*
surgeon [sə́·ʤən] N cirujano -na *mf*
surgery [sə́·ʤəri] N cirujía *f*; (room) quirófano *m*
surgical [sə́·ʤɪkəl] ADJ quirúrgico
Surinam, Suriname [súrɪnam(ə)] N Surinam *m*
Surinamese [sʊrɪnɑmíz] ADJ & N surinamés -esa *mf*
surly [sə́·li] ADJ malhumorado, hosco, arisco
surmise [sə·máɪz] VT conjeturar, suponer; N conjetura *f*, suposición *f*
surmount [sə·máʊnt] VT superar
surname [sə́·nem] N apellido *m*
surpass [sə·pǽs] VT superar, sobrepujar
surplus [sə́·plʌs] N excedente *m*, sobrante *m*, sobra *f*; (of funds) superávit *m*
surprise [sə·práɪz] N sorpresa *f*; VT sorprender
surprising [sə·práɪzɪŋ] ADJ sorprendente
surrealism [səríəlɪzəm] N surrealismo *m*
surrender [səréndə·] VI (accept defeat) rendir(se), darse por vencido; (give oneself up) entregarse; VT entregar; N rendición *f*
surreptitious [sə·əptíʃəs] ADJ subrepticio
surrogate [sə́·əgɪt] ADJ sustituto; — **mother** madre de alquiler *f*
surround [səráʊnd] VT rodear, circundar; (a city) sitiar
surrounding [səráʊndɪŋ] ADJ circundante; —**s** alrededores *m pl*, inmediaciones *f pl*
surveillance [sə·véləns] N vigilancia *f*
survey [sə·vé] VT (evaluate) evaluar; (measure) medir; (contemplate) contemplar; (poll) encuestar; [sə́·ve] N (inspection) reconocimiento *m*, inspección *f*; (measure) medición *f*; (overview) panorama *m*; (poll) encuesta *f*, sondeo *m*; — **course** curso general *m*
surveyor [sə·véə·] N agrimensor -ra *mf*
survival [sə·váɪvəl] N supervivencia *f*, sobrevivencia *f*; (subsistence) subsistencia *f*; **the — of the fittest** la supervivencia del más apto
survive [sə·váɪv] VI/VT sobrevivir (also live longer than); (subsist) subsistir
survivor [sə·váɪvə·] N sobreviviente *mf*
susceptible [səséptəbəl] ADJ susceptible; **to be — of proof** poderse demostrar; **to be — to pneumonia** ser propenso a la pulmonía
suspect [sʌ́spɛkt] N sospechoso -sa *mf*; [səspɛ́kt] VT sospechar, barruntar, recelar

suspend [səspénd] VT suspender
suspenders [səspéndə·z] N tirantes *m pl*
suspense [səspéns] N (uncertainty) incertidumbre *f*; (in movie) suspenso *m*; *Sp* suspense *m*; **to keep in —** mantener en suspenso, tener en vilo
suspension [səspénʃən] N suspensión *f*; (of a ban) levantamiento *m*; — **bridge** puente colgante *m*
suspicion [səspíʃən] N sospecha *f*, barrunto *m*
suspicious [səspíʃəs] ADJ (causing suspicion) sospechoso; (experiencing suspicion) suspicaz, desconfiado
sustain [səstén] VT (weight) sostener, sustentar; (pretense, effort) mantener; (an injury) sufrir; (an objection) admitir; (a musical note) sostener
sustenance [sʌ́stənəns] N sustento *m*, alimento *m*
suture [sútʃə·] N sutura *f*
swab [swab] N hisopo *m*, bola de algodón *f*; VT pasar un hisopo sobre
swagger [swǽgə·] VI (walk) pavonearse, contonearse; (boast) fanfarronear; N (walk) pavoneo *m*, contoneo *m*; (bluster) fanfarronería *f*
swallow [swálo] N (drink) trago *m*; (bird) golondrina *f*; VI/VT tragar; **to — up** consumir
swamp [swamp] N pantano *m*, ciénaga *f*; —**land** cenagal *m*; VI/VT (flood) inundar(se); (overwhelm) abrumar(se), agobiar(se)
swampy [swámpi] ADJ pantanoso, cenagoso
swan [swan] N cisne *m*; — **dive** salto del ángel *m*; — **song** canto de cisne *m*
swap [swap] VT cambiar, canjear; N cambio *m*, canje *m*
swarm [swɔrm] N enjambre *m*; VI (of bees) salir en enjambre; (of people, tourists) pulular, hormiguear; **to be —ing with** ser un hervidero de, abundar en
swarthy [swɔ́rði] ADJ trigueño, moreno
swat [swat] VT (a person) pegar; (flies) aplastar; **to — at** manotear; N manotazo *m*
sway [swe] VI/VT (move to and fro) balancear(se), bambolear(se); (move hips) menear(se); (influence) influir (en); N (movement) balanceo *m*, vaivén *m*, bamboleo *m*; (influence) influencia *f*; **to hold — over** dominar
Swazi [swázi] N suazi *mf*
Swaziland [swázilænd] N Suazilandia *f*
swear [swer] VI/VT (vow) jurar; (use profanity) decir palabrotas; *Sp* soltar tacos; **to — in** (give oath) juramentar; (take oath) prestar

juramento; **she —s by canned peaches** para ella no hay nada como los duraznos enlatados; **to — off** renunciar a; **to — to** jurar por

sweat [swet] VI (perspire) sudar; (ooze) exudar, sudar; (worry) preocuparse; N sudor *m*; **—shirt** sudadera *f*; **—suit** equipo deportivo *m*; *Sp* chándal *m*; **no —** no hay problema

sweater [swédə-] N suéter *m*, jersey *m*

sweaty [swédi] ADJ sudoroso, sudado

Swede [swid] N sueco -ca *mf*

Sweden [swídn] N Suecia *f*

Swedish [swídɪʃ] ADJ sueco

sweep [swip] VI/VT (clean with broom, scan) barrer; (dredge) dragar; VT (touch) rozar; (search) rastrear; VI (spread) extenderse; **to — away** llevar, arrastrar; **to — down upon** caer sobre, asolar; **to — off** limpiar; **to — into** (majestically) entrar majestuoso; (quickly) entrar rápidamente; **to — up** recoger; N (cleaning) barrida *f*; (extension) extensión *f*; (movement) barrido *m*; (search) rastreo *m*

sweeping [swípɪŋ] ADJ (statement) (demasiado) general; (victory) aplastante

sweet [swit] ADJ (in flavor, personality) dulce; (in smell) bueno, fragante; **—and-sour** agridulce; **—heart** querido -da *mf*; **— pea** *Sp* guisante de olor *m*; **— potato** batata *f*, boniato *m*; *Mex* camote *m*; **to have a — tooth** ser goloso; N dulce *m*, golosina *f*; **my —** mi vida, mi alma; **to —-talk** halagar

sweeten [swítn] VI/VT (a food) endulzar(se); (an experience) dulcificar(se)

sweetener [swítnə-] N endulzante *m*, edulcorante *m*

sweetness [swítnɪs] N (of personality) dulzura *f*; (of taste) dulzor *m*

swell [swɛl] VI/VT (limbs, with pride) hinchar(se), henchir(se); VI (river) crecer; (population) crecer, engrosar(se); VT (make grow) hacer crecer, hacer aumentar, engrosar; N (of ocean) oleaje *m*; ADJ estupendo, bárbaro

swelling [swɛlɪŋ] N hinchazón *f*

swelter [swɛltə-] VI sofocarse de calor

swerve [swɜ-v] VI/VT (in a car) virar; (from a goal) desviar(se); N viraje *m*

swift [swɪft] ADJ ligero, veloz, raudo; N vencejo *m*

swiftness [swɪftnɪs] N velocidad *f*, rapidez *f*

swim [swɪm] VI/VT nadar; (float) flotar; **to — across** atravesar nadando; **my head is —ming** me da vueltas la cabeza; N **—ming pool** piscina *f*; *Mex* alberca *f*;

—suit traje de baño *m*; **to take a —** ir a nadar, dar una nadada

swimmer [swímə-] N nadador -ra *mf*

swindle [swɪndl] VT estafar; N estafa *f*, trapacería *f*

swine [swaɪn] N puerco *m*, cerdo *m*; (person) *offensive* puerco -ca *mf*, sinvergüenza *mf*

swing [swɪŋ] VI/VT (on a swing) columpiar(se); (move to and fro) balancear(se), bambolear(se); VI (change) virar; VT (make turn) hacer girar; (influence) influir sobre; (baseball, golf) dar un swing con; **to — a deal** concretar un negocio; **to — around** dar vueltas; **to — open** abrirse; **I can't — a new car** no me puedo dar el lujo de comprar un auto nuevo; N (playground toy) columpio *m*; (oscillation) balanceo *m*, vaivén *m*, bamboleo *m*; (in golf, baseball, music) swing *m*; (change) cambio *m*; **in full —** en su apogeo; **to get into the — of things** agarrarle la onda a algo, cogerle el tranquillo a algo

swipe [swaɪp] VT (steal) afanar, sisar; (slide) deslizar; N (insult) insulto *m*; **to take a — at someone** (physical) tirarle un manotazo a alguien; (verbal) insultar

swirl [swɜ-l] VI/VT arremolinar(se); (dancers) girar; N remolino *m*; (smoke) espiral *f*

Swiss [swɪs] ADJ & N suizo -za *mf*; **— cheese** queso suizo *m*

switch [swɪtʃ] N (change) cambio *m*; (electrical) interruptor *m*, llave *f*; (stick for whipping) varilla *f*; (on railways) agujas *f pl*; **—blade** navaja automática *f*; **—board** centralita *f*; **—man** guardagujas *m sg*; VI/VT cambiar (de); (traincars) desviar; **to — off** (current) cortar; (light, TV) apagar; **to — on** encender, prender

Switzerland [swítsə-lənd] N Suiza *f*

swivel [swívəl] N pivote *m*; **— chair** silla giratoria *f*

swollen [swólən] ADJ hinchado

swoon [swun] VI desvanecerse, desmayarse; **to — over someone** morirse por alguien; N vahído *m*

swoop [swup] VI **to — down upon** abalanzarse sobre; N descenso súbito *m*; **at one fell —** de un tirón

sword [sɔrd] N espada *f*; **—fish** pez espada *m*

sycamore [síkəmɔr] N sicomoro *m*

syllable [síləbəl] N sílaba *f*

syllabus [síləbəs] N programa (de estudios) *m*

syllogism [síləʤɪzm̩] N silogismo *m*

symbiosis [sɪmbiósɪs] N simbiosis *f*

symbol [símbəl] N símbolo *m*

symbolic [sɪmbálɪk] ADJ simbólico

symbolism [símbəlɪzəm] N simbolismo *m*

symmetrical [sɪmétrɪkəł] ADJ simétrico

symmetry [símɪtri] N simetría *f*

sympathetic [sɪmpəθέDɪk] ADJ (compassionate) compasivo; (understanding) comprensivo; (favoring) favorable; (nervous system) simpático

sympathize [símpəθaɪz] VI (be compassionate) compadecer(se); (be understanding) comprender; **to — with** estar a favor de

sympathy [símpəθi] N compasión *f*, comprensión *f*; (condolence) condolencia *f*, pésame *m*; **to extend one's —** dar el pésame

symphony [símfəni] N sinfonía *f*; **— orchestra** orquesta sinfónica *f*

symposium [sɪmpóziəm] N simposio *m*

symptom [símptəm] N síntoma *m*

synagogue [sínəgɑg] N sinagoga *f*

synchronize [síŋkrənaɪz] VI/VT sincronizar(se)

syndicate [síndɪkət] N sindicato *m*; [síndɪket] VI/VT (form a syndicate) sindicar(se); VT (sell rights) vender los derechos de

syndrome [síndrom] N síndrome *m*

synonym [sínənɪm] N sinónimo *m*

synonymous [sɪnánəməs] ADJ sinónimo

synopsis [sɪnápsɪs] N sinopsis *f*

syntax [síntæks] N sintaxis *f*

synthesis [sínθəsɪs] N síntesis *f*

synthesize [sínθəsaɪz] VI/VT sintetizar

synthetic [sɪnθέDɪk] ADJ sintético

syphilis [sífəlɪs] N sífilis *f*

Syria [síriə] N Siria *f*

Syrian [síriən] ADJ & N sirio -ria *mf*

syringe [səríndʒ] N jeringa *f*

syrup [sírəp] N (food) almíbar *m*, jarabe *m*; (medicine) jarabe *m*

system [sístəm] N sistema *m*

systematic [sɪstəmǽDɪk] ADJ sistemático

systematize [sístəmətaɪz] VI/VT sistematizar

systemic [sɪstémɪk] ADJ sistémico

Tt

tab [tæb] N (on typewriter) tabulador *m*; (on index cards) pestaña *f*, ceja *f*; (bill) cuenta *f*; **— key** tecla de tabulación *f*

table [tébəł] N (furniture) mesa *f*; (list) tabla *f*; **— lamp** lámpara de mesa *f*; **— of contents** tabla de contenido *f*, índice *m*; **at —** a la mesa; VT posponer

indefinidamente, dar carpetazo a; **—cloth** mantel *m*; **—spoon** (spoon) cuchara grande *f*; (measurement) cucharada *f*; **—spoonful** cucharada *f*; **— tennis** tenis de mesa *m*; **—ware** vajilla *f*, servicio de mesa *m*

tablet [tǽblɪt] N (pill) pastilla *f*, tableta *f*; (paper) bloc *m*; (stone) tabla *f*, lápida *f*; (portable writing surface) tablilla *f*

tabloid [tǽblɔɪd] N (paper size) tabloide *m*; (type of press) prensa amarilla / sensacionalista *f*

taboo [tæbú] N tabú *m*

tabulate [tǽbjəlet] VT tabular

tachometer [tækɑ́mɪDə-] N tacómetro *m*

tacit [tǽsɪt] ADJ tácito

taciturn [tǽsɪt͡ɜ·n] ADJ taciturno

tack [tæk] N (nail) tachuela *f*; (stitch) hilván *m*; (heading of a boat) rumbo *m*; (course of action) táctica *f*; (equipment for a horse) arreos *m pl*; VT (to nail) clavar con tachuelas; (to stitch) hilvanar; **to — on** agregar; VI virar, cambiar de rumbo

tackle [tǽkəł] N (for fishing, hoisting) aparejo *m*; (in rugby, football) placaje *m*; (person) atajador *m*; VT (a problem) enfrentar, abordar; (a task) emprender; (a horse) poner arreos; VI/VT (rugby, American football) placar, atajar; **the cowboy —d the calf** el vaquero tiró al suelo al becerro

tacky [tǽki] ADJ (in bad taste) de mal gusto, chabacano; *Sp* hortera *inv*; (sticky) pegajoso

tact [tækt] N tacto *m*

tactful [tǽktfəł] ADJ que tiene tacto

tactics [tǽktɪks] N táctica *f*

tactile [tǽktəł] ADJ táctil

tactless [tǽktlɪs] ADJ falto de tacto

tag [tæg] N (label) etiqueta *f*; (question) coletilla *f*; (nickname) apodo *m*; **to play —** jugar al pillapilla; VT etiquetar; (in the game of tag) pillar; **to — along** acompañar; **to — on** agregar

tail [teł] N cola *f*, rabo *m*; (of a shirt) faldón *m*; (pursuer) perseguidor -ra *mf*; (buttocks) *vulg* culo *m*; **—bone** rabadilla *f*; **— end** (of a concert) final *m*; (of a procession) cola *f*; **to —gate** seguir demasiado de cerca (a otro coche); **—light** luz trasera *f*; **—pipe** tubo de escape *m*; **—s** (of a coin) cruz *f*; (tuxedo) frac *m*; **—spin** barrena *f*

tailor [télə-] N sastre *m*; **— shop** sastrería *f*; VT hacer a medida; (adapt) adaptar

taint [tent] N (stain) mancha *f*; (contamination) contaminación *f*; VI/VT (stain) manchar(se); (contaminate) contaminar(se)

Taiwan [taiwán] N Taiwán *m*

Taiwanese [taiwaníz] ADJ & N taiwanés -esa *mf*

Tajik [tɑʤík] ADJ & N tayiko -ka *mf*

Tajikistan [tɑʤíkɪstæn] N Tayikistán *m*

take [tek] VT (carry) llevar; (conduct) conducir; (steal) robar, llevarse; (subtract) restar; (prisoner, medicine, measures, a course) tomar; (one of a set) elegir, coger; (a bribe) aceptar; (a prize) recibir; (advice) seguir; (a walk) dar; (a vacation) irse; (a trip) hacer; (a piece of news) recibir; (remove from) sacar; (a photo) sacar; **to — a bath** bañarse; **to — a chance** arriesgarse, correr un riesgo; **to — after** salir a, parecerse a; **to — a fancy to** entusiasmarse con; **to — a look at** echar un vistazo a; **to — a nap** dormir la siesta; **to — a notion to** ocurrírsele a uno; **to — an oath** prestar juramento; **to — apart** desarmar, desmontar; **to — aside** apartar; **to — away** (carry away) llevarse; (steal) sustraer; **to — back** devolver; **to — back one's words** retractarse; **to — by surprise** tomar desprevenido; **to — care of** (a person) cuidar de; (a matter) atender a; **to — charge of** encargarse de; **to — down in writing** anotar, apuntar; **to — effect** entrar en vigencia; **to — exercise** hacer ejercicio; **to — in** (include) incluir; (comprehend) absorber; (deceive) embaucar; (orphans) albergar; (a dress) tomar, achicar; **to — leave** despedirse; **to — off** (a coat) quitar(se); (to jail) llevar; (discount) rebajar; (an airplane) despegar; **to — offense** ofenderse; **to — office** asumir un cargo; **to — on** (accept) asumir; (hire) tomar, contratar; (acquire) adquirir; **to — out** (withdraw) sacar; (carry out [food], take on a date) llevar; **to — place** tener lugar; **to — revenge** vengarse; **to — stock** hacer un balance; **to — stock in** tener confianza en; **to — the floor** tomar la palabra; **to — to heart** tomar a pecho; **to — to one's heels** poner pies en polvorosa; **to — to task** reprender, regañar; **to — up a matter** tratar un asunto; **to — up space** ocupar espacio; **I — it that** supongo que; **it —s ten minutes** lleva diez minutos; **the vaccination didn't —** la vacuna no prendió; N (profits) ingresos *m pl*; (of fish) pesca *f*, captura *f*; (of a film production) toma *f*; (opinion) opinión *f*; (approach) enfoque *m*; **—off** (of an airplane) despegue *m*; (parody) parodia *f*; **—over** (of

a government) toma de poder *f*; (of a company) adquisición *f*

talcum [tǽlkəm] N talco *m*; **— powder** polvo de talco *m*

tale [teł] N (story) cuento *m*, relato *m*; (lie) mentira *f*

talent [tǽlənt] N talento *m*

talented [tǽləntɪd] ADJ talentoso

talk [tɔk] VI/VT hablar; (chat) charlar; VT (nonsense) decir; (French) hablar; (politics) hablar de; **to — back** contestar con impertinencia; **to — down to** hablar con arrogancia a; **to — someone into something** convencer a alguien para que haga algo; **to — out of** disuadir de; **to — over** discutir; **to — up** alabar, hacer propaganda; N (formal speech) charla *f*; (gossip) habladurías *f pl*; (lingo) habla *f*; **— of the town** la comidilla del pueblo *f*; **— show** programa de entrevistas *m*

talkative [tɔ́kǝdɪv] ADJ hablador, parlanchín, charlatán

tall [tɔł] ADJ alto; **— order** misión imposible *f*; **— tale** cuento chino *m*, patraña *f*; **six feet —** de seis pies de altura; **how — are you?** ¿cuánto mides?

tallow [tǽlo] N sebo *m*

tally [tǽli] N (account) cuenta *f*; VT llevar la cuenta; **to — up** sumar; **to — with** concordar con

tambourine [tæmbǝrín] N pandereta *f*

tame [tem] ADJ (docile) manso, dócil; (domesticated) domesticado; (dull) aburrido; VT (make docile) amansar, domar; (domesticate) domesticar

tamper [tǽmpǝ] VI **to — with** (a jury) sobornar; (a lock) intentar forzar; (a document) alterar, amañar

tampon [tǽmpɑn] N tampón *m*

tan [tæn] VI/VT (cure) curtir(se); (sunburn) broncear(se), tostar(se); VT (cure) adobar; (spank) zurrar; N color tostado *m*; (of skin) bronceado *m*; ADJ (car) color tostado; (skin) bronceado, tostado

tandem [tǽndǝm] N tándem *m*; **in — with** en colaboración con

tangent [tǽndʒǝnt] ADJ & N tangente *f*; **to go off on a —** salirse por la tangente

tangerine [tændʒǝrín] N mandarina *f*; Am tangerina *f*

tangible [tǽndʒǝbǝl] ADJ tangible

tangle [tǽŋɡǝł] VI/VT enredar(se), enmarañar(se); N enredo *m*, maraña *f*; (in hair) nudo *m*, enredijo *m*

tank [tæŋk] N tanque *m* (also military), depósito *m*; VT guardar en un tanque; **to — up** (with gasoline) llenar el tanque;

(with alcohol) emborracharse

tannery [tǽnəri] N curtiduría f, tenería f; Am curtiembre f

tantalize [tǽntlaɪz] VT atormentar con tentaciones

tantamount [tǽntəmaunt] ADJ **to be — to** equivaler a

tantrum [tǽntrəm] N berrinche m, perrera f, rabieta f

Tanzania [tænzəníə] N Tanzania f

Tanzanian [tænzéniən] ADJ & N tanzano -na mf

tap [tæp] N golpecito m; (repeated) golpeteo m; (with the hand) palmadita f; (faucet) llave f; Sp grifo m; **— dance** claqué m; **— water** agua de llave f; VI/VT (once) tocar; (repeatedly) golpetear; (with fingers) tamborilear; (utilize) explotar; (draw off liquid) extraer; **to — a tree** sangrar un árbol; **to — a telephone** intervenir un teléfono

tape [tep] N cinta f (also adhesive); **— measure** cinta métrica f; **— recorder** grabadora f, grabador m; **— recording** grabación f; **to —-record** grabar; **—worm** lombriz f, solitaria f; VT (tie up) atar con cinta; VI/VT (record) grabar

taper [tépər] N (diminished size) estrechamiento m; (candle) vela f, candela f; VI/VT afinar(se); **to — off** (become smaller) afinar(se); (diminish) ir disminuyendo

tapestry [tǽpɪstri] N (wall hanging) tapiz m; (art, industry) tapicería f

tapioca [tæpiókə] N tapioca f

tapir [tépər] N tapir m

tar [tɑr] N alquitrán m, brea f; VT alquitranar; **to — and feather** emplumar

tarantula [tərǽntʃələ] N tarántula f

tardy [tɑ́rdi] ADJ **to be —** llegar tarde

target [tɑ́rgɪt] N blanco m; **— practice** tiro al blanco m

tariff [tǽrɪf] N tarifa f, arancel m

tarnish [tɑ́rnɪʃ] VI/VT (metal) deslustrar(se), empañar; (reputation) manchar(se)

tart [tɑrt] ADJ (fruit) agrio, ácido; (remark) mordaz; N (pie) tarta f; (woman) pej fulana f

tartar [tɑ́rdə] N (in wine) tártaro m; (on teeth) sarro m; **— sauce** salsa tártara f

task [tæsk] N tarea f, labor f, quehacer m; **to take to —** reprender, regañar; **— force** fuerza de tarea f; **—master** tirano -na mf

tassel [tǽsəl] N borla f

taste [test] VT (perceive) sentir el gusto/sabor de; (try) probar; (try wine) catar; VI **to — of onion** saber a cebolla; **it —s sour** tiene un sabor agrio; N (sense, esthetic judgment) gusto m; (flavor) sabor m; (small amount of food) bocadito m; (small amount of drink) sorbo m; **— bud** papila gustativa f

tasteless [téstlɪs] ADJ (with no taste) soso, desabrido; (in bad taste) de mal gusto

tasty [tésti] ADJ sabroso

tatter [tǽɾə] N andrajo m, harapo m, pingajo m

tattered [tǽɾə-d] ADJ harapiento, andrajoso

tattle [tǽɾl] VI acusar; **to — on** acusar a; N **—tale** alcahuete -ta mf, acusetas mf sg

tattoo [tætú] N tatuaje m; VT tatuar(se)

taunt [tɔnt] VT provocar, burlarse de; N provocación f, pulla f

taut [tɔt] ADJ tenso, tirante

tavern [tǽvə-n] N taberna f, cantina f

tawdry [tɔ́dri] ADJ (affair) sórdido; (outfit) charro

tax [tæks] N impuesto m, contribución f, gravamen m; (burden) carga f; VT (a product) gravar; (a person) cobrarle impuestos a; (patience, resources) poner a prueba; **—-deductible** desgravable; **—-exempt** no gravable, exento de impuestos; **—payer** contribuyente mf; **— return** declaración de impuestos f; **— shelter** refugio fiscal m

taxation [tækséʃən] N (result of taxing) impuestos m pl; (act of taxing) imposición de contribuciones f

taxi [tǽksi] N taxi m; VI ir en taxi; (an airplane) rodar por la pista; **—cab** taxi m

taxidermy [tǽksɪdə-mi] N taxidermia f

taxonomy [tæksánəmi] N taxonomía f

tea [ti] N té m; **— bag** bolsita de té f; **—cup** taza de té f; **—kettle** tetera f; **— party** té m; **—pot** tetera f; **—spoon** (spoon) cucharita f, cucharilla f; (measurement) cucharadita f; **—spoonful** cucharadita f; **—time** hora del té f

teach [titʃ] VI/VT enseñar; **to — a class** dar clase

teacher [tíʧə] N (primary school) maestro -tra mf; (secondary school) profesor -ora mf; **—'s college** (escuela) normal f

teaching [títʃɪŋ] N enseñanza f; **—s** enseñanzas f pl

team [tim] N equipo m; (of yoked animals) yunta de bueyes f; (of horses) tiro m, enganche m; VI **to — up** unirse, formar un equipo

teamster [tímstə-] N transportista mf, camionero -ra mf

tear [tir] N lágrima f; **—drop** lágrima f; **— gas** gas lacrimógeno m; **to burst into**

—s romper a llorar; [tɛr] VI/VT rasgar(se); (rip a hole) hacer(se) un siete; VT (snatch) arrancar; (disrupt) desgarrar; **to — along** ir a toda velocidad; **to — apart** (rip up) romper, destrozar; (separate) separar; **to — away** apartar(se); **to — down** (a building) demoler, derribar; (a machine) desarmar, desmontar; (a person) denigrar; **to — one's hair** arrancarse los cabellos; N desgarrón m, desgarradura f, rasgón m

tearful [tírfəł] ADJ (look) lloroso; (farewell) triste

tease [tiz] VT (make fun of a person) molestar, fastidiar; (tantalize sexually) provocar; (comb wool, hair) cardar; **to — out** sacar; N provocadora f

teat [tit] N teta f

technical [téknɪkəł] ADJ técnico

technician [tekníʃən] N técnico -ca mf, perito -ta mf

technique [tekník] N técnica f

technology [teknáləʤi] N tecnología f, técnica f

tectonics [tektánɪks] N tectónica f

tedious [tídiəs] ADJ tedioso, aburrido

tedium [tídiəm] N hastío m

tee [ti] N (T-shirt) camiseta f; (golf ball support) tee m; (start of hole in golf) punto de salida f

teem [tim] VI **to — with** abundar en, estar lleno de

teenager [tíneʤɚ] N adolescente mf

teens [tinz] N (teenage years) adolescencia f; (numbers 13–19) números de trece a diecinueve m pl

teethe [tið] VI **the baby is teething** al bebé le están saliendo los dientes

teetotaler [títódlɚ] N abstemio -mia mf

telecast [téləkæst] N teledifusión f

telecommunications [telɪkəmjunɪkéʃənz] N telecomunicaciones f pl

teleconference [télɪkanfɚəns] N teleconferencia f

telegram [téləgræm] N telegrama m

telegraph [téləgræf] N telégrafo m; VI/VT telegrafiar

telegraphic [teləgræfɪk] ADJ telegráfico

telemarketing [teləmárkɪdɪŋ] N telemercadeo m, telemarketing m

telepathy [təlépəθi] N telepatía f

telephone [téləfon] N teléfono m; **— book** guía telefónica f; **— booth** cabina telefónica f; **— number** número telefónico m; **— operator** telefonista mf; **— receiver** auricular m, tubo de teléfono m; VI/VT telefonear, llamar por teléfono

telescope [télɪskop] N telescopio m; VI

plegarse

television [téləvɪʒən] N (medium) televisión f; (device) televisor m; **— viewer** televidente mf

tell [tɛł] VI/VT (the truth) decir; (a story) contar; **to — apart** distinguir; **to — on someone** acusar a alguien; **to — someone off** regañar a alguien; **to — time** decir la hora; **I can't — if he's old or young** no sé si es viejo o joven; **his age is beginning to —** se le comienza a notar la edad; **a —tale sign** una señal reveladora; **he is a —tale** es un acusica

teller [télɚ] N (narrator) narrador -ora mf; (in a bank) cajero -ra mf

temerity [təmérɪdi] N temeridad f

temper [témpɚ] N (hardness) temple m; (bad humor) mal genio m; VT templar; **to keep one's —** mantener la calma; **to lose one's —** perder los estribos, encolerizarse

temperament [témpɚəmənt] N temperamento m, genio m, talante m

temperance [témpɚəns] N (moderation) templanza f, temperancia f; (abstinence from alcohol) abstinencia de bebidas alcohólicas f

temperate [témpɚɪt] ADJ (weather) templado; (opinions, habits) moderado

temperature [témpɚətʃur] N temperatura f; **to have a —** tener fiebre

tempest [témpɪst] N tempestad f

tempestuous [tempéstʃuəs] ADJ tempestuoso

temple [témpəł] N (church) templo m; (side of the forehead) sien f

temporal [témpɚəł] ADJ temporal

temporary [témpɚeri] ADJ temporal, provisional

tempt [tempt] VT tentar

temptation [temptéʃən] N tentación f

tempting [témptɪŋ] ADJ tentador

ten [ten] NUM diez

tenacious [tənéʃəs] ADJ tenaz

tenacity [tənǽsɪdi] N tenacidad f

tenant [ténənt] N inquilino -na mf, arrendatario -ria mf

tend [tend] VT (care for) cuidar; **to — to** ocuparse de; VI (lean toward) tender, inclinarse

tendency [téndənsi] N tendencia f

tender [téndɚ] ADJ tierno; (painful) sensible; N (offer) oferta f; (legal currency) curso legal m; (person who tends) cuidador -ra mf, vigilante mf; VT presentar, ofrecer

tenderness [téndɚnɪs] N (of feeling) ternura f; (of meat) terneza f, ternura f; (sensitivity to pain) sensibilidad f

tendon [téndən] N tendón m

tendonitis [tendənáɪdɪs] N tendinitis f
tendril [téndrəl] N zarcillo m
tenement [ténəmənt] N casa de vecindad f
tenet [ténɪt] N principio m
tennis [ténɪs] N tenis m; — **court** cancha de tenis f, pista de tenis f; — **player** tenista mf; — **shoes** tenis m pl
tenor [ténə-] N tenor m
tense [tens] ADJ tenso; N tiempo m
tension [ténʃən] N tensión f; (tautness) tirantez f
tent [tent] N tienda de campaña f; (circus) carpa f; VI acampar
tentacle [téntəkəl] N tentáculo m
tentative [téntədɪv] ADJ tentativo
tenth [tenθ] ADJ & N décimo m
tenuous [ténjuəs] ADJ (light, color, cloth) tenue; (peace) frágil; (rarefied) enrarecido
tenure [ténjə-] N (of professorship) titularidad f; (of an office) ocupación f
tepid [tépɪd] ADJ tibio
terabyte [térəbaɪt] N terabyte m
term [tɜ-m] N (word, mathematical expression) término m; (period) período m; (time in office) mandato m; (semester) semestre m; (trimester) trimestre m; (set date for payment) plazo m; — **paper** trabajo final m; —**s** condiciones f pl; **at** — a término; **to be on good** —**s** estar en buenas relaciones; **not to be on speaking** —**s** no hablarse; **to come to** —**s** aceptar; VT denominar
terminal [tɜ́-mənəl] ADJ terminal; N (of airport, computer) terminal mf; (electric) terminal m
terminate [tɜ́-mənet] VI/VT terminar(se)
termination [tɜ-mənéʃən] N terminación f; (of an employee) despido m
terminology [tɜ-rmənáləʤi] N terminología f
termite [tɜ́-maɪt] N termita f
terrace [térɪs] N terraza f, escalón m; VT poner terrazas en, escalonar
terrain [tərén] N terreno m
terrestrial [təréstriəl] ADJ terrestre
terrible [térəbəl] ADJ terrible, tremendo
terrier [tériə-] N terrier m
terrific [tərífɪk] ADJ estupendo
terrify [térəfaɪ] VT aterrar, aterrorizar, espeluznar
territory [térɪtɔri] N territorio m
terror [térə-] N terror m
terrorism [térə-ɪzəm] N terrorismo m
terrorist [térə-ɪst] N terrorista mf
terse [tɜ-s] ADJ lacónico
test [test] N (trial, experiment) prueba f; (of intelligence, multiple choice) test m; (examination) examen m, prueba f; **to** —**drive** probar; — **pilot** piloto de pruebas m; — **tube** tubo de ensayo m, probeta f; —**tube baby** bebé de probeta mf; **to undergo a** — someterse a una prueba; **to take a** — dar un examen; **to give a** — poner un examen; **to put to the** — poner a prueba; VT (try) probar, poner a prueba; (give an exam) poner una prueba, examinar; VI **girls** — **better than boys** en los exámenes salen mejor las niñas que los niños
testament [téstəmənt] N testamento m; (testimony) testimonio m
testicle [téstɪkəl] N testículo m
testify [téstəfaɪ] VI testificar; (confirm) dar fe
testimony [téstəmoni] N testimonio m
testosterone [testástəron] N testosterona f
tetanus [tétṇəs] N tétano(s) m
Teutonic [tutánɪk] ADJ teutónico
text [tekst] N texto m; —**book** libro de texto m; — **editor** editor de texto(s) m
textile [tékstaɪl] ADJ textil; N textil m, tejido m; — **mill** fábrica de tejidos f
texture [tékstʃə-] N textura f
Thai [taɪ] ADJ & N tailandés -esa mf
Thailand [táɪlænd] N Tailandia f
Thailander [táɪlændə-] ADJ & N tailandés -esa mf
than [ðæn] CONJ que; **I have more** — **you** tengo más que tú; **more** — **once** más de una vez
thank [θæŋk] VT dar las gracias, agradecer; **to have oneself to** — **for** tener la culpa de; INTERJ — **heaven!** ¡gracias a Dios! — **you** gracias; N —**s** gracias f pl
thankful [θǽŋkfəl] ADJ agradecido
thankfulness [θǽŋkfəlnɪs] N gratitud f, agradecimiento m
thankless [θǽŋklɪs] ADJ ingrato
thanksgiving [θæŋksgívɪŋ] N acción de gracias f; — **Day** día de acción de gracias m
that [ðæt] ADJ (something nearer the speaker) ese, esa; (something more remote from speaker) aquel, aquella; — **dog** ese/aquel perro m; — **one** (nearer) ese, esa; DEMON PRON (nearer to speaker) ese, esa; (more remote from speaker) aquel, aquella; (neuter) eso, aquello; — **is my daughter** esa/aquella es mi hija; — **was a nightmare** eso/aquello fue una pesadilla; REL PRON que; **the bike** — **disappeared** la bici que desapareció; **the pen** — **I was writing with** la lapicera con la que/cual escribía; — **is** es decir; CONJ que; **she said** — **she would come**

dijo que vendría; ADV tan; **it's not — far**
no queda tan lejos; **— much** tanto; **she
was — tall** era así de alta

thatch [θætʃ] N paja f; Am quincha f; VT
techar con paja; Am quinchar; **—ed roof**
techo de paja m; Am quincha f

thaw [θɔ] VI/VT (food) descongelar(se); (ice
and snow) derretir(se); (relations,
refrigerator) deshelar(se); N deshielo m

the [ðə, ði] DEF ART (singular) el m, la f; **—
boy** el chico m; (plural) los m, las f; **—
girls** las chicas f pl; **— good thing** lo
bueno; ADV **— more I work, — less I
accomplish** cuanto más trabajo, menos
consigo

theater [θíɑɾə] N teatro m

theatrical [θiǽtɹɪkəl] ADJ teatral

theft [θeft] N hurto m, robo m

their [ðer] POSS ADJ **this is — dog** es es su
perro, este es el perro de ellos

theirs [ðerz] PRON **this book is —** este libro
es suyo, este libro es de ellos/ellas; **these
things are —** estas cosas son suyas/de
ellos/de ellas; **— is bigger** el suyo/la
suya/el de ellos/la de ellos es más
grande; **a friend of —** un amigo suyo,
un amigo de ellos

them [ðem] PRON los m pl, las f pl; **I see —**
los/las veo; **I talk to —** les hablo a ellos;
I went with — fui con ellos/ellas

thematic [θɪmǽɾɪk] ADJ temático

theme [θim] N tema m; (essay) ensayo m,
redacción f; **— park** parque temático m;
— song tema m

themselves [ðemsélvz] PRON **they — built
their house** ellos mismos se
construyeron la casa; **they are not —
today** hoy no son los mismos de siempre;
they were sitting by — estaban
sentados solos; **they looked at — in the
mirror** se miraron en el espejo; **they
talk to —** hablan solos; **they bought —
a yacht** se compraron un yate

then [ðen] ADV (at that time) entonces, en
aquel tiempo; **it was cheaper —** era más
barato en aquel tiempo; (after) luego,
después; **from — on** a partir de entonces;
now and — de vez en cuando; **until —**
hasta entonces; **I ate, — I paid** comí,
luego pagué; ADJ entonces; **the —
president** el entonces presidente; CONJ
entonces; **if not, — you should stay** si
no, entonces deberías quedarte; **now —**
ahora bien; **are you sorry —?** ¿estás
arrepentido pues?

theology [θiálədʒi] N teología f

theoretical [θiəɹéDɪkəl] ADJ teórico

theory [θíəɹi] N teoría f

therapeutic [θeɹəpjúdɪk] ADJ terapéutico

therapist [θéɹəpɪst] N terapeuta mf;
(psychologist) psicólogo -ga mf

therapy [θéɹəpi] N terapia f

there [ðer] ADV ahí; Am allí; (more remote)
allá; Sp allí; **—abouts** por ahí, más o
menos; **—after** (after) después;
(subsequently) de allí en adelante; **—by**
así, de ese modo; **— ensued a war** a
continuación hubo una guerra; **—fore** por
consiguiente, por lo tanto; **—in** en eso,
allí; **— is, — are** hay; **— goes the bus**
ahí va el autobús; **— —** bueno, bueno;
—of de eso; **—on** (on that) encima; (after)
luego, después; **—upon** (after) luego,
después; (for this reason) por consiguiente;
(upon that) encima; **—with** (with that)
con eso; (after that) luego, en seguida;
who's —? ¿quién es? **is Mary —?** ¿está
María? **we got — at 5** llegamos a las 5

thermal [θə́məl] ADJ termal; **— energy**
energía térmica f

thermodynamic [θə́modainǽmɪk] ADJ
termodinámico

thermometer [θəmámɪdə] N termómetro m

thermonuclear [θə́monúkliə] ADJ
termonuclear

thermos [θə́məs] N termo m

thermostat [θə́məstæt] N termostato m

thesaurus [θɪsɔ́ɾəs] N (synonym dictionary)
diccionario de sinónimos m; (large
dictionary) diccionario m

these [ðiz] ADJ & PRON estos, estas

thesis [θísɪs] N tesis f

they [ðe] PRON ellos, ellas

thick [θɪk] ADJ (slice) grueso; (fog, soup)
espeso; (accent) marcado; (wit) torpe; **one
inch —** una pulgada de espesor; **— as
thieves** como carne y uña; ADV
—-headed estúpido; **—-set** grueso;
—-skinned insensible; N **the — of the
fight** lo más reñido de la pelea; **through
— and thin** pase lo que pase

thicken [θíkən] VI/VT espesar(se), trabar(se);
the plot —s la trama se complica

thicket [θíkɪt] N soto m, matorral m, boscaje
m

thickness [θíknɪs] N (of paper, wood) espesor
m, grosor m; (of soup) lo espeso; (of lips)
lo grueso; (of a beard) lo tupido; (of hair)
lo abundante

thief [θif] N ladrón -ona mf

thieve [θiv] VI/VT hurtar, robar

thigh [θai] N muslo m

thimble [θímbəl] N dedal m

thin [θɪn] ADJ (ice, wire) delgado, fino;

(person) flaco; (vegetation, beard, hair) ralo; (voice) tenue, fino; (air) enrarecido; (excuse) débil; (soup) aguado; VI/VT (paint, soup, sauce) diluir; (hair) entresacar; **to — out** (hair) ralear; (crowd) dispersarse

thing [θɪŋ] N cosa *f*; **there's no such —** eso no existe; **that is the — to do** eso es lo que hay que hacer; **the — about Mary** lo que pasa con María

thingamajig [θíŋəmədʒɪg] N chisme *m*, coso *m*

think [θɪŋk] VI/VT (reason) pensar, razonar; (believe) creer, opinar; **to — about** pensar en; **to — back** recordar; **to — it over / through** pensarlo bien, reflexionar sobre; **I'm —ing of you** pienso en ti; **what do you — of Mary?** ¿qué piensas de María? **I thought of a plan** se me ocurrió un plan; **to — up an excuse** inventar / elucubrar una excusa; **I don't — so** no creo; **who does he — he is?** ¿quién se cree que es? **to — well of** tener buena opinión de; **she —s nothing of spending $1000** no le importa nada gastar $1000; **to my way of —ing** a mi parecer

thinner [θínɚ] N disolvente *m*

thinness [θínnɪs] N (of ice, person) delgadez *f*, flacura *f*; (of hair) escasez *f*; (of air) enrarecimiento *m*; (of soup) fluidez *f*

third [θɚd] ADJ tercer(o); **— chapter** capítulo tercero *m*, tercer capítulo *m*; ADV tercero; N tercio *m*; (gear, musical interval) tercera *f*; **— person** tercera persona *f*; **—-rate** de poca categoría; **— World** Tercer Mundo *m*; **the — of March** el tres de marzo

thirst [θɚst] N sed *f*; VI tener sed; **to — for** tener sed de, estar sediento de

thirsty [θɚsti] ADJ sediento; **to be —** tener sed

thirteen [θɚtín] NUM trece

thirty [θɚDi] NUM treinta

this [ðɪs] ADJ & PRON este *m*, esta *f*, esto (neuter); **— one** este perro; **— is a disaster** esto es un desastre

thistle [θísəl] N cardo *m*

thong [θɔŋ] N (strip of leather) correa *f*; (garment) tanga *mf*; (shoe) chancleta *f*

thorax [θɔ́ræks] N tórax *m*

thorn [θɔrn] N (sharp growth) espina *f*; (plant) espino *m*

thorny [θɔ́rni] ADJ espinoso, escabroso

thorough [θɚ-o] ADJ (exhaustive) exhaustivo, minucioso, detenido; (conscientious) concienzudo

thoroughbred [θɚ́-əbrɛd] ADJ de pura sangre; N purasangre *m*

those [ðoz] ADJ & PRON (nearer) esos *m*, esas *f*; PRON (more remote) aquellos *m*, aquellas *f*; **— of you** los de vosotros / ustedes; **— that / who** los / las que

though [ðo] CONJ aunque; **as —** como si; ADV sin embargo

thought [θɔt] N (act, product of thinking) pensamiento *m*; (idea) idea *f*; (opinion) opinión *f*; (concern) consideración *f*; **to be lost in —** estar abstraído; **to give it no —** no darle importancia; **the very —** la mera idea; **at the — of** ante la idea de; **on second —** pensándolo bien; **my —s are with you** te acompaño en el sentimiento

thoughtful [θɔ́tfəl] ADJ (considerate) considerado, atento; (well thought out) bien pensado; (reflective) pensativo, reflexivo

thoughtfulness [θɔ́tfəlnɪs] N consideración *f*

thoughtless [θɔ́tlɪs] ADJ (inconsiderate) desconsiderado; (careless) descuidado; (not reflective) irreflexivo

thoughtlessness [θɔ́tlɪsnɪs] N (lack of consideration) desconsideración *f*; (carelessness) descuido *m*; (lack of reflection) falta de reflexión *f*

thousand [θáuzənd] NUM mil

thrash [θræʃ] VI/VT (whip, defeat) zurrar, vapulear, apalear; (thresh) trillar, desgranar; **to — around** revolverse, agitarse; **to — out a matter** ventilar un asunto

thread [θrɛd] N hilo *m*; (on a screw) rosca *f*; **—bare** raído; VT (a needle) enhebrar; (beads) ensartar; (a screw) enroscar; **to — one's way** abrirse paso

threat [θrɛt] N amenaza *f*

threaten [θrétṇ] VI/VT amenazar

threatening [θrétṇɪŋ] ADJ amenazador

three [θri] NUM tres; **—-dimensional** tridimensional

thresh [θrɛʃ] VT trillar

threshold [θréʃhoɫd] N umbral *m*

thrift [θrɪft] N economía *f*

thrifty [θrífti] ADJ económico, ahorrativo

thrill [θrɪɫ] VI/VT emocionar(se), ilusionar(se); N emoción *f*, ilusión *f*

thrive [θraɪv] VI prosperar; (plants) florecer

throat [θrot] N garganta *f*

throb [θrɑb] VI latir, palpitar; N latido *m*, palpitación *f*

throes [θroz] ADV LOC **in the — of war** en plena guerra; **in the — of death** agonizando

throne [θron] N trono *m*

throng [θrɔŋ] N muchedumbre *f*, turbamulta *f*; VI apiñarse, llegar en tropel

throttle [θrádl] N (of a motor) válvula reguladora/de aceleración *f*, regulador *m*; (of a motorcycle) puño giratorio del gas *m*; **— lever** palanca del regulador *f*; VT ahogar, estrangular

through [θru] PREP por, a través de; (as intermediary) por medio de; **Monday — Friday** de lunes a viernes; **all — the night** toda la noche; ADV (completely) de un lado a otro; (from beginning to end) de principio a fin, de cabo a rabo; **loyal — and —** leal a toda prueba; **an aristocrat — and —** un aristócrata de pura cepa; **to carry —** llevar a cabo; ADJ (ticket, train) directo; **to be —** (with a task) haber terminado; (in a profession) estar acabado; **we're —!** (with a boyfriend) ¡se acabó entre nosotros!

throughout [θruáut] PREP (all through) por todo; (during) a lo largo de, durante; ADV (duration) de principio a fin; (space) por todas partes

throw [θro] VI/VT (a ball) tirar, lanzar; (a light, voice) arrojar; (a switch) conectar; (a pot on a wheel) modelar en un torno; (a punch) lanzar; (a wrestler) tumbar; (a game for a bribe) dejarse perder; (a rider) desmontar; (a party) dar, organizar; **that really threw me** eso me confundió; **to — away** (dispose of) tirar, arrojar; (squander) malgastar; **to — down** tirar al suelo; **to — in** añadir; **to — into gear** engranar; **to — in the clutch** embragar; **to — out** (garbage) tirar, arrojar; (unruly guest) echar; **to — up** vomitar, devolver; N (act or instance of throwing) tiro *m*; (of dice) tirada *f*; (shawl) chal *m*; (blanket) manta *f*

thrush [θrʌʃ] N tordo *m*, zorzal *m*

thrust [θrʌst] VT (stab) clavar; (shove) empujar; **to — oneself upon** meterse en; **to — a task upon someone** imponerle una tarea a alguien; **to — aside** echar a un lado; **to — someone through** atravesar a alguien; VI (push) dar un empujón; (stab at) lanzar una estocada; (push through) empujar para pasar; N (stab) estocada *f*; (force of a jet engine) empuje *m*; (shove) empujón *m*; (military assault) arremetida *f*, acometida *f*

thud [θʌd] N golpe sordo *m*; VI caer con un golpe sordo

thug [θʌg] N matón *m*

thumb [θʌm] N pulgar *m*; **under the — of** bajo la bota de; VT hojear; **to give the**

—s up aprobar; **—tack** chinche *f*, tachuela *f*

thump [θʌmp] N golpe sordo *m*; VI hacer un ruido sordo

thunder [θʌndɚ] N trueno *m*; VI tronar; **—bolt** rayo *m*; **—head** nubarrón *m*; **—storm** tormenta eléctrica *f*, tronada *f*

thunderous [θʌndɚəs] ADJ atronador, estruendoso

Thursday [θɝ́zde] N jueves *m*

thus [ðʌs] ADV así; **— far** (space) hasta aquí; (time) hasta ahora

thwart [θwɔrt] VT frustrar

thyme [taɪm] N tomillo *m*

thyroid [θáɪrɔɪd] N tiroides *m sg*

Tibet [tɪbét] N Tíbet *m*

Tibetan [tɪbétn] ADJ & N tibetano -na *mf*

tic [tɪk] N tic *m*, manía *f*

tick [tɪk] N (sound of a clock) tic tac *m*; (cover of a pillow) funda *f*; (check mark) marca *f*; (insect) garrapata *f*; VI hacer tic tac; **to — off** (check off) marcar; (anger) enojar

ticket [tíkɪt] N billete *m*; Am boleto *m*; (slate of candidates) candidatura *f*; (summons) multa *f*; (tag) etiqueta *f*; **— office** taquilla *f*; VT (give passage) vender billetes; (give summons) multar

tickle [tíkl] VT (poke) cosquillear, hacer cosquillas; (amuse) dar ilusión; VI picar; N picazón *f*, cosquilleo *m*

ticklish [tíklɪʃ] ADJ (prone to tickles) cosquilloso; (delicate) delicado

tidal [táɪdl] ADJ **— wave** (tsunami) maremoto *m*; (large wave) marejada *f*

tidbit [tídbɪt] N (snack) golosina *f*; (gossip) chisme jugoso *m*

tide [taɪd] N marea *f*; (of opinion) corriente *f*; **—water** (water) agua de marea *f*; (land) marisma *f*; VT **to — over** cubrir

tidy [táɪdi] ADJ (orderly) ordenado; (large) considerable; VI/VT arreglar; **to — oneself up** arreglarse

tie [taɪ] VI (fasten) atarse; (make same score) empatar; VT (fasten) atar; (make a knot) hacer un nudo; (make same score as) empatar con; **to — down** atar; **to — in** cuadrar; **to — one on** emborracharse; **to — tight** atar fuerte; **to — up** (bind) atar; (hinder) bloquear; (occupy) ocupar; (moor a ship) amarrar; N (cord) cuerda *f*; (relations) lazo *m*, vínculo *m*; (cravat) corbata *f*; (score) empate *m*; (railway) durmiente *m*, traviesa *f*

tier [tɪr] N nivel *m*

tiger [táɪgɚ] N tigre *m*

tight [taɪt] ADJ (knot, nut) apretado, ajustado;

(clothes) ceñido, ajustado; (control) firme, estricto; (race) reñido; (stingy) tacaño, mezquino; (drunk) borracho; —**-fisted** agarrado; —**rope** cuerda floja f; —**wad** tacaño -ña mf; **to be in a** — **spot** estar en un aprieto; ADV bien, herméticamente; **to hold on** — agarrarse bien

tighten [táitn̩] VI/VT (knot, nut, belt) apretar(se); (control) estrechar(se)

tightness [táitnɪs] N estrechez f; (stinginess) tacañería f

tile [taɪl] N (on a roof) teja f; (on a floor) baldosa f; (on a wall) azulejo m; — **roof** tejado m; VT (roof) tejar; (floor) embaldosar; (wall) azulejar

till [tɪl] PREP hasta; CONJ hasta que; VI/VT labrar, arar; N caja f

tilt [tɪlt] VI/VT ladear(se), inclinar(se); N (act or instance of tilting) ladeo m, inclinación f; (incline) declive m; (joust) justa f; **at full** — a toda velocidad

timber [tímbɚ] N (cut wood) madera (de construcción) f; (trees) árboles para madera m pl; (beam) viga f; —**line** límite de la vegetación arbórea m; — **wolf** lobo gris m

timbre [tímbɚ] N timbre m

time [taɪm] N (past, present, future) tiempo m; (hour) hora f; (occasion) vez f; (period) período m, momento m, época f; —**bomb** bomba de tiempo f; —**keeper** cronometrador -ra mf; — **out** descanso m; —**piece** reloj m; — **signature** compás m; —**table** horario m; — **zone** huso horario m; **at** —**s** a veces; **at the same** — a la vez, al mismo tiempo; **at this** — en este momento; **behind** — atrasado; **lunch**—hora del almuerzo f; **from** — **to** — de vez en cuando; **for the** — **being** por el momento; **in** — a tiempo; **in no** — en seguida; **it's about** — ya era hora; **on** — puntual; **to buy on** — comprar a plazo; — **after** — una vez tras otra; **to do** — cumplir una condena; **to have a good** — divertirse; **what** — **is it?** ¿qué hora es? VT (a race) cronometrar; (a test) fijar la duración de; (one's arrival) fijar la hora de; **to** — **an attack well** atacar en el momento oportuno

timeless [táɪmlɪs] ADJ eterno

timely [táɪmli] ADJ oportuno

timer [táɪmɚ] N (person) cronometrador -ra mf; (device) reloj m

timid [tímɪd] ADJ tímido, apocado

timidity [tɪmídɪdi] N timidez f, apocamiento m

timing [táɪmɪŋ] N (measurement)

cronometraje m; (synchronization) sincronización f; **that was good** — lo hiciste en el momento oportuno

timorous [tímɚəs] ADJ timorato

tin [tɪn] N (metal) estaño m; (tin plate) hojalata f; — **can** lata f; — **foil** papel de estaño m, papel de aluminio m; VT estañar

tincture [tíŋktʃɚ] N tintura f

tinder [tíndɚ] N yesca f

tinge [tɪndʒ] VT (tint) teñir; (hint) matizar; N (of color) tinte m, matiz m; (of taste) dejo m; (of irony) matiz m

tingle [tíŋgɫ] VI sentir hormigueo, hormiguear; **to** — **with excitement** estremecerse de entusiasmo; N hormigueo m

tinker [tíŋkɚ] VI ocuparse, entretenerse; **to** — **with** toquetear, hacer ajustes

tinkle [tíŋkɫ] VT (ring lightly) tintinear; (urinate) hacer pipí; N tintineo m

tinsel [tínsɫ] N (Christmas trim) espumillón m, guirnalda f; (tawdry decoration) oropel m

tint [tɪnt] N (hue) matiz m; (for hair) tinte m, tintura f; (for glass) coloreado m; VT (hair) teñir; (glasses) colorear

tiny [táɪni] ADJ diminuto, chiquito

tip [tɪp] N (point) punta f; (gratuity) propina f; (piece of advice) consejo m; VI/VT (tilt) inclinar(se), ladear(se); (give a gratuity) dar propina (a); **to** — **a person off** advertir a alguien; **to** — **one's hat** sacarse/quitarse el sombrero; **to** — **over** volcar(se)

tipsy [típsi] ADJ alegre

tiptoe [típto] N punta del pie f; **on** —**s** de puntillas; VI andar de puntillas

tirade [táɪred] N diatriba f

tire [taɪr] N neumático m, cubierta f; Mex llanta f; Am goma f; VI/VT cansar(se), fatigar(se); **to** — **out** cansar, fatigar; ADJ —**d** cansado, fatigado; —**d out** cansado, fatigado

tireless [táɪrlɪs] ADJ incansable

tiresome [táɪrsəm] ADJ aburrido, pesado, plasta inv

tissue [tíʃu] N (cell aggregate) tejido m; (handkerchief) pañuelo de papel m; — **paper** papel tisú m

tit [tɪt] N (bird) paro m; (breast) vulg teta f

titanic [taɪténɪk] ADJ titánico

titanium [taɪténiəm] N titanio m

tithe [taɪð] N diezmo m; VI pagar el diezmo

titillate [tídlet] VT excitar; (interest) despertar interés

title [táɪdl] N título m; (of a picture) rótulo m; — **deed** título de propiedad m; — **page** portada f

TNT [tientí] N TNT *m*

to [tu] PREP **I gave it — you** te lo di a ti; **to count — ten** contar hasta diez; **I called — find out** llamé para averiguar; **— my surprise** para mi sorpresa; **a quarter — five** las cinco menos cuarto; **bills — be paid** cuentas por pagar; **things — do** cosas que hacer; **frightened — death** muerto de susto; **from house — house** de casa en casa; ADV **— and fro** de acá para allá; **to come —** volver en sí

toad [tod] N sapo *m*; **—stool** seta *f*, hongo no comestible *m*

toast [tost] VI/VT (brown) tostar(se); VT (congratulate) brindar por; N tostada *f*; (congratulation) brindis *m*

toaster [tóstə˞] N tostadora *f*; **— oven** horno tostador *m*

tobacco [təbǽko] N tabaco *m*

today [tədé] ADV hoy; (nowadays) hoy día

toddler [tádlə˞] N niño -ña pequeño -ña *mf*

toe [to] N dedo del pie *m*; (of shoe, sock) punta *f*; **—nail** uña del dedo del pie *f*; VT (touch with toe) tocar con el dedo del pie; **to — the line** hacer buena letra, entrar en vereda

together [təgéðə˞] ADV (in union) juntos; (at the same time) al mismo tiempo; **— with** junto con; **all —** todos juntos

Togo [tógo] N Togo *m*

Togolese [togəlíz] ADJ & N togolés -esa *mf*

toil [tɔɪl] N esfuerzo *m*, trabajo *m*; VI trabajar, esforzarse, bregar

toilet [tɔ́ɪlɪt] N (bowl) inodoro *m*; (lavatory) aseo *m*, lavabo *m*; **— paper** papel higiénico *m*; **—trained** que ya no usa pañales

token [tókən] N (symbol) señal *f*; (keepsake) recuerdo *m*; (coinlike metal piece) ficha *f*; **— payment** pago nominal *m*; **as a — of friendship** en prenda de amistad

tolerance [tálə˞əns] N tolerancia *f*

tolerant [tálə˞ənt] ADJ tolerante

tolerate [tálə˞et] VT tolerar

toll [tol] N (of bells) tañido *m*; (payment) peaje *m*; (charges) tarifa *f*; (of victims) balance *m*; **— bridge** puente de peaje *m*; **— road** carretera de peaje *f*; VI/VT tañer (a muerto)

tomato [təmédo] N tomate *m*

tomb [tum] N tumba *f*, sepulcro *m*, sepultura *f*; **—stone** lápida *f*

tomboy [támbɔɪ] N marimacho *m*

tomcat [támkæt] N gato macho *m*

tomorrow [təmóro] ADV & N mañana *f*; **— morning** mañana por la mañana *f*

ton [tʌn] N tonelada *f*

tone [ton] N (pitch) tono *m*; (of a speech) tono *m*, tónica *f*; VI **to — down** moderar, matizar

toner [tónə˞] N tóner *m*

Tonga [táŋgə] N Tonga *m*

Tongan [táŋgən] ADJ & N tongano -na *mf*

tongs [tɔŋz] N tenazas *f pl*

tongue [tʌŋ] N (body part, language, of a flame) lengua *f*; (of a shoe) lengüeta *f*; **to —-lash** reprender; **to be—-tied** tener trabada la lengua; **on the tip of my —** en la punta de la lengua; **to hold one's — callarse la boca; — in cheek** irónicamente; **— twister** trabalenguas *m sg*; VI tocar con la lengua

tonic [tánɪk] ADJ tónico; N (medicine) tónico *m*; (water, key note) tónica *f*; **— water** agua tónica *f*

tonight [tənáɪt] ADV esta noche

tonsil [tánsəl] N amígdala *f*

tonsillitis [tansəláɪdɪs] N amigdalitis *f*, anginas *f pl*

too [tu] ADV (in addition) también; (excessively) demasiado; **— bad!** ¡qué lástima! **— many** demasiados; **— much** demasiado

tool [tul] N herramienta *f*; **—box** caja de herramientas *f*; **—shed** cobertizo para herramientas *m*

toot [tut] VI/VT (horn) sonar; (whistle) pitar; (trumpet) tocar; **to — one's own horn** darse autobombo; N (of horn, trumpet) toque *m*; (of horn) bocinazo *m*; (of whistle) pitido *m*

tooth [tuθ] N (front) diente *m*; (back) muela *f*; **—ache** dolor de muelas *m*; **—brush** cepillo de dientes *m*; **— decay** caries (dental) *f sg*; **— fairy** ratoncito Pérez *m*; **— mark** dentellada *f*; **—paste** pasta dental *f*, pasta dentífrica *f*; **—pick** mondadientes *m sg*, palillo de dientes *m*; **to fight — and nail** luchar a brazo partido; **to have a sweet —** ser goloso

toothed [tuθt] ADJ dentado

toothless [túθlɪs] ADJ desdentado

top [tap] N (of a mountain) cumbre *f*, cima *f*; (of a page) parte superior *f*; (of a jar) tapa *f*; (of a convertible) capota *f*; (of a table) superficie *f*; (of a tree) copa *f*; (toy) trompo *m*, peonza *f*; (blouse) blusa *f*; **he's at the — of his class** es el mejor de su clase; **at the — of one's voice** a voz en cuello; **filled up to the —** lleno hasta el tope; **from — to bottom** de arriba abajo; **on — of** encima de; ADJ (officer, floor) superior; (shelf, step) más alto; **—coat** abrigo *m*; **to be — dog** ir a la cabeza; **—**

dollar precio exorbitante *m*; **— hat** sombrero de copa *m*; **—-flight** de primera; **—-heavy** desbalanceado; **—-most** superior; **—-notch** de primera; **at — speed** a velocidad máxima; VT (a tree) desmochar; (a list) encabezar; (a performance) superar; (a level) exceder; **to — off** (an action) rematar; (a tank) llenar hasta el tope; **that —s everything!** ¡eso es el colmo!

topaz [tópæz] N topacio *m*

topic [tápik] N tema *m*, materia *f*

topical [tápikəl] ADJ (of medicine) tópico; (current) de actualidad

topless [táplis] ADJ topless; **— swimsuit** monokini *m*

topple [tápəl] VT (knock over) derribar; (overthrow) derrocar; VI (fall) volcarse; (lose power) caer; **to — over** volcarse

topsy-turvy [tápsitɝvi] ADJ & ADV patas arriba

torch [tɔrtʃ] N antorcha *f*

torment [tɔ́rment] N tormento *m*; [tɔrmént] VT atormentar, martirizar

tornado [tɔrnédo] N tornado *m*

torpedo [tɔrpído] N torpedo *m*; **— boat** torpedero *m*; VT torpedear

torpor [tɔ́rpɚ] N letargo *m*, torpor *m*

torque [tɔrk] N par de torsión *m*

torrent [tɔ́rənt] N torrente *m*

torrential [tɔrénʃəl] ADJ torrencial

torrid [tɔ́rid] ADJ tórrido

torsion [tɔ́rʃən] N torsión *f*

torso [tɔ́rso] N torso *m*, tronco *m*

tortoise [tɔ́rdis] N tortuga *f*

tortuous [tɔ́rtʃuəs] ADJ tortuoso

torture [tɔ́rtʃɚ] N tortura *f*; VT torturar

torturous [tɔ́rtʃɚəs] ADJ torturante, torturador

toss [tɔs] VT (a ball, coin) tirar; (one's head) echar, tirar; (a salad) revolver; **to — aside** echar a un lado; VI (waves) cabecear; (in bed) dar vueltas; (of coin, ball) tiro *m*; (of head) sacudida *f*

total [tódl] ADJ & N total *m*; **— amount** importe total *m*, montante *m*

totalitarian [totælitériən] ADJ totalitario

totter [tádɚ] VI tambalear(se), titubear

touch [tatʃ] VI/VT tocar; (move deeply) conmover, enternecer; (compare with) compararse con, igualar; (affect) afectar; **to — down** aterrizar; **to — off** provocar; **to — up** retocar; **to — upon** mencionar; N (contact) contacto *m*, roce *m*, toque *m*; (sense) tacto *m*; (knack) mano *f*; (slight amount) poquito *m*; **—-and-go** precario; **a woman's —** un toque femenino;

—screen pantalla táctil *f*; **—stone** piedra de toque *f*; **—-tone** de botones; **finishing —** toque final *m*; **to keep in — with** mantener(se) en contacto con

touching [tátʃiŋ] ADJ conmovedor

touchy [tátʃi] ADJ hipersensible

tough [taf] ADJ (leather) fuerte, resistente; (fighter) duro, fuerte; (steak) duro, correoso; (situation) difícil; (neighborhood) bravo

toughen [táfən] VI/VT (leather) curtir(se); (meat) endurecer(se); (person) endurecerse

toughness [táfnis] N (of leather) resistencia *f*; (of a fighter, steak) dureza *f*; (of a situation) dificultad *f*; (of a neighborhood) lo bravo

toupee [tupé] N peluquín *m*

tour [tur] N (professional, artistic) gira *f*; (touristic) tour *m*, excursión *f*; (of a building) visita *f*; VI/VT (artistic, political) hacer una gira (por); (touristic) hacer un tour

tourism [túrzəm] N turismo *m*

tourist [túrst] N turista *mf*; **— class** clase turista / turística *f*

tournament [tɝnəmənt] N torneo *m*

tourniquet [tɝnikit] N torniquete *m*

tow [to] VT remolcar; N (pull) remolque *m*; (fiber) estopa *f*; **—rope** cuerda de remolque *f*; **— truck** remolque *m*, grúa *f*; **in —** a cuestas

toward, towards [təwɔ́rd(z)] PREP (in the direction of) hacia; (for) para; **— four o'clock** a eso de las cuatro; **to feel angry —** estar enojado con

towel [táuəl] N toalla *f*

tower [táuɚ] N torre *f*; VI elevarse; **to — over** dominar, descollar

towering [táuɚiŋ] ADJ (tall) elevado, muy alto; (excessive) desmedido

town [taun] N (large) ciudad *f*; (small) pueblo *m*, localidad *f*; (downtown) centro *m*; **— hall** ayuntamiento *m*, municipio *m*; **out of —** de viaje

toxic [táksik] ADJ tóxico

toxin [táksin] N toxina *f*

toy [tɔi] N juguete *m*; **— poodle** caniche enano *m*; VI **to — with** (fiddle with) juguetear con; (consider) considerar

trace [tres] N (path, mark, footprint) huella *f*; (mark) rastro *m*, traza *f*; (vestige) vestigio *m*; (strap) tirante *m*; VT (a plan) trazar; (history) examinar; (an image) calcar; (a criminal) rastrear

trachea [trékiə] N tráquea *f*

track [træk] N (of a heel, animal) huella *f*; (of a wheel) rodada *f*; (for racing) pista *f*;

(path) senda *f*, sendero *m*; (of a railroad) vía *f*; (on a record) surco *m*; (of study) orientación *f*; **— and field** atletismo *m*; **— meet** encuentro de atletismo *m*; **to be off the** — estar descarrilado; **to keep — of** seguir el hilo de; VI/VT (a criminal) rastrear, seguir la pista de; (an aircraft, a student, progress) seguir; VI (wheels) estar alineado; (stylus) seguir los surcos; **to — down** perseguir; **to — in mud** traer lodo en los pies

tract [trækt] N (of land) terreno *m*; (political) octavilla *f*; (digestive) tubo *m*

traction [trǽkʃən] N tracción *f*

tractor [trǽktɚ] N tractor *m*; **—-trailer** tractocamión *m*

trade [tred] N (buying and selling) comercio *m*, trato *m*; (industry) industria *f*; (swap) canje *m*, cambio *m*; (manual labor) oficio *m*; (profession) profesión *f*; (people in a business) gremio *m*; **—-in** entrega como parte de pago *f*; **—-off** compensación *f*; **—mark** marca registrada *f*, marca de fábrica *f*; **— name** (of product) nombre comercial *m*; (of company) razón social *f*; **— school** escuela industrial *f*; **— union** sindicato *m*; VI/VT (buy and sell) comerciar, negociar; (exchange) canjear; (traffic) traficar; **to — in** entregar

trader [trédɚ] N comerciante *mf*; (at fairs) feriante *mf*; (of slaves) tratante *mf*

tradition [trədíʃən] N tradición *f*

traditional [trədíʃənəł] ADJ tradicional

traffic [trǽfɪk] N (of drugs) tráfico *m*; (of vehicles) tránsito *m*, tráfico *m*; **— light** semáforo *m*; VI traficar

tragedy [trǽdʒɪdi] N tragedia *f*

tragic [trǽdʒɪk] ADJ trágico

trail [treł] VI/VT (drag) arrastrar(se); (follow in a race) ir detrás (de); (track) seguir la pista (de), rastrear; VT (leave a trace) dejar una estela / un reguero de; **to — off** desvanecerse, apagarse; N (trace) rastro *m*, huella *f*; (path) trocha *f*, sendero *m*, senda *f*; (of smoke) estela *f*; (of blood) reguero *m*; **— bike** motocicleta de trail *f*

trailer [trélɚ] N (of a truck) remolque *m*; (house) caravana *f*; (of a film) sinopsis *f*, trailer *m*, avance *m*

train [tren] N (railroad) tren *m*; (of a dress) cola *f*; **— of thought** hilo de pensamiento *m*; VI/VT (worker) capacitar(se); (troops, athlete) adiestrar(se); *Am* entrenar(se); VT (an animal) amaestrar; (a child) educar, formar; (a cannon) apuntar; **to — on** (a camera, eye) enfocar

trainee [trení] N aprendiz -iza *mf*,

practicante *mf*

trainer [trénɚ] N (of animals) amaestrador -ora *mf*; (of workers, troops, athletes) entrenador -ora *mf*

training [trénɪŋ] N (of animals) amaestramiento *m*; (of workers, troops, athletes) adiestramiento *m*, entrenamiento *m*; (of children) educación *f*

trait [tret] N rasgo *m*, seña *f*

traitor [trétɚ] N traidor -ora *mf*

trajectory [trədʒéktɚi] N trayectoria *f*

tramp [træmp] VT (trample) pisar; VI andar con pasos pesados; (roam, as a hobo) vagabundear; N (hobo) vagabundo -da *mf*; (promiscuous woman) *fam* fulana *f*; *Sp fam* golfa *f*

trample [trǽmpəł] VT pisotear; **to — on / over** pisotear, atropellar; **to — out** apagar de un pisotón

trampoline [trǽmpəlín] N trampolín *m*, cama elástica *f*

trance [træns] N trance *m*

tranquil [trǽŋkwɪł] ADJ tranquilo

tranquility [trænkwíłɪɾi] N tranquilidad *f*

tranquilizer [trǽŋkwɪlaɪzɚ] N tranquilizante *m*

transact [trænzǽkt] VT hacer, llevar a cabo

transaction [trænzǽkʃən] N transacción *f*, negocio *m*; **—s** actas *f pl*

transatlantic [trænzɪtlǽntɪk] ADJ transatlántico

transcend [trænsénd] VI/VT trascender

transcendence [trænséndəns] N trascendencia *f*

transcendental [trænsɛndɛ́ntł] ADJ trascendental, trascendente

transcribe [trænskráɪb] VT transcribir

transcript [trǽnskrɪpt] N transcripción *f*

transfer [trǽnsfɚ] VI/VT (bus, train) trasbordar; (a prisoner, worker) trasladar(se); VT (loyalty, rights, money) transferir; (property) traspasar; N (of loyalty, rights, money) transferencia *f*; (of a prisoner, worker) traslado *m*; (of property) traspaso *m*; (on a bus, train) trasbordo *m*; **— of ownership** traspaso de propiedad *m*

transferable [trænsfɚ́əbəł] ADJ transferible

transfix [trænsfíks] VT (paralyze) paralizar; (impale) traspasar, atravesar

transform [trænsfɔ́rm] VI/VT transformar(se)

transformation [trænsfɚ-méʃən] N transformación *f*

transformer [trænsfɔ́rmɚ] N transformador *m*

transfusion [trænsfjúʒən] N transfusión *f*

transgress [trænzgrɛ́s] VT transgredir; **to —**

against pecar contra; **to — the bounds of** traspasar los límites de

transgression [trænzgréʃən] N transgresión f, pecado m

transient [trǽnziənt] ADJ transeúnte, pasajero; N transeúnte mf, vagabundo -da mf

transistor [trænzístə-] N transistor m

transit [trǽnzɪt] N tránsito m; **in —** en tránsito, de paso

transition [trænzíʃən] N transición f

transitive [trǽnzɪDɪv] ADJ transitivo

transitory [trǽnzɪtɔri] ADJ transitorio, pasajero

translate [trænzlét] VI/VT traducir

translation [trænzléʃən] N (rendering in different language) traducción f; (movement) translación f

translator [trǽnzlenə-] N traductor -ora mf

transmission [trænzmíʃən] N transmisión f

transmit [trænzmít] VI/VT transmitir

transmitter [trænzmíDə-] N transmisor m

transom [trǽnsəm] N travesaño m, montante m

transparency [trænzpérənsi] N transparencia f

transparent [trænspérənt] ADJ transparente; **to be —** traslucirse

transpire [trænspáɪr] VI (happen) ocurrir; (become known) descubrirse; VI/VT (perspire) transpirar

transplant [trænsplént] VI/VT trasplantar; [trǽnsplænt] N trasplante m

transport [trænspórt] VT transportar, acarrear; [trǽnspɔrt] N (moving) transporte m, acarreo m; (airplane) avión de transporte m; (rapture) éxtasis m; (of freight) flete m

transportation [trænspə-téʃən] N transporte m

transpose [trænspóz] VI/VT (letters) transponer; (a song) transportar

transsexual [trænsékʃuəł] ADJ & N transexual mf

transverse [trænsvə́-s] ADJ transversal; (flute) transverso

transvestite [trænzvéstaɪt] N travestí mf, travesti mf, travestido -da mf

trap [træp] N trampa f; (for hunting) trampa f, cepo m; (under a sink) sifón m; **— door** trampilla f; VI/VT (to capture animals) cazar con trampa, atrapar; VT (to pinch) atrapar; (to pin) aprisionar

trapeze [træpíz] N trapecio m

trapezoid [trǽpəzɔɪd] N & ADJ trapezoide m

trash [træʃ] N basura f, desechos m pl; (people) pej gentuza f; **— can** cubo de

basura m

trashy [trǽʃi] ADJ ordinario

trauma [trɔ́mə] N (physical) traumatismo m; (psychological) trauma m

traumatic [trəmǽDɪk] ADJ traumático

travel [trǽvəł] VI/VT viajar (por); VI (sound waves) propagarse; N (traveling) viajar m; **— agency** agencia de viajes f; **—s** viajes m pl

traveler [trǽvələ-] N viajero -ra mf; **—'s check** cheque de viajero m

traverse [trəvə́-s] VI/VT atravesar, cruzar; (skiing) bajar en diagonal; N (crossbar) travesaño m; (crossing) travesía f

travesty [trǽvɪsti] N farsa f

tray [tre] N bandeja f

treacherous [trétʃə-əs] ADJ traicionero, alevoso

treachery [trétʃəri] N traición f, alevosía f

tread [trɛd] VI/VT (trample) pisar, pisotear; VI (walk) andar, caminar; N (step) paso m; (on tire) banda de rodadura/ rodaje f; (on shoe) dibujo m; **—mill** cinta rodante f

treason [trízən] N traición f

treasure [tréʒə-] N tesoro m; **— hunt** búsqueda del tesoro f; VT atesorar

treasurer [tréʒərə-] N tesorero -ra mf

treasury [tréʒəri] N tesorería f, tesoro m; **Secretary of the —** Ministro -tra de Hacienda mf

treat [trit] VI/VT tratar (de); **I —ed myself to ice cream** me di un festín de helado; N (pleasure) placer m; (gift) regalo m; **my —** yo invito

treatable [tríDəbəł] ADJ tratable

treatise [tríDɪs] N tratado m

treatment [trítmənt] N trato m, tratamiento m; (artistic handling) interpretación f

treaty [tríDi] N tratado m

treble [trébəł] ADJ (triple) triple; (of higher clef) de tiple; **— clef** clave de sol f; N tiple m; VI/VT triplicar

tree [tri] N árbol m; **— hugger** ecologista mf; **—top** copa de árbol f; **up a —** en aprietos

treeless [trílɪs] ADJ pelado, sin árboles

trek [trɛk] N expedición f; VI viajar con dificultad

tremble [trémbəł] VI temblar; N temblor m

tremendous [triméndəs] ADJ tremendo

tremor [trémə-] N temblor m, sacudida f

tremulous [trémjələs] ADJ trémulo

trench [trɛntʃ] N (military) trinchera f; (for pipes) zanja f; (on sea floor) fosa f; **— coat** trinchera f, gabardina f

trend [trɛnd] N tendencia f

trendy [tréndi] ADJ de moda

trespass [tréspæs] N (illegal entry) entrada

ilegal f; (religious) deuda f; vi (enter illegally) entrar ilegalmente; **to — against** violar; (sin) pecar; **no —ing** prohibida la entrada

triage [triáʒ] N triaje m, clasificación f

trial [tráɪəł] N (testing) ensayo m, prueba f; (attempt) tentativa f; (affliction) aflicción f; (in a court of law) juicio m, proceso m; **— balloon** globo sonda m; **— by fire** prueba de fuego f; **— flight** vuelo de prueba m; **— run** ensayo m, prueba f; **by — and error** por ensayo y error

triangle [tráɪæŋgəł] N triángulo m

triangular [traɪǽŋgjələ] ADJ triangular

tribe [traɪb] N tribu f

tribulation [trɪbjəléʃən] N tribulación f

tribunal [traɪbjúnəł] N tribunal m

tributary [tríbjəteri] ADJ & N tributario m, afluente m

tribute [tríbjut] N (tax) tributo m; (testimonial) homenaje m

triceps [tráɪsɛps] N triceps m sg

trick [trɪk] N (ruse) treta f, trampa f, trapisonda f; (magician's) truco m; (prank) broma f; (in cards) baza f; (of a prostitute) fam chapa f; **to be up to one's old —s** hacer de las suyas; **to play a — on someone** gastarle una broma a alguien; **to turn —s** slang prostituirse; slang hacer chapas; vt hacer trampa, engañar; **to — someone into something** hacer que alguien haga algo por medio de artilugios

trickery [tríkəri] N engaños m pl, argucias f pl

trickle [tríkəł] vi gotear; **to — in (out)** llegar (irse) de a poco; N goteo m

trickster [tríkstə] N embustero -ra mf

tricky [tríki] ADJ (artful) mañoso; (difficult) complicado

tricycle [tráɪsɪkəł] N triciclo m

trifle [tráɪfəł] N (worthless thing) fruslería f, nadería f, bobada f; (cheap purchase) bagatela f; (small sum) miseria f; vi **to — with** jugar con; **to — away** perder

trigger [trígə] N gatillo m; vt desencadenar; (suddenly) disparar

trill [trɪł] vi/vt (birds) trinar; (musical instrument) tremolar; (the r sound) pronunciar con vibración; N (of birds, etc.) trino m; (of the r sound) vibración f

trillion [tríljən] N billón m

trilogy [tríləʤi] N trilogía f

trim [trɪm] vt (adorn) adornar, guarnecer; (an edge) bordear; (fingernails, hair, threads) recortar; (hedge) podar; (airplane) equilibrar; (a wick) despabilar; ADJ (neat) cuidado; (slim) delgado; (fit) en buen

estado físico; N (embellishment) adorno m; (of sails) orientación f; (cutting of hair) recorte m; (cutting of hedge) poda f; (of an airplane) equilibrio m

trimming [trímɪŋ] N (act of cutting) recorte m; (on a uniform) orla f, ribete m; **—s** (embellishments) adornos m pl; (food) guarniciones f pl; (parts cut off) recortes m pl

Trinidad and Tobago [trínɪdædəntəbégo] N Trinidad y Tobago f

Trinidadian [trɪnɪdǽDiən] ADJ & N trinitense mf

trinket [tríŋkɪt] N chuchería f, baratija f

trio [trío] N trío m

trip [trɪp] N (journey, drug-induced condition) viaje m; (experience) experiencia f; (light step) paso ligero m; (accidental stumble) tropezón m; (throwing down) zancadilla f; vt (cause to stumble) hacer una zancadilla a; (cause to make error) confundir; (release a catch) soltar; (blow a fuse) hacer saltar; vi (stumble) tropezar; (skip) andar con paso ligero; (make a mistake) equivocarse; (hallucinate) viajar; (blow a fuse) saltar

triphthong [trípθɔŋ] N triptongo m

triple [trípəł] ADJ & N triple m; vi/vt triplicar

triplet [tríplɪt] N trillizo m

tripod [tráɪpɑd] N trípode m

trite [traɪt] ADJ trivial, trillado

triumph [tráɪəmf] N triunfo m; vi triunfar

triumphant [traɪʌ́mfənt] ADJ triunfante

trivial [tríviəł] ADJ trivial, baladí, fútil

trolley [trúli] N (electric bus) trole m, trolebús m; (on tracks) tranvía m

trombone [trámbon] N trombón m

troop [trup] N (of scouts) tropa f; (of soldiers) escuadrón m; (of tourists) horda f; **—s** tropas f pl

trophy [trófi] N trofeo m

tropic [trápɪk] N trópico m

tropical [trápɪkəł] ADJ tropical

trot [trat] vi trotar; vt hacer trotar; **to — out** sacar a relucir; N trote m; **the —s** fam cagalera f

trouble [trʌ́bəł] vt (make turbid) enturbiar; (afflict) aquejar; vi/vt (bother) molestar(se); (disturb) preocupar(se); N (problem) problema m; (difficulty) dificultad f, sinsabor m; (disturbance) disturbio m; (effort) molestia f; (ailment) enfermedad f, trastorno m; (mechanical breakdown) avería f, desperfecto m; **to be in — estar en un aprieto; it is not worth the —** no vale la pena; **—maker** agitador -ra mf, revoltoso -sa mf; **—shoot**

solucionar problemas; **—shooter** solucionador -ra *mf*, localizador -ra de averías *mf*; **to make —** causar problemas

trough [trɔf] N (for food) pesebre *m*, comedero *m*; (for water) abrevadero *m*, bebedero *m*; (of weather, on ocean floor) depresión *f*

trousers [tráʊzɚz] N pantalones *m pl*

trousseau [trúso] N ajuar *m*

trout [traʊt] N trucha *f*

trowel [tráʊəl] N (for mortar) llana *f*, paleta *f*; (for digging) desplantador *m*

truant [trúənt] N alumno -na que falta a clase sin permiso *mf*

truce [trus] N tregua *f*

truck [trʌk] N (vehicle) camión *m*; *Mex* troca *f*; (dealings) trato *m*; (vegetables) hortalizas *f pl*; **— driver** camionero -ra *mf*; *Mex* troquero -ra *mf*; VI/VT transportar en camión; *Mex* transportar en troca

trudge [trʌdʒ] VI andar con dificultad; N caminata difícil *f*

true [tru] ADJ verdadero; (story) verídico; (copy, translation) fiel; (well) a plomo; (wheel) alineado, centrado; **—blue** leal; **—false test** prueba de verdadero o falso *f*; **his dream came —** su sueño se hizo realidad

truly [trúli] ADV (surprisingly) verdaderamente; (sincerely) sinceramente; (actually) en realidad, realmente; (accurately) fielmente; **very — yours** su seguro servidor, atentamente

trumpet [trʌ́mpɪt] N trompeta *f*; VI/VT trompetear; (an elephant) barritar

trunk [trʌŋk] N (of tree, body) tronco *m*; (receptacle) baúl *m*; (of elephant) trompa *f*; (of a car) maletero *m*, *Mex* cajuela *f*; **—s** traje de baño *m*

trust [trʌst] N (responsibility) confianza *f*; (hope) esperanza *f*; (credit) crédito *m*; (charge) cargo *m*; (firm) trust *m*; (fund) fondo fideicomiso *m*; VI/VT (rely on) confiar en, fiarse de; VT (believe) creer; (hope) esperar

trustee [trʌstí] N (person holding property of another) fideicomisario -ria *mf*; (administrator) administrador -ra *mf*

trusteeship [trʌstíʃɪp] N (position of holding property) fideicomiso *m*; (administrative position) cargo de administrador *m*

trustful [trʌ́stfəl] ADJ confiado

trusting [trʌ́stɪŋ] ADJ confiado

trustworthy [trʌ́stwɚði] ADJ fidedigno, digno de confianza

trusty [trʌ́sti] ADJ leal

truth [truθ] N verdad *f*

truthful [trúθfəl] ADJ (account) verídico; (person) veraz

truthfulness [trúθfəlnɪs] N veracidad *f*

try [traɪ] VT (attempt) tratar de, intentar; (test, taste) probar; (strain) poner a prueba; (put on trial) procesar, enjuiciar; **to — on** probarse; **to — one's luck** probar fortuna; **to — and** tratar de; **to — out** (test) probar; (for a team) presentarse para; **—out** prueba *f*; N intento *m*, tentativa *f*

trying [tráɪŋ] ADJ penoso

tryst [trɪst] N cita romántica *f*

T-shirt [tíʃɚt] N camiseta *f*

tub [tʌb] N (for bathing) bañera *f*; (for butter) envase *m*; (for washing) tina *f*

tuba [túbə] N tuba *f*

tube [tub] N tubo *m* (also electronic); (television) televisor *m*

tuberculosis [tubɚkjəlósɪs] N tuberculosis *f*

tubular [túbjələ] ADJ tubular

tuck [tʌk] VT (stick in) meter; (make fold) alforzar; **to — in one's shirt** meter la camisa dentro del pantalón; **to — into bed** arropar; **to — something under one's arm** meterse algo bajo el brazo; N alforza *f*

Tuesday [túzde] N martes *m*

tuft [tʌft] N (of feathers) penacho *m*, copete *m*; (of hair) mechón *m*; (of plants) mata *f*

tug [tʌg] VI/VT (pull) tirar, jalar; (drag) arrastrar; **to — at** tironear; N tirón *m*; (boat) remolcador *m*

tuition [tuíʃən] N matrícula *f*

tulip [túlɪp] N tulipán *m*

tumble [tʌ́mbəl] VI (fall) caer; (collapse) venirse abajo; (do handsprings, etc.) dar volteretas; **to — down** rodar; **to — dry** secar en la secadora; **to — over** tropezarse; (fall) caída *f*; (gymnastic trick) voltereta *f*

tumbler [tʌ́mblə] N (glass) vaso *m*; (person) acróbata *mf*

tummy [tʌ́mi] N barriguita *f*

tumor [túmə] N tumor *m*

tumult [túmʌlt] N tumulto *m*

tumultuous [tumʌ́ltʃuəs] ADJ tumultuoso

tuna [túnə] N (fish) atún *m*, bonito *m*; (prickly pear) tuna *f*

tune [tun] N (melody) tonada *f*, aire *m*; (electronic adjustment) sintonía *f*; **to be in —** (in pitch) estar afinado; (adjusted) sintonizado; **to be out of —** estar desafinado; VT (engine) afinar; (musical instrument) afinar, templar; (radio) sintonizar; **to — in** sintonizar; **to — out** ignorar; **—up** afinación *f*

tuner [túnə] N afinador -ra *mf*; (electronics)

sintonizador *m*
tungsten [tʌ́ŋstən] N tungsteno *m*
tunic [túnɪk] N túnica *f*
Tunisia [tuníʒə] N Túnez *m*
Tunisian [tuníʒən] ADJ & N tunesino -na *mf*
tunnel [tʌ́nəl] N túnel *m*; (for traffic) viaducto *m*; VI cavar; VT hacer un túnel
turban [tɝ́bən] N turbante *m*
turbine [tɝ́baɪn] N turbina *f*
turbocharger [tɝ́boʧɑrʤə] N turbocompresor *m*
turbojet [tɝ́boʤɛt] N turborreactor *m*
turbulent [tɝ́bjələnt] ADJ turbulento
turd [tɝd] N *vulg* zurullo *m*, mojón *m*
turf [tɝf] N (lawn) césped *m*; (peat) turba *f*; (track for horseraces) pista *f*; (territory) territorio *m*; VT cubrir con césped
Turk [tɝk] N turco -ca *mf*
turkey [tɝ́ki] N pavo *m*; **— vulture** buitre pavo *m*
Turkey [tɝ́ki] N Turquía *f*
Turkish [tɝ́kɪʃ] ADJ turco; **— bath** baño turco *m*
Turkmen [tɝ́kmən] ADJ & N turcomano -na *mf*
Turkmenistan [tɝkmɛnɪstǽn] N Turkmenistán *m*
turmoil [tɝ́mɔɪl] N confusión *f*, agitación *f*
turn [tɝn] VT (corner) doblar, dar vuelta; (wheel, key) girar, dar vuelta; (page) dar vuelta; (soil) labrar; (stomach) revolver; (ankle) torcerse; (a river) desviar; VI (change color) cambiar de color; (become) ponerse; (rotate) girar; (change direction) girar, dar la vuelta; (be nauseated) revolvérsele a uno; **to — against** volverse en contra de; **to — around** dar la vuelta, girar; **to — away** (face) volver; (eyes) apartar; (person) rechazar; **to — back** (return) volver; (a clock) atrasar; **to — down** (offer) rechazar; (radio) bajar; (request) rechazar; **to — in** (hand in / over) entregar; (go to bed) acostarse; **to — inside out** dar vuelta al revés; **to — into** convertir(se) en; **to — off** (light) apagar; (faucet) cerrar; (a road) salir de; (person in general sense) disgustar; (person in sexual sense) quitarle las ganas a alguien; **to — on** (light) encender, prender; (faucet) abrir; (person) excitar; **to — out** (light) apagar; (people) expulsar; (product) producir; **—out** concurrencia *f*; **to — out well** salir bien; **to — over** (car) volcar(se); (engine) arrancar; (thought, idea, etc.) dar vueltas a; (criminal, weapon, etc.) entregar; **—over** (of employees) renovación *f*; (of merchandise)

volumen *m*; (pastry) empanada *f*, pastelito *m*; (of a ball) pérdida *f*; **—pike** autopista *f*; **—stile** torniquete *m*, molinete *m*; **—table** plato giratorio *m*; **to — to** (have recourse to) acudir a, recurrir a; (become) volver(se); **to — up** aparecer; **to — up one's nose** desdeñar; **to — up one's sleeves** arremangarse; **to — upside down** dar vuelta; N (rotation) vuelta *f*, revolución *f*; (change of direction) giro *m*, vuelta *f*; (change in condition) cambio *m*; (curve) recodo *m*, curva *f*; (opportunity) turno *m*; **— of mind** actitud *f*; **— of phrase** giro *m*; **— signal** intermitente *m*; **at every —** a cada paso; **bad —** mala pasada *f*; **good —** favor *m*; **it's my —** me toca a mí; **to take —s** turnarse
turnip [tɝ́nɪp] N nabo *m*
turpentine [tɝ́pəntaɪn] N trementina *f*, aguarrás *m*
turquoise [tɝ́kɔɪz] N turquesa *f*
turret [tɝ́ɪt] N (small tower, gun tower) torreta *f*; (on a ship) torre *f*
turtle [tɝ́dl] N tortuga *f*; **—dove** tórtola *f*; **—neck** cuello vuelto *m*
tusk [tʌsk] N colmillo *m*
tutor [túɾə] N profesor -ora particular *mf*; VI/VT dar clases particulares
Tuvalu [túvəlu] N Tuvalu *m*
Tuvaluan [tuvəlúən] ADJ & N tuvaluano -na *mf*
tuxedo [tʌksído] N esmoquin *m*
TV (television) [tíví] N tele *f*
twang [twæŋ] N (in music) tañido *m*; (of speech) nasalidad *f*; VI (vibrate) vibrar; VT hacer vibrar; VI/VT (speak nasally) ganguear
twangy [twǽŋi] ADJ gangoso
tweak [twik] VT (pinch) pellizcar; (adjust) ajustar; N (pinch) pellizco *m*; (adjustment) ajuste *m*
tweed [twid] N tweed *m*
tweezers [twízɝz] N pinzas *f pl*
twelve [twɛlv] NUM doce
twenty [twɛ́nti] NUM veinte
twerp [twɝp] N idiota *mf*, papanatas *mf sg*
twice [twaɪs] ADV dos veces
twig [twɪg] N ramita *f*
twilight [twáɪlaɪt] N crepúsculo *m*, ocaso *m*; **— zone** zona gris *f*
twin [twɪn] ADJ & N mellizo -za *mf*, gemelo -la *mf*; **— bed** cama individual *f*
twine [twaɪn] N cuerda *f*; VI/VT (twist) enroscar(se); (interlace) entrelazar(se)
twinge [twɪnʤ] N punzada *f*
twinkle [twíŋkəl] VI (star) titilar, parpadear; (eyes) brillar; N (of stars) titileo *m*,

parpadeo m; (of eyes) brillo m

twirl [twɜ-l] vi/vt girar, dar vueltas (a); N giro m, vuelta f; (of ice cream) espiral m

twist [twɪst] vi/vt torcer(se); (distort) tergiversar(se); (writhe) retorcer(se); (coil) enroscar(se); N (of an ankle) torcedura f; (in a road, coil) vuelta f; (unforeseen event) vuelta de tuerca f; (distortion) tergiversación f

twister [twɪstə-] N tornado m

twitch [twɪtʃ] vi/vt crispar(se), mover(se); N (tic) tic m; (pang) punzada f; (tug) tirón m

twitter [twɪ́də-] vi gorjear; N gorjeo m

two [tu] NUM dos; **—-bit** de chicha y nabo; **my — cents' worth** mi opinión f; **—-edged** de doble filo; **—-faced** (with two faces) de dos caras; (hypocritical) hipócrita, falso; **—-fisted** pendenciero; **—-way** de dos sentidos

tycoon [taɪkún] N magnate mf

type [taɪp] N tipo m, índole f; vi/vt (a letter) escribir a máquina, mecanografiar; vt (blood) determinar el grupo sanguíneo; **—script** texto escrito a máquina m; **to —set** componer; **to —write** escribir a máquina; **—writer** máquina de escribir f; **—writing** mecanografía f; **—written** escrito a máquina

typhoid [táɪfɔɪd] N tifoidea f; **— fever** fiebre tifoidea f, tifus m

typhoon [taɪfún] N tifón m

typical [típɪkəl] ADJ típico

typist [táɪpɪst] N mecanógrafo -fa mf

typographical [taɪpəgrǽfɪkəl] ADJ tipográfico; **— error** error de imprenta m, errata f

typology [taɪpálədʒi] N tipología f

tyrannical [tɪrǽnɪkəl] ADJ tiránico

tyranny [tírəni] N tiranía f

tyrant [táɪrənt] N tirano -na mf

Uu

ubiquitous [jubíkwɪdəs] ADJ ubicuo

U-boat [júbot] N submarino m

udder [ʌ́də-] N ubre f

UFO (unidentified flying object) [juefó] N OVNI m

Uganda [jugǽndə] N Uganda f

Ugandan [jugǽndən] ADJ & N ugandés -esa mf

ugliness [ʌ́glinɪs] N fealdad f

ugly [ʌ́gli] ADJ feo; (incident) deplorable; (mood) de perros

uh-huh [ʌhá] INTERJ sí

Ukraine [jukrén] N Ucrania f

Ukrainian [jukréniən] ADJ & N ucraniano -na mf

ulcer [ʌ́lsə-] N úlcera f

ulterior [ʌltíriə-] ADJ ulterior; **— motive** segunda intención f

ultimate [ʌ́ltəmɪt] ADJ (destination) último, final; (authority) final, máximo; (principle) fundamental; (vacation) perfecto; N súmmum m

ultimatum [ʌltəmédəm] N ultimátum m

ultralight [ʌ́ltrəlaɪt] ADJ & N ultraligero m

ultramodern [ʌltrəmádə-n] ADJ ultramoderno

ultraviolet [ʌltrəváɪəlɪt] ADJ & N ultravioleta m

umbilical cord [ʌmbílɪkəlkɔrd] N cordón umbilical m

umbrella [ʌmbrélə] N paraguas m sg

umpire [ʌ́mpaɪr] N árbitro m; vi/vt arbitrar

unable [ʌnébəl] ADJ **to be —** to no poder

unaccented [ʌnǽksɛntɪd] ADJ sin acento

unacceptable [ʌnɪkséptəbəl] ADJ inaceptable

unaccustomed [ʌnəkʌ́stəmd] ADJ (not used to) no acostumbrado; (uncommon) insólito

unadulterated [ʌnədʌ́ltəredɪd] ADJ puro

unaffected [ʌnəféktɪd] ADJ (sincere) natural, sincero; (unpretentious) sin afectación

unanimity [junənímɪdi] N unanimidad f

unanimous [junǽnəməs] ADJ unánime

unarmed [ʌnármd] ADJ desarmado

unassuming [ʌnəsúmɪŋ] ADJ modesto, sin pretensiones

unattached [ʌnətǽtʃt] ADJ (piece of paper) suelto; (person) soltero

unavoidable [ʌnəvɔ́ɪdəbəl] ADJ inevitable

unaware [ʌnəwér] ADJ inconsciente; ADV **to be — of** ignorar; **—s** sin darse cuenta

unbalanced [ʌnbǽlənst] ADJ desequilibrado

unbearable [ʌnbérəbəl] ADJ inaguantable, insoportable

unbeatable [ʌnbídəbəl] ADJ imbatible

unbeaten [ʌnbítn] ADJ invicto

unbecoming [ʌnbɪkʌ́mɪŋ] ADJ (inappropriate) impropio; (unflattering) que no queda bien

unbelief [ʌnbɪlíf] N incredulidad f, descreimiento m

unbelievable [ʌnbɪlívəbəl] ADJ increíble

unbeliever [ʌnbɪlívə-] N descreído -da mf

unbending [ʌnbéndɪŋ] ADJ inflexible

unbiased [ʌnbáɪəst] ADJ imparcial

unbounded [ʌnbáʊndɪd] ADJ ilimitado

unbridled [ʌnbráɪdld] ADJ desenfrenado

unbroken [ʌnbrókən] ADJ (intact) intacto; (not tamed) indomado; (uninterrupted) ininterrumpido

unbuckle [ʌnbákəl] VT desabrochar

unbutton [ʌnbátn] VI/VT desabotonar, desabrochar

uncalled-for [ʌnkɔ́ldfɔr] ADJ injustificado

uncanny [ʌnkǽni] ADJ inexplicable, misterioso

uncertain [ʌnsɚ́tn] ADJ incierto

uncertainty [ʌnsɚ́tnti] N incertidumbre f

unchanged [ʌntʃéndʒd] ADJ inalterado

uncharitable [ʌntʃǽrɪɾəbəl] ADJ duro, poco caritativo

uncivilized [ʌnsívəlaɪzd] ADJ incivilizado

uncle [ʌ́ŋkəl] N tío m; **to say —** darse por vencido

unclean [ʌnklín] ADJ (dirty) sucio; (impure) impuro

uncomfortable [ʌnkámfɚ-Dəbəl] ADJ incómodo

uncommon [ʌnkámən] ADJ (unusual) poco común; (extraordinary) extraordinario

uncompromising [ʌnkámprəmaɪzɪŋ] ADJ (intransigent) intransigente; (unfailing) incondicional

unconcerned [ʌnkənsɚ́nd] ADJ indiferente

unconditional [ʌnkəndíʃənəl] ADJ incondicional

unconscious [ʌnkánʃəs] ADJ inconsciente

unconstitutional [ʌnkanstɪtúʃənəl] ADJ inconstitucional

uncontrollable [ʌnkəntróləbəl] ADJ (movement) incontrolable; (urge, laughter) incontenible

unconventional [ʌnkənvénʃənəl] ADJ poco convencional

uncouth [ʌnkúθ] ADJ tosco

uncover [ʌnkávɚ] VI/VT descubrir(se); VI (remove bedcovers) destaparse

unctuous [ʌ́ŋktʃuəs] ADJ untuoso, zalamero

uncultivated [ʌnkʌ́ltəvɛDɪd] ADJ (talent) inculto, no cultivado; (land) no cultivado

uncultured [ʌnkʌ́ltʃɚd] ADJ inculto

undaunted [ʌndɔ́ntɪd] ADJ impávido, intrépido

undecided [ʌndɪsáɪDɪd] ADJ indeciso

undeniable [ʌndɪnáɪəbəl] ADJ innegable

under [ʌ́ndɚ] PREP (below) bajo, debajo de, abajo de; (in a ranking) por debajo de; (less) menos de; **— the democrats** durante el mandato de los demócratas; **— a pseudonym** bajo un seudónimo; **— cost** a menos del costo/coste, por debajo del costo/coste; ADV (below) debajo, abajo; (less than) menos; **to be —** estar inconsciente

underage [ʌndɚéɡ] ADJ menor de edad; **— drinking** consumo de alcohol por menores de edad m

underarm [ʌ́ndɚɑrm] N axila f

underbrush [ʌ́ndɚbrʌʃ] N maleza f

underclass [ʌ́ndɚklæs] N subproletariado m

undercover [ʌndɚkávɚ] ADJ clandestino, secreto

undercut [ʌndɚkát] VT (undermine) socavar; (sell for less) vender por menos que

underdeveloped [ʌndɚdɪvéləpt] ADJ subdesarrollado

underdog [ʌ́ndɚdɔɡ] N el/la de abajo

underemployed [ʌndɚemplɔ́ɪd] ADJ subempleado

underestimate [ʌndɚéstəmet] VT (person) subestimar; (price) subvalorar

underfed [ʌndɚféd] ADJ desnutrido

underfoot [ʌndɚfút] ADJ (beneath the feet) bajo los pies; (in the way) estorbando

undergird [ʌndɚgɚ́d] VT reforzar

undergo [ʌndɚgó] VT (an operation) someterse a; (a change) experimentar, sufrir

undergraduate [ʌndɚgrǽdʒuɪt] N estudiante de pregrado mf; **— course** programa de pregrado m

underground [ʌ́ndɚgraund] ADJ (under the earth) subterráneo; (secret) clandestino; N resistencia f, grupo clandestino m; ADV (under the earth) bajo tierra; (secretly) en secreto

underhanded [ʌndɚhǽndɪd] ADJ (secret) secreto, solapado; (illicit) ilícito

underlie [ʌndɚláɪ] VI/VT subyacer (a)

underline [ʌ́ndɚlaɪn] VT subrayar

undermine [ʌndɚmáɪn] VT minar, menoscabar

underneath [ʌndɚníθ] PREP bajo, debajo de, abajo de; ADV debajo, abajo; N la parte inferior

underpants [ʌ́ndɚpænts] N (for men) calzoncillos m pl; (for women) Sp bragas f pl; Mex pantaletas f pl; RP bombacha f

undersecretary [ʌndɚsékrəteri] N subsecretario -ria mf

undersell [ʌndɚsél] VT (to sell at a low price) malbaratar; (to sell cheaper than) vender a menos precio que

undershirt [ʌ́ndɚʃɚt] N camiseta f

underside [ʌ́ndɚsaɪd] N parte inferior f

undersigned [ʌndɚsáɪnd] N abajofirmante mf, infrascrito -ta mf

underskirt [ʌ́ndɚskɚt] N enaguas f pl

understaffed [ʌndɚstǽft] ADJ falto de personal

understand [ʌndɚstǽnd] VI/VT comprender,

entender; **I — you're leaving** tengo entendido que te vas; **to — about** saber de/entender de

understandable [ʌndə-stǽndəbəl] ADJ comprensible

understanding [ʌndə-stǽndɪŋ] N (comprehension) comprensión f, entendimiento m; (tolerance) comprensión mutua f; (agreement) acuerdo m; ADJ comprensivo

understate [ʌndə-stét] VT minimizar

understood [ʌndə-stʊd] ADJ entendido; (implicit) sobreentendido

understudy [ʌndə-stʌdi] N suplente mf, sobresaliente mf; VI/VT servir de sobresaliente (para), suplir (a)

undertake [ʌndə-ték] VT emprender, acometer; **to — to** comprometerse a

undertaker [ʌndə-tekə-] N director -ra de funeraria/pompas fúnebres mf, funerario -ria mf

undertaking [ʌndə-tékɪŋ] N empresa f

under-the-table [ʌndə-ðətébəl] ADJ ilícito, bajo cuerda

undertone [ʌndə-ton] N (low voice) voz baja f; (undercurrent) tónica f

undertow [ʌndə-to] N resaca f

underwater [ʌndə-wɔtə-] ADJ submarino; [ʌndə-wɔtə-] ADV por debajo del agua

underwear [ʌndə-wer] N ropa interior f

underweight [ʌndə-wet] ADJ de peso insuficiente

underworld [ʌndə-wɜ-ld] N (of criminals) hampa f; (netherworld) el más allá

underwrite [ʌndə-raɪt] VI/VT (finance) financiar; (sign) suscribir; (insure) asegurar

undesirable [ʌndɪzáɪrəbəl] ADJ indeseable

undisturbed [ʌndɪstɜ-bd] ADJ (unworried, uninterrupted) tranquilo; (unspoiled) virgen

undo [ʌndú] VT (reverse an action) deshacer; (unfasten) desabrochar, desabotonar; (destroy) destruir; (loosen hair) soltar

undoing [ʌndúɪŋ] N (reversal) deshacer m; (destruction) destrucción f, perdición f; (of buttons) desabrochar m

undone [ʌndán] ADJ (unfinished) sin terminar; (ruined) perdido; (unfastened) desabrochado; **to come —** (clothing) desabrocharse; (person) desquiciarse

undoubtedly [ʌndáʊdidli] ADV indudablemente, sin duda

undress [ʌndrés] VI/VT desnudar(se), desvestir(se)

undue [ʌndú] ADJ (inappropriate) indebido; (excessive) excesivo

undulate [ʌndʒəlet] VI/VT ondular

undying [ʌndáɪɪŋ] ADJ imperecedero, eterno

unearth [ʌnɜ́-θ] VT desenterrar

uneasiness [ʌnízinɪs] N (feeling) inquietud f, desasosiego m, desazón f; Sp grima f; (of peace) precariedad f; (of silence, situation) incomodidad f

uneasy [ʌnízi] ADJ (feeling) inquieto; (peace) precario; (silence) incómodo; (situation) molesto; (sleep) agitado

uneducated [ʌnédʒəkeɪd] ADJ inculto, ignorante

unemployed [ʌnɛmplɔ́ɪd] ADJ (jobless) desocupado, desempleado, parado; (unused) ocioso

unemployment [ʌnɛmplɔ́ɪmənt] N desocupación f, desempleo m, paro m; **— compensation** seguro de paro m; Sp paro m

unending [ʌnɛ́ndɪŋ] ADJ interminable

unequal [ʌníkwəl] ADJ desigual; **to be — to a task** no ser capaz de cumplir una tarea

unequivocal [ʌnɪkwívəkəl] ADJ inequívoco, tajante

uneven [ʌnívən] ADJ (rough) irregular, accidentado; (inequitable) desigual; (not uniform) disparejo; (odd, of numbers) impar

uneventful [ʌnɪvéntfəl] ADJ sin incidente

unexpected [ʌnɪkspéktɪd] ADJ inesperado

unexpressive [ʌnɪksprésɪv] ADJ inexpresivo

unfailing [ʌnfélɪŋ] ADJ (inexhaustible) inagotable; (dependable) infalible

unfair [ʌnfér] ADJ (measure, price) injusto; (competition) injusto, desleal

unfaithful [ʌnféθfəl] ADJ infiel

unfamiliar [ʌnfəmíljə-] ADJ (unknown) poco familiar, desconocido; (unacquainted) poco familiarizado

unfasten [ʌnfǽsən] VI/VT desabrochar(se), desprender(se)

unfavorable [ʌnfévə-əbəl] ADJ desfavorable

unfeeling [ʌnfílɪŋ] ADJ insensible

unfettered [ʌnfɛ́tə-d] ADJ desatado

unfinished [ʌnfínɪʃt] ADJ (matter) inacabado, inconcluso; (business) pendiente; (wood) sin barnizar; (task) inconcluso, sin terminar

unfit [ʌnfít] ADJ (unsuitable) no apto; (incapable) incapaz

unfold [ʌnfóld] VT (open out) desdoblar, desplegar; VI (happen) desarrollarse; (appear) extenderse; (reveal) revelarse

unforeseen [ʌnfɔrsín] ADJ imprevisto

unforgettable [ʌnfə-gédəbəl] ADJ inolvidable

unfortunate [ʌnfɔ́rtʃənət] ADJ desgraciado, desafortunado, desventurado

unfounded [ʌnfáʊndɪd] ADJ infundado

unfriendly [ʌnfréndli] ADJ (forces) hostil;
(person) antipático

unfurl [ʌnfɔ́ɨl] VI/VT desplegar(se)

unfurnished [ʌnfɔ́ɨnɪʃt] ADJ sin amueblar,
desamueblado

ungainly [ʌngénli] ADJ (ungraceful)
desgarbado, desmadejado; (clumsy) torpe

ungrateful [ʌngrétfəɨ] ADJ ingrato,
desagradecido

unguarded [ʌngáɨdɪd] ADJ (incautious)
descuidado, desprevenido; (unattended)
sin vigilancia; (defenseless) indefenso; an
— moment un momento de descuido

unhappiness [ʌnhǽpinɪs] N infelicidad f

unhappy [ʌnhǽpi] ADJ (sad) infeliz,
desdichado, desgraciado; (dissatisfied)
insatisfecho; (infelicitous) poco afortunado

unharmed [ʌnháɨmd] ADJ ileso

unhealthy [ʌnhéɨθi] ADJ (climate, food,
lifestyle) malsano, insalubre; (complexion,
obsession) enfermizo

unheard-of [ʌnhɔ́ɨ-ɒv] ADJ inaudito,
desconocido

unhinge [ʌnhíndʒ] VT desquiciar

unholy [ʌnhóli] ADJ (noise) infernal;
(alliance) nefasto

unhook [ʌnhúk] VT (disentangle)
desenganchar; (undo) desabrochar

unhurt [ʌnhɔ́ɨt] ADJ ileso

uniform [júnəfɔɨm] ADJ & N uniforme m

uniformity [junəfɔ́ɨmɪdi] N uniformidad f

unify [júnəfaɪ] VI/VT unificar(se)

unilateral [junəlǽɖə-əɨ] ADJ unilateral

unimportant [ʌnɪmpɔ́ɨtn̩t] ADJ
insignificante, sin importancia

uninhabited [ʌnɪnhǽbɪdɪd] ADJ deshabitado

uninhibited [ʌnɪnhíbɪdɪd] ADJ desinhibido,
desenfadado

uninspired [ʌnɪnspáɨrd] ADJ poco inspirado

unintelligible [ʌnɪntélɪdʒəbəɨ] ADJ
ininteligible

union [júnjən] N unión f; (labor) sindicato m,
gremio m; — labor mano de obra
sindicalizada / agremiada f; — leader
dirigente sindical mf

unionize [júnjənaɪz] VI/VT sindicar(se),
agremiar(se)

unique [juník] ADJ único, singular; that
feature is — to the South ese rasgo es
peculiar del sur

unisex [júnəseks] ADJ unisex

unison [júnəsən] ADV LOC in — al unísono

unit [júnɪt] N unidad f

unite [junáɪt] VI/VT unir(se)

United Arab Emirates [junáɪdɪdǽrəbémə-ɪts]
N Emiratos Arabes Unidos m pl

United Kingdom [junáɪdɪdkíŋdəm] N Reino
Unido m

United States [junáɪdɪdstéts] N Estados
Unidos m pl

unity [júnɪdi] N unidad f; (concord) unión f

universal [junəvɔ́-səɨ] ADJ universal; — joint
acoplamiento universal de cardán m

universe [júnəvɔ-s] N universo m

university [junəvɔ́-sɪdi] N universidad f; —
degree título universitario m

unjust [ʌndʒʌ́st] ADJ injusto

unjustifiable [ʌndʒʌstəfáɪəbəɨ] ADJ
injustificable

unkempt [ʌnkémpt] ADJ (uncombed)
desgreñado, despeinado; (messy)
desaliñado

unkind [ʌnkáind] ADJ antipático, poco
amable

unknown [ʌnnón] ADJ desconocido; —
quantity incógnita f; it is — se ignora

unlawful [ʌnlɔ́fəɨ] ADJ ilegal

unleaded [ʌnlédɪd] ADJ sin plomo

unleash [ʌnlíʃ] VT desatar

unless [ənlés] CONJ a menos que, a no ser
que

unlicensed [ʌnláɪsənst] ADJ sin permiso,
ilícito

unlike [ʌnláɪk] ADJ distinto, diferente; he is
— me es diferente de mí; PREP a diferencia
de; how — you to forget! ¡me extraña
que te hayas olvidado!

unlikely [ʌnláɪkli] ADJ (improbable)
improbable; (not realistic) inverosímil;
(exotic) exótico; I am — to come es
improbable que venga

unlimited [ʌnlímɪdɪd] ADJ ilimitado

unload [ʌnlód] VI/VT (take cargo from)
descargar; VI (pour out one's feelings)
desahogarse; (sell) liquidar

unlock [ʌnlák] VI/VT abrir con llave

unlucky [ʌnláki] ADJ (unfortunate)
desafortunado; (ominous) aciago, funesto;
an — number un número de mala suerte

unmanageable [ʌnmǽnɪdʒəbəɨ] ADJ (crisis,
situation) inmanejable; (person) poco
dócil

unmanned [ʌnmǽnd] ADJ (deprived of
courage) achicado; (with no crew) no
tripulado

unmarried [ʌnmǽrid] ADJ soltero

unmask [ʌnmǽsk] VI/VT desenmascarar(se)

unmistakable [ʌnmɪstékəbəɨ] ADJ
inconfundible

unmitigated [ʌnmídɪgedɪd] ADJ absoluto

unmoved [ʌnmúvd] ADJ (unflinching)
impasible; (indifferent) indiferente

unnatural [ʌnnǽtʃə-əɨ] ADJ (contrary to
nature) no natural; (unloving)

desnaturalizado; (monstrous) monstruoso; (affected) afectado

unnecessary [ʌnnésəseri] ADJ innecesario

unnoticed [ʌnnóʊɪst] ADJ inadvertido, desapercibido

unobserved [ʌnəbzə́ːvd] ADJ inadvertido

unobtrusive [ʌnəbtrúsɪv] ADJ discreto

unoccupied [ʌnákjəpaid] ADJ (house) desocupado; (territory) no ocupado

unofficial [ʌnəfíʃəl] ADJ extraoficial, no oficial

unoriginal [ʌnəríʤənəl] ADJ poco original

unorthodox [ʌnɔ́rθədaks] ADJ heterodoxo

unpack [ʌnpǽk] VT (a suitcase) deshacer, desempacar; (a carton) desembalar

unpaid [ʌnpéd] ADJ (debt) impagado, por pagar; (work) no remunerado

unpleasant [ʌnplézənt] ADJ desagradable

unpleasantness [ʌnplézəntnɪs] N (quality or state of being unpleasant) lo desagradable; (unpleasant episode) desavenencia f, disgusto m

unplug [ʌnplʌ́g] VI/VT desenchufar

unpopular [ʌnpápjələ˞] ADJ (decision) impopular; **she was — in school** tenía pocos amigos en la escuela

unprecedented [ʌnprésɪdentɪd] ADJ sin precedente, inaudito

unpredictable [ʌnprɪdíktəbəl] ADJ impredecible, imprevisible

unpremeditated [ʌnprimédɪtedɪd] ADJ impremeditado; (murder) sin premeditación

unprepared [ʌnprɪpérd] ADJ (surprised) desprevenido; (not ready) no preparado

unpretentious [ʌnprɪténʃəs] ADJ modesto, sin pretenciones

unprincipled [ʌnprínsəpəld] ADJ sin escrúpulos, falto de principios

unprintable [ʌnpríntəbəl] ADJ impublicable

unproductive [ʌnprədʌ́ktɪv] ADJ improductivo

unprofessional [ʌnprəféʃənəl] ADJ poco profesional

unprofitable [ʌnpráfɪtəbəl] ADJ no rentable

unpublished [ʌnpʌ́blɪʃt] ADJ inédito, sin publicar

unqualified [ʌnkwáləfaid] ADJ (worker) no cualificado; *Am* no calificado; (support) incondicional; (disaster) absoluto

unquestionable [ʌnkwéstʃənəbəl] ADJ incuestionable, indiscutible

unravel [ʌnrǽvəl] VI/VT (a rope) desenredar(se); (a sweater) destejer(se); (cloth) deshilachar(se); (a plan) deshacer(se); VT (a mystery) desentrañar

unreal [ʌnríəl] ADJ (not real) irreal; (unbelievable) increíble

unreasonable [ʌnrízənəbəl] ADJ (excessive) exagerado; (irrational) irracional, poco razonable

unrecognizable [ʌnrɛkəgnáɪzəbəl] ADJ irreconocible

unrefined [ʌnrɪfáɪnd] ADJ (oil, sugar) no refinado; (behavior) inculto, grosero

unreliable [ʌnrɪláɪəbəl] ADJ (person) informal; (machine, information) *Sp* poco fiable; *Am* poco confiable

unrest [ʌnrést] N malestar m, agitación f

unroll [ʌnróɫ] VI/VT desenrollar(se)

unruly [ʌnrúli] ADJ (students) indisciplinado, revoltoso, díscolo; (country) ingobernable; (hair) rebelde

unsafe [ʌnséf] ADJ (uncertain) inseguro; (dangerous) peligroso

unsatisfactory [ʌnsæDɪsfǽktəri] ADJ no satisfactorio, insatisfactorio

unscrew [ʌnskrú] VT desatornillar, destornillar

unscrupulous [ʌnskrúpjələs] ADJ sin escrúpulos

unseasonable [ʌnsízənəbəl] ADJ impropio de la estación

unseat [ʌnsít] VT derribar

unseen [ʌnsín] ADJ invisible, oculto

unselfish [ʌnsélfɪʃ] ADJ desinteresado

unselfishness [ʌnsélfɪʃnɪs] N desinterés m

unsettled [ʌnsédld] ADJ (situation) desordenado; (life) sin domicilio fijo; (wilderness) sin colonizar; (case) pendiente; (weather) variable

unsightly [ʌnsáɪtli] ADJ feo, antiestético

unskilled [ʌnskíɫd] ADJ (not trained) inexperto; (not qualified) *Sp* no cualificado; *Am* no calificado

unsophisticated [ʌnsəfístɪkeɪd] ADJ sencillo, no sofisticado

unsound [ʌnsáund] ADJ (argument) erróneo, falso; (body) enfermizo; (mind) demente; (foundation) poco sólido; (investment) poco seguro

unspeakable [ʌnspíkəbəl] ADJ indecible

unstable [ʌnstébəl] ADJ inestable

unsteady [ʌnstédi] ADJ (walk) inseguro, inestable; (flame) tembloroso; (pulse) irregular

unsuccessful [ʌnsəksésfəl] ADJ sin éxito, infructuoso

unsuitable [ʌnsúdəbəl] ADJ (person) no apto; (place) inadecuado, inapropiado

unsuspected [ʌnsəspéktɪd] ADJ insospechado

untenable [ʌnténəbəl] ADJ insostenible

unthinkable [ʌnθíŋkəbəl] ADJ impensable

untidy [ʌntáɪdi] ADJ (dress) desaliñado,

desastrado; (room) desordenado

untie [ʌntái] vi/vt desatar(se), destrabar(se)

until [ətít] PREP hasta; CONJ hasta que

untimely [ʌntámli] ADJ (ill-timed) inoportuno; (premature) prematuro

untiring [ʌntáirɪŋ] ADJ incansable, denodado

untold [ʌntóld] ADJ (riches) incalculable; (suffering) inaudito

untouched [ʌntátʃt] ADJ (not injured) ileso; (not affected) no afectado; **he left his dessert** — no tocó el postre

untrained [ʌntrénd] ADJ (worker) *Sp* no cualificado; *Am* no calificado; (animal) no amaestrado; (eye) inexperto

untried [ʌntráid] ADJ (untested) no probado, no ensayado; (not taken to trial) no juzgado

untrue [ʌntrú] ADJ (incorrect) falso; (unfaithful) infiel; (disloyal) desleal

untutored [ʌntútʊə·d] ADJ (unschooled) sin instrucción; (unsophisticated) inculto

untwist [ʌntwíst] vt desenroscar

unused [ʌnjúzd] ADJ sin usar; (unaccustomed) no habituado

unusual [ʌnjúʒuəł] ADJ (infrequent) desacostumbrado, raro; (highly abnormal) inusitado, insólito

unvarnished [ʌnvárnɪʃt] ADJ (without varnish) sin barnizar; (straightforward) puro

unveil [ʌnvéł] vt (remove a veil) quitar el velo a; (reveal) descubrir

unwarranted [ʌnwɔ́rəntɪd] ADJ injustificado

unwelcome [ʌnwéłkəm] ADJ (untimely) inoportuno; (unpleasant) desagradable; (poorly received) mal recibido

unwholesome [ʌnhółsəm] ADJ malsano

unwieldy [ʌnwíłdi] ADJ poco manejable, difícil de manejar

unwilling [ʌnwílɪŋ] ADJ **to be** — **to** no estar dispuesto a

unwise [ʌnwáiz] ADJ imprudente

unwonted [ʌnwɔ́ntɪd] ADJ inusitado, inacostumbrado

unworthy [ʌnwɔ́·ði] ADJ indigno

unwrap [ʌnrǽp] vt desenvolver

unwritten [ʌnrítn] ADJ no escrito; (agreement) de palabra

unzip [ʌnzíp] vt abrir la cremallera

up [ʌp] ADV (position) arriba; (direction) hacia arriba; ADJ levantado, derecho, erecto; (assembled) armado; (finished) terminado, concluido; **—-and-coming** prometedor; **—-to-date** actualizado; **—-front** (paid in advance) inicial; (frank) franco; **he's — for reelection** se presenta para la reelección; **I'm feeling** — me siento

optimista; **I'm — for golf** tengo ganas de jugar al golf; **prices are** — los precios han subido; **that is** — to **you** queda en tus manos, es cosa tuya; **the children are already** — ya se levantaron los niños; **the moon is** — salió la luna; **the wheat is** — germinó el trigo; **time is** — se terminó el tiempo; **to be** — on **the news** estar al corriente de las noticias; **to be** — **to one's old tricks** hacer de las suyas; — **and down** de arriba para abajo; — **against** enfrentado con; **what's** —? ¿qué pasa? PREP — **the current** contra la corriente; — **the river** río arriba; — **the street** calle arriba; — **to now** hasta ahora; N —**s and downs** altibajos *m pl*; vi **he** — **and went** agarró y se fue

upbeat [ʌpbit] ADJ optimista

upbringing [ʌpbrɪŋɪŋ] N crianza *f*

update [ʌpdét] vt actualizar

upend [ʌpénd] vi/vt (stand on end) poner(se) de punta; (defeat) derrotar

upgrade [ʌpgred] vt (facilities) mejorar; (computer) actualizar; N (facilities) mejora *f*; (computer) actualización *f*

upheaval [ʌphívəł] N trastorno *m*

uphill [ʌphił] ADV cuesta arriba; [ʌphił] ADJ penoso, arduo

uphold [ʌphółd] vt sostener, apoyar; (legal decision) refrendar

upholster [ʌphółstə·] vt tapizar

upholstery [ʌphółstəri] N tapicería *f*

upkeep [ʌpkip] N mantenimiento *m*

uplift [ʌplíft] vt (physically) elevar; (spiritually) edificar

upload [ʌplod] vt cargar

upon [əpán] PREP sobre, encima de; — **arriving** al llegar; **once** — **a time** érase una vez

upper [ʌpə·] ADJ (higher) superior; (high) alto; **to have the** — **hand** dominar, llevar la ventaja; N (of shoe) pala *f*; (of berth) litera superior *f*; — **class** clase alta *f*; — **crust** flor y nata *f*; —**case** mayúsculo; —**cut** gancho al mentón *m*; —**most** (highest) de más arriba; (most important) mayor; —**s** dentadura postiza superior *f*

uppity [ʌpɪdi] ADJ presumido

upright [ʌprait] ADJ (posture) erecto, erguido; (position) vertical; (just) íntegro, recto, cabal; — **piano** piano vertical *m*; N (column) montante *m*; (piano) piano vertical *m*; (post) poste *m*

uprightness [ʌpraitnɪs] N rectitud *f*

uprising [ʌpraizɪŋ] N alzamiento *m*, levantamiento *m*

uproar [ápɾɔr] N tumulto *m*, alboroto *m*, bulla *f*

uproarious [ʌpróriəs] ADJ (tumultuous) tumultuoso; (funny) graciosísimo

uproot [ʌprút] VT arrancar de raíz, desarraigar

upscale [ápskeł] ADJ de lujo

upset [ʌpsét] VI/VT (overturn) volcar(se), tumbar; (distress) trastornar(se), perturbar(se), alterar(se); VT (in sports) derrotar al favorito; ADJ (overturned) volcado; (ill) indispuesto; (distressed) disgustado, enojado; [ápset] N (overturning) vuelco *m*; (unexpected defeat) derrota inesperada *f*; (emotional state) trastorno *m*, disgusto *m*; (illness) malestar *m*

upshot [ápʃat] N consecuencia *f*

upside [ápsaɪd] N (upper part) parte superior *f*; (positive prospect) lo bueno; **— down** al revés, patas arriba

upstage [ápstéʤ] VT eclipsar

upstairs [ápstérz] ADV (location) arriba, en el piso de arriba; (movement) (para) arriba; [ápsterz] ADJ de arriba; N piso de arriba *m*

upstart [ápstart] N advenedizo -za *mf*

uptake [áptek] N **quick on the —** listo; **slow on the —** duro de entendederas

uptight [aptáɪt] ADJ (nervous) nervioso; (conventional) estreñido

upturn [áptɚn] N (prices) aumento *m*, subida *f*; (markets) tendencia alcista *f*

upward [ápwəd] ADV (toward a higher place) hacia arriba; **— of** más de; ADJ ascendente; N **— mobility** ascenso social *m*

uranium [juréniəm] N uranio *m*

urban [ɚbən] ADJ urbano; **— blight** tugurización *f*; **— legend** leyenda urbana *f*; **— renewal** renovación urbana *f*; **— sprawl** expansión urbana *f*

urchin [ɚtʃɪn] N pilluelo -la *mf*, guaje -ja *mf*

urethra [juríθrə] N uretra *f*

urge [ɚʤ] VT (exhort) exhortar, urgir; (beg) rogar; (propose) propugnar; **to — on** animar; N impulso *m*, gana *f*

urgency [ɚʤansi] N urgencia *f*

urgent [ɚʤant] ADJ urgente

urinal [júrɪnəł] N urinario *m*, mingitorio *m*

urinary [júrəneri] ADJ urinario

urinate [júrɪnet] VI/VT orinar

urine [jórɪn] N orina *f*

URL (Uniform Resource Locator) [juɑréł] N URL *m*

urn [ɚn] N urna *f*

urologist [jurólaʤɪst] N urólogo -ga *mf*

Uruguay [júrəgwaɪ] N Uruguay *m*

Uruguayan [jurəgwáɪən] ADJ & N uruguayo -ya *mf*

us [ʌs] PRON nos; **she saw —** nos vio; **he came with —** vino con nosotros; **he gave it to —** nos lo dio (a nosotros)

USA (United States of America) [juesé] N EEUU *m sg/pl*

usable [júzəbəł] ADJ utilizable, aprovechable

usage [júsɪʤ] N uso *m*, costumbre *f*

use [juz] VT usar, utilizar (also exploit); (consume) gastar; (take advantage of) aprovecharse de; VI **I —d to smoke** antes fumaba, solía fumar; **to — up** gastar, agotar; [jus] N (application) uso *m*; (utilization) empleo *m*, utilización *f*, aprovechamiento *m*; (usefulness) utilidad *f*; **it is of no —** es inútil; **out of —** en desuso; **to have no — for** no soportar; **to make — of** usar, utilizar; **to put to — utilizar; what is the — of it?** ¿para qué sirve?

used [juzd] ADJ usado; [just] **to be — to** estar acostumbrado a

useful [júsfəł] ADJ útil

usefulness [júsfəłnɪs] N utilidad *f*

useless [júslɪs] ADJ inútil, inservible

uselessness [júslɪsnɪs] N inutilidad *f*

user [júzɚ] N usuario -ria *mf*; **—-friendly** fácil de utilizar

usher [áʃɚ] N acomodador -ra *mf*; VT conducir, acompañar; **to — in** (a person) acompañar; (an era) anunciar, marcar el comienzo

usual [júʒuəł] ADJ usual, habitual; (of clothes) de todos los días; **as —** como siempre; **she wasn't her — self** no era la de siempre; **the — thing** lo normal; **more than —** más que de costumbre

usurp [jusɚp] VI/VT usurpar

usury [júʒəri] N usura *f*

utensil [juténsəł] N utensilio *m*, útil *m*

uterus [júɾəəs] N útero *m*

utilitarian [jutɪlɪtériən] ADJ utilitario

utility [jutíłɪti] N utilidad *f*; (public service) empresa de servicio público *f*; **— furniture** muebles prácticos *m pl*; **— program** programa utilitario *m*; **— room** lavadero *m*

utilization [judlɪzéʃən] N utilización *f*

utilize [júdlaɪz] VT utilizar

utmost [átmost] ADJ (extreme) sumo, extremo; (farthest) más distante; N máximo *m*; **he did his —** hizo cuanto pudo; **to the —** al máximo

utopia [jutópiə] N utopía *f*

utter [áɾɚ] VT (emit) dar, proferir; (say) decir, pronunciar; (make circulate) poner en circulación; ADJ absoluto, completo

utterance [ʌ́Dᴈᴈns] N (of words) enunciado m; (of money) emisión f
uvula [júvjᴈlᴈ] N campanilla f, úvula f
Uzbek [ʊ́zbɛk] ADJ & N uzbeko -ka mf
Uzbekistan [ʊzbékɪstæn] N Uzbekistán m

Vv

vacancy [vékᴈnsi] N (job) vacante f; (room in hotel) habitación libre f; no — completo
vacant [vékᴈnt] ADJ (position) vacante; (expression) vacío; (seat, room) libre
vacate [véket] VI/VT (a room) desalojar, desocupar; (a contract) anular; (a position) dejar vacante
vacation [vekéʃᴈn] N vacaciones f pl
vaccinate [vǽksᴈnet] VI/VT vacunar
vaccination [væksᴈnéʃᴈn] N vacunación f
vaccine [vǽksín] N vacuna f
vacillate [vǽsᴈlet] VI vacilar
vacuum [vǽkjum] N vacío m; — cleaner aspiradora f; —-packed envasado al vacío; — tube tubo de vacío m; VI/VT aspirar, pasar la aspiradora
vagabond [vǽgᴈbɑnd] ADJ & N vagabundo -da mf
vagina [vᴈʤáɪnᴈ] N vagina f
vagrancy [végrᴈnsi] N vagancia f
vagrant [végrᴈnt] ADJ & N vagabundo -da mf
vague [veg] ADJ vago, indistinto
vain [ven] ADJ (futile) vano, hueco; (proud of appearance) vanidoso; in — en vano
valentine [vǽlᴈntaɪn] N (card) tarjeta del día de San Valentín f; (person) querido -da mf; —'s Day día de San Valentín m, día de los enamorados m
valet [vælé] N (manservant) criado m; (in a hotel) mozo de habitación m; (car parker) aparcacoches m sg
valiant [vǽljᴈnt] ADJ valiente
valid [vǽlɪd] ADJ válido, valedero
validity [vᴈlíDɪti] N validez f
valise [valíz] N maleta f, valija f
valley [vǽli] N valle m
valor [vǽlᴈ] N valor m, valentía f
valorous [vǽlᴈᴈs] ADJ valeroso, valiente
valuable [vǽljᴈbᴈl] ADJ valioso, preciado; N —s objetos de valor m pl
valuation [væljuéʃᴈn] N (value) valoración f; (appraisal) tasación f, valuación f
value [vǽlju] N valor m; VT valorar
valve [vǽlv] N válvula f; (on mollusks) valva f

vamp [væmp] N vampiresa f; VT seducir
vampire [vǽmpaɪr] N vampiro m
van [væn] N camioneta f
vandal [vǽndl] N vándalo m
vane [ven] N (for weather) veleta f; (of a fan, windmill) aspa f; (of propeller) paleta f
vanilla [vᴈnílᴈ] N vainilla f
vanish [vǽnɪʃ] VI desaparecer, esfumarse
vanity [vǽnɪDi] N vanidad f; — table tocador m
vanquish [vǽnkwɪʃ] VT vencer
vantage [vǽntɪʤ] N — point mirador m
Vanuatu [vɑnuátu] N Vanuatu m
Vanuatuan [vɑnuátuᴈn] ADJ & N vanuatuense f
vapor [vépᴈ] N vapor m, humo m
vaporize [vépᴈ-aɪz] VI/VT vaporizar(se)
variable [vériᴈbᴈl] ADJ & N variable f
variance [vériᴈns] N discrepancia f, desacuerdo m; to be at — no concordar
variant [vériᴈnt] N variante f
variation [vériéʃᴈn] N variación f
varicose [vǽrɪkos] ADJ varicoso; — veins Sp varices f pl; Am várices f pl
varied [vérid] ADJ variado, vario
variegated [vériɪgeɪd] ADJ variopinto
variety [vᴈráɪɪDi] N variedad f
various [vériᴈs] ADJ vario
varnish [várnɪʃ] N barniz m, charol m; VT barnizar, charolar
varsity [vársɪDi] N equipo universitario m
vary [véri] VI/VT variar
vascular [vǽskjᴈlᴈ] ADJ vascular
vase [ves] N jarrón m; (for flowers) florero m
vasectomy [vᴈséktᴈmi] N vasectomía f
Vaseline™ [vǽsᴈlín] N vaselina f
vast [væst] ADJ vasto, inmenso
vastly [vǽstli] ADV radicalmente
vastness [vǽstnɪs] N inmensidad f
vat [væt] N tina f, barrica f
Vatican City [vǽDɪkᴈnsíDi] N Ciudad del Vaticano f
vaudeville [vɔ́dvɪl] N vodevil m
vault [vɔlt] N (arched structure) bóveda f; (burial chamber) panteón m; (place for valuables) cámara acorazada f; (jump) salto m; VT (cover with a vault) abovedar; VI/VT saltar
VCR (videocassette recorder) [visiár] N video m; Sp vídeo m
VD (venereal disease) [vidí] N enfermedad venérea f
veal [vil] N ternera f; — cutlet chuleta de ternera f
veer [vir] VI/VT virar; N virada f
vegan [vígᴈn] ADJ & N vegan mf
vegetable [véʤtᴈbᴈl] N (food) verdura f,

hortaliza *f*; (plant, paralyzed person) vegetal *m*; — **garden** huerto *m*; (large) huerta *f*; — **kingdom** reino vegetal *m*; — **oil** aceite vegetal *m*

vegetarian [veʤətériən] ADJ & N vegetariano -na *mf*

vegetate [véʤətet] VI vegetar

vegetation [veʤətéʃən] N vegetación *f*

vehemence [víəməns] N vehemencia *f*

vehement [víəmənt] ADJ vehemente

vehicle [víikəl] N vehículo *m*

veil [vel] N velo *m*; VT velar

vein [ven] N (blood vessel, style) vena *f*; (small deposit of ore) veta *f*; (large deposit of ore) filón *m*

veined [vend] ADJ veteado; (leaf) nervado

velocity [vəlásɪdi] N velocidad *f*

velvet [vélvɪt] N terciopelo *m*; ADJ (of velvet) de terciopelo; (like velvet) aterciopelado

velvety [vélvɪdi] ADJ aterciopelado

vendetta [vendédə] N vendetta *f*

vending machine [véndɪŋməʃin] N máquina expendedora *f*

vendor [véndɚ] N vendedor -ora *mf*; (in a stall) puestero -ra *mf*

veneer [vənír] N (layer of wood) chapa *f*; (outward appearance) barniz *m*; VT chapar, enchapar

venerable [vénəɹəbəl] ADJ venerable

venerate [vénəret] VT venerar

veneration [venəréʃən] N veneración *f*

venereal [vəníriəl] ADJ venéreo; — **disease** enfermedad venérea *f*

venetian blind [vəníʃənbláɪnd] N veneciana *f*

Venezuela [venɪzwélə] N Venezuela *f*

Venezuelan [venɪzwélən] ADJ & N venezolano -na *mf*

vengeance [vénʤəns] N venganza *f*; **with a —** (violently) con furia; (energetically) con ganas

vengeful [vénʤfəl] ADJ vengativo

venison [vénəsən] N carne de venado *f*

venom [vénəm] N veneno *m*

venomous [vénəməs] ADJ venenoso

vent [vent] N (outlet for air) ventilación *f*; (opening of a volcano) chimenea *f*; **to give — to anger** desahogar la ira; VI/VT desahogar(se), descargar(se)

ventilate [véntlet] VI/VT ventilar(se)

ventilation [ventléʃən] N ventilación *f*

ventilator [véntledɚ] N ventilador *m*

ventricle [véntrɪkəl] N ventrículo *m*

venture [vénʧɚ] N (adventure) aventura *f*; (business enterprise) empresa *f*; — **capital** capital de riesgo *m*; VI/VT aventurar(se), arriesgar(se)

venue [vénju] N lugar *m*

veranda [vərǽndə] N porche *m*, terraza *f*

verb [vɚb] N verbo *m*

verbal [vɚ́bəl] ADJ (linguistic, related to verbs) verbal; (not written) oral

verbatim [vəbédəm] ADJ textual; ADV textualmente

verbiage [vɚ́bɪʤ] N palabrerío *m*

verbose [vəbós] ADJ verboso

verdict [vɚ́dɪkt] N veredicto *m*

verge [vɚʤ] ADV LOC **on the — of** al borde de, a punto de; VI **to — on** rayar en, lindar con

verification [verəfɪkéʃən] N verificación *f*, comprobación *f*

verify [vérəfaɪ] VT verificar, constatar

veritable [vérɪdəbəl] ADJ verdadero

vermillion [vəmíljən] ADJ & N bermellón *m*

vermin [vɚ́mɪn] N bichos *m pl*

vermouth [vəmúθ] N vermú *m*

vernacular [vənǽkjələ] ADJ vernáculo; N (plain language) lengua vernácula *f*

versatile [vɚ́səɾəl] ADJ versátil

verse [vɚs] N verso *m*; (stanza) estrofa *f*; (line of poem) verso *m*; (in Bible) versículo *m*

versed [vɚst] ADJ versado

version [vɚ́ʒən] N versión *f*

versus [vɚ́səs] PREP contra; (in sports) versus

vertebra [vɚ́dəbɹə] N vértebra *f*

vertebrate [vɚ́dəbrɪt] ADJ vertebrado

vertical [vɚ́dɪkəl] ADJ vertical

vertigo [vɚ́dɪgo] N vértigo *m*

very [véri] ADV muy; — **many** muchísimos; — **much** muchísimo; **it is — cold today** hace mucho frío hoy; ADJ (same) mismo; (mere) mero

vessel [vésəl] N (container) vasija *f*; (duct) vaso *m*; (ship) nave *f*

vest [vest] N chaleco *m*; VT conferir; —**ed interests** intereses creados *m pl*

vestibule [véstəbjul] N vestíbulo *m*, zaguán *m*

vestige [véstɪʤ] N vestigio *m*

vet [vet] N (veterinarian) veterinario -ria *mf*; (veteran) veterano -na militar *mf*

veteran [védəɹən] ADJ & N veterano -na *mf*

veterinarian [vedəənériən] N veterinario -ria *mf*

veterinary [védəəneri] ADJ veterinario; — **medicine** veterinaria *f*

veto [víto] N veto *m*; VT vetar

vex [veks] VT molestar, irritar

via [váɪə, víə] PREP (by way of) vía; (by means of) por

viable [váɪəbəl] ADJ viable

vial [váɪəl] N ampolla *f*, frasco *m*

vibrate [váɪbret] VI/VT vibrar

vibration [vaɪbréʃən] N vibración f
vibrator [váɪbreɾɚ] N vibrador m
vicarious [vaɪkérɪəs] ADJ indirecto
vice [vaɪs] N vicio m
vice-president [váɪsprézɪɾənt] N
vicepresidente -ta mf
viceroy [váɪsrɔɪ] N virrey m
viceroyalty [vaɪsrɔ́ɪəlti] ADJ virreinato
vice versa [váɪsəvɚ́-sə] ADV viceversa
vicinity [vɪsínɪɾi] N vecindad f, cercanías f pl,
aledaños m pl
vicious [víʃəs] ADJ (having vices) vicioso;
(violent) violento, sanguinario; (evil)
maligno, perverso; (malicious) malicioso;
— **circle** círculo vicioso m; — **dog** perro
fiero m, perro bravo m
vicissitude [vɪsísɪtud] N vicisitud f, peripecia
f
victim [víktəm] N víctima f
victimize [víktəmaɪz] VT (make victim)
victimizar; (dupe) estafar
victor [víktɚ] N vencedor -ora mf
victorious [vɪktórɪəs] ADJ victorioso
victory [víktəri] N victoria f
video [vídɪo] N Am video m; Sp vídeo m;
—**cassette** Am video m; Sp vídeo m;
—**cassette recorder** videocasete m;
—**conference** videoconferencia f; —
game videojuego m; —**tape** Am cinta de
video f; Sp cinta de vídeo f
vie [vaɪ] VI competir; **to — for power**
disputarse el poder
Vietnam [vietnám] N Vietnam m
Vietnamese [viːtnəmíz] ADJ & N vietnamita
mf
view [vju] N (field of vision) vista f; (opinion)
opinión f; (panorama) visión panorámica
f; —**point** punto de vista m; **in — of** en
vista de; **to be within —** estar a la vista;
with a — to con el propósito de; VT (see)
ver; (consider) enfocar
viewpoint [vjúpɔɪnt] N punto de vista m
vigil [víʤəl] N vigilia f, vela f; **to keep —**
velar
vigilance [víʤələns] N vigilancia f
vigilant [víʤələnt] ADJ vigilante
vigor [vígɚ] N vigor m, pujanza f, dinamismo
m
vigorous [vígɚəs] ADJ vigoroso
vile [vaɪl] ADJ (evil) vil, ruin; (foul, bad)
pésimo
villa [vílə] N quinta f, casa de campo f
village [vílɪʤ] N aldea f, villa f
villager [vílɪʤɚ] N aldeano -na mf
villain [vílən] N villano -na mf
villainous [vílənəs] ADJ vil, villano
villainy [víləni] N villanía f, vileza f

vindicate [víndɪket] VT reivindicar, vindicar
vindictive [vɪndíktɪv] ADJ vengativo
vine [vaɪn] N (grapevine) vid f; (decorative)
parra f; (stem) sarmiento m; (climbing
plant) enredadera f
vinegar [vínɪgɚ] N vinagre m
vineyard [vínjəd] N viña f, viñedo m
vintage [víntɪʤ] N (act or season of
gathering grapes) vendimia f; (harvest of
grapes) cosecha f; (year) año m; ADJ (wine)
añejo; (classic) excelente; (old) antiguo, de
colección; (typical) típico
vinyl [váɪnəl] N vinilo m
viola [vɪólə] N viola f
violate [váɪəlet] VT violar; (a law) violar,
quebrantar
violation [vaɪəléʃən] N violación f; (traffic)
infracción f
violence [váɪələns] N violencia f
violent [váɪələnt] ADJ violento
violet [váɪələt] N (flower) violeta f; (color)
violeta m; ADJ violeta inv
violin [vaɪəlín] N violín m
violinist [vaɪəlínɪst] N violinista mf
viper [váɪpɚ] N víbora f
virgin [vɚ́-ʤɪn] ADJ & N virgen f;
(uninitiated) no iniciado -da mf; —
Islands Islas Vírgenes f pl
virginal [vɚ́-ʤɪnəl] ADJ virginal
virile [vírəl] ADJ viril
virility [vɚrílɪti] N virilidad f
virtual [vɚ́-tʃuəl] ADJ virtual; — **reality**
realidad virtual f
virtue [vɚ́-tʃu] N virtud f
virtuoso [vɚ-tʃuóso] ADJ & N virtuoso -sa mf
virtuous [vɚ́-tʃuəs] ADJ virtuoso
virulent [vírələnt] ADJ virulento
virus [váɪrəs] N virus m
visa [vízə] N Am visa f; Sp visado m
vis-à-vis [vizavíɪ] PREP con respecto a
visceral [vísəɹəl] ADJ visceral
viscous [vískəs] ADJ viscoso
vise [vaɪs] N tornillo de banco m
visible [vízəbəl] ADJ visible
Visigoth [vízɪgɑθ] N visigodo -da mf
vision [víʒən] N (sense, apparition) visión f;
(eyesight) vista f
visionary [víʒəneri] ADJ & N visionario -ria
mf
visit [vízɪt] VT visitar; (afflict) infligir; VI estar
de visita; **to — with** charlar con; N (stay)
visita f; (chat) charla f
visitation [vɪzɪtéʃən] N (apparition) visitación
f; (punishment) castigo m; (parental right)
régimen de visita m
visitor [vízɪɾɚ] N visita f, visitante mf
visor [váɪzɚ] N visera f

vista [vístə] N (visual) vista *f*; (mental) perspectiva *f*

visual [víʒuəł] ADJ visual

visualize [víʒuəlaɪz] VT visualizar, imaginar

vital [váɪd] ADJ vital; — **signs** signos vitales *m pl*

vitality [vaɪtǽlɪdi] N vitalidad *f*

vitamin [váɪdəmɪn] N vitamina *f*

vituperation [vaɪtupəréʃən] N vituperación *f*, vituperio *m*

vivacious [vaɪvéʃəs] ADJ vivaz, vivaracho

vivacity [vaɪvǽsɪdi] N vivacidad *f*

vivid [vívɪd] ADJ vívido, vivo

vivisection [vívɪsɛkʃən] N vivisección *f*

vocabulary [vokǽbjəlɛri] N vocabulario *m*

vocal [vókəł] ADJ (musical) vocal; (outspoken) vociferante; — **cords** cuerdas vocales *f pl*

vocalic [vokǽlɪk] ADJ vocálico

vocation [vokéʃən] N vocación *f*

vociferous [vosífə·əs] ADJ vociferante

vodka [vádkə] N vodka *m*

vogue [vog] N boga *f*, moda *f*; **in** — en boga, de moda

voice [vɔɪs] N voz *f*; — **mail** contestador automático *m*; VT expresar

void [vɔɪd] ADJ (devoid, empty) vacío; (not binding) nulo, inválido; —**ed check** cheque anulado *m*; — **of** desprovisto de; N vacío *m*; VT (intestines) evacuar; (a check) anular

volatile [váladł] ADJ (liquid) volátil; (political situation) explosivo; (stock market) voluble; (temperament) cambiante

volcanic [vɑłkǽnɪk] ADJ volcánico

volcano [vɑłkéno] N volcán *m*

volition [volíʃən] N volición *f*; **of one's own** — por su propia voluntad

volley [váli] N (of firearms) descarga *f*; (of protests, arrows, stones) lluvia *f*; (of balls) volea *f*; VI/VT (bullets) descargar; (balls) volear; —**ball** voleibol *m*, balonvolea *m*

volt [voʊt] N voltio *m*

voltage [vóʊtɪʤ] N voltaje *m*

volume [váljəm] N volumen *m*, tomo *m*

voluminous [vəlúmɪnəs] ADJ voluminoso

voluntary [váləntɛri] ADJ voluntario

volunteer [valəntír] ADJ & N voluntario -ria *mf*; VI/VT (offer) ofrecer(se), brindar(se); RP comedir(se); VI (do volunteer work) trabajar de voluntario -ria

voluptuous [vəláptʃuəs] ADJ voluptuoso

vomit [vámɪt] N vómito *m*; VI/VT vomitar

voodoo [vúdu] N vudú *m*

voracious [voréʃəs] ADJ voraz

vortex [vórtɛks] N vórtice *m*

vote [vot] N (right, ballot) voto *m*; (act of voting) votación *f*; VI votar; VT (a bill) aprobar; (a party) votar a/por; **to** — **to do something** votar por hacer algo

voter [vódə·] N votante *mf*

vouch [vaʊtʃ] VI **to** — **for** dar fe de, salir de fiador a, fiar a; VT **to** — **that** dar fe de que

voucher [váutʃə·] N (receipt) comprobante *m*; (coupon) vale *m*; (person) fiador -ra *mf*, garante *mf*

vow [vaʊ] N voto *m*; **to take a** — prometer; VT jurar

vowel [váuəł] N vocal *f*

voyage [vɔɪʤ] N viaje *m*; (by sea) travesía *f*; VI viajar

voyeur [vɔɪr] N mirón -ona *mf*

vulgar [válgə·] ADJ (rude) ordinario, grosero, soez; (popular, vernacular) vulgar

vulgarity [vʌlgǽrɪdi] N ordinariez *f*

vulnerable [válnə·əbəł] ADJ vulnerable

vulture [váłtʃə·] N buitre *m*

vulva [váłvə] N vulva *f*

Ww

wacky [wǽki] ADJ (person) chiflado; (idea) descabellado

wad [wɑd] N (for artillery, for filling) taco *m*; (ball) pelota *f*, pelotón *m*; (of money) rollo *m*, fajo *m*; VI/VT (a firearm) atacar; (a piece of paper) hacer una pelota (con)

waddle [wádł] VT anadear, andar como un pato; N anadeo *m*

wade [wed] VI andar por el agua; **to** — **through a book** leer con dificultad un libro

wafer [wéfə·] N (cookie) oblea *f*; (in Catholic ritual) hostia *f*; (computer) lámina/oblea de silicio *m*

waffle [wáfəł] ADJ Sp gofre *m*; Am wafle *m*; — **iron** Sp plancha para hacer gofres *f*; Am waflera *f*

waft [wæft] VI flotar; VT llevar por el aire; N (of air) ráfaga *f*; (of odor) ola *f*

wag [wæg] VI/VT menear(se), mover(se); **to** — **the tail** colear; N (movement) meneo *m*, movimiento *m*; (joker) bromista *mf*

wage [weʤ] N — **earner** asalariado -da *mf*; (paid daily) jornalero -ra *mf*; —**s** salario *m*; (daily) jornal *m*; — **scale** escala salarial *f*; VT (war) hacer; (battle) librar

wager [wéʤə·] N apuesta *f*; VI/VT apostar

wagon [wǽgən] N (horsedrawn) carro *m*; (covered) carreta *f*; (toy) carrito *m*; **to fix**

someone's — vengarse de alguien; **to be on the** — abstenerse de las bebidas alcohólicas

wail [weł] VI lamentar; N lamento *m*

waist [west] N cintura *f*; (of garment) talle *m*; **—band** pretina *f*; **—coat** chaleco *m*; **—line** talle *m*, cintura *f*

wait [wet] VI/VT esperar; **to — for** esperar; **to — on** servir; **to — tables** trabajar de camarero -ra; N espera *f*; **to lie in — for** estar en/al acecho de

waiter [wédɚ] N camarero *m*, mozo *m*, mesero *m*

waiting [wédɪŋ] N espera *f*; **— list** lista de espera *f*; **— room** sala de espera *f*

waitress [wétrɪs] N camarera *f*, moza *f*, mesera *f*

waive [wev] VT (rights) renunciar a; (rule) hacer una excepción

waiver [wévɚ] N (of rights) renuncia *f*; (of rules) excepción *f*

wake [wek] VI/VT despertar(se); **to — up** despertar(se); N (at death) velatorio *m*; (of a ship) estela *f*, surco *m*; **in the — of** después de, detrás de; **—-up call** (in a hotel) llamada del servicio despertador *f*; (to action) llamada de atención *f*

wakeful [wékfəł] ADJ (awake) despierto; (insomniac) insomne

waken [wékən] VI/VT despertar(se)

Wales [welz] N Gales *m sg*

walk [wɔk] VI andar, caminar; (to a place) ir a pie; (go away) marcharse; **to — back** volver a pie; **to — down** bajar a pie; **to — in** entrar caminando; **to — out** (to go out) salir caminando; (to abandon) dejar; (to strike) declararse en huelga; **—out** huelga *f*; **to — up** subir a pie; VT (to cause to walk) hacer caminar; (to trace on foot) recorrer; **to — the streets** callejear; N (period of walking) paseo *m*, caminata *f*; (pace) paso *m*; (gait) andar *m*; **— of life** condición *f*; **to take a —** pasear, dar un paseo

walker [wɔkɚ] N (to aid walking) andador *m*; (one who walks) caminante *mf*; (in sports) marchista *mf*

walking [wɔkɪŋ] ADJ andante; **— papers** despido *m*; **— stick** bastón *m*

wall [wɔł] N (interior) pared *f*; (garden) muro *m*, tapia *f*; (fort) muralla *f*; (of silence) barrera *f*; **to have one's back to the —** estar entre la espada y la pared; **to drive someone up the —** sacar a alguien de quicio; **I was climbing the —s** me moría de aburrimiento; **—-to-—** de pared a pared; **—flower** alhelí *m*; **she was a**

—**flower** no la sacaban a bailar; **—paper** papel de empapelar *m*; **to —paper** empapelar

wallet [wálɪt] N cartera *f*

wallow [wálo] VI (roll) revolcarse; (indulge oneself) regodearse

walnut [wɔ́łnʌt] N nuez *f*; **— tree** nogal *m*

walrus [wɔ́łrəs] N morsa *f*;

waltz [wɔłts] N vals *m*; VI valsar

wand [wɑnd] N (rod) vara *f*; (magic) varita *f*

wander [wɑ́ndɚ] VI/VT vagar (por), errar (por); **to — away** perderse; **my mind —s easily** me distraigo fácilmente

wanderer [wɑ́ndərɚ] N vagabundo -da *mf*

wane [wen] VI menguar, flaquear; N mengua *f*; **to be on the —** ir menguando

wannabe [wɑ́nəbi] N imitador -ora *mf*

want [wɑnt] VI/VT (desire) querer; **he —s judgment** le falta juicio; **he's —ed in Texas** se lo busca en Texas; N (desire) deseo *m*; (lack) falta *f*; (scarcity) escasez *f*; **to be in —** estar necesitado; **— ad** (aviso) clasificado *m*

wanting [wɑ́ntɪŋ] ADJ (lacking) falto; (deficient) deficiente

wanton [wɑ́ntən] ADJ (immoderate) desenfrenado; (immoral) lascivo; (senseless, unprovoked) gratuito

war [wɔr] N guerra *f*; **— crime** crimen de guerra *m*; **— games** juegos de guerra *m pl*, simulacro de batalla *m*; **—head** ojiva *f*; **—ship** acorazado *m*; VI guerrear, hacer la guerra

warble [wɔ́rbəł] VI gorjear; N gorjeo *m*

warbler [wɔ́rblɚ] N (European) curruca *f*; (American) arañero *m*

ward [wɔrd] N (district) distrito *m*; (of a building) pabellón *m*; (of a tutor) pupilo -la *mf*; VI **to — off** resguardarse de, conjurar

warden [wɔ́rdn] N guardián -na *mf*; (of prison) alcaide *m*

wardrobe [wɔ́rdrob] N (room) guardarropa *m*; (furniture) ropero *m*, armario *m*; (garments) vestuario *m*, guardarropa *m*

warehouse [wérhaʊs] N almacén *m*, depósito *m*

wares [werz] N mercancías *f pl*

warfare [wɔ́rfer] N guerra *f*

warlike [wɔ́rlaɪk] ADJ bélico

warm [wɔrm] ADJ (bath) caliente; (clothes) abrigado; (weather) caluroso; (colors, reception) cálido; **—-blooded** de sangre caliente; **—-hearted** de buen corazón; **it is — today** hace calor hoy; VI/VT calentar(se); **to — over** recalentar; **to — up** calentar(se), templar(se); **—up**

precalentamiento *m*; **it —s my heart** me
alegra el corazón; **she —ed to the idea**
se entusiasmó con la idea

warmth [wɔrmθ] N calor *m*, tibieza *f*

warn [wɔrn] VI/VT (advise of danger) advertir;
(urge to behave) amonestar

warning [wɔ́rnɪŋ] N (of danger) advertencia
f; (of punishment) amonestación *f*

warp [wɔrp] N (yarn) urdimbre *f*; (curve)
comba *f*, alabeo *m*; VI/VT (wood)
combar(se), alabear(se); (character)
deformar(se); **he has a —ed personality**
tiene una personalidad retorcida

warrant [wɔ́rənt] N orden *f*; **a — for his
arrest** una orden de arresto contra él; VT
garantizar

warranty [wɔ́rənti] N garantía *f*; VT
garantizar

warrior [wɔ́riə] N guerrero -ra *mf*

wart [wɔrt] N verruga *f*

wary [wɛ́ri] ADJ cauteloso, cauto; **to be — of**
desconfiar de

wash [waʃ] VI/VT lavar(se); **to — down** bajar;
to — out (clean) quitar; (demolish)
destruir; **to — up** lavarse; **he was —ed
away by the waves** fue arrastrado por
las olas; **his excuse won't —** su excusa
no va a colar; **the bottle was —ed up
on the shore** la botella fue traída por el
mar; **—-and-wear** de lava y pon, de no
planchar; **—ed-up** fracasado; **—ed-out**
desteñido; **—out** (erosion) derrubio *m*;
(failure) fracaso *m*; N (act of washing)
lavado *m*; (clothes to be washed) ropa
para lavar *f*; (washed clothes) ropa lavada
f; **—cloth** toallita para lavarse *f*; **—room**
lavabo *m*, lavatorio *m*

washable [wáʃəbəl] ADJ lavable

washer [wáʃə] N (washing machine)
máquina de lavar *f*; (ring) arandela *f*; **—
woman** lavandera *f*

washing [wáʃɪŋ] N lavado *m*; **— machine**
lavadora *f*, máquina de lavar *f*

wasp [wasp] N avispa *f*

WASP (white Anglo-Saxon Protestant)
[wasp] N persona blanca, anglosajona y
protestante *f*

waste [west] VI/VT (squander resources)
malgastar, desperdiciar; **to — away**
consumirse; VT (squander time) perder;
(murder) liquidar; N (of resources)
desperdicio *m*, malgasto *m*, derroche *m*;
(of time) pérdida *f*; (refuse) desperdicios *m
pl*, desechos *m pl*; **to go to —**
desperdiciarse; **—paper basket** papelera
f; **— products** productos de desecho *m
pl*; **—land** tierra yerma *f*, páramo *m*; **to**

lay — to asolar

wasted [wéstɪd] ADJ (squandered)
desperdiciado; (debilitated) consumido;
(drunk) borracho

wasteful [wéstfəl] ADJ despilfarrador,
gastador; (method) antieconómico

watch [watʃ] VI (look) mirar; (be careful)
cuidarse; (be vigilant) vigilar; VT (view)
mirar, ver; (observe) observar; (tend)
cuidar; **— out for the cars!** ¡cuidado con
los coches! **to — for** estar a la espera de;
to — over proteger; N (timepiece) reloj *m*;
(period of wakefulness) vela *f*, vigilia *f*;
(vigilant guard) guardia *mf*; (duty shift)
guardia *f*; (lookout) centinela *m*; **—band**
pulsera *f*; **—dog** (type of dog) perro
guardián *m*; (organization) organismo de
control *m*; **—maker** relojero -ra *mf*;
—making relojería *f*; **—man** vigilante *m*,
sereno *m*; **—tower** atalaya *f*, torre de
vigilancia *f*; **—word** (password)
contraseña *f*; (motto) consigna *f*, lema *m*;
to be on the — estar alerta; **to keep —
on / over** vigilar a

watchful [wátʃfəl] ADJ alerta, atento

water [wɔ́də] N agua *f*; **—bed** cama de agua
f; **—bird** ave acuática *f*; **— buffalo**
búfalo de agua *m*; **—color** acuarela *f*;
—cress berro *m*; **—fall** (small) cascada *f*;
(large) catarata *f*; **—front** muelles *m pl*; **—
heater** calentador de agua *m*; **— lily**
nenúfar *m*; **—logged** empapado;
—melon sandía *f*; **— pistol** pistola de
agua *f*; **— power** energía hidráulica *f*; **—
proof** (fabric) impermeable; (watch)
sumergible; **to —proof** impermeabilizar;
—shed vertiente *f*; **— ski** esquí acuático
m; **to —-ski** hacer esquí acuático; **—
softener** ablandador de agua *m*; **—
sports** deportes acuáticos *m pl*; **—spout**
(pipe) tubo de desagüe *m*; (tornado)
tromba *f*; **— supply** abastecimiento de
agua *m*; **— table** capa freática *f*; **—tight**
hermético; **— vapor** vapor de agua *m*;
—way vía navegable *f*; **my — broke** se
me rompieron las aguas, se me rompió la
fuente; VT (irrigate) regar; (dilute) aguar;
VI/VT (animals) abrevar; **—ed-down** (with
water) aguado; (simplified) simplificado;
(softened) suavizado; **my eyes are —ing**
me lloran los ojos; **it makes my mouth
— se** me hace agua la boca

watery [wɔ́dəri] ADJ (watered-down) aguado;
(like water) acuoso; (boggy) húmedo

watt [wat] N vatio *m*

wattage [wádɪdʒ] N vataje *m*

wave [wev] N (of radio) onda *f*; (of water,

heat, fashion) ola *f*; (of disgust, of people) oleada *f*; (with the hand) saludo *m*; **—length** longitud de onda *f*; VI/VT (flag) ondear; (hair) ondular(se); VI (greeting) saludar con la mano; **to — good-bye** decir adiós con la mano

waver [wévɚ] VI (hesitate) vacilar, titubear; (falter) flaquear

wavy [wévi] ADJ ondeado, ondulado

wax [wæks] N cera *f*; (for seals) lacre *m*; — **paper** papel encerado *m*; VT encerar; (defeat) derrotar; VI crecer; **to — poetic** ponerse poético

way [we] N (road) camino *m*; (manner) modo *m*, manera *f*; — **in** entrada *f*; — **out** salida *f*; **to —lay** (wait in ambush) estar al acecho de; (attack) asaltar; (stop) detener; **—farer** caminante *mf*; **—out** estrafalario; **—s** costumbres *f pl*; **—side** borde del camino *m*; — **through** paso *m*, pasaje *m*; **a long — off** muy lejos; **by — of London** por Londres; **by — of comparison** a modo de comparación; **by the —** a propósito; **in no —** de ningún modo; **on the — to** rumbo a; **to get out of the —** apartarse; **to go out of one's —** desvivirse por; **to look the other —** hacer la vista gorda; **to lead the —** ir a la cabeza; **to be in a bad —** hallarse mal de salud; **to give —** (yield) ceder; (break) quebrarse; **to get one's —** salirse con la suya; **to make — for** abrir paso para

wayward [wéwɚd] ADJ (disobedient) desobediente; (willful) porfiado

we [wi] PRON nosotros -as *mf*

weak [wik] ADJ débil; (deficient) flojo; — **force** fuerza débil *f*; **—kneed** achicado; — **sister** (coward) cobarde *mf*; — **link** parte más delgada del hilo *f*

weaken [wíkən] VI/VT debilitar(se), quebrantar(se)

weakling [wíklɪŋ] N alfeñique *m*

weakness [wíknɪs] N debilidad *f*, flaqueza *f*; (deficiency) flojedad *f*

wealth [wɛlθ] N riqueza *f*

wealthy [wɛ́lθi] ADJ rico, adinerado, pudiente

wean [win] VT destetar; **to — oneself of** quitarse el vicio de

weapon [wépən] N arma *f*

wear [wer] VT (have on) llevar, tener puesto; (dress in habitually) usar; VI/VT (waste away) desgastar(se); **to — away** gastar(se), desgastar(se); **to — down** (a person) agotar; (a pencil) desgastar; **to — off** perder efecto; **to — on** prolongarse; **to — out** (make unfit) gastar(se), degastar(se),

sobar(se); (expend) agotar; **it —s well** es duradero; N (use) gasto *m*; (clothes) ropa *f*; (durability) durabilidad *f*; (deterioration) desgaste *m*; — **and tear** desgaste *m*

weariness [wírinɪs] N cansancio *m*, fatiga *f*

wearing [wérɪŋ] ADJ (causing wear) desgastante; (causing fatigue) cansado

wearisome [wírɪsəm] ADJ fastidioso

weary [wíri] ADJ cansado, fatigado; VI/VT cansar(se), fatigar(se)

weasel [wízəl] N comadreja *f*

weather [wéðɚ] N tiempo *m*; (storm) tempestad *f*; **—beaten** desgastado/ curtido por la intemperie; — **bureau** oficina meteorológica *f*; — **conditions** condiciones atmosféricas *f pl*; **—man** meteorólogo *m*; **—proof** resistente a la intemperie; **—vane** veleta *f*; **it is fine —** hace buen tiempo; **to be under the —** estar enfermo; VI/VT gastar(se); (skin) curtir; **to — a storm** capear un temporal

weave [wiv] VT (cloth, basket) tejer, entretejer; (to put together) urdir, tramar; **to — together / into** entretejer, entrelazar; **to — one's way** zigzaguear; N tejido *m*

weaver [wívɚ] N tejedor -ra *mf*

web [web] N (of a spider) telaraña *f*; (of lies) sarta *f*; (membrane) membrana *f*; **—foot** (foot) pata palmada *f*; (animal) palmípedo *m*; — **page** página web *f*; **—site** sitio web *m*

wed [wed] VI/VT casarse (con); VT casar a

wedding [wédɪŋ] N boda *f*, casamiento *m*; — **day** día de boda *m*; — **dress** traje de novia *m*; — **ring** anillo de boda *m*

wedge [wedʒ] N cuña *f*; **to drive a — between** separar; VT acuñar, meter cuñas; **to be —d between** estar apretado entre

Wednesday [wénzde] N miércoles *m*

wee [wi] ADJ chiquito, pequeñito

weed [wid] N mala hierba *f*; (marijuana) hierba *f*; **—killer** herbicida *m*; VT deshierbar, escardar; **to — out** eliminar

week [wik] N semana *f*; **—day** día de semana *m*; **—end** fin de semana *m*; **a — from today** de aquí en una semana

weekly [wíkli] ADJ semanal; ADV semanalmente; N semanario *m*

weep [wip] VI llorar, lagrimear

weeping [wípɪŋ] ADJ lloroso; — **willow** sauce llorón *m*; N llanto *m*

weevil [wívəl] N gorgojo *m*

weigh [we] VI/VT pesar; (consider) ponderar, sopesar, barajar; **to — anchor** levar anclas; **to — down** agobiar, abrumar; **to — on one's conscience** pesar en la conciencia de uno

weight [wet] N (heaviness, importance) peso *m*; (for clocks, scales, barbells) pesa *f*; **—lifting** levantamiento de pesas *m*, halterofilia *f*; **— training** levantamiento de pesas *m*, halterofilia *f*; **—watcher** persona a dieta *f*; **to put on** — engordar; **to lose** — adelgazar; VT (add weight) añadir peso; (in statistics) ponderar; **to — someone down** agobiarle a uno

weightless [wétlɪs] ADJ ingrávido

weighty [wédi] ADJ importante

weird [wírd] ADJ (strange) extraño; (supernatural) misterioso

weirdo [wírdo] N bicho raro *m*, ente *m*

welcome [wélkəm] N bienvenida *f*; ADJ bienvenido; **—!** ¡bienvenido! **— mat** alfombrilla *f*, felpudo *m*; **— rest** descanso agradable *m*; **you are —** no hay de qué, de nada; **you are — here** estás en tu casa; **you are —** a tus órdenes; VT (friendly) dar la bienvenida, acoger; (unfriendly) recibir

weld [weld] VI/VT soldar(se); N soldadura *f*

welfare [wélfer] N (good fortune) bienestar *m*; (public assistance) asistencia social *f*; **— state** estado de bienestar *m*

well [wel] ADV bien; **— then** pues bien; **—being** bienestar *m*; **—bred** bien educado; **—-defined** bien definido; **—-done** (steak) bien cocido; (a task) bien hecho; **—-fed** bien alimentado; **—-fixed** adinerado; **—-founded** bien fundamentado; **—-groomed** bien arreglado, aseado; **—-heeled** adinerado; **—-informed** bien informado; **—-known** (of a fact) bien sabido; (of a person) bien conocido, notorio; **—-made** bien hecho; **—-meaning** bien intencionado; **—-nigh** casi, muy cerca de; **he is — over fifty** tiene mucho más de cincuenta años; **—-off** adinerado, acomodado; **—-read** leído, educado; **—-rounded** completo; **—-spoken** bien hablado; **all is —** todo está bien; INTERJ ¡bueno! ADJ (healthy) bien de salud, sano; N (of water, oil) pozo *m*; (of staircase) caja *f*; **—spring** fuente *f*, manantial *m*; VI **tears —ed up in her eyes** se le llenaron los ojos de lágrimas

wellness [wélnɪs] N (health) salud *f*; (health care) medicina preventiva *f*

welsh [welʃ] VI **to — on** (a debt) no pagar; (a promise) no cumplir

Welsh [welʃ] ADJ & N galés -esa *mf*

welt [welt] N verdugón *m*

west [west] N (cardinal point) oeste *m*; (hemisphere) occidente *m*; **— Berlin** Berlín occidental *m*; **— Indies** Antillas *f pl*; **— wind** viento del oeste *m*; ADV (direction) hacia el oeste; (location) al oeste

western [wéstən] ADJ occidental, del oeste; N película del oeste *f*

westerner [wéstənə] N occidental *mf*

westward [wéstwəd] ADV hacia el oeste; ADJ occidental

wet [wet] ADJ (drenched) mojado; (damp, rainy) húmedo; **—back** *offensive vulg* espalda mojada *mf*, mojado -da *mf*; **— blanket** aguafiestas *mf sg*; **— dream** sueño húmedo *m*; **—land** humedal *m*; **— nurse** nodriza *f*; **— paint** pintura fresca *f*; **— suit** traje de buzo *m*; VI/VT mojar(se); (dampen) humedecer(se)

wetness [wétnɪs] N humedad *f*

whack [hwæk] VI/VT golpear, pegar; **to — off** (cut) cortar; (masturbate) *vulg* hacer(se) una paja; N golpazo *m*; *Sp* hostia *f*; **to take a — at** hacer un intento de; **out of —** descompuesto, averiado

whale [hwel] N ballena *f*; VI pescar ballenas

wharf [hwɔrf] N muelle *m*, embarcadero *m*

what [hwɑt] INTERR PRON N & ADJ qué; **— did you say?** ¿qué dijiste? **— books did you want?** ¿qué libros querías? **—'s the matter?** ¿qué pasa? **— for?** ¿para qué? **and —not** y demás; REL PRON lo que; **come — may** venga lo que venga; **take — books you need** toma los libros que necesites; **any place —soever** en cualquier lugar; ADJ qué; **— happy children!** ¡qué niños más felices! **— luck!** ¡qué buena suerte! INTERJ cómo, qué; **so —?** ¡y qué?

whatever [hwɑtévə] PRON lo que; **— do you mean?** ¿qué demonios quieres decir? **do it, — happens** hazlo, pase lo que pase; **— you may think** pienses lo que pienses; ADJ **any person —** una persona cualquiera/cualquier persona; **no money —** nada de dinero; INTERJ ¡lo que sea!

wheat [hwit] N trigo *m*; **— germ** germen de trigo *m*

wheel [hwil] N (disc) rueda *f*; (of cheese) horma *f*; (for pottery) torno *m*; (for steering a car) volante *m*; (on a ship) timón *m*; **—barrow** carretilla *f*; **—base** batalla *f*, paso *m*; **—chair** silla de ruedas *f*; **—s** coche *m*; VT (a round object) hacer rodar; (a person, bicycle, wheelchair) empujar; VI **to — out** sacar rodando; **to — in** entrar rodando; **to — around** girar sobre los talones

wheeze [hwiz] N resuello ruidoso *m*; VI resollar

when [hwen] ADV & CONJ cuando; INTERJ, ADV & N cuándo

whenever [hwenévə-] CONJ — **I see him** cada vez que lo veo; ADV — **you arrive tomorrow** cuando llegues

where [hwer] ADV, N & INTERR PRON dónde *m*; (direction) adónde; CONJ donde; (direction) adonde

whereabouts [hwérabauts] N paradero *m*; INTERR ADV dónde

whereas [hwerǽz] CONJ mientras que; (in preambles) visto que, considerando que

whereby [hwerbái] ADV por lo cual

wherefore [hwérfɔr] ADV por lo cual

wherein [hwerín] ADV en donde

whereof [hweráv] REL PRON de que; INTERR PRON de qué

whereupon [hwerəpán] ADV después de lo cual

wherever [hwerévə-] ADV dondequiera que

wherewithal [hwérwiðɔl] N medios *m pl*, fondos *m pl*

whet [hwet] VT (sharpen) afilar; (stimulate) estimular; —**stone** piedra de afilar *f*

whether [hwéðə-] CONJ — **we like it or not** nos guste o no nos guste; **I doubt — we can do it** dudo (de) que lo podamos hacer; **he asked — I was coming** me preguntó si venía

which [hwɪtʃ] INTERR PRON cuál(es); — **do you want?** ¿cuál(es) quieres? REL PRON que; **the apple — I just bought** la manzana que acabo de comprar; **the book — I was talking about** el libro del que / cual estaba hablando; **that — you don't know can hurt you** lo que no sabes puede hacerte daño; INTERR ADJ qué, cuál(es) de; — **house is it?** ¿qué casa es? ¿cuál de las casas es?

whichever [hwɪtʃévə-] PRON & ADJ (no matter which) cualquiera (que); — **you choose, you'll regret it later** elijas el que elijas, te arrepentirás después; (anyone that) el que / la que; **choose — you like** elije el que quieras

whiff [hwɪf] N (waft) soplo *m*; (odors, scandal) bocanada *f*, tufillo *m*; **to take a** — oler

while [hwaɪl] N rato *m*; **a short** — un ratito; **a short — ago** hace poco; CONJ (during) mientras; (whereas) mientras que; (even though) aunque; VT **to — away** pasar

whim [hwɪm] N capricho *m*, antojo *m*

whimper [hwímpə-] VI/VT lloriquear, gimotear; N lloriqueo *m*, gimoteo *m*

whimsical [hwímzikəl] ADJ caprichoso, antojadizo

whine [hwaɪn] VI (whimper) gemir; (complain) quejarse; N (whimper) gemido *m*; (complaint) quejido *m*

whiner [hwáɪnə-] N llorón -ona *mf*, quejica *mf*

whiny [hwáɪni] ADJ quejoso, quejica, ñoño

whip [hwɪp] N azote *m*, látigo *m*, rebenque *m*; VT (hit with a whip) azotar, fustigar; (spank) zurrar, dar una paliza; (beat to a froth) batir; (defeat) vencer; **to — out** sacar; **to — up** (prepare) preparar rápidamente; (incite) incitar

whipping [hwípɪŋ] N zurra *f*, paliza *f*; — **cream** crema para batir *f*

whir [hwɜ-] VI zumbar; N zumbido *m*

whirl [hwɜ-l] VI girar; **to — around** arremolinarse; **my head —s** me da vueltas la cabeza; N (rotation) giro *m*; (of water) remolino *m*; —**pool** remolino *m*; —**wind** torbellino *m*, remolino de viento *m*; —**wind tour** gira relámpago *f*; **my head is in a** — me da vueltas la cabeza; **to give it a** — probarlo

whisk [hwɪsk] VT (sweep) barrer; (beat) batir; **to — away** llevarse de prisa; VI **to — by** pasar rápidamente; N (broom) escobilla *f*; (beater) batidor *m*

whisker [hwískə-] N (hair of beard) pelo de la barba *m*; (sideburn) patilla *f*; (of animals) bigote *m*

whiskey, whisky [hwíski] N whisky *m*

whisper [hwíspə-] VI/VT (voices) cuchichear, secretear; (leaves, water) susurrar; N (voices) cuchicheo *m*; (leaves, water) susurro *m*; **to talk in a** — cuchichear en voz baja

whistle [hwísəl] VI/VT silbar; (loud) chiflar; (in protest) rechiflar; VI (referee, train) pitar; **to — for someone** llamar a uno con un silbido; N (sound) silbido *m*; (loud sound) chiflido *m*; (of a referee) pitido *m*; (instrument) silbato *m*, pito *m*; — **blower** acusador -ora *mf*

white [hwaɪt] ADJ (of color, ethnicity) blanco; — **blood cell** glóbulo blanco *m*; — **bread** pan blanco *m*; —**bread** soso; —**caps** cabrillas *f pl*; —**collar** administrativo, de cuello blanco; — **gold** oro blanco *m*; — **hair** cana *f*; — **lie** mentirilla *f*; — **noise** ruido blanco *m*; — **trash** *offensive* sureño -ña blanco -ca pobre *mf*; **to —wash** (paint) blanquear, enjalbegar; (cover up) encubrir; —**wash** (paint) lechada *f*; (cover-up) encubrimiento *m*; N blanco *m* (also ethnicity); (of egg) clara f

whiten [hwaɪtn̩] VI/VT blanquear(se), emblanquecer

whiteness [hwáɪtnɪs] N blancura f

whitish [hwáɪdɪʃ] ADJ blancuzco, blanquecino

whittle [hwídl̩] VI/VT tallar; **to — away** ir gastando; **to — down expenses** reducir los gastos

whiz [hwɪz] VI zumbar; **to — by** pasar zumbando; N (sound) zumbido m; (ace) as m; VI hacer zumbar; **— kid** niño -ña prodigio mf

who [hu] REL PRON quien(es); INTERR PRON quién(es); **he —** el que

whoa [hwo] INTERJ (to express amazement) ¡jo! (to stop a horse) ¡so!

whoever [huévə⸳] REL PRON (whatever person) quienquiera que, el que; INTERR PRON (who) quién

whole [hol] ADJ (complete) completo, íntegro; (unbroken) entero; (uninjured) ileso; **—-grain** integral; **—-hearted** sincero; **—-heartedly** de todo corazón; **— milk** leche entera f; **— note** redonda f; **—sale** (in bulk) al por mayor; (massive) masivo; **—saler** comerciante al por mayor mf, mayorista mf, almacenista mf; **—sale slaughter** matanza f; **—-wheat** integral; **the — day** todo el día; **to go — hog** tirar la casa por la ventana; N todo m; (for amounts) totalidad f; **—sale** venta al por mayor f, mayoreo m; **as a —** en su totalidad; **on the —** en general; ADV **—sale** al por mayor; VI/VT **to —sale** vender al por mayor

wholesome [hólsəm] ADJ sano

whom [hum] REL PRON a quien(es); INTERR PRON a quién(es); **for / with —** para / con quien

whoop [hwup] N (shout) grito m; (gasp) respiración convulsiva f; VI (person) gritar; (owl) ulular; **to — it up** armar jaleo

whopper [hwápə⸳] N (large thing) cosa enorme f; (lie) mentira f, trola f

whopping [hwápɪŋ] ADJ enorme

whore [hor] N offensive puta f; **—house** vulg casa de putas f

whose [huz] REL PRON cuyo; **the man — son is here** el hombre cuyo hijo está aquí; INTERR PRON de quién; **— book is this?** ¿de quién es este libro?

why [hwaɪ] ADV & CONJ por qué; **that's the reason — he left** es por eso que se fue; N porqué m; INTERJ **—, of course!** ¡pero, claro!

wick [wɪk] N mecha f, pabilo m

wicked [wíkɪd] ADJ malvado, perverso

wickedness [wíkɪdnɪs] N maldad f, perversidad f

wicker [wíkə⸳] N mimbre m; **— chair** silla de mimbre f

wide [waɪd] ADJ (broad) ancho; (of great range) amplio; (spacious) vasto, extenso; **— apart** muy apartados; **—-awake** muy despierto, despabilado; **— body** avión de fuselaje ancho m; **—-eyed** ojiabierto, con los ojos bien abiertos; **— of the mark** lejos del blanco; **—-open** abierto de par en par; **—spread** (over a wide area) extendido; (among many people) generalizado; **to — open** — (a door) abrir de par en par; (one's mouth) abrir bien; **two feet —** dos pies de ancho

widely [wáɪdli] ADV **it is — known that** es bien sabido que; **he is a — known artist** es un artista muy conocido; **he is — read** es muy leído; **— different versions** versiones muy diferentes

widen [wáɪdn̩] VI/VT ensanchar(se), ampliar(se)

widow [wído] N viuda f

widower [wídoə⸳] N viudo m

width [wɪdθ] N ancho m, anchura f

wield [wild] VT (power) ejercer; (tool) manejar; (weapon) blandir, esgrimir

wife [waɪf] N esposa f, mujer f, señora f

wig [wɪg] N peluca f

wiggle [wígəl] VI/VT (hips) menear(se); (toes) mover(se); N (of hips) meneo m; (of toes) movimiento m; **— room** flexibilidad f

wigwam [wígwam] N tienda indígena f

wild [waɪld] ADJ (animals, savages) salvaje, bravío, bronco; (plant) silvestre; (party) desenfrenado; (conduct) alocado; (storm, temperament) violento; (hair) desordenado; (look) extraviado, descasajado; (enthusiasm) delirante; **— boar** jabalí m; **— card** comodín m; **—cat** gato montés m; **—-eyed** de mirada extraviada, con los ojos desencajados; **—fire** fuego arrasador m; **—flower** flor silvestre f; **— goose chase** búsqueda inútil f; **—life** fauna f; **I'm just — about Mary** estoy loco por María; **not in your —est dreams** ni lo pienses; **to drive someone —** volver loco a alguien; **to talk —** decir disparates; N **—s** regiones salvajes f pl

wilderness [wíldə⸳nɪs] N (near mountains) monte m; (desert) desierto m; (jungle) jungla f

wile [waɪl] N artimaña f, treta f

will [wɪl] VT (use will power) conseguir a

fuerza de voluntad; (bequeath) legar,
dejar; v aux **if you —** si quieres; **she —
come** va a venir, vendrá; **this
motorcycle — go 100 mph** esta
motocicleta puede hacer 100 millas por
hora; **in spite of everything, he — not
stop complaining** a pesar de todo, no
deja de quejarse; **she — just sit for
hours doing nothing** se pasa horas
sentada sin hacer nada; **that — do** basta;
N (wish) voluntad f; (testament)
testamento m; **—power** fuerza de
voluntad f; **at — a** discreción, a voluntad

willful, wilful [wílfəł] ADJ testarudo,
porfiado

willies [wíliz] N escalofríos m pl

willing [wíluŋ] ADJ dispuesto, voluntarioso

willingly [wíluŋli] ADV de buena gana,
gustoso

willingness [wíluŋnıs] N buena voluntad f,
buena gana f

willow [wílo] N sauce m

wilt [wıłt] VI/VT (plant) marchitar(se); VI
(person) languidecer

wily [wáili] ADJ astuto, artero

wimp [wımp] N pelele m

win [wın] VI/VT ganar; VT (support, fame,
affection) ganarse; (victory) alcanzar,
conseguir; **to — out** ganar, triunfar; **to —
over** conquistar; **a ——— situation** una
situación beneficiosa para ambas partes

wince [wıns] VI hacer una mueca; N mueca f

winch [wıntʃ] N cabrestante m, torno m

wind [wınd] N (air) viento m; (gas) gases m
pl; **—bag** charlatán -ana mf; **—breaker**ᵗᵐ
cazadora f; **—fall** ganancia inesperada f;
— instrument instrumento de viento m;
—mill molino de viento m; **—pipe**
tráquea f; **—shield** parabrisas m sg;
—shield wiper limpiaparabrisas m sg;
—sock manga de viento f; **—surfing**
windsurf m; **— tunnel** túnel
aerodinámico m; **to get — of** enterarse
de; **to break —** ventosear; **to catch
one's —** recobrar el aliento; ADJ **—ward**
de barlovento; ADV **—ward** hacia/a
barlovento; [waınd] VT enrollar; (watch)
dar cuerda a; VI (take a bending course)
serpentear; **to — around** enrollarse; **to
— down** (relax) tranquilizarse; (come to a
conclusion) irse terminando; **to — up**
(string) enrollar; (a clock) dar cuerda; (a
project) completar; (in jail) acabar; N
(turn) vuelta f; (bend) recodo m; **—up**
conclusión f

winding [wáındıŋ] ADJ sinuoso; **— staircase**
escalera de caracol f

window [wíndo] N (in building) ventana f;
(in car, plane) ventanilla f; (in a shop)
escaparate m; Am vidriera f; **—pane** cristal
m, vidrio m; **— shade** visillo m; **—sill**
alféizar m

windy [wíndi] ADJ ventoso; **it is —** hace/
hay viento

wine [waın] N vino m; **— cellar** bodega f;
—glass copa f; **—grower** viticultor -ora
mf, viñatero -ra mf; **— industry** industria
vinícola f; **—skin** odre m; **— tasting** cata
de vinos f

winery [wáınəri] N bodega f

wing [wıŋ] N ala f (also of building, table,
army); **— nut** tuerca (de) mariposa/
palomilla f; **—span / spread** envergadura
f; **—tip** extremo del ala m; **in the —s** en
los bastidores; **under one's —** al amparo
de alguien; **to take —** levantar vuelo; VI
volar; VT (transport) transportar por aire;
(wound slightly) herir en el ala/brazo; **to
— it** improvisar

wink [wıŋk] VI/VT guiñar; **to — approval**
guiñar en aprobación; **to — at** hacer la
vista gorda; N guiño m, guiñada f; **I
didn't sleep a —** no pegué un ojo

winner [wínə] N ganador -ora mf

winning [wínıŋ] ADJ (successful) ganador,
vencedor; (charming) atractivo; **—s**
ganancias f pl

wino [wáıno] N borracho -cha mf

winter [wíntə] N invierno m; **— weather**
clima invernal m; VI invernar

wintry [wíntri] ADJ invernal

wipe [waıp] VT (sweat, tears) enjugar; (wet
surfaces) secar; (dry surface) limpiar; **to —
away** enjugar; **to — off** limpiar; **to —
out** aniquilar; **to — up** limpiar

wiper [wáıpə] N limpiaparabrisas m sg

wire [waır] N (filament) alambre m;
(telegram) telegrama m; **by —** por
telégrafo; **— fence** alambrado m; **—tap**
intervención del teléfono f, pinchazo m;
to —tap intervenir un teléfono, pinchar
un teléfono; VT (an appliance) alambrar; (a
house) electrificar; VI/VT (a message)
telegrafiar; (money) girar; **to — together**
atar con alambre

wired [waırd] ADJ (installed) alambrado;
(tied) atado con alambre; (electrified)
electrificado; (enthusiastic) sobreexcitado

wireless [wáırlıs] ADJ inalámbrico

wiring [wáırıŋ] N cableado m

wiry [wáıri] ADJ (skinny) nervudo; (like wire)
crespo

wisdom [wízdəm] N (moral) sabiduría f;
(scholarly) saber m; **— tooth** muela del

juicio f

wise [waɪz] ADJ (discerning) sabio; (prudent) sensato, prudente; (erudite) erudito; **—ass** sabihondo -da mf; **—crack** broma f, chiste m; **— guy** sabihondo m; **the Three — Men** los Tres Reyes Magos; N **in no —** de ningún modo; VI **to — up** avisparse

wish [wɪʃ] VT desear; **I — you were here** ojalá estuvieras aquí; **I — you the best** te deseo lo mejor; **to — for** pedir; **to — upon a star** pedir un deseo; N deseo m; **to make a —** pedir un deseo; **best —es** saludos

wishy-washy [wíʃiwaʃi] ADJ indeciso

wistful [wístfəɫ] ADJ (pensive) pensativo; (nostalgic) nostálgico

wit [wɪt] N (intelligence) agudeza f, ingenio m; (verbal humor) gracejo m, sal f, chispa f; (person) persona aguda f, persona ingeniosa f; **to be at one's —s' end** no saber qué más hacer; **to live by one's —s** vivir de su ingenio; **to lose one's —s** perder el juicio; **to use one's —s** valerse de su ingenio

witch [wɪtʃ] N bruja f; **—craft** brujería f; **—hunt** cacería de brujas f

with [wɪθ, wɪð] PREP con; **rice — chicken** arroz con pollo m; **the man — glasses** el hombre de gafas; **I left my son — Mary** dejé a mi hijo al cuidado de María; **to be — it** está al día; **— me** conmigo; **— you** contigo, con usted

withdraw [wɪðdrɔ́] VI/VT retirar(se)

withdrawal [wɪðdrɔ́əɫ] N (of troops) retirada f; (from public office) alejamiento m; (from a bank) Am retiro m; Sp retirada f; **— (symptoms)** síndrome de abstinencia m

wither [wíðɚ] VI/VT (of a plant) marchitar(se); (of a person) consumir(se); **she —ed him with a look** lo fulminó con la mirada

withhold [wɪθhóɫd] VT (approval) negar; (funds) retener; (truth) ocultar

withholding tax [wɪθhóɫdɪŋtæks] N impuesto deducido del salario m

within [wɪðín] PREP dentro de; **— five miles** a menos de cinco millas; ADV dentro, adentro

without [wɪðáut] PREP sin; **— my seeing him** sin que yo lo vea; ADV fuera, afuera

withstand [wɪθstǽnd] VI/VT resistir

witness [wítnɪs] N (person) testigo mf; (testimony) testimonio m; **to bear —** atestiguar; VT (see) presenciar; (sign) firmar como testigo

witticism [wídɪsɪzem] N ocurrencia f

witty [wídi] ADJ ocurrente, dicharachero

wizard [wízɚd] N (sorcerer) mago m, brujo m, hechicero m; (genius) genio m

wobble [wábəɫ] N bamboleo m, tambaleo m; VI/VT tambalear(se), bombolear(se)

woe [wo] N aflicción f; **— is me!** ¡pobre de mí!

woeful [wófəɫ] ADJ lamentable

wok [wak] N wok m

wolf [wʊɫf] N lobo m; **— spider** araña lobo f

woman [wúmən] N mujer f; **a —'s touch** un toque femenino; **women's lib(eration)** movimiento de liberación femenina m; **women's rights** derechos de la mujer m pl

womanhood [wúmənhʊd] N (condition) condición de mujer f; (group of women) las mujeres f pl

womanizer [wúmənaɪzɚ] N mujeriego m

womankind [wúmənkaɪnd] N las mujeres f pl

womanly [wúmənli] ADJ femenino

womb [wum] N (uterus) útero m, matriz f; (insides) vientre m; (center) seno m

wonder [wándɚ] VI/VT preguntarse; **to — at** admirarse de, maravillarse de; **I — what time it is** ¿qué hora será? N (marvel) maravilla f; (surprise) asombro m; (miracle) milagro m; **it's a — that** es asombroso que; **it's no — that** no es de extrañar que

wonderful [wándɚfəɫ] ADJ maravilloso, estupendo

woo [wu] VI/VT cortejar

wood [wʊd] N (material) madera f; (firewood) leña f; **—cutter** leñador -ora mf; **—louse** cochinilla f; **—pecker** pájaro carpintero m; **—s** bosque m; **— shaving** viruta f; **—shed** leñera f; **—sman** leñador m; **—winds** maderas f pl; **—work** carpintería f, maderaje m; **to come out of the —work** salir de la nada

wooded [wʊ́dɪd] ADJ arbolado

wooden [wʊ́dn̩] ADJ (of wood) de madera; (lifeless) inexpresivo

woody [wʊ́di] ADJ (with trees) arbolado; (like wood) leñoso

woof [wʊf] N trama f; INTERJ ¡guau!

wool [wʊɫ] N lana f; **— sweater** suéter de lana m

woolen [wʊ́lən] ADJ de lana; N **—s** (fabric) tejido de lana m; (clothes) ropa de lana f

woolly [wʊ́li] ADJ lanudo

word [wɝd] N (lexical unit) vocablo m; palabra f (also promise); (news) noticia f, aviso m; (order) mandato m, orden m;

may I have a — with you? ¿podemos hablar? **— processing** procesamiento de textos *m*; *Sp* tratamiento de texto(s) *m*; **by — of mouth** de palabra; **—s (of a song)** letra (de una canción) *f*; **to eat one's —s** tragarse/comerse las palabras; **— for —** palabra por palabra; *VT* (oral) expresar; (written) formular

wordy [wɔ́ɾDi] ADJ verboso, prolijo

work [wɜ˞k] N (effort) trabajo *m*; (employment) empleo *m*, trabajo *m*; (artistic product, fortification) obra *f*; **—book** cuaderno/libro de trabajo *m*; **—day** día laborable *m*; **—force** mano de obra *f*; **—load** cantidad/carga de trabajo *f*; **—man** obrero *m*; **— of art** obra de arte *f*; **—place** lugar de trabajo *m*; **—shop** taller *m*; **— station** terminal de trabajo *m*; **—s** fábrica *f*; **the —s** todo; **—week** semana de trabajo *f*; **he's hard at —** está trabajando duro; *VI* (labor) trabajar; (function) funcionar; *VT* (change) efectuar; (metal, land) trabajar; (a crowd) manipular; (a mine) explotar; (employees) hacer trabajar; **to — in(to)** introducir; **to — loose** soltarse, aflojarse; **to — on** (repair) arreglar; (improve) tratar de mejorar; **to — one's way through college** pagarse los estudios trabajando; **to — one's way up** ascender a fuerza de trabajo; **to — out** (a plan) urdir; (a problem) resolver; **he —s out every day** hace ejercicio todos los días; **it all —ed out** al final todo salió bien; **to be all —ed up** estar sobreexcitado; **to get —ed up** agitarse

worker [wɔ́˞kə˞] N trabajador -ora *mf*; (in a factory) obrero -ra *mf*; (in an office) oficinista *mf*

working [wɔ́˞kɪŋ] N (act of someone who works, shaping of metals) trabajo *m*; (operation) funcionamiento *m*, operación *f*; (of a problem) cálculo *m*; (of a mine) explotación *f*; ADJ (class) obrero, trabajador; (majority) suficiente; **— class** clase obrera/trabajadora *f*; **— lunch** comida de trabajo *f*; **—man** obrero *m*

workmanship [wɔ́˞kmənʃɪp] N (skill) habilidad *f*, destreza *f*; (quality) confección *f*

world [wɜ˞ld] N mundo *m*; **—view** cosmovisión *f*; **— war** guerra mundial *f*; **—wide web** web *f*, red (mundial electrónica) *f*; ADJ **—class** de categoría mundial; **—shaking** trascendental; **—wide** mundial

worldly [wɔ́˞ldli] ADJ (mundane) mundano,

temporal; (sophisticated) de mundo, corrido; (material) material

worm [wɜ˞m] N gusano *m*; ADJ **—-eaten** comido por los gusanos, carcomido; *VT* desparasitar, quitar las lombrices; **to — a secret out of someone** extraerle/ sonsacarle un secreto a alguien; **to — oneself into** insinuarse en

worn [wɔɾn] ADJ desgastado, usado

worrisome [wɔ́˞risəm] ADJ preocupante

worry [wɔ́˞i] VI/VT preocupar(se), inquietar(se); VT (harass) atacar; VI **to — with** juguetear con; N preocupación *f*, inquietud *f*, zozobra *f*; **—wart** preocupón -ona *mf*

worse [wɜ˞s] ADJ & ADV peor; **— and —** cada vez peor; **— than ever** peor que nunca; **from bad to —** de mal en peor; **so much the —** tanto peor; **to be — off** estar peor que antes; **to change for the —** empeorar(se); **to get —** empeorar(se)

worship [wɔ́˞ʃɪp] N (act of worshiping) adoración *f*; (ceremony) culto *m*; VT (revere) adorar, venerar; VI (attend services) asistir al culto

worshiper [wɔ́˞ʃɪpə˞] N (one who worships) adorador -ora *mf*; **—s** fieles *mf pl*

worst [wɜ˞st] ADJ & ADV peor; **the — one** el/ la peor; **the — thing** lo peor; **—-case scenario** el peor de los casos; VT derrotar

worth [wɜ˞θ] ADJ **to be — a dollar** valer un dólar; **to be — hearing** ser digno de oírse; **to be —while** valer la pena; **it's — doing** vale la pena hacerlo; N valor *m*, valía *f*; **ten cents — of** diez centavos de; **to get one's money's — out of** aprovechar al máximo

worthless [wɔ́˞θlɪs] ADJ (useless) inútil; (despicable) despreciable

worthy [wɔ́˞ði] ADJ digno, meritorio; (esteemed) benemérito; **— cause** causa noble *f*; **— of praise** digno de elogio; N notable *mf*

would [wʊd] V AUX **I — do it if I could** lo haría si pudiera; **— you please open the door?** ¿podrías abrir la puerta por favor? **he said he — do it** dijo que lo haría; **as a child, I — play all the time** de niño, jugaba todo el tiempo; **— that she were alive!** ¡ojalá estuviera viva!

wound [wund] N herida *f*; VI/VT herir; (with an arrow) flechar

wow [waʊ] VT impresionar; INTERJ ¡huy!

wrangle [ɾǽŋgəl] VI/VT (quarrel) discutir; (obtain) agenciarse de; VT (herd) juntar; *Am* rodear; N riña *f*, pendencia *f*

wrangler [ɾǽŋglə˞] N vaquero -ra *mf*

wrap [ræp] vt envolver; **to — up** (a present) envolver; (a baby) arropar; (a task) terminar; (against the cold) abrigar(se); **to be wrapped in** estar envuelto en; **to be wrapped up in** estar absorto en; N (coat) abrigo m; (shawl) chal m; **—up** (summary) resumen m; (end) final m

wrapper [rǽpə] N envoltura f, envoltorio m

wrapping [rǽpɪŋ] N envoltura f; **— paper** papel para envolver m

wrath [ræθ] N ira f, cólera f

wreak [rik] vt **to — havoc** hacer estragos

wreath [riθ] N corona f; **— of smoke** espiral de humo f

wreck [rɛk] N (building) ruina f; (car, plane) restos m pl; (a ship) pecio m; (shipwreck) naufragio m; (person) desastre m, ruina f; (accident) accidente m; vi tener un accidente; vt (a ship) naufragar; (a car, totally) destrozar; (a car, with minor damage) chocar; (a building) demoler

wreckage [rɛkɪdʒ] N (of a car, plane) restos de un accidente m pl; (of a ship) pecio m; (of a building) escombros m pl

wrecker [rɛkə] N (tow truck) grúa f, camión de remolque m; (worker) obrero -ra de demolición mf

wrench [rɛntʃ] vt torcer, retorcer; **to — off / out** arrancar de un tirón, arrebatar; N (twist) torcedura f; (pull) tirón m; (tool) llave de tuercas f

wrest [rɛst] vt (pull) arrancar; (take away) arrebatar

wrestle [rɛsəɫ] vi/vt luchar (con / contra); N lucha f

wrestler [rɛslə] N luchador -ra mf

wrestling [rɛslɪŋ] N lucha libre f

wretch [rɛtʃ] N miserable mf, infeliz mf

wretched [rɛtʃɪd] adj (unfortunate) desdichado, infeliz; (despicable) vil, miserable, arrastrado; (inferior) pésimo

wriggle [rɪɡəɫ] vi culebrear, serpentear; vt menear, retorcer; **to — out of** escabullirse de

wring [rɪŋ] vt (twist) torcer, retorcer; (extract) arrancar; **to — one's hands** retorcerse las manos; **to — out** escurrir

wrinkle [rɪŋkəɫ] N arruga f, surco m; (problem) problema m; vi/vt arrugar(se)

wrist [rɪst] N muñeca f; **—watch** reloj (de) pulsera m

writ [rɪt] N auto m, mandato m

write [raɪt] vi/vt escribir; **to — back** contestar; **to — down** apuntar; **to — off** cancelar; **to — out** escribir en forma completa; **to — up** hacer un reportaje sobre; **it's written all over his face** se

le ve en la cara; **she —s for a living** es escritora; N **—up** reportaje m

writer [ráɪdə] N escritor -ora mf, literato -ta mf

writhe [raɪð] vi retorcerse

writing [ráɪdɪŋ] N (act of writing) escritura f; (handwriting) letra f, escritura f; (style) estilo m; **— desk** escritorio m; **— paper** papel de escribir m; **—s** obra f; **to put in — poner por escrito

wrong [rɔŋ] adj (incorrect) incorrecto, equivocado; (improper) inapropiado; **what's — with you?** ¿qué te pasa? **you are —** estás equivocado; **the — side of a fabric** el revés de una tela; **— side out** con lo de adentro para afuera; **to be on the — side of the road** ir a contramano / en sentido contrario; **that is the — book** ese no es el libro; **it is in the — place** está fuera de lugar; adv mal; **to go —** salir mal; N (evil) mal m; (injustice) injusticia f; **to be in the — (not be right) estar equivocado; (be to blame) tener la culpa; **to do —** hacer mal; vt perjudicar

wrought [rɔt] adj forjado; **— iron** hierro forjado m

wry [raɪ] adj (smile) torcido; (remark, humor) irónico; **to make a — face** hacer una mala cara

Xx

xenophobia [zɛnəfóbiə] N xenofobia f

Xerox[tm] [zíraks] N fotocopia f; vi/vt fotocopiar

x-rated [ɛksrɛdɪd] adj pornográfico

x-ray [ɛksre] N rayos X m pl, radiografía f; vi/vt radiografiar

xylophone [záɪləfon] N xilofón m, xilófono m

Yy

yacht [jɑt] N yate m; vi navegar en yate

y'all [jɔɫ] pron ustedes mf; Sp vosotros -as mf

Yankee [jǽŋki] adj & N estadounidense del norte del país mf

yard [jɑrd] N (measure) yarda (0.9144m) f;

(spar) verga *f*; (courtyard) patio *m*; (grassy area) jardín *m*; **—stick** (stick) vara de medida (de una yarda) *f*; (criterion) patrón *m*, norma *f*

yarn [jɑrn] N (material) hilo *m*; (story) cuento *m*

yawn [jɔn] VI bostezar; N bostezo *m*

year [jir] N año *m*; **—book** anuario *m*; **—-round** de todo el año

yearling [jírlɪŋ] N animal de un año *m*; (of cows) añojo -ja *mf*

yearly [jírli] ADJ anual; ADV anualmente

yearn [jɝn] VI anhelar, suspirar por

yearning [jɝnɪŋ] N anhelo *m*

yeast [jist] N levadura *f*

yell [jɛl] VI/VT gritar; N grito *m*

yellow [jélo] ADJ (color) amarillo; (coward) cobarde; **—fever** fiebre amarilla *f*; **—jacket** avispa *f*; **—pages** páginas amarillas *f pl*; N amarillo *m*; VI/VT poner(se) amarillo, amarillear

yellowish [jéloɪʃ] ADJ amarillento

yelp [jɛlp] VI gañir, aullar; N gañido *m*, aullido *m*

Yemen [jémən] N Yemen *m*

Yemeni [jéməni] ADJ & N yemení *mf*

yen [jɛn] N (currency of Japan) yen *m*; (desire) anhelo *m*; VI anhelar

yes [jɛs] ADV sí; **—no question** pregunta de sí o no *f*

yesterday [jéstə‑de] ADV & N ayer *m*; **the day before —** anteayer

yet [jɛt] ADV & CONJ **are they here —?** ¿ya llegaron? **they aren't here —** todavía no llegan, aún no han llegado; **— another** otro más; **ugly — charming** feo pero encantador; **as —** todavía, aún

yield [jild] VI/VT (surrender, give in) ceder, plegar(se); (produce) rendir, redituar; **to — five percent** dar un cinco por ciento de interés; N (production) rendimiento *m*, producción *f*; (of stocks) rédito *m*

yodel [jódḷ] VI cantar a la tirolesa; N canto tirolés *m*

yoga [jógə] N yoga *m*

yogurt [jógɚt] N yogur *m*

yoke [jok] N (crossbar) yugo *m*; (pair of animals) yunta *f*; (on a shirt) canesú *m*; VT uncir

yolk [jok] N yema *f*

yonder [jándɚ] ADJ aquel; ADV (location) allá; (direction) hacia allá

yore [jɔr] N **in days of —** antaño

you [ju] PRON **— came** (sg informal) tú viniste; (sg formal) usted vino; (pl informal) Sp vosotros vinisteis; Am ustedes vinieron; (formal) ustedes vinieron; **I see**

— you (sg informal) te veo; (sg formal) lo veo; (pl informal) Sp os veo; Am los veo; (pl formal) los veo; **I talk to —** (sg informal) te hablo; (sg formal) le hablo; (pl informal) Sp os hablo; Am les hablo; (pl formal) les hablo; **I went with —** (sg informal) fui contigo; (sg formal) fui con usted; (pl informal) Sp fui con vosotros; Am fui con ustedes; (pl formal) fui con ustedes; **it's for —** (sg informal) es para ti; (sg formal) es para usted; (pl informal) Sp es para vosotros; Am es para ustedes; (pl formal) es para ustedes; **this is how — make bread** así se hace el pan

young [jʌŋ] ADJ joven; **— man** joven *m*; **— people** gente joven *f*; **— woman** joven *f*; N (offspring) cría *f*

youngster [jʌ́ŋstɚ] N muchacho -cha *mf*, jovencito -ta *mf*

your [jɔr] POSS ADJ **this is — dog** (sg informal) este es tu perro; (sg formal) este es su perro; (pl informal) Sp este es vuestro perro; Am este es su perro; (pl formal) este es su perro

yours [jɔrz] PRON **this book is —** (sg informal) este libro es tuyo; (sg formal) este libro es suyo/de usted; (pl informal) Sp este libro es vuestro; Am este libro es suyo/de ustedes; (pl formal) este libro es suyo/de ustedes; **— is bigger** (sg informal) el tuyo/la tuya es más grande; (sg formal) el suyo/el de usted/la suya/la de usted es más grande; (pl informal) Sp el vuestro/la vuestra es más grande; Am el suyo/el de ustedes es más grande; (pl formal) el suyo/el de ustedes es más grande; **a friend of —** (sg informal) un amigo tuyo; (sg formal) un amigo suyo/de usted; (pl informal) Sp un amigo vuestro; Am un amigo suyo/de ustedes; **— truly** atentamente

yourself [jɔrsɛ́lf] PRON **you — wrote the letter** (sg informal) tú mismo escribiste la carta; (sg formal) usted mismo escribió la carta; **you yourselves wrote the letter** (pl informal) Sp vosotros mismos escribisteis la carta; Am ustedes mismos escribieron la carta; (pl formal) ustedes mismos escribieron la carta; **you are not — today** (sg informal) hoy no eres el mismo de siempre; (sg formal) hoy no es el mismo de siempre; **you are not yourselves today** Sp hoy no sois los mismos de siempre; Am hoy no son los mismos de siempre; (pl formal) hoy no son los mismos de siempre; **you were sitting by —** (sg informal) tú estabas

sentado solo; (sg formal) usted estaba
sentado solo; **you were sitting by
yourselves** (informal) *Sp* vosotros estabais
sentados solos; *Am* ustedes estaban
sentados solos; (pl formal) ustedes estaban
sentados solos; **you look at — at the
mirror** (sg informal) tú te miras en el
espejo; (sg formal) usted se mira en el
espejo; **you look at yourselves at the
mirror** (pl informal) *Sp* vosotros os mirais
en el espejo; *Am* ustedes se miran en el
espejo; (pl formal) ustedes se miran en el
espejo; **you bought — a house** (sg
informal) te compraste una casa; (sg
formal) usted se compró una casa; **you
bought yourselves a house** (pl
informal) *Sp* os comprasteis una casa; *Am*
se compraron una casa; (pl formal) se
compraron una casa
youth [juθ] N (person) joven *m*; (young age)
juventud *m*
youthful [júθfəł] ADJ juvenil
yo-yo [jójo] N yo-yo *m*
yucca [jákə] N yuca *f*
yuck [jʌk] INTERJ puaj, puaf
Yugoslavia [jugosláviə] N Yugoslavia *f*
Yugoslavian [jugosláviən] ADJ & N
yugoslavo -va *mf*
Yuletide [júłtaɪd] N Navidad *f*
yummy [jámi] ADJ delicioso; INTERJ ¡qué rico!
yuppie [jápi] N yuppie *mf*

Zimbabwe [zɪmbábwe] N Zimbabue *m*
Zimbabwean [zɪmbábweən] ADJ & N
zimbabuo -a *mf*
zinc [zɪŋk] N cinc *m*, zinc *m*
zip [zɪp] VI/VT cerrar/abrir con cremallera; **to
— by** pasar volando; **to — over** ir
corriendo; N cero *m*; **— code** código
postal *m*
zipper [zípɚ] N cremallera *f*, cierre
(relámpago) *m*
zirconium [zɚkóniəm] N circonio *m*
zodiac [zóDiæk] N zodíaco *m*
zombie [zámbi] N zombi *mf*
zone [zon] N zona *f*; VT dividir en zonas
zoo [zu] N zoológico *m*; *Sp* zoo *m*; **—keeper**
guardián -ana del zoológico *mf*
zoological [zoəládʒɪkət] ADJ zoológico
zoology [zoáłədʒi] N zoología *f*
zoom [zum] VI zumbar; **to — off** salir
zumbando; N zumbido *m*; **— lens**
teleobjetivo *m*, zoom *m*
zucchini [zukíni] N calabacín *m*
zygote [záɪgot] N cigoto *m*, zigoto *m*

Zz

Zambia [zǽmbiə] N Zambia *f*
Zambian [zǽmbiən] ADJ & N zambiano -na
mf
zany [zéni] ADJ absurdo
zap [zæp] VT liquidar
zeal [ził] N celo *m*, fervor *m*
zealot [zélət] N fanático -ca *mf*
zealous [zéləs] ADJ celoso, fervoroso
zebra [zíbrə] N cebra *f*
zenith [zínɪθ] N cenit *m*
zephyr [zéfɚ] N céfiro *m*
zeppelin [zépəlɪn] N zepelín *m*, dirigible *m*
zero [ziro] N cero *m*; **there's — possibility
that he'll come** las posibilidades de que
venga son nulas
zest [zɛst] N entusiasmo *m*
zigzag [zígzæg] N zigzag *m*; ADJ & ADV en
zigzag; VI zigzaguear, andar en zigzag; VT
hacer zigzaguear